BARRON'S
Guide to the
Most Competitive
COLLEGES

Fifth Edition

Edited by the College Division Staff of
Barron's Educational Series, Inc.

All inquiries should be addressed to:
Barron's Educational Series, Inc.
250 Wireless Boulevard
Hauppauge, NY 11788
www.barronseduc.com

Library of Congress Catalog Card No. 2007017853

ISBN-13: 978-0-7641-3760-0
ISBN-10: 0-7641-3760-3

Library of Congress Cataloging-in-Publication Data

Barron's guide to the most competitive colleges / edited by the College Division Staff of Barron's Educational Series, Inc. — 5th ed.
   p. cm
  Includes index.
  ISBN-13: 978-0-7641-3760-0 (alk. paper)
  ISBN-10: 0-7641-3760-3 (alk. paper)
  1. Universities and colleges—United States—Directories.
  2. College choice—United States—Handbooks, manuals, etc.
  I. Barron's Educational Series, Inc. College Division.

L901.B2656 2007
378.73—dc22

                     2007017853

PRINTED IN THE UNITED STATES OF AMERICA

9 8 7 6 5 4 3 2

❏ CONTENTS ❏

❑ INTRODUCTION ❑

We are proud to present this fifth edition of *Barron's Guide to Most Competitive Colleges*. A school's inclusion is based in the standards of Barron's Selector Ratings in the comprehensive *Profiles of American Colleges*. These schools accept only the best and brightest students.

In the fourth edition, published in 2005, 69 out of 70 eligible institutions were included. In this edition, we are happy to present 74 schools. Two of the schools listed in the last edition no longer qualified. Since the last edition, eight schools have been added to the elite group. Essays for seven of these schools appear in this edition. One school declined to participate.

We turned to recent graduates or (in several cases) soon to be graduates of each of these institutions and asked them to write an essay on what it's *really* like on campus. We requested them to comment specifically on those aspects of campus life that would be of most concern to a college-bound student trying to decide which institutions should be sent applications.

Essays for schools previously listed were either rewritten by new writers or the factual information was updated by the schools to ensure its accuracy.

Geographic locations of the colleges range from California to Maine. Some are large, others small. Most are private, but state universities are also represented. And several of the service academies are represented as well.

In addition to the college essays, we have included some advice that will be helpful to the prospective college applicant—from first applications while still in high school to study habits after enrolling.

The Most Competitive chart beginning on page 1061 shows at a glance how each of the most competitive schools stacks up against one another in areas such as acceptance numbers, test scores, and other comparisons.

Thumbnail sketches of each of the colleges that are profiled here are in a special section, as are short bios of the contributors. And finally, for quick geographic locating, the book concludes with an index by state.

It is our hope that these perceptive essays will be helpful in guiding the college-bound reader to intelligent choices in the major decision-making area of college applications.

The College Division Staff
Barron's Educational Series, Inc.

PLEASE NOTE

At press time, historical information regarding SAT scores for many of the colleges was only available for classes who were admitted based on the older version of the SAT exam.

That exam contained only two sections, verbal and math, with a total score of 1600. However, this information should provide you with a good basis for estimating the scores that these most competitive schools look for on the newer SAT, which contains an additional 800-point essay section, for a total score of 2400. Some schools have provided historical data for recent classes which took the new SAT test. Also, for definitive information about a particular school's admission requirements, including the ACT, SAT and the SAT Subject Tests, we recommend you visit the school's web site or contact the school's admissions office directly.

THE MOST
COMPETITIVE COLLEGES

AMHERST COLLEGE

Amherst College Photo

 Amherst College
Amherst, MA 01002-5000

 (413) 542-2328
Fax: (413) 542-2040

 E-mail: *admission@amherst.edu*
Web site: *http://www.amherst.edu*

 **Enrollment**

Full-time ❏ women: 819
❏ men: 831

INTRODUCING AMHERST

The Freshman Quad at Amherst, flanked by plain-faced brick dorms and the clock tower of Johnson Chapel, is the hub of this small college located in the Pioneer Valley. Whether those on its shady lawn are reading, playing Frisbee, strumming guitars, throwing snowballs, walking to class, or trudging from the gym to the dining hall, Amherst students appear to be experiencing the quintessential New England liberal arts education. However, to get a fuller picture of life at "The Fairest College," all visitors have to do is turn to see the churchless Stearns Steeple, the yellow Campus Center, the tile-green string course of the computer center or the view of the Holyoke Range from Memorial Hill and they'll see that Amherst provides the excellent education it is known for—and then some. An Amherst education is founded on the ideals of a liberal arts curriculum and is layered in diversity of thought, expression, and character.

Amherst has a reputation as one of the country's best colleges academically. But academics alone are not what makes so many people apply or why students who are there like it so much or why alumni still come back every year for Homecoming. It's the balance of academics and the social aspects; it's the people you meet and the conversations you have.

Amherst provides its students with a solid education in all disciplines, but its strength and energy come from its liberal arts philosophy—an Amherst student learns *how* to listen, think, analyze, and question. An Amherst student learns not only how to formulate ideas, but how to express and defend them. An Amherst education does not end in the classroom; students learn as much from the background and diversity of their classmates as they do from their top-notch professors.

Amherst, with an enrollment of approximately 1,600, is small. Everyone, eventually, knows everyone else. This familiarity truly makes Amherst not just an academic institution, but a community. Not only do students form close friendships with each other, but professors, coaches, administrators, and staff take an active interest in students. It is not unusual to see someone from the Dean's Office rooting on the sideline of a field hockey game. It is not uncommon to hear a cafeteria employee inquire about a student's latest all-nighter. It is not strange for a student to drop into the Office of the Dean of Students to chat or to have dinner at a professor's house. Amherst students don't just attend class and head straight for the library; they live, work, and play at Amherst, and it quickly becomes their second home.

Amherst is not perfect. Occasionally, an Amherst student, like anyone else anywhere else, will have a bad day (or two). The college has both formal and informal support systems. The Dean of Students Office, the Counseling Center, peer and disciplinary advocates, and the resident counselors, coaches, professors, and friends form a network to help students in many different ways at many different levels.

Amherst students are aware of the college's imperfections, but the difference between Amherst and other academic institutions is that Amherst students do not just sit and grumble—Amherst students take action and Amherst administrators listen. The college paper sometimes seems entirely made of Op-Ed letters. Students often meet with Dean of Students Ben Lieber or other administrators including President Anthony W. Marx, and represent student opinion on committees. In the past few years student concerns about issues of academic and personal responsibility led to the formation of an honor code. As in many other instances, these changes and actions were rooted in student opinion and executed by their peers. Amherst is a community, and its students recognize their responsibility toward making it their own.

You first realize it when you go home for vacation that first time. You begin thinking about Amherst differently—it's not just your school, it's your space, it's where you are starting to build your own life. When you first catch a glimpse of the campus on your way back from break, you feel in some way as if you are returning home.

The Amherst experience is different for every individual and every class, but in each case it is a solid education, made rich by its emphasis on thought and expression and made deep by the people who are the "College on the Hill."

ADMISSIONS REQUIREMENTS

Recently, Amherst received 6,142 applications for roughly 433 spots, making it one of the most competitive liberal arts colleges in America. While academic achievement is the most important factor for admission, it is not the only one. Nor is there any set formula—Amherst staffers do not sit around plugging your test scores, extracurriculars, or class rank into a computer to determine a winning applicant. Instead, they read through each application looking at the whole profile.

Of course there are some general requirements: the SAT and SAT Subject tests or the ACT. There are also some recommendations: four years of English, math through precalculus, three or four years of a foreign language, two years of history and social science, at least two years of natural science (including a laboratory science).

Amherst staffers read each application contextually. Realizing that students bring to the table different backgrounds and experiences, and that each student has been presented with various opportunities that others haven't, Amherst admissions officers look at *how* students made use of where they were and what they were offered. Amherst seeks multifaceted students who will not only give their intellects, energies, and talents to the school, but who will also gain the most from the Amherst education and experience. Many of those who work in the Admissions Office are Amherst grads themselves; they know what being an Amherst student is like, and thus know what kind of applicant is best suited for the school.

Admissions staffers warn that when filling out your application, elaborate strategizing is a waste of time. Instead, they say, spend the time figuring out if Amherst is the best school for you. If the answer is yes, then use your application to express your many dimensions as a student and as a person.

ACADEMIC LIFE

Amherst has no core curriculum, giving students the freedom to construct their own course of study. Although there are requirements in each major, the only general required course is the First-Year Seminar, an interdisciplinary course taken by all freshmen in their first semester. The lack of a core follows in the true liberal arts philosophy of the school. Students can take classes in a wide range of disciplines: an art history major can take a physics class, a premedical student can major in English, a psychology major can double in music. So while the bulk of a student's studies may be in one subject, he or she has the luxury of being able to dabble in another discipline, often stumbling across a passion for art, science, philosophy, or language that might have been otherwise undiscovered.

Even as a psychology and economics double major, I was able to take a variety of classes, from The Social Organization of Law to Autobiographies of Women to The Catastrophe of Cancer and AIDS. It was the lack of core classes that allowed me to experience the true meaning of a liberal arts education.

Amherst students work hard. Classes are demanding. Students spend long hours in the libraries and at their computers. Amherst students are always writing—in every discipline. Yet, for the most part, students are engaged in their work. While not every class and every professor is well loved by every student, there are many that are. Class discussions are not restricted to the classroom, but are carried back to the dorms and dining hall.

> *Don't get me wrong, I learned a tremendous amount from my classes and my professors, but it was the conversations in the hallways or dorms or around a Valentine lunch table that taught me how to really listen and how to be confident in speaking my own mind.*

While Amherst is an extremely competitive environment, it is not cutthroat. Though it varies from department to department, students often work in study groups and are usually willing to help each other. The first few weeks can be intimidating to the freshman who, used to being at the top of the class in high school, realizes that he or she is now with the 400 other top students, but after a while Amherst's collaborative atmosphere dispels these worries.

Professors

Professors, for the most part, are not out to get you. They have office hours and expect students to make use of them whether they are having trouble with the class or not. Most classes are small enough so that professors get to know each student personally. The class size very often makes it impossible to hide; students are expected to participate in class discussion.

> *It's very hard to fail out of Amherst—professors want you to do well and are willing to help point you in the right direction. They expect you to work hard, but they also expect you to speak up when you don't understand something.*

Surrounding Colleges

If, after a while, the classes at Amherst don't hold that same thrill, or if you're looking for a change of scene, make use of the surrounding four colleges: Smith's art department, museum, and library draw Amherst students to its Northampton campus. The other all-women's school in the valley, Mount Holyoke, also offers various classes not offered at Amherst. Looking for an experience in alternative education? Try taking a class at Hampshire College down the road. Or maybe you'd like to see what a large university has to offer; if so, take a class at UMass. Still looking for something new and different? Almost half the junior class spends a semester or two abroad or takes advantage of the Twelve-College exchange program.

Amherst veterans advise making use of office hours, the Writing Center and the Quantitative Skills Center. And don't be afraid to use the add/drop period at the start of each semester—there's no sense wasting a class on a blah professor or boring subject when Amherst has so many other incredible ones.

The Amherst academic program is a rigorous but rewarding one. At its cornerstone is the exchange of ideas between students and professors of various backgrounds and disciplines.

SOCIAL LIFE AND ACTIVITIES

At Amherst, we work hard and we play hard.

Just as Amherst students dedicate themselves to their studies, they dedicate themselves to their playtime. School-sponsored theme parties, which usually feature a DJ or band, have become increasingly popular in recent years: Madonna TAP, the Luau and Casino, to name a few. But for those of you who think that Amherst social life is limited to theme nights, think again. Parties not sponsored by the school, but by students, often kick off the evening. At Amherst, parties are usually open to everyone and they are usually free. The five neighboring colleges provide concerts, theater, sports, and a range of other events. Amherst and neighboring Northampton offer a wide variety of restaurants, great movie theaters, and clubs.

The student-run Social Council and Program Board work hard to plan all-campus events. There's bound to be a concert (most likely *a cappella*) or play either on campus or in the surrounding valley. And if you're not watching something, chances are you're helping to run it. Between the publications, musical groups, volunteer organizations, clubs, and athletics, Amherst students are always involved with something.

Publications and Organizations

Stacked in the lobby of the dining hall, floating from round green table to round green table of the Campus Center, or stuck into a backpack, Amherst publications abound. Besides the weekly newspaper, *The Student*, *The Indicator*, and *Prism* keep the flow of debate and opinion alive. *The Amherst Review* and *A Further Room* round out the literary magazines.

Amherst has been called the "Singing College," and with good reason. Not only does the school have five *a cappella* groups, but men's and women's choruses, as well as many instrumental ensembles. There are also tons of clubs to join including Hillel, the Newman Club, Christian Fellowship, Noor, Pacific Islander Club, the Debating Club, WAMH Radio, and others, not to mention the many organizations that are active around campus: The Center for Community Engagement, Habitat for Humanity, Global Rights of Women (GROW), and the Pride Alliance.

WHERE TO EAT IN AMHERST

Coffee Shops:
○ The Black Sheep, Rao's, Starbucks

Non-Valentine Cheap Eats:
○ Antonio's, Bueno y Sano, Bub's BBQ, La Veracruzana

Dining Out:
○ Judie's, Bertucci's, Pasta E Basta, Panda East, Lone Wolf

Parents' Weekend:
○ Del Raye, Carmelina's, Chez Albert

Ordering In:
○ DP Dough
○ Wing's

Northampton Restaurants:
○ Spoleto's
○ Eastside Grill
○ Brasserie 40
○ Herrell's Ice Cream

Worth the Trip:
○ Atkins Farms
○ The Whately Diner
○ The Book Mill
○ Summit House

Athletics

Amherst is an athletic college. While not everybody is a member of a varsity team, most students take part in some athletic pastime, whether it be a workout in the gym or a walk through the beautiful bird sanctuary. Amherst may be small, but its teams are mighty, regularly making it to the ECAC, NESCAC, and NCAA tournaments. Not only does Amherst offer a strong varsity program, but it also offers club and intramural teams as well. The women's and men's rugby clubs are among the best in the Northeast. Other club teams are the ski team, men's volleyball, water polo, tae kwan do, and Ultimate Frisbee.

Students also participate in school activities on other levels. Many students serve in the student government, others sit on committees, while others act as liaisons between the administration and students. The peer advocates, disciplinary advocates, and resident counselors play an active role in student life. Indeed, central to the character of Amherst social life is the residential aspect of the school. Students get to know each other well through common classes, interests, and living situations. And often how you know someone will overlap. Your next-door neighbor can be in your chem lab, your teammate can also be a member of your magazine staff, your RC may be in your English class. Amherst students get to know each other on many levels in many environments.

> *Sometimes the stupidest things will bring a floor or building together, like trying to fit an oversized couch through a door or having an impromptu study break or water fight. Then, when we really need to help each other out with the serious stuff, the bonds are already there.*

There is always something to do at Amherst, whether it be a keg party or a theme party, a night at a concert or a play, or an evening spent at the movies or in a coffee shop. Amherst students spend time working and playing together, social interactions that help to build friendships that last well past graduation.

FINANCIAL AID

Amherst makes its need-blind admission policy a priority. Indeed, the recent Amherst College campaign raised $35 million toward continuing need-blind admission. Those in the Development Office estimate that Amherst ranks among a dozen or so institutions that admit students without regard to financial need, and, more important, maintain the aid for all four years. Currently, fifty-two percent of students in the freshman class receive financial aid; the average amount offered is $32,892. There are plenty of jobs available on campus even if you aren't in a work–study program. Although many jobs are posted, many are obtained from word of mouth, and the new Student Employment Office helps provide a central source for job postings. Students work in Valentine and the library, as well as in the Keefe Campus Center and administrative offices, physical plant, and custodial shop. Not only do students earn spending money, but they are given the chance to get to know the staff of the college as well as the ins and outs of running the school.

I never really understood how strong the ties to Amherst were until I went to my first Homecoming as a graduate. I was surprised and thrilled at how genuinely happy I was to see everyone again. There's always a big turnout for Homecoming, and now I know why—as corny as it sounds, it really is like coming home.

Amherst graduates are an interesting bunch. They can be found in many professions in many parts of the globe. You read their names in newspapers, you randomly run into them in restaurants, you meet them at Homecoming. Amherst grads all seem to have taken their education and run with it, though not in the same direction.

Amherst does have a strong on-campus recruiting program for banking, consulting, and other careers, as well as a strong network in the nonprofit, education, and publishing fields. Amherst grads find what they are looking for—many are gainfully employed, many are in graduate school, many are pursuing fellowships and grants. Whatever they are doing, Amherst grads are not sitting still; they are active and energetic, armed with their Amherst education and their enthusiasm for learning at all levels.

The Amherst alumni are deeply connected to the school, contributing to its strong professional network as well as in the school's large endowment. About two-thirds of Amherst grads give to the school, the highest percent nationally. And when asked in a survey if they'd do it all over again, approximately ninety-two percent said they'd choose Amherst again.

The Amherst experience is one that is taken with you past graduation and built upon; the school, for many, is the bedrock of graduates' professional skills and personal outlooks.

PROMINENT GRADS

- Henry Ward Beecher, 1834, Preacher, writer, and thinker
- Melvil Dewey, 1884, Inventor of the Dewey Decimal System
- Calvin Coolidge, 1885, President of the United States
- Clarence Birdseye, '10, Inventor of Frozen Foods
- Lloyd Conover, '45, Inventor of Tetracycline
- Stansfield Turner, '45, Director of CIA
- William Webster, '45, Director of FBI
- Joseph Stiglitz, '64, Nobel Prize-winning economist
- Scott Turow, '70, Author
- Susannah Grant, '84, Screenwriter
- David Foster Wallace, '85, Author
- Dan Brown, '86, Author
- Jeffrey Wright, '87, Tony-Award winning actor

I did not realize how extensive the Amherst network really was until my senior year. Whether it be chatting on the sidelines of a football game or in the corner office of a New York City firm, I was amazed at the amount of time Amherst alums spent answering questions and offering advice to students on future career choices.

SUMMING UP

Amherst, with an enrollment of about 1,600, is a small school. Students, faculty, and staff get to know each other well in many different arenas and in many different capacities, making the school not just an academic institution, but a community. You'd have to look far and wide to find a school that would match Amherst's academic record, commitment to a liberal arts philosophy, and diversity of students and faculty. It'd be difficult to find a group of more enthusiastic and intellectually curious students, more caring and supportive faculty and administration, and more loyal and generous alumni.

Amherst admission officers do not look for perfect students; instead, they look for those who will gain the most from an Amherst education while at the same time contributing to the experiences of others. Amherst students learn from this diversity of thought and background just as they learn from their challenging classes. They learn from the shared experience of first-year anxieties, from the conversation at the lunch table or during a professor's office hours, from a tough loss on the playing field or from an exhilarating victory. They learn from the common experience of getting a paper back loaded with criticism, or spending the wee hours of the morning in the computer center, or even spending all night at a party. They learn from discussions with graduates, lectures from experts and authorities, talks with the building and grounds crew.

And while all this learning is going on, Amherst students are having fun, taking each opportunity that comes along. Amherst students know when and how to work hard, but they also know when and how to take the time to play.

When Amherst students graduate, they do not graduate as perfect people. They may be better versed in many different disciplines; they may have discovered a passion for art, or a love of economics; they may have questioned and challenged and reenforced their beliefs; they may have found their voices. What they have learned at Amherst will be used every day—how to communicate, to think, to question. They will be able to contribute their Amherst-honed talents while knowing how to experience all the world has to offer.

❏ *Molly Lyons, B.A.*

BARNARD COLLEGE

 Barnard College
3009 Broadway
New York, NY 10027

 (212) 854-2014
Fax: (212) 854-8220

 E-mail: *admissions@barnard.edu*
Web site: *http://www.barnard.edu*

 Enrollment

Full-time ❑ women: 2,296

Part-time ❑ women: 60

INTRODUCING BARNARD COLLEGE

With applications soaring and physical plant renovations springing up all over the place, Barnard College is moving and shaking in all sorts of ways. President Judith Shapiro is spearheading a major campaign for "Barnard of Tomorrow," the benefits of which are already being felt on campus.

Recently, the greenhouse, gymnasium, and major lecture halls were refurbished and upgraded, student computer consultants are available around the clock in each residence hall, and Elie Wiesel and alumna Suzanne Vega (among others) appeared before large and enthusiastic audiences. Not bad for a college whose mission is to educate and support the growth of some 2,300 students, all of whom are motivated and talented, all of whom are women.

Paradoxically, it is easy to forget that Barnard is a women's college, what with the intellectual excitement and the variety of activity on the campus. Barnard's unique relationship with Columbia University means that Barnard's women have access to a coed experience at all times, but on their own terms. It also means that the Barnard faculty and administration have as their main focus and attention the female Barnard student body, not the coed masses across the street (literally—Columbia's campus is just on the east side of Broadway). Therefore, the Barnard student is taught by faculty members rather than teaching assistants. These scholars are experts in their fields and have immeasurable resources that they share with their students. Or, as one young alumna put it:

As a graduate student at [Ivy League School X], I advised undergrads on their senior theses. I tried to be helpful, but I only know so much. My thesis advisor at Barnard was the chair of her department, a wealth of information, and an all-around inspiration.

Add to this wonderful mixture Barnard's New York City location—now considered the safest major city in America by the FBI—and one begins to see what all the fuss is about. A stroll down Broadway, a bus ride uptown, or a subway trip to Greenwich Village enables students to experiment in the most diverse cultural laboratory this side of the United Nations (where students regularly intern). The glamor of Fifth Avenue and the glitter of Broadway are equally accessible. And, as in any urban setting, opportunities abound to make a difference in the community: Barnard women serve as legal advocates to the homeless, tutors in the America Reads program, and providers of hot meals through the Community Lunch Program. So nice they named it twice, New York is a great college town.

Barnard is, quite simply, "hot," which is both exciting and daunting. Everybody and her sister seems to be applying, creating a stir among prospective students and the admissions staff. In recent years, the college has barely utilized its waiting list, indicating that the "yield" of students initially offered admission has gotten to a point where the ideal number of new students can be attained in one fell swoop. Barnard's applicant pool has increased by 162% or 2.6 times larger than in 1991, making it the most sought-after women's college in America.

Getting into Barnard isn't all that easy, but there is no single criterion a student can point and know, "THIS is the reason I was admitted." The application process is the usual, including personal data, high school transcripts, official copies of standardized test scores (either the ACT or the SAT plus two SAT Subject tests, and three recommendations—one from a principal or counselor and two from teachers (preferably in academic subject areas). To apply to Barnard, students must submit the Common Application in addition to the Barnard College supplement. If Barnard is the student's first choice, she may apply for Early Decision (ED); the deadline is November 15. Applicants may be deferred to the general application pool if they are denied admission. The regular deadline for application is January 1.

The admissions staff at Barnard works hard to make sure that each student offered admission will thrive in her own way. The ideal applicant to Barnard has a solid record, pursues diverse interests, and shows promise that she will take advantage of the breadth and depth of experiences the college and New York City will offer her.

The High School Record

The high school record is the single most important part of the application. While overall achievement (that is, high grades) is important, the admissions staff makes it very clear that they care about a student's demonstrated effort to challenge herself in the classroom. This means an A in a less rigorous class doesn't mean as much as a B+ in one that is more rigorous. In addition, course availability is taken into consideration. For instance, if a particular high school offers twenty-five ways to exceed the minimum graduation requirements, and an applicant avails herself of only one or two, she doesn't seem to indicate that she'd take advantage of the thousands of opportunities that await her upon matriculation at Barnard. On the other hand, an applicant taking the only two AP courses available at her high school can't be expected to do any more, but those courses are important measures of her success. In addition, because the college expects students to study a broad range of subjects, evidence of that interest—four years of English, social studies, and math and at least three years of science and foreign language—is very important.

Other Criteria

That is not to say that the Barnard experience is solely an academic one! The college takes pride in the amazing collective talent of its actors and athletes, debaters and dancers. Indeed, its strength comes from its unparalleled diversity—students hail from forty-eight states and forty countries, from around the corner and around the world. One in three Barnard students identifies herself as Asian American, African American/Black, Latina, or Native American. Participation and leadership in extracurricular activities—clubs, teams, youth groups, or community service opportunities—are part of the admissions picture. Holding down a part-time job is also considered in this category, as some high school students are active contributors to their family's overall earnings. Multiyear commitment to an activity is always a plus; it shows your ability to stay with something for longer than it takes to get your picture taken for the yearbook. A liberal arts college wants to educate students to be good citizens, not simply good scholars. Participation in the community, which often translates into activity and volunteer participation, is a reality at Barnard, a positive reality.

Standardized Tests and the Essay

Now, about those pesky standardized tests. They are required, they count for something, and it's a good idea to do your best on them. They are the one measure that can be used to compare students no matter where they're from. That said, as the official admissions materials state, "no preconceived profile of an ideal student population limits the number of applicants accepted from any one group." So when it's time to fill out the personal part of the application, students should feel free to show some personality and let their individual quirks and interests peek through. The essays are a student's golden opportunity to express herself, her views, and her goals—and not knowing exactly what to do with one's life is a terrific place to start as a Barnard first-year student!

ACADEMIC LIFE

The admissions staff brings in class after class of students who dive into the curriculum. Graduation requirements ensure that a Barnard degree means something; all students must be competent in writing, quantitative reasoning, and in a foreign language. Beyond the depth provided by a major field (from which there are about sixty to choose, or students may combine or design their own), distribution requirements guarantee exposure to the humanities, social and natural sciences, visual and performing arts as well as to a variety of cultures and societies. Several of the requirements overlap, however, and students always have a choice as to how to fulfill them. Although all students must take First-Year English, there are several topical areas from which to choose (American Identities and Writing Women's Lives are two of them). Its companion course, First-Year Seminar, is taught by faculty from all departments, allowing every first-year student the opportunity to discuss and write about subjects ranging from The Woman Warrior to The Psychology of Communication and from The Existence of Evil to The Crisis of Authority. Both of these courses are limited in size to promote active participation, lively discussion, and plenty of personal attention from the professors.

Faculty

Again and again, Barnard students and alumnae praise their academic experiences at the college.

> *Faculty members are great. They provide so much encouragement, are more than willing to provide a recommendation or just some encouragement and ideas. One history professor even helped me get my first real apartment!*

This kind of testimonial is available from virtually every Barnard student. Their close and productive relationships with the highly acclaimed Barnard faculty make Barnard a singular institution. Barnard students frequently collaborate with faculty as research assistants, so it is not unusual to hear a senior describe her work with an anthropology professor, or a junior discuss her experiences in the biology laboratory. Not long ago, a Barnard first-year student was asked to spend a semester at an astronomy station on Nantucket Island, where the other participants in the program were all graduate students.

During their first two years, Barnard students receive counseling from members of the faculty and the Dean of Studies Office.

> *My advisor helped me figure out what courses would be most useful to me in choosing a major and at the same time satisfying my general requirements. He also suggested I become a calculus tutor and helped me secure a summer internship at CBS news.*

Advisors are well versed in Barnard's policies and regulations, working closely with the Deans' Office and the Registrar to ensure that all students are on the right track for graduation. At the end of the student's second year, advisors are prepared to assist with the transition into the major. From then on, students are advised by a faculty member in their major department; a double major will have two advisors. Students can decide whether they want to establish a close relationship with their advisors or keep it strictly business. Advisors are prepared to provide the necessary and required parts of the job, but they have chosen this role because they want to be available to students in a more personal way. It is therefore not unusual for an advisor to write graduate school or other critical recommendations for students they never actually taught, but who they have come to know well over the course of several years together.

Partnership with Columbia

Barnard's partnership with Columbia means that the curricular offerings of one of the country's top research universities are available for the asking; courses in all departments are available for cross-registration. About equal numbers of Barnard and Columbia students do this, indicating a true academic parity between the two schools. Some celebrated professors have become major attractions; for example, Barnard's Richard Pious and Dennis Dalton are quite sought after, both as noted scholars in their fields (the American presidency and Gandhi, respectively) and as regular teachers of first-year students in introductory courses. Barnard students especially join their Columbia counterparts in courses taught by luminaries such as Robert Thurman in religion. While some departments are particularly focused on one campus or the other (theater at Barnard, for example, or computer science at Columbia), the offerings by popular departments such as English, history, and political science amount to nearly twice the number of courses as would be available otherwise. In every case, academic advisors can help students make informed choices about their course selection.

Senior Theses or Projects

Each Barnard student's academic endeavors are capped off by a significant culminating experience, which comes in the form of a senior thesis, project, or exam in her major. Preparing for and completing this terminal work presents true challenges, but that's part of the Barnard way. It understandably unifies the class; the buzz of activity in the library, labs, and studios keeps the midnight oil burning senior year. The idea is that if a student can succeed in such a project, she can do it in just about any field she chooses after Barnard. All things being equal, an art history major could just as easily land a financial services job as an economics major; they both certainly have the verbal, research, and critical thinking skills such a position might require.

Joint Programs

Other academic attractions include joint programs with the Juilliard School and the Manhattan School of Music, the Jewish Theological Seminary, and various graduate and professional schools of Columbia University such as the School of Engineering, the School of International and Public Affairs, the Law School, and the Dental School. While entrance into these programs is quite limited and often extremely competitive, the students who participate in them not only benefit themselves, but they contribute an extra degree of depth and diversity to their Barnard classrooms.

Exchange and Overseas Programs

About thirty percent of Barnard's graduates participated in study abroad, whether it was for a semester or two. Barnard's official exchange programs in the United States include Spelman College and the Columbia University-Howard University Exchange Program, while overseas programs are located in more than thirty-five countries, including Argentina, Australia, Cuba, England, France, Germany, Italy, Japan, Kenya, Russia, and Spain. These programs are structured so that, for example, students may bring their financial aid packages with them; however, Barnard students' diverse interests take them to such far-flung places as Russia, Israel, the Cameroons, Nicaragua, and Australia. The world, as they say, is their oyster. The Dean of Study Abroad meets with students individually and in groups, providing information and guidance before and after the experience.

After spending the spring term at the London School of Economics, I was feeling rather "out of the loop" at Barnard. When I attended Dean Szell's special meeting in the fall, my advisor helped me realize that I wasn't the only one feeling this way.

These kinds of touches mark the Barnard experience from start to finish. Whether it's the personal letter sent by the first-year class dean upon matriculation or the handshake from the college's president at graduation, the Barnard faculty and administration make a concerted effort to ensure that each student's experience at Barnard is individual and special.

SOCIAL LIFE AND ACTIVITIES

The past president of Barnard College, alumna Ellen Futter, often characterized Barnard by saying, "This is *not* a cloistered enclave," thus coining a slogan for the ages. While students find campus activities galore, they have never-ending access to the unquantifiable offerings of what is arguably the world's greatest city; moreover, the college tries to make the city's offerings affordable for the usually cash-strapped undergrad. Discount vouchers to first-run films and the performing arts supplement the popular Urban New York program, which takes students to events such as *Wicked* on Broadway, opening day at Yankee Stadium, the New York Philharmonic, and even the circus, all for the price of the subway ($4.00 round-trip). Each trip is escorted by a member of the college or university faculty or administration, providing an extra opportunity to get to know a key member of the community in a relaxed, sometimes unconventional, setting.

Most students worry, to some degree or other, about making friends in college. If they can be generalized in any way, Barnard friendships are built to last. That said, the need for privacy inherent in living in New York City means that personal space is valued and respected. People don't run right up to you to get to know you here, but don't mistake that for unfriendliness. Attend any club meeting, event, or party and you're sure to make a new acquaintance. Whether it's the woman in your sponsor group during orientation, the friend of a friend from high school or summer camp who lives down the hall, or the person who wants to have coffee after orchestra practice, student life lends itself to the friendship-making process.

Housing

Barnard's residential focus means a great deal of programming takes place in the dorms. First-year students are clustered together in the quad, a grouping of (surprise!) four halls that situated on the south end of the main campus houses a total of about 900 students. The main dining room is located here, in Hewitt Hall, and the Quad Café is open late into the evening for that much-needed burst of energy courtesy of Starbucks Coffee. Beyond the quad, which primarily features the traditional corridor style of dormitory living, upper-class students live in suites of various configurations in seven other residence halls surrounding the main campus. In every hall, Resident Assistants (RAs) sponsor floor programs and study breaks to foster social connections; movie nights and guest appearances by various peer education groups and speakers offer something for just about everyone. After the first year, students select their own living space through a lottery process. In addition, they may enter the lottery in groups, sometimes with their Columbia friends, for suite living on either campus. Another more competitive option is to participate in Special Interest Housing, meaning that students come together around a theme such as Community Service, Foreign Language, or Environmental Awareness, and sponsor programs in their residence hall for everyone's benefit. The Housing Office offers forums early in the spring semester to help explain the various options.

Outside Groups

The amount and quality of activity sponsored by and for the college is inspiring. While the faculty and administration present lectures and readings by prominent and emerging scholars and artists, students themselves create and invite a great deal of programming. Thus, you're likely to find both a classical musical recital and a concert by an alternative band, with a *Barnard Bulletin* (a news weekly) reporter on hand to interview the talent and audience as well. Barnard's radio station, WBAR, broadcasts a college/alternative format and there are traditional activities such as the yearbook and student government (called SGA), which is responsible for the eighty or so student organizations. Cultural organizations and various other community groups come under SGA's umbrella.

That said, there are at least as many groups at Columbia, giving Barnard students the opportunity to work on a daily paper (the *Spectator*) or a jazz-oriented radio station (WKCR), to get involved in religious, volunteer, and political organizations (most of which are jointly sponsored by Barnard, but whose offices are physically located on the Columbia campus), and clubs galore.

The Greeks

The Greek system, including both sororities and coed fraternities, is open to Barnard students who want to experience more "traditional" collegiate life. Those who take part in them tend to rave about their experiences; however, the SGA constitution prohibits groups that limit their membership and therefore does not recognize the Greek system. There's hardly a more concrete example of how student life at Barnard offers something for everyone!

Productions

Dance, theater, and musical productions abound. From improv comedy to *a cappella* singing, Barnard women regularly appear on stage. Two annual events are Acapellooza, an *a cappella* jamboree hosted by Barnard's own Bacchantae, which features groups from the university and selected others and results in a professional-quality CD, and Broadway Tonight, a benefit performance of Broadway selections that teams up Barnard students with professionals from the Great White Way. Off stage, students provide technical support and packed houses. This is one talented group of students, and a group appreciative of the efforts of their peers.

Athletics

Those who prefer their thrills on a court, arena, or stadium can participate on a number of levels. Barnard varsity athletes compete in Division I archery, basketball, soccer, field hockey, crew, tennis, lacrosse, cross-country, track and field, swimming and diving, softball, fencing, golf, and volleyball as part of the athletic consortium with their counterparts from Columbia College and the School of Engineering. We're talking Ivy League here—no athletic scholarships, just sheer love of the game. Club sports such as Ultimate Frisbee, sailing, and rugby offer unique opportunities for intercollegiate competition and comraderie. Intramurals provide a great way to let loose, either in soccer, basketball, or even bowling (at Barnard's on-campus alley). Finally, many students work out on their own or with friends by running in Riverside Park, taking a student-led aerobics class, or swimming a few laps in the Barnard pool. While obviously not an outdoorsy, let's-go-skiing-this-afternoon campus, Barnard students enjoy breaking a good sweat.

Off Campus

And, all right, let's not forget Barnard's location. From poetry readings to film screenings, cafés and restaurants to galleries and museums, concert halls to night clubs, this is the city that never sleeps and always has something to offer. Parades, street fairs, festivals, and impromptu concerts are year-round occurrences. Professional sports teams have crosstown rivals, bookstores have cappuccino, and there's nothing quite like a trip to Central Park, whether it's for a visit to the zoo, rollerblading around the Loop, or ice-skating at Wollman Rink. Even the lifelong New Yorker will find herself traveling to new places and trying new foods with her Barnard friends—and a welcome number of area restaurants deliver to the residence halls for snacking on sushi, tandoori, pizza, lo mein, or simply a nice deli sandwich.

FINANCIAL AID

Private colleges are expensive. Barnard's tuition falls in line with its peer institutions, but that doesn't make the bill much easier to swallow. Unlike many schools, however, Barnard admits students on a need-blind basis, meaning that students are admitted regardless of their ability to pay. Moreover, they are met with a full-need financial aid package in keeping with the federal government's formulas—once the Financial Aid Office has calculated the amount that a student and her family are able to contribute, it offers a package to make up the difference. Approximately fifty-three percent of the student body receives some form of financial assistance.

Generally speaking, this package has three parts. First, all students are expected to borrow money, but Barnard does not expect both the student and her parents to take out loans. Next, students are asked to work during the school year to contribute to their own education, with work-study awards focused on first-year and sophomore students in particular to assist in their getting to know the campus and its functionings; upperclass students are encouraged to find off-campus jobs relating to their majors or career interests. Summer earnings are also expected after the first year. Finally, the college provides grants—funds that need not be repaid—to bridge the gap. Forty-one percent of the student body receives grant monies from Barnard.

New York state residents who meet certain financial and academic criteria may apply as Higher Education Opportunity Program (HEOP) students. This program, sponsored by New York State but largely funded by the college itself, provides intensive preenrollment preparation for Barnard academics as well as special counseling and support during all four years. About twenty-five students are admitted each year under the HEOP program and their graduation rate is on par with the overall Barnard student population.

GRADUATES

Barnard women are staunch and loyal supporters of their alma mater, leading to an "old-girl" network that spans the country and the world. Organized Barnard Clubs in many regions sponsor faculty lectures and receptions for admitted students, but even more prevalent is the individual connection—the women who make themselves available to assist current students and fellow alumnae through informational interviews, internships, job contacts, and relocation support.

Several times a year, alumnae appear on panels to discuss their career paths, in fields ranging from psychology to law, from education to arts management. The BEST program, sponsored by the Career Development Office, not only organizes these panels and helps seniors with résumé and interview tips, but also offers workshops on building a business wardrobe, following proper etiquette at business meals, and even how to find a New York City apartment.

Thanks especially to the high standards and personal encouragement of the faculty, Barnard is one of the leading producers of Ph.D.s in the country. The most recent study of private undergraduate colleges and universities (done by Franklin and Marshall College for the period between 1920 and 1995) ranked Barnard third overall—second in the fields of psychology and foreign languages, third in anthropology and sociology, and fourth in English—in the number of its graduates receiving PhD.s. Not women graduates, *all* graduates. In terms of medical doctors, Barnard ranks fifth in the country in the number of women who become physicians, behind much larger institutions such as Cornell, Harvard, Stanford, and the University of Michigan. While no studies have been done on the field of law, Barnard boasts a remarkable array of graduates who go on to become lawyers and judges.

A recent graduate who is currently earning her Master's in International Affairs at Columbia recently said, "At Barnard, I learned I could do anything!" and this sentiment seems to echo through the generations. Barnard alumnae have authored more than 4,100 books and such best-selling novelists as Erica Jong, Mary Gordon, and Edwidge Danticat are among the ranks. In journalism, eight Barnard alumnae have won or shared the Pulitzer Prize, including Anna Quindlen and Natalie Angier at *The New York Times*, Eileen McNamara at the *Boston Globe*, and most recently, Jhumpa Lahiri for her book, *Interpreter of Maladies*. In broadcast news, Cable News Network's Maria Hinojosa and National Public Radio's Susan Stamberg are prominent contributors to their fields.

PROMINENT GRADS

- Helene Gayle, Assistant Surgeon General of the United States
- Zora Neale Hurston, Author
- Atoosa Rubenstein, Editor-in-Chief, *Seventeen Magazine*
- Jeane Kirkpatrick, United Nations Ambassador
- Margaret Mead, Anthropologist
- Joan Rivers, Comedienne
- Martha Stewart, Author, Television Personality
- Twyla Tharp, Choreographer
- Suzanne Vega, Singer, Songwriter

Former Dean of the College Virginia Gildersleeve helped to charter the United Nations; alumnae Jeane Kirkpatrick and Sylvan Foa became its first female ambassador for the United States and its first female spokesperson, respectively. While their names may be less recognizable, the women who lead Rockefeller and Company and the Ford modeling agency, the presidents of Bank Street College and the American Museum of Natural History, and one of the founders of the National Organization for Women all graduated from Barnard. But whether they have made big names for themselves or have pursued goals more privately, Barnard women make a difference in the world, an aspiration inculcated in them during their years on campus.

SUMMING UP

Barnard's unique position as a small independent college for women closely linked to a first-rate research university and located in one of the world's major cities offers an extraordinary and unparalleled opportunity for those young women smart and savvy enough to avail themselves of it. The internship possibilities and cultural offerings of New York City are second to none, and the intimacy of the Barnard campus and student body provides a perfect home base from which to explore Manhattan. It is a literal and metaphorical oasis, a place where students can relax and learn to express themselves more and more fully.

Often described as "the best of both worlds," Barnard students have the advantages of a women's college—its nurturing and inspiring faculty, the sisterhood that stems from a unity of purpose in studying the liberal arts—while at the same time having full access to the facilities, activities, and social life of a large, coed, multipurpose university. Columbia provides research facilities, graduate programs, and a diversity of talents and backgrounds that no other small college can offer.

A recent article in *Town and Country* magazine featured women from the colleges still affiliated by their Seven Sister history. The interviewer asked a Barnard senior which one part of her education she would use most if she were stranded on a desert island. The student's response?

Barnard does not educate women to live on desolate islands. Barnard educates women to make a real difference in the real world.

As this particular alumna now holds a master's degree in Public Policy and is currently spending a year in China as a Luce Fellow, she is certainly living up to the ideal she expressed.

Whether your interests lie in the humanities, the social and natural sciences, or the arts, Barnard College offers a fertile training ground for young minds and ideas. If the current generation has been described as apathetic, you'd never know it by meeting Barnard students or visiting the campus. The intellectual debates that begin in the classroom and extend into a dining hall or dorm room are reflective of the involvement and curiosity of the student body. Close academic relationships with faculty and peers, and a supportive environment that actively and tacitly provides a foundation for the intellectual and social development of an extraordinary group of young women makes for a wonderful home base from which to explore Columbia University, Morningside Heights, New York City, and the world. Small wonder it is experiencing such a surge in interest and excitement!

❏ Catherine Webster, B.A.

BATES COLLEGE

Photo by Phyllis Graber Jensen

 Bates College
Lewiston, ME 04240

 (207) 786-6000
Fax: (207) 786-6025

 E-mail: *admissions@bates.edu*
Web site: *http://www.bates.edu*

 **Enrollment**

Full-time ❑ women: 855
❑ men: 829

INTRODUCING BATES

Choosing the right college or university is often thought of as a difficult task. One obvious reason for this perception is that many college applicants are preoccupied with the academic, social, and athletic rigors of their senior year in high school. Deeper examination may reveal that the student is struggling with the important task of discovering exactly who they are. The successful choosing of the right college, in fact, involves a recognition and understanding of the true identity of an individual. It is also a reflection of what he or she wishes to become.

My college selection process was probably very similar to many other prospective students of the small liberal arts colleges in New England. I had interviews at many top schools and had a chance to walk around several campuses with students. My visit to Bates was definitely different than the others. From the beginning, the people at Bates made me feel very welcome and important. After my interview and tour I wandered into the science building to see the biology facilities (I was pretty sure I wanted to be a bio major). Walking down a hall with my family, we happened by an open door where a student was doing research. This student welcomed us into his lab and proceeded to tell us what he was doing and asked if we had any questions about Bates. I remember vividly this student's willingness to help me find the biology labs, but more importantly, what I took away from this conversation was the student's genuine interest and warmth. I also met with the lacrosse coach, and even though I was not a recruit and had just met him, he talked with me and my parents for over an hour, took us to lunch in the dining hall, and even walked us to our car. Of all the top schools I had visited, Bates was the one that felt right. With so many fine academic colleges to choose from, I went with a gut feeling that Bates was the best for me. I applied early and never looked back.

Bates College is a highly selective liberal arts college located in Lewiston, Maine. The school is known for its excellent academics, internationally distinguished debate team, competitive athletics, and its history. The college was founded in 1855, as the college course catalog states, "by people who felt strongly about human freedom and civil rights. Bates is among the oldest coeducational colleges in the nation, and from its beginning the college admitted students without regard to race, religion, national origin or sex."

From its creation, the college has never had fraternities and sororities. College activities are open to all its students. These long-held values of Bates pervade every aspect of the college, and are what makes it unique. Walk on the campus and talk to the students, the faculty, and the staff . . . talk to the people who make up what Bates is today. In these conversations, the values and ideals upon which the school was founded become obvious. There is a warmth in the interaction, a "friendliness" that over the years remains a characteristic of the typical Batesie.

I asked a friend about his college selection process, and his response often echoes what other students say of Bates:

I loved Bates from the first time I set foot on the campus. There is something about the college, the feel of the quad, the people who inhabit this place, that makes Bates so inviting—that makes Bates "friendly." In the summer before my senior year of high school, I visited about fifteen schools in several different regions of the country. In pursuit of a good education, and following my heart, I decided to apply Early Decision. I liked the obvious reasons for wanting to attend Bates, which were advertised in the viewbook, but I also liked the excellent facilities, the small size that allows one to get to know a lot of different people well, and also gives everyone the opportunity to make a difference. I also liked the cohesiveness of Bates, which can be seen in the absence of fraternities and sororities—thus helping to remove social barriers— and in the committed and accessible faculty.

Bates has much to offer its students. In addition to its human resources of faculty and staff, Bates continues to be committed to providing the latest equipment and finest facilities for its students. The new $35 million Dining Commons is under construction. Pettengill Hall opened in the fall of 1999. This five-story building is the home of the social science departments with classrooms, offices, and an atrium overlooking Lake Andrews or, as the students call it, "the puddle." There are lots of opportunities for research with faculty. In a 2003 senior survey, more than twenty-five percent of respondents reported that they participated in a faculty member's research project.

The Bates-Morse Mountain Conservation Area is 574 acres of salt marsh and rocky forested terrain adjacent to one of the last undisturbed barrier beaches where Bates students and faculty can study geology, botany, and zoology. In addition, the college owns eighty acres of freshwater habitat just north of the conservation area.

From electron microscopes to the Olin Arts Center, from the Davis Fitness Center to having the entire campus hooked up to a computer network and being Internet ready, Bates provides an environment in which students enjoy the benefits of attending a large university, while getting the personal educational experience of a small college.

ADMISSIONS REQUIREMENTS

Bates continues to be highly selective in its admissions process. Currently listed as one of the nation's Most Competitive colleges by *Barron's Profiles of American Colleges*, and similarly ranked by other major college review publications, the school's reputation for academic excellence draws highly motivated and talented students from all over the country and around the world. One big difference between Bates and most top schools is that, in its admissions process, standardized test scores are not required. Although most students do submit these scores and do very well, Bates recognizes that these tests are not always a true indicator of aptitude and future achievement. Admissions readers are more interested in the entire high school record. In addition to grades, evidence of a student taking challenging courses, the essays that are required with the application, extracurricular activities and interests, and recommendations by teachers and other school officials, are all carefully inspected by admissions personnel.

Bates, throughout its history, has recognized that diversity in its student body is a crucial requirement for an educational environment. Bates was coeducational before being coed was popular. Bates also makes great efforts to attract students from diverse cultures and backgrounds.

Interviews

An on-campus visit and interview are strongly encouraged. If this is not possible, in most cases an alumni interview can be scheduled. An interview is the opportunity for an applicant to link a personality with an application in the mind of an admissions reader. Often, this impression on an interviewer makes a difference in deciding on many applicants who have similar credentials.

Early Decision and Other Admissions Plans

Although not for everyone, the Early Decision admission plan is one way to separate yourself from other applicants. By applying Early Decision, prospective students declare that Bates is their first choice and, if accepted, they will withdraw all other college applications. When looking at it from an admissions point of view, they want students who know that they love Bates and have decided that this is the school that they want to attend. It is this type of applicant who will most likely get involved and improve the educational experience for others.

Many applicants are not willing or able to decide early, of course. In addition to the regular admissions process, other possibilities include: Deferred Admission, January Admission, Transfer Admission, and the option to attend Bates as a visiting student.

If you get the chance to drive up the Maine Turnpike and stop into Bates for a visit, you would notice that the academic buildings in which students attend classes are very close to each other around the tree-filled quad. A short walk through some of these buildings, such as Carnegie Science, or Pettengill Hall, would give a visitor a realistic impression of Bates.

Although Bates is one of the most competitive colleges in admissions, students have a collaborative work ethic and competition within themselves. They are self-motivated and, at times, the library becomes more familiar than one's room. Bates graduates leave confident they can handle any grad school. In the class of 2003, ninety-two percent of students completed a senior thesis or senior project. They also can handle the world. In the class of 2003, seventy percent of the graduates applied credit for study outside the United States.

Faculty

The Bates faculty makes the campus and the student body part of its life. Although time in the classroom makes up the majority of the time in which students interact with their professors, it is certainly not the only time. The Bates faculty is a central part of one's Bates experience inside *and* outside the classroom. Whether it is a departmental barbecue outside one of the residence halls, an all-campus barbecue during the fall or the spring, or even at the President's Gala, the faculty interacts with students and makes connections that enrich the educational experience. Better yet, all courses are taught by faculty members, not teaching assistants. All professors have office hours, which allow a student to meet one-on-one, but they will also make appointments with a student outside of these hours, if necessary. Most professors stay well after class to talk with students and explain any difficult material of that day's lecture, and give their home phone numbers out on the first day of class. Although at first this can be an intimidating way to get help, after a short time one comes to realize that members of the Bates faculty are happy to be available. They never leave the "teacher" role in their office; rather, they are teachers who are more than eager to aid a student who shows a willingness to learn.

Courses

The Bates academic year follows a 4-4-1 calendar. Students take four courses (the normal course load) during the fall and winter semesters, and for at least two of the four years take a five-week-long intensive course during the spring. This session, called Short Term, allows professors to have more freedom and creativity in designing each course and in many cases allows the class to leave the campus to study a subject by touching it and seeing it rather than just reading about it. Short Term courses allow geologists to study geologic history from inside a kayak in the intercoastal waterways of Maine; biologists study evolution by learning about the finches of the Galapagos Islands, as Darwin did from the *Beagle.*

> *In one of the first days of my Russian literature class, Tolstoy and Dostoyevsky, I realized that I was the only science major in the class. I found myself frustrated in the first few weeks because the professor turned the class over to the students for discussion of the stories instead of lecturing and telling us what the author meant. As the semester progressed, however, I came to value each student's opinion and realized that the process of thinking about what the passages meant to me, and to others who had read it, was as educational as the memorizing of facts that I was used to.*

The Harvard Center for Community Partnership

The Harvard Center for Community Partnership leads Bates' efforts in community involvement, including strong programs in service learning, community volunteerism, and environmental stewardship. The center aims to work with community partners to meet community needs and, in the process, to integrate civic engagement with the Bates educational experience. The Center offers short- and long-term grants to faculty, staff, and students, and provides summer support to pursue community-based research and work-study. The Harvard Center works with more than 125 partners, from schools and cultural institutions to grassroots community groups.

- **Academically-Based-Service-Learning.** The Harvard Center supports courses and projects that activate liberal learning to make a difference in the world. From oral history projects to pollution monitoring of the Androscoggin River to literacy research with local immigrants, some fifty percent of Bates students incorporate community work into their studies.

- **Community Volunteerism.** The center coordinates Bates' community volunteer programs. Led by a team of undergraduate Volunteer Fellows, the program enables Bates students to serve as school mentors or tutors, to work in senior centers or environmental conservation areas, even to plant community gardens and build ski trails. Each year, two thirds of the students on campus take part in volunteer services.
- **Environmental Stewardship.** Committed to environmental stewardship, the Harvard Center for Community Partnership oversees the Bates-Morse Mountain Conservation area, a six-hundred acre coastal preserve that protects rare salt marsh and dune beach ecologies for research and public use.

Degrees

Bachelor's degrees are fulfilled after completion of thirty-two courses and two Short Term units. A degree can be conferred after three years. This accelerated program requires completion of thirty courses and three Short Term units.

General Education Requirements

Bates College emphasizes a broad-based liberal arts education, encompassing the social sciences, humanities, mathematics, sciences, and the arts. There are no core courses required of all students; however, there is a structured menu of options allowing students to extend, focus, and connect areas of interest.

Students enroll in two General Education Concentrations (GECs) outside their major, exposing students to a variety of disciplines. A GEC is a group of four linked courses. A GEC may focus on one topic or area of inquiry, with courses coming from different disciplines, or a GEC may focus on a topic within a single department, program, or major. The faculty is developing an array of GECs. Some interdisciplinary examples being considered are: *Sound, Hearing and Music; Legal Studies; Coastal & Watershed Systems; Architectural Studies: Urbanism and Constructed Spaces; Diasporas; Evidence: Documentation & Reality; Indigenous Responses to Globalization;* and *Sports, Competition and Culture.*

Three goals serve the larger liberal arts objectives:

1. Teach every student how academic disciplines complement one another, providing a sophisticated perspective on how to pursue knowledge.
2. Teach every student to write correctly and persuasively.
3. Give students college-level instruction in the methods and findings of the sciences and in quantitative analysis.

Bates provides an environment that allows a student to achieve. I remember coming into my first year having little confidence about my writing ability. After one of the first writing assignments, my professor suggested that I make an appointment at the writing workshop. That experience was invaluable. We talked about my ideas and how I could change my paper to more clearly convey them. The instructor offered to read a second draft that afternoon. I returned a number of times during all of my four years. The assistance I received not only helped me get better grades in that class, but also gave me the organization and confidence to succeed in writing throughout my college career.

SOCIAL LIFE AND ACTIVITIES

Sports

While students are conscientious about their work, there are very few who don't have several extracurricular activities keeping them busy. Bates supports thirty varsity teams and twelve club sports teams. For many students, athletics are a very important part of the Bates experience. Two-thirds of the current student population participated in varsity and club sports. Bates' athletic teams compete in the New England Small College Athletic Conference (NESCAC). Without a doubt, the most intense rivalries are between Bates and Bowdoin and Colby, referred to as the BBC. One of the goals of every team is to become champs of this "mini-conference" for bragging rights of Maine.

In addition to these intercollegiate programs, Bates students can be found playing intramural sports all year long. Intramural sports are coed and include soccer, ice hockey, basketball, and softball. Intramurals are open to students of all abilities and are a great way to get away from the books for an hour. Although Bates athletics are competitive and successful, student athletes are constantly reminded that they are students first. Participation in athletics provides the student with a classroom in which the subject is character, leadership, tenacity, and teamwork. At Bates, academics and athletics are not separate entities, but are considered to be complementary to one another in a student's education and intellectual growth.

Clubs/Activity Groups

Bates also supports more than seventy activity groups on campus, including art, chess, choir, dance, drama, gay-lesbian-bisexual alliance, international, jazz band, newspaper, orchestra, political, radio and TV, religious, social, and student government. Students can also start a group. One example is the Bates Aviators Club, which was started by a student who came to Bates already experienced in piloting. Closely entwined with Bates' history is its debate society. Bates was the first American college to engage in international debate. It has produced such eminent Americans as statesman Edmund Muskie and civil rights pioneer Benjamin Mays.

One popular group is the Bates Outing Club. Founded in 1920, the second oldest only to that of Dartmouth, the Bates Outing Club sponsors outdoor activities almost every weekend and provides outdoor recreational equipment for students to use. The club sponsors student-run trips throughout the year including backpacking, skiing, snowshoeing, climbing, hiking, mountain biking, and kayaking.

Social Life

The social life at Bates is definitely "alive." Social activities are primarily on campus due to the fact that ninety percent of all students live on campus. Students can take study breaks at the Den or meet with classmates at the Ronj, an entirely student-run coffeehouse where students perform music and read poetry. Some like to play pool or Ping-Pong in Chase Hall. During the weekend, campus-wide parties, film club movies, and dance and theater productions give the students almost too many choices.

Bates activities and social events are open to all students. This is not only an administrative policy, but something that Bates students support and enforce. There are no fraternities or sororities at Bates, and all college-sponsored parties are open to anyone. Student groups sponsor parties every weekend and an occasional Wednesday night, and the college itself sponsors a number of social events. One of the biggest events is the annual President's Gala, to which the entire college community is invited, where big band orchestras and jazz bands perform. The Chase Hall Committee, a student-run activities group, does a great job of getting big-name bands to come and play on campus; past groups include Counting Crows, Trey Anastasio of Phish, eminent singer-songwriters Ellis Paul and Edie Carey, Guster, and perennial alt-favorites, Yo La Tengo.

Off-Campus Activities

Being in the metropolitan area of Lewiston-Auburn also provides students with a number of options. Several multi-screen cinemas, shopping malls, and restaurants, accessible by student-run shuttle vans throughout the weekend, give students an off-campus release when needed. Add in the fact that the Maine coastline, Portland's Old Port, and hiking and skiing are all less than an hour away, and one recognizes the opportunities students have to enrich their Bates experience.

Alcohol

The social scene at Bates in many ways revolves around alcohol, as at any other college. Bates students are expected to observe state liquor laws at college-sponsored parties. On-campus parties that serve alcohol employ outside caterers to effectively reduce underage drinking at Bates. On weekends the Den turns into a pub that serves great food and, for students who are twenty-one, fine beer. Off-campus bars are also a part of upperclass social life, the most popular being The Blue Goose, the Cage, The Midnight Blues Club and Muddy Waters Cafe. The Goose is well loved by Batesies for the low prices and great atmosphere, as well as for the foosball table.

Short Term

While this five-week session is a unique period of learning, it is also an opportunity for students to enjoy the spring and *socialize*. For seniors, Short Term offers a last chance to live it up before they are forced into the real world. Weekly barbecues on the quad, outdoor parties, intramural softball, picnics at nearby Range Pond or Popham Beach state parks, and the annual Outing Club-sponsored clambakes, give students plenty of opportunities to procrastinate.

FINANCIAL AID

In recent years, about forty percent of all first-year and continuing students received some form of financial aid. Although the Financial Aid Office has federal rules and guidelines to follow, it deals with families individually when putting together an aid package. In addition to aid through scholarships, which are need-based, students can take out loans and have the opportunity to hold part-time jobs on campus. Recently, average first-year packages, which include scholarships, loans, and work-study, totaled more than $27,545. Even if a student does not qualify for need-based aid, student loans and part-time work are available. Half of the student body works. On-campus jobs range from lifeguarding at the pool to driving the shuttle vans to the nearby mall. In my experience, even more students could work if they wanted to; there are always jobs at the student employment office.

Each semester I worked between five to eight hours per week as part of the work-study portion of my financial aid. During my first semester, I took a job cleaning glassware for the biology department and another job monitoring the entrance to one of the athletic facilities. I soon learned that there were some jobs that required less attention than others. While the glassware job was easy and offered a sometimes needed break from the books, the monitoring job demanded much less attention and during those three hours a week I could read or study while getting paid.

Other jobs have slow periods during which students can study. Thus, part-time work covers the weekly expenses during a semester, and rarely encroaches on the time needed for coursework.

GRADUATES

Mention Bates to older alumni, and there is a certain sparkle in their eyes when they talk to you. Bates is a special place with so much proud history and such bright promise. It has a special place in the hearts of its alumni, and being a fellow Batesie connotes a special bond, a bond of values and morals, a bond of shared memories of place and common interests that upon realization is priceless to its graduates.

Talking to Bates alumni about their college experiences reveals that over the years Bates has stayed the same in many ways. Even with the addition of modern dormitories and academic buildings, and of new majors and faculty, the impressions and impacts made on students over the years—more importantly, the values and the character of the students that the institution attracts—are remarkably similar. When fellow Bates alumni meet, there is an obvious passion and loyalty they feel toward the school. Perhaps the best physical example of this feeling is the commitment alumni show in the number of them who come back every fall for the Homecoming weekend, the number of admissions interviews that alumni conduct, or the number of graduates who stay and make Bates a part of their life as well as a career.

Bates alumni share a strong bond with one another, and the alumni network is similarly strong. From the regional clubs that keep Bates grads in touch, to the alumni who volunteer their time to help a student or recent grad explore their career, being a Batesie lasts well beyond commencement.

In my fourth year, the lacrosse team went on a winter break trip to North Carolina. After one of the two games that we played, we had a tailgate party with Bates alumni who were living in the area. I remember standing with the recent grads whom I knew and the alumni who brought their children to the game and realizing that, as happy as we were to have the support, they were equally happy to reconnect with Bates and talk to the students whether they were old friends or not.

Perhaps the beauty of the liberal arts degree is the vast possibility that lies ahead of its recipient. Graduates leave Bates on paths that lead all over the world, and use their education in all sorts of careers. Bates students are not "trained" for jobs, but are rather educated in how to think and how to educate themselves. From breakthrough research scientists to professional athletes, government officials to television personalities, musicians to founders of the civil rights movement, Bates grads share a belief in hard work to achieve their goals, and a sense of moral responsibility with which they enter the world.

For many, a Bates education is a motivating step to pursue further education. Bates students learn the liberal arts and gain a moral responsibility, but they also gain a passion for the process of learning. More than two-thirds of Bates graduates continue on to graduate school within five years of commencement. This high number reveals the quality of the students that Bates admits, as well as the education and inspiration that the college provides.

SUMMING UP

The college selection process can be difficult, there are many fine institutions. A person trying to make a decision based on academic reputation and "numbers" would be hard-pressed to differentiate between many of the schools in the "Most Competitive" category. Bates distinguishes itself with the characteristics many visitors cite: openness, warmth, inclusiveness, and respect for the members of its community. Throughout its history, Bates has been a role model for its peers in its policies and programs for students. From its beginning, Bates admitted students without regard to race, gender, religion, or nationality. Today, its admissions policies (SAT scores optional), study abroad programs, and service-learning program are all examples of Bates' values and leadership.

Bates is an environment in which students can excel. The small size, great facilities, and committed faculty provide students with resources on a par with large universities, yet support that can only be found in a small college. Fellow students at Bates are equally supportive.

While some might say that Bates's location is a drawback, there are many positives in being in Lewiston, Maine. In fact, many Bates students cite Bates's location as a major reason for choosing the school. Although not located in a major metropolitan area, Bates is urban enough so that students can easily get to many activities, stores, and businesses. For many, the absence of a large city is a positive. Maine has much to offer in the areas of outdoor activity and beautiful landscapes. Bates is within an easy drive of Portland, the coastline, and the ski slopes.

Another possible complaint about Bates is its small size. There are positives and drawbacks to both large and small schools that must be considered in the selection process. Even though Bates is considered small, it is very unlikely that a student could get to know everyone at the school and feel limited socially. On the contrary, the familiarity of a small school in many ways allows students to make more friendships than at a larger school. Even so, most Bates students study abroad or at some other college or university in the United States for at least a semester and get to experience the big school scene. The small size at Bates is hardly viewed as a drawback academically. No classes are taught by graduate students, and students find it very easy to build a relationship with their professor in even the largest classes.

So come on up to Bates, and see for yourself. Talk to the students on the Quad and observe a class. After a little while, you might get that gut feeling too, and realize that the academic excellence, warmth, and egalitarian values that can be seen in the Bates community are qualities reflected by you.

❏ *Christopher Byrne, B.S.*

Photo by Gary Gilbert

)	**Boston College** **Chestnut Hill, MA 02467** (617) 552-3100 / (800) 360-2522 Fax: 617-552-0798	**Enrollment**
&	E-mail: *ugadmis@bc.edu* Web site: *www.bc.edu/admission*	**Full-time** o women: 4,705 o men: 4,314

INTRODUCING BOSTON COLLEGE

Boston College's distinctive approach to undergraduate education can be best understood through the motto of the University: "Ever to Excel." For more than 135 years, Boston College has maintained a commitment to excellence through the experiences and opportunities it offers its students both inside and outside the classroom. "Men and Women in Service for Others" has long been a phrase used to describe the focus of a Jesuit education, and the influence of the Jesuit focus is evident in all aspects of the university. Academically, in addition to maintaining the highest standards for its faculty and its students, Boston College's curriculum is focused on helping its students develop a consciousness of their identities and their responsibilities in today's society. Socially, Boston College seeks to provide a diversity of opportunities for its students to discover their abilities and their calling, including dozens of clubs and organizations representing artistic, athletic, cultural, ethnic, religious, and political interests; professional internships; volunteer programs; international study; and leadership opportunities.

Boston College draws inspiration for its academic and societal mission from its distinctive religious tradition. As a Catholic and Jesuit university, it is rooted in a worldview that encounters God in all creation and through all human activity, especially in the search for truth in every discipline, in the desire to learn, and in the call to live justly together. In this spirit, Boston College regards the contribution of different religious traditions and value systems as essential to the fullness of its intellectual life and to the continuous development of its distinctive intellectual heritage. While highlighting its Jesuit and Catholic traditions and principles, Boston College recognizes the importance of a diverse student body, faculty, and staff, and maintains a firm commitment to academic freedom, as the university encourages a communal effort toward the pursuit of its mission.

Location

Boston College's main campus is located on the border between the city of Boston and the city of Newton, six miles from downtown Boston, in a village known as Chestnut Hill. BC's location is one of its most attractive features. Students enjoy having the ability to live and study on a quiet campus featuring green lawns and beautiful English Collegiate Gothic buildings, and at the same time, to have easy access to one of America's greatest cities. The Green Line of Boston's mass transit system, "the T," begins at the base of the main campus, and transports travelers to all parts of the city for only $1.70.

In addition to offering a plethora of opportunities for shopping, sightseeing, nightlife, professional sports, research, volunteering, internships, and employment, Boston is also America's largest college town. Boston College students often become acquainted with students from several of the neighboring universities, including Harvard, M.I.T., Tufts, Boston University, and Northeastern.

Boston College also features a Newton campus, located approximately one-and-a-half miles west of the Chestnut Hill campus. The Newton campus is the home of Boston College Law School, and also the home to more than 800 students in the freshman class. Shuttle buses travel between the two campuses several times each hour, providing for convenient access between them. Although undergraduate classes are always held on the main campus, freshmen living on the Newton campus enjoy the unique "freshman-only" community that the separate location affords them.

Size

In the fall of a recent year, 9,019 undergraduate students were enrolled at Boston College. However, the number studying on campus is somewhat smaller because many students choose to spend a semester studying abroad. Regardless, Boston College is best classified as a "medium-size" university. Although the student body is much larger than any student would have experienced in high school, the overall population is much smaller than that of most of America's leading universities. In addition, the large number of full-time faculty at Boston College allows class sizes to be kept small; the student-faculty ratio is 13:1.

ADMISSION REQUIREMENTS

Boston College features four undergraduate colleges: the College of Arts and Sciences, the Carroll School of Management, the Lynch School of Education, and the Connell School of Nursing. Although applicants do not have to declare a major when they apply, they must designate the school to which they are applying.

Students who apply to Boston College are usually those who have pursued challenging academic goals in high school; most have taken Advanced Placement classes, participated in numerous cocurricular and extracurricular activities, and have scored well on the SAT or ACT exams. Even among these students, Boston College is very selective. For the undergraduate class entering recently, more than 26,000 students applied for 2,250 places.

While specific courses in high school are not required, students are recommended to pursue a strong college preparatory program, which should include four years of English, mathematics, foreign language, laboratory science, and social studies. Students applying to the School of Nursing are *required* to complete at least two years of laboratory science, including one year of chemistry.

There are two standardized testing options. Students may either take the SAT test and two SAT Subject Tests; or, they may take the American College Test (ACT). Applicants must take all standardized tests by the December test date of their senior year of high school, and each applicant must have his or her test scores sent directly to Boston College. These scores must be received by December 15. For the class admitted to Boston College in a recent fall semester, the middle fifty percent of applicants scored between 1900 and 2100 (out of 2400) on the SAT, and/or between 27 and 31 on the ACT.

As mentioned before, the Boston College community reflects a diversity of talents, attitudes, backgrounds, and interests. Although diversity is sought in these areas, one common characteristic sought among applicants to Boston College is a demonstrated interest in the Jesuit ideals of commitment and service to others. Therefore, the Committee on Admission looks for applicants to demonstrate not only their academic abilities, but also their intellectual curiosity, strength of character, motivation, creativity, and devotion toward personal growth and development.

Freshman Applicants

To apply to Boston College, students must complete both the Common Application and the Boston College Supplemental Application. For students seeking to begin their academic career at BC in the fall semester, there are two admission pools: a nonbinding Early Action pool, and the regular admission pool.

Freshman applicants with superior academic credentials who view BC as a first choice should consider applying for Early Action; both admission forms, along with the $70 application fee, are due by November 1. Early Action candidates will be notified of their admission decision before December 25.

Forms and fees for the regular admission pool must be received by January 1. Candidates will be notified of their admission decision between April 11 and 15.

Students wishing to enter as freshman in the spring semester must submit all forms and fees by November 1.

Transfer Applicants

Boston College accepts transfer applicants each semester. Transfer candidates must also complete both the Common Application and the Boston College Supplemental Application. Students wishing to transfer into BC beginning in the spring semester must submit their application forms and the $70 fee by November 1; those students seeking to transfer into BC beginning in the fall semester must hand in the forms and fee by April 15. In addition to high school records and standardized test scores, transfer applicants must furnish transcripts from all postsecondary institutions they have attended.

The Core Curriculum

Perhaps the most distinguishing feature of a Jesuit undergraduate education is the core curriculum, a tradition that Boston College has embraced and defended since the school's founding in 1863. Rev. Timothy Brosnahan, S.J., who served as President of Boston College from 1894 to 1898, wrote the following in a statement justifying BC's reliance on common requirements for all of its students:

> *Education is understood by the Jesuit Fathers, in its completest sense, as the full and harmonious development of all those faculties that are distinctive of man. It is not, therefore, mere instruction or the communication of knowledge. In fact, the acquisition of knowledge, though it necessarily accompanies any right system of education, is a secondary result of education. Learning is an instrument of education, not its end. The end is culture, and mental and moral development. . . .*

Although the university has undergone many changes since Fr. Brosnahan's time, questions that have traditionally stood at the center of intellectual debate have remained salient. Many of these questions focus on issues such as the origin and destiny of existence, the principles of the physical world, the characteristics of human nature, the state of our society, and our attitudes toward the past. Because of the relevance of these questions to all academic pursuits, Boston College has retained its integrated core curriculum, allowing its students to examine all of these questions during their years at the university.

Because each academic discipline examines these questions from a unique perspective, the core requirements are dispersed among the university's many departments. All students are required to take a full year of theology, philosophy, natural science, social science, and modern European history. In addition, one semester of study is required in fine arts, cultural diversity, English literature, English composition, and mathematics. The College of Arts and Sciences and the Carroll School of Management also require each student to demonstrate proficiency in a foreign or classical language. As students proceed through the core, the above-mentioned questions are addressed in depth, with particular issues often revisited in several courses. Thus, the core experience challenges undergraduates to constantly formulate and reformulate their positions on the questions and issues that shape their lives as students, as professionals, and as human beings.

When talking with friends over a break during freshman year, we inevitably ended up discussing the classes we were taking. Some of them were surprised that BC's core curriculum involved so many areas of study. I remember one friend saying, "I'd rather just take classes in subjects that I'm interested in, and not have to be forced to take all that other stuff." At the time, I wasn't sure what to think—I had never taken classes in philosophy or theology before, and wasn't sure how they would compliment what it was that I thought I wanted to do. But looking back, I find that my interests (academically, professionally, and otherwise) have changed a great deal since I was a freshman in college. Had I filled my schedule with classes to prepare me for the career I sought when I was eighteen, I would have been quite disappointed when my path eventually changed course. But through the classes I took for the core, I was exposed to ideas that complimented all of the other classes I took in college, and in my grad school and law school coursework as well.

Faculty

One of Boston College's greatest assets is the quality of its faculty. Although BC prides itself on their research accomplishments, the professors, lecturers, and instructors at Boston College possess a common characteristic: all are devoted to the importance of their primary responsibility—teaching undergraduates. Unlike other research universities, at which many of the lower-division classes are taught by teaching assistants or part-time faculty, the bulk of the classes required in Boston College's core curriculum are taught by full professors. These faculty members are distinguished in their field, and most have decades of experience in undergraduate instruction.

In lower-division "survey" classes in the history, natural science, and social science departments, classes are taught by full professors in a lecture hall setting two days a week, and are then broken up into smaller discussion groups on a third day. This format allows for general information to be communicated *en masse*, but also gives students and faculty a weekly opportunity to discuss what has been presented and to relate the material to more specific topics. In other departments such as theology, philosophy, English, foreign languages, mathematics, and fine arts, classes are intentionally kept small to maximize the student's ability to comprehend and discuss the subject matter with students and faculty members alike.

As students move from the core requirements to their upper-division electives, they find that the class sizes become even smaller. Every semester, each department offers seminar classes in which a professor and small groups of students examine specific academic issues in detail; the departments also allow students to earn class credit for "Readings and Research" in a one-on-one project with a faculty member. A popular cocurricular employment opportunity offered by all four schools is the Undergraduate Faculty Research Fellowships, in which students can earn money as they assist faculty members with their research.

Course evaluations and surveys of graduating seniors demonstrate that Boston College students are quite satisfied with their professors; many have indicated that the student-faculty relationship at BC often transcends the classroom experience, as professors and students develop friendships that last well beyond the student's graduation.

Although BC boasts a beautiful campus and first-rate facilities, in my opinion, the school's greatest asset is its faculty. You can tell that the reason they are at BC is because they want to teach undergraduates. My sophomore year, I had a history professor who had a reputation as a very tough grader. After receiving a grade on a paper that was lower than I expected, I went to his office to ask him for advice. I didn't expect the meeting to last more than five minutes. He invited me into his office, and after discussing the paper for a minute or two, he began to ask me questions about my academic interests and the career path I was considering. At the time, I wasn't sure, and I told him so. His response was brilliant. He said, "Well, that's the reason you're here! One of the purposes of a liberal arts education is 'to liberate' you from the restrictions placed on your ability to learn about the world once you leave school and focus on a career. Use your time here to explore all that you can—you may not have many chances like this ever again." I took his advice, and outside of my major, I took classes on Shakespeare, American architecture, Beethoven, World War II, and other areas in which I had a curiosity. That professor and I became close friends, and are still in touch today. Not only did I get an A in his class, the advice he gave me about how to approach my college career was among the best I had ever received.

Academic Resources

Boston College students have access to a multitude of resources to assist them in their academic pursuits. The university's network of libraries features the Thomas P. O'Neill, Jr. research library, along with seven other libraries featuring art collections, rare books, and professional resources for education, social work, and law. These facilities also provide students with access to the Web and other on-line databases and applications, private small-group study rooms, and audiovisual equipment. Additionally, Boston College's Academic Development Center, located in the O'Neill Library, provides free tutoring to students in all subjects, along with specialized services for students with learning disabilities.

Boston College's Student Affairs division includes several offices that serve students seeking academic support. Included among these is the Learning Resources for Student Athletes office, and the Learning to Learn program, which helps students improve their critical thinking, and develop learning skills necessary to succeed in college.

Over the past fifteen years, the university has refurbished many buildings on campus to accommodate state-of-the-art classrooms, laboratories, computer facilities, and meeting rooms. These renovations are readily apparent as students undertake their coursework in the natural science departments of biology, chemistry, geology and geophysics, and physics, where laboratory facilities have been carefully designed to facilitate interaction between faculty members, researchers, and students. Students studying management, education, and nursing also reap the benefits of the recent construction, as the main buildings for the three professional schools have been given a face-lift in recent years, in an attempt to provide every Boston College student with a learning environment that complements the subject matter being taught.

Cable Television

Although often viewed as a resource for entertainment or communication, Boston College's cable television, telephone, and Internet network is also an important academic resource. At the beginning of each student's BC career, he or she is issued an e-mail address and a private telephone number with a voice mailbox, which remains the same until the student graduates. All dormitories are wired so that each resident student has his or her own hook-up for telephone, Ethernet, and cable television. All three of these are used by faculty and students alike. Professors and classmates share class distribution lists for e-mail and voice mail, allowing for mass transmittals of important class information. Faculty members and student groups utilize Boston College's own cable television channels to provide students with an opportunity to view movies, lectures, and other presentations on their own time. These resources were put in place in 1994, and continue to be developed and improved upon each year, demonstrating Boston College's commitment to providing its student body and its faculty with access to the latest innovations in communication technology.

SOCIAL LIFE AND ACTIVITIES

Student Groups

While Boston College students share much in common when it comes to dedication to academics and service, the diversity of the student body is most recognizable in the multitude of student clubs, musical groups, and organizations on campus. Not only is there diversity in the types of organizations, which include groups devoted to athletics, music, culture and ethnicity, religion, politics, dance, literature, charities, social action, and community service, but diversity is also found among the groups within each genre. For example, for musical ensembles, there are *a cappella* groups, jazz bands, gospel choirs and liturgical music groups, a symphony orchestra, a marching band, and the university chorale.

Many student groups have also been formed to assimilate students of a particular culture or ethnicity on campus; clubs exist for students whose heritage descends from Africa, Brazil, Cape Verde, the Caribbean, China, Cuba, Eastern Europe, Greece, Hong Kong, Indonesia, Italy, Japan, Latin America, Korea, the Philippines, Puerto Rico, South Asia, Southeast Asia, Thailand, and Vietnam. In addition to providing a sense of community for many students, these groups serve another important function at the university; they provide a form of "education outside the classroom" for both the students involved in them, and for the faculty, staff, and student body who experience the events sponsored by these organizations.

Athletics

No BC student can deny that varsity athletics—especially football, basketball, and hockey—have a profound effect on the culture of the university. Freshmen find this to be the case when they experience the first home football game on a Saturday afternoon in September. The campus erupts in maroon and gold, the marching band can be heard from the early hours of the morning, barbecued food can be smelled everywhere, and students, alumni, and fans from around New England and around the country descend onto campus to cheer on the Eagles.

Boston College's athletics programs serve many important functions at the university. For those who play sports, participation on these teams provides many students with opportunities to display their talents to a national audience, as all of BC's twenty-nine varsity teams compete at the NCAA Division I level. But even for those who cannot play on these teams, athletic events draw the campus community together, contributing to a spirit that is quite unique to Boston College. Among many other distinguishing characteristics, the presence of strong, major conference, Division I athletic teams, is yet another feature that allows Boston College to stand out among the other elite Catholic universities in the United States.

Recent success among many of BC's teams also plays a role in the popularity of athletics among Boston College students. In 2000, the Boston College men's ice hockey team won the national championship. In 2003, the football team played in the San Francisco Bowl, the men's and women's basketball teams were nationally ranked and earned berths in the NCAA tournament. In the past five years, BC's teams have won Big East conference regular season and playoff championships in men's basketball, women's basketball, women's field hockey, men's ice hockey, and women's softball. But at BC, excellence goes beyond the playing field, for Boston College maintains one of the highest graduation rates of any Division I university in the nation.

Many opportunities to participate in athletics are available for students who do not play varsity sports. Intramural and club leagues are sponsored by the university for more than thirty men's, women's, and coeducational sports. In Summer 2001, Boston College's main student athletics facility, the Flynn Recreation Complex, was given an $8 million face-lift, providing renovations to the pool, basketball and tennis courts, indoor track, weightlifting facilities, and locker rooms. Free weights are also available in the residence halls on the Chestnut Hill campus on the Newton campus.

Residence Life

Most students admitted to Boston College are offered three years of on-campus housing. The usual path followed is to live on campus for freshman, sophomore, and senior year, while spending junior year studying abroad or living off campus in a neighboring apartment.

There are many on-campus housing options at Boston College. Most freshmen live in traditional dormitories with one or two roommates in a single bedroom. These residence halls are located on the Newton campus and on Chestnut Hill campus. Most sophomores live in four-, six-, or eight-person suites, featuring two, three, or four two-person bedrooms, a common living room, and a kitchenette. Most seniors live in four- or six-person apartments, which have two or three bedrooms, as well as a full kitchen.

There are no fraternities or sororities at Boston College, a fact the vast majority of BC students are proud to announce. The freshman residence halls on both the Newton and Chestnut Hill campuses are arranged so that students not only feel as though they are part of a community in their dormitory, but also in their class. As students group together in suites and apartments as upperclassmen, socializing is moved to on-campus apartments, off-campus apartments, and into downtown Boston.

The most popular senior housing option is in the Modular Townhouses, better known as "the mods." Located near the football stadium, this community of seventy-eight two-story homes is often the center of Boston College's undergraduate social scene. Although only a small percentage of students get to live in a mod, all students have a common area in their suite or apartment in which they can host parties and gatherings.

Students living off campus experience college life from a different perspective. Although additional responsibilities are an inherent part of living off campus, most students also enjoy the additional freedoms and opportunities that living off campus allows. Because leases usually run for a full year, living off campus gives students a place to stay in the summer, an obvious benefit for students seeking jobs or internships in Boston during the summer before they graduate. Additionally, the large number of students living off campus adds another dimension to the Boston College social scene, providing an opportunity for students to get together away from school.

Students frequently ask about a student body's "diversity" when they are looking at schools. I've always found the term hard to define. The friends I made at BC came from all over the country. Some of their parents were business owners, some were teachers, some were in the military, some were farmers, and some were professionals. My friends were Catholic, Eastern Orthodox, Protestant, Mormon, Jewish, Hindu, and nonpracticing. Their ancestors were from North America, South America, Europe, the Middle East, Africa, and Asia. Some friends were more liberal, others more conservative; some politically active, and others not as involved. Today, my friends are doctors, teachers, lawyers, financiers, musicians, nurses, professors, students, college administrators, and computer programmers. This kind of diversity—in backgrounds, interests, beliefs, motivations, and aspirations—can't be appropriately expressed by a statistic. However, while there was no doubt that we were diverse in our differences, the best part of the BC student body was something we all had in common. The "typical BC student" is bright, well rounded, ambitious, and concerned, and spending four years with people with these kinds of common characteristics was what made BC a great place to learn and grow over the course of my college career.

Boston

Although Boston College is not located in the heart of downtown Boston, the ease with which students can access all that Boston has to offer makes the city a virtual extension of the campus. While events are always occurring on campus, the presence of a neighboring metropolis gives students opportunities to reach beyond the college environment. Boston's restaurants, concert halls, dance clubs, theaters, bars, and sporting events, are as much a part of the BC social scene as the campus-sponsored events.

Students interested in Boston College, but unfamiliar with the city of Boston, should be sure to visit the campus and the city. Unlike other big cities, many of which appear cold and unfriendly to the typical college student, Boston is "America's college town." Renowned for its history, its beauty in all four seasons, its diversity, and for its quality institutions of higher education, the city of Boston is a perfect complement to the history, beauty, diversity, and quality of education offered at Boston College.

FINANCIAL AID

BC is committed to admitting its students solely on the basis of their academic and personal accomplishments, and without regard to financial need. With the exception of the Presidential Scholars Program, which offers full-tuition four-year scholarships to fifteen incoming freshmen, all financial aid at Boston College is given on the basis of demonstrated need.

To demonstrate need, students and families must fill out the Free Application for Federal Student Aid (FAFSA) and the Profile form, published by the College Scholarship Service. Boston College also asks parents and students to provide the university with copies of their tax returns and W-2 forms. Because of the limited amount of financial aid available, it is important for parents and students to follow the instructions carefully, and to provide the university with the information requested by the specified deadlines.

Boston College has recently consolidated its offices of student financial aid, student accounts, bursar, and registrar into one department. This new division, now called the Office of Student Services, is prominently featured in the center of campus in completely redesigned facilities, providing students with quick and convenient access to answers for all of their financial and academic questions. Each student is assigned a counselor who works in the Office of Student Services, all of whom are willing to discuss specific cases with parents and students. Although the application process is structured and formal, the financial services counselors at BC take a personal approach to help students and families afford their education at Boston College.

GRADUATES

In 2000, Boston College's endowment surpassed the $1 billion mark for the first time. Much of the recent growth in the endowment can be attributed to the donations of many successful graduates who have given back to the school that gave so much to them.

As mentioned before, Boston College places a great deal of emphasis on service to others. For Boston College graduates, the theme of service is reflected in the career paths chosen by its graduates. In business, education, research, nursing, social work, politics, law, entertainment, or community service, Boston College graduates stand out as leaders in their fields.

The successes of Boston College alumni are beneficial, not only for the university, but also for current students looking for jobs and internships in the "real world." A common characteristic among BC graduates is a strong sense of loyalty to their alma mater. This loyalty is often expressed through the willingness of BC graduates to help current students, especially through job networking and career counseling.

SUMMING UP

Boston College stands out among its peers in American academe because of a distinctive approach to higher education. While upholding the standards of excellence that are expected of the nation's finest colleges and universities, Boston College's mission articulates another set of expectations for its faculty, staff, and students.

As Fr. Brosnahan wrote many years ago, "The acquisition of knowledge . . . is a secondary result of education." To the administrators, faculty, and staff at Boston College, the personal development of every member of the BC community is the primary result. Because of this belief, Boston College emphasizes its dedication to the philosophy of *cura personalis*, or "care for the whole person." This dedication is recognized through the university's commitment to employing a learned faculty devoted to teaching undergraduates; through the resources it makes available for education outside the classroom; through the academic, social, and recreational facilities it makes available to all members of its community; and through the holistic perspective it offers from its broad-based, spiritually focused, liberal arts curriculum.

Dedication to these goals, combined with the university's commitment to excellence in all aspects of its operation, has given Boston College recognition, not only as one of the nation's leading Catholic universities, but as one of America's finest providers of an undergraduate education.

o *Matthew J. Kita, A.B.*

Photo by Dean Abramson

Bowdoin College
Brunswick, ME 04011

(207) 725-3100
Fax: (207) 725-3101

E-mail: *admissions@bowdoin.edu*
Web site: *http://www.bowdoin.edu*

 Enrollment

Full-time ❑ women: 958
❑ men: 892

Part-time ❑ women: 5
❑ men: 3

INTRODUCING BOWDOIN

Bowdoin enjoys a reputation for academic prestige and rigor, but what truly distinguishes this small liberal arts college is its location in Maine. Just twenty-five miles up the coast from the comfortable city of Portland, Bowdoin's idyllic campus provides unique opportunities for an independent-minded student body. For more than 200 years, Bowdoin's world-class resources and tight-knit community have balanced tradition and innovation, a combination that continues to shape principled world leaders in every field.

Bowdoin is in the heart of Brunswick, a small town at the hub of several ocean peninsulas where retirees, fishermen, and pilots from the nearby naval air station make for an interesting milieu. Students and locals alike can take pride and enjoyment in the college's well-respected museums, frequent guest speakers, and outstanding hockey team. Bowdoin's dining service, recognized as one of the best in the country, puts on annual lobster bakes. Juniors and seniors can find great seaside cottages off campus, or choose from among a wide variety of housing options, which include dormitories with quads and singles, a sixteen-story tower of single-rooms, and college-owned houses and apartments. "The bricks" are the six mid-campus dorms that house all first-years and foster tremendous class unity. Fraternities were recently abolished in 2000, and Bowdoin has now acquired all of the houses; today these houses have been renovated, and make up the College House system, a unique social and residential opportunity.

Thanks to ambitious fund-raising in the nineties, there are also handsome new dining, library, and Outing Club facilities. President Barry Mills, himself a Bowdoin graduate, arrived in 2001 and has worked to expand and diversify the student body. In recent years, as at many other colleges, the activist spirit ebbed; now, with political turbulence at home and abroad, Bowdoin is reemerging as a place of intense political discourse.

In addition to the 200-acre campus—known for its beauty—the college owns 118 acres of forest, fields, and wetlands along the shore of the Atlantic just eight miles from campus. This site, on picturesque Orr's Island (a short bridge connects the mainland) features Bowdoin's Coastal Studies Center, for research in ecology, geology, ornithology, and marine biology.

Bowdoin prides itself on its excellent faculty and its cutting-edge information and technology resources. There is plenty here to guide a motivated student in his or her explorations. Likewise, this is a place of many extracurricular passions. Sports are a popular of college life here, but so are the Outing Club, the campus radio station, and a variety of volunteer programs.

Nevertheless, this is primarily a venue for intense academic rigor (though the cutthroat mentality is virtually unheard of here). Although Bowdoin students do play hard, the spirit of the college—evident in the admissions criteria, academic program, and alumni achievements—is independent thinking. Bowdoin students are encouraged to choose their own paths, and that freedom of choice generates true intellectual growth.

ADMISSIONS REQUIREMENTS

Gaining admission to Bowdoin gets harder each year. In 2006, Bowdoin accepted 1,167 of 5,401 applicants. That's less than twenty-two percent. Of those accepted, 483 matriculated—a full forty of them high school valedictorians. Since 1969 Bowdoin has made it optional to submit one's SAT scores, although most accepted students do, and the average score of that group is pretty high.

Bowdoin's admissions committee reviews grades, a personal essay, awards and honors, extracurricular activities and accomplishments, and teacher recommendations. Of special interest to the committee is a demonstrated willingness to seek out intellectual challenges in Advanced Placement and Honors courses. Interviews, while not required, are strongly encouraged, and can be arranged during a campus visit or in one's hometown with an alumni interviewer. If supplementary materials such as musical tapes or works of art help to flesh out one's basic application, then the committee encourages the applicant to submit these.

MATRICULATION BOOK

During the first week on campus, every new Bowdoin student signs the Matriculation Book. The book itself is laid out in the president's office on the desk of Henry Wadsworth Longfellow (class of 1825). Each new student meets the president before signing his or her own name. There is also a little bit of time to peruse past volumes, which are arrayed around the room, opened to the signatures of Hawthorne (1825) and former Secretary of Defense William Cohen (1962), themselves once fresh-faced and eager new students.

The entire admitted class begins in the fall, and generally includes only a very small handful of students who have transferred from other institutions. Some will have spent a day and night on campus the year before in order to sample the classes, the social scene, and the famously good food. Many will be international students, actively recruited by the college.

Early Decision

In addition to the Regular Decision program, there are two Early Decision programs at Bowdoin. The first requires that application materials be postmarked by November 15, and an applicant will receive notification a month later in mid-December. The second program has the same deadline as Regular Decision (January 1), but those applying under this program receive notification by mid-February. Both Early Decision programs are binding, and ask for one's signature to ensure that one enrolls at Bowdoin if admitted.

ACADEMIC LIFE

"To carry the keys of the world's library in your pocket, and feel its resources behind you in whatever task you undertake" is part of *The Offer of the College*, a sort of proto-Mission Statement, ubiquitous within the community ever since a former Bowdoin president penned it a century ago. Bowdoin remains true to this liberal arts ethos, with an academic program designed to broaden the range of the intellect rather than stuff it with facts.

Of the total, students must take one course on mathematical, computational, or statistical reasoning; one course on inquiry in the natural sciences; one course on "exploring social differences;" one course on "international perspectives;" and one course in the visual and performing arts. Courses are designed to help students hone their written and analytical skills, deepen their aesthetic judgments, use varied forms of informational resources, and create multifaceted solutions to complex problems.

ADMIRAL PEARY

Admiral Robert E. Peary made explorations of the Arctic, and found the North Pole. He and his assistant, Admiral Donald B. MacMillan, were Bowdoin graduates, (class of 1877 and 1898, respectively). Hence, the school mascot is the Polar Bear. The campus is home to the Peary-MacMillan Arctic Museum. Perhaps these reasons, plus Bowdoin's northern location, explain why Arctic Studies is stronger here. Students have approached that field from angles of environmental science, geology, and anthropology.

In addition, students are required to take one first-year seminar by the end of their second semester. These seminars provide an opportunity for students to take a small, seminar-style class about a topic of interest that is also directed toward building students' writing, critical reading, research, and analytic skills. The courses range widely; a few examples include: *Mass Media in American Politics; Seekers' Live; Dreaming in the Middle Ages; Non-Violence, Nukes and Nationalism.*

Students are allowed to direct their own studies, taking classes in many different fields outside their major. Pursuing two majors is not all uncommon. Requirements for the major vary, but eight to ten courses is a rough standard.

Of the forty-two majors and forty minors available at Bowdoin, the most statistically popular are government, English, and biology. Most students would agree that the film students, artists, and economics majors are discernable groups, and that there are some beloved professors in the Africana Studies and religion departments. Recent changes in the academic structure include the creation of two new programs: Latin American Studies and Gay and Lesbian Studies. New interdisciplinary majors have sprung up (English and Theater is just one), and for a small college in Maine, there are particularly strong departments of Asian studies, neuroscience, and computer science (some interesting work with robots and artificial intelligence here has caught international attention).

Several years ago the campus theater underwent renovation, and is now a vibrant center for theater and dance on campus, as well as a big draw for the Brunswick community. In

> *I used the pass/fail option only once, in my first semester, because I wanted to try some unfamiliar subjects before I got too serious. I did have a friend who used it junior year, in a fifth class he took by special arrangement with the dean. This meant that in the spring of our senior year he had to take only three classes, which allowed him to spend the extra free time making trips up to ski at Sunday River, which was about ninety minutes away. I had an AP credit, so I also had just three classes; I joined my friend a few times, but mostly used that extra time working on finishing my honors project.*

2007, the college's landmark Walker Arts Building will reopen after a two-year, $20 million renovation. The building is the home of the Bowdoin Museum of Art, a teaching museum with a collection of more than 14,000 objects. It is one of the oldest collegiate art collections in the United States with works from the ancient world to the present. Also in 2007, Bowdoin will open a new 290-seat state-of-the-art recital hall. And in the 1990s a donation by Stanley Druckenmiller (class of 1975) made possible a new, state-of-the-art science building that is successful both as a research center and as an architectural triumph.

Along with introductory-level courses (average size of 30), freshmen (known as "first years" at Bowdoin) may end up taking the regular course offerings that are the bread-and-butter of upperclassmen. These classes have an average size of sixteen. Toward the end of the Bowdoin experience, most students are back in senior seminars—the small, upper-level classes designed primarily for majors. Students are permitted to take up to four classes on a "credit/fail" basis, which allows for a greater opportunity for pressure-free academic exploration.

Independent Study and Honors Projects

Independent study is very popular at Bowdoin, chiefly owing to the motivation of the students and accessibility of the professors. Such projects allow the student (typically a junior or senior, but not always) to choose a topic, set specific goals and schedules, and work closely with a professor. An independent study usually replaces one of the four classes the student would normally take, and works like a class credit toward graduation and, if applicable, the major.

RECENT INDEPENDENT STUDY

○ Economics: "Patterns of Land Use, and Land Values, in Three Atlantic Coastal Regions"

○ English: "The New Journalism: True-Crime Novels of Norman Mailer and Truman Capote"

○ Sociology: "HIV/AIDS and Poverty in South Africa"

○ Chemistry: "Gas-Phase Hydrolysis Reactions of Ester of Methyl-Substituted Glutarates: Effect of an Alpha Methyl Group."

○ History: "Representations of Race in American Professional Baseball"

○ Biology: "Effects of Fetal Alcohol Syndrome on Cell Death and Cell Death Gene Expression in the Developing Brain."

○ Russian: "Existentialism, Social Realism, and Formalism in the Novels of Chernyshevsky, Turgenev, and Dostoevsky."

○ Coastal Studies: "Burial Depth of the Soft-Shell Clam, *mya arenaria*, in Response to Food Availability and Chemical Cues from the Green Crab *carcinus maenas*: a Behavioral Response to Confliction Needs."

Many projects begin as an extension of work that a student and professor explored earlier—or had to pass up—in a traditional classroom course. Sometimes students with similar interests will band together, find a professor, and use the independent study model to create what is for all intents and purposes a private class. Popular professors have been known to direct three or four projects in one semester, in addition to their classroom duties.

Some independent studies evolve into Honors Projects. This last feature of the curriculum, however, is much more involved than an independent study; a typical Honors Project spans two semesters, involves periodic oral defenses before the academic department, and may culminate in the publication of scientific data or a hundred-page paper. An Honors Project is always a solitary endeavor, and each department at Bowdoin encourages only the most motivated (i.e., graduate school-oriented) students to pursue such a project.

Independent studies and Honors Projects are among the most attractive features of Bowdoin College. It is rare, even at the highest academic levels, for students to enjoy such unfettered access to world-class faculty. Such close-quarter interaction is why intellectuals are drawn to small, elite colleges such as Bowdoin, and it is why they leave equipped with superior critical-thinking skills and broad knowledge of cultural, historical, and scientific fields.

Off-campus Study

Many Bowdoin students (about sixty percent) study off campus, usually abroad, for a semester or two of their junior year. Bowdoin sponsors a well-respected program known as the Intercollegiate Sri Lanka Education. Students participate in more than one hundred additional approved study-abroad programs.

Students less exotically inclined may also choose to study for a year at one of the schools in the Twelve College Exchange: Amherst, Connecticut, Dartmouth, Mount Holyoke, Smith, Trinity, Vassar, Wellesley, Wesleyan, Wheaton, and Williams.

Other possibilities, for students who want both a large university's resources as well as the liberal arts milieu, are the 3-2 engineering degree programs with Columbia and the California Institute of Technology or the 3-2 law program with Columbia.

Writing at Bowdoin

Naturally there is plenty of ambient literary energy at the school that produced Hawthorne and Longfellow, as well as hip, younger writers such as Jason Brown and Willing Davidson.

The Writing Project is a tutoring program in which students recognized for excellent writing serve as editors for their peers. These students are there to receive first drafts of papers and return them, prior to the due date, with nonjudgmental advice for revision.

SCIENCE BUILDINGS

Alongside a strong literary tradition, Bowdoin is also home to cutting-edge science. In the late nineties, Stanley Druckenmiller ('75) donated tens of millions for the renovation of Bowdoin's science buildings. Among the state-of-the-art research tools available there is a confocal laser-scanning microscope, made available in 2003 through a National Science Foundation grant. Bowdoin professors are leading scientific authorities on robotics and oil-spill cleanups, and places such as Caltech and Harvard Medical School always boast a handful of Bowdoin alums.

In addition to Hawthorne and Longfellow, another icon of eighteenth-century American literature has roots at Bowdoin. Harriet Beecher Stowe wrote *Uncle Tom's Cabin* here in Brunswick (her husband was a Bowdoin professor). The book, which stirred the North's condemnation of institutional slavery, can be said to have done as much to have precipitated the war as another Bowdoin graduate did to end it; Joshua Chamberlain, class of 1852, accepted the Confederate surrender at Appomattox. Long famous among Civil War buffs as one of the only unambiguous heroes of the conflict, Chamberlain's bayonet defense of Little Round Top was popularly dramatized in *The Killer Angels*. The novel, by Michael Shaara, was the basis of the movie *Gettysburg*, in which Jeff Daniels, playing Chamberlain, gets big cheers around Brunswick when he mentions Bowdoin College.

The *Bowdoin Orient*, the student newspaper, enjoys the distinction of being the oldest continuously published campus weekly in the country; *The Quill* is a student-run literary magazine; and the *Bowdoin Forum*, initiated in the late nineties, is an annual compilation of essays by students, faculty, alumni, and staff, and its primary focus is an analysis of international events. Several underground newspapers have come and gone, and the conservative *Bowdoin Patriot* has recently reemerged as a counterweight to what it calls Bowdoin's generally liberal tendencies.

In addition to all of these outlets, the English department continues to be recognized as first-rate. Scholars such as Pete Coviello, Ann Kibbie, Anthony Walton, are outstanding in their fields, and the Pulitzer-Prize-winning novelist Richard Ford was recently signed on to teach a semester's creative-writing course here.

SOCIAL LIFE AND ACTIVITIES

All kinds of off-campus activities are available within a short distance of the campus. Bowdoin is a short walk from downtown Brunswick, where students' favorite stops are two Indian restaurants, a small music store, a popular bar called Joshua's, and a small movie theater filled with sofas and featuring indie films. A ten-screen cinema is a few miles from campus.

The Outing Club arranges canoe trips, hiking, skiing, biking, and other outdoor activities. Many incoming students participate in preorientation trips that last three or four days, at which time new students bond with their classmates and enjoy Maine's woods and water.

All students at Bowdoin are allowed to have a car on campus, although first-years are last in the parking-sticker pecking order. Those students who do bring cars to Bowdoin frequently find themselves leading trips to Freeport, just fifteen minutes down a country road. There students find a wide array of outlet shops, but the main draw is L.L. Bean, legendary for its gadgets, indoor fish pond, and for operating twenty-four hours—the midnight trip to Bean's is an age-old finals-week tradition.

On campus, the Smith Union is undeniably the hub of campus life. Here are the campus post office and bookstore, a café, and a three-story pub (bring ID). The building itself is an architectural masterpiece (former college president Robert H. Edwards (1990–2001) called its early-nineties renovation one of the highlights of his tenure), with a spacious central lounge filled with couches and sofas. Guest speakers are frequent here, as are musical performers and petition drives. Encircling this lounge is a ramp that takes students past art exhibits, the campus bookstore, a game room, and meeting rooms. Smith Union is where Bowdoin feels smallest, and many students go there simply to socialize, since the whole student body seems to cycle through continuously.

Athletics

Bowdoin is passionate about athletics. One of the most striking aspects of the college culture, according to visitors, is how many students participate in intercollegiate and intramural sports. The school's gyms see a lot of daily use too; many men and women jog and lift weights.

There are thirty varsity intercollegiate sports teams here; thirty-five percent of students participate. There are brand-new squash facilities, a new astroturf field, a boathouse, and indoor and outdoor tracks. Diving, swimming, and water polo teams share a sixteen-lane swimming pool. Cross-country and squash are dominant in their competitions. The ski team is Division I, but the hockey team, which plays in the quaint shabbiness of Dayton Arena (slated to be replaced by a new arena in 2008), is central to Bowdoin pride. Many Bowdoin graduates cherish the memory of crowding into Dayton on grim winter nights and joining in ribald cheers with a crowd of students and local Mainers alike. The Colby-Bowdoin matchup is not to be missed.

Club sports like crew and rugby are also popular, and intramural competition (usually dorm vs. dorm) is common on Bowdoin's thirty-five acres of fields. Bowdoin is not a "jock" school, but it's fair to say that there aren't many idle bodies here.

I lived off campus my senior year, in an old hunting lodge that had been rented to Bowdoin seniors since the seventies. We were on our own island, attached to the mainland by a causeway that flooded and stranded us only once or twice a month. We paid $1,500 a month, among six of us, which was a little bit more than what seniors paid on campus, but which was totally worth it. We got solitude and social autonomy and a great venue for some unforgettable parties. We made sure to pass the lease off to kids we knew so that we could come visit after graduating.

The Social Scene

When Bowdoin phased out the fraternity system in 2000, the change turned the college social scene and housing situation upside down (over a third of the student body had been involved with the system, which was coeducational by the end). The college acquired most of the vacated houses, did extensive renovations, and turned them into the nonexclusive College House System, which provides students with many of the benefits of the old fraternity system, such as leadership opportunities, party venues, self-governed houses, and links with students of all four classes.

Now, from the day students set foot on the campus, they are affiliated with one of the "Social Houses"; each House is paired with one of the first-year dorms. First-years use the house as a gathering place, and have the option to live there over the next three years.

Although parties no longer revolve around fraternities, beer remains a staple of the Bowdoin social landscape, both at the Social Houses and several off-campus residences. Drugs are uncommon at Bowdoin, in comparison to many colleges. A popular student bowling league rounds out the party scene.

Living on the Water

Aside from the first-year dorms and the College Houses, Bowdoin has a broad spectrum of housing opportunities. Every spring a lottery system, complicated but fair, determines where students will live. Many sophomores end up in apartments in self-selected

> *I made a lot of money one summer working on a lobster boat. I was a sternsman (all lobstering vessels have a captain and a sternsman) and I hauled up traps, checked them, and baited them. I woke up according to the tides, and I perpetually reeked of rotten fish bait, but it was an incredible experience; I ate a lot of seafood, got to be around Brunswick through a summer, and made a pile of money. I also got to see the coast of Maine from a native's perspective; this is something that you sometimes miss when you're wrapped up in campus life, which gets pretty insular.*

groups of three and four. Most of the students living in the sixteen-story Coles Tower (there are four suites per floor, with four rooms in each) are juniors. Seniors often live in one of two clusters of condominium-like apartments, located beside the athletic fields, and nestled in the pines.

Students are also encouraged to explore off-campus housing opportunities. There are literally hundreds of seaside cottages within twenty minutes of the campus, and many of these are owned by retirees who spend only the summer in Maine. That means relatively low rent and a once-in-a-lifetime opportunity to live on the coast. A handful of coveted leases are handed down perennially between Bowdoin students, but a little searching is generally rewarded.

FINANCIAL AID

The college is committed to making a Bowdoin education available to students regardless of their financial situation. Financial aid at Bowdoin is *need-based*, which is to say that award packages are not dispensed according to academic or athletic merit. These packages include some combination of grants, loans, and student employment.

For the class of 2010, for example, forty-one percent of all Bowdoin first-years received need-based scholarship aid. The average first-year award for that year was $30,525. The average portion that was in the form of a grant was $26,395, the average loan portion was $2,650, and the average work contract was for $1,480.

- ○ Franklin Pierce, President of the United States
- ○ Nathaniel Hawthorne, Novelist
- ○ Henry Wadsworth Longfellow, Poet and Linguist
- ○ Major General Oliver Otis Howard, Union Army Officer and Founder and President of Howard University
- ○ Brigadier General Joshua Lawrence Chamberlain, Savior of the Union and Governor of Maine
- ○ Admiral Robert E. Peary, First Man to Reach the North Pole
- ○ Harold Burton, Chief Justice of the U.S. Supreme Court
- ○ Alfred Kinsey, Author of Seminal Works of Sexual Psychology
- ○ William S. Cohen, Secretary of Defense in the Clinton Administration
- ○ George Mitchell, Diplomat and Former Senate Majority Leader
- ○ Joan Benoit Samuelson, Gold Medal Winner in the First Women's Olympic Marathon
- ○ Kenneth Chenault, Chairman and CEO, American Express
- ○ Cynthia McFadden, Co-Host, ABC News Nightline
- ○ Reed Hastings, Founder and CEO, Netflix

The amount of financial aid given to each individual student is dependent on the financial situation of the student's family. Need is determined by an evaluation of financial-resource statements that the applicant submits to the Student Aid Office, and decisions are made annually on an individual basis. Financial aid extends to the semesters during which a student recipient studies off campus (in the United States or abroad). Furthermore, the college is able to offer some scholarships for postgraduate study at other institutions.

Some sixty percent of Bowdoin students work in part-time jobs on campus. Clerical work in an academic department, shelving books in the library, and driving the campus shuttle are some examples. There are plentiful off-campus jobs too.

The deadline for financial aid applications is February 15.

GRADUATES

Bowdoin conferred 424 bachelor degrees in 2006. Most students stay on a pretty regular course through the school (eighty-three percent graduate in four years, and ninety percent in five). In one recent class, eighty-two percent of graduates responding had either enrolled in graduate school or found employment in their field.

So it can safely be said that in addition to intangible rewards, the Bowdoin degree opens a lot of doors in the academic and professional world; the small class size means that Bowdoin's reputable professors are able to offer warm recommendations for their departing students.

The Career Planning Center

The Career Planning Center offers a wealth of resources for job searches, graduate school applications, and underclassmen seeking summer internships. The staff helps Bowdoin students refine their résumés and interviewing skills. One-on-one interview training with alumni, which might include videotape posture analysis, is also available. The Center indexes research on thousands of internships across the country. Even for students without specific ambitions there are workshops to help make important postgraduate decisions. The CPC publicizes the visits of recruiters and hosts review test-prep courses for the GRE, LSAT, and MCAT. At the Center, alumni offer job counseling, networking, and informational interviews. Even after graduation, alumni can still use the Career Planning Center resources, such as a newsletter with job postings and contacts within the alumni network.

SUMMING UP

Every other Friday at noon, the Bowdoin community convenes to hear a faculty member or guest speaker deliver a talk. The question-and-answer period that follows is often animated and memorable. Recent speakers have included Robert Reich, Doris Kearns Goodwin, George Will, Judy Fortin, Salman Rushdie, Paul Rusesabagina, Robert F. Kennedy, Jr., and Bill Bradley. This "Common Hour" is emblematic of the ideal for which Bowdoin has strived for over two centuries: a place where a variety of people can engage each other directly in intellectual exploration.

Bowdoin College is the perfect choice for young men and women who want more from an education than simply grabbing a credential and moving on. Working much more closely with their professors and peers than most of their Ivy League counterparts get to do, Bowdoin students learn to develop and explore previously untapped academic, cultural, political, and artistic interests that they retain for the rest of their lives. Bowdoin students also can enjoy pinetrees, snowstorms, and quick jaunts to the craggy shoreline, while staying connected to the world at large.

A "first-year" who enters Bowdoin today will find a school with strong traditions such as lobster bakes and hockey. That same student will also find that the abolition of fraternities has left the student body with a unique opportunity to determine the shape of the school's social scene and residential plan.

Students who benefit the most from Bowdoin are those who seek out new challenges and opportunities, who are willing to take risks, and who take pride in achieving their goals. The student community is competitive but the cutthroat careerism of some of the larger schools of this academic caliber is unheard of at Bowdoin. Students at Bowdoin know how to relax, look around, and appreciate the gifts of place and community.

After more than two centuries of shaping the world's leaders in business, diplomacy, education, social activism, medicine, and law, the school has perfected the craft of offering a rigorous, broadening curriculum to students from diverse backgrounds. Bowdoin graduates walk away with something special.

❏ *Nathaniel Vinton, A.B.*

BRANDEIS UNIVERSITY

Mike Lovett

✉ **Brandeis University**
Waltham, MA 02454

☎ (781) 736-3500
Fax: (781) 736-3536

Enrollment

Full-time ❑ women: 1,838
❑ men: 1,442

Part-time ❑ women: 18
❑ men: 6

INTRODUCING BRANDEIS UNIVERSITY

Founded in 1948, Brandeis is one of the youngest top-tier universities in the nation that is rated most competitive. In this respect and others, Brandeis has achieved in decades what other universities have taken centuries to accomplish. The university is named for the late Louis Brandeis, the first Jewish associate justice of the United States Supreme Court, and reflects the ideals of academic excellence and social justice he personified. These principles continue to shape every aspect of the university's character.

- 235 acres
- 99 buildings
- One castle
- Commuter train stop on campus connects with public transit in Boston and Cambridge
- Free weekend shuttle bus takes students to various points in Boston

One of the many reasons Brandeis has rapidly risen through the ranks is because its founders, including Albert Einstein, modeled it after the best of three centuries worth of American colleges and universities. It balances the feel of a small liberal arts college with the resources and faculty of a major research university. As a result, Brandeis students not only have remarkable faculty, but they actually have the opportunity to create personal and close working relationships with them, something few other colleges can offer to the same degree.

STUDENT POPULATION/LOCATION

- Located in Waltham, Massachusetts, nine miles west of Boston
- One of fifty colleges and universities within fifty miles of Boston
- Brandeis's athletic complex is one of the largest concert venues in the Boston Area
- 3,200 undergraduate students
- 1,800 graduate students
- Students from all fifty states and one-hundred and one foreign countries
- Seventy-five percent of undergraduates from outside Massachusetts
- Twenty percent of undergraduates are American students of color
- Seven percent of undergraduates are international students

This balance between a small liberal arts college and large research university is reflected again in both Brandeis's student population and its location. The Brandeis paths are filled with familiar smiles, but the undergraduate population is big enough to meet new people daily. While the community is fairly small, every state and over one hundred countries are represented at Brandeis. Since more than eighty percent of students live on campus, there is extraordinary exposure to a wide variety of different cultures, backgrounds, and perspectives. The campus is surrounded by the safe streets and great restaurants of Waltham, Massachusetts, but with easy access to Boston, including free shuttles and a train stop adjacent to campus, giving students the best of the big city as well.

No description of Brandeis would be complete without paying homage to the rich activist history and to the student body's dedication to social justice. Brandeis was a frequent destination of Martin Luther King Jr and others during the civil rights movement because of its activism. Brandeis students led the National Student Strike to protest American Foreign Policy during the Vietnam War. The history of Brandeis is filled with passionate students advocating change. The traditions of social activism and social services continues today.

Brandeis students work hard and play hard. While Brandeis has been able to rise through the ranks with the highest of academic standards, extracurricular activities, athletics, and parties have a presence on campus that can entangle even the strongest of wills. One factor that distinguishes extracurricular life at Brandeis from many other schools is that while nearly every conceivable interest is available on campus, students can be actively involved in multiple activities, not just one: A student can be an editor of *The Justice,* the independent student newspaper, play soccer with the Brandeis Football Club, and be a class senator, all at the same time. If you matriculate to Brandeis, regardless of your major you will attend at least one Pachanga—a clublike party put on by the International club that frequently attracts well over a third of the student body—see the statue of Louis Brandeis transmogrified into a variety of different characters such as a giant chicken or WWF wrestler during your stay, and sled down a snowy hill on a cafeteria tray in the dead of winter.

The founders of Brandeis succeeded in creating a university modeled after the best parts of other universities. Strong academics, a commitment to social activism, a robust student life, and a great community all contribute to the wonderful experiences and bountiful opportunities Brandeis offers. While other universities have multiple-century head starts, Brandeis continues to rise because of the quality of the experience.

LIBRARIES

- 1,090,000 print volumes
- 885,000 microform resources
- 385,000 government documents
- 30,000 audio recordings
- 6,000 print journal subscriptions
- 1,000 electronic journals and resources
- Annual Circulation 250,000
- Total seating: 800
- Computer Clusters: 5
- 100+ PCs and Macintosh computers with printers for student use
- Networked data jacks for laptop users

ADMISSIONS REQUIREMENTS

The Brandeis admissions process is designed to attract exceptional students with a broad range of interests and backgrounds. Brandeis looks for accomplished students who possess special talent or individuals who have used their resources well. Brandeis seeks students who are best prepared to embrace the university's academic rigors and contribute to campus life in diverse ways.

Qualified candidates tend to take the most challenging courses their secondary schools offer. The Admissions Office looks closely at involvement with Advanced Placement and Honors classes. The admission committee carefully considers recommendations from professors, headmasters, or other mentors. They are also interested in applicants' extracurricular involvement and/or volunteer work.

Admission into Brandeis is very competitive. Approximately ninety-three percent of Brandeis matriculants are from the upper quintile of their high school class and the median SAT score is 1367 (based on 1600). In a recent year, Brandeis had approximately 7,600 applicants and each undergraduate class is comprised of only 700–750 students. If Brandeis is your unwavering first choice you will find yourself in good company upon arrival. Last year, approximately twenty percent of the incoming students were accepted Early Decision.

The Office of Admissions

The members of the Admissions staff at Brandeis are very friendly and helpful. They know applying to college can be stressful, so they do what they can to make it as "applicant-friendly" as it can be. Tours are offered year-round and are given by student volunteers who try to give prospective students and their families a feel for life on campus. Visitors can sit in on classes and can stay overnight with student hosts. The university also hosts a yearly Open House that exhibits a sample of life at Brandeis through discussion panels with professors, a mini club fair, and presentations on what prospective students might expect.

The Application

The application attempts to glean the most information it can from applicants while steering clear of unnecessary forms or requirements. Brandeis accepts the Common Application on-line and in hard copy.

The university pays close attention to the secondary school record and, in general, recommends a course of study that includes the following:

- Four years of English
- Three years of foreign language (including, whenever possible, study in your senior year)
- Three years of college preparatory mathematics (prospective science concentrators should study mathematics for four years)
- A minimum of one year of science
- A minimum of one year of history

Aside from a student's academic record, Brandeis requires the following four components from students who are applying:

1. SAT and two SAT Subject tests OR the ACT
2. An essay
3. Two letters of recommendation
4. An interview (recommended)

Academic records and standardized test scores should be taken seriously because they are an important tool for admission; however, Brandeis is looking for students who have more depth than these numbers alone might communicate. Recommendations and the personal statement are important windows for the Admissions Office into the character of applicants. A strong recommendation and well-written personal statement will add depth to your application and, in turn, the Admissions Office's understanding of you.

Brandeis encourages but does not require a personal interview with a member of the admissions staff. Meeting with an admissions officer gives applicants a chance to learn more about specific opportunities of personal interest at Brandeis. At the same time, the interview lets an admissions officer get to know an applicant better by giving applicants an opportunity, through informal conversation, to communicate aspects of themselves that may not have an appropriate outlet in the written forms and school transcripts. If an on-campus interview is not possible, applicants can arrange to meet with an alumni admissions counselor. Alumni conduct interviews on campus and in cities throughout the world, and communicate their impressions to the Brandeis Admissions Office.

Finally, Brandeis has a need-blind admissions policy. This means that applying for financial aid does not influence Brandeis's decision regarding a domestic student's admission to the university during the Early Decision and Regular Decision admissions cycle. The Brandeis Office of Admissions reaches its decision, then notifies the Office of Financial Aid if the student has been admitted. Even Brandeis's admission policies reflect the philosophies its founders set forth. The university is committed to bringing together a student body that embodies excellence, social activism, inclusiveness, and a reverence for learning regardless of financial background.

FACULTY/CLASS SIZE

- 352 full-time faculty
- Ninety-six percent of full-time faculty hold a Ph.D. or the highest degree in their field
- Forty-one percent of faculty are women
- Twenty-four fellows of the American Academy of Arts and Sciences (thirteen emeriti)
- Nine members of the National Academy of Sciences (five emeriti)
- Three members of the Institute of Medicine, National Academy of Sciences
- Twenty-two fellows of the American Association for the Advancement of Science (fourteen emeriti)
- Five Howard Hughes Medical Investigators
- Three MacArthur Fellows
- Student-to-faculty ratio: 8 to 1
- Two thirds of all courses at Brandeis enroll nineteen or fewer students; median class size is seventeen

Academic life is one of the aspects of Brandeis that make it really shine in comparison to other top-rated colleges and universities. Brandeis attracts the most prestigious professors because of the attractiveness of its resources as a research institution. In a major study of higher education, "The Rise of American Research Universities" by Graham and Diamond, Brandeis was named the number one rising research university in the nation. When normalized for size, the Brandeis faculty rank number two out of the 3,000 colleges in the United States in the percentage of faculty who are members of the top three scholarly societies in America, namely the Academy of Science, the American Academy of Arts and Sciences, and the American Association for the Advancement of Science. However, prestigious faculty are not the only factors in making Brandeis stand out: The intimate learning environment that students share with their accomplished professors is exceptional. Other universities may have prestigious faculty, and other liberal arts colleges may have small classes, but having top professors in a small classroom is a rare luxury.

The one-on-one experiences with professors are really what makes the Brandeis experience special. I was able to attend a conference on Civic Engagement with one of my professors and at the conference present a paper I wrote to his peers. While a grad student is frequently common, my thesis advisor was also the chair of the department. The relationships with professors and peers contributed to the best learning experiences of my life.

This dynamic between professor and student translates into the classroom and beyond. World-renowned professors doing research at a university with small classes means exceptional research opportunities. Brandeis offers first-year students the unusual opportunity to be able to participate in a research lab assisting professors. Through students' stays at Brandeis they are presented with a number of opportunities to participate in research with their professors. Some examples that extend beyond the lab include working with national and international organizations and traveling to other countries to assist in the field. The product of this cooperation between professor and student is an opportunity-filled academic experience. Brandeis is the youngest institution to earn recognition by Phi Beta Kappa, in part, because of this successful dynamic.

The Curriculum

The College of Arts and Sciences (CAS) is the core of the University. CAS is comprised of twenty-four departments and twenty-four interdepartmental programs, which offer thirty-nine majors and forty-four minors. The departments and interdepartmental programs are divided among four schools forming broad groupings among the disciplines: the School of Creative Arts, Humanities, Science, and Social Science. Interdepartmental programs provide structured opportunities to explore areas of study that are interdisciplinary in scope. The broad range of departments and interdepartmental programs offer students and faculty the opportunity and formal structures needed to explore fields in-depth and across disciplines. The structure and offerings of CAS encourage and inspire students and faculty to pursue a true liberal arts education through university requirements and continuing research endeavors. The CAS's offerings are bolstered by the university's established graduate schools whose classes are open to undergraduates.

This broad range of offerings provide classes in almost every conceivable discipline. For students who aren't sure what they want to major in, Brandeis provides variety that smaller liberal arts colleges can rarely offer. For students who know (or think they know) exactly what they want to major in on their first day of class, the depth of the course selection will more than fulfill their interests.

Requirements

Flexibility and an interdisciplinary approach characterize the entire curriculum at Brandeis. Studying ideas from a variety of academic perspectives gives you the ability to form your own critical viewpoint and synthesize knowledge in new ways. To earn a Bachelor of Arts or Bachelor of Science degree at Brandeis, students must complete thirty-two semester courses, which include the required courses of your major and the general university requirements:

- One university seminar
- Three writing-intensive courses (one of which may be a writing-intensive university seminar)
- One quantitative reasoning course
- A three-semester foreign language sequence (or the equivalent)
- One course in nonwestern and comparative studies
- Two semesters of physical education
- At least one course from each of the four schools at the university—Humanities, Social Science, Science, and Creative Arts. (Courses taken to fulfill requirements listed above may also count for this requirement.)

The University Seminar in Humanistic Inquiries (USEM) is a hallmark of the Brandeis curriculum, designed specifically for first-year students and intended as a foundation for their studies at Brandeis. USEMs are small seminar-style classes, taught by distinguished faculty. They are interdisciplinary in subject matter and develop critical thinking and writing skills through close analysis of significant texts. They typify the intimate classroom environments with accomplished faculty that Brandeis works hard to create.

At Brandeis, you can design an academic structure for yourself, combining majors and minors that can either focus your interests through a multidisciplinary approach to a particular area of study, or broaden your view by exploring an eclectic array of interests in a personal journey of academic discovery. It is possible to earn two degrees simultaneously—a dual bachelor's/master's degree—in most programs at Brandeis that offer graduate study.

Brandeis also has an expansive study abroad program. It is not required, but more than twenty percent of juniors study abroad. Brandeis offers students from all majors opportunities to study in more than sixty-two countries, in many centers of learning that have centuries-old reputations for academic excellence.

Brandeis's requirements are not difficult to fill. Courses can double count for the core curriculum, distribution, and concentration requirements. This allows for many courses taken to be elective courses. In comparison to other universities, Brandeis's requirements are light, but they ensure that students leave with a true liberal arts education.

SOCIAL LIFE AND ACTIVITIES

Central Perk, the coffee shop in the Emmy Award winning show "Friends" (created and produced by Brandeis graduates Marta Kauffman '78 and David Crane '79) is modeled after Cholmondeley's, the campus coffeehouse at Brandeis. How many colleges have a social scene that receives nods on prime-time television weekly (daily if you include reruns)? It is located in Brandeis' genuine castle that serves as a residence hall for upperclass students and whose unique wedge-shaped rooms overlook Boston. While students probably won't see Jennifer Anniston or King Arthur on campus, students have a good chance of finding lifelong friends, their knight in shining armor, and much more.

Location

Brandeis is in the city of Waltham, an inner suburb of Boston, located nine miles upstream on the banks of the Charles River. The city is a popular dining location for residents of Boston and Brandeis students alike because of the wide variety of ethnic restaurants in its downtown. A cinema in town, specializing in independent and foreign films allows students to catch the best of Sundance as well as French, Italian, and Japanese films. For students who would like to spend some time in a big city, Boston is just a shuttle ride or commuter rail away. An on-campus commuter rail stop provides access to the Boston subway system all day seven days a week. Starting Thursday and running until Sunday, Brandeis provides free shuttles to and from Cambridge and downtown Boston.

Residence Life

Although students visit Boston many times during their four years at Brandeis, most are quite content to stay on campus because it is almost always bustling with activity. Approximately ninety-nine percent of first-years and eighty-two percent of all students live on campus in Brandeis's twenty-four residence halls in nine quads. Rooms range from traditional dorm rooms (lofted rooms and doubles) to suites, townhouses, and apartments. First-year students at Brandeis are housed either in Massel or North Quadrangle, right on campus, convenient to classroom and dining options. Each quad is supervised by a professionally trained director, assisted by resident advisors who are upperclass Brandeis students. Most residence halls are coed, though single-sex areas are available. First-year students are housed in either double or lofted rooms. Upperclass students are eligible to live in single rooms, suites, or apartments, including the castle. Part of the reason campus living is so popular is because more than half of the rooms on campus are singles. A brand-new residence hall housing 220 students is scheduled to open in the fall of 2003—perfect timing for the lucky incoming class.

In the residence halls a variety of programs are offered—movie nights, ice cream parties, and informational talks on subjects such as safe sex, current events, and local issues. Big screen TVs, kitchens, and foosball tables can be found in nearly every quad lounge, which are popular hang-out spots well into the wee hours of the morning. In first-year quads, milk-shakes, smoothies, and snacks are also available well into the night. Most students become confident that the quad, building, and even the hall they live in is the best in the university. Playing fields and basketball courts are adjacent to many of the residence halls, creating a perfect environment for pick-up games at virtually any hour. Every dorm room is equipped with a high-speed Internet connection, ideal for accessing multimedia, playing multiplayer computer games, or accessing Brandeis's 1,000 electronic journals and publications.

Dining

It will probably be difficult to find college food that is as good as home cooking, but Brandeis will certainly give your folks a run for their money if not for the food, for the convenience. Usdan Cafe and The Boulevard, located in the Usdan Student Center offer cook-to-order, "grab-and-go stations," and late night pizza delivery. If students are really hungry, they can go to Sherman Dining Hall's all-you-can-eat facility, which serves both kosher and nonkosher foods. All the dining locations provide generous vegetarian options and a station in Sherman always provides vegan food. Brandeis accommodates every dietary restriction; students need only speak with the dining staff. Some dining options include the ability to order from off-campus restaurants such as Dominoes. By using "Who Cash" in participating area restaurants, students add even more variety to the Brandeis diet.

The newly renovated "Stein," located above the Sherman Dining Hall, is a modern pub serving lunch and dinner entrees, as well as sandwiches, soups, salads, and homemade desserts. Students can celebrate their twenty-first birthday at The Stein with a sampling from a microbrewery or a glass of wine. Weekly Stein nights are hosted by various campus organizations and usually pack the house providing one of many outlets for the university's academic rigors.

Clubs and Organizations

The new Carl and Ruth Shapiro Campus Center, a $25 million addition to Brandeis's already dynamic campus, is the hub for student activity on campus. Open around the clock, seven days a week, it houses a cafe, a state-of-the-art student theater, lounges, function rooms, computer clusters, and offices for student organizations, all built around a soaring art-filled atrium.

At most campuses students must choose between serious involvement in one club or involvement in many with a selection of clubs to choose from. For example, at a big school being an editor of the student newspaper is often the exclusive post a student can hold. In contrast, a small school might welcome participation in many clubs, but might not have a selection that includes a radio station or the resources a bigger school might have to make the experience as worthwhile. Brandeis manages to deftly walk this line, making clubs and organizations an exceptionally popular outlet to have fun and learn. With more than 175 clubs and organizations, it is safe to say that every student participates in club life in some way.

CLUBS AND ORGANIZATIONS

- ○ Total student clubs and organizations: 250+
- ○ Community service clubs: six
- ○ Cultural awareness groups: twenty-one
- ○ Performing groups: thirty-two including three comedy troupes, six dance troupes, ten instrumental groups, and thirteen vocal groups
- ○ Religious groups: five
- ○ Sports and games clubs: thirty-nine
- ○ Student leadership/activism groups: twenty-three
- ○ Student publications: eleven
- ○ Student service organizations: thirteen
- ○ Television station BTV and radio station WBRS

It seemed that there was always something happening on campus. Whether it was a famous speaker, a club meeting, a party, an a cappella performance, or a rally, there was always some event to go to.

Students can write for *The Justice*, the independent student newspaper, or one of the ten other student publications. They can join the campus radio or television station and host a live talk show. They can join the debate team and win first place again in North American parliamentary debate. Students who dare can go skydiving, scuba diving, or mountain climbing all with a full or partial subsidy from Brandeis. The entertainment of theater groups, comedy troupes, and about a dozen *a capella* groups is enjoyed daily. Multicultural events fill the academic calendar and add richness to campus life. They include: Asian Awareness Week, Black History Month, Caribbean Week, Chinese New Year, Culture X, Hispanic Heritage

Month, Kwanza, Mela, and the Vietnamese Spring Festival. Dozens of athletic clubs provide instructors that will show students how to improve their game in everything from rugby and Ultimate Frisbee to Tae Kwon Do and kick boxing. Religious groups provide everything from a gospel choir and Friday night shabbat dinners to a Muslim prayer room.

With almost two dozen activist groups, students will find a strong and active community with a great history of national advocacy. Brandeis students led The National Student Strike against the Vietnam War and convinced the Board of Trustees to be one of the first universities to divest from apartheid South Africa.

When Charlton Heston visited campus, I can still remember that well over 1,000 students were either standing in line for the event, chanting in protest or support, or pretending to lie dead on the ground with blood-stained shirts to dramatize gun violence. The best part was after he left when students and NRA members engaged in long and productive discussions about gun rights and gun control. The event really captured both the openness to ideas and dedication to fostering dialogue that Brandeis cherishes.

Athletics

Brandeisians love athletics. If you are looking for Division I athletics Brandeis is not for you, but if you are merely looking to enjoy either competitive or recreational play Brandeis will more than suit your needs. More than 1,000 students participate in intramural and club sports every year. Brandeis has ten men's varsity sports, ten women's varsity sports, and one coed team (sailing). The Gosman Center is one of the largest multipurpose indoor athletic facilities in the East. It has a 70,000-square-foot field house; a 200-meter six-lane track, three indoor tennis courts, ten outdoor tennis courts, squash courts, weight training rooms, and fencing, dance, and aerobic facilities.

Creative Arts

Students interested in the arts will find a supportive community with top-notch resources. Brandeis's music department was founded by Leonard Bernstein and there are seventy musical performances annually. The theater department hosts six major productions each year and several student-run theater groups put on productions each semester as well. With two major state-of-the-art theaters (one opened last year) and several minor spaces, the university has quality theater resources. The Rose Art Museum, an art destination of many Bostonians, is located on campus, making museum openings especially convenient for Brandeis students. The museum boasts the largest, finest, and most comprehensive collection of twentieth-century modern and contemporary art in New England. Beyond the museum, the campus is dotted with sculpture by professionals and students alike year-round through permanent exhibits and art festivals.

The college experience can in many ways teach you more than your classes. Brandeis's supportive environment, so full of opportunities, virtually assures that you will maximize your college experience.

FINANCIAL AID

Approximately sixty percent of incoming undergraduates received some form of need-based financial aid during a recent academic year. Need-based financial aid is a combination of loans, work-study, and grant awards that are offered to students whose families demonstrated financial eligibility for assistance. Need-based aid is available from federal, state, and private sources, including Brandeis. To apply for need-based financial aid, students must submit the CSS/Financial Aid PROFILE and, if applicable, the

FINANCIAL AID FOR THE CLASS OF 2006

○ Fifty-eight percent received scholarship or grant assistance from Brandeis
○ Average need-based grant: $15,300
○ Total need-based financial assistance: seven million
○ Total scholarship funds awarded: $2.2 million
○ Total grant funds (scholarship and need-based) awarded $28 million

Business/Farm Supplement and Noncustodial Parent's Statement along with their application.

In addition to its deep commitment to need-based financial aid, the university maintains its own strong scholarship program. Brandeis scholarships are based primarily on academic merit and are used to enroll the very best class possible with the scholarship funds available. To be eligible, applicants must complete the CSS Profile.

Financial aid counselors work with students and their families to create a financial aid package that suits their needs. If necessary, they help find additional scholarships or loans to supplement Brandeis grants. Approximately 200 students in a recent first-year class of 837 received scholarship awards ranging from $5,000 per year for four years, up to $27,000 per year

○ Mitchell Albom, '79 Author of
Tuesdays with Morrie

○ Paula Apsell, '69 Executive Producer
of "NOVA"; Winner of Eight Emmy
Awards

○ Angela Davis, '65 Civil Rights Activist

○ Thomas L. Friedman, '75 Foreign
Affairs Columnist for *The New York
Times* and Winner of Three Pulitzer
Prizes

○ Ellen R. Gordon, '65 President of
Tootsie Roll Industries

○ Christie Hefner, '74 Chair of Playboy
Enterprises

○ Abbie Hoffmann, '59 Civil Rights
Activist

○ Margo Jefferson, '68 Theater Critic for
The New York Times; Winner of the
Pulitzer Prize for Distinguished
Criticism

○ Marta Kauffman, '78, David Crane,
'79 Creators, Writers, and Executive
Producers of Emmy Award-Winning
"Friends"

○ Debra Messing, '90 Costar of NBC's
"Will & Grace"

○ Letty Cottin Pogrebin, '59 Author
and Political Activist; Founder of
Ms. Magazine

○ William Schneider, '66 Senior
Political Correspondent for CNN

○ Judith Shapiro, '63 President of
Barnard College

○ Stephen Solarz, '62 Former Member
of U.S House of Representatives

for four years. In a recent year Brandeis awarded undergraduate students more than $27.9 million in scholarship/grant assistance.

GRADUATES

The ability to think creatively, solve problems logically, and communicate effectively defines a liberal arts education. A bachelor's degree from Brandeis signifies exceptional achievement in all of these skills compounded with a commitment to social justice. The successes of Brandeis alumni suggest that this is a winning formula.

Alumni can be found in nearly every profession or field of work. Notably, eighteen alumni serve as presidents of colleges or universities in the United States or abroad. Ten percent of Brandeis alumni are physicians. Brandeis graduates are presidents of fifty hospitals or HMOs. Of the 2,300 Brandeis alumni in the legal profession, seventy-five are district attorneys and thirty have gone on to become judges.

Brandeis graduates are among the highest echelons of graduate school applicants. In a recent year, Brandeis seniors achieved an eighty percent acceptance rate to medical school, while the national average is forty-seven. They also enjoyed a ninety-four percent acceptance rate to law school, besting the national average of seventy-eight percent. Brandeis graduates were accepted to an average of four law schools of their choice, as compared to the national average of 2.3.

One small part of graduates' success is the assistance they receive from the Hiatt Career Center. It provides career counseling and a range of services for undergraduates and alumni.

It directs students to internships related to their interests during the academic year and throughout the summer. The Center hosts Alumni Network Events at Brandeis during which students can meet with alumni to explore a wide variety of postgraduate careers; a Shadow Program allows students to spend a day in the workplace with a Brandeis graduate to explore a particular career field; the Hiatt Alumni Career Network gives students access to thousands of alumni volunteers who offer to share advice about utilizing a liberal arts degree in a broad variety of careers; and Alumni Network Events on campus and in New York offer prearranged interview days in Boston, New York, and Washington, D.C. Beyond all this, Hiatt offers resources and assistance on standardized tests, résumé preparation, interview techniques and much more.

SUMMING UP

While most American universities were named for a location or major benefactor, Brandeis was given its name seven years after Justice Louis Brandeis died. He is the namesake solely for who he was and the ideals for which he stood. In design, Brandeis was modeled after the best parts of the best American colleges and universities. The founders managed to combine the best qualities of location, size, offerings, and campus life to maximize the university's potential. As a result, in its short life span it has been able to create an experience that places it among the best colleges. The university fully embraces the mission of a liberal arts college with renowned research. The success of its graduates is perhaps the best indicator. A Brandeis degree can take its graduates anywhere they want to go. While not a household name in America, it is a name that is known and respected in both academic and professional circles. It is a name that allows its graduates to compete for the most sought-after jobs and most selective graduate schools. However, the value of a college experience is not in the diploma that hangs on the wall; it is based on the quality of the experience.

❏ *Joshua F.A. Peck, B.A.*

BROWN UNIVERSITY

Photo by William Mercer

 Brown University
Providence, RI 02912

 (401) 863-2378
Fax: (401) 863-9300

 E-mail: *admission_undergraduate@brown.edu*
Web site: *www.brown.edu*

 **Enrollment**

Full-time ❏ women: 3,127
❏ men: 2,737

Part-time ❏ women: 157
❏ men: 88

INTRODUCING BROWN UNIVERSITY

Brown University a unique member of the Ivy League, is a high-caliber institution that is low on pretension. With no core requirements, Brown's innovative curriculum takes academic decisions out of the ivory tower and puts them in the hands of students. Each student becomes the architect of his or her own education. The result is a community of self-motivated learners who relish the chance to discover and explore their true passions.

On the whole, Brown students are more collaborative than cutthroat. The university attracts some of the highest achievers from the United States and abroad, but in the Brown environment, these students value learning from and working with their peers over vying for grades. Brown students can also be an eclectic, creative bunch. The typical Brown student is atypical. As one student puts it:

"The main thing I love about Brown is that everyone is here to learn. There is a lot of passion in the student body. People come here because they have a love of learning and want to expand their minds—consequently, grades are not considered as important as they might be at other schools."

—*Elizabeth Gilbert*
Class of 2008

For some, the academic and social freedom can be intimidating, but Brown works hard to provide a system of advising to help students find their way. Students get the most support through one-on-one mentoring relationships with faculty members. Professors are easy to approach and devote considerable personal attention to undergrads. It is not uncommon for students to form close bonds with professors and stay in touch with them long after they graduate. And with University President Ruth J. Simmons's plan to hire one hundred new full-time faculty over the next five years, the level of meaningful interaction between students and faculty will only improve.

Students also tend to form close ties to Brown's locale, Providence, Rhode Island. An artsy, midsized city, Providence has undergone a transformation over the past decade. The refurbished downtown area boasts a beautiful walkway along the Providence River, several small-scale concert venues and theaters, and the easily accessible Providence Place Mall, complete with a movie megaplex and a vast array of shops and restaurants. All of these entertainments are within walking distance or a short trolley ride from College Hill. Closer to campus, students frequent the coffee shops and eateries on Thayer Street and Wickenden Street and enjoy the brick sidewalks and large Colonial and Victorian houses that give this section of Providence, known as the East Side, a distinctly New England feel.

Many students first get to know Providence through community service projects. Nearly seventy percent of Brown students contribute time and skills to the local community. This community involvement is a hands-on form of student activism, as students work to effect change locally through grass roots organizing.

Large-scale political activism is rare or nonexistent on Brown's campus. While Brown's liberal curriculum attracts a predominantly liberal student body, both sides of the political spectrum are represented, and protests are few and small. Students are most vocal about issues directly affecting the Brown community. In recent years, students successfully campaigned for the adoption of need-blind admissions procedures.

Campus activities and clubs offer another outlet for students' diverse interests. From musical groups and sports teams to campus newspapers and literary societies, Brown students make involvement in extracurricular activities a major part of their educational experience.

"The thing that I love most about Brown is that, as with any top college, the people here are extremely intelligent and talented. For the most part, they are also surprisingly modest. I never knew, for example, that my friend was a guitar prodigy until I heard her playing in the dorm one day. Brown is full of wonderfully talented people who are also easy to get along with and who impress you daily without even trying."

—*Amanda Nagai*
Class of 2005

Freshmen and sophomores usually dabble in a variety of clubs. By junior year, many students have focused their involvement on one or two organizations where they take on leadership positions such as team captains or editors. Alternatively, many students add to the activities on campus by starting their own organizations.

Brown offers bright, self-directed students the freedom and support they need to realize their full academic potential. Students shape their own learning experience while enjoying collaborative working relationships with professors and peers alike. They also know how to balance rigorous academics and community involvement with a social life for a well-rounded collegiate experience. It's no wonder then that ninety percent of respondents to a 2002 student life survey said they would choose Brown again.

ADMISSIONS REQUIREMENTS

Each year Brown's admissions process seems to get more selective. In a recent year, Brown accepted 2,555 of 18,316 applicants. Students seeking admission must meet high academic standards. Nearly half of the current freshmen were in the top ten percent of their high school classes, and SAT scores average 1400 (based on 1600).

But meeting these requirements alone does not ensure acceptance. There is no one formula for gaining admission to Brown. Admissions officers look at many different aspects of an applicant's profile in addition to his or her academic record. Brown, like most competitive colleges, looks for students who have the whole package—exceptional academics, leadership in outside activities, commitment to the community, and a certain intangible spark that can come across in an applicant's essay or recommendations.

Geographic and Ethnic Diversity

Brown's admissions committee also tries to foster geographic and ethnic diversity in the student body. For this reason, students who come from underrepresented regions, such as the Midwest, may have an easier time getting in than students from the Northeast. The university also actively recruits international students and values the diverse perspectives they bring to the community. At present, Brown enrolls approximately 5,900 undergraduates from all fifty states and almost seventy countries.

The university has an equally strong commitment to promoting ethnic diversity. About thirty percent of undergraduates are people of color. Over the years, the university has established programs to provide a network of support for the minority community on campus. Minority Peer Counselors or MPCs are a group of Arab, Asian, Black, Latino, Multiracial, and Native American undergraduates who provide academic and personal counseling to first-year students of color. They also conduct workshops in freshman dorms throughout the year to promote understanding on campus.

Student groups based on cultural background are another source of support and community for minority students and are very popular. They provide a venue for students from similar backgrounds to hang out and get to know each other, and they also host events on campus, such as performances or panel discussions, that let students share their heritages and raise awareness about issues affecting their community.

Application Process

Brown's application process is fairly standard. Applicants submit academic transcripts, recommendations, test scores for the SAT or ACT, two SAT Subject Test scores, and a personal essay.

Once students have assembled all of their materials, they can submit their applications to Brown by one of two deadlines: the Early Decision deadline or the Regular deadline. Students choosing the Early Decision option apply by November 1 and receive decisions by mid-December. This option is reserved for applicants who have selected Brown as their first-choice college and will attend Brown if admitted as an Early Decision candidate. The Regular admissions deadline is January 1.

What I like best about Brown is the open curriculum. Brown is great because it trusts its students to make their own academic decisions. Having the experience of choosing my classes based on my own interests and not those of some far-off administrator will help me to make my own decisions after Brown.

—Lisa Dietz
Class of 2005

ACADEMIC LIFE

Requirements

Brown stands out from other competitive colleges in its emphasis on student choice. While most schools have distribution requirements that all students must take to graduate—usually a series of introductory-level courses in different fields of study—Brown has no core curriculum requirements. There are requirements only within a student's concentration (Brown's term for a major). To graduate, students need to pass thirty courses, demonstrate competency in writing, and complete the requirements for their concentration.

Some might fear that students would abuse this system and miss out on all that a liberal education has to offer. But Brown students are inherently motivated and the school provides academic advisors to help them consider their academic programs carefully. The thought students invest in this process gives them more ownership over their course of study. Even without requirements, most students choose a well-rounded selection of classes, and they are more eager to put time and energy into classes they've chosen.

At the end of the sophomore year, students begin to focus their studies on one field by declaring a concentration. Requirements for concentrations vary greatly. Some departments, such as history, have as few as eight required courses, while other programs may require as many as twenty courses. Students also have the option to double-concentrate or create their own concentration in collaboration with a faculty advisor.

Applying Early Decision to Brown was the best choice I ever made. My experience here at Brown has been everything I hoped it would be. There is an incredible support system in place for freshmen that makes them feel welcome and at home when they arrive, and a rich student and campus life with opportunities for all students to get involved with whatever they are interested in. All the students I have met here are bright, interesting, and passionate people, the kind of people I want to be surrounded by and live with for four years.

—Beth Enterkin
Class of 2007

Academic Advising and Support

While Brown students enjoy tremendous freedom in shaping their course of study, they do not have to go it alone. All incoming first-year students are assigned an academic advisor, a faculty member with whom they meet during orientation and throughout the year. Most academic advisors teach in the Curricular Advising Program (CAP). This program allows freshmen to take a class with a professor who will also serve as their advisor.

The CAP program has garnered mixed reviews from the student body. While CAP advisors are generally encouraging and supportive, they often know a lot about their department but are less helpful when giving advice about courses outside of their area of specialty. Also, since students take their CAP course during the first semester of their freshman year, sometimes the CAP advisor's expertise and the student's interests don't mesh in the long run.

Fortunately, there are many other opportunities for students to receive guidance. Brown faculty members, on the whole, are accessible and eager to help students. Many advising relationships develop informally as students get to know their professors. Faculty Fellows, who host study breaks and social gatherings in their homes, can provide support and mentoring.

Fellow students are also on hand to help. Resident Counselors, upperclassmen who live in freshman dorms, have already navigated through their first year of decisions, and they can be an invaluable resource to the freshmen they mentor. Sophomores get an added level of support through Randall Counselors, faculty members who work particularly with sophomores to review their educational goals. And once students declare a concentration, concentration advisors help students further hone their course of study.

Classes

Class size and format vary at Brown depending on the department and type of course. Most classes are small in size (about thirty to forty students) and are taught in a seminar style with an emphasis on student participation. Introductory lecture classes and lab classes for sciences tend to be larger (one hundred students or more) but usually include smaller section meetings during the week where students can get more individual attention.

A shopping period at the beginning of each semester allows students to check out a variety of classes before finalizing their schedule for the semester. Students often use the shopping period to compare different courses and see which professors they prefer.

As with concentrations, students also have the opportunity to design their own classes. Student-created classes develop as collaborations between a small group of students and a faculty advisor and are known as Group Independent Study Projects, or GISPs. GISPs are a perfect example of what happens when you give motivated students the freedom and

> *The students really make the difference at Brown; there are so many smart, creative, and dedicated students that you learn as much from working with your peers as you learn in class.*
>
> *As a biology concentrator, Brown is big enough to have first-rate researchers and offer graduate-level science classes to undergrads, but small enough so that you can really get to know the professors teaching your courses.*
>
> *I've had phenomenal success getting medical school interviews so far as a senior from Brown.*

—*Nat Smilowitz*
Class of 2005

resources to pursue their true passions. Many GISPs encompass several fields of study and result in innovative research or help extend Brown's interdisciplinary course offerings.

Brown also offers cross-registration with RISD (pronounced Riz-dee), the Rhode Island School of Design, a top-level art school that is Brown's neighbor on College Hill. Visual Arts concentrators make the most use of this option. In the past several year, both schools have committed to raising academic collaboration to a new level.

RECENT INDEPENDENT CONCENTRATIONS AT BROWN

○ Physics and Religion: The Search for Understanding
○ New Media Publishing
○ Immigration Studies
○ The Culture of Medicine
○ Computer Graphics and Film

Grades

Most Brown students are inherently motivated to take their studies seriously, but they are not overly concerned with grades. Overall, grading at Brown is fair. Students receive an A, B, or C for passing work and an NC, or No Credit, for failing work. Professors maintain high standards for A and B level work in all disciplines, though professors in the sciences may grade more harshly.

Pass/Fail Grades

The S/NC grade option at Brown, which stands for satisfactory/no credit, is intended to encourage academic risk taking. Since students can opt to take any course S/NC, they are more likely to venture outside of their comfort zones academically without fear of sullying their transcripts with a low grade. For example, a history concentrator may decide to take a competitive physics course S/NC or an economics concentrator might try art history without having to worry about grades. Most students view the S/NC system as a nice option but still take the majority of their courses for a grade. Very few students abuse the system.

PLME

One final aspect of academic life at Brown is the Program in Liberal Medical Education (PLME). This program provides a unique path to medical education. Students apply to PLME as high school seniors and, if accepted, are guaranteed spots in Brown's medical school upon graduation, provided they maintain a certain GPA. As undergrads, PLME students are just like other members of the class. They are encouraged to take full advantage of Brown's liberal arts offerings, and many end up concentrating in the humanities before continuing on to medical school. Ultimately, this eight-year continuum of liberal arts education and medical education encourages PLME students to develop into well-rounded scholars who view medicine as a humanitarian pursuit rather than a trade.

SOCIAL LIFE AND ACTIVITIES

Units

The freshman unit marks the beginning of every Brown student's social life. It comprises forty to sixty students who live together in the same freshman dorm. Brown intentionally tries to maximize diversity in these groups, so students from one unit represent many different ethnicities, geographic backgrounds, and interests.

People tend to bond quickly with their unit mates, and units often travel as a pack during the first few months of freshman year. Members of the same unit will eat together in the campus cafeterias or turn out in large numbers to support one of their unit mates at a performance or sporting event.

Many Brown students make lifelong friends in their freshman unit, and some even meet their future spouses. Overall, the unit setup provides first-years with a feeling of community and gives students a chance to make a diverse group of friends whom they might not otherwise encounter.

As a first-year student at Brown, I was a little worried about coming to Providence from deep south Texas. But I soon found that social life is just as active on campus as off. Comedy, parties, music, movies on the green—anything you might want can be found at Brown University. You never have to leave the campus!

—*Meagan Brooke Garza*
Class of 2008

Fraternities and Sororities

Units are the first social group at Brown, but it isn't long before students begin to find their way to other campus groups and activities, such as fraternities and sororities. Unlike many college campuses, Greek life plays a small role in Brown's social scene. Ten percent of students belong to the ten fraternities and three sororities on campus. Of the fraternities, two are coed and tend to throw less traditional frat parties around themes such as swing dancing. The more traditional frats and sororities throw the majority of big public parties on campus. These parties can draw a crowd, but many students move on to other social options after their first year or two on campus.

THINGS TO TRY AT LEAST ONCE BEFORE GRADUATING

- ○ Dress up for the midnight organ concert on Halloween.
- ○ Undress for the annual "Naked Party" at Watermyn Coop.
- ○ Rub the nose of the statue of John Hay for good luck.
- ○ Sing your stress away at Karaoke Night in the cafeteria during finals period.
- ○ Nap on the couches in the Absolute Quiet Room in the John D. Rockefeller Library, AKA "The Rock."
- ○ Star gaze at the Ladd Observatory.

Other Social Activities

The alternatives to frat parties are as diverse and creative as Brown's student body. Cultural events are a particularly big draw. Students pack theater productions, dance performances, *a cappella* concerts, and improv comedy shows. There is also an on-campus bar and music venue called The Underground. Funk night at The Underground is popular among freshmen and sophomores, while upperclassmen frequent the Graduate Center Bar, known for its dungeonlike atmosphere, pool tables, and dart tournaments.

> *No matter how much you stood out in high school, at Brown you blend right in. For many people Brown will be the one time in their lives they will be just like everyone else around them for a change.*

—*Michael Thompson*
Class of 2007

STREET-LEVEL GUIDE TO PROVIDENCE

- ○ Thayer Street—the main drag, home of the Brown Bookstore, the Avon movie theater, and countless restaurants and coffee shops
- ○ Wickenden Street—like Thayer, but artsier and a few blocks farther from campus
- ○ Atwells Avenue—Providence's answer to little Italy
- ○ Waterplace Park—downtown's stage for free concerts and drama
- ○ Blackstone Boulevard—a road near campus with a great jogging path

Off Campus

Off campus, students enjoy the cultural and culinary offerings of Providence. A near-perfect college town, Providence is small enough to feel homey but large enough so there's always something going on. Recently, Providence has gone through a much-touted cultural renaissance. There's a thriving arts community that plays host to many quality theater productions and offbeat performance art. There are also several concert venues and jazz clubs and, for more mainstream entertainment, the massive Providence Place Mall has a megaplex movie theater as well as an Imax theater.

Providence is also home to some of the best restaurants in New England. Freshmen find that Parents Weekend is a perfect time to try some of the city's pricier establishments, such as the famed Italian restaurant Al Forno, while seniors who are off meal plan frequent South Providence's pan-Asian hangout, Apsara.

Dating

The dating scene at Brown is somewhat lacking; it seems that people are either in a serious relationship or they're single. There's not a lot of casual dating. Brown students tend to hang out in groups, and couples usually stay connected with their group of friends.

But there's always help for those who wish they were dating. Several years ago, one enterprising student created an on-campus matchmaking service called HUGS, Helping

Undergraduates Socialize. Each year at Valentine's Day students can fill out a questionnaire and, for a small fee, receive a list of their ten most compatible and five least compatible matches on campus. Then they wear out the pages of the class face books checking out the photos of their potential matches.

Sports

Brown offers a wide range of varsity sports (thirty-seven different teams) and has decent facilities for a school its size. In general, sports at Brown, like Greek life, are in the background. Attendance at games is low. Athletes tend to support other athletes and students support their friends who play sports, but rarely does the whole campus rally around a sporting event.

There is, however, a strong sense of community among athletes, and students who do attend games get caught up in the school spirit and cheer loudly. Many games are also attended by the very enthusiastic Brown band. The world's first ice-skating band, the Brown band performs postgame ice shows that are a highlight of the hockey season.

Groups

In addition to athletics, students can participate in a wide variety of activities. There are more than 200 student organizations at Brown including theater and dance ensembles, music groups, community service organizations, faith-based groups, student government, and much more. Involvement in campus groups is a major part of the Brown experience. Most clubs give students the option to get involved in a small or large way, and most students are actively involved in at least one club or volunteer activity. Students enjoy the opportunity to try new things, and they often find that campus groups provide their first introduction to a potential career path. For example, Andrew Barlow, class of 2000, served as a writer and editor for the campus humor magazine during his years as a student, and since graduation, he has published humor pieces in *The New Yorker*.

FINANCIAL AID

Beginning with the class of 2007, Brown implemented its new need-blind admissions policy. This means that an applicant's financial need will not affect whether or not a student is selected for admission. Another recent policy change replaced the freshman work-study requirement with one-year scholarships. Now, freshmen who receive financial aid won't have to work to contribute to their packages during their first year. Without the pressure of earning part of their aid, freshmen are free to fully explore and enjoy all that Brown has to offer.

Students receive financial support both through financial aid and scholarship grants. Nearly forty percent of Brown students receive some sort of aid. For the class of 2007, the average financial aid package totaled over $26,630.

Many students work part-time jobs as part of their work-study program or to make some extra spending money. Food service jobs are the most common, but there are also job opportunities in academic departments, libraries, or other campus facilities. On-campus jobs pay an hourly wage that typically increases as a student logs in a number of hours or rises to leadership. The average yearly earnings from campus employment is approximately $1,300.

The deadline for submitting financial aid forms is November 1 for Early Decision applicants and February 1 for regular applicants, and financial aid awards must be renewed each year.

GRADUATES

Over ninety-four percent of Brown students graduate, then they are faced with the anxiety of figuring out what to do next. Fortunately, Brown provides a support network to help seniors make postgraduation plans.

About a quarter of Brown graduates go directly to graduate or professional school after graduation. These students receive guidance from professors in the field and often attend the top schools in their discipline.

Having the Brown name on my resume has opened doors for me, even in fields completely unrelated to what I studied as an undergrad. Employers see that I went to Brown and they figure that I can learn whatever they need me to learn to do the job. It's a nice foot in the door.

—*Bonnie Boyd*
Sc.B. Human Biology, '99

Deans

For students who pursue professional tracks in law or medicine, there are deans at Brown who specialize in counseling prelaw and premed students. They guide students through the process of deciding whether or not law school or medical school is the right next step for them, and if students decide to apply, they help them navigate the involved application and interview processes.

There is also a dean who helps students apply for scholarships or fellowships. Historically, this support has helped Brown students fare very well in competitions for highly selective postgraduate awards, such as the Rhodes and Marshall scholarships.

Job Hunting

Career Services is the most valuable resource for students who look for employment directly after graduation. Each year, many finance and consulting firms recruit Brown seniors through interview sessions at the Career Development Center. Additionally, Brown provides excellent resources for the large number of students who wish to pursue noncorporate tracks with their "Careers in the Common Good" speaker series. And in recent years, Brown has assembled contact information for alumni who have agreed to talk with students about their jobs and how they got to where they are today. This vast alumni network gives Brown students an inside track to information about a wide variety of career options.

PROMINENT GRADS

- Mary Chapin Carpenter, Country Singer-Songwriter
- Ira Glass, Host of National Public Radio's "This American Life"
- John Hay, Personal Secretary to Lincoln and Secretary of State under Presidents McKinley and T. Roosevelt
- John Heisman, the Trophy's Namesake
- Charles Evans Hughes, Chief Justice, Supreme Court
- John F. Kennedy, Jr., Publisher
- Laura Linney, Oscar-Nominated Actress
- Horace Mann, Educator
- Joe Paterno, Football Coach
- Tom Scott and Tom First, AKA "Tom & Tom," Creators of Nantucket Nectars
- John D. Rockefeller, Jr., Philanthropist
- Ted Turner, Media Mogul
- Thomas Watson, Jr., Former IBM Head

SUMMING UP

Brown University provides bright, self-directed students with the freedom and resources to realize their full academic potential. By removing the confines of a core curriculum, Brown

This place will pick you up and spin you around like Dorothy in a Kansas twister. When you touch down again, though, the world appears in Technicolor. You are indeed somewhere over the rainbow, in a magic place of deeper awareness. The bumps and bruises of discovery are well worth the beauty Brown allows you to find in yourself and in the wider world.

—*Keally DeWitt*
Class of 2004

lets students, with the help of faculty advisors, select a course of study that best matches their interests and passions. From the beginning of their college careers, students learn how to discover and pursue their academic interests.

As students explore Brown's offerings, they have access to the full resources of the university, most notably, the faculty. One hundred percent of Brown faculty members teach undergraduates, and students develop close mentoring relationships with their professors. There are even university grants designated for undergraduate research with professors, a benefit usually reserved for graduate students.

Although Brown students are high achievers who embrace academic rigor, they are more collaborative than cutthroat. Brown's liberal curriculum and grading system help create an atmosphere where students value learning for learning's sake and enjoy working with their peers rather than competing for grades.

Brown students also know how to balance their studies with extracurricular and social activities. Involvement in campus groups lets students try things they've never done before, such as hosting a radio show or organizing a political rally. Brown students are also willing to try new things socially. While many schools' social scenes revolve around drinking and partying, Brown's social options are as diverse and creative as the student body itself.

Brown is a school that nurtures the student as an individual. Students are encouraged to chart their own course, and the professors who help them along the way also get to know them as people. Students graduate from Brown with a stronger sense of who they are and the conviction and skills to go on to pursue their true passions.

❏ *Michelle Walson, A.B.*

CALIFORNIA INSTITUTE OF TECHNOLOGY

Caltech Photo

California Institute of Technology
Pasadena, CA 91125

(626) 395-6341
Fax: (626) 683-3026

E-mail: *ugadmissions@caltech.edu*
Web site: *http://www.caltech.edu* (general)
      http://www.admissions.caltech.edu
      (Undergraduate admissions)

 Enrollment

Full-time ❏ women: 277
       ❏ men: 636

INTRODUCING CALTECH

Caltech's scientific reputation ranks it among the world's elite research universities, but with only 300 professorial faculty and 913 undergraduates, Caltech's small size sets it apart from its peers. Caltech is the place where Linus Pauling determined the nature of the chemical bond, where Theodore Von Kármán developed the principles that made jet flight possible, where Charles Richter created a logarithmic scale for the magnitude of earthquakes, where

Nobel Laureate in physics Richard Feynman—one of the most original thinkers of the twentieth century—spent the better part of his preeminent career, and where physicists and engineers are currently working toward the first detection of gravitational waves. However, Caltech is also a place where more than half of students participate in on-campus research before they graduate, where eighty-five percent of students participate in intramural or intercollegiate athletics, and where students have lived under a student-run honor system since the 1920s. The Caltech undergraduate experience is a fusion of two seemingly incompatible institutions: a multibillion-dollar research university and an intimate small-school community.

As a high-powered research institution, Caltech has produced some of the greatest scientific achievements of the past century. Caltech's undergraduate program trains scientists and engineers for the great discoveries of the next. In class, you don't just learn the answers to questions in your textbook; you learn to ask your own questions and are challenged to find the answers. Professors often treat students as intellectual peers and while this creates a very demanding curriculum, it also gives students the opportunity to actively participate in cutting-edge research. Many undergraduates work as research assistants on campus, and more than 300 participate in the Summer Undergraduate Research Fellowships program each summer. Many of these students will be named as authors or coauthors of articles in major scientific journals, a rare honor for undergraduates. This unadulterated exposure to the real world of science means that Caltech graduates are well prepared for a career in research. A higher percentage of Caltech graduates go on to receive Ph.D.s than do graduates of any other university.

Although the science at Caltech is very serious, student life at Caltech is laid back and a little quirky. Almost all students at Caltech are members of one of the seven houses on campus. The house, the modern-day remnants of long-lost fraternities, perpetuate a long list of offbeat traditions and are the center of year-round intramural sports competitions. The beautifully landscaped campus of open lawns, cool ponds, and winding pathways fosters a relaxed Southern California lifestyle. On an average day, you might find professors and students sharing coffee at an outdoor table or students teaching each other to juggle. At night, you might find a game of Ultimate Frisbee on the athletic fields or students grabbing a midnight snack at the student-run coffeehouse. There are more than eighty student clubs on campus, eighteen varsity sports, two jazz bands, a symphony orchestra, a concert band, numerous choral groups, and an active theater arts program. Caltech students work very hard on academics, but they're also very good at finding diversions and, fortunately, there's no shortage of activities from which to choose.

ADMISSIONS REQUIREMENTS

Caltech is not for everyone, and getting in is not easy. By campus tradition, the target size of the freshman class is always 215—the number of seats in the physics lecture hall. Compare that to the fact that 2,760 applications were received and the 551 letters of admission that were sent in 2005; do the math and you'll see that it is a highly selective process. Although there are no strict requirements for test scores, the academic achievements of the freshman class are always very high. The middle SAT I scores range from 700–770 Verbal and 780–800 Math; eighty-eight percent graduated in the top tenth of their high school class.

As a Caltech alum, I often speak to high school students about admission to Caltech, and they always ask, "How can I be sure that I will get in?" My answer, of course, is that there is no sure way, but there are definitely things that you can do to increase your chances. Take the most challenging courses offered at your high school. Look for ways that you can express your love of science outside of school. Ask for recommendations from teachers who really know you and what makes you tick, and who are willing to write about you in depth. And finally, spend time on your application essays! Your essays speak for you to the admissions committee, and they want to hear what you have to say, not what you think they want to hear.

—Debra Tuttle, B.S. '93—Literature

Although those numbers look daunting, there is no blueprint for getting in to Caltech. The admissions process at Caltech is not formulaic. The Undergraduate Admissions Office has only six admissions officers, but they get help from faculty and students in reading applications. The Freshman Admissions Committee includes sixteen faculty and sixteen undergraduate students. Each member of the Admissions Committee brings his or her own personal experiences of Caltech, and they work together to find and admit those students who fit best with Caltech. There are a few qualities that Caltech always looks for in its applicants: a strong *interest* in mathematics, science, or engineering, high academic *ability*, and demonstrated *initiative* in their approach to learning.

> *Caltech admissions has a knack for evaluating applicants for the intangible quality of being a good scientist, and in such cases can overlook blemishes in grades or test scores.*

—David Moore, '03—Electrical &
Computer Engineering

The goal of the Admissions Committee is to admit students who will become the "creative type of scientist" that Caltech seeks to produce. Members of the committee find these students by carefully reviewing the more subjective parts of the application—essays, choice of high school curriculum, extracurricular activities, and teacher evaluations. Caltech also encourages prospective students to attach a research paper to their application, which is one of the best ways to evaluate how well an applicant will do in a research-oriented environment. Caltech loves to find students who take an active role in their own education, and who pursue opportunities to learn both in and out of the classroom.

The only absolute requirement for coming to Caltech is a passion for science. Through Caltech's core curriculum, students who enroll don't get to choose whether or not they take science classes. This does not mean that applicants need to be one-dimensional; Caltech students are actually required to take more humanities courses than science majors at most other schools. A strong love of science is a must, though; those with just a casual interest need not apply.

> *The key to admission to Caltech is passion. An applicant must demonstrate a passion for learning, for life, and for science through activities outside the classroom. We focus more on how you spend your free time than on your test scores and class rank, because being successful at Caltech takes more than brains and more than diligence; it takes a love for what you are doing.*

—*Jialan Wang, '04—Mathematics and Economics*

ACADEMIC LIFE

The academic experience at Caltech is unlike that of any other university in the world. Every student has to learn the fundamentals of each major aspect of science while staying well rounded with a required number of humanities courses. Homework is done in collaborative groups and tests are almost all take-home. Participation in scientific research is easily accessible to every undergraduate and world-renowned faculty members interact with students on a daily basis. With big-time scientific research happening in an intimate small-school environment, the academic environment at Caltech is like no other.

When freshmen arrive at Caltech, they are all enrolled in math, physics, and chemistry courses. This is the beginning of the core curriculum, which is the heart of a Caltech education. Every undergraduate, whether majoring in biology, economics, literature, or chemical engineering, has to take five terms of physics, two terms of chemistry, one term of biology, one term of chemistry laboratory, one term of another introductory laboratory, one term of science communication, twelve terms of humanities and social sciences, three terms of physical education, and one term of astronomy, geology, or number theory.

AWARDS AND HONORS FOR CALTECH FACULTY AND ALUMNI

- Nobel Prize: 31 recipients, 32 prizes
- Crafoord Prize: 4 recipients
- National Medal of Science: 47 recipients
- National Medal of Technology: 11 recipients
- California Scientist of the Year: 14 recipients
- Fellow, American Academy of Arts and Sciences: 78 faculty
- Member, National Academy of Sciences: 71 faculty
- Member, National Academy of Sciences, Institute of Medicine: 2 faculty
- Member, National Academy of Engineering: 43 faculty

Options

At the end of the freshman year, students must declare an option, Caltech's version of the major. There are options in every aspect of science and engineering, with the most popular being physics, engineering and applied science (which includes computer science), biology, chemistry, mechanical engineering, mathematics, and electrical engineering. A few students each year graduate with degrees in history, economics, or literature, but they are very different from their peers at other universities—through the core curriculum, all humanities and social science majors will have taken differential equations and quantum mechanics. Changing options is generally very easy, and double options are pursued by a few students each year. Every few years, a student designs his or her own curriculum and graduates under the Independent Studies Program.

Classes

The major distinguishing characteristic of academics at Caltech is that it's very hard. Often unnoticed is the fact that Caltech students tend to take more classes than their peers at other universities. Caltech operates on a trimester system, with three terms a year that are each eleven weeks long. In addition, Caltech students take an average of five classes each term, while students at other universities generally take only four classes. After four years at Caltech, students almost always find themselves well ahead of their peers in the first year of graduate school.

I've heard rumors that at other colleges, students are very competitive. They are protective of their class notes, homework, and lab books and only care about how well they do. I've heard horror stories of students stealing each other's notes and sabotaging lab experiments. That doesn't happen here—we all want to help each other do well in our classes. It's comforting to know that your fellow students, even those you don't even know, are looking out for you.

—*Janet Zhou, '04—Electrical Engineering and Business Economics and Management*

The Honor System

The fast pace of Caltech is more than almost any student can handle on his or her own, but fortunately, nobody is expected to study without help. Collaboration with peers is strongly encouraged under Caltech's eighty-year-old Honor System. Instead of strict rules handed down from the administration, Caltech students are held responsible for their own actions and are on their honor not to cheat, plagiarize, or steal.

The greatest benefit of the Honor System is the fact that no tests are proctored. In fact, almost all quizzes, tests, and exams are take-home. The professor will set some ground rules for each test, and each student is responsible for respecting the given time limit and whether the test is open- or closed-book. Students are allowed to take tests wherever and whenever they want; some students sit in the privacy of their own rooms with their favorite CD or album playing, some prefer the quiet desks in the library, and some even take their tests out on the lawn or at the beach. Rather than having to wake up at 9:00 A.M., students can take their tests after dinner or even late at night; the professor won't care as long as it is turned in by the stated deadline.

The Honor System also applies to homework, where students are generally free to share their answers with each other. As long as each student understands everything written on his or her own paper, the professor will give full credit. This atmosphere of collaboration virtually eliminates competition between students for grades. Every Caltech student is happy to help a friend with a lab or homework assignment because some day, he or she may need the favor returned.

Scientific Research

This training in the Honor System is part of Caltech's strong focus toward scientific research. In the scientific community, researchers share their results openly and are held on their honor to conduct experiments with integrity. Undergraduates can experience this firsthand in numerous research opportunities on campus. The most popular way to do research at Caltech is through the SURF (Summer Undergraduate Research Fellowships) program. SURF provides grants of $5,000 to students who want to do research with a faculty member over the summer. Each "SURFer" must write his or her own proposal, submit progress reports through the summer, write a final paper, and present his or her research on SURF Seminar Day. Over the years, SURF has become an integral part of the Caltech experience. Last summer, more than twenty-five percent of the student body stayed on campus as part of the ten-week SURF program. In the most recent graduating class, more than fifty-nine percent of students had spent at least one summer in the SURF program.

Staying on campus over the summer is not the only way Caltech students can do research. The SURF program also pays for students to go to other universities over the summer—every year a few take this opportunity to travel to Europe. Caltech has recently instituted exchange programs with Cambridge University and the University of Copenhagen, which allow students to spend a term studying abroad. Students can stay on campus and receive hourly pay as research assistants during the school year or over the summer, and many labs are happy to hire undergraduates. Students can also earn academic credit by doing research as a senior thesis or to displace another requirement in their major. With so many laboratories at Caltech doing high-level research every day, the opportunities for undergraduates are seemingly limitless.

Laboratories

Some of the most advanced laboratories in the world are run by Caltech. The Jet Propulsion Laboratory (JPL) is the largest of these facilities. Located about fifteen minutes northwest of campus, JPL is NASA's center for robotic exploration of the solar system. It has been run by Caltech since the 1930s and is the place where *Voyager I* and *II*, now leaving the solar system, were designed and built. JPL also produced *Galileo*, currently orbiting Jupiter, and the highly successful *Cassini*, which is now orbiting the rings and moons of Saturn. JPL was also in the news for the multiple probes it has sent to Mars: *Global Surveyor*, the *Pathfinder*, *Odyssey*, and rovers *Spirit* and *Opportunity*. A van runs daily between Caltech campus and JPL, and many undergraduates make the trip throughout the summer.

Telescope Facilities

Caltech also operates several telescope facilities, including the Palomar Observatory north of San Diego housing the 200-inch Hale Telescope, and the Keck observatory on the summit of Hawaii's dormant Mauna Kea volcano, home of the world's largest optical and infrared telescopes. Caltech also operates the Owens Valley Radio Observatory, a collection of radio telescopes 250 miles north of campus. On the Caltech campus, there are 0.35-meter and 0.25-meter telescopes atop the Caltech astrophysics buildings that are used for undergraduate classes. Also, plans are underway at Caltech, in collaboration with the University of California, to design and build the Thirty-Meter Telescope, the worl's most powerful telescope.

LIGO

In conjunction with MIT, Caltech operates the Laser Interferometer Gravitational Wave Observatory (LIGO), a facility dedicated to the detection of cosmic gravitational waves. LIGO is the largest project ever funded by the National Science Foundation, and consists of two widely separated installations within the United States—one in Hanford, Washington, and the other in Livingston, Louisiana. They are each massive L-shaped structures with four-kilometer-long arms held in a vacuum, the largest high vacuum ever constructed. A one percent-scale prototype sits on Caltech campus, and a few undergraduates work there every summer, experiencing the cutting edge of experimental physics.

Other Facilities

Caltech is also home to Nobel Laureate Ahmed Zewail's Laboratory for Molecular Sciences, the headquarters of the Southern California Seismic Network, and a new initiative to improve voting technology. A new nanotechnology center and a state-of-the-art MRI facility are two more projects that are keeping Caltech at the forefront of scientific research.

Caltech students have the unique privilege of learning in the midst of advanced scientific research. Many other universities perform high-level research, but nowhere else can students so easily walk into the laboratories. On a campus where the Ph.D.s outnumber the undergraduates, anyone who wants to participate in research needs only to ask. Research experience is the best possible training for those going to graduate school, and Caltech students have an easy time gaining that edge.

SOCIAL LIFE AND ACTIVITIES

Tech is not full of people who lock themselves in their rooms and study. There is something for everyone here. Plenty of people go out clubbing on the weekends, and yet these are the same people who do interesting summer research in cutting-edge fields like quantum computing.

—*Kutta Srinivasan, '04—Computer Science and Economics*

Houses

Social life is generally not one of the reasons a high school student chooses Caltech, but every year, freshmen are surprised to find an active social scene centered around the seven undergraduate houses. Blacker, Fleming, Lloyd, Page, Ricketts, Dabney, and Ruddock

House are descendants of fraternities that dominated the campus in the 1920s. This fraternity lineage is most obvious at family-style house dinners each night. Student waiters set the tables, serve food, and refill drinks; everyone must ask permission to get up from the table, and dinner ends with announcements from the house officers. Dinner is certainly not a formal affair though; each house adds its own quirky rules; for example: no "nerd talk," and no freshmen sitting at corners. Breaking the rules results in a variety of interesting punishments and the nightly ritual serves as an entertaining diversion that makes each house seem more like a family.

During the first week of classes each year, freshmen are assigned to houses in a process known as rotation. A toned-down version of a fraternity rush, each freshman visits each of the seven houses and submits a list of preferences at the end of the week. Upperclassmen from each of the houses then get together and assign each freshman to a house in an all-night meeting. The end of rotation marks the beginning of a week of initiations, when freshmen can be found trading water balloons, and moving furniture across campus at the request of upperclassmen. This gives freshmen their first taste of Caltech pranking, and after this shared experience, each house is drawn together as a tight community.

The houses are microcosms within Caltech. There are enough different personalities within the houses that almost everyone can find someplace to fit in. I have found that the house system is a wonderful way to establish a family-like support network. Even from the beginning, I have felt like I was a part of what was going on and that people cared about what was going on in my life.

—*Aimee Eddins, '04—Biology*

Getting into a house gives each freshman an instant circle of friends and a constant source of social activity. Each house hosts one large "interhouse" party during the year, as well as many smaller parties. Every house elects a social team that plans other events such as ski trips, concerts, and trips to various L.A. tourist locations, but most social activity isn't incredibly organized. Nightly, students can be found relaxing and socializing in the common areas of the house, getting to know the group of people who will be their neighbors for four years.

California Institute of Technology

Athletics

While academic competition is almost nonexistent, the seven houses engage in constant competition through a year-round schedule of interhouse sports. The houses play softball, soccer, swimming, track, basketball, tennis, Ultimate Frisbee, and football, earning points for compiling the best record in each sport. The house with the most points at the end of the year wins the interhouse trophy. The games are competitive, but everyone gets a chance to play—eighty-five percent of students play in interhouse sports before they graduate.

Intercollegiate sports are open to almost any student who can commit to daily practices, and almost thirty percent of the student body plays on Caltech's eighteen NCAA, Division III teams. There is cross-country, soccer, basketball, baseball, fencing, and more, but for over a decade now, no football team. There are also a wide variety of physical education classes for students to fulfill their PE requirement, ranging from traditional sports to yoga, scuba diving, and rock climbing.

Other Activities

Many Caltech students happen to be talented musicians, so the school sponsors a variety of music and arts programs. There is a concert band, two jazz bands, chamber music, a symphony orchestra, men's and women's glee clubs, and a theater program that performs three shows every year. A growing number of arts programs at Caltech are now being organized by students. There are several *a capella* groups, multiple rock bands, dance troupes, and a literary magazine, all run entirely by students.

EXTRAORDINARY OPPORTUNITIES FOR A SMALL STUDENT BODY

- ○ Intercollegiate Sports: 1 sport for every 50 students
- ○ Clubs: 1 club for every 10 students
- ○ Student Government: 1 position for every 5 students
- ○ Summer Research Fellowships: 2 fellowships for every 3 students
- ○ Professors: 1 professor for every 3 students
- ○ Course Offerings: 1 class for every 2 students

Just because we're a small school doesn't mean we don't have talented musicians or poets or athletes or actors. It just means people came here to do science. Academics are rightly going to come first, but when people make time for extracurriculars, they typically put their souls into them. I've been singing in choirs since elementary school, so when I had some time in my schedule I signed up for the women's glee club. It's great! Where else on campus do you see 45 women, ranging from undergrads to faculty and staff to members of the community, all together? We're not just talking about singing here—the women's glee club is a force, a sisterhood, a philosophy lesson on living. People tend to stick with the club for all four years, so you make many friends. Not only is it a time to socialize; it challenges you in other ways. You learn with a different part of the brain, and it revitalizes that creative side.

—*Martha-Helene Stapleton, '03—Physics*

These groups are just a sampling of the more than ninety student clubs on campus—that's one club for every ten students! Caltech students run a cheerleading squad, chess team, entrepreneur club, student investment fund, amateur radio club, science fiction club, ethnic organizations, religious groups, and many more. Recently, a group of Caltech students started an undergraduate research journal that is now distributed at numerous universities across the country.

Whatever you want to do, Caltech will always be very understanding and supportive. If you're interested in extracurricular activities, it's simple to get involved in clubs or student government. If you're interested in sports, you can participate on a team or just play recreationally in interhouse sports. If you have a hobby that isn't already at Caltech, you can easily start a new club. Since there are so few students, one person can make a big difference. While I've been here, I've seen students start an undergraduate research journal, a cheerleading squad, and a community service group that didn't even exist when I was applying.

—*Janet Zhou, '04—Electrical Engineering and*
Business Economics and Management

Student Government

All these clubs operate with little or no oversight from the faculty or administration and are an example of Caltech's long tradition of student self-governance. Many aspects of this self-governance have been alluded to elsewhere in this essay, and it is an integral part of student life at Caltech. Student government bodies decide who lives in the dorms, discipline students in cases of cheating, fund the majority of student activities, and choose representatives that help read admissions applications.

Student government is centered around a non-profit organization known as the Associated Students of Caltech (ASCIT), Inc. Completely independent of the Institute, ASCIT publishes the student newspaper, yearbook, student handbook, and literary magazine. ASCIT is also in charge of administering the Honor System: suspected cases of cheating are investigated and adjudicated by the Board of Control, a committee of twelve students. Student representatives, along with faculty members, also sit on the Conduct Review Committee, which rules on disciplinary matters for undergraduates. Those students are just a few of the more than sixty student representatives on various Caltech committees that review academic policies, set the dinner menu, make admissions decisions, award merit scholarships, and determine academic ineligibility, to name a few examples. Caltech students are allowed to participate in almost every administrative decision that affects student life, which is a rare privilege in the present-day big business of higher education.

Traditions

This level of influence allows students a high degree of independence from Caltech administration. Over the years, students have been able to shape their own unique way of life without much administrative interference. This has created many quirky traditions, one of the wackiest being senior Ditch Day, which was featured on the *Tonight Show*'s "Jaywalking" in the summer of 2002. One day every May, all the seniors ditch their classes and leave campus. Many years ago, underclassmen began to prank seniors' rooms while

---

HISTORY OF CALTECH PRANKS

○ **1961:** The Rose Bowl crowd is surprised when the cards under their seats are raised to spell, "Caltech."

○ **1977:** The *Voyager I* and *II* spacecraft are launched with the letters "DEI/FEIF," mottos of two Caltech student houses, inscribed on a package plate

○ **1980:** Residents of Fleming House borrow a 1.3-ton cannon from Southwestern Military Academy.

○ **1984:** The final score on the Rose Bowl scoreboard reads "Caltech 38, MIT 9"

○ **1987:** In Hollywood's centennial year, the famous Hollywood sign is modified to read "CALTECH."

---

they were gone. The seniors countered by "stacking" their rooms, creating barriers to keep students from getting in on Ditch Day. Over the years, these stacks have become more elaborate, and now most take the form of an all-day scavenger hunt, where students run around campus collecting clues that will unlock the seniors' rooms. The Institute has relented to the students, and now cancels classes every year for Ditch Day. Every year, this creates some unexpected sights, which can really be understood only by those going through it. Ditch Day is somewhat representative of the entire student experience at Caltech; it is quirky and unpredictable, and is exactly what Caltech students enjoy.

FINANCIAL AID

I knew that Caltech would be expensive, but the good thing is that Caltech's price tag includes everything: tuition, room and board, student fees, health insurance, money for books, extra meals, and personal expenses, even travel money if you live far away. There aren't any hidden costs.

—*Debra Tuttle, B.S. '93—Literature*

Caltech financial aid has long held to a simple policy: "If you are an admitted student whose family has insufficient financial resources to pay for all or part of your educational expenses, Caltech will provide you a financial aid award that will meet Caltech's calculation of your financial need and so make it possible for you to attend." This has created a tradition of Caltech providing unparalleled opportunities to excellent students, regardless of their families' economic circumstances.

Applying for first-time financial aid is a simple process that mirrors that of other universities. Every applicant must fill out the Free Application for Federal Student Aid (FASFA) and the College Scholarship Service (CSS) Financial Aid PROFILE Application. These documents enable the Financial Aid Office to determine the amount that the student and his or her family can reasonably be expected to contribute toward a Caltech education. Any difference between that amount and the cost of attending Caltech is considered the student's financial need, and the Financial Aid Office will prepare a student aid package consisting of a combination of scholarships, grants, loans, and work study that will fully meet that need.

The sum of a student's contribution along with the financial aid award covers the entire cost of attending Caltech: tuition, room and board, student fees, health insurance, money for books, extra meals, and personal expenses, even travel money if you live far away. There aren't any hidden costs.

Caltech tuition is already well below the cost for its peers, but the Financial Aid Office makes the additional effort to make it affordable for everyone. Most students are very satisfied with their financial aid package.

Caltech strives to be fair and generous with its financial aid. A student's financial standing never factors into the admissions decision. The admissions process is completely "need blind" for domestic students and applications are evaluated separately from financial aid applications. Caltech also never uses financial aid as a bartering tool to attract students. All awards are based on need alone, and no award will ever be increased to match an offer from another school. If a student receives an outside scholarship, it will go toward reducing a student's loan or work study, rather than reducing scholarship or grant awards. If a student's financial circumstances change, Caltech is very willing to reevaluate the family's current, revised financial status.

Work-Study

Many students receive federal work-study as part of their financial award, and it is very easy to find opportunities to work on campus. The number of job opportunities far outnumbers the number of students on campus. The Financial Aid Office is very flexible with switching between loans and work-study, and many student work off a significant portion of their costs before they graduate. Some of the best-paying jobs are research assistant and teaching assistant. Students can also earn work-study by performing community service such as tutoring, reading to kids, or feeding the homeless. Other students work as office assistants, tour guides, ushers, or waiters. Many of these jobs have very flexible hours and pay reasonably well.

Scholarships

Caltech gives many scholarships that are need-based, but in recent years, several donations have allowed Caltech to give a limited number of merit-based scholarships to incoming freshmen. These merit awards come in a range of values. There is no separate application for the merit awards; all admitted students are automatically considered. There are also a number of upperclass merit awards given to sophomores, juniors, and seniors on the basis of academic excellence. These awards cover up to the full cost of tuition, and the Scholarships and Financial Aid Committee awards them to many outstanding continuing students each year.

GRADUATES

Thirty-two Nobel Prizes have been awarded to Caltech alumni and faculty. A Caltech education primes students for a career in scientific research, and a majority of graduates follow that path. On average, about half of Caltech graduates go on to earn a Ph.D., which is a significantly higher percentage than any other university. These are the students that Caltech is designed for—those who will dedicate their lives to the study and teaching of scientific knowledge. Caltech graduates are very successful in competing for fellowships and more than twenty each year win national and international awards.

Most freshmen enter Caltech dreaming of a professorship or a career in scientific research, but by the time graduation comes around, many find their interests are elsewhere. These students go into a variety of fields they never considered when they were in high school.

PROMINENT GRADS

- Frank Capra, Film Director
- Linus Pauling, Chemist, Political Activist, two Unshared Nobel Prizes: Chemistry and Peace
- Arnold Beckman, Chemist, founder of Beckman Instruments, Inc.
- Vernon Smith, Economist, Nobel Prize for Economics
- Ben Rosen, Cofounder of Compaq Computer Corporation
- Gordon Moore, Cofounder of Intel Corporation
- David Ho, Biologist and Physician

About twenty-five percent of graduates each year go straight into the workforce. Even when the economy is down, Caltech students don't have much trouble finding excellent jobs. More than one hundred companies recruit on campus each year; in a recent year graduates received offers that averaged about $61,000 and several graduates received offers in excess of $80,000. Most job offers come from the engineering and computer science industries, but an increasing number of recruiters come from the financial sector, insurance industry, and management consulting firms. More and more companies have found that the problem-solving skills, technical background, and mathematical ability of Caltech graduates apply to a wide range of activities.

This still leaves a group of graduates that doesn't fit into a particular mold. Although Caltech does not have a premedical program, each year graduates get into the top medical schools and go on to earn M.D.s. A growing number of graduates are applying to law school even though there are no prelaw majors. A few students each year join the Peace Corps, travel around the world, go into teaching, or start their own businesses. The rigorous education that Caltech provides does more than train students for scientific research; it teaches skills that are valuable in almost any field.

To graduate from Caltech is to be part of an elite club of a little more than 20,000 living alumni. As an extension of the intimate culture of Caltech, the alumni network is very close-knit and supportive. Many Caltech alumni look to hire other alumni, and all are happy to help in job searches or provide business contacts. Many graduates find their way back into the Caltech community; twenty-five current faculty members earned their undergraduate degrees at Caltech.

SUMMING UP

Most things at Caltech are not truly unique; there are many small schools where under-aduates live in an intimate environment, and there are many world-class research institutions where undergraduates have the opportunity to learn science and do research. However, Caltech is the only place where these two ideas coexist on a single campus. They come together with great success, as Caltech consistently ranks among the top schools in the world. This makes the California Institute of Technology truly special and very difficult to describe on paper.

One big thing that nobody realizes until they step onto campus is how beautiful the land-scape is. The student houses are flanked by brick pathways lined with orange trees on one side and olive trees on the other. Palm trees dot the campus and quiet ponds are home to lily pads, turtles, and bullfrogs. Every few weeks, a couple takes advantage of this scenery and gets mar-ried on campus; many more use Caltech as a backdrop for their wedding photos. This may have inspired the producers of *The Wedding Planner* to bring Jennifer Lopez on campus recently. Caltech students also recognize their campus in *Legally Blonde*, *Orange County*, and many other movies, as well as a host of TV shows. Located a few miles from Hollywood, Caltech is a prime site for filming on location. The northern and western sides of campus are decorated with roses, which reveal another often forgotten aspect of Caltech: It is located in Pasadena, California, home of the Tournament of Roses. Each year, the Rose Parade marches within a few blocks of campus and all Caltech women are eligible to enter tryouts for Rose Queen.

This tiny school is filled with surprises, and four years isn't nearly enough time to uncover them all. Caltech is a small school where there is big science. Its students are high achievers, but forego competition for an Honor System. Its beautifully landscaped campus shares space with cutting-edge scientific facilities. It is a place where Nobel Prize winners are spotted wearing shorts and T-shirts. It has innumerable extracurricular activities. It employs more Ph.D.s than there are undergraduates. It requires its literature and economics majors to learn quantum physics. It provides a top-notch education and charges less tuition than most peers. Can all of that exist at one place? At Caltech, it has existed for more than 100 years.

Coming to Caltech is certainly not for everyone, but for those who truly love science, there is no better place. The Caltech undergraduate experience is a wild and amazing ride, and there is never a shortage of things to do. Four years at Caltech forever changes the way every student looks at himself or herself, and most graduates agree that it is one of the most exciting periods of their lives. The shared journey bonds students together, and many make friends that last a lifetime. For all graduates, it is an experience they will never forget—once a Techer, always a Techer.

❑ *Ted Jou, B.S.*

Carleton College
Northfield, MN 55057

(507) 646-4190
Fax: (507) 646-4526 (800) 995-CARL

E-mail: *admissions@carleton.edu*
Web site: *www.carleton.edu*

 Enrollment

Full-time ❑ women: 1,033
❑ men: 925

INTRODUCING CARLETON COLLEGE

Driving down rural Highway 19 in southeast Minnesota amidst farms and cornfields, it's hard to imagine that one of the country's best liberal arts colleges lies just out of sight. Nestled in the small town of Northfield, Carleton attracts a talented, diverse, and intelligent group of students, many of whom were initially considering matriculation at the Ivies. In fact, what sets Carleton apart from its East Coast counterparts is that the campus atmosphere, while intensely intellectual, is at the same time laid-back and friendly. Strangers really do smile at each other in passing, and even in the middle of finals or midterms, Carls can be seen tossing a frisbee in the middle of campus or building snow forts in the subarctic Minnesotan winters.

In typical Carleton style, the college just celebrated the 140th anniversary of its founding with celebratory cupcakes during the half-time of its homecoming football game. Although the rural college still maintains its Midwestern humility, its student body hails from forty-nine states, the District of Columbia, and more than thirty foreign countries. Carls come from a wide range of socioeconomic, ethnic, religious, and cultural backgrounds, so there really isn't a "typical" Carleton student. Carls often discover their classmates' unique perspectives not just in the classroom but also in late-night conversations with their roommates, over a team dinner after sports practice, or on walks with friends in the college's arboretum.

ADMISSIONS REQUIREMENTS

For a small private college in the Midwest, Carleton has boasted acceptance rates in the past few years that are as selective as those of its East Coast counterparts. Getting into the college is not an easy feat, and in 2005, around thirty percent of people who applied to Carleton were admitted. What does it take to get into such a place—high SAT scores? Perfect GPAs in Advanced Placement classes? Good recommendations? Maybe. Since the college prides itself on its diverse and well-rounded student body, admissions officers don't just look for one outstanding quality in an applicant.

There are, however, certain qualities in any application that admissions officers do look for, and aspects about an accepted student that will set him or her apart from less qualified applicants. In order to select a group of students for an incoming class who will take full advantage of all that Carleton offers, admissions officers will review applicants' academic backgrounds, standardized test scores, school and community involvement, and other unique accomplishments. Regarding the application-reading process, Dean of Admissions Paul Thiboutot reflects, "If I think about twenty-plus years of reviewing, there is an interplay among our evaluation of the strength of curriculum taken and grades obtained, impressions from the essay and overall assessment of the person's engagement in the larger life of their school."

One of the most important parts of any student's application is his or her high school transcript. Admissions officers want to see that a student has taken challenging academics like honors, International Baccalaureate, or Advanced Placement classes, even if it means that the student has a lower GPA than if he or she chose to take easier courses. A broad range of harder courses on a transcript shows that an applicant is academically curious, can handle a Carleton-size course load, and is up for a challenge. Good grades aren't everything, but they are something, and admissions officers will take them into consideration. Want to secretly hide away all of your ninth grade English and history grades? Take heart, admissions officers also look favorably upon academic improvement over the course of an applicant's high school career. Keep in mind that officers also note any declining grades, especially in applicants' senior years, so don't succumb to any acute cases of "senioritis" yet.

Dean Thiboutot stresses that another extremely important aspect of the application is the essay. He states, "I know that a lack of effort in writing an application essay can have a negative impact in those final close deliberations or vice versa," since it allows admissions officers to really "get a glimpse" of the applicant's interests, sense of humor, ideas, and perspective on life. The essay also is a chance for applicants to show that they can communicate well in writing—a skill that will become invaluable at Carleton, even for budding math and science majors. You don't have to produce a work worthy of a Pulitzer, but it would be a good idea to enlist a few teachers, parents, and/or friends to read through your essay before you submit it.

Despite what some students may think, Carleton is not just about academics. It makes sense then that students' extracurricular activities and involvement in their school and neighborhood communities are also important parts of their applications. Carleton will probably not accept a student just because of perfect grades and a perfect SAT score if the student doesn't show that he or she has other interests besides coursework. A perfectly "well-rounded" student doesn't have to be the editor of the school newspaper, a varsity team captain, or the founder of a neighborhood charity organization (although it helps if you are any one of these), what is important is that a student shows a genuine interest in his or her community and/or enjoys helping and teaching others. Dean Thiboutot stresses that the admissions staff tries to undertake "a holistic evaluation of an individual, keeping in mind that we are not admitting some robot-like academic machine, but a human being with a host of interests, talents, and qualities that will be developed in the classroom and beyond at Carleton, from dining room conversations to exchanges while tossing a Frisbee."

Admission officers also consider teacher recommendations, the college counselor recommendation, and standardized test scores. Carleton requires either the SAT or the ACT with writing and recommends that students take the SAT subject tests (scores on these tests can generally only help an applicant). Students for whom English is a second language should take the TOEFL.

If you can visit Carleton or contact an alumni admissions representative in your area, a good idea would be to schedule an interview. Carleton encourages but does not require admissions interviews, and the absence of an interview is not held against an applicant in any way. The interview is "a chance to meet someone who knows the Carleton experience well and can share reflections on that experience and answer question and hopefully deepen a prospective applicants understanding of the college," Dean Thiboutot explains. Because of this purpose, interviews are pretty informal meetings and are definitely more like conversations than interrogation sessions. When preparing for an interview at Carleton, forget about your canned answers and instead think about what really interests you and why you care about it so much because that's what your interviewers will really want to know about you.

Early Decision

Carleton has two Early Decision options for those who are certain that Carleton is their top-choice school. Early Decision is a binding agreement, and accepted Early Decision students will have to withdraw all other applications and not submit new ones. The Fall application deadline is November 15, and decisions will be mailed by December 15. The Winter deadline is January 15, the same as the Regular Decision deadline. Winter Early Decision will be notified by February 15. Regular Decision will be notified by early April, and no later than April 15.

ACADEMIC LIFE

Academics are at the heart of students' liberal arts experience. Since Carleton is solely a full-time undergraduate institution, its academic programs are of course focused on undergrads, unlike many prestigious universities. Carls can choose from thirty-four majors and have the option of choosing one of sixteen concentrations, which is similar to an interdisciplinary minor. All Carls graduate with a Bachelor of Arts degree.

Distribution Requirements

Since Carleton is a college of liberal arts and sciences, students are expected and required to complete a wide range of courses in varied subjects. The college's distribution requirements are designed with the intention that all students' four-year academic experience will have breadth as well as depth. Everyone must take two courses in arts and literature (art and art history, dance, English, music, theater, classical and modern literature), two courses in humanities (history, philosophy, and religion), three courses in the social sciences (economics, educational studies, linguistics, political science, psychology, sociology, and anthropology), and three courses in math and the natural sciences (biology, chemistry, geology, physics and astronomy, mathematics, computer science, and specific psychology courses).

Students must also pass a writing requirement by taking a designated writing-intensive course and submitting a portfolio of samples of their writing by the end of their sophomore year. Carls also must fulfill the RAD (Recognizing and Affirming Differences) requirement, which basically means taking a class that focuses on a subject from a non-Western European perspective. Finally, all students must take four physical education courses, which can range from rock climbing to contact improvisation to ice skating.

"Distros," as these requirements are commonly called, represent about a third of the classes students will take at Carleton. Many Carls fulfill the distribution requirement without even thinking about it, and since there aren't any specific classes that all Carls are required to take, each student's course schedule can be incredibly personal and flexible.

Working Toward a Major

While distros are a great way for students to achieve a good breadth of knowledge, the major is an opportunity for them to study extensively in one subject that truly interests them. Many students have very vague ideas about a potential major when they arrive at college. Thankfully, Carls don't have to declare a major and an optional concentration until the spring of their sophomore year, so they have plenty of time to dabble.

Every major and concentration has its own distro requirements and required number of credit hours. Most majors require students to complete introductory courses (100 levels) in order to take intermediate (200 levels) and advanced courses (300 levels). Most students will also have to complete a methods course in their major during their sophomore or junior years and a Senior Seminar. Some will have to go through a petition process to complete a special major and/or double major. All students will meet with an assigned advisor from the faculty in their major to further discuss and plan their academic path.

The Senior Integrative Exercise, or "Comps"

In their senior year, students will cap off their major by completing a senior integrative exercise, or the comprehensive project. Carls fondly call this beast "Comps." Comps can take on many different forms, even within a certain major. They can be long exams, an in-depth research paper, an original thesis, a body of original artistic work, or student-conducted scientific or psychological research. Seniors love to gripe about comps, but secretly most enjoy the challenge of an extensive project that culminates their four years of academic study.

Academic Strengths

In the past decade, Carleton has been known for its strength in the physical sciences, and biology in particular has been one of the most popular majors with recent classes. About eleven percent of students in the class of 2006 were biology majors, and fifty-three percent of that entire class took at least one biology course during their Carleton careers. But biology isn't the only popular major at Carleton; political science/international relations, economics, English, and psychology also regularly make their way onto the top majors list. These top five majors are popular for a reason: students are attracted to the depth of study in which they can engage in each department, and the quality of professors and the breadth of subjects they teach.

Geology, a small but very strong department, has the amazing ability to attract students to its major. Few students come to Carleton intending to major in geology, but after taking a few introductory classes filled with plenty of hands-on field trips, many are hooked. The geo majors are a tight-knit group, and one can expect to see many of them literally camped out in their lab in the first floor of the Mudd Science Hall, entrenched in their research.

The arts of Carleton are receiving much attention. The initiatives being discussed will tie the arts into other aspects of the curriculum and provide new facilities. A planning committee has recommended the college create a center for visual and narrative arts featuring classrooms for campus-wide use: support services for visual and narrative production, studio arts, art history, cinema and media studies, English, and theater and dance; and a teaching art museum. The committee has also proposed the Perlman Learning and Teaching Center. The recommendation also calls for the development of an integrated music building that combines the teaching of music with performance space. Cinema and media studies (CAM) is now a major and will increase its course offerings and study-abroad programs.

The Trimester System

Carleton differs from the semester schedule of many other colleges of its size and caliber, and instead operates on a three-term system. The terms, conveniently named

"Fall," "Winter," and "Spring," are ten weeks long, and students will usually take three classes each term. Three classes seem like it would make for a relatively "light" course load, but when a semesters-worth of information is crammed into ten weeks, most Carls will agree that three classes is more than enough. The advantage of the trimester system is that it allows students to focus intensely on a few subjects for short bursts of time instead of spreading out their concentration to four or five classes that seem to last forever. Classes usually meet three days a week for seventy minutes or twice a week for an hour and forty-five minutes, so each class is incredibly important and bring something new to the course of study.

For four years, Carleton students will look at the world in ten-week increments: the first week is always an adjustment period, the fifth week is "crunch time" for midterm papers and exams, and things really pick up during the eighth and ninth week in anticipation of finals. The great thing about trimesters is that Carleton students are rewarded at the end of each term with a significant break. A six-week long break follows fall term, spanning from Thanksgiving to the beginning of the New Year. A two-week long spring break follows winter term, and, of course, the end of the spring term marks the beginning of summer.

The Classroom Environment

Since classes do meet for a significant amount of time, many students feel a particularly strong bond to their classmates and professors after ten weeks. Statistically speaking, the student-to-faculty ratio is nine-to-one, and the average class size is seventeen, with thirty-nine percent of classes having thirteen or fewer students. These stats show that Carleton students will (whether they like it in some cases or not) be an integral part of each class they take. Some introductory courses are more lecture-based classes and will have upwards of fifty students, but students in these large classes are split up into much smaller groups for the more hands-on laboratory sections.

Most classes are, however, discussion-based classes where each student is expected to participate regularly. In these classes, students help each other learn and will often meet in groups outside of classes to help each other study for exams or to critique each others paper's or projects.

> *One of the best things about an introductory religion class I took was the study group that a few other students and I formed. We'd meet regularly in the library or at a local coffee shop and just discuss the material until we knew it all inside and out. We even met a few times without studying in mind, just to catch up.*

Most Carleton professors are "accessible," meaning that they schedule ample time outside of class to meet with students and discuss anything from an upcoming paper to a theory that was glossed over in the last class. Some professors will even require their students to meet with them at least once so that they can connect and make the subject meaningful to everyone. Even though Carleton profs are brilliant and often critically acclaimed experts in their fields, most have chosen to teach at a small liberal arts school because they want to teach and interact with their students.

Learning Outside of the Classroom

When most people think of college academia, they usually conjure up visions of students sitting at desks in front of chalkboards, furiously taking notes, or students holed up in the college library, practically drowning in papers and books. While you can see plenty of scenes to match these visions at Carleton, much of the learning that occurs at the college happens in nontraditional settings, like on field trips, in study groups, or even in conversations that take place at a professor's house. Environmental biology courses will often take frequent trips to study the ecology of Carleton's 880-acre arboretum (or Arb), geology students will take frequent trips to South Dakota's "Badlands," educational psychology students will tutor in area schools, and sculpture students will install their works in public spaces across campus and in downtown Northfield.

Even Farther from the Classroom: Study Abroad

If there's one thing that Carleton students like to do, it's explore. About two thirds of students study abroad at least once during their time at college in over a hundred programs in forty-five different countries. It's not that Carls are dying to get away from campus (although doing tropical field research in Costa Rica might beat trudging to class in a Minnesota winter), it's probably more that Carls value a challenging, real-life experience away from the comforts of home. Many students choose to go on Carleton-sponsored programs, and each year faculty members lead groups of fifteen to thirty students to destinations around the world for ten weeks. These programs let students take a wide range of classes that help to fulfill requirements in their major, while at the same time allowing them to experience the subject they are studying on a more first-hand basis.

> *My favorite class was a program run by a Carleton professor in Ireland; we worked with an Irish scholar on James Joyce's* Ulysses. *It was one of the greatest intellectual challenges I've ever had, and I learned so much about Ireland, Joyce, and crazy indecipherable prose.*

> —*Derek Zimmerman,*
> *'07, English major*

If you want to get a little farther away from Carleton for a term, your options certainly aren't limited to the college's programs. Carleton is a member of several off-campus consortia, like the Associated Colleges of the Midwest and the Higher Education Consortium for Urban Affairs. You can also choose to participate in one of the many national and international college abroad schools, and programs like the Sea Education Association and The School for International Training are popular among students. Since the majority of Carleton students do go abroad, the Off-Campus Studies Office is very experienced at answering questions related to anything from credit transfers to host families to passports.

Technology Inside and Outside the Classroom

If you get a chance to walk around campus between classes, you'll probably see a fair number of students running to check e-mail at one of the many public computer labs around campus, or pulling out laptops to surf the net at Wi-Fi hubs in the Sayles-Hill Student Center or in the McKinley Gould Library, also known as the Libe. Many students will be rushing to post comments for a class on Moodle, Carleton's course-management system. Through Moodle, classes can create on-line forums for further discussion or questions outside of the classroom. All Carls also have access to a central server where they can access useful course materials, and more and more students can access most or all of their readings for certain classes on-line.

Carleton is both Mac- and PC- 'friendly,' although most classroom computers are Macs. Most students do own a computer, and laptops are useful, especially when they want to escape from distracting roommates and retreat to the depths of the Libe to write a paper. There are, however, plenty of computers around campus for student use, although finding an unused one can become quite a challenge during finals. If computers decide to revolt right before comps are due, workers at the Student Computing Information Center, or the SCIC, are there to help.

Academic Intensity—What to Expect

Most students at Carleton are academically curious and came to the college with the goal of satisfying that curiosity, not the goal of making straight As or being in the top of their class (although someone's got to do it). For some, this atmosphere is a dramatic shift from their cutthroat college-prep high schools, but in most cases, it's a welcome change. Students do worry about doing well in their classes, but "doing well" means really learning and manipulating the subject matter. Carleton has been called "a work hard, play hard" school, and it is not uncommon to see the student center filled with people typing furiously on their laptops or groups putting together a presentation at four in the morning during a finals period, or even during a particularly busy week. Another strange phenomenon about Carleton is that the person you least expect to be a physics whiz or heart-wrenchingly good writer, often is.

CARLETON CAMPUS "SLANG" 101

- Carl—A Carleton Student. "I met a Carl from '89 the other day at the gas station."
- Prospie—A prospective student. "How many prospies are you hosting this weekend?"
- Convo—A public talk/performance given by a notable speaker every Friday morning in the Skinner Memorial Chapel. "Hey, did you go to Convo last week?"
- Townie—A Name given to students and others around campus who are Northfield residents. "My roommate's a townie, so I'm going over to her house for dinner."

(Continued)

Social Life and Activities

If you think that the process of "getting an education" at Carleton only applies to hours spent in the classroom or studying in the Libe, think again. Much of the "learning" that happens at Carleton occurs during the conversations between classes with a floor-mate, in late-night broomball competitions, or while trying to organize a campus-wide event with a group of friends. But really, what does happen when you get a community of almost 2,000 incredibly interesting and talented young people together? Something pretty interesting.

Residence Halls

Carleton is first and foremost a residential campus, so all first-year students and the majority of all students live in the nine residence halls (or dorms) on campus. Every dorm is coed and mixed by class year. Freshmen will live in one of seven dorms (they don't live in two dorms because their layout isn't conducive to proper freshmen "floor bonding") and will be assigned to one or two roommates. Living in close quarters with a diverse group of people for an entire school year can be a challenging, yet ultimately rewarding experience. Dorm floors become small communities of their own, and many of them band together in intramural broomball games or as cast and crew of an annual campus-wide video-making competition called DVD Fest.

The chief overseers of the floor living communities are Resident Assistants, or RAs. RAs are upper-class students who have all applied for the job and have been trained to handle many of the situations that might arise in a dorm environment. Two RAs are assigned to live on each dorm floor, and they are good resources for first-year student making the transition to life at college.

Upper-class students progressively get more living options as their seniority grows. After their first year, students can apply to live in special interest houses like the Sustainable Living house or the Jewish Interest house. Some juniors and seniors can apply for Northfield Option, which means that they can live in privately owned houses or apartments in town. A few lucky seniors (and maybe some very lucky juniors and sophomores) get to live in college-owned townhouses, the cushiest campus living.

- **The Arb**— Carleton's 880-acre Arboretum located around and near the college. "I'm going running in the Arb—I'll be back in an hour."
- **The NNB**—The Noon News Bulletin—a general campus event calendar, also features lost and found, wanted, for sale, and general campus announcements. "I hope I can sell my 12-CD Barry Manilow set if I place an ad in the NNB. It's only slightly used."
- **S/C/NC or "Scrunch"**—In simple terms, a limited "pass/fail" option that students can use toward classes that do not "count" toward their major requirements. "I really want to take Linear Algebra, but I'd feel better about the class if I pre-scrunched it."
- **Comps**—A Comprehensive exercise that seniors have to complete in their major. "I haven't seen him very much this winter, I think he's really into his comps these days."
- **9th and 10th week(end)**—The final weeks of a Carleton term. Crunch time. "Why did I ever think it was a good idea to leave my 30-page history project for 9th weekend?!"

Clubs and Activities

At the beginning of every school year, each student is given a *Lagniappe*, Carleton's very own daily planner. It's a good thing to have around campus because schedules can get

CARLETON STUDENT INTEREST HOUSES

○ **Wellstone House of Organization and Activism**—seeks to create a diverse community of students with experience in a variety of different areas of grassroots political or social movements who can foster organization and activism at Carleton.

○ **Queers and Allies House**—helps to foster the growth of the LGBTA community on campus and to provide an alternative living situation that is comfortable for members of the LGBTA community.

○ **F.I.S.H. House**—a place to share the Christian faith by living the Christian faith.

○ **Culinary House**—a resource for culinary learning and experience.

○ **CANOE House**—enhances appreciation and the exploration of the outdoors through adventure-type experiences.

○ **La Casa Del Sol**—educates the Carleton and Northfield communities about the many questions, concerns, and cultural traditions of Latinos in the United States as well as Latin America.

○ **Green House**—brings together diverse individual and group environmental interests, serving as a central gathering place to address environmental issues.

○ **Farm & Parr House**—fosters awareness and appreciation of sustainable agriculture and sustainable living.

(Continued)

complicated very quickly. Besides class periods, assignment due dates, and readings to follow, a Carleton student will probably want to keep track of things like club meetings, performances, volunteer events, intramural games, and dates to hang out at the local coffee shop. All students are part of the Carleton Student Association (CSA), and elected officers form a student government that influences college policy and allocates funding to student organizations. There are over 150 "official" student organizations on campus to satisfy just about everyone's interests, whether it be religious, athletic, political, artistic, cultural, intellectual, or just plain goofy. If there isn't a club for a particular group of Carls, they can easily start their own.

Students often find a sense of camaraderie in the club that they join because they are drawn together by a collective enthusiasm, and sometimes passion, for a particular subject or cause. Because students have a broad and often unique range of interests, it's hard to peg people into certain groups. The captain of the rugby team might also be involved in the outdoor enthusiast association and the campus alliance against gun violence, or the awkward guy who helps you out with your calculus homework is also a member of a comedy improv group.

Being Nigerian means so much to me and I wanted to make sure that I did not forget that when I went to college. Joining AFRISA [African Students Association] was like meeting all of my brothers and sisters and getting to know a place I had not seen in so long. Its role is to make sure that the spirit of Africa that lives inside every African student on campus has a voice . . . and that voice is heard.

—Love Anani, '07, biology major

Community Involvement

Northfield's population of just over 17,000 people includes students from the town's two colleges, and this inclusive measurement goes to show how much the town relies upon college students to be involved residents. But what does it mean to be a Carleton student and also live in a small town in the middle of cornfields? First off, there's plenty of opportunity to get invested in a small but vibrant community. Carleton's Acting in the Community Together (ACT) office is a place that helps students find service opportunities in the Northfield area. From playing with puppies on Friday afternoons at the local animal shelter to traveling to rural Arkansas to help out with a Habitat for Humanity project during spring break; the ACT office gives Carls plenty of opportunities to get involved and stay involved.

- Jewish Interest House—serves to provide Jewish students with a culturally comfortable space and to educate all Carleton students about the Jewish culture.
- Womens Awareness House— explores and celebrates the diversity of women and their special needs in the Carleton Community.
- Multicultural Center—is a comfort zone and social area for students of color as well as an educational space for those majority students interested in multicultural concerns.
- Science Fiction House—offers a variety of Sci-Fi-related activities such as book discussions, craft projects and movie nights.
- Language House—housing and programming space for French, Spanish, German, Russian, Japanese, and Chinese languages.
- ASIA House—sustains Asian students and community members and serves to educate the general public at Carleton and in Northfield about issues facing the diverse Asian-American community.
- Freedom House—serves both to provide African-American students at Carleton with a culturally comfortable space and to educate all Carleton students about African-American cultures and issues.

Many students work as peer leaders in many different offices on campus. Carleton's Resident Advisors, Intercultural Peer Leaders, Gender and Sexuality Center Associates, Student

Wellness Advisors, Chaplain's Associates, and Student Departmental Advisors are constantly working to make Carleton a welcome and inclusive campus for all students. They frequently host guest speakers, panel discussions, open houses, movies, and other events to educate and inform the entire campus community.

Fine Arts

Two of the largest student organizations are KRLX, Carleton's very own radio station, and Ebony II, a dance troupe open to anyone (like just about all Carleton groups). Over 200 students are involved in each club each term—as DJs, newscasters, and engineers for the round-the-clock FM station, or as dancers in one or many of the Ebony II shows that debut near midterms. Students wanting to get more involved in dance can try out for Semaphore Repertory Dance Company, take classes ranging from ballet to moving anatomy, or even apply for a special major. Every year a few students also apply for special majors in theater, and there are many opportunities for Carls with a wide range of abilities and interest levels to get involved in theatrical productions. Every year students write, direct, and perform in a program of one-act plays or put on larger faculty-directed Players shows that go up in the large Arena Theater. Students can also participate in a number of CSA-sponsored theatrical and comedy groups that usually perform several times a term.

If there's one thing there isn't a lack of on campus, it's singing groups. There are seven a cappella groups, many of which you can sometimes hear practicing in dorm stairwells singing anything from The Postal Service to traditional Irish airs. There are also a number of choir ensembles, as well as an orchestra, a symphony band, a jazz ensemble, an African drum ensemble, and many other smaller groups for those who are musically inclined. Those who are interested can learn how to play the sitar, as Carleton offers music lessons to both beginners and advanced musicians for many different instruments.

Carleton offers a wide range of publications to inform, entertain, and educate the student body. The campus' weekly newspaper, *The Carletonian*, has been an independent source of news since 1877. From the wacky and often cynical articles in the *Carleton Literary Association Paper* (the *CLAP*) to the heated political debates published in the *The Observer*, there's something for everyone. There are also several more artistic and literary journals around campus for students to debut and share their work.

Athletics

A good majority of students will play varsity, club, or intramural sports during their time at Carleton because, really, Carls would rather be *in* the action than just watching it.

Whether its varsity soccer or intramural dodgeball, Carleton students will support their teammates and make lasting friends inside and outside the field, court, or pool.

There are twenty-one NCAA Division III varsity teams at Carleton who compete in the Minnesota Intercollegiate Athletic Conference, one of the strongest Division III sports conferences in the country. Men's and women's basketball, men's and women's swimming and diving, and women's soccer and volleyball have been particularly successful in the past few years. While varsity sports are a large commitment, student athletes are no different than their classmates—they're still the students singing in a cappella groups, finishing late-night projects in the lab, and laughing with friends over French fries in Sayles. Some sports teams can be a bit insular, but many athletes would argue that sports teams become close groups of friends, almost families of their own.

If a sport isn't played at the varsity level at Carleton, it's probably a club sport. Club sports range in intensity, but most seem to strike a balance between serious competitive play and just having fun. Some of the most intense club sports are the Ultimate Frisbee teams. Both Syzygy, the women's squad, and CUT, the men's squad, have made it to the national championships year after year. Other popular club sports are men's and women's rugby, cycling, hockey, lacrosse, and equestrian teams.

Most students get involved in intramural leagues, which are truly open to any student with any type of sports ability. Many students get involved in intramurals through their dorm floor teams, and others get involved through academic department squads. One of the most beloved intramurals is broomball—the perfect excuse to run around late at night in subfreezing weather and not feel cold. For those not wanting to brave the cold more than they already have to, there are also frisbee, sand volleyball, 3 on 3 basketball, dodgeball, indoor soccer, and tennis intramural leagues as well.

Many students will do a pilgrimage to Carleton's fairly new Recreation Center, especially in the winter months. The Rec Center features a fully equipped fitness center, as well as a climbing wall, a bouldering gym, multipurpose courts, racquetball and squash courts, and a dance/yoga studio. Students can sign up to take classes like yoga and kick boxing through the Rec Center. There are also two lap-swimming pools on campus available for student use. In the fall and summer months, Carls will take advantage of the seemingly endless running trails in the 880-acre Cowling Arboretum, or Arb (President Oden claims to have run on every single one of them). In the winter, students can check out cross-country skis from the Rec Center and explore the miles of trail while hurling a few snowballs at friends. Whatever the sport, Carleton students will stay active all year long and make like they're having fun doing it.

CARLETON TRADITIONS—WHAT MAKES CARLETON CARLETON

○ **Late Night Breakfast:** On the last night of reading days before the first day of finals, staff members, like the Dean of Students, serve all Carleton students plates of scrambled eggs, pancakes, and cinnamon rolls to refuel those needy brain cells.

○ **Schiller:** Forty years ago the bust of Friedrich von Schiller was stolen from the Office of the President. Students steal the bust from one another, knowing that whoever has possession of it must show it at campus events. Rumor has it that Schiller's taken trips around the world in his 40 year vacation.

○ **Rotblatt:** In 1964, a group of sophomores created a new intramural softball league and named it after ex-White Sox pitcher Marvin J. Rotblatt. The tradition of playing an annual game of one inning for every year Carleton has been in existence began in 1967. Every spring assorted loonies still gather in an attempt to complete a marathon game.

○ **Dacie Moses House:** Dacie Moses, a long-time employee at Carleton, was known for inviting students to her house for cookies and conversation. She donated her house where, now, two students live each year. It is still a shared gathering spot. Whether to bake cookies (which must be left for all to enjoy), share brunch, or maybe catch one of the a cappella groups practicing, this house provides a sense of "home" for many.

Making the Most of Campus

Since Carleton is a full-time residential college, the social scene is very campus-centric. In any given week or weekend, there are countless speakers, exhibits, community meetings, movies, presentations, gatherings, festivals, performances, and parties to attend. Sometimes it can be quite overwhelming. If there's one thing Carls know how to do, it's how to have fun, both inside and outside of academic activities.

Carleton does a good job of providing various types of events and social opportunities for its eclectic student body. The social atmosphere on campus is pretty laid back, and most feel that they're free to do what they want, with whom they want, and when they want. On a Friday night, Carls can watch and talk about Anime movies, sled down icy hills on lunch trays, or catch up with friends at a party, among a million other activities. There aren't any sororities or fraternities on campus, and the vast majority of social events on campus are open to all students. Members of the CSA-sponsored "Party Crew" will even help any group of students put on a unique all-campus party, whether it's a Bar Mitzvah or a Luau on Mai Fete Island.

The social atmosphere on campus is pretty liberal, and xenophobic, homophobic, sexist, and racist attitudes are not tolerated inside or outside the classroom. But students aren't just tolerant, and the college itself makes an effort to help student organizations that foster campus inclusiveness. In fact, Carleton was one of the first colleges in Minnesota, and perhaps the United States, to give institutional support to a campus Gender and Sexuality Center and the Queers and Allies

House. Since Carls are such a diverse bunch, it can sometimes be difficult to truly understand a roommate or a classmate, or even a group of peers, but it's a challenge that students want to tackle (and do) on a daily basis.

FINANCIAL AID

Regardless of what a prospective student is looking for in a school, a college's financial aid policy can sometimes outweigh almost any other aspect of the institution when that student is deciding to apply. Carleton knows this fact, and the Office of Student Financial Services claims that no student should hesitate to apply to the college because of its cost.

Carleton has a need-based financial aid policy, meaning that there is an expectation that the family will contribute as much as they can toward the cost of education. Of course, this contribution varies with each family. For the 2006–2007 school year, all Carleton students who demonstrated financial need had those needs met. Half of Carls receive need-based aid, and more than $33.5 million was awarded to Carleton students in 2005–2006. Nearly two thirds of that money was funded by Carleton grants and scholarships, which do not have to be repaid. Outside aid comes from federal and state grants and national, regional, and local scholarships. In each class, Carleton sponsors seventy-five or more National Merit and National Achievement Scholarships. Carleton does not, however, offer scholarships for athletics, the arts, or academic performance, since most students would be eligible for one of those anyway. Carleton also participates in the Federal Supplemental Education Opportunity Grant (SEOG), Federal Pell Grant, Academic Competitiveness Grant (ACG Grant), and National SMART Grant programs, as well as the Perkins Loan Program, the Stafford Student Loan program, SELF Loans, and a number of other loan programs.

Most of Carleton's financial aid packages consist of grants from Carleton and outside sources, a loan, and a work contract. About three fourths of all students work on campus, most as a part of the work-study program through their financial aid. First-year students don't work more than eight hours a week, and upper-class students don't work more than ten hours a week. Most students find that their work is manageable and often a rewarding part of their overall Carleton experience. From working in the Burton dining hall dishroom to writing press releases for the Media Services office, students are an important part of the "nuts and bolts" of the colleges' operations. Because students only work part-time and loans are generally between $2,500 and $3,500, the bulk of financial aid awarded to students comes from Carleton's grants—a testament to the fact that the college seeks to provide educational opportunities to academically qualified students, regardless of their financial situations.

GRADUATES

After four years at college, students sometimes struggle to realize that they will have to continue with life outside of the "Carleton bubble." After initially having to get over the fright of reality beyond dorm life, ten-week terms, and dining hall meals, most Carleton alums realize that their undergraduate education has provided them with the tools to succeed in "the real world."

PROMINENT GRADS

- Thorstein Vehlen, 1884, Economist
- Pierce Butler, 1887, U.S. Supreme Court Justice
- Michael Armacost, '58, Former U.S. Ambassador
- Barrie Osborne, '66, Film Producer
- Dr. Mary-Claire King, '67, Medical Genetics Researcher/Professor
- Jane Hamilton, '79, Novelist
- Jonathan Capehart, '89, Pulitzer Prize-winning Journalist

More than half of all Carleton alumni earn advanced degrees, with approximately seventy percent going on to graduate schools within five years of getting their Carleton diplomas. Many Carleton grads do not go straight to grad school and instead decide to enlist in programs like the Peace Corps, AmeriCorps, and Teach for America. They also might work for a few years to gain some practical experience before considering more school. Some Carls see the few years after graduation as a time to pursue a passion that they discovered and fostered while at Carleton. Many Carls also take advantage of postgraduate fellowships, like the Watson, Mellon, and Fulbright fellowships. These competitive opportunities are definitely once-in-a-lifetime experiences.

Mostly, I feel really lucky to have something in my life that I'm that passionate about and to be able to really pursue it. I don't feel like I chose—I didn't have a choice. I can never not be dancing—it's like I'm addicted to taking dance classes. When I realized I could never go even for a couple weeks at winter or spring break without dancing, I realized this was maybe something I should consider making the focus of my life.

—*Laura Grant, '06, political science/international relations major*

Carleton College

Carleton alumni have a strange, yet wonderful, knack for congregating in certain areas around the United States, including the Minneapolis area, New York City, and San Francisco. In fact, Carleton's alumni network is incredibly strong, and the fact that Carleton continually ranks high among the nations' private liberal arts schools in alumni giving shows how much Carls care about their college community, even after leaving Northfield. The alumni network is an amazing resource for recent grads to have, no matter where in the world they're living or what kind of career they decide to pursue.

SUMMING UP

I was deciding between Carleton and [a top university]. I'm a horrible decision-maker, and for about a week, this one was driving me crazy—keeping me up at night, totally distracting me from the rest of my life. And then I was going for a run one day and I just said to myself, "I'm going to Carleton." And it felt good. And at the end of my run, it still felt good. And a couple hours later, it still felt good. I think what it came down to was, "what kind of person do I want to be/become?" I am so, so glad that I chose Carleton—I've never regretted it— for that reason: the person I became there and am continuing to become.

—*Laura Grant, '06, political science/international relations major*

My mom really wanted me to go to a school in the Midwest, and I wanted to get away from Nebraska; we were looking at schools and I figured that Carleton was probably the best school in the region. My grades weren't stellar, so I figured I'd apply early decision to Carleton and if I got in, then that would be a great stroke of luck. And voila, I matriculated.

—*Derek Zimmerman, '07, English major*

The decision to come to Carleton is different for every student, but whatever the reason, not many people end up at the college by mistake. Some students will arrive for the first day of their freshman year in full Knights apparel, knowing the ins and outs of the academic system and the Ultimate Frisbee team's record since 1983. Others will need time to adjust to the small college community and the Minnesota winters. Regardless of background, Carleton is a great fit for students who want a small liberal arts college atmosphere, and a student body filled with a diverse, eccentric, and fun-loving people.

Prospective students who visit the campus in the summer will have a hard time envisioning what the college is all about because Carleton is really defined by the students, staff, and faculty who populate it. All of these people come together to make the college a supportive, intellectual, and challenging environment in which to live and learn. Carleton students don't just "get" an education, they have to make it their own—but there is no dearth of peers, professors, and other members of the Carleton community to help students on their way. Graduating seniors and alumni know that there is a great deal of truth in President Oden saying that "from the first day forward, you become a part of Carleton, and Carleton becomes a part of you."

❏ *Erika Lewis, B.A*

CARNEGIE MELLON UNIVERSITY

 Carnegie Mellon University
Pittsburgh, PA 15213-3890

 (412) 268-2082
Fax: (412) 268-7838

 E-mail: *undergraduate-admissions@*
andrew.cmu.edu
Web site: *www.cmu.edu/admission*

 Enrollment

Full-time ❏ women: 2,174
❏ men: 3,320

Part-time ❏ women: 44
❏ men: 68

INTRODUCING CARNEGIE MELLON

The atmosphere at Carnegie Mellon is one of the most eclectic of any school. The name "Carnegie Mellon" is often associated with computers and engineering; others think of it as a school that specializes in art and drama. All of these people are right. And when you add outstanding programs in the sciences, the humanities and business administration, you've got the basic academic view of Carnegie Mellon. The students here are as different from each other as you can get, yet everyone still finds ways to interact. There are students here from halfway around the world; there are students here from two miles away. There are students from all fifty states and over forty foreign countries. Some people are here building complex electronic devices, and some are making beautiful art. The one thing that everyone does have in common is that they're committed to what they're doing, and they work hard.

Carnegie Mellon, located about five miles from downtown Pittsburgh, is surrounded by three culturally active, residential neighborhoods. Pittsburgh has come a long way since its industrial past. Today, the city, a top twenty-five arts destination, has cultural activity and diversity, and there is no shortage of things to do and learn. This serves as the perfect setting for one of the fastest growing universities in the country.

In 1900 Andrew Carnegie, a Pittsburgh industrialist and philanthropist, founded Carnegie Institute of Technology and Margaret Morrison Women's College to educate the sons and daughters of local working class families. In 1967 Carnegie's institutions merged with Mellon Institute, founded by Andrew Mellon, and formed Carnegie Mellon University. In 1968 Margaret Morrison was closed and the College of Humanities and Social Sciences was founded, forming the basic model of Carnegie Mellon that is seen today. There are now six colleges within the university: Carnegie Institute of Technology (engineering) (CIT), Mellon College of Science (MCS), School of Computer Science (SCS), Tepper School of Business (Tepper), College of Humanities and Social Sciences (H&SS), and College of Fine Arts (CFA).

Carnegie Mellon has an incredibly distinctive history and, luckily, many of the traditions live on. Directly inside the doors of Baker Hall is a portrait of the profile of Arthur Hamerschlag, the first president of the university. Legend has it that it's good luck to rub his nose. Although they wouldn't admit it, many students have been caught rubbing the nose during exam time.

One of the rituals that students would not deny taking part in is the painting of the fence. When Carnegie Mellon was still divided between men and women, the two schools were literally separated by a ravine. The one footbridge that connected the two campuses was where all of the men and women met in their free time. Then, when the College of Fine Arts building was built, the builders leveled a hill and filled in the ravine. The students of both schools were so disappointed that the administration built a fence in the bridge's place, but this was not a good idea because the fence really had no point. The night before it was to be torn down, a group of fraternity brothers painted the fence to advertise a party. The party was such a huge success that it became a tradition to paint the fence. Today, anyone can paint the fence. The only rules are that the fence must be painted, with a paintbrush, between 12:00 A.M. and

5:00 A.M., and whoever paints the fence must guard it for twenty-four hours or as long as they want their painting to stay. The fence paintings range from messages from fraternities advertising parties to happy birthday wishes to friends.

Carnegie Mellon is also one of the only universities that uses bagpipes to greet its freshmen on the first day and say farewell to graduates at commencement. Carnegie's Scottish heritage is celebrated even today. The name of our marching band, the Kiltie Band, says it all; every member of the band wears authentic Scottish garb (yes, including kilts). Carnegie Mellon is one of the few schools in the United States that offers a music degree in bagpiping. If you're not interested in majoring in it, there's also a bagpipe club (no kidding).

> *I never realized how different my college experience was from that of my friends. I never knew how many different people could live together on one campus. Like a lot of other people that have never really left home, I just figured everybody would be more or less like me. I was so wrong. But I've learned so much from just being here that I wouldn't trade it for anything.*

ADMISSIONS REQUIREMENTS

What does it take to get into Carnegie Mellon? The Office of Admission looks at a lot of different elements when choosing who gets in. Basically, the admissions counselors are trying to get a feel of who you are and what you've done. Unlike many people think, it isn't only your transcript that admissions counselors look at. Of course, high school grades are important, but they are definitely not everything. The Office of Admission also looks at your standardized test scores (SATs or ACTs) and SAT Subject Tests, your essay, activities you've been involved in, personal recommendations, a portfolio or audition depending on your major interest and your interview (recommended not required).

There is no set formula for how people get accepted. In some cases, one element (like test scores) may not be as strong as you'd like, but something else (like extracurricular activities) will make up for it. What admissions counselors look at also depends heavily on what your intended major is. For example, if you are applying to be a math major, they will concentrate on your math grades and scores more than on other things.

However, what they *are* looking for is a well-rounded student who will take full advantage of the opportunity to come here. Your best bet is to do your best in everything and, above all, get involved! Most Carnegie Mellon students are involved in much more than just class work—the admissions counselors want to find people who will be willing to take part in other things. This doesn't mean just sports or clubs. Your activities can be interests or hobbies.

There is no grade or score that will get you in or keep you out of Carnegie Mellon. The decision comes from a number of different considerations that the counselors use to decide whether Carnegie Mellon is right for you.

To apply to Carnegie Mellon, you can call or write and request an application for admission. You can also submit the Common Application online. Once you're on the mailing list, the university will send you all the information you need. When you apply, you must indicate which college within the university you'd like to apply to. If you're still not sure what you want to major in (which college), you can apply to more than one college for no additional charge. Keep in mind that it is possible to be admitted to one college and rejected from another.

Requirements for Majors

The classes that you need to have taken in high school depend on what you're planning on majoring in. Each major has slightly different requirements, so be sure to check on that. Every major requires that you take four years of English; beyond that, it depends on the major. Of course, as long as you carry a normal high school course load, you should fulfill all of the requirements. You must submit scores from either the SAT or the ACT. In most cases, you also need to take two SAT (subject tests). Students applying to art, design, drama, or music are not required to take the SAT Subject Tests.

Interviews

Recommendations and interviews are two of the best ways to show the Office of Admission who you really are. Interviews are suggested, but not required. They not only give an admissions counselor an opportunity to learn more about you, but give you an opportunity to learn more about the school. For those students who are too far away to come to campus for an interview, the school also offers hometown interviews. These interviews serve the same purpose as campus interviews (although you won't see the campus). Alumni interviews in your hometown are available as well.

The students of Carnegie Mellon come from a number of different backgrounds. The one thing that everyone has in common is that they have worked hard to get here. Most of the students come from the top of their high school classes. At first, many of them are surprised that they are not necessarily in the same position here; however, they soon realize that they are gaining something even more valuable than a class rank. They are surrounded by people and situations that challenge them and inspire them to work harder.

Nobody ever said that being a student at Carnegie Mellon was easy, but it is certainly not impossible. You may be working hard and studying more than you'd expected, but so is everybody else. People understand what their colleagues are going through and they help each other.

When I was getting ready to come here, I was really worried because I thought I wouldn't be able to handle the work load. All I had heard was how hard it was and how much everybody had to work. Now that I look back on it, I do have a lot of work to do, but it was as if I was eased into it. I'm used to it. Plus, all of my friends have the same amount of work to do, so I don't feel that I'm the only one studying so much.

Although Carnegie Mellon is an extremely competitive school, students learn early that they need to help and support each other to succeed. People are willing to explain a difficult concept or give constructive criticism because they know that at some point they will probably need the same favor.

For every class, there is a study session offered before a test. In many cases, the professor or a teaching assistant will organize a review session to help members of the class. In addition to this, many students take it upon themselves to start their own study groups. In addition to helping and being helped by their peers, many students find this to be a good way to get to know people in their classes.

Classes and Faculty

The faculty/student ratio is ten to one; the average class size is between twenty-five and thirty-five students. This also takes into consideration the larger lectures. The largest lecture hall on campus seats 250, which is relatively small compared to other universities. Most of the classes that have lectures this size are introductory classes that many students are required to take. In classes with lectures this size, there is always a recitation offered with the lecture. The recitation is a smaller group (ten to twenty people) led by a teaching assistant (TA) or graduate student who discusses the concepts and subjects covered in the lecture. In all cases, the TA and professor will always have office hours for people who may need extra help, and, in most cases, they will also give the class members (no matter how many) their office (and sometimes home) telephone number and e-mail address. Some professors even host social gatherings to become better acquainted with their students.

When I was looking at schools, I was intimidated by Carnegie Mellon's reputation. I came for a visit and was really surprised to find that the students were normal people—their rooms were messy and they procrastinated, just like me! Since I've been here, I've found teachers and classmates to be very supportive. It's an intense environment, but I don't feel I'm in it alone.

The course load and the kind of work you do depends on what college you're in and what you're majoring in. Computer science majors will obviously spend a lot of time at their computers, while architecture majors will spend a lot of time in their studios. While one person is working on problem sets every night, another will be writing a long paper. Everyone will say that his or her work is the hardest, but the truth is that everyone is doing the kind of work they enjoy (or they should be). It's impossible to classify the class work here into one category. Every class has its own pattern.

No matter what a person's major is, he or she will have a few classes in other areas. For example, computer science majors are required to take non-computer related electives (such as an English class), people in the humanities are required to take a math class and two science classes, and every freshman is required to take a Computer Skills Workshop course, Introduction to World History, and an introductory English class.

Computers

Any student at Carnegie Mellon would tell you that this is a very computer-oriented campus. Almost everything, from communicating with professors to signing up for classes is done over the Internet. One of the first things students are taught when they come here is how to use the campus network, Andrew. Every freshman is required to pass a class called Computer Skills Workshop (CSW), which covers everything from e-mail to ethics. Almost everything is announced over the Internet. Most classes and student organizations have their own electronic bulletin boards to make announcements and have discussions.

Students aren't required to have their own computers, but many have them. There are computer clusters in many of the dorms and in every academic building. Every dorm room has ethernet hookups in case the students do have a computer of their own, so they have access to the Internet from their rooms. Carnegie Mellon was the first university campus to offer wireless networking in all administrative and academic buildings. Wireless Andrew, the largest installation of its type anywhere, connects over 5,000 students, faculty, and staff across campus—and that number is growing. The wireless network is now available in all administrative, academic, and residential buildings across campus. The network is also accessible from outdoor areas on campus due to wireless leakage around buildings and through access points mounted on the exterior of some buildings. Users are able to access Wireless Andrew by purchasing a WaveLan card from the campus computer store and inserting it into their laptop or portable computer. The need for a computer depends on the major. Some people, who have a lot of work to do on computers, find it convenient to not have to leave their room to get their work done. Others, who don't do a lot of work with computers, don't have any need for them. Your best bet is to wait until you get to school and figure it out then (if you don't already have one).

SOCIAL LIFE AND ACTIVITIES

The Campus

Carnegie Mellon is technically in a city. The campus is self-contained and surprisingly open for a city campus. There's grass and trees and (if you're in the right dorm) you never have to cross the street. The campus is also fairly safe. Pittsburgh's crime rate is relatively low compared to the national average. With relative security and other cultural benefits, Pittsburgh has continually been named one of the country's most livable cities. Because the Carnegie Mellon campus is so self-contained, it's even safer.

The university has about fifty security employees. About half are sworn police officers who have the power to make arrests; the other half are security guards. These guards and officers patrol the campus (on foot, bike, and in cars) twenty-four hours a day. If something does happen on campus, the campus police will hang up "crime reports" on all of the bulletin boards and in all of the dorms to keep everybody informed.

In addition to the campus police, there are many student-run safety organizations. There is an escort shuttle bus (driven by students) that runs within two miles of the campus and will bring you home if you don't want to walk off campus alone. If you feel unsafe walking across campus alone, you can call Safewalk and two students will come and walk you wherever you need to go.

Unwinding

Although the academic environment can get fairly intense, Carnegie Mellon students definitely know how to unwind. After a full week of classes and schoolwork, everybody's ready to relax and have some fun. A common stereotype of Carnegie Mellon students is that they can never tear themselves away from their computers. While everybody here has probably had a few weekends when they spent much of it working, it is much more common for students to find other, non-work-related things to do.

When I got here, upperclassmen kept telling me about how they had pulled all-nighters and had gone days without sleep. I got a little scared, and then I got worried because I was sleeping (I thought maybe I was doing something wrong). Finally I realized that it was said to psyche each other out. I've noticed that people say they haven't slept as a way to brag about how much time they've spent working. I'm a junior now, and I can honestly say that I've never pulled an all-nighter. I've had a few very late nights, but those are spent just as much talking with friends as they are working.

Off Campus

A lot of students jump at the chance to get off campus on the weekends. The Carnegie Mellon campus is situated in the middle of three major shopping areas: Oakland, Shadyside, and Squirrel Hill. Between these three areas you can find shopping, restaurants, movie theaters, coffeehouses, museums, and nightlife (and this is all within walking distance). Beyond that, it is easy to catch a city bus going downtown or to a nearby shopping mall. Students have free access to public transportation with their ID card. Pittsburgh is full of things to do, from the cultural to the just plain fun. You can go to the symphony one night and then go to a Pittsburgh Penguins game the next. The possibilities are endless.

Athletics

Of course, you don't need to leave campus to find something to do. Carnegie Mellon has seventeen varsity sports (nine men's, eight women's). There are also many more intramural and club sports (these range from very competitive to strictly for fun). Even if you're not interested in participating in one of these sports, you'll probably have at least one friend who does. Around eighty percent of the student body participates in an intramural or club sport at one point or another.

Organizations

Beyond sports, there are more than 130 student organizations on campus. The student body of Carnegie Mellon is incredibly diverse, so it is obvious that the list of clubs would be just as diverse. From organizations celebrating ethnic heritage to clubs based on political views to clubs made up of people who like to play chess, there is a club here for everyone. And even if there isn't, all you have to do to start one is find a few people with your common interest and apply to the student senate to be recognized. Student organizations recognized by the senate are open to any student and vary in size from a few people (usually the newer clubs have fewer members) to a lot of people.

I had been involved in drama in high school, but I knew I wouldn't be able to take part in the drama productions here because I wasn't a drama major. I was so excited when I found out about Scotch and Soda, a group of nondrama majors who put on shows throughout the year. I've met some of my best friends through S&S.

Scotch and Soda, an amateur theater group, has a long tradition at Carnegie Mellon. Throughout the year the group produces two full-length shows and several one-act plays. The playwrights of both Godspell and Pippin were not only Carnegie Mellon alumni, but Scotch and Soda members.

Fraternities and Sororities

Throughout the year, the eleven fraternities and five sororities on campus plan various events open to the entire campus. These events have, in the past, included talent shows, dance marathons, and the annual Mr. Fraternity contest. The Greek system (fraternities and sororities) make up about fifteen percent of the campus. Many of those involved in the Greek system enjoy it because it gives members a chance to get to know other students and to take part in large social events (each fraternity and sorority also takes part in several charity events), but the number is low enough to not overwhelm the campus. If a student chooses not to join the Greek system, he or she will still have no problem having a social life. It is also very common for people to interact with many people in an organization without being a member.

Spring Carnival

Each spring, the campus comes together for Carnegie Mellon's annual Spring Carnival. This three-day event includes shows, concerts, and contests. The two biggest elements of Spring Carnival are Booth and Buggy. Each organization has the opportunity to build a booth corresponding to the carnival's theme, and each structure includes a game in which all of the money raised goes to charity. These booths are often quite large and quite elaborate.

These same organizations build buggies, high-tech soapbox derby cars, to race through Schenley Park. The buggies look like torpedoes on wheels and are driven by the smallest student (usually a female) that the organization can find. People push the buggies up the hill and then let them coast through the park (some get up to speeds of thirty-five to forty miles per hour).

Buggy has been one of the highlights of my life at Carnegie Mellon. At first, I wasn't sure about it. Everyone seemed to know exactly what they were doing but I had no clue. However, the first time I pushed, the whole team ran along beside me cheering—after that first push, I felt like a pro. I've also made a lot of friends through Buggy. There's a lot to be said about the friends you can make getting up at 5:00 A.M. on a weekend.

FINANCIAL AID

The total cost of a year at Carnegie Mellon, including tuition, room and board, books, etc., during a recent year was $46,308. With a price tag like this, it's obvious that many students will need some kind of financial aid. Depending on your financial need, your financial aid package might include a combination of grants, loans, and work-study. About seventy percent of the freshmen who entered in a recent year received some sort of financial aid. The average need-based package was $23,597. Although you are not guaranteed financial assistance, most people who are eligible and in need receive it.

Work-study gives students the opportunity to have on-campus jobs in order to make money to pay some of their college expenses. These jobs include positions in offices, food service, the child-care facility, and the library, to name a few. These jobs usually don't take up more than ten to fifteen hours a week and they allow the student to make extra money that they might need to buy books or for other necessities. Since there are so many jobs available, students may work on campus even if they don't qualify for need-based work-study.

My parents own a small business and don't have a lot of extra money. When I applied to Carnegie Mellon, I was worried that the cost would be too high for them to afford. If it wasn't for the financial aid, there is no chance that I would be here. I've talked to several of my friends about this and many of them are in the same position.

GRADUATES

There are almost 68,000 Carnegie Mellon alumni spread out all over the world. The goals achieved and backgrounds of these alumni are as diverse as when they began their careers at Carnegie Mellon. There is no one category that all graduates fit into. There are Carnegie Mellon alumni who have become great actors, writers, artists, and scientists, over 2,000 alumni are presidents or vice-presidents of corporations, more than 1,400 teach as professors at universities, and thirty are deans.

Very few of these people graduate and go immediately to the top; however, many of these graduates are used to working hard to achieve their goals. After four years at Carnegie Mellon, these people know how to get the job done. Because of Carnegie Mellon's reputation for preparing students with real-world and practical experience, employers are eager to hire recent Carnegie Mellon graduates. About seventy-five percent of graduates get job offers within six months of graduation, while another twenty-two percent go on to graduate school immediately after commencement.

There is a large network of Carnegie Mellon graduates organized all over the world. This network helps fellow alumni who decide to relocate or need advice concerning a job. It is also an invaluable resource for meeting people in your field. The one thing that all Carnegie Mellon alumni do have in common is the pride and tradition of being part of this network. You could go anywhere in the world and be able to chat with alumni about Spring Carnival or Schenley Park. Although alumni may have complained about their classes or other things while they were here, very few can admit that being a student at Carnegie Mellon did not help them in the long run.

SUMMING UP

Carnegie Mellon has, in a word, everything—there is nothing that you could not find at Carnegie Mellon. Walking across the Cut (the grassy area in the middle of campus), you can see people studying, playing Frisbee, reciting poetry, sleeping . . . the list could go on and on. The people who end up coming to Carnegie Mellon are from all over the world, with different cultures, different beliefs, and different interests. But they all exist together. People say that going away to college is as educational outside of the classroom as it is inside. This has never been more true than it is at Carnegie Mellon.

Being from Pittsburgh originally, I was worried when I came to Carnegie Mellon because I thought that I'd miss out on the experience of going to a college out of state, but I've met so many interesting people, not only from all over the country, but all over the world! Even though I didn't leave Pittsburgh, I feel that I've learned more than I would have if I had gone away to another school.

There is so much here, it can be very intimidating at first. Where do I go? What do I do? How do I make friends? It's impossible to know exactly how to approach it. Fortunately, somebody has already planned this. For the first week that freshmen are on campus they are involved in, as many students would tell you, the best orientation anywhere. Through the entire week, students take part in planned activities, learn how to deal with being away from home, and meet more people than they could ever remember. This orientation is just the beginning of the series of support systems that exist here. No matter what you're doing, there will always be somebody there to help you. There are programs here ranging from peer tutoring to peer counseling. If you have a problem that you don't think a peer can help you with, the professors and other staff are always willing to try to help you. Basically, no matter what's going on, if you look for help, you'll find it.

The students that attend Carnegie Mellon are motivated, driven, and goal-oriented. Everyone here knows that everyone else has worked hard to get here. They're all in the same boat, and this brings everyone closer together. College is about the things you learn and the friends you make in the process. You'll have both at Carnegie Mellon.

There isn't anybody who goes here—or has ever gone here—who won't tell you that everything about this place is intense. People work hard. They have goals and dreams. But they also have friends and fun. Don't ever let anybody tell you that it's too hard.

❏ *Jessica Demers, B.A.*

CASE WESTERN RESERVE UNIVERSITY

 Case Western Reserve University
Cleveland, OH 44106

 (216) 368-2000 (general information)
(216) 368-4450 (admission)
Fax: (216) 368-5111

 E-mail: *admission@case.edu*
Web site: *http://www.case.edu*

Enrollment

Full-time ❏ women: 1,500
❏ men: 2,214

Part-time ❏ women: 103
❏ men: 132

INTRODUCING CASE WESTERN RESERVE UNIVERSITY

Case Western Reserve University has seen many large-scale improvements, including those to the undergraduate general education requirements. Most students, including me, dread having to take classes in which they have absolutely no interest, but are required to receive their degree. It can be especially hard for freshmen to adjust to the competitive, high-intensity learning atmosphere at Case while lost in undergraduate classes with hundreds of other students. Starting fall 2005, all incoming students are enrolled in the SAGES curriculum, an undergraduate requirement program enabling students to make selections among diverse course choices, as well as enjoy close personal attention from professors in smaller classes sizes.

In addition to the curriculum, the physical campus itself is getting a major face-lift. Currently, Euclid Avenue, one of Cleveland's major streets, cuts the campus in half, effectively dividing the undergraduate population by a thirty-minute walk between North and South Residential Villages. Work was completed summer 2005 to centralize the separate residential areas in a massive complex on the North Side of campus, allowing classmates to more easily interact and creating a much more cohesive atmosphere and culture on campus.

Location

When considering which school to attend, location usually factors into the final decision, so why pick Cleveland? There are no mountains, no rolling green fields or glittering lakes flanked by glaciers, and no antiquated academic buildings smothered in ivy, but there are myriad other things of more value than stereotypical campus aesthetics. Case is integrated into the city of Cleveland and located in the center of University Circle, home to a multitude of excellent cultural institutions, such as the Cleveland Museum of Art, Severance Hall, and the Cleveland Institute of Art and Cleveland Institute of Music. A massive medical complex is positioned in the center of campus, home to university hospitals and the medical, dental, and nursing Schools. The famed Cleveland Clinic is just blocks away.

The architecture is as impressive as the culture, exemplified by the sturdy, modern style of Kelvin Smith Library's spiral stairways and flowing open spaces, and the eccentrically designed Peter B. Lewis building, which looks, honestly, like a titanic soda can exploded and warped the brick building on which it sits. While it may not be the most classically picturesque campus to choose, it is absolutely jammed with every type of institution possible and all within walking distance of student housing.

Majors

Case is known mainly as an engineering school, but lurking within that blanket reputation is a thriving liberal arts community. Case is about variety, with its four undergraduate colleges (nursing, business management, engineering, and arts and sciences), and offers students plenty of opportunity to explore whichever educational options may be tugging at their intellects. Sitting in an English class, you may be surprised to discover that nearly half the students are electrical engineering majors, some of whom are double-majoring in world literature, and others who are pursuing a political science degree. At Case, there is no need to stress over knowing exactly what subject to major in on the first day because there is so much opportunity to try different educational avenues. If you don't like the direction you're headed, or want to pick up an extra major, then you are free to do exactly that. In fact, it's encouraged; double-majoring is far from uncommon. It's not unusual to pass by a Japanese class and see a math major, or computer science classes and spot several philosophy majors, because it's that type of explorative, open-minded mindset that Case cultivates.

ADMISSIONS REQUIREMENTS

Case accepts a large percentage of its applicants, accepting seventy percent of the pool in a recent year. This doesn't mean Case opens the floodgates to anyone who submits a completed application, but it's certainly worth applying if your high school career went well, especially considering the dollars available from financial aid. Case's student body is comprised largely of highly qualified applicants. Sixty-three freshmen in a recent class finished first in their high school, eighty-seven percent of the current freshmen finished in the top fifth of their class, and ninety-eight percent finished in the top two-fifths. Of the new freshmen there were sixty National Merit Finalists. More than one-third of students accepted at Case score 700 or above on the SAT Verbal section and more than half scored 700 or better on the SAT Math section. More than seventy percent scored above 27 on the ACT. In addition to either of those tests, Case strongly recommends students take any three SAT Subject Tests. Those planning on pursuing science, engineering, or mathematics should take the Math Level I/IC or IIC. Applicants are required to submit a writing sample and a recommendation. As a bonus, the application fee of $35 is waived for those who apply online. But admission to Case isn't all grades. The Admissions Department takes into account Advanced Placement or honors courses taken as well as extracurricular activities and leadership qualifications. Generally, a score of 4 or above on an AP exam receives college credit.

There are more options available to incoming students than just applying to Case's undergraduate programs. Case allows prospective students to put in for a B.S.N. degree at the Frances Payne Bolton School of Nursing, a double major through the Cleveland Institute of Art or Cleveland Institute of Music, or the Preprofessional Scholars Program (PPSP). The PPSP allows applicants, if accepted and able to maintain a certain grade point average, to be conditionally accepted at Case's medical, dental, or law schools, as well as Case's Mandel School of

Applied Social Sciences. Given the difficulty of getting into such professional schools, competition is more heated and admissions requirements more stringent for PPSP applicants. Applicants are free to apply to any school or program they choose, but , if accepted, PPSP applicants always have a reserved spot in one of Case's professional schools.

Applicants have the opportunity to be admitted during the fall, spring, and summer. Standardized tests should be taken by the fall of your senior year in high school, though Case recommends you take them during your junior year. For fall entry, admissions materials need to be filed by January 15th and applicants will be notified of a decision by March 1st.

ACADEMIC LIFE

While you may find freshmen sitting in the morning dark, staring at computer monitors with fingers poised over the keyboard as the hour of class registration draws near, you won't find any upperclassmen doing the same. The fact is, none of Case's classes are that crowded, and only a handful actually fill up within the first few days of registration, so there is no need to stress about signing up at the earliest possible moment. As a freshman, the introductory math and sciences classes are generally the most populated, but no student should have trouble getting in. If a student does get locked out of a class, there's always plenty of variety left to choose from.

SAGES

This variety has been further expanded with the implementation of the Seminar Approach to General Education and Scholarship program, or SAGES. Incoming students enroll in what is called a First Seminar. These courses are small, limited to seventeen students. Every course will be taught by a Case faculty member who will function as the students' advisor for the freshman year. That way, instead of being immediately thrust into an open-ended college environment, students will be in close contact with someone who can give advice and help map out the academic path their students wish to follow, which is certainly helpful given the myriad opportunities available. Instead of sitting around and listening to droning lectures for hours, like so many other freshmen courses, First Seminars promote student discussion allowing peer interaction and letting students express their ideas and experiences. The three hours a week dedicated to the First Seminar will be accompanied by "fourth-hour activities" that incorporate the cultural and scientific institutions around University Circle, including the Cleveland

Natural History Museum, Cleveland Museum of Art, and the Western Reserve Historical Society, allowing students to get out of the classroom for a change.

First Seminar courses are followed in the students' later years by University Seminars, Departmental Seminars, and a Senior Capstone course, all of which let students concentrate on and study what interests them. Aside from the main SAGES courses, students are free to experiment with the course selection to fulfill their breadth requirements, which range across Case's wide variety of subjects. SAGES is designed to focus on students' writing as well. Instead of taking an introductory writing course, SAGES classes will, in addition to Case faculty, be staffed with writing teachers, usually graduate English students, to give each student close attention to their content and style.

Aside from SAGES, Case's undergraduate students benefit from a great deal of freedom. Instead of requiring students to be admitted to specific undergraduate colleges such as an engineering college or a physical sciences college, students are free to study whatever subjects they feel like pursuing. This translates to a theater major being able to take an electrical engineering course with no more hassle than clicking the "add course" button through Case's online class registration system. While some may not feel the need to experiment with their course selections, the fact that the option is available is useful, just in case something really interesting pops up in a subject that is not your major. Physical education is also part of the curriculum, where students can golf, play racquetball, practice tennis, or keep up their running regimen.

College Scholars Program

Students have the opportunity to apply to the College Scholars Program (CSP) during their freshman year. If accepted, they would take one CSP course for three credits per semester for the remaining three years of their undergraduate study. CSP courses emphasize student-directed study and service learning, and allow groups of students to meet and discuss issues with professors and, often, distinguished guests such as, in the past, Kurt Vonnegut and Ralph Nader. The program also provides the option to live in CSP-specific housing consisting of single rooms and fully equipped kitchens.

Internships

Because Case is embedded in a metropolitan setting, it's easy to get some real-world experience through internships. Whether it is with an engineering firm or an independent newspaper, Cleveland companies are eager for student workers, and look to Case to turn out capable candidates. This provides an opportunity for students to gain knowledge that can't be

I was originally planning on majoring in physics. I ended up with an English degree. Because of Case's open-ended course selection structure I was able to discover and fully explore English after initially taking two semesters aimed at physics, and earn my B.A. within the allotted four years in addition to minors in philosophy and psychology. Ironically, it was at Case, a school known for its engineering, that I discovered my interest in writing for the first time. The courses offered in the two subjects through the English department and the humanities courses in general are excellent, thanks to the dedicated faculty and the intelligent, driven student community.

learned in the classroom. One hundred and sixty employers offer students co-op programs that may be alternated with classroom study. Also available are study abroad programs, a Washington semester, and work-study programs, as well as accelerated degree programs, B.A./B.S. degrees, student-designed and dual majors, 3-2 binary engineering degrees, nondegree study, and independent study.

SOCIAL LIFE AND ACTIVITIES

A lot of people like to knock Cleveland for being a run-down city with nothing to do, but they obviously have never been here or looked around very hard. Cleveland is absolutely brimming with opportunities for entertainment, whether you are looking for cinema, music, food, art, theater, anything, it's pretty much right around Case's campus.

Off-campus Places of Interest

Since Case is located directly in the center of University Circle, students are a short walk away from the Cleveland Museum of Art, Cleveland Museum of Natural History, the Cleveland Botanical Garden, Severance Concert Hall, which is home to the Cleveland Orchestra, and many more cultural institutions. While those things are great for a Saturday afternoon or a quiet evening, or just impressing your parents, Cleveland is ripe with opportunities for college students to toss the books out the window and have some fun.

Cleveland has a thriving cinema scene, and not just a group of theaters showing the latest *Spider Man* or *Harry Potter* releases (though they also exist). The Cedar-Lee Theater is minutes away from campus and regularly shows smaller-scale releases from more independent studios that many times you've never even heard of, yet that doesn't mean they're not good, it's a great place to go when you're in the mood for something different. For more eclectic tastes, the Cleveland Cinematheque is located right on campus inside the Cleveland Institute of Art, which shows just about every type of film you could ever imagine. From the latest releases around the world to classics from the early ages of films to the most obscure films that maybe only a handful of people have ever heard of, it's all there, all the time. It's a pity to overlook the opportunity to acquaint yourself with global film trends and a true big picture of the medium's history.

One of the first things that usually comes to mind when a person mentions Cleveland, is the Rock and Roll Hall of Fame. And that's great to visit. Once. In all honesty, it's a bland tourist attraction, but it seems to be a beacon that brings in some of the best music acts. It's amazing how many bands make Cleveland one of their stops, and there are plenty of places for them to play as well, all located fairly close to campus. These aren't just big, headliner bands playing at major venues, but also popular underground bands and others more obscure. You'll find music and see acts in Cleveland that you'd never have the opportunity to see on other campuses.

The school's shuttle service, small buses oddly called "Greenies" (they're not green at all), cart students around campus and the near vicinity. One of their regular routes is to Coventry, about a two-minute drive from campus, where students can find dingy stages that boast an incredibly diverse lineup of live acts. Any night of the week, if the books are getting to be too much, which is more than likely to happen (students at Case *will* spend most of their time studying), students can shuttle over and catch a music show—be it death metal, psychedelic electronics, or folk music—then walk right down Coventry and get a burrito, or a fine Chinese dinner. They can shop for trendy clothes, buy a video game or DVD, browse for antiques, buy a classic novel, pick up milk and cereal for tomorrow morning, and do their dry cleaning. Or students could walk over to Little Italy, pretty much right on campus, for fine dining, drinks, doughnuts, or to browse through art galleries. Or, if students feel adventurous, they could step onto the RTA, Cleveland's transit system, for a ten-minute ride downtown to see professional baseball, football, and basketball games, or yet more shopping, fine dining, and entertainment.

But more likely, you'll be sequestered in your dorm room, poring over books and battling the urge to flip on your computer to distract yourself. Again, students at Case study a lot. Those who aren't ready to fully commit themselves to their academics drop out fast. The SAGES program might make it a little easier to transition into Case's environment, but without the understanding of school as the main priority, things can start to pile up pretty quickly.

Clubs and Organizations

As one might expect from a group of motivated students, new groups and organizations are being created and expanded all the time. Whether it is philanthropy, media, or honorary groups, Habitat for Humanity, Mortar Board, or Ignite (Case's student-run television station), in addition to academic, performance, political, ethnic, religious, and athletic groups, there is plenty of opportunity for students to get involved. There's also a thriving Greek community on campus, in which thirty percent of Case's students actively participate. In fact, Greek Week, along with the Hudson Relays and Springfest, is among the most popular events on campus.

CAMPUS GROUPS

Like to get involved around campus and in the community? Case has a wide range of groups organized to give every student a chance. On campus you'll find:
- 10 honorary societies
- 16 athletic clubs
- 37 special-interest organizations
- 12 religious groups
- 4 political organizations
- 5 social service clubs
- 9 performance groups
- 23 ethnic clubs
- 5 competitive teams
- 33 academic groups
- 8 media organizations
- 25 fraternities and sororities
- 5 governing organizations

The Network

One thing Case is particularly proud of and what students may find most appealing is what is referred to as The Network. Case students' computers are linked to each other through a switched-gigabit connection that allows blazing fast transfer speeds of any file types. In total, about 12,800 locations are linked to each other around Case including libraries, residence halls, laboratories, and pretty much every other building on campus. This allows for the material and handouts of many courses to be posted online and remain easily accessible, which is certainly a welcome alternative to lugging around binders bursting with files and those pesky course syllabi that seem to consistently escape through holes in students' backpacks. What's even more impressive is that Case's network has gone wireless. This makes it possible to head out to one of the many parks in the area with your computer on a clear day and type that essay that's due next week without being stuck inside. Having a computer on campus, whether it's a desktop or a laptop, really makes things easier.

Residences

Though many students like to knock the dorms for being for dorks, few will have reason to do so with the construction of the new residential village. Case is completely revamping how it houses its students, placing them now in what is being dubbed the NRV (North Residential Village). The first phase features three building complexes comprised of seven residential "houses" that is home to approximately 750 upper-class students who get to bask in the apartment-style housing. The actual living quarters boast several bedrooms, each with its own double bed and closet, a bathroom for every two students, and a kitchen with full-sized stove, refrigerator, and microwave. Freshmen and sophomores will certainly have something to look forward to.

Athletics

Though at Case you might not expect it, there are plenty of competitive sports and facilities on campus. Intercollegiate sports for men and women total nineteen, with sixty intramural sports for both genders. Dotted around campus are multiple athletic facilities, providing students with tennis courts, all-weather tracks, wrestling, fencing and weight rooms, racquetball courts, facilities for badminton, basketball, volleyball, and squash, as well as an archery range, softball diamonds, baseball, football, and soccer fields. But keep in mind, Case's focus is academics.

I used to be that guy, sitting around the dorms complaining about having to constantly study and how there was nothing fun to do. So I went Greek, like many of the people I knew in my dorm. I think the entire floor in my dorm went Greek. It turned out to be a great decision, putting me in touch with a large network of like-minded individuals and leading to my finding some of my closest friends in school. It helped to show me that there was more to the experience than slaving over study. Now that I've graduated, there's a far-reaching network of fellow alumni I can easily get in contact with, which is more valuable than some may think. For anyone who finds the idea of going Greek to be revolting, a way to "pay for friends" (which I admit I initially thought too until I experienced it firsthand), Case has plenty of other opportunities to get involved with other students for study and socially.

FINANCIAL AID

Ask any undergraduates about why they decided to attend Case and you'll hear one common answer: money. To the students who are accepted it's true, Case hands them a respectable chunk of money, whether it is in financial aid grants or scholarships. Most recently, ninety-two percent of undergraduate students at Case received financial aid, the average financial aid package being $23,458, which, needless to say, is a lot. There are many varied scholarships available to freshmen, including President's, Trustee's, National Merit, and Creative Achievement scholarships, all of which are awarded on the basis of achievements and credentials.

Students, much like me, will find it necessary to work during school just so they're not completely without a little pocket money. For that, Case offers work-study awards as part of the financial aid packages. There is a wealth of jobs available to students on work-study, most with flexible hours that can be worked around class times since employers recognize education as students' priority. All positions anywhere, even if you're just handing out towels at the Veale Athletic Center, pay really well. It's without a doubt an option worth looking into, even if you're not a student with a work-study award, though the work-study students are given priority.

GRADUATES

Then there's graduation. When it comes time to don ridiculous robes and hats and walk across the stage, the degrees you might hear being called out most frequently are in management, biology, and mechanical engineering, which together make up about twenty-five percent of Case's graduates' majors. A little more than half of the students will graduate in four years or less, and close to seventy-five percent will graduate in five years or less.

Coming out of college, around forty percent of graduates in a recent year enrolled in graduate school within six months of graduation; the other approximately sixty percent found jobs or had other plans. Aiding students about to graduate is the Career Center, an on-campus office students are free to visit anytime for advice on what opportunities exist. They can put you in touch with alumni among Case's 95,000 graduates who volunteer their contact information and invite students to ask them about finding jobs. Students can contact those who work in similar fields of interest and set up informational interviews, inquire about what sorts of skills are needed for that type of work, or discover who else might be a good and helpful person to talk to. This sort of networking is crucial in finding the best opportunities, and is readily provided by the Career Center.

Additional resources include E-Compass, an online campus job search engine where employers post positions and student internships. All the contact information is easily accessible and students are able to create a profile and resumes and cover letters, which they can use to apply to positions or post online and make available for employers to read. For writing the materials necessary for job application, students can set up appointments with Career Center staff for tips on interviewing, help with career assessments, and insight on the job search process.

SUMMING UP

Experiences at Case can range from brain meltingly boring to rocket-propelled merry-go-round exciting. It depends on who you are and what you're looking for. If you're looking to sit down every night with your studies and dedicate yourself fully to your grades, then you will get good grades. A lot of students at Case make the decision to do this, which is, in part, why Case gets a reputation for being a "nerdy" school. This is unfortunate—tragic almost—given the opportunities available to students. Apply and attend and you will be surprised as long as you want to be surprised. Opportunity is here for an amazingly unique experience that is not just academic, but social and cultural and anything else you can think of. You just have to be willing to get off the couch and go find it.

❑ *Charles Onyett, B.A.*

CLAREMONT MCKENNA COLLEGE

 Claremont McKenna College
Claremont, CA 91711

 (909) 621-8088
Fax: (909) 621-8516

 E-mail: *admission@claremontmckenna.edu*
Web site: *http://www.claremontmckenna.edu*

 **Enrollment**

Full-time ❑ women: 530
❑ men: 610

INTRODUCING CLAREMONT MCKENNA

Recognized as one of the nation's most prestigious liberal arts colleges, Claremont McKenna College sets itself apart from its counterparts by its focus on leadership. The college's mission statement is to train "leaders in the making" and leadership is stressed everywhere, from the classroom to dorm life to athletics. Many students pursue the "Leadership Sequence," which includes courses focusing on leadership across disciplines, in addition to their major.

> *CMC is academically different because it provides its students with so many opportunities outside of the classroom for them to gain experience and knowledge that textbooks simply cannot offer. There are countless numbers of fellowships and scholarships for students that will pay for interning in another country, working for a nonprofit organization, starting up businesses, and study trips.*

—*Joanna Respold*
Class of 2007

One of the admissions criteria is leadership potential and the "typical" CMC student excelled academically in high school and also participated in some sort of leadership role, whether yearbook editor, swim team captain, or orchestra section leader. Students selected for the McKenna Scholars program are chosen for their leadership activities in high school.

Consequently, CMC students are "doers." They apply what they have learned in the classroom at one of the college's eleven research institutes or through internship programs. They participate in more than 180 student organizations that support student activities from skiing to vegetarian cooking. They play on one of CMC's twenty Division III athletic teams. They study abroad in more than forty countries internationally and have performed volunteer work at a high rate compared to other colleges nationwide.

With especially strong programs in economics and government, the college excels in preparing its students to pursue careers in business, government, and the professions. CMC's economics department is ranked first among liberal arts colleges and more than thirty percent of students graduate with a degree in economics. However, CMC's liberal arts curriculum requires that students complete a broad distribution of courses across departments, including mathematics, literature, and foreign language. More than half of students choose to pursue dual or double majors, often combining fields as disparate as economics and literature.

Employers note that CMC students are prepared for the work world. They are trained to think analytically and to present their ideas both orally and in written form. Writing skills are stressed from the freshman writing seminar through the mandatory senior thesis, in which students present their senior research project in a paper which may range from fifty to hundreds of pages. Also, CMC students are taught to present their ideas orally through oral exams and research presentations, as well as through in-class debate with professors or fellow students.

With approximately 1,050 students on its campus, CMC has a community feel. It is not uncommon to attend a class dinner at a professor's home in the nearby Claremont village, and strong friendships are formed between students, starting from the ten-day freshman orientation including WOA (Wilderness Orientation Adventure) and lasting far beyond graduation day. More than ninety-five percent of students live on campus for all four years and the dorms serve as hubs for on-campus social life, hosting various themed parties throughout the year, and for student government. The Associated Students of Claremont McKenna College (ASCMC) is one of the most popular on-campus organizations, as more than one-third of the student body serve in student government as dorm presidents, class representatives, and student senators.

Location and the Claremont Consortium

Claremont McKenna is located on a fifty-acre campus in the convenient and safe college town of Claremont, thirty-five miles east of downtown Los Angeles. CMC is close to two major freeways, and for beach lovers, Laguna Beach and Santa Monica are each about an hour away; nature enthusiasts often head to Joshua Tree National Park for camping and hiking; and on weekend evenings many students make the forty-minute drive west to Hollywood or Universal City. It also is not uncommon for students to take weekend trips to San Francisco, San Diego, or even Las Vegas!

THE "ATH"

Host to a year-long dinner and lecture series Monday through Thursday evenings, as well as the much-beloved afternoon tea, the Marian Miner Cook Athenaeum is a crown jewel of the college. The "Ath" hosts lectures four nights a week open to all students, faculty, and Claremont community members. Lectures are preceded by a gourmet dinner, prepared by the Ath's chefs and student assistants. Seating with the featured speaker is limited exclusively to students, who in recent years have had the opportunity to rub elbows with speakers including the former President of Ireland, Mary Robinson, Janet Reno, director Spike Lee, author Michael Cunningham, and former Speaker of the House Newt Gingrich. The speaker's presentation is introduced by the student Athenaeum Fellows who work actively with the director to choose the year's program. After a presentation the floor is opened for a question-and-answer period during which students' questions have priority.

CMC is also unique through its inclusion in the Claremont Colleges consortium. As part of the consortium—a group of five undergraduate colleges and two graduate institutions—located in one square mile—the atmosphere is that of a small college within a larger university. Students take classes, socialize, and participate in activities across the greater Claremont community but always have the home base of CMC. The consortium makes CMC an ideal choice for students who want a small college experience academically but also want the resources that a larger university would provide. Dining halls and libraries are open to all students and it is easy to take classes that may not be offered at CMC at one of the consortium colleges.

ADMISSIONS REQUIREMENTS

CMC is highly selective and traditionally accepts approximately twenty percent of applicants. What is this selectivity based on? There are the usual traits—each entering class includes its fair share of valedictorians and National Merit Finalists, and the median combined SAT score is around 2100. In addition, though, CMC seeks students who will be engaged learners and active members of the CMC community. Admissions officers look for students who have shown leadership potential, self-motivation, and interpersonal skills, and emphasis is placed on extracurricular involvement and how these activities could translate into success in the classroom and in the CMC community.

> *We're not trying to maximize pure intellectual performance. Certainly, we want to have good grades, test scores, and recommendations, but we balance it a lot with other considerations. It is ultimately important whether or not the student is a good fit for CMC, and vice versa.*

—*CMC Dean of Admission Richard Vos*

CMC's small size allows the Admission Office to build a comprehensive class made up of individuals who will be well suited to the CMC community and CMC's educational style. The admissions officers will try to "get to know you" as they consider your admissions materials. The components of your application that allow your personality to shine through, such as your essays, along with other factors such as your test scores, will all be considered. One recent graduate recalled being amazed when, during her first semester at CMC, one of the admissions officers approached her in the dining hall to tell her how much she had enjoyed the student's personal statement.

It is equally important for you as an applicant to get to know CMC to determine that CMC is the best fit for you.

The Admission Office regularly offers tours of the campus and it is also possible to arrange an overnight stay in a dorm. Those who may be unable to visit the campus can write directly to current students with any questions that they may have by using the "Ask a Student" section of the Admission Office Web site.

Curriculum and Standardized Tests

An applicant's high school education must have included four years of English, three to four years of math, at least three years of a foreign language, at least two years of science, and one year of history. All high schools are different however, and the availability of advanced, honors, or AP classes at your school will be taken into account. Steady improvement over the high school career is considered, and slacking during the senior year is not viewed favorably. Admission Dean Vos said, "That last year is crucial because students who carry their grades through to the end will likely be people who see projects through and complete tasks to the best of their ability."

The SAT is required. The median SAT score for the entering class in 2006 was 700 on the Critical Reading portion and 700 on the Math portion. These are median scores, however, not hard-and-fast standards that all candidates must achieve and the Admission Office requests that applicants submit all scores earned for each and every time that an applicant has taken the SAT. Interested students should plan to take the exam during their junior year, or between October and January of the senior year.

Recommendations and Essays

It is also necessary to include three recommendations, one from a high school guidance counselor and two from teachers. Two essays must also be included. These essays include a personal statement and an analytical essay, and are one of the most important components of your application. The personal essay is an opportunity to show your personality and highlight your special achievements or personal experiences. The analytical essay should identify a person who has shaped current events and culture.

It is also highly recommended that all applicants complete an interview with either an admission officer or with an alumnus of the college in their city. This interview is another opportunity for applicants to demonstrate the qualities that can set them apart from other candidates.

Admission Plans

There is a binding Early Decision plan for students who view CMC as their top choice; it should be filed by November 15th. Eighty Early Decision candidates were accepted into the 2006–2007 class. Regular fall semester applicants should submit their applications by January 2.

ACADEMIC LIFE

CMC students know that big is not necessarily better. The small size of Claremont McKenna allows for an academic environment that is rigorous, yet personalized, as students can count on a great deal of interaction with their professors. In fact, student participation is expected at CMC, where the average class size is sixteen students (the average in a laboratory is eighteen).

Majors

CMC students are known for their eclectic choice of majors as many students pursue a double major or a dual major. (A student with a double major fulfills all course requirements in both majors while a student with a dual major fulfills slightly fewer courses than a full major in both departments.) Students are also allowed to complete a major at one of the other Claremont Colleges that may not be offered at CMC. Another option is the self-designed major, which must be planned with direction from a faculty advisor.

Requirements

CMC has various general education requirements that all students, regardless of major, must fulfill. These include three semesters of social sciences, two semesters each of science and humanities courses, and one semester of literature, math (calculus-based), and world civilization. Additionally, all students must either demonstrate proficiency in a foreign language or complete three semesters of foreign language study.

An additional requirement for all CMC students is the senior thesis, a major research paper or project designed by the student. Normally completed during the senior year and overseen by a faculty advisor, this one- or two-semester venture is usually on a topic of interest within the student's major field of study. Social science and humanities students usually write thesis papers ranging from thirty to hundreds of pages, science students design and carry out experimental research, and often students choose to do a creative project such as a short film or a novel.

Professors

Do not choose CMC if you want to go through four years of college as an anonymous student in the back of the classroom. The vast majority of CMC professors want to hear your ideas and opinions, they want you to ask questions, they hope that you will come to their office hours, and they would like to know how you are doing outside of school as well. It is not uncommon to find professors eating lunch with students in the dining hall and students are often invited to professors' homes for class gatherings.

> My professors introduced me to fundamental schools of thought that bend my mind and make me feel more engaged in the rest of my life. The best classes here leave me thinking about the basic values and truths of the world after I leave the classroom. They also spark conversations about anything and everything with my friends."

—*Ethan Andyshak*
Class of 2006

Comparing this school with what I have heard about other colleges from friends, CMC demands more hours of work than most colleges, but it repays me for my pain.

—*Ethan Andyshak*
Class of 2006

Feedback

However, the payoff may not be initially in terms of grades. The bar is set high and new students may not also receive the straight As that they earned in high school. Students must challenge themselves to master material and improve their knowledge and they do so in an environment that is collaborative and supportive. Competition with one's fellow student is virtually unheard of and most CMCers note that there is a sense of solidarity when exam or term paper time rolls around.

Grades at CMC are based on a 12-point, rather than 4-point scale, with 12 being an A, 11 equal to an A–, 10 is a B+, and so forth. The Dean's List credits students who have achieved a GPA of 10.0 or higher during the previous semester, and the Distinguished Scholar List is a mark of achievement for those who earned a GPA of 11.0 or higher.

Because there is a special emphasis on writing as part of a CMC education, first-year students may be dismayed when they receive their first papers back. CMC professors work to improve their students' writing through the application of proper grammar, the use of effective techniques, and clear structure. A popular government professor requires first-year students to review effective writing techniques before writing their first paper of the semester, and one literature professor in recent years required that his students write an essay on the correct usage of the word "like." The Writing Center is a unique resource that offers writing help and specialized workshops for students who would like extra help. Writing at the college level can seem daunting at first but CMC grads report that their training in writing has served them well in their professional lives.

Throughout their college career students can count on the advice and guidance of their faculty advisor. Students are assigned faculty advisors in their interested field of study at the beginning of their first year.

Research and Other Programs

CMC students have more opportunities to participate hands-on in original research than at any other liberal arts college nationwide. While a number of American universities house research centers, work at these centers is usually reserved for professors and graduate students. Students at CMC are able to gain valuable experience in their chosen field by initiating research projects, supervising fellow student researchers, publishing in academic journals, organizing and participating in conferences, and attending group study trips organized by the research institutes.

RESEARCH INSTITUTES

○ **Family of Benjamin Z. Gould Center for Humanistic Studies.** Studies the major forces that have gone into and are still at work in the formation of the modern world, integrating knowledge from the humanities, social sciences, and science.

○ **H.N. and Frances G. Berger Institute for Work, Family, and Children.** Examines economic, public policy, and child development questions relevant to contemporary family and work issues.

○ **The Center for the Study of the Holocaust, Genocide, and Human Rights.** Explores the causes of genocide and human rights abuses, as well as policies and processes necessary to oppose those conditions.

○ **Reed Institute for Applied Statistics.** Where students solve practical problems posed by business and government, using mathematical models and forecasting techniques.

○ **Henry Kravis Leadership Institute.** A center for teaching and research in the areas of leadership, entrepreneurism, and organizational effectiveness.

○ **Keck Center for International and Strategic Studies.** Promotes research, debate, and undergraduate education in the problems and effects of strategy and diplomacy in the world, particularly in Europe and the Asia-Pacific region.

○ **Roberts Environmental Center.** Where faculty-student teams conduct multifaceted environmental projects involving biological and physical science, government, industrial, and environmental standards and economics.

○ **Lowe Institute of Political Economy.** Focusing on the study of public policy issues, the Institute's current research targets such topics as NAFTA, APEC, international financial crises, and impacts of globalization.

○ **Henry Salvatori Center for the Study of Individual Freedom in the Modern World.** Concentrates research efforts on the nature and effects of moral authority, the concepts of intellectual freedom and organizational behavior.

○ **Rose Institute of State and Local Government.** Advances knowledge about politics and government, and provides services that make the political process more viable.

I studied in Oxford and had a wonderful time. This was my first trip outside the United States, and it really showed me what the United States is like from a different cultural viewpoint. Being in the UK for the election as well, showed me how they see and interpret the U.S. and U.S. policy abroad, especially in Europe.

—*Justin Levitt*
Class of 2006

Off-Campus Experiences

Students may exchange at one of the following liberal arts colleges in the United States: Colby, Haverford, Morehouse, or Spelman Colleges. The Washington, D.C. Semester includes a full-time internship with an elected official, government agency, or public interest group, courses with CMC faculty, and a major research paper requirement. This experience infects many students with the "DC bug" and has led to the start of many students' future careers in Washington.

Study abroad programs are offered in more than fifty cities in Europe, Asia, Africa, Latin America, Australia, and the Middle East.

CMC also offers students many opportunities to complete internships in cities around the world, in Washington, D.C., and in locations closer to home through opportunities such as the McKenna International Internship program, the Community Service Internship program, and other internship opportunities offered through the various research institutes.

Special Degree Programs

CMC offers many special degree programs that allow students to combine fields of study or to accelerate the completion of their undergraduate and postgraduate degrees through various partnership programs. Politics, Philosophy, and Economics (PPE) is an interdisciplinary major modeled after an Oxford University program in which students participate in small seminars and tutorials with faculty. The Environment, Economics, and Politics (EEP) major is a unique interdisciplinary program that trains students to analyze and develop policy solutions for environmental issues. CMC sponsors cooperative programs with graduate schools that allow CMCers to combine their study at CMC with eventual post-graduate study. CMC offers several accelerated degree programs including: the Robert A. Day 4+1 B.A./M.B.A. with the Drucker School of Management at Claremont Graduate University; a 3+2 B.A./M.S. in Applied Biology with Keck Graduate Institute of Applied Life Sciences, and a 3+3 B.A./J.D. with Columbia Law School. Additionally, students interested in engineering may participate in accelerated programs in Economics/Engineering or Management/Engineering by combining a B.A. from CMC with a B.S. from a top engineering school like Cal Tech or Claremont Consortium partner Harvey Mudd College. Another unique degree program is the Management Engineering program in which CMC students can earn a B.A. from CMC and a B.S. in engineering from schools including Cal Tech or Claremont Consortium partner Harvey Mudd.

SOCIAL LIFE AND ACTIVITIES

It is often said that Claremont McKenna students study hard and play hard too. Extracurricular activities and social life at CMC are part of the experience. They are a way to meet new people, develop friendships, take a break from studying, follow hobbies, and develop a support system.

Clubs and Organizations

There are a wide variety of clubs, sports teams, and other organizations for CMC students to choose from. Everything from orchestra, to Debate Club, to religious and ethnic organizations, to the student newspaper, to karate, is available.

It is also always possible for students to develop new clubs themselves if they find that a niche is lacking at CMC. Students can apply for money from the student activity fund and charter a new organization. In recent years, students have founded clubs and organizations focused on everything from human rights to vegetarian cooking to boxing.

CMC also hosts International Place (I-Place), the heart of the international program at The Claremont Colleges, which provides support to international students and hosts weekly luncheons with presentations on international politics and culture.

The Associated Students of CMC often hosts concerts in Claremont Bridges Auditorium. Recent concerts have included Claremont native Ben Harper, the Black Eyed Peas, and George Clinton.

Community Service

Many CMC students take part in community service, ranging from tutoring to working on Habitat for Humanity projects. CMC clubs and sports teams are also active in service projects. An annual community service project is also part of the freshman orientation.

Every year two students serve as community service coordinators organizing service projects in the local community.

Dorms

CMC does not have fraternities or sororities and the vast majority of students (over ninety-five percent) choose to live on campus. As a primarily residential campus, the heart of CMC social life is the college's twelve dorms. Divided into North Quad, Mid Quad, and South Quad, each grouping of dorms has a different feeling and most students develop an allegiance to one residential area. In their fourth year, students can choose to live in on-campus student apartments located on the eastern edge of CMC's campus. Dorms often host parties that range from simple gatherings to themed affairs including disco parties and costume parties. Popular themed parties include Mardi Gras and Monte Carlo, complete with blackjack tables. Another popular event is the semiannual SYR ("screw your roommate") dance in which students set their roommates up on blind dates.

Off-Campus

The "Village" of Claremont is only a five-minute walk from campus and offers restaurants, coffee shops, shops, and a local farmers market. All that southern California has to offer is only a car or train ride away from Claremont. Weekends often find students heading into L.A. (forty minutes away by freeway and by Metrolink commuter rail train) or to nearby beaches. Claremont is served by Ontario International Airport—only fifteen minutes from campus—so going home for vacations is never a problem.

FINANCIAL AID

Claremont McKenna has a need-blind, meet-all-need admission policy, a practice shared by only thirty-five colleges and universities nationwide. Your application for admission will be reviewed without regard for your ability to pay, and all admitted students' determined financial need will be accommodated.

Financial aid supports sixty percent of students who are enrolled at the college. While most student aid is need-based there are also merit scholarship programs. One exciting scholarship is the McKenna Achievement Award, a $10,000 scholarship renewable for all four years, which is awarded to thirty incoming first-year students who have demonstrated outstanding academic and personal achievements during their high school careers. The average need-based financial-aid package in 2005–2006 was $26,650. Family incomes of students qualifying for financial aid range from $0 to six figures.

All students who wish to apply for financial aid must file the Free Application for Federal Student Aid (FAFSA) and the Financial Aid PROFILE form that is processed by the College Scholarship Service (CSS) in order to be considered eligible. The deadline for these forms usually occurs soon after the admission application is due.

Though it may seem a long way off now, CMC graduates leave Claremont with less debt than the average college graduate. The average need-based loan debt of students in the 2004 graduating class was $10,769—less than ten percent of the four-year tuition bill.

GRADUATES

CMC graduates leave Claremont with a sense of direction as they move into the workforce or on to graduate or professional degree programs. On-campus recruiting by firms, graduate schools, and the local and national government takes place throughout the senior year and the majority of CMC students have a job lined up by the spring.

CMC students are also competitive in the field of postcollege scholarships and fellowships such as the Fulbright, Rhodes, Marshall, and Truman. Claremont McKenna College has been ranked third, nationally, among undergraduate colleges for the number of

In talking with students who attend top colleges across the country, I have yet to encounter a similar degree of generosity and support for the interests of students. CMC seeks to make leaders that will leave their mark on society and thus do all that they can to provide students with a well-rounded education that can hardly be gained anywhere else.

—Joanna Respold
Class of 2007

- Betsy Berns, President, Bvision Sportsmedia
- Robert Day, Chairman of the Board, Trust Company of the West
- David Dreier, U.S. Congressman and Chairman of the House Rules Committee
- Ray Drummond, Acclaimed Jazz Bassist
- Donald Hall, Chairman and CEO, Hallmark Cards, Inc.
- Mike Jeffries, Chairman and CEO, Abercrombie & Fitch
- Henry Kravis, Founding Partner, Kohlberg Kravis Roberts & Co.
- Robert Lowe Chairman and CEO, Lowe Enterprises
- Nancy McCallin, President, Colorado Community College System
- Harry McMahon, Vice Chairman, Merrill Lynch & Co.
- Thomas Pritzker, Chairman and CEO, The Pritzker Organization
- George Roberts, Founding Partner, Kohlberg Kravis Roberts & Co.
- Karen Rosenfelt, President of Production, Paramount Pictures
- Tasia Scollinos, Director of Communications, U.S. Department of Justice
- Julie Spellman Sweet, Partner, Cravath, Swaine & Moore
- Julie Wong, Deputy Mayor for Communications, City of Los Angeles

Fulbright Scholars it produces, according to a national ranking just published by *The Chronicle of Higher Education.* Seven CMCers from the class of 2004 were awarded Fulbright scholarships that year.

The CMC Career Center is a helpful resource throughout the process. Professional career counselors and student assistants are on hand to help fine-tune resumes, practice interviewing skills, search for internships, and also keep alumni informed about career development opportunities.

CMC alumni stay in close touch through the Alumni Office, which organizes nationwide events, publishes a newsletter, and sponsors class reunions.

SUMMING UP

What kind of college education do you want? Claremont McKenna College is not for everyone; it is for students who would like to be challenged, who would like to know their professors and have their professors know them; it is for those who hope to build relationships in a small setting, but still have all of the options that a larger university would afford them, it is for students who are considering a career in public service and the professions and who would like to attend a school that will teach them the leadership skills and ethics to pursue such a career. And the sunshine of Southern California doesn't hurt either.

CMC students are smart and many of them had their choice of top-ranked schools. But they chose CMC. Students choose CMC because they believe that it will be the best school for them, in terms of education and environment. This is apparent when you meet the students—they are active in campus life. The campus is crowded on weekends, attendance at Ath lectures and sporting events is high, and—a rarity on some college campuses— students attend class regularly. They also know that CMC supports them, their education, and their future career development.

❏ *Sarah Ciaccia, B.A.*

COLBY COLLEGE

 Colby College
Waterville, ME 04901-8841

 (207) 859-4800, (800) 723-3032
Fax: (207) 859-4828

 E-mail: *admissions@colby.edu*
Web site: *http://www.colby.edu*

 Enrollment

Full-time ❏ women: 1,001
       ❏ men: 864

INTRODUCING COLBY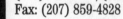

At first glance, Colby doesn't seem all that different from its NESCAC brethren. Like New England's other small, private, liberal arts colleges, the manicured lawns are gorgeously pastoral, the student body enthusiastic and friendly (indeed, Colby's students have been rated the "happiest" in the nation), the academics rigorous, and the faculty first-rate. To stand on the steps of the ivy-laced Miller Library, perched regally atop Mayflower Hill, and offering a sweeping view of the entire 714-acre campus (and seemingly the entirety of Maine itself), is to experience the very quintessence of "collegiate"—in every sense of the word, because Colby prides itself not only on its handsome veneer, but its commitment to academics and to the community as well. Therein lies the difference.

Community may be a buzzword these days, but at Colby it's truly in evidence. Chalk it up to the long winters, the Maine location, or the fact that its Greek system was abolished in 1984, but whatever the reason, Colby manages to cultivate a sustaining, enmeshed environment. This does not mean that every single student is indeed happy, and that there aren't cliques. What it does mean is that, though Colby is still committed to a goal of true multi-culturalism, its populace is already diverse in many ways. This is because Colby students are given not only free rein, but also the necessary support and encouragement, to pursue their disparate interests, whether academic, creative, or recreational.

And surprisingly enough, they do. "I had so many friends doing so many different things," Colleen Creeden, class of 2002, remembers. "Some sang in *a capella* groups; others loved art, or skiing, or specialized in partying." Colby may be a famously athletic campus—its impressive field house is home to thirty-two varsity sports teams and nine intramural sports clubs—but look beyond the Patagonia outerwear and you'll also see a hodgepodge of rugged individualists: musicians, poets, activists, actors, painters, potters, long-distance runners, and on and on. As Michael Cobb, class of 1995, says, "Interesting countercultures abound in a place where everyone seems to be 'the middle.'" Colby may be tucked away in the center of Maine, closer to lakes and mountains than to any urban center, but nonetheless it teems with life and energy. When asked to sum up his Colby experience in one word, Cobb exclaimed, "Electric!"

ADMISSIONS REQUIREMENTS

Colby goes to great pains to create a student body that will best enhance the community, which means that the selection process is highly competitive—for years now the acceptance rate has hovered around thirty-five percent—and difficult to predict. One graduate, for instance, remembers her surprise upon learning that a high school classmate with better grades and test scores than hers, and with equivalent athletic accomplishments, but with fewer creative and volunteer pursuits, was turned down while she was not. The majority of students tend to be not only academic high achievers, but creative and athletic standouts as well. A recent incoming class, for example, boasted thirty-three languages spoken, 160 high school varsity captains, the Kentucky state chess champion, the youngest recipient ever of the EPA's Environmental Excellence Award, and a Portuguese-Chinese translator in Brazil.

The application process itself is fairly standard, calling for essays, recommendations, transcript requests, and personal data, save for the requirement of SAT or ACT scores, which Colby's peer schools in Maine no longer require. Mean test scores among successful applicants are, most recently, 680/680 (Verbal/Math) for SAT I and 29 for the ACT. (Note: International students must also submit a TOEFL score of 600 or higher.) Other important considerations include AP and honors courses, leadership, and extracurricular and volunteer accomplishments, as well as less tangible factors such as character and intellectual promise. An interview is not required but is highly recommended, both as an extra measure by which the college can judge candidates and an opportunity for candidates to better assess the college. Of course, given that a remarkable number of alumni say they "just knew" Colby was right for them as soon as they saw the place, campus visits are decidedly in the college's advantage. And in fact, judging by the steady increase over the years in Early Decision candidates, the number of visitors that "just knew" keeps rising. Of a recent pool of 4,242 applicants, 459 had applied Early Decision. Though only 217 were accepted, they did make up almost half of the class of 475.

Colby has a pronounced commitment to attracting applicants who represent diverse geographic and racial backgrounds. While its central Maine location has long drawn a mostly Caucasian, Northeast-based population, the percentage of international students in recent incoming classes has increased to ten percent and the number of domestic minority students to eleven percent. Fifty percent of incoming students were from New England and fifty percent from other states, territories, and abroad. Among them, eighty-three percent were white. The male/female ratio, however, has long remained relatively equal. Also fairly consistent over time is the breakdown between public and private high school—in a recent class, fifty-eight percent of the students had graduated from public schools and the remaining forty-two percent from private schools, with a small percentage from parochial schools.

As a Midwesterner from a rural community, I was forced at Colby to really figure out who I was. After first discarding my Midwesternness, because it certainly didn't belong at Colby, I eventually came to embrace it, because it makes me who I am. That sounds like a cliché, but it was a surprisingly hard lesson to learn.

—*Lynne Moss, class of 1995, B.A.*

Colby's academic environment is as rigorous as the weather—giving credence to Oscar Wilde's idea that "wisdom comes with winters." Whether in spite of or because of its snowy winter months, rare is the student who gradutes without somehow being academically transformed. Though the school's three most popular majors—Economics, Biology, and English—reflect its commitment to the liberal arts, the sciences may be the school's strongest suit, particularly the biology, chemistry, and physics programs. The International Studies and Environmental Policy majors and the Environmental Science and Neuroscience options available in several majors all earn praise. That said, the creative writing program is the one most often remembered among graduates for its "eye-opening," "extremely challenging," and "head-spinning" writing workshops.

Though the school encourages experimenting with different sorts of courses before settling into a major, it should be noted that Colby's conditions for graduation are strict, so planning how to best use the four years of study is important. Along with the coursework for their major, students must fulfill a foreign language requirement and take English composition as well as two courses in the natural sciences and one course each in the arts, historical studies, literature, quantitative reasoning, and the social sciences. Two courses, one internationally focused, constitute a diversity requirement, and students must meet Colby's wellness requirement by attending five of seven First-Year Supper Seminars.

I was enormously challenged at Colby, mainly because I was given the space to become a deliberate learner who could generate intellectual questions and desires, and translate them into provocative intellectual projects. I particularly found the Religious Studies and Women's Studies departments to be some of the most exciting departments—small strengths that cultivated an intense political and intellectual engagement, and helped me grow and transform and engage the world more substantively than I had before I arrived at Colby.

—*Michael Cobb, class of 1995, B.A.*

SOME FAVORITE COURSES

- Nikky Singh's Sihkism seminar
- Deborah Campbell's "Contemporary Western Theology"
- Lyn Mikel Brown's "Women and Girls and the Culture of Education"
- Phyllis Mannochi's "Art and Oppression"
- Anything with Cedric Bryant, especially "African-American Literature" and "The American Gothic"
- Any chemistry course with Das Thamattoor
- Robert Weisbrot's "Crisis and Reform: America in the 1960s"
- Ira Sadoff's "Modern American Poetry"
- Poetry workshops with Peter Harris
- Tom Tietenberg's "Environmental and Natural Resource Economics"
- Russ Cole and David Firmage's "Problems in Environmental Science"
- Margaret McFadden's "Alternative Popular Cultures"

Faculty

"Colby gave me a superb education," Michael Cobb, class of 1995, remembers, "mainly because of the exquisite, smart faculty, who cared enough to push my thinking in new, critical, and politically engaged ways." Colby's faculty is far and away the school's strongest asset. Between the student/professor ratio of ten to one and the fact that professors spend a great deal of time on the snug campus (some even living there), close relationships between faculty and students are easily engendered. Office hours are flexible, home phone numbers are widely available, and faculty are guaranteed to be present at athletic contests and cultural happenings. "I used to stop by my advisor's office all the time, often without an appointment, just to talk about something I'd read, and I can't remember a time when he wasn't in and completely willing to see me," Erika Troseth, class of 1995, recalls. Moreover, once students get past the large introductory lecture courses common to the first two years of study, class sizes are small and intimate. "Before Colby, I wasn't aware that I could perform at such a high academic level," says Alyssa Severn, class of 2002. "I realize now that I did it out of respect for my professors as individuals, not only professors. I became so engaged, motivated, and interested in the content of their courses that I didn't even pay much mind to the grades I received." And the relationships don't stop with graduation. Many alumni keep in touch with their professors, whether with occasional visits or letters.

Programs

Colby offers B.A. degrees in fifty-three majors running the usual liberal arts gamut from African-American/American studies to physics to theater and dance. Some majors offer specific concentrations. An art major, for example, may choose to concentrate on art history or studio art. Likewise, a biology major may focus on environmental science or neuroscience.

And if none of the available options appeal, a student may propose an independent or combined major of his or her own choosing. (Mike Daisey, a 1996 graduate, writes about his independently created aesthetics major—a combination of theater and creative writing— in his book *21 Dog Years: Doing Time @ Amazon.com*.) Those students who don't want to limit themselves to declaring one major can declare two—twenty-three percent of a recent graduating class fulfilled double majors—or augment their studies by electing a minor. In a recent graduating class, thirty-six percent had at least one minor, and sometimes two. Of the thirty-two minors available to choose from, most can be found on the list of majors, though there are a few unique additions, such as Administrative Science, Indigenous Peoples of the Americas, and Jewish Studies.

COOT

COOT, which stands for Colby Outdoor Orientation Trip, is Colby's way of introducing first-year students to Maine, Colby, and each other. Soon after they arrive on campus, students leave with ten or twelve of their classmates and two trained upper-class student leaders for four days of outdoor adventuring of their choosing, such as hiking, fly fishing, road biking, or sea kayaking. Those students who don't have much interest or experience in roughing it can opt for Excursion, a low-impact option involving more leisurely day trips, Theater/Improv, which entails lots of lakeside improvisational theater and relaxing, Civic Engagement/Volunteerism or Trail Work/Service for students interested in doing volunteer work. Upon returning to campus, each COOT group becomes a team to assist students as they transition to campus life.

COOT really works. Even if you don't become best friends with your COOT-mates, and odds are you won't, they do provide a nice base of stability from which to launch into Colby. Familiar faces in a new place cannot be overrated. And your COOT leader will be there for questions or support for as long as he or she remains on campus.

Off-Campus Study

Colby is rightly proud of its popular off-campus and exchange programs—more than two-thirds of the student body spend at least one full semester away from Waterville in one of scores of approved destinations. Colby maintains its own programs in Cork, Ireland; Salamanca, Spain; Dijon, France; and St. Petersburg, Russia. Additionally, students may enroll in programs offered by peer institutions centered in large and small towns around the world, both domestically and internationally. "The most important gift Colby gave me was my year abroad. I grew up a lot that year and was challenged at all levels," claims Lynne

Moss, class of 1995. Though the benefits of traveling abroad are obvious, some graduates complained that leaving the academic rigors of Colby to study in a foreign—and often less challenging—program disrupted their intellectual momentum, and they wished they had saved their traveling for after graduation.

Integrated Studies Program

This intensive, semester-long program was designed to explore an era or aspect of world civilization from the perspective of several disciplines. Structured around clusters of courses, the program is open to all classes. Recent offerings have been "The Green Cluster," which deals with environmental ethics, literature, and biological science, "The Holocaust and the Religious Response," studying the Holocaust from historical and religious viewpoint, "Death in the Renaissance," focusing on Dante's Inferno in Italian and Art courses.

January Semester

One of Colby's innovative programs continues to be the long-standing January Program—or Jan Plan, as it's known—that not only breaks up the long winter, but allows students to devote a month to nearly anything of their choosing. With virtually limitless boundaries, except for the requirement that students must complete three Jan Plan programs, students have trekked across African countries researching gender relations, learned woodworking, immersed themselves in a new language, and interned in nearly every imaginable professional role in preparation for life after Colby. Staying on campus has its appeal—skiers take full advantage of the relaxed schedule to frequent nearby Sugarloaf Mountain, and for the less active there's something cozy about hunkering down in the middle of Maine with only one course or project to concentrate on—but some students complain that it gets claustrophobic, and recommend leaving campus as much as possible. Colleen Creeden, class of 2002, says that her second-year Jan Plan trip to Guadeloupe to live with a family was a turning point.

The experience was so colorful and different from anything I had known before. I hiked up to a waterfall barefoot in the rain, met several native authors, learned so much more about the social and economic conditions in the Caribbean, and became very excited about language. When I returned to Colby in February, I declared my French Studies major.

Public Affairs and Civil Engagement

In 2004 the Goldfarb Center for Public Affairs and Civic Engagement was formed to connect teaching and research with contemporary political, economic, and social issues. The Goldfarb Center provides a venue in which students and faculty can think and work across disciplinary boundaries to develop creative approaches to complex local, national, and global challenges. The center is a clearinghouse for ties with the community, including civic engagement courses and volunteer opportunities; it serves as an intellectual forum, sponsoring lectures, seminars, and visiting scholars, and it helps students with internships and research projects that expand their learning beyond the classroom.

SOCIAL LIFE AND ACTIVITIES

Residences

Because Colby's location is somewhat remote—Portland, the only Maine city of significant size, is an hour's drive away—and ninety-four percent of the students live on campus, campus life revolves around the residence halls. There are three dining halls (students are free to eat in any dining hall they wish), the buildings are primarily classical neo-Georgian—lots of red brick, in other words—save for the two starkly modern, glass-paned complexes nestled in the woods on the edge of campus. First-year students are dispersed evenly throughout every residence hall on a random basis, except for those who request chemical-free or "quiet" housing, all of whom are accommodated, after which they are free to request any dormitory they'd like. Most rooms are doubles or triples, though students can opt to live in large group suites and singles upon request. In 1999, a new apartment building open to senior class members only was added to the mix and almost every dorm has been part of a $44 million upgrade. Because all of the halls are pleasant, well-maintained, and completely wired—every room has an individual Ethernet connection and a cable television outlet—it's nearly impossible to have anything but a comfortable residential life. By senior year, some students choose to live off campus, whether in downtown apartments or lake houses several miles away, but this is the exception and not the rule.

Where a student lives greatly influences his or her social experience, as each residence cluster tends to have its own personality. The south end of each campus, for instance, usually houses the artsy, crunchy types, while Roberts Row, on the other side of campus, is favored by the jock community. Though incoming students have little say in where they'll be placed, by the end of their first year most people have a sense of where they'd like to live, and generally find themselves there.

Cotter Union, the student center, is the physical and organizational heart of the campus, and a $10-million expansion underway in 2006-07 would add the Pulver Pavilion to create a "living room" for students. The building houses a central meeting and social area with a coffee bar and The Spa, Colby's snack bar. It also contains the student post office, and ATM, and the Page Commons, a large function room for all-campus events. Attached to the Student Center is The Pugh Center, "a common ground in which students of all races, cultures, and religions have a stake." It contains offices for multicultural student organizations, a kosher kitchen, and a large lounge or meeting space.

Campus Expansion

Colby recently completed a new 15-acre campus expansion, the Colby Green, and elliptical lawn that is the site of the admissions building, the alumni center, and the new Diamond Building for social science and interdisciplinary studies programs. Another academic building for the sciences, also is planned on the Colby Green.

Athletics

Rare is the Colby student who doesn't take part in some sort of athletic activity, whether this means the occasional walk through the arboretum, a weekly jog, a season spent playing on an intramural soccer team, or four years of committed varsity competition. Those who aren't prone to being active might change their minds when confronted with the first-class Alfond Athletic Center. Boasting over 197,064 square feet of fitness, weight training, and exercise areas, four locker rooms, a full-sized gymnasium, a hockey rink, a twenty-five-yard by twenty-five-meter swimming and diving pool, and an indoor field house for tennis, track, and indoor practices, it is one of the most comprehensive athletic centers in New England. And that's not counting the campus's fifty acres of fields for outdoor sports, or the new synthetic turf field, installed in 2004–2005.

Roughly one third of the student body competes as White Mules in the NESCAC conference, whether on one of the college's thirty Division III intercollegiate teams, or the Division I Nordic and Alpine ski teams. And they are consistently competitive. In recent years, the women's crew won the 2003 Division III national championship, men's basketball has earned trips to the NCAA tournament, the volleyball team won the New England NCAA Division III Championship and went to the national "Sweet 16" tournament, and in 2005–2006, twenty-eight

All-American honors were won by sixteen students in various sports. All of this is done without the benefit of athletic scholarships, which are banned in Division III.

Meanwhile, for the more laid-back competitor, there are a plethora of I-PLAY (intramural sports) and club team programs. Students of both sexes can often be seen throwing axes for the Woodsmen's team, battling in a scrum at the Swamp during a rugby match, or tossing the disk for the Ultimate Frisbee club.

Finally, for those students interested in the great outdoors, there is all of Maine to explore. Students are constantly taking off for the mountains, and the scenic Maine coastline, which can be reached within about an hour. On weekends, skiers flock to nearby Sugarloaf Mountain and Sunday River, hikers trek out to Mt. Katahdin and Acadia National Park, and water lovers head off to Camden, Rockport, or the nearby Belgrade Lakes for canoeing and sailing, and the Kennebec, Dead, and Penobscot rivers for whitewater adventure.

> *During my freshman year I volunteered at an elementary school reading to children. Sophomore year I made soup and sandwiches once a week in the basement of a church for families that were barely getting by. During my senior year I volunteered in the office of the Maine International Film Festival. It was certainly beneficial for me to mix with the larger community on a weekly basis, and Waterville's population can benefit greatly from an active Colby student body.*

—Colleen Creeden, class of 2002, B.A.

Extracurricular Activities

As if in recompense for its small size and out-of-the-way location, Colby is *teeming* with extracurricular activities, which go a long way in making up the backbone of student life on campus. There are more than 100 clubs catering to a multitude of cultural, political, religious, and volunteer agendas, from a feminist Women's Group to the college's literary magazine, *The Pequod*. The most popular is The Colby Outing Club. Particularly popular also is the campus radio station, WHMB, where students host their own radio shows. On any given Sunday afternoon, students can be found throwing pots in the pottery studio, practicing for a dance recital, or relaxing in the student-run coffeehouse.

From the COOT trips to the Hume Center to the Outing Club Cabin on Great Pond, you shouldn't leave Colby without sleeping outside, watching a sunrise from Runnals Hill, or taking a walk through the Arboretum. If you miss the coast, you can reach Popham Beach in an hour. If you love to ski, you will always have someone to go with any weekend during the winter... and the drive there can be just as much fun. If you want to try outdoor sports, you will find someone who shares the same enthusiasm to learn with you, or be your guide.

—*Colleen Creeden, class of 2002, B.A.*

Maine worked its way into my heart—the spectacular fall foliage, the jagged little coastline, the Belfast co-op, and Portland's coffee shops, bookstores, and restaurants all allowed me to dwell in zones of Down East feeling. And I could easily drive to Boston and New York City whenever the isolation pushed me over the edge.

—*Michael Cobb, class of 1995, B.A.*

Volunteer Activities

The student-run Colby Volunteer Center has established many programs devised to get students involved in the Waterville school system, soup kitchens, and rape crisis and the Colby Cares About Kids program, which pairs more than 300 Colby students as mentors to local children. What is usually only a one-day-a-week commitment can prove to have tremendous personal payoff.

Environmental Awareness

Colby has been recognized by the U.S. Environmental Protection Agency and Maine officials for its commitment to environment stewardship, both in academic programs and in practices adopted on campus. The college's environmental studies program, begun in the

1970s, remains one of Colby's strengths. An Environmental Advisory Group, composed of students, faculty, and administrators was founded in 2000. Now, with recycling programs, conservation, environmentally friendly electricity production, a new alumni center that uses geothermal heating and cooling, and other initiatives in place, Colby has become a leader in adopting sustainable practices.

Fraternity Ban

In 1984 Colby's Board of Trustees abolished the college's long-standing fraternity system. In protest, students burned furniture in the quad between Roberts Union and the library, and were slow to take to the commons-based, college-sponsored social system that sprung up in its wake. For a while—and perhaps even to this day—now-illegal fraternities stubbornly persisted underground. But more than twenty years later, almost all traces of any Greek adherence have disappeared, and most students agree that the campus is far better off for it.

Alcohol

Gone, too, are the beery bashes of yore. This is not to say that drinking isn't a big part of student life, but as a result of increasingly strict alcohol enforcement, most alcohol consumption is done in off-campus student houses and bars. Twenty-one-year-olds are allowed to host parties, but because they are held accountable for underage drinking violations, most tend not to take on the responsibility.

Student-Sponsored Events and Other Activities

Colby students are uncommonly assiduous when it comes to organizing social activities. From free plays, concerts, and readings, to improv performances, to cheap second-run movies in Lovejoy Hall, there is always something to do on a weekend night. Each year the student government sponsors one or two headline acts—recent years have seen Ben Folds, Margaret Cho, Matisyahu, and Mavis Staples—as well as frequent dance parties and semi-formals. An increasingly popular place to congregate is the student-run coffeehouse, which hosts innumerable open-mic nights and poetry readings, aside from just being a nice place to chat with a friend over a cup of coffee. A much quieter cultural oasis is The Colby College Museum of Art, which houses the works of Alex Katz, an extraordinary permanent collection of American art, and frequent traveling exhibitions.

Off Campus

Waterville (pop. 16,000) is no urban center, but it does have its share of bowling alleys, pool halls, movie theaters, restaurants, and shops. Though owning a car isn't essential to getting around—there is a shuttle bus that runs from campus to the heart of downtown—there aren't any limits to automobile ownership on campus, and those students who can take advantage of this flexibility, do. Having a car means being able to take a shopping trip to Freeport, a weekend getaway to Boston, or simply taking a car ride through Maine's gorgeous landscape.

FINANCIAL AID

With a price tag of $44,080 a year (2006–2007), Colby isn't cheap. But it does all it can to help students meet that cost. Approximately one third of all Colby students receive financial aid in the form of scholarships and grants, with an average first-year aid package of $28,493 (2005–2006) for one year. More than two thirds receive financial assistance through loans and/or work-study jobs on campus. By working ten to twelve hours per week in the library, bookstore, dining halls, athletic complex, administrative offices, academic departments, mailroom, and computer center, students may earn a portion of their college expenses and/or spending money. Most students use this income to defray the costs of personal expenses and books, which run at about $1,500. Most parents report that the Financial Aid Office was very helpful and pleasant to work with, which made what can sometimes be a difficult and complex process much easier.

> *I'm actually surprised at how often I am in touch with Colby friends and alumni. Colby people seem to be everywhere, and are always so willing to help.*

> —*Alyssa Severn, class of 2002*

GRADUATES

It's not easy to leave a place like Colby. The "real world" can seem downright barren when compared to this haven of intellectual stimulation, close friends, fun diversions, and first-rate facilities. Fortunately, Colby's sense of community extends far beyond Mayflower Hill. The Office of

Career Services maintains an alumni network that can be an invaluable resource when looking for job leads or advice, especially given the range of professions Colby graduates go on to excel in—from the glitz of Hollywood and Wall Street to the challenges of community activism. A handful of recent alumni include a carpenter, a college English professor, a published poet, and a biochemist, to name a few. Nearly twenty percent of graduates enroll directly in graduate medical, business, or law school, and two thirds of Colby's alumni seek further education within five years of graduation.

SUMMING UP

It's been said that there are so many colleges, and so many of them so similar to one another, that it hardly matters which one you end up attending. But if Colby proves anything, it's that each small liberal arts college really is a world unto itself. The homogenous student body may fool people into thinking that there's not much diversity, but in fact the campus hosts all manner of contradictions. At the same time a basketball game is being played before 500 fans in a packed gymnasium, there's a guy at the other end of campus snuggling down for the night in his homemade snow fort, or a group of students huddled around a table in the Student Center, penning a manifesto.

Though Colby's commitment to community may give its students ample room to flex their critical and creative muscles, it's true that the small size can get, well, too small. What's cozy to some is cliqueish to others. At the end of four years, what once felt supportive and nurturing can feel downright oppressive. But truth be told, a bit of chafing is probably necessary—otherwise, a person might never feel compelled to leave.

❏ *Kate Bolick, B.A.*

COLGATE UNIVERSITY

 Colgate University
Hamilton, NY 13346

 (315) 228-7401
Fax: (315) 228-7544

 E-mail: *admission@mail.colgate.edu*
Web site: *www.colgate.edu*

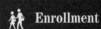 **Enrollment**

Full-time ❑ women: 1,345
❑ men: 1,402

INTRODUCING COLGATE UNIVERSITY

Just a short drive off of historic Route 20 in upstate New York, travelers are bound to pass by rustic farms, cozy villages, and robust antique fairs. As the Chenango valley opens, visitors find themselves at the doorstep of Colgate University: a beautiful hill crested by the golden dome of the Memorial Chapel, gracefully surrounded by 550 acres of lake, oak lined drives, willow lined footpaths, and sprawling landscapes. Walking onto campus is really like walking onto the quintessential northeastern university. Taking in the limestone academic buildings, the classical English garden, and the grand staircase ascending the Colgate hill and watching the annual torchlight processionals, one truly feels a connection to the first students at Colgate back in 1819. However, after spending a little time with the people of this liberal arts university, Colgate reveals itself as an institution where tradition and innovation coincide.

Colgate's academic philosophy is driven by the tradition of a liberal arts core curriculum. This core includes two literary courses about the foundations of Western culture and the post-Enlightenment challenges to Western thought, as well as an in-depth look at a non-Western culture and an exposure to the forefronts of science. While a student is having these academic experiences in a wide range of topics, Colgate as a research university further challenges students to delve deeply into their major course of study. So, what is a typical Colgate day? Students might discuss Gilgamesh over breakfast, undertake multivariable calculus before lunch, practice yoga (reading Nietzsche in the downward-facing dog pose), and finish up with a scientific discussion about Atlantis before heading over to the Picker Art Gallery to work on a thesis paper. Mental yoga may become necessary to develop this academic flexibility.

The Colgate community reflects this sort of academic challenge: meet the Renaissance student. The 2,800 undergraduate students that bustle across Colgate's beautiful campus are hard-working, outgoing, and community-minded. Colgate students love to be challenged, whether as star of the hockey team, double majoring in math and physics with a senior thesis in computational mechanics, or as a creative writing and theatre double major dividing time between a fraternity, Ultimate Frisbee practice, and a volunteer organization working with local children. Colgate students love to be busy, as evidenced by more than 120 student-run organizations coordinated through the Center for Leadership and Student involvement. While students keep the campus calendar alive with performances, lectures, athletic contests, festivals, and parties, Colgate provides opportunities for reaching out to the surrounding community through the Center for Outreach, Volunteerism, and Education (COVE). The COVE advises groups that tutor, build houses, and build ties with the Hamilton community and beyond, sending spring break groups to New Orleans to assist with Hurricane Katrina relief. The students at Colgate continue traditions in the Greek houses on Broad Street and the Colgate Memorial Chapel but also create on the cutting edge in state-of-the-art biology labs and digital recording studios.

A world-class faculty motivates Colgate's well-rounded education. The distinguished scholars that teach in Colgate's halls are working at the forefront of their fields, publishing and conducting research on campus. However, all of Colgate's classes are taught by the faculty, never by teaching assistants. These are individuals who truly love to work with undergraduate students. This creates a stimulating academic environment for the Colgate student: a professor that challenges with high expectations yet is available to help and listen during at least four posted office hours every week. There are also opportunities to conduct research alongside Colgate faculty year-round, on campus or abroad from France to Australia, Great Britain, and Mexico.

The community the university calls home further shapes the Colgate experience. The village of Hamilton is a cozy rural community à la Bedford Falls in *It's a Wonderful Life*. From the newly renovated movie house and Colgate Bookstore to New York Pizzeria (affectionately termed "Slices" by Colgate students), and the Barge Canal coffee shop, students become part of a tightly knit community (of which they are half the population). Colgate contributes an active arts and athletic calendar to the Hamilton community. Colgate is the venue for more than one hundred student artistic events each year, including nearly ten full-scale theatrical productions, musical performances, art exhibits, and an annual week-long arts festival, complete with ice sculptures, guerrilla performances, and lectures by visiting artists. Meanwhile the mighty Colgate Raiders (charter members of the Division I Patriot league) compete year round, with more than eighty percent of Colgate's students participating in some form of athletics, from the club and intramural to the varsity teams.

Colgate University continues its connection to a proud history with an active network of successful alumni, who simply love their school, and each year a new class of students with groundbreaking, altruistic, and gregarious ideas continue to further the character of this institution with a strong tradition and an exciting future.

ADMISSION REQUIREMENTS

With each entering class of Colgate students, the application to be one of 720 first years becomes more and more competitive. Over 7,800 applications were submitted from all fifty states, Washington, DC, and 112 countries to become a part of the Colgate class of 2010. Roughly one third of those who applied were admitted to Colgate, and eight percent of the applicants were Early Decision. The standardized test scores were impressive, with the average SAT I Verbal and Math components at 690, and the composite ACT score reaching 31. In the classroom, a staggering ninety-five percent of the class of 2010 finished in the top twenty percent of their high school class. Every accepted applicant was lauded by outstanding teacher recommendations as well.

While scholastic and testing achievements are an important factor in the admission to Colgate, there is no formula for the way an application is analyzed. Accompanying the numerical expression of a student's academics, Colgate is looking for applicants with a strong record of participation and community involvement. The school wants to know that you have challenged yourself with a rigorous course load including honors or Advanced Placement courses, and that you have explored your interests by engaging in outside activities and your community. Colgate seeks to accept a well-rounded class of creative, inquisitive, and motivated individuals with diverse backgrounds, experiences, and passions. The admission staff is developing the future of the Colgate student culture with each admission decision, so they are seeking students who will develop, expand, and energize the activities and initiatives that exist on campus. Each application is reviewed several times, as the admission staff considers the applicant as a whole person, not merely a sum of statistics.

Early Decision is a fantastic decision for the prospective students who have fallen in love with Colgate and are positive that Colgate is their first choice (the decision is binding). Applications for Early Decision I must be filed by November 15, and a decision will be mailed out approximately one month later. Candidates can also be considered for Early Decision II until January 15 on a rolling basis, or may change their application to Early Decision after submission up until March 1. An admission decision is made approximately four weeks after the submission of all application materials. Over half of all Early Admission applicants were accepted into the Class of 2010, comprising forty-six percent of the entire class.

The Admission Office offers a number of on-campus programs to provide a taste of the Colgate experience. Prospective students and families are invited to take the scenic tour of campus with a knowledgeable Colgate student or to take part in personal informational interviews and group information sessions. All interviews are non-evaluative in the admission process, and allow a prospective student to ask questions of an admission officer or senior intern in a one-on-one setting. The forty-five-minute to one-hour group information session led by an admission officer provides a nice overview of Colgate life and an opportunity for students and family members to have questions answered. Perhaps the most enlightening experience for the prospective student is the overnight visit program coordinated by the Admission Office. Current undergraduates host prospective students in their dorm rooms and give the prospective students the opportunity to attend a class, eat in the dining halls, and participate in student life.

2,747
- The Number of Undergraduates Attending Colgate

1385
- Average Combined Math and Critical Reading SAT Score for the Current First-Year Class

100
- Percentage of Classes Taught Only by Professors

51
- Number of Majors Offered

32
- Number of Courses Required to Graduate

18
- Average Class Size

13 (A Colgate Tradition)
- Men with $13: The Founders of Colgate, Each of Whom Had $1

10-to-1
- The Student-to-Faculty Ratio

4
- Number of Years Spent at Colgate to Learn, Create, and Grow into a World Citizen

ACADEMIC LIFE

Every Colgate student will complete thirty-two courses in order to graduate, and anywhere from eight to sixteen of those courses will complete a major course of study. Colgate offers fifty-one concentrations known commonly as majors, and twelve additional minor programs to its undergraduates.

Colgate classes are not an opportunity to turn on one's linear tape recorder and later transcribe fifty to seventy-five minutes worth of lecture. Faculty at Colgate typically employ a Socratic style in the classroom. Colgate students enter the door prepared to engage in a many-voiced discussion, encouraging the student to develop answers and find an individual intellectual voice. True to liberal arts form, graduation requirements include four general education courses, a first-year intensive seminar, and six distribution requirements drawing from natural sciences and mathematics, the humanities, and the social sciences. Colgate students can explore a wide variety of intellectual pursuits before deciding their educational path.

First-Year Seminars

Each incoming first-year student selects three courses for his or her first Colgate semester, plus a first-year seminar. First-year seminars are offered in topics as widely spread as "British Comedy" and "The Atlantis Debate." Taught by professors from every academic division, first-year seminars are the Colgate student's first opportunity to delve into their primary academic love or explore a new and intriguing field.

Every first-year seminar class bonds together through orientation activities and events alongside an upper-class link leader, creating a social relationship to complement the educational demands during the transition to collegiate work. Regardless of the central topic of each first-year seminar, every course provides intensive training in writing at the university level. The ins and outs of the university library system and strategies for studying are approached in a group setting. The professor becomes the student's academic advisor until the student declares a major during sophomore year.

Professors

The warmth that one feels from the faculty at Colgate is created by a genuine interest in the well-being of the students. The faculty will arrange to meet students out at the Barge coffee shop for exam review or invite a whole class into their homes to encounter food and music from a different culture. Colgate professors also routinely invite undergraduate students to participate in their own academic research and projects, conducting studies during the school year and also during the winter and summer breaks. Colgate professors will not, however, accept less than what they believe is a student's best work. Through a series of challenges, from intense classroom discussions to probing essay topics to demanding projects, Colgate professors lead each student to realize his or her own capabilities within a subject.

While Colgate professors maintain high expectations for their students, the students are not left to sink or swim. Professors at Colgate are known for their accessibility. Not only does each professor post between two and four office hours every week, often professors make themselves available by appointment as well. One of the hallmarks of the Colgate education is the degree of investment that every professor, staff member, and administrator has in every student's success. Colgate professors are available to help at any stage of the work process, giving assistance in whatever may be causing difficulties for the student.

I have worked with legendary professors studying Mayan ruins in Copan and learning the local folk traditions of rural Indian villages. Only at Colgate could I bring experiences like that to both my economics course and to theatrical endeavors to come to a deeper level of understanding of both subjects. The professors that I have studied with are the kind who are at once quoted in the footnotes of Shakespeare texts and still enthused enough about teaching that they will gladly meet me for coffee to chat about a scene we did not even cover in class.

—*Dani Nolan, '07, theater and Asian studies*

Workload

The Colgate education is highly valued as a foundation for one's adult life because academic success at Colgate is achieved through hard work. The Colgate student experiences a highly interactive classroom environment. Since Colgate is one of the nation's leading liberal arts universities, there is a continual challenge set by both the volume and the complexity of coursework and studies. Students on campus tend to be incredibly self-motivated to continuously improve and achieve personal goals. Therefore a prospective student should expect to feel driven to succeed by his professors and by his personal ambitions.

Support is available at every stage of the academic process. Students have access to free tutoring in any subject, a student-operated writing center open six days a week, and a student staffed twenty-four-hour tech support service, to name only a few resources. Of course, each student needs to seek a balance in managing free time to complete assignments and coursework. The O'Connor Campus Center (the Coop) is an excellent location on campus to observe the status of work and rest. The student typing feverishly at a term paper in front of the large central hearth is coexisting with the student enjoying a smoothie with her friends in the dining lounge. The study spaces on campus, from the scenic window bridge of Persson Hall to the Keck Humanities Center, host both study groups and the ubiquitous napping student.

Students tend to balance their workload requirements with classes in contrasting fields. One's four classes a semester may include everything from "Modern Theatre" to "Mega Geology" to "Chaucer." Students will also typically enroll in a physical education class to help fulfill their requirements, adding golf or spinning class to complete a well-rounded day.

Core Curriculum

Colgate's commitment to tradition is quintessentially expressed in the liberal arts curriculum. Colgate has one of the oldest liberal arts core curriculums in the country, including four general education courses. Two courses consist of the origins of Western thought and the philosophical revolution of the nineteenth century: Western Traditions and Challenge of Modernity. The scientific perspectives course and non-Western culture course allow Colgate students to experience a topic on the cutting edge of interdisciplinary science and explore the history and traditions of a culture in Africa, Asia, or the Americas. The six-course distribution reinforces the Colgate goal of providing a broad base of intellectual experience. Students will take two courses in three disciplines: humanities, social science, and the natural sciences and mathematics.

Study Abroad

In keeping with the university's goal of developing world citizens with a global perspective, Colgate offers a robust study abroad program. Students are encouraged to study off campus for a semester with one of twenty-three programs. Approximately sixty-eight percent of Colgate students will study off campus during their four years. A professor will lead each program, teaching a course and aiding the study group to fully assimilate the study abroad courses into their Colgate transcript. Study abroad programs are offered in fourteen different countries, including Australia, Switzerland, Japan, and Spain, and also four domestic locations, Santa Fe, San Francisco, Washington, DC, and the National Institutes of Health in Bethesda, MD.

SOCIAL LIFE AND ACTIVITES

At Colgate, one of the great advantages of living in a community with so many diverse, ambitious, and interested students is participating in the student culture on campus. Colgate students complement their rigorous academic life with a stimulating involvement in student-organized groups and the community.

> *When I first arrived at Colgate, I knew I wanted to major in astronomy, but I had no idea that by the time I would graduate I would study economics, philosophy, and British Comedy. I really threw myself into trying new things: I learned how to fence, I joined the Ballet Club and Swing Dancing Club, having never taken lessons, and I volunteered at the Hamilton Food Cupboard and worked with local kids through the organization Sidekicks. I had a valuable opportunity to learn about my hidden capabilities on campus.*

The Center for Leadership and Student Involvement (CLSI) helps to coordinate more than one hundred student-organized groups on campus. At the beginning of each semester, underclassmen are invited to the Student Involvement Fair, where they can collect information and join the mailing list for incredibly diverse groups, from the artistic and performance initiatives to club sporting teams to cultural and political groups to fund-raising and volunteer organizations.

Downtown Hamilton

Recently, Colgate's hometown of Hamilton has witnessed a number of revitalizations and renovations. The cuisine of the town includes Greek and Italian at Numero Uno, sushi at Sushi Blues, traditional American fare in Nichols & Beale and The Colgate Inn, and Chinese at Main Moon. This list is hardly exhaustive, as it omits the two staples of a collegiate diet: pizza and coffee. Colgate students can be seen any day sipping a bubble tea and highlighting textbooks at the Barge Canal Coffee Shop or taking in the Midnight Movie (complete with a slice of pizza) at the beautifully renovated Hamilton Movie House.

Downtown also presents a center for cultural happenings, from the Hamilton Music Mix every summer to art gallery showings to book signings at the Colgate Bookstore. Hamilton also hosts many options for nightlife, including dancing at The Old Stone Jug, and more convivial options for students and community members of age.

Greek System

Colgate's Greek system is a strong part of campus tradition. Though not the predominant social force on campus, the fraternities and sororities that line Broad Street play an important role in philanthropy in the Hamilton area, hosting pumpkin-carving events and rubber ducky races for charity. Regardless of one's Greek affiliation or independent status (as two-thirds of the campus identify), all Colgate students have equal access to the social events at all of the Greek and non-Greek upperclassmen housing.

Colgate operates a delayed recruitment system, so Colgate students must wait until their sophomore year before deciding to join a Greek organization. This leaves the entire first year free to explore all aspects of social life that Colgate offers. While fraternity and sorority life has been lampooned and lauded in entertainment media, Colgate works to maintain a healthful and functioning Greek system. Colgate owns all Greek and non-Greek housing on campus and works with its students to register and coordinate all social functions. Though the majority of Colgate students are not Greek, Colgate continues to foster the Greek system and to provide the most diverse social and residential options to its students.

As a freshman, I became deeply involved with theater through my first year seminar at Colgate. Although that has yielded some of my closest friends, joining a sorority has allowed me to broaden my horizons past anything I could have done on my own. I've made friends not only with girls in my own sorority, but girls from all four of them. It is so great to know that there is always someone there for me, whether she's in my sorority or in another. That's something that the Greek system guarantees for me.

—*Ally Dall, '09, classics*

Athletics

Sports are near and dear to the spirit of every Colgate Raider, but not necessarily all at the Division I level. Colgate's student athletes have one of the highest graduation rates in the country. Colgate's varsity teams are Division I, with men's hockey and basketball and women's soccer and volleyball among the standouts. Hamilton residents, students, and alumni are often found crowding Starr Rink during hockey season to cheer on the team.

In keeping with the Colgate spirit, students are more apt to be found participating in sports than just watching from the sideline. Whether one chooses to participate through the club and intramural sports programs or join various sports interest groups, there is an athletic outlet for everyone.

Colgate also hosts a very active Outdoor Education program that sponsors activities such as spelunking, wilderness survival, and moonlight canoe trips during the fall and spring and snowshoeing and telemark skiing in the winter months. With the Adirondack Mountains a short drive from campus, the setting for outdoor sporting is absolutely perfect.

During the spring of my senior year, I was in the middle of the Varsity basketball season as the team co-captain and I was cast in a lead role for the Spring theatrical festival. Being able to balance academics and having an artistic extracurricular and athletics as well, really pushed my threshold. I never in a million years thought I would do all three of those things at once. Doing all three sums up what Colgate is all about. Colgate challenges you, but you learn you can go further than what you previously thought your limits were.

—*Alvin Reed, '06, political science*

Student Diversity

One quarter of the class of 2010 is comprised of students from multicultural backgrounds. With a fifth of the entire campus identifying as multicultural students, the range of culturally based events and groups abound in student life. The ALANA (African, Latino, Asian, and Native American) Cultural Center is a flagship for many of these organizations, sponsoring food tastings by groups like the China Club in its full kitchen and hosting workshops such as Skin Deep to promote awareness of racism, discrimination, and ethnocentrism in its large meeting room and lounge area. Student groups provide banquets and invite speakers to increase campus cultural visibility, such as the Banghra nights hosted by the South Asian Culture Club and speakers brought by The Brothers (a group based on relaying Black heritage) such as the Reverend Jesse Jackson and Spike Lee.

Additionally, the Office of LGBTQ (Lesbian, Gay, Bisexual, Transgender, Queer, and Questioning) Initiatives provides support to the LGBTQ community and programs for the whole campus to enjoy. The initiative coordinates groups such as WorkOut for faculty, staff, and community members who are not out and Rainbow Alliance to support the students who are. The community and advocates throw events such as Big Gay Weekend, participate in Sex Week, run Safe Zone training events for student leaders and administrators, and sponsor lectures such as "Some Version of the Gay Cowboy" to inform and enliven the campus culture.

Artistic Life

Students profoundly express their ideas and create a campus dialogue through art. In support of the excellent art, theatre, and music departments on campus, the students coordinate an active calendar of events through the student groups in the arts initiative. The Colgate 13 are a sixty-five-year-old all-male a capella tradition, who annually perform around the country and record new albums. In addition, the all-female Swinging Gates and the coed Resolutions and the Dischords make beautiful music on campus. Musical performance opportunities abound from the Colgate Orchestra to the University Chorus to the Jazz Band.

Alumni members of the Colgate 13, or "Crusts" as they are known within the 13, are actively involved in maintaining the success of the group. Crusts help in setting up concerts, providing food and shelter on the road, and have established an endowment to provide transportation for the 13 in the form of "The Grunt," a stretch limo that seats 13 and has become a symbol of the group's touring achievements. Crusts constantly go out of their way to tell stories and folklore of the group, and to provide opportunities for current and future generations to create memories of their own.

—*Dennis Wong, '06, political science*

The Theatrical Season is coordinated every year through the cooperative efforts of the University Theatre program and the Masque & Triangle, Colgate's historic student dramatic society on campus. Between large main-stage productions, full-scale ballets, smaller poetry release nights, and One Night Stands (staged readings), there is a theatrical offering for every taste on any given weekend. The student artists on campus routinely display innovative work in the gallery-style Little Hall and present unexpected installations all over campus. The student media at Colgate also represent a fine tradition, with the oldest college weekly in the country, *The Colgate Maroon News*, and creative programming on the campus radio station WRCU, and CUTV, appropriately broadcast on channel 13.

The culmination of all campus artistic efforts is the annual student-coordinated "arts! Festival." This weeklong celebration every spring offers performances, visiting artists, presentations of the improv comedy troupe Charred Goosebeak, and workshops for Colgate artists. The entire campus is awash with color and excitement, with beautiful lighting installations and ice sculpture on the quad, an arts bazaar in the COOP, and monochrome one-inch buttons adorning every lapel.

Volunteerism and Civics

Now celebrating its fifth year in operation, the COVE serves as a home for Colgate's community service-based organizations. More than seventy percent of the student body is involved in the numerous service projects throughout the community, devoting their time to groups such as Sidekicks (a big brother/big sister mentoring program), Habitat for Humanity, SOMAC (the volunteer ambulance corps), Students for Environmental Action, and the Food Salvage Program.

To amplify the lively political debate and intellectual discourse on campus, CLSI has recently founded the Colgate Speaking Union (CSU). The CSU is composed of the Debate Team, Model United Nations, Mock Trial, and the Student Lecture Forum. The groups themselves are totally autonomous and run by students. In addition to competing domestically and abroad, the Debate Team helps to run a public discourse workshop during orientation, while regularly hosting showcase debates with various departments, including International Relations, Peace and Conflict Studies, and Women's Studies. Since the inception of Colgate's chapter of Model UN, the delegates have attended conferences at Georgetown, Yale, Penn, Oxford, Edinburgh, McGill, Harvard, Beijing, and Geneva. Colgate delegates have received awards ranging from Verbal Accommodation to Best Delegate. The Student Lecture Forum also provides students the opportunity to develop academic papers and lectures in an extracurricular setting, and also to compete in an annual contest with a monetary prize. Colgate's education really works to develop the student's role as a citizen, inside and outside the classroom.

FINANCIAL AID

As everyone knows, college is an investment. Colgate's education is a sound investment that should benefit the graduate throughout his or her entire life. Of course, the worrisome part is always trying to figure out how to pay for a private, highly selective, liberal arts university like Colgate. This is where Colgate financial aid comes in.

Colgate does not offer any merit-based aid, but for those who demonstrate need, Colgate does offer assistance. In a recent first-year class, forty percent of students receive an average of $28,000 in scholarship or grant—which does not need to be paid back—and the average total package comes in at $33,500 with student loans and other campus jobs. All applicants who applied for financial aid and demonstrated need for the class of 2010 had their need met in full. For those students who do rely on student loans, the total debt incurred after graduation averages just over $12,000—much lower than most of Colgate's peer institutions.

Colgate also offers a variety of awards, such as the Stafford Loan, Perkins Loan, Pell Grant, Federal Work Study, and institutional grants. To apply for financial aid, prospective students must file the PROFILE application for financial aid with the College Scholarship Service (CSS). Also to be completed is the Free Application for Federal Student Aid

(FAFSA) to be filed with the federal processor upon matriculation. Both applications can be completed and filed on-line.

GRADUATES

Colgate alumni are supportive, enthusiastic, and interesting people. They define school spirit, showing up on campus to cheer on the athletic teams, but they are also personally interested in the daily life on campus. The time spent at Colgate is so special and impactful, that simply seeing someone walk down the street with a Colgate sweatshirt will instantly evoke a deep bond within the alumni/student community.

Alumni are continuously advocating for the current Colgate students, exemplified chiefly in the "Colgate Connection," a volunteer network of over 3,000 alumni and parents coordinated by the Center for Career Services. These individuals provide career counseling and networking opportunities for current undergraduates, coming to campus to provide mock interviews and to participate in career exploration panels and simply being available by phone to inquisitive students.

Careers

Colgate is very serious about making each student's liberal arts degree an essential springboard to a successful adult life. Typically, seventy-five percent of recent graduates are employed full-time after one year, and nearly twenty-one percent are attending graduate schools. Colgate's Career Services Center brings more than 200 employers to campus every year to recruit current undergrads. Additionally, Career Services works to make sure Colgate students are prepared for employment opportunities as they arise, by leading cover letter writing workshops, offering workshops about careers in the modern market, and providing one-on-one appointments for resume writing, internship searches, and fellowship applicants. Careers in finance and consulting have tended to be popular among Colgate graduates;

PROMINENT GRADS

Charles Evans Hughes, 1884, Chief Justice of the Supreme Court

Broken Lizard, '90, '91, '92, Comedy Group of Super Troopers and Club Dread Fame

Gloria Borger, '74, Journalist and CBS Television Commentator

William Rogers, '34, Former Secretary of State

Andy Rooney, '42, Television Commentator

Francesca Zambello, '78, Opera and Theater Director

Adona Foyle, '98, Center for the Golden State Warriors and Founder of "Democracy Matters"

Ed Werner, '71 and John Honey, '70, Creators of *Trivial Pursuit* however, there are also a growing number of alumni working in education, public service, and the nonprofit sector. The Colgate student who wishes to experiment intellectually and attempt new sports, hobbies, and art forms will invariably become the Colgate alumna or alumnus who seeks a challenging and fulfilling career after graduation. Luckily, there are more than 28,000 alumni and a committed staff on campus that are able to help realize a successful future.

SUMMING UP

Colgate University is the perfect setting for an undergraduate experience. Students are challenged both in the classroom and in extracurricular activities and community involvement. Colgate provides an ideal environment for students to find their intellectual voice, as they dabble in many different subjects, experience many cultures, and explore the world not only through discourse and study but also firsthand. Colgate students learn the value of integrity and competition, both academic and athletic.

As students work toward their liberal arts degrees, professors approach their classroom in an interdisciplinary and personal way. Professors consistently publish and discover at the forefront of academia, while drawing out the maximum performance from each of Colgate's 2,800 students. The liberal arts education prepares each Colgate student for a multifaceted future, whether he or she becomes an improv comedian working as an environmental lawyer or an athlete engaged in public service.

Support and resources are available to all students as they continue the entrepreneurial spirit of Colgate in the classroom and in the residence hall. Students at Colgate are hard-working and ambitious, developing new organizations and communities to add to the one hundred currently operating groups on campus. While students continue to build campus culture, Colgate continues to build facilities, introducing an updated library and a state-of-the-art interdisciplinary science building. Colgate is always growing, but the traditions on campus keep the university grounded to a very proud history.

Colgate graduates are outgoing, confident, flexible, and incredibly engaging individuals who build companies and families and constantly change the world for the better. The experience of four years on the hill of Colgate is transformative, creating leaders out of students with incredible potential, intellect, and motivation. Colgate is an invaluable experience, a launching point for a truly successful and wonderful adult life.

❏ *Stephanie Wortel, B.A.*

THE COLLEGE OF NEW JERSEY

 The College of New Jersey
Ewing, NJ 08628

 (609) 771-2131, (800) 624-0967
Fax: (609) 637-5174

 E-mail: *admiss@tcnj.edu*
Web site: *http://www.tcnj.edu*

 **Enrollment**

Full-time ❑ women: 3,293
❑ men: 2,432

Part-time ❑ women: 63
❑ men: 107

INTRODUCING THE COLLEGE OF NEW JERSEY

Just a few miles from the state capital of Trenton, New Jersey, TCNJ is an oasis of ideas and enthusiastic energy. Stepping onto campus, visitors immediately get lost in the ultimate collegiate environment: lush, manicured landscaping, Georgian Colonial architecture, criss-crossing pathways. Benches abound and on a warm fall day, blankets and books and footballs and Frisbees fill the velvety lawns surrounding the dorms.

I originally had my heart—and my money—set on a large, prominent university in the Midwest. Growing up a small town girl, I had every aspiration of moving on to bigger and better things, and I thought that going far away for school would enlighten me about the rest of the world. However, when my mother informed me that if I went to the Midwest I wouldn't be able to come home for Thanksgiving, I quickly realized that "bigger and better" didn't necessarily mean moving far away. Choosing TCNJ gave me the best of both worlds: I had the opportunity to live away from home in an active collegiate environment, but at the same time, I was close enough to easily get home for the family get-togethers that I simply couldn't live without.

ALL IN A NAME

Since its establishment in 1855, the institution currently known as The College of New Jersey, has undergone five name changes:

1855—New Jersey State Normal School
1908—New Jersey State Normal School in Trenton
1929—New Jersey State Teachers College and State Normal School at Trenton
1937—New Jersey State Teachers College at Trenton
1958—Trenton State College
1996—The College of New Jersey

Starting out as a teachers' college, the name changes have reflected the institution's progression into the state academic powerhouse it is today.

Established in 1855 by the state legislature as the New Jersey State Normal School, the College has always been grounded in the finest traditions of higher learning. Starting out with only fifteen students in its first year of existence, the school now boasts a student body of more than 6,500. Originally housed in a small building in downtown Trenton, the college is now comprised of thirty-eight buildings. Despite being a smallish school in a relatively obscure part of central New Jersey, TCNJ is quickly making a national name for itself and is hardly dwarfed by some of the neighboring "big name" schools.

The campus itself—289 tree-lined acres in suburban Ewing—is closed to outside traffic. Secluded from the outside world with the help of the Hillwood Lakes—Lake Sylva and Lake Ceva—that border the campus, students are given the experience of being a world away, even if home is nearby.

With a heavy emphasis on community, TCNJ quickly becomes a home away from home. When you move into your freshman dorm, you'll be greeted by your CA—Community Advisor—who is an upper-class student in charge of your area of the residence hall. Your CA will introduce you to the inner workings of campus life as well as provide you with helpful tidbits such as which Chinese food delivery restaurant won't make you sick, and who you should call if your light fixture in your room unexpectedly falls off the wall.

Play Fair

The most exciting thing to look forward to when moving in as a freshman is Welcome Week, the five "freshmen only" days prior to the start of classes when first-year students get free use of the campus before the rest of the students arrive. Despite all of the activities, lectures, meetings, and hang-out time allotted during those five days, "PlayFair" is hands-down the main attraction of the week. PlayFair is the first time that all 1,200 members of that year's freshman class come together. Gathering on a warm August night under the stars on the Astroturf in Lions' Stadium, PlayFair can quite possibly be considered the world's largest ice-breaker, complete with team-building activities that are too much fun to pass up. It is here that students come together as one community, and where the first college friendships are made.

Traditions

TCNJ students are proud to take part in the college's long-standing traditions, but relish in the fact that they can also take an active part in developing new traditions. Recent classes can also brag that they've left their mark on the school by finally giving a name to

I knew the first time I visited TCNJ that I wanted to go there. Besides having an amazing reputation for a great price, it felt like college was supposed to. It has a beautiful campus without being too uptight and it's relaxed and fun while still upholding high academic standards. "At other schools I felt like people were more concerned with money and clothes than they were with being in college, but at TCNJ, people seemed to have their priorities in order. It just felt comfortable. I definitely made the right choice and I was absolutely right about the school."

—*Eileen D. Nagle, Class of 2003*

the longtime unnamed Lion mascot, now dubbed "Roscoe" as a tribute to former College President Roscoe L. West.

TCNJ even has its very own commemorative ice cream! In honor of the school's sesquicentennial anniversary, the *SesquiMINTennial* flavor was dreamed up by a student and made a reality by a husband and wife alumni team who are the proprietors of a successful local artisan ice cream shop.

With a retention rate of ninety-five percent, it certainly seems that the students who choose to embark on their college journey at TCNJ are happy with that choice. For many, parents and prospective students alike, all it takes to cement their decision is one visit to the campus.

My younger sister was one of the "I just know" applicants. Visiting my dorm and attending classes and campus activities with me and my friends gave her a firsthand taste of life at TCNJ well before her college application process even started. Campus visits, official or unofficial, should be an integral part of any college search process, and TCNJ encourages interested students to come and check out the campus. To my knowledge it isn't a proven fact, but having that gut feeling about a school usually points you in the right direction. If your gut tells you that you're in the right place, listen to it. If you can't see yourself as a member of a college's community after your campus visit, chances are you should keep searching. Find a school that feels so right that you "just know" that that's where you should be.

ADMISSIONS REQUIREMENTS

Many students "just know" that they want to attend TCNJ, and they spend their high school years preparing themselves to submit the "perfect" application. For other students, a campus visit is really what it takes to bolster the decision to apply.

For many, the admissions process starts during a campus tour or Open House, where prospective students have the opportunity to meet with and have their questions answered by current students, faculty, and staff. Deciding if you can see yourself having a successful future at TCNJ is ultimately the first thing that needs to happen in order to get the admissions process rolling.

Over the past few years, the school has become much more selective and competitive. With more and more of the area's brightest choosing to apply, the SAT I combined scores of recent entering classes have climbed to an average of over 1300. TCNJ aims to have an incoming freshman class of 1,200; with an applicant pool hovering around 6,300 applicants; slightly less than half of those are offered admission.

But don't give up hope—test scores are hardly in charge of your fate.

Application Process

As with any college, there isn't an exact combination of GPA, test scores, and extracurriculars that will guarantee admission to TCNJ. Instead, TCNJ admissions counselors look very carefully at an applicant's high school transcript. To the admissions office, a high school transcript is the best indicator of an applicant's academic intensity and drive, as well as the best predictor of success in college. Course selection and difficulty, grades, GPA, and class rank are all weighed heavily in the decision-making process, more so than standardized test scores. Eighty-seven percent of freshmen are in the top one-fifth of their high school class, and 98 percent are in the top two-fifths.

The application process itself is relatively standard, requiring prospects to submit a transcript, test scores (SAT or ACT), several letters of recommendations, a personal essay, and a list of extracurricular activities. TCNJ also offers the Early Decision option for those students who wish to take advantage of it. TCNJ's Web site is an easily accessible and easily navigable wealth of information, so if you're looking for specific deadlines and details, surf over to *www.tcnj.edu/~admiss*.

In recent years, TCNJ has made concerted efforts to increase the diversity of its student body. The college offers several programs (such as the Educational Opportunity Fund, detailed in the Financial Aid section) that aim to encourage and foster the development of those students throughout their college careers.

ACADEMIC LIFE

With seven schools and a variety of majors to choose from, the academic experience at TCNJ has been labeled an Ivy League education for a state school price. Rarely, if ever, will you find yourself having your regular class meetings in the enormous lecture halls you see in the movies. The average student-to-faculty ratio is 17:1.

I spent quite a bit of time having casual chats with my department chair, who I still keep in contact with through e-mail despite the fact that I have since graduated and he has since retired. Take the time to get to know your professors and make connections with whomever you can; you never know who you might need to turn to for academic guidance, a letter of recommendation, or just a shoulder to lean on.

The small class size at TCNJ is a really big plus. You never get lost in the mix and the professors always get to know you on a personal level. More than just lecturing in the classroom or facilitating your student research project, TCNJ professors make it their personal duty to do whatever they can to help you succeed inside and outside of the classroom. Members of the faculty and staff at TCNJ are truly mentors to the student body.

Curriculum

Having undergone a recent curriculum transformation, an essential liberal learning curriculum is now in place at TCNJ. What does that mean? For starters, TCNJ's redesigned curriculum means fewer, more intensive courses, and more options for interdisciplinary study. The liberal learning program helps ensure that students learn the fundamentals of reasoning, communicating, and living in today's world. There is still a list of requirements that students must complete, but students now get to choose from a wide selection of courses to fulfill each requirement. One obligation of all first-year students is the completion of a First Seminar. The students get to pick their own seminar, with a broad selection of topics ranging from Walt Whitman to tourism and the American identity, from cultural history and the science of food to early philosophical cosmology. The choice is yours, and there are many!

Community Service

Community service, or civic engagement, is also a built-in part of the First Year Experience (FYE) at TCNJ. Each first-year student has the chance to participate in his or her choice of more than thirty social service agencies in the Ewing/Trenton area. It is in the program that many students find a niche in society and a genuine interest in giving to their community.

Internships and Independent Study

Internships are another great opportunity to get out in the "real world" and get hands-on, practical experience. Though not required by every department, internships are strongly encouraged, not to mention that they are a great way to make connections and expand your network. Students at TCNJ can apply their internship for up to six credits (sometimes more, in special cases that vary from department to department). Internships, both paying and nonpaying, can often be found directly through your professors and departments, the Office of Career Services, or on your own through some of the many online internship databases.

When my career interests led me in the direction of public and media relations, I decided that finding an internship in such a field would be the best practical way for me to get more experience and decide if that field was really where I wanted to be. A fan and season ticket holder of a local professional sports team, I got over my fear of phones and cold-called the team's public relations manager to ask him about internship opportunities with the team. An hour later, I had secured an interview for a game night internship and the next week I began working in the press box at all the home games. By the end of that semester, I had earned three credits toward my degree, made unbelievable contacts in the sports industry, gained valuable experience in my field of interest, and not to mention made some great friends. Four seasons later, I still volunteer my time for the team!

Hand in hand with internships are independent study and research projects. There are plenty of opportunities for students to work on (and get credit for) their own research interests, as well as assisting professors in their research projects. Whether it's a lab assistant, library researcher, interviewer, or other type of data gatherer, TCNJ's curriculum is fluid enough that students can literally "design their own courses" by way of independent study or research assisting.

Organizations and Honor Societies

There are also a variety of academic organizations and honor societies to participate in, including Phi Kappa Phi, Leadership in Public Affairs (LPA), and Women in Learning and Leadership (WILL). An on-campus tutoring center provides opportunities for students to enhance their classroom experiences through drop-in and scheduled tutoring in math, science, and the humanities, single-session writing conferences, and study groups, and foreign language conversation hours.

Other helpful resources and facilities on campus include, of course, the Roscoe L. West Library, named for a former College president, state-of-the art science labs, a planetarium, observatory, and the Instructional Technology Services (ITS) office. ITS is TCNJ's answer to a late-night copy shop, providing such services as:

- CD burners
- Scanners
- Photo-quality color printers
- Image editing/desktop publishing software
- Copying
- Binding
- Laminating
- Transparencies
- Labeling
- Large-format printing
- Support for instructional Web sites
- Digital cameras
- Digital scanning
- Slide production

There truly are more resources on campus than can even be listed. Explore, talk to people, ask questions, seek out and soak up information. Those are the underlying—and encouraged—elements of a successful academic experience at TCNJ.

SOCIAL LIFE AND ACTIVITIES

TCNJ is located in Ewing, New Jersey, a suburb of the state capital of Trenton. The campus is closed off from the outside world, encompassed by a 2.5-mile road that is largely utilized by runners and power-walkers at any time of day or night. Though most of the students—ninety-five percent—are from the Garden State, TCNJ is moving away from its long-standing image as a suitcase school. More than sixty-five percent of students live on campus, and freshmen and returning second-year students are guaranteed housing. Though first-year residents are not permitted to have cars on campus, a regularly running shuttle bus is available to students who wish to visit the local shopping centers. There is also an NJ Transit bus stop at the Brower Student Center that provides easy access to area attractions, as well as the local train station for those students who wish to enjoy a day in New York City. Philadelphia's art museums and concert venues are also just a few miles away, as well as a variety of attractions on both sides of the Delaware River.

Off-campus or On-campus Events

However, you don't have to travel to another state to have a good time if you're a TCNJ student. Trenton plays host to an AA affiliate of the New York Yankees—the Trenton Thunder—and an ECHL hockey team—the Trenton Titans, the affiliate of the Philadelphia Flyers. Not to mention the fact that there is always something happening on campus, whether it is a student organization-sponsored lecture or a College Union Board concert or late-nighter. These events are always publicized in a weekly e-mail list so students are always in-the-know.

OUTSIDE ACTIVITIES

Think there's nothing fun to do in or around New Jersey? Think again! New Jersey is a hub of activity, nestled between two of the country's most entertaining and educational cultural hotspots: New York City and Philadelphia. Professional sports abound (both major and minor league), Madison Square Garden is an hour away, the Jersey shore is thirty minutes away, and the Poconos are a ninety-minute drive. Or you can stay very local and visit the twenty-four-seat-auditorium movie theater with stadium-seating, go mini-golfing, or out for a night of sampling fine Italian cuisine in Trenton's historic Chambersburg. You can visit any of these places during the day and still make it home in time for your favorite primetime TV show!

Some of my favorite TCNJ memories involve road trips with my friends. We were always up for a trip to Philadelphia's South Street for a good cheese steak, or a late-night adventure to Atlantic City. Being in the center of such a culturally active part of the country gave us limitless educational and entertaining options to pass the time. However, nothing quite beat the time we spent having perpetual sleepovers (ah, the joys of being able to wear your pajamas 24/7!) and video game competitions in each other's dorm rooms, eating dollar pints of ice cream from the local dairy, and staying up until all hours of the night forging forever friendships and eating microwaveable macaroni and cheese. Those are the times at TCNJ that I will always remember, and will always be thankful for.

Men's
- ⭕ Baseball
- ⭕ Basketball
- ⭕ Cross-Country
- ⭕ Football
- ⭕ Golf
- ⭕ Soccer
- ⭕ Swimming and Diving
- ⭕ Tennis
- ⭕ Indoor Track and Field
- ⭕ Track and Field
- ⭕ Wrestling

Women's
- ⭕ Basketball
- ⭕ Cross-Country
- ⭕ Field Hockey
- ⭕ Lacrosse
- ⭕ Soccer
- ⭕ Softball
- ⭕ Swimming and Diving
- ⭕ Tennis
- ⭕ Indoor Track and Field
- ⭕ Track and Field

Athletics

There is nothing better than pulling on your favorite college hoodie, grabbing some friends, and planting yourself in Lions' Stadium for a traditional Saturday afternoon of football. If you're an athlete or sports buff, be sure to note that TCNJ is an NCAA Division III powerhouse. Since 1979, TCNJ has amassed a total of thirty-six Division III crowns in six different sports. In addition, TCNJ has posted twenty-nine runner-up awards, giving the college the best record nationally in these categories. As impressive as the overall record is, the college's accomplishments as a leader in women's sports are even greater. Since NCAA Championships were initiated for women in 1981, only TCNJ has won as many as thirty Division III team championships. Intramural sports are also very popular among the students, providing a fun way to relax and unwind from the stresses of schoolwork. Ice hockey, flag football, volleyball, basketball, softball, and dodgeball are just a sampling of some of the intramurals that TCNJ students enjoy.

One of TCNJ's biggest and best-attended events occurs the very first night of classes. "LollaNobooza" is a campus-wide welcome back party where student organizations team up to host an all-nighter full of events and activities that promote making healthy choices. On a warm summer night, students pour into Lions' stadium to participate in athletic skills tests, obstacle courses, bull-riding, pie-throwing, root beer pong, live music, free food, and a variety of other free, fun activities.

Clubs and Organizations

If you're looking to get involved with Greek life, TCNJ has two local and five national fraternities, and seven national sororities. The campus proper doesn't host any Greek houses, but there is an off-campus presence if that's your cup of tea. If Greek isn't the way you want to go, not to worry: there are more than 180 campus clubs and organizations to get involved in, ranging from musical ensembles, the school radio station, and the Ayn Rand Society, to the Video Game Design and Appreciation Club, Circle K, and the Flying Lions Adventure Club. If by chance you can't find your niche in one of the existing clubs, you can even start your own. Fostering community development is key at TCNJ and it is encouraged in all facets of campus life.

FINANCIAL AID

Comparatively speaking, TCNJ offers an education that far exceeds its price tag. However, the Financial Aid Office is frequented by many students. Nearly half of all full-time freshmen receive some form of financial aid. Financial aid at TCNJ is allotted largely on a need-based scale, and filling out the Free Application for Federal Student Aid (FAFSA) is the first step. The easiest way to fill out and track your FAFSA application is by accessing the application on the Internet (*www.fafsa.ed.gov*), but it is also available in paper form. After the application and all supporting documents are submitted to TCNJ's Office of Student Financial Assistance, you'll be notified about the maximum amount of need-based aid for which you qualify, which is usually a combination of scholarships, grants, work-study, and loans.

Many students come into the college with a bank of private scholarships supporting them, most of which students find by searching through online scholarship databases and with the assistance of their high school guidance counselors. Work-study is also available at TCNJ, with a variety of jobs that suit the diverse talents and interests of the students who need them. The average annual on-campus salary is $750, and there are jobs (mostly in residence life) that offer free room and board. Ninety-five percent of all undergraduate students (receiving aid or not) work part-time for extra cash or to pay for their tuition or textbooks and other supplies.

IMPORTANT VISITORS TO TCNJ

Think big-name academics and big-name celebrities visit only big name schools? Here's a list of the people TCNJ students have welcomed to campus in recent years:

- ○ Bill Cosby
- ○ Maya Angelou
- ○ Naomi Tutu
- ○ Sugar Ray Robinson
- ○ Ben Folds
- ○ Anna Quindlen
- ○ Spike Lee
- ○ Dave Chappelle
- ○ Lewis Black
- ○ Jill Sobule
- ○ The Bacon Brothers
- ○ Salman Rushdie
- ○ Lani Guinier
- ○ John Leguizamo
- ○ Carson Kressley
- ○ Cornel West

Wanting to stay debt-free for as long as possible, I somehow managed to make my way through four years of undergraduate schooling without a single loan. Fortunately, I had the strong support of my parents, but they had an educational payment plan behind them! My father enrolled in the Academic Management Services (AMS) installment plan, the only payment plan authorized by the college. By setting up a schedule with payments they could handle, paying for my four years of tuition and room and board was a little easier to swallow. There are a variety of ways to pay your tuition, and worrying about paying shouldn't deter you from considering TCNJ; the Financial Aid Office and the Office of Student Accounts are readily available to assist you in any way. For more information about AMS, visit their Web site at www.tuitionpay.com.

EOF Program

Finally, the Educational Opportunity Fund (EOF) at TCNJ is a support package that many state residents take advantage of. More than just financial support, the program offers academic and personal support to students who, without the EOF program, would not have found themselves in college. According to its mission statement, the EOF program is designed for students who are from backgrounds of "historical poverty" and who have lacked access to quality educational preparation to attend college. EOF maximizes the participating students' chances for success in college by providing academic support, mentoring, supplemental instruction, and financial assistance. For information about the EOF program, e-mail *eofp@tcnj.edu*.

GRADUATES

A degree from TCNJ is an investment that will carry you above and beyond anywhere you've dreamed of. More than 600 companies recruited on campus in a recent year, and TCNJ also has a comprehensive Office of Career Services that helps students create a resume, build a portfolio, research jobs, hone their skills, and apply for positions. Students can also take advantage of videotaped mock interviews, ongoing career counseling

Though my commencement was a chilly and drizzling day in May, all I can remember were blue and gold banners and streamers and bright smiles everywhere. Filing into Lions' Stadium with a thousand of my peers, I realized how full-circle my TCNJ experience had been. Four years earlier at Welcome Week, we stepped onto that field as strangers. At commencement, we were stepping onto the field and filling up the stadium as a proud community of learners, leaders, and more importantly, friends.

PROMINENT GRADS

- James Florio, Former Governor of New Jersey
- Guy Chiarello, Chief Technology Officer for Morgan Stanley
- Susanne Svizeny, Regional President of Wachovia Bank
- Thomas McCarthy, Philadelphia Phillies Announcer

resources, as well a service that will easily maintain and send your letters of recommendation should you need them for graduate school or a potential employer. LionsPro, powered by MonsterTRAK, is TCNJ's on-campus recruitment program. When students are ready to look for a permanent position or an internship, the LionsPro system is one of the most convenient and productive means by which to do so. The program allows students and alumni to submit resumes online to potential employers and/or interview one another regarding possible employment opportunities.

In a recent year, more than eighty percent of students were employed within six months of graduation, and sixteen percent were enrolled in a graduate program within six months.

TCNJ grads go on to medical school, law school, and graduate schools in almost every discipline. Many grads are also lined up with jobs well before they graduate, and some are lucky enough to find out about a job offer on graduation day. Graduates work in a variety of fields, some of the most popular being education, business, and computer science.

Recent graduates have opened ice cream shops, work in publishing, write children's books, own marketing agencies, and become Rotary International World Peace and Conflict Resolution Fellows. A TCNJ graduate can apply his or her degree to anything and be taken seriously in any field.

SUMMING UP

College, like any experience, is what you make of it. There are two kinds of people in the college world: those who considered TCNJ and those who didn't. TCNJ is not the little suitcase school of past years. TCNJ is proud of its roots as New Jersey's state teachers' college, but it is also bravely, enthusiastically, and quickly embracing its new position as one of the nation's leaders in higher education. TCNJ students are driven go-getters with a passion to excel in all aspects of their lives. Your time spent at TCNJ is what you make of it, so take full advantage of the small classes, become friends with your professors, join some clubs, meet people, try something new. The only guarantee is a world-class faculty, state-of-the-art facilities, and a learning environment dedicated to the success of its undergraduates. Combine that with an unforgettable residential experience and social activities galore, and students get a truly remarkable place, full of all the resources and opportunities they need to achieve their loftiest goals and make their wildest dreams a reality. TCNJ gives you the tools and materials; what you build with them is up to you.

❏ *Emily L. Weiss, B.A.*

COLLEGE OF THE HOLY CROSS

 College of the Holy Cross
Worcester, MA 01610-2395

 (508) 793-2443, (800) 442-2421
Fax: (508) 793-3888

 E-mail: *admissions@holycross.edu*
Web site: *http://www.holycross.edu*

 Enrollment

Full-time ❑ women: 1,535
❑ men: 1,255

INTRODUCING HOLY CROSS

The only Jesuit Catholic college in the country to offer an exclusively undergraduate liberal arts education, Holy Cross enjoys a well-deserved reputation as one of the preeminent schools in the United States. Small class sizes, devoted faculty members, and a challenging curriculum have made the college an increasingly popular choice for many top-notch high school students. Others are attracted to the beautiful campus, active student body, and friendly living/learning environment. Whatever their reasons for choosing Holy Cross, few students are disappointed when they arrive, as evidenced by the school's ninety-five percent freshman retention rate and overwhelmingly positive student satisfaction statistics.

Holy Cross has grown in both size and stature since it was established in 1843 as an academic community where the Jesuit ideals of educational integrity and social justice could flourish among its male students and faculty. Founded by Benedict Joseph Fenwick, the second bishop of Boston, the school originally comprised only one wooden building and a half-finished brick structure on a hill overlooking the largely unsettled town of Worcester, Massachusetts. There was little evidence to suggest that such a prominent college would eventually arise from this undeveloped setting.

Coeducational since 1972, the college is today home to nearly 2,800 young men and women and the campus is widely recognized as one of the most impressive in the country. Driving through the black, wrought-iron gates that form the entrance to Linden Lane, the tree-lined passageway that leads through the Holy Cross campus, visitors are immediately struck by the school's beautiful architecture and perfectly manicured grounds, which are spread over 174 acres. Ivy-covered residence halls and open green spaces are intermixed with technologically advanced academic buildings and state-of-the-art athletic facilities. There are three well-endowed libraries, two multi-sport recreational facilities, a recently renovated campus center, and a comprehensive art complex. Completed in 2001, Smith Hall, located in the center of the campus, is the home of the college's Center for Religion, Ethics, and Culture, as well as the philosophy and religious studies departments, the Center for Interdisciplinary Special Studies, information technology services, and the registrar's office. The Center's primary public space is the two-story Rehm Library, which provides space for hospitality, lectures and events, quiet space for reading and reflection, and enhanced library resources on religion and spirituality. With its outdoor sculptures and idyllic flower gardens, the award-winning campus is both peaceful and picturesque. Few who visit the school are disappointed by its physical surroundings.

Perhaps more impressive than the campus, however, are the strong traditions and deep loyalties that have taken root here for many generations. Each year, young men and women from all over the country come to Holy Cross to participate in a vibrant academic and residential community where the Jesuits' founding principles continue to flourish. These students experience an educational environment where intelligent dialogue is encouraged and scholarly exploration is rewarded. Along the way, they become part of a close-knit social atmosphere where lifelong friendships are fostered. Holy Cross graduates carry these meaningful lessons and experiences with them by continuing to seek ways to integrate their faith, their lives, and their value-centered education.

ADMISSIONS REQUIREMENTS

In recent years, Holy Cross annually receives applications from more than 7,000 students who are competing for only 700 places in the first-year class. Though the Admissions Committee considers many factors before making its decision, those students who demonstrate a pattern of superior academic performance in high school do a great deal to improve their chances of gaining acceptance to the college. This is confirmed by the fact that nearly all of the entering students graduated in the top twenty percent of their high school class and an overwhelming majority come with Advanced Placement or honors coursework on their transcripts. In recent years, the average SAT I score has exceeded 1280 (based on 1600), though few on campus consider this statistic a meaningful measure of success in either the admissions process or the school's curriculum.

Besides a high level of academic achievement, other characteristics that have been identified as common among those students offered admission to Holy Cross are an openness to different veiwpoints and ideas, a willingness to become engaged in the life of the college outside the classroom, a desire to grow not only intellectually, but socially and spiritually as well, and a commitment to helping others, both within the college community and beyond.

Unlike larger schools that rely on formulaic methods to make admissions decisions, the admissions staff at Holy Cross tries to remain focused on each individual and his or her unique talents. Before going through "committee," where the final decision is made, each application is read by at least two (and sometimes three) staff members who try to determine how well the applicant utilized the academic and extracurricular resources available in his or her high school. In this way, the team hopes to identify those students who will not only excel academically, but who will also make positive contributions to the vibrant intellectual, social, and spiritual life of the campus.

Requirements

Since 2005, submission of standardized text scores (SAT or ACT) is optional. In addition, prospective students are asked to write an essay on a question chosen by the Admissions Committee. Interviews, while not required, are highly recommended and should be considered an excellent opportunity to share additional insights about one's personality.

Early Decision

For those who have made Holy Cross their first choice, the school recommends applying Early Decision, which allows the Admissions Committee to spend more time reading the application and getting to know the student. An additional advantage of this option is the convenience of hearing a decision within three or four weeks of the school's receipt of all required application materials. One should be aware, however, that Early Decision applications are binding and therefore require accepted students to immediately withdraw all pending applications at other colleges.

Children of Alumni

Recognizing that there is no greater compliment paid to a college than an alumnus/a who wishes to send a son or daughter to his or her alma mater, Holy Cross does give special consideration to those children of alumni who are seeking admission to the school. The fact that more than ten percent of the student body qualify as such legacies offers testimony to the loyalty of Holy Cross graduates.

Minority Students

While the college has been home to a distinguished and proud list of minority alumni including U.S. Supreme Court Justice Clarence Thomas, and James Healy, the Church's first African-American Bishop—recruitment of ALANA (African-American, Latin American, Asian-American, and Native American) continues to be a challenge. The faculty, administration, and students support the notion that increasing diversity is a college-wide issue, and the responsibility of all members of the community. This collaborative effort has had a positive effect on the college's ability to enroll greater diversity. Seventeen percent of the Class of 2010 are ALANA students, compared to thirteen percent five years ago.

ACADEMIC LIFE

The academic atmosphere at H.C. is one of cooperation rather than cutthroat competition. Although some have complained that As are becoming increasingly scarce and, therefore, more highly coveted, most students are quick to assist their fellow classmates who are struggling with a concept. During exam periods, it is not uncommon to see large study groups congregating in Dinand Library's social lounge (often referred to as the Blue Room) or classmates sharing ideas in the Hogan Campus Center. As one premed student pointed out:

The great thing about the sciences at Holy Cross is that they are not as competitive as you might find at other colleges. Instead of competing with each other, we work as groups and encourage one another to do well. There is a real sense of teamwork among the students here. The professors also contribute to this environment by always being there for anyone who is seeking further elaboration on a lesson or an answer to a question.

Faculty

The Holy Cross faculty receives high marks from the student body. Recent surveys reveal that students find their professors to be both very intelligent and highly accessible, traits not often shared in today's academic world where scholars face increasing pressure to conduct research and publish regularly. While scheduled office hours for student visits are required by the college, most professors maintain an open-door policy and encourage their students to drop in frequently throughout the semester. Furthermore, it is not uncommon to hear of a professor holding class in his or her living room over wine and cheese or a home-cooked meal. Such hospitality is not lost on the students, who appreciate the opportunity to get to know their instructors outside the classroom and get away from the cafeteria for an evening. Just as it is a love of teaching that leads most faculty members to the college, it is this informal sharing of knowledge and ideas that makes H.C. so appealing to its students. As one senior commented:

I truly appreciate the philosophy of education at Holy Cross. My professors are more like friends. It's a shared intellectual atmosphere, and that is what makes this school such a great place to learn. It's not just learning for the sake of learning—it's learning for the sake of applying knowledge.

Common Requirements

This mature and open-minded attitude toward learning is the cornerstone of a liberal arts education. Though there is no core curriculum or specific set of classes required by the school, students must fulfill flexible common requirements entailing the selection of ten courses from nine areas of study:

- The Arts, Language and Literature (one course in each)
- Religious and Philosophical Studies (one course in each)
- Historical Studies (one course)
- Cross-Cultural Studies (one course)
- Social Science (two courses)
- Natural and Mathematical Sciences (two courses, one of which must be a natiural science)
- Language Studies (two courses in a language other than the one in which they possess native fluency)

Within this academic framework, students are encouraged to take classes that will both interest and challenge them. The curriculum trains students to think critically and independently, write succinctly and cogently, and communicate effectively. Holy Cross recognizes that these fundamental skills will provide graduates an educational foundation that is necessary to build successful careers in nearly any occupation.

One of the strengths of a liberal arts education is that it helps you to tie together fields as diverse as the classics and mathematics. It connects certain themes through all subjects of study and all themes of life. Many things seem to coincide. It's nice to step back every once in a while and look at the big picture, which is what an education like this enables you to do. I can go to law school, medical school, or become an engineer. Holy Cross really has provided me with many options and has expanded my intellectual capabilities.

Students take four courses a semester, which does not seem too overwhelming until one considers the weighty reading list that usually accompanies each class syllabus. Athough students may spend fewer than fifteen hours a week in class, they are expected to do a great deal of reading and learning outside the classroom. While some majors (English, history, political science) are definitely more "reading/writing intensive" than others, it is not uncommon to hear of economics professors using seven or eight texts in a semester. As a result, most Holy Cross students either develop strong time-management skills early on or become very accustomed to pulling "all-nighters."

Classes

With class sizes that average fewer than twenty students and many with fewer than fifteen, professors are able to offer their students highly personalized instruction and individual attention. In return, students are usually expected to not only show up for class, but to come prepared to discuss that day's topic in some detail. Upper-level seminars are particularly interactive, with professors often only facilitating the exchange of well-developed student commentary. Students rarely complain about H.C.'s faculty or curriculum, except to lament the lack of "gut" courses that might be taken to enhance one's GPA.

Research Projects and Internships

The faculty and administration grant a high level of academic autonomy to those students who are seeking opportunities to learn outside the classroom. By their junior year, many students are collaborating with H.C. professors on extensive research projects that are often presented at national symposia or in academic journals. Others gain valuable work experiences through school-sponsored internships that are offered either locally or in Washington, D.C. Additionally, each year more than 140 students study abroad and immerse themselves in the cultures and traditions of foreign lands.

Computers

In recent years, the admininstration has made a significant effort to enhance the school's technological capabilities by implementing new state-of-the-art information systems in the classrooms, libraries, and residence halls. As a result, there are now more than 4,000 locations on campus offering fully networked computer hookups.

SOCIAL LIFE AND ACTIVITIES

Although a heavy workload keeps most Holy Cross students fairly occupied, evenings and weekends serve as a welcome opportunity to relax, catch up with friends, and explore Worcester. Crossroads Grill offers great food and free on-campus musical entertainment until

2:00 A.M. For those who are of age, the Pub provides a convenient and comfortable place to catch the latest sporting event or enjoy a beer with friends. Students display their purple pride at the Hart Center, where they cheer on the Crusaders in Division 1 Basketball and Hockey. Following the game, students migrate to Caro Street for a celebration at any of the several off-campus apartments. Fortunately, a mature and laid-back attitude toward drinking prevails at the school and few students report pressure to imbibe from their peers. When not on campus, students can be found dining in the fine eateries of Worcester's Italian section or exploring the night life downtown.

Dances and Shows

Holy Cross offers numerous social or entertainment options for almost any personality. Throughout the year, each dorm class sponsors a semiformal dance. Also well attended are the student-produced theater productions, popular concert performances, and stand-up comedy acts that are regularly sponsored by the Campus Activities Board. Those looking for something a little quieter (or cheaper) often decide to take in a show at the on-campus Kimball Theater where first-run movies can still be seen for free.

Whether tailgating at home football games or just going out for pizza and a movie, Holy Cross students tend to socialize in large groups. With everyone taking a diverse courseload and most participating in multiple extracurricular activities, acquaintances are made easily and friendships forged quickly.

Off Campus

If one is in need of a change of scenery, the school's central New England location offers plenty of convenient day trips and adventurous outdoor excursions. Boston, with its excellent shopping and diverse cultural opportunities, is less than an hour away. Free bus service is provided from the college on weekend evenings. The beautiful beaches and quaint villages of Cape Cod offer another popular weekend escape for those who are feeling land-locked in Worcester. For those hoping to become one with nature, there is exciting skiing, challenging rock climbing, and excellent camping, all within short driving distance from campus.

Athletics

Holy Cross athletics have regained headlines in recent years. Since 2002, the field hockey, women's soccer, men's ice hockey, and men's and women's basketball teams have all appeared in the NCAA Tournament. The men's and women's basketball teams captured national attention when they both made appearances in the tournament's round of sixty-four teams in 2007. There is a long and proud tradition of sports at Holy Cross. Many older alumni remember earlier decades when eventual NBA legends Bob Cousy and Tommy Heinson achieved tremendous success on the basketball court and helped the school win an NCAA championship in 1947. Others recall the Crusader football teams that dominated the college gridiron in the 1980s behind the offensive and defensive play of two-time All-American Gordie Lockbaum, a finalist for the Heisman Trophy in both his junior and senior years.

Most of the college's twenty-seven varsity teams maintain strong winning traditions and loyal student followings in spite of being one of the smallest schools to compete at the Division I level. With nearly twenty-five percent of Holy Cross students participating in NCAA intercollegiate athletics, and many more participating in intramural competition, there are usually plenty of sports fans in the stands cheering their friends to victory.

Giving to the Community

Holy Cross students also find time to give something back to their neighbors in the Worcester community. Having heard the Jesuit mantra "Men and Women for Others" numeorus times while at Mass or on retreat, students recognize the moral obligations inherent in a values-based education. More than thirty percent of the student body routinely volunteers time to those who are less fortunate. Most choose to do such work through Student Programs for Urban Development, an umbrella organization composed of twenty-five student-run outreach activities. As the largest extracurricular club on campus, with more than 350 participants, SPUD offers students the opportunity to serve food to the homeless, tutor in the public schools, visit the elderly, or counsel domestic violence victims. Moved by these experiences and the lives that they have touched, many participants choose to spend their spring breaks working on Appalachian service projects building homes for the poor.

Faith

Students actively contribute to the faith life of the college community. Though attendance at mass is no longer required as it was years ago, about half of the students choose to regularly attend the on-campus liturgies. The Jesuit priests and lay chaplains recognize the integral role that spirituality plays in a Holy Cross education and they typically deliver inspiring and thought-provoking homilies on topics or issues that resonate with young adults. As a result, it is not uncommon to see nearly the entire library empty out on Sunday evening as students attend the two crowded Sunday evening services. Also popular are the five-day silent retreats known as the Spiritual Exercises of St. Ignatius, which are led twice a semester by the chaplain's office. Many consider this week of solitude, prayer, and reflection to be among the most meaningful and rewarding experiences offered at the college.

FINANCIAL AID

Tuition, room, and board fees total $42,893; the cost of attending the college, however, should not deter anyone from applying. The college has a comprehensive financial aid program, with more than fifty-seven percent of the student body receiving some form of assistance. Holy Cross makes every attempt to meet the demonstrated financial need of every admitted applicant through a mix of scholarships, work-study, and loans.

To apply for assistance, an incoming student must indicate on the admissions application that he or she would like to be considered for Holy Cross financial aid. Also, a student must file both a Free Application for Federal Student Assistance (FAFSA) and register with the College Scholarship Service by filing a PROFILE document to be considered for both Federal Student Assistance and Holy Cross scholarships. The Financial Aid Form must be submitted as soon after January 1 as possible, and no later than February 1.

GRADUATES

Holy Cross students are frequently asked, "So what exactly do you do with a liberal arts degree?" An appropriate response to this question might be, "What can't you do with such an education?" A glance at the school's list of alumni reveals success in a diverse range of occupations.

Law, medicine, and business are the most common professions pursued after graduation. The college's science program maintains an excellent reputation among medical schools, which accept H.C. graduates at a rate of eighty-two percent, or nearly twice the national average.

Having enjoyed their time spent in service to others, many students choose to continue their social service work in a full-time capacity after graduation. Of the nation's twenty-eight Jesuit colleges and universities, Holy Cross consistently sends the highest number of students to serve in the Jesuit Volunteer Corps, a year-long postgraduate national service program. Many graduates also go on to volunteer through other organizations such as the Peace Corps, VISTA, and Teach for America.

By any measure, Holy Cross alumni are among the most loyal of any college in the country. They are also very generous with alumni participation in the school's annual fund-raising campaign, routinely placing it among the nation's top twenty undergraduate institutions. Another way in which they express their love for their alma mater is with the professional assistance they provide through the extensive alumni network. The school's Career Placement Office routinely puts both young and old job seekers in touch with fellow alumni who can offer guidance on a possible field or even identify specific employment opportunities. Their connection to Holy Cross has proven to be an invaluable resource for many alumni.

PROMINENT GRADS

- Robert J. Cousy '50
  Retired Boston Celtics basketball player and professional basketball coach
- Anthony S. Fauci, M.D. '62
  Director, National Institute of Allergy and Infectious Diseases, National Institutes of Health
- Billy Collins '63
  U.S. poet laureate, 2001–2003
- Robert C. Wright '65
  President and CEO, NBC
- Hon. Clarence Thomas '71
  Associate Justice, U.S. Supreme Court
- Edward P. Jones, '72
  2004 Pulitzer Prize-winning author of *The Known Word*
- John J. "Jack" Higgins '76
  Editorial cartoonist for the *Chicago Sun Times*, winner of a Pultizer Prize in 1989
- Mary Agnes Wilderotter '77
  President and CEO, Citizens Communications
- Mary G. Berner '81
  President and CEO, Reader's Digest Association

SUMMING UP

Holy Cross offers a superior values-centered, liberal arts education in the Jesuit tradition. Students here are bright, accomplished, and highly motivated. They are also excited by the diverse academic and social options that are available to them during their four years at the college. Many will take advantage of the opportunity to explore new interests and cultivate hidden talents. Some will discover that faith and spirtuality mean much more than simply attending mass.

Through their active participation in the intellectual, social, and spiritual life of the college, these students will receive a challenging and well-rounded education that provides a firm foundation for successful careers and productive lives. Along the way, they will also gain many wonderful experiences and loyal friendships that they will carry with them for the rest of their lives.

At the end of four years on campus, most will recall with great fondness their education on Mount Saint James. Like thousands who came before them, these students will recognize and appreciate the lessons that were learned and the values that were formed as a result of their experiences at Holy Cross.

❏ *Tim Keller, A.B.*

COLLEGE OF WILLIAM AND MARY

 College of William and Mary
Williamsburg, VA 23187-8795

 (757) 221-4223
Fax: (757) 221-1242

 E-mail: *admiss@wm.edu*
Web sites: *http://www.wm.edu*

 Enrollment

Full-time ❏ women: 3,200
         ❏ men: 2,500

Part-time ❏ women: 45
         ❏ men: 50

INTRODUCING COLLEGE OF WILLIAM AND MARY

Visitors and tourists alike wander through William and Mary's campus on a daily basis. They amble around old campus walking under a canopy of trees and on top of hundred-year-old bricks. Everyone stops to admire the Crim Dell, W&M's supremely photogenic lake in the middle of campus. Surely, anyone who visits Williamsburg and has a look at William and Mary's campus leaves knowing that it is a gorgeous and pleasant place; that it's the home of one of America's oldest and finest universities.

And these visitors are correct. W&M is the second oldest college in America, founded in 1693. It is known as the "Alma Mater of a Nation" as the Tribe credits four American presidents and sixteen members of the Continental Congress in the ranks of alumni. These visitors will also certainly notice that W&M is not stuck in the past. Anyone who walks around campus will hear tales of our thirty-nine Fulbright Scholars since the year 2000. A tourist might stroll past a club meeting, ranging from Belly Dancing to the Harry Potter appreciation club. They'll even see evidence of the Tribe athletic teams truly defining the term "student athlete," winning championships and scholarships at the same time.

Yet, these visitors, most people who come to look at William and Mary, are missing the best part of campus! Actually, it's hard to blame them, since the best part of William and Mary can't be experienced just by a casual stroll through grounds. In fact, the best part about William and Mary isn't even visible at all. What defines the William and Mary experience, what will make your next four years outstanding beyond imagination, is the community spirit that reaches from every person to every corner of campus.

This family spirit lies in the interactions between students and professors. The relationships formed extend far beyond the classroom, reaching into real collaborative research and lasting friendships. W&M students aren't confined to doing menial research; they regularly publish professional articles side-by-side with their professors.

The W&M life-blood pulses and thrives in our residence halls, governed by a policy of self-determination. Self-determination allows your hall, the people you live with, to determine the rules that you will live by. I'm sure Thomas Jefferson, Class of 1762, is smiling at this adaptation of democracy to the policies governing your new home.

The community shows its strength in our students helping friends and strangers, on campus and off. One doesn't have to look far to find students volunteering and helping others; the majority of W&M students volunteer on a regular basis. But the students' volunteering interests aren't confined to typical pursuits; it reaches even to the incoming freshman each year. Hundreds of upperclassmen move down to Williamsburg a week early for the sole purpose of helping incoming freshmen carry their things into their rooms, and settle in their new homes!

Our community shows off its muscle in our athletic teams. Our varsity athletes truly define the phrase "student athlete." The Tribe is *the* Colonial Athletic Association (CAA) powerhouse among all sports, having won more than eighty conference championships. But this athletic prowess does not come at the expense of academic success, no not at all. The Tribe athletic teams can claim a 95 percent graduation rate, fifth best among all universities in the country. "Student-Athlete" indeed.

But, what if a student isn't interested in participating in sports at a varsity level, just for recreation? No problem. The campus recreation center has just finished a renovation project that doubled its size. Last year, *Men's Health & Fitness Magazine* ranked W&M as the seventeenth fittest college in the country, highlighting our healthy options available at all dining halls. Our spirit certainly runs strong through many different kinds of athletic endeavors.

W&M's community spirit whips through campus like a winter wind. It moves, it morphs, it pervades. It runs from every dorm to classroom to concerts to coffeehouses. The spirit burns inside every member of the Tribe, bursting through in the form of smiles, laughs, and friendships formed. This community spirit shows in our acceptance and tolerance of others. There is no other university in the country like William and Mary. It is singularly unique in the combination of personal attention, extraordinary academic opportunities, research capability, and on-campus student community.

The community spirit, the fire inside William and Mary students' hearts, can be yours. But just touring the college, just visiting and admiring the pretty buildings, won't reveal to you the true extent of our community. This spirit, this fire, is best experienced from within, as a member of the Tribe.

ADMISSIONS REQUIREMENTS

Admission procedures at William and Mary take into account many different factors from your high school years. But simply put, William and Mary is looking for the best students in the world who are looking to challenge themselves and grow in all facets of their life. The classes you took and the grades you earned are important, but so are the characteristics that tell us more about the kind of person you will grow to be, like leadership, creativity, and character.

Many students ask, "What classes should I be taking?" William and Mary does not have a magic formula of the specific classes you need to be taking to gain admission. However, the typical admitted William and Mary students challenge themselves in every opportunity during their high school years. Most admitted students take the strongest and most rigorous course of study their high school offers. This usually includes four years of English, four years of math, four years of a foreign language, three to four years of history, three to four years of science, and other elective courses. Honors, Advanced Placement, and International Baccalaureate courses all entail rigorous study and are therefore recommended whenever possible. The Admissions Office recognizes that course offerings are not consistent between schools so exceptions to this rule of thumb always exist.

All applicants must take the SAT or ACT as part of a complete application. SAT subject tests are fully optional. All testing must be completed by January of the senior year so that scores will be reported to William and Mary in time. Students who enter William and Mary must also meet proficiency requirements in foreign language and writing by time of graduation. However, you can exempt yourself from these ordinarily required courses if you have already satisfied the requirements in high school! You can satisfy the foreign language requirement by successfully completing four years of one foreign language or a minimum score of 600 on the SAT Foreign Language subject test (650 on the Latin test). A student can gain exemption from the writing requirement by scoring well on the AP or 1B English Exam.

But these aren't absolutely the most important parts of the application. William and Mary knows that you are more, so much more than just classes, grades, and test scores. You have a whole life outside of classes where you have done some amazing things. To William and Mary, the intangibles that make you *you* are just as important as grades and scores. The admissions committee certainly takes this into account when considering each student's admission. But the committee needs your help. In the application, you should present your activities, accomplishments, interests, and values. Try to really convey who you actually are and what you will add to William and Mary's community of scholars. A large opportunity for this is the essay section. The Common Application (of which William and Mary is an exclusive user) essay section is also a large opportunity to creatively and appropriately enlighten us about your intangibles.

I must confess something here. I was not an All-Star college applicant in my senior year of high school. 4.0? Nope. 1600? Not even my bank account was that high, let alone my SAT. I suppose I am living proof of the Office of Admissions' policy of really considering who you are what you could bring to the W&M community, rather than just looking at me as a number. And was the Office of Admissions right in their decision? I'd have to say without a doubt, yes. I was a leader in multiple campus groups, finished with better grades in college than I had in high school, and was the speaker selected to represent all graduates at the 2006 Commencement. In short, I thrived at William and Mary. And it is all because the Admissions Committee had the foresight to see past my less-than-impressive numbers. That's why you should believe me when I say: they really look at you as more than a number. Believe me, I know.

For the simple fact that William and Mary is included in this book, you know that we are labeled "Most Competitive." Each undergraduate class is comprised of between 1,200 and 1,500 students, of which 65 percent are Virginians. In recent years, the Admissions Office has received over 10,000 applications for each class. While those numbers might be intimidating, don't be discouraged. The Admissions Office encourages everyone to apply!

If you have decided that William and Mary is the only place for you, that it is your absolute first choice, and that you want to become a new member of the Tribe more than anything else, then you might want to consider our Early Decision plan. Early Decision at William and Mary is binding, which means that if you are accepted, you agree to attend. The application deadline for Early Decision is November 1, and notifications will be sent one month later, on December 1.

Regular Decision applicants must postmark their applications by January 1 for freshman, February 15 for fall-term transfer applicants, and November 1 for spring-term transfer applicants.

ACADEMIC LIFE

A university's charge is not just to teach facts, formulas, and procedures. The true mark of a university is how well it can help to mold and meld the nubile minds of freshmen into cogent, prepared, and mature adults ready to start the path towards leading the future. Many universities accomplish this, but to varying degrees. William and Mary meets this charge to the highest degree.

Here, in our school's academic setting, you will, without a doubt, be challenged on a daily basis. However, do not confuse the word "challenged" with "unbelievably difficult." Believe me, if you are admitted, we know you can do the work that lies ahead of you. But at William and Mary, challenging means more than this. It means you will have extremely dedicated faculty members seeking to draw out your best. It means you will have peers who are just as excited as you are about classes and studies. It means you will have the opportunity to, and many times be expected to, develop original and innovative research that is graduate level at many other schools. In short, the academics at William and Mary will challenge every inch of what you can do.

Faculty

William and Mary encourages students to develop a very well-rounded educational base while at the college. It requires that students take classes in all of the different types of disciplines, but leaves the students a lot of flexibility when it comes to choosing which specific courses to take. For example, the requirements don't say students must take one course in the English department; one of the requirements is for students to take one course in literature and history of the arts, of which many English department courses qualify.

Because of William and Mary's smaller size, most classes are small enough for students to interact regularly with the professor and with fellow classmates. The student-to-faculty ratio is eleven-to-one, one of the lowest of any public school in the country! Here are some more stats to further set your mind at ease: Introductory courses are taught by professors, not graduate students, the majority of classes have between ten and thirty students, and your professors are really committed to teaching you, not just to completing their research. These are all things that might not be true at larger universities. See, you really won't be just a number at William and Mary!

Special mention must go to our professors. The dedication of the William and Mary faculty to teaching was recently ranked third in the country, and first among public schools in a national poll. For W&M professors, research and publication are important, but teaching always comes first. William and Mary undergraduates do the kind of research and work with their professors that is rarely seen at other universities until work begins for the Ph.D.

Another special facet of the William and Mary education is the freshman seminar, guaranteed and required for all first-year students. The classes, taught by full-time professors, are all topical in nature and work to greatly advance students' writing and critical thinking skills while also providing an in-depth examination of the subject. One of the best facets of these seminars is that the maximum number of students allowed in them is fifteen. Past years have seen seminars like "Reading the Romance Novels," "The Literature of Baseball," and "J.R.R. Tolkien's World." Many graduates have fond memories of their freshman seminar, and many credit it with introducing them to their major, research interest, or faculty advisor.

My freshman seminar was in the music department and was called "Sound and Image." The course explored the relation between the two, specifically sound and music used in movies. We watched plenty of films for the course and spent time training our brains to listen to movies rather than watch movies. It was a fascinating process, and I can credit that course with advancing my writing and critical thinking skills more than any other course I took at W&M.

Majors

William and Mary offers about forty undergraduate majors, as well as an opportunity for students to create their own major combining various disciplines. There are also many opportunities to explore personal interests in one's major through independent study, senior honors projects, and even collaboration on scholarly publishing with professors. Recently, the most popular majors have been in the School of Business Administration, psychology, government, English, history, and biology.

Also, in William and Mary's academic system, students are encouraged to explore all facets of our academic offerings. This also makes it very easy for students to double major or have a minor and still graduate in four years. Double majoring is very popular at W&M and allows many students to gain a more specific skill-set that might take a graduate degree at other colleges.

SOCIAL LIFE AND ACTIVITIES

Obviously, the focus of transforming and molding young minds into educated adults is not contained within the classroom walls. A large part of learning in college comes outside of the classroom. What you do outside of those fifteen to twenty hours a week you spend in class really matters and can truly have an impact on the kind of person you develop into. Simply put, ordering pizza, watching movies, and playing video games is not the best way to spend all of your extracurricular time as an undergraduate. Thankfully, William and Mary recognizes this and has more than you could possibly ask for to make your life at college more fun than you can even imagine.

One of the most popular ways to enrich your life outside of classes is by getting involved with any of our more than 300 student organizations, most of which are organized and run solely by students. William and Mary has a wide and varied selection of

FRESHMAN MOVE IN-DAY

Without doubt, one of the most exciting days of the whole school year at William and Mary is freshman move-in day. All 1,350 or so freshmen, in the peak of Virginia's summer heat, move into their campus dorms at the same time; sounds stressful and hectic right? To make the process easier for you and your family, hundreds of William and Mary upperclassmen move back down to campus early just to come and help incoming freshmen move in. They wear shirts that say "Sweating for you!" and will gladly help carry all of your things from the curb up to your dorm. This lets you take a little load off and organize your room, while your parents can grab some much-deserved cold lemonade in the shade. It's just another example of the amazing community spirit at W&M and shows the volunteer spirit that runs strong in the members of the Tribe.

groups to capture the interests of most students. Walking across campus, you might run into the Club cross-country team out for a run, an a capella team staging an impromptu concert, the geology club digging up some treasures, or even the Harry Potter fan club staging a mock-quidditch game! W&M also has several service-oriented clubs, cultural groups, social fraternities and sororities, literary magazines and newspapers, yearbook, student government, and many performing groups. The point is William and Mary has a club for every kind of interest you could have. If by some chance we don't, then you have the opportunity to create the club with some friends.

Something else that must be mentioned: William and Mary is not a commuter school; that is to say, on the weekend, our students do not vacate the grounds to go back home. People live here, stay here, and have their friends here on campus. The residence hall is the basic organizing unit of W&M dormitories, and coincidentally, it is where most students meet their best friends. Many students spend the weekend hanging out and relaxing with their friends all over campus and off campus too.

In your freshman year you'll have a roommate that is usually matched up with you by the Office of Residence Life. It's a scary thought to live with somebody you haven't met yet, but they have a great track record and do an amazing job of matching up roommates.

My roommate and I had talked a few times on the phone over the summer, but we met for the first time on move-in day. I'm a big guy, about six feet tall, strong, and have a body type similar to a refrigerator. My roommate was maybe five feet six inches tall with a distance runner's body. We certainly looked like an opposite and odd pair at first, but everything turned out great through the year! We were great friends all through university, and Joe and I remain great friends to this day. We are one of thousands of examples of the Office of Residence Life doing a fantastic job of matching up freshman roommates!

The largest source of weekend events is the campus events programming group, UCAB. They are responsible for bringing hundreds of events to the campus with something going on every weekend and most weeknights. Every year, UCAB brings comedians, hypnotists, prominent speakers, entertainers, new movies, debates, and lots of concerts to campus. Recent years have seen bands like Wilco and The Roots, comedians like Jon Stewart and Dave Attell, and speakers like Former UN Secretary General Kofi Annan and Archbishop Desmond Tutu come to Williamsburg!

William and Mary performing arts also doesn't disappoint when it comes to social life fun. The theatre department puts on several high-quality productions each year, including many that are student-directed. The campus also has a wildly popular improvisational theatre group (think *Whose Line Is It Anyway?*) that perform all over campus, much to the delight of students, faculty, and staff. William and Mary is also fortunate enough to have so many student-run a capella student groups that you might think there is a concert going on every night of the week!

For students interested in Greek organizations, William and Mary does not disappoint. About one quarter of the William and Mary student body is in one of fifteen social fraternities or twelve social sororities. Think you know all there is to know about Greek organizations after watching some Hollywood movies? Think again! William and Mary Greek organizations not only serve a social purpose but also commit large amounts of time to philanthropic endeavors. Every Greek organization puts on philanthropy events all through the year. These events are hugely popular and regularly raise thousands of dollars for the organizations' charities.

Athletics at William and Mary are also a big draw for students. Students at W&M say they all have Tribe Pride running through their veins and bleed William and Mary's colors, green and gold! At the varsity level, the Tribe is, statistically and historically, the best overall team among all sports in our conference, the Colonial Athletic Association. In the past years, you might have seen many of our teams streaking up the Division I Top 25 in men's and women's cross country, men's gymnastics, women's field hockey, men's and women's soccer, and women's tennis. Not interested in varsity sports? No problem. There are opportunities for you to compete against other colleges in our club sport program, or just relax and have some fun with intramurals. Overall, 85 percent of W&M undergrads participate in intercollegiate sports, club sports, and/or intramural programs. Also, *Men's Health* recently named William and Mary students some of the fittest in the country.

For off-campus entertainment, there is more than you might think. True, Williamsburg is no New York City. But there is much more to the town than just touristy Colonial Williamsburg. Some of the more popular and student-friendly places in town are the delis. These three bars/restaurants are right off campus and, according to the students, have the best submarine sandwiches and cheese fries for miles around! They are great places to hang out with friends and watch a game, listen to live music, or just talk and unwind from the school week. Williamsburg also has numerous coffee shops, movie theatres, and restaurants, all right off campus. And how many colleges can claim to have Busch Gardens right in their backyard!

Of all of W&M's many service organizations, one stands out from the crowd. Each year, the William and Mary campus unites behind The Annual Alan Bukzin Memorial Bone Marrow Drive. William and Mary's bone marrow drive is the largest on-campus bone marrow drive in the country and the second largest overall in the country! Since its inception at the college, almost 10,000 people have been added to the national registry, which has led to roughly sixty life-saving matches and donations.

The main reason why W&M's drive is so special is that, on that day, it is free to join the registry. Normally, it costs $65 for someone to join the registry. This cost is a big deterrent for many people who could be saving lives. The Bone Marrow Drive committee makes it their goal to raise enough money so that all who wish to join the registry can do so free of charge. To this end, they will raise $55,000 this year!

You want a night out in the big city? No problem: Norfolk, Virginia Beach, and Richmond are all less than an hour's drive away.

Finally, one of the biggest extracurricular pursuits for W&M students is community service. More than 70 percent of William and Mary students participate in public service activities during their time on campus, contributing over 150,000 volunteer hours every year. W&M students' character really shows through when you see that our largest fraternity on campus is actually a coed service fraternity that is dedicated to service projects on campus and off.

FINANCIAL AID

One of the things that makes a William and Mary education so special is not only the benefits outlined above, but also its comparatively low price tag in relation to schools of the same caliber. As an example, *Kiplinger* recently ranked William and Mary third on the 50 Best Values in Public Colleges!

Nonetheless, the cost of a college education today is a difficult burden to bear for many families. Many students rely on financial aid for assistance in their quest for higher education.

At William and Mary, financial assistance can come in different forms, but most aid is distributed in the form of grants, loans, and work-study opportunity packages. William and Mary uses the Free Application for Federal Student Aid (FAFSA) to determine each student's unique need. Each student's financial need is not just based on family income. It also takes into account family size, number in college, assets, and many other variables. Early Decision applicants should turn in their forms by November 1; Regular Decision applicants should turn in the FAFSA between January 1 and February 15.

William and Mary has three main merit scholarships. The William and Mary Scholars Award is available to twenty to twenty-five entering students who will greatly enhance the diversity of the student body. Awards are equal to the value of Virginia tuition and fees for four years. The second main award is the Monroe Scholars program. Between 8 and 10 percent of the entering freshman class is designated as a Monroe Scholar. Beyond academic benefits, recipients are provided a $3,000 research grant to pursue a specific academic interest. Both of these programs require no separate application.

The third main award is the Murray Scholars Program. Endowed by a multimillion dollar alumni gift, the Murray Scholars Program will provide four students per year with extensive benefits, including in-state tuition, fees, room and board annually, two separate $2,500 research grants towards their academic research interests, and the kind of academic attention reserved at most universities exclusively for graduate students. Murray Scholars candidates must be nominated by their guidance counselor, submit an additional essay, and submit their completed application by December 1 (for Regular Decision).

Federally funded grants such as the Pell Grant and the Supplemental Educational Opportunity Grant are available at William and Mary, as are federally sponsored loans such as the Perkins Loan and the Stafford Loan. The State Council of Higher Education for Virginia (SCHEV) awards the Virginia Transfer Grant for minority transfer students. Some academic departments give scholarships to students who demonstrate outstanding scholarship in that field. There are several other unique opportunities for assistance such as $1,500 scholarships offered by the Order of the White Jacket for students who are working in food service to help put themselves through school.

GRADUATES

It is quite understandable that your immediate focus is on getting in to William and Mary, and not particularly on what you will do after you graduate. However, the opportunities available to you post-W&M, and how we help prepare you for that time, is an important facet to consider in any school. William and Mary, in fact, does not disappoint in this respect.

To be competitive after graduation these days, more is required than just a diploma and good grades. Nobody will hand you a job just for that. Sorry. You must develop and demonstrate skills that do not come easily: leadership as well as humility, self-reliance and also the ability to work in a team, self-awareness while also being internationally knowledgeable. William and Mary is the place where you can learn and develop these skills. Memorizing some formulas won't cut it, in the real world or at William and Mary. Here, students are given the well-rounded background they need to live life to the fullest once they graduate.

Carter Braxton, Signer of the Declaration of Independence

Glenn Close, Actress

Benjamin Harrison, Signer of the Declaration of Independence

Thomas Jefferson, Third President of the United States

Linda Lavin, Actress

James Monroe, Fifth President of the United States

Darren Sharper, NFL Football Player for the Minnesota Vikings

Jon Stewart, Comedian, host of *The Daily Show with Jon Stewart*

John Tyler, Tenth President of the United States

George Wythe, Signer of the Declaration of Independence

John Marshall, Supreme Court Justice

Robert Gates, Former Director of CIA, Current U.S. Secretary of Defense

Perry Ellis, Fashion Designer

Mark McCormack, Founder of IMG, World's Largest Sports Marketing Agency

As for what our graduates do after graduation, William and Mary students are known for their passion in learning and education. Towards this end, between one third and one half choose to go directly to graduate school. Acceptance rates for graduate schools (including medical schools and law schools) hover in the 75 to 80 percent range, well above any national average. Students with a B or B+ average have a 75 to 85 percent acceptance rate for medical school, far above the national average.

Interested in a job after graduation? The college will give you more help than you can imagine in finding one. The Career Center brings approximately 750 employers to recruit on campus each year. They also host over a hundred sessions each year to help students with resume and cover letter writing as well as job searching. Not ready for graduation you say? They also coordinate internships on campus and will help you prepare for and land that connection-making summer internship you can only now dream about. Also, many of the companies who recruit at William and Mary have a large body of W&M grads already employed. They know the caliber of our students and come looking for more!

SUMMING UP

The current President of William and Mary, Gene R. Nichol, loves to end all of his speeches, e-mails, and official communication with the phrase "Hark Upon the Gale." The phrase comes from the refrain of William and Mary's Alma Mater:

William and Mary loved of old, Hark Upon the Gale!
Hear the thunder of our chorus, Alma Mater Hail!

The word *hark* can be interpreted two ways, as "to listen" and "to think back on something." The word *gale* is usually defined as a "very strong wind" but can also mean "a noisy outburst." So one can interpret this in two ways, both seem quite appropriate to the college. Hark Upon the Gale! Listen to the strong wind! Remember our actions! Put in more direct terms: Feel our impact!

William and Mary is a university that has a very strong impact: an impact on the nation and local community, the alumnae, the current students, and you, the future students.

William and Mary has the nickname of "Alma Mater of a Nation" for a reason: Our litany of successful alumnae from Thomas Jefferson to Jon Stewart and everyone in between has truly shaped the history of our great nation. The strong scientific and research contributions made not only by our professors, but also our undergraduate students (a rare combination for any university) has also made an impact felt throughout academic circles.

Students who consider William and Mary are looking for a university that isn't so large that they become lost in the crowd or just another number passed from one teaching assistant to another. They want a school that is big enough for a diverse student population and for a variety of academic and social options to be available. They want a school that has a personal touch and has a staff that is there to help with any problems the students face. Yet, they also want a school that allows its students the personal freedom to decide what classes to schedule and when, when to come and go from residence halls, and when to study and when to play.

This is a special kind of place that has a palpable and tangible soul. You can literally *feel* the college as you are walking around. The history, the community, the scholarship, and the excitement: It is all here for you to feel and experience. I invite you to apply and join the William and Mary family. It's a dynamic community, one where you will certainly have the opportunity to be a leader in our collective "gale," our impact. Join us, and be a part of our great impact on the world. Let William and Mary also impart her wisdom on you, for this is a place where you will grow to achieve your potential. "William and Mary loved of old, Hark Upon the Gale!"

❏ *Matt Scranton, B.A.*

COLUMBIA UNIVERSITY/COLUMBIA COLLEGE

 Columbia University/Columbia College
212 Hamilton Hall
New York, NY 10027

 (212) 854-2522
Fax: (212) 854-1209

 Web site: *http://www.columbia.edu*

 Enrollment

Full-time ❑ women: 2,195
❑ men: 2,030

INTRODUCING COLUMBIA

*I first stepped onto Columbia's campus at nighttime. I was a senior in high
school, visiting my cousin in the engineering school and had just arrived from
Los Angeles. The sun had just set, but the campus buildings were brightly lit and
aglow with white haze. They were intimidating with their red bricks and copper*

roofs and appeared as academic-looking as I had expected. My first thought was, "What's a poor girl from a Mexican neighborhood in L.A. doing at Columbia? It's Ivy League." Almost seven years later, graduated with both a bachelor's and a master's degree from Columbia, and with a good job in New York, I now know there was nothing I couldn't accomplish in college. I am the strong-willed free-thinker Columbia wanted me to become and New York is where I truly found myself.

Columbia University is a city within the City. Columbia College, one of four undergraduate schools on the university's Morningside Heights campus in upper Manhattan, is a small college within a large academic setting. Its liberal arts tradition, based on its unique core curriculum, aims to produce students learned not only in factual knowledge, but in the ways of the world, the social and political issues that affect people, and the critical thinking required for today's young leaders.

Founded as King's College in 1754, when America was still a cluster of colonies ruled by England, the school was the first institution of higher learning in the then province of New York. Its first alumni included John Jay, who would later become the first chief justice of the United States, and Alexander Hamilton, who would later become the first secretary of the Treasury.

Suspended during the American Revolution, the school reopened in 1784 as Columbia College, this time rechartered without ties to church or state. It remains the country's oldest independent institution of higher education.

THE SIXTEEN COLLEGES AND SCHOOLS WITHIN COLUMBIA UNIVERSITY

- ○ Columbia College
- ○ College of Physicians and Surgeons
- ○ School of Law
- ○ The FU Foundation School of Engineering and Applied Science
- ○ Graduate School of Arts and Sciences
- ○ Graduate School of Architecture, Planning and Preservation
- ○ School of Nursing
- ○ School of Social Work
- ○ Graduate School of Journalism
- ○ Graduate School of Business
- ○ School of Dental and Oral Surgery
- ○ School of Public Health
- ○ School of International and Public Affairs
- ○ School of General Studies
- ○ School of the Arts
- ○ School of Continuing Education

Today, the face of Columbia's student body is as variegated as autumn leaves in Central Park. Going coed in the early 1980s, the students come from all fifty states and more than forty different countries. Every race, culture, and religious background is represented, which makes for a school founded on tolerance and understanding that knows how to celebrate its diversity. All this resides within the framework of New York City, the original melting pot of the nation.

Beyond Columbia's wrought iron gates lies a city brimming with energy, culture, and unforgettable, real-life experiences waiting to happen. Museum Mile, Restaurant Row, Lincoln Center, Broadway, Wall Street, Greenwich Village—upon arriving in New York City, the feeling that it is the center of the world becomes overwhelming! Which is why New York City becomes the perfect accompaniment to an education at Columbia; in many ways, it becomes its own classroom. An arts humanities class (one of the core requirements) might opt to study cathedral architecture inside the Cathedral of St. John the Divine, which is just down the street from campus and which happens to be the world's largest Gothic-style cathedral. A music humanities class (another core requirement) might understand opera a little better by attending Puccini's *La Bohème* at the famed Metropolitan Opera House. A student can visit the New York Stock Exchange to understand the mechanics of economics, and a drama student might learn something about acting technique by catching any number of off-Broadway plays.

But one need not venture outside Columbia's campus to breathe in a little culture or excitement. The surrounding Morningside Heights neighborhood is home to many ethnic restaurants, bookstores, and bars, where one can catch live jazz, stand-up comedy, or a local band any night of the week. There is a twenty-four-hour bagel shop and the all-night diner, of *Seinfeld* fame that has hosted many nocturnal cram sessions. There are poetry readings at cafes, used books being sold at every corner, and perhaps the largest slice of pizza anywhere in the city.

Columbia's students fit right into the neighborhood's bustle. During a leisurely stroll down College Walk, the school's main thruway, one might pass two students disagreeing over an interpretation of hell in Dante's *Inferno*, or a group of students jamming to hip-hop music on the steps of Low Library, the school's main administration building.

Such diversity at Columbia is a very valued component of its student body; therefore, the college's admissions process allows prospective students many opportunities to let themselves, their interests, and their aspirations shine through.

ADMISSIONS REQUIREMENTS

> *I think what matters more than aptitude to Columbia admissions officers is attitude. I was never a high scorer on standardized tests, and didn't do amazingly well on the SATs, but I was an active student in high school: I played two sports, was a member of a poetry club, and a class vice president. I did well in my English classes and knew right away that I would take a more literary path in college. I had some direction and think that I came off well in my admissions interview and that really helped me.*

Columbia College values a student body filled with people from varying geographic, social, economic, and ethnic backgrounds because of the spectrum of perspectives and ideas each student will bring to a class. Therefore, Columbia's admissions selection of an applicant is based on a number of quantitative and qualitative factors. Aside from good grades in high school, the admissions officers are looking for extracurricular activities, an applicant's maturity and leadership capabilities, and his or her personal interests, talents, or hobbies.

This past year, 15,000 applications were received; of that amount, only 1,633 were accepted (a 10.9 percent admit rate). The odds are tough, but the general rule-of-thumb is that the more intellectualy passionate, the better the odds. Students with a strong interest in physics, chemistry, math, and astronomy are also strongly encouraged to apply.

The comprehensive application is designed to allow students many opportunities to document their achievements, interests, and goals. The regular admission deadline is January 1, and notification of the admissions office's decision gets mailed in April.

Recommendations for Admission

While the admissions office doesn't require a minimum SAT or ACT score or have strict requirements on high school classes an applicant should take before applying, it does have some recommendations:

- four years of English, with an emphasis on writing
- three or more years of math
- three years or more of a foreign language
- three, but preferably four, years of social science
- three years or more of a lab science like chemistry (however, a student interested in science or medicine should take as much math and science—particularly chemistry and physics—offered in high school)

The required standardized tests are the SAT Reasoning Test or the ACT Assessment test, and three SAT Subject tests (one of which must be the Writing test). For students taking the new SAT with writing, or the ACT with writing, students are required to take two additional SAT Subject tests. The school recommends that these tests be taken in October or November of an applicant's senior year, but will accept scores taken during the junior year.

The Admissions Office will also heavily weigh an applicant's recommendations from a school principal, headmaster, counselor, and teachers, who are asked to comment on the applicant's personal qualities as well as academic stature and involvement in school activities. Interviews are also available with Columbia College alumni located worldwide. Candidates are contacted by Alumni Representative Committee members after the first part of the application is received.

Early Decision

Candidates can also submit their application for Early Decision consideration for admission. Columbia must be the first choice, and completed applications must be in by November 1 of the senior year. Applicants vying for Early Decision will hear from the Admissions Office by mid-December, at which point they are obliged to accept the admission offer and withdraw applications at other colleges.

Columbia College occasionally accepts transfer students entering their sophomore or junior year, who are admitted with advanced standing. The college also has a visiting student program that welcomes students from other colleges to spend all or part of an academic year in New York. However, the program is open only to students other than freshmen.

Once admitted, a Columbia entering class is designed to bring fresh, diverse ideas and opinions to its rigorous academic requirements.

ACADEMIC LIFE

The tie that binds Columbia's varied student population is the college's core curriculum, a rigorous series of required classes based on the contributions of Western civilization to the modern world. Through the core—which was developed after World War I and patterned by many other schools shortly thereafter—students are exposed to the works of Homer, Plato, Beethoven, and Picasso, among other greats.

What makes the core classes a more powerful exposure to the world's great achievements in literature, history, philosophy, art, music, and science, is class size—no seminar class holds more than twenty-two students. In such an intimate setting, students are expected to engage in intellectual observation, argument, comparison, and analysis, all in preparation for the life of the worldly freethinker Columbia would like all its students to become.

The two cornerstones of the core—Literature Humanities and Contemporary Civilization, or Lit Hum and CC as they are popularly called—are year-long classes that are usually taken during the first two years at Columbia. While students may complain about the vast amount of reading they'll do for homework, or each course's length (two-hour classes twice a week for an entire year!), they will in the same breath wish there was more time to spend with each work.

I made the mistake of taking CC during my first year at Columbia, before taking Lit Hum as it is recommended. You could say I delved into the course's subject matter more out of fear and intimidation than sheer intellectual curiosity. The sophomores in my class, well-prepared from their first year of Lit Hum, were assured, effective debaters of their own points and those of the authors we studied. I flopped with my first term paper and was asked to do it over again (perhaps because I did it in a few hours the night before it was due). But with my revision, I learned hard and quick how to dissect Plato's Republic *and find a point that I actually understood. I had to change completely the study habits that got me by in high school, and with that, realized I was no longer one of the elite, smart crowd in school—everyone at Columbia was smart and we were all peers that way.*

Lit Hum is designed to take a close examination of the most influential literary texts of Western culture. The class is light on lecture and heavy on the sometimes heated discussion of a text's themes that is expected in every class. Students soon enough find that to properly discuss a text, they must also be good listeners—listening to their instructor as well as their classmates.

CC was created in 1919 as a war-and-peace-issues course and has evolved into a class preparing students for lives as active, socially-minded citizens, indispensible members of a democratic form of government. Intense class discussions centered around the works of some of the world's most influential political thinkers will engage students for most of their class time.

Often, teachers for both Lit Hum and CC will invoke the Socratic method to teach a point, provoking the "disputatious learning" so favored at Columbia. Along with the exploration of literary themes and philosophy that students will do as a class by sharing ideas and opinions, students on an individual basis will learn very quickly how to defend their own points of view. And defend them well, which is why it is always painfully obvious in class if a student didn't do the reading.

The rest of the Core is composed of:

- the art and music humanities classes, formally called Masterpieces of Western Art and Masterpieces of Western Music (one semester each)
- three semesters of approved science courses
- Frontiers of Science, which introduces students to exciting ideas at the forefront of scientific research and develops the habits of mind characteristic of a scientific approach to the world.
- intermediate proficiency a foreign language
- one semester of a comprehensive writing class
- one year of physical education and a mandatory seventy-five-yard swimming requirement
- one year of "Major Cultures" classes, an introduction to those major civilizations not included in the core.

Both art and music humanities courses aim to produce visually and musically literate students. In Art Hum, students observe and also analyze the style and motifs of many great paintings, sculptures and monuments of the Western world, like the Greek Parthenon, Picasso's "Guernica," and Frank Lloyd Wright's Guggenheim Museum. Class lectures are supplemented by visits to many of New York's famed museums, galleries, and buildings.

In a similar way, Music Hum—a class that chronologically follows music from its origins to the creation of symphonies, opera, and jazz—is enhanced by the city's constant rhythm and beat. Students are expected to attend at least one musical performance, (and of course there are many to choose from in the Big Apple), and write about it for class.

After the Core

In addition to the Core Curriculum, students will also explore a field of interest via any one of the school's approximately ninety majors in fifty-five departments and interdisciplinary programs, each having their own rigorous set of requirements. Majors range from Comparative Literature and Society and African-American Studies to Neuroscience and Behavior and Film Studies. The college's departments most popular with students are English, history, and political science. Columbia College also has a strong history and vibrant offerings in the sciences, mathematics, languages, and the arts.

Academic life for the Columbia student will include an average of about five classes a semester. But the college expects each student to balance school life with an active campus life and benefiting from the social and cultural resources of the city.

Faculty

Whichever major a student chooses, he or she can expect to learn from the experts in that field. Columbia boasts a faculty that includes forty-one members of the National Academy of Sciences, 1 of 3 fellows of the American Academy of Arts and Sciences, twelve recipients of the National Medal of Science, and seventy-two Nobel Laureates, who now or at one point taught at or attended the university. All faculty in the Arts and Sciences teach undergraduates.

The Library

Here is some information about Butler Library, Columbia's main library:

- It currently holds one third of the university's seven-million books (the remaining four million books can be found in any of the school's twenty-two other libraries).
- Butler is also home to the Rare Book and Manuscript Library that contains twenty-four million manuscripts and a half million rare books.
- Each semester at the stroke of midnight before the first day of finals (and whether you like it or not), the notorious Columbia Marching Band storms Butler Library and cajoles everyone present into singing the school's fight song, "Roar, Lions Roar."
- The library was named after former University President Nicholas Murray Butler, who coincidentally was the main force behind the development of the SAT.
- The names of renowned writers are etched onto Butler's facade: Homer, Herodotus, Sophocles, Plato, Aristotle, Vergil, Dante, Shakespeare, Cervantes, Voltaire.
- In a recent student poll, Butler Library was ranked as the most favorite place to study.

SOCIAL LIFE AND ACTIVITIES

During my first year at Columbia I joined three clubs, did volunteer work with children in Harlem, and played intramural volleyball. Through many student organizations I met other students just like myself and, more importantly, learned from others completely unlike me. What I learned from Columbia's diversity matched what I learned in class. What was interesting was that, despite my involvement outside the classroom, my grades never suffered. I got the best of both worlds, socially and academically, that Columbia had to offer.

At Columbia College, there's a student organization or club for just about everyone—frisbee throwers, community volunteers, jugglers, *a cappella* singers, debaters, and aspiring comics alike. There are also groups representing just about every ethnic and religious background, political party, and career interest. Student groups plan social and fundraising events, but are also there to foster friendship and support among students who are dealing with being away from home and the things with which they identify. In all, there are over 300 organizations, which include fraternities and sororities, and student-run media outlets, including a daily newspaper, radio station, and cable television channel.

Athletics

Columbia, as part of the Ivy League, also competes in NCAA Division I sports. Men's varsity teams compete in baseball, basketball, crew (both heavy and lightweight), cross-country, running, fencing, football, golf, soccer, swimming, tennis, diving, wrestling, and track and field, as do women's varsity teams in archery, basketball, crew, cross-country, diving fencing, golf field hockey, lacrosse, soccer, softball, swimming and diving, tennis, volleyball, and track and field.

There are also intramural opportunities in flag football, basketball, racquetball, soccer, softball, squash, swimming, tennis, Ultimate Frisbee and volleyball.

I came to Columbia with my high school best friend and we agreed to dorm together our first year in Carman Hall. We ended up on the thirteenth floor, in room 1313, and while I thought that was a bad omen in the beginning, I could not have been proven more wrong. All of us on the thirteenth floor became one huge family, a giant pack that would dine together every night at the John Jay cafeteria, hop from party to party on Friday nights, and hold all-night cram sessions in the hallway of our floor. I've managed to keep in constant touch with some of those friends since graduation three years ago.

Housing

At Columbia, you will find your home to be a vibrant and lively place in a supportive residence hall community. A dedicated team of Residential Programs staff, class center staff, deans, faculty, and students ensure that your education extends beyond the classroom. Through programs and activities, study sessions, academic advisement, and mentoring, students and professionals join you in making CU an exciting and memorable academic and residential experience.

New York Life

Beyond Columbia's undergrad dorms is a whole other world—New York City—to explore. Students from big cities will find in New York more of what they enjoyed back home—impressive museums, large sporting events, concert venues, and the like. Those from more suburban homes will find the vast amount of things to do in the Big Apple exhilirating. But every student will find the city invigorating for culture, internships, and unparalleled nightlife.

• •

True to the song, New York is the city that never sleeps. Nowhere else can you go to see a movie at one in the morning (and that's not the late show!), catch a variety of live bands on a single street (a good place to start is the Village), or dance the night away in any of the city's famed nightclubs.

More and more, however, students are finding enough things to do in Morningside Heights, Columbia's surrounding neighborhood. It's entirely possible during a quick study break to 1) grab a slice of pizza, 2) hear a set of jazz, and 3) play a round of pool, and return in time to finish one's work.

At times, a student will go an entire week without setting foot off campus. Besides classes and homework, there are plenty of student-sponsored coffeehouses, musical performances, and drama productions to attend; the options never stop, not for at least four years!

THINGS TO DO IN NEW YORK CITY (WHEN NOT STUDYING)

- Ice skate in Rockefeller Center.
- Throw a Frisbee on Central Park's Great Lawn.
- Make a wish atop the Empire State Building.
- Take a quick round trip on the Staten Island ferry at sunset (it's only fifty cents!).
- Shop at Macy's, the world's largest department store.
- Stroll across the Brooklyn Bridge.
- Eat dim sum in Chinatown.
- Catch a Broadway musical (discount tickets are always easy to buy).

FINANCIAL AID

Columbia's admissions policy is need-blind, meaning the school accepts students solely on their academic, personal, and extracurricular merits before even looking at their ability to pay for tuition and costs (however, this policy only applies to students who are U.S. citizens, permanent residents or Canadian citizens). The foundation of the college's funding program is its full-need financial aid package, meaning it tries in any way to match a student's demonstrated financial needs. Approximately half of all enrolled students at the college receive some form of financial aid, whether in the form of grants, loans, or work-study jobs (funding is more limited for transfer students).

Columbia made great pains to match what my parents and I needed to cover tuition costs. I was happy to bear most of that responsibility with Stafford and Perkins loans, and money I earned from my work-study job at the Graduate School of Arts (which was a whole other tremendous learning experience). Sure, now I owe a pretty sizable amount on my loans, but I know I'll pay them off gradually, like a habit, and will hardly notice when I'm done. It's a small cost to pay every month for what Columbia gave me—not only knowledge, but self-assurance, maturity, and loads of memories!

Determining a student's eligibility for financial aid is a multilayered process that requires your family to provide a great deal of financial information in a timely manner. A student's demonstrated financial need is the difference between tuition and other related costs, and the amount the family can contribute. The family contribution, which includes what both the student and the parents will give, is determined by taking a close look at parents' income and assets, the family size, and the number of family members already attending college.

All entering students receiving financial aid are expected to work during the summer and save a certain amount of money to be used toward their contribution ($1,600 for first-year students, $1,800 for sophomores, $2,000 for juniors and $2,100 for seniors). Once at Columbia, students will usually also earn an expected amount of money from an on-campus work-study job.

To receive grant aid (money from Columbia's trust that need not be repaid), students must stay enrolled for eight terms of undergrad study and register for a minimum of twelve points (usually four classes) each term.

Government-funded, low-interest loans (either the Stafford or Perkins loans) can be another source of funding in a student's package. After graduation, a student has a grace period (usually six months) before having to start paying back the loans in increments. The payback time is generally spread over ten years. Because the federal government allows upper-classmen—juniors and seniors—to borrow larger amounts of money, Columbia will usually increase the amount of government loans in their financial aid package.

Every year a student must reapply for financial aid, and any change in income or assets from the previous year will be accounted for in the financial aid package. Students will remain on financial aid only if they continue to do well academically.

GRADUATES

Applying to graduate schools during my senior year happened almost by rote—I just knew there was no other immediate path for me to take. Of course, I wavered on whether I'd get in, so I hoped for the worst from the two schools to which I applied. If I got accepted from either, I'd call it a "pleasant surprise." That acceptance phone call was an ecstatic climax to my four years. I'm halfway through getting my MFA in photography at the School of Visual Arts, and when I'm done with this, I'll start on my master's in art history at Columbia. My dream is to open up my own photo gallery in New York City that will spotlight younger, struggling artists. I'd say I'm off to a great start!

Ninety percent of Columbia College graduates eventually go to graduate school, either right after their four years, or after a few years of working. Which path a student takes can vary as much as Columbia's diverse student population.

The college's Office of Career Education hosts a comprehensive recruiting program, where many New York-based companies recruit graduating students for outstanding jobs in fields as diverse as publishing, marketing, moviemaking, and engineering.

Students also, get aggressively scouted by many of Wall Street's brokerage firms and investment banks, where they can look forward to careers as stockbrokers, analysts, management trainees, or consultants. Many of them eventually wind up in business school, working on MBAs that will further advance their careers.

No matter what, Columbia alums always come back to their alma mater, some in bigger ways than others. In 1987 John Kluge donated $25 million for a minority-aid program. Morris Schapiro gave $5 million for the construction of Schapiro Hall, one of the newer dormitories which overlooks the Hudson River. And some alums give back to Columbia and its students by returning to campus to mentor students, give on-campus seminars, and talk to students about their professional work.

The Young Alumni Club, created to bring together alums from the previous ten years, has brought many newer, younger alumni back to Columbia as well, by organizing a variety of social and professional events.

SUMMING UP

The combination of Columbia College's rigorous academics, esteemed faculty, diverse student body, and location within New York City makes Columbia a truly unique option for higher education. At least, this is the sentiment felt among everyone on campus. From the minute students step onto College Walk for the first time, to the moment they step onto Broadway as newly-minted graduates, the whirlwind four years they've just spent will be filled with academic triumphs, unforgettable New York experiences, and relationships with professors and friends that will outlast those first few years in the professional world.

The core curriculum, designed to engage each student in the innermost workings of the world's greatest literature, art, music, and political and philosophical thinking, is matched by the world of knowledge waiting outside the school's wrought-iron gates. Required assignments of visiting some of the greatest art museums in the world or taking in a musical performance at any number of famed venues will hardly feel like tedious homework. Plus, the core is ultimately matched by the college's wide-ranging academic majors taught by the intellectual leaders in their fields.

Nary a moment is wasted in four years. The Columbia student knows how to balance schoolwork with the myriad social and student on-campus activities, as well as the vast number of goings-on in the city at any given moment.

Students are graduated with factual knowledge as well as street smarts. One student may have spent hours working on differential equations, but also balanced that with tutoring an inner-city high school student in algebra. Another might have composed a thesis on presidential-congressional relations while campaigning for a spot on the college's Student Senate. Columbia's legacy of student involvement and activism, recorded in the school's rich history, is unmatched by any other high-caliber institution of higher learning.

Columbia seeks out the nation's young leaders—those high school seniors who have made great strides in their school and community. The comprehensive admissions application is a canvas on which prospective students paint a picture of themselves, their goals, hopes, and interests. Once admitted, Columbia's Office of Financial Aid and Educational Financing will make sure all possible avenues are taken to finance a first-year student's education, and will continue to do so for the remaining three years.

Four years at Columbia College breeze by. Perhaps this is best reflected by the number of grads who stick around to pursue graduate work in any one of the university's remaining fifteen schools, or by the number of grads who pursue jobs in New York City. But far and wide, Columbia College alums share that everlasting something special—four years in which they were urged to find themselves and become freethinkers, ready to serve as leaders in their communities and beyond.

❏ *Anna Lisa Raya, B.A.*

COLUMBIA UNIVERSITY/SCHOOL OF ENGINEERING AND APPLIED SCIENCE (SEAS)

  Columbia University/SEAS
212 Hamilton
New York, NY 10027

(212) 854-2522
Fax: (212) 854-1209

 Web site: *http://www.engineering.columbia.edu*

 Enrollment

Full-time ❏ women: 388
❏ men: 1,048

INTRODUCING SEAS

    Columbia's tradition in engineering and applied science education traces back to the chartering of King's College in 1754. Steamboat inventor John Stevens graduated from the college a few years before the Revolutionary War, and DeWitt Clinton, the statesman responsible for the Erie Canal, earned his Columbia degree in 1786. Columbia's legacy of engineering instruction continued in the nineteenth century and was formalized in 1864 with the founding of the engineering school, the third oldest in the country.

As the Engineering School has diversified and grown, it has built an enduring reputation as a center of research excellence in select fields and as Alma Mater to generations of alumni who have shaped academic departments and industrial research programs across the country. In 1997, Z.Y. Fu and The Fu Foundation announced a gift of $26 million, designed broadly for "support of engineering excellence at Columbia," and more specifically for support of faculty and the enhancement of interdisciplinary research in areas of emerging strength.

Retrospectively, I appreciate Columbia far more than I thought possible; conversations with friends, both recent graduates and not-so-recent graduates, seem to indicate that this is the norm. It is rare that one appreciates the intangible lessons and experiences of life—especially as an undergraduate—while they are being taught; rather one looks back to treasure the good times and internalize the experiences. SEAS exposed me to a rigorous technical engineering program, as well as an insightful liberal arts curriculum, but it also taught me to be resourceful and to be prepared to walk through any doors leading to opportunity.

An immediate measure of the benefits of the naming gift from The FU Foundation has been the addition of more than forty-five new faculty members, representing a fifty percent increase within the past decade. While the faculty has grown, class size has not increased, so an already impressive student-to-faculty ratio has gotten even better, and now stands at 10:1.

ADMISSIONS REQUIREMENTS

Admission to Columbia University's FU Foundation, School of Engineering and Applied Science (SEAS) is highly competitive. Either SAT or the ACT is required. Additionally, SAT Subject Tests are required in the areas: Mathematics (either level I or II), Chemistry or Physics, and Writing. For students taking the new SAT with writing, or the ACT with writing, students are not required to take the SAT II Subject Writing test. In addition to the standardized examination requirements, it is expected that each applicant has had sufficient preparation in high school to maintain competitive standings while enrolled at Columbia. It is recommended that the high school preparation courses include:

- mathematics courses including calculus
- one year of chemistry
- one year of physics
- four years of English
- three to four years of history or social science
- two to three years of a foreign language

In addition to coursework requirements, in consideration for admission to SEAS, a written evaluation from a guidance counselor or college advisor is expected. Also expected as part of the applicant's file are two recommendations from teachers of academic subjects, including one from a mathematics teacher. A personal essay is also a required part of the application.

As in most other aspects of life at Columbia, admission is based on balance. Academic standing alone is not the only attribute used to measure a student's potential to be a successful and integral member of SEAS. While Advanced Placement or honors placement in high school are important factors, also weighted is the applicant's extracurricular activities record as well as evidence of special talent. Further, a substantive and sincere interest in engineering should be demonstrated.

> *Life as a student at CU was probably far different than life would have been had I attended any other school. Before joining the CU community, I thought college would simply be an extension of my academic career. I had visited the atypical New York City green campus only a few times, but for some reason I always felt comfortable and excited while on campus. Columbia has prepared me academically and socially. Most of all, Columbia has been responsive to both technological changes and social changes providing effective tools to approach life with an open mind and great enthusiasm.*

ACADEMIC LIFE

Since the founding of the school in 1864 as the nation's first engineering school within a liberal arts college, the University has always placed engineering and applied science in its broadest intellectual context. The school's graduates, shapers of industrial and academic programs across the country, have been educated, not trained.

From their first days as undergraduates, Columbia's engineers work to master scientific fundamentals, problem-solving, and original thinking. To give the broad perspective necessary for a successful career, first and second year undergraduate students take courses from different disciplines within the University that include Columbia's famed Core Curriculum in the humanities as well as professional courses in individual engineering disciplines. Columbia SEAS is committed to educating the whole person to ensure students have both the fundamental technical knowledge and the professional skills required to participate in this rapidly changing technological environment. This integrated approach to engineering education begins from the start of the first year.

Engineering Design and Community Service

The course *Design fundamentals using advanced computer technologies*, also known as the Gateway Lab course, is the epicenter of the engineering student's early experience at SEAS. All first-year students take this course, either in the first or second semester. Taking advantage of the many nonprofit organizations within New York City, students have the opportunity to learn significant technical, professional, and communications skills while working on real-world projects for the community. Columbia Engineering is the only engineering school in the country that has a required first-year course with a community service component. Some of the projects so far have included designing playground equipment for children with disabilities, developing a mixed-use bus stop that monitors the environment for asthma-related causes, and a space design for a recording studio in a local community technology center.

The course focuses on the fundamental engineering design processes and application of computer technologies (such as three-dimensional graphics and Web applications) using the Botwinick Gateway Laboratory, a multimedia interactive facility with gigabit of network speed at each desktop. In addition to learning the technical components of design, students develop specific professional skills, such as making compelling and precise presentations, problem-solving, project management, collaboration, and team management. Students experience what they would be doing as engineers in various fields.

Professional Courses

Choosing a branch of engineering or applied science is an important decision for both the student's academic program and future professional career. To support these important decisions, SEAS students focus on five major areas of technical inquiry: engineering, mathematics, physics, chemistry, and computer science. To support their decision process, students are required to take at least one professional-level course. The courses are designed to acquaint SEAS students with rigorous intellectual effort in engineering and applied science early in their academic careers. Among the courses are:

- Physics of the human body
- Introduction to computational mathematics and physics
- Engineering in medicine
- Molecular engineering and product design
- Design of buildings, bridges, and spacecraft
- Earth resources and the environment
- Introduction to electrical engineering, with laboratory in circuit design
- Engineering graphics
- Atomic-scale engineering of new materials
- Mechanical engineering: micromachines to jumbo jets

Undergraduate Research Involvement Program

At SEAS, the faculty takes an active role in research, which is funded by both private and government sources. Faculty members view student involvement in research as part of the educational process and actively encourage it. By becoming involved in research programs, students develop critical skills necessary to participate in future research endeavors. Each year, the list of research opportunities grows and the choices across all engineering and applied science programs are numerous. Recent research opportunities have included topics in

- nanoscience and nanotechnology
- in vivo mechanical signal transduction in bone tissue
- design and characterization of enzyme-catalyzed proton exchange membrane fuel cells
- developing high-performance durable fiber-reinforced concrete products for both architectural and structural applications
- software and hardware projects in the Columbia Robotics Lab
- prediction of flood, hurricane, and drought risk using climate forecasts
- video compression and streaming for interactive TV and Internet-based applications
- creation of novel atomic-scale magnetic materials
- design and fabrication of instrumentation for testing of MEMS devices and other micro-systems.

Undergraduate Departments

One of the great attractions of an undergraduate education at a research university is the range of resources it provides, including the vast array of programs of study it offers. SEAS currently offers fifteen majors, several disciplinary and interdisciplinary minors, and the ability to choose either engineering or liberal arts minors.

Departments and Majors:

- Applied Physics and Applied Mathematics. Majors: Applied Physics, Applied Mathematics, Materials Science and Engineering
- Biomedical Engineering
- Chemical Engineering
- Civil Engineering. Majors: Civil Engineering, Engineering Mechanics
- Computer Science. Majors: Computer Science, Computer Engineering
- Earth and Environmental Engineering. Majors: Earth and Environmental Engineering, Materials Science and Engineering
- Electrical Engineering. Majors: Electrical Engineering. Computer Engineering.
- Industrial Engineering and Operations Research. Majors: Engineering and Management Systems, Industrial Engineering, Operations Research
- Mechanical Engineering

Nonengineering Minors

In response to student interest, Columbia Engineering now offers minors in several liberal arts subjects as well as the opportunity to qualify for New York State Teacher Certification through the Barnard College Education Program. Currently, nonengineering minors are available in the following additional areas of study: American Studies, Architecture, Art History, Economics, Education, English and Comparative Literature, French, French and Francophore Studies, Greek or Latin History, Music, Philosophy, Political Science, Psychology, Religion, Sociology, and Spanish.

SOCIAL LIFE AND ACTIVITIES

The engineering curriculum at Columbia is definitely demanding. Equally as demanding is participating in all of the extracurricular activities that might catch your eye. In addition to all of the commonly available activities on college campuses, such as sports—both varsity and intercollegiate—group publications, and student government, there are many active, thriving groups on campus. Various cultural groups, which welcome all students, organize spectacular fashion shows, buffet dinners, and dances that are known to sell out. There are also drama, comedy improv, and *a cappella* groups on campus to help satisfy your yearning to perform.

In addition to activities that offer entertainment and cultural education, there are groups that enable CU students to fulfill their need to help others. The Community Impact programs organized on campus are not only an important part of CU's community but the Morningside Heights community as well, providing tutoring to younger students of the neighboring schools, peer counseling, and numerous other services.

My social life was easily extended beyond the borders of our green campus bounded by the iron gates. The theater is only minutes from campus. Cuisine of almost any culture is only a hop, skip, and jump away. Any music—from classical at Lincoln Center to jazz down in the Village to rock played by various CU bands just across the street at the local hangout—can be heard in a heartbeat. Major sports arenas are just a subway ride away. The abundance of activities available in New York City always left me wishing I could be in more than one place on a Saturday evening.

FINANCIAL AID

Admissions is need-blind for U.S. citizens, U.S. permanent residents, Canadian citizens, and persons granted refugee visas by the United States. This means that applications are reviewed without regard to whether students are able to pay for the total cost of attending Columbia.

SEAS is committed to meeting the full need of all applicants admitted as first-year students. Certain limitations apply, however, in the case of transfer students. Although transfer admission is need-blind, financial aid resources for transfer students are limited. Therefore, SEAS is unable to meet the full need of transfer applicants, with the exception of students who enter the Combined Plan Program and those who transfer from Columbia College.

The Combined Plan Program for undergraduates offers students from affiliated schools across the country the opportunity to earn both a B.A. in a liberal arts field from their home institutions and a B.S. in engineering from SEAS in five years.

SEAS assesses the information applicants provided to the Office of Financial Aid and Educational Financing to determine how much a family is expected to contribute to college costs. The resulting "family contribution" will include both a "parental contribution" and a "student contribution." If the calculated family contribution is less than the cost of attendance, aid is awarded to make up the difference.

Only students who demonstrate financial need are eligible for financial aid. Except for the unsubsidized Federal Stafford Loan, all institutional and federal aid is need-based. The financial aid package may contain a combination of Federal Stafford Loans, Federal Work-Study, and Federal Perkins Loans.

There are no academic, athletic, or talent-based institutional scholarships. While Columbia students are often the recipients of merit-based scholarships from outside organizations, nothing merit-based is offered directly from the school.

Foreign students should note that the admissions process is need-blind only for U.S. citizens, U.S. permanent residents, Canadian citizens, and persons granted refugee visas by the United States. At this time, financial aid for foreign students who do not fall into one of these categories at SEAS is very limited. However, each year several foreign aid students are admitted to Columbia with a financial aid package that covers one-hundred percent of educational expenses. Because the SEAS community is so small, foreign applicants who need financial aid must be considered on a case-by-case basis; candidates should be aware that such awards may not be possible every year.

GRADUATES

Graduates of Columbia University's Engineering School pursue various endeavors after completion of their undergraduate degrees, the most obvious being the practice of various disciplines of engineering. Many of the SEAS graduates go on to graduate school to continue their engineering education or to obtain professional degrees. Numerous SEAS alumni also can be found in business consulting and Wall Street positions. The education offered at the School of Engineering and Applied Science is far more than information handed to its students, rather it is a tool provided to each of its graduates enabling them to acquire, process, analyze, and dispense information given any circumstance.

PROMINENT GRADS

- ○ Jeffrey Bleustein, President and CEO of Harley Davidson, Inc.
- ○ Ed DiGiulio, President, Cinema Products Corp.
- ○ Joseph Hoane, Software Engineer for IBM's Deep Blue Development Team
- ○ Robert Merton, 1997 Nobel Laureate in Economics
- ○ Pete Slosberg, Founder, Pete's Brewing Company
- ○ Greg Smith, Chief Investment Strategist, Prudential Securities
- ○ C.J. Tan, Senior Manager of IBM's Deep Blue Development Team

I don't think students realize what they are getting each day that they are sitting in class, studying in their rooms, programming in Gussman lab, or just talking with their professors. Only five months after graduating, I experienced a tremendous epiphany: Columbia has intensified my desire to learn and share my knowledge with all those around me. Everyone at Columbia has a thirst for knowledge, but you will know you have chosen the right place to continue your education when you can say your desire for knowledge has grown.

SUMMING UP

Many doors were opened for me as a result of attending Columbia. I not only earned a B.S. in biomedical engineering, I also received an education from an institution that demands its graduates enter the world with knowledge beyond the confines of their discipline. When talking with friends about Columbia, it was unanimous—being part of Columbia is a huge milestone in each of our lives.

Entertainment and relaxation are definitely important aspects of a Columbia education, but taking a break from lectures, laboratories, and studying does not necessarily mean defaulting to the neighborhood bar or campus party. The Columbia experience truly encompasses the principle of diversity in every sense of the word.

❏ *Kelly Lenz, B.S.,*
Joseph Kennedy, Columbia University

CONNECTICUT COLLEGE

 Connecticut College
New London, CT 06320

 (860) 439-2200
Fax: (860) 439-4301

 E-mail: *admission@conncoll.edu*
Web site:
http://www.connecticutcollege.edu/admissions

 Enrollment

Full-time ❏ women: 1,084
❏ men: 724

Part-time ❏ women: 54
❏ men: 24

INTRODUCING CONNECTICUT COLLEGE

If indeed there are ten thousand worlds for the choosing as Cormac McCarthy wrote in *All the Pretty Horses*, Connecticut College gives you access to each of them. The opportunities are endless. CC students are their own breed—intelligent and inventive souls with a strong commitment to social justice. Fewer than 2,000 students from all parts of the world (a surprisingly large majority from "outside of Boston") come together to partake in a four-year journey—academic, social, and personal transformations. Connecticut College is a highly competitive coeducational liberal arts college where the classes are like exotic lands of thought that you enter at your own will, the people—your tour guides. With a tradition of shared governance, social activism, and an Honor Code, it promotes an academically strong, socially conscious home base from which to embark on the inevitable adventures to follow beyond the undergraduate years.

Resting on what is referred to as "the hill" in historic New London, Connecticut, the picturesque campus is located halfway between New York City and Boston and overlooks the Long Island Sound. "What college is supposed to look like," my father remarked the first time we stepped foot on the green. Our eyes widened to the casual gait of students moving from one class to another, tossing Frisbees across the green, and two dozen more students sitting under a blossom tree by the sun dial, engaged in what was their 2:30 P.M. Writing the Short Story course. Yes, I felt, this *is* it.

Connecticut College is committed to empowering students to take charge of their own education; the faculty works to provide students with the necessary tools to implement their ideas. My experience with professors goes unmatched. With a student-to-faculty ratio of 10-to-1, I never felt short of attention from professors! It is common for professors and faculty to host students to do everything from watching "Rosewood" and eating nachos, to sitting around a backyard picnic table discussing existentialism, or whether or not our D3 basketball team would make it to this year's NCAA basketball tournament.

The Connecticut College education in a nutshell? That is the point: There is no nutshell. Each individual brings a different spark to the campus community. Because of this, there are infinite ways any one student can work to take advantage of opportunities such as international study, research with faculty, paid internships, self-designed studies, and community action. While the CC Experience may encompass a set of core values and ideals, opportunities, and experiences each serving as colors on a palette, no one student colors his or her canvas the same. This is the greatest part about CC—you can truly develop yourself as a scholar and as an individual.

ADMISSIONS REQUIREMENTS

Admission to Connecticut College is competitive. Know this: the Admissions staff at Connecticut College seeks bright individuals, and they are cognizant that there is more than one way to reveal this. While CC has experienced an increasing number of applications in the last few years, the "criteria" remain such that any dedicated, thoughtful applicant has the opportunity to compete. Connecticut College is looking for students with passion and with a commitment to pursuing academic excellence through a rigorous academic program and selective travel and work experiences.

Common Application

Connecticut College uses the Common Application. A college application is made with the following basic building blocks: Your biographical information and extracurricular activities, a high school transcript, standardized test scores, an essay, recommendations, and perhaps an interview. In addition, each applicant must submit the Supplement to the Common Application. The supplement is due by December 15 with the Common Application and other admission materials due by January 1 with notification by April 1. Submission of the SAT Reasoning Test is optional, but all candidates for admission must choose one of the following testing options: results of three SAT Subject Tests or the results of the American College Testing Assessment (ACT). Beginning with the class of 2010, which marks the introduction of the new SAT with the writing component, either the ACT or two SAT Subject Tests will be required. Submission of SAT scores will still be optional. Interviews are not required but are highly recommended as part of the application process. Interviewers see the conversation as a time to exchange information and personalize what can often seem like an impersonal process to students.

Early Decision

Many of my good friends at CC applied Early Decision. The college offers two Early Decision options, both of which are binding. Early Decision Round I has an application deadline of November 15 with a notification date of mid-December. Early Decision Round II has a supplement deadline of December 15 and all other application materials are due January 1. The notification date for Early Decision Round II is mid-February.

> *My vision of college was a nebulous one before my freshman year. I never imagined that "learning" could take place while sitting among my classmates in the living room of one of my professor's houses and discussing issues of the "Other" or the problem of choice in a pluralistic society. I never imagined that so much of my education would be attributed to long talks in dorm hallways late at night while procrastinating challenging assignments. And I surely never imagined that my college experience would endow study abroad or work experiences in a dozen different countries.*

Distribution Requirements

Take the *liberal* in liberal arts college seriously. Students choose from fifty-five majors, with the option of self-designing a major as well. Yet that's not to say that the academic program falls anywhere short of demanding and powerful. Connecticut College's academic program within the major is extensive with its requirements. In addition, there are seven General Education requirements (seven courses from seven different academic areas), a language requirement, and a writing across the curriculum requirement.

Students must take a foreign language course at the intermediate level or study a new language for two semesters. Placement at the intermediate level is achieved by passing a college-administered oral and written proficiency exam during orientation. I found that many students took advantage of the plethora of language study programs and services offered by the college (see Study Abroad section).

Connecticut College students have the unique opportunity of applying to a number of centers and programs that are designed to integrate a student's major with a service project, domestic or international internship, intensive science research, or other technologically

Some people consider spending a semester or a summer in New York City as an international experience. In many ways I found this to be true while interning at Ms. Magazine in downtown Manhattan for a summer. Professor Blanche Boyd in the English Department and the Office of Career Services helped me earn an internship at the prominent feminist magazine. Suddenly I was in the working world (or at least I was trying it out), and I had research deadlines and editorial meetings where Gloria Steinem would frequently make an appearance. I learned as much from her as I did from the incredibly brilliant staff of women working at Ms. They answered questions I hadn't even proposed yet about the world.

advanced research project. This hands-on experience is designed to complement curriculum with practical experience often reserved for graduate students at larger academic institutions. Basically, of all the competitive colleges and universities I looked at as a senior in high school, not one offered such distinct, creative opportunities as the ones described below.

The Toor Cummings Center for International Studies and the Liberal Arts (CISLA)

A Connecticut College gem is its Toor Cummings Center for International Studies and the Liberal Arts, a program to which students apply in the fall of their sophomore year to work toward completing an integrative research project relative to their major. The center funds an international internship the summer before the senior year. In addition, students are required to complete two International Studies courses, with a focus on the following questions: What are the origins and dynamics of contemporary society? What is the relevance of the past in understanding the present and the possibilities of the future? What are the material, spiritual, and ethical challenges of modernity?

The Toor Cummings Center for International Studies and the Liberal Arts is indeed one of the most highly regarded international studies programs in the country. Officially, it aims for its students to leave prepared for a lifelong reflection on study and learning as a journey to wisdom that one shares with others. Unofficially, it is the coolest program at Connecticut College. The plethora of independent research projects can include conducting environmental field research in Bali, researching media studies while interning at CNN in Berlin for a summer, and examining the effects of Amnesty International's human rights work in Santiago, Chile. These experiences, combined with the solid academic foundation of a liberal arts college, in addition to the large realm of study and work experiences in all parts of the world, surely make for profound, diverse classroom discussions.

The most challenging and rewarding experience I had as a Connecticut College student, by far, was my CISLA internship. As a member of the Center for International Studies and the Liberal Arts, I was able to complete my international internship at the United Nations Development Fund for Women (UNIFEM) in Lagos, Nigeria, where I interviewed women and wrote articles on the various projects that UNIFEM implements in Nigeria and Ghana.

In short, I had a dream internship. Monday through Friday, my host family's driver would take me to the United Nations headquarters in Lagos. The actual drive was a whirlwind of smoky cars, motorbikes, women holding baskets on their heads, babies crying, kids skipping, adults standing in line at the various European and American embassies, lethargic policemen in military uniforms, and then occasional homeless people on the street asking for money or food. By the time I got to work, my mind was already full. I signed in every day and was handed an "Official Consultant" badge (I never got used to the idea). Nonetheless, I worked at UNIFEM.

Amazed at how the UNIFEM-Lagos team (a staff of eight people) was able to balance friendliness and professionalism in their day-to-day work schedules, I felt immediately comfortable in the work environment. I shared an office with one of the Program Officers, and fortunately I was supplied with a laptop. On my first day at work the Regional Program Director (my boss) said to me, "So why don't you look through the UNIFEM literature that we have and then make a list of stories you want to write about, people you'd like to interview, and then make a time table for it all—oh and be specific, work on what you're interested in, because frankly, I don't want to waste your time." And so the summer began.

My original CISLA project proposal was to study the dynamics of UNIFEM and the ways in which it promotes growth and empowerment in women in the three areas of governance, economics, and human rights. Really, I was able to see the backstage aspect of development programs and of the United Nations in general. The internship experience was a huge leap in that it gave a practical meaning to my academic major of International Relations. Also, in publishing articles in the UNIFEM monthly publication, The UNIFEM Currents *and the* United Nations Partnership of Nigeria *quarterly magazine, I feel that my writing not only strengthened but that I was able to attain a certain level of legitimacy in my work.*

The Ammerman Center for Arts and Technology

Students can weave their academic, personal, and artistic expression together through the college's Center for Arts and Technology. The Ammerman Center links studio art, music, dance, theater, writing, film, and museum studies with the world of mathematics and computer science. Students study the symbiotic relationship between technology and the arts while exploring such areas as computer graphics, animation, music composition, recording technology, and virtual reality. In addition, students of this center have the opportunity to undertake projects such as designing a program to conduct a virtual music ensemble, exploring 3-D visualization to enhance scientific learning, and designing interactive web sites. Like the other distinguished interdisciplinary centers at Connecticut College, The Ammerman Center offers funded internships. For example, working at a high-technology firm during the summer can complement a student's key knowledge gained in the way of coursework and involvement in the center.

The Goodwin-Niering Center for Conservation Biology and Environmental Studies

The location of Connecticut College—on Long Island Sound and the Thames River—attracts a faculty that includes some of the world's leading experts on wetland ecology, water quality, tidal marsh vegetation, and bird migration. Goodwin-Niering Center internships have included studying production and environmental sustainability on an organic banana farm in Costa Rica; studying a component of Vitamin E found in palm oil in Malaysia; and working for the Oregon Environmental Council. Many students choose to use their extensive research experience and copublish their results with faculty members. In the past, students have won environmental awards for their presentations at national conferences.

The Holleran Center for Community Action and Public Policy (CCAPP)

Connecticut College provides a supportive environment in which students take advantage of many volunteer or community service opportunities. Indeed, CC is a school that pushes students to walk their talk, so to speak, when it comes to issues of social justice. With students committing as many as 30,000 hours a year to organizations in the surrounding area, the Holleran Center for Community Action and Public Policy builds on CC's longstanding tradition of working to address issues of poverty, inequality, and racial/ethnic conflict. This remarkable center also sponsors the Program in Community Action, otherwise known as PICA, which has formed many community partnerships and public policy initiatives with local and national causes and their organizations. Through the Holleran Center, students have completed internships at the Harvard University Medical School, U.S. Department of Housing and Urban Development in Washington, D.C., Save the Children in Bolivia, and the Georgia O'Keeffe Museum in Santa Fe, New Mexico.

Study Abroad

The second semester of my sophomore year I studied abroad in Hanoi, Vietnam, on the SATA program. SATA, the College's Study Away Teach Away Program, enables CC students to travel to another country and study with CC professors. It is a unique program that works to broaden experiences of both students and professors, with the goal of having them bring back what they learned to the greater CC community. It was through taking classes in government, economics, and even Vietnamese, that my major of international relations was first actualized for me. For the first time I felt I could see the answers to questions we asked in class and the certain effects that a government could have on a nation. From riding my bicycle through the maze of streets on a daily basis to talking to new Vietnamese friends, I felt I was able to gain a greater understanding of Vietnam.

- **The Office of National and International Programs.** Whatever happened to regular study abroad? The Office of National and International Programs at Connecticut College helps to place students in a number of different study abroad programs around the world according to their personal and academic interests, independent of the college's unique centers and programs. These more traditional study abroad programs include L'Institute d'Etudes Européenes in Paris, France; London School of Economics; University of Cape Town in South Africa; or a semester abroad in Sydney, Australia. Other study abroad opportunities take the *regular* term to a new dimension however.

The first semester of my junior year I studied abroad in Paris, France through L'Institute d'Etudes Européenes. I learned about this study abroad program through the Connecticut College Office of National and International Programs, which works to place students in a number of different study abroad programs around the world according to their personal and academic interests. While taking courses in the French language and living with a French family, I learned to value the French way of doing things, and I also earned a new perspective on government policy and immigration issues in France. Through an IES program, I had the opportunity of participating in a Model European Union program in Freiburg, Germany. I was able to propose questions to other EU member state leaders and answer on behalf of France's position. By far, this opportunity served as an eye-opener of the way states interact with each other in the international arena.

- **Study Away Teach Away (SATA).** An unmatched study abroad opportunity offered to Connecticut College students, this program enables students to travel to another country and study *with* Connecticut College professors. Both students and professors work together to explore the host society, thereby broadening their experiences on a multitude of levels. The greater goal of having them bring back what they learned to the greater college community is icing on the cake. Among students on campus, widely recognized SATA countries include Vietnam, Egypt, Morocco, India, Greece, Italy, and Czech Republic.
- **Travel and Research Immersion Program (TRIPS).** TRIPS, Connecticut College's Travel and Research Immersion Program, is an unparalleled academic opportunity. This fairly new program allows students and their professors in designated courses to travel outside of the classroom in order to enhance what they are learning in the classroom. Take these words literally: *outside of the classroom.* TRIPS can take you to Ellis Island for the weekend with an American Literature class, or to Jerusalem for two weeks with an Introductory to Religious Studies class. This is by far one of the most outstanding programs CC offers.

I was fortunate to be able to travel to Spain during Thanksgiving break of my senior year with Professor Kushigian of the Hispanic Studies Department and several classmates as part of our advanced Spanish Literature course, "Orientalism." While in Madrid, I interviewed an eighty-three-year-old woman who spoke of her experience in the Franco era. She offered a great and serious insight into Spain, as she solidified my own passion for writing and journalism.

SOCIAL LIFE AND ACTIVITIES

Students make or break a college social environment. Nowhere else is this as true as Connecticut College. With students representing forty-five states and thirty-five foreign countries, and approximately ninety-eight percent of undergraduates living on campus, the social scene can be lively and varied. A Friday evening may include attending a dance performance in Cummings Arts Center, followed by a Comedy Club routine in the student center. Parties are to follow, of course, although Saturday night's roar is usually heard the loudest.

With more than fifty-five student organizations on campus, students never fall short of ways to be involved. If you do, then feel free to start the fifty-sixth student organization! Join Student Government, or the Ballroom Dance Club. Start your own jazz band or contribute to *The College Voice* (the college newspaper), or better yet, one of several student-run magazines. Engage in dynamic discussions in La Unidad, the Latino/a-American student organization, or UMOJA (African/African-American student organization). Make your voice heard; participate in Feminist Majority, or pitch in on the college's own radio station, WCNI-FM.

In addition, the dance, theater, music, and studio art departments pride themselves on outstanding student performances, yet Connecticut College works to include other ways of artistic expression under the umbrella of "the arts." For example, in recent years film studies, museum studies, architectural studies, and the nation's first undergraduate certificate program in art and technology are increasingly popular among Connecticut College students. And there are a number of ways to let your creativity flow. Connecticut College hosts a number of guest artists throughout the year as well. Situated between Boston and New York City, Connecticut College rests in a prime spot to attract artists and performers of every kind.

Dorm Life

With ninety-eight percent of Connecticut College students living on campus, and all four classes living together in each student residence, housing is a breeze. The college has no Greek system (no fraternities or sororities) but there are theme houses as well as traditional residence halls. Some of these include Knowlton (cultural/language house), Blackstone (substance-free house), Plant (quiet house), Unity House (multicultural house), Earth House (environmental house), and Abbey House (co-op house). Each of the twenty-one dorms has a Housefellow; basically he or she serves as a person to count on for personal or academic matters or concerns undergrads may have. The College's Honor Code values come into play in residential life as well.

My senior year I lived in Knowlton Dormitory, an old-fashioned high-ceiling building, now a cultural/language house. Students who wish to immerse themselves in a second language apply to live in the dorm. For example, as a French Studies minor I chose to apply to the French section of the dorm. Although casual, I enjoyed speaking French with the people in my hall and I was submerged in a living environment where hallmates had an appreciation for French culture. The hardwood floors were great, too.

Athletics

Connecticut College is a member of the New England Small College Athletic Conference (NESCAC) and is a Division III member of the National Collegiate Athletic Association (NCAA). The Camels compete in twenty-eight intercollegiate varsity sports (fifteen—women, twelve—men, one coed) including soccer, basketball, hockey, lacrosse, and water polo. Men's basketball, women's soccer, women's rowing, and women's lacrosse have each qualified for NCAA Championship competition in the past. With a broad range of intramural, club, and athletic sports to choose from, ninety percent of the student body participates in intercollegiate, club, intramural, recreational, or physical educational athletics. In addition to the usual tennis, hockey, golf, and volleyball, other club sports such as Ultimate Frisbee, karate, and cricket are also offered. Nothing beats cheering for the Camels during weekend games for both men's and women's soccer and lacrosse, while sitting on the campus green and enjoying a view of the Long Island Sound too.

FINANCIAL AID

Connecticut College invests in its students. The Financial Aid Services Office works diligently to make the CC experience affordable to anyone based on need. The entire college works from a foundation of true scholarship; this is evident in the student body. In recent years more than forty-five percent of all Connecticut College students have received financial aid. For more information, visit Financial Aid Services Web site at *www.connecticutcollege.edu/offices/financial-aid.*

GRADUATES

PROMINENT GRADS

- James Berrien '74, President, Forbes Magazine Group
- Allen Carroll '73, Chief Cartographer, *National Geographic*
- Michael Collier '76, Poet Laureate of Maryland and Director of the Bread Loaf Writers' Conference
- Anita DeFrantz '74, Olympic Medallist and Member of the International Olympic Committee
- David Foster '77, Ecologist, Author, and Director of the Harvard Forest
- Agnes Gund '60, President Emerita, The Museum of Modern Art
- Bruce Hoffman '76, Terrorism Expert, Rand Corporation
- Peter Som '93, Fashion Designer
- Susan Kronick '73, Vice Chairman, Federated Department Stores
- Dr. S. Harvey Moseley Jr. '72, Senior Astrophysicist, NASA Goddard Space Flight Center
- Estelle Parsons '49, Academy Award-winning Actress and Artistic Director of The Actors Studio
- Dr. Ellen Vitetta '64, Cancer Researcher and Director of the Cancer Immunobiology Center at the University of Texas
- Patricia Wald '48, Former Chief Judge on the U.S. Court of Appeals (D.C.)
- Amy Gross, Editor-in-Chief, *O, The Oprah Magazine*

Some of the best mail you'll ever receive after college comes in the form of *Connecticut College Magazine*. It's downright fascinating to see what your fellow grads are up to these days. Without a doubt, they are doing something amazing and demanding. On any given page, I can read about a fellow CISLA (Toor Cummings Center for International Studies and the Liberal Arts) scholar heading a development project in West Africa, or learn news of a CC couple starting a school in western Massachusetts.

The advantage of going to a small school is clear in this regard—the alumni network is booming with successful social and professional relationships. And the pool is so eclectic due to the varied interests of the diverse student body. It is not uncommon to find many double majors, too.

A key benefit of going to a small liberal arts college such as Connecticut College surfaces here. Because your education at CC is so personal and individualized, you are able to gain the skills and make the professional contacts as an undergraduate that will put you ahead of the rest in what is becoming a more and more competitive job search. When applying to any given field—professional and academic—sure enough, you will find a CC alumnus involved in some way. With more than 20,000 alumni and nearly 600 of them living abroad, if you wanted to, say, apply for an international fellowship in Timbuktu, it's guaranteed that current undergraduates or Connecticut College alumni have been there—and they are willing to help you, too.

CELS

Also willing to help you in your job search is the staff of the college's Career Enhancing Life Skills (CELS) program. They provide everything from résumé writing one-on-one conferences, workshops on job search-related skills, as well as a number of resources and alumni contact information for specific fields of interest. In addition, CELS offers a unique e-Portfolio system that allows students to keep an on-line record of their career and academic planning processes and accomplishment during their undergraduate years at Connecticut College. This creative and sophisticated manner of documenting academic information as well as cocurricular experiences serves as a vital tool in the job search.

Connecticut College students are doing meaningful work in their fields, and are often publishing or presenting the results before they go on to graduate school or their first real job. Funded internships, international study, the use of technology, and collaborative research with other students and faculty all help to build résumés for Connecticut College students before they graduate. An impressive number of graduates choose to pursue competitive post-graduate programs such as the Thomas J. Watson Fellowship, the Fulbright, the Peace Corps, or Teach for America, thereby continuing their adventure in education.

Other graduates pursue fields such as medicine/science, law, journalism, fine arts, education, and business. With a strong liberal arts background developed in classrooms, in extracurricular activities, in conversations with professors and debates over dinners, in venues across campus and around the globe, students acquire the ability to see the particular as part of a larger phenomenon, to understand people from different backgrounds and cultures, to acquire skills in negotiation and problem-solving and to critically evaluate new ideas. These are skills that make CC alumni valuable in whatever profession they choose. The value of a liberal arts degree from Connecticut College lasts a lifetime.

The Connecticut College experience is a metamorphosis. Each semester unfolds an organic undergraduate experience for students. As freshmen, CC students may come in wide-eyed and idealistic, questions in hand. As graduates, they leave only to embark on another journey. Now, however, they have the tools to create answers of their own. Nothing could begin to compete with the altruistic qualities of the curriculum at Connecticut College, the spirit of philanthropy among its students and faculty.

Like a pebble tossed in a pond, CC's ripple effect can be felt literally all over the world. From the Adult Education ESL classes in downtown New London to the maze of streets in Hanoi, Vietnam, where dozens of CC students have completed a Study Away Teach Away semester accompanied by CC professors. Professors conduct research in countries all over the world and an impressive number of students have been able to copublish along with them. Without a doubt, the extraordinary study and work experiences the college offers through its unique centers and programs are what make CC stand out from the rest.

When I first stepped on campus, I had no idea what a carpet ride I would embark on during the next four years. As an undergraduate, I was able to travel to twelve different countries including Vietnam, France, and Nigeria. If the spine of my college experience at Connecticut College is a liberal arts curriculum, then the flesh is international experience. Still, what makes CC stand out from the rest is just that—each CC experience unfolds for itself, thereby making each CC student a valued part of the greater Connecticut College Camel community.

During the entire college process—from looking at colleges as a junior in high school to facing graduation day as a Connecticut College senior. I asked myself many questions. How do I choose a major? What kinds of people will I spend four years with? Where will I study abroad? How will I be able to take my college education and transform it into an actual job? Honestly, it was through contemplating the core questions of such programs like Freshmen Focus and CISLA, that I continued to realize just how important it is for a student to take authority over his or her education, and to steer and clear his or her own path when necessary. And to know that to assume the role as an educated person means acting responsibly with that education—to question the essence of what and why we learn. Connecticut College fostered so many of my life goals in a few short years. And yet I know none of these experiences would have been possible without the perfect combination of my curiosity and will, and Connecticut College's plentiful collection of opportunity and encouragement. For this reason, I know I made the right decision in coming to Connecticut College.

❏ *Jennifer De Leon, B.A.*

COOPER UNION FOR THE ADVANCEMENT OF SCIENCE AND ART

	Cooper Union for the Advancement of Science and Art New York City, NY 10003	 Enrollment
	(212) 353-4120 Fax: (212) 353-4342	**Full-time** ❏ women: 336 ❏ men: 611
	Web site: *http://www.cooper.edu*	**Part-time** ❏ women: 2 ❏ men: 0

INTRODUCING COOPER UNION

The founder of Cooper Union, Peter Cooper, had a vision to offer an education that was "as free as water and air." Established in 1859, Cooper Union is the "only private, full-scholarship college of higher learning in the United States dedicated exclusively to preparing students for the professions of architecture, art, and engineering."

Cooper Union sits in the heart of the East Village of Manhattan and offers more than an exceptional classroom education to its students of art, architecture, and engineering. The institution's campus *is* New York City, a city alive with the sounds, smells, and events of the culturally, ethnically, and racially diverse population. It is not uncommon for a professor's assignments to extend outside of the classroom and incorporate different aspects of the city. During my freshman year, the assignment for my engineering design class was to design an effective system to allow for subway transfers on one subway line in lower Manhattan. Architecture students are often given assignments of photographing buildings and bridges for class. Art students frequently take class trips to view different installations in the plethora of great museums, studios, and galleries of Manhattan.

From helping in local soup kitchens, to the sorority's annual scavenger hunt, to dinners in Chinatown, the various student organizations also offer students the chance to experience New York City. Cooper students become a part of New York City by giving back to their community; it's not uncommon for a student organization to sponsor a volunteer outing or a food/toy drive to benefit New York City residents. After September 11, students organized a "penny drive," which raised over five hundred dollars for the local fire company. Aside from having its students explore the city, Cooper brings the city's culture to the school with various lectures in its historic Great Hall and Wollman Auditorium, and art and architecture exhibits in its galleries.

The education in each of the three schools—Engineering, Architecture, and Art—is stellar. The professors succeed in bringing out each student's creative problem-solving abilities in different ways. At Cooper, it wasn't only what I learned, but how I learned, and how I learned to think and analyze. The professors and administration actively reach out to their students. It's not uncommon for a professor to help a student in the evening or for faculty to attend a basketball game or a student performance. After my four years, I realize that the professors and administration really care; they are an integral part of the Cooper community.

As a high school senior, I was told by my guidance counselor to contact the deans and department chairpersons of schools that I would like to attend. I contacted quite a few schools, and I must admit that the attention I received from the chair at Cooper was exceptional. Since I had swimming practice after school, the chair set aside time at night to speak with me. I had mentioned that I wanted to visit the grounds over the weekend and the chair called me back a few days later to give me instructions on obtaining access to the buildings and gave me his home number in case I had any trouble entering the buildings. Early the following week, he called to ask me what I thought and to see if I had any questions. Consistently throughout our conversations, I could tell that the chair really cared about the students and the institution.

The Cooper community is quite diverse; the students represent different ethnic, religious, racial, socioeconomic, and geographical backgrounds. This diversity is represented in the multitude of clubs and organizations that represent the student body's various interests and range from ethnic and religious clubs, to professional societies, to sports, to special interest groups.

Peter Cooper's legacy lives on as Cooper Union continues to provide students with the unique opportunity of attending a distinguished full-scholarship small institution with all the benefits of the wonderful big city!

ADMISSIONS REQUIREMENTS

Admission to Cooper Union is highly selective. Most students, albeit bright, intelligent, and talented, when asked why they think they were accepted, will most likely say they fell through the cracks! However, deep down, we Cooper students know that each one of us was hand-picked for our special talents in our chosen field. The key to being accepted to Cooper Union is showing that you posses the skills and qualities necessary to excel in this first-rate academic institution, skills and qualities that range from talent, to intelligence, to motivation, to dedication.

Admissions requirements for each school vary; however, all applicants must take the SAT or ACT, complete sixteen to eighteen high school academic credits, and graduate from an accredited secondary school. In addition, engineering applicants must take SAT Subject Tests in mathematics I or II and physics or chemistry. Applicants must also complete an application with essays that enable them to describe themselves to the admissions committee. Art and Architecture applicants must complete a home test that shows their unique abilities to the admissions committee.

ACADEMIC LIFE

Cooper Union is comprised of these schools— Engineering (The Albert Nerken School of Engineering), Architecture (The Irwin S. Chanin School of Architecture), and Art, each offering an unparalleled undergraduate education. Cooper Union grants the following bachelors degrees: B.S., B. Arch., B.E., and B.F.A. The engineering school also offers a masters program in some areas of study. The engineering school has B.E. degrees in chemical, civil, electrical, mechanical, and interdisciplinary engineering. The art school offers a B.F.A. , which provides both a general visual arts education and a focused preparation for future artists and designers. The architecture school offers a five-year program leading to the Bachelor of Architecture, the first professional accredited degree. Cooper Union's engineering school is ABET-accredited, the architecture school is NAAB-accredited, the art school is NASAD-accredited. It is quite a challenge, although not impossible to switch between schools so you should choose wisely, and know that whichever school you study in, you are getting a first-rate education.

GREAT HALL

The Great Hall, "opened in 1858 . . . quickly became a Mecca for all interested in serious discussion and debate of the vital issues of the day." Since opening its doors many notable people have spoken from its podium, including:

- President Abraham Lincoln
- President Ulysses S. Grant
- President Grover Cleveland
- President William Howard Taft
- President Theodore Roosevelt
- President Woodrow Wilson
- President Bill Clinton
- P. T. Barnum
- Mark Twain
- Henry Ward Beecher
- Sidney Hook
- Mortimer Adler
- Jacques Barzun
- Norman Cousins
- H. V. Kaltenborn
- Orson Welles
- Malcolm Cowley
- Lionel Trilling
- W. H. Auden
- William Carlos Williams
- Dylan Thomas
- William Jennings Bryan
- Samuel Gompers
- Booker T. Washington
- Andrew Carnegie
- W.E.B. DuBois
- Victoria Woodhull
- Frederick Douglass
- Salman Rushdie
- Bill Cosby

Joint Program

In addition to the majors offered at Cooper, Cooper has a joint program with Cardozo Law School. This program offers students the opportunity to apply to law school in their junior year. If accepted, students can complete their first year of law school during the summer between their junior and senior years of undergraduate studies. This summer program is offered to accepted students at no charge provided the student continues to study at Cardozo.

Faculty

Professors at Cooper are scholars in their field who have graduated from excellent institutions worldwide—many even graduated from Cooper themselves! Aside from their academic merit, professors care about their students. Their relationship with students motivates and drives the students. For the most part, professors are easily accessible and ready to help. It's not uncommon to see professors in the halls on a weekend, or to e-mail a professor a question on a weekend and get a quick response. In fact, I was visiting my architecture roommate in the "studio" where all architecture students "live" during their Cooper years, and walking through this large room, with desk upon desk upon desk, was one of their professors ready to help if anyone needed it. One of my professors agreed to hold early morning study sessions so we could get a head start before the lecture, and hold study sessions in the evening too, so we could review and ask questions. Although this was not my best or favorite subject, his willingness to help motivated me to continue studying.

Fellow Students

Student relationships with one another also drive motivation. Due to small class sizes, students become very fond of their classmates; they are usually their study partners, as well as their best friends. As a freshman, I was told, the only way to survive at Cooper is to work with others—and that was true. So, I give that same advice to freshmen. Students at Cooper want to help each other. It's rare to find a student who will not share notes or help. After being sick, I returned to school to find that a classmate had already photocopied the class notes and put them in my mailbox. That's camaraderie! I fondly remember my study sessions with my peers as we worked hard trying to solve problem sets. Today they are my closest friends.

Throughout the three schools class sizes are extremely small, which helps foster the unique teacher-student relationship. Additionally, classes rarely have TAs, and if a class has a TA, the TA is only there to complement the professor and help. In my years at Cooper, I had only one TA!

Core Classes

Each school sets its own core classes for each major; the humanities department also has a set of core liberal arts classes required for each student, regardless of the major. These classes include literature classes and history classes. Additionally, students are required to take a certain number of elective humanities and social science courses. For some majors, humanities elective credit may be fulfilled with a language course. Cooper Union offers a wide range of language courses from the traditional French and Spanish to the more unusual Japanese or Hindu. Students may also participate in courses at the New School University. Although Cooper is not a liberal arts institution, it places great emphasis on the humanities and social science courses, and hires professors from prestigious liberal arts institutions to teach classes.

In the engineering school certain core classes are required for every engineering student, including: physics, chemistry, physical chemistry, calculus, probability, differential equations, computer programming, and design principles. Students are given the opportunity to perform research in such areas as chemistry, environmental engineering, and biomedical engineering. Art students must be proficient in such courses as drawing, color, two-dimensional design, and three-dimensional design. Architecture students are required to take such courses as design structures, mathematics, and physics. For some majors, electives within the major are required. Study abroad programs for summer and semester study are available for more majors and provide a unique and interesting way to continue studying your own discipline while exploring a new culture.

Graduation Requirements

The requirements for graduation in each school vary. Art students must complete 128 credits, including 38 liberal arts credits. The five-year architecture program requires 160 credits, with 30 in liberal arts and electives. The engineering requirements include 135 credits, with 24 credits in liberal arts and social sciences.

Since Cooper prides itself on a fair education for all, there is no grade inflation. If you graduate above 3.0, you are definitely in the minority. After a few tests, where the class average is only forty or fifty percent, you quickly learn that it's not the grade on your exam that matters, but what you will be able to accomplish with what you've learned when you are faced with challenges outside of the classroom setting.

Senior Project

Each school requires a senior project. Engineering senior projects range from designing an ethylene plant to designing a car, and anything and everything in between. Some of these projects are entered in competitions, and many receive recognition. Each art student is given the chance to display his or her work in a senior show. Students present work ranging from paintings, to drawings, to movies. In their fifth year, architecture students enroll in their senior thesis class, which prepares them for work after graduation.

With small classes, friendly helpful professors, plenty of research opportunities, and bright and helpful peers, the opportunities for academic growth are endless.

SOCIAL LIFE AND ACTIVITIES

It's true that the workload at Cooper is challenging, but Cooper students do know how to have a good time. I can honestly say I was never bored at Cooper—between academics, campus organizations, and exploring Manhattan, every minute was occupied.

Housing

The Cooper residence hall, home mostly to freshmen, with a few upperclassmen, gives students their first opportunity to build a community at Cooper. Friendships start in the dorm and last a lifetime. Housing is apartment-style with three-, four-, and five-person apartments. The dormitory has a recreation room where many organizations hold meetings, a study lounge with the Hall and Resident Assistant offices, and a laundry room. Ethernet access is available in all the apartments. Resident Assistants with extensive training are available in an emergency, or simply to talk. During the first few weeks of the semester, RAs help bring out the community within the dorm, and try to foster that throughout the year with various activities and meetings.

Like a rite of passage, after the first year, most students move out of the dorm into apartments in the surrounding areas. Some students venture into Brooklyn or Queens. Living off campus affords students freedom, but not without many new added responsibilities. Having your own apartment, paying rent, electricity, and phone bills can be quite an adventure, and a lot of responsibility too! But, it is a growing experience, preparing oneself for the "real world."

Activities and Organizations

Campus events and activities range from lectures, to plays, to gallery openings, to Greek parties sponsored by the various student organizations. Student organizations and clubs range from student government, to literary and artistic groups, to religious and cultural organizations, to Greek societies, to professional societies.

Every year, the South Asia Society, along with other ethnic and cultural clubs, organizes the Annual Culture Show, where student groups perform pieces representing world cultures, and there is also an international food fair, where students can sample food from different parts of the world. Donations collected during this event are given to UNICEF. South Asia Society also holds a Diwali Celebration for the Indian New Year with traditional Indian food and music. Hispanic Heritage night is a popular event sponsored by the Society of Hispanic Professional Engineers and !Enclave! Café Night, a relaxing night of varied performances from Cooperean and city residents, is sponsored by the Black Student Union. Also popular is the Soulsa Dance sponsored by Enclave and the Black Student Union, with Caribbean and Latin food on the menu. Kesher-Hillel, the Jewish Student Union, also draws a large crowd as it holds its semiannual Shabbaton to celebrate the Jewish Sabbath.

From the beginning of the year, many students look forward to Dean Baker's annual ski trip at Mount Sutton in Canada. Over a hundred students and their friends cross over the

American-Canadian border for a week of skiing and fun. This trip was so popular that the dean started an alumni trip during President's Day weekend.

The February Celebration is also a favorite among Cooper Students. It's the annual semiformal where students get the chance to dress up and dance the night away with their friends.

The Cooper Dramatic Society works hard to put on a performance each semester.

Greek societies usually provide a social outlet for students. There are two national fraternities—Zeta Psi and Tau Delta Phi—and one local sorority—Delta Eta on campus. Usually, there is one Greek-sponsored party on campus per semester. But the Greeks tend to throw off-campus parties too. Greeks sponsor events such as TechnoBowling, Chilli Night, and Lipsync.

Students appreciate the larger community and do give back to the community with penny drives, fund-raising activities, and various volunteer opportunities.

Athletics

Cooper students play as hard on the field as they work in the labs and studios. As Dean Baker puts it, Cooper students have: "No gym. No courts. No fields. No pool. No time. No money. No EXCUSES!!" Yet, year after year, Cooper receives many accolades for its athletic programs; Cooper teams and players have been featured in the *New York Times*, ESPN Magazine's *The List*, *Glamour* Magazine, and on HBO's "Real Sports with Bryant Gumbel."

There are both intercollegiate and intramural sports. There are five intercollegiate men's teams and two women's teams. There are twelve intramural coed teams. The basketball team makes its annual trip to California to play Caltech. Some home basketball games honor a graduating senior, and these games are followed by food and festivities. The soccer and tennis teams also draw small crowds of cheering fans.

Off Campus

Cooper Union is located in the best city—a city that never sleeps. Off-campus adventures can be exciting. The opportunities to explore New York are endless; trips to Chinatown or Little Italy can be culturally stimulating. Additionally, students frequent coffee shops, restaurants, museums, galleries, bookstores, movies, theaters, and concerts. There are farmers markets in Union Square, and street performers in Washington Square Park. Street fairs line the streets throughout Manhattan during the spring, fall, and summer. And, with New York's public transportation, you can be anywhere in just a few minutes.

> *"I wouldn't want to be anywhere else. I wouldn't be able to do all the things I've done at another place."*

—*Diana Santos, Civil Engineering Student*

FINANCIAL AID

Cooper Union is a private institution; however, thanks to Peter Cooper who believed education should be as "free as water and air," Cooper is tuition free. All U.S. resident students are admitted under a full scholarship, which covers the $27,500 tuition. However, there is an additional student fee that must be paid each semester. Students must also pay for housing (dorms or off-campus apartments), food, books, and expenses.

The financial aid counselors really help to ensure that students receive the most aid possible so that they can attend Cooper without having to worry about how they will finance their education. In fact, almost half of the incoming freshmen receive financial aid, and a substantial number of upperclassman receive aid. The average financial package is approximately $3,712. (Remember, each student also receives a full-tuition scholarship.) Aid is offered in the form of scholarships and need-based grants, loans, and work-study programs. Approximately one-quarter of the students work part time on campus, and some also work off campus. The average financial indebtedness of the 2006 graduate was $10,743.

GRADUATES

Students graduating from each school pursue different paths, but what's true for graduates from any major at Cooper is that upon graduation, they have attained the necessary skills in their field to conquer anything the future may bring. Cooper provides the basis for which all future possibilities are endless. Some students continue their education at Cooper and pursue a master's degree. Others enroll in other prestigious universities to pursue higher-level graduate education in the arts or engineering fields. Others enter medical school or law school. Many return to school for M.B.A.s after working for a few years. Some students begin applying their newly acquired skills and find jobs in the "real world."

Cooper has a career counseling department actively helping students find jobs upon graduation. Also, the Career Services department helps underclassmen find summer intern-

Engineers

○ Thomas Alva Edison, 1875–79, Inventor

○ Joshua Lionel Cowen, 1875–79, Inventor (Lionel Toy Trains)

○ Felix Frankfurter, 1898, Former Justice of U.S. Supreme Court

○ Daisy Brown, '04, Educator, First Black Female to Graduate from a School of Engineering in the United States

○ Arthur C. Keller, '23 Acoustical Engineer, Inventor of First Stereophonic Recording System

○ Dr. Albert Carnesale, '57, Chancellor, University of California, Los Angeles, past Academic Dean, Harvard University, Chief of the Defense Systems Division, U.S. Arms Control and Disarmament Agency

○ Richard Schwartz, '57, President and CEO, Alliant Techsystems, Expertise in America's Aerospace Program

○ Stanley Lapidus, '70, President, EXACT Laboratories, Inventor of Screening Techniques for Early Detection of Colon and Uterine Cancer

○ Dr. Russell Hulse, '70, Principal Research Physicist, Plasma Physics, Princeton University, Recipient of the 1993 Nobel Prize for Physics.

○ Thomas Campbell, '71, Founder and President, Coastal Planning and Engineering, Boca Raton, FL

○ Genghmun Eng, '72, Research Scientist, The Aerospsce Corporation

○ Angelica Forndran, '72, Chief of Engineering and Scientific Services, NYC Department of Environmental Protection

○ Dr. Barbara Schwartz, '74, Vice President, Future Development, Ethicon (a Johnson & Johnson Co.)

○ Marisa Lago, '75, Director, Office of Internal Affairs, U.S. Securities and Exchange Commission

○ Thomas Driscoll, '76, Director of Stock Research, Salomon Brothers, Inc.

ships and school-year internships; these internships will be valuable assets in preparing students for work upon graduation. During the 2005–2006 academic year, 100 companies recruited on campus and others recruited through the school's on-line recruiting system. Alumni are also active in the recruiting process. Many students find jobs through a network of alumni who return and recruit graduates. Alumni return each year to help in the annual Networking Dinner and Mock Interview nights sponsored by various professional societies and Career Services. Career Services sponsors the ever-popular Etiquette Lunch, where graduating seniors learn the art of interviewing while eating.

Those who do not find jobs right away may travel and explore new and exciting areas, others apply and receive Fulbright scholarships, twenty in the last six years alone. Some join various organizations helping others. One engineering student in my graduating class went to teach English in Japan.

As I said, for Cooper graduates the possibilities are endless.

SUMMING UP

Cooper Union in the heart of Manhattan's East Village is a small school with a community atmosphere. Its excellent teachers and wonderful opportunities provide its students with an unrivaled education. Its classrooms, labs, and studios are filled with top students who come to develop into top scholars in their fields, without compromising their social science and humanities education. In addition to the education, students are exposed to new and exciting people, cultures, events, activities, and experiences, which enable them to grow and learn socially. After graduation, the Cooper connection continues to help its alumni grow and develop in their major; the strong Cooper Union network of alumni helps students find job placement in the engineering, art, and architecture circles. As you can see, the name Cooper Union is the key to success in the art, architecture, and engineering worlds.

❑ *Dalia Levine*, B. E, Ch E

CORNELL UNIVERSITY

Photo by Charles Harrington

 Cornell University
Ithaca, NY 14853

 (607) 255-5241

 E-mail: *admissions@cornell.edu*
Web site: *http://admissions.cornell.edu*

 Enrollment

Full-time ❏ women: 6,729
 ❏ men: 6,786

INTRODUCING CORNELL

Whenever my schedule got way too crazy and it seemed like I wasn't going to make it, I took the time to put everything in perspective. Sitting at the top of Libe Slope and taking in the breathtaking view of Ithaca and Cayuga Lake, or standing in the middle of the suspension bridge and jumping up and down to make the whole thing shake while watching water cascade over the falls, was the best cure for anything that was getting you down.

When the name Cornell comes up in conversation, people who've been there usually exclaim, "It's so pretty there," and after a visit, it is easy to agree. Cornell sits on founder Ezra Cornell's farm, overlooking Cayuga Lake, in the Finger Lakes region of New York State. The campus covers 745 acres with classic ivy-covered buildings and contemporary research labs. Ezra Cornell's educational philosophy, "I would found an institution where any person can find instruction in any study," is the guiding force throughout campus where any person is free to found any organization, play any sport, practice any religion, and do just about anything they want without too much trouble.

Cornell students are proud of the fact that the university has been open to all kinds of students from the beginning. By 1870, Cornell was the first major university in the eastern United States to admit women. And Cornell led the way in welcoming students of varying ethnic backgrounds as well. The nation's first African-American fraternity, Alpha Phi Alpha, was founded at Cornell in 1906. In addition, Ezra Cornell was determined that Cornell graduates would enter the world both well educated and useful, accounting for the university's emphasis on a superb liberal arts program and equally outstanding applied programs in areas such as engineering, business, and agriculture.

○ A copy of the Gettysburg Address handwritten by Abraham Lincoln in 1864, one of only five copies in existence.

○ A vellum copy of the 13th Amendment to the United States Constitution, signed by Abraham Lincoln and members of the Senate and House who voted for the joint resolution, one of three copies known to exist.

○ A complete set of the Shakespeare folios.

○ The "Jade Book" of the second Manchu emperor K'ang-hsi (reigned 1662–1722), inscribed in Chinese and Manchu in blue and gold on ten tablets of solid jade.

○ A witchcraft collection containing 3,000 books and manuscripts, one of the most comprehensive collections available for the study of European witchcraft.

○ Five manuscript volumes of the famous Chinese fifth-century encyclopedia, *Yung-lo ta-tien.*

○ Cornell's Human Sexuality Collection, established in 1988 to record and preserve the cultural and political aspects of sexuality, one of the few collections of its kind.

In fact, Cornell offers seven undergraduate colleges: the College of Agriculture and Life Sciences; the College of Architecture, Art and Planning; the College of Arts and Sciences (the traditional liberal arts college); the College of Engineering, the School of Hotel Administration; the College of Human Ecology; and the School of Industrial and Labor Relations. Students in all the colleges come from a wide range of backgrounds, and from all fifty states and more than 120 countries. It's a high energy, eclectic mix that gives Cornell its distinctive flavor.

Libraries

The twenty on-campus libraries provide the best places for studying in whatever kind of atmosphere suits you best. The two most popular libraries are Mann and Uris. Mann is located on the Ag quad and is most frequented by students in Ag and Hum Ec. Uris Library is located on the corner of the Arts quad looking down the hill, affectionately known as Libe Slope. Uris can get pretty social at night, but within the library, the A.D. White Library, with its balconies and alcoves, provides a classic academic aura for studying. It's nice and quiet studying among the books in the stacks. The best-known spots in Uris are the Fishbowl and the Cocktail Lounge where wine isn't served, but wines may be studied.

ADMISSIONS REQUIREMENTS

Here's what it boils down to: If Cornell accepts you, you can make it. Every fall, thousands of applications pour into the Admissions Office. Over 28,000 students apply for admission to one of the seven colleges. The Undergraduate Admissions Office collects and keeps track of all the applications and, once they are complete, funnels the applications to admissions offices in each college for decisions. The Common Application and short Cornell Supplement are used in all the colleges (interviews and portfolios are required for some). An applicant's first encounter with the uniqueness of Cornell's colleges is at this stage when applicants must decide which of the colleges to apply to. For example, one can major in biology in both the College of Agriculture and Life Sciences and in the College of Arts and Sciences. In the Ag school, bio focuses on the natural world. In Arts and Sciences, biology can be studied with anything from classic civilizations to anthropology to linguistics. (Don't worry—internal transfer between schools is possible if you decide you don't want to study biology and want to try meteorology or theater arts instead.)

Requirements for admission vary by school and program, but basically excelling in any college preparatory course load in high school is a step in the right direction. The SAT or ACT with writing is required. SAT Subject tests are specified by college and division. AP credits are accepted but will count differently depending on your major and score, so don't think you're home free just because you got a 5. Applicants who go to small high schools that don't offer AP classes shouldn't be concerned about being at a disadvantage. Some freshmen arrive with fifteen to twenty AP credits under their belt, and yes, they will probably be able to start out in

The transition to Cornell was not easy. I knew that my classes were going to be much more difficult than in high school. For the first semester, I struggled a little and did my best. A number of my friends also found the course work challenging, but we stuck together and gave each other confidence. The foundation of support has led to great friendships, and these friendships are what make the Cornell experience so great.

higher level classes or maybe finish a semester early, but the majority of students have only a few, if any, AP credits and still graduate in good standing after four years.

Important Factors

One of the best things about Cornell admissions is that they look beyond the numbers. Special talents and leadership records are just as important as your SAT scores. Three percent of incoming students with an exemplary leadership record in high school are selected as Meinig Family Cornell National Scholars. Students who held jobs during their high school academic year may be selected as Cornell Tradition Fellows, an undergraduate loan replacement fellowship. In order to continue to be a Fellow, students must work, keep a certain GPA, and be involved in public service activities. Upperclassmen can apply to be Cornell Tradition Fellows in the spring of each year. The Hunter R. Rowlings III Cornell Presidential Research Scholars program is designed to recognize, reward, and encourage students who have demonstrated academic excellence and true intellectual curiosity. These scholars are assigned a faculty mentor in freshman year and are given special opportunities (some paid) to participate in research as undergraduates.

Interviews

Regardless of whether the college you're applying to at Cornell requires an interview or not, the Cornell Alumni Admissions Ambassador Network offers the opportunity for applicants to meet with alumni in their local area for a casual exchange of information.

The most important thing to remember is that if you get accepted to Cornell, the people who read the application believe you can make it and be a success. There's no need to change from the person you were in high school. Your record there led admissions officers to believe you would be a success at Cornell, too.

Regardless of which undergraduate college you technically enrolled in, you can take classes from every school on campus, and there's no need to search in order to find the popular ones. The legendary Psych 101, incessantly discussed in tours and information sessions, is held in Cornell's biggest classroom, Bailey Hall, with a mere 2,000 of your closest friends. Despite its size, Psych 101 is educational and interesting. Offered only in the fall, one class in the semester is a live demonstration of a psychic telling one student everything about his or her life.

When I took Psych 101, Professors Bem and Maas selected Mindy from the class for their demonstration. Four years later, I would still hear people say, "There's that girl from Psych 101." In a class of 2,000, who says you don't get to know your classmates? Interested? It's offered Mondays, Wednesdays, and Fridays at 10:10 A.M.

Other popular classes, though smaller in size, are Human Sexuality offered in Human Ecology, and Introduction to Wines in the Hotel School, which once a week offers an hour of tasting wines from around the world.

I would always see people carrying around these little black cases on Wednesdays. It seemed like they were everywhere. I had no idea what they were used for until one day, a senior opened up her case and I saw the three nicely packed wine glasses. From that moment on, I couldn't wait to have my own little black box.

Class Size

Cornell is big, and you have to accept this fact to be happy there. Classes vary in size, but in freshman year, you will most likely have a couple of classes with at least 200 people. Depending on what you are studying though, it is possible that you may never have a class bigger than fifty people. Popular intro classes, such as Government 111 and Chemistry 207, can easily have 400 or more students in the class, but, as you move into upper-level classes, the numbers get much smaller. Language classes and first-year writing seminars usually aren't much bigger than twenty students per section. Most large intro classes will also have a mandatory discussion section held during the week, led by a TA (teaching assistant) or the professor, with many fewer students, rarely over twenty-five per section. These sections provide students with a time to ask questions and get to know the teaching assistants. TAs can be very helpful and are usually very willing to meet with and help the students in their section. Being nice to your TA will come in very handy when you need help on papers or problem sets. Faculty are accessible and friendly too if you make the effort to get to know them. Don't be shy!

Degrees

There are seemingly, to quote late Cornell professor Carl Sagan, "billions and billions" of programs of study at Cornell. There are more than eighty majors at the university, and you can graduate with a B.A., a B.S., a B. Arch, or a B.F.A., or any combination. Bachelor's degrees are awarded to any field from animal science, and operations research, to ancient civilizations, textiles and apparel, and mechanical engineering. The largest enrollments (by major) are in biological sciences, applied economics, and engineering.

Believe it—you can major in anything and any combination of things you can find. Friends of mine had majors in classic civilizations, historic preservation, and linguistics and psychology.

Clearly, there are no boundaries to what you can study, even if it includes subjects that have never been put together as a formal major or your areas of interest are in more than one at Cornell college. That's one of the benefits of going to a school with a great deal of academic flexibility.

Required Courses

As for what's actually required of all students, the list is pretty short. Entering freshmen must take and pass the swim test, take two semesters of first-year writing seminars and two semesters of physical education. Now, there's no need to worry about these three requirements in the least. Seminars offered across the curriculum by the award-winning Knight Institute for Writing in the Disciplines are as varied as majors. Writing seminars are offered on such topics as:

- African-American Women Writers
- The Personal Essay
- From Fairy Tales to the Uncanny
- Contemporary Moral Problems

There are just as many phys ed classes to choose from to fulfill that requirement including the (extremely popular) ballroom dancing, tae kwon do, rock climbing, intro to ice skating, badminton, squash, Swedish massage, yoga, scuba diving, running, skiing, golf, and riflery.

Study Away

Getting tired of being on campus but think transferring is a little too drastic? It's easy to study somewhere off campus and still graduate on time. You can study abroad in more than fifty countries, such as Spain, Sweden, Australia, and France. Engineers can take part in a co-op program and spend a semester and a summer earning some serious money in real-world work experiences. The Cornell in Washington program gives students in any college the opportunity to live inside the beltway at Dupont Circle in the Cornell Center (a four-story building with three floors of apartments and one of classrooms and a computer lab), take classes with Cornell faculty and visiting professors, and have an internship in the nation's capital. Urban Semester gives students a chance to spend a semester in New York City working and studying.

One friend of mine spent a semester in Sweden and traveled all around eastern Europe. Four days after she got back for the summer, she headed to D.C. for an internship and stayed at the Cornell Center. I spent a fall semester with the Cornell in Washington program, and interned at PBS Online. Being from Maine, it was my first time living and working in a big city. I took the Metro to work and experienced what rush hour traffic really meant! Other cool D.C. experiences were seeing the lighting of the Christmas tree, watching Bobby McFerrin conduct the National Symphony Orchestra, seeing the AIDS Quilt laid out in its entirety on the Mall, and spending an afternoon at the Supreme Court talking with Cornell alum and Supreme Court Justice, Ruth Bader Ginsburg.

You can also spend a summer at Shoals Marine Lab on Appledore Island off the coast of Maine. Undergraduate students can earn a semester's worth of credit studying topics related to marine biology and ocean ecology, and participate in research projects—sometimes on the station's research vessel. Adventurous Cornellians also take part in archeological digs around the world and more locally in New York State.

Undergraduate Research

Cornell is one of the top research universities in the world, and hundreds of undergraduates participate in faculty research projects every year. It isn't hard to find a project. It can be as easy as talking with a faculty member after class about getting involved in his or her research. There are also structured undergraduate research programs on campus, such as the Hughes Program in biology or the research teams (such as Robocup) in the engineering college. Some students even get their names on research papers and present their results at conferences. It's a wonderful way to meet professors and other student researchers, and it looks great on your résumé!

SOCIAL LIFE AND ACTIVITIES

Housing

All freshmen have a similar first-year housing experience, living together in residence halls located on North Campus. Some returning students elect to live in residence halls on West Campus, but about half of Cornell students live off campus in sorority or fraternity houses, in Collegetown, and in the surrounding areas. There are a variety of off-campus options to choose from, from high-tech (and expensive) apartment buildings to three-story Victorian houses with six apartments that include oddities like oval windows, sinks in hallways, and sit-down showers.

CORNELL FIRSTS

- ○ Cornell's chimes, dedicated in 1868, were the first to peal over an American university.
- ○ Cornell awarded the first Bachelor of Veterinary Science in 1871, the first Doctor of Veterinary Medicine in the United States in 1876, and the first DVM degree to a woman in 1910.
- ○ Cornell granted the first Bachelor of Mechanical Engineering degree in 1871.
- ○ Cornell appointed the first professor of American history in an American university in 1881.
- ○ Cornell endowed the nation's first chair in American literature.
- ○ Sigma Xi, the national science honor society, was founded at Cornell in 1886.
- ○ Alpha Phi Alpha, the nation's first black fraternity, was founded at Cornell in 1906.
- ○ Cornell offered the first college-level course in hotel administration in 1922.
- ○ Cornell established the first four-year school of Industrial and Labor Relations in 1945.
- ○ Cornell developed CUinfo, the first campus-wide information system, in 1986.

I guess I was a little naive about housing because I had never really looked into it—I just assumed everyone lived in dorms for all four years. Once one person mentioned apartment hunting, the race began. Those of us not living in fraternities and sororities started finding roommates and looking for apartments. As I look back, I'm now thankful for the chance to live off campus. My folks helped out with the bills, since they weren't paying for Cornell housing, but I got a sense of what it was going to be like after graduation. Off-campus living was one of the most practical experiences I had at Cornell, which successfully prepared me for the real world of bills, rent, and late fees.

Parties

The university offers a lot of music, theater, dance, and films, but if you're looking for other social activities, trust me, you'll find plenty. As each weekend approaches, one is faced with an immense variety of choices. Since one-third of the campus is Greek (fraternities and sororities), there are always a collection of fraternity open parties, crush parties, after hours, and formals to attend. Fraternities are housed both off and on campus in just about every direction, so there is bound to be one nearby. Many other options exist outside of the Greek realm and cater to many different interests. Cornell supports more than 600 student organizations and clubs—and if you can't find one you want to join, you can create your own! In addition, Cornell's very extensive intramural sports programs will help you let off steam in competitions involving everything from giant slalom skiing to inner tube water polo.

Campus Activities

Just glance at the *Daily Sun* on Friday and you'll find a plethora of activities going on all over campus. On any given weekend, you can attend a concert, a varsity sporting event, intramural games, an ethnic festival, or listen to a speaker. Because of its size, there are always lots of people at whatever event you attend, and you'll definitely meet someone with interests similar to yours:

- Diwali, a celebration of the Indian New Year—"the festival of lights"—takes place every fall. It's put on by the Society for India and the Cornell Indian Association and features traditional Indian food and a performance of skits, traditional and modern dance, and instrumental music.

- In the spring, the Festival of Black Gospel brings famous gospel singers to campus and unites regional gospel choirs, like Cornell's own Pamoja Ni, in song and spirit.
- One weekend in every year, Lynah Rink is packed solid to watch the hockey team play their biggest rival, Harvard. Smuggled in under jackets and in shirts, fish of every size and color as well as some frozen fish sticks and lobsters become airborne when Harvard players skate onto the ice.
- Some years, Bailey Hall is packed with over 1,800 *a cappella* fans for Fall Tonic, the all-male Hangovers annual concert. Visiting *a cappella* groups who perform during Fall Tonic are undoubtedly amazed at the number of people at the concert and often mention that there are more people in the audience than students at their own school. We are dedicated fans and strongly support the groups or teams we enjoy!

Volunteering

Volunteerism runs like a raging river through Cornell as thousands of Cornellians find extra time in their crazy schedules to help others. The Public Service Center, mobilizes over 3,000 student volunteers each year in both one-time and ongoing projects. That's over 170,000 hours each year of service to the community. During Into the Streets, a national day of service, there are close to 500 volunteers who work with thirty local agencies. On that one Saturday alone, Cornellians do over 2,500 hours of service in the greater Ithaca area. Cornell's record of public service is one of the things that Cornell's president admires most about the university.

Movies

In the evening and weekends, Cornell Cinema offers at least four different films, playing either in the theater at the Straight (Willard Straight Hall, the student union) or in Uris Auditorium. Both are on central campus and are a short walk from any dorm or apartment. The movies can be classics that you never thought you would see on the big screen, movies that have just left theaters across the country, and foreign films. Every so often, the student film classes show their own interesting (and often experimental) work.

Sports

Sports at Cornell may not draw the television coverage of the Big Ten, but there are many teams doing an excellent job representing Cornell, and you have to admire student athletes for their hard work and hectic schedules. Hockey tickets are the only tickets that aren't free to students, and many games sell out. Cornell has varsity teams in basketball, cross-country, indoor and outdoor track, soccer, squash, tennis, polo, lacrosse, field hockey, rowing, gymnastics, and hockey. Known as the Big Red, Cornell teams are of championship quality.

FINANCIAL AID

Cornell's need-based admissions policy makes it affordable to attend. Paying for college is often a burden for a family, and Cornell's philosophy is that the burden shouldn't be one that kills you. About sixty-five percent of Cornell undergrads receive some form of financial aid. Students always gripe about financial aid, but on the whole, Cornell assists those families who really need help paying for college. There are also plenty of on campus and off campus jobs to be had as well as temporary jobs for crunch times.

The simplest way to think about it is this: If Cornell accepts you, they will find a way for you to meet your financial obligations. Financial aid packages are usually made up of some combination of grants, loan, and work study. Adjustments can also be made to your financial aid package during the school year if your family's financial situation changes.

Cornell's financial aid system is 100% need based. Cornell (and all other schools in the Ivy League) doesn't give merit or athletic scholarships. Cornell is also 100% need-blind when it comes to admission. Your need for financial aid does not influence your admission decision at all at Cornell.

The most important thing to remember is that paying for college isn't meant to be easy. It can put a strain on your resources. But you will receive a top-quality education, and as alums will tell you, the name alone will take you far in life.

> *My financial aid package was excellent. I was a Cornell National Scholar and came out owing only $5,000. But my parents made sacrifices and so did I. My mother went to work while I was in school to help pay for my college. (She hadn't worked before.) Yes, I was in debt. My take on it is this: Education's supposed to be hard; not impossible, but not a free ride.*

Need-based aid also gives Cornell the kind of diverse community it needs to be a great institution. The mix of income levels and socioeconomic backgrounds at the university makes it a truly interesting and stimulating place.

Work-Study

When parents think about paying for college, work-study is always on the top of their lists. Work-study is a great thing. Your employer only has to pay half of your wage; the other half is paid by the government. Therefore, employers LOVE work-study students, and there are usually enough jobs to go around. Granted, it may not be your dream job, but in most jobs, there is plenty of room for advancement, and your salary usually advances, too. If the job is in research or something related to your major, it gives you additional experience that makes you even more marketable once you leave. There's a student employment office to help you out, and job postings on CUinfo, Cornell's computer information system.

When I first started hunting for a job, it was the worst. Every place I inquired at was full and none of the available jobs fit in with my class schedule. It seemed hopeless. I called my mother in tears and told her I didn't want to be on work-study anymore. Then I found a job at the Undergraduate Admissions Office as an administrative assistant. The job had great (and flexible hours), and an understanding staff. I stayed there for the rest of my four years, became a student personnel assistant—which meant I hired and coordinated all the students for the building—and still had a job after taking a semester off to go to Washington. The job gave me excellent experience that I put to good use after I left Cornell.

During the senior class campaign, I found that many of my friends on financial aid were much more willing to donate to the university and to the scholarship our class was establishing than those students who weren't. Financial aid recipients are thankful for the assistance they received to come to Cornell and were willing to give back to Cornell at the drop of a hat.

GRADUATES

Friends who have had long hair since freshman year are getting haircuts and buying suits. Résumés are spilling off printers everywhere, and reality is starting to set in. What time is it? It's the fall of senior year, and recruiters are swarming over the campus. There are job fairs and information sessions every week, and everyone is talking about how to survive an interview. Cornell brings in recruiters from more than 700 nationally prominent companies and 160 grad and professional schools each year.

PROMINENT GRADS

- Adolph Coors, '07, Beer Baron
- E.B. White, '21, Author
- Allen Funt, '34, TV Personality
- Harry Heimlich, '41, Developed the Heimlich Maneuver
- Kurt Vonnegut, Jr., '44, Author
- James McLarmore, '47, Burger King Founder
- Ruth Bader Ginsburg, '54, Supreme Court Justice
- Toni Morrison, '55, Author, Nobel Prize Winner
- Janet Reno, '60, Former U.S. Attorney General
- Lee Teng-Hui, '68, Former President of Taiwan
- Christopher Reeve, '74, actor
- Pablo Morales, '94, Olympic Medalist

Of those who aren't interviewing for jobs, many of them are interviewing for graduate school. People are leaving left and right to go to med school, grad school, and vet school interviews—senior year of high school all over again, except much more intense. There's a breather after all the applications and interviews are over, but the decision letters start coming in the spring. There will be much rejoicing, but there may be disappointment, too.

In addition to the main Career Services Office, each of the undergraduate colleges also has a career services center where students can go for career planning and information, job search strategies, and advising. Cornell alumni around the world network with current students to help them find jobs and offer externships to sophomores, juniors, and seniors who want to experience the real world of work. Placement rates into medical, veterinary, and law schools are considerably higher at Cornell than the national average for other colleges and universities. Cornellians are definitely successful, and their years of hard work pay off well when they go job hunting.

Public Service Continues After Graduation

Cornell's record of public service holds true after graduation as well as during the undergraduate years. Cornell traditionally ranks in the top ten schools nationally in the number of alumni who are accepted into Peace Corps training. Many more work with AmeriCorps and VISTA in their postgraduate years. There are thousands of opportunities out there, and Cornellians are experiencing them every day.

SUMMING UP

Seven undergraduate colleges; 4,000 courses to choose from; more than eighty majors. After four years at Cornell, anyone is prepared to be a success in the real world. With the help of faculty and your fellow students, you'll find yourself evolving intellectually and personally throughout your years at the university into a person ready to take on any challenge. You may travel far after graduation, but you will always be a member of the Cornell family. The opportunities provided to you on 745 beautiful acres are unique and unlike those available anywhere else. Cornell has been called by more than one Cornellian, "the best place on earth to be."

Cornell gave me three priceless things. First, I got an amazing education. Second, I had a broad range of experiences that helped me grow into an independent adult. And finally, Cornell gave me an incredible bridge to the future. I will always look back on my days at Cornell with fondness and pride.

❑ *Laura Barrantes, B.A.*

DARTMOUTH COLLEGE

Photo by J. Mehling

 Dartmouth College
Hanover, NH 03755

 (603) 646-2875

E-mail: *admissions.office@dartmouth.edu*
 Web site: *http://www.dartmouth.edu/apply*

 **Enrollment**

Full-time ❏ women: 2,016
❏ men: 2,034

INTRODUCING DARTMOUTH

If you're thinking of going to Dartmouth, the only Ivy League school to call itself a college, here's a few things to expect:

- First, you'll love green eggs and ham (and the color green, in general).
- You'll be tempted to learn new languages and you'll probably study abroad at least once.
- You'll always be taught by a professor.
- Your summer vacations are portable. You can transfer your "Leave Term" to the winter to

avoid New Hampshire weather or compete for an internship in the fall and then return in the summer to study.

- If you learn to ski, you'll do it at the Dartmouth skiway.
- You'll wonder why every school doesn't have a version of "Camp Dartmouth" on a mandatory summer term.

Founded in 1769 by the Reverend Eleazar Wheelock for the expressed purpose of educating Native Americans and all those seeking education, Dartmouth is the ninth oldest college in the United States. It's also one of the most beautiful. Nestled between the White Mountains of New Hampshire and the Green Mountains of Vermont, the 200-acre campus has its share of picture-perfect scenery. In fact, visiting the campus for a commencement address in 1953, Dwight Eisenhower commented that "this is what a college ought to look like." Affectionately termed "the college on the hill," Dartmouth's central green is adjacent to the cozy town of Hanover, New Hampshire. On campus, brick dorms and administrative buildings are adorned with ivy, and Baker Library's tower presides majestically over it all. If you listen carefully, every day at 6:00 P.M. the bell tower plays a recognizable melody. Selections range from show tunes to Beethoven.

Dartmouth, however, has a lot more going for it than aesthetics. A bona fide "college" rather than university, Dartmouth prides itself on this distinction. The whole issue was decided in 1819, during the now-famous "Dartmouth College Case," in which Daniel Webster, class of 1801, successfully convinced the Supreme Court that Dartmouth should remain a private institution instead of becoming a property of the state of New Hampshire. In what is an oft-quoted line around campus, Webster summed up his argument by saying, "It is, sir, as I have said, a small College, but there are those who love it." From then on, Dartmouth has fondly referred to itself in the same way.

ADMISSIONS REQUIREMENTS

Dartmouth's admissions process is selective. Dartmouth saw the highest surge of applications in the Ivy League in a recent year, and of the 13,938 students who applied for admission, only 2,186 (more than fifteen percent) were accepted. The middle fifty percent of the class had scores between 1350 and 1550.

Admissions, however, is not based on book smarts or academic standing alone. What distinguished the exceptional applicants admitted from the thousands of other qualified candidates is intellectual curiosity, and academic or extracurricular passion, and an eagerness to be a positive member of a diverse and international community. In essence, Dartmouth is looking for students who will add to the community, inside or outside of the classroom.

Dartmouth has eliminated the college application and now uses the Common Application for admissions. There is one particularly unique supplement to the Common Application that Dartmouth requires, however. In addition to two teacher recommendations, you'll also need to solicit one of your more eloquent friends to write a peer evaluation. Dartmouth realizes that the best way to understand how you might interact in our community is to see how your peers in your own environment evaluate your contributions.

Alumni Interview

Conducted by one or more alums in the applicant's home district, this personal conversation allows the student to convey their interests in the admissions process in ways that a written application might not easily facilitate. Dartmouth does not require an interview, nor does it favor students who have one with alumni.

I am still convinced that part of the reason I got into Dartmouth was because I wore a green shirt to my alumni interview. This was completely unplanned, but because the interviewers thought I was totally gung-ho, our session got off to a great start. We talked about everything from Clinton's presidency to my SAT scores. I even told them I felt that I could chat with them for hours! Afterwards, one of the interviewers called me to congratulate me on doing so well. Dartmouth scored very big points with me that evening.

Early Decision

Finally, here's one more bit of advice. If you're completely psyched to go to Dartmouth, apply Early Decision by November 1. If admitted, you'll be finished with the entire college application process in time for the holidays. Keep in mind that the Early Decision admissions process is binding, meaning that you have to go if you are admitted. Although the percentage of applicants accepted for Early Decision is typically slightly higher than that of the normal applicant pool, the selection process is comparably competitive.

Despite three top-notch professional schools (the Dartmouth Medical School, The Amos Tuck School of Business Administration, and the Thayer School of Engineering), as well as twenty-four other graduate programs in the arts and sciences, Dartmouth prides itself on what seems to be an almost singular focus on undergraduates. Dartmouth students, consequently, have a unique advantage. Alone in the Ivy League, all classes are taught by professors with Ph.D.s, and not graduate students. Not surprisingly, Dartmouth consistently gets high rankings for its quality of teaching, as well as for the level of interaction between faculty and students.

The Dartmouth Plan

The Dartmouth plan is a unique year-round calendar that was instituted in 1972 when the school became coed—nearly thirty years ago. Dartmouth's academic year is divided into four ten-week quarters (called fall term, winter term, etc.), and students typically take three classes in each. This schedule works particularly well because not only is it difficult to get bored after a mere ten weeks, but students enjoy being able to focus on just three subjects at a time.

In order for the logistics of this to work out, students are required to spend at least nine terms on campus, including fall, winter, and spring of their freshman and senior years, as well as the summer between sophomore and junior year. Often a favorite term, summer allows for a less crowded campus, afternoons of studying outside in weather that's finally warm, and something called Tubestock where students float around the Connecticut River on inner tubes for the afternoon. Students then get to decide what they want to do with the other terms; choices range from staying on campus to doing a transfer term at another university to taking part in one of Dartmouth's forty-seven off-campus programs in nineteen nations. International destinations include Prague, Costa Rica, and Beijing, and sixty percent of the student body will go abroad at least once during their four years.

I chose Dartmouth in large part because of its Russian department, and spent the spring of my sophomore year on the Dartmouth Foreign Study Program at St. Petersburg University in Russia. We were in Russia at a time when the country was changing every day and it was an unbelievable experience to witness these changes firsthand—and to have the language ability to speak to people about how their lives were affected. After it was all over, I came back to Hanover and shared what I had learned with my classmates.

The year-round D plan is a ubiquitous force in the academic life of the college. Not only does it structure the length and duration of the classes, but in all honesty it makes students hyper-aware of how much their studies relate to the seasons. This translates into such attitudes as, "It's winter term and it's really cold and I'm going to study really hard." It's always funny to see how students pick and choose classes based on what term they're offered in. Summer term, generally, is a popular time for some students to take only two courses as opposed to the standard three.

Distribution Requirements

The other important academic policy is Dartmouth's recent implementation of a structured set of graduation requirements. As a liberal arts college, Dartmouth has a set of distribution requirements so that students are able to think critically in a wide variety of disciplines and make intellectual connections between them. Approximately one third of the thirty-five courses for graduation are spent on distributive courses across all departments. The second third of courses are usually within a major, with the final third used for electives. There is no core curriculum, so the program allows flexibility in choosing a course from a set of departments. The requirements can overlap, but are as follows:

- As always, students need to take a first-year writing seminar and demonstrate proficiency in at least one foreign language.
- Students also need three courses in world culture—one Western, one Non-Western, and one on culture and identity. A class such as Literature and Business (jointly taught by an English professor and one at the Tuck School of Business) satisfies this requirement, as do others dealing with such topics as computerized music or the current health care system. The final component of the new curriculum also requires ten classes in the following areas—one art, one literature, one from either philosophy, history, or religion, one deemed international or comparative, two on social analysis, one considered quantitative or deductive, two natural sciences, and one technology or applied science. Additionally, one of the natural or applied science classes must have a lab.

Finally, students are now expected to engage in a "culminating experience" within their major, which can take the form of an honors thesis, an independent study project, an exhibition, or a performance. These new requirements, albeit more extensive than those of the past, were set up with an eye to making sure that the curriculum really did reflect the liberal arts focus that Dartmouth so prides itself on.

> *When I realized that I needed to fulfill an art distributive, I wasn't sure what I was going to do. I'm not exactly artistically inclined, but I found the perfect class. I enrolled in Greek Tragedy, which provided a unique alternative. Instead of creating or studying art in the forms of paintings or sculptures, we studied the art of performance in Ancient Greece. It suited me perfectly.*

Faculty

Dartmouth has an incredibly strong faculty and student-faculty relationships are excellent. Classes for the most part are small. In fact, more than 75.5 percent of the 1,350 courses offered in a recent year had enrollments of fewer than thirty. Also, the most popular departments at Dartmouth tend to be the strongest, so you can expect to find a lot of history, English, government, chemistry, and language majors.

Foreign Language Program

One particularly innovative academic program is Dartmouth's unique approach to foreign language instruction. The brainchild of famed professor John Rassias, the program is designed to make students comfortable speaking their new language. Each day, in addition to a regular class period, students have a one-hour "drill," which meets at 7:45 each morning. (Those who can't hack the early hours can elect to take a 5:00 P.M. drill instead.) There, they meet with an upper-level teaching assistant who puts them through the rigors of conjugating verbs and practicing dialogue. The session, accented by liberal amounts of pointing and clapping on the part of the instructor, is incredibly fast-paced and lively.

> *Although taking—and then teaching—drill got me up at 6:30 A.M. for most of my college career, I'm convinced that Dartmouth is an ideal and nurturing environment for anyone hoping to learn another language. Hundreds of students flock to drill each day to witness Professor Rassias's unique "in your face" approach, which is probably part of the reason I fared so well in my foreign language classes. It gave me such a good foundation, in fact, that now I'm fluent in French, in graduate school for Spanish literature and education, and learning Italian in my spare time.*

Intellectualism and Special Programs

Another important part of the Dartmouth "character" is a continuing interest in intellectualism.

In keeping with this effort to increase intellectualism, a number of campus-wide programs have been implemented. In 1990 the Women in Science program began, specifically designed to encourage freshmen women who like biology, chemistry, or physics. (It was started after Dartmouth noticed the discrepancy between how many women arrived at Dartmouth intending to be science majors versus how many actually became science majors.) Thanks to the program, approximately 400 first-year women are paired with a faculty member to conduct "hands-on" scientific research. Another popular option is the Presidential Scholar Program, which was recently endowed with enough money to keep it a permanent fixture on campus. The program allows approximately eighty to ninety juniors to work directly with professors and assist with research. After aiding the professor for two terms, most Presidential Scholars complete a senior thesis on the same, or a related, topic.

As a Presidential Scholar research assistant, I had the opportunity to assist my government professor on an article he was writing about the timing of presidential economic initiatives. He involved me almost every step of the way, providing me with first-hand exposure to the correct methodology for conducting political science research. I am currently using this knowledge to further my own research on media coverage of women gubernatorial candidates. In fact, my thesis proposal on this topic was accepted at the Midwest Political Science Association's Annual Meeting, and I presented my results at their annual convention in Chicago.

Dartmouth also has a number of Senior Fellowships, usually awarding around twenty. Senior fellows spend their entire senior year doing research, and then complete a large-scale project—a book, film, or full-length production. (The big bonus here is that senior fellows get their own offices in the main library, instead of a lowly carrel where most honors students toil.)

Participating in the Senior Fellowship Program allowed me to study the life and work of a woman named Theodate Pope Riddle, one of the nation's first women architects. Because I was required to take only a couple of classes during the year, I had the chance to visit Riddle's buildings and travel to museums to do archival research. I also learned a lot from my advisor, a professor who specialized in architectural history. By the end, I had written a biography that was more than 200 pages long and produced an accompanying video documentary.

Research Funding

It's not just senior fellows who fare well with research, either. As students will attest, funding at Dartmouth for almost any sort of academic endeavor is readily available. Much money is doled out by the Rockefeller Center, named for Nelson Rockefeller, class of 1966. The center houses the departments of economics and government, and has financially supported everything from internships at the U.S. Embassy in Ecuador to research on Dartmouth's role in the Civil War. The center also draws a number of prominent speakers for panels and discussions. In recent years, it has hosted former Prime Minister of Israel Ehud Barak, chairman of the Pakistan Press International Foundation Owais Aslam Ali, Pulitzer-prize winner Laurie Garrett, and former Secretary of Labor Robert Reich, '68.

DARTMOUTH MAKEOVER

Thanks to a $27 million donation from John W. Berry '44, the Baker Library (the largest on campus) has recently been expanded by about 125,000 square feet. The Baker-Berry Library now has expanded rooms for books, maps, and manuscripts; a multimedia reserve room; new carrels and computer workstations; high-tech classrooms; and even a cafe. Five hundred new beds have been added in two new residential clusters.

Libraries

The final thing to know about Dartmouth academics is that students spend a lot of time in one or more of Dartmouth's nine libraries, which contain over two million printed volumes. Baker is the largest and is an architectural wonder. The wood-trimmed Tower Room is a popular studying spot, as is the reserve corridor, which is framed by the murals of

Mexican artist José Clemente Orozco. Painted between 1932 and 1934 when Orozco was the artist-in-residence, the famed murals depict the barbaric nature of the colonization of the New World. Dartmouth also has related libraries for biomedical science, math, business, physical science, engineering, art and music, and English. One thing to check out is the Sanborn English Library in midafternoon; every weekday at 4:00, students break for tea, cookies, and talk.

SOCIAL LIFE AND ACTIVITIES

"BLITZ ME"

Before freshman week is over, Dartmouth students are baptized into one of the school's most unique traditions—blitzmail. The Dartmouth version of e-mail, the on-line system is so incredibly popular—in part because everyone on campus is required to bring a computer or purchase one prior to matriculation. As a result, phone calls between Dartmouth students are virtually obsolete. Instead of phoning your friend to see if she's free for dinner, you blitz her a message. (The fact that the word *blitz* is used as both noun and verb could cause linguistic confusion, yet oddly it never seems to. Dartmouth students think it perfectly natural to get a *blitz,* and then *blitz* that person back.)

With everybody going to and fro so often, it might seem that Dartmouth would have a hard time fostering a sense of community on campus. Ironically, the opposite is true. Bonding begins early, in fact, before students even officially matriculate at Dartmouth. Over ninety percent of the incoming class elects to participate in a first-year trip sponsored by the Dartmouth Outing Club. Each group of eight to fifteen "first-years," led by an upperclassman, faculty member, or school administrator, take to the woods for three days of hiking, canoeing, biking, and rock climbing. There are few rules, but one remains firm: no showers. After the three days are over, students convene at the Moosilauke Ravine Lodge on Dartmouth's Mt. Mousilauke (still no showers) to practice singing the alma mater, learn the Salty Dog Rag, and pay tribute the Theodore Geisel, a.k.a. Dr. Seuss, class of 1925. (This is also where the green eggs and ham come into play.)

Dorm Life

Besides first-year trips, Dartmouth has an impressive network set up to unite incoming students. Organized by residence, each dorm floor has a U.G.A. (undergraduate advisor) who organizes movies and ice cream sessions, plus dorm formals and barbecues. Dorm life tends to be incredibly social during first year, although it undoubtedly lessens as the years go on. Surprisingly, however, even after first year, eighty-seven percent of students remain in the dorms. Many Dartmouth students are surprised to find that the dorms, for the most part, are far more spacious than other living quarters. More than one person typically would share more than one room, and private bathrooms (although not showers) are not uncommon. Plus, many have fireplaces, which is an especially appealing feature as you're living through a long Hanover winter.

As if freshman trips, hall-bonding, and a host of common interests weren't enough, there's one more thing that tends to unify a diverse group of undergraduates: a fondness for their school. Student satisfaction ratings are among the highest in the country, and tend to breed an odd phenomena: the "I-love-everything-that's-green-and-related-to-Dartmouth" mentality. At first, anyway, it seems exceedingly hard to find anything you *don't* like. Of course, Dartmouth students do not love it blindly. In the past years, issues of race and sexuality have sparked debates, as has the age-old issue of whether or not the Greek system should be abolished. And despite impressive numbers of students of color (they compose more than twenty-seven percent of the student body) and international students (they compose more than six percent of the student body), Dartmouth continually strives toward a communal balance of supporting affinities and interests with the institutional need of integrating students to enrich the intellectual discourse. As a perfect example, Dartmouth supports affinity housing (such as Cutter-Shabazz for students interested in learning more about African-American issues), but has the housing available to all students with genuine interest. Though Dartmouth issues reflect the issues in society, the sense of community yields a dialogue that is open and respectful. It is safe to say that Dartmouth students have a very real affinity for their school—not only during the years they attend, but in the years to follow.

Sports

More than seventy-five percent of the campus participate in either intercollegiate, club, or intramural sports programs. The athletic center's modern facilities include two pools, basketball courts, squash and racquetball courts, an indoor track, a weight-training room, a ballet studio, and a gymnastics area. Outside, there are tennis courts, an outdoor track, and the football stadium. Dartmouth also has its own skiway about twenty minutes from campus, and buses run to and from it six days a week during the winter. If you decide you want to ski, you can get a season pass to the skiway, a seasonal bus pass, and rent skis, all for about $200.

> *My skiing lessons were Tuesday mornings, and as I was headed up the lift, I always used to think how crazy it was that I was here skiing, when almost everyone else I knew was either in class or at work. Was I spoiled!*

Tucker Foundation

A host of other popular programs falls under the auspices of the Tucker Foundation, which organizes all the volunteer activities on campus. About one-third of the students devote time to programs like Big Brother/Big Sister, Adopt-A-Grandparent, Students Fighting Hunger, and Habitat for Humanity. To facilitate volunteering, the Tucker Foundation has cars that students can use to travel to their activities.

> *I see the Tucker Foundation as one of the moral and spiritual centers of Dartmouth. I volunteered as a book buddy, reading to and with a young boy, and then in the Adopt-A-Grandparent program, visiting a woman in a local nursing home. Both of these experiences taught me a great deal about the world beyond campus and also inspired me to spend a leave term volunteering full time. Funded by a Tucker grant, I worked at a legal services organization in Los Angeles. There I helped Holocaust survivors apply for reparations and counseled low-income people in need of free legal advice.*

In addition to organizing—and often funding— volunteer activities, Tucker is also the umbrella under which all the campus religious organizations fall. Most recently, Dartmouth dedicated the new Roth Center for Jewish Life, which will provide space for Jewish religious services, an annual Holocaust commemoration, and social events.

Racial/Ethnic Groups

Dartmouth students also spend a lot of time participating in groups organized by particular racial or ethnic affiliations. Groups such as the Afro-American Society, The Dartmouth Asian Organization, The Korean-American Student Association, Africaso, Al-Nur, La Alianza Latina, and Native Americans at Dartmouth all have large memberships.

The Dartmouth Rainbow Alliance, Dartmouth's gay and lesbian organization, also tends to be a vocal force on campus.

Publications

Working on student publications is also popular. *The Dartmouth*, said to be the oldest college newspaper in the country, resides in the same building as Dartmouth's AM and FM radio stations, which are completely student-run. The newspaper is supplemented by a number of specialty publications, including the *Stonefence Review* and *Snapshots of Color* (both literary magazines), *Sports Weekly*, *Easterly Winds* (the Dartmouth Asian Organization's publication), and *Black Praxis* (the Afro-American Society's publication). One recent interesting trend is the introduction of electronic magazines. Currently, there are two: *Sense of Place*, an environmental magazine, and *SANDpaper*, which is about the arts. *The Dartmouth Review*—the reason that so many outsiders mistakenly think of Dartmouth as a conservative bastion—is the mouthpiece of a small, but vocal few, but interest in it has been declining in recent years.

Campus Committees and Groups

Students also serve on campus committees, in the student government, and in organizations that try to educate the campus about problems that affect the Dartmouth campus, such as alcoholism, sexual assault, and eating disorders.

I was a member of SAFE, Students Against the Abuse of Food and Exercise. College-age women are so vulnerable about feeling that their bodies aren't good enough, and they fall victim to eating disorders. We wanted to get the word out that the campus has excellent resources, which include nutrition experts and body image counselors.

Many also sing in one of the eight *a cappella* groups on campus. For those who don't sing, attending their shows is a favored pastime. (About now, you're probably beginning to understand why that daily planner comes in handy.)

Hopkins Art Center

The Hopkins Center, or the "Hop," designed by the architect who was responsible for both Lincoln Center and the U.N., is the hub of the arts on campus. Interestingly, it's also the home of the campus mailboxes. They were put there, goes the rationale, so that students would be forced to take notice of all of the Hop's artistic offerings. Besides housing three departments (art, music, and drama) and a jewelry studio, the Hop has incredible films, plays, and concerts. In a recent term, for example, the Hop played host to:

- Ang Lee (on campus for the U.S. debut of *Crouching Tiger Hidden Dragon*)
- Wynton Marsalis
- Itzhak Perlman
- Oliver Stone

The hop also features movies; for a $20 pass, you could conceivably see about thirty-plus films per term.

Hood Museum

Dartmouth's other cultural center is the Hood Museum, which houses over 60,000 college-owned artifacts. The collection, which draws over 40,000 visitors annually, is particularly strong in African and Native American Art, nineteenth- and twentieth-century painting, and contemporary art.

Parties, Carnivals, and Fun

OK, so Dartmouth students are busy, you say. But do they have any fun? The resounding answer to that question is yes. Dorm parties are a big deal first year, as are Homecoming (fall), Winter Carnival (winter), and Green Key Weekend (spring). Each fall, it's the responsibility of the first-year class to build a big wooden structure in the center of the green—and make sure that it's still standing on Friday night for the big bonfire. On that night, there's also an alumni parade, many speeches no one hears, and lots of parties. Winter Carnival, perhaps Dartmouth's most famous social tradition, is complemented by a huge snow sculpture on the green, and for the very brave, a dip in the local pond.

Besides the dorms, fraternities, sororities, and coed houses there are central party areas. First-years are banned from houses during their first term, but after that, anyone can go to almost any party (there are few "closed" events on campus). No one joins a fraternity, sorority, or coed house until sophomore year, however, but those who do generally form close relationships with the people in them. The merits of the primarily single-sex Greek system are heavily debated on campus, although for the time being it seems to be here to stay.

For those who aren't into the Greek scene, there is a host of other social opportunities. The college often sponsors comedy clubs, hypnotists, concerts, and something called "casino night," which tends to be incredibly popular with the high rollers on campus. And, contrary to popular belief, people do date at Dartmouth. However, the on-again, off-again nature of the D-plan—you're there for nine months, and then gone for six—has been known to put a crimp in many a budding romance. Sorority and fraternity formals are popular date functions. Finally, right outside campus is the quaint town of Hanover, which has one good movie theater, a few bars, and a ton of reasonably affordable restaurants.

> *People always asked me what I found to do in Hanover, but the truth was, I was busy all the time. I loved the fact that my friends and I couldn't go anywhere particularly exotic: it made us all so much closer to one another. Had there been the distraction of a big city, I'm not sure I would have formed the fabulous friendships that I did.*

FINANCIAL AID

First, the bad news. Dartmouth is *really* expensive, as in, you could take a few trips to Europe and buy a new car for the price of going to school there for one year. Thankfully, though, there is some good news. Not only will Dartmouth meet 100 percent of your demonstrated financial need, but they have a need-blind admissions policy. That means your application is kept separate from your financial aid forms, so that admissions decisions are in no way based on how much you can or cannot pay. Basically, if Dartmouth wants you there, they'll make sure you're able to afford it.

In fact, approximately fifty percent of each entering class receives money from the college or other sources. These funds come in the form of grants, loans, and/or work-study. Just to give you an idea of what kind of figures we are talking about, the average scholarship grant for a recent class was over $28,000. Another interesting note: Dartmouth does not award academic, merit, or athletic scholarships. All aid is based solely on need.

Between my 10-hour-a-week work-study job in the cafeteria, student loans, and my family contribution, we were able to survive the first year at Dartmouth. The deal I worked out with my parents was that they'd cover the cost of the college bills not covered by loans, but books and spending money were my responsibility. I think it was a fair trade; they never sent me money, but I kept all that I earned.

Thanks to the fact that every incoming freshman is required to purchase a computer (or prove they have one compatible with Dartmouth's system), expect your freshman year bill to be particularly high but well worth the expense. Not only does Dartmouth have a good deal worked out with the computer company to get you really good prices, but it's virtually impossible to survive on campus without one.

Another thing that can complicate your financial future is the D-plan. Some students end up going to school for over a year without a summer break, and/or go abroad without having had sufficient time to earn extra money for the trip. Don't worry. A financial aid officer can work with you to increase your loans or scholarship for that time period, or figure out some other way for you to meet costs. Extra money is often allotted for students on financial aid to study abroad.

When I found out that my summer internship in publishing was virtually unpaid ($25 a week doesn't go far in New York), I had a meeting with my financial aid officer. Together, we worked out a schedule so that my loans would be a little higher for the coming term. I also spent two weeks in the spring working with Dartmouth's commencement and reunions. This gave me a lot of overtime, which was exactly what I needed.

GRADUATES

A few years ago, a rumor floated around campus that the average Dartmouth graduate makes $80,000 a year. While the figure was never completely confirmed, it's probably not far off base. On average, Dartmouth churns out large numbers headed for lucrative jobs in investment banking and consulting; recently, more than 200 companies looked to Dartmouth to recruit prospective employees.

Of course, not everyone from Dartmouth heads off to the world of big business. Medical school and law school are both popular options for many recent grads, as are M.A.- or Ph.D.-tracked graduate programs. In a recent year, about twenty-five percent of the senior class was headed right back into school. Additionally, by the time they've been out of school for five years, about seventy-three percent will have gone back to some school.

The working crowd, meanwhile, tends to be attracted to jobs in education, social services, advertising, and publishing. Others teach English in foreign countries or head off to parts unknown with the Peace Corps.

Even with so many varied directions , the one thing you can be almost sure of with most Dartmouth graduates is that they'll come back to Hanover at some point. Dartmouth has an incredibly strong alumni network, and Homecoming and reunions are always well-attended. The alumni magazine is one of the strongest in the country. Each class produces a newsletter several times a year.

Dartmouth graduates don't just stay in touch with each other, either. They also stay in touch with the college. Over two-thirds of alumni contribute to Dartmouth's alumni fund, making Dartmouth's endowment one of the largest in the country. Alums also keep up with recent graduates. Dartmouth's Career Services keep extensive files on alumni who are willing to be contacted about their jobs, and the networking connections are consistently strong. Dartmouth graduates tend to like their school, and like others who went to their school.

PROMINENT GRADS

- Salmon P. Chase, Former Secretary of State
- Louise Erdrich, Author
- Robert Frost, Poet
- Buck Henry, Film Director
- Laura Ingraham, TV Commentator
- C. Everett Koop, Former Surgeon General
- Norman Maclean, Author
- Robert Reich, Former Secretary of State
- Nelson Rockefeller, former U.S. Vice President
- Dr. Seuss (Theodore Geisel), Author
- Andrew Shue, Actor
- Paul Tsongas, Former Senator
- Daniel Webster, Orator and Statesman

Since I've been out of college for over a year, I'm surprised in a way by how involved I still am with Dartmouth. I recently attended the twenty-fifth Anniversary of Coeducation and was heartened simply by the sight of so many bright, articulate women who shared my alma mater. Dartmouth has exposed me to so many wonderful ideas and people that I'm realizing it's something I never want to give up.

SUMMING UP

If Dartmouth isn't the ideal campus, it's pretty much as close as you can reasonably get. With its northern location, year-round calendar, and focus on the undergraduate experience, Dartmouth is perhaps the most comfortable of the Ivy League schools. Its intimate atmosphere breeds some of the highest student satisfaction rates in the country, which is probably partly due to the fact that everything balances so well. Dartmouth students are some of the smartest in the country, but they also like to have a lot of fun. The Dartmouth community is incredibly close-knit, yet, thanks to the fact that different students and professors come and go each term, it never feels stifling. Hanover is a beautiful, rural locale, yet the school manages to attract first-rate speakers, performers, and intellectuals. In fact, you'd probably be exposed to about as much culture at Dartmouth as you would in any major metropolis. It's just that Hanover is a heck of a lot quieter. Student activities see high participation rates, but the school is small enough so that you never get lost in the crowd. And finally, the school has just enough surprises so that even when you're feeling stressed, there's always something to appreciate.

Finally, Dartmouth is an intellectual powerhouse that offers incredible on-campus and international opportunities. Besides those tangibles, however, Dartmouth offers something ineffable. As evidenced by the fact that everyone puts their arms around one another as they sing the alma mater, there is something very special about going to school up in the mountains. Perhaps, in fact, this appeal is best summed up by the alma mater's cryptic last line, which speaks to the permanency of the Dartmouth experience. Dartmouth students, it proclaims, find themselves with "the granite of New Hampshire in their muscles and their brains." Go to Dartmouth, and by the end, you'll understand what that phrase means. I know I do.

❏ *Suzanne Leonard, B.A.*

Photo by Billy Howard

 Davidson College
Box 7156
Davidson, NC 28035

 (1-800) 368-0380, (704) 894-2230
Fax: (704) 894-2016

 Web site: *http://www.davidson.edu*

 Enrollment

Full-time ❑ women: 843
❑ men: 840

INTRODUCING DAVIDSON COLLEGE

Founded in 1837 with the belief that a strong liberal arts education prepares students for lives dedicated to leadership and service, Davidson continues to instill a sense of honor and responsibility in each individual who passes through its hallowed halls. Retaining the highest degree of selectivity and scholarship, Davidson enrolls students with academic promise, strength of character, dedication to service, and an open-minded diversity of interests. Students exhibit enthusiasm for learning not only in the classroom, but also in the everyday adventures that shape a college experience. A single day may transport a Davidson student from reflections in a discussion-based Gandhi seminar to the neuroscience lab for cutting-edge research on Alzheimer's disease. After class, community organizations welcome students as mentors to local children and volunteers at a free medical clinic. And whether scoring on the Division I playing field or rolling kayaks on the lake, Davidsonians are constantly on the go, thriving in an environment that encourages vigorous and engaged learning both inside and outside the classroom. Although faculty, staff, and community provide an invaluable support network, Davidson students are independent, creative individuals who thrive on giving back to their community.

Situated on a 450-acre arboretum in a picturesque town of 7,100 residents, Davidson's ideal location draws a geographically diverse student body of approximately 1,650 students from forty-six states and thirty-three countries. Students celebrate opportunities for meaningful relationships and cross-cultural discussion. Close proximity to the booming metropolis of greater Charlotte balances the benefits of a small college town setting with easy access to all the cultural and professional opportunities that the city has to offer. The school's ideal location on Lake Norman offers a network of cross-country trails, and central access to both the mountains and the Carolina coast. In addition, approximately seventy percent of the student body will study abroad at some point during their Davidson career. Extensive travel, study, and service encourage students to reflect on their position as local and global citizens.

THE CITY OF CHARLOTTE

Charlotte's vibrant community allows students to retain a global perspective in their daily lives. Attending cultural events and professional sporting contests, and taking advantage of internship opportunities creates an ideal balance for students between their home base in Davidson and the resources of the city. Whether serving the greater Charlotte community of 1.3 million at Urban Ministries, catching a movie at the IMAX theater, or racing in the annual Reindeer Romp, students find themselves with plenty of opportunity to take advantage of all Charlotte has to offer.

Davidson's Honor Code serves as the foundation for a strong environment of academic and personal freedom. Take-home tests and self-scheduled exams enhance classroom study by combining an interactive, discussion-based classroom atmosphere with an evaluation based on knowledge and thought, not test-taking know-how. A signature on the Honor Code pledge represents dedication to a place where unlocked doors signify the immense trust that governs each interaction; through the Code students cultivate a unique sense of responsibility to the greater community.

My favorite Honor Code story happened in the Baker Sports Complex. Over my four years at Davidson, I swam laps in the pool in the Sports Complex each morning. I kept my goggles, swimsuit, and towel in a locker in the locker room and I never thought to put a lock on my locker. In the rush of graduating, I forgot to clean out my locker. When I returned two years later for Homecoming, I went to visit my old locker. Although a little dusty after two years, I discovered all of my belongings just as I had left them. Indeed, the most important aspect of my four years at Davidson was the Honor Code. There is an immense sense of freedom derived from living and learning in a community where you know that you are trusted and you know that you can trust those around you.

E. H. Little Library houses extensive resources including 591,325 volumes and an inter-library loan system that allows students to have access to virtually any resource their academic explorations may require. Periodicals number 2,788 and a comprehensive collection of journals is housed on-line, permitting students to access resources from personal Internet connections in their room or a library computer. High-tech music and art slide libraries complete with sound recordings, music scores, music reference works, multimedia listening stations, DVDs, and videotapes supplement the main library. The brand-new Sloan Music Center, complete with sound-proof practice rooms, electronic music and recording studios, and performance space complements the light-filled visual arts center and Duke Family Performance Hall. Students drawn to the sciences thrive in extensive research facilities and state-of-the art laboratories. Internet access is comprehensive, with two wireless facilities and personal Internet ports for each student. Nationally recognized for its careful roommate pairing system (welcome to the world of the Myers Briggs personality test), Davidson's highly residential campus houses ninety-two percent of the student body in doubles, singles, suites, and apartments.

ADMISSIONS REQUIREMENTS

Davidson seeks to gather an intellectually rigorous, well-rounded, open-minded community of learners with the highest degree of academic achievement and promise. In evaluating a student's application for admission, the Office of Admission and Financial Aid examines both academic performance and potential. Each application is carefully reviewed, with special attention paid to the rigor of the high school record, contributions to school and community, recommendations from teachers, counselors, and peers, essays, and test scores. Admission to Davidson is highly selective with about one third of the applicants earning a place.

Nearly three-quarters of first-year Davidson students have graduated in the top tenth of their high school classes, with a strong academic curriculum of at least sixteen credits (four English units, three units of math, two units of the same foreign language, two units of history/social sciences, and two sciences). Suggested high school courses may include additional courses in science, history, mathematics (ideally through calculus), and foreign language, with competitive candidates acquiring twenty academic credits during high school. The middle fifty percent of those accepted score 640–740 (writing), 650–750 (critical reading), and 650–740 (math) on the SAT; the middle fifty percent of ACT scores fall between 27 and 31. Standardized test scores continue to play a role in the admission process but are not used as a single factor in the decision-making process. While SAT Subject Tests are not required, they are recommended, with one in mathematics and one other of your choice strongly encouraged.

Students may receive credit for AP classes with a score of a 4 or a 5 in the academic areas (or a 3 in Calculus AB and BC) or for A-level examinations in the International Baccalaureate Program.

An important factor in the evaluation of a student's high school curriculum is the amount of rigor present. While a strong GPA certainly plays a role in the evaluation process, course choice has significant impact on the evaluation of the application. Strong applicants also demonstrate a loyal commitment to school and community activities. As an applicant approaches the Davidson admission process he or she should understand that admission counselors seek not only academic motivation and potential but also personally compelling students who will contribute significantly to the Davidson community both inside and outside the classroom. Thus, in addition to placing emphasis on academics, each admission counselor works to evaluate the whole person in areas including leadership, personal character, service, and motivation. Personal recommendations often contribute keen insight to this side of the admission process. In an ever-increasingly diverse society, counselors are also aware of students who represent diverse ethnic, cultural, economic, and religious backgrounds as well as evaluating the differences among secondary schools.

Davidson's highly personalized approach in the admission process was essential in my decision-making process. The obvious care and attention played not only a significant role in my visit to campus but my final decision to attend. Faced with several options, I wrestled for days until a personal phone call from an admission counselor. The fact that the school cared enough to check in with me during perhaps the most important decision of my life sealed my already strong gut feeling that among all my choices, Davidson was different—not only a place where I could receive a stellar education but one where I would be encouraged to reach for the highest personal ideals as well. I've yet to be disappointed.

Decision Plans

Because first-year students are admitted for the fall semester, standardized tests should be taken no later than January of the senior year. Students are welcome to apply to Davidson under either one of the two Early Decision Plans or under Regular Decision. Both Early Decision Plans are binding, and therefore, students who make Davidson their first choice are encouraged to apply. Early Decision candidates should take standardized tests no later than October of their senior year. The first Early Decision deadline is November 15, with notification in mid-December. The second Early Decision Plan deadline is January 2, with notification in early February. A requirement of the Early Decision plan is the Early Decision candidate's agreement stating that Davidson is the student's first choice and if accepted he or she will enroll and withdraw any other applications from other colleges and universities. The Regular Decision plan requires that students submit application materials to Davidson no later than January 2; admission decisions are mailed by the first week of April. In addition to accepting its own application, available in both a paper and electronic form, Davidson encourages the use of the Common Application, provided the student completes the necessary supplementary information.

Campus Visits

Although Davidson does not require a campus visit for admission, it is strongly recommended. Sometimes the deciding factor in the college decision, the campus visit provides valuable insight to a student's process and allows him or her to have direct contact with members of the Admission and Financial Aid staff. The Office is open from 8:30 A.M. to 5:00 P.M., Monday through Friday, and selected Saturdays throughout the year. Students are encouraged to call and schedule an appointment ahead of their visit. Tours and information sessions are offered daily in both group and individual settings.

Prospective applicants are welcome to visit classes and encouraged to have conversations with faculty, coaches, and current students. Seniors are invited to stay overnight in the residence halls on selected evenings. To schedule time on campus, please call the Office of Admission and Financial Aid at least one week prior to your planned visit.

ACADEMIC LIFE

Dedicated to a traditional liberal arts and sciences curriculum combined with the most up-to-date methods in research and technology, Davidson's academic strength lies in an inter-disciplinary course of study. Students, motivated by strong ambition and inspiring faculty, choose from a myriad of academic opportunities. With special emphasis placed on writing, analytical and critical thinking, and eloquent communication skills, classroom learning extends beyond the traditional college lecture into a rare undergraduate experience of intellectual discourse.

A strong core curriculum encourages students to choose initial courses in literature, foreign language, writing, history, natural sciences, mathematics, social science, religion and philosophy, and fine arts. In addition, a cultural diversity and physical education requirement remind students of Davidson's dedication to the whole person. Thorough and rigorous examination of each area in a discussion-based environment affords students the opportunity to not only strengthen their academic foundation, but also discover new areas of intellectual pursuit. Flexibility and individualized guidance characterize an advising system that works with students from orientation to postgraduation. Cutting-edge research gives students a competitive margin over their counterparts with exposure to graduate study technique and methods in a fully undergraduate environment.

At Davidson, learning is approached as a lifelong endeavor, placing great importance of molding students into global citizens with the skills to lead in whatever field they choose to pursue after graduation. Challenging the mind and engaging the heart make Davidson's classroom environment a unique and highly stimulating place to pursue academic study. The results are priceless; not only do students leave with an exceptional liberal arts education, but they are highly sought after by businesses and graduate, and professional schools, and regarded as some of the most highly competitive candidates in the workplace and beyond. Davidson students truly are the "go-to" leaders in their communities.

● ●

Students choose their major from twenty-one disciplines by the end of their sophomore year, with the possibilities of double majoring or minoring in a second area.

Concentrations provide the opportunity to pursue more specific interests through interdisciplinary study in an area such as Gender Studies, Applied Mathematics, Computer Science, Genomics, and International Studies. In addition to the strong traditional liberal arts curriculum, Davidson offers students the opportunity to engage in professional programs in the areas of Prelaw, Premedicine, Preministerial, Education, and the dual degree Engineering Program.

CENTER FOR INTERDISCIPLINARY STUDIES

The Center for Interdisciplinary Studies offers students the opportunity to develop individualized courses with faculty or design their own interdisciplinary majors in areas such as: International Development Studies, Computational Genomics, Film and Media Studies, Peace Studies, Neuroscience, Biophysics, Poverty and Development, Environmental Policy, Gender Issues in Reproductive Health, Medical Humanities, Bioethics, and Contemporary German Studies. Interdisciplinary seminars and tutorials are also offered through the Center.

Faculty

Although some students will tell you that the most passionate intellectual discussion often takes place at 3:00 A.M. in the residence halls, an outstanding faculty is truly the core of what makes Davidson a premier institution of higher education. Noteworthy achievements and credentials aside, the most exceptional characteristic of each faculty member is an absolute passion for and dedication to undergraduate learning. Full professors in each classroom (ninety-eight percent of whom hold Ph.D.s in their area of study) facilitate learning in a dynamic discussion-based environment. The absence of teaching assistants and graduate students creates an atmosphere of engaging intellectual challenge that encourages students to pursue their interests to the highest degree.

Individual attention heightens the effectiveness of Davidson's average class size of fifteen students, with some seminars numbering as few as five. Independent research projects ground students in a practical experience, which few of their counterparts at larger colleges and universities can boast; students geared toward graduate study and other postgraduate pursuits benefit greatly from an in-depth approach to study alongside accomplished faculty scholars.

Open office hours, meetings held at the local coffeeshops, and faculty and staff who serve as activity advisors fully incorporate educators into the Davidson student life. Students find their professors accessible and eager to engage their minds in the current issues of the day and the past events that have shaped history. A student-to-faculty ratio of 11:1 ensures highly personalized attention with relationships that often stretch beyond the classroom walls. Several students note professors' willingness to open up their homes for dinner discussion and advising meetings. From the moment students set foot on campus their Davidson experience is shaped with the help and insight of a faculty advisor. Each works to ensure success from class selection to the graduate study that eighty-five percent of alumni undertake at some point.

I arrived at Davidson with the study skills to make the grade; I left with a fiery passion for the written word. My advisor was not only an accomplished scholar in her chosen area of study but a true mentor who listened, challenged, and led me in an intellectual journey to push toward the outer reaches of my potential.

STUDY ABROAD

In addition to a plethora of options available through agreements with other colleges, universities, and international programs, several students choose to study on one of Davidson's own programs: fall semester in India and Nepal; year or semester in Tours, France; year in Wurzburg, Germany; summer in Cambridge, England; summer at The University of Cape Coast, Ghana; summer premed program in Kikuyu, Kenya; summer program in Mwandi, Zambia; summer archeological dig in Cyprus; summer in Moscow, Russia; summer in Monterey, Mexico; spring semester in Classical Humanities in Greece, Sicily, Italy

Off-Campus Study Programs

In a community where a global perspective is valued, seventy percent of students are eager to pursue a portion of their studies abroad. Davidson sponsors a wide variety of programs, taking students from the monasteries and museums of India and Nepal to the storied history of Cambridge University and over to Kenya for medical studies and volunteer work. Although Davidson programs span the globe, students are permitted to enroll in non-Davidson programs through the Office of Study Abroad, an important part of the Dean Rusk International Studies Program. The Dean Rusk International Studies Program, named for former Secretary of State and Davidson graduate Dean Rusk, supports a wide variety of international opportunities both on and off campus. Throughout the year, the community is enriched by visits from international speakers and government officials and conferences organized through the Dean Rusk Program. A generous monetary pool also allows students to dream up independent global adventures and academic experiences with more than $35,000 in grants given annually for international pursuits.

SOCIAL LIFE AND ACTIVITIES

Davidson students' only limitation to the pursuit and cultivation of their passions is the short twenty-four hours in each day. Building on a diverse array of interests and talents, the Davidson student body dedicates time and energy to lead over one hundred student organizations. Active in a variety of ways, students learn not only the importance of community involvement, but effective leadership skills through involvement in student government policy, campus life, the organization of campus events, and promotion of social causes and multicultural interests.

Supported by outstanding facilities, student activities and gatherings are enhanced by the recently opened Alvarez College Union. Fueled by a constant buzz of activity, this student haven boasts a twenty-four hour a day workout facility, a rock-climbing wall (part of the popular Davidson Outdoors organization, which hosts a variety of trips and training sessions in everything from hang gliding on North Carolina's Outer Banks to skiing in West Virginia to canoeing in the Everglades), the Duke Family Performance Hall (which hosted the Royal Shakespeare Company in an ongoing campus residency), and a cafe and grill open to students and the surrounding community. The Union Board works to keep minds engaged outside the classroom with recent speakers including: Gloria Steinem, Cornel West, Marian Wright Edelman, Jane Goodall, and Annie Proulx. Music enthusiasts also find a haven in the concert committee, active in not only bringing local acts to campus but also supporting diverse acts from Ludacris to Counting Crows. Tuesday nights the infamous 900 Room opens its bar for the beloved "Twenty-One-Year-Old Night" and the Friday Afternoon Club brings faculty and students together for casual interaction outside the classroom. Both the *Davidsonian* and *Libertas,* Davidson's premier publications, hold offices in this space. From an active SGA that governs everything from the tax activities council to the Vamonos Van, students have endless opportunities for involvement.

Perhaps the best thing about Davidson is not the opportunities that already exist, but those that you, with a little determination and creativity, create on a daily basis. As a prospective student I searched out female a cappella groups on each campus I visited. Although Davidson was the only campus without an existing group, I wasn't deterred. By the end of my freshman year The Davidson Delilahs were headlining concerts alongside the established male a cappella group and by midway through my junior year I was working in a recording studio on our first CD!

SAMPLES OF DAVIDSON STUDENT ACTIVITIES

Club Sports, College Democrats and Republicans, Davidson Outdoors, Prelaw Society, Premedical Society, Phi Beta Kappa, Organization of Latin Students (OLAS), AIDS Project, Amnesty International, GSA (Gay-Straight Alliance), Gender Resource Center, Jewish Student Union, Catholic Campus Ministries, Reproductive Rights Alliance, Model United Nations, Mock Trial, *Hobart Park* (literary magazine), WALT (radio station), Interfaith Fellowship, Honor Council, Symphony Orchestra, Peace Dialogues, Davidson Dance Troupe, etc.

Patterson Court

Comprised of thirteen houses, the self-selecting Patterson Court social system is unique to Davidson College. Unlike a traditional Greek system, students join houses through a self-selecting process that invites each student to spend time in the houses before choosing membership in an organization. The majority of houses (seven national fraternities for the men and four eating houses for the women) are single-sex, with two of the houses offering open membership to both sexes (one coed house and the Black Student Coalition). Houses offer the opportunities for social interaction, shared meals, and service projects. The houses also support court-wide projects such as the annual Project Life Pasta Dinner (to benefit Bone Marrow Transplants) and the recent Habitat for Humanity Gala (in conjunction with the Union Board and several other campus organizations to support a Davidson College Habitat House). About seventy percent of the women and forty percent of the men choose to join a house.

Music and Theater

Bolstered by state-of-the-art facilities in both music and theater, the performing arts enjoy great popularity at Davidson. Supported by brand-new facilities, Students gain valuable performing experience through active participation in the writing, directing, and producing of theatrical productions. An annual visiting Artist Series and plethora of events enhance the cultural community. Through ensembles, performances, lectures, individual instruction, and academic courses, the theater and music departments provide both the college and the community with invaluable resources that strengthen the human spirit and intellect. Whether jamming with a group of friends on your freshman hall or listening to the *a cappella* concerts under the stars, participating in an opera workshop, or performing in the improv comedy group, there is a hardly a student that remains untouched by the vibrant cultural pulse of these departments.

Community Service

Davidson's commitment to community service is reflected in the twenty-six student-run programs that comprise United Community Action. From day one, the Freshman Service Experience introduces students to service in and around the Davidson community with a focus on poverty, the environment, children, and senior citizens. Reflecting the diversity of the student body, opportunities range from scaling roofs with Habitat for Humanity, translating for recent immigrants at a local medical clinic, and working with CROP to organize an annual hunger-awareness week. Four annual grants for environmental service and summer programs total upwards of $75,000 to make student projects a reality.

Athletics

Success and high levels of performance stretch beyond the classroom walls to the Division I playing field. Twenty five percent of Davidson students engage in rigorous competition with the same tenacity that they approach their academic studies. Davidson students balance their hard work with fierce efforts on the fields; eighty percent are involved in athletics at either a club or intramural level. Size doesn't stunt the high level of performance students bring to the playing field, evidenced by the thirteen conference championships captured by Davidson varsity teams in the past

PROJECT LIFE

Project Life was formed in 1989 by a group of students honoring a friend who had a bone marrow transplant. This exemplary Bone Marrow Registration program enables the typing of all new students through the raising of $25,000 annually. In thirteen years, Davidson has added over 4,000 names to the national registry, with at least eighteen matches as a result. Project Life serves as a model program for other colleges.

five years. Often pitted against larger universities, Davidson succeeds in not only making the Division I experience a reality but coupling it with the finest academics around.

FINANCIAL AID

As an institution that practices need-blind admission, Davidson is committed to making education affordable to all qualified applicants, thereby supporting a diverse community from which all students benefit. In accordance, all application decisions are made without regard for a student's financial situation.

Davidson offers both need-based and merit-based financial aid to its applications. Approximately one third of the student body receives some sort of need-based aid, usually in the form of grants, loans, and work-study positions. At the heart of Davidson's financial aid philosophy is a desire to keep loans as low as possible, while making a Davidson education a reality. Financial aid is renewable each year, provided that students stay on track for their degree, and their family's financial situation does not change significantly.

To apply for financial aid, applicants will complete the College Scholarship Service/Financial Aid PROFILE Application and the Free Application for Federal Student Aid (FASFA). These forms are available through high school guidance offices and Davidson sends these forms to each applicant. The timetable for need-based aid is as follows:

| Early Decision: | CSS/Financial Aid PROFILE Application | November 15 |
| Regular Decision: | CSS/Financial Aid PROFILE Application | February 15 |

Merit scholarships are also available in varying dollar amounts to stellar applicants, regardless of need. Characteristics including outstanding academic and leadership potential, ability, character, and potential contributions to the Davidson community all play a role in the selection process. No application is necessary for general merit aid. A small pool of special application scholarships recognize excellence in specific academic and art areas that require the submission of a portfolio, writing sample, or an audition or interview, which take place during Scholars Weekend in April.

I currently work for a hedge fund based in Hong Kong that makes investments across the Asia-Pacific region. My coverage countries include Thailand, Indonesia, and the Philippines, so I visit those countries often to evaluate investment opportunities for the fund. I love my job for a lot of reasons but mainly because I learn an outrageous amount every day about a part of the world that is new to me. My goal is to go to business school, then eventually create a unique hybrid organization that will target world problems using the for-profit incentive. As I reflect on my time at Davidson, I realize I had so much fun that I actually feel secretly guilty that they let me hang out there for four years. No kidding.

In an increasingly educated and specialized society, some question the value of a liberal arts education; citing the pressure to specialize in one single track, thereby imaginably increasing their marketability in the professional world. At Davidson, the community remains fiercely loyal to the ideals of a liberal arts education, which allows students to not only build skills in a highly focused area but also attain a broader foundation that makes them both versatile and desirable in today's society.

To ask what the "typical" Davidson graduate pursues in his or her post-Davidson life is to open a floodgate; graduates pursue innumerable paths but share the common motivation not only to reach for the highest realms of the professional world but also to give back to the community. Although popular professional paths center on traditional fields such as medicine, law, and business, a strong number of students also pursue the ministry, academia, and nonprofit fields. Graduates are often known as the "go-to" people in their communities, emerging as leaders and facilitators—they are the people who others look to in order to get things done. With strong writing and communication skills, extensive leadership experience, and a vested interest in their communities, Davidson alums find themselves recruited by the top organizations in a spectrum of industries. A rich history of graduate fellowships also paves the way for students (twenty three Rhodes Scholars!) to make possible the continuation of their studies at the graduate level.

An extensive alumni network and access to a shared job database allows students maximum exposure to opportunities for internships and jobs both during their Davidson experience and in their postgrad lives. Beginning in the freshman year and continuing through graduation, Career Services plays a significant role. Offering career workshops, alumni panels, and professional job fairs throughout the year increases the exposure students have to the working world and allows them to explore various fields while still under the guidance of the professional Career Services Staff. In addition, the extensive and varied experience of the faculty lends itself to concrete career advising.

Fortunately for current students and the institution, Davidson alums are passionate about their alma mater and are notorious for their willingness to help fellow Davidson graduates explore different career and life paths. A Davidson connection is one of the strongest a graduate can have and a strong ally in an anonymous world.

SUMMING UP

Davidson's application asks two simple short answer essay questions. The first deals with its foundation: the Honor Code. The second cuts straight to the heart of it all: Why Davidson? Why, after all the colleges and universities you have explored; why, when there are so many fine institutions of higher education available to you; why will you choose Davidson? The answer? It is not in the million dollar facilities for art, sciences, and athletics. It is not in the fully wired network that allows students access to equipment, materials, and facilities rare at institutions ten times our size. It is not even the fact that Davidson does your laundry (although, admittedly, that doesn't hurt . . .).

It is the people. At the true heart of what makes Davidson unique is the community. There is no question, from the staff that rise before the sun to the students who dance until dawn, that the individuals that Davidson draws from all over the country are unique. Without these extraordinary human beings, dedicated to "lives of leadership and service" the physical beauty of the Davidson campus would be just that, fleeting, ephemeral, and empty. With these individuals, Davidson becomes a remarkable microcosm of society in which people truly believe that they can make a lasting difference in the lives of others.

Grounded in the ideals of Honor Code and anchored in a tremendously talented faculty, Davidson retains simple, basic values that embrace a commonality of spirit and celebrate the differences of each individual. *Let learning be cherished where liberty has arisen* continues to serve as Davidson's motto and perhaps even more true for those who have studied in its halls, liberty arises through the mind-opening collaboration and challenge this dedicated group of scholars brings to daily life.

As a student who didn't know a whole lot about Davidson before visiting, I sometimes wonder what life would have been like had I stayed on my New England-centered path in the college search. The thought that I would have chosen otherwise makes me more than grateful that Davidson entered my life when it did. Simply put: Davidson is different. Without hesitation I wholeheartedly encourage you to seriously consider Davidson, but be forewarned—it may just change your life.

❏ *Page Neubert, A.B.*

DUKE UNIVERSITY

Photo by Les Todd

 Duke University
Durham, NC 27708

 (919) 684-3214
Fax: (919) 681-8941

 E-mail: *undergrad-admissionse@duke.edu*
Web site: *http://www.duke.edu*

 Enrollment

Full-time ❑ women: 2,977
❑ men: 3,267

Part-time ❑ women: 32
❑ men: 27

INTRODUCING DUKE

If Duke University's location in Durham, North Carolina, conjures up images of a staid institution in a lethargic southern town, a closer examination of Duke will change those impressions. Set in the middle of the state, this 8,000-acre campus exudes the energy and entrepreneurial spirit of the Research Triangle Park area, Duke's home. Just as the region is a relatively recent hotbed for economic development and growth, Duke is a relatively young university that pulses with activity and enthusiasm.

Complemented by eight graduate and professional schools, Duke's Trinity College of Arts and Sciences and the Pratt School of Engineering have climbed to the top tier of undergraduate programs.

There is a sense on campus that the best is yet to come. That expectation translates into energetic students and faculty pouring themselves into bettering the university and themselves.

Duke is an institution full of surprising and pleasant contrasts. The most dramatic and immediately apparent contrast is the widely divergent architecture of Duke's West and East Campuses. West Campus features the soaring 210-foot-tall chapel framed by Gothic buildings, creating an inspiring picture of intense academic pursuit.

On the other hand, the Georgian architecture and long, lush lawns of the East Campus convey a sense of relaxation and peace. Weekends on East are often filled with outdoor concerts, Frisbee on the quad, and sunning students.

In the same way that the architectural styles of the campuses work together to create a magnificent place to grow academically, emotionally, and spiritually, the intense nature of Duke's academic program is enhanced by a sense of balance and perspective as students engage in a wide array of interesting activities and events.

With eighty-six percent of the student body coming from outside North Carolina, and a significant international and minority presence, the university is a model of diversity. Student backgrounds vary from America's top prep schools to large public schools in some of the country's most impoverished areas. In the midst of this divergence of experiences, however, Duke has created a unique sense of "family" among its community members. This closeness is evident in the informal chatting of students crossing Duke's pristine quads or in the chaos of the Cameron Crazies cheering for Duke's revered basketball team.

Perhaps the men's basketball program has contributed to a "team mentality" among the students. It's great to feel a part of something bigger during your college years.

Some students cite Duke's friendly environment as the reason for such a close-knit community. Others believe that the students attracted to Duke represent multi-dimensional, engaged individuals with common desires to excel in every activity while they develop lasting relationships in the process.

> *It is not uncommon to walk from one end of the main quad to another and know the first names of most of the people around you.*

This camaraderie often stops at the campus gates during athletic seasons, however, since Duke is in close proximity to two of its primary athletic rivals, North Carolina State University and the University of North Carolina at Chapel Hill. Outside of sports, however, Duke utilizes its relationships with these schools to benefit its students.

An interlibrary loan program allows the three schools to share resources, enhancing Duke's impressive library collection of more than 4.8 million volumes. In addition, Duke students can cross-register at the other campuses, greatly expanding the number of available courses. These relationships have also translated into a large number of local internships available to students during the academic year or the summer.

Faculty

The rigor of Duke's academic program is intense. The Duke faculty represents a demanding group of individuals who are known to expect incredible academic performance from students. In the midst of this push, however, Duke's faculty is made up of a group of caring and interested scholars, many of whom are available for lunches with students so they can get to know the students personally.

A faculty associates program pairs top faculty with specific resident halls to encourage collaboration and student-faculty interaction. Most students also take on independent research with Duke's faculty members to develop relationships and experiences.

> *Faculty mentoring and interaction with the students seem to be genuine goals of the university administration. Many resources are funneled into creating opportunities to build relationships.*

With its natural beauty and eye-catching architecture, dedicated faculty, and friendly environment, Duke is an invigorating, friendly, competitive, challenging, and beautiful place to spend the undergraduate years.

ADMISSIONS REQUIREMENTS

It works to Duke's advantage that the Admissions Office hosts its accepted students weekend in mid-April when the North Carolina spring is in full bloom. Flowers are everywhere, students are studying outside, and the sweet Southern air hovers at about seventy degrees. It is perfect weather, and the students who attend are appreciative because they have made it through a tough cut.

Each year, around 18,000 students from around the world apply to Duke for a class of 1,665. Applications come from every state in the country, with eighty-five foreign countries represented in the Duke student body.

While admitted students at Duke have impressive academic credentials, like most top-tier institutions, grades and test scores are far from the only factors in the admissions process.

Duke students are amazing. They are leaders, and they possess a resilience that excites others around them.

Applicants are evaluated on talent and active participation in learning. The Admissions Office focuses on six areas:
- quality and rigor of secondary school academic program
- academic record
- recommendations from teachers and counselors
- extracurricular activities and accomplishments
- standardized testing (SAT, ACT)
- application essays

To be admitted, most students must possess strengths in each of these areas. While these six areas are used to evaluate the candidates overall, Duke does a good job of assessing applicants in the context of their individual circumstances. Through school profiles and guidance counselor reports, Duke attempts to get a picture of the strengths of each high school to understand the differences in the rigors of secondary school programs. As one admissions officer has said, "We admit students, not schools." Therefore, a student's ability to excel in his or her own high school environment is of utmost relevance.

Duke's student body is active and engaged. The application should reflect a real desire to actively partake in the life of the community. Recommendations should point to a depth of interest in academics and an ability to translate intelligence and leadership into understanding among others in the university.

A group of undergrads helps provide visitor programs and tours of the campus. These students give wonderfully honest assessments of the university and also complement daily group information sessions offered by the Admissions Office. Those sessions are consistently praised as friendly and helpful.

My tour guide at Duke made the difference as I toured college campuses. He was positive, yet frank. When I enrolled, I felt I had a better sense of what to expect.

The Admissions Office can also arrange overnight stays with current students at certain times during the school year. This provides prospective students with a chance to stay in the dorms and get a clearer picture of the undergraduate experience.

Although the admissions process is extremely competitive, as in many other top-tier institutions, the university has done a good job of making the process as friendly and helpful as possible. Under the leadership of Admissions Dean Christoph Guttentag, Duke has been able to recruit a first-rate group of scholars and leaders, while ensuring an open and encouraging applications process.

Duke's motto, *Eruditio et Religio* (Erudition and Religion), signifies the university's commitment to infuse learning with moral responsibility, and to use the educational experience to enlighten others and help communities.

Students at Duke enter the Trinity College of Arts and Sciences or the Pratt School of Engineering. Both schools provide stimulating curricula that allow students to experience different courses across departments. In the first and second years, Duke's Pre-Major Advising Center encourages students to explore areas of potential interest.

I was really encouraged to use my first two years as an opportunity to get into some of the departments in which I had some interest. This opened my eyes to new ways to think about using the major.

ABOUT ACADEMICS

In a constant push to keep academics alive and relevant, Duke has worked diligently to attract "Professors of the Practice" to add new dimensions to classroom study.

Former White House advisor David Gergen and Pulitzer Prize-winning columnists William Raspberry and David Broder are famous people who made their way into Duke classrooms. Rather than coming to campus simply to make speeches, these "professors" teach weekly classes, have office hours, and become an active part of the university community.

Some professors are not celebrities but are experts in specialized fields. For example, Tony Brown, former chief operating officer at CS First Boston, complements the public policy curriculum by teaching courses in business leadership and public-private partnerships. Students love these courses because of their relevance and applicability to situations they will encounter after Duke.

Majors

By the end of the second year, Duke students choose one or two concentrations from thirty-six arts and sciences majors or five engineering majors, or arts and sciences students can pursue one of their own devising with faculty guidance. The diversity of these offerings is complemented by a selection of minors and certificate programs ranging from neurosciences to markets and management studies. While most students take approximately eleven courses within the major, there is plenty of room to fulfill Duke's requirement of courses in five areas of general knowledge (arts, literature and performance, civilizations, natural sciences, social sciences, and guidance studies) as well as requirements in a broad spectrum of focused areas, including writing and foreign language, ethical and cross-cultural inquiry, research and science, and technology and society.

Credits

To graduate, Duke students must fulfill thirty-four semester courses, which makes a normal semester load for undergraduates four courses and occasionally five. While this often seems like few courses to new students, the amount and difficulty of the reading and work quickly prove this to be a rigorous course of study.

> *Students should come here ready to work. Professors expect a certain level of excellence that requires not only keeping up with the reading but adding creativity and new ideas to class discussions. It's an intense experience.*

Faculty and Programs

The faculty at Duke is made up of renowned scholars who are surprisingly accessible to students. Formal office hours and after-class question periods are supplemented by regular meals together and informal meetings. Some students complain that professors are sometimes burdened, but most faculty members are willing to connect with students if students make the effort to stop by and get to know them.

Some of the first-year courses are large introductory lectures, with discussion sections run by teaching assistants. Others, like those in Duke's more than forty-five First-Year Seminars, are courses for no more than fifteen students taught by senior faculty in specialty fields. A former Duke president and the dean of the college are regular participants. Freshmen build lasting relationships with faculty members and are encouraged to begin specialty research projects early in their academic life.

Duke has made its freshman Focus Program an integral part of its offerings. A quarter of the first-year students participate in one of eleven to fourteen semester-long programs. For example, in the Game2Know Program, students take courses in virtual culture with an eye toward understanding the impact of computer gaming and modeling on real-world data manipulation. In the Exploring the Mind Program, students examine how the brain functions from the perspectives of philosophy, computer programming, and visual perception as a way to understand the brain's contribution to the human experience.

The Focus and First-Year Seminar programs are dynamic. Our small group studies the same materials, has fabulous interaction with leading faculty, and meets weekly for dinner discussions. This is what I came to college for!

A final, unique trait of Duke's curriculum deals with its emphasis on experiential learning and independent study. Rather than simply studying under Duke's faculty, students are encouraged to join with faculty members in independent research. The students are also given ample opportunities to take the ideas of the classroom into the Durham community and into the world. Community service, internships, and summer experiences are all used by the faculty to drive home lessons begun in the classroom. The vibrancy of the student body and faculty is demonstrated every day in the intense quest for learning, both in and out of Duke classrooms.

SOCIAL LIFE AND ACTIVITIES

After Duke students leave the classroom, day planners and tight schedules are the norm as students balance their wonderfully intense academic, extracurricular, and residential lives.

In any week the pulse of Duke's campus is energetic. Almost 400 clubs and organizations meet at different times during the week. *A cappella* singing groups and orchestras rehearse. Students work in hospital internships, and community service groups plan outings into the local community. Duke is a busy place, with something to match every interest.

There is so much to do here. If an activity that interests you doesn't exist, the student government provides seed money to get the event up and running. My best college memories have been dashing from meeting to meeting making new friends.

During basketball season, the famed tents that make up Krzyzewskiville pop up outside Cameron Indoor Stadium. Students camp out for the best seats in the house as Duke takes on the finest teams in the Atlantic Coast Conference and the country. Tickets are free, but there is heavy demand for those courtside seats.

As students wait for games, study groups meet in the tents, while some students put on musical performances, and others get caught up on neglected reading. Coach K is known to send pizzas out to the students waiting for the big game.

Consider having your parents visit during this time. It may convince them that you have resorted to living in a tent because they do not send you enough cash. The money will start flowing in!

Sports

Many students choose to participate in athletics, from fitness or recreational programs to intercollegiate sports. Although many of Duke's athletic teams are of national-championship caliber (and students love to support them), other teams exist at the club and intramural levels. This array of opportunities gives students the chance both to stay physically fit and to be spectators of first-rate athletics. State-of-the-art athletic facilities are located on West Campus and East Campus.

Residences

Residential life at Duke is another draw for many of the students who choose to be a Blue Devil. Around eighty-five percent of the students elect to live on campus for all four years, and on-campus living is required for the first three years as long as space is available. So campus life is a crucial part of the undergraduate experience. All of the freshmen live together on Duke's East Campus. Activities, meals, and special campus programs are tailored to build comfortable interaction for Duke's newest community members. Many students cite class unity and quality of life as the best traits of the East Campus experience. To help students become acclimated to Duke and Durham, upperclass FACs (Freshmen Advisory Counselors) are assigned to the first-year students to help them adjust. In addition, upperclass "quads" adopt freshmen houses as a way to introduce first-year students to the intricacies of campus life.

My freshman year was incredible. Imagine living with 1,600 of your classmates on a campus that allows you to know almost everyone's first name! It is wonderful to "come home" to our campus every night and find a comfortable place to grow. We had movie nights, arts events, and the all-too-often all-night academic discussions. It was a great transition into college life.

Most upperclass students including all sophomores, live on Duke's West Campus where they are assigned to sections of university housing. Most of the sections are randomly distributed through a lottery system. Extensive dining choices are available to replace the board plan of the first-year campus, and some students feel a letdown moving from the bonded first-year community to the larger, more individualized feel of West. As one way to counter this feeling of upperclass autonomy, Duke offers traditional fraternities (some of which are residential), sororities (which are not residential), and selective living opportunities (which are residential).

Duke isn't a "Greek or geek" campus. Most of the students interrelate with each other at sporting events, weekend trips, and open campus parties.

While a majority of the students do not belong to Greek organizations, it is one outlet of community building at Duke. Most students feel at home in the various organizations, groups, and residence halls on campus. Social life at Duke is vigorous and open-ended as most campus groups encourage all students to attend their parties. Durham is booming with new restaurants, a revitalized Ninth Street, Satisfaction's, and the Durham Bulls Athletic Park (home of the Durham Bulls AAA baseball team), but the city doesn't provide a particularly active college social scene. Students have many options for on-campus activities, many of which are expressive of their creativity. Movies, Broadway at Duke, Springfest, and large quad events highlight the social calendars of Duke students each year.

FINANCIAL AID

Duke's president and Board of Trustees repeatedly stress their belief that the undergraduate admissions process should be "need-blind." Your family's ability to pay is not a factor in determining your admission to Duke. Therefore, when you apply to Duke, one form goes to the Financial Aid Office while the application goes to the Admissions Office.

Once accepted, the cost of attending is one of the factors students (and their families) take into account as they decide where to go to college. Students receive their financial aid analysis with their acceptance letters. Duke admits students on the basis of academic ability, then provides one-hundred percent of their demonstrated financial need for U.S. citizens and permanent residents. The university has also made need-based financial aid available for a limited number of foreign students who are not U.S. citizens or permanent residents. It is important for accepted students and parents to remember that their perception of need may be different from the "demonstrated need," which is calculated using federal and institutional guidelines. Fortunately, the Financial Aid Office at Duke works well to alleviate this shock by putting together manageable financial aid packages to make a Duke education accessible for most accepted students.

> *Once I was accepted, the Financial Aid Office did everything possible to creatively work with my family to design a package to meet our needs.*

More than forty-two percent of Duke undergrads receive financial aid of some sort. Aid usually consists of a package combining:
- federal and university grants
- loans
- work-study funds

Students and parents have the ability to pick and choose from the funding options offered to them.

The process for applying for financial aid can be a cumbersome one. Parents and students will find themselves filling out many forms throughout the four years at Duke. (Aid is granted one year at a time, so students must reapply annually.) On the whole, though, the Financial Aid Office at Duke is friendly and easy to work with. If a family situation changes during the year, the Financial Aid Office tries to adjust packages. In addition, good counselors often explain packages and changes to students and are accessible to parents. In this challenging process, it is good to have helpful assistance.

Payment Plans

One of the recent developments in financial aid at Duke has been the increasing number of commercial payment plans available to parents and students. Rather than paying the bursar's bill in large, semesterly chunks, Duke has contracted with vendors to allow parents or students to spread out their payments to the university over ten to twelve months. Duke's bursar's office has an extremely resourceful and diligent staff. Clerks as well as the bursar are willing to sit down with parents and students to help them in choosing options that work best with individual needs.

Merit Aid

Students often are curious about merit scholarships at Duke. While many of the students who are accepted to Duke are eligible for scholarships at other schools, they often are not offered a scholarship at Duke because of the quality of the student body and the relatively few scholarships available. All applicants are considered for each scholarship that is appropriate based on their qualifications. Full-tuition scholarships include the A. B. Duke Scholarship, B. N. Duke Scholarship, Reginaldo Howard Scholarship, University Scholars Program, and the Robertson Scholars Program.

Students at Duke are also very resourceful when it comes to finding further financial aid. Many look for outside scholarships from local organizations. Students will find that the Duke name brings much attention from local organizations that provide scholarships funds.

Once my local Rotary Club found out I had been accepted to Duke, my chances for receiving its scholarship improved greatly.

While figuring out the financing of a Duke education may be one of the more difficult parts of the four years, most students find the process bearable by tapping into the university's many resources.

GRADUATES

Duke's reputation has led to a demand for its graduates in the work force and at leading professional schools. As senior year approaches, most students don suits for job interviews or get ready to take graduate or professional school entrance exams. In the process, most find that the Duke name on their résumé can take them far.

All of the large management consulting, investment banking, and accounting firms flock to Duke each year hoping to pick up future grads. The students' well-rounded background and personable style serves them well in

PROMINENT GRADS

- Shane Battier, NBA Star
- Elizabeth Hanford Dole, U.S. Senator for North Carolina
- John Mack, CEO of Morgan Stanley
- Charlie Rose, Talk Show Host
- William C. Styron, Author
- Judy Woodruff, Anchor, CNN

interviews and most students have very little trouble finding jobs. One of the recent trends at Duke has been the increase of small, entrepreneurial companies recruiting at Duke. The nontraditional style of many of these start-up firms seems to be a good match for the energetic, motivated students at Duke.

> *Many of my friends decided to look for jobs at firms that allowed for maximum independence and creativity. I don't know if this is a need for most of our generation or a special characteristic of Duke students.*

Most students get word of job offers in late February or March, so a pleasant euphoria settles on the senior class for its final months in Durham. Seniors enjoy the peaceful spring months in North Carolina—after graduation, many will flock to Washington, D.C., New York, and Boston to begin careers in these large urban areas.

Graduate and Professional Schools

For those choosing to go to graduate or professional school, Duke offers exceptional counseling and preparation that allows the students to compete for spots at America's top graduate schools. Duke boasts a ninety-nine percent acceptance rate for those applying to law school. Duke pre-law students are well advised under the tutelage of Dean Gerald Lee Wilson, the pre-law advisor. Dean Wilson gets to know these students well and is very effective at steering them to a law program best suited for them. He then becomes a grand advocate for helping the students gain acceptance. Once accepted, Dean Wilson aids students in choosing the school they should attend. The dean and his assistants are well known around the campus as being extremely helpful and comforting to stressed pre-law students trying to figure their way through the law school maze.

> *Dean Wilson has the ability to comfort you yet challenge you about law school decisions. After my sessions with him, I knew I wanted to go to law school, and I knew where to go. He helped others realize that law school wasn't the best choice for them.*

For pre-meds, the rate of acceptance is slightly lower—around eighty-five percent, or about double the national average. Due to fewer, more competitive spaces for medical schools, Dean Kay Singer, Duke's health professions advisor, is extremely effective at assessing students' options, helping them choose schools by applying strategies to bolster their acceptance chances. Her organized and efficient style helps students stay on track in the process. Deans Wilson and Singer are excellent examples of effective advising of pre-professional students.

Students desiring to go to business school have access to the Pre-Business Advising Office as well as resources at the Career Center.

SUMMING UP

The energy and electricity of the Duke experience is reflected in and, in many ways, created by the dynamic leadership of Duke's most recent presidents. President Richard H. Brodhead came to Duke in July 2004 from Yale University, where he taught for thirty-two years and served as dean of the undergraduate college for eleven years. President Brodhead succeeded Dr. Nannerl. O. Keohane, who served as president of Duke from 1993 to 2004. Both President Brodhead and former President Keohane have been actively involved in undergraduate affairs and have worked to improve the quality of the academic and co-curricular programs at Duke.

The active, inclusive climate at Duke has given the campus a feeling of constant change. Students are encouraged to share ideas and participate in the affairs of the university. There is a sense that Duke is not interested in resting on its laurels but constantly and creatively thinks about ways to grow and develop.

While Duke's Trinity College traces its origins to 1838, Duke University was created in 1924. Because of its relative youth as a university, Duke does not boast graduating Revolutionary War heroes or America's earliest presidents. However, alums like Judy Woodruff, Elizabeth Dole, Gary Wilson of Northwest Airlines, and Phil Lader, founder of the famed Renaissance Weekends and an ambassador to Great Britain, represent the current generation of political and corporate leadership. Duke is fast becoming a training ground for top participants in American and international affairs. The Terry Sanford Institute's Hart Leadership Program is a special program that brings together classroom, extracurricular, and internship experiences to prepare students from different majors to think about lessons of ethics and leadership. This is just one way that Duke instills a sense of responsibility and challenge in its graduates as it continues to produce tomorrow's leaders.

Duke has been a growing experience. Instead of being a part of a university community, I learned to become an active participant. Duke taught me to act after thinking, to encourage, and to constantly push.

Duke is uniquely positioned to provide students who want the opportunity to develop and learn. No other school in the country has such a strong sense of possibility throughout its campus. Under the leadership of President Brodhead, it is certain to become the leader in higher education for the century. This aggressive positioning involves and excites students who are working to make Duke's vision of excellence a reality. In this move to preeminence, however, Duke never loses sight of its commitment to develop and foster personal relationships among students, faculty, and the entire university community. It is common to find Duke grads congregating at parties or events around the country, watching Blue Devil basketball and sharing stories of their student days. Their loyalty to the university speaks volumes of the power of the Duke undergraduate experience.

Every March, I feel a strong urge to pack my bags and flee to Duke. My memories of the friendships I made, the classes I struggled with, and the ways I grew are intense and sweet. Returning to the glorious campus with friends reminds me of how we all grew up in those four years.

In the end, Duke is transforming. Students who are fortunate enough to enter the "gothic wonderland" will find challenge and reward. On the road to gaining these rewards, however, students also build the kind of relationships that last and will encounter opportunities to actively lead in all settings—laboratories, classrooms, athletic fields, organizations, and living groups.

After four years, you will feel refreshed, renewed, and ready to excel in new settings with a cadre of "family" members to assist you on the way. I can hardly think of more precious experiences to gain from college.

❏ *John Tolsma, B.A.*

 Emory University
Atlanta, GA 30322

 (1-800) 727-6036
Fax: (404) 727-6709

 E-mail: *admiss@emory.edu* or visit
www.emory.edu/ADMISSIONS
Web site: *http://www.emory.edu*

 Enrollment

Full-time ❑ women: 3,329
❑ men: 2,396

INTRODUCING EMORY

The white marble buildings and manicured lawns are the first clue when walking onto Emory's campus that it's not a typical college. Aside from the gorgeous setting that's fifteen minutes northeast of downtown Atlanta, Emory's combination of diversity and academic excellence drives its students to work hard and play hard. Since its inception as a small Methodist college in Oxford, Georgia, in 1836, Emory has become a nationally ranked university. The school offers a broad liberal arts education and sets students on a track for

At Emory, there's an abundance of clubs and organizations. With more than 100 school-sponsored activities to choose from, extracurriculars run the gamut, from the emblematic Student Government Association to the not so mainstream Revolutionary Knitters. Here's a look at three of the unique clubs at Emory.

○ **Ngambika.** This organization is geared toward freshman females who seek to promote community service through their African identity. The group is known for its riveting step-show performances that showcase dynamic attitude for the Emory community through a cultural dance medium.

○ **Rathskellar.** If enjoying a good laugh or making people laugh is the mission, consider it accomplished through Rathskellar. This comedy improvisation group leaves show-goers and its performers in hysterics and is a good stress reliever during academic crunch times.

○ **Outdoor Emory Organization:** The largest of Emory's clubs, OEO helps students get outside and away from the everyday drone of college. Whether it's a water-skiing trip an hour away, a weekend trip to the Smoky Mountains for hiking and camping, or a longer getaway to Baja Mexico, OEO lets students explore the outdoors with colleagues and promises an abundance of fun.

success in various fields and concentrations. Emory's connections to highly accredited businesses and organizations in Atlanta, such as the Centers for Disease Control and Coca-Cola, help the university attract applicants from more than fifty countries and rank among the nation's elite. Emory is known for its commitment to creating positive transformation in the world—it expects its students to do well and also do good for the world.

Emory's always changing and that's directly seen by the constant construction on campus. The University continues its commitment to providing students with state-of-the-art facilities, including compensation of a $14.8 million expansion/renovation of the Cox Dining Hall, and a $20-million Sorority Housing Complex that opens this year on Fraternity Row. Additionally, ground has been broken on a brand new freshman residence hall, which will open in August 2007. This facility will eventually be part of a ten-building freshmen residential complex with a focus on new housing initiative and "learning communities." The recently finished Cox Hall computer lab lets students create interactive projects with SmartBoards and DVD production software, and the new Math and Science Center helps students study constellations in the high-tech planetarium. The forty-two-acre Clairmont Campus offers apartment-style housing to juniors and seniors, equipped with a washer/dryer unit, full kitchen, and individual rooms with full-size beds. The Student Activity and Academic Center on Clairmont Campus lets students soak up rays beside the Olympic-size, heated outdoor pool, play sand volleyball, or study on the plush leather couches. The 90,000-square-foot Schwartz Center for the Performing Arts allows students to enjoy an orchestra concert, dance performance, or theater reading. These additions combined with the pedestrian-friendly, auto-restricted zones makes Emory accessible and unique for all its students.

Aside from the innovative buildings and designs, the students' serious drive for excellence sets Emory apart from other schools. Almost 300 undergrads double-major in one of the college's nine major academic divisions and 840 students play a varsity or club sport. Many come to Emory already sure that they want to pursue a terminal degree, and sixty-five percent of a recent graduating class went on to a graduate program in medicine, law, business, sciences, or the humanities within six months of graduation.

Students enjoy Emory outside of the classroom as well. There's always an on-campus lecture by a renowned writer, a unique sub-Saharan art exhibit, or a band concert featuring popular artists, such as Common, The Roots, and Guster, that students can attend. Undergrads can also step off campus to attend a Falcons game, visit the Atlanta Botanical Gardens, or enjoy a meal at a trendy restaurant in smart Buckhead or the Virginia Highlands. For weekends and breaks, Emory's location makes it convenient for students to take road trips to the coast of Georgia, the Panhandle of Florida, or the Louisiana bayou. Whatever the event, Emory students are seldom bored and can always find the perfect mix of academic, cultural, and entertaining events on or off campus.

> *During my four years at Emory, it always astonished me how people reacted when they heard I attended this university. Whether it's my father's coworker or a random person I met at an internship or in a doctor's office, the "wow" reply never ceased to amaze me. People were taken aback by Emory, and recognized the institute as a respected, forward-thinking school. I am proud to say I attended one of the top twenty schools in the nation. As a graduate now, I constantly run into people through my new job who ask where I went to college and still receive that "wow" or "great school" comment. There's nothing better than hearing a stranger be impressed by my collegiate choice.*

ADMISSIONS REQUIREMENTS

Emory's admission process is fairly standard. Applications must include test scores (SAT or ACT), an essay, and recommendations. Since little of the numeric information conveys much about a student's personal ambitions, passions, or interests, it's vital for an applicant to give the admissions committee some sense of his or her personal qualities in the essay portion of the application. What sets an Emory student apart isn't so much his or her academic strengths, since all of Emory's accepted applicants are strong students, but the combination of talent, energy, and ambition that's apparent in Emory's student body. The admissions committee often looks for advanced placement or honor courses, along with a varied extracurricular portfolio, in a student's application.

For the 2005–2006 year, 14,222 students applied and 32 percent were admitted. Of those, 96 percent were in the top fifth of their class, 80 were National Merit finalists, 59 percent scored above 30 on the ACT, and the SAT I average was 680/verbal, 700/math.

Decision Programs

The Regular Admission deadline is January 15, but many students choose to apply through Emory's Early Decision program. In a recent year, thirty-four percent of all enrolled students were admitted through Early Decision, and eleven percent of admitted students were Early Decision. Early Decision applicants have two chances to apply: the first deadline is November 1 and the second is January 1. This flexibility allows applicants to consider all aspects of other schools before making their decision. Last year, 488 of the 4,535 students accepted were chosen through the Early Decision process. Applicants should mull over their decision to apply early, because both Early Decision options are binding and Emory expects accepted applicants to withdraw their remaining applications. Although the Early Decision option is a big commitment, it's also a good way for a student to demonstrate his or her desire to attend Emory. Students will hear from the Admissions Office by December 15 if they applied in November, and by February 1 if they applied during the second Early Decision round. (Don't forget that your financial aid forms must also be filed early if you choose this path.)

Campus Visit

The Admissions Committee and most Emory students agree that a visit to Emory's campus is essential for prospective students, as it gives them a chance to get a sense of the school before making a decision. The Admissions Office can help those interested in visiting by arranging class visits or meetings with specific professors or program directors. For those who want to just tour the campus, the admissions staff prefers to schedule visits between Sunday and Thursday, so that students can get a sense of a collegian's weekday schedule. If applicants can't actually visit Emory, the Admissions Office can send those interested a "Video Visit," or students can take a virtual campus tour on the Web. Be sure to check out the new Schwartz Center and Clairmont Campus while online. For a virtual tour visit *www.emory.edu/WELCOME/VirtualEmory*.

I remember getting a slip of paper during an art history class in February of senior year, saying my mother had called regarding Emory. I returned her call, my heart beating, while I dialed the number. When she answered, she sounded excited. "You got in; you know where you're going," she said. I shouted with joy and ran to tell my friends. I still remember how relieved I felt, knowing I had an excellent college to attend in the fall. When the rest of my friends worried in April, I was able to sit back and await their decisions, without worrying myself.

ACADEMIC LIFE

At Emory, students take their academics seriously and professors expect a lot from them. With a student-faculty ratio of seven to one, students have abundant access to their professors, whether it occurs during office hours or individual appointments. Professors are more than willing to work with students' schedules and genuinely care about their pupils' performances. Expert faculty who love to teach choose Emory for the opportunity to work with intelligent and ambitious students. The academic environment is friendly, albeit competitive, as students support and push one another to execute their best. Students can always find a colleague to commiserate with regarding a sociology paper, or consult an upperclassman or teaching aid about a math quagmire. With the recent technology additions, Emory professors are implementing more group projects, allowing students to split up work and present innovative projects that incorporate programs such as Powerpoint and Dreamweaver. The university's Writing Center continues to be a successful part of Emory's academic life and allows students to bring outlines or rough drafts to selected undergrads and graduate students to help them sharpen their writing skills.

What's more, Emory knows how much its students like to be connected, and have stationed kiosks around campus to allow students to stop and check their e-mail or surf the Web briefly between classes. The school's computing services help students sift through various computer quandaries and will make on-campus trips to your dorm room to personally fix your computer glitch. The new EPASS (Emory Pathways to Academic Success for

Students) program offers online study tips, individual academic consultation, and science mentoring. Whatever a student needs academically, Emory offers a plethora of support that is easily accessible and shows the university's commitment to educating its students.

Advising Systems

To further help collegians, Emory offers extensive advising systems that students can tailor to their majors and minors. Upon entering the college, freshmen are assigned to FAME (Freshman Advising and Mentoring at Emory) groups, in which older students, a faculty member, and staffer help first-years choose their schedules, discuss transitioning to Emory's environment, and take field trips around Atlanta to a Braves baseball game or a symphony concert. This system allows freshmen to start on the right track in a cohesive atmosphere and a group's faculty member remains their advisor until they declare a major. Once students choose their program of study, they often find one or two professors to advise them in the appropriate field. Professors devote a lot of time to their advisees and are more than willing to write recommendations for internships, scholarships, and jobs. They also offer personal advice about coping with stress, managing time, and making the most of Emory. Students can always pop their heads in to professors' offices for a chat or a quick question.

Majors

Emory students' majors and minors run the gamut, as four of the university's nine academic divisions offer undergraduate degrees in almost any concentration. Emory College is the largest with 5,000 students, offering liberal arts classes with popular majors like biology, political science, and history. Students can attend Emory College freshman through senior years. Oxford College has 700 students and is on Emory's original campus in Oxford, Georgia, about forty miles from Atlanta. Students go here for freshman and sophomore years, and most continue on to Emory for junior or senior years. The Nell Hodgson Woodruff School of Nursing has about 220 juniors and seniors pursuing a bachelor of business administration degree; you can apply here from Oxford or Emory College after your sophomore year. Emory is known for producing future doctors and lawyers, along with students who pursue Ph.D.s in the humanities or start nonprofit organizations. The diversity among majors and concentrations is indicative of the school's vicissitude and its study abroad components further demonstrate students' desires to explore global places. With the help of CIPA (Center for International Programs Abroad), 724 students studied abroad last year, either for a semester or over the summer. CIPA offers comprehensive assistance in planning a student's time abroad. Advisors help students make sure credits transfer, visas are granted, and help organize any immunizations that are required. They're available to talk about cultural differences and help students immerse themselves and readjust to the Emory community before and after their experiences abroad. Emory's programs allow collegians to spend a semester in D.C., China, or Africa, or summers in England, Chile, or Spain. Wherever one chooses, Emory can help make studying abroad a life-altering experience.

> *Days before I left for Nairobi, I contacted my study abroad advisor to double-check that I had everything in order. She was so helpful in making sure my credits would transfer, my visa was granted, and I had received the multiple shots needed for my four months in Kenya and Tanzania. With the help of Emory, I was able to go abroad and not have to worry about the red tape surrounding my experience. Somewhere between sleeping in a dung hut on goatskins, helping commercial sex workers reform their ways, and hiking an active volcano, I realized how lucky I was to have had the opportunity to study abroad. I wouldn't have been able to do it without Emory's encouragement to go out and explore the vast lands of East Africa.*

SOCIAL LIFE AND ACTIVITIES

There are plenty of activities to keep Emory students entertained, both on and off campus. Collegians have been known to work and play hard and numerous organizations help them maintain a good balance of academics and amusement. Students perform through Theater Emory, write opinions for *The Emory Wheel*, and read books to inner-city children through Volunteer Emory. Off campus, students can intern at the Carter Center or CNN or spend an autumn afternoon at Six Flags Over Georgia. Well-known guests are invited to speak year-round; Maya Angelou, Naomi Wolf, and Kenneth Cole have made recent appearances on campus. One of the special events specifically orchestrated for freshmen is the annual Carter Town Hall Meeting, in which former president Jimmy Carter addresses questions asked by the new students about foreign policy, national issues, and local politics in a relaxed environment. He's also been known to lecture to certain political science classes and offers many internships to Emory students through the Carter Center, located a few miles from campus.

Athletics

There's a long-standing joke among Emory students that the football team is still undefeated. That's because Emory, a Division III school in the NCAA, doesn't have a football team. But that doesn't stop students from gearing up for sporting events. There are sixteen intercollegiate sports at Emory, including basketball, soccer, swimming, and diving. Emory's varsity athletic successes have proved that the college is both an academic and athletic powerhouse. Emory has been in the Top 10 in the Sears Cup since 2000–2001. It finished number four in the nation among 418 NCAA Division III schools in the NACDA Directors' Cup Standings and secured three national championships! Teams placing in the top 10 nationally were women's tennis (first), men's tennis (first), women's swimming and diving (first), men's swimming and diving (third) women's volleyball (fourth), golf (eighth), and baseball (ninth).

For those not on varsity teams, Emory has over forty intramural or club sports for students to engage in. The competitive intramurals can make any student think he or she is at a championship game, as fraternities, sororities, and other organizations go head to head in flag football, soccer, and softball. Sometimes these are the most exciting games to watch!

The primary gym boasts an Olympic-size swimming pool, a 3,000-seat gymnasium with four basketball courts, an indoor and outdoor track, rock climbing wall, and an impressive array of exercise equipment. Students can take yoga, step aerobics, kick boxing, and spinning classes, as well as dance and weight training through the university's physical education system. On the new Clairmont Campus, basketball courts, outdoor tennis courts, sand volleyball courts, and a weight room equipped with cardiovascular machines, that's open until midnight, let students sweat a bit at any hour they need a break.

Unofficial Mascot

To spur school spirit, Emory's students flock to Dooley, the unofficial mascot. Though the Emory Eagle is the official mascot, Dooley illuminates students' enthusiasm through his unexpected and impromptu visits all over campus. Dooley is a skeleton that is always accompanied by black-clad, white-gloved bodyguards who relay his messages to the student body. The saga says that Dooley was adopted in the early years of the university when some Emory students developed an unusual attachment to a lab skeleton in one of their classrooms. Ever since, Dooley has been the spirit of students and he always dons a skeleton-painted shirt, dapper top hat, and long black cape. His identity is a strictly kept secret and students never know when or where he'll appear. He's present at major student events, leaning on his cane while crossing the floor, and will show up unannounced in any classroom during the school's annual Dooley's Week. During his week, he's given license to release any class he chooses with a slow wave of his arm and a message from one of his escorts. If a professor refuses to excuse his or her class, the teacher will hear groans from discontented students and receive a water-gun assault from Dooley himself. He always departs with the same motto: "Students may come and students may go, professors may come and professors may go, presidents may come and presidents may go, but Dooley lives on forever."

Greeks

Another aspect of Emory's activities is the Greek system. Thirty-three percent of under-grads pledge one of the fifteen fraternities or thirteen sororities. Emory's Greek life is known to be laid back, fun, and productive, as Greeks often are seen organizing a run for cancer, cooking dinners for ill children, and raising money for various charities. Students go through Greek recruitment second semester, which gives collegians the chance to make plenty of friends outside of an organized social group when they first arrive on campus. The unique thing about Emory's Greek life is that it's not exclusive; many students who pledge an organization say their best friends aren't in a fraternity or sorority.

Activities On and Off Campus

Aside from Greek organizations, Emory offers a plethora of activities for undergrads to enjoy on campus. Students go to parties, attend film screenings, and see concerts on campus. Undergrads can always find a friend to toss a Frisbee with and watch a band concert on McDonough Field, or nosh on free food at a club meeting. For a break, students can grab a gourmet cup of coffee in the recently renovated café on the top floor of the Michael Graves-designed Michael C. Carlos Museum, or listen to a poetry reading outside Cox Hall. Off campus, Atlanta provides plenty of adventures for undergrads. Students can go to Six Flags Over Georgia for the day, dance at a trendy club in Buckhead, grab eclectic food on Ponce de Leon, or attend a show at the Fox Theater. Some of the most popular off-campus activities include attending a Braves game, visiting the local Sweetwater Brewery and wandering around the High Museum of Art.

FINANCIAL AID

Emory is committed to helping its students find a way to finance their education. Last year, fifty-nine percent of freshmen and sixty percent of continuing students received some sort of financial aid. Through on-campus jobs, grants, loans, or scholarships, the Emory administration works with students to help them finance their education with as little stress as possible. If you hope to receive financial aid, be sure to fill out the CSS/Profile or FAFSA forms by the appropriate deadline. Early Decision applicants must turn in their forms with their applications. The average freshman financial aid awarded last year was $26,335. Of that amount, $21,616 was need-based aid. Emory encourages its applicants to spend the time to apply for financial assistance and devotes a portion of its sizable resources to student support in the financial realm.

Merit Scholarships and Programs

One of Emory's financial aid strengths is the plethora of merit scholarships it makes available to students each year. The most prominent of these is the Emory Scholars program, which students must be nominated for, and includes the most prestigious award, the Woodruff Scholarship. The Woodruff Scholarship offers selected students full tuition, room, and board for their four collegiate years. Emory scholars receive extremely generous

DON'T DRINK A PEPSI ON CAMPUS

Emory's large endowment can be credited to the Candler and Woodruff families, the early owners of the Atlanta-based Coca-Cola Corporation. The university has been associated with the families and the company ever since Atlanta pharmacist Asa Griggs Candler sent a keg of Coca-Cola syrup to his son at Emory in 1895. Today, several buildings on campus are named after members of the Candler and Woodruff families and Emory doesn't serve any beverages that aren't Coke-produced on campus. An urban legend still circulates among students that a couple of seniors placed a Pepsi vending machine on the quadrangle one year, sending the administration into a frenzy, and they immediately ordered the removal of it. Resident Advisors even joke that they'll make periodic dorm raids to make sure that students are drinking the "right" cola.

awards and the university program currently has 377 students in the Scholars program. The Admissions Office receives more than 2,000 nominations for the scholarships that are renewed each year for students' four-year stints at Emory. Scholars have access to a number of special academic and cultural opportunities, ranging from research grants and funding for study abroad programs to small "coffee talk" discussions with speakers invited to Emory. They frequently attend events in Atlanta, such as the Atlanta Symphony and Ballet, as well as sporting events, concerts, and funded group dinners.

For those not initially selected as Scholars, there's also the possibility of becoming an Emory Scholar after one's freshman or sophomore year by receiving the Goodrich C. White Scholarship. Around sixty of these scholarships are available each year, and recipients usually have a college G.P.A. of 3.9 or higher.

One of the other unique programs available at Emory is the Kenneth Cole Fellows Program. Emory alum and world-renowned fashion designer Kenneth Cole built the program with social consciousness in mind to give undergraduates the opportunity to help build communities and spur social change in the Atlanta area. The twelve-month program gives students the opportunity to work with professors and community partners to rebuild inner-city neighborhoods and promote community initiatives.

Aside from Emory scholarships and programs, the school acknowledges National Merit Scholarships, the HOPE Scholarship for Georgia residents, and funding for summer and study abroad programs. For seniors, the Robert T. Jones Scholarship enables recipients to live and study in St. Andrews, Scotland, for one year. In addition to this internal award, Emory works hard to help students win outside scholarships, such as Fulbright fellowships, Luce scholarships, and James Madison scholarships.

In addition to offering scholarships, Emory holds copious meetings throughout the year to coach interested students in the scholarship/award application process. Emory students can engage in mock interviews, essay workshops, and hear from scholarship recipients on how to strengthen their applications. Emory's administrators, professors, and career counselors are more than willing to help students throughout the processes and students are encouraged to apply for these awards. Those interested in learning more about these programs and others can visit *www.college.emory.edu/current/achievement/careers*.

The Atlanta Ballet, a Counting Crows concert, the NCAA Elite Eight games, and stimulating conversation at the Atlanta Fish Market with other scholars are just a few of the occasions I enjoyed while participating in the Emory Scholars program. Emory Scholars have an impeccable academic background and drive, which the program supports through an array of academic, research, and study abroad opportunities. I received supplementary scholarship money to study abroad the summer before my senior year, and I applied this toward linguistic studies in Spain. The program allows Scholars to leave an individual, lasting mark; by the time I graduated, I had sat on the advisory board, created new Emory Scholars events, and interviewed potential incoming scholars. These qualities make the Emory Scholars program truly unique among the merit based scholarship programs offered at the country's top schools.

—*Rachel Loftspring, Emory Scholar and 2004 Graduate, B.A.*

GRADUATES

Emory graduates are among some of the most successful alumni nationwide. Many graduates go on to become doctors and lawyers, while others pursue Ph.D.s in the humanities, join the Peace Corps, or work on political campaigns. Emory's Career Center is very active and can assist students by hosting career fairs, to critiquing personal resumes, to helping Emory's graduates attend the school or land the job of their dreams. The Center also helps students find summer or semester internships that can lead to potential full-time jobs. Whatever the desire, the Center helps undergraduates and alumni get in touch with the staff and make use of their resources. More than 250 companies recruited on campus each year, and motivated students can usually find a post-graduation position in Atlanta or beyond. Or, if a career isn't the initial desire of grads, the Center helps student hone in on postcollegiate study. Of the 2005 graduating class, sixty-five percent were enrolled in graduate school within six months of graduation. Whether it is medical school or graduate school for art history, the Center will keep students' recommendations on file and send them out when requested to help ease the application process. For more information on these services, visit the Career Center's Web site.

During January of my senior year, I still wasn't sure what I wanted to do. I'd attended job fairs, applied for positions online and wasn't sure what would be my next path. The Career Center counselors helped me focus on several options. I applied and was admitted to graduate school for international affairs and landed a summer job prior to graduation. I couldn't have done this without the resume critiques and advice from the Career Center. My summer job has turned into a full-time position and it's nice to say I'm now able to pay my own bills!

SUMMING UP

Emory offers a unique, fantastic education to those who're ready for a diverse and demanding education. Although Emory is probably not for everyone, students who seem to thrive on full schedules, big ambitions, and a work-hard, play-hard attitude will find themselves at home here. Emory offers a challenging, but supportive environment with great intellectual and cultural resources. Students learn a number of theories, but most important, they learn how to think critically and for themselves.

But facts and figures can offer only so much information; it's impossible to describe the special atmosphere at Emory. Students find it difficult to quantify fond memories of ordering Dominos pizza at three in the morning while procrastinating for studying for a midterm, grabbing a drink with friends to celebrate a new job, or caravaning to the Coast for a weekend getaway. Graduates will always have a soft spot for something—a cold Coke or a burrito from Willy's—that reminds them of their alma mater. Emory is more than a college education; it's a glimpse into the copious opportunities of the real world that are framed by an outstanding network of professors, researchers, athletes, and artists. Whether a student wants to become an archeologist, doctor, politician, or writer, a solid Emory education will get him or her on the right track. The diversity of the school in the heart of Atlanta produces the comfort and adventure of a quintessential college experience that lucky students will have the chance to encounter.

I don't think I could've landed such a good first job if it hadn't been for my experience at Emory. I learned how to think for myself and be aware of my surroundings. After four years at Emory, I emerged as a confident and inquisitive woman with a new vision of what I wanted to do in life and what mattered, both professionally and personally. My only regret is not getting to spend more time at Emory. During senior year, I wish I wasn't so antsy to graduate and begin working, because if I could, I'd be back there in a heartbeat.

❑ *Alyssa Abkowitz, B.A.*

Emory University

THE GEORGE WASHINGTON UNIVERSITY

 The George Washington University
Washington, DC 20052

 (800) 447-3765
(202) 994-6040
Fax: (202) 994-0325
E-mail: *gwadm@gwu.edu*
 Web site: *http://ww.gwu.edu/~go2gw*

 Enrollment

Full-time ❑ women: 5,511
❑ men: 4,230

INTRODUCING THE GEORGE WASHINGTON UNIVERSITY

Washington, D.C. is most certainly the cultural capital of the world. In addition to the countless foreign embassies and international organizations present in D.C., the city serves as home to the full spectrum of values, beliefs, and tastes inherent to our own nation. And within the District there is no greater single embodiment of this cultural, ideological, and individual diversity than The George Washington University campus. Situated next door to the

State Department, three blocks from the White House, across the street from the World Bank, and minutes from Downtown, GW offers unparalleled access to some of the most powerful institutions in the world—not that you would know it from the games of barefoot Frisbee out on the University Yard, or creative writing classes sitting out on Kogan Plaza. What makes GW truly remarkable is its ability to foster an engaging student environment in the center of the most international city in the world, simultaneously offering students new ideas or skills as well as the perfect setting in which to put them into practice.

The Campus

Such has been the case ever since the university was chartered by Congress in 1821. Originally known as the Columbian College, the University moved to its current location in Foggy Bottom early in the 1920s. GW currently occupies a vibrant section of Northwest D.C. stretching from Virginia Avenue to 19th Street, and from E Street north to K Street, the heart of the financial district in the city. In 1998, GW offered several satellite campuses in Northern Virginia and a sister campus known as Mount Vernon—located amid the rolling green hills of Foxhall Road. While the name and location may have changed over time, the university's commitment to providing quality academics has not. With a student body that hails from all fifty of the United States, Puerto Rico, the Virgin Islands, and some 136 foreign countries, GW encourages scholarly research and learning that encompasses many perspectives. Each of the 10,000 undergraduates can choose from over 100 different major fields of study in any of seven different schools—from the Columbian College of Arts and Sciences to the world-renowned Elliot School of International Affairs.

Organizations and Tradition

When it's time to take a study break, students can check out the activities going on in one of more than 350 student organizations ranging in focus from ethnic and religiously affiliated groups, to academic honor societies, to Xbox gaming clubs. Students watch the fall colors spread across the National Mall while playing intramural football or club lacrosse. Freshmen members of the Watergate Living and Learning Community learn about the 1972 political scandal while living in the building where it took place. Colleges from all over D.C. and the mid-Atlantic region gather in sold-out Lisner Auditorium to cheer on their own students at Step and Bhangra dance competitions. Exam week finds thousands of students in their pajamas migrating to the J Street eatery to enjoy Midnight Breakfast together. Seniors cheer the Graduation Countdown Clock at Lindy's Red Lion, a popular hamburger joint just off campus. These represent just a fraction of the traditions that build a true college spirit in the middle of D. C.

Beyond Campus

For those ready to venture beyond campus, the city also represents the ultimate playground for college students. Less than five minutes from campus, students can attend free concerts every night on the Millennium Stage of the Kennedy Center. The Foggy Bottom area is surrounded by neighborhoods known for their own culinary treats and tasteful stores—just spend an afternoon walking through Dupont Circle, Adams Morgan, or Georgetown and you'll find it hard to resist the smells of Malaysian, Italian, Indian, Moroccan, Thai, and Spanish cuisine. Hop the Metro on Saturday evenings to U Street and Cardoza for some of the best jazz on the East Coast, not to mention Latin dancing; right around the corner you'll find the legendary 9:30 Club, home to the most popular bands, seven days a week. Grab the Blue Line on Sunday mornings to Eastern Market and browse among fresh seafood, vegetables, pastries, and fine local artwork. Socially or professionally, the city offers an infinite number of possibilities; for those students willing to seek them out, something truly happens here.

ADMISSIONS REQUIREMENTS

Admission to GW is highly competitive, with more than 20,000 applications for 2,400 spaces. The school is one of only sixteen private schools with over 15,000 applications per year, and one of only a handful of private institutions with more than 20,000. Quality academics, an unparalleled location, and amazing professional opportunities combine to make the school very attractive to students all over the country and the world. This mass appeal provides for the incredible diversity found at the University—diversity in thought, in religion, in demographics, and in disciplines, a fitting match for one of the most culturally diverse places in the world. Such appeal also ensures that the thirty-eight percent of applicants who are accepted represent the most qualified students possible. Sixty-five percent of those admitted rank in the top ten percent of their graduating class, and ninety-two percent of freshmen ranked in the top twenty-five percent. The middle fifty percent of incoming freshmen score between 1240 and 1390 on their SAT tests, with 37 percent of those admitted scoring above a 28 on the ACT.

Requirements

The Admissions Office looks at a number of other factors in determining acceptance. High school transcripts, recommendations from teachers and counselors, standardized test scores, and personal essays are required. Emphasis is placed on performance, involvement, and excellence in academic pursuits. Applicants may interview with an Admissions representative. For those who are certain that GW is the best fit for them, two Early Decision options are available—ED I and ED II, with deadlines in mid-October and early December (respectively).

Special Programs

The University offers a number of honors and integrated programs to which students can apply. These opportunities are designed to increase the academic challenge for students while promoting an interdisciplinary approach to learning. Several offer a chance to jumpstart professional and graduate education by collaborating with the GW Law School or the School of Medicine.

Many of these programs require additional credentials; please consult the Admissions Web site for specific requirements.

SPECIAL PROGRAMS

These programs include

- University Honors Program
- Seven-Year Integrated B.A./M.D. Program
- Six-Year Integrated B.A./J.D. Program
- Science Scholar Program
- Integrated Engineering and Law Program
- Integrated Engineering and Medicine Program
- Presidential Arts Program in Theater, Dance, Music, and Fine Arts
- Elizabeth Somers Women's Leadership Programs

Visiting GW

For those students with an interest in having a truly engaging college experience and living in one of the most vibrant cities in the world, the university offers year-round campus tours and information sessions. These visits encompass a range of activities, including guided walks through the Foggy Bottom and Mount Vernon Campuses led by STARS (Student Admission Representatives), and tours of District monuments and sights aboard the GW Trolley. Interested students should consult the admissions Web site for current schedules. Don't stop with GW though; the Visitor Center can also provide plenty of maps and suggestions for local events going on in the District that will help make your visit even more enjoyable.

> *I'll never forget my campus visit to GW—that's what really sold me on the university. The folks at the Visitor Center were incredibly helpful, not only in terms of answering my questions, but making sure I had my itinerary straight for the rest of the day and knew how to get to my appointments. I grabbed lunch with a couple of STARS, watched a large political debate taking place outside the Marvin Center, had a personal meeting with Financial Aid, and left the campus that evening convinced that this was the place for me.*

ACADEMIC LIFE

The foundation of any university is the quality of its academic programs. This quality, reflected in the accomplishments of its students, is generated by the faculty through their innovative teaching methods and their commitment to the furthering of knowledge by investigative research. GW faculty excel on both fronts: GW professors have proven a commitment to generating new information and being on the forefront with knowledge that benefits not only their students, but their society as a whole. Additionally, GW professors constantly seek a problem-based approach to learning that takes advantage of the numerous experiential opportunities available in the city. For instance, the School of Engineering and Applied Science (SEAS) recently undertook an initiative to place every incoming freshman in an internship that would provide real world experience, as well as offer a unique perspective on the applications of the student's discipline. This type of initiative help students take advantage of Washington's many professional opportunities and provide unique methods of integrating academic pursuits with life experiences. Professors encourage students to get out of the bounds of campus while doing research by using the resources at the Library of Congress or visiting one of the dozens of museums in the city within walking distance, or meeting any number of international experts who call D.C. home. This integrated approach not only benefits student academic performance, but provides students with vast networks of contacts and resources that benefit them both professionally and personally.

Faculty

More than ninety-two percent have a doctorate degree. Students also benefit from a wealth of adjunct faculty in the D.C. metropolitan region who are often considered experts in their fields. Lawyers, politicians, lobbyists, artists, engineers, and many other profes-

○ **The Business of the Olympics. Since 1992, Associate Professor of Tourism and Sports Management Lisa Delpy Neirotti has made a biannual tradition of taking her Sports and Event Management students across the country and the globe in an effort to expose them to the largest sports management event on earth—the summer and winter Olympic games. After completing related coursework and research, students spend several weeks meeting event managers, athletes, officials, and conducting on-site market research. The courses have taken students to Barcelona (1992), Lillehammer (1994), Atlanta (1996), Nagano (1998), Sydney (2000), Salt Lake City (2002), and Athens (2004), where they cheered on several GW students competing in the games.**

○ **The Only Vaccine of Its Kind. Thanks in part to a generous donation from the Bill and Melinda Gates Foundation, Professor and Chair of Microbiology and Tropical Medicine Peter Hotez, M.D., Ph.D. is currently developing one of the only vaccines in the world designed to prevent infection from hookworms. Affecting one billion people worldwide, this disease is particularly damaging to children. Dr. Hotez's work utilizes the cutting-edge area of genomics in trying to decrease the prevalence of this global disease and increase the quality of life for a significant number of people—most of whom reside in developing parts of the world.**

○ **Finding Armageddon. With undergraduates students, Chair and Professor of Classical and Semitic Languages and Literatures Eric Cline, Ph.D., journeyed recently to Megiddo, Israel to work on an excavation of what is believed to be King Solomon's temple. The project focuses on characters from ancient Hebrew texts. Dr. Cline facilitates his courses in a manner that gives old-world context and meaning to current situations in the Middle East and other important regions. In addition to eighteen seasons of excavation and numerous publications, Dr. Cline has provided appearances on television for National Geographic, the BBC, and both the Discovery and History Channels.**

Created in 1997, the School of Public Health and Health Services is one of only thirty-six accredited schools of Public Health in the country and the only one in the District of Columbia. As such, D.C. officials, federal officials, and members of large international development organizations such as the World Health Organization and the World Bank rely heavily on its faculty for research and expertise.

sionals share their knowledge and expertise with students in a number of specialized courses designed for students with a particular interest in a certain subject. No matter what area students are hooked on, they're certain to find it among the nearly 100 majors available to undergraduates through GW's seven schools:

- Columbian College of Arts and Sciences
- School of Media and Public Affairs
- School of Business
- Elliott School of International Affairs
- School of Engineering and Applied Science
- School of Medicine and Health Sciences
- School of Public Health and Health Services

Classrooms and Facility Space

To facilitate learning, GW pays special attention to the classroom and facility space available to students. The last three years have witnessed the opening of several new teaching facilities, including the Media and Public Affairs building—home to Jack P. Morton Auditorium and permanent CNN offices, 1957 E Street—home to the Elliott School of International Affairs and The George Washington University Hospital. The University also completely remodeled Mount Vernon Campus science laboratories and will soon celebrate the opening of Duques Hall, future home to the School of Business. This explosive growth has been accompanied by the installation of the newest teaching technologies available, providing laptop hook-ups, multimedia equipment, LCD projectors, and microphones standard in all lecture halls. Such developments allow GW students to enjoy a learning environment that offers smaller class sizes and more intimate discussions. Almost fifty percent of the undergraduate courses have fewer then twenty students and almost twenty-five percent have fewer than ten students.

Resources

The university offers a number of resources in support of its academic mission for undergraduate students. The Gelman and Eckles libraries offer more than two million volumes, subscribe to hundreds of print and online periodicals, and offer a number of study and group meeting spaces. Additionally, the local consortium of libraries gives GW students access to a total of more than five million volumes in the D.C. area. The Study Abroad Office is a resource for individuals who are interested in academic challenges abroad. Last year, some 870 students participated in study abroad programs that took them to fifty different countries. Additionally, the Writing Center on campus is

In an effort to help students prepare for their academic careers and create a more scholarly environment in class, the university recently instituted a new writing initiative. The program includes courses for freshmen designed to introduce students to the norms of academic and publishable writing, as well as upper-level classes for juniors and seniors known as Writing In the Discipline courses. These classes focus on the particulars of writing in certain fields and provide students with the practice needed to be comfortable participating in scholarly research, publication, and peer review during their careers.

a free student resource that uses peer mentoring and collaborative learning to help students improve their own writing. For international students, the International Student Office provides invaluable service in helping students transition to their new home comfortably.

SOCIAL LIFE AND ACTIVITIES

Any University located in the heart of a large metropolitan area will have a plethora of social activities available to help students enjoy the extracurricular aspects of their college experience. What makes GW unique is how many of those metropolitan activities actually occur right on campus—primarily a result of the fact that GW students are active, concerned, and passionate about the causes they believe in. With a Metro station literally right in the middle of campus, those that need to get off campus for a while can, but those that stay behind are in for a treat.

Along with academic and cultural diversity, a myriad selection of student life options exist across both the Foggy Bottom and Mt. Vernon campuses. The fun begins within the residence halls; the Community Living and Learning Center not only provides some of the most attractive and modern residence halls in the country, complete with computer labs and apartment-style living options, but also hosts a number of in-house programs for freshmen. In particular, students can choose to take part in Living and Learning Communities. These communities are theme-based, providing funding and leadership for students to get to know one another and conduct activities around a certain subject; recent options have included the Residential Arts Community (the RAC Pack), the Culinary Arts Community, the Outdoor Adventure Community, and the Elections and Campaign Strategy Community.

Athletics

The Lerner Health and Wellness Center, less than two years old, is a state of the art wellness and workout facility with everything from Pilates and yoga to weightlifting and squash. Two top-floor basketball courts provide amazing nighttime views of the Lincoln Memorial and National Mall. The facility provides a perfect place to work on skills for the wide range of intramural and club sports available for students. Those interested in training for NCAA sports will be pleased to see the selection GW offers—from basketball and gymnastics to crew and softball. With a brand-new suspended scoreboard, the Smith Center hosts some of the most exciting basketball action in the D.C. area. Students can join the "Colonial Army" and become one of the thousands of fans sporting a yellow foam hat and cheering on our women's and men's teams.

In the past year I had the chance to hear addresses from Senator John Kerry, former Secretary of Homeland Security Tom Ridge, Senator Hillary Clinton, Al Franken, "Daily Show" host Jon Stewart, and Vermont Governor Howard Dean—twice! Only at GW...

Student Organizations

Those looking for more ways to get involved can choose from the nearly 300 student organizations present on campus. From academic honor societies to *a cappella* music groups, students are provided funding, meeting space, and support to create their own unique communities. Additionally, GW is home to nearly thirty Greek chapters whose members account for approximately fifteen percent of the student body. Recently, the university proudly opened Townhouse Row, a collection of Greek-only housing options boasting special features such as large common areas for chapter meetings.

Arts and Entertainment

Arts and entertainment options abound on campus as well. Venues such as the Hand Chapel, Lisner Downstage, and the Mitchell Hall Theater host student-led theater productions nearly every weekend. The Program Board is responsible for bringing big-name acts to campus for events including Fall Fest and Spring Fling; recent headliners have included the Black Eyed Peas, Jimmy Eat World, Busta Rhymes, and Dana Carvey. Those interested in art, theater, and dance are treated to a continuous host of performances in Lisner Auditorium, one of Washington's most popular venues. Whether it's the classic jazz of world-renowned artists such as Dave Brubeck, or side-splitting comedy from The Second City improv comedy troupe, students are constantly amazed at the performers who appear on campus.

GW IN THE CITY

Visitors to campus will no doubt hear some impressive statistics about the university's role in D.C. Not only is the university the largest private employer in the city, it's also one of the largest private landowners. What most visitors may not hear is an even more impressive set of statistics—GW's service to the city:

○ GW provides over 100,000 hours of community service annually to District residents.
○ More than 2,300 students each year take part in volunteer opportunities.
○ GW partners with some fifty community agencies and four domestic agencies to match willing volunteers with needy residents.
○ For six years in a row, GW has entered the largest team in the annual AIDS Walk, raising more than $4,000 last year alone.

D.C. Life

If all of those options aren't enough, D.C. lies just beyond the bounds of campus. Students can attend groundbreaking Supreme Court proceedings or watch Congress in session. The nearby neighborhoods of Dupont Circle, Adams Morgan, and Woodley Park provide some of the best restaurants, shopping, and entertainment in the metropolitan area. One of the best ways to see the city is to join a project through the Office of Community Service; whether volunteering at a homeless shelter or tutoring underserved children, students become more familiar with the city and form intimate connections with their friends and neighbors in other parts of the District. Hundreds of miles of bike and running trails along and over the Potomac River provide a perfect backdrop for those looking to play outside.

As everyone applying to college knows, tuition costs continue to rise even while students are in school, thus making tuition more expensive each year and increasing the burden of aid that students must seek as they continue their education. GW is one of the first schools in the nation to offer a fixed-tuition plan that promises students a fixed-tuition amount throughout all four years of college. What students pay their freshman year will be the same amount they pay as seniors. This approach allows families to more accurately budget college expenses and eases the burden on students to find increased funding while still in school.

FINANCIAL AID

The university administers more than $85 million in aid each year to students, with the average aid package totaling around $21,800 per student. The office of Student Financial Assistance works tirelessly to help students secure aid in the form of institutional and federal grants, work study, and federal loans. To be considered for financial assistance, students must submit the Free Application for Federal Student Aid (FAFSA) and the CSS Profile. Incoming freshmen are encouraged to submit these materials as early as possible. In addition to the aid provided by the Federal government, the University also offers a number of academic and need-based awards, which include the University Alumni Award, The George Washington Guaranteed Grant, and more than 100 various University Scholarships.

Students can check eligibility, learn about specific requirements, and obtain application materials by visiting the office of Student Financial Assistance web site.

GRADUATES

GW graduates typically go on to be as active, concerned, and committed as they were as undergraduates. Many stay on to pursue advanced degrees from among the university's top-ranked graduate programs, including the Graduate School of Education and Human Development (ranked 24th nationally), the Law School (ranked 20th nationally), or the School of Medicine. Others go on to put their passion to work in politics; currently, the United States House of Representatives includes eight GW alumni and the Senate four more, including Senate Minority Leader Harry Reid, J.D., '64. Numerous other congressional staffers and employees hold degrees from the university. In addition, the United States Supreme Court currently employs three Law School alumni as clerks, part of a tradition that includes some twenty-eight.

GW students are also among those routinely considered for prestigious postbaccalaureate fellowships including Fulbright, Rhodes, Marshall, and Truman Scholars. The Office of Graduate Student Assistantships and Fellowships coordinates efforts to secure such awards and works closely with students to ensure that their applications are among the most competitive. In addition, the Career Center provides professional development tools and resources, and oversees a large database of available positions and jobs on behalf of employers across the country and the globe. The Career Center employees work with students throughout their undergraduate careers to prepare for internships, part-time or full-time work, and postgraduate plans. Second, the GW Alumni Association provides outreach and support for grads no matter where they end up. Chapters across the United States—from Seattle to Miami to New York—and across the globe host social events, organize members, and look forward each year to attending the annual Colonials' Weekend alumni gathering.

- Secretary of State Colin Powell, M.B.A., '71
- President, Fisk University Carolyn Reid Wallace, Ph.D., '81
- Senate Minority Leader Harry M. Reid, J.D., '64
- President, NASD Securities, Inc. Mary L. Schapiro, J.D., '80
- Governor, State of Virginia Mark Warner, B.A., '77
- President, D.C. Board of Education Peggy Cooper Cafritz, B.A. '68, J.D., '71
- President and CEO, Motion Picture Association of America Dan Glickman, J.D., '69
- Managing Director, Goldman, Sachs & Company Abby Joseph Cohen, M.A., '76
- Secretary of the Treasury John W. Snow, J.D., '67
- Former Ambassador to the Dominican Republic Charles T. Manatt, J.D., '62
- Delegate to Congress, U.S. Virgin Islands Donna M. Christensen, M.D., '70
- Independent Counsel, Kenneth W. Starr, B.A., '68
- Jacqueline Kennedy Onassis, B.A., '51

SUMMING UP

The George Washington University is an institution constantly moving forward. A strong academic reputation continues to grow thanks to a strong commitment to education and innovation. The opportunities available to students for social and professional engagement are constantly growing due to the university's premiere location. The diversity and culture present in Washington, D.C. is echoed by the liberal and engaging learning environment that GW's faculty create, offering to students a college experience that challenges, motivates, and equips students to enter successful careers at home and abroad. GW visitors often hear "Something Happens Here." This sentiment is no stranger to students at all levels on campus; the feeling in the air is of more excitement, more success, and more achievement about to come. It goes beyond the new buildings, classrooms, and halls that provide space for students to live, learn, and play. It encompasses something far more intangible—a feeling that to succeed, to achieve your goals and dreams, to learn, requires an element of risk. It requires an understanding of the diversity of our nation and our world, a desire to learn from the various cultures and perspectives encountered. GW offers students a glimpse of the innumerable cultures and perspectives present around the globe, instilling in them the confidence and the skills necessary to face challenges and accept the risks that learning and life offer, to build airplanes no matter where they go. Something has always happened here, but as anyone on campus will tell you, even greater things are getting ready to happen.

❑ *Jeremiah Davis, B.A.*

GEORGETOWN UNIVERSITY

 Georgetown University
Washington, DC 20057

 (202) 687-3600
Fax: (202) 687-5084

 E-mail: *guadmiss@georgetown.edu*
Web site: *http://www.georgetown.edu*

 Enrollment

Full-time ❑ women: 3,497
❑ men: 3,007

Part-time ❑ women: 122
❑ men: 93

INTRODUCING GEORGETOWN

"My earliest memory of Georgetown begins with crossing the Potomac River and driving into the District of Columbia. The lampposts lining the Key Bridge were adorned with flying blue and gray balloons—I felt like the entire city was

welcoming the new class of Hoyas! And so began my Georgetown experience, a time of challenging classes and professors, life-changing relationships, and inspiring conversations and events. From the time I spent my days in New Student Orientation until the day that I walked across the Commencement stage, Georgetown remained the driving force behind my development as a reflective human being dedicated to a life of service to others."

The nation's oldest Catholic university, Georgetown University, is a vibrant, student-centered institution dedicated to educating a diversity of students in the Jesuit tradition. Committed to engaging people in open dialogue, Georgetown considers the undergraduate experience a vital component of its mission. Georgetown is one of the few schools of higher education that effectively combines the benefits of a large research university with the community and uniqueness of a small liberal arts college.

Georgetown offers a superb faculty and cutting-edge research opportunities while encouraging intentional reflection on questions of faith, meaning, and truth. Drawing on their broad exposure to the liberal arts, students engage the faculty and each other through critical thinking and thoughtful debate. Georgetown's four undergraduate schools include the Georgetown College of Arts and Sciences, the School of Nursing and Health Studies, the Walsh School of Foreign Service, and the McDonough School of Business. Academic life at Georgetown is rigorous and driven by a belief in holistic education. The institution focuses on the whole person, simultaneously fostering intellectual, spiritual, and social development.

Drawing students from all fifty states and more than 120 countries, Georgetown continues to fulfill its foundational commitment to diversity. By encouraging spiritual inquiry and development in all faiths, it has attracted students of every religious tradition and background since its founding in 1789. Georgetown University offers academic programs in arts, humanities, sciences, international relations, nursing and health studies, business administration, law, and medicine. In addition, Georgetown prides itself on a multitude of volunteer opportunities and student activities complete with cultural, political, academic, and social organizations.

Due to its prominent position overlooking the Potomac River, Georgetown University is often affectionately called the Hilltop. It sits on 104 acres of land, a mere mile and a half from downtown Washington, D.C. Although Georgetown relishes its appeal as an urban institution, it still provides the feel of a small residential campus. Its sixty buildings include six libraries with over two million volumes, two dining halls, athletic facilities, and residence halls and apartment complexes featuring high-speed Internet access. Washington, D.C. is a fantastic city for students, offering museums, galleries, libraries, theaters, concerts, sports events, and festivals—many of them free-of-charge and easy to access via Georgetown transportation shuttles and public Metro system. Of course, Georgetown students are often drawn toward the political action in the city. Rallies, protests, political campaigns and activities, and internships abound in our nation's capital, and Georgetown often plays host to American and world leaders and international summits.

ADMISSIONS REQUIREMENTS

Georgetown is one of the most selective universities in the country, and it has seen a consistent increase in the number of applications over the last ten years. In 2006, 15,070 applications, and 3, 367 applicants were accepted. Approximately forty percent of accepted students ranked first, second, or third in their high school class. An outstanding high school academic record, challenging academic program, solid SAT or ACT scores, leadership and extracurricular experience, and a unique and sincere essay are necessities. Most applicants also utilize the alumni interview as a way to demonstrate their distinctiveness and desire to enroll. Georgetown is definitely looking for more than an exceptional academic background; the school is seeking creative students with a diversity of interests.

Applicants must choose one of the four undergraduate schools when applying. The application essay and other admissions requirements may differ with each school. In general, applicants' secondary school education should include a full program in English, a minimum of two years each of social studies, modern language, and mathematics, and one year of natural science. There are additional school-specific recommendations as well. Applicants are also asked to submit the results of at least three SAT Subject Tests. Candidates for the Walsh School of Foreign Service or the Faculty of Languages and Linguistics (a part of the Georgetown College), for instance, should include a modern language test among these two.

Georgetown University is proud of its "need-blind" admissions policy; an applicant's ability to pay tuition costs is not a factor in the admission's process. This ensures that all qualified persons have access to a Georgetown education, regardless of financial status. All regular decision applications must be received by January 10; transfer applications are due by March 1. Georgetown also offers an Early Action Program for interested students; these applications are typically due by November 1. Although the students accepted through the Early Action Program will be notified of their admission in December of their senior year, they, too, have until May 1 to decide if they will enroll, and they are not obligated to accept the offer of admission. Students not accepted in the Early Action program are included among the regular decision applicant pool. Generally, fifteen percent of these applicants are accepted after the regular decision review. First-year accepted students are also given the option to defer their enrollment for one year.

I still remember the first time I walked through the Healy Gates to visit Georgetown's campus. It was alive with activism and discourse. Students read along Copley Lawn, faculty members walked through the hallways engaged in debate, and the Healy Clock Tower provided a symbol of Georgetown's international presence. I knew without a doubt that I would attend Georgetown. It remains one of the most significant decisions of my life.

The Office of Undergraduate Admissions provides daily campus tours and information sessions for students and families. The student-led tours are an excellent way to get a sense of the Georgetown campus and overall student life. You can sit in on a class, eat a meal in one of the dining halls, or just chat with students, faculty, and staff. Applicants may download information and an application from the Office of Undergraduate Admissions web site (*http://www.georgetown.edu/undergrad/admissions*).

ACADEMIC LIFE

Georgetown consists of four undergraduate schools: the Georgetown College of Arts and Sciences, the School of Nursing and Health Studies, the Edmund A. Walsh School of Foreign Service, and the Robert Emmett McDonough School of Business. All of these schools also offer graduate degrees. In addition, there are graduate programs at the Georgetown University Law Center and the Medical Center. Despite their enrollment in one undergraduate school, students enjoy a shared educational community, taking courses in other schools and living and socializing with students from every major and background. Although required to remain in their chosen school for at least one year, students may opt to transfer to another undergraduate program. Most students, however, spend the entire four years in their original school.

> *Georgetown educates women and men to be reflective lifelong learners, to be responsible and active participants in civic life, and to live generously in service to others.*

—*Georgetown Mission Statement*

The Jesuit tradition ensures that students are instilled with a sense of responsibility for their community—both local and global. Accordingly, Georgetown is committed to offering students a comprehensive liberal arts education, not mere preprofessional training. All Georgetown students are required to complete the six-course liberal arts core curriculum. This includes two courses each in English, Philosophy, and Theology. There are additional school-specific course requirements as well. The Walsh School of Foreign Service, for instance, requires two courses in a regional history and four courses in economics; the McDonough School of Business, for example, requires two courses in Accounting and a course in the Social Responsibilities of Business.

Majors

Although all are shaped by Georgetown's commitment to a liberal arts education and social responsibility, the four undergraduate programs offer a variety of majors and concentrations. The Georgetown College offers majors in: American Studies, Anthropology, Arabic, Art History, Biology, Biochemistry, Chemistry, Chinese, Classics, Comparative Literature, Computer Science, Economics, English, French, German, Government, History, Interdisciplinary Studies, Italian, Japanese, Linguistics, Mathematics, Medieval Studies, Philosophy, Physics, Political Economy, Portuguese, Psychology, Russian, Sociology, Spanish, Studio Art, Theology, and Women's Studies. The College also offers minors in a variety of disciplines including Art, Music, and Theater, Environmental Studies, and Justice and Peace Studies to name a few. This diversity of offerings allows students to engage in a wide range of ideas and values.

The School of Nursing and Health Studies offers both a Nursing major and a Health Studies major that includes Science, Health Systems, and International Health tracks. Like all of the undergraduate programs, there is an emphasis on the liberal arts and sciences in conjunction with theory and clinical practice. Celebrating its centennial in 2003, the School of Nursing and Health Studies continues to produce the future leaders of the health care industry.

Established in 1919, the Walsh School of Foreign Service, the oldest school of its kind in the United States, offers concentrations in: Culture and Politics, International Economics, International History, International Politics, International Political Economy, Regional and Comparative Studies, Science, Technology and International Affairs, and individualized courses of study. All of these concentrations are multidisciplinary, engaging fields that range from economics, history, and government to sociology, philosophy, and the fine arts. The school also features extensive certificate programs that are open to students enrolled in the other three schools. These may be region-specific such as the Latin American Studies Certificate program, or discipline-related such as the International Business Diplomacy Certificate program.

The McDonough School of Business offers concentrations in: Accounting, Finance, International Business, Management, Marketing, and individualized courses of study. Business students are highly encouraged to obtain a minor within liberal arts as well. Above all, the McDonough School produces socially responsible women and men within the business community.

Faculty and Class Size

Georgetown faculty members are both cutting-edge researchers and top-notch teachers. All professors keep weekly office hours and meet regularly with students. Average class sizes echo this commitment to students by boasting an introductory lecture average of thirty-four, a laboratory average of eighteen, and a regular course average of twenty-nine. There are virtually no courses taught by graduate students, although smaller discussion sections for larger classes might be led by teaching assistants.

Georgetown's location in the nation's capital ensures that it will attract some of the world's most notable politicians, scholars, and humanitarians. It is not unlikely to see former ambassadors or world-renowned linguists teaching undergraduate courses. Georgetown's faculty boasts some of the world's leaders in all fields, and their expertise is often solicited by congressional hearings, foreign governments, and the media. Above all, however, our faculty members are widely recognized for their commitment to undergraduate teaching.

Study Abroad Opportunities

The study abroad experience is one that many Hoyas decide to pursue. With more than ninety summer, semester, and academic programs worldwide, Georgetown's division of Overseas Studies offers extensive international programs with direct matriculation, that is, students are enrolled in their host university as normal students. This creates a more authentic cultural immersion. Drawing from the Jesuit philosophy, these overseas opportunities encourage students to reflect on their identities and on their roles as responsible citizens of the world. Approximately fifty percent of the junior class opts to study abroad for at least part of the junior year. Many programs include a home-stay option for interested students, and others may travel to one of the two Georgetown-owned villas in Florence, Italy, or Alanya, Turkey. These programs offer students a chance to study with Georgetown's own professors in another country.

I had the extreme good fortune to study for a semester in Auckland, New Zealand. It was truly a life-changing experience; one in which I learned more about myself and other cultures that I had previously thought possible. Many of my friends still refer to their time abroad as wonderful periods in their lives, allowing genuine reflection and practical learning opportunities.

SOCIAL LIFE AND ACTIVITIES

Georgetown is fortunate enough to combine the benefits of an active campus life with the opportunities of a vibrant city like Washington, D.C. The Georgetown neighborhood alone provides countless restaurants, bars, and shops. The nation's capital provides an abundance of cultural and political activity with the Smithsonian Institution, the Kennedy Center for the Performing Arts, the Cherry Tree Blossom Festival, art exhibits, concerts, protests, rallies, and lectures. Many students expand their educational pursuits by obtaining internships in nonprofit organizations, media organizations, congressional offices and committees, think tanks, and a variety of other institutions. Washington, D.C. also features professional sports teams and seven other colleges and universities. Although Georgetown does not have any social fraternities, sororities, or eating clubs, the vibrant social scene centers on student organizations and campus events and the surrounding Washington, D.C. communities.

One of my fondest memories of Georgetown and Washington, D.C. begins with obtaining free tickets to a Kennedy Center performance of Harper Lee's To Kill A Mockingbird. *A few friends and I received free tickets from the university president's office, and we trotted down to the theater. As we made our way to our seats, we began to realize that everyone around us was wearing a congressional pin. We had managed to get ourselves into the congressional viewing of the play! They had even postponed the congressional session so that the members could all attend; we were as mesmerized by the performance as we were by our fellow theater-goers.*

There is a high level of student activism signified by the more than 180 student organizations registered through the Office of Student Programs. There is an abundance of cultural, political, intellectual, and social groups on campus. Georgetown students participate in more than four campus media publications, a television station, and a radio station. Georgetown's Outdoor Education program offers rock-climbing, kayaking, hiking, and outdoor training programs. In addition, the Georgetown Program Board serves as the main source of campus entertainment by providing free weekly movies, large-scale concerts, comedy shows, and trips around the D.C. area. Students certainly have no trouble finding a group to suit their interests.

As mentioned above, student organizations often have a significant social component. Events such as the Holiday Gala, Business School Ball, D.C. A Cappella Festival, Late Night at Leavey, the Halloween screening of *The Exorcist* (which was filmed at Georgetown), and Diplomatic Ball are just a few of the annual events that mark a typical Hoya's semester. Georgetown also serves as a host to a myriad of lectures, panel discussions, and forums through the student-run Lecture Fund. Past speakers include former President Bill Clinton (SFS '68), Senator Hillary Rodham Clinton, Dikembe Mutumbo (COL '91), Hamid Karzai, Patricia Ireland, Reverend Al Sharpton, Former Secretary of State Madeline Albright, and Justice Sandra Day O'Connor. All of these events are open to all Georgetown students.

The Georgetown University Student Association functions as the student government on campus. Its representatives and committee members serve as the liaison between the student body and the university administration. One of the greatest aspects of Georgetown is the amount of student ownership over the campus culture. For business-minded undergraduates, there is a multimillion dollar corporation, Students of Georgetown, Inc., that remains the largest completely student-run company in the country.

The Office of Performing Arts houses a number of student arts-related organizations. There are dance companies, an improv troupe, numerous *a cappella* groups, bands, the orchestra and choir, and three dramatic societies that produce multiple shows per semester. There is a one-act festival for student-authored scripts, an Independent Film Festival, and an annual HoyaStock battle of the bands. In addition, cultural organizations such as the South Asian Society produce performances like their Rangila show. Its 700-seat venue sells out within minutes every year!

In keeping with the Jesuit philosophy of service to others, Georgetown's Center for Social Justice contains the Volunteer and Public Service Center (VPS) where students can engage in a variety of volunteer activities. Students tutor at area schools and community centers, work at soup kitchens and shelters, and build houses through Habitat for Humanity and the Spring Break in Appalachia program. VPS is definitely one of the more active areas of campus, with more than twenty-five community service organizations. Indeed, more than 1,400 students are currently involved in weekly service projects in Washington, D.C. alone. Georgetown also provides the opportunity for service-learning credit by combining community service with academic coursework.

The last day of classes during each spring semester has been declared "Georgetown Day" by the entire campus community. It is one of the most lively days of the year, full of celebration and activity. Student performers take multiple stages, grills produce burgers and hot dogs, faculty's children jump and play within the Moon Bounce, and pride fills the air. The Hilltop community comes together in celebration of all that is wonderful about Georgetown. We plant blankets along the lawn, watch and listen to our fellow Hoyas, and chat with friends. Year after year we remark, "It never rains on Georgetown Day." Indeed, it never will.

The Jesuit tradition is one that values diversity and the spiritual development of students of all faiths and backgrounds. Accordingly, the Hilltop also has a very active Campus Ministry with full-time chaplains including Catholic priests, Protestant ministers, Jewish rabbis, and a Muslim imam. Students can join any number of Campus Ministry organizations centered on particular religious affiliations. There are also vibrant retreat programs with a variety of faith-based and non-faith-based retreat opportunities.

Athletics

The Georgetown athletics department boasts twenty-two varsity sports teams. These include women's basketball, crew, field hockey, golf, lacrosse, sailing, soccer, swimming/diving, tennis, track, and volleyball. The men's varsity programs include baseball, basketball, crew, football, golf, lacrosse, coed sailing, soccer, swimming/diving, tennis, and track. Although well known for the men's varsity basketball program, Georgetown has an honored athletic tradition in multiple sports. A member of the Big East Conference in our Division I programs, the Georgetown Hoyas are always serious contenders and thrive on their academic excellence.

Georgetown students also enjoy an active intramural sports program. Indeed, over forty percent of all Georgetown students participate in an intramural sport at some point in their college career. There are a number of club sports teams as well. These include lacrosse, rugby, soccer, volleyball, water polo, field hockey, softball, and Ultimate Frisbee. Yates Field House serves as the main recreational facility with indoor tennis, basketball, squash, racquetball, and volleyball courts, an indoor track and swimming pool, golf practice facilities, free weights, cardiovascular equipment, weight machines, saunas, and a wellness center. There are aerobics, spinning, cardio-kickboxing, and yoga classes on a regular basis. All of these facilities are available to all students.

FINANCIAL AID

As previously mentioned, Georgetown is proud of its "need-blind" admissions policy. Once a student is accepted, Georgetown is committed to meeting his or her full financial needs. Thus, the university wants qualified students to attend and enrich the Georgetown community, regardless of their ability to pay for tuition and other associated costs. Although yearly tuition is about $30,000 (for a recent year) with room and board costs of approximately $10,000, students usually receive grants, loans, and federal work-study opportunities to alleviate the financial burden. In fact, each year, more than fifty-five percent of the undergraduate students at Georgetown receive some form of financial assistance. In a recent year, Georgetown undergraduates received $38 million in grants, scholarships, employment, and loans. The average Georgetown-funded grant award per recipient was $17,325.

Georgetown University is proud to be among the few educational institutions in the United States that practice need-blind admissions and meet 100 percent of the demonstrated financial need of eligible undergraduates. We believe these programs help us to enroll and retain the most talented students who enhance the Georgetown educational community in endless ways.

—Patricia McWade
Dean of Student Financial Services

Like most institutions, applicants are asked to complete the FAFSA and PROFILE forms and indicate Georgetown University as a recipient of the processed information. The Office of Student Financial Services also helps families plan to allocate existing family resources. The Office offers monthly payment plans, low-interest supplemental loans, and updated links to external scholarship programs.

GRADUATES

A Georgetown education is definitely a significant investment—one well worth the time, heart, and energy. Graduates leave the Healy Gates as intellectual, thoughtful, and reflective critical thinkers. Hoyas live out the Jesuit philosophy through their actions as responsible citizens of global society. Many graduates enter the Peace Corps, Jesuit Volunteer Corps, or programs such as Teach for America. Others head to Wall Street or Capitol Hill. Most alumni eventually go on to graduate work and become lawyers, doctors, and scholars.

○ *William Jefferson Clinton (SFS'68), Former President of the United States*

○ *Antonin Scalia (C'57), Supreme Court Justice*

○ *George Tenet (SFS'76), Former Director of Central Intelligence Agency*

○ *General James Jones (F'66), Commandant, Marine Corps, NATO Commander*

○ *Andrew Natsios, (C'71), Administrator, U.S. Agency for International Development*

○ *Gloria Macapagal Arroya (SFS'68), President of the Philippines*

○ *Francis A. Keating II (C'66), Governor of Oklahoma*

○ *Charles Cawley (C'62), Chairman and CEO, MBNA Bank of America*

○ *Ted Leonsis (C'77), President and CEO, AOL Interactive Properties; Majority Owner, Washington Capitals Hockey Team*

○ *Philip Marineau (C'68), President and CEO, Levi Strauss & Co.*

○ *Stuart Bloomberg (C'72), Chairman, ABC Entertainment*

○ *Jonathan Nolan (C'98), Author of* Memento

○ *Margaret Edson (G'92), Pulitzer Prize-Winning Author of* Wit

○ *Maria Shriver (C'77), First Lady of California and best-selling author*

○ *Malcolm Lee (C'92), Director,* The Best Man *and* Undercover Brother

○ *Antonia Novello (Hospital Fellow '75), Physician, Former U.S. Surgeon General*

○ *John J. Ring (C'49; M'53), Former president, American Medical Association*

○ *Solomon Snyder (C'59, M'62), Neuroscientist*

○ *Joan Claybrook (L'73), President, Public Citizen*

○ *Robert M. Hayes (C'74), Founder, Coalition for the Homeless*

○ *Anthony Shriver (C'88), President, Best Buddies International*

○ *Paul Tagliabue (C'62), Commissioner, National Football League*

○ *Carmen Policy (L'66), Former President, Cleveland Browns Football Team*

○ *Patrick Ewing (C'85), Professional Basketball Player and Coach*

○ *Alonzo Mourning (C'92), Professional Basketball Player*

○ *Dikembe Mutombo (SLL'91), Professional Basketball Player*

Prominent Hoya alumni can be found as leaders in business, politics, social action, education, entertainment, the media, and professional sports. Graduating from Georgetown University insures life-long membership in the global Hoya community. The Georgetown family offers any number of benefits and connections. Most importantly, however, it links you to the mission of Georgetown and its reputation as a premier institution of higher learning.

SUMMING UP

With its exhilarating location and a milieu characterized by activism, diversity, open dialogue, and academic rigor, Georgetown University offers students an unique opportunity. There is a vibrant campus life with volunteer programs, athletic teams, performing arts, and student organizations, in addition to the countless social and educational opportunities in the greater D.C. area. Whether interested in arts, humanities, sciences, international relations, nursing and health studies, or business administration, Georgetown emphasizes the benefits of a liberal arts education. With a student-centered mission, Georgetown offers a premier faculty dedicated to teaching. Its superb academic programs, dedication to service, commitment to diversity, and location in our nation's capital, ensure that Georgetown will attract the country's most outstanding applicants.

Attending Georgetown is an amazingly formative experience. It is marked by significant relationships, personal challenges, and incredible learning opportunities. Georgetown prepares its students as leaders—people with a strong moral character, a reflective nature, intellectual prowess, and the tools necessary to tackle both the personal and professional tensions of life. Grounded in the Catholic and Jesuit tradition, the Georgetown community is committed to diversity and the holistic development of students from all faiths and backgrounds. Membership in the Georgetown family ensures meaningful friendships, professional connections, and a common dedication to a life of service to others.

❏ *Meaghan M. Keeler, B.S.*

HAMILTON COLLEGE

 Hamilton College
Clinton, NY 13323

 (315) 859-4421 or (800) 843-2655
Fax: (315) 859-4457

 E-mail: *admission@hamilton.edu*
Web site: *www.hamilton.edu*

 Enrollment

Full-time ❏ women: 902	
❏ men: 897	
Part-time ❏ women: 9	
❏ men: 8	

INTRODUCING HAMILTON COLLEGE

No matter when you arrive at Hamilton College, your first drive up College Hill Road will make a significant impression on you. If it's summertime, you'll probably be amazed by the number of people you see bustling around. Many students choose to stay on campus during the summer to conduct research with professors, work in one of the offices, or help out with the various camps that Hamilton hosts. If your arrival takes place during the spring or fall, you'll likely be caught off guard by Hamilton's breathtaking campus—the tree-lined paths and stone and red brick buildings are especially gorgeous when flowers are blooming and leaves are either sprouting or turning an astonishing blaze of reds, oranges, and yellows. And if it's wintertime, you're definitely just praying your car triumphs over the snow and makes it up the hill! But whatever the season, you'll probably be greeted by at least one passerby on campus, and you may begin to understand exactly what it means to be a part of the Hamilton College community.

Hamilton College is a small liberal arts institution set atop a rather large hill in the middle of Central New York. Because of its location, Hamilton almost demands that its students become part of a vibrant and close-knit campus community. At Hamilton, there's no big city full of distractions to pull you away from the dorms (where you'll likely live for all four years), and there's nowhere near enough people on campus to let you even consider being anonymous. At times, particularly during the winter, this situation can be a bit frustrating, to say the least. But, because it absolutely necessitates that students get to know each other and become involved in campus life, it is also precisely this situation that leads to the creation of the unique Hamilton community that many Hamilton grads yearn for even years after they've left the Hill.

History, Tradition, and the Future

As a newcomer walking around Hamilton's campus, you'd probably notice that the parts of campus you see on your left look quite

---

THE SACERDOTE SERIES: GREAT NAMES AT HAMILTON

Established by the family of Alex Sacerdote, Class of '94, the Sacerdote "Great Names" Series provides the opportunity for Hamilton students, faculty, and staff, as well as the surrounding community, to benefit from the insight and opinions of some of the world's most prominent individuals. Once or twice a year, these noteworthy personalities come to Hamilton to give a speech, participate in a question-and-answer session, meet with selected students, and, generally, teach a class or two. Students, faculty, and community members alike have been encouraged to think critically and discuss openly the opinions and positions of the following individuals:

2005—Tom Brokaw, NBC News

2004—William Jefferson Clinton, Former President of the United States

2003—Bill Cosby, Comedian, actor, and author

2002—Madeleine Albright, Former Secretary of State (March)

—Rudolph Giuliani, Former Mayor of New York City (September)

2001—Jimmy Carter, Former President of the United States

2000—Desmond Tutu, Archbishop of Capetown, South Africa

1999—Lady Margaret Thatcher, Former Prime Minister of the United Kingdom

1998—F.W. de Klerk, Former President of South Africa (April)

—B.B. King, Musician (October)

1997—Elie Wiesel, Author

1996—Colin Powell, Former Secretary of State (April)

—James Carville and Mary Matalin, Political Strategists (October)

---

different from those that you see on your right. This is because College Hill Road once ran between two separate colleges. On the right lies the north side of campus and the origins of Hamilton College. Founded by Samuel Kirkland in 1793 as the Hamilton-Oneida Academy and chartered as Hamilton College in 1812, the Hamilton of today (which was once all male) is the third-oldest college in New York State. On the left lies the south side of campus, which used to be Kirkland College, an independent, experimental, all-female college that was founded by Hamilton in 1968. The two schools merged in 1978, but the vastly different architecture—stone and red brick vs. poured concrete—makes their history hard to forget.

Hamilton does not encourage its students to forget its long history. Hamilton has worked hard to preserve and promote the ideals of both Hamilton and Kirkland Colleges. From the Hamilton side comes the current emphasis on developing writing and speaking skills, and a strong association with science, social science, and government service. From the Kirkland side comes a keen interest in the arts, a more liberal view of what a college education should include, and a strong emphasis on interdisciplinary studies. In many ways, Kirkland complemented Hamilton very well, and students today benefit from a greater diversity of academic offerings due to Hamilton's continuous incorporation of both schools' strengths.

Despite its strong ties to the past, though, Hamilton persists in looking toward the future. Its new, $56 million science center was completed in 2005, it is investing over $60 million in renovating and expanding facilities for the social sciences, the arts, and student activities, and it is constantly examining and reinvigorating its academic offerings. One of Hamilton's biggest assets is its careful blend of tradition and progress—it is truly a college that knows where it has been and eagerly anticipates where it is going.

Hamilton Students

So, if Hamilton is moving rapidly toward the future, who is going to take it there? The answer: its 1,800 students, sixty percent of whom come from public high schools and forty percent of whom come from private high schools. Hamilton students originate in forty-three U.S. states and forty countries, and the student body is 5.3 percent international, 4.3 percent African-American, 0.9 percent Native American, 6.6 percent Asian/Pacific Islander, 4.2 percent Hispanic, and 71.0 percent Caucasian. Although Hamilton is admittedly lacking in racial and ethnic diversity, it is taking steps to attract and admit a wider array of students by engaging in a more concentrated recruiting effort.

Basically, regardless of their backgrounds, Hamilton students have several traits in common and, as such, comprise a unique group. They tend to be fairly conservative people who highly value a strong liberal arts education and a commitment to excellence. They appreciate being seen as individuals, and not just as numbers, in a close-knit and vibrant community. And they have a wry sense of humor about, and a curious appreciation of, their rural surroundings and often less-than-favorable climate. Ultimately, they are intelligent, well-rounded people who tend to look back fondly on their time "on the Hill."

ADMISSIONS REQUIREMENTS

Hamilton is a small liberal arts institution that takes great pride in its commitment to personal instruction and independent research. As such, the size of each entering class is kept relatively small, with a target of 470 students. At the same time, because Hamilton is growing in notoriety, the number of applications the Admissions Office receives each year keeps increasing, and Hamilton's acceptance rate is now around thirty-three percent.

So, how do you get yourself noticed (and accepted!)? When making its decisions, Hamilton's Admissions Office looks first and foremost for students with a proven record of academic achievement and for those with strong academic potential. In fact, eighty-one percent of accepted students ranked in the top ten percent of their high school classes.

Not to worry, though, if your GPA isn't quite as high as you'd like. Hamilton also seeks out well-rounded and involved students, so a strong activity resume demonstrating your leadership skills, extracurricular involvement, athletic accomplishments, or community service may make up for a slightly lower GPA. Additionally, it never hurts to showcase your special talents or interests, so if you have tapes of your athletic, theatrical, or dance performances, or if you have samples of your art, photos, poems, stories, or music, feel free to send them along. (Contact the Admissions Office or check the Admissions pages on Hamilton's web site for the preferred format of these submissions.)

In terms of actual admission requirements, Hamilton is like most colleges in that it accepts the Common Application and requires an application fee ($50 that can, at times, be waived), a school counselor evaluation, a teacher evaluation, a personal statement, your choice of standardized test scores, and a midyear grade report. Hamilton also requires that students submit a graded sample of their expository writing, such as an analytical essay or a research paper (but not lab reports or creative writing), and that they complete Hamilton's own supplement to the Common Application. An interview is not required, but is strongly recommended.

Hamilton is unlike many schools, however, in the recent decisions it has made about standardized test scores. Because Hamilton believes that students can demonstrate their academic potential in a variety of ways, it no longer requires that applicants submit scores from the SAT I test (though the middle fifty percent of accepted students have submitted scores between 1320 and 1480, based on 1600). Instead, for students applying, Hamilton now simply requires either the SAT, ACT, or three AP/IB, or SAT Subject Test scores: one that reflects quantitative skills, one that reflects verbal and writing skills, and one test of the student's choice. (The Admissions Office can provide a list of tests that satisfy the quantitative and verbal requirements.) And when in doubt, you can submit a variety of tests and The Admission Committee will select the best scores from among them.

ACADEMIC LIFE

At the heart of Hamilton's academic mission lie two main goals:

1. Develop well-rounded, accomplished, critical-thinking individuals who continually thirst for knowledge and who are ready for nearly any challenge the "real world" might throw at them.
2. Produce students who are able to express themselves clearly and effectively through written and oral communication.

No small challenge. But Hamilton has a long history of accomplishing both of these goals, chiefly through its dedication to the quintessential liberal arts education. At Hamilton, students are encouraged to take a wide variety of courses in a number of disciplines so that they may develop the most balanced, informed perspective on life they can. In so doing, they become better prepared to meet life's challenges because they are able to examine and analyze almost any issue from a variety of viewpoints, which is far more effective than seeing only one.

Consequently, although Hamilton students select their concentrations (typically one or two subject areas out of about forty options) and their minors (one discipline out of about forty-five options) during the second semester of their sophomore year, many spend their first couple of semesters—and many semesters beyond that—taking a variety of courses, a good number of which probably seem entirely unrelated to their intended or declared concentrations. An economics concentrator, for example, may take dance or biology classes, and a religious studies major might find himself or herself in a calculus or a French class. The excitement and challenge for most students is figuring out how these seemingly disparate disciplines overlap, and the biggest reward tends to come when they realize they're using information or perspectives they gained in one area of study to inform or improve upon their work in another.

The Hamilton Plan for Liberal Education

In a continuing effort to help students acquire the most solid education possible, Hamilton recently examined its academic requirements and instituted the Hamilton Plan for Liberal Education. Under this plan, Hamilton did away with distribution requirements and, instead, established a series of recommended academic goals for students. In this way, students have more responsibility, as well as more freedom, in obtaining the education they desire. Hamilton also began strongly encouraging students to participate in a variety of first- and second-year proseminars. These proseminars, which are comprised of no more than sixteen students, introduce students to Hamilton's culture of close professor-student relationships and emphasize the development of strong writing, speaking, and study skills via these relationships. Furthermore, Hamilton also began strengthening the advising system, placed renewed importance on writing skills, and created the Sophomore Program.

The Sophomore Program

As part of the Sophomore Program, each Hamilton student must participate in an inter- or multidisciplinary seminar at some point during his or her second year. These Sophomore Seminars are limited to twelve students per faculty member and culminate in a final project with a public presentation that once again emphasizes the interconnectedness of seemingly different disciplines. Many students find these classes to be quite challenging, but also quite interesting, because they tend to pair professors and subjects that normally wouldn't seem to belong together. *Food for Thought: The Science, Culture and Politics of Food; Freaks* (which examines what has been considered "normal" by social, biological, and psychological standards throughout history); *It's About Time* (which examines the concept of time from a physics, as well as a literary, standpoint); and *1968: Pop Culture in the Age of Sex, Drugs and Rock 'n Roll* are just some of the Sophomore Seminar options available to second-year students.

Writing Skills

Because one of Hamilton's primary objectives is to produce students who write well, all students are required to pass at least three writing-intensive classes, each taken during a different semester, during their first two years of study. In these classes, the majority of grades that students accumulate tend to come from writing papers, and students generally have the opportunity to revise most, if not all, of these papers to ensure that they understand the processes and principles behind good writing.

Because Hamilton is so committed to the concept of a liberal arts education, it offers—and strongly encourages—a variety of options to get students off the Hill and out into the world. Three of the most noteworthy are described below:

○ STUDY OFF-CAMPUS: Approximately forty percent of each junior class studies away from campus, and Hamilton has its own programs in Paris, Madrid, Beijing, New York City, and Washington, D.C. Hamilton also encourages its students to seek out other schools' programs if they wish to go elsewhere in the world. As Katie McLoughlin, '05, a government concentrator, notes, "Acquiring permission and processing the paperwork for spending my semesters in Washington, D.C., and Athens, Greece, was one of the easiest things I've done at Hamilton. The school is very nonbureaucratic, and there is very little red tape standing between you and your abroad experience."

○ ALTERNATIVE SPRING BREAK: To do something philanthropic with one-half of their two-week spring break, several groups of ten or so Hamilton students take school-owned vans to poverty-stricken areas and work to make a difference for a week. Regardless of whether they are painting churches or volunteering with local Boys and Girls Clubs, almost everyone who participates in these trips comes back raving about the bonding experiences they had, the people they met, and how good helping out felt.

○ ANTARCTICA: Each year (since 1988), geology professor Eugene Domack takes several students to Antarctica to conduct research funded by the National Science Foundation. Hamilton is the only U.S. college with this type of program.

The Writing Center

In the event that students need or want more support in developing their writing skills, they may visit the Nesbitt-Johnston Writing Center. At the Writing Center, students bring in any piece of writing they're working on—from essays for class to cover letters to senior theses—and meet one-on-one for an hour with a peer tutor. Usually, these conferences focus on grammar, organization, structure, ideas, or the writing process in general, and many students find that their writing improves dramatically over their four years, provided they invest the effort.

Hamilton also provides a variety of other kinds of academic support to students. The Quantitative Literacy (or Q-Lit) Center, for one, provides peer-tutoring services to students who are taking classes that require math/quantitative skills. Students may drop into the Q-Lit Center for assistance or they can make appointments for more ongoing help. In addition, the college maintains more than 4,200 high-speed Ethernet connections around campus, is working on expanding wireless Internet access throughout campus, and provides free use of more than 400 public computers and printers.

The Libraries

The Burke Library, the Media Library, and the Music Library together possess 610,000 volumes, subscribe to 22,000 periodicals, in print and electronic form, and participate in an interlibrary loan program that enables students to obtain books and periodicals that Hamilton does not own from other nearby libraries. The Burke Library also houses a Rare Book Room that owns a good deal of material related to religion, classics, local history, the Adirondacks, and Civil War regimental histories. Additionally, they possess a particularly extensive collection of Ezra Pound's work that literature and Modernism scholars have yet to fully explore.

Academic Atmosphere

The Honor Code

Because Hamilton is a school that takes academics quite seriously, all incoming students must sign the school's Honor Code, which basically says that students pledge to maintain academic honesty at all times. Students are thereby treated more or less as adults and their honesty is trusted and respected. As a result, professors do not generally feel obligated to police exams and may assign take-home exams that students are on their honor to complete fairly.

Collaborative Atmosphere

At the same time, although the Honor Code is quite serious and academics are rather rigorous, the general academic atmosphere on campus is far more collaborative than it is competitive. Many students hold themselves to high academic standards, so a certain degree of competition is created that way, but few, if any, students engage in the type of cutthroat academics that are rumored to be typical of many academically prestigious institutions. Hamilton students are much more likely to get together at Café Opus, the campus

In terms of academics, the thing I like best about Hamilton is my relationship with my professors. Because it's a small school, professors and students get to know each other really well. And because it's solely an undergraduate institution, the professors aren't there to do research while some grad student teaches their classes. They're there because they truly want to be teaching undergrads. Consequently, I find my relationships with a lot of my professors to be collaborative. It feels more scholar-to-scholar than teacher-to-student. This relationship keeps me invested in my coursework because I feel like my professors truly value my thoughts."

—Ann Horwitz, '06

coffeehouse, for a group study session or to lend each other their notes to study from than they are to steal each others' class materials. Because of this cooperative atmosphere, many students make some of their best friends by working on group projects or having late-night study sessions.

And this cooperative atmosphere tends to extend to professor-student relationships as well. In fact, as previously mentioned, close professor-student relationships are one of the hall-marks of a Hamilton education. Currently, Hamilton employs 180 full-time faculty (95 percent of whom hold the most advanced degree in their fields), and maintains a student-faculty ratio of 9.7:1. Accordingly, one-third of all classes have ten or fewer students, and three-fourths have twenty or fewer students. Students therefore have ample opportunities to engage in their education and almost have no choice but to participate in class. After all, it's hard to slip through the cracks or fade into the background in a class of fifteen students!

"The brochures the college sends out might seem cheesy with their over-the-top anecdotes about how much time students spend drinking coffee with their advisors or having a review session at a professor's house, but they're true. Some of the best conversations I had at Hamilton took place in my professors' homes. Professors became more friends than teachers at times like these, and discussing academics, careers, or life in general tended to be easier and more interesting outside the formal atmosphere of classrooms and offices. Meeting a professor's family is a very pleasant and personal aspect of a small college—and when I discovered that my French professor's nine-year-old twins spoke French ten times better than I did, it motivated me to work much harder in her class."

—Jane Simmons, '04

SOCIAL LIFE AND ACTIVITIES

Hamilton students know that mixing work and play is the key to a rich, fulfilling college experience, and it is this universal commitment to balance that makes Hamilton the vibrant community that it is. Although Hamilton students take their studies seriously, most are involved in at least one extracurricular activity that gets them out of the library at crucial times and allows them to meet other students with similar interests.

Athletics

For about thirty-five percent of the student body, the extracurricular activity of choice is playing on a sports team. Hamilton sponsors twenty-eight varsity sports (fourteen men's, fourteen women's), which are affiliated with the NCAA Division III, the New England Small College Athletic Conference, the Liberty League, the Eastern College Athletic Conference, and the New York State Women's Collegiate Athletic Association.

One group that always makes its presence known at sporting events is a rambunctious crowd of students known as the Dawg Pound. This group, which is comprised largely of other athletes, dons ridiculous costumes, amps up Continental spirit, and heckles the opposing team. To be honest, though, despite the Dawg Pound's enthusiasm and the talent of many of Hamilton's athletes, Hamilton's athletic events are generally not that well attended. True, some sports, such as men's hockey and basketball, tend to be a little more popular than others, but, on the whole, Hamilton is not known for having throngs of people at football or field hockey games. That being said, however, student spirit *has* seemed to be on the upswing in recent years and the games are generally free and open to the public, should you have the desire to cheer on Hamilton's dedicated Conts.

And even though Hamilton's organized athletics do not dominate life on campus, approximately sixty percent of students participate in intramurals at one point or another. Hamilton sponsors about fifteen intramural activities and over a dozen club sports each year, and because Hamilton is such a small school, it is relatively easy for anyone to set up an intramural league or pick-up game.

Clubs and Organizations

> *"Activities are very accessible to everyone on campus. Unlike at larger schools where you can't work on the newspaper unless you're a journalism major or you can't debate unless you're pre-law, at Hamilton hard work and interest can usually make up for no prior experience."*
>
> —Alex Sear, '05

Other students occupy their time by joining one (or several!) of Hamilton's approximately 110 clubs and organizations. These groups cover just about any interest under the sun, so there really is something for everybody. These clubs and organizations plan and participate in their own events, and many also hold a variety of social functions—both with alcohol and without—that are open to the entire campus.

In addition, because Hamilton is so small and nonbureaucratic, if a particular interest isn't already represented by a club or organization, a dedicated student should have no trouble *starting* a group to reflect that passion. Within the past several years, for example, over two dozen new groups have cropped up. In fact, Hamilton students are so open-minded about extracurriculars that interested students have started up a "varsity streaking team" that actually travels to other colleges and (for better or worse!) has gained national attention. On the other hand, though, because the school is so small, when interest in some of the smaller organizations begins to wane, certain groups may go dormant until someone new revives interest.

Entertainment

Because Central New York is not exactly an entertainment Mecca, many groups work to bring diversions to campus. The Emerson Gallery, Hamilton's on-campus art gallery, for example, spices up its regular offerings of primarily American, British, and Native American work by bringing lecturers and special exhibitions, and the Department of Theater and Dance brings a variety of solo performers and ensemble groups. (Note, too, that student exhibitions in art and performances in theater and dance are also quite common, either as part of class requirements or as part of the fun had by some of the more artistic extracurricular groups.) Moreover, a variety of student groups work to bring guest-lecturers that pique their own interest and that might not correspond with the offerings of any one particular department.

Movies

If the silver screen is your thing, the Samuel Kirkland Film Society brings both classic and relatively current movies to campus several times a semester and shows them multiple times over the course of a given weekend. Many students enjoy recruiting their friends, popping a bag of popcorn, and going to watch these free films, which are shown movie-theater style in one of the larger lecture halls on campus.

Music

The Campus Activities Board (CAB) generally brings comedians and larger-name musical acts to the Annex, and those coordinating the Acoustic Coffeehouse series ensure that interested students can sip free coffee while taking in the soulful stylings of well-known artists as well as up-and-coming stars. Within the past few years, the likes of Guster, They Might Be Giants, Jason Mraz, Naughty by Nature, Dar Williams, Dropkick Murphys, Howie Day, Lucy Kaplansky, and Ellis Paul have all graced the Hamilton stage.

Music makes its way to the Hill in a variety of ways outside of CAB and Acoustic Coffeehouse events, too. The Music Department brings visiting artists and lecturers, the school runs eight different ensemble groups that perform regularly, and students taking classes in the music department also give the occasional recital. Additionally, Hamilton is home to four student-run *a cappella* groups that perform several times each semester: Special K (all female), the Hamiltones (coed), Tumbling After (all female), and the Buffers (all male).

THE WEATHER OUTSIDE IS FRIGHTFUL . . .

No doubt about it—Hamilton can be a cold place. In fact, from October until at least March, there's a very good chance of there being a heaping helping of snow on the ground. The following are some Hamilton favorite ways to stave off a whopping case of Seasonal Affective Disorder.

- Recruit some friends and build a snowman...or snowwoman.
- Rent some gear from the Hamilton Outing Club and go snowshoeing in Root Glen.
- Take bets on the amount of time that will pass before the next avalanche of snow careens off the roof of Kirkland, Dunham, or Root Hall.
- Two words: snow angels.
- Ski.
- Steal (er, borrow) one of the plastic trays from the dining hall and go sledding behind Bristol Campus Center.
- Snuggle up in your dorm room with a warm blanket, a cup of hot chocolate, and a good book.
- Watch the snow fall. Wax poetic.
- Get involved in "Feb Fest," Hamilton's annual winter carnival. The week of festivities features concerts, snow-sculpture contests, snoccer (snow-soccer) and snow-football tournaments, all-campus snowball fights, wine/beer/chocolate tastings, and a variety of other events that all aim to alleviate the winter blues.

Greek Life

Currently, the school recognizes ten fraternities and seven sororities, some of which are national and some of which are local. Unlike at many colleges, though, frats and sororities at Hamilton do not have their own houses, a situation that some students feel is beneficial for Hamilton's social life because it means that societies do not tend to isolate themselves from the rest of the campus community by having friendships, living arrangements, and social events that revolve entirely around the society. On the other hand, some students *do* feel that there is a real divide between Greek-affiliated students and Independents. This ongoing debate creates an interesting Greek/non-Greek dynamic on campus at times, and conversations revolving around fraternities and sororities can become quite heated. Regardless, fraternities and sororities do tend to contribute substantially to Hamilton's social scene by throwing parties, coordinating lectures, and organizing philanthropic events.

Parties

In terms of the late night social scene, there are usually a variety of parties—both with and without alcohol—that students can attend. As mentioned before, many different clubs and organizations hold parties, and most of these gatherings tend to be open to the entire campus. They also very often have a theme, and many Hamilton students seize the opportunity to venture out to the local Salvation Army for appropriate (and cheap!) attire for the evening.

Bon Appétit!

You might not think about it much—or you might not have considered it at all—but the quality of the food in the dining halls is a very important aspect of college life. After all, you're most likely going to be eating this food two or three times a day, at least five or six days a week, for four years. That's a lot of meals. Fortunately, Hamilton's food service

> *"College may be your last time to act like a kid, and parties are often a lot more fun when you and your friends can laugh about the fact that you're dressed like a farmer for the Farm Party, a devil for Heaven and Hell, or a disco diva for Studio 54."*

—Marla Nasser, '04

provider, Bon Appetit, does a great job of making a variety of fresh and largely healthy dishes for the Hamilton community. Sure, they have some "misses," but the majority of the time the food is quite good, particularly for college standards.

But what's even more impressive about Bon Appetit is its connection to the students. If you have a favorite recipe from home that you're just dying to have on campus, bring it in and Bon Appetit will look into making it. If you're sick of seeing only apples, oranges, and bananas as your fruit options, let them know and you might walk in to find kiwis, mangos, plums, and pears the next day. And if you and your friends want to have a picnic in the pavilion, just give Bon Appetit the meal card numbers of everyone involved and they'll set you up with hamburger patties for grilling, buns, chips, sodas…the whole shebang.

It's a small detail, but it's just one more aspect of Hamilton that makes the on-campus community feel a little more like home.

The Little Pub

One location on campus that generally tends to attract a crowd both on the weekends *and* during the week is the Little Pub. In addition to serving lunch during the week, the Pub serves wine and beer in the evenings and is host to Monday Night Football, live jazz music on Wednesday, happy hour on Friday, bimonthly karaoke nights, and monthly "senior nights," during which liquor is

Although Hamilton and the surrounding area certainly can't offer the same variety of restaurants as, say, New York City, Hamilton students have nevertheless found some surprisingly unique and tasty places that are great for a study break, a relaxed Sunday brunch, or a weekend dinner out with family or friends.

○ **The Only Café:** Comfort food prepared in a home-y setting. There's no set menu; the chef makes what he feels like making that day, from mac 'n' cheese to pulled-pork pizza.

○ **The Phoenician:** Family-owned restaurant with authentic Lebanese food.

○ **The Mason Jar:** Big portions of hearty food—think Frisbee-sized pancakes, steak and eggs, and biscuits and gravy. Very popular on Saturday and Sunday mornings.

○ **La Petite Maison:** Fine, sophisticated French cuisine. Popular on Family Weekend.

○ **The Rio Grande** (or "Tex Mex," as it is more commonly known around campus): Moderately priced Mexican food. Perfect for Friday and Saturday night dinners.

○ **Nola's,** formerly the Adirondack Coffeehouse: Small café and coffeehouse with homemade soups and salads. Located just down the Hill on Park Row in Clinton.

○ **Breakfast at Tiffany's:** Known for its hit-the-spot, early morning (think 2 A.M.) eats.

○ **O'Connor's Alexander Hamilton Inn:** Another Family Weekend hotspot. The restaurant upstairs is fairly upscale; the pub downstairs is more low-key.

○ **Piggy Pat's Barbecue:** Their motto is "Put some South in Yo' Mouff"…'nuff said.

And if you've got a craving for Italian or Indian food, just take a drive into Utica and explore the many options the city has to offer.

served and only students who are twenty-one and older may enter. Many students cite the Pub as being their favorite on-campus place to relax and hang out with friends.

Local Bars

Should a curious Hamilton student have the desire to venture off campus for his or her entertainment, though, Don's Rok and the Village Tavern are the two main watering holes down in the village of Clinton. And, in an effort to keep students safe at night, Hamilton runs free jitneys (twelve-person vans) between the village and the center of campus well into the night so that students are not tempted to drive up and down the Hill.

The Diner

Finally, whether Hamilton students stay on campus or venture off at night, many ultimately find themselves at Hamilton's Howard Diner after the festivities.

> *"The on-campus diner serves breakfast late night until 5 A.M., and is somewhat of an early-morning pilgrimage on the weekends as students straggle in from the bars on a quest for bacon, egg, and cheese sandwiches with a side of hash browns."*

—*Céline Geiger, '04*

FINANCIAL AID

Admittedly, Hamilton is an expensive school. Very expensive. Fortunately, though, every year, Hamilton offers financial aid to about fifty-five percent of its students via scholarships, loans, and campus jobs. In 2006–2007, for example, the average financial aid package for an incoming first-year student was $27,502. This award was paid toward an estimated student budget of $45,500, and was calculated to take into account expenses such as books, personal needs, and travel, in addition to tuition, room, and board.

If you have your heart set on going to Hamilton and you need financial aid, though, you should seriously consider applying Early Decision. Hamilton is unable to be "need-blind" during the last five percent of its application decision process; however, the college is committed to meeting 100 percent of the demonstrated need for any student it admits. At the same time, although you may have a less nervewracking time obtaining financial aid if you apply Early Decision, the amount of your award will be the same whether you apply via Early or Regular Decision.

GRADUATES

Thanks to their broad liberal arts backgrounds, Hamilton graduates go on to engage in a wide variety of pursuits. In terms of statistics, in recent years, around seventy-two percent of graduating seniors chose to take jobs and about twenty-three percent chose to enter graduate or professional school immediately after graduation and three percent pursue fellowships (Watson, Fulbright, etc.). About fifty percent entered graduate school within five years of graduation.

The Career Center

One resource that helps prepare students for their post-Hamilton pursuits is the Career Center. Students may make appointments at the Career Center at any point during their time at Hamilton and, in fact, are encouraged to do so as

- Elihu Root, 1864, U.S. Senator, U.S. Secretary of War, Secretary of State, Winner of the Nobel Peace Prize
- James S. Sherman, 1878, Vice-President of the United States
- William M. Bristol, 1882, cofounder, Bristol-Myers Co.
- Ezra Pound, 1905, poet
- B.F. Skinner, 1926, behavioral psychologist
- Sol M. Linowitz, 1935, former Ambassador to the Organization of American States, Chairman of the Board of Xerox, Co-Negotiator of the Panama Canal treaties, recipient of the Presidential Medal of Freedom
- Paul Greengard, 1948, 2000 Nobel Prize Winner in Physiology or Medicine
- Thomas E. Meehan, 1951, Tony Award-winning playwright (*The Producers, Hairspray*)
- Robert Moses, 1956, Leader of the Civil Rights Movement (1960s), currently a pioneer in algebra education (The Algebra Project)
- Edward S. Walker, Jr., 1962, Professor at Hamilton, Former U.S. Ambassador to Israel, Egypt, and the United Arab Emirates
- Terry Brooks, 1966, author, *Star Wars: Episode I: The Phantom Menace*
- Barry Seaman, 1967, Former Special Projects Editor and Former White House Correspondent, *TIME* Magazine
- A.G. Lafley, 1969, President and CEO, Procter & Gamble
- Kevin Kennedy, 1970, Managing Director, Goldman, Sachs & Co.
- Melinda Wagner, 1979, 1999 Pulitzer Prize in Music Composition
- Mary Bonauto, 1983, Civil Rights Attorney (gay marriage amendment)
- Stephen R. Foley, 1984, Commander, U.S. Navy Flight Demonstration Squadron (Blue Angels)
- Guy Hebert, 1989, Former Goalie, Anaheim Mighty Ducks; 1998 U.S. Olympic hockey team

> *"It was so nice having someone to talk to at work during those first weeks, and I think Andrew's gesture really exemplifies what's so special about Hamilton—that shared sense of community and history you feel with other Hamilton grads even when you're nowhere near campus."*

—Elizabeth Backer, '04

early as their first year of studies. During these appointments, students meet one-on-one with either a career counselor or a Career Center intern, depending on their needs, and they discuss a wide variety of topics, including career assessment materials, graduate school applications, cover letters, interview strategies, finding an internship, and networking to find a job. If students so request, they may schedule a "mock interview" to prepare for either graduate school or professional interviews.

The Career Center also offers a variety of recruiting opportunities, workshops, and lunches throughout the year that students are encouraged to attend. The workshops often center around choosing the right graduate school, crafting a resume, writing a cover letter, or learning computer skills such as Microsoft Excel, and the lunches often feature Hamilton alumni who have returned to campus to talk about their current careers, how they have gotten to this point in their careers, and the industry in which they work in general. The workshops and lunches not only help prepare students for continuing their education or entering the professional world, but they provide valuable networking experiences as well.

Alumni Relations and the "Hamilton Connection"

These meetings are not the only way that members of the Hamilton community network with each other, however. Hamilton has alumni associations that plan outings and events in many large cities throughout the United States. And because Hamilton is such a tight-knit community, alumni actually attend these events, which is not always the case with alumni of larger colleges and universities. These events are great ways for recent grads to make contact with older, more established alumni, and they provide a venue in which newer alums can network to find a job, make new friends, or learn about the city to which they have just moved.

Other times, older alumni will simply make the effort to connect with more recent grads on their own. When Elizabeth Backer, '04, a public policy concentrator, began her first day of work at a market research company in Boston, for example, the company's HR department sent out an e-mail introducing her as a new hire. Within hours, Liz received an e-mail from Andrew Stockwell, '96, a new colleague who wanted to take Liz out to lunch based purely on their Hamilton connection.

When I think of what being from Hamilton means, I am brought back to a Friday afternoon I spent at a skating rink in Aspen, Colorado. I spent a winter out there, and every day the local ice rink opened up for noon hockey. One Friday, there were eight of us playing, and I happened to be wearing a Hamilton jersey. One by one, the guys came up and asked if I went to Hamilton, and then told me what year they graduated. Five of the eight skaters that day were alums, ranging from '99 (I had just graduated that May) to sometime in the early '60s. Three of them were retired, and only one of them was old enough to truly be retired by rite. I think it says something about the school, the lifestyle it fosters, and the people who attend the school in snowy Upstate New York that five skaters show up for noon hockey in Aspen on a workday. It made me smile that Hamilton alums have both success and enough knowledge to enjoy it.

—Ari Fingeroth, '99

SUMMING UP

The bottom line is this: Your Hamilton experience is what you make of it. If you intend to spend your four years shuffling to and from class with your head down, making the occasional trip to the library or dining hall, and staring forlornly out your window at the snow, you're going to have a miserable and isolating time indeed. But if you're willing to take some risks, join some groups, go to some parties, and really, truly engage with some professors (inside *and* outside of class), you're almost bound to have a rewarding experience. You'll grow from being an uncertain, and perhaps unhappy, freshman to a senior who has gained some incredible friends and experiences and loves where you are.

It's the things that weren't expected or immediately perceived at Hamilton that were the most important to me. It's the four-hour-long dinners in the dining halls that no one wanted to be the first to leave…the first walk in Root Glen in the spring…the sentence that your professor casually tosses over her shoulder that makes you adopt academia as your new religion…the omelet that you waited 30 minutes in line for on a Sunday morning because the Omelet God was working that day. It's the late nights spent chatting with friends, the sound of TVs booming over the Dark Side when The Bachelor *or* The Real World *was on, the play you buy tickets to so you can cheer on your friend who you ran lines with for three months…I never imagined myself doing stand-up comedy, working in Admissions, or majoring in a subject that would require me to learn another language and use quantum physics, but four years on the Hill can encourage you to take some bizarre, wonderful, and relatively risk-free challenges that can change your life. Go Conts.*

—*Jane Simmons '04*

❏ *Jennifer Kostka, B.A.*

 Harvard College
Cambridge, MA 02138

 (617) 495-1551
Fax: (617) 495-8821

 E-mail: *college@harvard.edu*
Web site: *http://www.harvard.edu*

 Enrollment

Full-time ❏ women: 3,135
❏ men: 3,505

INTRODUCING HARVARD COLLEGE

Tour guides leading visitors around the Harvard campus are quick to mention that Harvard, founded in 1636, is the oldest college in the United States. In historic Harvard Yard, tour guides explain that Hollis Hall, a red brick structure built in 1763, housed Washington's troops during the Revolutionary War. In front of Widener Library, tourists learn that Harvard's library system is the largest university system in the world, containing more than ninety libraries, more than fourteen million volumes, and some 100,000 periodicals.

Harvard's age and outstanding physical resources are among the college's most distinctive features. Yet, few Harvard alumni will say that the best part of their Harvard experience was the fact that the college is the oldest in the country. It is more likely that they will mention the environment of daily life as the distinguishing aspect of their experience, an environment characterized by the cities of Cambridge and Boston, a unique residential life system, and the people who make Harvard tick.

LIBRARIES AT HARVARD

- ◯ Harvard's Widener and Pusey Libraries contain millions of volumes on more than 57 miles of bookshelves.
- ◯ Harvard's libraries contain more than just books: a set of Harry Houdini's handcuffs; Charles Dickens's walking stick and paper knife; T.S. Eliot's panama hat; a set of George Washington's pistols.

Harvard has called Cambridge, Massachusetts, home for all of its 360-plus years. Cambridge, located along the Charles River a few miles from downtown Boston, boasts beautiful tree-lined streets as well as numerous shops, cinemas, restaurants, music stores, coffeehouses, bars, theaters, and bookstores.

In addition, the city of Boston is only a $1.25 trip away on the subway. The Boston area is home to more that forty colleges and universities and some 200,000 college students, five professional athletic teams, and all of the resources of a large city in a historic, scenic, and pedestrian-friendly package.

Boston was a considerable factor in my search for a college. Throughout high school, I'd said that I want to go to college in Boston because there are just so many colleges there. I really like Harvard's location because, while there are many opportunities and resources on campus, the entire Boston area is also still available. Public transportation makes it so easy to get to practically anywhere, and it's safe and inexpensive. Harvard Square in Cambridge is great for coffee, food, shopping, and even street entertainment; there just never seems to be a dull moment. I really like Boston for the cultural events that are there: I saw four musicals and one ballet last year in Boston. I'm from a large city, and I wanted to attend college in a place that would provide all the opportunities and experiences to which I was accustomed. I have yet to be disappointed.

Harvard students also enjoy the world beyond metropolitan Boston. The mountains of New Hampshire and the Maine seacoast are each a short drive away to the north; the beaches of Cape Cod are a short drive south of Boston.

Harvard students are amazing in the diversity of their backgrounds, interests, and perspectives. Students come from all fifty of the United States as well as more than seventy foreign countries, and nearly seventy percent of them come from public high schools. The college is entirely coeducational and has been since 1977, when Harvard and Radcliffe joined forces in a unique partnership. (Radcliffe was completely assimilated by Harvard in 1999.) Students hail from many different religious, ethnic, and socioeconomic backgrounds. It is impossible not to feel energized by the presence of so many different people and ideas.

> *I think the best thing about student life at Harvard is that, in a typical discussion, the topics of conversation could be anything from Kant's philosophy on morals to the thorough pummeling the New England Patriots received at the hands of the Green Bay Packers in last week's football game. It is really gratifying to be able to engage in a serious intellectual conversation whenever and with whomever one pleases. Also, because the Harvard community is saturated with such amazing talent, the atmosphere of high achievement and hard work around campus tends to motivate each of us to strive to be our very best.*

Harvard's location, its residential system, and its many human resources create a unique environment for the college years. Regardless of your interests or goals, daily life in this environment is challenging, inspiring, and, in Boston-speak, "wicked fun."

ADMISSIONS REQUIREMENTS

Getting into Harvard is extremely competitive. Only ten to twelve percent of the applicants in the past few years were admitted, yet more than eighty-five percent of the applicants were academically qualified. Harvard attracts some of the best students in the world: most admitted students rank in the top ten to fifteen percent of their high school graduating classes, with over 2,500 applicants for the class of 2010 being valedictorians of their high school classes. Statistics like these can be intimidating, but remember that a little over 2,000 people received good news from Harvard last year. It's hard to get in, but it's not impossible.

If you decide to apply, do your best to present yourself to the Admissions Committee with a complete, concise application. Keep this in mind if you are thinking of applying:

- Harvard accepts only the common application, and does not even have its own institutional form. The common application is fairly straightforward: send a transcript, write an essay on a topic of your choice, fill in some biographical information, provide a summary of your extracurricular life, and ask two teachers and a counselor to fill out recommendations. An alumnus interview is also a required component of the application. After you send in your application, a volunteer from your local area will contact you to arrange the interview. Harvard requires students to submit either the SAT or ACT and any three of the SAT Subject Tests. Finally, a Secondary School Report and Mid-Year School Report must be filled out by your college advisor or school counselor.

- Harvard College no longer offers an Early Action program, as of fall 2007. The Regular Action deadline is January 1; decisions are mailed in early April.

- In making its decisions, the Admissions Committee considers all aspects of a person's candidacy. You will be evaluated on your academic performance and potential, your extracurricular talents, and your personal strengths. First and foremost, the committee wants to be confident that you can handle the Harvard coursework. Your high school transcript is important here; take the toughest classes your school offers and that you can do well in. Once it has been determined that you could swing it in Harvard's classrooms, the committee will look for what distinguishes you from the thousands of other qualified candidates. Some applicants set themselves apart from the rest of the pool based on their extraordinary academic promise. Others are distinguished because of their well-roundedness or their specific talents beyond the classroom. Personal qualities are important in every decision.

There is no formula through which one is admitted to Harvard. The committee reads every application with great care and strives to identify and admit those students who will make an impact during their college years and beyond. Be yourself on the application and in the interview and let your strengths, talents, and accomplishments speak for you. You certainly can't get in if you don't apply.

Students at Harvard enjoy a great variety of academic offerings and resources. Pursuing their A.B. or S.B., undergraduate students choose from about 3,500 classes every year and over forty fields of concentration (or majors). Throughout the course of eight semesters, students are required to take and pass thirty-two semester-long courses to graduate. The concentration accounts for roughly half of the course load over the four years. Students major in such fields as engineering, folklore and mythology, computer science, linguistics, economics, history and literature, and biological sciences, to name just a few. Some students design their own concentrations or pursue joint concentrations in two different disciplines.

The Core Curriculum

The remaining half of the curriculum is divided between electives and the core curriculum. Through the core, students are able to explore seven semester-long courses that have nothing or very little to do with their concentration. With the help of your advisor, you decide when to take the core courses and which ones to take. Many students end up taking more classes in the core curriculum than they are required to take for their diploma. The core courses are lively and interesting; they provide an opportunity to explore areas outside of your concentration.

Electives

The last part of the curriculum is composed of electives, which allow students to explore any other interests they might have. For example, some students concentrate in a nonscience discipline and use their electives to complete the premedical requirements. Others become fluent in a foreign language or take studio art classes as electives. Many students use their electives to take classes that will be fun and that will provide them with a different academic experience.

The curriculum offers students a great deal of choice and flexibility, and it includes special opportunities such as cross-registration at M.I.T. and study

EXAMPLES OF CORE CLASSES

- ○ Caribbean Societies: Socioeconomic Change and Cultural Adaptations
- ○ Individual, Community, and Nation in Vietnam
- ○ Medicine and Society in America
- ○ The Warren Court and the Pursuit of Justice
- ○ Tragic Drama and Human Conflict
- ○ The Modern Jewish Experience in Literature
- ○ Majesty and Mythology in African Art
- ○ The Hero of Irish Myth and Saga
- ○ Ethics and International Relations
- ○ Matter in the Universe
- ○ The Biology of Trees and Forests
- ○ Children and Their Social Worlds

abroad. In a recent year, Harvard students studied in thirty-five different countries in Europe, Asia, Africa, and Latin America. Physical resources, such as the world's largest university library system, enhance the curriculum by providing students with world-class facilities. Yet it is the human resources, namely the faculty and students at Harvard, that have the largest influence on the academic experience at the college.

Faculty

The student body benefits from a great human resource—the faculty. For the most part, the professors are kind, approachable people, as well as remarkable scholars. They make themselves available to students through office hours, by leading students in research, and by chatting informally before or after class or in the Yard during the school day. The enthusiasm of the professors is a perfect complement to that of the students they teach.

My favorite professor is Peter Burgard, who is also the Head Tutor for my concentration (German Cultural Studies). As a freshman, I took one class each semester with Professor Burgard. He really seemed to care about what we thought of the class by periodically asking the students for feedback. Professor Burgard encouraged us to see him during office hours, which I frequently did. He was always very helpful in answering my questions, and he helped me to think about which classes would be most beneficial for my interests, in addition to providing information on study abroad programs.

The Harvard professors are terrific scholars, but they also prove to be caring and devoted teachers. Ninety-eight percent of the faculty teach undergraduates, and the average class size is smaller than you might imagine (about sixteen or seventeen students, according to a recent survey). Students take advantage of the small class sizes provided by numerous seminars and tutorials. Many students are involved in research at some point during their college years, which might include one-on-one work with a professor. A senior thesis project is an option for most concentrations, although a few of the departments do require a thesis.

Freshman Seminars

Freshman Seminars bring together faculty members and small groups of freshmen to investigate specialized topics. About a quarter of the entering class takes advantage of this early opportunity to work closely with professors in an area of mutual interest. Some recent Freshman Seminars:

- Childhood and Its Literary Cu
- The Genome and Society
- Bob Dylan
- African Musical Tradition
- Nationalism in Modern Western Europe
- Wrongdoing in Russian Literature
- AIDs in the Caribbean

Academically, the experience at Harvard depends to a certain degree on what you decide you want to do with your time in Cambridge. Small classes, accessible, friendly professors, helpful advisors, and top-notch physical resources are yours to enjoy; ultimately, it's up to you to take full advantage of the opportunities.

SOCIAL LIFE AND ACTIVITIES

Residences

The exciting atmosphere of the area surrounding Harvard's campus complements the college's unique residential system. Students are guaranteed on-campus housing for each of their four years at the college, and about ninety-eight percent of them choose to live on campus. First-year students live in Harvard Yard, the historical, academic, and administrative center of the campus. This first year is fun, and living with all of your own classmates in the heart of the campus is a great way to create class unity and to adjust to college life in a friendly, supportive environment.

The housing system is an enormous part of my life here. I have forged some of the most wonderful friendships with the people from my freshman year entryway. The house masters and tutors really create a family atmosphere. It's a good feeling to be able to go to the dining hall and know among all those eating there—there is certainly not a dearth of friends.

Sophomores, juniors, and seniors reside in one of the twelve residential houses, which are large dorms accommodating 350 to 500 students. Each House has its own dining hall, library, computer lab, weight room, music practice rooms, and other facilities. Faculty members are in residence as well as a team of advisors or tutors. House spirit is strong, as students represent their houses on intramural sports teams and spend hours socializing in the house dining halls and common areas. In sum, while students at Harvard College enjoy all of the resources of a university, the residential system provides the feeling of a smaller college. The communities of the Yard and of the houses give students access to one another, and to the educational benefits of the college's diverse population.

I have absolutely loved the way [freshman] housing is done. Because so much effort went into arranging first-year rooming groups, I got along really well with my suitemates (I had four). My entryway—the people who lived near me in the same dorm—was really close, and we often went to meals and to Boston together. My proctor always had his door open, and he made the transition into college life a lot easier. I also really felt that I was able to get to know people in my class who were not in my dorm or classes because all freshmen live and eat together. I doubt that I would have had as much class pride if it weren't for this factor.

Everyone in my blocking group this year was from my entryway last year. Now that I am in a house, I am still with wonderful people, plus there are the benefits of having numerous tutors, an extremely helpful house staff, and a library right in the house.

Harvard Square

The second tier of social life, after the houses, is Harvard Square and Cambridge. On the weekends, students flood the Square, taking full advantage of this unique urban atmosphere. Even during the week, the Square offers a refreshing break from the books; a study break might include a movie, a cup of coffee with a friend, or an hour of listening to Cambridge's fantastic street musicians.

The City of Boston

The final tier of the social life at Harvard is the city of Boston, where students might attend the theater, go to museums or concerts, visit other local colleges, or walk and shop in the city's historic neighborhoods. While the Harvard campus itself provides all students with social options, many do like to explore the surrounding environment in their free time.

Student Organizations

Harvard students like socializing and relaxing, but they also tend to be busy, as most are involved in two or three extracurricular activities. All told, there are more than 300 official student organizations on campus, including five orchestras, two jazz bands, a marching band, a gospel choir, a glee club, over ten *a cappella* groups, a daily newspaper and dozens of other political and literary publications, more than eighty theater productions per year, and student government, debate teams, religious groups, and minority public service organizations.

I'd like to say I chose Harvard because I thought it was the best fit for me in terms of size, location, student-professor ratio, etc. I have to honestly admit, however, that I came here mostly because of Harvard's reputation. I knew my academic needs would be met here but was actually worried I wouldn't be musically stimulated. My worries were unfounded, however, because Harvard gave me musical opportunities that I probably wouldn't have found at another institution. Not only was I able to sing a lead in an opera, but was able to sing solos with full orchestras and tour around the world. Only at Harvard are undergraduates given this much opportunity at such a young age.

Athletics

Harvard boasts forty-one varsity athletic teams, more than any other college or university in the country. If you don't think of Harvard as a jock school, think again. In recent years, Harvard athletes have won Ivy League championships in men's and women's soccer, women's basketball, men's tennis, baseball, football, men's and women's squash, and men's and women's crew. Harvard athletes have earned NCAA Division I championships in women's lacrosse, men's and women's hockey, crew, and squash. In addition, intramural, club, and recreation-level sports are extremely popular; about two-thirds of undergraduates are involved in some sort of athletic endeavor. You can take aerobics, learn a martial art, row novice crew, or play soccer for your house or dorm intramural team. Even if you are a non-athlete, you'll probably enjoy the Ivy League rivalries and the school spirit they inspire. The Harvard-Yale football game continues to be one of the highlights of the school year.

The example of athletics demonstrates the scope of extracurricular life at Harvard; it is astounding if not sometimes overwhelming. You will probably never be able to take part in as many activities or groups as you would like; however, you can rest assured that the opportunities for involvement will be numerous regardless of your level of ability.

The energy of Harvard's campus is one of its most distinctive features. That energy originates from the wide range of extracurricular and cocurricular activities and from the committed, enthusiastic students who keep them going. Some people perceive all Harvard students to be "grinds," interested only in their academic pursuits. This is one of the biggest myths about Harvard. Daily life is full of occasions for involvement, and it's hard, if not impossible, to find a Harvard student who isn't passionate about something beyond school work.

> *My problem is trying to narrow down what I really want to do extracurricularly because there are so many groups and programs that interest me. I am currently involved in varsity cheerleading, the Black Students Association, undergraduate recruiting, and the Undergraduate Admissions Council. I have also been involved in the Harvard Entrepreneurs Club and tutoring elementary school students. I find that I need to be involved in activities; it's just an important aspect of who I am.*

FINANCIAL AID

Harvard is committed to a need-blind admissions process. This means that an applicant's candidacy for admission will be evaluated without regard for the family's ability to pay. So, let's say you've been admitted; now, how to foot the bill? College is expensive, and Harvard is certainly no exception. Fortunately, Harvard is also generous in its use of funds to support students.

Once you have been admitted, Harvard will meet your family's demonstrated need to make it possible for you to matriculate. All of the financial aid is based solely on need. Harvard believes that all of its students make valuable contributions to the college; therefore, the college offers no merit-based scholarships. In addition, as part of the Ivy League, Harvard offers no athletic scholarships.

Approximately seventy percent of Harvard students receive some form of financial assistance. In recent years, the average scholarship was $32,000; the average financial aid package, including a grant, a loan, and a campus job, totaled over $36,000. In 2007–2008, Harvard will distribute more than $135 million in financial aid, including over $100 million in direct need-based scholarships to undergraduates.

Applying for Financial Aid

Logistically, it's important to have your act together and to submit all of the forms required for a financial aid application on time (by February 1 of your senior year).

- You will need to fill out the CSS Profile, a form that you actually file directly with the College Scholarship Service. Don't forget to designate Harvard as one of the schools to which you are applying.
- You need to fill out the Free Application for Federal Student Aid (FAFSA), a form that is available in your school guidance office.
- You are also required to submit your own and your parents' federal income tax returns.
- Students applying from countries other than the United States should fill out Harvard's own Financial Statement for Students from Foreign Countries instead of the CSS Profile. This is the only difference for international students in the financial aid process.

The financial aid officers are some of the most helpful people at Harvard. They want to work with you and your family to make it possible for you to come to Harvard once you have been admitted. Stay organized so that you always give the Financial Aid Office the most accurate, up-to-date information. It's also a good idea to photocopy all of the forms you submit as part of your financial aid application.

GRADUATES

The commencement ceremony is Harvard's most spectacular annual event. I remember every detail of that day vividly—the beautiful crimson, black, and white flags and banners in Harvard Yard, the music, the smiling graduates draped in caps and gowns, my own friends and family sharing in my excitement.

This extraordinary celebration of the university community was the perfect way to end the college experience.

Students leave Harvard well prepared to head off in many different directions. Many of my own close friends went into graduate programs; some went right to work. They pursued work in investment banking, consulting, advertising, and teaching. Now that we have been out of college for a few years, many of my close friends are starting to make changes, such as going back to school for an M.B.A. or graduating from medical school and beginning their residencies. It is exciting to see all the different opportunities my classmates are pursuing.

PROMINENT GRADS

- John Adams, President of the United States
- John Quincy Adams, President of the United States
- Leonard Bernstein, Composer, Conductor
- e. e. cummings, Poet
- W.E.B. DuBois, Educator, Writer
- T. S. Eliot, Poet
- Ralph Waldo Emerson, Writer, Philosopher
- Al Gore, former Vice President of the United States
- Oliver Wendell Holmes, Jurist
- Henry James, Author
- Tommy Lee Jones, Actor
- John Fitzgerald Kennedy, President of the United States
- John Lithgow, Actor
- Yo-Yo Ma, Cellist
- Franklin Delano Roosevelt, President of the United States
- Theodore Roosevelt, President of the United States
- George Santayana, Author
- Henry David Thoreau, Writer
- Paul Wylie, Skater

Harvard's liberal arts curriculum provides students with a base on which to build their futures. Students graduate from Harvard with a comprehensive understanding of their concentrations, and with an appreciation for other disciplines. In recent years, the most popular concentrations have been economics, government, and biology. This may reflect many students' interest in business, law, and medicine, respectively. But many graduates who were government concentrators are not aspiring lawyers; they are pursuing various career paths. The message here is that it is impossible to generalize about Harvard students and graduates.

Students receive excellent career counseling from the Office of Career Services, where they are encouraged to explore possible career paths. More than 300 companies recruited on campus in a recent year. These facts illuminate the degree to which students are exposed to different possibilities before they leave Harvard.

SUMMING UP

When you think of Harvard, think of its many resources, both human and physical. Think of Cambridge and Boston and New England. Think of the vibrant extracurricular life. Think of the special benefits of the residential system.

At the same time, Harvard isn't the ideal school for everyone. For one thing, Harvard is urban and it might not be a good place for those looking for a small, quiet, college town. Cambridge has a lot of trees and lawns and a beautiful river, but it also has traffic and a lot of general activity. Harvard might not be great for those who want a small college environment. Although the college is considered medium-sized, you probably won't be able to learn everyone's name. Moreover, although you will work closely with an advisor, Harvard is more suited to those who are excited about taking some of the responsibility and initiative to make their education a success. Finally, Harvard might not be a good choice for you if you have a clear idea of what field you want to pursue in college and want to pursue a strictly professional program. Having said that, come visit Harvard. It's worth seeing as an historic site even if you never decide to apply.

What is so great about Harvard? More important than the prestige (though perhaps because of it), it is the resources and opportunities that Harvard places within your reach that shrink your four years into fleeting moments. What you have at Harvard is an unmatched opportunity to discover and rediscover, in and outside class, who you are and what motivates you.

❏ *Brooke Earley, A.B.*

HARVEY MUDD COLLEGE

Photo by Chuck Chaney

Harvey Mudd College
Claremont, CA 91711

(909) 621-8011
Fax: (909) 607-7046

E-mail: *admission@hmc.edu*
Web site: *http://www.hmc.edu*

 Enrollment

Full-time ❏ women: 213
       ❏ men: 516

INTRODUCING HARVEY MUDD COLLEGE

Harvey Mudd College is a highly selective private coeducational undergraduate college of engineering, mathematics, and science that could well be billed as "one of the best colleges in America that most people have never heard of." The college does not show up in the Final Four or try to market itself as the Harvard of anywhere. What it does do is attract some of the nation's brightest students and offers them a unique, rigorous, and liberal technical education that is as good as or better than the more famous colleges that some turn down to matriculate here. There are three key aspects of HMC that set it apart from other top colleges and give the school its often touted "one-of-a-kind" status: Harvey Mudd College is an intensely small college; it has a narrow academic focus on engineering, science, and mathematics, and it prides itself on having humanities and social sciences requirements that it hopes will produce "leaders with an understanding of the impact of their work on humanity."

For most prospective students Harvey Mudd College seems like a big enough place engulfed in the larger Claremont Colleges Consortium. In reality, HMC is a close-knit community, a place where everybody knows your name, or at least everyone recognizes your face. The entire student body of around 730 "Mudders" is smaller than the high school graduating class of many incoming students. With ninety-six percent of the school living in the eight dorms (and the other four percent often crashing with friends on campus), getting to know your fellow Mudders is not difficult. The core math and science curriculum ensures that most freshmen are taking a nearly identical set of classes. All of this community interaction means that the same group of people you sit with in class in the morning will be eating with you in the dining hall at lunch, dropping by your room to work on homework that evening, playing intramural inner-tube water polo with you later that night, and going out to have a good time together on the weekend. And it stays that way for four years. With this amount of inter-campus intimacy, Mudd is a good place to make great friends and a terrible place to make any enemies.

With no graduate students, no TAs, and a faculty dedicated to a high level of student interaction, few Mudders fall through the cracks or blend into the woodwork. Even the administration and staff take an active role in campus life. The chef in the dining hall and the building attendants on the night shift are some of the best-liked and most well-known personalities on campus, regularly chatting with students. Faculty/staff/student interaction is supported on all levels through "Friday Forums" (where all are invited to discuss current campus and world issues) and the Activities Planning Committee (APC for short), a student group that sponsors trips to cultural and fun events throughout Southern California that are open to all members of the HMC community. It is common for a student—any student—to be seen working out with the president of the college, playing Frisbee with a professor, or dropping in to the office of the dean of students to talk about which campus policies need to be reformed. This camaraderie and immediate access to the people who make the college run (from the maintenance staff to the professors to the president) gives Harvey Mudd College a sense of community unthinkable in the large research-oriented institutions that most Mudders turn down to come here.

Some students find HMC's small size a bit smothering, and most students need to take a break from the college every now and then. For these Mudders, the other four undergraduate colleges in Claremont provide a convenient distraction from the unique culture and atmosphere that make up HMC. Within the five undergraduate colleges and two graduate institutions in Claremont, there are innumerable clubs, organizations, concerts, art shows, sports teams, and coffeehouses to take your mind away from the academic rigor of a small engineering and science school. Anyone with a car has the unlimited distractions of Los Angeles just a quick freeway drive away. Students looking for nationally televised football games, fraternity/sorority parties, and large government-funded research laboratories, however, will be sorely disappointed if they come to Harvey Mudd College. What can be found instead are afternoon pick-up football games, impromptu dorm parties, and small well-stocked labs where talented faculty involve their undergraduate students in every aspect of their research.

ADMISSIONS REQUIREMENTS

Getting into Harvey Mudd College can be as much fun (and as difficult) as graduating from the place. Over the past several years, HMC's Admission Office has worked hard to put a human face on the sometimes cold and judgmental world of college admissions. The school's clever "Junk Mail piece" (a satirical mailing introducing Harvey Mudd College to prospective students), adds much needed levity to the college recruiting process, poking fun at the way most schools try to market themselves, while at the same time drawing in the type of savvy but not humorless student that Harvey Mudd seeks to attract.

I got way more personal attention from the Admission Office at Harvey Mudd College than any other college I applied to. I liked the fact that every letter I received was signed in ink, not laser printed or photocopied. Any time I had questions I was able to talk to someone directly and not just get brushed off in favor of some pamphlet dropped in the mail. I felt that I was a welcome part of the college before I ever saw the campus.

Harvey Mudd College is a highly selective college and the applicant pool is dominated by students in the top ten percent of their high school class. Each year around one-fourth of the incoming class is made up of National Merit scholars. As opposed to some larger schools, the HMC Admission Office avoids hard-and-fast admission minimums or formulas. Instead, the staff at HMC favors reading each application and determining if the individual applicant is the sort of student who will thrive at Mudd. The staff does, however, insist that every incoming freshman at Mudd has had chemistry, physics, and calculus as part of a rigorous and successful high school career.

SAT scores among applicants tend to be extremely high. Aptitude in math, as demonstrated by test scores and grades, is an important admissions criterion, as the science and engineering curriculum at HMC is, by necessity, very math-intensive. Verbal scores, however, are not neglected in the admissions process. The college seeks to educate scientists and engineers who can think, write, and express themselves, as well as perform laboratory research and engineering calculations.

The college has been successful in adding more diversity to its student body in the last several years; for example, the class of 2005 is made up of about thirty percent women students. Extracurricular activities, unique talents, interests, hobbies, and a diversity of geographic and cultural backgrounds are all taken into consideration in the admission process, although academic aptitude remains the essential component in each admission decision. Interviews are encouraged, although visiting the campus and experiencing its unique atmosphere is highly recommended for prospective students.

ACADEMIC LIFE

Although Mudders tend to be extremely talented and have widely varying interests and hobbies, everyone's course load at HMC revolves around a heap of rigorous courses in engineering, science, and math. The core curriculum demands that every student take courses in physics, chemistry, biology, computer science, engineering, and a lot of math. Coincidentally, these are the same six fields that you can choose to major in at Mudd. Students with a distaste for one of these fields will find themselves sitting in tough classes with high expectations, a motivated professor, a steep grading curve, and a room full of classmates who are engrossed in the subject matter. Almost everyone suffers through at least one such course during the freshman or sophomore year before settling into more comfortable classes required for their chosen major.

Humanities and Social Sciences

The significant humanities and social sciences requirement (around one-third of the total graduation requirements) makes the curriculum at Harvey Mudd College far more interesting and challenging than the typical tech school. Mudd has been described as "a liberal arts college of science and engineering." Indeed, the educational approach at Mudd is to provide young scientists and engineers with a broad, liberal education including courses in a variety of technical and nontechnical fields. Although no one without a strong affinity for the sciences and engineering should enroll at HMC, those who cannot stomach reading books and writing papers are well advised to stay away as well.

Few Mudders can fill the requirements for their technical classes anywhere other than HMC, but it is common for students to take advantage of the vast course offerings in the humanities and social sciences at the other four undergraduate colleges in Claremont. The Claremont Colleges Consortium provides Mudd students with a wide array of course offerings including music, fine arts, and foreign languages, which would otherwise not be available at HMC. The strong academic programs at the other colleges in Claremont allow Mudders to study nontechnical fields in depth and even double major if they so desire.

> *One of my classmates double majored in chemistry at Mudd and literature at Scripps College; another was the concertmaster for the Pomona College orchestra and double majored in music. Next to them I felt like an academic slacker completing my physics major from Mudd with an economics concentration.*

Some of the best and most interesting "HSS" (humanities and social sciences) professors in Claremont, however, teach right at Harvey Mudd College and every Mudder is required to take several of their classes from the HMC Department of Humanities and Social Sciences. Although students lament the limited selection that the on-campus HSS department can offer in any given semester, there are several extremely popular HSS courses at HMC, including an annual Shakespeare seminar, The Media Studio (a course in media production), and an economics course entitled Enterprise and Entrepreneurship. At the end of each semester the computer labs are filled through the night with as many students writing humanities term papers as students running computer simulations of chemical processes.

Majors

After three well-regimented semesters of the core curriculum, students complete their career at Harvey Mudd taking classes in their major and completing the humanities requirements. The six majors at Harvey Mudd are all academically broad in their own right. The most popular major, engineering, shuns the specialization seen in other top engineering programs for an emphasis on core design principals, mathematical modeling, and a cross-disciplinary "systems" approach to the ever-broadening field of engineering. The chemistry, physics and biology majors are largely focused on producing top-caliber graduate students who will go on to become career scientists, although in recent years more and more Mudd science majors are studying and pursuing applied fields. A math and computer science joint major and a mathematical biology major are widely recognized by top undergraduate programs, and a new "chemistry and biology" joint major leads students into an exciting and evolving new area of study.

All students at Mudd must have a concentration in a humanities or social sciences field in addition to their technical major. This concentration (which may as well be termed a minor) may be in any nontechnical field from dance to political science to religious history. The vast array of course offerings in Claremont gives Mudd students a lot of options in choosing their HSS course of studies, although students must take about half of their nontechnical courses from HMC faculty members.

Projects

During the junior and senior years, students are required to get involved in either a research or a Clinic project. The faculty at HMC has a variety of ongoing research projects, especially in chemistry, biology, and physics, in which students can get involved either as a summer job or toward a senior thesis. Many students, however, opt to organize their own research project for their senior thesis with a faculty advisor providing guidance and advice. Faculty and student research at Mudd ranges from analytical modeling and computational projects to field observation of wildlife and measurement of seismic activity. Laboratory and computer facilities at Harvey Mudd College are unrivaled among undergraduate institutions, and students have access to these facilities around the clock via passcode protected locks and the strength of the HMC Honor Code.

The Clinic Program (pioneered by HMC more than forty years ago) brings blue-chip corporate sponsors to campus to "hire" teams of four to six HMC engineering, math, physics, and computer science majors for one-year projects that solve a problem or fill a need for the company. The Clinic projects, both domestic and international, give students at Mudd the opportunity to deal with the real-world issues of working with a client, facing deadlines, writing reports, presenting and defending their work, and finding solutions to problems that do not appear in a textbook. The nature of the Clinic projects varies widely both in scope and in subject matter. Conceptual designs, research projects, detailed analysis, and software development are all common in Clinic projects that may incorporate mechanical, electrical, structural, or chemical systems, depending on the problem as defined by the Clinic sponsor. Biology, chemistry, and physics majors who are oriented toward professional careers often elect to participate in a Clinic project in lieu of a research project. Numerous patents have come out of work done by HMC Clinic teams over the years, and many companies return to sponsor Clinic projects year after year.

The Honor Code

The strong, student-administered Honor Code at HMC has broad implications on the academic aspect of the college. Cheating of any kind is not tolerated, but there is a high level of trust between the faculty and among the students due to the Honor Code. Open-book, proctorless, and take-home exams are all common at Mudd. Students are encouraged to study and work in groups, but are also instructed to acknowledge their classmates who help them on homework assignments. The horror stories that come out of some institutions of sabotaging lab experiments, classmates refusing to share lecture notes, and stealing homework assignments are foreign concepts at Mudd. Mudders scorn the cut-throat attitudes that mark some highly selective colleges, preferring cooperation and camaraderie.

Course Load

A typical course load at Mudd is five courses per semester. At least one lab per semester and one or two HSS classes per semester is the norm. Those who choose to double major often enroll in six classes each semester. Those who can get away with taking four classes (through summer school, advanced placement, or sheer luck) are teased by their friends for slacking off. At the other four undergraduate colleges in Claremont, and many other private colleges, four classes per semester is the accepted norm.

Grades

The grading scale at HMC can be brutally harsh, although most Mudders exaggerate the cruelty of their grades. GPAs average around 3.3 at graduation, although many fresh-men and sophomores suffer through much lower GPAs before pulling them up during their junior and senior years. Counter to the notoriously high grade inflation at some prestigious schools, at Harvey Mudd College students who do not perform in the classroom receive the appropriate grade—and that does not mean a B+!

Struggling through freshman physics was one of the best things that ever happened to me at Mudd. Although it was a real blow to my ego at the time, it forced me to get serious about my homework and not let things slide until an exam came along as I had in high school. The study habits I adopted in order to get through physics became part of my routine for every class and helped me keep my grades up for the rest of college—although to this day I still hate physics.

Midterms and finals, always administered proctorless under the HMC Honor Code, can be three-hour nightmares, designed to ensure that there is a broad range of scores and that no one aces the exam. Class average scores of fifty to sixty percent on an exam are common with some students who had 4.0s in high school scoring in the twenty to thirty percent range. Fortunately, most of the faculty at HMC grades on a sliding scale and there is an abundance of academic tutoring resources available for students who fall behind in their studies.

Freshmen at Mudd do not receive letter grades for their first semester classes in order to give incoming students a chance to adjust to the raised academic expectations of a fast-paced and demanding college course load. A new joint faculty-administrative position ensures that every freshman at Mudd makes it through the year without slipping through the cracks.

Students at Mudd are expected to work hard, study hard, and do an abundance of homework each of their four years at HMC (and few take more than four years to graduate). The work load is heavy, but the competition between students is not. Studying in groups is standard, peer tutoring is widely offered on both a formal and informal basis, and the faculty keep long office hours and offer extended review sessions before exams.

SOCIAL LIFE AND ACTIVITIES

Dorms

Social life at Harvey Mudd revolves around eight on-campus dorms in which nearly the entire student body resides.

HMC Dorms: The Quad:	East (Mildred E. Mudd Hall)
	West
	North
	South (David X. Marks Hall)
The new dorms:	Atwood
	Case
	Linde
	Sontag

Each dormitory at HMC has a distinct personality and set of traditions. The social atmosphere in any given dorm (and indeed on the entire campus) evolves somewhat with every group of new students, but there is a surprising amount of continuity in the types of students found hanging out in certain dorms at Mudd year after year. Dorm stereotypes are plentiful: West Dorm is rowdy, Case is secluded and quiet, South is eclectic, Atwood dorm is where the athletes live, etc. Mudders often identify themselves by which dorm they live in and hence what sort of people they socialize with. The dorm images are (like all stereotypes) only partially grounded in the truth. HMC is small enough (and homogeneous enough) that students are generally comfortable regardless of which foreign dorm they end up in for a review session, study break, or weekend party. Of course, many students take up residence in a dorm that is not their first choice, and Mudders tend to have friends scattered across multiple dorms; most students at Mudd reside in more than one dorm over the course of their four years.

The dorms are all coed and include a mix of students from all classes. Freshmen are required to live on campus with a roommate and are placed in all eight dorms. The quad dorms, the four older dorms on campus, are named for the four points of the compass although in a Mudd-esque twist of logic, South Dorm is north of West Dorm and west of North Dorm. The quad dorms are each constructed in the 1950s vintage cinderblock style that dominates the architecture on the campus. The atmosphere tends to be more social in the quad dorms, even if less aesthetic and less air-conditioned than the newer dorms, where suite arrangements are typical and students are more likely to stick with their closest friends and less likely to wander throughout the dorm. All of the dorms have central lounges with TVs and VCRs (perfect for weekend movie festivals), and all of the dorm rooms are hard-wired into the campus computer network for modem-free access to the central file servers and the Internet.

Proctors (seniors trained in first aid, crisis management, and handing out candy) are placed in each dorm. There is little non-student presence on campus after hours, except for one faculty member in residence and the bike-pedaling Claremont College campus safety force, and the campus is therefore largely egalitarian. There are a host of official and not-so-official student government organizations on campus that set student policy, organize events, discipline those who step over the line, and promote the general welfare.

Parties and Competitions

Parties of all sizes, from small spontaneous gatherings to well-hyped five-college extravaganzas, take place at frequent intervals in the dorms on the HMC campus. Mudd parties are reputed throughout The Claremont Colleges to be the biggest, most creative, and most fun parties in Claremont. As on all college campuses, alcohol is a part of the social fabric, although drinking and driving is not, since all of the parties are within walking distance on campus. In truth, HMC's rigorous academic curriculum ensures that students who do not understand when to stop partying and start studying will not last very long on the campus.

There is a sizable portion of the student body at Mudd that does not drink at all and there are always a myriad of nonalcoholic events at HMC including regular movies, concerts, and off-campus trips. "Jay's place," an on-campus pizza parlor and pool hall, is a popular hangout seven nights a week, occasionally offering up live music and other events. Mudders are as good at coming up with creative and unique extracurricular activities for themselves as they are at throwing parties. The Etc. (extremely theatrically confused) Players produce original plays as well as old standards as often as they can get a willing cast together (three or four times a year). Other Mudd clubs plan outdoor events like the Delta-H (which means "change in height") club, race the school yacht *Mildred* (a nineteen-foot class boat named for Mrs. Harvey Mudd), and coordinate volunteer opportunities for Mudders looking to use up the last remaining ounce of their valuable spare time.

The four-class competition is an annual event with little or no redeeming value besides being a great time. The event is a giant relay race that crisscrosses the campus with representatives from each class performing in such events as whistling with peanut butter in one's mouth, computer programming under pressure, running a seven-legged race, and stuffing a textbook into a milk bottle. Faculty and staff serve as judges for the events, although stretching the rules is a time-honored tradition. After the race is over (it takes about thirty minutes), the entire campus settles in for a picnic and celebration of all things great about being at Harvey Mudd College.

Dating

The dating scene at Harvey Mudd is as unconventional as the rest of the school. Students at Mudd frequently lament "the ratio," referring to the fact that Mudd is roughly two-thirds male. The Claremont Colleges Consortium is the saving grace that takes the edge off the ratio. Scripps, a women's liberal arts college, is literally across the street from HMC. Naturally, many Mudd men find dates at Scripps and Mudd women enjoy choosing from the men at Mudd or from the rest of the Claremont Colleges population.

Sports

Despite the emphasis on academics, Mudd is a very athletic campus. Many Mudders achieve in varsity sports, although for some students it is difficult to find time to participate in the NCAA Division III athletic program HMC shares with two of the other Claremont schools. Intramural sports are popular and help promote dorm rivalries. Pick-up games of volleyball, basketball, soccer, and softball are daily occurrences at Mudd, as most students are looking for any chance to put aside their homework, soak up some sun, and release some stress. HMC is near Mt. Baldy, one of Southern California's highest peaks, which means that quality mountain biking, hiking, and skiing are less than a half hour away.

Trips

Claremont is well located for weekend and spring break road trips. Los Angeles, Las Vegas, the Joshua Tree National Monument, Santa Barbara, San Diego, and Tijuana are all within three hours by car. San Francisco, the Grand Canyon, and resort towns in Baja are all popular locations, well within the reach of road-tripping HMC students with a few days break. Perhaps the most popular road trip among Mudd students, however, is to DonutMan (a.k.a. Foster's), home of world-famous strawberry donuts. Mudders make the fifteen-minute drive nightly, bypassing numerous other inferior donut shops along the way. This is the popular eating spot for Mudders who are studying late (or taking a break from studying late).

FINANCIAL AID

Harvey Mudd College is, unfortunately, an expensive place to go to college. The school is young (founded in 1955) and has an impressive endowment for its age, but does not bathe in the financial resources that much older institutions enjoy. However, most of the students (around eighty percent) receive financial aid of some form. As at other prestigious private institutions, students and parents alike often accrue a sizable debt over their four years at HMC. The consistency of Mudd graduates being placed in high-paying jobs and prestigious graduate school programs, however, makes all of this debt a little easier to stomach and faster to pay off.

Fortunately, HMC is the type of small institution that can give students personal attention, even in financial aid matters. It's common for parents to call and discuss their child's financial aid package with the college's Financial Aid Office or with the college vice president overseeing the financial aid office. Mudd will work with parents and students to adjust financial aid awards and to establish payment plans that help ensure that any student who has been admitted to HMC has every opportunity to attend the college.

GRADUATES

Perhaps the greatest testament to Harvey Mudd College is the success of its alumni body. Although the average age of the alumni body is between thirty and forty, Mudd has produced a greater percentage of graduates who go on to receive Ph.D.s (nearly forty percent) than any other undergraduate institution over the last several years. A respectable percentage of HMC alumni own their own businesses and alums litter the faculty ranks at top colleges across the country (including six who teach at HMC). HMC alumni have been astronauts, another produces the James Bond films, and still another currently serves as U.S. Ambassador to Israel. Not bad for a college with around 4,500 total alumni, fewer than many universities produce in a single year.

PROMINENT GRADS

○ **Richard Jones, Ambassador**
○ **Stan Love, Astronaut**
○ **Michael Wilson, Film Producer**

About forty percent of the students at Mudd step directly into the top graduate programs in the country. Students from all majors regularly make the choice to go immediately to graduate school out of Mudd, but the chemistry and biology majors are especially valuable commodities and generally can write their own ticket into the graduate program of their choice. In the past several years, numerous highly prized NSF fellowships, Churchill scholarships, Thomas Watson fellowships, and two Rhodes Scholarships have been handed out to Harvey Mudd College graduates.

Due to the HMC Clinic Program and the continuing success of Mudd alums in the work force, dozens of companies come to campus each year to recruit HMC engineering, physics, computer science, and math majors. Most of these companies are located in Southern California or the Silicon Valley although Mudd is gaining increasing national exposure in the professional world. HMC graduates leave college with a set of skills and experiences that are unique to the Mudd philosophy of education, and invaluable to employers. These experiences include working in randomly selected teams of peers, tackling open-ended problems with no clear solution, exploring the intersection of different technical fields, and generally working hard with limited resources under tough deadlines and related stress.

In my first year out of Mudd working for a big Silicon Valley software firm I was amazed at how most of the guys I started with would complain about the long hours and difficult project assignments that they felt were way over their heads. All I could think was "this stuff is fun and interesting and a hell of a lot easier to manage than my clinic project back at Mudd was." I was certainly challenged in my new job but I wasn't overwhelmed like the other new guys.

A few Harvey Mudd College graduates go on to business, law, or medical school, although most pursue more traditional careers in engineering, science, and math. Medical school applicants from HMC often face the disadvantage of a lower GPA than most of the competing applicant pool who have not endured HMC's rigorous curriculum and take-no-prisoners grading curve. A growing number of Mudd students are pursuing volunteer service appointments upon graduation including programs in the Peace Corps, AmeriCorp, and Teach for America.

SUMMING UP

Harvey Mudd College is a distinctly small school where some of the top undergraduates in America come together to study engineering, science, and mathematics in an academically rigorous, but extremely fun, environment. The technical curriculum is broad with an emphasis on the humanities and social sciences as well as core science, math, and engineering principals. The residential campus is vibrant with a student body that is widely talented, dynamic, and eccentric in addition to being academically gifted. HMC is bolstered by its participation in The Claremont Colleges Consortium, which gives Mudd students access to academic resources, course offerings, athletics, and other opportunities that could not otherwise be supported by a small technical college. The student-run Honor Code demands integrity and honesty from every student. In addition, the general pace and atmosphere of the college demands a healthy sense of humor in addition to a healthy work ethic and a strong affinity for engineering, science, and math.

❏ *Erik Ring, B.S.*

HAVERFORD COLLEGE

 Haverford College
370 Lancaster Avenue
Haverford, PA 19041-1392

 (610) 896-1350 (admission)
(610) 896-1000 (general info)
Fax: (610) 896-1338

 E-mail: *admission@haverford.edu*
Web site: *http://www.haverford.edu*

 Enrollment

Full-time ❑ women: 622
❑ men: 546

INTRODUCING HAVERFORD

Once a well-hidden gem tucked away in leafy, suburban Philadelphia, Haverford is breaking out of obscurity and into the forefront of the country's top liberal arts colleges. And why not? Haverford embodies what most people associate with college: an arboreal campus dotted with historic stone halls, professors and students chatting away on the steps after class, people reading or throwing a Frisbee on the main green. But there are many things about Haverford that go beyond that, that break the mold and make it a unique place. An Honor Code brings trust and respect to the campus community both in the classroom and at Saturday night parties. Only 1,100 students means that even intro courses average fifteen or fewer students, giving you close contact with a challenging and accomplished faculty. And Haverford has the top collegiate varsity cricket team in the nation (also the only one). It's no wonder Haverford is no longer a secret.

The college covers 204 acres about ten miles from Center City Philadelphia; however, you could easily be convinced that you were in the middle of nowhere. Shrouded by a wall of trees on all sides, the campus consists of rolling fields with buildings concentrated around a square in the middle. The campus itself is an arboretum, and there is a duck pond (complete with ducks). Founded in 1833 by members of the Society of Friends, Haverford was intended for Quaker men, but soon thereafter opened its doors to all comers (except women, who were admitted in 1980). The Quaker tradition is strong but not overbearing in typical Quaker fashion. Meeting is held weekly for those who choose to attend, and aspects such as consensus decision-making and the Honor Code are direct results of the Quaker background.

Liberal arts is the important thing to remember when talking about academics. Haverford is truly committed to the idea, meaning that physics majors cannot hole themselves up in lab for four years, just as philosophy majors will end up stepping into the Marian E. Koshland Integrated Natural Sciences Center more than once or twice during their college career. A few basic requirements, such as a year of foreign language, freshman writing, and a social justice class, are designed to ensure this, but don't prove to be restrictive. That's not to say Haverford students will do well only in Trivial Pursuit; the past few classes have produced prize-winning physicists and published economists, among others. Be prepared to roll up your sleeves right away—the work is rigorous to say the least. The thirty-page reading assignment that you were shocked to get in high school will seem like a night off.

Of course it's not all work and no play. Haverford offers a broad range of activities for such a small college. More than three quarters of the student body plays sports at either the varsity, club, or intramural level. Students can choose from more than 100 clubs and groups ranging from theater to the Zymurgy Club (beer-making). Haverford also has the highest per capita number of *a cappella* groups in the nation, making for a lot of harmony on campus.

The surrounding towns offer the usual fare of movie theaters, restaurants, book stores, and twenty-four-hour Wawa convenience stores, which come in very handy when you want a hoagie at 2:30 A.M. Downtown Philadelphia is a fifteen-minute ride away on the local train; Swarthmore and Bryn Mawr can be reached through regular van and bus service.

The Honor Code

Underlying life at Haverford is the Honor Code, one that goes beyond not copying off your neighbor's exam book. All incoming students have to sign the Code, pledging to live by the academic and social responsibilities it assigns to all students and faculty. What this translates to is take-home tests, and unproctored, self-scheduled final exams that can make the stress-induced angst of finals week a bit easier to take. The more blurry and controversial side of the Code is its social expectations. The basic premise is that all students must treat each other with respect and work out their differences through dialogue. Enforcing such a vague idea can be difficult. The social Honor Code has been a big topic of discussion the past few years at Plenary, the town-meeting style biannual gathering. The Code is a work in progress, constantly being changed and remolded by students who propose amendments and then plead their case at Plenary. All resolutions are put to a vote, and if passed, become part of the Code.

If what you are looking for is academic excellence combined with a strong sense of community, then look no further. A strong emphasis on the liberal arts and the trust and respect implicit in the Honor Code teach Haverford students not only how to be a complete intellectual package, but also how to be humane and thoughtful in their social interactions.

ADMISSIONS REQUIREMENTS

Gaining admission to Haverford is not an easy task, but it's also not one that should be discouraging. Fewer than thirty percent of the students who apply are accepted, but being in the top of your class with great SAT scores doesn't guarantee you a spot nor does that C+ you got in tenth grade geometry seal your fate. The Office of Admission uses the numbers as a benchmark, but is also interested in more than just an applicant's statistics. It is looking for students who will not only excel in the classroom, but also contribute to the Haverford community, either on the athletic field, on stage, at club meetings, or even in a conversation in the dining center. So keep up the piano lessons, join the French club, and maybe take a weekend day or two to volunteer.

Now for the numbers. A total of 3,358 students applied to Haverford during a recent year; for admission in the fall of 2006, 873 were accepted, from which 316 chose to attend. Of those who enrolled, ninety-three percent were in the top fifth of their high school class, and eighty-five percent were ranked in the top tenth. The median range for Verbal SAT I was 640–740; median range for Math was 640–720. Women make up fifty-five percent (174 students) of the class of 2010, and thirty-three percent of the class are students of color. Almost all the enrolled students have been officers of one or more school organizations or have lettered in a sport, illustrating the emphasis Haverford places on complete candidates. Volunteer service was also high among the class of 2010.

The Office of Admission requires the standard materials from applicants: SAT (or ACT) and SAT Subject Tests, high school transcript, recommendations, and a personal writing sample. Haverford uses the Common Application exclusively along with a one-page supplement. Interviews are required for students living within 150 miles of Haverford, and are strongly encouraged for those outside of the radius. Any additional material sent with an application is welcomed, but make sure it is relevant to your admissions information. You might want to hold onto the tape of you scoring the winning goal in last week's soccer game. If you're seriously considering Haverford, an overnight visit is also a good way to get a good feel for the place. Admissions has a cadre of nonthreatening hosts ready to show any prospective students around for a night.

Haverford has been making a concerted effort to increase the diversity of the college. Close to thirty percent of the students are students of color, and Haverford offers need-based scholarships such as the José Padín Fund for students from Puerto Rico and the Ira DeA. Reid Fund for minority students. The college has also been addressing other areas of diversity, including class differences while many Haverford students come from upper middle-class backgrounds, the Office of Admission is trying to affect change by seeking out talented students from lower income families. This is a difficult task because it means putting a heavy burden on the already limited amount of financial aid the college can provide, but one that Haverford has committed to.

ACADEMIC LIFE

The freshman orientation week used to include a session with a long-time chemistry professor on balancing work. The bow-tied chemist would break down, to the hour, the daily schedule of the average Haverford student in an effort to impress upon the freshmen the amount of planning they needed to keep up with their studies. Eight hours a day were allotted for sleeping, three for meals, four for class, and three for any extracurricular activities, which, according to his calculations, left a reasonable six hours of the day for homework. Needless to say, this left many already apprehensive freshmen wondering what they had gotten themselves into.

While few if any Haverford students follow these recommendations for time budgeting, they take their studies very seriously. There are no stereotypical students; the captain of the basketball team might also be a philosophy major who reads Kant when not at practice. The work load is heavy, and often the faculty members seem to forget that you aren't taking only one course each semester. The library is one of the most popular places during the week, which also makes it one of the most social spots on campus. Students looking for some serious studying can hole themselves up in one of the numerous carrels that are scattered throughout the stacks, leaving the main floor for those more interested in being seen.

The cutthroat competition that is rampant in high school does not carry over to Haverford. With the academic responsibility of the Honor Code as a backdrop, the academic life at the college is refreshingly noncompetitive; that is, people are only interested in their own work and don't snap their neck trying to see how their neighbor did on an exam. Haverford supports this by intentionally avoiding a competitive environment; there is no dean's list or honors program.

> *I remember the summer after my freshman year at Haverford, returning home after one of the most stressful years of my life. It was the first time that I had really been home since the school year began, and the first time I had seen many of my high school classmates since graduation. I was really taken aback when one person asked me what my GPA was. Maybe I was reacting as any Haverford student, not used to asking people about their grades, and not being asked about mine, or maybe I thought it was a judgment of my success in college. The fact is I had become part of a community in which grades are not the measure of a person's worth (nor a point of competition or separation within the student body), a community that looks at each member as an individual and values what that individual brings to the community. I am a lot more than the ten-page paper I stay up all night writing, and I am glad to be at a school where the community (and not just my close friends) realizes that.*

The Value of Liberal Arts

Haverford heavily stresses the value of liberal arts, meaning that there is a set of academic requirements. Students must take at least three credits (one class equals one credit) in each of the three major disciplines: the social sciences, humanities, and natural sciences. A semester of freshman English is required for all first-year students, and two semesters of a language are necessary to graduate unless a student can test out of the requirement. There is also an oft-forgotten gym requirement that can haunt seniors who need gym credits to graduate. Students can choose from thirty-two majors, including those at Bryn Mawr College.

The bi-college relationship with Bryn Mawr is designed so that the two colleges offer more together than they could individually. For example, Bryn Mawr offers a major in growth and structure of cities while Haverford provides astronomy. Some majors, such as comparative literature, are bi-college, sharing faculty and campuses. Class size is generally small, averaging fifteen to twenty students. Introductory courses can reach thirty and the occasional survey course can reach seventy-five students. However, by the time students are seniors, they have most likely been a part of more than one seminar that numbered from five to ten.

Faculty

Small classes mean that students come into close contact with professors, and Haverford has some of the best around. Not only are many at the top of their fields, but they are also interested in teaching as well as research. The biology faculty welcomes juniors into their labs over the summer to assist them in their research, and many biology majors use that experience as part of their thesis or to get published. Most Haverford professors encourage classroom discussion, which both enlivens courses and means that if you haven't done the reading for the day, there's nowhere to hide. Professors are very accessible, with ample amounts of office time, and they are willing to stay after class to talk. Many live on campus. Faculty members will invite students over to their homes for dinner, and some hold class in their living rooms.

The summer after I graduated, I drove across the country with five friends of mine from Haverford. We were crashing with friends as much as possible, but we didn't know any people in the Upper Midwest, so we called up one of the history professors who spends his summers in Montana. The seventy-year-old professor met us at the end of his dirt road on a dirtbike complete with boots and helmet. He put the five of us up for the night at his cabin in the middle of a national park and cooked us dinner and breakfast. He even took us on a tour of the woods and told us about the family of moose that lived nearby and the bear that tried to break down his door.

Study Abroad

By junior year, many students feel the urge to try something new for awhile and to meet some new people. Study abroad programs are enormously popular and the junior class is gutted each semester when students head off for all corners of the globe. The most popular programs are the European ones, but Haverford has also established ties with universities in Nepal, Ghana, Japan, and Chile, among others. Junior year abroad serves two purposes: students get to see the world, and they also tend to return to campus with a fresher view of the college after their time away.

SOCIAL LIFE AND ACTIVITIES

The Haverford experience begins with Customs Week, basically five days of intensified summer camp. Freshmen are divided into groups of ten to fifteen according to their dorm and hall, which becomes their Customs group. Upperclass students, usually sophomores, guide first-year students through a gauntlet of games, get-to-know-you activities, and general orientation to the college. The week includes a dorm Olympics, where each of the three freshman dorms compete against each other in games ranging from the human knot to egg tossing. Customs groups tend to be tight-knit during the first semester, usually traveling *en masse* to and from the dining center. This mentality can slow down the process of meeting new people, but it also is easier to make some close friends within the group.

Housing

For those who enjoy their personal space, housing at Haverford is ideal. Many of the dorms have single rooms, usually grouped together in suites with a common room. Except for freshman year, there is a good chance that a student can go through most of college without having to share a room. If you are looking for a college roommate with whom you can share stories at your twenty-fifth reunion, the several houses on campus and the Haverford College Apartments (HCA) are the way to go. HCA is a complex located on the edge of campus. It houses a third of the freshmen and a large part of the sophomore class. Apartments are shared by three or four students, each with two bedrooms, a bathroom, and a kitchen. The only drawback is that you have to clean the bathroom yourself. HCA develops its own social scene throughout the year, since the third of the student body that lives there creates its own special camaraderie.

Parties and Bars

Haverford has no Greek system, but party-goers still tend to gravitate toward the several houses on campus for their Friday and Saturday night activities or to Lloyd dorm for traditional Thursday night parties. The same scene can get old midway through the first semester, so the more adventurous and legal fun-seekers head out to some of the area bars. Actually, most don't make it any further than the five-minute walk to Roache and O'Brien, more affectionately known as Roaches. About the size of your average walk-in closet, Roaches is a bizarre mixture of seedy locals and Haverford students, complete with a life-size poster of Willie Nelson, a jukebox that hasn't changed a record in twenty years, and a bartender who dishes out insults along with drinks. It's no wonder why it is such a popular hangout. Bryn Mawr is also five minutes away by Blue Bus, the shuttle that runs between the two campuses. Haverford men have the distinct advantage of the famed 3:1 ratio, that is, three women between the two schools for each Haverman, although this is no guarantee that romance will be found. The dating scene can get a bit claustrophobic at a school as small as Haverford, and a general complaint is that there is no casual dating—most relationships tend to be intense. However, many students find their future spouses in the bi-college community.

Traditions

The college also has some long-standing traditions, the most notable being Class Night, a variety show in which classes compete with each other to put on the most ridiculous and often offensive skit. Alums will get teary-eyed remembering their Class Night shenanigans, but in the past few years, participation has flagged, and some classes don't get organized enough to put in an entry.

Going Off Campus

Finding places to go off campus is not too hard. Vans run between Haverford and Swarthmore every day, and UPenn is a twenty-minute car ride away. Right across the street from Haverford is a commuter train stop that goes directly into Center City Philadelphia, opening up a whole world of restaurants, theaters, clubs, sports, stores, parks, and, of course, historical Philadelphia. New York is also a one-hour ride away and Washington, D.C. can be reached in two hours. Or, if you're interested in risking your student job earnings, Atlantic City is only an hour away.

Sports

Athletics are a big draw at Haverford, ranging from the varsity athlete to the intramural badminton player. Forty percent of the students play intercollegiate sports and another fifteen percent play on club teams. There are twenty-one varsity teams that compete in the NCAA Division III and in the Centennial Conference, which includes schools such as Swarthmore, Bryn Mawr, and Johns Hopkins. While some teams are up and down each year, both the men's and women's track teams are perennial powerhouses, advancing to the national championships virtually every year. The college does not have a football team, so Haverford has a unique Homecoming with soccer as the centerpiece of the weekend's events. One requirement to play or watch sports at Haverford is a passionate hatred for Swarthmore. The academic camaraderie is left at the door whenever there is a game against Swarthmore, and the schools compete for the Hood Trophy, given annually to the winner of the most games.

Clubs or Groups

If you're looking for a club or group to join, there is a smorgasbord to choose from. Interested in boats? Sign up for the sailing club. Want to learn how to make films? Try the Bi-College Filmmaking Club. If you have an interest that you want to pursue or organize, the college will help you get it started.

For the past few years, people had been talking about how Haverford needs a pottery studio. Every now and then someone would put up a sign about organizing a club, but nothing ever got off the ground. Two friends and I decided to finally do something about the one wheel covered with dust in the basement of the dining center, and last year we began to organize a pottery club. We received a large donation from an alum to buy another wheel, and with budgeting funds from Student Council we bought a third wheel, a kiln, clay, glazes, and tools. When we advertised at the Student Activities Fair, 120 students signed up to use the room or learn how to throw on the wheel. It is tough to accommodate so many people with three wheels, but we try to let everyone use the studio and we can keep getting more equipment. It took a lot of time to go through all the necessary paper work and finances with the college to set this up, but it was definitely worth it. We finally have a completely functional pottery studio that anyone can use. I think we found out that if you want to make something happen at Haverford, you can do it as long as you organize.

Haverford shares a weekly newspaper with Bryn Mawr, and the entirely student-run *Bi-College News* is a favorite Saturday morning brunch reading material. Lighted Fools is a popular student theater group that produces several comedy skits each semester, and Horizons Unlimited Musical Theater puts on two musicals each year. Four campus *a cappella* groups regularly square off against each other in joint concerts as does the Bi-College Chorale.

In accordance with its Quaker roots, Haverford also encourages students to take part in service activities. The 8th Dimension Office is a resource for students looking to do some volunteer work, and the office has a goal of getting every student to take part in at least one activity before graduation. That goal has never been realized, but a good number of Haverford students do take time out to volunteer. This can simply be spending one Saturday afternoon helping to fix up an abandoned row house in Philadelphia, or a Big Brother/Sister pairing that lasts for all four years of college. The Quaker student group on campus also runs several service events and each spring break Haverford sends small groups of students throughout the country to help build or repair housing for low-income families.

FINANCIAL AID

Haverford is not cheap. With a price tag that is just over $40,000 a year, many students need help to cover their expenses. The Financial Aid Office is as generous as it can be, providing aid of some form for thirty-five percent of all freshmen and forty-one percent of the entire student body. Admission is need-blind, and financial aid is addressed only after a student has been accepted.

Financial aid decisions are made solely according to a need-based allocation formula developed by the college. In other words, Haverford does not offer any financial aid on the basis of academic, musical, athletic, or any other merits.

Financial aid at Haverford comes primarily in the form of grants and scholarships. The college has around 120 scholarship funds that students are awarded as part of their aid packages, and can be general or directed at students with particular interests. Campus jobs are plentiful, and range from monitoring the field house during evenings to writing press releases for the Public Relations Office. Students often use work-study as résumé-builders for summer internships or even jobs after graduation. Students receiving financial aid are given preference in hiring for campus jobs.

GRADUATES

The real test of the value of a Haverford education and experience comes after students walk across the stage to receive their diplomas. For some it is directly on to graduate or professional school, while others want to take some time to breathe before continuing their education. Roughly fifteen percent of all graduating seniors head straight for school right after college, with four percent attending law school and five percent going on to medical school. Another thirty-five percent spend some time in the work world before going back to school within five years of graduation. Those who do start the nine-to-five life do so in a wide variety of fields. Recent graduates tend to find jobs in business, education, scientific research, and journalism—basically most types of employment. Some students receive fellowships for overseas programs. Haverford is a perennial recipient of at least one Watson Fellowship, which provides money for a student to pursue a self-designed research project overseas. Recent grads on Watson Fellowships have played baseball in Russia and traveled throughout Scotland taking photographs.

PROMINENT GRADS

- John Whitehead, '43, Former Deputy Secretary of State
- Gerald M. Levin, '60, Former Chairman and CEO, Time Warner
- Joseph Taylor, '63, Nobel Laureate in Physics
- Norman Pearlstine, '64, Former Editor-in-Chief, Time Inc.
- Dave Barry, '69, Humorist

The bi-college career development office has a wealth of information on jobs, careers, and internships for those who get over the apprehension of even thinking about finding a job. Recruiters from many major companies and firms come on campus each year in search of future employees, and job-seeking students are also able to interview off-campus through programs established by career development. Those who try the word-of-mouth approach of networking can draw upon an alumni body of roughly 12,000, a small but tight-knit and very accomplished group eager to help out a fellow Haverfordian. Younger alumni tend to congregate in the major cities of the East Coast, a large contingent move a whopping ten miles away to Philadelphia, many succumb to the lure of New York, and Washington, D.C. is often referred to as Haverford's southern campus because of the large number of alumni living there.

I never really appreciated the effect that Haverford had upon me until I graduated. Comparing myself now to who I was when I arrived as a freshman is like looking at two different people. When I was a student, I never took the time to step back and realize what a fantastic experience I was having; I was more concerned with my work, my social life, the here-and-now. It wasn't until I left the comfort zone of college and joined the "real world" that I began to realize what Haverford had done for me. Not only was my brain crammed with more information than I knew what to do with, but I also had picked up a lot of valuable tools. I could write, express myself, carry on an intelligent conversation, and think critically. I found myself more aware of the world around me and how I could affect it. The Honor Code had opened my eyes not only to larger-scale social issues, but also to my interactions with people on an everyday basis. I would say the best thing Haverford did for me was to make me a complete person.

Haverford offers its students an experience that they will carry with them long after graduation. It is also a rare example of a school where the word community can be used without stretching the truth. With only 1,100 students, most of whom know everyone on campus, Haverford is like a small town, and even has Plenary, its own form of the old-fashioned town meeting. This is exactly what some students are looking for, while others find it too stifling. Whatever their perception on the size, most would agree that the best aspect of the Haverford community is the healthy environment, one with intelligent, thoughtful, and respectful people.

And let's not forget education—Haverford offers one of the best around. Top-notch professors challenge the limits of their students, and classes are intimate academic experiences only a small college can offer. Students work hard, but in return are given the best available resources, the opportunity for independent work, and a thorough education. Haverford will forever remain committed to the liberal arts, choosing to produce intelligent, capable people rather than those trained to occupy a niche.

Each year Haverford sends its graduates out into the world, and in the fall, welcomes another batch of freshmen. While the faces are constantly changing, the college remains the same, and so do the values and education it imparts to its students. Trust, respect, and excellence will forever be the cornerstones of the Haverford experience.

❑ *Steve Manning, B.A.*

THE JOHNS HOPKINS UNIVERSITY

The Johns Hopkins University
140 Garland Hall
Baltimore, MD 21218-2683

(410) 516-8171
Fax: (410) 516-6025

E-mail: *gotojhu@jhu.edu*
Web site: *http://apply.jhu.edu*

 Enrollment

Full-time ❑ women: 1,992
         ❑ men: 2,359

INTRODUCING JOHNS HOPKINS UNIVERSITY

Hopkins was the last stop on my long list of senior year college visits. New Haven, New York, New Jersey—up and down the Turnpike, these cities and the institutions within them each bore witness to the team of my mother's and my "positive attitude," and Polaroid camera respectively in tow. Although a large part of my visit to JHU was given over to an Admissions Office open house program, my decision ultimately hinged on the most quintessential of campus visit options: the overnight stay. Shepherded from a cappella concerts and improv comedy to an evening game under the lights and several late-night parties, I found myself mentally bumping Hopkins to unforeseen heights on my college hierarchy. Blame it on the eclectic energy and powerful voices of the Mental Notes, clad in their signature Hawaiian shirts; blame it on the oversized Blue Jay mascot stalking the sidelines. From the words of a winning departmental chair (who sold my mom) to the welcoming wisecracks of upperclassmen (who sold me), conversations with campus personalities radiated a warmth and sincerity far beyond what I expected from one of the nation's preeminent research universities. I believed it then and I believe it now, nearly six years later: While a Hopkins education may be considered a rarefied experience, the people are what make the place so extraordinary.

If one were to poll the 1,160 students in Johns Hopkins University's most recently admitted class, virtually every individual would name a different reason for selecting Hopkins. Some would doubtlessly cite top-ranked programs and world-class faculty, while others might offer up the lush campus grounds, the startling variety of activities, or simply the "feel" of the place. Contrary to popular opinion, there isn't only one select type of student who finds Hopkins fascinating. Similarly, there isn't only one select type of student for whom Hopkins is an excellent fit. While the university continues to conduct leading work in the field of medicine, budding scientists and future physicians are *not* the only intellectuals best served by the undergraduate experience; in fact, prospective students do themselves an injustice by stopping there! With numerous well-respected (and highly ranked) programs in the Humanities, the Social Sciences, and Engineering, a Johns Hopkins education promises excellence in every discipline.

Founded in 1876 by railroad magnate and philanthropist Johns Hopkins, the institution was the first of its kind in the United States. Curiosity and independence were the watchwords for this new establishment, headlining a tradition of exploration and inquiry that continues even more strongly today. Material examples of this educational philosophy are evident in the university's open curriculum, the availability of undergraduate research opportunity, and the amalgam of student organizations, ever in flux. This philosophy encourages students to take responsibility for their own education in a uniquely powerful way—those who are willing to ask questions and to dig deeply make the most of the Hopkins legacy.

Johnny Hop, the Hop, JHU...University nickberg nicknames are plentiful and prominent in campus-speak. Though most are viewed with a certain degree of fondness, the oft-maligned "John Hopkins" instills more ire (and more mockery) than any other. Why the extra "S" you ask? The university was named after Johns Hopkins, a young man blessed at birth with two last names. ("Johns" was actually the maiden name of his great-grandmother, Margaret Johns.) A favorite local fact, the source of the university's eclectic moniker will win you points with any campus tour guide!

The Campus

Hopkins undergraduates spend the majority of their four years on the Homewood Campus, a 140-acre swath of green in northern Baltimore City. Only three miles from the city center and tourist district, bordered by two busy thoroughfares, Homewood is an accessible, urban campus with a surprisingly rural feel. Georgian structures and fleets of sweeping marble stairs lend a collegial uniformity to the extensive, pedestrian grounds. Dotted with lampposts and a variety of flowering trees, the campus is an aesthetic triumph (and as such, is often a surprise to visitors expecting the raw, the gritty, or the hectic).

Boasting a modest population of approximately 4,400 undergraduates, Homewood houses both the Krieger School of Arts and Sciences and the Whiting School of Engineering. Relatively compact departments and their corresponding faculty cohorts create an intimate learning environment, lending courses the air of a much smaller liberal arts college.

While size wasn't a factor in my college search, it most likely should have been. Hailing from a small, private high school in Minneapolis, Minnesota, I was unprepared for the grand scale of many institutions on my list. In truth, I got lucky with Hopkins; 4,100 undergraduates was the perfect size for me. I was able to maintain a close-knit group of friends throughout all four years, while forming new relationships every single semester. These weren't the kids who spent all their time in the library; these were social, engaging students with majors and interests similar to my own.

The Hopkins Umbrella

Still, don't be fooled! New arrivals to Homewood will soon discover what locals have learned long ago: the "Hopkins umbrella" stretches far and wide, encompassing a good deal of Baltimore and the world beyond. Free shuttles run from Homewood to the Schools of

Medicine, Nursing, and the Bloomberg School of Public Health in East Baltimore, after making a stop at the Peabody Institute Conservatory of Music just south of campus. The Nitze School of Advanced International Studies (also known as SAIS) is based in Washington, D.C., and maintains campuses abroad in China and Italy. Students also have access to the School of Professional Studies in Business and Education (also known as SPSBE) and finally, the Applied Physics Laboratory. Some of these divisions offer specific undergraduate programs, while the remainder provides opportunities for independent research or employment. Ultimately, no interdivisional work is mandatory; however, if a student seeks adventure away from the Homewood quads, the rest of the university and all of its resources are waiting.

At Hopkins, students need not choose between the rural or urban, the small or expansive; the university somehow manages to provide and to be something slightly different for everyone. With that said, be forewarned: Hopkins students don't view these, or any other defining features, as "compromises." They fully feel as though the best of all worlds is accessible.

ADMISSIONS REQUIREMENTS

Over the past several years, the number of applications submitted to the Office of Undergraduate Admissions has increased approximately forty percent, making the highly selective process that much more challenging. Still, gaining admission to Hopkins isn't impossible and numbers aren't everything. In order to matriculate a highly diverse and well-crafted class each year, Hopkins admissions counselors have the luxury of reviewing each applicant individually. A 4.0 GPA and flawless standardized testing won't guarantee admission; students must demonstrate a promise of contribution in and outside of the academic arena. From artists and athletes to class leaders and community citizens, students with commitment and passion consistently prove most successful in the application process.

Applying

Prospective students have several application options and submission deadlines from which to choose. Hopkins accepts both its own application and the Common Application; both are available online and in paper form. Similarly, students can choose between an Early Decision and a Regular Decision program with deadlines of November 15 and January 1, respectively. While Regular Decision is much more flexible, Early Decision is binding, and thus best suited to those students who are sure Hopkins is their top choice.

Applications are evaluated using a number of specific components, some more academic and others more extracurricular in nature.

- Within the academic sphere, the transcript will prove the most helpful. Not only will it demonstrate how well a student has done, but also (and perhaps more importantly), it will indicate how challenging that student's course load has been. Raw grades and class rank don't tell the whole story; an assessment of rigor, or difficulty, in a curriculum demonstrates that student's investment in the act of learning.

- Standardized testing is also considered an academic component. Though by no means the final word on a student's intellect or abilities, the SATs and ACTs provide some consistency between applicants.

- The summation of extracurricular involvement is weighed very significantly in the selection process. While some students choose to use the space allotted in the application to detail their activities, others enclose a resume or extended list. Regardless of the method used, this description of involvement is an essential indicator of contribution at the collegiate level. The admission committee is looking for variety and diversity of activity, but also for leadership and commitment.

- Required essays, of late, have taken on a creative bent. The most recent offering is the following: "If you had a full day with no commitments, no homework, no home responsibilities, and only the money in your pocket, what would you do?" While this topic is certain to be exchanged for another eventually, the focus on originality and creativity will remain. Essays are the best opportunity to share something new or something unique that may not be readily available in other parts of the application. While admissions counselors hope to see strong writing, they are most concerned with content.

- Two recommendations are required, one from a teacher or instructor and one from a guidance counselor. These should supplement the essay in detailing the character of the applicant.

Keep in mind that the admissions committee takes great care to understand the differences between schools, towns, states, and regions. Not every student has access to the same opportunities; all the committee asks is that an individual has delved deeply in that which is available.

Within the School of Arts and Sciences and the School of Engineering, the philosophy of education manifests itself in numerous ways. Students are given the opportunity to both focus and expand their academic interests through traditional coursework, independent research, internships, and study abroad experiences. In and outside of the classroom, within Maryland or overseas, Hopkins students are hard at work fulfilling the mission of JHU's first president, Daniel Coit Gilman: "[t]he object of the university is to develop character... Its purport is not so much to impart knowledge to the pupils as to whet the appetite, exhibit methods, develop powers, strengthen judgment, and invigorate the intellectual forces." Once students have gained admission to Hopkins, it's up to them to best utilize what they've earned.

Open Curriculum

At Hopkins, work within the classroom is divided into two loosely defined areas: departmental requirements and distribution credits. Unlike many of its peer institutions, Hopkins doesn't instate any type of core curriculum. The only "must-take" classes fall within students' self-selected majors or minors, allowing individuals the opportunity to craft a changeable course of study that meets their needs.

Major and Distribution Credits

With thirty-six majors in Arts and Sciences, thirteen in Engineering, and more than thirty minors ranging from Ancient Law to Writing Seminars, students have a great deal from which to choose; however, due to the absence of a core curriculum, most aren't limited to one field or one major. More than two-thirds of Hopkins undergraduates complete a double major or minor in four years. It's also very easy to shift between majors or schools if the need arises. As Hopkins students become accustomed to the wide variety of academic options at their disposal, changes inevitably occur.

> *One of my good friends began his time at Hopkins with interests in computer science; however, after taking several Chinese language and cultural courses, he decided to add a double major in East Asian Studies. After graduating last May, he accepted a teaching position in Beijing, China, and loves it.*

While majors and minors encourage intellectual focus (and occupy the majority of students' time and energies), part of an average semester is usually given over to "distribution" credits. These courses, taken in areas outside of the major field of study, provide the opportunity to expand and explore. Though technically required, they maintain balance in a curriculum, offering the new, the diverse, and the challenging.

As an English and history of art double major, I was obviously oriented toward the humanities; however, I wasn't prepared to sacrifice my fascination with the natural sciences as I moved into college. Hopkins allowed me to do both. From "Gen. Bio." and Biological Anthropology to an engineering course on art historical preservation and conservation, I was able to self-tailor my curriculum to my interests.

Consequently, students do receive a liberal arts education at Hopkins; however, their collective experience is marked by greater freedoms and increased autonomy. The structure is there, but the specifics are up to them.

Satisfactory/Unsatisfactory

Another way in which the university encourages academic investigation is through the deeply entrenched and strongly supported system of covered grades.

During the first semester of freshman year, students will register for and participate in courses as they normally would; however, the final grades they receive will be covered, appearing on their transcripts as either "S" or "U," "satisfactory" or "unsatisfactory."

The rationale for this system is twofold: first and foremost, it encourages freshmen to sample a diverse array of courses without the threat of poor performance as a deterrent. Second, and perhaps more subtly, it supports the notion that college isn't just academics; it is an all-consuming, holistic experience and it should be treated as such. The first semester of freshman year is filled with stimuli. There are friends to meet, clubs to join, a campus to comprehend, and a city to explore, not to mention a series of rigorous courses with which to grapple. "S/U" gives students a break. It allows them to enjoy the immersion process while slowly, humanely, preparing them for their next seven semesters.

Research

There is little doubt that the average university student could be kept busy with courses alone, yet would class hours, problem sets, exams, and papers really provide enough intellectual fodder for the Hopkins undergraduate? From the look of it, apparently not—more than two-thirds of JHU students will conduct meaningful research by the time they graduate.

○ Anthropology: Women's Movement and Reproductive Health in India
○ Civil Engineering: The Qualifications of 19th-Century American Truss Bridges as Structural Art
○ Film and Media Studies: "2:37 A.M." A Film
○ History of Art: Visions of the Virgin
○ Near Eastern Studies: "The Investigation of New Kingdom Occupation at the Temple of Mut in Luxor, Egypt"
○ Neuroscience: The Role of Perivascular Cells in HIV Associated Dementia
○ Political Science: Thwarting the Terrorist Threat: Lessons from the Israeli-Turkish Experience
○ Writing Seminars: "Lost Writers and their Lost Works"

Research is the real meat of the undergraduate diet. Substantial, sustaining, it isn't just theorizing—it is the direct application, the fleshing out, of those theories. With a broadly based definition encompassing classical laboratory work, self-crafted classes, honors theses and capstone projects, internships, and study abroad experiences, an independent research opportunity is one of the university's signature offerings.

Hopkins undergraduates can become engaged in research as early as freshman year and in every major. Academic advisors, faculty, and departments all help students find topics and projects right for them. While some students choose to contribute to the work of a professor or colleague, others design their own projects with assistance from a faculty mentor.

Many undergraduate research projects are realized with help from fellowships, grants, and additional funding. Incoming freshmen have the opportunity to submit proposals for a Woodrow Wilson Undergraduate Research Fellowship when they apply for admission to the university. If selected, students receive a stipend of up to $10,000 to conduct original work. Current scholars benefit from the Provost's Undergraduate Research Awards, a program that sponsors around fifty students a year and provides grants of up to $3,000. Although these are only two examples, they demonstrate the administration's serious dedication to undergraduate research, both in theory and in practice.

○ Ballroom Dance
○ Day on the Street—Seminar in Financial Literacy
○ The Nature of Infinity
○ The Stand-Up Comic in Society
○ Tropical Biology and Ecology in Ecuador and the Galapagos Islands
○ Wine Appreciation (21 and over)

Internships, Study Abroad, and Intersession

Though internships and study abroad experiences aren't commonly categorized as research, they do incorporate the element of experiential learning so critical to a Hopkins education. By investigating a profession or exploring a city, a country, or a culture, Hopkins students can test what they've learned in the classroom through direct, on-site application.

The Office of Academic Advising and the Career Center each provide resources for students interested in pursuing formal internship programs or more casual career exploration. Examples of recent internships include work at Amnesty International, the Brookings Institution, J.P. Morgan Chase, the Metropolitan Museum of Art, National Public Radio, the United States Congress, and the World Health Organization. Internships can be conducted for university credit, for a salary, or simply, for the experience itself.

Study abroad opportunities, like internships, are easily coordinated and readily available. Hopkins students can work with the Office of Academic Advising or organize something independently; with several campuses abroad and more than 300 students living and working overseas each year, the university maintains a highly respected international presence.

While I didn't personally choose to study abroad, my junior year was filled with comings and goings as friends traveled to all parts of the globe. Glowing reports of art history in Scotland and robotics in Japan were sent via e-mail; others went rafting in Australia and hiked Machu Picchu in Peru on days when classes weren't in session. More than simply an academic experience, study abroad fostered a genuine kind of growth and change in those who chose to take it on. Even now, some just can't let it go—my suitemate who went to Barcelona is still talking about it!

For those students who feel as though adequate time for these options isn't available during the academic year, Intersession provides an excellent outlet. Similar to the "J-Terms" or "Wintersessions" offered at other institutions, Intersession is a three-week block of time tacked onto the end of mid-year vacation. Students can stay home if they wish; however, a good number choose to return to campus. One- or two-credit classes are offered, allowing students to lighten their course loads for spring; recreational courses are also available, along with time for research, internships, or short study abroad adventures. Popular offerings include a public health course in Cuba, a behavioral biology trip to the Galapagos Islands, and a financial course that culminates in a trip to New York City.

> *At every stage, on every level, Hopkins students are actively involved in the acquisition of knowledge. I wanted a place where the students were genuinely interested in learning…not just a place for people who were "smart." Here, professors don't expect you to [only] know what they taught. They expect you to take what they taught and teach yourself. It's a place where [people] are only limited by themselves."*

—Sarah David, 2007, International Studies

SOCIAL LIFE AND ACTIVITIES

Clubs and Organizations

With more than 350 clubs and organizations from which to choose, students are provided with everything and anything extracurricular. Offerings range from publications to political organizations and from cultural and religious groups to club sports teams and community service. Like their varying memberships, these activities reflect the diversity of the Hopkins community.

Founded, led, and governed by students, these organizations, not surprisingly, retain a great deal of autonomy. While there should be something for everyone, in the event that there isn't, any group of students, large or small, can obtain funding to begin a club of their own. As a result, the greater body of extracurricular activities is ever evolving. Introduced at an expansive, open-air fair that traditionally follows the week of freshman orientation, student groups vie for the attention of new members.

I don't believe I'll ever forget my first activities fair. As I browsed up and down the rows of folding tables, sense and sensibility were assaulted—literally! Back issues of The News-Letter *were thrust into my arms, already filled with flyers from the Outdoors Club, Student Council, and the Admissions Office. Dodging the oars extending from the crew team's table, I offered up my contact information in exchange for handfuls of Lifesavers or Tootsie Rolls, along with promises for fun times in the future. Though I probably signed up for too much, I soon became convinced that at Hopkins, there was rarely a dull moment.*

Arts and Music

With Peabody Institute just down the road and the Mattin Student Arts Center located right on campus, students are surrounded with opportunities for the fine arts at Hopkins. Although Peabody does offer several options for undergraduate degrees, interested students are able to pursue coursework, ensemble participation, and private lessons in a more informal way. Membership in the Hopkins Symphony Orchestra, the JHU Band, the assortment of *a cappella* groups, and other music organizations on campus is a popular pursuit and generally available by audition. In addition, concerts given at Peabody and at Homewood are available for Hopkins students free of charge. The Mattin Center, which opened in 2001, provides an assortment of art and dance studios, a black-box theater, darkrooms, a digital media lab, music practice rooms, and multipurpose meeting space for student groups. From the Hopkins Studio Players and Witness Theater, to the Gospel Choir and the Indian Cultural Dance Club, the variety of organizations dedicated to the arts fosters Homewood's collective creativity.

Athletics

With varsity, club, and intramural options available at two interconnected facilities on the north end of campus, athletics are a priority for more than three-quarters of the students at Hopkins. Twelve varsity teams for women and fourteen for men compete at the Division III level, while both men's and women's lacrosse contend in Division I. Despite excellent performances from many of its Division III teams, few Hopkins sports fans would argue with the fact that men's lacrosse, a perennial powerhouse, is the great love of the institution. From the opener straight through to Homecoming and the season's end, the Blue Jays pack the stadium; thousands upon thousands of pennant-waving, sign-wielding, blue-painted students, faculty, staff, and alumni fill the stands, ready to cheer their team to victory.

For the more casual participant, club and intramural teams offer numerous ways to get in shape or to stay active. With both traditional and more eclectic options available (wallyball and inner tube water polo come immediately to mind), competition is friendly and open to all. A *de facto* home base for these groups, the Ralph S. O'Connor Recreation Center offers basketball, volleyball, racquetball, and squash courts, weight and fitness rooms, several studios of various sizes, and a two-story climbing wall. Varsity and nonvarsity athletes alike have so embraced the space that it seems always to have been part of campus, despite its recent completion in 2002.

Campus Events

On several occasions throughout the academic year, Hopkins students convene as a community to learn, to listen, and on many occasions, to kick back and relax. On balmy days in the fall and spring, "the Beach," an extended, grassy space between the library and North Charles Street, is packed with students. Armed with blankets, books, radios, and Frisbees, groups convene to soak up the sun en masse. The Hopkins Organization for Programming, or the HOP, brings comedians and other performers to campus, while coordinating with Student Council to organize casino nights, club nights downtown, and concerts. Friday Night Films shows movies, often working in conjunction with the JHU Film Society.

Incoming students and upperclassmen alike anticipate Orientation, a week-long affair that precedes classes. Organized by a large executive staff and several hundred volunteers, its academic sessions and social events are well attended by all. The fall semester also witnesses a weekend-long Fall Festival, plus Culturefest and the Milton S. Eisenhower Symposium. Culturefest, a week-long series of lectures, discussions, and social activities, seeks to promote appreciation for diversity and tolerance, while the M.S.E. Symposium, the longest student-run lecture series in the country, increases campus and community awareness of national issues. Recent topics have included: "Changing Times: Who Are We? An Introspective Look at American Identity in the 21st Century"; "The Great American Experiment: A Juxtaposition of Capitalism and Democracy"; and "Rebuilding America: Peace and Prosperity at What Price?" Past speakers have included Maya Angelou, Rubin "Hurricane" Carter, Ann Coulter, Charlton Heston, Patricia Ireland, Spike Lee, Nelson Mandela, Bobby McFerrin, Michael Moore, Kurt Vonnegut, and Tom Wolfe.

The second semester at Hopkins is equally full as activities capitalize on Baltimore's temperate climes. Students enjoy socializing at Spring Fair, an enormous student-run carnival complete with rides, "fair food," craft booths, and live entertainment. The complexity of the event's many components requires assistance from a staff of sixty coordinators and more than 200 student volunteers. Traditionally following Fair weekend, Homecoming brings generations of alumni back to Homewood. Convening for brunches, luncheons, the big game, and a good dose of nostalgia, families and friends mingle with current students in celebrating Hopkins.

Greek Life

I came to Hopkins thoroughly ambivalent toward anything "Greek." With a mother who served as the president of her sorority years ago, I felt as though my own collegiate experience would be perfectly satisfying without the influence of sorority life. Though this mindset did follow me through to graduation, I was pleasantly surprised to find a much less intense, much more welcoming group of organizations than originally expected.

With eleven fraternities and twelve sororities, the Hopkins Greek System and its process of rushing and pledging is much more of a "match to be made" rather than a means of establishing one's social status. Events are usually open to everyone; weekend fraternity parties and community service activities include members and nonmembers alike. While naturally these groups attract different types of students and boast varying campus reputations, all seek to serve their members through academic, social, and community-minded outlets. As such, they provide well for those students seeking a Greek system; however, rarely is being "Greek" all that one is or all by which one will be defined.

Residences

For a student's first two years at Hopkins, on-campus housing is required and guaranteed. As a result, social activities tend to revolve around, or at least stem from, life in the dorms. Students are able to select their preferred living arrangements from a series of options: basic doubles, singles, and suite-style rooms are available during the first year, while larger apartments supplement the second year's offerings. During this time, individuals live, dine, study, and relax together; lasting friendships are made, strong social networks are formed, and commonalities are discovered, even between the most disparate of personalities. With the advent of junior year, most students move off campus to apartments or row houses with friends. Though university-owned housing is available, the Off-Campus Housing Office is accessible to assist students. Few residences are more than two or three blocks from Homewood, encouraging continued involvement in club meetings, concerts, sporting events, and parties. Still, the move off campus will have many upperclassmen looking increasingly toward greater Baltimore for the weekend's social activity.

Charles Village and Baltimore

Campus and all of its facilities are located in Charles Village, one of the many small neighborhoods that compose Baltimore City. Consisting of several main roads intersected by residential streets, the area caters to college students and local residents alike. Restaurants and small shops supply ready stomping grounds for those eager to grab a bite or a cup of coffee. The Baltimore Museum of Art, or the BMA, is adjacent to campus; with free admission for Hopkins students, there's really no good excuse for missing the latest exhibition.

Students also have access to greater Baltimore, an extensive yet easily navigable city. From the northern suburbs' malls and movie theaters to the historic neighborhoods near the harbor, students quickly learn what to do and where to go. Just south of campus, Mt. Vernon and the arts district house Peabody, the Meyerhoff Symphony, the Lyric Opera, and the Walters Art Museum. Further south, the Inner Harbor and tourist district lie within easy walking distance of Camden Yards, home of the Orioles, and M&T Bank Stadium, home of the Ravens. Canton, Federal Hill, and Fell's Point are favorite haunts of the fun-loving, each offering slightly different hybrids of the bar/club/restaurant mix. Finally, for the truly ambitious, Washington, D.C., Philadelphia, and New York City are only brief train rides away!

FINANCIAL AID

Though a Hopkins education could hardly be called inexpensive, the Office of Student Financial Services seeks to make the experience affordable for students and their families. Forty-eight percent of all undergraduates receive some kind of financial assistance. The university is committed to funding as much of a family's "demonstrated need" as possible, a figure determined using national and institutional criteria. Although the majority of aid offered is need-based in nature, limited merit scholarships are available. Approximately twenty Hodson Trust Scholarships of $23,000 are offered each year, along with two full-tuition Westgate Scholarships for engineering students. The university has also recently partnered with Baltimore City public schools in offering full tuition scholarships to eligible city students admitted to the university who are also city residents.

GRADUATES

Life after college isn't as terrifying a thing as it might appear; after years of working and living independently, most Hopkins students are more than prepared to meet postgraduation challenges. Assisted by the Office of Academic Advising, the Career Center, and the Pre-Professional Advising Office, students who know what they're looking for (and students who don't) are provided extensive resources to help them along.

The Hopkins emphasis on lifelong learning isn't a fiction; more than eighty percent of Hopkins students continue on to earn graduate or professional degrees within ten years of graduation, the highest percentage in the nation. Similarly, for students interested in professional institutions, the rate of acceptance is equally impressive. Approximately ninety percent of medical school applicants who participate in the premed advising process are accepted, which is more than twice the national average; similarly, ninety-two percent of those who apply to law school are accepted.

The Alumni Association for the Johns Hopkins Institutions provides numerous resources for the recent graduate. With career networking and professional development opportunities, social activities, and events for young alumni, the association is the tie that binds hundreds of thousands of members in more than thirty-five United States chapters and more than twenty international clubs. Wherever they go, wherever they find themselves, Hopkins alumni can always rely on support from their own. Indeed, as the T-shirts given out by the athletic association proudly read, each graduate is "forever a Blue Jay."

SUMMING UP

While most alumni would probably agree that Hopkins provided well for them both academically and socially, the university isn't resting on its laurels. Within the past several years, eight new buildings have been added to campus and several additional initiatives are well underway. From Clark and Hodson Halls to state-of-the-art new chemistry and computational sciences buildings, facilities for research and teaching have grown larger and glossier. Through the construction of the new arts and recreation centers, the rich extracurricular lives of Hopkins students have been not simply acknowledged, but commended and encouraged; their existence makes good on the notion that a Hopkins experience isn't solely academic. The university has also just completed construction on Charles Commons, a 300,000-square-foot housing, dining, and retail complex. Following almost immediately on its heels, a new quad area, complete with academic facilities and a university visitor center, fleshes out the south end of campus.

All told, these additions are indicative of a reflective, self-evaluative university that doesn't feel immune to critique. Hopkins embraces change per se, but perhaps more importantly, recognizes the need for an evolution that builds upon distinctive features and existing traditions. As noted by the second president of the university, Ira Remsen, in regard to campus construction, "[o]ur general plan should determine the style of architecture and arrangement of buildings appropriate to the gradual development of the campus so that in years to come the groups…will form a symmetrical whole." This passage is easily applied to the university at large; in reinventing its various parts, attention to the greater whole—the bigger picture—isn't just a priority, but a consistent practice.

PROMINENT GRADS

- Woodrow Wilson, Ph.D., 28th President of the United States
- John Astin, actor, Most Notably of *The Addams Family* (TV)
- Michael Bloomberg, Mayor of New York City; President and CEO of Bloomberg Financial Network
- Rafael Hernandez-Colon, Former Governor of Puerto Rico
- Russell Baker, *New York Times* Columnist and host of Masterpiece Theatre
- Antonia C. Novella, Former Surgeon General of the United States
- Wesley Craven, Director of *Nightmare on Elm Street* and the *Scream* films
- Jody Williams, 1984 Nobel Peace Prize winner
- Corbin Gwaltney, Founder-President of *The Chronicle of Higher Education*

There has never been a better time to become part of Hopkins. The changes my friends and I have witnessed are dramatic; there are obviously more to come. Still, these aren't the only reasons why I continue to so strongly support the university and all it has to offer. The resources, the endless opportunity, the collection of peerless faculty, colleagues, and friends with whom I've lived and worked combine to produce what can only be called an experience. As a result, I still have a difficult time conceiving of Hopkins as my "alma mater." The designation has such finality to it, such assurance. Yes, I've proudly walked across Homewood Field in Commencement 2003; certainly, I no longer question the validity of my diploma (such a flimsy piece of paper!). Still, "alma mater" connotes a degree of distance that, try as I might, I simply cannot feel. My time at Hopkins remains vibrantly, vividly alive—ever present—in all that I do and all that I am.

❏ *Amy Brokl, B.A.*

KENYON COLLEGE

 Kenyon College
Gambier, OH 43022-9623

 (800) 848-2468
Fax: (740) 427-5770

 E-mail: *admissions @kenyon.edu*
Web site: *www.kenyon.edu*

 Enrollment

Full-time ❏ women: 844
❏ men: 787

INTRODUCING KENYON COLLEGE

When Kenyon College founder Bishop Philander Chase first smoked the ham (smoked the what?!?), he had no idea what he was getting himself into.

It was the late 1820s and the location was Gambier, Ohio. The dinner Bishop Chase held that night for the handful of young men recently enrolled at this, the Bishop's fledgling college, would be the first of many intimate meals taken on this Midwestern hilltop. Today, 1,600 students from all over the world inhabit Kenyon, and as any current student will proclaim, intimate meals on the hilltop continue.

Kenyon, one of the strongest small liberal arts colleges in America, is a place where tradition and innovation constantly renegotiate their boundaries; a place where a professor of classics can attain the rock star status not seen since life in Ancient Greece; a place where "learning in the company friends" is not only reality, it is a bona fide credo.

Nearly eighty percent of students at Kenyon come from outside the state of Ohio. A roommate is more likely to hail from Boston than from Cincinnati. Students at Kenyon are an eclectic group, and the college does an excellent job of providing for its unique community. A vigorous and varied social life exists on the 1,000-acre campus, which stretches throughout the rolling hills and quaint farm towns of Knox County, Ohio. The city of Columbus sits forty-five minutes to the south, offering up the closest urban experience for students. And while taking advantage of the art museums, good ethnic food, and international airport located in the city is always tempting, Columbus is not a place students go on even a weekly basis. Students happily call the town of Gambier their home. Campus life is self-contained, and Kenyon is committed to funding the kind of intellectual and social activities that effectively pierce the serenity of the mid-Ohio calm.

Thoreau would have loved this place. Instead of using Walden Pond for leisurely walks and self-meditation, students make do with the nationally recognized Kokosing River and the surrounding Kokosing Valley, which serve as the natural centerpiece of Kenyon's strong environmental science program. To boost the quality of science research and instruction available to its undergraduates, Kenyon recently constructed a multimillion dollar science complex on campus. Both the natural surrounding and the man-made facilities that now exist demonstrate a strong commitment to science education at Kenyon. This has led to a host of multimillion dollar research grants from the likes of the Howard Hughes Medical Institute and the National Science Foundation, intended to promote collaborative research among students and faculty.

But of course, labs are not for everyone. In that case . . . there's always English. Nearly thirty percent of Kenyon students call the English department home, and for good reason; Kenyon's literary tradition dates to the 1940s and 1950s, when Kenyon served as the birthplace of modern literary criticism. The father of this movement, poet and critic John Crowe Ransom, as well as other imposing figures in the literary world, such as Peter Taylor '40, Robert Lowell '40, and E. L. Doctorow '52, all figure prominently in Kenyon's contributions to modern literature. One of the many legacies of this storied group of English giants can be seen in the *Kenyon Review*, one of the nation's foremost literary journals, known throughout the world for publishing the next generation of literary figures well before major publishers lavish them with book deals. The real plus for students is that the *Review* hires a number of interested students to assist with the publication of the journal. As one may imagine, this is a coveted position for any student seeking a future in the world of writing, and it's available only to Kenyon students.

There are many rites of passage at Kenyon. One of them is learning and singing the many Kenyon songs. They are learned and sung first as freshmen, and seniors must once again sing them in front of family and friends at graduation ceremonies four years later. One of the most familiar of those is "Kokosing Farewell."

Old Kenyon, we are like Kokosing,
Obedient to some strange spell,
Which urges us from all reposing;
Farewell, Old Kenyon, Fare thee well.

And yet we are not like Kokosing,
Which beareth naught upon its swell
But foam of motion's own composing
Farewell, Old Kenyon, Fare thee well.

But when we are far from Kokosing,
We still shall hear a calling bell,
When round us evening shades are
     closing;
Farewell, Old Kenyon, Fare thee well.

And see a river like Kokosing,
In meadows sweet with asphodel,
When mem'ry dwells dear past
     supposing;
Farewell, Old Kenyon,
Fare thee well.

As a liberal arts and science college dedicated to the intellectual and personal stimulation of undergraduates, Kenyon works hard to ensure that students are happy. In doing so, the institution places an emphasis on hiring staff and faculty who are committed to the college well beyond their standard nine-to-five work day. Kenyon faculty and staff members can often be seen attending football and basketball games with their spouses and children on the weekends, leading extra study sessions in the evenings prior to midterm exams, and attending the myriad lectures, concerts, and panel discussions held for students throughout the year. If Kenyon is about anything, it is about engagement on that most personal of levels: the human level.

ADMISSIONS REQUIREMENTS

My Kenyon interviewer did not ask me whether I had taken calculus or not, he asked me what I thought about why we study history and "what makes history so special anyway?" Honestly, I'd never thought of that before. I just studied it because it was what the teacher told me to do, and I thought that's what I had to do.

I realized then that Kenyon encourages students to think through even the most basic assumptions about life. If this was the admission officer talking, I couldn't wait for the professors. I submitted my application a week later.

Kenyon has seen a meteoric rise in applications in the last five years, and, consequently, it has had to become much more selective in its application process. Although the college now accepts around thirty percent of its applicants, it would behoove prospective students to do what Kenyon students already do best: be themselves.

Kenyon takes most of the typical things into consideration: scholastic record, extracurricular activities, letters of recommendation, and SAT or ACT exam scores. So, in other words, take hard classes, be a change agent, study for those standardized tests, and ask the teachers who like you to write you a recommendation letter or two. Oh, and don't miss the deadline. And even then, there is no guarantee.

Kenyon admission officers work hard throughout the year to recruit and shape a class that is diverse, inquisitive, talented, and earnest in their love of learning. Kenyon does not admit students based on specific departmental requirements; rather, it seeks students with wide-ranging intellectual curiosity. Students who do well in the admissions process at Kenyon are able to demonstrate that they have both the intellectual stamina to succeed in a classroom filled with discussion, and the social bravery to immerse themselves in a completely participatory community. Most students who are admitted have exceeded the minimum admissions requirements of four years of English and math, three years of foreign language, science and social studies, and one year of fine arts coursework. Most students have also visited the campus, either in the summer of their junior year or during the fall of their senior year, and many students interview, either on campus, or with an alumnus in the many cities around the country where they are offered.

> *My high school years brought a yearning to flee as far from home as possible, and so initially I decided Kenyon wasn't for me. That is, until I visited. When I visited, I sat in on an English class with Ellen Mankoff, and the vibrant discussion that she facilitated was amazing. This model of discussion mixed with lecture was what really impressed me most.*
>
> —Dayne Baughman, '08

If students have done particularly stellar work in an area of the performing or creative arts, the Admission Office will accept an arts supplement, such as slides or an audition tape for voice or instrumental music. These are optional and will be used in the review process if submitted. Kenyon pursues a holistic review process for its applicants. No stone is left unturned. Admissions officers are committed to thinking about whether students will benefit from four years in the Kenyon community and thus, "student fit" is an important X factor.

Quintessential Kenyon: Understanding Fit and Match

Kenyon students enjoy "the journey." They appreciate what it takes to be successful in life, and they know how to work hard to accomplish goals. But, they are not resume chasers. Internships might be important to some, but figuring out a personal *raison d'etre* is a far better use of time for most Kenyonites. They are thinkers of a grander sort; they are intellectual altruists. Above all, they are smart, thoughtful, and usually willing to see Kafka as just as good a potential roommate as their "buddy down the hall." This sort of intellectual thoughtfulness permeates the mind of every Kenyon student. It describes the physics major and the philosophy major alike—these idiosyncrasies are well understood by Kenyon admissions officers and they look for this "fit" in every applicant.

Visiting Campus

Visits are highly encouraged. Students interested in applying in one of the two Early Decision rounds of admission are strongly encouraged to visit campus prior to submitting an application. During a visit, prospective students can spend the night in the residence halls, sit in on classes where they have a particular curricular interest, have an interview, and/or watch an in-season team practice their sport. Kenyon admissions welcomes visitors all year round, and sponsors Visit Days programs during select weekends in the fall and spring of every year.

ACADEMIC LIFE

I remember very clearly that it was on September 7 of my sophomore year that I decided to be a history major. Professor Reed Browning had just brought in birthday cake for the celebration of the 467th birthday of Elizabeth I, and I thought, wow, this guy is crazy, I want him to be my advisor. So, I majored in history.

Academic offerings at Kenyon are broad and far-reaching. It is common for first-year students to sample many academic disciplines before deciding on a major. By the end of the second year, all students will have settled into a particular department and declared a major or two. But after choosing a specialty, professors expect students to draw from the various traditions, disciplines, and research projects conducted in more disparate academic areas when speaking up in class. Talk about Boaz in Playwriting 101. Talk about Lincoln in an English seminar. Talk about Pythagoras in a human sculpture class. Others will relate, connections will be made, and professors will smile.

Learning in the Company of Friends

The academic environment at Kenyon is a synaptic fireworks show. Kenyon is truly a place where students are not intimidated from talking philosophy in the lunch line and bioethics in the math lab. Interdisciplinary studies have seen an explosion of growth in the last few years, with programs such as scientific computing, law and society, and international studies, which allow students to pursue work at the intersection of multiple disciplines simultaneously. With a ten-to-one student-to-faculty ratio, a library with more than a million volumes, and wireless access all over campus, doing homework is hardly a problem.

Professors at Kenyon are loath to assign anything but an essay. Let something be stressed: at Kenyon you will learn how to write. Sure, there are some disciplines that will ask you to write less than others, but Kenyon's philosophy is very clear: even math majors need to communicate their theorems. In order to do that, they must learn the most basic art of communication: writing. Regardless of the topic of the class, writing is an essential component of doing well at Kenyon. It is very common to have at least two to three hours of homework for every one hour of class time during the week. In some upper-level classes or for a seminar class that meets only once a week, it might be three to four hours to every one hour of class. Kenyon faculty expect students to come to class prepped and ready to engage, and one way to ensure that this happens is to assign a lot of work between classes.

Advising

A good many Kenyon professors are great lecturers, but most would cringe at the thought that they would be known more for what *they* say rather than for what they get their students to say. Most Kenyon faculty members realize mentorship is a large part of the job description here. The classroom environment serves as an extension of the professor's office, and the college expects all professors to hold office hours at least twice a week. Additionally, virtually all work well with e-mail, and responses are generally timely.

In addition to the many formal academic departments and majors offered at Kenyon, there are interdisciplinary programs, all of which are frequently pursued by Kenyon students.

Interdisciplinary Programs and Majors
American Studies
Biochemistry
International Studies
Molecular Biology
African and African American Studies
Asian Studies
Environmental Studies
Integrated Program in Humane Studies
Law and Society
Neuroscience
Public Policy
Scientific Computing
Women's and Gender Studies

In addition to serving students in the classes that they teach, Kenyon faculty have advisees who are majors in their particular department, as well as first-year students who are entering the college without any clear direction.

Freshman advising takes up a large portion of a faculty member's time in the very early stages of every semester, but students are expected to make connections with a faculty advisor if they need assistance during another part of the year. Faculty are always available, and students are treated as adults. It's quite well known that setting up a meeting on campus is as easy as sending an e-mail. Professors will go out of their way to help. Kenyon faculty are teacher-scholars who uphold the teacher side first. They do not mind staying late after class. They do not mind being stopped in the bookstore. Most do not even mind a phone call at their home at 10 P.M. They *want* their students to get this stuff. They don't mind going the extra mile (or four) to make it happen.

In addition to faculty advisors, freshmen on campus also receive an upper-class counselor. These are current Kenyon sophomores or juniors who help acclimate new students. They work in tandem with faculty advisors to get students enrolled in their first two semesters' worth of classes. They also serve as an immediate social contact, helping introduce newbies to the social scene and plugging them in to any activities that they might wish to pursue. The upper-class counselor stays with a preselected group of four to six students for their entire first year at the college, meeting with them periodically throughout the year to check in on both academic and social concerns that new students may have.

Studying Abroad

As if living in rural Ohio isn't enough excitement, Kenyon also encourages students to go to other places, meaning . . . Madrid, Nanjing, and Cairo, among others. Study abroad, either in an international program or one located in the United States, is a popular option for Kenyon students, and nearly fifty percent of them will choose to participate. In addition to the 150 or so programs available to students, Kenyon runs three of its own programs that are tremendously popular. They are the Kenyon-Honduras program in anthropology and archaeology; the Kenyon-Exeter program, based in England and focusing on English literature; and the Kenyon in Rome and Florence program, devoted to the study of art history. Because the curriculum is developed by each department, and because the courses are led by Kenyon faculty themselves (unlike the other abroad programs), majors in the various departments frequently take advantage of these programs.

SOCIAL LIFE AND ACTIVITIES

"Bells, bells, bells, the tin tinabulation of the bells bells bells . . ."

—*Edgar Allan Poe really gets Kenyon College*

At five o'clock every Friday afternoon, the Kenyon peelers fill the air with sound. From high atop the steeple of the only chapel on campus, a relic from the days when Kenyon held close ties to the Episcopal Church, Kenyon students understand what it all means: The weekend is finally here.

The Weekend

Social life at Kenyon is best described as organized chaos. The weekend is essentially strung together via a patchwork of structured programming and spirited random events, all coalescing to create what amounts to a whirlwind of young bodies flowing in and out of campus buildings for a full forty-eight hours. After 4 P.M. on Sunday, though, it's usually study time.

And who says the middle of nowhere isn't fun? A given weekend in Gambier might include both a Chanticleer concert and a fraternity toga party, as well as a talk by *Times of London* columnist Andrew Sullivan and a sold out performance of Marsha Norman's play *Night Mother*. The great thing about this is that the same students will attend all four events. Kenyon students are an eclectic bunch, and they revel in the intellectual and social diversity that Kenyon's generous budgets allow. Whether it's bringing in major political speakers like John Kerry, sponsoring a weekend full of Diwali festivities, or paying for transportation to a community service activity, Kenyon administration is sensitive to the fact that, because everyone lives on campus, and, because it's not easy to get into a major city, that social life must be well funded. And it is.

> *Kenyon offers so many opportunities to get involved and to take on leadership responsibilities. What I loved about the activities at Kenyon is that you could be involved in a bunch of things that had nothing to do with one another and it was not only okay, it was celebrated. The clubs and activities are really the lifeline of Kenyon.*

—Taryn Myers, '03

It's Not All About Books: This Place Is Fun

Life on campus is helped along by the more than 150 clubs and organizations. Popular clubs include many publications, such as *The Kenyon Collegian*, the college's only weekly newspaper; *Persimmons*, a creative writing journal; and *The Observer*, Kenyon's more right-leaning political journal. Music-based organizations such as the Kenyon Chamber Singers and the ten other student music ensembles, including five strong a cappella groups, are also favored, as are drama and dance groups such as the Fools On the Hill and the Kenyon Musical Theater Society, and the community service clubs such as Circle K, Habitat for Humanity, and APSO, the Appalachian People's Service Organization, which sponsors a major service-learning trip to that region every semester. The local volunteer fire department sponsors Emergency Medical Technician (EMT) training to willing students and welcomes students who obtain EMT certification as members of the local ambulance and fire service. Student government is also a popular option. In addition to the First Year Council and Upper Class Council, current students are invited to participate on Board of Trustee committees, academic department student advisory boards, and administrative level committees that examine everything from study abroad policy to student activities budgets.

Greek Life

Nearly thirty percent of men and ten percent of women belong to a Greek organization on campus. These fraternities and sororities are frequent sponsors of campus social activities, and their parties are a fixture on the Friday night calendars of a majority of Kenyon students. Because of the close-knit nature of the campus community, parties are not usually exclusive, and the attitude is welcoming. Greeks at Kenyon view themselves not as secret "skull and bones societies" (my apologies to Yale) but rather as clubs and organizations just like any other on campus. While sometimes a bit cliquish in the dining halls, the vast majority of fraternity brothers and sorority sisters do not maintain exclusive ties with their organizations. Just like other Kenyon students, it is common to see frat boys running with a diverse circle of friends and serving in leadership roles within the Kenyon community that help to foster, rather than hinder, campus dialogue.

Athletics

There must be a word about fitness. The word is KAC. The Kenyon Athletic Center opened in January 2006 to applause from the entire community. This behemoth of a building is the center of the Kenyon athletic department. At the same time, it serves nearly 1,000 students who visit its 263,000 square feet of space every day for recreation and fitness purposes. It's kind of like a mothership with squash courts (and swimming pool, huge fitness room, full indoor track . . . well, you get the idea).

Varsity athletes—men are the Lords and women are the Ladies—compete within the North Coast Athletic Conference (Division III), the first conference in the country devoted to giving equal emphasis to men's and women's sports. Approximately thirty percent of Kenyon's student body participates on the twenty-two varsity sports teams, while nearly thirty-five percent more are involved in intramural competition. Kenyon leads all NCAA Division III institutions with a total of fifty national championship trophies and ranks second with forty-seven NCAA Postgraduate Scholarship award winners. Many of these championships belong to the Kenyon swim team, which has dominated for over two decades. The men's team has won twenty-seven consecutive NCAA Division III national championships, and the women have won twenty of the last twenty-two NCAA Division III national championships. And just in case anyone is wondering, the average GPA of a Kenyon swimmer last year was nearly a 3.5.

FINANCIAL AID

Let's face it, the cost of colleges like Kenyon can pose a challenge. The good news here is that Kenyon places a high value on making it affordable. And yes, there are scholarships. And yes, there are also loans.

The Financial Aid Office at Kenyon is a small, friendly office staffed with people who understand the phrase "extenuating circumstances." This is a good thing. It will mean that financial matters will not be maddeningly bureaucratic. It will mean mom and dad will be able to know someone's first name, so that making "that call" will be a bit easier.

I feel that financial aid is one of the places where Kenyon really shines. It was no more difficult applying for aid to study abroad than it was applying for aid any other semester. The staff was most helpful, and answered all of my many, many questions almost as quickly as I could ask them. In fact, there was a problem with one of my loans being credited to Kenyon—the bank scheduled disbursement weeks after I was set to leave for my study abroad in Spain—meaning that I would not have access to the money once I was overseas. But I called, and they were able to handle the problem in one afternoon and made sure that I had access to the loan funds before I left.

—Dayne Baughman, '08

Like most private colleges in America today, Kenyon sounds expensive. Total charges this year were about $42,000. Kenyon does meet one hundred percent of a family's demonstrated financial need, which means that, after all the dust clears, if you need money to attend Kenyon after mom and dad pony up their piece, then Kenyon will provide it in the form of a financial aid package.

In fact, nearly half of Kenyon students receive need-based financial aid, and the average package is about $30,000. U.S. residents must fill out two forms on-line: The Free Application for Federal Student Aid (FAFSA) and the CSS PROFILE, available from the College Board. International students must fill out the International Student Financial Aid Form, also available on the College Board web site.

Scholarships

Kenyon sponsors several of its own merit scholarship programs. The Kenyon Honors Scholarship, the Kenyon Science Scholarship, and the Kenyon Trustee Scholarship are all offered to students regardless of financial need. They range in dollar amounts from several thousand dollars up to half tuition. Additionally, Kenyon sponsors the Distinguished Academic Scholarships, which are separate and decent-sized merit scholarships awarded to students who have demonstrated excellent leadership in high school. Kenyon is also one of the few schools in the United States that offers aid to international students. There are different forms that must be filled out, but Kenyon's commitment to diversity is strong, and this commitment manifests itself in many forms, including international student financial aid.

GRADUATES

After leaving the somewhat coddled life on Gambier Hill, alumni are thrust into the real world of quarterly performance evaluations and monthly rent payments, all of which seemed completely unthinkable only six months earlier. Alumni quickly learn that Kenyon has taught them many things, but that chief among them, it has taught them to think critically and to communicate effectively.

One of the best things about being an alumnus of Kenyon is that it means one is not alone. The Kenyon alumni network includes over 15,000 other alums who are always eager to help younger alumni find jobs, apartments, and internships. Nearly eighty percent of graduates go directly into the workforce after graduation from Kenyon, while the rest go on to graduate school. However, within five years of graduation from Kenyon, a full seventy percent of Kenyon graduates reenter graduate school to work toward an advanced degree of some kind. Law, business, and medical degrees are common; Ph.D. programs are very popular as well.

And for those who don't work right away, there's always travel. Kenyon is frequently listed among the top ten Fulbright-producing colleges in the nation. In fact, in the last five years, Kenyon students have been named Coro Fellows, Fulbright Fellows, Truman Fellows, Marshall Scholars, Mellon Fellows, and Watson Fellows, allowing them to travel, teach, or attend graduate school at little or no cost.

> *When I went to graduate school and began working as a teaching assistant, I was immediately struck by how different the undergraduate experience of those whom I taught was compared to my own. They had great professors who were really smart, but who were also largely removed from them. I had very intimate relationships with professors who were also very smart, but who . . . pulled me aside to make sure that I was okay and to let me know how I was doing in their class. Looking back, that meant a lot to me.*

—James Lewis, '03

SUMMING UP

Kenyon is an institution where tradition still holds a coveted place in the hierarchy of things. The college does its best to ensure that matriculants understand that they are part of something bigger and more profound than themselves. Kenyon does pomp and circumstance very well. Kenyon maintains its modern sensibilities, but it does not mind being old fashioned if the reasons are warranted. It blends what it had with what it has. It constantly reminds students that life is not about having the right answers but about asking the right questions. It will turn the eighteen-year-old mind inside and out until it has been thoroughly cleansed of everything that it thought was true.

Kenyon is not a place for intellectual sponges. Do not attend a class just to soak up a professor's thoughts from the back of the classroom. Do not think that the dictionary, the thesaurus, or the lab coat are anathema to an education. Hiding is not an option. Be prepared to speak up. Be prepared to attend dinner in the home of a professor. Come equipped to argue over the finer points of things like Western values, nanotechnology, and the 2008 election. And don't worry, you'll find someone who knows a little about them all . . . guaranteed.

It is a place where students engage the community in an attempt both to add to it and to leave their mark. Kenyon celebrates the individual, and it encourages everyone to live an examined life. The Ohio calm will allow plenty of time for contemplation, relaxation, and maturation. Kenyon wants students in the classrooms and the laboratories by day and in the lecture halls, concert halls, and theatres by night. Kenyon is a place where putting forth great effort will meet with great reward. It remains a place where the students, the buildings, and the weather constantly change, but where the questions people ask do not. Kenyon College is a small place that likes to think big.

❏❶*Adam Sapp, B.A.*

Lafayette College
Easton, PA 18042

(610) 330-5100
Fax: (610) 330-5355

E-mail: *admissions@lafayette.edu*
Web site: *http://www.lafayette.edu*

Enrollment

Full-time ❑ women: 1,110
❑ men: 1,212

Part-time ❑ women: 23
❑ men: 36

INTRODUCING LAFAYETTE

There is a little known theory about Lafayette. It doesn't involve mathematics or chemistry, but it may describe the actions of thousands of people over more than a hundred and seventy-five years. No scientists, anthropologists, or philosophers have been consulted, but after reading this essay, the theory may get their support. The theory is simply this: There's a certain type of magic you will find at Lafayette. That's right—magic. There is no name for it, and no proof that the magic is in the water or in the air, but anyone who graduated from Lafayette knows it's there. How else can you explain why such miraculous things happen at this college?

The heart of the magic is that year after year, the most well-rounded students begin their college careers at Lafayette. And during their four years at the college, these students find the magic contagious, as they exchange their own interests, enthusiasm, and passions with other students. It's this magic, and the brilliance of the students, faculty, and administration that allows students to leave their mark, make a difference, and continue to contribute to the college long after graduation.

The Lafayette Experience

A few years ago, the college put into words what Lafayette was all about. Titled the *Lafayette Experience*, it truly was created to describe a student's experience, which includes

- student-focused teaching and mentoring by an exceptionally qualified faculty committted to each student's success.
- a challenging, broad-based academic curriculum that also offers strong programs in the liberal arts, sciences, and engineering.
- a small-college environment with large-college resources.
- a friendly community offering an exciting social life with a broad spectrum of extracurricular activities.

In fact, the Lafayette Experience is truly what students encounter on day one. Concerned and knowledgeable faculty advisors assist students in selecting classes, small classrooms make student-directed learning a reality, the finest and most sophisticated technology drives research in the lab and social interaction in the state-of-the-art recreation center.

In Easton, Pennsylvania, on top of a steep hill, sits a well-manicured, tradition-soaked 110-acre campus. Although its geographic location doesn't allude to it, Lafayette knows no boundaries—and neither do the students. That's what makes the college so magical.

As you drive up the hill to the college for the first time, you can only see hints of the old buildings hanging over the cliff. But once you reach the top, you become immersed in the Lafayette lingo and way of life. The school lets you grow but nurtures you at the same time.

ADMISSIONS REQUIREMENTS

There are hundreds of small liberal arts colleges sprinkled across the Northeast. For a long time the reputation of Lafayette was that the college was just one of the many schools to offer a solid academic experience on a beautiful campus. But over the past few years, Lafayette has broken away from that pack, and its national reputation has begun to truly represent the college's uniqueness in the academic world.

As Lafayette has gained national notoriety, however, the school still maintains the same sort of nurturing educational experience it always prided itself on. And that is why, to this day, the number of students hovers only around the 2,300 mark.

Here are the numbers that mean something to you:

- More than 5,800 apply to fill only 600 first-year class spots.
- The average SAT I score was Verbal—617, Math—647.
- Sixty-three percent of the first-year class was in the top ten percent of their graduating class.

But please realize that it isn't all about numbers at Lafayette. In fact, the Admissions Department indicates that aside from test scores and GPA, it is very interested in "evidence of special talent, and personality/intangible qualities." While you're calculating your highest combined SAT score, why not think about things that really matter at Lafayette:

- Can you make a difference?
- Are you ambitious?
- Do you have the makings of a student leader?
- How can you impact your academic department?
- How will you leave your mark?

Interviews

Although interviews are not required, you are encouraged to have one. While your application may mention the clubs and community service you participated in during high school, an interview is the perfect opportunity to let your personality and drive shine through. And even if you're not ready to be a future world leader or business tycoon, the Lafayette admissions staff is very adept at seeing the special sparkle in someone even before they recognize it themselves.

If you cannot get to the campus, Lafayette has more than 600 Alumni Admissions Representatives (AARs) who interview candidates in their home areas throughout the country. Interviewing with an alumnus may not only be more convenient for you, but it's a great way to see how influential the college has been on a student years after graduation.

Student Representative Program

The best way to see Lafayette is to participate in the Student Representative Program. A current student will be assigned to spend the day and night with you, taking you to classes, meals, and social activities. The Student Representatives volunteer to host prospective students overnight, with the hopes of sharing the magic of Lafayette with others. No doubt, after spending a day and night on campus, you will have a definite idea of whether the school is right for you.

Early Decision

If Lafayette is your first choice, you should consider applying for Early Decision. Decisions on such applications normally are made within thirty days of receipt of completed application forms on a rolling basis between November 1 and January 1. Applicants admitted under the plan must withdraw applications to other institutions. And if you are a financial aid candidate, you are bound to Lafayette only if your financial need is met.

While many Lafayette students do come from the northeastern United States, the student body represents forty states and fifty-four countries including Argentina, Australia, Bahamas, Brazil, China, Egypt, France, Ghana, Hungary, Kenya, Pakistan, Russia, Saudi Arabia, Sri Lanka, Turkey, and Zimbabwe.

ACADEMIC LIFE

To fully appreciate Lafayette, you really need to take advantage of all that the faculty has to offer. One of the greatest gifts that the faculty has given is student focused, student-directed learning. Lafayette is not about boring lectures and unavailable professors. Rather, Lafayette has built a strong reputation in the liberal arts, sciences, and engineering, because of its focus on the student. This unusual combination of strengths continues to define Lafayette's special role among the top liberal arts colleges in the nation.

Students can choose from forty-six majors in four main categories: engineering, humanities, natural sciences, and social sciences. If Africana Studies, Neuroscience, or Environmental Science don't interest you, you have the flexibility to design your own major. The current curriculum has been designed to allow students to experience greater depth in their learning, by requiring only four courses per semester.

One of the main focuses of the academic program is to create well-rounded thinkers. To accomplish this, Lafayette has introduced new areas of learning and has enhanced the current curriculum.

Faculty and Seminars

Small classes are one of the most valuable benefits of a small college, and at Lafayette, the professors are as dedicated to the introductory courses as they are to independent research. In fact, all senior faculty teach beginning as well as advanced courses. And the student/faculty ratio of 11 to 1 guarantees that no students have the opportunity to hide from interactive learning.

There is no better example of how important this attention to students is than the first-year seminars. Limited to sixteen students per seminar, this series of courses of varying topics are designed to introduce first-year students to the value of small-class learning. Furthermore, the courses give students an opportunity to be comfortable among their peers and prepare them for the many other student-directed learning experiences that are ahead of them.

In fact, students use these skills each year as they present papers at the annual Conference on Undergraduate Research. Lafayette's delegation is one of the largest among the 250 institutions that participate, including ones several times the size of Lafayette.

Renovations and Improvements

The college's impressive endowment of more than $688 million and the recently completed Lafayette Leadership Campaign of $213 million make renovations and improvements possible. New or renovated academic buildings completed in the last five years include: a $25 million Hugel Science Center for Chemistry, Physics and Biochemistry; a $22 million renovation of Skillman Library; a $10 million Oechsle Hall for Psychology and Neuroscience; a $3.5 million Williams Visual Arts Building; a completely renovated Acopian Engineering Center; a Ramer History House; and an $8.5 million Kirby Hall of Civil Rights for Government and Law. The Hugel Hall of Science and the renovation of Olin Hall has created a $25 million state-of-the-art complex for biochemistry, chemistry, and physics. Located adjacent to the biology and engineering buildings, the complex includes new classrooms, teaching laboratories, seminar rooms, offices, and lecture rooms that have the most modern equipment for teaching and research. Also featured are smaller research laboratories designed for student-faculty research and lounge/study areas where students and faculty gather for informal discussions.

The Kirby Hall of Civil Rights, home to government and law, was one of the first academic buildings to undergo renovations, and now features impressive state-of-the-art classrooms that will be replicated throughout the campus. In these "e-classrooms," learning is enhanced by equipment that enables faculty to use sound, film, video, live camera, and the Internet as well as display images, book pages, and three-dimensional objects. This technology allows professors to use the computer software to complement discussions and allows students to review presentations that are hot-linked to the Web.

Another new addition to the campus is the Williams Visual Arts Building, with studio and gallery space for student and community artists. This impressive facility has been built at the base of College Hill, where the campus meets downtown Easton.

TECHNOLOGY

Elmo isn't just from Sesame Street. Walk into any classroom, and you will probably hear students and professors talking about Elmos. Elmos are the electronic learning tools that are now being installed in all classrooms. They allow professors to easily access the Internet, give presentations, and digitally display any printed material, all with the press of a button. Furthermore, the technology allows students to bring PCs to class, and plug right into the system.

Only at Lafayette...
would an alumnus donate $50,000 so that a retiring professor could continue his work. That's right, former student R. Marshall Austin, class of 1971, donated $50,000 to honor Professor Bernard Fried. After thirty-seven years as a professor of biology at Lafayette, studying parasitic flatworms, Mr. Fried will be able to continue his studies in his retirement because of Mr. Austin's generosity. The reason for the gift? Mr. Austin believes it was the research that he published with Professor Fried that got him admitted into Duke University's M.D./Ph.D. program. Now that's magic.

Writing and Technology

No matter whether you decide to be an engineering, psychology, or business major, writing will be a major focus of your studies. The Writing Program is intended to help integrate the practice of writing into courses throughout the college. The program trains selected undergraduates as Writing Associates (WAs), assigning them to specific courses in the college's general curriculum and in a wide variety of disciplines. Through the Writing Program, everyone who graduates from Lafayette enters the world with an impressive understanding of the written word, and is able to leverage writing skills as an effective communication tool.

VAST values in science and technology courses provide an exploration of math/natural science and humanities studies that look at the way technology and science impact our world. The courses are designed to engage students in problem solving using a multidisciplinary perspective. In particular, there should be strong evidence of both humanistic and scientific approaches to the chosen problem or issue. In essence, VAST courses are less about teaching content, and more about teaching a process of thinking.

Special Programs

The EXCEL Scholars Program is Lafayette's paid research assistantship program. Students do undergraduate research working one-on-one with a faculty member. Each year, more than 150 students gain this invaluable experience. Besides the stimulating academic challenge, they have the opportunity to apply techniques and knowledge learned in class to a specific problem.

Lafayette encourages students to consider the international dimension as an integral part of their education. Lafayette students may select from several faculty-led programs offered in cooperation with European institutions. A Lafayette faculty member accompanies students and teaches one or two courses in these semester-long programs.

Another alternative learning opportunity is the Interim program. Last year, 170 students took seven courses on four continents including China, Africa, Israel, Germany, England, and the Bahamas. Subjects of study may be as tightly focused as techniques of botanical measurement, as broad as the New York jazz experience. Each interim course earns the same credit as a semester course.

Students at Lafayette are building their futures by participating in exciting and rare research experiences:

○ Professor of History Don Miller's students worked with him for a year writing the twenty-six-part PBS series titled *A Biography of America*.

○ Students who were part of the annual Lafayette Technology Clinic built a Drunk Driving Simulator, which was recently installed at the Weller Center in downtown Easton.

○ The research that students conducted with Professor of Economics and Business Susan Averett was featured on NBC's Today Show.

○ Lafayette's Engineers without Borders team was one of only six college and university teams nationally awarded an EPA grant in the Design Competition for Sustainability.

The fact that, as B.S. majors, we were required to take various liberal arts courses such as English and foreign languages was very beneficial. I have met many people who had very "narrow" educations from wonderful schools— extremely knowledgeable about science but very lacking in communication and writing skills.

SOCIAL LIFE AND ACTIVITIES

For the 2,300 students at Lafayette, there are more than 250 student-run organizations, nine fraternities, six sororities, and forty-four intramural sports, so the average student could easily be the photo editor of the newspaper *The Lafayette*, the drummer of the pep band, a DJ on the college radio station, and the vice president of a fraternity. In fact, ninety-two percent of all first year students end up graduating from Lafayette—and as any student knows, it's not just the academics that help retain students. Rather it's a combination of academics, recreation, leadership activities, and fun that makes college a well-rounded experience. And Lafayette makes sure that every angle is covered.

Sports

Most recently, Lafayette completed construction of the new $35 million Allan P. Kirby Sports Center. In addition to the already existing varsity sports area, the construction adds an additional 110,000 square feet for recreational sports. The new intramural area boasts two indoor basketball courts, an elevated jogging track, an indoor inline skating rink, six-lane indoor pool, thirty cardiovascular machines, spacious weightlifting area, a thirty-five-foot rock climbing wall, six racquetball courts, and a café. There is also an entire floor of the center dedicated to pool tables, foosball, and Ping-Pong. The most dramatic feature of the center is its wall of windows that face the varsity football field.

In addition to an impressive intramural program, there are twenty-three varsity sports for men and women. All Lafayette Leopards varsity teams compete in Division I except for football, which is I-AA. The records of the women's field hockey team, men's basketball team, and the football team outshine some of the other varsity sports. As soon as you come on campus in the fall, students will be already talking about the annual Lafayette-Lehigh matchup. This year marks the 142nd year of this game, making it the most-played football rivalry in the nation. And it is therefore one of the oldest college party events in the nation too, as students and alumni from both Lehigh Valley schools make it a day to remember.

Community Service

Lafayette has a very active Community Outreach Center, with numerous and diverse programs. You'll easily find one that fits your interests and schedule. Every year, more than 900 students give more than 33,000 hours of community service. Lafayette also participates in the America Reads program, providing reading tutors for young children. One of the most exciting programs is Alternative Spring Break. Groups of students travel to four locations during the January interim session or spring break such as Johns Island, South Carolina; a Navaho reservation in New Mexico; Atlanta, Georgia, and Honduras to help communities with painting, home repairs, tutoring, or environmental work. You can volunteer for any of the center's programs or create one of your own.

Greek Life

Part of the Lafayette Experience is Greek life. Although it no longer overwhelms the campus or first-year students, fraternities and sororities still hold an important place in the social scene. Twenty-five percent of men and forty-five percent of women are members of Greek houses, but that certainly doesn't limit non-Greeks from getting involved in the system. Part of the magic at Lafayette is that social events are hardly ever restricted, and those who are not Greek don't let that stop them from taking advantage of the parties and events that the houses sponsor. Furthermore, sorority and fraternity rush (the period of time when you learn about joining a house) doesn't take place until sophomore year, giving first-year students a whole year to get acclimated to college life before being thrust into the Greek system.

Off Campus

As the town of Easton continues to rebuild itself, more and more local pubs and bars are extending the social scene away from the fraternities and sororities and "down the hill." But there is much more to do on campus than go to parties. The award-winning activities planning organization, LAF, brings comedians, musicians, and other entertainers to campus each week. Recent shows have featured Bela Fleck and the Dave Mathews Band. And there are also the much talked-about yearly events, such as Homecoming, the Lafayette-Lehigh Football Game, and All-College Day, which all involve a lot of outdoor parties, bands, and Lafayette spirit.

On-Campus Living

Living at Lafayette has taken on a whole new meaning in the past few years. While everyone is guaranteed housing for all four years, the options for living continue to expand. An exciting addition to Lafayette's residential campus is the newly-opened Sullivan Lane complex of four buildings and a parking garage. Designed to promote a distinctive integration of living and learning, the buildings are particularly well suited for living groups that are centered on academic or cocurricular interests.

Year after year, the most desirable place for underclass students to live is South College, which underwent a $3.5 million renovation and modernization. But since everything is within ten minutes walking distance, you are never too far away from anything to make one residence hall more desirable than others. First-year students receive first choice for housing, and many of the top picks are South, McKeen, and Ruef Hall. Each room includes a bed, a desk, and a chest of drawers. As you can imagine, you will want to decorate your room to reflect your personality but any questions that you could ever have about your room and Lafayette in general can be answered by your Resident Advisor, an upperclass student who is highly trained and dedicated to making your experience complete.

After your first year, your living options increase to fraternities, sororities, college-owned off-campus houses, and specially designed learning-living houses. The most prominent of these houses is McKelvy House, which is home to the McKelvy Scholars Program. This program encourages academic excellence and facilitates the exchange of ideas among students. Students are nominated by the faculty to reside in the house, where students participate in discussions and other intellectual activities, including the production of a scholarly journal titled *The McKelvy Papers*. Living in the McKelvy House is highly coveted by students, and the program was featured on CBS News' *Sunday Morning*.

One of the best things about Lafayette is how responsive the college is to meeting students' needs. If you want to make something happen, all you need to do is ask. Lafayette is small enough that the faculty and administration are very responsive, and large enough to have the resources to get things done.

FINANCIAL AID

There is really no way around saying this: Lafayette is expensive, more than $30,000 a year. But that doesn't mean that affording Lafayette is impossible. In fact, about sixty percent of all students receive some sort of financial aid from the college, with about fifty percent receiving need-based aid. The president and trustees do realize that many families would have to channel some magic just to afford the school so the college is constantly increasing the amount of financial aid and scholarships that it awards to students. The average student is awarded $24,559.

Lafayette awards more than $38 million in financial aid and offers its own fully subsidized HELP loans up to $7,500 each year, $30,000 over four years. In the class of 2008, forty-nine percent received college-awarded financial aid in the full amount of demonstrated need. Some other students received aid in an amount less than demonstrated need or that did not include grant assistance. Awards ranged from $500 to $34,500 per year.

Even students whose families are expected pay the full cost of college can take advantage of special payment options that can result in savings, payment plans that apportion costs into more manageable monthly amounts, or loans with reasonable rates that provide cash-flow relief.

Lafayette offers special educational opportunities and more than $1 million in scholarships to the most academically promising applicants. These awards are offered to more than 300 accepted students who have demonstrated academic excellence and intellectual curiosity. These students may be designated as Marquis Scholars or receive a Trustee Scholarship. Marquis Scholars receive an annual minimum award of $16,000 (totaling $64,000 over four years) or a grant to the full amount of demonstrated need if need is more than $16,000. Other Marquis Scholars Program benefits include

- a college-funded, study-abroad course during January interim session.
- cultural activities in major U.S. and Canadian cities and on campus.
- mentoring programs with Lafayette faculty.

Trustee Scholarships provide an annual minimum award of $8,000 ($32,000 over four years) or a grant covering full demonstrated need if need exceeds $8,000.

GRADUATES

The Lafayette magic follows students even after graduation. Talk to Lafayette graduates and they can recount times when they have been in odd places and encounter other Lafayette alumni or stories of running into alumni almost every week in New York City, where many alumni seem to relocate to after graduation. But even more important, is that Lafayette grads continue on to do great things. In fact, Lafayette ranks second in the nation among the

PROMINENT GRADS

Because Lafayette students are so equipped to make a difference on campus, it's no surprise that they have made their marks post graduation. Here are some highlights.

- Philip S. Hench, '16, Nobel Prize Winner in Medicine
- H. Keffer Hartline, '23, Nobel Prize Winner in Medicine
- Peyton C. March, 1884, United States Chief of Staff
- Alan Griffith, '64, Vice-Chairman, Bank of New York

thirty top-ranked national liberal arts colleges in the percentage of alumni who are corporate leaders according to Standard & Poor's.

But you are not on your own after graduation. Lafayette helps you make specific plans for graduate or professional school and for the world of work. You will gain experience during your four college years in applying your knowledge through undergraduate research, independent studies, community work related to your academic field, and internships. Through this special four-year career development program, Lafayette students work with an advisor to create an action plan to help them achieve their goals. Through the Career Services office, Gateway provides a wide range of informational and counseling services as well as access to a network of Lafayette alumni who can provide practical advice based on their own experiences. Students who sign up for the program are paired with a professional career advisor. Together they work out an action plan based on the student's interests and goals. Students have the opportunity to be matched with alumni for work-related experiences and networking in a specific career field. In addition, students registered with Gateway are linked to JobAlert. Through this computerized job database, students will be notified when Career Services receives information about a job vacancy that matches their skills. Internships are an excellent way to gain experience in a field of interest. Most students participate in these during the summer or over the January interim session.

Faculty members and the Career Services office provide information on these opportunities, some of which offer academic credit. A major value of an internship is the on-the-job experience—an accomplishment sought by employers and graduate school admissions committees.

In addition to internship opportunities, Lafayette students have the chance to participate in a special program made possible by alumni volunteers. Lafayette alumni offer more than 200 on-site job experiences called "externships," which are short-term internships. Students spend four to seven days, during the January interim sessions, shadowing an alumnus or alumna in a profession that they are interested in pursuing. For instance, one student assisted the supervising researcher at the National Marine Fisheries Service in Honolulu, Hawaii; another spent a week with a pediatrician in New Jersey; and another reviewed civil cases and observed a trial with a New York City law firm.

Approximately thirty-seven percent of all Lafayette graduates earn advanced degrees. Some prefer to work before pursuing graduate study, but about one in five goes directly into a graduate or professional school.

All academic departments provide graduate school counseling for their majors, but the college also offers specific assistance to those headed for professional schools.

SUMMING UP

The best thing about Lafayette is that it will prepare you for your future in a way that no other college can. The sky's the limit; if you want to try something new, create a new organization, research with a professor, create a major, or travel abroad, people at Lafayette will encourage and help you.

Lafayette is the perfect mix of independence and nurturing. You will become an independent thinker, an amazing writer, act in a play, sing in the chorus, play new sports, and of course, make long-lasting friendships. Lafayette will teach you how to think, how to be resourceful, and how not to let any obstacle keep you from your dreams—and that's all part of the magic.

❏ *Jodi Morgen, B.A., M.A.*

MACALESTER COLLEGE

 Macalester College
Saint Paul, MN 55105-1899

 (800) 231-7974
Fax: (651) 696-6724

 E-mail: *admissions@macalester.edu*
Web site: *http://www.macalester.edu*

 Enrollment

Full-time ❏ women: 1,100
❏ men: 784

Part-time ❏ women: 21
❏ men: 13

INTRODUCING MACALESTER

In the 130 years since its founding, Macalester has come a long way from its Scottish roots. Affectionately nicknamed "Mac," Macalester seeks to educate thoughtful and responsible global citizens by integrating the traditional values of an academically excellent small liberal arts college with an emphasis on internationalism and civic engagement. Convincing Mac students of the importance of internationalism and civic engagement is simple—a visit to campus makes this instantly clear. Outside of Old Main and Carnegie

Hall, you will see students continuing classroom discussions about international economics with their professors. At the Campus Center, you will likely overhear students arguing about emerging U.S. policies in English and many other languages. On the sidewalk leading from the DeWitt Wallace Library to the Olin-Rice science complex, you will see colorful messages chalked by students about social/political rallies and student organization meetings. In the student newspaper, *The Mac Weekly*, you will read convincing but conflicting columns expressing opinions about proposed Macalester administrative decisions. At the Center for Civic Engagement, you might hear stories of a Mac student inspiring an immigrant child to take her studies seriously so that she might one day attend the college of her mentor. If you stay up past midnight, you might find a group of first-year Genetics students in "The Link" between the Library and Old Main working feverishly to finish a lab report for the next morning. However, Macalester is not just a constant barrage of academic and sociopolitical engagement. In fact, you are just as likely to hear students outside of Old Main discussing the outcome of last night's soccer game (Mac won by a landslide, of course). Outside of the Campus center, you might hear Jordanian and African students planning

Twin Cities: population 2.9 million
- Minneapolis (the largest city in Minnesota) and St. Paul (the state capitol) are divided by the Mississippi River
- The 15th largest metropolitan area in the nation
- Home to the Timberwolves (NBA), Twins (MLB), Vikings (NFL), and Wild (NHL) professional sports teams
- Second only to New York City in number of theater seats per capita
- Home to numerous museums, thousands of restaurants, concert venues, lakes, and parks

Macalester's Campus: population 1884
- Located on Summit and Grand Avenues in residential St. Paul
- Summit Avenue: the longest stretch of restored Victorian homes/mansions in the nation, including the former residence of F. Scott Fitzgerald and the governor's mansion
- Grand Avenue: home to forty-six restaurants, three bookstores, three bakeries, two grocery stores, two art galleries, and numerous specialty shops

a trip to the nearby Mall of America. Chalked messages around campus might advertise the coming Trads and Sirens concert, where students line up outside of the concert hall hoping to get a seat at the popular *a cappella* show. Or, you might be lucky enough to catch the biannual Mock Weekly, where *Mac Weekly* writers parody their normally serious journalism. In the Center for Civic Engagement, you might hear a student bragging about this year's massive yield at the community garden where they volunteer. And, if you visit the campus center just before midnight, you will find chatting students ordering chicken strips and smoothies during a late-night study break.

Late one Saturday morning, a few weeks after arriving at Macalester, I awoke to the distant sound of song. It wasn't long before I realized that the song was Mac's fight song "Scotland the Brave" played on our official instrument, the bagpipe. At the time, I knew the song only as a tune, but soon I was "loudly and proudly calling Scotland the brave" with my fellow Fighting Scots at any and every opportunity. I still regret not taking advantage of the free bagpipe lessons that Mac offers to any interested student so that I might have been able to make Macalester proud with my own piped rendition of "Scotland the Brave."

Because of its small size and location in a large city, Mac successfully combines the intimacy of a top-tier small liberal arts college with the excitement, engagement, and opportunities of a large metropolitan environment in a way that few other top liberal arts colleges can. Admittedly, Macalester's brand of liberal arts education is not for everyone. However, if you like the sound of a college where academics, internationalism, and civic engagement collide in the everyday life of students, then Macalester just might be the place for you.

ADMISSIONS REQUIREMENTS

As one of the top small liberal arts colleges in the nation, admission to Macalester is highly competitive. Dramatic increases in numbers of applications received, without concurrent increases in size of the student body, over the past decade have led to greater selectivity with each passing year. However, because Macalester's name recognition is not as widespread as many coastal schools with which it competes for students, applicants to Macalester are highly self-selected. Many applicants learn about Macalester because of the exceptional academic reputation that it holds within academic communities. Typical applicants to Macalester have put a great deal of thought and research into which colleges best suit their academic and cocurricular needs. The result of all of these factors is that, although admission to Macalester is academically competitive, the percentage of applicants who are admitted to Macalester remains high relative to the Ivy League.

Requirements

Macalester's application process is designed to give admissions officers at the college a view not only of the achievements of the applicant, but also of the passions, potential, and future goals of the applicant. For this reason, personal statements and the recommendations of teachers and counselors, along with the academic choices and accomplishments of the applicant, form the basis for selection of a student body. Because of the small size of the school, the admissions committee at Mac has the luxury of being able to review all applications completely and thoroughly. The statement that there are no formulas for admission or cutoffs is really true in the case of Macalester admissions. However, as one of the most academically competitive liberal arts colleges in the nation, outstanding academic and cocurricular performance in high school is certainly a prerequisite for admission; this necessity for academic excellence is reflected in the achievements of the entering class each fall. In particular, it is expected that applicants have taken full advantage of the academic and extracurricular opportunities afforded to them at their high school.

Macalester accepts either the Macalester-specific or the common application. However, students submitting a common application must also submit a supplement provided by Macalester. Either the SAT or ACT is required for admission, and SAT Subject Tests are recommended. Interviews for admission also are advised. An excellent interview can separate one applicant from a sea of otherwise academically similar applicants. One-on-one interviews are offered on campus from April through January. Off campus interviews are offered on selected dates in many U.S. cities and internationally.

ACADEMIC LIFE

Curricular Requirements

A cademic life at Mac can be at once overwhelming, exhilarating, and exhausting. Macalester is first and foremost an intensely academic environment, even outside of the classroom and laboratory. Showing a deep commitment to the liberal arts, Macalester requires students to undertake rigorous coursework in a variety of fields. Macalester's graduation requirements result in a curriculum that represents the best of the liberal arts; both breadth and depth of study are reflected in every student's coursework. The first requirement that entering Mac students encounter is the first-year course. The first-year course serves as a home base for the entering student. First-year courses are offered in every conceivable area of study, from "Big Bang Physics" to "Doing and Undoing Race in America." Many first-year courses are residential, meaning that the sixteen students in the course live together on the same dorm floor. In this way, the courses help foster friendships and provide instant study groups. The first-year course professor also acts as a student's academic advisor until a major is declared in the sophomore year.

Other unique requirements are the domestic and international diversity requirements. These requirements can be fulfilled by designated courses in a variety of departments, such as "Jazz and the American Experience" and "Medical Anthropology." Macalester was one of the first schools to institute diversity requirements, and they continue to blend in with Mac's emphases of internationalism and multiculturalism. Although Mac has many curricular requirements, and holds rigorous major requirements, many opportunities exist for students to broaden their education with elective courses. Whereas most students welcome the opportunity to expand their academic horizons, there are always a number of students who complain about certain "unnecessary" requirements. Invariably, they are the ones who, at graduation, express only regret about choosing to take another chemistry course rather than a Shakespeare seminar.

> *Choosing classes each semester was always a difficult task. With so many interesting classes to choose from, it constantly seemed like there were at least three times too few spots in my schedule. However, at the end of the process, I always felt that the mix of classes suited my needs perfectly."*

In short, it is the diversity and rigor of Macalester coursework that transforms high potential into great minds. However, both students and faculty are never completely satisfied with the college program. Because of this, requirements at Macalester are constantly evolving as students and faculty continue to improve the educational experience.

Classroom Experiences and Professors

The level of teaching at Macalester is outstanding. Mentorship relationships formed between students and professors are commonplace at Mac and are a critical part of the Macalester experience. Small classes at Mac mean that professors and students know each other well. Even classes that are normally taught lecture style, such as developmental biology, are enhanced by the inevitable discussion that results in classes smaller than ten or fifteen students. Professors at Macalester are deeply committed to undergraduate education, and it shows. Although all Macalester faculty members are accomplished scholars and scientists, their primary commitment is teaching undergraduates. This is the real distinction between a Macalester education and the education one might receive at a large institution. Professors motivate their students to achieve inside and outside of the classroom, and they truly care about the well-being of students.

Individualized Research

Mac's academic environment consistently fosters creative, critical thought and research among its students, as evidenced by the large number of Mac students who produce independent projects with their professors. The opportunities and funding for student research are tremendous and available to any qualified student. Nearly ninety students at Mac are awarded research grants each summer. As expected, Mac students produce, and often publish, works in classical liberal arts fields such as Literature, Religious Studies, and Classics. Possibly less expected, however, is Macalester's strength in the social, physical, and biological sciences, stemming from a strong teaching and research faculty and resulting in excellent student research. Also, the state-of-the-art research facilities are a plus. Because of Mac's excellent science professors and small class sizes, students are taught more than just facts—Mac students are taught how to be scientists, in that they are encouraged to be both critical and creative.

Opportunities for individualized interdisciplinary research at Macalester are also exceptional.

My senior year at Mac I created an interdisciplinary honors project that encompassed my studies in classics and political science. I looked at the influence of ancient religion and gender on modern war, not exactly your everyday subject matter. My professors at Mac, from both disciplines, wholeheartedly supported my research. They were always available to me for questions, advice, and creative criticism. They truly cared about my project and me. Having met professors from other schools and visited other college classrooms, I believe that the opportunity to pursue this kind of creative research with kind and encouraging faculty is rare at most schools. At Mac though, it is just part of our everyday experience.

Senior Honors Thesis

All majors require a senior capstone experience and many students choose to undertake a senior honors thesis. The senior honors thesis represents at least one full year of individualized research under the tutelage of one or more chosen thesis advisors. Many honors theses are the result of multiple years of research, especially in the laboratory sciences. The honor's thesis process culminates in public defense of the thesis to a committee of at least three faculty members. A completed thesis is bound and stored in the school library for use by future students.

Off-campus Study

The huge number of businesses, hospitals, and law and government offices centered in the Twin Cities provides students with endless opportunities for internships during the summer and academic year. Some typical sites for off-campus internships include 3M, Piper Jaffray, Merrill Lynch, the State House, and numerous hospitals and law firms. Approximately 300 students complete an internship through the internship program every year; some even receive academic credit for their work. Internships completed for academic credit range from apprentice papermaker (Art) and naturalist (Environmental Studies) to investment analyst (Economics) and architectural computer imaging intern (Computer Science).

Study Abroad

Furthermore, more than half of all Macalester students study abroad during their undergraduate career. The range of study abroad opportunities available to students at Mac is so vast that choosing just one can often feel overwhelming. However, the International Center at Mac is well equipped to match students with a study abroad program where they can fulfill their pre-med requirements, sharpen their German, and volunteer at a hospital in Hamburg. Approximately 250 students study abroad each year in nearly 50 countries, from Argentina to Vietnam. These students return from their journeys eager to share the unique perspective they gained through both service and cultural immersion. Study abroad is considered by Mac to be a critical component of educating global citizens.

Steering Committees

Students at Macalester are never shy about expressing their opinions on any and every possible subject, especially administrative decisions of the college. Fortunately, these opinions don't fall on deaf ears. Many students have the opportunity to serve on faculty selection, admissions, and curricular renewal committees (to name a few). Student involvement on decision-making bodies demonstrates that the school values the opinions of its students. Many students will tell you that they not only sat on these committees, but that they also influenced the course of action the committees took. Experiences like these are invaluable to students who will stay in academia and those who will go into the job market.

Location, Location, Location

Mac's leafy fifty-three acre campus in residential St. Paul looks like the traditional college campus. Campus buildings frame three large, grassy quads, where you are just as likely to see students reading Sartre as playing Ultimate Frisbee. Mac invests heavily in building and updating academic and residential structures; over eighty million dollars have been invested in the past ten years, including a new campus center that opened in 2001. Although this investment results in outstanding academic and nonacademic facilities, it is the world outside of campus that highlights the many advantages of Mac's location. At Mac's front door, Summit and Grand Avenues provide pleasant scenery for outdoor activities and more restaurants and shops than any student could possibly need. The many restaurants that line Grand Avenue range from dirt cheap to quite expensive. Literally feet from the campus, students can always be found studying at Dunn Brothers or Coffee News. You also might see someone grabbing a kebab at Shish, a Mediterranean grill. Occasionally, you will find students at the more expensive restaurants on a date or out for a nice evening with friends. Summit Avenue boasts incredible Victorian mansions, the best walking/jogging/biking route to the Mississippi River, and a view of the Minneapolis skyline. The greater Twin Cities, with a metro population of almost three million, provide students with endless volunteer, internship, and additional social opportunities.

Civic Engagement

SCOTTISH ROOTS

Official Macalester
- Mascot: The Fighting Scot
- Instrument: The Bagpipe
- Fight Song: "Scotland the Brave"
- Plaid: The Clan MacAlister Tartan
- Student Nicknames: Scots, Fighting Scots

Mac students are heavily involved in community service; over half of enrolled students participate each semester. One of the advantages of being in an urban environment is that there are numerous opportunities for different types of community service that positively impact the Twin Cities. The popular and well-run Center for Civic Engagement ensures that students get connected with the type of community service that interests them most, whether it be volunteering at the Center for Victims of Torture, teaching English as a Second Language to Somali immigrants, or tutoring middle-school kids in chemistry.

> *Macalester's Community Service Office was an invaluable resource for me as an undergraduate. Whether I wanted a one-time event or a weekly volunteering opportunity, a staff member was always available with opportunities to compliment my academic program and interests in child psychology. I took advantage of several one-time events in addition to volunteering on a weekly basis at an afterschool reading program for at-risk students, a residential treatment program for children with emotional and behavioral problems, and an experimental afterschool program to reduce weight stigmatization among fifth and sixth grade students.*

Through its commitment to civic engagement, Macalester instills the nobility of service in its graduates for a lifetime. In short, Mac is an environment that encourages engagement in sociopolitical action. The college succeeds in instilling its core values in students of all disciplines—thus, graduating a class of future leaders in science, politics, medicine, economics, and academia who share a commitment to service and value an international perspective in an increasingly global society.

Student Groups

Although the richness of the Twin Cities offers students both rewarding and fun activities, Macalester's own campus life offers many opportunities for students. More than eighty student organizations exist at Mac ranging from *a cappella* singing groups to the chemistry club. In tune with Mac's international emphasis, some of the most popular student organizations are Macalester International Organization (MIO) and Model United Nations. Notably, both organizations are open to domestic and international students. The men's and women's *a cappella* groups The Traditions (Trads for short) and The Sirens belt *a cappella* renditions of Madonna's "Like a Virgin," Ben Folds Five's "Kate" and some satirical originals. Groups such as the Macalester African Music Ensemble enjoy widespread recognition throughout the Twin Cities. Many students write, edit, or take photographs for the student newspaper *The Mac Weekly.* Mac also has a very active student government (MCSG) in which many students participate. MCSG, among other things, provides funds to form new groups, as evidenced by the recent forming of the coed *a cappella* group "Scotch Tape."

Internationalism and Multiculturalism

Macalester has one of the highest percentages of international students of any college in the nation; twelve percent of the student body hails from overseas (sixteen percent if you count dual citizens). Mac is also the first college in the country to fly the flag of the United Nations and is the alma mater of the current Secretary-General of the U.N. and recent Nobel Peace Laureate, Kofi Annan. The large number of international students at Mac provides a unique and diverse perspective that pervades the academic and social lives of students in all disciplines.

When choosing a college, I was looking for an academically excellent small liberal arts college in a major city. I was sure that I wanted to major in biology and chemistry, and was unconcerned with internationalism and service. However, I soon realized that the international diversity and commitment to service typified by Mac enriched my college experience and strengthened my understanding of the world. On my first-year dormitory floor, there were students from fifteen different countries. I vividly remember watching the 2000 presidential election with friends from Ethiopia, India, Bangladesh, Sweden, and China. On that night alone, I learned so much from my international friends about world views of American politics. Because of experiences like this, I realized how lucky I was to attend a college that provided outstanding educational and research opportunities in biochemistry, as well as talented, diverse, and involved peers.

The International Center at Mac is often the starting point of international activities on campus. However, it does much more than help international students acclimate to American life and arrange study abroad programs. It also reaches out to the global community by organizing programs such as the Macalester International Roundtable where top research scholars and Mac students and professors gather for a week of discussion and debate on an internationally relevant topic. The International Center also plays host to the World Press Institute where journalists from all corners of the earth have the opportunity to learn more about their craft in the United States through a competitive fellowship program.

As part of Macalester's focus on Multiculturalism, the Lealtad-Suzuki Center in the Department of Multicultural Life and a Dean of Multicultural Life position were created in 2002. Recently, selection of a Dean for the Study of Race and Ethnicity to head the new American Studies: Comparative Racial Formations department also was initiated. Although the center for multiculturalism plays a large role in making Mac an inviting place for students of color, it also focuses on welcoming any group of students that is traditionally underrepresented, such as students of varied religions, gender identities, cultural backgrounds, and their allies.

Athletics

Division III athletics at Mac are an important part of student life, of particular note are men's and women's soccer, cross-country, and men's basketball; each of which has featured All-American players and consistently compete in the postseason. Many club teams, such as men's and women's Rugby and Ultimate Frisbee are also popular among students. Although Mac values its students' athletic abilities, academics come first at Mac. Coaches are aware of the values of the school and the fact that students have chosen Mac for its excellent academic opportunities. They push their players hard to improve on the field, track, and court while maintaining excellence in the classroom. The consistent presence of "M Club" members (a club of Mac alumni who were scholar-athletes) at a variety of sporting events creates a sense of athletic history that benefits scholar athletes in business and in life.

Housing and Dining Options

Like many liberal arts colleges, first- and second-year students are required to live in Mac's dormitories to enrich the community experience among students. Dormitories are constantly being built or renovated by the college. On-campus housing is coveted by upperclassmen, who are not guaranteed spots. Housing for upperclassmen is offered on a lottery basis; approximately half of upperclassmen live in college-owned dorms, houses, and apartments. Fortunately, for students who do not get a high draw in the lottery, the Mac-Groveland neighborhood that surrounds the college offers many affordable rental properties within a few blocks of campus. The college also offers many specialty housing options. At the veggie co-op students cook their own vegan/vegetarian food. Hebrew House residents, who make up diverse faiths, immerse themselves in Jewish traditions, make kosher food, and host Shabbat services. French, Spanish, Japanese, Chinese, Russian, and German houses also are offered as places where students can live and dine with native speakers and be immersed in a foreign language.

Students who live on campus eat in Café Mac in the new Campus Center, where the dining options are palatable and abundant. Cuisine choices are split into the four corners of the compass, North (Smorgasbord and Mediterranean), East (Asian), South (Latin American and Subcontinental), and West (Burgers, Chicken, and Fries). Also included are fruit and cereal at all meals and a salad bar, fresh soup, and wood oven-baked pizza at lunch and dinner. From made-to-order omelets, French toast, and fresh strawberries in the morning, black olive and mushroom pizza and a fruit salad at lunch, to chicken curry, broccoli, and wontons for dinner, the culinary options really are endless. Vegetarian and vegan options are also available at every meal. Visitors to Café Mac are always impressed by the choices and quality of food served, and many students who live off-campus choose to eat at Café Mac during the day. Furthermore, many students and faculty get individually priced meals, coffee, smoothies, snacks, and desserts at the Grillé outside of the cafeteria.

Leisure Activities

Because there are no fraternities or sororities at Macalester, student get-togethers often consist of small- to medium-sized gatherings in dorm rooms or small- to large-sized gatherings off-campus. Although Mac students work hard, and there are always a substantial number of students who are studying on Friday and Saturday nights, Mac students also know how to relax and have a good time. Options for relaxation on the weekend vary from watching movies with a few friends at a Mac Cinema showing to attending a campus-wide event to a gathering with a group off-campus. First-year students quickly realize which types of activities suit them best and attend accordingly. Various student organizations host dances, concerts, and other cultural events during the week and weekend. Students also venture into the Twin Cities for entertainment. Many students visit museums, such as the Walker, attend concerts at First Ave, sporting events at the Metrodome, and plays at the Ordway. Some students explore the bar and club scenes of Minneapolis and St. Paul, ending up at noticeable places such as the Groveland Tap, W. A. Frost, the C.C. Club, or Bryant Lake Bowl. Either way, if one wants to escape the walls of the college, there are many different activities to be found.

The most referenced motto of Macalester admissions and financial aid is "excellence and access." Essentially, this means that the administration is committed to making a Macalester education accessible to all academically distinguished students. The bottom line is that if you are admitted to Macalester, the school will make sure that you can afford to attend, without draining your life savings or drowning in student loans. The cost of a Macalester education is subsidized by more than 16,000 dollars per student through the endowment; thus, even though tuition, room, and board totals 39,000 dollars per year, Macalester actually spends approximately 56,000 dollars per student, per year. Approximately sixty-five percent of students receive some form of need-based financial aid, totaling more than twenty-four million dollars a year (seventy-five percent of which is in the form of grants or scholarships). A financial aid package usually consists of a combination of grants, work-study, and loans. Work-study jobs can often be one of the highlights of a Mac education.

> *One of the best things about having a job on campus is how many great work-study opportunities exist. During my time at Macalester, I was able to act as a teaching assistant for four different classes in my major, and was offered other opportunities to act as an assistant outside my major. These experiences deepened my understanding of the subject matter, my relationships with professors, and strengthened my drive to continue my studies in pursuit of a professorship where I can teach undergraduates.*

Scholarships

Macalester offers only a few merit-based scholarships, amounting to less than ten percent of the cost of attending Mac. Although almost all students who are admitted to Mac would receive large merit scholarships from many other institutions, students choose Mac because they recognize the value of an excellent education that suits their particular needs. Money not spent on merit-based scholarships can be used to provide excellent faculty and facilities. Furthermore, forgoing most merit-based aid allows more money to be put into need-based financial aid, thus encouraging socioeconomic diversity on campus. Indeed, Mac is one of the most socioeconomically diverse top-tier liberal arts colleges in the nation.

Students and parents must fill out both FAFSA, and the more detailed College Scholarship Service (CSS) financial profile. Tax returns for both the applicant and applicant's parents also must be submitted. The Financial Aid Office then calculates an amount that the family can comfortably afford. Macalester figures out how to fill the gap between what the family can afford and the total cost using grants, loans, and work-study. Surprisingly, because of Mac's commitment to generous financial aid, the out-of-pocket cost of a Macalester education to many students can be less than that of a public university that does not have comparable financial resources and commitment to financial aid.

GRADUATES

Civic Engagement

Macalester, in its classes and social environment, instills in its students a feeling of responsibility to use their education and privilege to change the world for the better. Many recent graduates volunteer with AmeriCorps, Peace Corps, or Green Corps en route to their chosen careers. In the long term, many Mac graduates enter service-oriented professions such as nonprofits and government. However, this sense of commitment to a better world manifests itself in the career and life choices of all graduates. For example, an alumnus who enters the field of law might do *pro bono* work for an NGO, or for refugees; or a surgeon might join Doctors Without Borders, or volunteer his or her services to victims of land mines.

When applying to graduate school, I was a little bit nervous about the outcome. However, once I had met my competitors during interviews, I realized that no one had the depth and breadth of preparation I had received at Mac. Furthermore, professors at top schools noted that Mac's reputation, the recommendations I had gotten from Mac professors, and the many opportunities I had taken advantage of at Mac had pushed me to the very top of the applicant pool. I know for certain that I am not the only one to have this experience; I have so many friends from Mac at top graduate and professional programs that I can no longer keep track.

○ **Kofi Annan, '61, Nobel Peace Prize Laureate and Former Secretary-General of the United Nations**

○ **Walter Mondale, '50, Former U.S. Vice-President, Senator and Ambassador to Japan**

○ **Tim O'Brien, '68, National Book Award Recipient and Bestselling author of Several Novels on the Vietnam War, including *The Things They Carried***

○ **DeWitt Wallace '11, Founder of *Reader's Digest***

○ **Gary Hines '74, Founder, Director, and Songwriter for the Emmy Award-winning group *The Sounds of Blackness***

○ **Paul Light, '75, Vice-President and Founding Director of Government Studies at The Brookings Institution**

○ **J.J. and Jeremy Allaire, '91 and '93, Co-founders Allaire Corporation (Merged with Macromedia)**

Graduate and Professional Studies

Macalester education also prepares students for successful entry into graduate and professional education. Many Mac alums who have attended and excelled in these areas strengthen Mac's reputation at the best graduate and professional schools.

Macalester students attend the best graduate and professional schools, and they excel. There is no better preparation for graduate or professional study than the high-quality liberal arts education that one receives at Macalester. A Macalester education prepares students so well for graduate and professional study that top programs look for Macalester graduates during the selection process. Furthermore, a Macalester education instills excellent analytical and practical skills, as well as the creativity that is necessary to stand out in academia.

Career Paths

Macalester graduates follow many different paths after graduation. Mac graduates are leaders in academia, government, law, medicine, and business. A large number of graduates work for national and international nonprofit organizations and other nongovernmental organizations. Others stay in academia, enter government, and some enter the private sector. However, no matter what path they take, Macalester students invariably initiate and execute change for the better. Furthermore, no matter how far removed from Mac one becomes in distance or in time, the excellent Career Development Center at Mac is a great resource for all things related to finding a job in the "real world," including job listings, résumé preparation, interview skills, and alumni networking.

Global Networks

Alumni networking plays a powerful and positive role in the career paths of many Mac graduates. Mac students abound in major cities across the globe. The Macalester experience is so transforming, that alumni feel a lifelong bond. This leads to lasting business, academic, and personal relationships among Mac alums of different generations. Due to the international blend of students and international emphasis at Macalester, alumni connections are global. Because of the large number of international students at Macalester, and the penchant Mac grads have to pursue advanced degrees or careers abroad, you would be hard pressed to find a Macalester graduate who does not have friends in Africa, Western and Eastern Europe, Asia, and South America. Graduates will confirm that it is great to have a friend from Mac to visit while you are on business in Hong Kong, at a lecture in Stockholm, or working with Doctors Without Borders in Swaziland. As a graduate of Macalester, you will be continuously surprised with when and where you run into other Mac alums. A recent issue of the Mac alumni magazine includes letters from alumni reporting chance meetings of fellow Scots in Sweden, Iceland, New York, Oregon, and South Vietnam.

SUMMING UP

Macalester College is an academically distinguished small liberal arts college located in a friendly yet interesting neighborhood in St. Paul, one of Minnesota's Twin Cities. The combination of urban location, academic excellence, internationalism, and civic engagement make Mac unique among the top liberal arts colleges in the nation. Macalester's ideal environment, outstanding facilities and professors, and exceptional and engaged students create a vibrant milieu where the lines of classwork, community service, research, and play often blur. Although the resources and opportunities available at Mac would make any college great, it is the student body that makes Macalester truly exceptional. Mac students (and alumni) recognize the value of immersion in a traditional small liberal arts setting. They are deeply concerned with the affairs of their college, nation, and world, and they are committed to stewarding their college, countries, and continents, into a more promising tomorrow. Who knows that such a great college exists in the middle of St. Paul, Minnesota? Lots of people know, including other liberal arts college students and professors, as well as admissions officers at top medical, law, and graduate schools who enthusiastically admit so many Mac graduates. The thousands of alumni who are leaders in academia, government, medicine, law, business, and nonprofit organizations in every major city worldwide know, too. Undoubtedly, a Mac education is the ultimate preparation for success in graduate studies and any number of careers. But more importantly, Mac is an environment of life-altering enlightenment, life-changing experiences, and lifelong friendships.

❏ *Noah Palm, B.A.*

MASSACHUSETTS INSTITUTE OF TECHNOLOGY

Photo by Donna Coveney

Massachusetts Institute of Technology
Cambridge, MA 02139

(617) 253-4791
Fax: (617) 258-8304

Web site: *http://admissions.mit.edu*

 Enrollment

Full-time ❑ women: 1,747
❑ men: 2,258

Part-time ❑ women: 11
(special) ❑ men: 37

INTRODUCING MIT

The MIT educational experience is like a series of "ah-ha!" revelations that students build into an arsenal for attacking problems—and it will happen to you no matter what you major in. Everyone—this includes philosophy majors as well as physics majors—must take a year of calculus, a year of physics, a term of chemistry and a term of biology. There are other institute-level requirements (such as eight humanities, arts, or social science classes and a laboratory course) but it's really the science core that sets a quantitative ability standard for all undergraduates. This standard makes MIT students extremely attractive to graduate schools, professional schools, and potential employers. And it provides for an unusual sense of community—how many other schools can you name where *everyone* is able to solve a reasonably complex kinematics problem?

This doesn't mean that the only people who belong at MIT are mathematicians, physicists, and engineers. Quantitative thinkers don't necessarily manipulate equations for a living, and there's certainly a need for more of them in policy-making positions. John Deutch, an MIT alumnus and professor, lamented the lack of technical literacy in the higher levels of government during his tenure as Director of the CIA:

> *...probably two people in the Cabinet could solve quadratic equations. If you include deputies, you might have four. And three of them will have gone to MIT.*

ADMISSIONS REQUIREMENTS

> *From the time Early Action applications arrive in early November, until Regular Action decisions are made in early March, each admissions staff member will have read close to 950 applications. It seems that most MIT applicants have high standardized test scores and very good grades. Our pool is very self-selecting, so a lot of the applicants are quite similar. We turn down a surprising number of straight-A students.*

The take-home message is that you need to be distinctive. MIT is fortunate enough to be able to pick and choose from a very large pool of academically superior applicants. Distinction comes in many forms; athletes, musicians, chess players, and debaters are all distinctive if they achieve at a high level. Applicants who work on a farm for thirty hours a week and still manage to get straight As are distinctive. Students who have gone out of their way to take college courses or participate in independent research are distinctive. And of course, *extreme* academic talent or achievement is distinctive.

A word about how MIT defines "extreme" for academics—straight As and 800s on your SATs are *not* enough to guarantee admission (more than a third of MIT applicants have at least one 800). MIT is far more likely to admit a student with scores in the 700s, a few Bs in English classes, and an Intel science fair project that made it into the semifinals. Why? Because the Intel applicant has demonstrated initiative, a passion for learning, and a degree of competence in a very competitive field. That last bit is important. No matter how brilliant you are, if the Admissions Committee can't see your brilliance, then it won't help your application one iota. And the SATs alone are not enough to prove brilliance.

So, if you're truly gifted academically, make sure that the committee has some way of knowing that.

- Participate in the American Mathematics Corporation

- Get into an academic competition or science fair at the state (even better, national) level.

- Find a local university professor and get involved in independent research. It helps if you include a letter of recommendation from that professor with your application.

- For those of you who spend a solitary forty hours a week hacking on the internals of some compiler, *please* make sure that you have some way of providing verification of this work in your application.

- Get your independent programming projects supervised by teachers at your high school and then choose these supervisors to write your letters of recommendation.

This touches nicely on another point: how to present yourself in the application. Pick teachers who know you well (preferably, ones who like you) to write your evaluations. Ask them to relate some anecdote that they think captures you as a student. It's very difficult to get a feel for an applicant from a list of adjectives; "intelligent," "motivated," and "curious" all have different meanings, depending on who is using them. A story, on the other hand, provides context for the reader of the application, and has the nice side effect of making you appear more of a living, breathing, human being.

Description of Activities

Also, when you list your extracurricular activities, be very descriptive. The Admissions Committee probably doesn't know a lot of specifics about your high school, so if you write that you are the president of the National Honor Society, the reader doesn't know if there are five people in the NHS or 500. Detail is good. Detail is also important in writing your application essays. Expounding on some formative event in your life is a reasonable start, but remember that you're not just telling a story—you're trying to convince the reader why you belong at MIT more than 10,000 other students. Show off your creativity. If you choose to take a humorous route, be witty, not just funny. Above all, try to display some element of intellectual curiosity in your writing. Speak to the reader.

The Interview

As for the interview, it can be a mixed bag. In most cases, the interview lasts for about an hour and consists of fairly low-stress questions. The questions will probably be reasonably vague (as in, "Why do you want to go to MIT?"), so it helps to think about these types of questions in advance. You should also come up with a set of meaningful questions to ask, something beyond "How good is the food?" because it will indicate to the interviewer that you're serious about your decision to apply. Questions turn the interview into a two-way conversation, which will help to make it less stressful. In reality, a negative interview report is unlikely to hurt your application very much, but a good interview can give you an extra edge in gaining admission.

Highlights

There are a few more highlights you should probably know about the MIT admissions process.

- Of the 12,443 applications received in a recent year, 1,533 students were admitted, so competition is tough.
- MIT is Early Action, not Early Decision (if you're admitted early, you don't have to enroll).
- MIT admissions are need-blind, so the admissions staff has no idea how much your parents make or whether you're applying for financial aid.
- MIT has an affirmative-action policy, so all qualified underrepresented minorities (African American, Chicano Mexican American, Native American, Puerto Rican) who apply are admitted.
- Finally, international applicants go through a more competitive admissions process.

All of this factual information, plus a lot of other detail, can be found in the MIT admissions literature.

ACADEMIC LIFE

First, a general overview. MIT is divided into five schools: Architecture; Engineering; Humanities, Arts, and Social Sciences; Management; and Science. Within those schools there are twenty-two academic departments (such as Brain and Cognitive Science, Electrical Engineering, Computer Science, Mathematics). Most departments offer several majors, all of which are variations on a theme. Students aren't expected to declare a major until the end of their freshman year, so you don't need to apply to a particular school or department as an undergraduate; when you're admitted to MIT, you're admitted to all of MIT. Here's one student's perspective on the importance of this:

It didn't really occur to me that the lack of administrative hassle would turn out to be such a vital thing. I switched majors twice: from architecture to biology and from biology to chemistry, and each time all I needed to do was get a signature from my advisor. I was horrified to hear stories from friends at other colleges who needed to write a long petition to switch majors, or go through a mini-admissions process to get into another department. If I had been asked to choose a major straight out of high school, it would have been a random choice, at best.

This lack of bureaucracy pervades MIT's entire approach to education. With the exception of a few humanities courses, students never have to deal with being lotteried out of over-subscribed classes. You can add a class as late as five weeks into the term and drop a class as late as five weeks before the end of the term. After freshman year, there are no limits on the number of classes you can take per term or the number of majors you can declare, as long as your advisor approves the decision (which is a rubber-stamp process for students who are performing well). Many students double major. Undergraduates can also register for graduate-level classes, which offer a very different type of educational experience: most graduate courses meet in a small room with very few students and one professor. The topics in these courses are usually closely related to the professor's current area of research, and the class feels more like a discussion than a lecture.

Classes

As for the undergraduate classes, there's a lot of variation in the presentation format. Most of the freshman science core courses consist of three lectures and two recitation sections per week. Lectures for these courses have between 200 and 300 students, but recitations are limited to about twenty students per instructor, giving a lot of opportunity for individualized instruction. Departments also offer variants on the basic core courses, so while the standard freshman calculus class has the format described above, the theoretical version of freshman calculus has far fewer students in its lectures. In addition to the other flavors of the science core classes, MIT has different versions of the freshman year program itself. Concourse, the Experimental Studies Group (ESG), the Integrated Studies Program (ISP), and the Media Arts and Sciences (MAS) Freshman Program, all offer alternative, innovative approaches to teaching the freshman curriculum. These programs are limited in size (between twenty-four and sixty students in each) and are first-come, first-served, so if you're interested in learning more about them, do your research before showing up on campus.

Credit

The institute gives Advanced Placement credit for some classes if you score well enough on your AP exams, and in many cases will accept transfer credit from another college. Advanced standing exams are also offered by MIT, and if you pass them you receive credit. More than three-quarters of MIT's enrolling freshmen receive some sort of advanced credit, but no matter how much credit you have, MIT does not offer sophomore standing to first-term freshmen (although second-term sophomore standing is offered in the second term).

Grading

There is a limit on the number of classes freshmen can take and there is one other major difference between the first term of the freshman year and the remainder of the MIT undergraduate experience: Pass/No Record. This refers to the grading system used for freshmen. If you earn an A, B, or C in a course, it appears as a P on your transcript. Ds and Fs do not appear on the external transcript at all—it will simply look as though you had never even registered for the course. There are three reasons why MIT has this system of grading: to level the playing field for students from different high school backgrounds; to get students acclimated to the MIT way of thinking and problem solving; and to allow students to explore a little (academically or otherwise) without fear of receiving a bad grade.

Many prospective students want to know if the freshman year is difficult. "Different" would be a better word. Generally speaking, if you're bright enough to be admitted to MIT, you're more than bright enough to handle the material. For students with advanced high school preparation, most of the core classes will feel like accelerated versions of the material in high school with slightly more complicated homework, longer tests, and some interesting stories thrown into the lecture. If you're truly bored with the standard fare, try one of the theoretical versions of calculus or physics; even the brightest, most academically prepared students find these courses to be quite challenging.

Seeking Help

Students with less rigorous background training might have more of a shock; if you've never seen a vector before, freshman physics might appear somewhat alien to you at first. Here's a hint: If you don't understand something after fifteen minutes, ask someone. More often than not, it will take a knowledgeable person five minutes to explain something that could take you hours to extract from a book. MIT does offer one-on-one tutors for the science core classes, but it's usually easier to grab the first available upperclassman for help. In fact, upperclassmen often look for freshmen working on problem sets. That may sound bizarre, but there are a few reasons for this apparent selflessness:

- All upperclassmen have taken the core courses, so they are familiar with the material.
- There's no freshman dormitory, so upperclassmen and freshmen occupy the same living space.
- Realistically, all MIT students are a touch egotistical at heart; they enjoy being able to demonstrate their knowledge.

So even though they're not necessarily altruists, the upperclassmen are a fantastic resource for the freshman class.

After freshman year, it's difficult to make sweeping claims about academic life. What people choose as a major drastically affects their experience. Generally speaking, the classes become much smaller and more specialized. Engineering courses, design courses, and laboratory courses will be very different from anything you're likely to have seen in high school. They'll be more time consuming as well (some classes are notorious for this). One student had the following comment:

I had never touched a computer before coming to MIT, so the first time I took a programming class, I had a lot to learn: how to use a text editor, how to move files around—some really basic stuff. Many of the other students in the class had been programming for years, which was sort of intimidating, and on the first problem set, I spent all night (from 5:00 P.M. to 8:00 A.M.) in front of a computer and accomplished literally nothing. I was going to drop the class, but a friend offered to come in and show me the essentials, so I took her up on the offer. We spent about four hours working, and it was enough to give me an overview of what I needed to do. I stayed with the course, and ended up earning an A in it. Looking back, it's hard for me to imagine why I thought it was so complicated at first, but I guess that's because I actually learned something.

Programming

MIT classes tend to be heavier on the theory side than many people expect. This is the reason why a person with no programming experience can do as well as, if not better than, a veteran coder in the same class. MIT is one of the few places where students can major in computer science without being required to learn C or Java or any other programming language in popular use. Instead, they learn Scheme and CLU and languages that few people outside of academia have ever heard of. But all of these languages are chosen with a purpose: They are ideal for teaching good engineering principles and good design techniques. So MIT students find that when they go to learn a more common language it takes them very little time to do so because they are able to easily apply the fundamental ideas they've learned to a specific case. As a result, when technology changes, MIT graduates are able to adapt with it. This phenomenon isn't specific to computer science; the same holds true across all MIT disciplines.

Engineering Contest and Other Projects

Some MIT courses are so different, they're famous. One of the mechanical engineering design classes requires students to build a small robot, which they ultimately operate against other robots in a huge contest. This is a cult experience at MIT; many of the people who take the class are not even mechanical engineering majors! The contest itself is held in a large lecture hall in front of a packed audience, and it's televised for the viewers at home. There's an electrical engineering version of the same contest in which the robots must be equipped with an automatic controller. For one of the architecture design courses, students develop visual projects that they display publicly. So, for a few weeks during the term, sandboxes, statues, performance artists, and thought-provoking signs can be found everywhere on campus.

Nonengineering Classes

MIT is often thought of as primarily a science and engineering school, but in reality it's more of an analytical thinking school. MIT's economics, management, political science, and philosophy programs are all top-notch. In particular, economics and management are always ranked as one of the top three programs in the country. For some reason, math and music go hand-in-hand, so the music department is phenomenal; moreover, MIT students can cross-register for classes at both Harvard and Wellesley, so if you're really dying to take a course in Sanskrit, that's not an adequate reason to avoid MIT.

IAP/UROP

There are two other very unique elements to MIT academics: the Independent Activities Period (IAP) and the Undergraduate Research Opportunities Program (UROP). IAP takes place during January, and it's like a miniature, optional, month-long term. Students can decide for themselves whether they want to be at MIT for those four weeks, but the vast majority of students stay. Some students choose to do a wide variety of one-day seminars and projects, some students take classes (often for credit), and others work. Here's a small sampling of the noncredit activities offered last IAP: the 18th Annual Paper Airplane Contest, Basic Darkroom Techniques, Blackjack 101, Computers and the Human Genome Project, Hebrew Reading Literacy in Eight Hours, Intro to British Politics, Practical NMR Spectroscopy. For-credit classes included: Intro to Special Relativity, Special Problems in Architecture, IAP Japan Workshop (which included a three-week stay in Japan), Intro to Neuroanatomy, Experiencing Health Policy: A Week in D.C., Foreign Currency Exchange, Intensive German. There are hundreds of course offerings during IAP; for a complete listing of last year's activities as well as detailed descriptions of the events, check out *web.mit.edu/iap*.

The majority of students who work during IAP will probably do so through UROP, which is quite arguably one of the best things about MIT. In this program, undergraduate students work on a research project at MIT. UROP isn't limited to a select few, nor are the projects watered-down pedagogical tools. More than eighty percent of all students choose to get a UROP at some point in their undergraduate careers. The projects themselves are ongoing research efforts, so undergraduates work together with professors, graduate students, and "postdocs." With a little motivation, undergraduates can even coauthor research papers with the group, and there's no better way to cultivate a good faculty reference for later use. UROP enables students to interact with professors as colleagues, not just teachers; it also gives undergraduates an excellent sense for what graduate studies in a particular field would be like. On top of all this, students actually get paid for their work in UROP so they don't have to choose between meeting financial need and doing undergraduate research. For a listing of current UROP openings and their descriptions, look at *web.mit.edu/urop*.

The summer after my freshman year, I got a UROP with the Communications Biophysics Group working on a speech aid for deaf-blind people. We built a device that decomposed sound waves into different spectral regions, and then mapped each region to one of twelve buzzers. When you strapped the device on your forearm, you were able to "feel" people talking. The engineering was cool, but working with the deaf-blind test subjects was probably the most interesting part. They had been deaf and blind since birth, yet could speak pretty well and were able to "hear" me talk by placing their hand across my face. Listening to their perceptions of the world was absolutely fascinating.

SOCIAL LIFE AND ACTIVITIES

Housing

MIT's housing system has a lot to offer: a diversity of experiences; a place truly to call home; active communities, with opportunities to connect with undergraduate students of all years, as well as faculty and graduate students. But most of all, it offers the freedom to choose housing most appropriate to you and that best suits your personality and lifestyle.

All freshmen are required to spend their first year at MIT living in one of MIT's eleven undergraduate residence halls. However, this doesn't mean that the decision of where to live is going to be simple or boring—in fact, quite opposite is true. MIT has an amazingly diverse residential community. Each residence hall has a different flavor, and most floors within these houses have distinct cultures. For example, there is a brand new residence hall; an all-women's residence hall; a residence hall that is world famous for its architectural significance; a residential hall that wired its laundry and bathroom facilities to the Internet. There are also five cultural houses that celebrate the languages, foods, and customs of different cultures.

On-campus housing is guaranteed for freshmen and for upper-class students for eight consecutive semesters. After the freshman year, many students will take the opportunity to move into one of MIT's many fraternities, sororities, and independent living groups (FSILGs). Today, there are twenty-seven fraternities, five NPC sororities, five living groups and five NHPC fraternities and sororities. Each fraternity, sorority, and living group has its own unique characteristics. However, each group's primary purpose is to foster brother/sisterhood and camaraderie, and provide a supportive and healthy environment for its members.

Loyalty to one's living group is common at MIT. Undergraduates find that the residence halls and FSILGs are a great support network, academically, socially, and otherwise.

Athletics

MIT has an amazingly large athletics program—there are forty-one varsity teams at the institute. In many of these sports, MIT is quite competitive, even by national standards. Athletics at MIT are accessible; it is not uncommon for a person with no rowing experience to join the crew team as a freshman and then stay with it at the varsity level for four years (the Charles River is literally across the street from MIT). Club and intramural (IM) teams are also very common; at last count there were more than 1,000 IM teams participating in thirty different sports. D-league ice hockey is a great example of the IM spirit. It's hockey for people who don't necessarily know how to skate. The A-league teams, however, are considerably less forgiving.

Student Activities

There are more than 330 student activities at MIT, including cultural groups, student government, journalistic organizations, performance groups, and clubs for people interested in games. Getting involved at the institute is very easy—just ask. MIT students are about as anti-elitist as people can get; they're usually thrilled to find someone else who's interested in what they do. They're also enthusiastic teachers, so even if you know nothing about a particular game or skill, you'll probably be able to find someone who will spend hours showing you the ropes. Free of charge.

MIT students are famous for the elaborate practical jokes that they manage to pull off. Cars, telephone booths, makeshift houses, and plastic cows have all appeared on the tops of MIT buildings at various points throughout MIT history. While many hacks require what seems to be a small miracle of engineering, others are just really good ideas put into action:

> One of my all-time favorite hacks was pulled at a football game, but it's not the famous Harvard-Yale inflating balloon prank. Every day for several months before the game, an MIT student would show up at the stadium, blow a whistle, and then throw handfuls of seed onto the field. On the day of the game, right before play started, the MIT student blew the whistle. Hundreds of birds descended onto the field, delaying the start of the game for some time. Of course, in order to start the game they needed to blow a whistle again...
>
> I think that the simplicity of this hack is what appeals to me—the student didn't have to resort to complicated technology to pull this off, just raw cleverness and some birdseed.

FINANCIAL AID

MIT is expensive but the good news is that MIT is committed to meeting the financial need of all admitted students (although sometimes the institute's definition of "need" differs from the definition students' families have). More than three quarters of all undergraduates receive some sort of financial aid.

Packages

Unfortunately, there's no quick formula to give you an estimate of what your financial aid award would be. Evaluations are made by financial aid staff on a case-by-case basis.

If you disagree with the amount of aid offered, you can always contact the Financial Aid Office to try and renegotiate, but unless they've missed something egregious, this is unlikely to change your aid package very much. Bottom line: The median loan debt for students in a recent graduating class was $22,855. Even so, this seems like a staggering amount of money to many people.

You may think that you don't receive as much financial aid from MIT as you would have from other universities. This is not your imagination, and it doesn't mean that MIT cares less than other colleges about whether you enroll, but because MIT is committed to need-blind admissions, financial aid packages are very conservative. Moreover, MIT offers no merit scholarships of any kind—there are no academic, athletic, or music scholarships. MIT will accept outside scholarships, but then deducts fifty percent of the scholarship amount from whatever grant money was awarded to you. At this point, you're probably wondering when this gets better.

It eventually does, but you won't see the improvement until you leave the institute. Here's the upside: MIT graduates are absurdly employable people. Companies need to fight just to get space for a booth at MIT career fairs. The job placement rate, as well as the average starting salary for MIT students, is incredibly high in comparison to other universities; in a recent survey, students graduating with a bachelor's degree reported an average starting salary of $60,000. It's probably difficult to believe this when you're faced with the prospect of massive debt, but in all likelihood you won't have any trouble repaying your loans. MIT graduates have the lowest student loan default rate in the country. Read that sentence again.

GRADUATES

PROMINENT GRADS

- Richard Feynman, '39, Nobel Prize Winner in Physics
- I.M. Pei, '40, Architect
- Kenneth Olsen, '51, DEC Founder
- Sheila Widnall, '61, Former Secretary of Air Force
- Shirley Jackson, '68, U.S. Nuclear Regulatory Commission
- Kofi Annan, '72, UN Secretary General
- Benjamin Netanyahu, '75, Former Israeli Prime Minister

Many extraordinarily bright people have attended MIT. The institute has had more than its share of Nobel Laureates, National Medal of Science recipients, and the like. Rattling off a long list of MIT's all-time stars would be interesting but probably wouldn't tell you much about how the average graduate fares.

MIT students have very high acceptance rates into postbaccalaureate programs, and more than fifty percent of graduating seniors choose to go directly to graduate, medical, or law school. Industry and government employers heavily recruit students seeking jobs after graduation. A nice side benefit of MIT is the name recognition—simply saying you're a graduate commands a certain level of respect. Of course, it also sets a pretty high expectation level for your abilities.

MIT prepares its graduates to be more than just cogs in the machine, unless you like being a cog, in which case that's your choice. In 1997, the BankBoston Economics Department prepared a report titled "MIT: The Impact of Innovation." Here's what was reported.

If the companies founded by MIT graduates and faculty formed an independent nation, the revenues produced by the companies would make that nation the twenty-fourth largest economy in the world. The 4,000 MIT-related companies employ 1.1 million people and have annual world sales of $232 billion. That is roughly equal to a gross domestic product of $116 billion, which is a little less than the GDP of South Africa and more than the GDP of Thailand.

MIT graduates excel at whatever they choose to do, primarily because they can often think circles around people with less quantitative backgrounds. While they're here, students may complain about the work load, but it's unlikely that you'll ever hear the phrase "I regret getting an MIT degree."

SUMMING UP

If you're still trying to figure out whether MIT is the place for you, consider the following two questions: Does "fuzzy thinking" bother you? Do you want to learn how to critically assess problems in whatever discipline interests you (whether it's mechanical engineering or political science)? If you can answer both with an enthusiastic "Yes!" then there's no better place for you academically than MIT.

❏ *Stacy McGeever, B.S.*

MIDDLEBURY COLLEGE

Photo by John McKeith

Middlebury College
Middlebury, VT 05753

(802) 443-3000
Fax: (802) 443-2056

E-mail: *admissions@middlebury.edu*
Web site: *www.middlebury.edu*

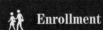 **Enrollment**

Full-time ❑ women: 1,256
❑ men: 1,151

Part-time ❑ women: 17
❑ men: 14

INTRODUCING MIDDLEBURY COLLEGE

Middlebury is among the finest liberal arts schools in the country. It also happens to be in one of the most beautiful settings. Prospective students are often taken by the million-dollar views and resort-worthy amenities, and that feeling of awe doesn't wane over four years of study. The landscape, hemmed in by the Adirondacks to the west and the Green

Mountains to the east, is a constant source of inspiration. As the sun sets over the jagged and usually snow-capped Adirondacks (or rises over the aptly named Greens), Middlebury students can't help but pause to ask themselves: Do I *really* get to go to school here?

In this idyllic place, students sample from a curriculum steeped in the liberal arts before honing in on a particular area. "Breadth and depth" of educational experience becomes something of a mantra. That could mean a chemistry major with a passion for Victorian literature or an English major with a knack for astronomy. Such unlikely combinations are the essence of the Middlebury experience. To think: A bookworm who relishes an afternoon of skiing at the college-owned Snow Bowl; a standout athlete who edits the arts section of *The Middlebury Campus* newspaper; or an environmental activist with a jazz show on 91.1 WRMC-FM, the college radio station. These are the students who populate the College on the Hill.

Versatility

So-called Midd-Kids place a premium on this brand of academic and extracurricular balance. They also value close student-professor interaction; they're all but guaranteed small class sizes and accessible professors. Speaking of which: Celebrated creative writing professor Jay Parini shoots hoops at Pepin Gymnasium most weekdays during lunch hour; President Ron Liebowitz, who also teaches geography, routinely dines with students at Ross Dining Hall; other professors grade papers at The Grille, a social hub on campus that serves up everything from fair trade coffee to "love me tender" chicken sandwiches. Still others bring their kids skiing at the Snow Bowl. No Middlebury experience would be complete without such informal interaction with faculty mentors. In fact, you'd be hard pressed to locate a Middlebury student or alum who doesn't count several professors (not to mention administrators) as personal friends.

> *When most students write a thesis, their advisor simply approves their topic in the beginning and then six months later reads it and throws on a grade. At Middlebury, my advisor met with me weekly, read every draft and was continuously giving me feedback and advice on how to make it a better paper.*

> —*Chesley Thurber, '04, an international studies major who studied abroad in Italy and was a senior editor at* The Campus *newspaper*

Location

The campus' location in rural Vermont fosters an uncommon sense of community. Burlington, Montreal, and Boston are all within striking distance, but most students' social life is centered on Middlebury, which makes for a lively oasis in the rolling hills and pastures of northern New England. The stats bear it out: ninety-four percent of students live on campus, and a quick glance at the weekend lineup is enough to convince even skeptics that there's a lot going on.

Resources

And despite the historic New England town that is the college's namesake, the campus' modern resources rival those of much larger schools. *Sports Illustrated* has called Middlebury a "wellspring" of success at the Division III level, thanks in part to athletic facilities that are the envy of D-I institutions. Add to that a state-of-the-art, $40 million library that opened in 2004 and an equally impressive science center constructed in 1999, and you begin to sense the investment the college has made in its students.

Yet, throughout the development of the Middlebury skyline, the college has retained the unique, close-knit character that most students cite as their reason for coming in the first place. Not surprisingly, alumni cite the same reason when explaining why Middlebury will always seem to them a second home. Welcome to Middlebury, Vermont, and welcome to Middlebury College.

ADMISSIONS REQUIREMENTS

To Choose and Be Chosen

If there were a formula that guaranteed admission to Middlebury, somebody would have cracked it by now. The committee considers a range of factors in making its ultimate decision, tilted to favor individual over empirical gauges of potential. But as a rough guide, Middlebury recommends that candidates complete the following college preparatory coursework to prepare for its rigorous academic expectations:

- Four years of English
- Four years of foreign language
- Three years of laboratory science
- Four years of mathematics and/or computer science
- Three or more years of social science
- Some study of art, music, or drama

Middlebury is among the few colleges that do not require the SAT for admission. Instead, the college allows applicants to designate a representative sample of standardized tests from among the SAT, ACT, AP, and International Baccalaureate exams that reflects their abilities in three areas—one qualitative, one quantitative, and one in an area of the applicant's choice. The policy suggests a whole-person view of the admissions process, one that anticipates the very ethos of the college applicants who vie to attend.

In that spirit, Middlebury welcomes varied perspectives on a candidate's ability beyond what is reflected in the usual portfolio of high school record, standardized test scores, and teacher recommendations. The college evaluates supplementary materials such as dance and theater videos, artwork, or music compilations. Those clues—as well as those gathered through an interview and admissions essay—often prove more illuminating than any class ranking or standardized test score.

Because Middlebury receives far more applications from qualified applicants than it can possibly accept, Dean of Admissions Bob Clagett has been known to send a note to prospective students explaining the difficult task before the Admissions Committee each year. He concedes that Middlebury turns away many applicants who would otherwise make significant contributions to the college community. Denial from Middlebury isn't a vote of no confidence in one's academic ability, according to the Admissions Director. It's a reflection of ever-escalating applicant volume at a college that's established itself as among the nation's finest.

Students' Backgrounds

Middlebury received 6,204 applications for admission to the class of 2010 and accepted 1,506 students, 1,339 to start in September and 167 to start in February. Of those admitted, thirty-eight were school or class presidents, thirty were publications editors, 194 were team captains and one was an oboe player. And despite a healthy supply of Vermonters and New Englanders—4.3 percent and twenty-four percent, respectively—the pool of admitted students also included representatives of thirty-six countries and forty-seven states.

Of course, age-old stereotypes die hard. Like many elite New England colleges, Middlebury was historically regarded as a haven for well-to-do, white Northeasterners. The college still contends with a reputation for rural seclusion and homogeneity, but new initiatives are accelerating the ever-diversifying student population. The Posse Program, now in its eighth year, handpicks standout students from urban settings and grants them the scholarships and institutional support they need to transition successfully into Middlebury's vibrant, if isolated and decidedly new, environment. And as the college continues to become a better version of itself through infrastructure improvements and curricular advancement, it inevitably attracts an increasingly varied population to its bucolic campus.

The college wants students from Nepal and North Dakota. It wants logrolling champions and competitive fly-fishers and cross-country skiing enthusiasts, not to mention standout ice hockey goalies and aspiring poets and all-state orchestra participants. The bottom line: Middlebury College wants students with broad-based interests, experiences, and backgrounds who will seize opportunities to propel and invigorate campus life—and themselves—across four years of study.

Decisions, Decisions

Regular applications are due December 15th. For candidates who know Middlebury is their first choice, the college offers a binding, Early Decision program that telegraphs one's commitment to Middlebury and offers the promise of early notification from the Admissions Committee, which may choose to accept, reject or defer a decision until the usual April 1 deadline. Early decision applications are due November 15th.

The Feb Program

Among countless boxes to check and blanks to fill in, Middlebury applicants will confront the "September preferred" and "February preferred" dilemma. The so-called Feb program emerged in the 1970s as a novel way to fill beds vacated by students studying abroad in the spring. It's evolved into a fixture of the Middlebury community, offering a fresh infusion of energy and talent at midyear. As the second semester begins and students grow wary of the sometimes-arctic chill, a vivacious group of 95 "Febs" energize the campus, bringing with them varied experiences amassed during a gap semester between high school and college. Febs swear by the experience. They say their time at Middlebury was enriched by travel, work, or study completed in the fall before launching their college careers. They also enjoy a lively camaraderie born of being midyear transplants to Vermont, often broadcast to the larger community by T-shirts bearing lettering such as "Febs—Curiously Strong (inscribed on an Altoids container) and "Febs come later and last longer," among other less suggestive slogans. The Feb experience culminates four years later in a winter celebration for the new midyear graduates, a ski-down process in mortarboards and gowns at the College-owned Snow Bowl, and of course, someone always wipes out on the slopes while donning traditional cap and gown.

Transfer Students

In addition to Febs and "Regs," as September students are often called, Middlebury enrolls five to ten transfer students selected from a pool of 200–250 applicants. All students hoping to matriculate at the college must complete the Common Application and a Middlebury-specific supplement. Application deadlines for transfer students are March 1 for fall admission, and November 15 for spring admission. A few weeks after dropping the package in the mail, don't be surprised if Clagett sends a detailed letter about the admissions pool that year in addition to acknowledging receipt of the material.

> *There's a phenomenon called the Middlebury Sibling. It happens like this: The elder chooses Middlebury, proceeds to rave about the experience, and so the younger chooses Middlebury as well. I know. It happened to my family. My younger sister, Jill, applied Early Decision to Middlebury and launched her career as I completed mine, and so we became the latest sibling pair of Midd-kids.*

FINANCIAL AID

A Genuine Commitment

Middlebury cushions the shock of its $44,330 comprehensive fee with an admissions process that is separate from the financial aid process. Need for financial aid has no effect on the admissions decision, and the college has a commitment to meet each student's full demonstrated need as calculated by the Office of Financial Aid. Even though additional expenses ranging from textbook bills to travel to and from Vermont may push price north of that figure, students and families can take heart in Middlebury's unwavering commitment to providing students with a financial aid package to put the cost of attendance within reach. Financial aid packages—typically combining grants, federal and institutional loans, and work—remain consistent over four years, provided that family financial circumstances do not change. The college requires the FAFSA in addition to its own financial aid supplement by January 15.

To calculate a family's expected contribution, the office evaluates family income and assets and then extends a financial aid offer based on need. In a recent academic year, forty-three percent of first-year students and forty-two percent of continuing students received need-based aid, and the average first-year grant totaled $27,471. Middlebury's reputation for solid financial aid packages is often credited with attracting a student body that includes representatives of more than seventy countries

It's worth keeping in mind, though, that Middlebury distributes aid dollars based only on need—there are no athletic or academic scholarships awarded through college channels. Students may still apply for outside scholarships to offset their college expenses.

Help Wanted

Whether for extra cash or to satisfy a financial aid condition, many students turn to on-campus job opportunities ranging from monitoring the music library to researching for a professor to sorting recyclables at the recycling center. Marcus Hughes, who transferred to Middlebury for his sophomore year and praised the college's commitment to aid, said he found two jobs within forty-eight hours of arriving on campus, one working in an administrative office and the other monitoring the fitness center. Other students venture into town and land jobs waiting tables at nearby restaurants or working in any of the string of boutiques that line Middlebury's tourist-friendly Main Street. Both on campus and off, the job market is flexible enough to accommodate all students who wish to work during their college experience.

ACADEMIC LIFE

The First-Year Seminar

For all of the campus' natural beauty and showcase facilities, students discover Middlebury's actual heart and soul in much more modest environs. It looks something like this: a classic seminar room with a full professor (no TAs here) and fifteen or twenty students clustered around a table, all engaged in a spirited discussion of that day's material. The curriculum sets the standard for close student-professor interaction early on. Writing-intensive first-year seminars, a rite of passage for all incoming students, enroll no more than fifteen students and often focus on a subject rooted in the professor's own research interests. Professor of Russian Michael Katz, a noted translator of Russian literature, teaches a course entitled "Art of Translation" that interrogates the artistic and technical role of the translator and challenges students to try their hand at the craft, drawing upon previous knowledge of a foreign language. Other seminars confront the political ramifications of September 11, explore the history of Tibetan and Buddhist art, or analyze *The Da Vinci Code*.

Students in first-year seminars are often situated in the same dormitory halls to foster friendship and academic collaboration outside the classroom. The first-year seminar professor also serves as students' academic advisor until they declare a major, but students often stay in touch with their first-year mentor throughout their undergraduate careers.

Faculty

The first-year seminar program is a microcosm of the larger Middlebury experience—meaningful relationships with professors who both awe students with their academic prowess and then meet them at The Grille to confer about an assignment over coffee. Therein lies one of the college's defining qualities: Middlebury is first and foremost a teaching institution, and although faculty members have impeccable scholarly credentials and make significant contributions to their fields, they remain committed to the core mission of instructing and interacting with students. That commitment extends to the upper ranks of the college leadership. The president, vice-president for academic affairs, dean of the faculty, and secretary of the college all began their careers as professors and continue to teach.

Middlebury transforms into an oasis of foreign cultures and foreign tongues each summer as the college's nine language schools convene for their annual sessions. The language schools' signature language pledge governs all interaction, both academic and social. In short, it says not to speak English for the duration of the program under penalty of expulsion. The same intensity of foreign language instruction comes through during the academic year (*sans* the *no English ever* part), and it motivates more than half of the junior class to take leave of Middlebury for either a semester or a year to pursue coursework and travel abroad. Many choose to immerse themselves in the language (or languages) they studied at Middlebury, often drawing on Middlebury's network of twenty-six C.V. Starr Schools Abroad with sites in Argentina, China, France, Germany, Italy, Mexico, Russia, Spain, Brazil, Chile, and Uruguay. Others opt for non-Middlebury programs in destinations as varied at the United Kingdom, New Zealand, Niger, and Turkey. The common ground in study abroad: Virtually everyone does it. In fact, students who remain on campus for all four years often find themselves explaining why they didn't seek personal and academic enrichment abroad.

And Middlebury's last president, who was drawn from the faculty, recently opted to return to a full-time teaching position in the history department after thirteen years at the helm.

Class Size

Although class size averages just sixteen, students occasionally contend with larger lecture sessions, particularly in popular introductory courses. In a Middlebury student's vocabulary, however, large class means anything over forty, a label that would surely confound peers at other schools who are accustomed to sports-arena seating in lecture halls. Even in the rare instance that class sizes edge toward forty or more, students typically divide into discussion sections once a week during which the professor meets with about twenty students at a time for a more interactive consideration of course themes.

Spectrum of the Liberal Arts

Middlebury's well-deserved reputation for foreign language study doesn't begin to capture the scope of its academic strengths. The college offers more than 850 courses in more than forty majors and encourages students to sample widely from the curriculum (breadth) before developing particular expertise in one discipline (depth). To guide students through the curriculum, the college requires at least one course in seven of eight core areas, including literature; the arts; philosophical and religious studies; historical studies; physical and life sciences; deductive reasoning and analytical processes; social analysis; and foreign languages. Before graduation, students also satisfy regional distribution requirements by studying the cultures of North America, Europe, Asia, Africa, or Latin America, and comparative studies. A caveat that allows students to satisfy two distribution categories with AP or IB scores keeps most from grumbling about the imposed structure. In fact, most students ultimately find the requirements quite flexible because one course may count toward multiple distribution areas.

For a school of only 2,420 students, Middlebury offers a considerable number of interdisciplinary programs in addition to the enduring lineup of liberal arts departments. The International Studies (IS) major, for example, combines foreign language study, regional specialization, time abroad and a disciplinary focus, which may range from political science to economics to sociology. IS majors often deliver a mouthful when asked for their major. Think: European studies with a human geography focus, paired with Italian language mastered during a semester abroad in Florence. In this sense, the IS department draws on Middlebury's longstanding reputation for foreign language instruction and fuses it with other aspects of the curriculum to create a wildly popular program.

> *Working in international public health in Latin and South America, my language skills have been one of my most valuable assets. The fluency I gained both at Middlebury and while studying abroad in Segovia, Spain, has set me apart from my co-workers and enhanced my contributions to our language-intensive work.*

> —*Thomas McMennamin, '04, neuroscience and Spanish double-major and varsity swimmer originally from Portland, ME*

Middlebury also pioneered the interdisciplinary field of environmental studies, launching the first undergraduate program in the country in 1965. The department remains a staple of the undergraduate curriculum and draws about fifty faculty members across twenty-six departments to offer a wide range of courses. Like IS majors, ES students also select a disciplinary specialization after completing a prescribed list of core classes. As one of the most popular departments at the college, ES attracts environmental chemists and economists, geologists, and literary analysts, all of whom tailor their coursework to suit their particular interest under the ES umbrella.

In keeping with its history of academic innovation, Middlebury's curriculum is ever-evolving to accommodate with the diverse research interests of its students. The IS department recently added regional specializations in African studies and Middle Eastern studies, while the language division added first-year Portuguese and Arabic to its slate of offerings.

A Home for the Sciences

> *Middlebury remains ahead of the curve with the Grille, new dorms, McCardell Bicentennial Hall, and the new library. This consistent adaptive environment works perfectly with the permanence of the surrounding mountains.*

—Doug Burdett, '87, English major, member of the English Department at the Upper School of the Brunswick School in Greenwich, CT, and son of Peg Stearns Burdett, '50, and Bruce Burdett, '50

Middlebury's facilities keep pace with its enterprising academic culture. Just where the campus gives way to rolling farm fields, McCardell Bicentennial Hall stands as a monument to Middlebury's commitment to the sciences. Completed in 1999 in time for the college's bicentennial anniversary, the building garnered numerous accolades from architectural groups but produced some distress among environmentalists and local residents who thought the imposing edifice overpowered the landscape. However, no one could argue with the Bi-Hall's well-equipped laboratories, or with the fact that the building confirmed Middlebury's ever-present commitment to the sciences as a vital component of liberal education. McCardell Bicentennial Hall houses the geography, psychology, chemistry, and biology departments, among others, in addition to the Armstrong Science Library and a rooftop observatory that regularly opens its doors to members of the local community, scientists and nonscientists alike. And to capture the western exposure to the Adirondack mountains, Bi-Hall boasts what's rumored to be the largest single pane of glass in the state of Vermont. The scale of Bi-Hall's academic resources is similarly impressive, with state-of-the-art laboratory space and lecture halls wired with the latest bells and whistles.

Winter Term

No Middlebury experience would be complete without the academic experimentation and winter-induced revelry of J-Term. As the temperatures take a Vermont-style turn in January, Middlebury students embark on the "1" component of the "4-1-4" academic calendar. The one-month interlude between the fall and spring semesters provides much-needed reprieve from the competing pressures of a full course load, freeing students to immerse themselves in a new discipline or to deepen knowledge of an established one. J-Term classes meet for at least ten hours per week and span the academic spectrum. Some are offbeat, others are traditional courses crammed into a four week-period. For example, students who begin a first-year language and hope to continue it in the spring semester must study that language over J-Term as a bridge between classes. Others may opt to jump-start their major requirements by taking a compressed version of organic chemistry or first-semester psychology in J-Term. But just as often, students take an academic risk and dabble in a yet-unexplored area of the curriculum. History majors take a dance class in the mechanics of movement, cotaught by a physics and dance professor. Neuroscience majors enroll in a crash course in local politics. And biology majors take a poetry writing workshop led by a noted faculty poet. To ensure a broad range of course offerings, the college draws on faculty talent as well as outside scholars, authors, and experts in crafting the academic lineup each year.

Although J-Term courses can be surprisingly demanding, students inevitably spend less time in the classroom. They migrate en masse to the college-owned Snow Bowl for an afternoon of skiing, or borrow snowshoes from the Middlebury Mountain Club and forge a fresh path in the snow-blanketed landscape. The Office of Campus Activities and Leadership also fields many workshop offerings during the J-Term. Recent examples: A student-taught Norwegian language and culture class, an introduction to wine tasting (yeah, ID required), figure skating 101, and tap dancing for beginners.

Students whose vision of college life looks something like Times Square should think twice before packing for Middlebury. But for those who crave the thrill of winter sport, an active and passionate student body, and a landscape ripped from the tourist brochures, follow signs for central Vermont.

SOCIAL LIFE AND ACTIVITIES

After about 8 P.M. an eerie calm descends over downtown Middlebury, save for the bustling (and alumni owned) Neil & Otto's pizza shop and the local pubs. Don't worry. A short stroll up the hill to campus reveals a different picture entirely. En route to a WRMC-91.1 FM-sponsored indie rock concert, you pass the French House on Franklin Street hosting a reception with hors d'oeuvres—and yes, all dialogue would be *in* French—that will later give way to a party, most likely after the faculty members call it a night. A little further up, conversation spills out of an open dormitory window on Old Stone Row, where students have gathered before heading to a midnight show in Hepburn's Black Box Theater. Then comes the pulsating sound of a McCullough—campus lingo for a dance party in McCullough Social Space, a former gymnasium transformed into a performing-cum-dance party venue attached to The Grille, the two-tier social hub that serves up chai latte and late-night quesadillas (surely there's a healthy crowd there, too). Continue past The Gamut Room where the African-American Alliance is sponsoring a slam poetry event featuring some of Middlebury's best, who enjoy celebrity status on campus. And then, out of breath and probably semi-frostbitten, you arrive at Coltrane Lounge and the sounds of the indie favorite The Decembrists surround you. Middle of nowhere, eh?

> *Because virtually all students live in college housing, campus life centers on—surprise!— campus. The result: a hotbed of activity amidst a patchwork of farms in a classic New England town. It's hard to be bored. You'd actually have to try.*

Greek à la Carte

Of course, no one could have taken that late-night stroll on a Saturday night without hearing a light rumble coming from a wooded grove on the far side of campus. Ever lively, social houses clustered in that area regularly throw parties open to the entire college community. In the early 1990s, the college banned single-sex fraternities and sororities and severed their national affiliations. So began the transition to a social house system regulated by a council of students, faculty, and staff as opposed to being beholden to national Greek networks. The result is a system that largely replicates the Greek experience of close-knit, extended-family-like houses that know how to throw a good party and how to support the community through volunteer service. Students may pledge a social house—which are all coed—after completing one semester at the college. Although each house has its own building, some members may opt to continue to live in the dorms while remaining active in house affairs. For some students, the social house system proves a key ingredient in their extracurricular and social life at the college. They may pledge a house, ascend to house leadership, and find a circle of friends through their involvement. Others treat the social houses as a destination for partying on a weekend night. Still others rarely interact with the social house system and seek out social options elsewhere. The basic outlook: It's there if you're interested, but not omnipresent if you're not.

A Commons Way of Life

No description of Middlebury's social landscape would be complete without mention of the Commons System. Upon arrival at Middlebury, students automatically become members of one of five Commons based on their residence hall assignment. Each Commons has its own dean, faculty head, self-governing council, and culture—or so the college hopes will ultimately be the case. The system becomes more firmly entrenched in campus life with each passing year, but as a product of 1990s innovation, it continues to find its stride. The Commons reflects Middlebury's prevailing belief that liberal arts education takes place continuously. The Commons System strives to foster close student interaction within a framework that includes support from an accessible dean and engagement by a faculty head who frequents Commons events and routinely invites students to his or her home. As a practical matter, the Commons dean serves as the go-to person when students are struggling with personal problems and is always available for informal counseling on academics or other topics.

The Commons also have considerable financial resources at their disposal, and they're regular sponsors of lectures, visiting performers, outings, and social events. Brainerd Commons takes students apple picking in the fall. Cook Commons hosts a cookout on Battell Beach (the field behind Cook-affiliated Battell Hall) in the spring. And Ross Commons throws a Viva Ross Vegas party in its newly constructed dining space that readily converts to a nighttime venue.

A Community of Joiners

If you're an environmental activist pining to campaign against gas-guzzling SUVs, there's the Environmental Quality activist group. For those who prefer a policy-oriented approach to promoting, say, energy efficiency in the dorms, there's an Environmental Council of students, faculty, and staff with similar concerns and policymaking authority. And if environmental awareness isn't your extracurricular focus, choose from more than

150 extracurricular options on campus, which are displayed at a campus-wide activities fair twice annually.

> *Middlebury students live at the edge of their abilities. And although most teeter at the brink of being overwhelmed by the collision of academic, social, and extracurricular pressures, they wouldn't have it any other way.*

Take off with African running choir Mchaka-Mchaka and chant traditional songs while running across campus at night, or help to build the symbolic closet the Middlebury Open Queer Alliance and Ally Group construct on the quad each year to mark Coming Out Week. The spectrum of extracurricular opportunity is broad, and includes everything from the campus Progressives to the juggling brigade to cultural groups like the Alianza Latinoamericana y Caribena and African-American Alliance, which enrich Middlebury life with regular cultural revues, speakers, and artistic performances.

If anything, Middlebury students over- rather than under-participate in extracurricular life, producing a somewhat frenetic environment that motivates every student to embrace a variety of extracurricular pursuits.

Athletics

> *Cheer, boys, cheer for Middlebury's here,*
> *Fight, boys, fight, fight with all your might,*
> *Cheer, boys, cheer, for Middlebury's here,*
> *It's going to be a hot time in the cold town tonight*
> *Hey, hey, hey!*

—*Middlebury College Fight Song*

Make no mistake—Middlebury fields some of the most competitive teams in the New England Small College Athletic Association (NESCAC), and athletics are a way of life for a considerable majority of Middlebury students. Whether skiing the slopes of the Snow Bowl, competing in Ultimate Frisbee, or joining a demanding (but very rewarding) varsity intercollegiate team, athletics figure prominently into the Middlebury experience.

The Panthers field thirty NCAA varsity teams that draw twenty-eight percent participation from the student body—and almost 200 athletes compete in more than one varsity sport.

To document Middlebury's athletic success in recent years, look no further than the trophy case: Middlebury has won national championships in men's hockey, women's lacrosse, men's lacrosse, women's cross-country, women's hockey, field hockey, and men's tennis.

Athletics also provide a rallying point for the community. The men's ice hockey team enjoys special status among spectators, luring full houses as it perennially advances toward championship matches with age-old rivals. Students, faculty members, locals, and dining hall workers sit side by side in Kenyon Arena to cheer on the team, periodically shouting the College Fight Song to invigorate the players on the ice.

Students who do not join varsity squads frequently take advantage of Middlebury's full slate of intramural athletics, including crew, rugby, Ultimate Frisbee, and many others. The Middlebury Mountain Club—billed as the largest club on campus—also provides a recreational outlet for students wishing to hike, ice climb, or snowshoe in Middlebruy's rugged surroundings. Whatever athletic option Middlebury students pursue, it tends to be characterized by a refreshing balance with academic and other cocurricular commitments.

I was constantly supported not only by my coach in my academic ventures, but also by my professors in my athletic competitions. Middlebury breeds a healthy coexistence of academics and athletics.

—Thomas McMennamin, '04

The Arts Beat

The Center for the Arts (CFA) is to music, dance, and theater what Bi-Hall is to the sciences. The architectural gem slightly removed from the hustle and bustle of central campus houses numerous havens for the artsy set, including an extensive music library, concert hall, and dance studio. The Museum of Art also makes its home in the CFA, as the campus shorthand goes. The Museum has featured a traveling exhibit of treasures from Iraq, and a special installation of story quilts from the New York City-based artist Faith Ringgold, in addition to a permanent collection well worth a visit. Students make tracks to the CFA regularly to see theater performances at Seeler Studio, cabaret revues, and classical music concerts from groups such as the Emerson String Quartet in the acoustically refined Concert Hall, or special exhibits on view at the Museum.

Of course, the art world extends beyond the CFA in the form of student-directed shows in black-box Zoo theater in Hepburn residence hall, student visual art installations at the Johnson academic building, and student-produced films at Dana Auditorium. Middlebury is also a hotbed of *a cappella* performance, with at least half a dozen groups delivering regular performances to capacity crowds. Other artistic contributions enrich the social fabric at the college, as well. Slam poetry, break-dancing, the "On Tap" troupe, "Riddim" world dance and regular cultural shows add intrigue to Middlebury's social scene and give students many choices when considering how to spend a weekend night in rural Vermont.

> *Middlebury probably has more theater per capita of any college around. And I'm not talking about "You'll never believe who he went home with last night" drama. With five performing spaces, there's an unparalleled opportunity to perform, direct, or simply take in a piece of theater at Middlebury.*
>
> —*Laura S. Rocklyn, '04, English and theater double major and a former arts editor of* The Middlebury Campus *newspaper, stage manager, and frequent performer in student and faculty shows.*

GRADUATES

> *In October of my freshman year, my new friends and I decided it would be a grand idea to hike along Long Trail of Vermont and pitch a tent next to a mountain pond. We did just that, but the temperatures took an unexpected turn for the worst overnight and we awakened to a snow-coated trail and iced-over pond, shivering beside each other. Somehow, this encapsulated the Middlebury experience. Somewhat chilled, but joined in a rare solidarity of academic pursuit and extracurricular enrichment that you carry with you into the professional world. It forever links you to those who shared in it, whether past or current students. (Oh, and in case you were worried, we lived to complete our undergraduate careers.)*

If brought together in one location, all of Middlebury's living alumni wouldn't fill Boston's Fenway Park, Major League Baseball's smallest stadium. But—to invoke the well-worn cliché—they make up in quality what they lack in quantity. A Middlebury degree signifies a special bond with all who came before and all who come after. That much is clear from any alumni mixer in any city nation- (or world-) wide.

○ Julia Alvarez, Author of *How the Garcia Girls Lost Their Accents* and *In the Time of the Butterflies*

○ Ari Fleisher, Former White House Press Secretary

○ Felix Rohatyn, Financier and Former Ambassador to France

○ Jim Douglas, Governor of Vermont

○ Frank Sesno, Former CNN Senior Vice-President and Washington, D.C., Bureau Chief

○ Aditya M. Raval, White House Producer, BBC News

○ Eve Ensler, Playwright, *The Vagina Monologues*

○ Chris Waddell, Para-Olympic Gold Medallist

○ Adrian Benepe, New York City Commissioner of Parks and Recreation

○ Paul R. Aaronson, Executive Managing Director, Standard & Poor's

○ Sabra Field, Woodcut Artist and Designer of the Best-Selling UNICEF Card and U.S. Postage Stamp

○ Donald Yeomans, Senior Research Scientist, NASA's Jet Propulsion Laboratory, and expert on asteroids and comets

○ James Davis, Founder of the New Balance Athletic Shoe Company

○ Rep. William Delahunt, Congressman from Massachusetts

○ Rep. Frank Pallone, Congressman from New Jersey

○ William Burden, Opera Singer

○ Charles Moffett, Vice Chairman of Impressionist, Modern and Contemporary Art, Sotheby's

○ John Martin, Former CEO, Taco Bell

○ Jacqueline Phelan, Three-Time National Championship Mountain Bike Racer

○ Hon. Robert T. Stafford, One of Only eighty-three Americans Elected by One State as Governor, U.S. Representative, and U.S. Senator

Middlebury alumni are found across industries and across the world. Consider that the Governor of Vermont, the White House senior at BBC News, a gold medalist Para-Olympian, an opera singer, a financier, an entry-level management consultant, and a Peace Corps volunteer are all linked by their Middlebury degrees. The strength of the alumni network shines through when students are looking for internships or jobs. With the help of the resourceful Career Services staff, students are linked into a web of contacts that yield superb opportunities to develop professional skills.

SUMMING UP

Middlebury students agree: There's no place quite like here. Middlebury students value the beauty of the campus, the depth of the academic resources, and the wealth of extracurricular opportunities to keep life frenzied and fulfilling. Similarly, they value the diversity of experience and background that their peers bring to seminar discussions, quick coffee breaks at The Grille, or intense late-night conversations in the dorms. Upon graduation, they can't help but look back nostalgically at all things Middlebury—even the winters.

❏ *Devin B. Zatorski, B.A.*

NEW YORK UNIVERSITY

 New York University
New York, NY 10011

 (212) 998-4500
Fax: (212) 995-4902

 Web site: *admissions.nyu.edu*

 Enrollment

Full-time ❏ women: 10,340
         ❏ men: 6,665

INTRODUCING NEW YORK UNIVERSITY

If you stroll through Washington Square Park, the heart of Greenwich Village and unofficial quad of the New York University campus, on any weekday morning, it's impossible to miss the hundreds of bright-eyed, energetic college students headed to their first class of the day. This image, coupled with a crisp chill in the air and a rustle of autumn leaves, evokes a purely collegiate feeling. If you squint just a little, it's almost possible to imagine this busy, urban "quad" to be in some rural area surrounded by endless miles of cornfields. If you stand on the southeast corner of the park, in the shadow of NYU's Bobst Library, you might just hear a century's worth of academic ghosts whisper, "This is college." For a moment, you think, "This is how I always dreamed college would be."

But then reality sets in and you realize that the voices you hear do not belong to former NYU scholars, but to performance artists slamming poetry near the park's fountain, and the imagined cornfields have dissolved into an unobstructed view of fabulous Fifth Avenue, with its impressive buildings and flurry of activity. NYU definitely offers a collegiate experience, but there is nothing typical about it. And NYU students don't want it to be. They are happy to exchange cows and barns for Broadway and Wall Street. Wrought iron and ivy become much less significant when prospective students learn about all that NYU and New York City have to offer.

NYU is a large, private research university set in the Greenwich Village neighborhood of New York City. The school was founded in 1831 by a group of citizens attempting to fashion New York in the likeness of London, the proclaimed cultural epicenter of the time. They knew, even then, that the way to maintain a steadily evolving modern society was through higher education. NYU has kept that tradition alive by offering more than 160 innovative and unique programs of study at its eight different colleges, which include The College of Arts and Science, The Stern School of Business, The Steinhardt School of Education, The Tisch School of the Arts, The Gallatin School of Individualized Study, The College of Nursing, The School of Social Work, and The School of Continuing and Professional Studies. Each college offers major courses of study in distinctive subject areas. The benefit of having such a wide range of programs to choose from is that students are allowed and encouraged to pursue seemingly disparate interests across the seven colleges.

The strength of each program at NYU attracts very driven and ambitious students to each discipline, which makes for an interesting and diverse student body. For instance, a few years ago a business student at Stern and a drama student at Tisch got together and created the Stern Tisch Entertainment Business Association (STEBA), a thriving NYU club that wants its members to learn about and make contacts in the entertainment industry. As different as these two camps of students may appear, they are truly members of a unified, academic community. NYU students like to recognize the traits they share and are proud of these qualities. The caliber and the personality of each individual, in addition to the open-minded and proactive nature of fellow students, makes NYU the amazing place it is and will continue to be.

So the next time you find yourself in Washington Square Park, take a closer look at the students who are on their way to class. They're probably a bit edgier and may walk with a bit more purpose than most college students. Just take a look around you to see why this is the case. These people have chosen to attend an institution in downtown Manhattan—they know what they want and know that NYU is the best place to find it. This time, don't squint and try to make the school and its neighborhood look typical. Open your eyes and take in the reality of what NYU is: a fantastic school in a city often described as the center of the universe. If cows are what you're looking for, you won't find any here, unless there is a bovine exhibit at the Met.

ADMISSIONS REQUIREMENTS

Applicants often seek definitive numbers and statistics to quantify an acceptable NYU student, but no such absolute profile exists. NYU aims to create a holistic application review process, learning as much as possible about a person from ten simple pieces of paper. That being said, NYU is still a highly competitive institution. Even well-rounded, three-dimensional students must be at the top of their high school class while enrolled in a challenging curriculum composed of honors, AP, and/or IB courses. Solid performance on the SAT or ACT is a must for all applicants, and two SAT Subject Tests are required except for applicants who must submit a portfolio or audition as part of their admissions requirements.

With just under 35,000 applications for a recent academic year, there certainly wasn't a shortage of qualified students. Many applicants are academically talented, so Admissions Officers must rely on personal characteristics to distinguish students within the applicant pool. They want to see hard evidence of leadership, commitment, and drive in how you choose to spend your free time. It does not matter if your preferred activity is ballet or babysitting, the committee would like to see applicants who have been seriously involved in extracurricular activities while in high school. Stellar letters of recommendation and a thoughtful, personal essay that showcases a meaningful aspect of the applicant will also help set you apart from the crowd.

Procedure

NYU offers two application processes for prospective students: Early Decision and Regular Decision. Students who know that NYU is their first choice school may want to consider Early Decision. It is a binding agreement, which means that if you are admitted to the university, you will withdraw all other applications and accept NYU's offer of admission. Students interested in applying Early Decision must submit all necessary materials to the Undergraduate Admissions office by November 1 and can expect to hear of their decision by mid-December. Regular Decision requires applications to be submitted by January 15. Notification of acceptance will arrive near April 1.

Certain programs at the university have unique components to their admissions process that other programs may not. Some require the submission of supplementary information, a portfolio or even an audition, so please read through your application instructions carefully. The goal of the admission process is to succeed in choosing students who will thrive at NYU and in New York City. Obviously, the best students start with the best applicants; those who submit a complete, correct, and intelligent application on time will make a favorable impression where it counts the most.

ACADEMIC LIFE

At NYU, I have not learned all the answers. Instead, I have realized what an insurmountable task that is. Instead of learning answers, I have learned how to ask the right questions. And I think this is infinitely more important. A plus B equals C, simple enough. NYU has taught me to say A plus B equals C—or does it? Am I sure? Can I support what I think? I have learned how to think for myself here, a pretty monumental lesson. My education is not about regurgitating information; it's about finding my own truth under the influence of some truly fantastic minds.

— *Mary Hershkowitz*
BFA, 2003

The academic environment varies widely depending on which school or college of the university students attend. While this is the case, all NYU students share one common experience—the work is intense. Whether a student is perfecting moves in a dance studio, teaching inner-city youth at a public school, or researching the genetic makeup of mutant worms, they are engaged in a rigorous learning environment for most of their waking hours. The amazing thing is that NYU students would not have it any other way. These fiercely independent students crave new ideas and constantly push themselves further. They want to learn in order to be successful, more informed people who are not afraid to put in the hard work it takes to achieve their goals.

Walk through the Tisch School of the Arts at night and find a surprisingly large number of students tucked away in studios, individually honing their craft. Stand in the atrium of Bobst

Library and notice twelve stories of students studying. Because their education means so much more to them than a letter grade ascribed to their work, NYU students are ambitious scholars, scientists, teachers, and artists of their own accord.

Core Curriculum

Regardless of school affiliations, most students at the university participate in the core curriculum called the Morse Academic Plan (MAP). Each college within the university uses this core a bit differently, but the structure that it provides is universal. While the aim of MAP is to provide a strong, liberal arts foundation, it also allows students the freedom to tailor their program to their individual interests—to experiment with and investigate what truly fascinates them. Requirements for the MAP program are broken down into specific subject areas. To fulfill the Expressive Culture requirement, for instance, students may choose from a variety of classes ranging from courses that deal with anything from Jewish culture, to political culture, or artistic culture. At NYU, students are encouraged to explore many different academic pursuits while laying a foundation for more complicated and specific coursework that accompanies their chosen major.

Internships

Internships play a huge role in the life of an undergraduate at NYU. Although few programs at the university actually require an internship to graduate, all programs do encourage and recommend them as an excellent way to preview a variety of professions. Eighty percent of students hold at least three distinct internships by the time they graduate. The Office of Career Services (OCS) manages CareerNet, a database of more than 7,000 internships available exclusively to NYU students and alumni. These internships are quality positions that offer real-world work experience, not simply making copies and getting coffee. OCS has forged relationships with major businesses, theaters, schools, community organizations, museums, and hospitals in order to make these opportunities accessible to students. Many of these organizations have a long list of past interns from NYU and they keep coming back for more.

Faculty

Primarily a research university, NYU attracts many prominent scholars and researchers in any given academic pursuit. Among them you'll find CEOs and Fulbright Scholars, as well as Nobel and Pulitzer Prize recipients and Oscar and Emmy Award winners. They are revolutionary scholars, experts, and working professionals who are very much immersed in their fields. These are the leaders who teach NYU's undergraduates. All faculty members teach at least one undergraduate course per year—even the current NYU president and former dean of the NYU School of Law John Sexton teaches a Freshman Honors Seminar. The NYU faculty enjoys and takes pride in teaching and advising its undergraduate students.

In the classroom, it's easy to recognize the faculty's commitment to their individual fields. They are enthusiastic while introducing new material and show a genuine interest in engaging class dialogue. They want to learn from their undergraduates and will often cite their students as a source of inspiration for a new article or project. It is not uncommon to hear a professor say, "I had never thought of it that way" during a round-table discussion with his students. Together, students and professors engage the material very seriously, which always makes class a worthwhile, and sometimes breathtaking, experience. While there may be lectures that students must take at the introductory level, the preferred method of instruction at NYU is the seminar, where a small group of students and a faculty member exchange thoughtful discourse.

STUDY ABROAD

In addition to the New York City campus, students can study at eight NYU campuses throughout the world in:
Accra (Ghana)
Berlin
Florence
London
Madrid
Paris
Prague
Shanghai
NYU also offers Global Exchange Programs with selected urban research universities across the globe.

Undergraduate Research

NYU has so many faculty members doing postgraduate research right on campus that undergraduates wanted in on the action. For example, the College of Arts and Science created the Dean's Undergraduate Research Fund (DURF), a program that lets undergraduates pitch research ideas to the DURF committee, and if the proposal is considered worthwhile, receive funding for the project. Research projects may be individual or done in conjunction with a faculty member. CAS students' research projects really run the gamut—they range from studying Irish Literature in Belfast or tracing neurons of rat amygdala, to an analysis of the stained glass art of John La Farge or the development of contour detection and how it affects our visual world. Students who are granted funding must write a paper on their findings, present it at the annual research symposium held on campus each spring, and publish their abstracts in *Inquiry*, the NYU research journal.

SOCIAL LIFE AND ACTIVITIES

There is *always* something to do at NYU. This is not an overstatement in the least; in fact, it may be an understatement. NYU resides in and is part of Greenwich Village, the most hip, vibrant, young, eclectic, bohemian neighborhood in all of New York City. Being a college student in this creatively charged neighborhood, in the city that never sleeps, is a win-win situation. Students at NYU are never bored; they never grapple with the age-old question, "What should I do tonight?" Instead, they are faced with the challenge of juggling a social life with schoolwork. The catch phrase here is time management—NYU students choose and create a social hierarchy, attempting to fulfill their overwhelming number of commitments by the end of the night.

A Typical College Experience

Students who yearn for the typical college experience can still find it at NYU. There is an on-campus Greek system that, because of the high premium placed on real estate in the city, operates from designated floors in NYU residence halls. Greek letters adorn sheets hung from windows in otherwise innocuous-looking buildings as opposed to being firmly mounted on the front porch of an *Animal House*-style frat house.

Although Greek life does not dominate at NYU, university clubs and organizations are hugely popular. The NYU Office of Student Activities boasts a roster of over 300 student-run clubs ranging from the more serious breed, such as community service organizations, religious clubs, and political activism communities, to the light-hearted and fun, including the yo-yo club, and the soap opera watchers club.

NYU also has sports. In fact, it has twenty-four intercollegiate teams that compete in the NCAA Division III. Throughout the year, the NYU Violets compete against other private, research universities such as Brandeis, Carnegie Mellon, and Emory. Students interested in sports may join the competitive level for maximum commitment or can choose from more than 165 recreational, intramural, and club sports for some exercise and fun. For a good workout, NYU students can take advantage of their membership to the Coles Sports Center and the brand-new Paladium Fitness complex, premier NYU recreation centers.

As well, many students at NYU, not just drama majors at Tisch, are interested in the performing arts. There are literally hundreds of opportunities for non-drama majors to be involved in theatrical productions. The College of Arts and Science has CAST, a theater group that is open to talented students within the college who, in addition to their studies, want to perform in a production. The Steinhardt School of Education invites students to join their *a capella* groups and jazz bands, and there is an all-university gospel choir. If you want to be involved in something extracurricular, and most NYU students are, there are plenty of outlets to do so.

An Atypical College Experience

At NYU, you will find many students who enjoy the traditional college experience. They love to curl up on a couch in the student lounge of their residence hall with a bunch of other pajama-wearing eighteen- to twenty-two-year olds, order pizza, and watch a bad movie. But at the same time, there is an entire world outside just waiting to be explored. The NYU neighborhood alone reveals countless treasures: art galleries and cafes, ethnic restaurants and gourmet food shops, secondhand bookstores and antique shops, specialty music stores, and art movies houses. Beyond the Village there are new neighborhoods to discover, each offering their own cultural surprises. You can shop on Fifth Avenue, catch a Broadway show in Times Square, attend an art gallery opening in SoHo, and see the latest exhibit at the Guggenheim in the same day. At NYU, all of New York City is at your doorstep; you just have to walk outside to experience it.

From the very first day of orientation, NYU encourages new students to venture out into New York City and conquer their fears of the great unknown. Students attend events and outings that make them feel comfortable in their new home away from home. The university does everything in its power to ensure that you are safe in your travels on and off campus. If the city ever seems too big, or feels unmanageable, students can always rest assured that there will be friends hanging out in lounges, eating cold pizza and watching bad movies. You are always welcome, and that is the beauty of student life at NYU.

FINANCIAL AID

No doubt everyone knows that NYU and New York City are expensive places to live and study. It should come as no surprise that tuition for one academic year (including room, board, fees, etc.) is around $45,000. Fortunately, the university understands that spending this amount of money on higher education is a major financial commitment. Therefore, NYU's financial aid policy is quite simple: If students find that NYU is the best institution to meet their educational needs and interests, the NYU Office of Financial Aid will work with students and their families to help make NYU an affordable option. In fact, over seventy-two percent of full-time undergraduates receive some form of financial aid.

Students seeking financial aid from NYU should apply for assistance by submitting one form: the Free Application for Federal Student Aid (FAFSA). Students are encouraged to fill out the FAFSA via the Internet, which is the fastest and easiest method of applying for financial aid. Around November 1, the FAFSA is also available in paper form at high school guidance offices. With the information you provide on the FAFSA, the U.S. Department of Education uses a federally mandated formula to assess a family's financial status and determine the amount of money the government feels each can contribute to higher education. The NYU Office of Financial Aid then creates an individual financial aid package based upon the amount of financial need estimated by the government. Packages can include need- and/or merit-based scholarships, state and/or federal grants, work-study, and student loans.

NYU gives hundreds of millions of dollars in aid to undergraduates each year. A large percentage of this aid comes to students in the form of grants and scholarships. NYU scholarships range from $1,000 to $25,000 per year. All admitted students are automatically considered for every scholarship they qualify for—there is no separate application process. NYU also honors all independent scholarships or other money that students have acquired from outside the university. NYU participates in a variety of payment plans. They range from interest-free prepayment plans, to extensive loan programs that allow families the option to finance the cost of an NYU education over many years.

When it comes to financial aid, the bottom line is that NYU really makes a conscious effort to help individuals and families offset the cost of higher education in any way possible. The staff at the NYU Office Financial Aid is friendly, extremely knowledgeable, and always willing to provide sound financial options.

GRADUATES

NYU graduates are doing some great things out there in the real world. The university's Office of Career Services reports that typically over ninety percent of the class are employed in full-time positions or enrolled in graduate programs upon graduation—a statistic that speaks volumes about the type of preparation NYU provides to its students.

A large percentage of NYU grads enter medical, law, or dental school, and with acceptance rates of eighty percent (twice the national average), they are obviously ready to attend some of the top schools in the country. Stern School of Business students often work on Wall Street and Madison Avenue for companies such as Citibank, JP Morgan Chase, and Goldman Sachs. Tisch School of the Arts is stocking Broadway with many recent grads and current students who perform in major roles on the stage. Every year Los Angeles receives a high influx of film grads working on major motion pictures or television shows. The Steinhardt School of Education stocks New York schools with accomplished grammar, high school, and special education teachers. Hospitals, nationwide, are staffed by graduates of the Nursing Program. These are just some examples of the kinds of futures NYU graduates are pursuing when they leave the university. No matter what your specific interest is, at NYU you'll learn what you want and how to get it.

PROMINENT GRADUATES

- Jill Bargonetti, Prominent scientist and professor
- Carol Bellamy, Executive director, UNICEF
- Clive Davis, Founder and director, Arista Records
- Hon. Betty Weinberg Ellerin, Justice, Appellate Division—First Department, Supreme Court of the State of New York
- Rudolph Giuliani, Former mayor of the city of New York
- Alan Greenspan, Chairman of the Federal Reserve Board
- Rita Hauser, Appointee to Intelligence Board by President Bush
- Ang Lee, Oscar-winning filmmaker
- Spike Lee, Filmmaker
- Dr. Jonas E. Salk, Late scientist, discoverer of the polio vaccine; AIDS researcher

Attaining these desirable positions and acceptances to top graduate programs are not simple tasks. For example, the preprofessional advising center in the College of Arts and Science helps to prepare future lawyers and doctors. Advisors meet with students throughout their four years at NYU, in order to help them secure positions in their graduate program of choice.

The NYU Office of Career Services (OCS) lends a helping hand to students interested in pursuing a career upon graduation. OCS believes that preparation for a career or an advanced degree does not begin during spring semester senior year, but starts as early as freshman year. Students get a taste of their field and how it functions in the real world through internships, which also allows them to network and make important connections with potential employers. Often, these internships lead to full-time positions after graduation. OCS also offers résumé building and interviewing workshops and hosts massive recruitment fairs on campus twice a year. They also maintain CareerNet, a database of more than 10,000 available on- and off-campus jobs. OCS really does as much as it can to prepare students for whatever path they may choose after graduation. It is common for NYU students to drop by the Office of Career Services and ask a counselor for help to secure a political position in Washington D.C. or a seat in the entering class of NYU School of Law. Without hesitation, students always receive valuable words of advice and a "let's do it" attitude.

SUMMING UP

NYU is a large, research university set in Greenwich Village, the heart of New York City. All its academic programs include a strong liberal arts foundation as well as many areas of pre-professional specialization. The academic, research, study abroad, and internship possibilities are endless. The social life is exciting and varied. NYU graduates are extremely successful. Taken alone, these facts somehow overlook the true essence of what NYU is really about. Is it important to know that you will receive a top-notch education? Yes. Should you be aware that your degree would land you a great job or acceptance into a graduate program? Yes. But there is so much more to NYU that can only be discovered once you set foot on campus.

> *First and foremost, NYU is about discovery. As a new freshman, I felt like Christopher Columbus leading the Nina, the Pinta, and the Santa Maria through uncharted waters to America. There was a whole new world out there I had never seen before, and NYU introduced me to it. It's here that you'll find what you care about, you'll find lifelong friends, you'll find the city, and hopefully you'll find yourself. And that's what college is all about.*
>
> *—Jeremy Godfrey*
> *BFA, 2002*

So I took my own advice and set foot on campus. I sat in the unofficial "quad" and tried to summarize NYU. But to harness all that NYU is and quantify it into something tangible is impossible, because NYU is not one thing. It's not simple or usual, and defies definition, which is the allure of this university. The fact that NYU does not lend itself to categorization is the exact reason why people want to attend. Those who consider themselves unconventional refuse to be defined. They are searching for an institution of higher education as avant-garde and open-minded as they are. At NYU, people find their passion and their voice, and begin to carve out a unique space in this world.

❏ *Eric Muroski, B.A.*

NORTHWESTERN UNIVERSITY

✉	**Northwestern University** **Evanston, IL 60204-3060**
☎	(847) 491-7271
🌐	E-mail: *ug-admission@northwestern.edu* Web site: *www.ugadm.northwestern.edu*

👥 Enrollment

Full-time ❏ women: 4,208 ❏ men: 3,781	
Part-time ❏ women: 93 ❏ men: 71	

INTRODUCING NORTHWESTERN

There's a T-shirt with a phrase on it that applies to most Northwestern University students: "Plays well with others." Although Northwestern undergraduates are unquestionably intelligent and academically driven—approximately eighty-three percent of them graduated in the top ten percent of their high school class—they are also a remarkably collaborative group.

As a result, you'll find Northwestern students working together on everything from scientific research projects with faculty members to a seemingly infinite number of *a cappella* and theater groups to the nationally known Dance Marathon, an annual thirty-hours of nonstop dancing fund-raising event for a designated charity. You'll also find students engaged in community service projects and internships throughout the Chicago metropolitan area where Northwestern is located.

Northwestern students value the challenging intellectual environment as much as they enjoy endless social outlets and easy access to one of the world's most exciting cities.

In my four years at Northwestern, I cheered wildly as the football team pulled off miracle upsets against Big 10 powerhouses, gussied up with girlfriends before sorority formals at the Sears Tower, and hopped on the "El" for class trips to the Chicago Shakespeare Theatre and the Lyric Opera. I also attended lectures by Margaret Thatcher and Tom Brokaw, pulled all-nighters to complete big assignments, and participated in the half-genuine, half-comic primal scream that kicks off every exam week.

Although I earned a degree in English Literature, my Northwestern education is characterized by a balance between the liberal arts, practical skills, and real-world experience. By the time I graduated, I knew how to write an airtight essay, a killer cover letter, a catchy press release, and a working web page. I also knew how to score cheap admission at the Art Institute and where to get the best hot dog in the country on the ride home.

Part of that cooperative ethic stems from Northwestern's academic culture, which encourages collaborative learning in an unusually broad range of disciplines for a school of its size. Students can explore academic subjects in any or all of six undergraduate schools, regardless of major, either through academic programs such as dual degrees or simply by taking electives. Regardless of academic discipline, you're likely to end up in classes where you'll not only have a chance to voice your opinion, you'll be expected to do so. That means you're an active participant in your education, not a passive note-taker.

So why is a private university in the Chicago metro area named Northwestern? When it was founded in 1851, the university's founders intended it to educate the children of those living in the states that had been carved out of the Northwest Territory, which was created by Congress in 1787. The vast region included all the land between the Ohio River, the Mississippi River, and the Great Lakes. The area ultimately became the states of Ohio, Michigan, Indiana, Illinois, Wisconsin, and a portion of Minnesota, and was known for decades as simply "the Northwest." Today Northwestern attracts students from all fifty states and approximately one hundred foreign countries.

And part of this sense of community also results from the often-unplanned interactions that occur when you get 8,000 intelligent, involved students together in one place. Whether it's debating the merits of a particular viewpoint in class, hanging out at any of Evanston's half-dozen coffeehouses near campus, or riding the "El" together to catch events in neighboring Chicago, Northwestern students generally cram as much into their lives as possible. If you want solitude, you can definitely find it at Northwestern—the campus' mile-long shoreline of Lake Michigan is a favorite place, especially in good weather—but if you're someone who enjoys "playing well with others," Northwestern is a good fit.

ADMISSIONS REQUIREMENTS

While I can't claim to know what goes on behind the closed doors of the Admissions Office, I can attest to the results of the process. It's one of the best universities in the nation, so I knew going in that my peers would be accomplished and intelligent. And, while I met my fair share of valedictorians, class presidents, and high school busybodies, my classmates consisted of much more than the credentials they listed on their college apps. The friends I made at Northwestern came from all sorts of places, and they were carried by all sorts of passions. Whether I hung out with an aspiring actress from Milan, a hopeful politician from Miami, or a baseball star from Madison, I constantly found myself both challenged and inspired by big personalities with big ambitions to match.

Admission to Northwestern isn't easy. The university accepts less than thirty percent of the 20,000 plus students who apply each year. Good test scores are a basic requirement, of course, but a more important factor is how well you did in a challenging high school program. If you've taken advantage of the most demanding courses offered in your school, such as AP and Honors courses, and excelled in them, that carries a great deal of weight. Northwestern wants to hear your individual voice. The essay is the place to express this. The essay is a chance for you to give Northwestern a better feel as to who you are and whether you'd be a good match for the university. Therefore, taking your time and doing a good job on the essay will definitely help. The application also includes an activity chart that allows you to show important interests you have outside the classroom, so be sure to complete that portion as well.

Admission to Northwestern is "need-blind," meaning that an applicant's ability to pay is *not* considered when the application is being reviewed. Approximately forty-two percent of Northwestern students receive university-funded need-based scholarships and sixty percent receive some form of financial aid: need-based scholarships, loans, and/or work-study jobs. All awards are based on financial need (see the Financial Aid section for more information).

Tests

Northwestern requires that you submit the results of either the SAT or ACT. The median score for admitted students is 720 for the SAT Verbal, 740 for the SAT Math, and 32 for the ACT. While not required, the results of any Advanced Placement, International Baccalaureate, or SAT Subject Tests that you have taken also are considered. If English is not your primary language, you must submit the results of the Test of English as a Foreign Language (TOEFL) as well.

Early Decision

If you believe strongly that Northwestern is the university you would most like to attend, you should consider applying by November 1 under the Early Decision plan, which allows you to receive a decision in December. Do this only if you're sure Northwestern is your first choice—by applying under this binding admission option, you agree to withdraw all applications at other colleges, initiate no new applications, and enroll at Northwestern if you're admitted.

NORTHWESTERN'S SCHOOLS AND COLLEGES (WITH YEAR OF FOUNDING)

○ Judd A. and Marjorie Weinberg College of Arts and Sciences (1851)
○ School of Communication (1878)
○ School of Continuing Studies (1933)
○ School of Education and Social Policy (1926)
○ Robert R. McCormick School of Engineering and Applied Science (1909)
○ Graduate School (1910)
○ Medill School of Journalism (1921)
○ School of Law (1859)
○ J. L. Kellogg School of Management (1908)
○ Feinberg School of Medicine (1859)
○ School of Music (1859)

Choosing Courses

With a full-time undergraduate population of about 8,000, Northwestern provides personal attention and flexibility that is rare in larger institutions. Students also benefit from superior academic advising, career counseling, and student services.

Yet the size of the student body and an easily navigated campus may be the only things about Northwestern that feel small. The broad range of academic opportunities is unmatched in other schools of similar size. In fact, students at Northwestern have a larger pool of courses to choose from—about 4,000 each year—than at most other institutions of comparable size. Undergraduates benefit from the fact that Northwestern is home to six strong and distinctive undergraduate schools that will prepare them for the work place or graduate study.

On the Sunday before finals week, the main library is the hottest scene on campus. Study groups crowd around tables littered with coffee cups, Coke bottles, and bags of M&M's. Everywhere you look, students are poring over textbooks, recopying notes, or squinting at computer screens. Around midnight, serious studiers with big exams make their way up to Core, the 35,000-volume "library-within-the-library," which is open twenty-four hours a day during finals. There they camp out with other diehards until the wee hours of the morning. If hunger strikes, tired students make the short trip to Norris University Center, where they break over chips, veggies, and dip at midnight or a full bacon and egg breakfast at 3 A.M.

Surprisingly, there's something fun and exciting about exam week at Northwestern. The buzz surrounding deadlines and due dates seems to inspire a collective outpouring of intellectual and social energy. Camaraderie accompanies stress, and you often see groups of friends chatting, giggling, and joking within the frantic atmosphere created by ten-page papers, class presentations, and cumulative exams.

Also making it easier to customize a Northwestern education is an academic calendar of three quarters each year (with a fourth quarter of optional summer study)—instead of two semesters—that allows you to take four courses per quarter. It's an ambitious curriculum that means that you have to hit the ground running in each of your courses. But it also ensures that you'll have a solid foundation in the liberal arts and a thorough education in your chosen field. And it allows you to explore interests and subjects you might not have thought about before you came to Northwestern.

As a prospective undergraduate, you'll apply to one of Northwestern's schools that offer undergraduate programs. At the center of Northwestern is the oldest, largest, and most comprehensive of the undergraduate schools, the Judd A. and Marjorie Weinberg College of Arts and Sciences. Enrolling more than half of the undergraduates, Weinberg combines the vigor of a leading liberal arts college with the resources of a major research university.

Northwestern's other colleges and schools—McCormick School of Engineering and Applied Sciences; School of Education and Social Policy; Medill School of Journalism, School of Communication; and School of Music—offer outstanding preprofessional programs in their respective fields. Regardless of what area you choose, you will enjoy an unusual degree of personal attention—in classrooms, around seminar tables, and in conversation with academic advisers from the university's many disciplines. You will also be able to work in the laboratories of prominent scientists, study with award-winning scholars, and engage with speakers from around the world.

Special Programs

UNDERGRADUATE RESEARCH

Northwestern students have the opportunity to engage in major research projects while still undergraduates. Following is a sample of some of the topics explored by undergraduates who received summer research grants recently:

○ Designing the American Metropolis: Buenos Aires and Chicago in the Early Twentieth Century
○ The Effects of Proliferin-Related Protein Absence on the Regulation of Angiogenesis During Pregnancy
○ The Influence of Maps on the Development of Childrens' Neighborhood Knowledge
○ Them! Dissecting the Cultural Aesthetics of the 1950s American Society
○ Drawing on Success: What AIDS Organizations in Kenya Can Learn from Uganda
○ The Studies of NOX and HNO_3 on Metal Oxide Surfaces
○ Women's History through Women's Words, 1770–1820
○ Dance and Cubism: Materializing a New Space
○ Role of Religious Ethics in Philosophical Ethical Debate: A Study of Charles Taylor and John Milbank

I don't mean to blow anyone's cover here, but it's pretty easy to get research money at Northwestern. When my thesis adviser suggested I apply for a research grant, I thought it was worth a shot. A month later, I was on a plane to Philadelphia for a weekend visit to Penn's Rare Books and Manuscripts Library. I spent my days fishing through Walt Whitman's personal letters and possessions, from the original scrawlings of Leaves of Grass *to a neatly trimmed lock of his long, white hair. I spent my evenings in a cultural tour of downtown Philly, checking out the sights and sampling the food.*

I returned to Northwestern with a new intimacy with Walt Whitman's text, a new premise to work into my thesis, and a new appreciation for authentic Philly cheesesteaks, all courtesy of the Office of Fellowships.

In addition to the opportunity to customize academic programs, Northwestern also offers several specialized programs for undergraduate students. Among these is the Honors Program in Medical Education, in which a select group of students complete three years of undergraduate study and in the fourth year are admitted to the entering

Northwestern University

class of Northwestern's Feinberg School of Medicine. Or students may apply to the Integrated Science Program or the program of Mathematical Methods in the Social Sciences, which combine small classes with courses from across those respective disciplines. Many students also take advantage of undergraduate research programs, which provide funds for students to conduct in-depth study, either during the year or over the summer, into a particular topic under the guidance of a faculty member.

> *When you think of a liberal arts education, the words "practical" or "pertinent" don't necessarily come to mind. But, by declaring a minor in Northwestern's Business Institutions Program in the College of Arts and Sciences, I was able to supplement my liberal arts coursework with tangibly applicable classes such as "Bargaining and Negotiation." In BIP, I created marketing plans, devised P.R. strategies, and analyzed case studies. I also learned how to negotiate my salary, reallocate a budget, and play the stock market.*
>
> *Northwestern's Business Institutions Programs provides an invaluable opportunity to acquire real-world experience and real-life exposure. It's a great way to feel out postgraduate possibilities while acquiring the skills you'll need in any profession.*

Study Abroad

Every year, nearly 600 students from all of Northwestern's six undergraduate schools participate in overseas educational opportunities. With affiliated programs at approximately 100 institutions, Northwestern students literally have a world of choices. While Europe remains a popular location, a growing number of students choose to study in Africa, Asia, and South America. Some programs are university-based, meaning that students live in one place and take courses at a university. Others are field-based, focusing more on fieldwork and independent research projects.

Faculty

> *In my 398 American Literature Seminar, skipping the reading wasn't an option. We were a class of six, and my professor wasn't one to tolerate silence when it came to discussion. We'd show up for class every Tuesday and Thursday, armed with texts extensively decorated with pink highlighters and yellow Post-its. For the next hour and a half, we'd pick apart the language of Emerson's* Nature *or Hawthorne's* The Scarlet Letter, *challenging one another to define words in new ways and defend unique textual interpretations. I found that the expectations that came with small class settings inevitably led to confidence, capability, and deeper understanding. When it's taboo to simply show up and clam up, and when you're expected to make pithy and valuable contributions, you make a point to read more closely and think harder as you prepare for class.*
>
> *Small classes are common at Northwestern, especially at the upper levels. Many professors strictly cap their classes at twenty students, and, though it's a drag to get shut out of a course you want, the challenges and rewards of learning in an intimate setting are worth it when you do make enrollment the following quarter.*

Northwestern has nearly 1,000 full-time faculty who teach in its undergraduate college and schools. One of the hallmarks of Northwestern historically has been that almost all faculty members teach undergraduate students; that remains true today. That means you'll be taught, mentored, and advised by Pulitzer Prize winners, MacArthur Fellowship recipients, and members of numerous honorary and professional societies.

SOCIAL LIFE AND ACTIVITIES

Lakefront Living

Most undergraduates at Northwestern live on the Evanston campus in one of the residence halls, residential colleges, sororities, or fraternities. Some of the halls and residential colleges, and almost all the fraternities and sororities, are in older, ivy-covered houses. Other residence halls and residential colleges are new and feature apartment-style suites with individual bathrooms. Several of the residence halls/colleges overlook Lake Michigan, and all are within easy walking distance of the main classroom buildings.

Regardless of where students live, they can enjoy Northwestern's beautifully landscaped lakefront campus that stretches for a mile along the shore of Lake Michigan. That location can bring some fairly chilly winds in winter, but it also means an endless horizon to the east, a private beach and boathouse where you can take sailing lessons, and plenty of open space where you can soak up the sun in the spring and fall.

RESIDENTIAL COLLEGES

Northwestern's eleven residential colleges provide housing and specialized programs that allow students and faculty to pursue a common interest outside the classroom. Here are some of the disciplines covered by res colleges:
- ○ Communication
- ○ Cultural and Community Studies
- ○ Humanities
- ○ International Studies
- ○ Performing Arts
- ○ Public Affairs
- ○ Science and Engineering
- ○ Women's Studies
- ○ Commerce and Industry

Activities

Over-opportunity-ed. That was how one student described her undergraduate experience at Northwestern.

There's something to do almost every night on campus—theater, music, all kinds of things. And if you want, you can go into Chicago. The problem here is that there are too many things to do, especially if you're worried about keeping your GPA up.

— Molly Browne, '04 from Washington, D.C.

MAKE A DATE WITH PLAN-IT PURPLE

Along with their daily planners, a key source for Northwestern students is Plan-It Purple (*www.planitpurple.northwestern.edu*), the on-line calendar that lists nearly every event that occurs at Northwestern. More than 600 organizations and on-campus entertainment venues list their events on Plan-It Purple (named for Northwestern's official color of purple). Students can even create their own customized version to remind them of their own meetings and events.

Northwestern students tend to be active, engaged, and involved. That means, at least for most students, that their most important accessory is their day planner (either paper or electronic), followed closely by their cell phones because they keep rescheduling all their commitments.

For many students, those commitments include not just academic studies, but other activities as well. Northwestern has more than 415 extracurricular groups on campus, ranging from cultural groups to religious and spiritual groups to dozens of music and small theater groups open to nonmajors. Every fall during the first week of classes, the Student Activities Fair showcases these organizations, giving new students a chance to find out more and choose which ones they'd like to join. With enthusiastic members promoting each group, it's easy to jump into lots of organizations. If you're really good at time management, you can pull it off, but be prepared for some late nights—many groups start their meetings/rehearsals/practices at 9 or 10 P.M.

> *I can still remember the look on my best friend's face when I told her I'd joined a sorority. "You!" she exclaimed with a chuckle, "a sorority girl?" I must admit, I never fancied myself as a Greek kind of a gal before coming to Northwestern; however, my experience in Northwestern's Greek system broke the mold of the superficial sorority stereotypes you see in the movies. My membership in Kappa Alpha Theta sorority opened the door for professional networking, community service, and internship opportunities. It was also a great way to make friends and a fun social outlet in what can be a very stressful environment.*
>
> *The Greek system is fairly big at Northwestern, but if you choose to join, it won't be the dominant force of your social life, and it won't distract you from academic pursuits. I know that the system has some cheesy implications, but at Northwestern, it's really worth a try.*

Community Service

Another key interest for Northwestern students is community service. Approximately 3,000 students perform some sort of community service each year, ranging from tutoring at local schools to service projects in Chicago. The largest student group on campus is the Northwestern Community Development Corps, which serves as an umbrella organization for many of the service groups on campus. In addition, the web site at *http://www.volunteer.northwestern.edu/* matches up students with volunteer opportunities in the community.

Athletics

Northwestern is a charter member of and the only private university in the Big Ten, one of the premier Division I athletic conferences in the country. Some of the nation's best teams, including Northwestern, play regularly on the Evanston campus and the football and basketball games provide a social experience for undergraduates, as well as great competition. Northwestern offers twenty-three intercollegiate athletic teams (ten men's and eleven women's). Sports at Northwestern are not just for watching, however, as club and intramural sports attract approximately 2,000 participants each year. The thirty-four club sports include crew, Ultimate Frisbee, ice hockey, equestrian, water polo, and a host of others, many of which compete at the highest levels. Intramural offerings range from casual softball leagues to competitive basketball, and many of the outdoor sports are played on Northwestern's lakefront fields.

Evanston and Chicago

One of the major factors that came into play when I was picking a school: location, location, location. And it's tough to beat Northwestern's prime turf on the North Shore of Lake Michigan. A short ride on the "El" can lead to a shopping extravaganza on the Magnificent Mile, a cultural afternoon at the Art Institute, or an evening full of laughs at Second City. When the big city seems daunting, downtown Evanston is full of cozy coffeeshops, cute boutiques, quality restaurants, and neighborhood bars. And, after spending the winter braving Chicago's infamous cold winds and snowstorms, nothing beats that first spring day when it's warm enough to study out on the lakefront.

Evanston isn't a typical college town. While Northwestern is a vital part of the community, it doesn't dominate the city of 75,000 that adjoins Chicago as a large university often does a small town. So you won't find a large area of somewhat shabby student apartments just off campus or rows of bars catering to the just-of-age (or perhaps not) crowd.

Instead, Northwestern's campus is bordered by a neighborhood of beautiful old homes and a vibrant downtown. Downtown Evanston has dozens of interesting locally owned shops and more than sixty restaurants, ranging from student budget-friendly cafés to fancier places that are great for Family Weekend. Within walking distance of the campus is an eighteen-screen movie theater, with six of the screens devoted to showing independent and foreign films. Best of all, the theater—and almost all the stores and restaurants downtown—offer a discount if you show your WildCARD, the Northwestern student ID.

Then there's Chicago, one of the world's truly great cities. The third-largest city in the country, a place with world-class museums, an incredible theater scene, ethnic restaurants, and nightlife galore. Students can take advantage of such great opportunities as the Chicago Art Institute's free admission day and student-discount tickets to the Chicago Symphony (as cheap as $10), and, of course, a Cubs game at Wrigley Field.

Getting to Chicago is easy. The CTA rapid transit ("the El") has three stops near campus and even runs express from Evanston during rush hours. In addition, the university runs a shuttle bus on weekdays between the Evanston campus and the Chicago campus (home to the law school, medical school, and part of the business school), which is only two blocks from Chicago's Michigan Avenue, one of the best shopping streets in the world.

FINANCIAL AID

Financial aid at Northwestern is awarded on the basis of family need, although the university does offer a limited number of merit-based scholarships.

There's no getting around the fact that a private school college education is a financial stretch for most families. In order to ease the burden for mine, I applied to spend my junior year as a Resident Assistant in a freshman dorm. It turned out to be a great deal. For a year of meeting great new people and taking on some pretty crazy situations and responsibilities, the university picked up my room and board.

Recipients of need-based financial aid come from a wide range of income backgrounds, so if you're not sure whether you'd qualify for need-based aid, go ahead and apply. To do so, you must complete the Free Application for Federal Student Aid (FAFSA) and the College

Scholarship Service Financial Aid PROFILE. Northwestern awards more than $63 million in grant assistance to undergraduate students each year.

GRADUATES

Northwestern alumni, and their employers, regularly comment on how much they value a Northwestern education. Of the most recently surveyed graduating class, fifty-four percent accepted full-time employment, thirty percent entered a graduate or professional program, and sixteen percent pursued full-time community service or volunteer work, an internship or fellowship, or other endeavors.

Few students view graduation as the end of their education, however. The majority of Northwestern's undergraduate alumni eventually go on to earn advanced degrees. Another survey found that sixty percent of a typical graduating class earned a higher degree within ten years of graduating. Of those alumni, twelve percent obtained M.B.A.s; eleven percent law degrees; nine percent M.D.s; and six percent Ph.D.s, while the rest received other graduate degrees.

Northwestern alumni, numbering approximately 160,000, include leaders in business, government, law, medicine, media, education, and the performing arts. In addition, alumni are engaged and active in their communities and their professions.

PROMINENT GRADS

- Greg Berlanti, Writer/Director
- Rod Blagojevich, Governor of Illinois
- Nick Chabraja, Chairman and CEO, General Dynamics
- Johnetta Cole, President, Bennett College
- Richard Gephardt, Former U.S. Representative, House Minority Leader
- Heather Headley, Tony Award–winning Actress; Star of *The Lion King* and *Aida*
- Brigid Hughes, Executive Editor, *The Paris Review*
- Sherry Lansing, Chairman, Paramount Pictures
- George McGovern, former U.S. Senator and Presidential Candidate
- David Schwimmer, Actor
- Ellen Soeteber, Editor, *St. Louis Post-Dispatch*
- Graham Spanier, President, Pennsylvania State University
- John Paul Stevens, U.S. Supreme Court Justice
- Mary Zimmerman, MacArthur Fellowship Recipient, Tony Award–winning Director, and Northwestern Professor of Performance Studies

Although NU arms its students with a variety of skills, perhaps the most valuable assets of a Northwestern graduate are confidence and capability. At Northwestern, there is no typical answer to the question, "What are your plans after graduation?" Six months after my graduation, I have friends all over the world engaging in all sorts of activities. Whether they're studying at the nation's premier graduate schools, trying out for Broadway plays, researching for a Fulbright, or working in the business world, my former peers are all deftly doing the things they've always wanted to do.

SUMMING UP

There really isn't such a thing as a "typical" Northwestern experience, mainly because there are so many different types of people here. That's probably a good thing, although it makes it hard to characterize the institution. In the end, Northwestern students can make their time here be pretty much anything they want, given the range of choices that exist. For most students, that means four years of a great education—and some really fun times with good friends.

Northwestern was my final stop on a coast-to-coast tour of the nation's top schools. After spending a freezing afternoon wandering around campus, talking to students, and sitting in on classes, Northwestern just felt right. Four years and one bachelor's degree later, I'd make the same choice.

Northwestern packs a lot of bang for the buck, which is something to consider when you're spending so many of them. It's a Big 10 school with top-ten academics, and it's not uncommon to bounce from the student section of the football stands to the study carrels of the library in the same afternoon.

As a Northwestern student, I had as much fun hitting the books in the library as I did hitting the parties on Friday night or hitting the streets of downtown Chicago, but the good times were just icing on the cake. As a Northwestern graduate, I have the skills I need to reckon with the "real world," and, in the end, that's what really counts.

❑ *Kristen Acimovic, B.A.*

Oberlin College
Oberlin, Ohio 44074

(440) 775-8411 or (800) 622-6243
Fax: (440) 775-6905

E-mail: *college.admissions@oberlin.edu*
Web site: *http://ww.oberlin.edu/coladm/*

 Enrollment

Full-time ❑ women: 1,537
❑ men: 1,218

Part-time ❑ women: 44
❑ men: 46

INTRODUCING OBERLIN COLLEGE

The most impressive aspect of an Oberlin College education is the genuine rapport that exists between the diverse student communities. Obies come from every corner of the globe to share an intellectually stimulating atmosphere, where they are encouraged to be socially and civically engaged through a myriad of extracurricular activities.

> *Oberlin gave me the chance to intern at a high-ranking senator's office my freshman year. It also gave me the opportunity to develop close relationships by way of easy access to my professors, many of whom are very highly respected in their fields.*

Think one person can change the world? So do we.

When a pair of Yankee missionaries founded Oberlin College in 1833, they envisioned an institution built on high intellectual standards, a liberal education for all, excellence in teaching, and a commitment to the social and moral issues of the day. For the past 171 years, Oberlin has honored this mission, encouraging students to use their liberal arts education and change the world, one Obie at a time.

Today, Oberlin College's 440-acre campus sits next to, and has inexorably meshed with, the city of Oberlin, Ohio. A small town by definition, Oberlin (with a population of 8,600) is thirty-five miles west of Cleveland, Ohio. At first glance, the town's tree-lined square and old-fashioned business district may evoke memories of a sleepy Mayberry, but the annual fall migration of college students revitalizes the town with their youthful energy.

The small-town atmosphere is an attractive draw for many students, who (because of the town's proximity to the college) often forge lasting bonds with local residents. Whether it's over a cup of coffee at the Java Zone, participating in annual events such as the Big Parade, or during a city- and campus-wide effort to register voters, students and "townies" band together to form an experience that is uniquely Oberlin.

Oberlin College's commitment to the surrounding community has introduced countless students to the idea of service and learning. In fact, the college's addition of academically based community service courses to the curriculum encourages students to take what they have learned in the classroom and apply it to real-world service situations. Students in these classes work with local community partners to strengthen the programs that are vital to Oberlin's diverse population.

With its emphasis on academics and social justice, it's no surprise that countless Oberlin grads have gone on to make a significant impact in the fights against poverty, racism, gender inequality, and other important social and political issues. Whether as doctors, lawyers, business executives, educators, politicians, or volunteers, Obies have left their mark on society by holding themselves to a higher standard and living Oberlin's ideals long after they've graduated.

Oberlin's founding fathers would be proud.

Oberlin's competitive admissions process attracts a cross section of intelligent, forward-thinking students, including the 5,824 who applied for one of the 742 coveted spots in the class of 2008. With sixty-seven percent of first-year applicants in the top tenth and eighty-five percent in the top quarter of their senior classes, prospective Obies have all their academic bases covered.

Oberlin's application process is fairly standard, calling for transcripts, recommendations, and a personal essay. The average test scores among successful applicants are 690/660 for the SAT I and 29 for the ACT. Oberlin requires the writing sections of both the SAT and the ACT. (Note: Oberlin requires either the SAT or the ACT, but recommends the SAT Subject Tests.) International students who apply to Oberlin must submit their TOEFL scores. Oberlin's admissions counselors (who are often Oberlin alumni) also consider a student's advanced placement and honors courses, leadership record, and extracurricular and volunteer accomplishments.

Although Oberlin does not require its prospective students ("prospies," as they are affectionately nicknamed) to schedule an on-campus interview, one is strongly recommended. Oberlin's admissions counselors are more likely to recognize the intangible qualities that define an Obie during a face-to-face interview. All prospies are encouraged to visit Oberlin during the academic year, to meet current students, and attend the classes that interest them. This candid look at campus life offers prospective students a clear picture of the Oberlin experience.

Students unable to schedule a campus interview can arrange one with Oberlin alumni in their hometown. Simply call Oberlin's Office of Admissions (1-800-622-OBIE) to request an off-campus interview or visit the office's web site (*http://www.oberlin.edu/coladm*) for further information. All alumni interviews must be scheduled by January 2.

Oberlin's Application

When applying to Oberlin, all prospective students must submit a two-part application. The easiest way to complete the first part of the application is to submit it online. But you can also submit an online request for information, e-mail an admissions counselor, or telephone the office directly to ask for an application packet.

The second part of Oberlin's application includes the Common Application and its personal essay, as well as the "Why Oberlin" essay and some supplemental forms. Prospies may submit the Common Application and the "Why Oberlin?" essay online.

Admissions Deadlines for First-Year Students

If Oberlin is your top college choice, consider applying as an Early Decision candidate. The admissions committee considers the enthusiasm of Early Decision candidates a plus during the selection process, giving these applicants a slightly better statistical chance of gaining admission to Oberlin than a Regular Decision candidate.

Oberlin offers two Early Decision options. Early Decision I candidates must submit their applications by November 15, while the applications for Early Decision II must be postmarked by January 2. Students applying under the first program will receive their notification (admission, deferral, or denial) by mid-December. Early Decision II applicants will receive their notification by February 1.

All first-year, Regular Decision candidates must apply to Oberlin by January 15. They will receive notification of their status from the Office of Admissions by April 1.

Admissions Deadlines for Transfer Students

Oberlin enrolls first-year students during the fall semester *only*; however, transfer students may enroll during either the fall or spring semesters. Oberlin College defines a transfer student, for admissions purposes, as a student who has been enrolled in a degree program at another college or university or who has earned more than thirty semester hours of college course credit.

Transfer applicants must apply to Oberlin by March 15 for enrollment the following fall and by November 15 for enrollment the following spring. Notifications for these applicants are mailed in mid-December and at the beginning of April.

Deferred Enrollment

Oberlin also offers a deferred enrollment plan. Students admitted to the Division of Arts and Sciences can request deferred enrollment for up to one year. A written request for this status should be submitted to the Dean of Admissions, detailing the student's plan for the coming year. Approved deferral requires the student's commitment to enroll, as well as a deposit to secure a place in the following year's class.

The Oberlin Conservatory of Music

In addition to the College of Arts and Sciences, the campus is home to the Oberlin Conservatory of Music. Founded in 1865, the Conservatory is known throughout the world as a professional music school of the highest caliber. It is the oldest continuously operating conservatory in the United States, and is the only major music school in the country linked with a preeminent liberal arts college.

The Conservatory provides preprofessional training in music performance, composition, music education, electronic and computer music, jazz studies, music theory, and music history to approximately 595 students. The Conservatory offers the following degrees: Bachelor of Music, Performance Diploma, Artist Diploma, Master of Music in performance on historical instruments, and unified five-year programs leading to the BMus and MM in conducting, teaching, education, and opera theater.

Oberlin also offers a double-degree program for students admitted to both the Conservatory and the College of Arts and Sciences. Students in the five-year program earn a BMus in the Conservatory and a BA in the College.

The Conservatory is housed in a complex of three soundproof and air-conditioned buildings designed by Minoru Yamasaki that includes Bibbins Hall (the teaching building), the central unit (the rehearsal and concert hall building), and Robertson Hall (the practice building). The central unit also houses the Conservatory Library—one of the largest academic music libraries in the country. It includes a collection of more than 121,000 books and scores, 47,000 sound recordings, forty-two listening stations, and six audiovisual listening rooms.

Admission to the Oberlin Conservatory of Music

Like students applying to the College of Arts and Sciences, those seeking admission to the Conservatory of Music must submit their scores from either the SAT or ACT exams. Applicants whose first language is not English should submit the results of the TOEFL exam. Unlike the College of Arts & Sciences, however, the deadlines for the Conservatory application, as well as all supplemental material are November 1 for Early Review and December 1 for Regular Review.

Prospective "Connies" must also audition as part of the application process. Students audition in their principal medium (instrument or voice) unless applying for admission as a composition or electronic and computer music major (in which case they must submit their original compositions). All applicants are encouraged to audition in person, but may, if necessary, attend any one of the regional auditions that are held throughout the country during the months of January and February. Prerecorded auditions are allowed if travel to Oberlin or a regional audition is cost-prohibitive.

ACADEMIC LIFE

Oberlin's many departments and programs offer a mind-boggling number of courses, allowing each student to design a personalized educational program. Students can choose from more than forty disciplines (majors), or create a specialized course of study through the Individual Majors Program.

Selecting a major encourages students to study a particular discipline in depth. At Oberlin, students are not required to declare a major until the end of their sophomore year, which gives them time to explore new areas of study and discuss their interests with faculty advisors. The most popular majors at Oberlin are English, politics, and biology.

Students in the College of Arts and Sciences are required to take and pass 112 credit hours before receiving their B.A. Approximately half of these credits must be earned in the student's major field of study, while the remaining half are divided between the Divisions of Arts and Humanities, Social and Behavioral Sciences, and Natural Sciences and Mathematics. In addition, students must earn writing and quantitative proficiency certification, take a minimum of three courses dealing with cultural diversity, and complete three winter term projects.

Faculty

Oberlin's professors are both scholars and teachers. Like professors at major research universities, they contribute to their discipline through writing and research. But unlike the faculty of major research institutions, Oberlin professors teach everything from first-year courses to advanced seminars, without the aid of TAs. All professors keep regular and frequent office hours, coordinate and supervise independent study projects, and view the education of undergraduates as the most important role of their careers.

Faculty members also act as mentors to their students, especially when guiding their academic development. Since the college's founding, countless professors have collaborated on important research projects with their students. Some of the more recent collaborations include the study of smog pollution, the use of three-dimensional imaging technology to reconstruct archeological finds, and the publication of a dictionary that traced slang usage on campus through a decade's worth of students.

> *In a liberal arts setting, research is a pedagogical tool—not always just an end product in itself. That research produces results is a good thing, but—more importantly—it offers me an opportunity to teach students the substance of the discipline, as well as its techniques.*

The Honor System

Every student at Oberlin is familiar with the college's Honor Pledge, which reads: "I affirm that I have adhered to the Honor Code in this assignment." This pledge, formal and archaic as the phrasing may sound, is a very real part of campus life.

Oberlin's Honor Code is part of its student-administered Honor System and is based on the assumption that academic honesty lies at the heart of academic enterprise. The system applies to all work submitted for academic credit, including quizzes, exams, papers, and laboratory assignments. Each assignment must include the Honor Pledge and the student's signature in order to affirm the integrity of their work.

First-Year Seminar Program

Oberlin's first-year seminar program (FYSP) gives students the opportunity to experience liberal arts learning at the onset of their college careers. Each seminar brings together faculty members with a small group of students to investigate specialized topics. This format encourages students to test new ideas, learn from their peers, and get to know professors well in a small classroom setting, while at the same time honing their critical thinking, writing, and discussion skills.

Winter Term

Oberlin students spend the month of January pursuing projects of their own design. Individual or group-oriented, on or off campus, career-related or just for fun, winter

---

term projects provide an opportunity to fully explore a unique educational goal. Winter term encourages students to discover the value of self-education by emphasizing creativity, intellectual independence, and personal responsibility. Many of the concerts, theatrical productions, films, lectures, forums, and discussion groups that take place during January are part of on-campus winter term projects.

RECENT WINTER TERM PROJECTS

- ○ Listening in Silence: Exploring Modern Day Monasticism
- ○ "I'm a Stranger Here Myself": Writing Across Cultures
- ○ Oberlin Shorts: An Original One-Act Play Festival
- ○ Winter Term Opera: *La Cambiale Di Matrimonio*
- ○ Practicum in Museum Education: Docent Training
- ○ Urban Sustainable Design Studio
- ○ Land Use in Japan
- ○ Introduction to Youth and High School Coaching
- ○ Intensive Greek
- ○ Spanish Poetry Workshop
- ○ Internship with Charles Barron's New York City Mayoral Campaign
- ○ Multiculturalism in the Global Arena

The Experimental College (ExCo)

Oberlin's Experimental College, or ExCo, began in 1968 as an experiment in alternative education. Four decades later, ExCo is still an integral part of campus life, with more than sixty courses offered each semester.

ExCo is a student-run organization, headed by a volunteer committee that is responsible for choosing the curriculum and maintaining the integrity of the program.

ExCo is open to everyone in the Oberlin community, including students, faculty and staff members, and townspeople. Likewise, anyone who proves to be an expert in a particular subject can teach a class, as long as it is judged to have educational merit and a reasonably serious purpose.

ExCo reflects the current academic, intellectual, social, ideological, philosophical, political, emotional, sexual, and fashion trends of the Oberlin community. The most recent ExCo curriculum has included courses on grassroots organizing, environmental justice, Cantonese language, Indian film, Hip-Hop dance, sketch comedy, vegetarian cooking, knitting, and rock climbing.

Students may receive up to five credits toward graduation through the Experimental College, or they may take as many courses as they'd like for no credit. ExCo instructors receive credit for teaching ExCo courses.

SOCIAL LIFE AND ACTIVITIES

Residence Halls

Oberlin is a residential campus; all first-year students and the majority of other students live in the residence halls on campus. Housing options include single-sex and coed dorms, on-campus apartments, language houses (i.e., French House), special-interest houses (i.e., Afrikan Heritage House), and co-ops (Tank Hall). On-campus housing is guaranteed for four years and is assigned by lottery.

Student Cooperative Housing (Co-ops)

The Oberlin Student Cooperative Association (OSCA) provides students with an alternative to traditional college housing and dining options. Student-owned and operated, Oberlin's co-ops cultivate community by encouraging members to take responsibility for their own living environments. Co-op members share cooking, housekeeping, and maintenance tasks, and use a participatory, democratic approach to settling co-op policy and resolving disputes. All co-op duties involve flexible hours and take into account students' class schedules, interests, and skills.

Athletics

Whether they're playing varsity sports or intramurals, Obies find the camaraderie, competition, and physical challenge of athletics the perfect complement to their academic pursuits. The College sponsors twenty-two varsity sports (eleven for women and eleven for men), fourteen club sports (including Ultimate Frisbee, scuba diving, martial arts, and cheerleading), and an ever-changing roster of intramural for both students and college employees.

VARSITY SPORTS AT OBERLIN

Oberlin is an NCAA Division III school playing in the North Coast Athletic Conference.

Men's Varsity Sports
- Baseball
- Basketball
- Cross-country
- Football
- Golf
- Lacrosse
- Soccer
- Swimming
- Tennis
- Track and field, indoor
- Track and field, outdoor

Women's Varsity Sports
- Basketball
- Cross-country
- Field hockey
- Lacrosse
- Soccer
- Softball
- Swimming
- Tennis
- Track and field, indoor
- Track and field, outdoor
- Volleyball

Student Organizations

With more than eighty student organizations to choose from, Oberlin has something for everyone. Students can write for *The Oberlin Review*, sing *a cappella* tunes with the Obertones, toss a Frisbee on Tappan Square with members of the Flying Horsecows, or get active in politics with the OC Democrats.

Many student groups celebrate the diversity of cultures, ethnicities, and identities that can be found on campus. At Oberlin, student groups exist for those of African, Caribbean, Chinese, Korean, Latino, and Philippine descent, as well as for those who are Muslim or Jewish. Other groups exist for those who identify themselves as lesbian, gay, bisexual, or transgendered.

Music at Oberlin

Music and Oberlin are practically synonymous. Each year, the Conservatory hosts more than 400 concerts, including performances by faculty members and students, as well as guest appearances by visiting artists. Oberlin's annual Artist Recital Series brings premier, internationally renowned performers to campus, while alumni musicians frequently return to perform or teach master classes.

But the Conservatory isn't the only musical game in town. The Student Union brings big-name acts such as Bela Fleck and Rufus Wainwright to Finney Chapel's stage, while the Cat in the Cream Coffeehouse opens its doors to popular folk artists such as Sujan Stevens as well as to local and campus bands. And don't forget the 'Sco, where Oberlin's Djs spin everything from rap to rock, and where '80s night has achieved near-cult status.

Films, Theater, and Dance

An average year at Oberlin includes more than 200 film showings, two operas, and more than 60 theater and dance productions. Aside from the performances sponsored by the Theater and Dance program, many student organizations stage their own productions, and student filmmakers regularly hold screenings of their original works.

Volunteer Activities

Oberlin's long history of social engagement lives on in today's students, fifty-five percent of whom participate annually in volunteer activities. The Center for Service and Learning (CSL) organizes many of these service opportunities by pairing student volunteers with local community partners. The CSL also develops programs that combine community involvement with students' intellectual and artistic pursuits, and sponsors conferences and other events to nurture the relationship between the college and community.

FINANCIAL AID

With a price tag of $43,146 a year, many applicants may think that an Oberlin education is out of reach. But that's not true. Oberlin's historic dedication to an economically diverse student body means that nearly all funding from the Office of Financial Aid has been committed to students and families in financial need. Financial aid at Oberlin is need-based. It includes a combination of grants, loans, and student employment.

In 2004–2005, approximately sixty percent of Oberlin's students received a total of nearly $40 million in need-based financial aid. The average first-year award for that year was $22,500, which included an average of $17,500 in grants and $5,000 in loans and work-study earnings. A student's financial aid eligibility extends for eight semesters (ten for double-degree students) or until graduation, whichever comes first.

Financial aid applications are mailed to all prospective students with Oberlin's admissions material. Oberlin uses the College Scholarship Service's (CSS) PROFILE form, as well as the Free Application for Federal Student Aid (FAFSA) to calculate family contributions and financial aid awards for all first-time applicants. The College also considers parental income and assets, benefits, noncustodial parent information (if appropriate), awards from outside agencies, and a student's expected savings from summer employment when awarding aid to each student.

Approximately fifty-seven percent of all Oberlin students work part-time jobs on campus or in the surrounding town. Many opportunities exist for students to fulfill their work-study contracts, such as shelving books in the library, doing clerical work in an academic department, or earning money by working in one of Oberlin's cafeterias.

The deadline for financial aid applications is February 15.

GRADUATES

Oberlin College graduates have gone on to make lasting impressions in the sciences and humanities, often receiving praise and recognition along the way. Oberlin can claim three Nobel Prize winners and seven MacArthur Fellows as alumni, as well as numerous Javits, Mellon, and Watson Fellows, Marshall and Goldwater Scholars, and Fulbright Grant recipients.

○ George Walker, '41 (Composer)
○ Carl Rowan, '47 (Journalist)
○ D.A. Henderson, '50 (Director of The Nation's Center for Public Health Preparedness)
○ Johnnetta Betsch Cole, '57 (President of Bennett College)
○ James Burrows, '62 (Television Director, *Cheers* and *Will and Grace*)
○ Richard Baron, '64 (President of McCormack Baron & Associates, Inc. and Champion of Innovative, Affordable Housing in Urban Neighborhoods)
○ William Schulz, '71 (Executive Director of Amnesty International)
○ Jerry Greenfield, '73 (Ice Cream Mogul)
○ Bill Irwin, '73 (Actor)
○ Julie Taymor, '74 (Director and Writer, Best Known for Directing and Designing The Theatrical Production of Disney's *The Lion King*)
○ David Zinman, '58 (Music Director, Zurich Tonhalle Orchestra)
○ Robert Spano, '83 (Grammy Award-winning Conductor of The Atlanta Symphony)
○ Stephen Issevlis, '80 (Internationally Renowned Cellist)
○ Richard Lenski, '77 (Biologist and MacArthur "Genuis" Award Recipient)
○ James McBride, '79 (Musician, Composer, and Author of *The Color of Water: A Black Man's Tribute to His White Mother*)
○ Billy Cohn, '82 (Heart Surgeon and Inventor of the Cohn Cardiac Stabilizer)
○ Tracy Chevalier, '84 (Best-selling Author of *Girl with a Pearl Earring and The Lady and The Unicorn*)
○ Denyce Graves, '85 (Opera Singer)
○ George Smith, '87 (ESPN Sportscaster)
○ Bi-khim Hsiao, '93 (Legislator with The Republic of China/Former Advisor and Interpreter to China's President Chen Shui-Bian)
○ Mike Heithaus, '95 (Marine Biologist and Host of The *National Geographic* Television Series "Crittercam")
○ Jennifer Koh, '97 (Violinist)
○ Sadhu Johnston, '98 (Assistant to the Mayor for Green Initiatives, City of Chicago.)
○ Josh Ritter, '99 (Folk Musician, *Golden Age of Radio and Hello Starling*)

Many Obies have gone on to earn Ph.D.s at the nation's most esteemed graduate and professional schools. In the last two decades, more Oberlin students received Ph.D.s than did students from any other predominantly undergraduate liberal arts college in the country. Not only do Obies attend the nation's top graduate schools, they teach there, too. Oberlin graduates can be found teaching at almost every one of the nation's top sixty colleges and universities.

SUMMING UP

Oberlin is a small community. On or off campus, it's easy to get to know your classmates and professors, and to form lasting ties with local residents. While some people might find a small-town atmosphere confining, a visit to Oberlin and the surrounding campus would most probably change their minds.

With a world-class Conservatory and some of the most forward-thinking members of their fields teaching in the College of Arts and Sciences, life at Oberlin is anything but dull. The constant stream of concerts, operas, theater productions, dance recitals, poetry readings, distinguished speakers, and other campus visitors creates a cosmopolitan climate that rivals that of a university in a big city. Not to mention all the impromptu gatherings and groups that evolve as students come and go, creating a vibrant, intellectually charged environment that is uniquely Oberlin.

An Obie's connection to campus doesn't stop after graduation. Oberlin alumni are a fiercely loyal crew, returning year after year to celebrate Commencement/Reunion Weekend and staying in touch with classmates through regional alumni groups. It's an old joke that an Obie can spot a fellow Obie a mile away, but there is some truth to that statement. Oberlin graduates can be found in all walks of life and at all corners of the globe, and they are always happy to share their memories about their alma mater with prospective students, or to reminisce about sunny afternoons in Wilder Bowl.

❏ *Sue Angell, B.A.*

For me, Oberlin has always felt like home. From the moment I set foot on campus, I knew that I had found a place where I could belong—even with my quirky ideas and esoteric interests. My professors nurtured me, yet pushed me to do the work they knew I was capable of doing. Oberlin was tough, but the experience was necessary. I can't even begin to imagine what I would be like today without the wealth of ideas and knowledge I accumulated as an undergraduate at Oberlin.

OCCIDENTAL COLLEGE

Occidental College
Los Angeles, CA 90041

(323) 259-2700; (800) 825-5262
Fax: (323) 341-4875

Email: *admission@oxy.edu*
Web site: *www.oxy.edu*

 Enrollment:

Full-time ❑ women: 1,017
❑ men: 777

Part-time ❑ women: 13
❑ men: 12

INTRODUCING OCCIDENTAL COLLEGE

The phrase "urban oasis" is often used to characterize Occidental, and in many ways it's an apt description of the liberal arts college situated on 120 acres in Los Angeles, just eight miles northeast of downtown. Students stroll about in nearly perpetual summertime and do their reading sprawled on the grass by the quad; classes often migrate outdoors. And yet insofar as "oasis" conjures a disconnect from the world beyond, it's misleading; Oxy students and faculty are deeply involved in wider cultural and civic life.

The beautiful campus feels like a private little enclave in the middle of all the hustle and bustle of Los Angeles. But what stood out to me my freshman year was the extent to which my professors engaged, and inspired us to engage, the larger community. My politics professor that year was Eric Garcetti, who is now the president of the Los Angeles City Council, and he encouraged us to attend Council meetings and would regularly ground his lectures with anecdotes about social and political concerns of the day. That spirit of community engagement pervades the campus.

—*Holly Smith, '04, history major*

Oxy graduates are rightfully proud of their intellectually rigorous and broad liberal arts education, and will tell you that the work here is highly demanding. Current students love to gripe—and alumni, to brag—about the comprehensive exams or theses that all thirty majors require prior to graduation. And yet learning at Oxy is far from a harsh and competitive exercise; with a student-to-faculty ratio of ten to one, and a faculty as stirred by teaching as by their own research, it's impossible not to get to know your professors on an individual level. Professors regularly mentor students who choose to embark on independent patterns of study, sponsor student research and grant applications, and hang out with students at barbecues or even invite them to holiday dinners. It's learning in the truest sense, the sort that mingles lectures with life, and an education here inspires in students real intellectual curiosity—a majority of students go on to attend grad school, and they are highly competitive for national honors and awards (Occidental is one of the country's top producers of student Fulbright Award winners).

At Oxy, professors knew me on a first-name basis. I had their home phone numbers and could call in the middle of the night, tell them I'm applying for this or that scholarship, last-minute, that I need a letter of recommendation. I developed this great relationship with the Bio chair; she didn't say, "You're an English major, you can't do a research project on biodiversity." I went to a sustainability conference in Vietnam. None of my requests to do undergraduate research were ever turned down.

—*Libby Evans, '06, English major*

First-time visitors to the picturesque Occidental College campus may encounter déjà vu—the place seems perennially familiar. This makes sense given that Oxy has been a popular film and TV location for more than eighty years, beginning with MGM's *Cup of Fury* in 1919. Its proximity to Hollywood and its unique and beautiful campus make Oxy a favorite of directors and location scouts. Students often drop by the shoots to watch the process unfold in front of their eyes—before seeing it again on-screen. You might recognize Occidental from such movies as (from old to new):

- *Horse Feathers* (1932) with the Marx Brothers
- *She Loves Me Not* (1934) with Bing Crosby and Kitty Carlisle
- *That Hagen Girl* (1947) with Shirley Temple and Ronald Reagan
- *Pat and Mike* (1952) with Katharine Hepburn and Spencer Tracy
- *The Tall Story* (1960) with Jane Fonda and Anthony Perkins
- *Midnight Madness* (1980) with Michael J. Fox and Pee Wee Herman
- *Real Genius* (1985) with Val Kilmer
- *For the Boys* (1991) with Bette Midler and James Caan
- *Clueless* (1995) with Alicia Silverstone
- *Jurassic Park 3* (2000)
- *Orange County* (2002) with Colin Hanks and Jack Black
- *The Holiday* (2006) with Cameron Diaz, Kate Winslet, and Jack Black

Or from such TV shows as *The L Word, Dragnet, The West Wing, Charmed,* and *Beverly Hills 90210.*

Diversity, in all its forms, is a fundamental value at Occidental, and its 1,819 person student body is one of the most racially, geographically, and socioeconomically diverse in the nation. In our increasingly interconnected world, intellectual muscle is most useful when combined with cultural and social literacy, and in this sense Oxy students learn much from each other. Roughly three quarters of students receive financial aid, and elite prep school graduates blend with those from inner-city public high schools. Almost every world religion is represented—more than a dozen Protestant denominations, plus Catholics, Jews, Muslims, Hindus, Buddhists, and Sikhs—and all are welcome to worship at the nondenominational Herrick Chapel. First-year students share a residence hall with the people in their core classes, and classroom discussions spill into the dorms. There is a feeling of community and camaraderie among students and a common desire to unite the intellect with the heart, theory with practice, to make a difference in the world.

Some seventy percent of students live on campus, while some upperclassmen choose to find housing nearby. Most venture out regularly into LA, on organized excursions or on their own, partaking in the endless panorama of music, theater, art, dance, food, nightlife, and culture. It's a quick drive to the coast—to some of the most famous beaches in the world—or to the Angeles National Forest where students often go to hike and perhaps take a dip in the natural pools around Switzer Falls. Campus, all the while, remains as busy as ever: a quarter of students participate in nineteen intercollegiate sports and hundreds more compete in intramural and club sports such as rugby, lacrosse, Ultimate Frisbee, and crew. Some one hundred clubs sponsor all manner of events. Theaters on campus hum with student plays, dance productions, and concerts.

ADMISSIONS REQUIREMENTS

This is the section that sets hearts racing and palms sweating. "*If only* I had started taking SAT prep courses in middle school," you think. "*If only* I had joined fifteen clubs and sports teams instead of twelve. *If only* . . . " As is the case with the rest of the schools listed in this book, the admissions statistics at Occidental are impressive and daunting. The acceptance rate currently hovers around forty-one percent and will likely continue to fall, as it has nearly every year for the past decade. Ninety percent of accepted students in the class of 2010 were in the top fifth of their high school class. Keep in mind, however, that a student's place on the statistical continuum is only one factor among many; Occidental evaluates applicants in a holistic manner that takes into account the whole person, the wide variety of passions and circumstances that GPA and SAT scores do not reflect. Students here often recall being pleasantly surprised by an admissions process that viewed them as human beings rather than reducing them to the sum of their statistically measurable parts.

I remember visiting UCLA on freshman admit day. We were given numbers and sent to different rooms, with 400 of us to a room. People who had the highest GPA and SAT scores had lunch in a special dining room, while everybody else ate in the cafeteria. We were already being divided up, and I thought, "maybe I don't want to go here anymore." The next day I visited Occidental; I walked into the Admissions Office without an appointment, and the woman at the front desk introduced me to Bill Tingley, the vice president in charge of admissions and financial aid. He knew offhand what I had written about in my application, and the financial package they had given me. I was impressed. I wanted to choose a school where I would be recognized as a person, treated as an individual.

—*Joel Key, '04, Spanish and studio art double major*

Occidental seeks to enroll students who bring to the table a wide variety of talents and experiences, and who possess the intellectual curiosity and muscle necessary to take full advantage of its rigorous and stimulating liberal arts education. Competition for admission to

Occidental and other top colleges is fierce and becoming fiercer, which can have the unfortunate effect of transforming high school into an anxiety-ridden experience. Too often in high school, frantic and shallow resume-building takes the place of other more valuable modes of exploration and maturation. Enrolling in every AP course and participating in a full load of extracurricular activities can be positive, certainly—but not if doing so impinges significantly on your ability to pursue your truer interests. Oxy is most interested in students who excel from a place of personal authenticity, rather than boilerplate candidates whose search for collegiate prestige undercuts their individuality. This does not imply that test and GPA scores don't count—they do—but there are also candidates who stand out from the crowd by capitalizing on their own uniqueness.

It goes without saying, then, that applicants to Occidental should opt for honesty and openness. Don't attempt to shoehorn yourself into the role you think Oxy wants you to play, which will inevitably cause you to come off as wooden and uninspired. Writing the essays will of course be challenging, but it shouldn't prove unduly painful. You've already done the heavy lifting—years of coursework, sports games, club meetings, living life—and here's your chance to tell your story to a friendly audience. The application for fall admission is due on January 10 and may be submitted by mail or electronically via the web site; the common application is also accepted and must be accompanied by a supplemental form. Early Decision applications should be filed by November 15. Either the SAT or ACT is required (average SAT verbal score was 640, math, 650; ACT, 29). High school course requirements include four years each of English and math, three each of foreign language and science, and two each of social studies and history. The writing sample and interview are voluntary, but they will help the admissions committee get to know you—and therefore are a very good idea.

ACADEMIC LIFE

Academic work at Occidental is consistently challenging, but not in a dry and overly cerebral way. Students are encouraged to integrate life experience into intellectual conversation and to apply academic ideas toward understanding and navigating our complex and interconnected world. The broad diversity of the student body is of great service in this regard, and all are encouraged to engage the alternate worldviews of their peers—particularly in first-year cultural studies seminars and colloquia, which set the tone for the rest of the Occidental experience. First-year students choose from seminars in a variety of disciplines, each designed to examine large liberal arts questions; recent subjects include: "Visions of the Floating World: Painting and

Prints of Edo Japan" (art history and the visual arts), "Urban Fictions: The Modern City in Literature and Other Arts" (English and comparative literary studies), "Whose Music Is It Anyway? Issues of Appropriation in Hip Hop" (music), and "The Taming of Infinity" (mathematics). Seminars are capped at 16 students, all of whom live together in a common dorm.

> *My freshman year I lived in a dorm at the top of campus, and in the morning a bunch of us would head down the hill together to our core seminar, an art history course called "Reading and Writing about Visual Experience." That stroll, and lunch afterwards in the quad, was as much a part of the seminar as was our time in the classroom. I don't mean to imply that we spent our days and nights engaged in a formal debate about Griselda Pollock's feminist critique of modernist art history—but rather that as our intellectual and personal lives intertwined, conversation bridging the two realms began to feel natural and fluid. Late on a Tuesday evening a few of us might've been tossing a Frisbee in the hallway at the dorm, laughing about an improv show we'd seen earlier that evening, and brainstorming ideas for a paper contrasting the scholarly worldviews of Michel de Certeau and Dick Hebdige. Occasionally, our professor would come to us instead of the reverse, trekking up the hill and holding class or office hours in the common room of our dorm—and we scarcely had to change out of our pajamas.*

The first-year cultural studies seminars and colloquia, and the communities surrounding them, are an essential part of the college's Core program, which is designed to support rich liberal arts values throughout the Occidental experience. Students at Oxy become conversant across a wide breadth of academic disciplines and learn to approach their chosen field from an interdisciplinary perspective that also takes into account the intermixture of cultures, languages, religions, and historical narratives that constitute the world today. One society or set of ideas is hardly understandable these days in isolation from its neighbors, as underscored by our increasingly effective and affordable technologies of communication and transportation, and postmodern interpretations of self and country. As such, the Core program emphasizes global literacy and requires that all students take at least three courses that touch on at least three disparate geographical areas, for instance, Africa and the Middle East; Asia and the Pacific; Europe; Latin America; and the United States. Further, all students fulfill requirements in the fine arts and in the sciences, mathematics, or other courses that address formal methods of reasoning; they also become proficient in one or more foreign languages. Finally, students must demonstrate proficiency in writing, a skill that develops organically given the large amount of writing that many classes require.

Of course, this liberal arts framework would be meaningless without stellar teaching, which is the fundamental ingredient of an Occidental education. Professors engage passionately in their own research, but their first and foremost responsibility is in the classroom. Consequently, Oxy attracts professors who genuinely love to teach and who bring with them an infectious enthusiasm for the subject at hand. Class size is small—average lecture size is 21; laboratory, 16; regular course, 20—and discussion is integral to many courses. No introductory courses are taught by graduate students. Professors are very much part of campus life outside of the classroom, and you will often find professors and students ambling about together, engaged in lively intellectual conversation. Few professors adhere strictly to posted office hours and will generally tolerate—if not welcome—unarranged knocks on their doors.

"The professors are the best part about Oxy. I went to a high school where my graduating class was nineteen kids. I was close to my teachers there, but I was even closer to my professors at Oxy. In fact, I still keep in touch with my professors, all the time, and they're still there for me two and a half years after I graduated. I have a couple of professors to thank for helping me get the job I have now, as an assistant producer at National Public Radio. They knew me well enough to make strong recommendations, and helped me get good journalism internships when I was in school. Of course, you have to show initiative—but if students show initiative, the support is there for them.

Oxy is in LA, which has so much to offer, and professors try to use that as much as possible. In theater classes, we would have outside directors and designers come in, people who were very accomplished in the LA film and theater industry, and they would work with us for a week or two on a show. I remember a politics class on Bill Clinton's foreign policy; I was actually going to drop the class, but when I approached the professor, he said, "That's fine, but you should really come to the first day of class. We have a special visitor." So I went, and it was President Clinton guest-teaching the class. I stuck around, and the next week we went to meet with former secretary of state Warren Christopher, at his law office. And then, Mickey Canter, who was Clinton's trade representative, came to class. Every week, it was all these luminaries.

—Ben Bergman, '04, politics major

Students at Occidental commonly seek out internships and independent research opportunities, and faculty serve as willing mentors and advocates. Over the past seven years, more than 700 Occidental students have received funding to undertake joint summer research with faculty, which often results in coauthored publications in peer-reviewed journals. Occidental traditionally sends more student presenters to the Southern California Conference on Undergraduate Research than any other participating school, and over the past three years has sent fifty-five students to make presentations at the National Undergraduate Research Conference. Undergraduate students from all majors are invited to pursue research opportunities that at larger universities are typically open only to high-achieving graduate students, and the college is routinely recognized for excellence in this realm, such as by the National Science Foundation, which conferred on Occidental its Integration of Research and Education Award in 1998. As far as internships go, opportunities in Los Angeles are limited only by the imagination, and students fan out to a wide array of organizations, such as the *Los Angeles Times*, NASA's Jet Propulsion Laboratory, UCLA Medical Center, and DreamWorks Studio.

RESEARCH OPPORTUNITIES

Students at Occidental have access to a wide breadth of research opportunities and funding sources as early as their freshman year. For instance, Oxy is one of only a dozen institutions selected to participate in the Richter Summer Research Program, which has awarded more than $1 million in research grants to students since 1969. Oxy students of all majors may apply to receive Richter grants to support independent research or creative work abroad; past projects include:

○ Geothermal Energy in Iceland— Applications in the United States
○ The Role of Indigenous Knowledge System in Fighting AIDS in Botswana
○ Act Like You Care: Photography and Leadership for Inner-city Girls, Los Angeles
○ The Fusion Music of the British Asian Dance Club and Concert: Contemporary Ethnic Identity of Anglicized Second Generation
○ Protestant Pentecostal Faith and Spirituality in Guatemala

As an institution dedicated to educating citizens of a pluralistic world, Occidental encourages all students to participate in off-campus study. Each year, roughly a third of the junior class heads off to more than fifty programs in dozens of countries; a student might study tropical biology at a field research station in Costa Rica, perhaps, or research international development and democratization in Hanoi, Vietnam. Some students choose to take part in domestic exchange options, such as the semester-long Occidental-at-the-United Nations program, the only of its kind in the country, in which students live and take classes in New York City while interning in the United Nations Secretariat or with a related institution. Students

---

who wish to pursue research abroad may also participate in off-campus summer research programs. Occidental is one of a dozen institutions selected to participate in the Richter Summer Research Program, which funds independent research projects or creative work; recent Richter projects by Occidental students include "Media Freedom in Post-1997 Hong Kong," "Illicit Asian Art Trade, London, England," and Ideology and Normalcy, Paris, France."

Even when abroad, students remain solidly connected to the Occidental community back in Los Angeles. Friends and professors clamor for updates—with pictures, if possible. It wasn't long ago, after all, that these savvy world travelers were arriving to that first freshman seminar, then heading back to the dorms with their sixteen pals. It's remarkable how enduring those friendships can be. And likewise, the Occidental ethos—defined differently by whomever you ask, but certainly including intellectual curiosity, cultural engagement, and service to the community—sticks with students and continues to influence them, whatever direction they may take.

SOCIAL LIFE AND ACTIVITIES

Living in Los Angeles is inextricably part of the Occidental experience, and even the most extroverted students find that by graduation they've exhausted only a fraction of the resources the city has to offer. A student interested in museums, say, might begin by exploring the Norton Simon Museum, home to one of the world's finest collections of European, American, and Asian art, situated just a few miles from Oxy in bustling Old Town Pasadena. In the months and years following, he or she might spend time at the LA County Museum of Art, the Museum of Contemporary Art, the Japanese American National Museum, the Getty Center and the newly redesigned Getty Villa, UCLA's Hammer Museum, the Museum of Neon Art, and countless other museums and art galleries throughout the city. The theater and music scenes are equally robust, as you might expect in a city brimming over with world-class actors and musicians. Thousands of restaurants serve up every possible type of cuisine, and bars and nightclubs run the gambit from kitschy karaoke dives to swanky Hollywood hot spots. Some students have cars, while others catch Bengal Busses—free shuttles named for the Oxy mascot, a Bengal tiger, that ferry students to and from rotating destinations throughout the city. An Oxy club, Arts L.A., sponsors biweekly outings to museum exhibits, plays, film festivals, and other arts events.

Walking is also a very good option. Occidental is nestled in the northeastern Los Angeles neighborhood of Eagle Rock, which has become increasingly hip in recent years, with colorful boutiques and eateries joining such long-time student hangouts as the burrito joint Señor Fish and the Italian restaurant Casa Bianca, serving arguably the best pizza in Los Angeles. (New restaurants aside, some Oxy students claim that the tastiest food comes from homegrown "taco trucks" that set up shop each evening on nearby avenues.) The area immediately surrounding Oxy is mostly residential, a multicultural and mixed-socioeconomic neighborhood where many professors choose to live. Students are actively involved in the Eagle Rock community, particularly those affiliated with the Occidental Urban and Environmental Policy Institute, a college major which also serves as an umbrella organization for a variety of research and advocacy programs addressing work and industry, food and nutrition, housing, transportation, regional and community development, and urban environmental issues.

Regardless of the many adventures to be had in this vast metropolis, however, the Oxy campus remains filled with life; drop by for a visit, and you'll understand why students choose to stick around. The campus itself is airy and beautiful, a pocket of tranquility amid urban sprawl, and given the small student body it's rare to go anywhere on campus without bumping into friends. Come mealtimes, students choose between two dining options: the Tiger Cooler, popular for lunchtime and late-night snacking, is a grill serving all manner of hot and cold sandwiches, wood-fired pizza, sushi, smoothies, and frozen yogurt. The Marketplace, where most students take dinner and breakfast, is organized by station; for instance, there are stations for deli, home-style, grill and wok, and pasta, as well as a bakery and a fully stocked salad bar. Much of the food at the Marketplace is cooked-to-order—try the salmon and asparagus over rice, a perennial favorite. Suffice it to say that students remain well and happily fed.

The college maintains a full schedule of programs and entertainment, such as student plays and other theater productions held in two large theaters or outside in a Greek-style amphitheater, movies, concerts given by students and professional musicians, wildly popular dance productions, a variety of lecture series, and on-campus parties such as the elaborate casino-style themed shindig, "Da Getaway." There are always plenty of unofficial parties and get-togethers on and off campus, including those thrown by Oxy's modest Greek community (six percent of men belong to fraternities; thirteen percent of women, to sororities). Clubs and groups meet all over campus; find your interest among

BIRTHDAY DUNKING

Students at Occidental learn quickly that when your birthday rolls around, it's best to wear something that will survive a drenching. You never quite know when it's coming, but at some point on your birthday, friends may nab you, carry you down to the Gilman Fountain at the front of campus, and gingerly (it's shallow!) toss you in. Campus safety officers apparently dislike this tradition, but they don't do much to stop it. The good news is that this is sunny Los Angeles, so you can air dry on grassy slopes nearby while you plot your revenge.

the many choices—chess, choir, orchestra, improv comedy, musical theater, either side of the political spectrum, student government, photography, forensics, Occidental College Radio (KOXY), religious communities. Student publications include the *Occidental Weekly* newspaper, yearbook, and various literary magazines. Students interested in investing can apply to serve on the board of the Blyth Fund, a six-figure portion of Occidental's endowment managed solely by students. Opportunities for quietude and relaxation mingle with the hustle and bustle; enroll in Tai Chi, actually a course in the theater department, or head down to the gym for a yoga class, kick back poolside, or stroll up a dirt pathway to the highest point on campus, a rustic plateau dubbed Mt. Fiji. Here you can listen to owls hoot and gaze out across the elegant downtown skyline, the San Gabriel Mountains, or the coast.

Student athletes abound at Occidental, and there are resources for athletes of every level. The college is a member of NCAA Division III, and some twenty-five percent of students participate in women's and men's varsity sports such as basketball, cross-country, golf, soccer, softball, baseball, swimming, tennis, track and field, volleyball, and water polo. Many others play in intramural leagues, and the fields around campus teem with all sorts of balls, sticks, and discs (rugby, lacrosse, Ultimate Frisbee). Surfers lug their boards seaward, and broomball players clear out residence hall common rooms for their gregarious and popular matches.

I ran cross-country for all four years in high school, and I was never the best of the best, but it was a good experience. So I decided to join cross-country at Oxy. My freshman year, we were a young, inexperienced team—so we set a goal that before we graduated, we would win a conference title as a team. We trained really hard for a sport that is challenging both mentally and physically; at its top, we were running about eighty miles a week. Of course, school always came first (usually it was sleep that was sacrificed). We definitely improved, and our junior year we won the title. A liberal arts education addresses the whole person, and I think sports are part of that.

—*Colleen Callahan, '04, urban and environmental policy major*

Athletics are an integral part of the well-rounded Occidental education—"the sweatiest of the liberal arts," one coach calls them—but even top varsity players are expected to keep scholarship on the front burner. Through all that studying, however, teams manage to excel—take the men's basketball team, for instance, which in 2003 became the first in the history of the NCAA Division III tournament to advance from Oxy's conference to the Elite 8. Oxy's football team has gone undefeated in conference play over the past three years. The Oxy athletic program has produced All-Americans numbering in the hundreds, dozens of Olympians, world record holders and national champions, and professional athletes and coaches. Alumni remain enthusiastic boosters of the athletic program and through the Tiger Club raise hundreds of thousands of dollars each year in support of Occidental athletics.

FINANCIAL AID

The price tag of an Occidental education can be intimidating, but keep in mind that over seventy percent of students receive some form of financial aid, which renders the cost comparable to those of public institutions. Oxy is dedicated to maintaining a socioeconomically diverse student body, and financial difficulties should not keep anybody from applying. Students hail from a smorgasbord of backgrounds, and those arriving via public high schools actually outnumber their prep school peers. Applicants are automatically considered for a variety of merit-based scholarships, from the Margaret Bundy Scott scholarship ($17,500 annually) to the Honor's Scholarship ($5,000 annually). Merit scholarships are highly competitive and are awarded to students who have demonstrated outstanding academic and extracurricular achievement. Need-based assistance comes in the form of grants, work-study, and student loans. It's important that applicants file the requisite forms on time; the Free Application for Federal Student Aid (FAFSA) and the College Scholarship Service (CSS) Profile are due on February 1, while the Cal Grant application, required of California residents, is due on March 2. In 2005–2006, the average freshman award was $23,949, and the average financial indebtedness of a 2005 graduate was $15,943.

My family was in an unusual financial situation when I applied to Occidental, and it looked on paper like we could afford to pay more than we actually could. If the financial aid office had relied strictly on numbers in putting together my award, I probably would not have been able to attend Occidental. Instead, a financial aid counselor suggested that we submit a letter fleshing out our financial picture, and then promptly responded with an award that was commensurate with the reality of our situation. As is the case with administrators and professors throughout the college, financial aid officers treated me as an individual and sought to understand the nuances of my circumstance. It felt as if we were working together to make this happen, with plenty of goodwill on both our parts.

Occidental alumni achieve highly in a range of fields and are generally united in their ambition to use scholarly expertise to address real-world problems and concerns.

Writers and Journalists:

○ Steve Coll, '80, a Pulitzer Prize-winning Staff Writer at *The New Yorker*

○ Bill Davis, '80, President, Southern California Public Radio

○ Erik Eckholm, '71, Bureau Chief, *New York Times*

○ Patt Morrison, '74, Columnist, *Los Angeles Times* and Emmy-winning Public Radio Host

○ Rosalind Wiseman, '91, Author of *Queen Bees and Wannabes: Helping Your Daughter Survive Cliques, Gossip, Boyfriends, and Other Realities of Adolescence,* which inspired the movie *Mean Girls.*

Business Leaders:

○ Stephen Cooper, '68, "Turnaround Specialist," Former CEO of Krispy Kreme Doughnuts

○ W. Don Cornwell, '69, CEO of Granite Broadcasting

○ Bruce Fabrizio, '74, President and CEO, Sunshine Makers, Inc.; Founder of EGBAR Foundation (Everything's Going to Be All Right), a National Environmental Education Curriculum for Children

○ J. Eugene Grigsby, '66, President and CEO of the National Health Foundation

GRADUATES

Describing Occidental alums is no easy task; just as the school seeks to enroll a rich diversity of students, so too do graduates head off to follow their bliss in every conceivable direction. While generalizations in this realm tend to be inexact, it is safe to say that most students leave Oxy with a keen sense of the world's multilayered complexity and a framework through which to navigate that complexity, an enduring intellectual curiosity, and a sense of empathy and social responsibility. The focus at Occidental on merging education with action, theory with practice, produces graduates who are raring to apply their expertise in the real world, and they are highly competitive in the workforce, landing top jobs throughout the public and private sectors. When given the choice, Oxy grads will often pass up a high-paying job for one offering a clear benefit to community and society, and each year a good many choose to exercise those muscles in the Peace Corps and in nonprofit organizations the world over.

While some graduates go directly into the workforce and stay there, a majority head to grad school, eventually winding up in academia, education, law, medicine—an array of professions too numerous to mention. Oxy students and grads also contend successfully for national fellowships such as the Fulbright, Marshal, Rhodes, Truman, Luce, Watson, and National Science Foundation Fellowships. Whatever students choose to do with themselves, involvement with Oxy rarely ends on graduation day. Freshman year dorm mates have evolved into lifelong friends, professors are now enduring mentors. These relationships will continue to mature and evolve. Alums form the backbone of Oxy GOLD (Graduates Of the Last Decade), whose chapters, spread across the nation, sponsor all manner of mixers, meals, and events. The Oxy Career Center and other on-campus organizations remain invaluable resources for graduates.

SUMMING UP

The college application process often evokes more angst than excitement about the future, and all that worrying can seriously dampen the high school experience—but need this be the case? One Oxy freshman published an essay in the *Los Angeles Times* arguing for a different vision: "This rat race deserves the rotten reputation it has earned. I've been in the trenches—I graduated from high school last year and am a college freshman now—and I'm here to say there is another way: Follow your heart *and* get into the college right for you." Most folks at Occidental would echo that sentiment. Students at Oxy are encouraged to appreciate the innate value and joy in education, rather than seeing it as merely a precursor to future prestige. High school students might consider embracing a similar mindset. At least, know that if you choose to apply to Occidental, you will be evaluated as a unique participant in a wonderfully complex world. There is no universal yardstick by which to measure us all.

Oxy is a small, diverse, vibrant intellectual community, set in one of the most stimulating and creative cities in the world. The combination of its mission and location produce "an institution with intimate scale and infinite scope," as former Oxy president Ted Mitchell describes it. Los Angeles serves at once as a playground and a laboratory for students and faculty, while campus remains alive with energy and activity. Students immerse themselves in a chosen discipline—and simultaneously receive wide liberal arts training that puts individual phenomena and ideas into context. They participate in a multitude of sports and clubs, conduct independent research, and study abroad all over the globe. It is a uniformly full and meaningful experience for most students. That said, no single college is right for everyone, and whoever is interested in Oxy is advised to come for a visit, if possible. Arrange with the Admissions Office for an overnight stay in the dorms, if you'd like, or just drop by and have a look around. Knock on doors, chat with students and professors, visit classes, lounge about on a bench with a book, and enjoy the sun.

❏ *Steven Barrie-Anthony, B.A.*

Photo by Philip Channing

**Pomona College
Claremont, CA 91711**

(909) 621-8134

E-mail: *admissions@pomona.edu*
Web site: *http://www.pomona.edu*

 Enrollment

Full-time ❑ women: 759
❑ men: 773

INTRODUCING POMONA

*I came to Pomona seeking an atmosphere that was ferociously intellectual,
but at the same time, more open and friendly than colleges back East.*

Pomona College is a coed, residential, nonsectarian liberal arts college located thirty-five miles east of Los Angeles. Its mission is "the pursuit of knowledge and understanding through study in the sciences and the humanities…[its curriculum prepares] students for lives of personal fulfillment and social responsibility in a global context." (*Pomona College Catalog*) Like most things in life, students get out of a Pomona education exactly what they put into it. They can spend four years thinking hard, taking a broad variety of classes, and stretching their intellectual experiences and capabilities, surrounded by other highly motivated people in one of the world's most pleasant climates.

Pomona was founded in 1887 by New Englanders affiliated with the Congregational Church. They named the school after the Roman goddess of the harvest, and conveniently forgot she was also a goddess of wine. The founders wanted to provide a liberal arts college "of the New England type" for the youth out West. They also took the then-radical step of making Pomona coeducational from the start. Today, students come from all over the country and some foreign countries as well, and the Congregational heritage survives only in some restriction of alcohol consumption on campus. People still have fun—they just do it without kegs. The educational goals have also been refined, most recently in 1994, when the college adopted new general education requirements aimed at giving students the skills "to live resiliently in a changing world." Pomona is the founding and largest institution of The Claremont Colleges, a consortium of five colleges and two graduate institutions. The Claremonts share some facilities and work together to provide students with expanded classroom and extracurricular opportunities.

Just looking at the beautiful campus, you could guess that Pomona offers a lot of resources to its students. The chemistry, biology, and physics labs are among the finest available to undergraduates anywhere. The Seaver Theatre complex has large and small stages, studios, and classrooms housing The Claremont Colleges' theater program. It's a stone's throw from the Oldenborg Center, a combination international study center and residence hall, with its own dining room and international film and colloquia series. Three computer labs, one on north campus and two south, provide students with word processing, printers, on-line course materials, and candy: free e-mail, Internet access, and multi-user games. Pomona's administration has housed itself in Alexander Hall, where students can walk in air-conditioned comfort from pleading for classes at the Registrar's Office, to pleading for money in Financial Aid, to pleading for time at the Business Office, to pleading for mercy from the Dean of Students.

ADMISSIONS REQUIREMENTS

If this sounds good so far, start planning for the application process. Applicants are required to submit an application form, recommendations, a transcript, and either ACT or SAT results. The admissions staff is interested in people who have done strong academic work, and have stretched themselves in some way. The high school transcript shows academic strength. Pomona expects applicants to have spent four years in high school English, three each in mathematics and foreign languages (but four is better), and two years each in laboratory sciences and social sciences. This doesn't leave much room for electives. Those nonacademic courses show that applicants have lots of interests, but grades from electives don't count in helping determine if they will do well at a demanding college. Admissions officers also consider whether they took Advanced Placement or honors courses if available.

The application form asks some basic demographic information, a few more personal questions, and requires two or three essays that indicate to the admissions staff the special things the applicant has done. They are looking for applicants who took on challenges, acted in a play, did community service, edited a publication—anything that asked the applicant to take on a new project and see it through. Not all Pomona students were valedictorians, but the vast majority of them played sports, participated in student government or community service, or were performing or studio artists in high school. Applicants can use the common application if they don't have Pomona's own, which is available on Pomona's Web site.

Recommendations

Three recommendations are also required, one from the applicant's high school principal or guidance counselor, and two from teachers in core academic subjects. Core academics are English, math, social sciences like history and anthropology, languages, and laboratory sciences like biology, chemistry, or physics. Applicants need recommendations stating that they are the most outstanding students ever encountered, because that's the caliber of the competition. The SAT or ACT is also required. The average incoming Pomona student had a verbal SAT I score of 730 and a math score of 730. Students submitting the SAT must also submit the results of two SAT Subject Tests.

Other things that are recommended, but not required, for applicants include interviews, visits to the campus, and supplemental application materials. Applicants can interview either with admissions officers on campus or with a Pomona alum in their area. In addition, applicants can send samples of what makes them special along with their applications.

Videotapes of their performances, clippings of news stories they wrote, slides or photographs of their paintings or sculptures will all stand out and help the admissions staff see the applicant as unique.

ACADEMIC LIFE

Before applying, students should know some of the demands Pomona will place on their time. Students at Pomona need to pass thirty-two courses to receive the Bachelor of Arts, the only degree Pomona confers. (Even science majors are BAs here. Then again, at Harvard, computer science majors receive the Bachelor of Arts, too.) The classic student will complete courses in four years, taking four courses each semester. Pomona doesn't count credit hours, but some nonacademic classes, such as foreign language conversation and physical education, count only as half a course. Time demands vary from subject to subject, instructor to instructor, but most students won't want to take much more than four courses at a time. There's extensive lab time for science classes, hours of language lab each week for introductory foreign language classes, and huge amounts of reading and writing (and rewriting) in almost every class. Classes are kept small so everyone gets plenty of attention from the instructor. After freshman year, most classes have ten or twelve students, the biggest classes having about twenty-five students.

General Education

Most colleges and universities require all of their students to demonstrate basic knowledge of a few academic subjects, and the choice of subjects and the level of achievement demanded varies from school to school. Some call it breadth of study, others general education. The Pomona faculty in 1994 defined a common core of intellectual experiences and skills their students should have. Supposedly, these skills in perception, analysis, and communication will enable students to explore ideas, evaluate evidence, draw balanced conclusions, and communicate their findings throughout their college career and in their life afterward. The ten skills are

- read literature critically.
- use and understand the scientific method.
- use and understand formal reasoning.
- understand and analyze data.

- analyze creative art critically.
- perform or produce creative art.
- explore and understand human behavior.
- explore and understand an historical culture.
- compare and contrast contemporary cultures.
- think critically about values and rationality.

Students are required to take one course in each of these areas: creative expression; history; values; ethics; cultural studies; the natural and biological sciences; mathematical reasoning; and social institutions and human behavior. Some of these courses will fall within their field of concentration, but they'll have to broaden their intellectual pursuits for others, at least for the four and one-half months it takes to complete the course.

Writing

Every Pomona student has to complete at least two writing-intensive courses, in which several drafts of every paper are submitted to the instructor for comment before a final grade is given. The required Critical Inquiry seminar every student takes in the first semester at Pomona counts for one of these.

My second writing-intensive course was Economic History with Professor Hans Palmer. There were only eight students in the class. Professor Palmer required us to turn in four drafts of every paper, and he reserved the right to require more revisions when necessary. I was in the second semester of my senior year, so I had plenty on my mind besides my courses and was a little taken aback when I got the first draft of my first paper back with three pages of comments and suggestions, in red ink. When the second draft came back with just as much red ink, I was downright dismayed. But my writing improved, and while I was rethinking my written ideas over and over, I was also sharpening my analysis of what I learned.

Foreign Language Proficiency

Another requirement for a Pomona degree is proficiency in a foreign language, defined as speaking and writing the language at the level of a third-semester course. Pomona is serious about this requirement, and it has even kept a few bright people from graduating on time. Plan ahead. Students can test out of this requirement by scoring a 650 or better on a language SAT Subject test, or by scoring a 4 or 5 on an Advanced Placement exam. Students are also required to complete one course defined as "speaking-intensive." This is a new requirement; the catalog defines it as "frequent, extemporaneous oral presentations, discussion, or debate that are carefully evaluated by instructors." With all these requirements, it would seem that there isn't much room to do your own thing, but in truth, a single course can often satisfy more than one graduation requirement. An advanced language class can also be writing- or speaking-intensive. A philosophy class can also involve learning about a modern or historical culture.

Majors

On admission, students are asked what academic subject they intend to study, and they may be assigned to a faculty advisor based on this initial concentration, or major. Don't worry too much about your initial choice. Pomona has a number of great academic programs, and you can change your mind a lot later in your college career than you think. If the introductory courses in a subject don't light your fire, you'll be taking classes in other subjects that might. No one will look back at your admissions essay when you declare an English concentration and say no, you can't do this, because you said you wanted to be a diplomat. Honest!

When you decide which subject you're interested in, choose a permanent faculty advisor who teaches in that concentration. Pomona offers top-notch courses in forty-one concentrations, in the natural and laboratory sciences, mathematics, social sciences, and humanities. Read the catalog for complete listings and course descriptions. The foreign language concentrations are also extremely demanding, so, as mentioned, plan to start studying the language in high school.

Studying Off Campus

Students can take up to eleven courses at the other Claremont Colleges during their four years, though in order to graduate there are a few courses they absolutely must take at Pomona. Some concentrations are offered jointly among all Claremont Colleges. If you choose to pursue Neuroscience, Women's Studies, Black Studies, Chicano Studies, Asian American Studies, Media Studies, or Science, Technology, and Society, you'll automatically be taking a number of your courses at other campuses. You'll become acquainted with new professors, new students, and new ways of thinking by doing so, and with any luck, your social life will also be enhanced.

If the Claremont Colleges don't offer enough variety of experience, students can also study as exchange students at Colby, Spelman, Smith, and Swarthmore colleges. Students can pursue five-year joint engineering degree programs with Caltech and Washington University in St. Louis. Every year, about twenty juniors and seniors spend a semester in Washington, D.C., where they serve as interns in government or national organization offices, write research papers, and attend seminars. There's also a semester internship with the California state government in Sacramento.

About half of Pomona's students choose to study abroad during their undergraduate years, for one or two semesters. The college strongly encourages study abroad, sponsoring forty programs in thirty-seven cities located in twenty-six foreign countries. At each of these sites, there's a program director who acts as an advisor to the students and a liaison between the foreign school and Pomona.

I went to Strasbourg, France, for a semester in a Pomona-sponsored program run jointly with Brethren Colleges Abroad. The American and French staff associated with BCA helped me register for classes, found housing for me, sent my friends to doctors and dentists who spoke English, held get-togethers that supplemented my pitiful food budget, and generally made integration into a new culture much easier. My Pomona liaison took us out to dinners, the opera, and local museums, all on Pomona's dime! I had a great experience studying abroad although it was tiring speaking another language all the time, and I had to think really hard about the business of everyday life. It wasn't just because of cultural differences, but also because I wasn't living on campus anymore, so I was doing a lot more on my own. I learned a lot.

In general, people have had a much easier time on study abroad by going on Pomona-sponsored programs. They don't require people to set up their own living arrangements; they usually involve taking real classes at real universities, and Pomona makes sure they're reputable. Truly adventurous students have found independent programs in places like the Dominican Republic, South Africa, and Indonesia, with widely varying results.

While I was studying abroad, I took a vacation in Ireland, and I stayed in a youth hostel in Limerick where I met up with a group of unlucky young Midwesterners whose study abroad program had promised them housing with local families, but hadn't delivered. For three months, they'd been staying in a dingy building, sleeping dormitory-style with total strangers every night, with no on-site laundry facilities. Every night, five or six of them would sit in the hostel lounge, tune the TV into Baywatch, and talk about how they couldn't wait to get home. What a waste!

SOCIAL LIFE AND ACTIVITIES

Life in a Pomona residence hall is nothing like a youth hostel. It's more like an elite summer camp. Everyone there was a high achiever in high school. Everyone wants to do something important in the world upon graduation. Almost no one is there because "Oh, well, Mommy and Daddy went here, and it's something to do between prep school and joining the family firm." People really think and talk about what they're learning, and are active in the community, on campus and off.

Housing

Everyone lives in residence halls as a first-year student. The first-year students are placed with a sponsor group of twelve to sixteen other first-year students and two sponsors, one male and one female, who are sophomores or juniors. The members of a sponsor group live in neighboring rooms, or adjoining hallways but men and women have separate bathrooms. Upperclassmen can always spot first-year students because they travel in packs. Entire sponsor groups arrive together at the dining halls, swimming pools, concerts, even dances.

My sponsor group lived in Oldenborg, the foreign language dorm. We had a great mix of people who had lived abroad, were first-generation Americans, spoke English as a second language, or were just interested in languages and international studies. My sponsors were great people. They spent a lot of time with us, clueing us in to all kinds of essential Pomona facts, and making the transition to a new lifestyle a lot easier.

There are a few important facts to know about the residence halls. Of course, they have developed personalities over the years. Oldenborg in particular has a reputation for being very insular. People enter "the Borg" and don't often come out, since it has its own dining hall, a library, and a movie theater in the basement. Walker residents live the closest to what most people imagine the Southern California college lifestyle is. They tend to be laid back, playing a lot of Frisbee in the day and partying hard into the night. Lots of stressed-out first-year students and sophomores choose to live in Mudd-Blaisdell because there's a computer lab in the court-yard; they can work late into the night and have a short walk back to their rooms.

Students can apply for permission to live off campus in their sophomore, junior, and senior years, but only a few students are permitted to go every year, and it's hard to stay involved with campus life if you do. However, there are a few good reasons to move off campus. If you live in the residence halls, you have to eat at the cafeterias, or at least pay for the meal plan, whether or not you eat there. Alcohol consumption in the residence halls is regulated. Private parties can have alcohol only in single servings—no kegs. So, if you want to throw wild parties, you can either move off campus, or register your event with the Office of Campus Life and hold it in one of the six designated social rooms on campus.

Off-Campus Life

It is a good idea to cultivate friendships with people who own cars, because the sidewalks roll up at 9:00 P.M. in the village of Claremont. There is no movie theater, fast food, late-night restaurant, or shopping mall in the village, though there are a few smart little clothing boutiques and a video store or two within walking distance, and the Rhino Records store and Starbucks, source of all good things. Anybody can have a car at Pomona, although registration is required and parking areas are restricted.

Sports

The administration realizes the limits placed on their students by the suburban location, so to keep them from stagnating in their personal development, any number of activities to keep them occupied outside of class have been organized. Pomona fields nineteen men's and women's intercollegiate sports teams. The sports facilities are really first-rate. The twenty-five-yard recreational pool behind Mudd-Blaisdell residence hall is a favorite spot for unofficial late-night visits, as are the Scripps and Harvey Mudd pools to the north. There's also an eight-lane all-weather track anyone can use and the Rains Center, a $16 million facility built in 1992 that houses the weight room and CV equipment, squash, racquetball, basketball, and volleyball courts, aerobics studio, and locker rooms and coaches' offices. The dance department has its studio on south campus, and students can cross-register for any physical education class at the other Claremont Colleges as well.

Student Union

Pomona opened a new Campus Center in fall 1999, which provides a centrally located space for student activities both organized and disorganized. The college has a full complement of performing arts, political, cultural, and community service groups, honor societies, and any other activities that you'd expect from an extremely wealthy small college. The Smith Campus Center also houses restaurants, a ballroom, and a 200-seat movie theater.

Clubs and Organizations

The hosts of clubs and organizations spend lots of time recruiting new members in the first few weeks of every semester. Most announce their activities to the wider community in *The Student Life*, Pomona's student-run newspaper; *Collage*, the five-college paper; online; and various flyers and posters around campus. KSPC, Pomona's student-run independent FM radio station, is also a good source of information about things to do.

Performances and Socials

Almost everyone joins at least one significant extracurricular activity, but there are plenty of other ways to pass time on campus. The Committee on Campus Life and Activities, made up of elected student representatives and staff from the Office of Campus Life, has a huge budget dedicated to making sure that students have a good time and occasionally expand their minds when they're outside class. They help sponsor performances on campus from such acts as The Dave Matthews Band, No Doubt, Indigo Girls, and the Kodo Drummers. They sponsor screenings of second-run films, parties and dances in the residence halls, the spring formal dance, the spring carnival, and even a few lectures here and there. Individual residence halls also sponsor their own activities, such as ice cream socials and movie nights.

There are six social rooms scattered among the residence halls that can be reserved in advance for any social event. There are a few social fraternities to join, but no sororities, although some of the fraternities are coed. No recognized Greek organizations are allowed to maintain houses for their members, so fraternity parties are also held in the social rooms, or off campus. Greek parties in the social rooms are subject to the same regulation as everyone else's, including a requirement to have security officers for events with more than fifty people.

Getting Away

If the attractions of Claremont wear thin, there are always the Pacific beaches, about an hour away by car. The San Bernardino mountains are an hour in the opposite direction, with camping, hiking, and even skiing at Big Bear. Adventures in downtown Los Angeles are also an hour's drive away, and Disneyland is just forty-five minutes away. L.A. has a wide variety of cultural, shopping, and entertainment experiences to offer, what you'd expect from a huge city filled with hundreds of ethnic and cultural groups.

FINANCIAL AID

If you are wise in the ways of the world, you have been asking yourself how much a college with so much to offer will cost. The budget (tuition, fees, room and board, and personal expenses) was about $43,000 a year in a recent year, which is comparable with costs at other private schools of its caliber. If you can afford this out of pocket, great! Skip ahead.

For the rest of the population, the Financial Aid Office will be a significant part of your college life. The Financial Aid Office at Pomona is extremely knowledgeable and helpful. Pomona is committed to meeting the financial need of all enrolled candidates, so applying for financial aid has no effect on admissions decisions.

Financial aid applicants file the Free Application for Federal Student Aid to determine their eligibility for federal programs such as Pell Grants and Perkins and Stafford loans, as well as Federal Work-Study funds. They also file the College Scholarship Service's Profile application to determine their eligibility for funds administered by Pomona. Pomona gives away or loans a lot of its own money every year to students who have financial need, which is a big help because there isn't much money available from the federal government. California residents also file the Cal Grant GPA Verification form. Students with divorced parents will be asked to send a Non-Custodial Parent's statement, giving financial information about the parent they do not live with, along with their Profile application.

The information gathered on all these forms shows how much money your family can contribute toward the costs of your education. If there is anything on any of these forms that confuses you (most likely, there will be), or if the picture of your family's finances that comes out of the form doesn't look right, contact the Financial Aid Office and ask them about it. They have seen thousands of students and awarded millions of dollars in aid. Chances are they will know exactly how to help you, as long as you keep them informed.

GRADUATES

Pomona graduates often go into public service—teaching, government, nonprofits, congressional internships—right after graduation. Then, when the thrill of working long hours for poverty-level wages wears off, they pursue advanced degrees and move into more lucrative fields, such as management consulting, medicine, and the law. Pomona is well represented in scientific research, publishing, and business marketing as well.

SUMMING UP

Pomona College is a coed, residential, nonsectarian liberal arts college located thirty-five miles east of Los Angeles. It is academically rigorous and attracts highly motivated people as students, staff, and faculty. Its location is both a blessing and a curse, with a great climate and easy access to mountains, beaches, and city life, but little activity in the surrounding town. The college is aware of this and outdoes itself providing on-campus activities and resources for students, funding student projects, building recreational facilities, and bringing distinguished performers and lecturers to campus. Graduates can rely on their skills to go anywhere they want and do whatever they dream.

❏ *Christina Caldwell, B.A.*

PRINCETON UNIVERSITY

Photo by Robert P. Matthews

 Princeton University
Princeton, NJ 08544-0430

 (609) 258-3060
Fax: (609) 258-6743

 Web site: *www.princeton.edu*

 Enrollment

Full-time ❑ women: 2,226
❑ men: 2,564

INTRODUCING PRINCETON

One of the leading universities in the world, Princeton is impressive on all levels and deservedly appears at or near the top of all of the ranking reports you might read. Like other Ivy League schools, competition to get in is stiff: in a recent class, ninety-eight percent of the enrolling students had been in the top fifth of their high school class and two-thirds of them had scores higher than 700 on both Math and Verbal SATs. Like other Ivy League schools, the faculty members represent the best in their fields, from professors whose novels win the National Book Award to those whose achievements in molecular biology win a Nobel prize.

I graduated from a public school in a small town where all the teachers were neighbors and not only knew the students, but knew the parents, too. I didn't have a lot of choice about courses, but I was used to getting high grades pretty easily and getting along with my teachers really well. When I first got to Princeton, I was nervous—the campus seemed huge, I was taking an introductory course in philosophy in a lecture hall with more kids than had been in my whole high school, and the professor was down on a stage and seemed as far away from me as a famous rock star in a concert. On top of that, I didn't do very well on my first paper. My roommate told me to go to see my preceptor for the course. My preceptor went through the whole paper with me, and helped me to broaden my thinking about how to tackle different concepts. She really cared about helping me learn how to learn. Not only did I write better papers after that, but I wasn't nervous anymore. Princeton wasn't so different from home after all.

What sets Princeton apart, however, is its dedication to undergraduate education. The undergraduate population of approximately 4,400 students comprises over seventy percent of the total student population. More than ninety years ago, Woodrow Wilson, as president of Princeton, implemented the preceptorial system; even the largest lecture courses meet in small class groups once or twice a week. As early as your first year you could find yourself sitting at a seminar table with only ten other students arguing the finer points of *Hamlet* with one of the world's leading Shakespearean scholars.

Not surprisingly, this commitment to undergraduates results in both flexibility in devising academic programs and greater access to faculty members for independent study. Between the two bachelor's degree programs (A.B. and B.S.E.), the university offers more than sixty department and interdepartmental programs. Students may also apply for independent concentration outside of the already existing programs. In fact, independent study is an important part of every undergraduate's academic life. For A.B. candidates, all departments require a combination of upper-level courses and independent study during both junior and senior years, and all A.B. candidates (as well as most B.S.E. candidates) must write a senior thesis. The thesis averages 100 pages and is the culmination of a year's study (outside of regular coursework) on a topic of your choice under the direction of a faculty advisor.

In a world where some colleges require no core courses and others require course plans structured toward practical applications, Princeton remains a fierce proponent of a balanced liberal arts education. All A.B. candidates must meet a one-term writing requirement and show proficiency in a foreign language. In addition, they must take one course each in the four distribution areas of epistemology and cognition, ethical thought and moral values, historical analysis, and quantitative reasoning, and they must take two courses each in literature and the arts, science and technology (with laboratory), and social analysis. Nor are engineering students off the hook. They too have to satisfy a writing requirement and take a number of (although not as many) courses in the various areas of study.

That Princeton's distribution areas are not traditional represents a conscious decision by the university to move with the twenty-first century. There are other signs, in both enrollment and governance, that the Princeton of today is not the elitist tradition-bound school of past portraits. The undergraduate student body comes from all fifty states and seventy foreign countries. American minorities (including African American, Latino, Asian American, and Native American students) make up twenty-seven percent, and an additional five percent are foreign citizens. Almost forty-five percent of all undergraduates receive some kind of financial aid. Students also play an active role in policy-making at the school, sitting on committees right along with faculty and administration. Each spring a graduating senior is elected to serve a term on the university's Board of Trustees.

Of course, you can still find plenty of tradition at Princeton, from Opening Exercises in the Gothic University Chapel to the locomotive cheer at football games to Class Day festivities on Cannon Green behind Nassau Hall, the home of the president's office and for several months (in 1783) the capital of the United States. Princeton seems to connect its preparation for the future with its affection for the past in so many ways that, no matter how diverse the community, anyone can find a place to feel at home there.

ADMISSIONS REQUIREMENTS

For an Ivy League school, Princeton is relatively small: it enrolls approximately 1,130 freshmen of the 1,700 it accepts. Yet nearly 15,000 applications come into the Admissions Office. In other words, almost ninety percent of those who apply will receive that dreaded thin envelope.

It's not easy to get into Princeton. Among those admitted, more than seventy-five percent had SAT I scores over 680, and one-third of those had scores over 780. On the other hand, Princeton has only three mandatory admission requirements—SAT, SAT Subject Tests in three subject areas, and the application form itself. While the Admissions Office recommends that applicants take four years each of English, math, and a language, as well as two years each of history and a lab science, it also insists that there are no fixed unit or course requirements that must be completed before admission. The school gives "full consideration to any applicant who has been unable to pursue studies to the extent recommended if the record otherwise shows clear promise."

Of course, the key words are "clear promise"—and the admissions process itself can seem far from clear. There is no formula for getting in. Like other highly competitive schools, Princeton wants to see how candidates have excelled, not only in their coursework but also in their extracurricular activities. Because Princeton is a residential university, the committee takes an interest in candidates' roles in their communities. Special talents are also considered, whether the talent is on the athletic field or on the stage. The Admissions Office encourages candidates involved in the performing and creative arts to submit audition tapes or portfolios. Legacies (children of alumni) are given a certain amount of special consideration. (In 1999, forty percent of the 451 alumni children who applied were admitted; seventy-nine percent of those admitted enrolled, accounting for 143 of the class of 2003.)

Decision Programs

Princeton has two decision programs: Early Decision and Regular Decision. (The university has discontinued its Early Action program. You may apply Early Decision only if you are not applying Early Decision or Early Action anywhere else.) Early Decision applications must be mailed by November 1. You will hear from the Admissions Office in December whether your application has been accepted, denied, or deferred for review in the Regular Decision process. All admissions are for September enrollment; however, Princeton allows you to defer enrollment to travel, work, perform military service, or participate in special year-abroad programs. You cannot request a deferral until you have actually been notified that you have been admitted.

My mother was a whiz at Latin in high school and got a really high score on the Latin Achievement Test. When she was accepted at Princeton, the Classics Department wrote her a letter saying that if she wanted to major in classics she could start as a sophomore. She said, "No way! I worked hard to get into Princeton and I'm not going to shortchange my time there by a year!"

Some students joke that it is harder to flunk out of Princeton than it is to get in. There is some truth in that. You could spend your four years cruising, making full use of pass/fail options and easier courses, doing the minimum amount of work, getting by with Cs. But what a waste that would be. Princeton has so much to offer that these can also be the most intellectually stimulating years of your life. If anything, the tough part for a new student is trying to absorb all of the information about department offerings, programs, and seminars.

The undergraduate course catalogue is more than 400 pages. Princeton has thirty-three departments, supplemented by twenty-nine interdisciplinary programs ranging from African American Studies to Musical Performance to Women's Studies. New students can start right in on their special interests through Freshman Seminars, small groups of students chosen on the basis of a short essay who meet with a professor on a specific topic. Recently there have been as many as forty-six freshman seminars, including The Aims of Education, led by the president of the university.

Off Campus

Princeton is flexible with off-campus opportunities. The Field Study Program lets students substitute, for one semester, a full-time job or research assignment closely related to their academic interests. For example, if you major in biology, you could apply to do biological research in a private lab. The field study doesn't have to be near Princeton: people have done work from San Francisco's Bay Area to the Woods Hole Oceanographic Institute on Cape Cod. Although Princeton doesn't run any of its own foreign study programs, the university will allow students to receive credit for a semester or a full year in an approved program. Students on financial aid even continue to receive support.

Special Schools

There are also some special schools on the undergraduate level. In addition to the School of Engineering and Applied Science, Princeton has a School of Architecture and the Woodrow Wilson School of Public and International Affairs. The official word is that the Woodrow Wilson School "prepares students for participation and leadership in public affairs on the local, national, and international levels." Most Princetonians will tell you, though, that it is a breeding ground for budding lawyers. The Woodrow Wilson School limits its enrollment to eighty students a year and the competition is pretty intense. (Good practice for trying to get into law school.)

Advisors

If this already seems like too much to take in, there is help. Academic advising is available to all freshmen and sophomores through the residential colleges. The masters and directors of studies in the colleges are also available for counseling.

I didn't pay any attention to my advisor my freshman year; I figured that all he had about me was a file. How could he know what I might want to do? Well, by sophomore year I realized that I had been pretty arrogant. He might not have known me, but he did know Princeton. The suggestions he had made would have been much more sensible for me. Instead, I just did my own thing and ended up taking some courses that were just not right for me. I wish I had paid more attention to him—and I sure wish now that I had that time back.

Graduation Requirements

Graduation requirements are based on the number of courses taken, not the number of credits. Students in the A.B. program must complete thirty courses. (Students in the B.S.E program must complete thirty-six courses.) Normally, students take four courses a semester during their first three years, and then three courses a semester during the senior year. Most students try to take care of the distribution requirements in the early years so that they can have as much flexibility as possible in structuring their majors. (Majors are usually declared in the spring of sophomore year.) Be aware: You may be able to use a high score on an Advanced Placement test or an SAT II: Subject test to satisfy the language requirement, but all students must take one of the university courses to satisfy the writing requirement—even if you did get a 5 on the English AP.

Classes

Courses usually meet three times a week, with two lectures and a class (precept). (Engineering and science courses may meet more frequently and have required lab periods.) You might notice, however, that as you start taking upper-level courses the size of the lecture gets smaller, or you have two precepts and only one lecture, or you meet as seminar groups. You will have more and more individual contact with professors, whose accessibility is one of Princeton's hallmarks. All professors have weekly office hours, open time when any student can go in and just talk.

Papers and the Thesis

You will get to know some of the professors in your department especially well during your junior and senior years when you are doing the required independent work with an advisor: the J.P. (Junior Paper) and the senior thesis. The J.P. is in many ways practice for the thesis. It is usually a long paper written each semester on a topic of your choice. Work on the senior thesis, part of Princeton's student lore, is intended to take the time you would spend on a course. (This is why seniors take only three courses per semester, not four.) Many students very diligently allocate their time that way, regularly holing up in a carrel in the basement of Firestone Library, accumulating several shelves of texts for references, filling out box after box of index cards, handing in chunks of a rough draft periodically to their advisors. Several unfortunate students have been known to endure some very unpleasant weeks with little or no sleep right before the spring due date for the thesis.

Faculty

Princeton has more than 700 full-time faculty members and all of them teach undergraduates, making the student-faculty ratio 7-1. The faculty is top-notch. At any one time there may be six Nobel Prize winners teaching, or eighteen MacArthur Fellows. (MacArthur Foundation grants are sometimes referred to as "genius grants.") And, yes, it can be exciting to bump into novelists Toni Morrison or Joyce Carol Oates coming out of the English department office. But it can be equally exciting to be on an adventure of discovery with a new assistant professor in the biology department. Because of its prestige, Princeton attracts the best and the brightest of candidates out of graduate schools, people who are doing the most up-to-the-minute research in their chosen fields.

I kept telling my roommate how much I enjoyed the preceptor of my United States and World Affairs course. She was young and had terrific energy and seemed to know everything. My roommate told me to invite her to dinner at our eating club. I didn't think she'd come, but I asked her anyway. She said sure! A bunch of us sat around a table with her, all talking at once and having a great time. For that hour or so she seemed just like one of us—only a lot smarter!

Facilities

Princeton's facilities are top-notch, too. The main library, Firestone, provides easy access to more than five million books and 30,000 periodicals as well as manuscripts, maps, coins, prints, and microform. All but the rarest of materials are in open stacks. There are an additional sixteen satellite libraries associated with various departments. Princeton has two museums on campus, the Princeton University Art Museum and the Natural History Museum, as well as a variety of exhibition spaces. There are four major venues for the cultural and performing arts, from a 200-seat recital hall to Tony Award-winning McCarter Theatre. Princeton also provides an extensive computing environment. Students can go to hundreds of workstations in two dozen computing clusters around campus. Students who bring their own computers can subscribe to Dormnet, a data service available in every undergraduate dorm room on campus that connects to campus and Internet resources. In 1999–2000, ninety-three percent of those eligible for Dormnet participated.

Academic life at Princeton can be as rich as you choose to make it. The array of opportunities is far more than you will be able to explore in your four years, and there is the danger that, in trying to do it all, you will feel stressed and pulled in too many directions. But it is all there for the taking, and the rewards are well worth the risks.

The hardest thing for me to get used to at Princeton was the different sense of time. In high school, my days and weeks were pretty structured (usually by someone else!) and we had specific assignments almost every night. At Princeton, courses meet only a couple times a week, sometimes leaving big blocks of time during the day. Many professors just hand out a syllabus at the beginning of the course and you are on your own to keep up with the reading and to remember when papers are due. At the end of each semester is "reading period"—about two weeks with no classes scheduled just before exams. At first it seemed as though I had unlimited free time, and I confess I spent a lot of my first semester goofing off. Then, when I had three papers due at once and got into a jam, I realized that it wasn't that it was free time; it was my time. I had to learn to be responsible for my own time now. No one else was going to do it for me.

SOCIAL LIFE AND ACTIVITIES

Whenever something exciting happens in the borough of Princeton (which is not very often), the newspapers always refer to it as a "genteel college town." The 300-year-old town (population of about 30,000) is charming. Shops range from the local hardware store to Laura Ashley and The Gap. More restaurants and coffee shops have appeared over the last twenty years as the area right outside of Princeton has become home to several corporate headquarters. Students can get fries at Burger King, and parents can splurge at a fancy French restaurant right around the corner.

But Princeton is not a party town. The few "hang-outs" are strict about checking IDs and they close early. New York and Philadelphia are only an hour away, with regular bus and train service to New York City, and the university often subsidizes student trips for various cultural and athletic events in both cities. Nevertheless, there is hardly a mass exodus to either city on the weekends, or at any time. Princeton really is a residential college, with more than ninety-seven percent of undergraduates living on campus, and it is on campus that most students experience their social life.

Residential College, Dorms, and Clubs

For freshmen and sophomores, life generally revolves around their residential colleges. Each college houses between 440 and 490 students and is made up of a cluster of dorms, a dining hall, lounges and study rooms, a library, computing facilities, and game and television rooms. Some of the colleges even have theaters and exhibit spaces, and all have an extensive intramural athletic program. Students themselves plan most of the activities, so that each college takes on the character of the group of students in it. This residential college system is relatively new for Princeton (it was instituted in 1982), and freshmen particularly like it. It's a lot easier to be a new person in a group of 440 than in a universe of 4,400.

Upperclass students live in dorms that are not part of the residential colleges, and seventy-five percent of juniors and seniors belong to one of the twelve eating clubs that line Prospect Avenue. Each club has between 120 and 180 members who meet and eat and socialize in large houses that the clubs themselves run. Run by student officers under the guidance of independent alumni boards, the clubs are more than simply a place to eat. While each club has study and computer areas, they really are a haven for a tight community of friends to relax together. On any given weekend, several—or all—of the clubs will be having parties and the Street (as Prospect Avenue is called) is alive with activity, windows lit up, music streaming out of open doors, groups of people wandering from one club to another to visit friends and to see who has the best band that night.

Alternatives to the clubs do exist. Upperclass students may choose instead a university-sponsored nonresidential dining facility on Prospect that has its own extensive social program and is open to juniors and seniors. They may also opt to remain in the residential colleges or to be independent—to make their own arrangements for meals. Several of the dorms have special facilities for independents who want to cook their own meals, including one house that has been converted to a dorm for those who want to shop and cook vegetarian meals as a co-op. The new 170,000-square-foot Frist Campus Center opened in the year 2000, providing food, meeting spaces, and activities of various kinds for undergraduates in all four classes, as well as graduate students, faculty, and staff.

Extracurricular Activities

Princeton provides a remarkable choice of extracurricular activities. In athletics alone, there are sixty teams and crews, men and women compete in thirty-seven varsity sports, and there are another thirty-one men's, women's, and coed club teams. Nearly forty-five percent of the undergraduate student body competes in intercollegiate sports. While Princeton may not be known as an athletic powerhouse, during the past several years the school's varsity teams have won eight national championships. *Sports Illustrated* recently ranked Princeton the number ten jock school in the country. The basketball, lacrosse, and squash and field hockey programs rank at the top of anyone's list.

One of Princeton's most famous extracurricular activities is Triangle Club. Each year students write and produce a musical that they perform in McCarter Theatre and take on tour. Prominent Triangle alumni include Josh Logan, Jimmy Stewart, and, of more recent vintage, Brooke Shields. Theatre Intime, one of three other student production facilities, offers a student-produced drama series every year. Students interested in music have numerous outlets for their talents: the Orchestra, the Opera Theatre, the Jazz Ensemble, the Band (well known for its irreverent attitude at football games), the Glee Club, the Chapel Choir, and the Gospel Ensemble. Nine *a cappella* singing groups perform their own arrangements regularly around campus and in concert tours during vacation breaks.

Publications

Writers will find all kinds of publications on campus. Students publish two regular newspapers, the *Daily Princetonian* and the *Nassau Weekly*. The *Nassau Literary Review* is the nation's oldest student-run literary magazine. There are at least ten other publications, from the yearbooks to *Business Today*, which has a national circulation. (Princeton also has its own radio station, WPRB, which is affiliated with the Associated Press.)

Organizations

The American Whig-Cliosophic Society (known as Whig-Clio) is the oldest college political, literary, and debating society in the United States. (When a school has been around for more than 250 years, it's bound to have many of "the oldest" organizations!) This organization brings about twenty speakers to campus each year and sponsors a variety of programs related to public affairs. Those thinking of going into public affairs themselves can practice by participating in the Undergraduate Student Government (USG). In addition, twelve undergraduates sit on the Council of the Princeton University Community. The Student Volunteers Council and Community House provide service opportunities in which more than a thousand students participate each year.

These organizations may be the largest, but they are not the only ones on campus. The Office of the Dean of Student Life recognizes more than 200 official student organizations, and new ones are started all the time. These include more than twenty minority organizations on campus. On a far larger scale, the Third World Center, founded in 1971, emphasizes the cultural, intellectual, and social issues of students of color. Its mission is to be a readily accessible resource to all students interested in minority and Third World issues. The International Center, the Center for Jewish Life, and the Women's Center all represent the university's commitment to educational, cultural, and social programs that speak to a diverse student body. The Dean of the Chapel and Religious Life and various denominational chaplains on campus provide many opportunities for religious inquiry and expression—and Princeton surely has one of the most glorious college chapels in the world.

As with the academic programs, there is something for everyone in the abundance of extracurricular activities. Just pick one…or ten.

I was scared about the workload at Princeton, so I decided that I wouldn't do anything else but study. I had a pretty dull freshman year, and my grades weren't even that good! Then I missed singing too much and decided to audition for Triangle and one of the a cappella groups. I got into both and started having fun. It also turned out that having other commitments helped me organize my study time better and—surprise!—my grades went up. That might not work for everybody, of course, but I have found since graduation that the people I keep in touch with most are the ones I sang with.

FINANCIAL AID

Princeton admissions are need-blind, and the university pledges "to provide aid to all enrolled students judged by the Financial Aid Office to be in need of assistance." In a recent year, Princeton allocated almost $23 million in direct support through endowed scholarships and general funds to more than 2,000 undergraduates. That's almost forty-five percent of the student population. The Financial Aid Office looks at not only the parents' contribution, but also the potential contribution from the student, from savings, student loans, summer jobs, and campus jobs. Princeton is also very flexible in helping families who are not typical candidates for financial aid. The Student Employment Office helps undergraduates find jobs on and off campus. Financial aid students are given priority, but there really are jobs for anyone who wants one and almost seventy percent of the undergraduate student body works part-time. There is also a Princeton Student Loan program for students who don't qualify for financial assistance. And there is even a loan program, called the Princeton Parent Loan, for high-income families who do not need financial aid but who want to extend their payments over a much longer time than the four years.

In other words, if you are admitted to Princeton, Princeton will work with you and your family to figure out a way to pay for your four years there.

My father was an alumnus of Princeton, and I was the first girl (woman!) in the family to be accepted. During the spring of my senior year in high school, he and I spent a lot of time going over the catalog and talking about all of the things we would do together. Then that summer my father died suddenly. Everything changed. Not only did I miss my father terribly, but it was also too late for me to apply for financial aid for that year. I knew my mother was worried about the costs. Instead of arriving on campus for Freshman Week bouncy and eager, I arrived sad and anxious. I hadn't been there more than a few days when I got a call from one of my father's classmates who was in the administration. I had never met this gentleman before, and I didn't remember my father ever having mentioned him as a good friend. Somehow, though, he had heard about my father's death and knew that I was starting at Princeton. He invited me to a home-cooked meal with his family. Within a few weeks he had helped me find the right people to talk to in the Financial Aid Office and had helped me find a part-time job. Later that year, he nominated me for a scholarship established by my dad's class. I was awarded that scholarship for my remaining three years. In June he invited me to stop by the class's tent at Reunions, where I met many of my father's college pals who made me laugh—and cry—with stories about my dad when he was my age. These men didn't know me at all, but they made me feel part of a family when the strongest link in my own family was gone.

I honestly believe no other school can claim the intense alumni loyalty that Princeton generates—loyalty both to fellow Princetonians and to Princeton itself. This speaks volumes about just how remarkable the Princeton experience is.

Over the past decade or so, there has been a slight shift in the postgraduate choices of Princeton seniors. The number choosing to go straight into the job market has steadily risen. In a survey of a recent graduating class, fifty-two percent said that they were going to get a job right away. Of the twenty-seven percent who answered that they were going to continue their education, half were going to graduate school and the other half to professional school. Of those choosing professional schools, most were going to medical school (twenty-four percent) or law school (twenty percent). Only a handful were going on for degrees in education, business, or public policy.

What do all these numbers mean? Because of its former elite reputation, Princeton is still often thought of as a place that churns out only doctors and lawyers. In fact, however, less than twelve percent of the Class of 1996 planned to go into those fields. Princetonians can be found in all walks of life, and the university has a number of resources to help graduates explore many kinds of prospects. Those interested in teaching or school administration can turn to the Program in Teacher Preparation, which maintains a placement service for all Princeton students and alumni. The Princeton-in-Asia program places interested students in short-term teaching assignments in China or Japan. Career Services offers a full range of programs and counseling, including workshops on résumé-writing and interviewing. Staff members can arrange interviews with representatives of professional schools and corporations. Career Services also coordinates with the Alumni Careers Network, which is made up of over 4,500 alumni around the world who have volunteered to give guidance and job-hunting assistance.

It's no surprise that Princeton has an incredibly loyal alumni body. Of the nearly 70,000 living Princeton alumni, both undergraduate and graduate, at any given time ten percent are involved in some kind of volunteer work for Princeton, whether in regional associations, the job placement network, or community service. More than 13,000 alumni keep up with the university and each other through an electronic alumni network known as Tigernet. And every spring more than 5,000 alumni return to Princeton on the weekend before Commencement for Reunions, to walk again the paths between the dorms, to catch up with classmates, and to parade through the campus, smiling at the cheers of current students and proudly wearing their orange and black.

SUMMING UP

Princeton University successfully combines the best of several possible worlds. It has a world-renowned faculty, yet its primary focus is on its undergraduates. It has a range of activities that rivals even the largest universities in the country, yet the undergraduate population of 4,400 gives it an intimacy similar to that of a small liberal arts school. The diverse student body is drawn from all corners of the United States and the world, yet the students all share one thing—the intellectual potential to achieve at the highest level.

This is not to say that Princeton is for everyone; however, the students who have been disappointed tend to be those who expected something that Princeton never attempted to offer. If you are a star running back and want to play your college football games in front of rows of scouts and national television audiences, Princeton is not for you. On the other hand, the Princeton Tigers regularly get to the NCAA Basketball Championships and have defeated such powerhouses as UCLA. If you want to get a B.F.A. in film or creative writing, Princeton is not for you. On the other hand, you could design your own interdisciplinary major under the auspices of the Film Studies Committee or write a novel for your senior thesis in the English department and go on to a career in entertainment or the arts.

What you can expect from Princeton is one of the finest educations in the country. In this you won't be disappointed. You will also get something more: experiences that will stay with you a lifetime. You may have the chance to hear a famous Chaucer scholar recite *The Miller's Tale* in Middle English to a packed lecture hall, making everyone laugh in the right places just by the judicious raising of an eyebrow. You may have the chance to work with a new preceptor in microbiology who will win the Nobel Prize in 2019. You may have the chance to dance in a Triangle Show kickline next to a skinny young man who will go on to become the next Jimmy Stewart.

The Princeton experience can be as unique as each student chooses to make it. Most graduates look back on their four years as a wonderful time of unlimited opportunities. This combination of the unique and the universal creates a bond among Princetonians that lasts far beyond graduation day.

❏ *Kathryn Taylor, B.A.*

REED COLLEGE

 Reed College
Portland, Oregon 97202

 (503) 771-7511
Fax: (503) 777-7553 or (800) 547-4750

 E-mail: *.admissions@reed.edu*
Web site: *web.reed.edu*

 Enrollment

Full-time ❑ women: 697
❑ men: 575

INTRODUCING REED COLLEGE

Reed means being smart. Smart, in the biggest, most complicated, inspiring, and open sense of the word. Smart in the sense of taking risks, of seeking challenges, and of seeing in any answer an infinite array of more interesting questions. Smart in taking nothing for granted, and asking every day, "What does it mean to learn, to communicate ideas, to seek understanding?"

The 1,350 students who congregate on Reed's 100-acre campus share a singular passion for learning in an academic environment that is as known for its intense intellectual rigor as it is for its out-of-the-box, open-minded, and liberal students. For many, Reed's mixture of classical learning and independent living seems like a contradiction in terms; for those who see college as an adventure for the mind, as a challenge for the self, and as an opportunity to learn not for profit but for the intrinsic value of knowledge, Reed makes perfect sense.

What, then, of a school that seeks to capture and cultivate smartness?

Intensity can exist without senseless competition. At Reed, grades exist, but they aren't reported on individual assignments or placed on report cards. Students produce work because they value success as a measure of understanding. Classrooms come into being as spaces for discussion, where professors, called by their first names, guide student-driven inquiry. There are no honors programs, no dean's lists, or any exclusive club, organization, fraternity, or sorority—no NCAA or varsity athletics, either.

Trust creates true community. Students, faculty, and staff alike are governed by the Honor Principle, an unwritten commitment that takes the place of arbitrary rules and regulations. You're expected to act honestly and with regard for the community in all matters, academic as well as social. From the college's founding, this has meant that tests and examinations need not be proctored; you're as likely to take your chemistry test in the library as you are to take it on the front lawn. In all matters, students must engage disagreement rather than support divisiveness. An all-student judicial board, chosen by student representatives, provides for true peer review.

Fun exists. Reedies take learning seriously, but they also, refreshingly, remember not to take themselves too seriously. There's a college newspaper as well as a comic book library. And each year, students celebrate the Seventh Annual Nitrogen Day, a tribute to that element's unique triple bond.

And while Reed can't claim responsibility for Portland, the city that hosts the college's splendidly green campus is also known for its smartness. An award-winning public transportation system connects you to a vibrant downtown and to the city's many neighborhoods, whether you want to eat a great meal, go to a concert, or explore Forest Park's many miles of hiking trails.

ADMISSIONS REQUIREMENTS

For more than ten years now, Reed has openly refused to participate in annual college rankings, a fact that captures the college's attitude toward admission. Rather than rely on arbitrary numbers, presumptions of status and prestige, and the notion that colleges, like toasters or television sets, can be ranked from best to worst, Reed wants to be judged on its merits and chosen by students with a true interest in the education it offers. There is no one single Reed, either, in numbers, guidebooks, or online message boards, so you should explore as many angles of vision as possible to discover the school's distinctive character. Ideally, a campus visit offers the most comprehensive picture. You can meet students, go on a tour, and find out that the food is actually quite good. During the school year, you can sit in on classes and spend a night in the dorms. If you're not able to get to Portland, you should see if an admissions representative is traveling to your area, as interviews are offered in cities across the country in late summer and throughout the fall. Alumni interviews are also widely available. Check out the school's Web site, including the newly redesigned virtual tour, as well as individual student and professors' pages. There are as many sorts of Reedies and Reed experiences as there are students on campus, so look to discover and enjoy both diversity and coherence in your explorations.

On the college's end, Reed seeks to admit students with the same desire and ability for smartness that underlies the existing community. For starters, this assures that getting in is not a numbers game. Nor is it a matter of finding that most perfectly "well-rounded" person, as if the spherical was somehow the most nobly lived life. Reed is notable for "taking risks" with applicants who may be far from perfect on paper, but who have demonstrated in any number of ways their readiness and ability for success at Reed.

What Is Important?

At the same time, there are some familiar truisms that, much more often than not, carry the day. The better you do in high school, especially taking the most challenging courses offered by your school, the better your chances for admission. There are no specific curricular requirements, though it's recommended that you have multiple years of coursework in all the major core subjects such as English, social studies, math, science, and foreign language. Involvement and extracurricular activities matter, though demonstrable passion, intellectualism, commitment, and thoughtfulness of involvement always triumph over resume building. Diversity of background, experience, and identity, including race, ethnicity, and gender play an important role in admission and in the larger Reed community.

> *When I was looking at schools, Reed was the one college that didn't try to impress me with how hard it was to get in, or to suggest that only some cadre of saintly elite might be worthy of admission. Everyone I spoke to wanted to know what I was interested in, how I thought about things, and why I wanted to go to college. Reed didn't mix up education with pretension or exclusivity; it just asked that I be interested in ideas, want to learn, and be willing to share in challenging work. It seemed so simple an idea yet Reed was the only place I could find such honesty. And they had fun, too.*

Applying

First-year students can apply to Reed under either the November 15 or January 1 Early Decision options, both of which are binding, or at the January 15 Regular Admission deadline. If you're certain that you want to attend Reed, applying Early Decision can give your application added advantage in demonstrating your commitment. All admission options require the general Common Application form and supporting materials such as teacher recommendations and so forth. Also required are results from either the SAT or ACT and the Reed supplement form, a graded writing sample, and an essay that answers, "Why Reed?" This last piece is quite important; you should use your essay to demonstrate your understanding of the school, most importantly by showing how you imagine yourself at Reed. You're not being asked to write propaganda; instead, have fun and describe the potential adventures, challenges, and successes that draw you to the college.

ACADEMIC LIFE

Legends abound as to the amount and the difficulty of the work at Reed. Some have used the metaphor of boot camp. Those less militaristic and more existential have offered the myth of Sisyphus. Don't be afraid, though, of the hyperbole. There's no doubt that the academics are hard, that expectations are high, and that people take thinking seriously. At the same time, you're aren't thrown in the deep end and expected to know everything on the first day of class. Above all, you need to be interested in and engaged by learning. With that in mind, you'll find the challenges and satisfaction of studying at Reed to be as amazing as anything you might imagine.

Reed values the classical model of a liberal arts education, based on a requirement structure meant to ensure both breadth and depth in each student's program of study. Tradition also reigns within the college's department structure, with very few "interdisciplinary" or topical majors offered. The professors at Reed feel seriously that students need a grounding in their chosen major, with a comprehensive introduction to the various methods and theories of that discipline, past and present. This preparation gives you a solid foundation for the challenges you'll face and the independence you'll be given in upper-division coursework. Such focused introductions don't breed singularity of thought, however. Instead, they provide the basis for seriously considering similarities and differences in the various ways scholars both ask and answer questions. With this preparation, it's no wonder that Reed graduates have such a fantastic track record for success in graduate school.

SERIOUS SCIENCE

Reed is the only undergraduate college with a nuclear reactor, one of the many resources that support the college's extraordinary science program. The 250 kW TRIGA research reactor is the only one in the world that is primarily operated by students (science majors as well as students of English and religion, among other departments), all of whom are licensed by the nuclear regulatory commission. Reed's reactor also has more licensed female operators than all other research reactors combined.

Classes, Professors, and Evaluations

One of the greatest parts of learning at Reed comes in the small, conference-based classroom environment that predominates on campus. Conferences at Reed average thirteen students, and all are taught by members of the faculty. You're expected to be as active, involved and engaged as anyone around the table, including the professor. For starters, you can abandon the high school foolishness of hand raising. All students, shy and extroverted alike, develop their skills as conference participants during their time at Reed. Each meeting offers its own vibrancy and originality, and above all, you are learning how to think in harmony with others, how to ask questions and articulate your ideas.

Faculty at Reed are called by their first names, and this openness exemplifies the interest and support they offer students. You have a faculty member as an academic advisor from the day you step on campus, and you can easily change advisors if your interests shift or you develop a connection with another professor. Every professor hosts many office hours each week, and e-mails receive quick yet thoughtful replies, sometimes even at two in the morning.

Because letter or number grades are not noted on your assignments, faculty evaluate your work with extensive and detailed comments. The criticism is as plentiful as it is constructive. You're called to task on the strength and logic of your arguments, on the evidence you used or might have used. And you're also given encouragement to further your strengths and develop your own original questions, in the classroom, library, and laboratory.

> *When I started at Reed, I figured I would check my grades at the end of first semester, just to get a sense of how I was doing. When the time came, though, I had no interest in asking. My whole sense of not only how I learned, but why I was in school, what it meant to be successful, had begun to change. After four years, I can't imagine what it would be like to know your grades while in school, to be in an environment where people talked about or even worse were competitive about them.*

Humanities 110

The summer before you arrive at Reed, the alumni association sends you a copy of Richmond Lattimore's verse translation of Homer's *Iliad*. With this text, new Reedies begin the shared and enduring experience of the required year-long introductory humanities course that focuses on ancient Greece in the first semester, and Imperial Rome and the rise of Christendom in the second. Course material consists mostly of primary sources in all classical fields, including art, with a minimum of secondary sources. Hum 110, as the course is known, has two distinct components. First, three times a week, the entire first-year class comes together for a lecture from one of the twenty or so faculty members drawn from a variety of departments who are teaching the course. You hear well-researched and thought-provoking talks that cover a given text or combination of works, offering useful contextual information as well as arguments on how you might develop your own interpretations. Second, each student is a member of a small, thirteen- or fourteen-student conference, led by one of the professors in the course. Conferences can vary in character

PAIDEIA

The Greek word for learning, Paideia also names the ten days before the start of spring semester at Reed, a time when students organize and teach a diverse program of classes and seminars on pretty much anything. Some of the hundreds of recent course offerings include: Tree-Sitting 101, Underwater Basket Weaving, Notebook Binding, Inside the Animal Mind, Bad Faulkner, Ben and Jerry's Appreciation, Introduction to Photoshop, Catapult Construction Competition, and Japanese Monster Movies.

depending on the home discipline of the professor, who might be a philosopher, political scientist, or art historian, yet all share the same syllabus and paper deadlines. In Hum 110, you learn as much about the classical humanities as you do about writing well, receiving academic feedback on your work, and participating in the conference environment.

Group Requirements

Part of attending Reed means having a broad interest in ideas and learning, and the curricular group requirements provide structure for ensuring breadth in each student's education. A total of eight of the thirty units required for graduation are given to these requirements; most semester-long courses are valued at one unit. Two units must be taken from one department within each of four groups: literature, arts, philosophy, and religion; history, the social sciences, and psychology; laboratory courses in physics, chemistry, or biology; and, mathematics or a foreign language. Though there is no specific order or timeline for taking these requirements, most students concentrate on them during their first two years at Reed, the advantage being that you gain exposure to a variety of different fields before choosing a major at the end of sophomore year.

Studying Off Campus

Close to thirty established foreign and domestic exchange programs allow Reedies the opportunity to study away from campus for either a semester or a full year. All of the programs are arranged in coordination with the faculty to support an aspect of the college's academic program. For instance, if you're studying Islam in the religion department, you might choose to take a semester intensively studying Arabic at the Al Akhawayn University in Morroco. Some programs offer more general opportunities for your exchange program, such as a year at Wadham College, Oxford, or at Ireland's Trinity College. Because each program has a direct tie with Reed, students are assured that they will have a meaningful experience, and years of established relationships give Reedies access to the fullest privileges at partner institutions. In addition, the International Programs Office will work with students to craft any number of additional opportunities that suit a student's particular interests. Unlike the established programs, however, those that you devise on your own are not covered by the college's financial aid packages. Because of the general curricular requirements that each student needs to complete, fitting a study abroad year into your time at Reed can take some planning, so it's worthwhile beginning to develop your plan for an exchange early on in your time at Reed. Many Reedies also choose to take time off to travel rather than participating in an official program, and the college is very flexible in granting leaves of absence. While a very different sort of experience, an independent adventure can often provide for some refreshing time away from the routines of a traditional academic semester.

The Junior Qualifying Examination

Before students can begin their senior year, they must pass a junior qualifying examination proctored by their major department. The "qual," as it's known, can vary widely in format from department to department, yet all are designed to test students' initial mastery of the skills and methods of their chosen field. The exams don't generally target a specific body of information that you need to cram into your brain in order to get through the test. Mostly, they are concerned with seeing if you've begun to get a handle on the way scholars in your department do research and communicate their findings, and the various methods and traditions that inform their work. Some departments, such as history and English, require specific Junior Seminar courses that play a role in preparing students for the exam. In all cases, the faculty of each department meets to discuss students' performance on their exams, as well as their work in the courses they've had up to this point. With solid focus and preparation, the vast majority of students pass their qual outright the first time they take the exam. Some receive what is called a conditional pass; in this case, you need to meet a specific stipulation, such as retaking a particular section of the exam or taking a class in a particular area. For students, the qual serves as a good time to think about your particular interests in your major, and look toward a topic you might like to explore in your senior thesis.

The Senior Thesis

Your thesis is a defining experience of your time at Reed. Along with two or three other classes in your senior year, you are given the opportunity to embark on a sustained and original piece of scholarship on a topic of your choice in your major. You have an advisor specifically for your thesis, and you're given the independence to shape your inquiry in a manner you find most engaging. Depending on your field, you usually complete one of three types of theses: experimental, research-analytical, or creative. Generally, those in the sciences take the experimental route; they get lab space for the year where they can base their work. If you're writing in literature, the humanities, or social sciences, you get a thesis desk in the library. Studio space in the art building or access to the theater or dance studio is given to those who do a creative thesis in the arts.

Wherever your thesis project lands you, the space inevitably becomes a home away from home, with decorations, stashes of food, reminders to call your family, and an accumulation of coffee cups that helps as a material reminder of your progress. There are also funds available if your project requires travel away from campus, such as visiting an archive, doing fieldwork, or using lab equipment that's not available at Reed.

Thesis means getting your hands dirty as a scholar, and Reedies produce amazing work that expresses their passion for thinking, for developing their ideas, and sharing them with others. Many a late-night conversation revolves around how everything in the world can be explained through your topic; the brilliance of this is that you present your case as eagerly as you listen to your friends explain theirs. Thesis gives you frustration and revelation and challenge, and ultimately, an unmatched experience for seeing how much you are able to accomplish through the cumulative education you've received in your time at Reed.

RENN FAYRE

Following the spring semester thesis parade, the entire Reed campus celebrates a weekend-long festival known as Renn Fayre. Inspired by the fairs of the European Renaissance, current Reedies transform the entire campus with decorations and continuous activities. Rooms are entirely filled with balloons for your romping pleasure, teams vie to win the softball tournament, and bands play day and night in the student union. Each year, Glo-Opera presents an after-dark performance animated entirely with glow-sticks, a humorous skit that creatively adapts in Reed spirit stories such as *Calvin and Hobbes*, *Where the Wild Things Are*, or *Harold and the Purple Crayon*. Creativity and imagination reign as Reedies pay tribute to the best of a modern Rabelaisian spirit.

All theses are due to the college registrar by three o'clock on the last day of the semester, an event that is marked by Thesis Parade, an extraordinary celebration in which the community fetes all the seniors who have completed their projects. In the spring semester, the annual weekend-long Renaissance (Renn) Fayre celebration follows this ritual event. Later, during exam week, all students present their work for oral examination by a panel or four or five faculty members, including their thesis advisor. Tradition dictates that students bring plentiful refreshments for their orals board, and respond to two hours of faculty questioning. Orals mark the final completion of your thesis, confirmed with a handshake and congratulations from your advisor.

SOCIAL LIFE AND ACTIVITIES

Reedies' passions extend far beyond the classroom, and the myriad of organizations, activities, and events occurring on campus testify to their creativity and involvement. Campus life occurs within these webs of interest, with people engaging one another in refreshingly genuine terms. With no exclusive clubs or organizations, such as fraternities, sororities, and NCAA athletics, community at Reed has a true sense of openness and opportunity.

Residences

Though it's not technically a requirement, pretty much every first-year student lives on campus. Dorms vary in size and location on campus, and generally the word actually designates the specific floor on which a student lives rather than an entire building. All dorms have students from every class year, and except for one all-women's floor, are coed. Most first-year students share what's called a "divided double," composed of an inner and outer room, the latter with a door to the hallway. On average, the rooms are generously large, and give you the benefit of both having a roommate and also getting your own space. Upper-class students have single rooms and participate in a housing lottery that decides who gets to pick their room on campus first—those with fireplaces tend to get snapped up early. Some dorms have designated themes, recently including film appreciation, community service, and one called "Running with Scissors" that sponsored lots of children's games. Language houses, each with a native speaker in residence, exist for the five modern languages taught at Reed. The college also owns a number of apartments on the west edge of campus, and this is a popular alternative to the dorms, one that doesn't require students to stay on campus. All dorms have upper-class students serving as house advisors, usually called dorm "moms" and "dads."

About a third of students live off campus, a number of them in "Reed Houses" near the school. Original names such as "The Fridge" or "Red Barn" offer testimony to their having been occupied by Reedies for as long as anyone can remember. Most students walk, bike, or bus to campus, but there are no restrictions on having a car. Reed provides a nightly van service that will take you to your off-campus house until 2:30 each morning.

Funding Poll

At the beginning of each semester, the student senate initiates a funding poll, and any organization that wants student body funds—new or well established—must submit an entry in the poll. Every student on campus has a chance to vote preferentially on all of the proposals. Groups that receive the most student support receive priority in presenting their ideas to the student senate during funding circus, which in turn divvies up close to $200,000 each semester. This open and directly democratic system reflects the autonomy given to students in governing campus life, and also assures that anyone with an idea has a chance to see it happen. Groups such as the campus newspaper, radio station, multicultural resource center, outdoor club, and political organizations always receive significant support. More exceptional groups have been created under banners such as the motorized couch collective, cookies for campus, and midnight theater.

I've always been amazed by how much goes on at Reed. It's sort of like an incubator for people's passions, and that means it's never boring. One weekend a group of students turned the student union into a Nerf palace. Another group brought a mechanical bull to campus, for anyone who wanted to give it a whirl. And these are the same people who are licensed to operate the nuclear reactor, who have spent time researching plant fauna in Nepal, who developed a community exchange with a town in Nicaragua. As involved as I was, I also would just smile at the fact that so many people where getting to see their ideas take shape and participate in so many different activities.

Athletics

Playing sports at Reed means having fun more than anything else. A few competitive teams exist, most notably the very successful female rugby team, along with Ultimate Frisbee, basketball, and squash. While there certainly isn't any jock culture on campus, Reedies do a good job of staying active, though generally through life sports such as tennis, squash, or hiking. Reed students must fulfill a general physical education requirement as well, and the available courses defy anything you might have found in high school gym class. Offerings include yoga, skiing at nearby Mt. Hood, canoeing, juggling, dance, SCUBA certification, and much more, assuring that there is something to suit everyone's interest.

Honor Principle

Reedies enjoy a remarkably large amount of freedom when it comes to campus life. Very few rules exist, and students respect this privilege by taking an active responsibility for their own conduct. The honor principle originated, and still thrives, as a hallmark of academic honesty. Professors opt not to proctor examinations, for instance, as an indication of the general trust extended to students for completing all of their work honestly and in good faith as assigned. More broadly, the honor principle has become a terms to designate the way of life agreed upon by all community members. Not a code of conduct to be adhered to—in fact, the honor principle isn't codified or written down at all—students instead have a responsibility for being aware of their actions and of the comfort and well-being of those around them.

The City of Portland and Beyond

One of the greenest, most vibrant, and livable cities in the country, Portland provides an exceptional backdrop to the experience at Reed. The college itself is located in a residential area about five miles from the city center. Downtown, along with the many great neighborhoods around the city, can easily be reached by public transportation. The city has also won awards for being one of the most bicycle-friendly in the world. Opportunities for cultural and artistic activities abound, from opera to Indy-rock, along with an almost endless number of great, inexpensive restaurants. Beyond the city, you can be skiing at Mt. Hood in about two hours, where the college has a cabin that's free for community members' use. Seventy-five miles east, the Oregon coast offers astounding views and lends itself to picnics and hiking adventures. From the Columbia River gorge to the many wilderness areas all around Portland, the opportunity for outdoor activities is beyond comparison.

REED CANYON

Over twenty acres of Reed's campus are dedicated to a natural plant and wildlife habitat forming the headwaters of Crystal Springs Creek, the only natural lake remaining in inner Portland. Currently, the college is engaged in an ongoing restoration project to remove invasive plant species and return the canyon to a more natural state. The canyon's waterway has been restored, including the installation of a fish ladder, in the hopes that salmon may again return to this site to spawn. Each year, Canyon Day brings members of the community together to get their hands dirty and celebrate this amazing part of campus. Every day, too, students enjoy exploring the canyon, whether for a biology research project or a relaxing and meditative middle-of-the day walk. To learn more, visit the canyon Web site at *web.reed.edu/canyon.*

GRAY FUND

In the early 1990s, Betty Gray, a long-time Reed benefactor, donated many millions of dollars for sponsoring fun activities on campus and adventures around the Northwest. A student, faculty, and staff committee plans events that have included bringing singer Ani DiFranco, historian and activist Howard Zinn, and spoken word poet Saul Williams to campus. Additionally, the Gray Fund sponsors trips almost every weekend, from white-water rafting adventures to trips to the Oregon coast or an afternoon at the art museum or movies. And the best part is, all trips are completely free—usually with an abundance of great food, too.

The best colleges and universities tend to be very expensive, and Reed is no exception to that rule. At the same time, the college is extremely committed to making its education accessible to students from all economic backgrounds. To do this, Reed offers entirely need-based financial aid that covers tuition, room, board, college fees, and other related expenses, and will meet one-hundred percent of the demonstrated financial need of all accepted students. Need is determined by the Financial Aid Office using information from the FAFSA and Profile forms. Over half of current students receive aid, which is composed primarily of grants; it also includes loans and, in addition, gives students the opportunity to use any campus job toward their small work-study contribution. The average aid package is well over $20,000. Another benefit of being a small school, Reed's Financial Aid Office can take the time to assist each student in maximizing the available resources for studying at Reed.

GRADUATES

Almost three years after finishing Reed, I am still struck by how transformative an experience I enjoyed while in college. The amount of possibilities I see in the world, the amazing diversity of friends I made who have found such interesting paths to follow, make me realize exactly how Reed empowers your education. The personal rewards of independent thinking, of being critically aware, provide a bridge between the academic and the practical, the theoretical and the everyday. That bridge isn't handed to you; it's something that you begin building at Reed and continue to recognize in everything you do, always finding innovation and insight in whatever challenges you confront, whether at your job, taking action in your community, or simply continuing to explore the world.

Reed graduates take on the world with the same intellectual, creative, and open-minded energy that defined their undergraduate education. Success for Reedies means finding satisfaction and fulfillment in the challenges of the world, and little judgment exists as to whether that ought to mean starting your own organic farm, becoming a professor, or making your way in the marketplace. While there are no business or preprofessional programs on campus, many alumni have made successful careers in business, law, and medicine. Nearly ten percent of alumni are practicing artists or have direct involvement in the arts. A large contingent of graduates work for nonprofit and non-governmental organizations, from international agencies such as the United Nations to smaller community-driven efforts. Most often, Reedies pursue careers in education at all levels and in any manner of ways.

No matter what path is chosen, Reed graduates more often than not attend graduate school, regularly gaining acceptance to the best programs in the country. In fact, nearly three out of every four alumni have earned a graduate degree, and one quarter of all graduates have a Ph.D. Reed's tremendous legacy of academic and intellectual achievement has included widespread recognition for its alumni, including thirty-one Rhodes Scholarships, sixty-one Watson fellowships, twenty-three Mellon awards, and two MacArthur "Genius grants."

Reed offers a distinctive liberal arts education for students who seek smartness in its many forms. First and foremost, you've got to enjoy academic work and find fulfillment through intellectual inquiry. Reed mixes irreverence, creativity, and a dedication to community in a way that makes education an ongoing and open question. The combination of classical learning with extensive personal freedom fuels a continuous creation of diverse and meaningful experience. Smart, liberal, and passionate, Reedies shun consumption and senseless competition and embrace production and collegiality, limited only by their imaginations.

❏ *Christopher Moses, B.A.*

 Rice University
Houston, TX 77005

(713) 348-RICE; (800) 527-OWLS
Fax: (713) 348-5952

 Enrollment

Full-time ❑ women: 1,427	
❑ men: 1,539	
Part-time ❑ women: 11	
❑ men: 11	

INTRODUCING RICE

Established in 1912, Rice University is one of the youngest and most dynamic of America's highly competitive universities. Although it may not boast the lengthy history of many of its peer institutions, it has taken advantage of the unique opportunity to create an ideal college environment by analyzing and emulating the successful attributes of its predecessors. Well before the first students matriculated, Rice's founders commissioned a study of the premiere educational institutions of the world. After visiting seventy-eight institutions in fifteen countries, the traveling party returned to Texas and combined the best attributes of each into their own vision of a utopian university on the outskirts of the young city of Houston.

The Rice of today has achieved international prominence among educational institutions by adapting itself to the needs of the twenty-first century while remaining loyal to the well-crafted vision of its founders. That vision focuses on three guiding principles:

- A focus on *undergraduate* teaching and research led by world-class faculty.
- A commitment to making the Rice educational experience affordable to all qualified students.
- Development of a vibrant yet close-knit academic and social community based on an inclusive residential college system.

FAMILY CONNECTION

Rice's connections to the Baker family have been instrumental in the establishment and development of the university, extending back to the school's dramatic beginning. When Rice's benefactor, William Marsh Rice, was murdered in 1900, his butler conspired to abscond with the family fortune until Mr. Rice's lawyer, Captain James A. Baker, uncovered the plot and preserved the endowment. As a tribute to his crucial role in the founding of the university, Baker College was later named in honor of Captain Baker.

Almost one hundred years after this valiant deed, Captain Baker's great-grandson, former Secretary of State James A. Baker III, established the Institute for Public Policy at Rice. The Institute now lends a meaningful voice to the debate on domestic and foreign policy issues while providing a multitude of exceptional resources to the Rice community, including campus visits from dignitaries such as Vladimir Putin, Kofi Annan, Nelson Mandela, and Colin Powell.

As a result, Rice students benefit from an atmosphere of learning that infuses the campus, both within and outside of the classroom, and that allows them to stimulate their intellectual curiosity while forging life-long friendships with classmates and faculty alike. Perhaps what makes Rice most revered by its students, however, is its ability to provide a challenging and rewarding academic environment without stifling the fun-loving nature of its 2,988 undergraduates. The administration is known for being particularly tolerant of the mischief that often results from the collaboration of some of the nation's most creative young minds.

The intensity and frivolity of the Rice experience are combined on a 300-acre wooded campus in the heart of Houston, the nation's fourth largest city. The campus itself, which is closed to through-traffic and is bounded by an eight-foot hedge and live oak trees, is surrounded by the world's largest medical center; an impressive museum district (offering student discounts); a city park that is home to a zoo, an outdoor amphitheater, and a public golf course; an upscale residential neighborhood; and a lively pedestrian shopping district that includes both conventional and quirky shops and a diverse array of restaurants and pubs. Though students do not have to set foot outside of the campus or the adjacent neighborhoods for learning opportunities or weekend entertainment, they do not hesitate to venture out to exciting venues throughout the lively and very navigable city of Houston. Whether students are enjoying the city's internationally-recognized performing arts scene, internship opportunities at Fortune 500 companies, research projects in the medical center, or live music at the city's numerous concert venues, they consider the city of Houston to be a very important partner in their Rice educational experience.

ADMISSIONS REQUIREMENTS

Rice prides itself on having a student body that is diverse in every sense—from ethnic, religious, and geographic backgrounds to socioeconomic status and political tendencies to musical and athletic prowess. As a result, admissions at Rice is a very individualized process that endeavors to compile a class of unique individuals who will challenge and learn from each other during their four years at Rice and throughout their lives.

First and foremost, Rice seeks to admit students who are intellectually prepared for and eager to participate in the Rice community. Although grades and test scores can be helpful in determining a student's likelihood of success, other factors that illustrate a student's motivation, such as course selection, teacher recommendations, and extracurricular involvement, are equally important. In fact, in its attempts to compile a diverse but symbiotic class, the Admission Committee may forgo a technically superior candidate in favor of another qualified individual with the capacity to make a unique impact on campus life. Thus, strong academic candidates who use their applications to tell their personal stories and demonstrate commitment and perseverance within and outside of the classroom typically have the best chance for success. Nonetheless, the competition is rigorous: of the 8,776 applicants for a recent freshman class, only 2,080 (twenty-four percent) received an offer of admission.

Rice requires its applicants to submit the customary application components: SAT or ACT test scores, two SAT Subject Test scores, an official high school transcript, recommendations from high school teachers and counselors, the Rice application, and a $50 application fee. An interview is also recommended and can add a personal touch to an application while providing the candidate an opportunity to learn more about life as a Rice student. Applicants to the schools of Architecture and Music are also required to submit a portfolio or perform a live audition, respectively.

The Rice application must be submitted in two parts. Part I, which requires perfunctory information such as name and address, must be filed well in advance in order to allow for ample time to receive and contemplate Part II, which must be postmarked by the application deadline. Part II provides students with multiple opportunities to express themselves, including several short-answer questions, a thought-provoking essay, and an empty two-dimensional box that applicants are asked to fill with something that appeals to them (an excellent opportunity to make an impression on a reviewer!). Rice also accepts the Common Application and requires a supplementary form be submitted as well.

Note: Each component of the application receives a thorough review, so be sure to answer each question carefully, choose conscientious teachers to write your recommendations, and watch those typos!

Decision Plans

To help alleviate the anxiety surrounding the college admissions process, Rice offers three decision plans for its applicants.

1. Students who are confident that Rice is their first choice school and would like to complete the application process early may apply via the Early Decision Plan by November 1. While awaiting the December 15 notification date, students may continue to prepare and submit applications to other schools as long as no other early decision applications are filed. Students admitted under the Early Decision Plan are required to either commit to Rice or withdraw their applications by January 2. Nonadmitted students may be deferred for later consideration or denied admission.

2. Rice's Interim Decision Plan provides a unique opportunity for students who are less sure of their college decision but would like more time to contemplate their opportunities. By submitting an application by December 1, Interim applicants will be notified of Rice's decision by February 10 but will have until May 1 to secure a spot in the class.

3. Students using the Regular Decision Plan must postmark their applications by January 10 and will receive notification by April 1.

Offers of admission must be accepted by May 1. In most years, a number of talented applicants are initially placed on the waiting list and later, a fair number receive an offer of admission, filling spaces that become available in May and June.

Rice/Baylor Medical Scholars Program

Each year, Rice and the Baylor College of Medicine offer a select group of students concurrent admission to an eight-year combined undergraduate and doctoral degree program. Admitted students enjoy access to special programs at Baylor during their four years at Rice and are offered automatic acceptance (i.e., no MCATs!) to Baylor College of Medicine upon their graduation. Interested students must apply to and be accepted by Rice through the Early or Interim Decision Plan in order to compete for the Medical Scholars Program.

Getting to Know Rice

One cannot fully appreciate the beauty and intimacy of the Rice campus without paying a visit to the university, so prospective students and their families are encouraged to schedule a trip to Houston if at all possible. The hospitable Admissions Office is open year-round, but visits during the school year can provide the best insight on campus life.

Visitors will quickly learn that one of the biggest indications of Rice students' love for their school is their enthusiastic participation in campus recruiting activities. Each year, more than one-third of undergraduates volunteer to host prospective students on overnight visits, lead campus tours, and visit high schools to share information about Rice. In addition, students coordinate the annual "Owl Weekend," when all admitted students are invited to spend a long weekend on campus to experience life as a Rice student. While you are considering Rice, these student volunteers will be one of your best sources of information, so be sure to ask the Admissions Office about these student-sponsored programs.

With less than two weeks remaining to make my college decision, I headed to Houston for Owl Weekend, utterly confused about my future. I was fortunate enough to have been admitted to several universities, but deciding among them seemed to be an even more monumental task than completing the applications. Once I reached the campus, however, I relaxed and allowed myself to become immersed in the Rice experience. I became fast friends with other prospectives, met enthusiastic students and professors, attended stimulating classes, and learned about the endless opportunities for campus involvement. It didn't take long for me to realize that I felt at home in the Rice community. The next morning, I called my mom and asked her to cancel my reservation at another college recruiting event that weekend—I had decided on Rice! Thanks to Owl Weekend, I was able to make a truly informed college decision that I have never regretted.

The aim of the Rice education is not simply to increase students' knowledge but to improve their capacity to learn and ability to think critically through teaching, research, testing, and experience. Whether students are studying in the schools of Engineering, Architecture, Music, Humanities, Social Sciences, or Natural Sciences, they are pushed toward this objective by accomplished faculty members who have come to Rice because they enjoy and are challenged by the exchange of ideas that takes place in its classrooms. A recent quote by Nobel Prize winner Professor Robert Curl typifies the attitude of the Rice faculty: "Teaching strengthens and nourishes research . . . [by] forcing one to think and rethink the very foundation of one's discipline, year after year."

The Rice Curriculum

The focus on producing well-rounded graduates who think independently is enhanced by the flexible Rice curriculum. Although students are asked to indicate a preferred area of concentration upon entrance to the university, Rice recognizes that intellectual development often leads to new ideas and new interests. Thus, the Rice education is designed to provide undergraduates with the maximum amount of flexibility to change their courses of study or pursue multiple and/or novel majors during their undergraduate careers.

I came to Rice fairly intent on majoring in political science and economics, and I entered my first academic advising session with a schedule full of poli and econ classes ready for the professor's approval. While acknowledging my eagerness, the professor shared with me the Rice philosophy of intellectual exploration and encouraged me to take a more diverse course load. Thanks to his advice, I broadened myself by enrolling in Introduction to Art History, Survey of African American Literature, Contemporary Moral and Legal Issues, and Sexuality and the Social Order, and developed a newfound appreciation for Rice's flexible curriculum.

Students are particularly encouraged to explore the university's diverse course offerings during their first two years on campus. In fact, they are not required to declare a major until the spring semester of their sophomore year, and many change majors well after that time.

With the exception of the Architecture and Music schools, there are no special entrance requirements, so changing majors can be as simple as submitting a form to the registrar. Even after students have declared a major, the relatively flexible degree requirements (particularly in the social sciences and humanities) allow them to continue to take classes in a broad array of disciplines or, in many cases, pursue a second or third major in other subjects. Other students find themselves intrigued by a multitude of interrelated fields and choose to pursue (or create!) an interdisciplinary major. As an added incentive to seek out academic challenges, Rice allows undergraduates to take up to four courses under the pass/fail designation.

SAMPLE LISTING OF INTERDISCIPLINARY ENDEAVORS AT RICE
○ Nanotechnology
○ Biomedical Engineering
○ Asian Studies
○ Chemical Physics
○ Study of Women and Gender
○ Medical Ethics and Health Policy

Regardless of their chosen field of study, all Rice students are required to complete at least twelve hours in each of the general disciplines of science, social science, and the humanities. Most satisfy this requirement effortlessly.

Student-Faculty Relationships

During my four years at Rice, I never encountered a class that was taught by a graduate student, and I was more likely to have a graduate student as a classmate than as a teaching assistant. In fact, one of my favorite classes was an upper-level political science class with only four students—two undergraduates and two graduate students. Each Monday afternoon I felt like I was participating in a friendly debate among colleagues that furthered, and challenged, my understanding of our political system.

Rice's esteemed faculty members teach ninety-two percent of undergraduate classes, and students benefit from a student-faculty ratio of five to one and a median class size of fifteen students. However, student-teacher interactions are certainly not limited to the classroom. The majority of professors are also affiliated with one of the residential colleges, thereby fostering more personal relationships between students and faculty. It is common to find faculty members playing on college softball teams, lunching in the college cafeterias, inviting students to their homes, and bringing their children to campus on Halloween night to trick-or-treat. In addition, professors' affiliations with the colleges facilitate academic advising for underclassmen. During orientation, freshmen are assigned to faculty members from their colleges who teach in their areas of interest and will counsel them on course selection and other scholastic matters until they declare a major at the end of their sophomore year.

Rice professors also collaborate with their students in the many research laboratories on campus. The university's size, resources, and reputation combine to create ample opportunities for undergrads to complement their classroom experiences with firsthand research opportunities in a variety of disciplines. Professors and students alike frequently work closely with researchers from the Texas Medical Center, NASA, other governmental agencies, and numerous private companies. Because so many research opportunities exist on campus, many students find that all they have to do to get involved is volunteer.

Largely because of the factors cited above—small classes, the residential colleges, and research opportunities—the faculty are integral members of the Rice community and are uncommonly accessible. Few students leave Rice without having connected with one or more professors either through classes, the college system, or research opportunities. Thus, most students have several academic mentors to consult for advice on course selection, recommendations for graduate school, and career guidance.

The Honor Code

The Honor Code is a distinct feature of academic life at Rice. All undergraduates are schooled in the expectations of the Honor Code during orientation, and they are required to sign a pledge to refrain from giving or receiving unauthorized aid on each assignment. The success of the Honor Code provides Rice students with uncommon freedoms, including unproctored tests, take-home examinations, and self-scheduled finals. To most students, the Code is indispensable because of the trusting, accommodating environment it produces.

The success of the Honor Code depends entirely upon student enforcement of its tenets. In the rare instances when students observe others violating the Code, they are required to report the infraction to the student-led Honor Council. The Council considers all alleged violations and imposes appropriate punishments, ranging from loss of credit on an assignment to suspension from the university.

Grades

The grade inflation that has been widely reported at other universities is unknown at Rice, and obtaining a Rice degree continues to be a challenge. However, while students should enter Rice expecting to work hard, they can also expect to find every possible resource to help them succeed, including a flexible curriculum, accessible professors, and a trusting environment. In addition, students will find a network of support among their peers, for the Rice environment has always favored collaboration over competition. In the end, Rice graduates are rewarded with the admiration of top-notch graduate schools and employers who recognize that a Rice degree is a symbol of aptitude for success.

SOCIAL LIFE AND ACTIVITIES

The Colleges

The Rice community revolves around and is distinguished by its unique residential college system. The colleges serve as Rice's alternative to the Greek organizations and social clubs typically found on other American campuses, which are expressly forbidden by the Rice charter.

The inclusive college system randomly assigns all new students to one of the nine colleges upon their acceptance to the university. In any given year, seventy to seventy-five percent of Rice students reside in their residential college, and the remaining students enjoy the benefits of membership despite their nonresident status. Since each college reflects the diversity of the entire student body, the system encourages friendships among students of different ages, races, backgrounds, and interests.

Each college is a separate physical structure similar to a dormitory that houses its own dining hall, computer lab, library, recreational lounges, and laundry room. In addition, a college is a self-governing body that provides opportunities for student leadership, innovation, and artistic expression through student government organizations, theatrical productions, athletic teams, social committees, and other activities.

The college system also facilitates student-faculty interaction. In addition to the nonresident faculty affiliates described above, each college has two resident associates and a college master who are members of the faculty or staff of the university. The RAs live in modified dorm rooms within the college itself, and the master, along with his or her family, lives in an adjacent house. All are present on a daily basis to enhance and participate in the college experience, not to patrol the activities of the residents.

My parents loved Rice almost as much as I did. They anxiously awaited the annual Families Weekends so they could attend classes, mingle with my professors at social events, and get to know my friends over dinner at Houston's fabulous restaurants. However, they first realized the true importance of the Rice community during the middle of my freshman year when my grandfather passed away unexpectedly. Having met the Resident Associate at my college several times before, they knew they could call on him to be there for me when I heard the news, provide transportation to the airport, and inform my professors of my absence. My Rice "family" made that difficult time a little easier for all of us.

From the minute Rice students set foot on campus during orientation week, they feel like part of their residential college family. Upperclassmen eagerly welcome their new "siblings" to Rice and coach them on their respective college traditions. The college bond continues to grow over the course of the Rice experience because members eat, study, compete, and relax together on a daily basis. Not surprisingly, the rivalries among the colleges are deep-rooted and fierce. The antagonism always begins with friendly pranks (called "jacks") that frequently occur between rival colleges during orientation week and continues through the annual spring ritual of Beer Bike, a bike-racing, beer and water (for underage competitors) chugging contest among the colleges.

Campus Clubs and Organizations

Rice is home to over 200 campus clubs and organizations, and because of the school's size, there are endless opportunities for campus involvement. It is not at all unusual to see motivated students assuming important campus roles such as newspaper reporter, radio disc jockey, or student association representative within just weeks of enrollment. Rice students also enjoy the advantage of an administration that expects and encourages student involvement in campus decision-making processes.

Athletics

Athletic events are some of the most popular activities on campus for both participants and spectators. Rice has the distinction of being the smallest university to compete in Division I-A athletics but remains competitive despite its size. In recent years, the baseball team has won six consecutive conference titles, made three trips to the College World Series, and won the NCAA National Championship in 2003. The women's track team has garnered several individual national titles, and the Owls have generally finished in the top tier of the previous Western Athletic Conference, and now in Conference USA, in the sports in which they compete including basketball, cross-country, football, golf (men), track, soccer (women), swimming (women), tennis, and volleyball (women).

Rice also offers varying levels of competitive sports for nonvarsity athletes ranging from the casual competition of intramurals to intra-college contests that aggravate rivalries to the club teams that compete against other universities. Spectating remains a popular sport as well—friendships developed in the residential colleges translate into support on the field, whether for a roommate in a championship game or a neighbor in his or her first intramural match.

Other Student Interest Groups

In addition to athletics, many campus activities revolve around traditional student interest groups such as religious and social groups, political affiliations, service organizations, and academic and artistic pursuits. However, students also busy themselves throughout the year with such off-the-wall traditions as the Marching Owl Band, the school's satirical *non-marching* marching band; Baker 13, a bimonthly campus run led by shaving cream-clad daredevils; the legendary Rally Club, the unofficial, raucous cheering squad for the Owl athletic teams; and elaborate theme parties, including the infamous Night of Decadence ("NOD") at Halloween.

Social Activities

Social life at Rice is as varied as the students themselves. On a typical weekend, a host of activities keep students entertained without ever leaving the campus, such as a theme party thrown by one of the colleges, a theatrical production, live music at the coffeehouse, a pool tournament at the campus pub, or an Owl athletic event. One reason why social life revolves around the campus is that students of legal age are allowed to drink alcohol at Rice. Although unusual, the "wet" alcohol policy is consistent with the school's emphasis on student responsibility and is supported by the Rice community because it discourages drunken driving. In addition, many students believe the open policy results in less peer pressure to drink.

When students do venture off campus, the dance clubs, theaters, sporting and concert venues, restaurants, and art galleries of Houston provide them with limitless choices for quality entertainment. On long weekends or special occasions, students are inclined to take road trips to the beach (less than an hour away), nearby state parks, or a college-student haven such as Austin or New Orleans.

PROMINENT GRADS

Bill Archer, '46 *Congressman since 1971, Chairman of House Ways and Means Committee*

Clay Armstrong, '56 *Neurobiologist, Member of National Academy of Scientists, Albert Lasker Award for Research*

Lance Berkman, '98 *Major League Baseball Player, Houston Astros, 2001 National League All-Star Team*

Garrett Boone, '66 *CEO and Founder of the Container Store, 1999 Retail Innovator's Award from the National Retail Federation*

William Broyles, '66 *Journalist, Screenwriter (including* Planet of the Apes)

Nancy Cole, '64 *Educator, Former President, Educational Testing Service*

Robert Curl, '54 *Nobel Laureate in Chemistry*

John Doerr, '73 *Venture Capitalist*

William Maurice Ewing, '26, '27, '31 *Geophysicist and Oceanographer; Laid Foundation for Plate Tectonics Concept*

Marshall Gates, '36 *Chemistry Educator, First to Synthesize Morphine*

Alberto R. Gonzales, '79 *White House Counsel to President George W. Bush*

James E. Gunn, '61 *Astrophysics, National Academy of Scientists, Gold Medal from Royal Astronomical Society, Heinemann Prize from American*

FINANCIAL AID

Rice is committed to attracting and retaining talented students regardless of their financial backgrounds, and it has established a three-pronged strategy to support this aim. Rice uses its large endowment to discount tuition for all students gaining recognition on a national level as being one of the best values in higher education. Rice administers a need-blind admission process so that students' applications for admission and financial aid are considered separately. Rice meets 100 percent of a student's demonstrated financial need through a combination of loans, grants, work-study programs, and scholarships. For families with less than $30,000 in total income, Rice meets all demonstrated need with grants and work study—no loans

GRADUATES

After four years of hard work, students graduate from Rice with a sharpened intellect, a true sense of accomplishment, and outstanding prospects for future success. Regardless of whether they elect to pursue graduate studies, international scholarship competitions, or employment opportunities, Rice grads can be sure that their undergraduate records will be held in high regard.

Graduate Studies

Past records show that approximately forty-four percent of graduates continue their studies immediately after Rice in some of the most prestigious graduate schools in the country. Often with the help of the preprofessional advising programs at Rice, these students have compiled impressive applications for graduate admissions and completed an undergraduate course of study that will enhance their graduate experiences. In fact, in a recent study, more than seventy percent of continuing students received an offer of admission to their first-choice graduate program, and eighty-nine percent of medical school applicants were accepted to at least one program. In addition, Rice students are becoming increasingly successful at winning prominent national and international scholarships such as the Rhodes, Fulbright, Marshall, and Watson scholarships.

Employment Opportunities

Other students choose to pursue employment opportunities after Rice, and the university helps them to be equally prepared for the demanding interview process. Each year, more than 250 companies and organizations come to the Rice campus to recruit, and hundreds more alumni volunteer to mentor graduates in their disciplines. Within months of graduation, Rice students discover that their classmates have spread across the globe to pursue their varied interests in computational engineering, nonprofit organizations, business, environmental research, and other worthwhile pursuits.

Regardless of where the road to success might take them, however, most graduates remain in contact with their beloved Rice throughout their lives.

SUMMING UP

Rice students enjoy many luxuries during their undergraduate careers, including small classes, personal interactions with professors, first-rate research opportunities, an inclusive social structure, and a collaborative student environment. But what students come to appreciate most during their years at Rice is the culture of personal responsibility and self-determination that pervades the campus. The Rice administration treats its students like adults from the very first minute of orientation week through the end of graduation day. This trusting environment is evidenced throughout all aspects of student life, from the Honor Code and the flexible academic curriculum to the emphasis on student government, the "wet" alcohol policy, and the absence of hall monitors and curfews in the residential colleges. Such freedoms provide students with the ideal environment to mature and develop as intellectuals and as human beings. Although there will certainly be stumbles and challenges along the way, Rice students leave campus as some of the happiest and most self-aware, confident, and capable college graduates in the country.

❑ *Michol McMillian Ecklund, B.A.*

Scripps College
Claremont, CA 91711

(909) 621-8149
Fax: (909) 607-7508 or (800) 770-1333

E-mail: *admission@scrippscollege.edu*
Web site: *www.scrippscollege.edu*

 **Enrollment**

Full-time ❑ women: 859

INTRODUCING SCRIPPS COLLEGE

The motto of Scripps College is *Incipit Vita Nova*, Here Begins New Life, and nothing could be closer to the truth. From their first academic day (usually spent listening to a required interdisciplinary Core I lecture) to their last (spent finishing the required senior thesis), students are challenged to grow intellectually and personally by faculty and fellow students alike.

The fact that Scripps is a women's college makes this growth all the more meaningful. From convocation onwards, students are not just encouraged to make a splash in the world—they are expected to, no matter what their field of study. While many students admit to a clear sense of self-determination, most find the all-female environment to be collaborative rather than competitive.

Situated thirty-two miles east of Los Angeles, the lush campus of Scripps opens up like a hidden oasis as soon as one steps through the western-facing Honnold Gate, welcoming entrants with a quote from Scripps College founder Ellen Browning Scripps: "The paramount obligation of a college is to develop in its students the ability to think clearly and independently, and the ability to live confidently, courageously, and hopefully." This driving mission ensures that Scripps women graduate with the ability to think, live, and succeed in an ever-changing world.

At its heart, Scripps is a residential college with ninety-eight percent of students choosing to live on campus. The original four residence halls, listed in the National Register of Historic Places, are each unique with tile-roofed Mediterranean architecture, fountains, and sprawling patios perfect for enjoying the California sun. With the exception of a few rainy days, students take advantage of the weather, studying and even taking naps outside on the large expanse of grass in front of the residence halls.

> *While I was moving into my hall as a first year, a woman came into our third-floor room and asked how everything was going. My parents just thought she was another parent, until she smiled and introduced herself: "I'm Nancy Bekavac, the president of Scripps College." My parents were shocked and impressed, but I just smiled, knowing I had chosen the right college.*

When not in class, students can be found participating in one or more of the fifty clubs and organizations on campus (including the newly formed Equestrian Club and a student investment fund), chilling out at the student-run Motley coffee house, or lounging by the outdoor pool.

Claremont Consortium

Scripps is also one of the founding members of the Claremont Colleges Group Plan, the initial vision of creating a group of independent colleges that share key resources. Today, the Claremont Consortium includes five undergraduate colleges and two graduate institutes. Claremont Consortium resources include the Honnold/Mudd library (housing over two million volumes) and the newly constructed Student Health Services building. Students are welcome to eat at any of the dining halls and are free to enroll in courses in any of the five undergraduate colleges.

The consortium approach gives each college its own unique social and academic flavor, but it also allows for students to meet people with vastly different experiences and views. Weekend socializing frequently crosses campus boundaries with parties and events advertised across the five undergraduate colleges.

The women at Scripps are all smart and independent, but they are not intimidating as a lot of powerful women are. They are honest and accepting and still hold familial values. I didn't much like the girls in my high school class so I was reluctant to go to a women's college, but I soon realized that women aren't the issue—it is how women act around men. In college, nobody has to act a certain way or feel pressure to convey a certain image around men. It is such a relief! Finally, I have women friends who are showing their true sides! And, if the idea of being around women all the time still does scare you, don't worry, there are still plenty of men around everywhere! The other campuses are right next door.

—Greer Grenley, '10, English

ADMISSIONS REQUIREMENTS

Gaining admission to Scripps becomes more and more competitive each year with over 1,956 applications sent in for the 223 spots in the class of 2011. Even before being admitted, however, each student is thought of as an individual who has the potential to enhance the Scripps community. The admission committee looks over each application a minimum of three times before any final decisions are made in hopes that the students admitted will become a truly unique and cohesive class come fall. The Dean of Admission has described this process as building a kaleidoscope, picking the brightest of all the beautiful pieces and colors.

Scripps enrolls students from all over the world, including women from Bangladesh, China, India, Iran, Singapore, and Thailand. This speaks to the commitment the college has made to establish a campus of diverse identities and ideas. The admission committee seeks out women with different cultural, economic, and political backgrounds in hopes that each woman's unique perspective will enhance the community as a whole.

> *Less than two percent of all college graduates come from women's colleges. I wanted to experience the road less traveled.*

While there are no hard and fast rules when it comes to securing a spot, applicants should show what they have to offer the campus intellectually and personally. Successful applicants usually have taken a rigorous high school course load including four years of English, three or more years of social sciences, at least three years of one or two foreign languages, three years of science, and three years of math. Students with a special talent or skill are encouraged to submit writing samples, art slides, or other additional materials that show off their abilities.

In addition to the standard application materials, Scripps requires two letters of recommendation from teachers and one from a guidance counselor. These should be written by teachers who know the student on a more personal level and can relate what she has to offer the collegiate community. To get a better sense of who an applicant truly is, the admissions committee also asks each student to list all the books she has read over the past year. This gives the committee a chance to see what engages a student and what she enjoys learning about.

Of course, applicants must also submit their SAT or ACT scores and are encouraged to submit any SAT II subject tests they may have taken. Over the past few years, Scripps has enrolled more National Merit Scholars than any other women's college in the country, with seventeen choosing to enroll in the class of 2010.

Prospective students interested in experiencing life as a Scripps student are welcome to stay overnight in a residence hall and attend classes with a current Scripps student in addition to the standard student-led tour of the campus. Interviews with an admissions counselor are not required but are strongly encouraged and are available for scheduling at both on- and off-campus locations.

Early Decision

Scripps offers two Early Decision deadlines, the first on November 1 and the second on January 1. Those applying under the earliest deadline should be notified as to their acceptance no later than December 15, while students applying under the January 1 deadline should hear from Scripps by February 15. Applicants accepted under the Early Decision program are expected to withdraw their applications for other colleges and enroll at Scripps.

Merit Scholarships

In order to be considered for one of many merit scholarships, including the James E. Scripps Scholarship worth half tuition for four years, applicants must submit their materials by

November 1. This deadline is separate from the Early Decision deadline and is completely nonbinding. When choosing recipients of these scholarships, the admissions committee looks for students who will become leaders and contributors to the Scripps community.

> *I not only enjoyed my interview, I actually idolized my interviewer. She was a recent alum from Scripps, and we had a long enjoyable conversation about Jane Austen. She was so intelligent, gracious, poised, fun, and beautiful, and I thought that if this was the kind of person that Scripps produced, I wanted to be a Scripps student. I wanted to be intelligent, gracious, poised, fun and beautiful too. I applied Early Decision a month later, and was accepted. I have loved every minute of my time at Scripps and I have become very passionate about the values of women's colleges. My decision was the right one for me!*

> —Laura Guaglianone, '07, double major studio art and English

ACADEMIC LIFE

Forget what high school teachers say about college courses: Attendance *does* matter at Scripps. When a class has only fifteen students (the average class size at Scripps), the professor knows when someone goes missing. In fact, regular participation usually accounts for at least ten percent of a final grade. This helps facilitate the process of students becoming more than just passive recipients of information and instead helps them become active agents in their own learning.

The small class sizes also ensure that the faculty creates meaningful connections with the students. It's not uncommon to see students and faculty enjoying a cup of coffee together in the Motley. Professors are also known to invite their classes to their houses for an end of the year barbeque or dessert celebration. Over fifty percent of Scripps professors are women, and ninety-nine percent of the faculty holds a Ph.D. or equivalent terminal degree.

> *All the women that I met at women's colleges were incredibly confident, poised, and intelligent—features that I rarely saw in girls at the coed schools I had visited. Moreover, I just felt more comfortable at women's colleges. I felt a great sense of support for women and women's intellectual capability than I did at coed schools.*

> —Laura Guaglianone '07, double major studio art and English

While students take many if not all of their classes at Scripps, students also have the option of enrolling in courses across the other five colleges. If Scripps does not offer a particular major that another college does offer, students are allowed to fulfill the major requirements of the other institution. Students are also allowed to fill their general electives with courses at the other colleges.

Core

The interdisciplinary focus of Scripps starts early with all first-year students required to take Core I "Culture, Knowledge, and Representation" in the fall semester. It is a course unlike any other in the country in that it brings together twelve professors and the entire first-year class to discuss seemingly disparate topics such as music, philosophy, and metaphysics. The history of Enlightenment intellectual thought is studied by reading primary texts written by thinkers like Rousseau, Descartes, and Darwin, and is then deconstructed through contemporary critiques. Students rotate between attending lectures (given by a different professor each week) and smaller discussion sections organized around the common goal of critically questioning knowledge production and dissemination.

The following semester, students enroll in one of six Core II offerings that are team-taught by two professors, teaching a total of between thirty and forty students in a more specific but still interdisciplinary subject. Past courses have included "Women in Greek Myth," "Communities of Hate: Genocide in the 20th Century," and "Literary and Psychological Approaches to the Fairy Tale."

The program culminates with a Core III course taken the following autumn. Students have fifteen courses from which to choose, but in all sections students are expected to transform their knowledge into a final self-designed project. One of the most popular Core III courses is the foreign language and culture teaching clinic, during which students teach another language to elementary school students in the nearby communities. Students, who must have completed at least one upper division language course, may teach Dutch, French, German, Japanese, or Spanish. In the past, students have also been able to submit a syllabus for their own Core III course and, upon approval from the Core convener, students undertake the course under the supervision of a faculty member.

> *The Core program provides us with a great basis for a modern, liberal arts education. I have taken the significant readings with me to other classes and endeavors in my life. The program also helps develop the critical thought processes that give you a real leg up in the "real world."*

—*Kathryn Densmore, '07, European studies*

General Electives

Besides the rigorous three-semester Core program, students are also expected to take a wide variety of general elective courses, including at least one course in letters, social sciences, natural sciences with a lab, fine arts, women's studies, and race and ethnic studies. Many students find they can count most courses for up to two requirements (for example, the course "Women and Music" would count for both women's studies and fine arts).

Students must also take at least three semesters of foreign language and pass a precalculus or statistics math course. During first-year orientation, entering students take placement tests and can pass out of one or both of these requirements. While some find the requirements to be daunting at first, some students take a course they wouldn't have otherwise taken and end up minoring or majoring in that very subject.

Joint Science Program

As a women's college, Scripps prides itself on encouraging its students to pursue scientific knowledge, whether that be in a nonmajor course such as "Energy and the Environment" or through a major field of study such as chemistry, biology, physics, or neuroscience. Students may also combine science majors or create one with a specific focus, including bioethics or environmentalism. Courses are offered through the unique Joint Science Program, linking the resources of Scripps, Pitzer, and Claremont McKenna Colleges to offer an outstanding, comprehensive education in the sciences.

The high level of thought that occurs in the science program can be seen through the Scripps students who produce award-winning research projects at conferences across the country. At an international conference on chromosomes last winter, one Scripps student presenter won an award typically given to graduate students. The projects undertaken by science majors ensure that upon graduation, students are more than prepared to pursue higher education in the sciences or continue on to medical school.

Majors

One of the strengths of the Scripps academic program is the ability for students to dual or double major in vastly different fields. Interested in neurobiology and studio art? Not only can a student major in both, but she would be expected to explore relevant connections between the two. Students also take advantage of the ability to create their own majors, with recent conceptions like bioethics and commercial communication and design.

No matter what their majors, all students must complete a senior thesis. For a chemistry major, this could mean undertaking a major experiment and then writing and presenting the

---

Knowledge knows no bounds when it comes to the Scripps College Humanities Institute. The institute is focused around interdisciplinary studies, focusing specifically on a different theme for each semester. Each theme brings prominent scholars and speakers to campus. "The New Documentary Impulse," for example, brought documentary filmmakers, war photographers, and radio journalists to campus to speak on the topic. Authors, think tank founders, activists, and artists have frequently been invited in other semesters.

While most institutes restrict their fellowships to graduate students, the Scripps Humanities Institute is unique in inviting undergraduate students to become Junior Fellows for a semester. Between ten and fifteen students are selected, meeting every week to discuss aspects of the theme as well as meeting with the speakers personally. While other classes may dally on what exactly an author meant in a sentence, Junior Fellows get the chance to ask the author herself.

results. English majors usually write at least sixty pages on any topic in literature (one recent grad wrote hers on Harry Potter). Requirements across disciplines vary, but in all cases the thesis must be a substantial undertaking, bringing together the knowledge and know-how of the previous three years of study.

Off-Campus Study

Over 60 percent of Scripps students choose to study offcampus sometime during their junior year for one or both semesters. The Office of Off-Campus Study offers approved programs in every continent (with the exception of Antarctica). While some programs require a certain language proficiency, many others teach language skills in the host country. Foreign language majors must study abroad for at least one semester in order to meet their graduation requirements.

The Office of Off-Campus Study guides students throughout the whole process from narrowing down continent and country options to deciding on whether a home-stay or dorm life is the best option for any particular student. Because of the extensive application process that Scripps requires, almost all Scripps students are accepted to their program of choice.

No matter what program a student chooses, she pays Scripps tuition, room, and board and in return the Office of Off-Campus Study covers the host program's tuition, room, and board as well as the cost of airfare to the host city. The Off-Campus Study program is anything but a semester long vacation—not only must students enroll in the equivalent of a full course load at Scripps, but all grades earned at the host institution are transferred as letter grades on the Scripps transcript. All the hard work generally pays off, and students come back more independent, mature, and culturally aware than they were before they left.

SOCIAL LIFE AND ACTIVITIES

Activities

The center of Scripps activities is located above the dining hall in SARLO (shortened from Student Activities and Residential Life Office). SARLO is the hub of Scripps Associated Students, or student council, as well as many of the other student organizations. It's also the place to go if you want to start your own club and need the paperwork to get it approved in order to receive funds from the college.

SARLO regularly organizes trips to Pasadena, Disneyland, the beach, and musicals in Hollywood, all usually at reduced prices. Students who file their driver's license on record can also apply to check out one of the two Scripps vans to organize their own excursions around Southern California.

I had visited the Claremont Colleges on vacation in California when I was in the ninth grade, and fell in love with the Scripps campus. With its beautiful orange groves and Mediterranean architecture, I was surprised to learn that I could actually spend my college years studying there. What could be more idyllic? I envisioned myself lying on the grass, eating oranges under the hot California sun, and reading novels. (In this respect, Scripps has not disappointed).

—Laura Guaglianone '07, double major studio art and English

Plenty of outdoor activities like hiking and horseback riding are offered by SOAP (Scripps Outdoors Activities Program) and are open to all Scripps students. Outdoor gear like

RUTH CHANDLER WILLIAMSON GALLERY

The Ruth Chandler Williamson Gallery is appropriately housed in a stucco building near the art department building on the Scripps campus and houses nearly 7,500 art pieces. Selections from the collection, including works by impressionist artist Mary Cassatt and Japanese artist Chikanobu, are put on view throughout the year in conjunction with themed gallery shows.

Every year the gallery hosts the Scripps College Ceramics Annual, the longest running exhibition of contemporary ceramics in the country. Artists' works are selected from across the country, and students are always invited to the opening reception and encouraged to attend the gallery throughout the year.

Scripps art students also make use of the gallery in April during the annual senior art show, showcasing the significant projects that senior art majors have worked on throughout the year.

Dedicated to expanding the knowledge and understanding of the countries of Europe, the European Union Center of California is based at the Scripps campus and brings influential speakers to discuss foreign policy and international affairs involving the European Union. The center hosts an annual state of the EU address and offers internships and research grants to students interested in working in the field of European studies.

tents and cooking supplies can be checked out from the SOAP office for a small refundable deposit for students interested in taking weekend camping trips to Joshua Tree National Park or the beach.

Students are also free to make use of the five-college resources such as the Office of Black Student Affairs, the Chicano Latino Office of Student Affairs, and the Office of the Chaplains, which offers weekly Catholic, Protestant, and Jewish services. Each office plans events throughout the year and offers mentoring and advising to any student who requests it.

Residential Life

Housing on campus has been cozy over the past couple of years in part because the Scripps residence halls are consistently named some of the most beautiful in the country and attract most students to live on campus year after year. Of the nine residence halls, four are listed in the National Register of Historic Places. Some students prefer the storage space and bathroom amenities of the newer dorms, but many can't resist the charm and mythology of the older buildings.

Accommodations vary from standard-issue double rooms, to suite-style living, to apartments for students who want to try their hand at cooking. Most first-year students live in double or triple rooms, but juniors and sometimes even sophomores can land a single room. Almost every room has its own sink, and many rooms on campus have an attached bathroom.

Students who are particularly interested in Spanish, French, German, or Italian have the option of living in one of four language corridors. Most of the rooms in the language halls are single rooms, but residents must sign an agreement to speak only the specified language when interacting with anyone else in the corridor.

Sports

The Southern California weather provides the perfect environment for students of all athletic inclinations. NCAA Division III varsity sports are offered in conjunction with Claremont McKenna and Harvey Mudd Colleges, with students from all three schools coming together to form a joint Claremont-Mudd-Scrips team. In total, nineteen teams comprise the CMS program. Female sports teams use the Athenas as their mascot, while the male teams are known as the Stags. Since the inception of the CMS women's teams into the Southern California Intercollegiate Athletic Conference (SCIAC), the program has won fifty-five SCIAC titles, the second most out of all SCIAC schools. The other two Claremont Colleges, Pomona and Pitzer, also share an athletic program, which creates quite the rivalry when CMS plays the Pomona-Pitzer team around homecoming.

Pick-up intramural sports are offered across the five colleges and have proved to be a reliable way of getting to know other students at the Claremont Colleges. Thanks to a revitalized interest in the program, the intramural program has become more than just volleyball and flag football and has started to include Texas Hold 'Em tournaments and bowling championships each semester. The program coordinator is also always open to student suggestions and is constantly adding new activities to interest participants.

Students who like to do their own athletic activities make use of the Scripps workout room, or the Claremont McKenna or Harvey Mudd gyms. Many students run in the open space trails just north of the colleges and others enjoy swimming at the Scripps outdoor pool, regularly staffed with lifeguards seven days a week. Construction is currently underway at Scripps to create a lacrosse field and a large gym and field house to connect to the pool. The project is scheduled to be finished by 2008.

Weekend Social Life

While the small town of Claremont has plenty of boutiques and coffee shops to fill any Saturday or Sunday afternoon, many students find the nightlife of Pasadena and Los Angeles more compelling. But for those without access to a car, the Claremont Colleges provide plenty to do on campus. Every weekend, one of the Claremont Colleges hosts at least one party, often focused around a seasonal theme. Scripps hosts an annual Oktoberfest

---

WEDNESDAY TEA

Continuing an age-old Scripps tradition, students gather around the Seal Court fountain (named for the two seals who grace the lily pads with a steady stream of water) every Wednesday and enjoy afternoon tea. In addition to the hot tea, hot chocolate, and flavored punches available for imbibing, the Malott Commons caters the weekly event with a new confection every week, whether it be cupcakes, cookies, or chocolate fondue. To keep it on the healthy side, vegetables plates with inventive dips are also available.

The tradition is far from a formal affair, but it provides a tasty break for socializing midweek. The event is usually sponsored by a different campus group or office each week, providing students with useful information and other free goodies.

party held in the courtyard of the Humanities building, as well as a handful of other parties throughout the year.

Outside of the party scene, each campus regularly has film screenings, performances, concerts, or college-organized weekend excursions to satisfy any taste. One of the five-college favorites is the improv group Without a Box that puts on monthly shows on Friday or Saturday nights at a different campus for each performance.

Even with all the activities available, many students find the weekend a perfect time to catch up on homework or just relax at the Motley or the pool.

FINANCIAL AID

Over sixty percent of Scripps students receive at least some type of financial aid, usually awarded in a combination of grants, loans, and work-study funds. The average grant or scholarship award for the 2005–2006 year was $22,350, with over $10 million awarded in grants or scholarships. Scripps students shoulder less debt than many other colleges with similar price tags.

Work-study jobs are very common on campus, and students have no trouble finding a job that fits into their course schedule. Many jobs are actually great resume builders, including internships in the offices of the President and the Dean of Students, as well as the Development offices. The Motley Coffeehouse and Student Store are also both completely student run and primarily work-study, offering managerial and product development positions that can serve as great business experience.

To be considered for financial aid, students need to submit the CSS PROFILE and the Free Application for Federal Student Aid (FAFSA), as well as signed copies of the most recent federal income tax return and W-2 forms for both the student and the student's parents. The PROFILE only needs to be completed once, but the FAFSA must be completed each year for financial aid consideration.

Scripps offers a monthly payment plan that allows tuition payments to be made over the course of eight months.

GRADUATES

With a friendly and resourceful Career Planning Resources (CP&R) office, Scripps gives its students the chance to get a headstart on post-Scripps life. The office offers tips on searching for jobs and applying to graduate schools and even provides the opportunity for a student to participate in a videotaped mock interview so she can get an idea of how she is presenting herself to prospective employers. A conference entitled "Life After Scripps" is presented for all students each year to get a glimpse of future possibilities. The CP&R Office also offers an alumnae networking service called "Life Connections" that allows any current student to contact alumnae who may be working in her particular field of interest.

A number of Scripps students are awarded the most prestigious national fellowships each year, including the Watson Fellowship, the Barry M. Goldwater Scholarship, the Rotary Ambassadorial Scholarship, and the Fulbright Scholar Program.

Many seniors apply to graduate programs across the country and are accepted into some of the most prestigious Masters and Ph.D. programs in the world. Scripps women are also accepted to law and medical schools in high numbers. Recent grads are currently working on pursuing graduate degrees at the University of Oxford, California Institute of Technology, Duke University Law School, and Columbia University.

MATRICULATION

Ellen Browning Scripps, the founder of the college, wanted desperately to visit the first entering Scripps class in 1927. But by that time, she was ninety-two years old and in no condition to travel. So instead, the first Scripps class each wrote their names and hometowns in a book and sent it down to La Jolla where Ms. Scripps lived.

That tradition has continued with entering students signing their name and hometown in a hand-bound book in the Denison library. The main steel doors of the library are only opened twice a year, once for new students to enter and sign, and again at graduation when students leave through the doors, glancing at their signed name on their way out. The ceremony represents the four years spent inside an institution of learning, and hopefully concludes with students exiting more enriched and enlightened than before they entered.

Scripps students are successful when it comes to job hunting as well. According to the survey that the CP&R office sends out to recent graduates, approximately fifty percent of graduates who start their job search during the spring of their senior year have a job by graduation.

Scripps College also has an energetic and active alumnae association that plans frequent reunions and social events throughout the country. Former Scripps students are always opening their doors to other former and current Scripps students, providing homes away from home across the entire world.

SUMMING UP

Scripps is a college where an independent and open-minded woman can thrive. She is sure to be challenged each and every day, and any obstacles she encounters are sure to make her grow into a stronger person. Students are constantly stretched to the full breadth of their ability and then urged to share what they know with others. Learning here is never over and is expected to continue long after a student dons her mint green graduation gown.

The campus is a community built on sharing ideas and expanding the scope of knowledge in every field. Students are never cornered into choosing only a single interest but are encouraged to explore every area of intrigue and connect them in their thinking. The staff and faculty also push students to take these interests outside of the Scripps walls by studying in another country or conducting research in the surrounding community. The learning process is only limited by what a student is willing to take on during her four short years here.

Best of all, the women of Scripps are able to engage in this high-level thinking within a lush and elegant campus. The residence halls are built to encourage community and the sharing of resources, and it is a daily occurrence to hear students carrying on a conversation about the Core I film *The Battle of Algiers*, or any other interdisciplinary subject, from lunch until dinner. Of course, Scripps women also know how to relax from time to time and are skilled at finding the perfect spots across Southern California from Mt. Baldy to the Pacific Ocean.

The women who graduate from Scripps enrich the world with their critical thinking skills and ability to communicate clearly and confidently. No matter where they may go in life, Scripps women pursue their dreams with a drive to make a difference.

❏ *Lindsey Galloway, B. A.*

SMITH COLLEGE

Smith College
Northampton, MA 01063

(413) 585-2500

E-mail: *admission@smith.edu*
Web site: *www.smith.edu*

Enrollment

Full-time ❏ 2,600
women

Part-time ❏ 30
women

INTRODUCING SMITH COLLEGE

While a number of women's colleges have begun admitting men or become absorbed into coeducational universities, Smith College has grown into the largest independent women's college in the country. In 1871, Sophia Smith founded the school to provide women with a liberal arts education as rigorous as the curricula of esteemed all-male institutions. In her will, she bequeathed her $400,000 inheritance so that women's "power for good will be incalculably enlarged." Today, Smith is one of the nation's preeminent liberal arts colleges. Its

Every year, the U.S. Department of State gives out the Fulbright award, a scholarship that supports student projects and academic endeavors in foreign countries. Smith has consistently ranked among the top liberal arts schools in the country to turn out Fulbright Scholars. In 2005–2006, Smith boasted the best success ratio in the country and topped the nation's list of bachelor's institutions producing students for the esteemed international exchange program. Seventeen of Smith's thirty-eight applicants taught English in South Korea, Germany, and France, while others engaged in academic research in countries including Italy, Nepal, and Bolivia.

roster of more than 60,000 alumnae are leaders in government, film, medicine, and academia, and the Northampton school counts First Ladies Nancy Reagan and Barbara Bush among its alumnae.

Smith sits on a 125-acre campus at the center of a town that enjoys a vibrant cultural scene. Though Northampton boasts a population of just 30,000, it offers many of the amenities of a major city like Boston, which is 90 miles to the east. Moroccan, Thai, Indian, Spanish, and Italian restaurants line Main Street, which bustles with activity, especially on warmer days and nights. Venues like the Pearl Street Night Club and the Calvin Theatre draw crowds from across the Commonwealth to sit in a cozy performance space and hear Bill Cosby's stories, Ani DiFranco's candidness, or Ray Lamontagne's soul-influenced sound.

Follow Main Street uphill, past the various clothing stores, salons, bookstores, and jewelry shops, and you'll come across the Grecourt Gates, erected in 1924 as a memorial to the Smith College Relief Unit who rebuilt ruined villages in France during World War I. The women refused to leave the war-torn country until they completed their mission. Similarly, the gates symbolize the responsibility of being a Smith College alumna, armed with the breadth of a liberal education and prepared to throw one's energies into world progress.

But the gates at the top of the hill invite the community to experience Smith, too. The scenic New England campus changes character with each season. Every fall, when New England bursts with sharp reds, yellows, and greens, students may hear a bell ringing at the Helen Hills Chapel signaling one day off from classes to enjoy the peak foliage by apple picking, picnicking, or hiking with housemates. On a cooler day in November, the administration dismisses afternoon classes to honor Otelia Cromwell, Smith's first known African-American graduate. Musical events, films, and workshops commemorate the event, which intends to address racism in a diverse and multicultural environment. On Election Day 2004, Lani Guinier, the first female tenured professor at Harvard Law School, delivered the keynote address titled "Race, Exclusions, and Political Elections." It was a timely lecture in which Professor Guinier's explanation of the political process helped ground the audience with the weight of another close election.

Between the first and second semesters, students enjoy a six-week-long winter break—an opportunity to work part-time or try out a new discipline in the classroom, through an internship or as a volunteer. Students may return to campus during the break, called Interterm, to enroll in extracurricular courses such as savvy socializing or bhangra. Others will opt for stricter lessons in a foreign language and in topical areas like "Changing Native American Representations in Film" or "The Unsung Heroes of the Civil Rights Movement." With fewer students on campus, housemates often veg out and drink cider by the fireplaces in common areas.

When students return to campus in January, layers of snow blanket the ground, and the once Ivy covered buildings are coated in white. Sledding becomes a predominant sport, as does skating on Paradise Pond, a body of water in center campus surrounded by hiking trails and redwood trees. The shallow pond becomes a center of campus activity in the spring with canoes and boats floating on its cloudless waters and joggers circling the natural paths. Professors often eschew the nineteenth-century brick buildings to hold class on green grass outside.

By commencement, a new generation of Smith alumnae leaves the familiar campus cycle to apply their interdisciplinary skills to new neighborhoods and workplaces. All Smith students, who fondly call themselves "Smithies," look forward to this momentous occasion when they can share Smith with their closest family and friends. Students work hard and cultivate strong friendships with their housemates, professors, and staff. Smith alumnae all share a bit of regret in having to leave what has been their second home.

A popular bumper sticker reads, "It's not a girl's school without men, it's a women's college without boys." It resonates with students less because it's catchy than because it fits.

The first time I saw Smith was as I was moving into my house, days before I would begin my first semester. Sitting in the backseat of my family's minivan, I watched my father follow the signs to Smith College, driving down exit 18 off Interstate 91. We arrived at an antique shop, a car wash, and an abundance of trees. I thought I had made a huge mistake. But as we drove closer to campus, more and more cafes, bookstores, theatres, and restaurants appeared. Main Street bustled with activity, and I received my first glimpse of Northampton's lively social scene. Soon, we were driving along the college campus, whose manicured lawns and aged brick buildings presented a weighty sense of history and import. This was a community that had much to offer, and I was excited to begin my career there.

ADMISSIONS REQUIREMENTS

Smith's application materials compare with those required of any similarly ranked institution. The college uses the Common Application exclusively and strongly suggests prospective students submit it on-line, an attractive offer considering the application fee is waived. The application may be accessed through the college's Web site, *www.smith.edu/admission*, or directly at *www.commonapp.org*.

Although some schools no longer require standardized test scores, Smith does. Prospective students should submit scores from either the SAT or ACT. However, the admission committee reviews a number of qualifying information, and a comparatively low SAT score, for example, isn't an obstacle to gaining admittance. The average combined SAT score for the 2005–2006 first-year class was a 1300 (based on 1600), with an average of 660 and 640 on the verbal and math components, respectively.

Taking a closer look at the standardized test scores of the 2005–2006 entering class shows just how varied a group they were. On the SAT verbal section, thirty percent of students scored above a 700, thirty-eight percent scored between a 600 and 700, seventeen percent scored between a 500 and 599, and just eight percent scored below a 500. In math, eighteen percent of entering students scored above a 700, forty-three percent scored between a 600 and 700, twenty-five percent scored between a 500 and 599, and just seven percent scored below a 500. With only twenty-seven percent of the entering class submitting ACT scores, the scores yielded an arguably smaller range, with fifty-three percent scoring above a 28, thirty-seven percent scoring between a 21 and 28, and ten percent scoring below a 21.

FIRST-GENERATION STUDENTS

Among the students who entered Smith in the fall of 2006, a record 22 percent were first-generation students, those from families in which neither parent has earned a bachelor's degree. That year, Smith received a historic number of undergraduate applications—3,427—and enrolled 696 students. Of those, 150 are first-generation college students. Smith guarantees to meet the full financial need, as determined by the college, of all the admitted students.

Besides the Common Application, and test scores, prospective students are required to submit a School Report, including a guidance counselor's recommendation and official high school transcript. The GED is accepted, too. Prospective students should also present two Teacher Evaluation Forms and a Midyear Report.

Regular applications are due by January 15 for fall entry, and notification is sent by April 1. Early Decision applications, which include a commitment form, should be filed by November 15. The college sends a notification to those applicants on December 15. The 2005–2006 first-year class included 164 Early Decision candidates. Of 531 applicants on the 2005 waiting list, 120 were admitted.

For transfer students, the admission committee requires similar criteria, except more emphasis is placed on the student's college record. Between 2004 and 2005, ninety-one transfer students enrolled at Smith. Once admitted, they were expected to successfully complete at least two years of academic work on the Smith campus for the bachelor's degree.

Finally, Smith is a diverse community recruiting and enrolling hundreds of international students. In a recent year, some 180 international students enrolled. These applicants must take and submit their scores from the TOEFL, the Test Of English as a Foreign Language, and the SAT or the ACT, if their language of instruction is English.

By applying to a smaller school, a prospective student can rest assured that the admission committee will review her entire application, and not just focus on the numbers. Important factors in the admissions decision are Advanced Placement or honor courses, recommendations by school officials and the student's leadership record. If admitted, the student will find herself among a group of intelligent, and highly qualified women. Among the 2005–2006 entering class, sixty-one percent of students ranked in the top tenth of their high school graduating class.

Furthermore, Smith highly recommends students complete four years of English, two years of history, and three years each of math, science, and a foreign language. SAT Subject Tests, particularly in writing, are strongly recommended, as are personal interviews either on campus or with a local alumna, a great way to put a face to the college, especially if a candidate is unable to make the trek to Northampton. If the prospective student can visit Smith, however, the college offers regularly scheduled orientations, including student-guided tours, four times a day between Monday and Friday when school is in full session, and on Saturday mornings between September and January. On-campus interviews may also be scheduled during these times. During most of the year, information sessions are offered twice daily. There are guided tours available for informal visits, and visitors may sit in on classes and stay overnight. To schedule a visit, contact the Office of Admission.

As a senior in high school, I had received a number of informational packets from Smith, but I didn't think that single-sex education was for me. However, after spending my freshman year at a large state university and becoming disenchanted with the cliques that seemed more appropriate in high school, I decided that I should apply to Smith, and see if an educational environment among women would be a better fit. I was somewhat nervous about transferring to a school where my class would have solidified friendships during its first year together, but the Smith community welcomed me and assured me I made the right decision. Today, as an alumna, I have no regrets about spending three rewarding and challenging years at Smith College. I just wish I gave single-sex education a chance earlier.

MAJORS

Bachelors Degrees are awarded in
Arts
Architecture
Dance
History of Art
Music
Studio Art
Theatre
Humanities and Language
Afro-American Studies
Classical Studies
Classics
Comparative Literature
East Asian Languages and Cultures
East Asian Studies
English Language and Literature
French Studies
German Studies
Greek
Italian Language and Literature
Italian Studies
Latin
Medieval Studies

ACADEMIC LIFE

Smith professors and students are often on a first-name basis. That's because most classes are small, allowing professors to take an active interest in their students' academic development. The average size of an introductory lecture, which can include hundreds of students at a large state university, is just twenty-four at Smith. These classes are taught by actual professors, not graduate students. The average size of a regular class includes sixteen students, and a laboratory class includes thirteen. In the smaller learning environment, students receive more personal attention, even when they are just beginning to explore a discipline.

Smith's open curriculum allows unlimited choices. There are literally hundreds of interesting and challenging courses at Smith, so students navigate their course of study with the help of a faculty advisor. When a student arrives for her first year, she is assigned a premajor advisor, who guides her through her course selection and helps her choose a balanced and varied curriculum each semester. Advisors make sure their students meet certain curricular guidelines such as enrolling their first-year students in a writing-intensive course of their choosing. Once the student has decided upon a major, sometime during her sophomore year, she chooses a major advisor within that department to guide her through her course selection for the rest of her Smith career. Advisors check that their advisees complete sixty-four credits outside their major and between thirty-six and sixty-four credits in their major. Distribution requirements are necessary for Latin honors eligibility. Students need 128 credits to graduate. They must also maintain a minimum of a 2.0 GPA in all academic work including during the senior year. A thesis is required to be eligible for departmental honors.

Besides keeping their students on track to graduate, advisors are great resources for information on internships, fellowships, and study abroad. Nearly half of the junior class studies abroad for at least one semester in countries including Italy, France, Germany, Switzerland, India, Japan, Russia, China, South Africa, Peru, Brazil, and Spain. After being away, students often return to Smith eager to catch up with their friends and share stories of living abroad. Some students opt to study at another university during their junior year, and may take advantage of cross-registration with the area's five colleges. Another option is to spend a semester in Washington, DC, either conducting research at the Smithsonian Institution through a program administered by the American studies department, or studying public policy in the Jean Picker Semester-in-Washington Program for government majors and those with the appropriate social science background. Students also may enter an exchange program with historically black colleges, other liberal arts colleges, BioSphere2, or an engineering degree program offered with Dartmouth College.

MAJORS

Philosophy
Portuguese-Brazilian Studies
Religion
Russian Civilization
Russian Literature
Spanish
Study of Women and Gender
Science
Astronomy
Biochemistry
Biological Sciences
Chemistry
Computer Science
Engineering
Geology
Mathematics
Neuroscience
Physics
Psychology
Social Sciences
American Studies
Anthropology
Economics
Education and Child Study
Government
History
Latin American and Latino/a Studies

Smith has an outstanding offering of courses in majors including biochemistry, Afro-American studies, and East Asian languages and culture, not to mention the opportunity to double major or design one's own major. Typically, the three most popular majors are government, psychology, and art, but with so many disciplines to explore, students are encouraged to expand their field of knowledge by taking courses in subjects they may know little about. There is no core curriculum at Smith, and half of a student's overall credits must come from outside of her major. Therefore, interdisciplinary education is not only encouraged; it is the essence of a Smith education.

In 1999, Smith launched the first engineering program at a women's college in response to a dearth of women engineers and the school's ongoing commitment to providing new opportunities. The engineering major is attracting a growing number of students. In spring 2007, Smith broke ground on Ford Hall, a 140,000-square-foot science and engineering facility that will be on the edge of campus. Students, under the tutelage of architects and mechanical and electrical engineers, designed elements of the facility, such as a unique combined power and cogeneration system.

The engineering program attempts to redefine traditional engineering education by marrying an engineering education with traditional liberal arts. In 2004, the first class of engineers—twenty women who represented thirteen states and two foreign countries—graduated and entered engineering programs at Harvard, MIT, Michigan, Dartmouth, Cornell, Princeton, Berkeley, and Norte Dame. Two received highly competitive National Science Foundation fellowships for postgraduate study in engineering at any U.S. university. And several had positions waiting for them at national firms in fields including information systems, finance, and construction management.

While Smith is a challenging environment, there are supportive services available such as counseling and tutoring in every subject. There is a reader service for the blind, and numerous services for students with learning disabilities, including note taking, oral tests, readers, books on tape, reading software, voice recognition, tape recorders, and extended-timed tests. Also, free and unrestricted wireless Internet access is available to all students.

Besides the numerous opportunities at Smith, students may also enroll in courses at the area's five colleges, a great way to learn more about a particular field, meet professors, and make friends at the other schools. It's also a great way to learn more about the community and gain a different perspective of the Pioneer Valley.

I didn't realize what a great asset a liberal arts education would be upon graduating from college. As a journalist, I have to know something about everything. Although completing internships has helped me perfect my writing and reporting skills and gain professional experience, my interdisciplinary education has occasionally been a competitive advantage against undergraduates who have studied one vocation.

SOCIAL LIFE AND ACTIVITIES

The range of social options at Smith can be multiplied by five, said Cristina Jacobs, a 2006 graduate. Web sites such as the Daily Jolt and Five Colleges post a range of events at the area's five schools. Students can attend a football game at the University of Massachusetts—Amherst, a popular Halloween party at Hampshire College, an art exhibit at Mount Holyoke, or a lecture at Amherst College. A range of cultural, athletic, and social events awaits students at the other schools, assuming they can tear themselves away from campus life at Smith.

There are more than one hundred student organizations on campus including academic, arts, cultural heritage, and language groups. The Student Government Association, of which every student is a member, supports the projects and programs of the numerous organizations. There are religious groups that provide transportation to area churches, and political action groups that attend rallies and

SOME SMITH TRADITIONS IN JOHN M. GREENE HALL

Convocation—The evening before the first semester's classes begin, all members of the Smith community, including the faculty, dressed in caps and gowns, gather in John M. Greene Hall to listen to an opening address and a performance by the Glee Club.

Rally Day—Students have a day off from classes to honor distinguished alumnae who are awarded Smith College Medals by the president. The day also marks the first time the seniors publicly wear their graduation caps and gowns. In recent years, however, the caps have been replaced by inventive hats of the students' choosing, and often of their own creation.

GET INVOLVED

Student organizations represent areas including art, chess, choir, chorale, chorus, computers, dance, debate, drama, ethnic connections, film, gay life, honors, international relations, literary magazine, musical theater, newspaper, orchestra, photography, politics, professional concerns, radio and TV, religious, social, community service, student government, symphony, and yearbook.

conferences across the state. A capella groups often perform during Family Weekend in October. The weekly student newspaper, *The Sophian*, publishes the latest news at Smith and in Northampton. There's always an event to attend or a group to join. Students seem to balance rewarding academic and personal lives.

Smith also offers state-of-the-art facilities, including a new fitness center, an indoor and outdoor track and tennis courts, two gyms, a climbing wall, an indoor swimming pool with one- and three-meter diving boards, two weight-training rooms, squash courts, and field hockey, soccer, lacrosse, and softball fields. There is a performing arts center, a concert hall, and dozens of practice rooms with baby grand pianos for music students.

Living in a house, and not a dorm, is an important and delightful aspect of the Smith experience. Every house, whose communities' range from 12 to 102 students, unites people from a variety of backgrounds and life experiences. There's housing for non-traditional-age students, and an apartment complex for a limited number of juniors and seniors. For students with disabilities, seventy-five percent of the campus is accessible, and there are services such as on-campus van transportation, an adaptive technology lab, and specially equipped restrooms available. Most students live on campus, and they are guaranteed housing for four years.

First-year students choose an area of campus to live, which dictates the type of community they will enter. For example, the houses on Green Street and Center Campus are some of the oldest. Between forty-three and seventy-one students live in each house, which are in close proximity to center campus. The Quadrangle, which students call "The Quad," houses the most students. These houses, three- and four-story red brick buildings, are about a ten-minute walk from center campus, and house between sixty-two and one hundred students. Some bedrooms provide a view of Paradise Pond, or the green courtyard where commencement is held every year. The largest number of Smith houses is on the edge of campus on Elm Street. These houses, which are a short walk to center campus and downtown

Northampton, range from former inns and boardinghouses to large brick buildings created specifically as Smith residences. They range in size to accommodate from twelve to eighty students.

Houses often host their own social events for the campus community, such as parties during Spring and Winter Weekends, which are designated each semester, and events for their own community, such as senior wine and cheese. Every house also holds tea, an opportunity to unwind at the end of the workweek, eat delicious treats, and catch up with housemates.

FOOD AND DINING

No matter where a student lives, she can dine in any of fifteen dining rooms on campus. Students can choose between Indian, Thai, and Mexican food on some nights. There's a vegan and vegetarian dining room as well as one serving kosher and halal meals to meet students dietary needs. All meals are prepared on-site, and residential students are on a full board plan, which entitles students to eat breakfast, lunch, and dinner six days a week. On Sunday, brunch and dinner are available. All meals are served buffet-style to accommodate busy student schedules. The exception may be Thursday dinner, when some dining rooms offer a family-style meal to which students can invite faculty or staff members.

CANDLELIGHT DINNERS

On Thursdays, students enjoy a candlelit dinner, a delightful tradition where students often invite faculty guests to enjoy family-style dining.

THE SMITH MASCOT

The first women's collegiate basketball game was played at Smith in 1893, which pitted the classes of 1895 against 1896. The score: 5 to 4, class of 1896. Today, the name of the school's athletic teams—the Pioneers—attempts to express the same spirit of leadership in women's athletics.

FINANCIAL AID

At a celebration the day before commencement exercises, Esi Cleland, a member of the class of 2006, delivered an address that expressed her gratitude to Smith alumnae for generously contributing to a scholarship that covered her entire Smith education. Cleland, who was raised in Ghana, said that her parents' combined total income was less than $13,000. A Smith education for one year is almost four times their earnings.

"Clearly, without the generous financial aid award, I would not be here now," Cleland told nearly 1,000 Smith seniors, alumnae, and members of the campus community.

A Smith education may come with a heavy price tag—$43,200 for combined tuition and room and board for 2006–2007—but the college offers need-based aid, and most students are receiving it in some form. Every year, sixty percent of all full-time students receive some form of financial aid. The average financial aid award in 2006–2007 was big—$32,035. Need-based scholarships and need-based grants averaged $21,665, the maximum being a full award.

There is available money for students in need, so applicants should not feel priced out of a Smith education. Cleland, for example, had never braved a New England winter. Funding from the Smith Student Aid Society enabled her to buy a winter coat. Moreover, a summer travel grant permitted her to travel to Germany to conduct biophysics research, and a Praxis stipend, offered to students who elect an internship funded by the college, allowed Cleland to further develop her interest in physics. Through that internship, Cleland coauthored a paper with a leading physicist and was invited to deliver an oral presentation at a medical imaging conference in San Diego, a trip Cleland afforded through a Smith College conference fund.

Students can obtain even more financial assistance through need-based self-help aid, such as loans and work-study jobs. If a student requires a non-need-based award, Smith has offered awards and scholarships that averaged $3,460. That generosity has continued. For the class of 2009, sixty-five percent of students are receiving some form of aid, fifty-five percent of them receiving need-based aid. The average Smith grant was $21,665.

"I wouldn't be standing here if I didn't think that my achievements illustrate to a large degree what many of us have learned and accomplished because of the generosity of Smith alumnae," Cleland told the audience.

"Vince Lombardi once said that luck is a matter of preparation meeting opportunity," she continued. "It seems to me that every time we have been prepared, Smith has met us halfway by providing us opportunities.

The average financial indebtedness of the 2005 graduate was $25,023. Unlike some private schools, Smith guarantees to meet the full financial need, as calculated by the college, of all admitted students who meet the published admission and financial aid deadlines.

Prospective students should file for financial aid by February 15 for fall entry. The CSS PROFILE or the FAFSA are required, as are copies of the student's and parents' most recent tax returns. Once an applicant submits her aid application, she may track it on Smith's Banner Web using a PIN number. Check the school Web site, or contact the Office of Admission directly, for other forms of financial aid and financing options.

GRADUATES

Smith instills a sense of purpose and social engagement that encourages each graduate to make a difference in her profession and community. Smith students enter numerous fields such as engineering, journalism, nonprofit work, and government. Over the years, Smith women have earned distinction as Pulitzer Prize winners, attorneys, political columnists, environmental researchers, film directors, physicians, venture capitalists, and more.

To help students as they enter the workforce, the Smith Student Aid Society offers seniors one time grants of up to $200 to assist with the expenses associated with interview travel and clothing, graduate and professional school applications, required entrance exams, and Fine Arts portfolios.

The Career Development Office (CDO) serves as a vital resource for all students in navigating their job search, learning successful interview strategies, and keeping abreast of career fairs and other opportunities. It's never too early to visit the CDO, and students are encouraged to drop by their first year. The office's services include individualized appointments, drop-in sessions, internship and summer planning, and graduate/professional school planning. Before graduating, students may even send their recommendation letters to the CDO, which will keep the letters on file until the student requests a copy.

PROMINENT GRADS

Julia Child, '34, Magazine Writer, Cookbook Author, Television Personality, Entrepreneur
Harriet Doerr, '31, Writer
Margaret Edson, '83, Playwright
Betty Friedan, '42, Writer.
Thelma Golden, '87, Curator
Meg Greenfield, '52, Journalist
Molly Ivins, '66, Columnist
Ann Kaplan, '67, Businesswoman
Yolanda King, '76, Actress, Producer-Director, and Lecturer
Lauren Lazin, '82, MTV Producer and Filmmaker
Anne Morrow Lindbergh, '28, Author
Sylvia Plath, '55, Author
Gloria Steinem, '56, Activist, Author and Politician

Ivy Day—On the day before commencement, alumnae escort the seniors in a
parade around campus. Then the
seniors plant and ivy vine for the class,
a visible symbol of the connection
between the college and its graduates.
Illumination Night—The night before
commencement, only colored paper
lanterns light the campus, and students
reminisce about their time at Smith.
Commencement Weekend—Parents,
friends, and seniors gather in the Quad
to hear a distinguished speaker—in
2006, it was U.S. Representative Jane
Lakes Harman—and observe the awarding of diplomas.

SUMMING UP

It's difficult to capture Smith through writing;
it's a place whose nuances, charms, and pleasures
require first-hand experience. The close relationships
with professors are only known through classroom
interactions and office hour visits where confusing
passages or mathematical formulas are explained.
Smith is a place where a particular grade still has
meaning, and students work hard to become successful leaders in their academic and extracurricular lives.
But one's personal life is cared for too. Not many people can say they practiced the piano in their house living room on weekends, or sipped tea with their housemates in front of the fireplace. At Smith, the entire
person is nurtured, challenged, and encouraged to
grow. And once the student graduates, her affiliation with the school has just begun. A network
of alumnae across the country and around the world will invite the new alumna to her neighborhood Smith club, so that together they can generate the same sense of support and hope.

❏ *April Simpson, B.A.*

STANFORD UNIVERSITY

Photo by Stanford News Service

 Stanford University
Stanford, CA 94305-3020

 (650) 723-2091
Fax: (650) 724-7489

 E-mail: *admission@stanford.edu*
Web site: *http://admission@stanford.edu*

Enrollment

Full-time ❑ women: 3,079
❑ men: 3,436

INTRODUCING STANFORD

I spent the summer after my senior year of high school vacillating between nervous anticipation of my upcoming life at Stanford and sheer terror at the huge transition I would soon make. Hailing from the border city of Tijuana, Mexico, I thought I was in for an enormous culture shock. I loved my rowdy home city, where the potent mix of tourists and travelers always guaranteed an interesting, if not scenic, ambiance. I was worried Stanford was nothing more than a conglomerate of libraries: wealthy in knowledge certainly, but perhaps alienated from the turbulence that made life colorful and challenging. Surpassing these cultural misgivings was the fear that I wouldn't measure up to Stanford's rigorous academic standards. I was in awe of Stanford; its reputation for academic excellence haunted my summer when I seriously doubted whether I belonged in such a place.

The first day of Freshmen Orientation proved my misgivings both right and wrong. As for my worry that Stanford would be too sheltered, I couldn't have been further from the truth. The first day of Orientation I realized I was now much more exposed to life than I had ever been. Meeting students from Africa, Asia, Europe, Latin America, and every region of the United States drove home the point that Stanford was offering me the world on a plate. I was now privy to as many cultures, ideas, and challenges as my mind could handle. Stanford was going to be anything but sheltered, and the colorful life I had known and loved in Tijuana would be surpassed by the remarkable diversity and experiences available to me at Stanford.

As for my awe of Stanford's academics, the first day of Orientation did not prove me wrong. If anything, meeting my peers confirmed how impressive Stanford students were. They were all so fascinatingly sharp that my fearfulness of Stanford's academic excellence quickly turned into a feeling of gratitude. I was glad Stanford students lived up to their reputation, and I knew I would only be the richer for having such a stimulating undergraduate experience, both culturally and academically.

Life at Stanford is about unlimited possibilities. Stanford students roam the art-filled halls in Paris's famed Musée d'Orsay, form part of the White House's work force, and command the attention of fifteen Nobel Laureates on the faculty. As a Stanford undergraduate, you can make the Galapagos Islands your classroom, or stay on campus and enjoy the more than eight million volumes in our libraries, not to mention the technical facilities that advance our nation's scientific knowledge daily. Stanford channels the world's resources into its students, transforming them into tomorrow's innovators. Stanford alumni are responsible for such household names as Yahoo!, Google, the laser, GPS Technology, *Grapes of Wrath*, and *One Flew over the Cuckoo's Nest*. The boundless resources at Stanford create a vibrancy on campus, infecting students with a sense of purpose and intellectual ambition. Stanford students have wildly differing interests: a single group of friends may include a computer scientist, a budding novelist, or a dedicated public servant, all of whom would be well served by Stanford's curriculum and extracurricular possibilities.

Balancing the unparalleled academic possibilities are Stanford's extracurricular activities. Stanford has received twelve consecutive Directors' Cups, an award recognizing the top all-around athletic program in the NCAA Division I. Stanford's stellar sports program not only injects its undergraduate body with some of the most dedicated and talented athletes in the country, but it also creates a powerful feeling of Stanford pride and unity among its students. Aside from its sports program, Stanford students have created more than six hundred student-led organizations, ranging from the SIMPS (Stanford Improvisers) to the yo-yo club, to hip-hop dance groups. Each quarter ninety-nine percent of the 6,600 undergraduates either reside on campus or are participating in one of nine off-campus studies programs sponsored by the university; residence life is an integral and vital aspect of the Stanford experience. Grouping so many young adults together leads to a rich variety of activities, clubs, and social events, guaranteeing that undergraduate life is anything but dull.

Best of all, Stanford students never have to put their activities (academic or extracurricular) on hold. Thanks to its gloriously mild weather, students literally enjoy Stanford every day of the year. Stanford's perennial sun also serves to highlight its beautiful campus of more than 8,000 acres located in the foothills of the Santa Cruz Mountains and less than an hour from San Francisco and the Pacific Ocean. Students also relish being near attractions such as Lake Tahoe, Monterey Bay, Big Sur, and Yosemite National Park.

STANFORD BY THE NUMBERS

Undergraduate students living on campus	95%
Number of undergraduate residences	78
Number of student organizations	>600
Number of varsity sports	35
Estimated number of bicycles on campus	12,000
Public service organizations housed at the Haas Center	64
Percentage of undergraduates who study overseas	40%
Stanford athletes, coaches, and alumni at the 2004 Olympic Games in Athens	42

ADMISSION REQUIREMENTS

The fall of senior year was a miserable time for me. As college pamphlets flooded over my desk and were strewn all over my bedroom floor, I grew more and more confused over my college prospects. I knew I was a good student, but I also thought that there were many good students out there competing for a small number of spots. Now I know that there are more than 3,000 colleges in the United States, and all that unnecessary stress did more damage than good. My advice to high school seniors is to stop putting all that excess tension into your life and consequently your family's life. This is the last year you get to live with your parents—don't let your family relationships fall prey to the college stress. Pick a few colleges that would be a good fit for you, and pour your heart out into their applications. The application process varies a little from college to college. Here's how Stanford's process works:

Every year Stanford's Office of Undergraduate Admission assembles a freshman class of 1,600 students out of about 22,000 applicants. Needless to say, getting admitted to Stanford is a complicated and layered process. The selection process weighs everything from extracurricular activities to personal qualities, but academic excellence is far and away the single most important criterion for admission to Stanford.

Each of the 22,000 applications is conscientiously reviewed by as many as five admission officers. The goal of the admission staff is to create a freshman class with a myriad of strengths; every student should contribute a valued talent or life experience to Stanford's undergraduate body, as well as proven academic excellence. The Office of Undergraduate Admission seeks to admit those students whose distinctions, whatever they may be, prove they would flourish at a place like Stanford. Stanford values both well-rounded and specialized students; it is important to remember that there is no cookie-cutter recipe for admission to Stanford. Stanford's admission process is truly a personalized one. The application relies heavily on short essays, which allow students to present themselves fully: their motivations, passions, and ideals should resonate throughout the application. Stanford admission officers thus have the privilege of getting to know applicants' personal strengths as well as their academic achievements and intellectual passions.

Examinations

All applicants, including transfer students and international students, must present official scores from either the SAT Reasoning Test or the ACT with the Optional Writing Test. Stanford also strongly recommends that students submit three SAT Subject Tests scores, specifically the Math IIC and two of the student's choice. Stanford has no minimum thresholds for grade point average (GPA), test scores, or rank in class. Although there will be plenty of students with perfect test scores and GPAs in its applicant pool, Stanford is looking beyond numerical figures: Stanford seeks to admit intriguing and passionate individuals who will contribute to campus life and take full advantage of the opportunities available to them, and who demonstrate an intellectual vitality that clearly states they derive pleasure from learning for learning's sake.

Stanford also values exceptional ability in both the arts and athletics. If you are interested in having these talents evaluated in the admission process, consider submitting samples of artwork or auditioning in music, drama, or dance, or communicating with a coach to see if your abilities are competitive within the Stanford Division I program. For information on pursuing these options, visit *http://admission.stanford.edu*. Please keep in mind that these talents will enhance your application only if you are otherwise well qualified; they will not earn you admission in and of themselves.

Single-Choice Early Action and Interviews

Stanford offers a Single-Choice Early Action option for those students who know clearly that Stanford is their first-choice school and have completed a thorough and thoughtful college search. This option will best serve students who are ready to be evaluated in terms of their high school career by the beginning of November of the senior year. Early candidates should feel confident in their sophomore and junior year programs, and should complete their standardized testing by the October of the senior year. Those offered admission have until May 1 to consider where they will enroll.

Stanford does not require and in fact does not offer interviews as part of the application process. Students and their families may register on-line for and attend "Discover Stanford," a two-part program consisting of a campus tour and a group information session.

Admission Statistics

The following chart gives some statistics on Stanford's entering freshman class for fall 2006. Keep in mind that these statistics do not quantify many of the criteria Stanford values in the admission process, including personal qualities, intellectual curiosity, and many other areas of excellence as described above.

High School Rank in Class	Percent of Applicants	Admit Rate	Percent of Admitted Class
Top 1–2% of Class	28%	18%	46%
Top 10% of Class	76%	13%	91%
Top 20% of Class	90%	12%	96%

Sat I Verbal	Percent of Applicants	Admit Rate	Percent of Admitted Class
700–800	44%	17%	59%
600–699	38%	9%	33%
500–599	14%	5%	8%
Below 500	4%	<1%	<1%

Sat I Math	Percent of Applicants	Admit Rate	Percent of Admitted Class
700–800	60%	14%	67%
600–699	30%	10%	29%
500–599	8%	5%	4%
Below 500	2%	1%	<1%

While Stanford accepts both the ACT and the SAT, we do not provide data for ACT results here, as the number of applicants submitting ACT scores in not statistically significant.

Stanford admits students of either sex and any race, color, religion, sexual orientation, or national and ethnic origin to all the rights, privileges, programs, and activities generally accorded or made available to students at the university. It does not discriminate against students on the basis of race, color, handicap, religion, sexual orientation, or national and ethnic origin in the administration of its educational policies, scholarship and loan programs, and athletic and other university-administered programs.

ACADEMIC LIFE

Stanford prides itself on its quality of education at the undergraduate level. More than seventy percent of undergraduate classes have twenty or fewer students, so the undergraduate experience is extremely personalized. Exclusive to freshmen and sophomores are more than 200 small-group seminars where students can enjoy close interactions with professors.

With a 7:1 student-to-faculty ratio, it's easy for both students and faculty to get to know each other. There are more than sixty majors from which to choose, including several interdisciplinary majors, and you can create your own major with the help of a faculty member. In addition, you are free to take any class at Stanford, including the Medical, Law, and Business schools. This freedom to explore beyond undergraduate classes allows students to get a glimpse into what graduate school might be like, thus letting them make informed decisions about their academic futures.

The summer before my sophomore year, I went back to Stanford a few weeks early to take a condensed seminar before the school year started. Sophomore College, as these three-week seminars are called, was one of my favorite classes. My classmates and I concentrated on the dichotomy of "God and Evil." Through philosophy and religious studies, we studied how people justified their idea of a benign god when evil was so clearly present in the world. The sessions were filled with passionate debate as my classmates and I all lived, ate, and breathed this frustrating yet fascinating dichotomy. Since we were just about the only students on campus, and we were all housed together, we developed into a close-knit community. Our professor took us on outings to San Francisco, and we all dedicated one Saturday to helping a local elementary school clean up its construction site. Sophomore College was a fabulous experience, one where I truly felt I was living the life of an intellectual and expanding that life beyond the classroom into the real world.

Overseas Programs

Stanford students can choose from among nine Stanford campuses around the world. Australia, Beijing, Berlin, Florence, Kyoto, Moscow, Oxford, Paris, and Santiago all host a Stanford campus complete with Stanford faculty. Students earn full Stanford credit while studying at these centers. Each center provides unique research and/or internship opportunities: While Florence and Paris are prime centers for art history research, Kyoto offers engineering students great hands-on skills. Archeology students benefit greatly from the Santiago program.

Aside from these overseas centers, Stanford also offers a myriad of seminars that have taken students to the Galapagos Islands, China, Korea, Russia, and Jerusalem.

Thanks to Stanford's Overseas Program, I spent six kaleidoscopic months in Paris. Every day I would head out into the city without a map, with the sole purpose of soaking in the city's ever-changing scenery. One can never fully know Paris; its hundreds of museums are constantly highlighting different cultural movements. Its streets are a revolving door for street fairs, open-air galleries, and impromptu celebrations. Paris is at once a place for introspection and exploration. After a full day of roaming, I would settle in at my favorite café and wonder how the rest of my life could possibly live up to the beauty of my days in Paris.

The following are among the scholars who will enrich your undergraduate research education:

○ Nobel laureates	15
○ Pulitzer Prize winners	4
○ MacArthur fellows	23
○ National Medal of Science recipients	21
○ National Medal of Technology recipients	3
○ American Academy of Arts and Sciences members	223
○ Wolf Foundation Prize for Mathematics winners	7
○ Koret Foundation Prize winners	7
○ Presidential Medal of Freedom winners	4

A Research Institution for Undergraduates

Stanford is a premier research institution, responsible for MRI technology, gene splicing, global positioning systems, DNA micoarray technology, and a host of other inventions contributing significantly to the world. As an undergraduate at Stanford, you will be invited to participate in this innovative research. Student research grants sponsored by the Undergraduate Research Programs provide undergraduates with about $4.1 million each year to pursue their intellectual passions. As with any researcher, students must submit a research proposal in order to receive these grants. Faculty members assist students in the organization and development of the project, but students have full ownership of their project.

With more than 130 research centers, Stanford provides students with the opportunities and resources to research just about any topic, anywhere. Some of the most renowned centers include:

- Hoover Institution on War, Revolution and Peace. Hoover boasts one of the largest collections of twentieth-century political materials.

- Hopkins Marine Station. Located ninety miles south of the campus, students can supplement their marine biology courses with research in this marine laboratory.

The summer after my sophomore year, having received a $3,000 research grant, I headed to Mexico City to study the modern-day pilgrims who travel to the Basilica of Guadalupe every year. Each day I maneuvered my way through the thousands of pilgrims, trying to understand the religious and cultural impact of and on these worshippers. Witnessing the devotion of the waves of people traveling to the Basilica every day brought a new understanding of the power of religion, and its unifying or destructive effects on cultures. My research also exposed me to the political, familial, and national implications of such popular devotional rituals. Although my research ended with more questions than answers, the research was an invaluable addition to my undergraduate experience.

- Jasper Ridge Biological Preserve. Twelve hundred acres within a short walk of campus, where protected flora and fauna can be appreciated or studied.
- Stanford Humanities Laboratory. Interdisciplinary humanities laboratory on campus.
- Stanford Linear Accelerator Center. Operated for the U.S. Department of Energy, researching particle physics.
- Stanford University Medical Center. Includes dozens of specialized clinics. Located on campus, undergraduates are free to attend classes at the medical school, and frequently become research assistants.
- Woods Institute for the Environment. An interdisciplinary center that serves as the hub for all environmental resaerch and education on campus.

SOCIAL LIFE AND ACTIVITIES

Residential Life at Stanford

More than ninety-nine percent of Stanford students live in Stanford housing or at a Stanford-sponsored off-campus study program each quarter. That translates into a community of 6,600 people under the age of twenty-six all living within a relatively small radius. Because of this, Stanford's campus is a vibrant residential campus, full of every imaginable student-led organization, from Greek life to political groups, to recreational clubs, to ethnic-cultural organizations and many more.

Looking back on my Stanford career, I miss the residential campus life the most. I will never again be able to walk down the hall and see every friend I love. The immediacy of having your friends next door made everything more exciting. Whether it was chatting happily about our upcoming social events, or ruminating over the uncertainty of our futures, our dorm halls were the epicenter of our friendships. The intimacy of my residential college life helped me form a new family at Stanford, one that will continue to be a central part of my life, regardless of whether we now live close by or not.

PROMINENT CARDINAL ATHLETES

- ○ **Football Players:** John Elway, former Denver Broncos quarterback; John Lynch, Denver Broncos wide receiver; and Jim Plunkett, Heismen Trophy-winner and former Oakland Raiders quarterback.
- ○ **Olympic Medalists:** Janet Evans, Eric Heiden, Misty Hyman, Bob Mathias, Pablo Morales, Summer Sanders, Debra Thomas, and Jenny Thompson
- ○ **Basketball Players:** Jennifer Azzik, Jason and Jarron Collins, Kristen Folkl, Brevin Knight, Mark Madsen, Kate Starbird, and Jamila Wideman
- ○ **Baseball Players:** Mike Mussina, and Cy Young-winners Jack McDowell and Jim Lonborg
- ○ **Golfers:** Notah Begay, Casey Martin, Tom Watson, and Tiger Woods

Stanford guarantees housing for the four years of a student's undergraduate career. Stanford's small-house system includes seventy-eight residences all located within ten minutes walking distance from the center of campus. The houses vary in size and theme, and include: all freshmen houses, sophomore houses, four-class houses, upper-class houses, apartments, crosscultural theme houses, and a handful of Greek houses. Approximately fifteen percent of students participate in the Greek system, making it a fun option for those who are interested, but not letting it command the undergraduate social scene.

Stanford Athletics—Go Cardinal!

Athletics flourish at Stanford. The glorious California weather, the 8,000 acres of open fields, and the Olympic caliber facilities all contribute to widespread popularity of athletics at Stanford. Not only has Stanford's athletic department captured the Directors' Cup for twelve years in a row, but also eight out of ten Stanford students participate in the athletic programs, whether it be at the varsity, intercollegiate, intramural, or club sport levels. Stanford's expansive campus and idyllic location also provide the perfect setting for hikers, campers, runners, or rock climbers.

A quick list of Stanford's major athletic facilities includes: Stanford Stadium, Arrillaga Family Sports Center, Artificial Turf field, Avery Aquatic Center, Cobb Track and Angell Field, Maples Pavilion, Stanford Golf Course, Taube Family Tennis Stadium, twenty-six tennis courts, a driving range, riding stables, and plenty of outdoor basketball and volleyball courts scattered throughout campus.

Stanford home games also provide a welcome release for students who relish the idea of showing Cardinal pride, often screaming themselves hoarse to the band music of the most irreverent and colorful band in college sports, the Leland Stanford Junior University Marching Band.

Traditions

Stanford traditions are priceless in their sheer wackiness. Incoming freshmen are accepted into the Stanford fold in the freshman right of passage, Full Moon on the Quad. During the first full moon of the quarter, departing seniors welcome incoming freshmen to Stanford with a kiss. The sight of more than 3,000 people kissing under a full moon is unforgettable. Serenaded by the crazy Leland Stanford Junior University Band, Full Moon on the Quad is one raucous night.

Stanford traditions are rooted in irreverence.

— *Libusha Kelly, class of 1997*

Every Sunday night, Stanford students put down their books to go enjoy a movie at Flicks, a student-run movie house. You can expect a rowdy paper fight during the movie's beginning credits as well as dorm chants and sporadic hissing from the crowd. Every student looks forward to the last flick of their undergraduate career, a free showing of Dustin Hoffman's *The Graduate.*

While this list is by no means exhaustive, here are a few Stanford alumni who have made amazing contributions to the world:

- ○ Vinton Cerf, Internet protocol co-author, "The father of the Internet"
- ○ Doris Fisher, Cofounder of Gap, Inc.
- ○ William Hewlett and David Packard, Founders of Hewlett-Packard Co.
- ○ Philip Knight, Chairman and CEO of Nike, Inc.
- ○ Ted Koppel, Television Journalist
- ○ Sandra Lerner and Leonard Bosack, Founders of Cisco Systems
- ○ Charles Schwab, Chairman and CEO of Charles Schwab Corp.
- ○ Chih-Yuan "Jerry" Yang and David Filo, Founders of Yahoo!
- ○ U.S. Supreme Court Justices: Stephen Breyer, Anthony Kennedy, Sandra Day O'Connor (former), and the late William Rehnquist
- ○ U.S. Senators: Max Baucus, Jeff Bingaman, Kent Conrad, Dianne Feinstein, and Ron Wyden
- ○ Ehud Barak, Former Israeli Prime Minister
- ○ Warren Christopher, Former U.S. Secretary of State
- ○ Fred Savage, Actor
- ○ Jennifer Connelly, Actress
- ○ Herbert Hoover, Former U.S. President
- ○ Sergey Brin and Lawrence Page, Google Founders
- ○ William Perry, Former U.S. Secretary of Defense
- ○ Alejandro Toledo, President of Peru

The Leland Stanford Junior University Marching Band traditionally dons wild, colorful costumes and sports uniquely decorated instruments. Known for their irreverent halftime shows, the Band is one Stanford tradition that keeps Stanford jumping. Backed by Stanford's ever-energetic mascot, the Tree, the Band is the wackiest of Stanford's wacky traditions.

GRADUATES

Stanford students go on to accomplish whatever they set their minds to. Stanford's broad liberal arts education imbues its students with an education applicable to any number of disciplines. Among Stanford's alumni are world leaders, technological innovators, and people of great influence.

Career Development Center

While a tremendous number of Stanford young alumni go on to pursue graduate studies, some set off into the real world with the help of Stanford's Career Development Center (CDC). The CDC provides individual counseling at all stages of a student's career planning and hosts a strong recruiting program, where industries and employers come to campus each quarter to recruit new graduates. Stanford alumni are also a fantastic resource for young alumni and recent graduates.

Stanford Alumni Association

The personal and academic connections students enjoy at Stanford continue to flourish after graduation. For those alumni who wish to continue their academic growth after graduation, the Stanford Alumni Association (SAA) offers an education series entitled "Stanford Reads." Designed to connect Stanford alumni throughout the world, "Stanford Reads" includes an on-line book salon hosted by a Stanford professor. For those alumni who wish to reconnect with their Stanford peers in recreational ways, there is a yearly Reunion Homecoming weekend full of Cardinal activities, as well as opportunities to vacation with fellow alumni in various locations around the world. These Stanford vacations have included such destinations as the Arenal Volcano of Costa Rica, the Amazonian rain forests, and the mountains of Tibet.

FINANCIAL AID

Tuition, room, and board at Stanford costs approximately $43,400 annually. Books and personal expenses are estimated at about $3,200 annually. Stanford is need-blind in its admission process, meaning that applying for financial aid does not affect the admission decision. This policy applies to students who are U.S. citizens or permanent residents of the United States. International students should refer to the following section. Stanford is committed to providing a financial aid package that will meet the full demonstrated financial need of every admitted U.S. student or permanent resident of the United States.

The process of applying for financial aid requires filing the Free Application for Federal Student Aid (FAFSA), available on the Web. Stanford also requires all students applying for financial aid to submit the College Scholarship Service (CSS) PROFILE. The university also considers the financial means of the noncustodial parent for applicants whose parents are either divorced or separated. In these cases, the CSS Noncustodial Parent PROFILE must be filed as well.

More than seventy percent of students at Stanford receive financial aid from internal and/or external sources. Stanford financial aid comes in the form of self-help and gift aid. Self-help refers to student loans and part-time work-study eligibility. While this might sound daunting, the university does not expect anyone to work more than ten hours a week, and the standard loan debt per year is around $4,000. Gift aid is financial support in the form of scholarships and grants, and does not need to be repaid.

Stanford also allows students to earn their work-study portion of their financial aid package through community service. This alleviates incoming students' concern that they will be placed in unfulfilling jobs. Instead, Stanford's service organization, the Haas Center for Public Service, helps students find rewarding part-time jobs. The popularity of these community service job accounts for the more than 3,000 students who participate in Haas-sponsored activities. In fact, Stanford has ranked first among top universities in dispensing federal work-study money for community service. The Haas Center also works with faculty to combine community service with classroom teaching. These school-based service programs complementing a student's curriculum include the School of Engineering Precollege program, the East Palo Alto Community Law Project, the Stanford Medical Youth Science Program, and the School of Education's Stanford/Schools Collaborative.

Financial Aid for International Students

Stanford does not practice need-blind admission for international students, which means the need for financial aid is a consideration in admission. Some international students may be offered admission on the condition that they finance their Stanford education. Financial aid is available to international students on a limited basis.

For more information on Stanford's financial aid program, visit *http://financialaid. stanford.edu.*

SUMMING UP

Stanford is committed to offering its undergraduates an education that is unrivaled among research universities. Recognized as one of the world's leading research and teaching institutions, Stanford has one of the most renowned faculties in the nation. Stanford's extraordinary students—men and women of all races, ethnicities, ages, and experiences—are distinguished by their love of learning and desire to contribute in a significant way to the greater community. From their first day on campus, students explore virtually limitless opportunities that fuel their intellectual passions and help them fulfill their academic and personal promise. They are encouraged to share their interests with members of all campus communities, resulting in a vigorous intellectual life outside the classroom as well as inside.

Let us not be afraid to outgrow old thoughts and ways and dare to think on new lines as to the future work under our care.

—*Jane Stanford*

The entrepreneurial spirit that inspired Leland and Jane Stanford to establish the institution and that later helped shape the discoveries and innovations of Silicon Valley, located right at Stanford's doorstep, cultivates an environment of intense creativity. Students at Stanford learn from policy makers, inventors, entrepreneurs, and scholars involved in the most pressing issues facing the world and in turn become involved themselves in discovering new knowledge that will inform the future.

Simply put, the ways you will think and live tomorrow are being shaped at Stanford today.

❏ *Gabriela Gutierrez, B.A.*

SWARTHMORE COLLEGE

 Swarthmore College
Swarthmore, PA 19081

 (610) 328-8300
Fax: (610) 328-8580

 E-mail: *admissions@swarthmore.edu*
Web site: *http://www.swarthmore.edu/
admissions*

 Enrollment

Full-time ❑ women: 772
❑ men: 705

INTRODUCING SWARTHMORE

When I first came to Swarthmore, a lot of little things around the campus struck me as very intellectual. Phrases like "Use well thy freedom" and "To thine own self be true" were carved into the walls of its buildings. Every tree, shrub, and flower on the campus was labeled—in Latin. And best of all, there were dozens of fantastic places on campus to sit alone and read, the grandest of which was the amphitheater, with its grassy terraces and canopy of ancient trees.

But even though I basically had the right idea about Swarthmore—that it was, indeed, very intellectual—I hadn't a clue what that meant, or what four years at a place like that might mean. What I didn't get yet was this: Being genuinely committed to learning isn't about sitting alone under a tree absorbing the wisdom of the masters. It isn't about sitting at all. It's much more than that. Swarthmore, for me, was about arguing passionately, questioning constantly, pushing my limits, failing, and, eventually, succeeding. And it happened among the students themselves as much as between the students and the professors—in the dorms, on the playing fields, and in late-night meetings of virtually every imaginable activity, Swatties teach each other, and they pull each other through.

Founded by Quakers in 1864, Swarthmore College is a diverse community of some 1,500 students and 165 professors in southeastern Pennsylvania. Despite being an easy twenty-minute commuter-rail ride from Philadelphia, the campus itself is a lushly suburban, 357-acre arboretum. And even though it might look like a country club, its clientele isn't quite the country club set—students from all fifty states, more than forty foreign countries, and an exceptionally broad range of backgrounds call this green haven home. They also call it, affectionately, "Swat."

Swat is small by design. When you sign on as a Swattie, you commit to four years of what might be called, for better or for worse, intimacy. On the bright side, classes are usually marvelously small. With a student:faculty ratio of eight to one, everyone can speak in class and everyone can claim a sizable hunk of the professor's attention. On the slightly dimmer side, everyone at Swat seems to know everything about everybody else. Questions like, "Hey, did you hear that thing about Dave?" are usually answered in the affirmative.

Swat does liberal arts like no one else does liberal arts. This is due, in part, to the exceptional range of courses, majors, and concentrations that are available, from Interpretation Theory to Psychobiology. While majors like English and biology seem to be perennial favorites, it's never unusual to see students double-majoring in physics and philosophy, or creating their own majors. In addition, unlike most other liberal arts colleges, Swat has a very highly regarded engineering program.

As you might have heard, Swat is tough. The unbridled pursuit of knowledge seems to be, in fact, its primary purpose for existence. The two main libraries on campus probably get more foot traffic per day than those of most schools twice its size. Professors are very accommodating; students collaborate rather than compete, which takes the edge off stress. Raising the stress factor, around thirty-three percent of all Swatties elect to undergo the unique External Examination Program, taking tiny, double-credit seminars for their last two years, and facing ultimate evaluation at the end of their senior years by experts from other universities.

Yet, as much as Swatties lament the amount of work they have to do, it's tolerable; virtually everyone makes it through just fine. Despite what some jaded seniors might tell you when you first arrive, you don't have to spend every weekend behind the bars of McCage (proper name: McCabe Library). But there is no denying that being a student at Swarthmore is an intense experience. The intensity spills out of the classroom and into the hallways after class, into political debates in dormitory lounges, into numerous campus activities and activist organizations, and into energetic athletic rivalries. And as far as interests go, there seems to be something for everyone (not to mention someone for everyone, considering that nearly one in five Swatties eventually marries another Swattie).

If students who come to Swarthmore have anything in common, it's that they want to be in the middle of things academically. They have intentionally avoided the anonymity of large universities because they want to know each other, and their professors, very well. It becomes clear over the course of four years that this is a school where everyone has an opinion on everything. During the course of four years, you will develop an opinion on everything, too. At Swarthmore, you cannot hide. You also cannot ever be lost.

ADMISSIONS REQUIREMENTS

There's a rumor afloat that the hardest thing about some prestigious schools is just getting in—the four years thereafter, presumably, are a breeze. Though few graduates would argue that this is the case at Swat, the competition for admission may still seem daunting to potential applicants. One recent freshman class's average SAT verbal and math scores were both around 700, and ninety-five percent of them were in the top fifth of their high school class. But it's hardly a lost cause; not as many people out there have heard of Swat as have heard of the big Ivies, so year after year, Swat accepts about twenty percent of those who give application a try.

The secret to admission is being yourself, and being it in excruciating detail. The admissions officers aren't just number crunchers. They ask for the usual stuff, of course, like an essay, recommendations, transcript, and SAT and SAT Subject Tests. But beyond that, they look for students with remarkable talent, creativity, passion, or motivation. You may impress them if you're a student council president or a valedictorian, but you may impress them a lot more if you taught yourself Greek or started a community organization or took college physics for fun while still in high school. Or, they may see something in you that you don't even see quite yet—a significant proportion of Swatties spend their first year wondering why exactly they were admitted to this assembly of minds at all.

If you're considering a four-year immersion in Swat, you may want to test the waters for a couple of days first. The Admissions Office encourages applicants to visit the campus, sit for an interview, observe classes, and maybe most importantly, stay the night in a dorm with real, live Swatties to see what the place is all about. Prospective students, dubbed warmly "prospies," regularly make their way to parties, club meetings, and (of course) the cafeteria alongside their Swattie hosts. If you can't visit campus, you might want to schedule an interview with an alumnus or alumna who lives near you. In general, the Admissions Office wants applicants to find out as much about Swarthmore as Swarthmore wants to find out about them.

When I was considering Swarthmore in my senior year of high school, I stopped by Swat's table at a local college fair. I approached reluctantly, expecting to be intimidated. When it became clear to the man from the Admissions Office that I didn't really know what I was supposed to ask, he started asking me questions: what I wanted to study, what I liked to do outside class, and what I was looking for in a college. More at ease, I had a nice discussion with him and left feeling good about the school. I felt even better when, to my surprise a week later, I got a packet in the mail with more information about everything we had spoken about, and a handwritten personal note from him, thanking me for my interest.

Tucked in a little pocket of suburban Philadelphia, Swat is home to precious few students actually from Pennsylvania. Though the mid-Atlantic states are well represented, Swatties hail from every state in the union and from more than forty foreign countries. Many first-year roommates and hallmates find that they come from almost different worlds. Unlike at many other top private colleges, around sixty-five percent of the student body comes from public high schools. And, also unlike at many other top private colleges, approximately thirty-five percent of the students, not including foreign students, which are six percent of the student body, are nonwhite, due in part to the college's extraordinary outreach efforts.

Decision Plans

Fully eighty-three percent of students accepted at Swat in a recent year applied in the regular admissions round, in which applications are due January 2. The remaining students applied through one of two available Early Decision plans: the fall plan, in which applications are due November 15 and decisions made by December 15, and the winter plan, in which they're due January 2 and decisions are made by February 15. If Swat is indeed the one and only school that you want, it is generally in your favor to demonstrate it to the Admissions Office by applying early. Of course, these Early Decision plans are binding, so you need to be very sure about your decision. You are required to withdraw all of your other applications if you're admitted to Swat and can afford to attend—it may be a strict policy, but it gives you the pleasure of sending Princeton and Harvard a few rejection letters of your own.

ACADEMIC LIFE

If you're really serious about applying to Swarthmore, you probably turned to this section first—after all, this is what it's all about. Swatties think; therefore they are. They elect to spend their college years at a school that has a long-standing, well-deserved reputation for being academically grueling, and most of them love it. Well, perhaps more accurately, most of them have a love/hate relationship with it.

Luckily, there are enough things to study that most students can find something they really want to devote hours to. The curriculum is disproportionately large—more like what you'd see at a school with 2,000 or 2,200 enrollment. Swat offers B.A. degrees in the more than two dozen fields in the arts and sciences and a B.S. degree in engineering, just about six percent of the student body pursues (usually a very bonded and very clever group, the engineers posed on stage at graduation a few years ago with a large sign that read, "Now our B.S. is official.") In addition, students can add one of almost fifty minors onto their majors, with themes like public policy, women's studies, peace and conflict studies, and black studies. If none of the above appeal to them, they may also work with faculty members to create their own interdisciplinary special majors. The most populated departments on campus seem to be English Literature, Political Science, Economics, History, Mathematics, and Biology. Almost half of all students choose to escape Swat altogether for at least a semester, either studying abroad in the country of their choice or participating in a domestic exchange.

Of course, students are required to try a little of everything first. In addition to taking at least twenty classes outside their majors, Swatties have to take at least three courses in each of the three divisions—humanities, social sciences, and natural sciences. Three of these classes must be W(writing) courses or seminars, and those three must include work in at least two divisions. Students are also required to complete a Natural Science and/or Engineering practicum/lab course. Before graduation, Swatties also have to pass a swimming test (we're not kidding), and complete phys ed classes.

Class Size and Professors

While some first-year classes can have thirty students or so, most classes and labs have fifteen or fewer. Due in part to the quality of the students and in part to the efforts of the professors, the classroom experience is both challenging and familiar. A majority of classes are quite small, discussion- and question-oriented, and heavy on reading and writing. Swatties pass a common milestone the first time they discover that they have to read not just particular sections from a book, but the entire book, before the next class. In addition, professors assign frequent papers, with which students often find competent help from Swarthmore's Student Writing Associate Program, the largest of its kind at comparable liberal arts schools.

Academics at Swat are very personal, in part because of the extraordinary way students and professors relate. Professors choose to teach at Swarthmore because they are more interested in their students than in potential research opportunities at a larger university. Over the course of my four years at Swat, I formed genuine and lasting friendships with many of my professors. Because they really have respect for their students, discussions with them often seem more like an interchange of ideas between equals than a lecture from someone who knows to someone who doesn't. Since I've graduated, I've found that Swarthmore professors look out for their former students more than I could have possibly anticipated. They invest a lot in them and want to see them do well. They honestly see maintaining these connections with students as one of the great joys of their jobs. That's part of what makes my Swarthmore education the most valuable experience I've ever had.

External Examination Program

About one-third of students choose to spend the last two years at Swat in the External Examination Program, a plan of study unique to Swarthmore that's colloquially called "honors." Instead of regular classes, honors students take half their courses as double-credit seminars (and often write double-credit theses and create their own double-credit class combinations), usually with fewer than eight students per seminar. Sometimes held in special seminar rooms and sometimes in professors' living rooms, seminars meet once a week for several hours, focusing discussion on papers written by the seminar participants. Between weekly meetings, students are usually assigned upwards of 500 pages of reading and are encouraged to explore all of the other literature on the special shelves in the library reserved for their seminars. After two years of this, the program culminates in one very manic, anxious week when professors from other universities administer both oral and written tests to honors students. Although honors students do receive grades from their professors every semester, the final level of honors they graduate with (highest honors, high honors, honors, or none) is determined entirely by these outside examiners.

The honors program has its pros and cons. As an introduction to the kind of writing and thinking students will need to do in graduate school, it's second to none. Students develop a kind of intellectual independence through the program that's hard to come by elsewhere, and the program is well known and respected among graduate schools. Because seminars are so uniquely student-led, seminar quality depends less on the professors and more on the quality of the students who choose to take them. Plus, the final week of exams is nerve-racking. Emphasizing depth over breadth, the program offers students the absolutely unique educational experience of sitting in a professor's living room with one another for five hours every week, eventually arguing their way to their own personal truths.

SOCIAL LIFE AND ACTIVITIES

The first person to say, "Life is what happens while you're making other plans" must have been a Swattie. At Swarthmore, social life is what happens while you're doing everyday things like checking your mail in Parrish at noon or gathering around the dinner table at Sharples in the evening, both of which you can expect to do upwards of a thousand times in four years. It also happens in dorms (in which ninety-five percent of all students live), in the midst of meetings of all kinds of organizations, at weekend parties, and at sports matches and practices. As a rule, socializing is both informal and intimate.

Even outside of classes, Swarthmore challenges its harried students' convictions in every way possible. It's not uncommon for a classroom discussion to spill over into an analogy-filled debate in the dining hall about topics as common as income taxes and as obscure as exactly how mimsy were the borogroves. Because Swat is such an academic institution, its whole atmosphere is born of the students' shared need to learn and to teach.

Student Organizations

On this campus of some 1,480 people, there are just over 100 student organizations. As a point of comparison, Penn State University's main campus has 30,000 undergrads and 400 student organizations. Of course, like everything at Swat, many of its organizations are pretty small. Vocal and instrumental music groups, student publications, and ethnic and gay/lesbian groups attract a loyal following, as do less traditional groups such as men's and women's rugby, the volunteer firefighters, Motherpuckers (ice hockey club), Swarthmore Warders of Imaginative Literature, Vertigo-go (improvisational comedy), and Ultimate Frisbee. Every fall, these and other campus organizations gather at the Activities Fair, where they set up their tables in a big circle and recruit new students. This happens, like most everything else at Swat, on Parrish lawn, or beach, as the locals like to call it. It gets its name in part because people tend to read, sleep, and sunbathe on it in the warmer months, and in part because it's equipped with massive white Adirondack chairs in which to see and be seen.

In general, campus clubs and organizations thrive because they involve almost everyone. Aspiring professional musicians and actors obviously won't be turned away, but most people who participate in these activities are aspiring doctors, economists, and writers who just happen to be amateur singers and actors.

Politics

When they're not studying or playing, some Swatties are off trying to change the world. By any measure, Swarthmore is politically active. Environmental, human rights, and women's groups write letters and organize boycotts while several volunteer groups travel to nearby Chester and Philadelphia to offer food and tutoring to those in need. Politically, the students (and faculty) are legendary for leaning to the left. In a case that amused the local press a few years ago, there was heated debate among the students over whether to raise an American flag over Parrish; some students said it represented values they didn't share. Of course, some groups, like the Swarthmore Conservative Union, aim to change the world by first changing Swat. Through their organization, such prominent conservatives as William F. Buckley, Jr. and Phyllis Schlafly have made their way to campus on speaking tours.

Sports

More than twenty percent of students find time to compete on one of twenty-two varsity teams in the NCAA's Division III. Needless to say, these aren't nationally televised games, but many of the teams advance to regional and even national competitions. Just as impressive is the fact that almost a third of the campus competes in interscholastic play. The swimming, men's and women's tennis, field hockey, and men's lacrosse have seen post-season play in recent years, and many other teams have been competitive. There are varsity teams, club teams (which compete with other colleges and clubs, but are student-run) and a whole host of intramural sports on campus. All students who don't participate in interscholastic sports are required to spend two semesters taking such physical education classes as weight training, swimming, or dance.

Parties

Finally, Swatties let off steam every weekend at parties. As with on-campus lectures, performances, and other events, parties at Swat are almost always free of charge. Most parties are hosted by clubs or informal groups of friends. (There are two fraternities on campus, but they're tiny, nonresidential, and nothing like *Animal House*.) As far as parties are concerned, the good news is that there are several interesting get-togethers each weekend, and the bad news is that they are usually at the same half dozen places with all the same people. During your first few years at Swat, you will probably enjoy these places and these people and everything will work out fine. Sometime around junior year, you and your friends may choose instead to spend your precious free time at off-campus parties and in coffee shops in Philly, a short ride away on the train. And, in case you wondered, there's little in the way of bar-hopping to do in the village of Swarthmore.

There are some interesting places to explore at Swat when you're not in the library.

○ The extensive Crum Woods, featuring Crumhenge, a large circle of stones that are there for no particular reason.

○ The nineteenth-century Sproul Observatory, featured in the film *Addicted to Love* with Matthew Broderick and Meg Ryan.

○ The verdant Scott amphitheater, in which everyone eventually gets a diploma.

○ The Arboretum's prized rose garden outside Parrish.

○ The "ruins garden" outside Kohlberg, built where the old Parrish Annex once stood.

○ Philadelphia and the surrounding suburbs, via Swat's on-campus train station.

Swarthmore has been nicknamed "the Quaker matchbox," but that's not entirely accurate—even though the college maintains some Quaker philosophies and traditions, I've noticed few actual Quakers here, and even though some people make matches and go on to marry each other, there is very little casual dating. In general, I think Swatties would probably rather spend two hours talking about the business environment in Hungary with a friend from their economics seminar than head out to a fraternity for a few beers. That doesn't mean we don't have social lives; it just means our social lives are a little unusual at times.

FINANCIAL AID

With an over $1 billion endowment and a commitment to completely need-blind admissions, Swarthmore's not a bad choice for those whose finances aren't quite as stellar as their SAT scores. As part of its commitment to diversity, Swat tries to attract bright students from all kinds of financial backgrounds, and retain them with rather generous aid. In fact, more than half of the student body—including many international students—receives some kind of financial aid, whether in the form of grants, loans, or work study. And the campus jobs students use to pay the bills aren't that bad either; working as research associates with their professors, at the libraries, as tour guides, and as assistants in administrative and academic departments, students get pretty useful work experience along with much-needed cash.

The average financial aid award at Swat is $30,126—most of it in scholarships. To give you an idea of how far this aid goes, in 2006, tuition, fees, room, and board together totaled $43,532. The average amount parents of aided students are expected to pay is $13,281 (median is $11,960). The loan component of Swarthmore's aid awards is intentionally low—an average of $2,332 each year—so that students will be free to make decisions about major and career without worry about debt repayment. Because the load burden is so low, a significant number of Swarthmore students are able to go on to careers in teach, research, social service, and the like.

In addition to regular aid, Swat offers two major scholarships: The McCabe Achievement Awards and Evans Scholarships are given every year to incoming students with superior leadership qualities. The Lang Opportunity Grants for Social Action (part of the $50 million Eugene Lang has donated to date) provide support for social service projects, for students with strong community service backgrounds to sophomores.

GRADUATES

Having made the transition to adulthood together in classrooms, dorm rooms, and Sharples dining hall, Swatties tend to grow in the same directions even many years after graduation. About a quarter of current alumni have chosen academic careers of some kind, be they as professors, researchers, teachers, or authors. Others land jobs in government, medicine, journalism, and business, often in offices and agencies alongside one another. Whatever their individual experiences may have been at Swat, most alumni expect that students coming out of Swarthmore are first-rate; a lot of Swatties get their first jobs (and even summer internships) from older Swatties. It may be a kind of nepotism, but it's not a bad route to take.

Immediately after graduation, about twenty percent of grads go directly to graduate and professional schools. Among those who don't go to graduate school right away, jobs in research, consulting, and teaching are popular. The college's Career Services Office has extensive resources and coordinates several rounds of on-campus recruiting for seniors. Within five years, a stunning over half of Swatties are back at the books, whether at graduate school, law school, medical school, or business school. Clearly a cerebral bunch, alumni of Swarthmore include five Nobel

- Michael Dukakis, Former Governor of Massachusetts and Presidential Candidate
- Eugene Lang, Founder of the I Have A Dream program
- Carl Levin, U.S. Senator
- James Michener, Author
- Alice Paul, Suffragist, Author of the Equal Rights Amendment
- Molly Yard, Former President of the National Organization for Women

Laureates, nineteen recipients of MacArthur genius grants, thirty-six members of the prestigious National Academy of Sciences, and more Ph.D.s per capita than almost any other school in the country. Not bad for a group of 18,000.

Just as admirable is the fact that alumni all over the country regularly make their names and addresses available to other, especially young, alumni who may want a place to stay while traveling through. They're a closely knit crowd, probably because there just aren't that many intensely studious, liberal, somewhat neurotic people out there in the general public.

Every June, approximately 350 people join the ranks of Swarthmore alumni. A few leave intellectually exhausted, wondering whether they might not have fared better as bigger fish in smaller ponds. But despite being pushed to their limits, most Swatties are energized by the experience, and roll that energy into building promising careers.

SUMMING UP

As with most everything else in life, what you get out of Swarthmore depends a lot on what you put into it. Intimate, liberal, and intense in every way, Swarthmore requires of its students a very personal, four-year investment of time, creative energy, and, above all, self. In return for this investment, Swatties get a diploma, a set of friends for life, an acute understanding of themselves and their fields of study, and a profound sense of accomplishment at having done it all. That's the deal.

That said, it is perhaps just as important to understand what you *won't* get at Swat. Even though Swat was recently number one on *U.S. News & World Report*'s list of liberal arts colleges, a Swarthmore degree won't command the kind of immediate respect from the general public that a degree from a big Ivy League school will. If you choose Swarthmore, you won't always feel confident, and you won't leave college with exclusively sunny memories of carefree days and wild parties. And no matter how much Swatties try to explain their experience to friends and colleagues, some people out there will never appreciate what a challenge this little Pennsylvania college can be. In general, if you want to get the greatest acclaim for the least possible pain, you might want to avoid Swat. Similarly, if you don't really enjoy losing yourself in your reading, your writing, or your calculations, Swarthmore isn't the place for you.

But despite what you hear from guidebooks like this one, there's a lot more than just dry studying going on on this campus. Beyond the memories of papers, exams, and stress, Swat alumni treasure the memories of certain little ceremonies and traditions, some of which are so much a part of everyday Swat that they go unappreciated until after graduation. For instance, at midnight the night before finals begin every semester, all 1,479 people on campus lean out their dorm windows and join the primal scream. Every April Fool's Day, a set of students (often the engineers) puts together a programmatic plan of pranks that affect—and amuse—the whole campus. At the end of every semester, professors invite all of the students in their seminars to their houses for homemade seminar dinners. And every year on graduation day, the seniors pick roses from the Arboretum's prized rose garden and pin them onto their graduation gowns.

When it's all said and done, Swarthmore remains highly admirable year after year primarily because of the special batch of young people it attracts. Energetic, diverse, imaginative, and always inquisitive, the students of this little college consistently teach each other—and often their professors—a lot about both books and life.

> *When things got tough academically, and they did get tough, my father liked to remind me why I had chosen Swarthmore in the first place. I wanted, for the first time in my life, to be average. I wanted to be around people who performed better than I did, people from whom I could learn. I wouldn't recommend Swarthmore to everyone, but for those made of Swattie material, it's right, and it feels like coming home.*

> ❏ *Sylvia Weedman, B.A.*

Tufts University
Medford, MA 02155

(617) 627-3170
Fax: (617) 627-3860

E-mail: *admissions.inquiry@ase.tufts.edu*
Web-site: *http://admissions.tufts.edu/*

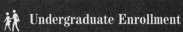 **Undergraduate Enrollment**

Full-time ❑ women: 2,492
❑ men: 2,446

Part-time ❑ women: 34
❑ men: 23

INTRODUCING TUFTS UNIVERSITY

Founded in 1852, Tufts University has grown from a small, regional college to a world-renowned, major research university whose 5,000 undergraduates come from more than sixty-five countries. Regardless of where they are from, Tufts students, staff, and faculty all share the common goal of using their intellects to better the world, whether it is working in rural Ghana to stop the spread of parasitic diseases found in local water sources or volunteering in Boston as translators for recent Vietnamese immigrants.

A Tufts education "will inspire [you] to get out into the world and shake things up, tear things down, and make things better."

—Kyle Halle-Erbe,'10

Referred to by President Larry Bacow as a small university with a sense of intimacy, Tufts nurtures the development of global scholars and leaders by combining the best aspects of small liberal arts colleges—discussion and inquiry-based classes; close relationships with professors—and the best attributes of large research universities—funding and support for undergraduate research; award-winning, internationally recognized faculty. Emphasizing the importance of intellectual exploration and interdisciplinary education, Tufts fosters the growth of poetry-writing engineers, political activist premed students, and environmentally conscious entrepreneurs. Although students are enrolled in either the school of engineering or the school of liberal arts, classes in each school are open to all undergraduates. Undergraduate students also benefit from the resources and research opportunities available at Tufts' eight graduate schools, including the School of Medicine, School of Dental Medicine, School of Veterinary Medicine, Nutrition School, and Fletcher School of Law and Diplomacy, the nation's oldest and arguably most prestigious graduate school in international relations.

A national leader in active citizenship, Tufts is home to the Jonathan M. Tisch College of Citizenship and Public Service. In May 2006, six years after its founding, Tufts alumnus Jonathan M. Tisch's generous $40 million endowment gift ensured the college's future as a university fixture. Integrating active citizenship into the curriculum, Tisch College facilitates collaboration between civic-minded students and faculty who aspire to solve complex real-world problems. Recent student-initiated projects include biomedical engineers utilizing light spectroscopy for breast cancer screening and studio art students examining art and social change as reflected through graffiti.

Located just five miles northwest of Boston, Tufts' beautiful 150-acre New England college campus rests upon Walnut Hill and overlooks the city skyline. The campus is a short walk or shuttle bus ride from Davis Square, a bustling social center that is home to independent coffee shops, live music venues, delicious ethnic food, and one of Boston's best used-bookstores. Davis Square, located on the Red Line of the subway, also provides students with easy access into Boston, where students often grab dinner in the North End (Boston's "Little Italy"), visit the Museum of Fine Arts (where Tufts students receive free admission), or catch a Red Sox or Celtics game.

Although students appreciate Boston's accessibility, the heart of undergraduate life is found on campus, home to more than 3,300 students and 200 thriving student-run organizations. Students who live on campus have the option of choosing between single-sex and coed dormitories, on-campus apartments, fraternity and sorority houses, and numerous culture units, including the Africana, Latino, Asian American, International, Jewish, Muslim, Spanish, French, German, Russian, Arts, Crafts, and Substance Free Culture Units. All first- and second-year students are required to live on campus; many third- and fourth-year students choose to live with friends in off-campus apartments immediately surrounding the university.

Construction vehicles and hard hats have been a common site on campus recently. Two major construction projects were recently completed. Sophia Gordon Hall, an environmentally friendly "green" dormitory that houses 125 seniors, opened its doors in the fall of 2006. The university's new music building, home to the music department and a new 300-seat, acoustically engineered, recording-quality auditorium, was completed in January of 2007. Other campus improvements within the past couple of years include the construction of a $2 million boathouse on the Malden River for Tufts' crew teams, the renovation of West Hall, a residence hall since 1872 that is a favorite amongst students and known for its spacious rooms and prime location on the academic quad, and the revamping of Cabot Auditorium and the Fletcher School of Law and Diplomacy.

Tufts is an eclectic and dynamic community of passionate students from a wide variety of geographic, racial, ethnic, socioeconomic, religious, and cultural backgrounds. Students of color and international students make up more than a third of the undergraduate study body. It is not unusual for a first-year student from Chicago to be roommates with a student from Seattle and neighbors with a student from Hong Kong and a student from Texas. The diversity within the undergraduate student body creates a stimulating, intellectual community in which students are constantly learning in the classrooms from their first-rate professors and outside the classroom from their eclectic classmates.

ADMISSIONS REQUIREMENTS

Once a moderately selective regional college, Tufts has transformed itself over the past twenty-five years into a most-selective international university. Students applying to Tufts are required to submit the Common Application and the Tufts Supplement form. Last year twenty-seven percent of the 15,300 applicants were offered admission to either the school of liberal arts or the school of engineering. The fact that the admissions process is highly selective should not discourage applicants from applying since the application review process at Tufts is holistic.

As Dean of Admissions Lee Coffin likes to say, a student's application is made up of two parts: the "data" (a student's academic performance) and the "voice" (a student's extracurricular activities, recommendations, and essays). According to the admissions office, the vast majority of Tufts applicants are academically "qualified" to succeed in the classroom. With that in mind, it is important for applicants to realize that although the data certainly does play an important role in the admissions process, the voice is just as, if not more, important.

The data portion of a student's application consists of the high school transcript and standardized test scores. In addition to reviewing students' grades, Tufts evaluates each applicant's curricular rigor and gives preference to students who have challenged themselves by taking AP, IB, and honors classes, or the most demanding classes available to them.

The university also requires students to submit either the SAT exam and two additional SAT Subject Tests or the ACT exam with writing. Students applying to the school of engineering who submit the SAT should submit an SAT Subject Test in math and a Subject Test in either physics or chemistry. For students accepted into the class of 2010, the mid-50 percentile range for the SAT math, critical reading, and writing exams was 680–760, and the mean composite ACT score was 31. Although the admissions committee does take standardized testing into consideration, it is but one of many factors in the admissions process. Students who fall within or exceed the mid-50 percentile are not guaranteed admission and students who score below the mid-50 percentile may not be denied admission. Students who do not speak English as a first language are required to submit the Test of English as a Foreign Language (TOEFL) exam as well.

The voice portion of a student's application is often what distinguishes him or her from the thousands of other Tufts applicants. Admissions officers rely on extracurricular activities, recommendations, essays, and an optional alumni interview to get a better sense of who the applicant is and how he or she would add to the Tufts campus.

Given the importance Tufts places on active citizenship and leadership, admissions officers want to know what students have been up to outside of the classroom. Be it community service, music, athletics, arts, entrepreneurship, or employment, Tufts places an emphasis on the quality of a student's involvement rather than the number of activities in which a student has participated.

Students are required to submit one recommendation from a teacher in a major subject area (math, science, social studies, English, foreign language) that they have had in either their junior or senior year. The best teacher recommendations come from teachers who know students well and are able to share stories, fond memories, and personal anecdotes with the admissions committee. A strong teacher recommendation can carry considerable weight with the admissions committee and almost always strengthens the voice of the application. Additional recommendations are welcomed if the student believes that the extra recommendation will add new information to the application.

Perhaps the most important part of the voice, student essays play a significant role in the application review process. In addition to submitting a 250- to 500-word personal statement, applicants are given the option to write a few short essays in response to creative and innovative questions that change annually. Past prompts include: "A high school curriculum does not always afford much intellectual freedom. Describe one of your unsatisfied intellectual passions. How might you apply this interest to serve the common good and make a difference in society?" and "Create a short story using one of the following topics: The end of MTV; Confessions of a Middle School Bully; The Professor Disappeared; The Mysterious Lab." Students are discouraged from writing essays about banal topics, such as a community service trip, the "big game" or "big shot," or one's love for grandma and grandpa.

All interviews for Tufts are optional and are conducted by local area alumni who are part of the Tufts Alumni Admissions Program (TAAP). After a student submits the Tufts Supplement Form, the admissions office will notify an alumni interviewer in the students' local area who will in turn contact the applicant to schedule an interview. Interviews often take place at coffee shops, bookstores, libraries, and other public locations agreed upon by both the applicant and interviewer. The purpose of the interview is twofold: first, to provide students with another opportunity to add to the voice of their application and, second, to learn more about Tufts through the experiences of the alumni interviewer. In a typical year more than 10,000 interviews are completed by dedicated TAAPers who volunteer hours of their time to remain connected to the university and to advocate for applicants from their local area. Since interviews are optional; students who are not able to complete an alumni interview are not at a disadvantage in the admissions process.

Students have the option of applying to Tufts Early Decision (ED) I, Early Decision (ED) II, or Regular Decision. Both Early Decision rounds are binding, meaning that if admitted the applicant is required to attend Tufts and withdraw any applications to other colleges. The only difference between Early Decision I and Early Decision II is the application deadline (November 1 for ED I and January 1 for ED II). Students who apply Early Decision are notified of their admissions decision approximately one month after the application deadline. The Regular Decision application deadline is January 1, and all applicants are notified of their decision by April 1. The current application fee is $70. Students who are unable to pay the application fee should contact their guidance counselor or the Tufts admissions office to inquire about obtaining a fee waiver.

Whether it is meeting with a student during office hours, grabbing coffee at the library's Tower Café (where beverages are on the house when a student and professor go in together), or inviting students to their houses for dinner or a barbecue, Tufts professors take a genuine interest in the lives of undergraduates, both inside and outside of the classroom. With an average class size of twenty and a student-to-faculty ratio of seven-to-one, classes tend to be discussion- and inquiry-based and require students to come to class prepared and ready to contribute to the learning process.

With an aim of providing students with a broad-based liberal arts and engineering education, Tufts students are encouraged to explore their academic interests by taking classes in any academic department within the university. The most popular majors within the school of liberal arts are international relations, English, political science, and psychology. Tufts is also recognized for its first-rate programs in history, philosophy, child development, biomedical engineering, and community health. Mechanical engineering and electrical engineering are the two most popular majors within the school of engineering, though the biomedical engineering program has experienced tremendous growth and has increased in popularity in recent years. More than forty percent of students—across disciplines—will choose to spend a semester or a year studying abroad on one of the ten Tufts programs or one of the 200 preapproved non-Tufts programs throughout the world. All undergraduates, in both the school of liberal arts and the school of engineering, are encouraged to engage in undergraduate research.

What distinguishes Tufts from many other schools when it comes to research is that rather than doing research *for* a professor, Tufts students play an active role in doing research *with* a professor. Rather than joining an already existing research project, students are strongly encouraged to develop their own projects and to delve deeply into their field. Research takes place across all disciplines, from the sciences to the humanities to the arts. Initiatives such as the Summer Scholars Research Program give undergraduates the opportunity to engage in funded one-on-one research with a faculty member at any of the university's eight undergraduate or graduate schools, including the schools of liberal arts and engineering, the medical school, veterinary school, dental school, nutrition school, and the Fletcher School of Law and Diplomacy. Recent Summer Scholars projects include a drama major that worked with a professor to recreate the costumes and clothing for a PBS documentary on the French and Indian War set in eighteenth-century Pennsylvania, and a community health major who analyzed the problems of asthma and obesity in immigrant populations. Hands-on research is a core element of the undergraduate experience at Tufts and often culminates in a senior honors thesis or further study in graduate school.

At Tufts, whether you like it or not, you are going to get to know your professors. For most students, myself included, that is a good thing. My professors, expert scholars and teachers, were all down-to-earth and inspired me to achieve more than I ever thought possible. I formed meaningful professional relationships and friendships with my professors that have lasted well beyond graduation, and I still correspond with many of them on a regular basis, whether it is to ask for advice or just to catch up.

The amount of time and effort Tufts professors devote to their students never ceased to amaze me. During my senior year, I wrote a political and intellectual biography of comedian and civil rights activist Dick Gregory for my senior honors thesis. My advisor, a bibliophile, would oftentimes be at a bookstore in Boston and see a book he thought might be helpful to me and my research on Dick Gregory. He would buy it for me and give it to me the next day. That happened on more than one occasion. We also attended numerous Celtics and Red Sox games together and formed a life-long bond during my four years as an undergraduate. Another professor of mine, a Pulitzer Prize-winning historian with whom I'm still in close contact, invited our entire seminar class to his home and treated us to a mouth-watering salmon dinner he had prepared.

Tufts professors are much more than top-notch scholars and teachers; they are role models, mentors, and friends.

The Experimental College

Founded in 1964, the Experimental College has been an integral part of the Tufts curriculum for more than forty years. The Experimental College, or ExCollege, is more of an academic department than an actual separate college within the university. Known for offering innovative, imaginative, and interdisciplinary courses that don't necessarily fall into any one academic department, the ExCollege has been a favorite amongst students since its inception.

A unique aspect of the ExCollege is that courses are usually taught by outside professionals rather than university professors. Many of the outside professionals who teach in the ExCollege enrich the learning environment by bringing invaluable real-world experience—and contacts—into the classroom. Recent hits include a course taught by the former general manager of the Celtics on "The Business of Sports: A History of the NBA"; a course on forensic science and crime scene investigation led by a twenty-four-year veteran police inspector of the Connecticut State Attorney's office; and a class on "Producing Films for Social Change" taught by an Academy Award-winning documentary filmmaker. In 2005 Tufts students in the "Producing Films for Social Change" class won a College Emmy Award for *From the Fryer to the Freeway: Alternative Energy Today*. In addition to taking classes in the ExCollege, students also have the ability to teach pass/fail classes in an area of their own personal expertise. All ExCollege courses count for credit toward graduation, and some count as credit toward various majors.

The Dual-Degree Programs

Tufts has two special five-year dual-degree programs with other schools in Boston. The first is a five-year B.A./B.F.A. program with the School of the Museum of Fine Arts, located next to the Museum of Fine Arts in downtown Boston. The second is a five-year B.A./B.Mus. program in which students earn a Bachelor of Arts degree from Tufts and a Bachelor of Music degree from the New England Conservatory, one of the country's most prestigious conservatory programs. A shuttle bus takes dual-degree students back and forth between campuses, though many opt to ride the easily accessible subway as well.

Both dual-degree options are highly selective and are meant for students who are serious academicians and dedicated and talented artists. To apply for either program, students must submit an application to Tufts and a separate application to the other institution. Students should indicate on each application that they would like to be considered for the dual-degree program.

Early Acceptance to Tufts' Professional Schools

During a student's sophomore year at Tufts, he or she may apply for early acceptance to the Tufts School of Medicine, School of Dental Medicine, or School of Veterinary Medicine. In order to be seriously considered for the program, students must meet two criteria: they must be on track to fulfill the required pre-health science requirements (coursework in biology, chemistry, organic chemistry, physics, etc.) within four years and they must have maintained a high level of academic performance during their first two years.

None of the programs are meant as acceleration programs, though some students may be able to complete the combined dental medicine program in seven years. All students accepted early to the medical or veterinary school, and most of those accepted early to the dental school, will still spend four years completing their undergraduate studies and four years in professional school. The benefit of the early acceptance program is that they will know by the end of their sophomore year whether or not they have been admitted into a top-notch health science graduate program. The early acceptance programs are not binding, and students have until the end of their junior year to decide whether or not they will accept the offer of admission.

Institute for Global Leadership

The Institute for Global Leadership (IGL) provides undergraduates with an opportunity to examine a multitude of complex global issues through course work, on-campus lectures and symposia, and funded in-the-field research. The IGL encourages student-centered learning and pushes students to connect theory to practice by "getting their hands dirty" through funded international research. Recent student trips sponsored by the IGL include a trip to the United Arab Emirates to attend a conference on women's rights and a trip to Zimbabwe to research the problems that country faces as a result of its scarce water resources.

Home to a wide range of initiatives, the IGL's signature program is Education for Public Inquiry and International Citizenship (EPIIC), a year-long colloquium exploring a major global issue. Past EPIIC themes include "Race and Ethnicity," "Sovereignty and Intervention," and "America's Role in the World."

More in depth information about the Institute for Global Leadership can be found at *http://www.tufts globalleadership.org/*.

SOCIAL LIFE AND ACTIVITIES

Something that Tufts students understand very well is that a lot of learning in college takes places outside of the classroom. Though students' primary reason for being at Tufts is to excel inside the classroom, a healthy balance exists between coursework, extracurricular activities, and a student's social life.

STUDY ABROAD

- Did you know that . . .
- More than forty percent of students choose to study abroad, placing Tufts among the top ten research universities for percentage of students who study abroad.
- Tufts has a campus at the foot of the French Alps in Talloires, France. During the summer, students have the opportunity to live with a French family while taking six-week-long classes with Tufts professors in an eleventh-century Benedictine priory.
- Tufts' ten study abroad programs are located throughout the world in Chile, China, Germany, Ghana, Hong Kong, Japan, London, Oxford, Paris, and Spain. There are also more than 200 preapproved non-Tufts programs.

Even though Boston is just a short T ride away, the heart of the undergraduate social life is found on campus. Students build time into their schedules to participate in some of the more than 200 already existing student organizations, ranging from the Multiracial Organization of Students at Tufts (MOST) to Traveling Treasure Trunk, a children's theater troupe.

Given the university's emphasis on integrating active citizenship into the curriculum, it is no surprise that the most popular student organization is the Leonard Carmichael Society (LCS), an umbrella community service group that is home to nearly forty outreach initiatives. Students interested in media and communications are often active in Tufts University Television (TUTV); Tufts' radio station, 91.5, WMFO; the *Observer*, a biweekly news magazine; and the most widely read publication on campus, *The Tufts Daily*. Tufts is one of the smallest colleges in the country to have a daily newspaper. Performing artists can sing in one of the six a cappella groups, sing in the choir or gospel choir, play in the wind ensemble or the big band, or dance in Spirit of Color, Sarabande, Tufts Dance Collective, TURBO (a breakdance troupe), or one of the university's step teams.

Many students are involved in the cultural organizations that are collectively known as The Group of 6: the Africana Center, Asian/Asian-American Center, International Center, Latino Center, Lesbian Gay Bisexual Transgender Center, and the Women's Center. There are also active religious organizations and groups on campus, including the Protestant Ministry, Catholic Center, Hillel, and the Islamic Center. Students who find that their interests are not met by one of the already existing organizations always have the opportunity to petition to create a new organization.

Athletics

Students interested in participating in athletics at Tufts may do so at the varsity, club, or intramural level. The Tufts Jumbos boast twenty-nine Division III varsity athletic teams that compete in the New England Small College Athletic Conference (NESCAC). Arguably the most competitive Division III conference both athletically and academically, NESCAC foes include Amherst, Williams, Wesleyan, and Middlebury.

Tufts teams compete at the highest level and placed sixth out of 281 Division III schools in the 2005–2006 Sports Academy Directors' Cup, an annual ranking of the best overall intercollegiate athletic programs in the country. Though many teams had great success in 2005–2006, of particular note was the women's soccer team's Final Four appearance, the men's basketball team's Sweet 16 showing, and the track team's Fred Jones capturing the national triple jump title at the NCAA Outdoor Track and Field Championships.

Popular club sports include a nationally ranked Ultimate Frisbee team, rugby, flag football, and table tennis. Those simply looking to stay in shape can take advantage of Tufts' 40,000 pounds of free weights, new nautilus equipment, indoor pool, and the Gantcher Family Sports and Convocation Center's elevated indoor 200-meter track and indoor tennis courts.

Greek Life

Approximately fifteen percent of Tufts students are Greek. With twelve fraternities and five sororities, the Greek system at Tufts is a legitimate social outlet for those interested in taking part in Greek life. At the same time, there is no pressure to join a fraternity or sorority given the numerous opportunities for social stimulation both on campus and in Boston. Even if a student is not directly involved in Greek life it doesn't necessarily exclude him or her from attending parties, dances, fund-raisers, or other events organized by a fraternity or sorority.

Please visit *http://www.tuftslife.com* for more information about student life and a daily listing of campus events.

FINANCIAL AID

One of the first questions on many high school students' and parents' minds is, "How am I going to pay for college?" As the cost of attending college continues to rise, this question gains more and more validity. At Tufts, admissions and financial aid officers work closely with students' families to ensure that finances are not the factor that prevents a student from attending the university. In 2006, President Larry Bacow launched a $1.2 billion capital campaign, with a primary goal of maximizing the university's financial aid resources.

MAJOR GIFTS PUT ENDOWMENT OVER $1 BILLION

- ○ **$100 million—Pierre and Pamela Omidyar.** Tufts alumnus and founder of eBay Pierre Omidyar made the largest gift in university history. In doing so, he and his wife Pamela established the Tufts-Omidyar Microfinance Fund. The entire gift is dedicated to providing small microfinance loans to entrepreneurs in developing countries with the hope that the loan will help them work their way out of poverty. Half of the returns will be reinvested, and half of the returns will be used to increase financial aid and help in the recruitment of faculty.
- ○ **$50 million—William Cummings** endowed the Tufts University School of Veterinary Medicine, solidifying its place as one of the premier veterinary schools in the country.
- ○ **$40 million—Jonathan M. Tisch** endowed the Jonathan M. Tisch College of Citizenship and Public Service, emphasizing the importance Tufts places on integrating active citizenship and leadership into the curriculum.

Financial aid at Tufts is need-based and the university is dedicated to meeting 100 percent of a student's financial need, as determined by the Free Application for Federal Student Aid (FAFSA), the College Scholarship Service (CSS) Financial Aid Profile, and the family's tax returns. The only form of merit-based aid are awards from the National Merit Scholarship Corporation. ROTC scholarships are also available to students. Each year students resubmit their financial aid forms so that the university can recalculate and adjust their financial aid package as needed.

Financial aid packages usually include three types of aid: grant, loan, and student contribution. However, the vast majority of aid is in the form of grants, or money that the student does not have to repay. Of the $12.8 million in aid given to the class of 2010, more than $10 million was in the form of grants. The average grant was $23,907 and the average total award was $26,300. Student contribution, or work-study, provides students with an on-campus job during the academic year. Though a variety of jobs are available, the most highly sought after jobs are those that allow students to study or do work while on the clock. The foreign language lab, gymnasium, and library media center are a few of the most popular places to be employed. In addition to working on campus, some students decide to take advantage of the plentiful job opportunities in Boston to help pay for school.

GRADUATES

Given the geographic diversity of the undergraduate student body and the emphasis on educating tomorrow's global leaders, it is no surprise that Tufts graduates can be found throughout the world. There are more than 80,000 Tufts alumni living in places as close as Boston and New York and as far as Botswana and New Delhi. Current undergraduates and recent graduates greatly benefit from the Tufts Alumni Association, an active network of alumni who are eager to offer advice, resources, and contacts.

Upon graduating from Tufts, around half of all students will go directly to graduate school, though within five years of graduating more than eighty percent of all graduates have already completed a graduate degree or are in graduate school. Approximately a quarter of the graduating class will engage in volunteer opportunities or complete prestigious scholarships and fellowships. Each year Tufts is one of the top schools of its size to send students on to be Fulbright Scholars and Peace Corps Volunteers. Other recent graduates have also been recognized as Marshall Scholars, Truman Scholars, Udall Scholars, and recipients of the Jack Kent Cooke Foundation's Cooke Scholarship. The remaining quarter will enter into the workforce in fields including public service and government, investment banking, consulting, teaching, and journalism among others.

When people ask me what my friends did after we graduated, I usually don't know where to start.

Kate, whom I met during our weeklong freshman orientation community service trip in Boston, won a Fulbright Scholarship to do research on the HIV/AIDS epidemic in sub-Saharan Africa and then went on to work for UNESCO in Paris before doing a master's degree in international public health.

Steve, whom I lived with all four years of college, recently received his master's degree in Islamic and Middle Eastern Studies in Israel and has also been working full-time for a leading conflict resolution nonprofit. Steve's connections at Tufts led to a once-in-a-lifetime opportunity the year after we graduated. That year, he traveled to India as part of a three-person delegation sent to meet with the Dalai Lama and advise the Tibetan government in exile in their dealings with the Chinese.

My other friends are doing equally impressive things across the country and throughout the world, ranging from Ph.D. and professional degree programs to opening up a bookstore on the Greek island of Santorini to working in postconflict areas such as Rwanda and Northern Ireland.

SUMMING UP

Most students are drawn to Tufts because they are looking for a challenge—both inside and outside of the classroom. Tufts provides students with a high-quality education where the learning extends far beyond the walls of the classroom. Tufts students appreciate the diverse student body, beautiful campus, access to a major city, and community in which students take their academics seriously, yet lead healthy and balanced lives.

Originally from the small, rural town of Schulenburg, Texas, Michelle Eilers, '10, chose Tufts because she wanted to attend a school where students learned just as much from their peers during political debates in the dining hall and late-night discussions about global dilemmas in the dorms as they did from their professors. She wrote, "I want to meet people with whom I have nothing in common and argue about values and beliefs. I want to interact with people involved in making real world contributions, because I want to make meaningful contributions of my own." In Tufts, Michelle and many other like-minded students have found a perfect match.

Unlike many other prestigious universities, Tufts is a dynamic and innovative institution of higher learning whose president, professors, and students use academic and social capital to make tangible differences in the world. Under the leadership of President Larry Bacow, the university has heightened an already impressive academic profile by attracting top-notch students and faculty. Robert Sternberg, former president of the American Psychological Association and one of the world's foremost experts on the topics of creativity and intelligence, assumed the position of Dean of Arts and Sciences in 2005. Linda Abriola, a member of the National Academy of Engineering and a universally recognized specialist in water allocation and water resources, became one of the few female Deans of Engineering in the country when she accepted that position in 2004.

Scholars and students alike recognize that Tufts is a special school—a university on the forefront of both research and teaching, a campus defined by intellectual curiosity and hands-on learning, and a community of scholars and leaders who want to "shake things up, tear things down, and make things better."

❑ *Adam Goodman, B.A.*

TULANE UNIVERSITY

 Tulane University
New Orleans, LA 70118

 (504) 865-5731
Fax: (504) 862-8715 (800) 873-9283

 E-mail: *undergrad.admission@tulane.edu*
Web site: *www.tulane.edu*

 Enrollment

Full-time	❏ women:	4354
	❏ men:	4448
Part-time	❏ women:	1006
	❏ men:	798

INTRODUCING TULANE UNIVERSITY

You'll know why students love Tulane University the moment you step off of the St. Charles streetcar onto the azalea-filled campus in "uptown" New Orleans. Since its founding in 1834, Tulane, aided by the mystique of the Mississippi River city that surrounds it, has been both educating and entertaining students for generations. Tracing its roots back to the Medical College of Louisiana, Tulane owes its name to a wealthy New Jersey merchant, Paul Tulane, who earned his fortune in the crescent city. After more than a century as one of the most prominent features of the city of New Orleans, Tulane is an even more integral part of the city after surviving the challenge of Hurricane Katrina in 2005. Now, students are flocking to Tulane to experience the rebirth of an amazing cultural center, as well as to be educated in a world-class research environment.

The students at Tulane are diverse, intellectual, and very social. Boasting more than 250 campus groups and situated in the heart of one of the most culturally important cities in the country, Tulane offers students more than just a top-tier liberal arts education, it offers an amazing collegiate experience. "Work hard, play hard" doesn't even begin to describe it. As President Scott Cowen leads the university through the challenges created by Hurricane Katrina, the community of Tulane has come together to embrace what has made city and the school unique and to make sure new students can experience Tulane for years to come. "Only at Tulane. Only in New Orleans" has become the unofficial school motto that is invigorating campus activities, stimulating educational programming, and encouraging the student body to be a part of the rehabilitation of the coastal region.

The culture is just one of the many reasons students love being located in the heart of New Orleans. Public service opportunities, internships with local business and sports teams, full-time employment, and religious communities are all just minutes away. Students can enjoy the history of the French Quarter, the Spanish architecture, the Creole food, and the location of the birth of jazz while surrounded by a university with a renewed focus on educational excellence and a commitment to public service.

At the heart of the campus stands the Lavin-Bernick Center for University Life, the hub of extracurricular activities at Tulane. Under construction until just recently, this brand-new building opened its doors in January of 2007 and puts a fresh face on the forty-year-old University Center (affectionately known as the UC). This hub holds dining and meeting facilities, a large bookstore, and the offices of both student programming faculty and student organizations. This building is the heart of the campus and a popular meeting place for groups and individuals alike. Fanning out from the UC is the 110-acre campus, complete with a new business school building—one of the most advanced in the nation—a new $7.5 million baseball stadium, freshly renovated dorm buildings, and lines of historic oak trees that are almost evergreen in the tropical climate of the Deep South. The university has constructed, on average, one new building a year for the past dozen years, with plans in place for further construction among campus' oaks, magnolias, and occasional banana tree or bamboo grove.

On campus, students study at one of ten schools and colleges, depending on their major and degree. Undergraduates start their Tulane career at the recently reorganized

Newcomb-Tulane College. This undergraduate college was created by joining the H. Sophie Newcomb Memorial College for Women, which was established as part of Tulane in 1886, with the undergraduate men's arm of Tulane College. As the first coordinate college in a university setting to grant degrees to women in the entire nation, Newcomb and Tulane draw students in with their rich history and innovative programming.

Tulane would not be the institution that it is, however, without the philosophies and customs of the city of New Orleans. The charm, hospitality, and pace of the city are undeniably seen in the culture of the university as well. The traditions of both are woven together, and as the leadership and students of Tulane step up and embrace the tasks of rebuilding the city, the futures of the city and the school are inextricably linked. The strength and passion of the city is carried over into the determination and excitement of the students and their educational and personal goals.

ADMISSIONS REQUIREMENTS

Immediately after Hurricane Katrina and the cancellation of the 2005 fall semester, Tulane students were spread to over 600 schools in all fifty states. When the campus reopened in January of 2006, eighty-seven percent of these students chose to return to Tulane to continue their education. This enthusiasm to attend Tulane continues to be very strong in new applicants as well.

Tulane has been growing more and more competitive over the past several years. A trend of increasing applications has continued, despite the interruption of Hurricane Katrina. As a testament to this trend, the 2006 application season, the first after the storm, presented the largest number of applications in the school's history. Now ranked as one of the nation's most competitive colleges, the last academic year before the hurricane saw 17,572 applications, of which, 7,867 were accepted, leading to a freshman enrollment of just over 1,600. Although the entering class size has become smaller in the past year, the student body has remained a compilation of the nation's top high school graduates. According to university statistics, approximately fifty-one percent of enrolling freshmen in 2006 were ranked in the top ten percent of their high school classes; nearly seventy-five percent in 2006 ranked in the top twenty-five percent; and ninety-six percent in 2006 were in the top half of their class. In addition to being strong academically, Tulane's typical freshman class is both geographically and ethnically diverse. A surprising number of students come to Tulane from great distances—over seventy-five percent of the typical entering freshman class hails from more than 500 miles away from the school. This diversity ensures that students are not only learning from their academic programs, but also from each other.

Application Requirements

Scores from either the SAT or the ACT are required to apply. The average SAT score for the 2006–2007 freshman class was 1294 (based on 1600) (ACT equivalent of 29), which was 285 points above the national average. The ACT Optional Writing test is also required and SAT subject tests, such as math, writing, and science, are recommended for placement purposes. The school recommends taking the SAT, which includes a standard writing section. Equally important for placement and honors program consideration are Advanced Placement (AP) credits, which are enthusiastically accepted. Factors that demonstrate to the admissions team your unique qualities are AP and honors courses, recommendations, and extracurricular activities records, along with a personal essay. For architecture applicants, a portfolio is recommended as well. Students are encouraged to have completed four years each of high school English and math, and three years each of foreign language, social studies, and the sciences.

Campus Visits

Tulane Students who visited the campus the spring of their senior year in high school all attest to the power of seeing the campus in bloom and experiencing New Orleans in such beautiful weather. All applicants are encouraged to visit the campus for one of the prospective students activities in the spring, but they will also be accommodated at any point during the year. Daily campus tours are given by passionate Green Wave Ambassadors, often seen on campus walking backwards in flip-flops in front of a crowd of prospective students and parents. Ambassadors also host prospective students on overnight visits where the prospective student can join them in attending classes, meeting friends and professors, and participating in campus activities or sporting events. Efforts are made to make sure that visiting students experience both academic and social life at Tulane before, or after, they make their final decision to attend. To contact an Ambassador, learn more about the visit schedule, or book your tour with the on-line reservation system, visit *www.tulane.edu/~admiss/prospective_students/entering/visit_campus.html.*

Tides

First-year students participate in the Tulane InterDisciplinary Experience Seminars (TIDES) program, which connects them to other students who share similar interests. These seminar courses include speakers, trips, social events, and special programs that link to one of fifty chosen topics. Possible choices include: "The Music and Culture of New

Orleans"; "Hurricanes, Human Rights, and History"; "Philosophy of Public Service"; "The Cultures of Food"; "Reading and Writing Women"; and many more. These programs were developed to introduce students to the city, the school, and each other by linking them up with faculty, activities, and other new students who share similar personal interests.

ACADEMIC LIFE

Top students come to Tulane to get a world-class education in a unique setting. Academic opportunities, therefore, are embraced by all students. All undergraduates enter through the Newcomb-Tulane Undergraduate College, where a core curriculum ensures academic breadth as they begin their collegiate career, a TIDES course connects them to students with similar passions, and the public service requirement fulfills the mission of Tulane to produce graduates with cultural knowledge who are "good citizens of the world."

Faculty

All courses at Tulane are taught by professors who both teach and conduct research—not teaching assistants. All professors hold open office hours and are more than willing to spend time with students individually. The student-to-faculty ratio of nine-to-one ensures that classes are kept small and students are all given individual attention. The academic environment is influenced by the culture of the surroundings and is more friendly and encouraging than competitive.

One of my most memorable times during my freshman year at Tulane was my French 102 class. Taught by the Vice President of Academic Affairs herself, the class was only twelve people, which allowed us to do things I would have never guessed a freshman in college would get to do. Sitting, with my classmates, on a rooftop deck overlooking the Mississippi River, enjoying an authentically made French dinner with one of the university's top officials, I realized that I would have never gotten such an opportunity at a larger school. This type of experience was repeated many times throughout my Tulane education, with many different professors. Not only were these activities educational, they also led to some of my most cherished college memories.

1. Tulane's Newcomb College, joined to the university in 1886, was the first coordinate college to grant degrees to women.
2. Tulane's study abroad program is one of the oldest in the country.
3. Tulane's School of Social Work has its roots in the very first training program for social workers in the Deep South.
4. The Community Action Council of Tulane University Students (CACTUS) is the oldest and largest student-led community service organization in the country.
5. Tulane's School of Public Health and Tropical Medicine, founded in 1912, is one of the oldest such schools in the country.
6. Founded in 1964, the Tulane National Primate Research Center is one of the oldest and largest of the eight federally funded primate research centers in the United States.
7. The Newcomb College Center for Research on Women is one of the nation's oldest and most prominent research centers of its kind.

Schools, Programs, and Libraries

Outside of the core programs, students will choose majors from the five undergraduate schools: School of Liberal Arts, which awards Bachelor of Arts (B.A.), Bachelor of Science (B.S.), or Bachelor of Fine Arts (B.F.A.) degrees, depending on the choice of major; School of Science and Engineering, which awards a B.S.; A.B. Freeman School of Business, which confers the Bachelor of Science in Management (B.S.M.) degree; School of Architecture, in which students receive the Master of Architecture I degree; and the School of Public Health, where students receive a Bachelor of Science in Public Health. Students may also pursue cross-registration with other universities in the area, and are able to use these additional resources and libraries to their advantage.

Tulane also offers many joint degree programs that combine undergraduate and graduate/professional degrees. Cross-registration in different schools and "4+1" programs are also available. Students can also choose from flexible study options, such as student-designed, dual, and interdisciplinary majors. Because Tulane is nationally recognized in many of its academic programs, a large percentage of students take advantage of more than one academic department for their concentrations.

Academic and research resources available to students are second to none. The main library on campus, Howard-Tilton Memorial, is not only home to five floors of "stacks" and study spaces but also the Latin American Library and the Maxwell Music Library, where students have access to some of the greatest music in the world. Special collections of the university include the Hogan Jazz Archive, Southeastern Architectural Archive, and the Louisiana Collection. Other special libraries on campus span the fields of architecture, botany, business, law, mathematics, natural history, primate research, race relations and ethnic history, and women's studies (home to an impressive collection of historical local cookbooks).

Advisors

Students are assigned to an academic advisor when they arrive at Tulane. These advisors take time to understand a student's goals and passions, and align those with the opportunities and coursework at the different schools. Advisors assist in planning for special programs such as joint degree, personal research, and study abroad. They also suggest courses based on personal interest and coordinate with professors. Once a major is declared, a major advisor is also chosen to assist with field-specific goals, thesis research, and degree planning.

During my junior year at Tulane, I was struggling to find the perfect class to fill one of my last elective requirements. My academic advisor suggested that I take a break from my heavy academic workload and sign up for modern dance. At first, I was completely taken aback, but after I attended one class, I was hooked. The opportunity to step outside of my comfort zone and learn something new was amazing. My advisor knew it was exactly what I needed to augment my studies, and I have her to thank for such a perfect suggestion.

Another advising resource at Tulane is the Career Services Center, which helps students at all levels of their collegiate career. The center advises students on everything from resume writing and interview skills to choosing the right major with resources to help understand not only the curriculum, but also the related career paths. The center offers free workshops, sponsors career fairs, and connects students with internship and job opportunities, as well as offers counselors to critique application essays and cover letters. On-line self-assessments and tools offer advice to students on their schedule.

Tulane's Education Resources and Counseling Center, another facet of the university's advising system, offers both academic and personal counseling services. The center teaches academic skills and tutoring sessions free of charge while also providing personal counseling such as support groups, crisis counseling, and individual therapy.

Beyond the Campus

A significant number of Tulane students participate in the study abroad program. Tulane's Junior Year Abroad (JYA) program is one of the oldest of its kind in the country. Students can choose from full-year or semester programs, Tulane-sponsored programs, or trips coordinated with other schools, or they can develop their own overseas experience with the help of advisors at the Center for International Studies. Tulane has programs in over twenty countries spanning Europe, Latin America, Africa, Asia, and Australia, in addition to a variety of faculty-led summer study-abroad programs for both undergraduates and graduates. Also offered are Washington, DC, semesters for students interested in politics, policy, and public service. All Tulane-sponsored study-abroad programs allow students to keep their specific scholarships and financial aid packages, which removes many barriers often present when studying at another school as a visiting student.

Growing up in a small town in the south, I always knew I wanted to travel abroad at some point during my college education. So, it was imperative when I was conducting my college search that I find a school that not only had great academic programs on its campus, but had great programs with other schools around the world. When I learned of Tulane's historic study-abroad programs, the number of students who studied in other countries, and the fact that scholarships and aid would transfer seamlessly, Tulane became one of my top choices. Once at Tulane, I worked with my academic advisors and the Center for International Studies to create a program overseas that would fit in with my major. Before I entered Tulane, I had never left the U.S., and now, thanks to the university's great programs, I've not only lived in another country, but traveled through nine countries in all.

To complete the public service graduation requirement, students engage with the Center for Public Service to take a service-learning course, coordinate with faculty-sponsored service programs, design a study-abroad experience with a service component, or complete a public service honors thesis. All students at Tulane get outside the classroom to participate in the revitalization of New Orleans and the Gulf Coast. Building houses, painting elementary schools, volunteering for education and health programs, and raising awareness of the region's challenges are examples of ways students get involved.

SOCIAL LIFE AND ACTIVITIES

Tulane University is located in the heart of uptown New Orleans. From listening to world-class musicians at renowned jazz clubs to throwing a Frisbee on the grassy park at the levee, New Orleans offers activities that simply can't be found at other cities. The social life of Tulane, therefore, is inextricably linked with the city that surrounds it. Jazz musicians perform at Tulane events, shuttle bus service takes kids around the city free of charge, students attend professional sporting events, movies shot in the city have their red-carpet premiers on campus, and freshman year officially starts on a paddle boat on the Mississippi River. Throughout a student's years at Tulane, this continues to be the case. Most of the "social life" of the school is rooted in and around the city's activities and big events. Some New Orleans festivals and events most popular with Tulane students include Mardi Gras, the weeks of carnival season associated with large parades throughout the city; New Orleans Jazz & Heritage Festival ("Jazz Fest"), a two-weekend blowout of world famous bands and performing artists, arts and crafts, unique cuisine and late-night concerts; Voodoo Music Experience, a large annual music-festival; and the annual Sugar Bowl college football game.

Student Organizations

On campus, there are over 250 student organizations that create the social scene. Except for a select few, groups are open to all students and range from activism to sports. The oldest program on campus is the Community Action Council of Tulane University Students (CACTUS), which organizes community service activities of all kinds and involves almost every Tulane student at one point in his or her college experience. In addition to CACTUS, there are honors and professional societies, club and intramural sports, a healthy student government system, and a multitude of multicultural, political, performance, and religious groups. Campus media includes the *Hullabaloo*, the student-run newspaper that is published once a week; a student-managed television channel; and the immensely popular WTUL radio station. Student DJs man the airwaves in two-hour shifts at all hours of the day and night and have shows ranging from rock to folk.

Greek Life

Another dimension to campus life is the Greek system. There are fifteen national fraternities and ten national sororities on campus. Of all students, thirty percent of men and thirty-five percent of women belong to one of these chapters. Greek parties are open to all students, however, and the social scene is not dominated by these events.

In fact, fraternities and sororities are some of the most active service organizations on campus and provide a great way to get involved in the community. The Greek recruitment, "Rush," is deferred until a first-year student's second semester on campus, giving the student the chance to make friends, understand the social scene, and join other organizations before committing to a fraternity or sorority. Most students who pledge do not live in organized housing, opting instead to live among friends not involved in the same Greek chapter.

Living on Campus

All freshman and sophomore students at Tulane are required to live on campus and are guaranteed space in one of the university's many dormitories or apartment complexes. Many junior, senior, and graduate students also opt to live on campus, as it provides them with a convenient, safe housing situation. Special living arrangements include female single-sex houses; theme living situations, such as honors, special interest, and international student houses; and the "Leadership Village"—a gathering of the university's top student government and organizational leaders. Campus resources include a plethora of dining alternatives, a barbershop, several bank branches and ATMS, a copy center, post office, bookstore, grocery store, and several laundry facilities.

Campus Programming

Tulane University Campus Programming (TUCP) is a very active group on campus. This student-run club is responsible for bringing chart-topping bands and performers, well-known comedians, and political figures and speakers to Tulane. TUCP also runs a cinema program—which shows new releases on campus for a fraction of the price of movie-theatre admission—and organizes an annual spring carnival.

Mardi Gras

The highlight of every spring semester at Tulane is the arrival of Carnival season. The weeks between Epiphany (January 6) and Ash Wednesday (40 days before Easter) are filled with parades, crawfish boils, parties, and concerts. You will see Tulane students enjoying the parades on St. Charles Avenue, riding on floats with social groups, and marching in parades with the Tulane Marching Band. The university has special programs to maintain the safety of its students during this exciting time of year, including special safety and awareness programs and a registration system to track students visiting campus during Mardi Gras.

Athletics

The Tulane Green Wave is a member of Conference USA in athletics and participates with teams in several NCAA Division 1-A sports, including football, basketball, and track, to name a few. Students receive free admission to all home games of all sports, and transportation is provided. The Louisiana Superdome, home to the Saints Football franchise and the Sugar Bowl, also hosts the Green Wave football team, which has recently produced NFL quarterbacks J. P. Losman and Patrick Ramsey. It is not unusual to be seated at a football game next to President Cowen, who is known to spray paint his hair bright green and paint his face for games!

Perhaps Tulane's most successful sports team is men's baseball, which earned its second trip to the College World Series in the 2005 season. The recent renovation of Turchin Stadium, one of the largest and most impressive collegiate baseball fields in the country, will be complete in April 2007. Tulane's student athletes are also recognized as successful scholars, with one of the largest percentages of graduating student athletes in the country.

FINANCIAL AID

Tulane is committed to offering a great education to all students, regardless of financial situation. In a recent year, eighty-two percent of all full-time freshmen received some form of financial aid. Financial aid packages include grants, government loans, merit-based scholarships and awards, and student employment opportunities both on and off campus. Tulane has a robust work-study program and about forty-five percent of undergraduates work part-time at some point in their college careers. Athletic and ROTC scholarships are also available to students who qualify.

As a member of the College Scholarship Service (CSS), the CSS PROFILE or Free Application for Federal Student Aid (FAFSA) are required to apply for financial aid. The average award for the 2006–2007 year was $25,224, with an average annual earnings from campus work at $2,500. Upon enrollment, all students are assigned a financial aid counselor, who is committed not only to designing a financial aid award package that is tailored for each student but also to being available on a daily basis for questions about deadlines, forms, procedures, and options.

My freshman year, I was awarded a work-study campus job in my financial aid package. I began doing administrative work for the Levy Rosenblum Institute of Entrepreneurship (LRI) during my free time between classes. After four years at LRI, I had built relationships with local business owners, gotten to know business school faculty personally, and participated in amazing programs. The experience led me into business school at Tulane, where I graduated with an MBA. The experiences I had, consulting for non-profits, improving family-owned regional businesses, and planning events for national figures, could not have been gotten anywhere else.

Merit-Based Aid

The university offers many merit-based scholarships that are awarded based on a student's proven academic record and commitment to community involvement. A special application must be filled out for students applying for the Deans' Honor Scholarship. This merit-based full-tuition scholarship is awarded to a few select students each year. The application includes THE BOX—a blank square on the application that you must fill as creatively as you can. Also requiring a separate application is the Community Service Scholarship, which awards up to full tuition to those students who can illustrate how they have dedicated exceptional time and effort to their communities. All students, regardless of application type or deadline, are automatically considered for other merit-based awards that do not require a separate application, with scholarships that range from $14,000 to $22,000 per year. Financial aid counselors will also work one-on-one with students accepted to Tulane who have received merit-based scholarships from outside organizations or government entities.

GRADUATES

Graduates of Tulane University are equipped not only with a fantastic liberal arts education but also with a great respect for the world's cultures and an understanding of the importance of public service. Tulane produces citizens of the world who are bright and energetic about solving problems, but who are also compassionate and hard-working when it comes to their communities. Tulane grads have pioneered heart transplant and knee reconstruction surgeries; they have changed the world of entertainment; and they have invented software and tools, such as Netscape and Yahoo!, that have transformed our digital world.

In a recent year, 1,504 bachelor's degrees were awarded. Popular majors included business, social sciences, and engineering. In the 2004–2005 school year, 134 companies actively recruited on campus. Since the hurricane, Tulane has revived its commitment to its students to find jobs after graduation. The recent launch of the all-encompassing web site *www.hiretulane.com* helps connect students, employers, counselors, and alumni in a strong network that supports the career paths of Tulane students. Separate career centers for the A. B. Freeman School of Business, the Tulane University School of Law, and the Tulane School of Public Health focus on recruiting, internship, and full-time job opportunities for their students; however, students in these schools are free to use the university career center as well.

SUMMING UP

A Tulane education provides more than just a degree. Academically, Tulane's faculty will prepare you to solve problems, challenge you with new theories, and support your personal research and endeavors. The cultural education you will obtain, however, is like nothing else in the nation. The history of New Orleans, added to the unique cuisine, music, traditions of the city, and the rebuilding process combine to form a truly unmatched collegiate experience. Students who choose to attend Tulane now will not only be studying at a great university, they will be an integral part of rebuilding an American treasure after one of the most devastating natural disasters of our time.

Tulane students all agree that their education is special—architecture students can study Spanish, French, and British influences right in their backyard; English majors can regularly visit places they read about in novels; business students are trusted to invest the school's own money in one-of-a-kind programs; and students studying music have some powerful acts to follow.

The size and location of Tulane make it the perfect combination of opportunity and individuality. Small enough to offer personal support yet large enough to provide research and internship experiences, it offers Southern hospitality coupled with big-city activities to meet the needs of a very diverse student body that hails from all fifty states, and one hundred countries.

No other school in the country offers as great of an academic experience coupled with just as great of a cultural one. Tulane not only gives you the tools to make your own decisions, it grants you the humor to cope with your mistakes. It rewards you for working hard, while teaching you that work isn't everything. You would be hard-pressed to find another school in America where you can learn as much about life from the surroundings as you can learn inside the classroom.

Taken from Casey Haugner's commencement address at the 2006 graduation ceremony

❏ *Casey Haugner, '05*

UNITED STATES MILITARY ACADEMY AT WEST POINT

 United States Military Academy at West Point
West Point, NY 10996

 (845) 938-4041
Fax: (845) 938-8121

 E-mail: *admissions@www.usma.edu*
Web site: *http://www.usma.edu/admissions*

 Enrollment

Full-time ❑ women: 627
❑ men: 3,739

INTRODUCING WEST POINT

What do I remember most about West Point? It would be impossible for me to choose just one event. Perhaps it was marching with my class onto the parade field at the end of the very first day and taking the oath as my family and friends watched anxiously from the stands. Or maybe it was the exhilarating feeling of parachuting from an airplane 1,250 feet in the sky and the shock of seeing my parents waiting for me on the drop zone! Or it may very well have been the day I found out I passed physics. Or perhaps the day we beat Navy in football for the fifth straight year. Or the day I scored two goals in our Army-Navy lacrosse game and we won by one goal in the last second. Or it could have been when I was a squad leader and my squad successfully completed squad stakes competition and found our way home. Or perhaps the day I became platoon leader at CTLT (cadet troop leader training) at Fort Campbell, Kentucky. Or it might have been when I shook the hand of the President of the United States after receiving my diploma. Now that was a day to remember. …

Founded in 1802, West Point is our nation's oldest service academy. Graduates of West Point "serve this nation honorably, sharing a strong sense of purpose, pride, and satisfaction that comes from meaningful service to others."

Attending the United States Military Academy is a wonderfully unique and challenging experience. West Point is a four-year college with a mission to develop leaders of character for our army—leaders who are inspired to careers as commissioned officers and lifetime service to the nation. The students of West Point (called cadets) are selected from the most talented, energetic, and well-rounded young people in the country. Located on 16,000 acres in the scenic Hudson Valley region of New York State, West Point is conveniently situated just fifty miles north of New York City. The year-round pageantry and tradition make the Military Academy a national treasure and a popular tourist spot. People come from all over the world to see cadets in action, and there is so much to see.

Choosing West Point opens the door to countless opportunities. Cadets receive a top-notch education, training in leader development, and numerous professional opportunities. They learn first how to be a follower, and then to be a leader—skills that will carry them in all of their life endeavors. Not to mention the fact that they are guaranteed a five-year job in the military.

So what makes West Point such a special place? West Point is more than a school; it is a tightly knit community. The officers and noncommissioned officers who serve as instructors at West Point share a special bond with the cadets. The students and their instructors at West Point are members of the same profession and are dedicated to the same principles of "duty, honor, and country."

Cadets at West Point live under an Honor Code that states that "a cadet will not lie, cheat, or steal, or tolerate those who do." The penalty for those who violate this code is serious. The Honor Code is meant to develop cadets into true leaders of character. Cadets internalize the importance of living honorably and carry this value with them into the army.

ADMISSIONS REQUIREMENTS

Admission to West Point is highly competitive, and the application process is much more involved than that of a civilian school. Of the approximate 12,000 candidates who start files each year, only about 1,500 are offered admission. While most colleges and universities look primarily at a student's academic background, West Point is interested in the whole package. Not only must candidates be of high academic caliber, they must qualify physically and medically as well. Candidates must also earn a nomination from a U.S. representative, senator, the president, vice president, or from the Department of the Army (these nominations are service-related).

The admissions committee seeks students who are bright, athletic, and have "demonstrated leadership potential" throughout their high school years. To determine the academic strength and potential of a candidate, the admissions committee examines both the high school transcript and the SAT/ACT scores. To determine the physical fitness and potential of a candidate, the committee looks at the athletic activities in which the candidate participated during high school. In addition, candidates are required to take a physical aptitude examination (PAE), which consists of several events such as a 300-meter run, pull-ups, and a broad jump, designed to determine athletic ability and potential.

Leadership Potential

Because West Point strives to be the premier leader development institute in the world, it is important that the academy admit cadets who have leadership potential that can be built upon. With that in mind, the admissions committee looks for students who were part of the student government in their school, primarily student body or class president. Other indications of exceptional leadership potential might include participation in boys/girls state, scouting, debate, school publications, and varsity athletics. In a typical class of about 1,200 new cadets, more than 1,000 earned varsity letters in high school and about 750 were team captains. Over seventy-five percent of the class graduated in the top fifth of their high school class. The mean SAT I score for a recent class was 630 Verbal and 647 Math, 28 on the ACT, and some 237 earned National Merit Scholarship Recognition.

Candidates must also be at least seventeen and not older than twenty-three years of age on July first of the year they enter the academy. They must also be U.S. citizens, be unmarried, and not be pregnant or have a legal obligation for child support.

Steps in Applying

There are several steps in applying to West Point.

- Make a self-assessment. Determine if you qualify for West Point and if this is something that you would be interested in doing.
- Start a candidate file. This is done by contacting the USMA Admissions Office.
- Seek a nomination from the representative in your district and your senators.
- You must complete all of your SAT and ACT testing, as well as your physical and medical examinations.
- You then have the option of visiting West Point and spending the day with a cadet on a candidate orientation visit. This is optional, but highly recommended. An orientation visit is the best way to get a feel for academy life and if it's for you.
- If you complete all of these steps and are admitted into the incoming class, your final step is to enroll in the academy on Reception Day.

For those candidates who consider USMA to be their top college choice and are interested in applying early, West Point offers an Early Action plan. Under this plan, applicants are informed of their admissions status by January 15. Persistence is "key," as about thirty percent of each incoming class are second-time applicants.

ACADEMIC LIFE

I'll never forget my first day of classes as a plebe (freshman). I was astonished to see that each of my classes had only about fifteen cadets in it, about half the size of my high school classes. The first thing each professor did was write his or her home phone number on the blackboard. "Call me at home anytime, day or night," each one said. The classroom experience at West Point is unlike any other. There simply are no crowded lecture halls or graduate assistants. Each class is taught by an instructor whose primary responsibility is to teach cadets. Each class has a maximum number of eighteen students. You just can't get that kind of personal interaction at other universities—many of my friends at other schools had as many graduate assistants as they did professors. My professors taught every lesson, were available for additional help at all hours of the day or night, and even came out to support me at my athletic matches!

The Core Curriculum

Academics at West Point are tough, but with the amount of assistance available, cadets are set up for success. The overall curriculum contains classes in both science and the arts. Unlike most colleges and universities, the core curriculum is very extensive. In other words, during the first two years, there is not much flexibility in course selection. The core curriculum consists of thirty-one courses. This broad base of classes serves several purposes. Cadets not only get a solid foundation before specializing in one area, but have also studied in all of the academic departments and have a sound basis for selecting one of forty-two majors. Besides their major or field of study, all students take what is called a five-course engineering sequence. This sequence strengthens the cadet's engineering background and in a sense gives him or her a second major. The engineering sequences include electrical engineering, environmental engineering, civil engineering, mechanical engineering, nuclear engineering, systems engineering, and computer science. All graduates receive a bachelor of science degree. The United States Military Academy introduced a "major with honors," which contains a minimum of twelve courses, an individual research requirement, and requires a minimum academic program score cumulative (APSC) of 3.0 in the core curriculum and a 3.5 in the major.

Resources

The resources available to cadets are very impressive. The library contains over 600,000 volumes of resources and 2,000 academic journals and newspapers. All cadets have desk-top computers in their room and full access to the Internet. In addition, the Center for Enhanced Performance assists cadets in achieving their potential in all aspects of academy life, offering classes, open to all students, in reading efficiency and student success. One-on-one additional instruction is available to cadets from their instructors and is what sets the military academy apart from other schools.

Physical Education and Military Development

Part of the overall curriculum includes physical education and military development. The physical education curriculum spans the four years. Physical education classes are incorporated into the grade point average, which highlights the importance of physical fitness in the army. Cadets receive grades in each physical education class as well as the Army Physical Fitness Test and the Indoor Obstacle Course Test. The physical program is quite challenging, but rewarding and fun as well.

Military development is also part of the curriculum. Cadets are graded based on military performance within their cadet companies as well as their performance during summer training and military intersession. The heart of the military training takes place during the summer. During their first summer, new cadets are introduced to the academy through the rigors of Cadet Basic Training, a six-week experience that transforms the new class from civilians to cadets, and gives the upper two classes the opportunity to practice small unit leadership. During Cadet Basic Training—also called "Beast Barracks"—new cadets learn what it means to be a cadet as well as what it means to be a soldier.

The summer after plebe or freshman year, cadets participate in Cadet Field Training. At Camp Buckner, sophomores or "yearlings" complete seven weeks of advanced military training including weapons, tank, and aviation training. During this time, cadets are also introduced to the different branches of the army and how their focus contributes to its overall mission. They apply the skills they learned in the classroom as they practice tactical exercises in small units. Like Cadet Basic Training, upperclass cadets serve as the cadre for this training.

Camp Buckner is also a time for recreation and class bonding. During the summers before junior ("cow") and senior ("firstie") year, opportunities for cadets broaden significantly. During these summers, cadets must participate in either Cadet Troop Leader Training or Drill Cadet Leader Training. This involves being assigned to an active army unit for six weeks and acting as either platoon leaders or drill sergeants. For most cadets, it is their first experience in the regular army and it is both exciting and rewarding. A cadet must also serve as a leader or cadre member for either Cadet Basic Training or Cadet Field Training during one of these summers.

This leaves two periods open for cadets to participate in Individual Advanced Development (IADs). Some military IADs include Airborne School (parachuting), Air Assault School (rappelling out of helicopters), Combat Engineer Sapper School, Mountain Warfare School, and Special Forces Scuba School. There are also physical IADs such as training at the U.S. Olympic Center and Outward Bound. Very popular among cadets are academic IADs. These are similar to internships students at civilian colleges might participate in. Some academic IAD cadets participate, including duty with the Supreme Court, Crossroads to Africa, the Foreign Academy Exchange Program, NASA, and the National Laboratories.

Perhaps this is a curriculum unlike any you've ever seen. A cadets total QPA (quality point average) is based on fifty-five percent academics, thirty percent military, and fifteen percent physical. Cadets must be well rounded. The curriculum is meant to develop "enlightened military leaders of strong moral courage whose minds are creative, critical, and resourceful." It was Thucydides who said "The Nation that makes a great distinction between its scholars and its warriors will have its thinking done by cowards and its fighting done by fools."

SOCIAL LIFE AND ACTIVITIES

A few years ago, a couple of seniors painted "West Point is a party school!" on the side of their R.V. in an attempt to rouse spirit among the corps. The irony of this statement roused more than a few chuckles, because cadets know that nothing could be further from the truth, but, while the rowdy fraternity party scene is not alive and well at West Point, don't be fooled into thinking that being a cadet isn't fun. With the number of available activities, it can be an absolute blast!

One of the toughest things about being a cadet is deciding what activities to become involved in. From sports to dramatics to religious activities, West Point truly has it all.

Athletics

Because "every cadet is an athlete, and every athlete will be challenged," all cadets must participate in sporting activities throughout the year. West Point has a highly competitive varsity program, with sixteen men's varsity sports and eight women's, each competing at the Division I level. More than twenty-five percent of the corps participates at this level. Some examples of varsity sports are football, basketball, baseball, softball, soccer, track, lacrosse, and swimming. For those cadets not involved in varsity athletics, there are twenty-nine competitive club sports. Some examples of club sports are crew, equestrian, fencing, mountaineering, rugby, sport parachute, marathon, martial arts, skiing, team handball, water polo, and women's lacrosse. Competitive club sports are great leadership opportunities as cadets do the majority of the planning and executing of team practices and events.

Yet another portion of the corps is involved in intramurals. Intramural competitions occur twice a week at 4:00 P.M. and are between teams fielded by each cadet company. There are seventeen different intramural sports for cadets to choose from. Intramurals foster company spirit, sportsmanship, and competition. Whichever level of sports a cadet chooses to participate in, each cadet is truly challenged. Sports at West Point are highly competitive, a great deal of fun, and a welcome break from the rigors of the academic day. School spirit and support for sporting teams at West Point are outstanding.

Every athletic facility you can think of is available for your use at West Point. Many of these facilities compare favorably with those found in the nation's top colleges and universities. Michie Stadium is the home of the Army football team with a seating capacity of over 39,000. There are capacity crowds throughout the fall season. Holleder Center houses 5,000-seat Christi Arena for basketball and 2,400-seat Tate Rink for hockey competition. The Arvin Cadet Physical Development Center, which features five gymnasiums and three swimming pools, begins a major renovation soon. It features Crandall Pool, an Olympic-size 50-meter pool. There are numerous special purpose rooms for squash, handball, racquetball, wrestling, and weight training. Gillis Field House is used for varsity and intramural indoor track competition. There is an all-weather outdoor track oval and football field at the renovated Shea Stadium complex that is used for daylight and evening competitive events. Lichtenstein Indoor Tennis Complex is the newest of the athletic facilities at West Point. There are also pistol and rifle ranges, numerous outdoor tennis courts, a ski slope, and an 18-hole golf course, which has also been redesigned.

Clubs

In addition to sports, there are countless other activities for cadets to enjoy. For instance, there are over 100 recreational clubs for cadets to participate in:

- There are clubs that support the corps such as the cadet band and the cadet radio station.
- There are clubs that are academic in nature such as the debate club.
- There are clubs that are geared toward the arts such as the Theatre Arts Guild.
- There are numerous religious groups and activities. Religion plays a large part in the lives of many cadets and cadets are the backbone of the churches on post. From singing in the choir, to teaching Sunday school, cadets find plenty of time to grow in their spirituality both personally and as a member of the larger community. Almost all religious denominations have services on post for cadets to attend.

There are also many social activities for cadets to attend. There is an on-post movie theater, frequent dances, a golf course, a ski slope, a bowling alley, boat rides, and tailgates. You'll very rarely ever hear a cadet say that he or she is bored!

FINANCIAL AID

Because there is no tuition cost associated with attending the United States Military Academy, all students have an equal chance of attending. This creates a diverse population within the corps of cadets. Because we wore the same uniforms and none of us paid tuition, we really didn't know how well-off our fellow cadets were, nor was it our concern. We accepted one another for who we were, not for our family's background.

All cadets at West Point are active-duty soldiers in the regular army. As such, they receive approximately $10,000 a year in pay. They are provided medical and dental care, and room and board. For this, cadets perform assigned duties and agree to serve as commissioned officers for a minimum of five years following graduation. From the cadet salary, deductions are made in order to pay for uniforms, textbooks, a desk-top computer, laundry, grooming, and similar necessities. Upon acceptance of the appointment, cadets are asked to make a one-time, nonrefundable deposit of about $2,900. The total cost of a cadet's full education is about $275,000. This is quite an impressive national investment!

GRADUATES

Some of my fondest memories of West Point involve marching in the alumni parades. Marching along an endless line of distinguished alumni and trying our hardest not to let them down was just an awesome experience. I recall one time when I was moved to tears as an "old grad" in a wheelchair struggled to his feet as my company marched by. We were his old company, and he was not going to sit in his wheelchair as we passed his position. As he applauded and cheered, "Looking good H-4! Go Hogs!" I could not help but get choked up. I was so proud to be even the smallest part of this amazing place. I was part of a tradition, part of history, and someday I too would be standing there facing the corps, recalling my days as a cadet, and cheering them on.

Graduates of West Point tend to be very proud of their alma mater; it seems that the older they get, the prouder they become. Alumni weekends are always very inspiring and very

- Robert E. Lee, 1829
- Ulysses S. Grant, 1843
- George Goethals, 1880
- John J. Pershing, 1886
- Douglas MacArthur, '03
- George Patton, '09
- Omar Bradley, '15
- Dwight D. Eisenhower, '15
- Matthew Ridgway, '17
- Leslie Groves, '18
- Maxwell Taylor, '22
- Creighton Abrams, '36
- Doc Blanchard, '47
- Glenn Davis, '47
- Alexander Haig, Jr., '47
- Brent Scowcroft, '47
- Frank Borman, '50
- Fidel Ramos, '50
- Edward White, '52
- H. Norman Schwarzkopf, '56
- Peter Dawkins, '59
- Mike Krzyzewski, '69

crowded. Grads come decked out from head to toe in paraphernalia that indicates their year of graduation. The alumni are known as "old grads" and the funny thing is, one is referred to as an "old grad" the second he or she tosses that hat in the air on graduation day. The common joke is that "old grads" are always complaining that the structure and discipline at West Point is simply not as rigid as when they were cadets. But most agree, it is the values and traditions that make West Point an enduring national treasure.

West Point has had more than a handful of distinguished graduates. Much of the U.S. Army leadership since the Civil War were members of the Long Gray Line—and the tradition continues. West Point graduates have, and will continue to make wonderful contributions to our nation. More than 100 graduates have competed on various U.S. Olympic teams. West Pointers have served as everything from presidents of corporations to presidents of the United States. Service is what West Point is all about, and our graduates serve our nation well.

SUMMING UP

West Point is indeed a special place. Where else can you eat virtually every meal in less than twenty minutes with the entire student body? Where else can you march into a stadium on national television and be a part of the Army-Navy rivalry? Where else can you stop on the way to class and pose for a picture with tourists? Where else can you make so many friends for a lifetime? At no other school does the word classmate mean so much. The bonds that are formed at West Point are unparalleled. On the very first day cadets are advised to "cooperate and graduate." This mantra follows them through victories and defeats, through successes and failures, from reception day until graduation day. The West Point Experience prepares cadets for all that life has to offer. When they throw their hats in the air, they are truly ready to be all that they can be.

❏ *2LT Megan Scanlon, B.S.*

UNITED STATES NAVAL ACADEMY

 United States Naval Academy
Annapolis, MD 21402-5018

 (410) 293-4361
Fax: (410) 293-4348

 Web site: *http://www.usna.edu/admissions*

 Enrollment

Full-time ❑ women: 600
❑ men: 3,600

INTRODUCING THE UNITED STATES NAVAL ACADEMY

*If life is measured by unique experiences, you just can't pick a better place.
In my four years, I went to Navy firefighting school, spent six-weeks of one summer in San Diego training on an amphibious vessel, sang for the president five
times as a member of the Men's Glee Club, skippered a forty-four-foot sailboat from
Annapolis to Newport, Rhode Island, and back, spent another month one summer*

with an F/A-18 squadron in Virginia Beach, went to Dublin, Ireland, to watch the Navy football team play Notre Dame, got my scuba qualifications, was in four musical productions, did aerobatics in a T-34 (one of the Navy's training planes) in Pensacola, Florida, and went under the waves in a submarine for a few days. Sound fascinating and eclectic? It was. And I recommend it to any of you.

The United States Naval Academy was founded in 1845 to provide a place where young men could learn the ways of the sea and the necessary traits of a future combat leader in an environment where a misstep could be tolerated here and there. *Here and there*, mind you. Not often. More than 150 years later, Navy offers both men and women undergraduate degrees in nineteen majors. While math and engineering receive the primary emphasis academically, there are several majors offered in the social sciences and humanities, including history, political science, and English. Everyone who is offered an appointment to Navy is admitted on full scholarship. The Navy pays for your room and board, tuition, medical and dental bills, and even gives you a modest monthly stipend. The academy has baccalaureate accreditation with both ABET and CSAB to go along with its regional accreditation. The Nimitz Library, built in 1973, acts as a second home for many of the academically taxed midshipmen at the Naval Academy. It has 636,500 volumes and subscribes to 2,000 periodicals, as well as possessing such computerized library sources and services as the card catalog, interlibrary loans, and database searching.

Special learning facilities include a learning resource center, planetarium, wind tunnels, radio station, propulsion laboratory, nuclear reactor, oceanographic research vessel, towing tanks, flight simulator, and a naval history museum called Preble Hall.

Mission

The Naval Academy has a unique clarity of purpose, expressed in the school's official mission: "To develop midshipmen morally, mentally, and physically, and imbue them with the highest ideals of duty, honor, and loyalty in order to provide graduates who are dedicated to a career of naval service and have potential for future development in mind and character to assume the highest responsibilities of command, citizenship, and government." That puts everyone—faculty, staff, and midshipmen—on the same wavelength. It also encourages a sense of spirit and pride found at few other schools.

The Campus

The Navy campus, known by the Brigade of Midshipmen as the "Yard" is located in Annapolis, a small Chesapeake Bay sailing mecca and the capital of Maryland. The city is located about thirty miles southeast of Baltimore and thirty-five miles east of Washington, D.C. The Yard covers 338 acres, and is home to twenty-five historic buildings including Bancroft Hall, in which all midshipmen live, which happens to be one of the single largest dormitories in the United States (4.8 square miles of hallway).

Classmates

One thing you can look forward to if you become a midshipman at the Naval Academy is making some of the best friends of your life. Your classmates will hail from all fifty states and more than twenty foreign countries. A recent high school graduate will have classmates here who have spent some time at other colleges or in the operational Navy as enlisted sailors or marines. The diversity is extraordinary, and refreshing. Religiously, many midshipmen practice traditional Judeo-Christian religions. Every major religion in the world is represented within the Brigade. Whatever else may happen, you can be sure that your horizons will expand tremendously.

ADMISSIONS REQUIREMENTS

Requirements for getting into the Naval Academy are much stiffer even than those at many of the nation's other top schools, because, at least in part, Navy looks at other things. While other institutions will examine you closely academically, the academy, because of its affiliation with the federal government and the U.S. Navy, will want to know more about what they are getting. To enter, you have to be between the ages of seventeen and twenty-three, unmarried, with no children, and pass the Department of Defense Medical Review Board physical exam. You must also score high on SAT or ACT. Of the 14,423 applicants for the class of 2008, only 15.2 percent received offers of admission. Of those finally admitted, fifty percent had scored higher than 600 on the Verbal section of their SAT and eighty-eight percent had done at least that well on the Math section (thirty-five percent exceeded 700 on the Math). The combined average SAT scores for the class of 2008 was 1320.

The Nomination

Once you've met these requirements, the next step is to attain a nomination. This can be done through a couple of different sources, the most common of which is the congressional nomination. This means that you put your name and information in the hands of your congressman and both of your senators, and they decide whether or not to grant you an interview. If you are successful in gaining an interview, you may receive a nomination. If a nomination is offered, it is up to the academy whether or not they will give you an appointment, which is the final acknowledgment of admission. (Note: if you are the child of a career military officer or enlisted person, or if your parent was disabled or killed in the service of our country, there are special categories under which you can be nominated; more information is available on this from the Office of Admissions web site: *www.usna.edu/admissions*). One little hint: you will put yourself in the best position to get a good look from your congressman and senators and the academy if you get your admissions materials in early.

What to Submit

There are a few things that you need to submit. In the spring of your junior year of high school you should write to the Candidate Guidance Office at the academy and ask for a Preliminary Application. They will send you one, and when you complete and return it, if scholastically qualified, you will officially be on the list of potential candidates. Then, sometime in the late summer or early fall of your last year in high school, you will receive the rest of the academy's admissions packet. Send it back quickly and you will jumpstart the process.

Extracurricular Activities

To make yourself most competitive for a nomination and subsequent appointment to the Naval Academy, there are a few things you can do. First of all—and this is true for all the good schools—get involved in all that you can and do it well. Prove in various activities that you have what it takes to be a leader. Load up your plate with Advanced Placement and Honors courses and perform favorably in them. These courses, along with faculty recommendations from your high school, play a sizable role in the selection process. Also, play varsity sports. The vast majority of each class entering the academy each year lettered in at least one sport in high school. These accomplishments, combined with good grades, show that you are a well-rounded individual, just the kind of person the military is looking for to make up its corps of officers.

Suffice it to say, if you are seeking academic challenge, you won't be at all disappointed by the Naval Academy—it is undoubtedly one of the most stressful and taxing academic programs found in our country. On top of that add the fact that military activities take up much of your free time, and you have a true time-management challenge. Study time simply isn't plentiful, and it takes a great deal of self-discipline to maximize your effectiveness. Over time you learn to cope, however, and are a better person for it.

There is also a great deal of academic opportunity at Navy.

Degrees

The Naval Academy offers the Bachelor of Science degree in three major areas. Engineering, Mathematics and Sciences, and Humanities and Social Sciences. Every midshipman is required to complete 140 semester hours to graduate, and to pass core courses in mathematics, engineering, natural sciences, humanities, and social sciences.

Physical Education

Physical Education is another staple of the curriculum, with everyone taking three semesters of swimming, a semester of boxing and wrestling, a semester of martial arts, and three semesters of free electives. The Physical Readiness Test (PRT) is taken each semester and tests the midshipmen's fitness by measuring their performance in push-ups, sit-ups, and a one-and-a-half-mile run. All midshipmen also take mandatory professional development courses during their four years that include Naval Leadership, Ethics and Law, Seamanship, and Navigation. Class attendance is mandatory for all midshipmen.

Class Size and Faculty

Class size and student-to-faculty ratio are advantages that you will truly appreciate if you attend the Naval Academy. The largest plebe chemistry lecture section may consist of thirty-five people. The average size for an introductory lecture is twenty-three students; for a regular course it's about fifteen, and for a lab, ten. The student-to-faculty ratio is seven to one.

The faculty, you'll find, is impressive in its own right. It is composed of both civilian professors and military officers, with ninety percent of its members holding Ph.D.s.

Educational Options

Last but not least, if you make it through all the rigors of the program and come out with top grades, there are several special options open to you at the academy. First, a group of seniors begin graduate work at educational institutions in the Washington, D.C./Baltimore area like Georgetown and Johns Hopkins each year. This is called the Voluntary Graduate Education Program, and is a great deal for the academically motivated. A small number of midshipmen are also named as Trident Scholars, allowing them to spend their last two semesters doing an independent research project. The Trident program culminates in a presentation given by the Scholars, attended by the faculty of their department, and open to the public. There are ten national honor societies active at the Naval Academy, and five of the departments on the Yard have honors programs in their majors.

SOCIAL LIFE AND ACTIVITIES

Want to be busy? Don't worry about that for a second if you receive an appointment to the Naval Academy. Activities aren't even really an option—they're an imperative. Everyone marches in parades, everyone plays a sport (either intramural or intercollegiate), everyone attends all home football games, everyone attends guest lectures by high-level speakers—everyone takes an active role in the moral, mental, and physical development as a future Navy or Marine Corps Leader of Character.

Sports

On the athletic front, the possibilities are endless. Everyone must participate in a sport, whether at the varsity, club, or intramural level. Navy offers nineteen different intercollegiate sports for men, ten for women, and three coed. Men's and women's basketball, water polo, men's lacrosse, football, and swimming, and crew are some of the sports in which Navy has traditionally been very strong.

In the fall, the football team is the center of all nonacademic activity. Before every home game, midshipmen march to the stadium and conduct a brief parade on the field; after the game they hold tailgaters. But during the game, they sit as a group. There is no sight quite like that of more than 4,000 young men and women in full uniform leaping up and down in celebration of a big play by the team. And keep in mind that the chance to cut loose only comes once in a blue moon at the academy. It gets crazy at Navy-Marine Corps Stadium in the fall, and, in the last couple of years there has been plenty to cheer about. In 2004, the team finished 10–2 and defeated the University of New Mexico in the Emerald Bowl in San Francisco. And since we're on the subject of football, we must mention the annual Army-Navy game. Is it a big event? Read this and you'll see. Both West Point and Navy pack their *entire* student body into buses and cart them to Philadelphia. So you've already got 4,200 plus students from each school there in uniform. Add countless alumni from both schools and national television coverage and you have a truly BIG event. More celebrations of even higher intensity ensue if Navy wins. If it's not a Navy win, the weekend usually takes a major downswing and becomes a time of commiseration with friends. Either way, it's an unforgettable thing to witness. And the game is ALWAYS great. It seems that every year, no matter what the records, rankings, or anything else, the game is a grudge match that comes down to the wire.

Club sports of the more exotic variety like rugby, ice hockey, and karate are also available and are part of some intercollegiate competition as well.

Organizations

Nonathletic activities at the Naval Academy are just as varied as the athletic offerings, if not more so. For the adventurous spirit (as are many that look into attending one of the service academies) there are organizations like the Alpine Racing Club and the Cycling Club, offering basic training sessions as well as more advanced opportunities to their members. Those interested in the fine arts will find the program, especially in the field of vocal music, significantly more rewarding than they might have expected at a service academy. The Men's and Women's Glee Clubs are two of America's best-known and critically acclaimed groups of their type, and Navy's annual winter musical productions are the largest drawing nonprofessional theatrical events in the Baltimore-Washington area. Gospel Choir and Protestant and Catholic Chapel Choirs round out the varied offerings for singers at Navy.

Players of brass instruments and percussion may find a home in the Naval Academy's Drum and Bugle Corps, which generally travels with the football team on road trips and plays every day for a flock of tourists as the Brigade of Midshipmen marches in from noon meal formation.

The Masqueraders are the Naval Academy's thespian troupe; they present a full-length dramatic production in the fall of each year.

If none of this sounds good, maybe mountaineering, cheerleading, competing in triathlons, or one of the host of other options available will. The possibilities are nearly endless.

Social Life

Now to your social life at the Naval Academy. USNA is not a party school. It should be said right off the bat that if your goal at college is to strengthen your liver and go to wild parties five days out of the week, while appearing only to take your exams each semester, Navy is *not* the place for you. Consistently ranked highest in the nation for sobriety and zero tolerance of drugs. Of course, you are reading this book, so this is not presumably the path you have chosen. You won't be highly successful at any of the other schools in this book by modeling your life after John Belushi's character in *Animal House*, but depending on your innate ability and resourcefulness you might be able to graduate. Forget it at Navy. You will be challenged with the restrictions, and the academic demands, accompanied by the fact that you have to stay in pretty darned good physical shape throughout your four years.

With that little disclaimer out of the way, the best way to explain social life at the academy is that you start out with none and it slowly gets better. One of the intentional pillars of the rigid training that one undergoes at the academy is self-sacrifice, and one of the big ways that this is hammered into you is through the withdrawal of many social privileges during your four years. You start out as a plebe (freshman) and go through your summer of basic training (known as Plebe Summer), in which you are not allowed to leave the Yard at all. Then the year starts.

An average day as a plebe? How about a morning? Wake up at 5:30, study your rates (required memorization), read the three newspaper articles that you'll be asked to report on at meal, go report your knowledge to your upperclass at 0630, fix your shoes and uniform for formation, do a chow call (stand out in the passageway and scream out the breakfast menu, officers of the watch, and a million other memorized items), and run off to 0700 formation. Morning classes feel more like sanctuary than a grind, since they mark the only time when you can sit quietly. Relax in Bancroft and an upperclassman will gladly remind you of the laundry bags to be delivered, newspapers to be collected for recycling, and various other menial jobs to do. Some plebes escape to the library during their free periods but there aren't any bells there, and fourth class midshipmen are notorious for dozing. Nod off in Nimitz and you might sleep through the rest of your classes for the day...and a plebe on restriction is significantly more unhappy than a plebe delivering laundry. The gist of all this: the kinder and gentler era we live in has had no effect on the level of activity that punctuates an academy plebe's mornings.

As a plebe during the academic year, you can go out only on Saturday afternoons and evenings. When you do venture away from the Yard, you can't drive, have to wear your uniform, and can only go a certain distance away from the grounds of the academy. Pretty limiting.

During sophomore year, known as youngster year, midshipmen can go out on Saturdays and Sundays. Once or twice a semester, they are allowed to leave on a Friday afternoon and to return that Sunday evening.

Weekday and weekend liberty is granted for first and second class midshipmen, based upon academic, athletic, and military performance.

Social Opportunities

While social life is, to say the least, not traditional, there ARE some social opportunities at the academy that are quite impressive. Every year popular music groups as well as renowned classical musicians come into Alumni Hall, the Naval Academy's arena and theater complex. Popular concerts of the past few years have included shows by Hootie and the Blowfish, Brooks and Dunn, Third Eye Blind, and the Goo-Goo Dolls. The Baltimore symphony, the St. Petersburg State Ballet Theatre, and the Moscow Virtuosi Orchestra, and the traveling company of the New York City Opera have recently appeared as part of the Distinguished Artists Series, a classical program conducted each year in Alumni Hall.

Dances

Some of the traditionally highly anticipated nonperforming arts social events of each year are just as impressive. The Ring Dance, which takes place at the end of the second class year to celebrate the new firsties' right to put on their class rings for the first time, is basically super-prom. It's a formal dance, and the second class midshipmen spend much of the year prior to the event agonizing about who they will bring, often from all the way across the country, to the event. The night includes dancing, a formal dinner, and fireworks to top it all off. Most people arrive in limos and stay at luxurious hotels in Washington, D.C., or Baltimore for the weekend. It's a nice reward for three years of hard work—and good motivation to put up with one more.

Commissioning Week

Then there is Commissioning Week, an indescribably exciting time each year that leads up to the graduation ceremony and the hat toss that mark the end of the road for the departing seniors. It's a week filled with formal parades, concerts, ship tours, a special performance by the Navy's Flight Demonstration Team, the Blue Angels, and many other nice events. Annapolis is so packed with people during Commissioning Week that it is advisable for parents to get hotel reservations at least one year in advance.

NOTABLE ACCOMPLISHMENTS OF NAVAL ACADEMY GRADS

- ○ 1 President of the United States
- ○ 2 Cabinet Members
- ○ 6 Ambassadors
- ○ 19 Members of Congress
- ○ 5 State Governors
- ○ 5 Secretaries of the Navy
- ○ 1 Secretary of the Air Force
- ○ 3 Chairmen of the Joint Chiefs of Staff
- ○ 3 Vice Chairmen of the Joint Chiefs of Staff
- ○ 25 Chiefs of Naval Operations
- ○ 9 Commandants of the Marine Corps
- ○ 2 Nobel Prize Winners
- ○ 73 Medal of Honor recipients
- ○ 52 Astronauts
- ○ 39 Rhodes Scholars
- ○ 15 Marshall Scholars
- ○ 84 Olmsted Scholars
- ○ 23 Fitzgerald Scholars
- ○ 766 Burke Scholars

FINANCIAL AID

Financial aid at the United States Naval Academy is a given. Everyone at the school has room, board, and tuition paid for all four years by the federal government. Midshipmen even receive a modest (very modest) stipend each month for any extraneous expenses. At the end of the second class year, all members of the Brigade are eligible for the "career starter loan." This is a loan of up to approximately $25,000 (the ceiling gets a little higher every year) that you pay back at incredibly low (in the neighborhood of one percent) interest rates over the time that you serve in the Navy or Marine Corps after graduation. And that brings up another point: in exchange for these various little perks, all graduates of the Naval Academy owe the Navy or Marine Corps at least five years serving as officers in the operational force.

GRADUATES

The effect that graduating from a place like the academy has on a person is interesting and a bit humorous. You spend four years grousing and complaining at every turn about the limitations that have been put on you and how you wish you could just be "normal" and such. Then you toss your hat up into the azure skies on graduation day and develop an instant and puzzling fondness for almost everything about the place. Navy grads are like a huge extended family. They can be found in all walks of life and are always ready to lend friendship and a helping hand to another alum. And, as it might seem would be the case, they've got more exciting stories to tell than the average grad from a "normal" school. Where the average homecoming gathering at another school will undoubtedly be filled with tales of business deals and house remodelings, a Navy homecoming is filled with anecdotes concerning such topics as night landings on aircraft carriers, being shot at by surface-to-air missiles, or a weekend spent on liberty in Bahrain. It's a whole different world. . . .

SUMMING UP

What the academy did for my classmates and me was that, through all of its stifling regulations and regimentation, it set us free on the playground of life. It opened up to us a wealth of opportunities that will take some of us to the top of the military profession and to the highest levels of government, and others in altogether different but exciting directions. And we all set out on our journeys armed to the hilt with weapons not often found in our society today: self-awareness, self-reliance, and determination. We were forged in the fire of four years by the waters of the Chesapeake Bay, four years that often hurt, but also purified and strengthened the good in us, and gave us the tools to attack life and its hurdles with gusto and confidence.

Attending the United States Naval Academy is a decision that, if you come expecting a challenge, you will never regret. It is a small, insulated, often unforgiving place that pushes you to your limits. For twenty-three hours, fifty-five minutes a day in a regular school week during your four years there you might hate it. But that other five minutes comes about once a day when something happens that reminds you of how much you owe to the place. Maybe it happens walking to class in the morning and looking out at the beautiful campus for a minute, or seeing one of the many close friends you've made there, or going into Memorial Hall and seeing the memorial register of past graduates who sacrificed their lives for our country in all of the major wars that America has been involved in since 1845. Those moments are special. They make it all worthwhile.

And let's face it...there are more pluses than you could hope for at most other schools: Your education is paid for, you are in a great and historic town, you make lifelong friendships, visit exotic places, try things you've never previously dreamed of, and get a degree out of all of it. You'll have all the tools you need to be a success once you are done here. So how could you really go wrong?

The single biggest thing that attracted me to Annapolis was my awe for the extraordinary heroism that so many graduates of the school had exhibited throughout our nation's history. Only a few of us will ever be called on to perform in situations that dire. But the way we prepare for that is the same way that we must prepare for roles more typical but no less important. The essential thing is that we ready ourselves, whether we are preparing to give our life for our men and women or just be a figure that works for general improvement in the quality of life in our community. This preparation must be intrinsic, but there are a few institutions left in America that can give you invaluable tools with which you can further sculpt yourself into that which you ultimately desire to be. The Naval Academy is one of them, because no matter what one's personal experience, good or bad, it is a place that you leave self-aware. You know what your strengths and weaknesses are, and you know that you can put up with a great deal of hardship compared to the average person you run into on the street who spent four years at fraternity or sorority parties, having the time of his or her life. Any way you slice it, if one is serious about making a difference, whether it be as a sub-mariner, a pilot, a businessperson or in any other career, this is still the best school in the United States to attend. There's no question in my mind.

❏ *Ensign Anthony Holds, B.S.*

UNIVERSITY OF CALIFORNIA, LOS ANGELES (UCLA)

 University of California, Los Angeles (UCLA)
Los Angeles, CA 90095

 (310) 825-3101
Fax: (310) 206-1206

 E-mail: *ugadm@saonet.ucla.edu*
Web site: *www.admissions.ucla.edu*

 Enrollment

Full-time ❏ women: 13,524
❏ men: 10,326

INTRODUCING UCLA

UCLA is like a city within a city, drawing more than 60,000 people daily to its 419-acre campus, nestled in the hills of west Los Angeles five miles from the Pacific Ocean.

I love the view from the top of Janss Steps. Looking west, you can see the residence halls rising above the green athletics field and Drake Stadium. In the distance are the Santa Monica Mountains. Looking east, you face the heart of campus, where Royce Hall and Powell Library, the campus' oldest and most famous buildings, stand majestically. Between them is a beautiful quad area and a brick fountain. Just breathtaking!

The "metropolis" of UCLA includes some ten libraries, two museums and an art gallery, three gardens, an elementary school, day-care facilities, residential complexes and buildings that house nearly 7,000 people, several theaters and performing arts auditoriums, stores, restaurants, gyms, a basketball arena, and a hospital. Additionally, the campus has its own police department, a chiller/cogeneration plant that assures the campus of low-cost power, hot water, and efficient cooling, its own postal system, a fleet of buses, and several newspapers.

In fact, UCLA and Los Angeles have nurtured one another through the years, ever since the precursor to UCLA, a two-year teaching college, was established in the little pueblo town of Los Angeles in the 1880s. As Los Angeles grew, so did UCLA. Founded in 1919, the university moved to its current Westwood home in 1929.

From then on, both the school and the city enjoyed phenomenal growth and development. Today, Los Angeles has the second largest population in the United States, and UCLA educated 37,000 students and is the most popular university in the United States among applicants.

In just over eighty years, the university has earned a worldwide reputation for the excellence of its programs and the achievements of its students and faculty. It has distinguished itself as the only campus among the nation's top ten research universities that was established in the twentieth century.

UCLA is a large and complex institution devoted to undergraduate and graduate scholarship, research, and public service. Known for academic excellence, many of its programs are rated among the best in the nation, some among the best in the world.

For more information, please visit *www.ucla.edu*.

ADMISSIONS REQUIREMENTS

If you decide to apply to UCLA, you're in good company: No other university in the nation receives as many applications for freshman admission as UCLA, making it the country's most popular school among applicant four years running with more than 44,000 applications received for a recent freshman class. Of those applicants, UCLA admitted 10,455 and enrolled 4,257. Because of the sheer number of students hoping to be admitted to UCLA, getting in has, predictably, become extremely competitive.

Grades and Test Scores

Here's a sense of what it takes in terms of grades and test scores: The overall grade point average of those students admitted for the same freshman class, including extra weight given to honors and advanced placement courses, was 4.23. The raw grade point average, without calculating extra points for honors and AP courses, was 3.77. The median SAT I score of admitted students was 1,322. And admitted students took an average of 18.2 honors and advanced placement courses.

Academic Performance and Personal Achievement

While strong academic performance is exceedingly important and at least half the entering class is selected solely on academic criteria, UCLA does admit some students on a combination of academic performance and personal achievement. Personal achievement includes leadership and initiative in school or community organizations, special talents, ethnic/cultural awareness, and overcoming general life challenges particular to the student's environment, personal/family situation, social or economic difficulties, or lack of educational opportunities.

The vast majority of Bruins come from California, though students hail from all over the nation and world. In fact, UCLA is considered one of the most racially, ethnically, and culturally diverse universities in the country and, as such, is especially committed to recruiting top underrepresented high school students.

Personal Essay

In addition to requiring the SAT or ACT standardized tests and two SAT Subject Tests—in two different subject areas—UCLA also asks applicants to submit a personal essay. No topic is specified for the essay; its purpose is to give admissions officers a better, more personalized feel for the applicants since UCLA does not conduct interviews as part of the admissions process. The personal statement also gives applicants a chance to provide information about themselves complementary to the rest of the application.

Application Filing

The application filing period for freshmen applying for fall admission of the following year is November 1–30. Application forms are available from California high school and community college counseling offices and at University of California campuses. Prospective students may also print an application or enroll on-line at *http://www.ucop.edu/pathways*, the

University of California's comprehensive admissions web site. One application can be used to apply for any of the University of California's eight campuses that offer undergraduate instruction. The application cost for each school is $40. Notification of admission is sent out in March.

Transferring

Another, and somewhat less cutthroat, way to get into UCLA is by transferring from a community college. A lot of partnership programs are in place between UCLA and California community colleges that help facilitate the transfer process.

ACADEMIC LIFE

As with anything, academic life at UCLA is all about balance. It's about choosing a balanced class load, balancing class and work schedules, and balancing schoolwork and extracurricular activities.

It's very easy, especially with new students, to lose that balance—for an active social life (i.e., partying) to leave no room for studying—or, at the other extreme, to become too overwhelmed with schoolwork to enjoy the recreational and extracurricular activities that are so important to a well-rounded college experience.

It often takes a while for students to find the groove that works for them—the best times to take classes, the best ways to study, how to approach test-taking, how to get away with the minimum amount of work—but trying to find that balance early on can be a real boost.

Orientation and academic counselors are available to help students plan class schedules and give advice about ways to lead a balanced college life. The campus also offers some academic skills and support workshops that can help as well.

The Basics

Unlike most schools, UCLA operates on a three-quarter, not a two-semester, system. This means more classes overall and less time per class, as instruction lasts only ten weeks a quarter plus one week for finals.

Students generally take three to four classes per quarter. Most lower-division classes earn five units each; undergraduates need a minimum of 180 units to graduate. Class time averages four hours a week per course. Grades are based on a four-point, letter-grade scale.

Students will take a combination of upper-division and lower-division coursework. Lower-division courses tend to be broad, introductory courses taken by first- and second-year students to satisfy general education requirements or major prerequisites. These are often large lectures with a smaller discussion section. Upper-division classes are more focused classes that tend to be taken usually during the junior and senior years of school by those majoring in the department.

The majority of UCLA's 25,300 undergraduates choose majors from departments in the College of Letters and Science, which is the intellectual core of the campus with thirty-eight academic departments and thirty-seven specialized programs offering 103 majors. Additionally the campus has eleven professional schools, four of which grant undergraduate degrees: the arts and architecture, engineering, nursing, and theater, film, and television.

The members of the faculty at UCLA are some of the most distinguished in the world; among them are Nobel Laureates, Guggenheim fellows, Fulbright scholars, and members of the National Academy of Sciences and the American Academy of Arts and Sciences. Students will find them to be very knowledgeable and passionate about their subject matter, and most take a genuine interest in their students. The discussion sections and some seminar classes are usually led by graduate student teaching assistants.

Class grades are usually determined by some combination of midterms, finals, quizzes, paper, research or other projects, homework assignments, and participation.

Students must declare a major by their junior level of school. The average time to graduation is four years and a quarter.

North and South Campuses

There exists at UCLA a healthy rivalry between its liberal arts and its science majors. An invisible line separates the north campus from the south campus, which indicates not just a physical distinction but an academic one as well: The north campus houses the arts, theater, film and television, the humanities, and the social sciences, while engineering, the medical complex, and the life and physical sciences call the south campus home.

General Education Clusters

Students are required to take, usually during the first couple of years of study, a set of general education (GE) courses intended to introduce them to the richness and diversity of the various academic departments and broaden their intellectual perspective. Taking GE courses is also a way for students in search of a major to explore different academic areas.

UCLA recently revamped its general education requirements by reducing the number of required courses to focus on writing, discussion, and broad theory in three "foundation" themes: arts and humanities, society and culture, and scientific inquiry.

Entering freshmen can gain invaluable academic experience by taking a Freshman Cluster course. Each cluster course spans three quarters and is team-taught by faculty members from various disciplines across campus. Each course focuses on a common theme, such as the global environment, and presents students with an interdisciplinary perspective for approaching certain problems. Freshmen get priority in the new Fiat Lux Program which provides seminar courses for small groups of students (15) with UCLA's top faculty in a broad range of subjects.

Taking a cluster course is also a good way for incoming students to meet other freshmen and develop a sense of academic connectedness during the first year, get introduced to a variety of disciplines, and form relationships with faculty early on, as well as sharpen writing, quantitative reasoning, critical thinking, and information literacy skills that they need to excel at UCLA.

Undergraduate Research

UCLA is devoted to providing interested undergraduates with opportunities to conduct research, either alongside faculty or on their own projects. Several renowned programs support undergrads in independent research or partner students with faculty mentors in valuable research training and experience for advanced work and preparation for graduate school.

The Undergraduate Research Centers, which support scholarly, critical, and creative undergraduate research in the college, provide individual counseling, administer stipends and scholarships, sponsor the undergraduate research journals, and organize campuswide undergraduate research events, among other roles.

Additionally, students can engage in research for academic credit by enrolling in classes with a research component. This can include classes where a research assignment or paper is part of the coursework; special classes or programs within a department with a focus on research; or the departmental honors program, which awards honors to students who complete two quarters of individual research culminating in a senior thesis.

Many students also find jobs in labs or as assistants to professors, which is also a great way to gain exposure to research.

Research has provided me with a very rewarding way to not only learn about science, but also contribute to its body of knowledge. Most importantly, it has fostered my independence. From presenting work at professional conferences to the writing of papers and abstracts, I was forced to do many things on my own which were quite different from my classroom work.

Other Educational Opportunities

For those with personal or professional interests outside of Los Angeles, or a sense of wanderlust, there are several ways for students to combine education with travel.

The most obvious choice is to spend a year abroad. The UC system's Education Abroad Program (EAP) offers study opportunities at more than one hundred universities in thrity-six countries. Students continue to be registered at UCLA and receive university units, grades, and financial aid.

If the year-long program is too much of a commitment, EAP also has one-term programs and summer programs in a variety of countries. UCLA Summer Sessions also offers summer programs abroad. In these programs, UCLA faculty members teach UCLA courses in a foreign city that is relevant to the subject matter.

The Center for American Politics and Public Policy, which sponsors the Quarter in Washington, D.C. Program, and the EXPO Internship and Study Abroad Services are two other sources for national and international study opportunities. The Center for Community creates opportunities for students to enhance their studies with work in the community or government agencies.

SOCIAL LIFE AND ACTIVITIES

UCLA is one of the most populated campuses nationwide, with several times the number of students as at a small, liberal arts college, so for a new student, being just one of so many faces in the crowd can be intimidating. But who's got the time to feel out of place or lonely when there are so many different ways to meet people and get involved?

Granted, it's not always easy to meet other students in a 200-person lecture, so the key to a large social circle at UCLA is really to break the campus down to its component parts. Again, think of the campus as a large city, and go out and find a sense of community in smaller-group situations, whether it's through involvement in a community service group, participation in recreation class, or working on the student newspaper. Small group settings can be found in most classes. More than half of all classes have twenty-five students or less.

The great thing is that you'll make friends across the campus, and through those people meet more and more people. Ninety percent of freshmen live on campus, and the vast majority of all undergrads live within a half-mile of UCLA.

So it really doesn't matter if you don't know anyone, you soon will. Just have fun doing the things that interest you—UCLA and Los Angeles certainly aren't lacking for activities, just read on!—and before you know it, you'll be making friends and leading an active social life.

Dorm and Apartment Life

The best way to feel a part of the college social community is to live on or near campus. The majority of the noncommuting student population lives either in residence halls, suites, and complexes, which are situated at the northwest part of campus, or in Westwood apartments located in a pocket southwest of the campus.

For freshmen, social life tends to revolve around the dorms. At UCLA, about ninety-three percent of incoming freshmen live on campus, so it's really the best way to meet others during the first year. Students will have close contact with their roommates and those on their floor, and will tend to make many friends—some lifelong—from this group.

Students also have the option of choosing a "theme" floor, in which all those on the floor share a similar interest, such as the great outdoors, the arts, or health and fitness. All residence halls and complexes are coed except for designated single-sex theme floors.

UCLA's Office of Residential Life offers a variety of academic and social programs for residents, while formal and informal gatherings, outings, parties, and other activities are always taking place, as well.

> *Looking back at my freshman year in the dorms brings back many fond memories. There was the time when eight or nine of us packed in a pickup truck to go to the USC football game. I remember my friends singing karaoke on my stereo to the Grease soundtrack. I was so happy when some twenty people piled into my dorm room at midnight and sang "Happy Birthday" to me when I turned eighteen. I remember us ordering Thai food when late-night hunger struck. I remember us throwing water balloons out our sixth-story window at unfortunate passersby. I'll never forget creating gross concoctions with our left-over foods and daring each other to eat them. And I'll always remember a gaggle of us girls having long, serious talks, giving each other makeovers, and getting ready to hit the town.*

While apartment life is less social and structured than living in the dorms, many students by their second or third year have their groups of friends, have found their interests and niches, and feel the need to be more independent. Most often, four students share a two-bedroom apartment, and social life tends to revolve around roommates and friends, hanging out at the apartment, or going out to parties or Westwood.

Parties and Nightlife

The apartments are the setting for a lot of the parties students attend. Usually several apartment parties take place each Friday and Saturday night, and the students who hold them often make them open to anyone who wants to come.

Fraternity houses usually hold parties every Thursday night for members and invited and female guests. Each house also has one or two big theme parties a year that are open to most students. Fraternities and sororities also often have private parties, exchanges, and other activities for their members.

By the time the students who used to frequent parties reach the age of twenty-one, they can often be found hanging out at Westwood bars and restaurants, where the big student nights tend to be Tuesday, Thursday, Friday, and Saturday.

The students who have cars and find that Westwood has grown too small for them often explore the nightlife offered by Santa Monica, Hollywood, and Manhattan and Hermosa Beach hotspots. UCLA is a designated "transportation hub" for three major municipal bus services. The campus is served by hundreds of bus stops each day.

Students can also often be found catching a new movie being shown at one of Westwood's numerous theaters or hanging out at restaurants and coffeehouses in Westwood.

Campus Life

With more than 850 campus clubs and organizations, from student government to sports clubs, cultural organizations to fraternities and sororities, one would be hard-pressed not to find a group to join. But if so, then with a minimum of three people, students can start and register their own campus group.

Here is just a sampling of the variety of campus groups and programs available to students.

- Aspiring writers, journalists, photographers, and designers may find invaluable experience working on the student paper, the *Daily Bruin*, which is one of the largest daily newspapers in Los Angeles.
- The talented and the spirited might find a spot with the UCLA Marching Band or on the Spirit Squad as a cheerleader or yell leader.
- The Undergraduate Students Association Council has six elected offices (president, internal vice president, external vice president, three general representatives) and seven student commissions (Academic Affairs, Campus Events, Community Service, Cultural Affairs, Facilities, Financial Supports, and Student Welfare). How about running for office or joining the staff of an elected student official?
- The Community Service Commission serves Los Angeles through more than twenty programs to help disenfranchised groups such as juvenile inmates, the homeless, the

mentally and physically disabled, the impoverished, and the abused. More than 2,500 students offer their services on a volunteer basis. Numerous other opportunities for volunteer work and community service exist across campus.

- Help bring entertainment and cultural programming to campus by joining the Campus Events Commission or the Cultural Affairs Commission. Campus Events is responsible for bringing speakers such as Bill Gates, David Letterman, Whoopie Goldberg, Jesse Jackson, and Matt Groening to campus, as well as bands such as Rage Against the Marchine, Green Day, 10,000 Maniacs, and No Doubt for concerts. Cultural Affairs sponsors WorldFest, a celebration of campus diversity, and the annual Memorial Day weekend Jazz/Reggae Festival.
- UCLA has an active Greek system. More than forty organizations, many with their own houses, provide members with multiple opportunities for social and academic support, leadership development, community service, and networking. At various times during the year, but particularly during the fall and spring, the various houses launch a series of "rush" events to recruit new members. About ten percent of the student population takes part in Greek life.

Feeding the homeless through Hunger Project was one of my greatest memories of UCLA. I feel like I made a true contribution to society. I took action in a cause that I truly believed in. Being at UCLA opened that door of opportunity for me and motivated me to create change.

ATHLETIC LEGENDS

- ○ Kareem Abdul-Jabbar, basketball
- ○ Troy Aikman, football
- ○ Arthur Ashe, tennis
- ○ Jimmy Connors, tennis
- ○ Gail Devers, track
- ○ Florence Griffith Joyner, track
- ○ Eric Karros, baseball
- ○ Jackie Joyner-Kersee, track
- ○ Karch Kiraly, volleyball
- ○ Reggie Miller, basketball
- ○ Jackie Robinson, baseball
- ○ Bill Walton, basketball

Athletics

Sports fans rejoice! With more national championships in men's and women's sports than any other university, UCLA is unsurpassed in the world of college athletics. When one talks about UCLA sports, one talks about winning championships, breaking records, and creating legends. UCLA has under its belt a total of 107 national championships, among them eighty-six NCAA team titles, the highest in the nation. Legendary coach John Wooden made UCLA a basketball institution when he led UCLA to a record-setting eighty-eight straight wins and ten national titles in twelve seasons.

UCLA has also been a consistent powerhouse in the Olympic Games. At the 2000 Sydney games, fifty-eight Bruins—alumni and current and incoming students—competed in fifteen sports, the most of any university. UCLA also ranked number one among all universities in gold medals (eight), overall medals (eighteen), number of different gold medalists (eight), and number of different medalists (seventeen). In fact, UCLA students and graduates have won so many gold medals that, as a group, they've consistently made the top ten on a country-by-country ranking. In a tally of gold medals, UCLA was the third most-decorated "country" in the 1984 Los Angeles games, the fourth in 1988 in Seoul, the ninth in 1992 in Barcelona, and the seventh in 1996 in Atlanta.

What does all this mean for UCLA students and Bruins sports fans? Come football season each fall, it means treks to the Rose Bowl in Pasadena, the nation's most famous college football stadium and home to UCLA's football team, for tailgating and barbecuing, exciting sports action, and suffusing feelings of school spirit and pride—just take a look at the alumni families in full Bruin regalia and you'll understand. The annual UCLA vs. USC crosstown rivalry game is probably the most anticipated single annual sporting event. It's highlighted by "Beat USC" week activities, including a huge pep rally and bonfire two nights before the game.

I remember when UCLA's basketball team won the national championships in 1995. It was the most amazing, unforgettable feeling. My friends and I watched it on television and after the victory, we all walked into Westwood, where it seemed as though the whole school had gathered. So there we were, hundreds and thousands of proud and joyous Bruins celebrating, yelling, screaming, cheering, laughing, and hugging. It was my proudest Bruin memory ever!

Basketball season induces similar bouts of Bruin fanaticism. The most diehard students regularly camp out overnight in front of the ticket office to get the best student seats in the house—arena level at Pauley Pavilion. At the games you'll find the atmosphere and the clapping, cheering, and chanting traditions infectious. Don't worry if you can't watch the games live: There is a good chance that a group of Bruins will be yelling and cheering, crowded in front of a television at someone's apartment or at a bar, especially during "March Madness." As the name would suggest, college basketball fans across the nation get a little insane for about two weeks every year during the NCAA basketball tournament, in which UCLA is a regular contender.

Those whose idea of sports enjoyment runs more toward the likes of volleyball, tennis, baseball, gymnastics, water polo, and track and field will still find plenty to cheer about at UCLA, which is also a national leader in those sports. Additionally, UCLA, on occasion, hosts major sporting events in its arenas. For example, the Mercedes-Benz Tennis Cup, which draws the world's top male tennis players, is held annually at UCLA's Los Angeles Tennis Center.

For more information, visit *www.uclabruins.com*.

Recreation

For those who enjoy playing sports as much as watching them, enter UCLA Recreation. The comprehensive recreation center includes facilities such as a weight room, tennis and racquetball courts, swimming pools, and a rock-climbing wall; programs such as martial arts, tennis, dancing, Tae-Bo and yoga classes; outdoor adventure trips; sailing, kayaking, and surfing lessons through the UCLA Marina Aquatic Center; private lessons; and refereed intramural sports competitions. Working out at the gym, taking some of the classes, or going on a trip are great ways to get in shape, let out some of that stress, and meet other students. It can also be a way to try new sports or discover one that can last a lifetime.

There are also plenty of opportunities at UCLA Recreation for student employment or involvement, from umpires for the IM tournaments to counselors for Bruin Kids summer camp; from lifeguards to class instructors and trip leaders. In most cases, the recreation center provides training for these positions.

Enrolled students do not have to pay anything extra for use of the facilities. A pass to take the drop-in fitness classes costs $45 a year. Some classes require a small fee. Classes at the marina and outdoor trips tend to be somewhat steeper, but still a bargain.

For complete information, go to *www.recreation.ucla.edu*.

Los Angeles—Entertainment, Culture, and Beyond

Located in one of the largest, most vibrant, and well-known metropolitan cities in the world, UCLA offers its students Los Angeles as their backyard and playground. For those who love the outdoors, Los Angeles is just steps from the ocean, mountains, forests, rivers, and deserts, which means that activities such as surfing, rafting, snowboarding, hiking, camping, or just getting out of the city and looking at the stars in the clear night sky are less than a couple of hours drive away.

For another type of stargazer, Los Angeles is the place to be. Celebrities regularly come on campus to perform, give a talk, walk their dog, use the track, watch Bruin sports, or even get treated at the medical center. The campus has also hosted such events as rock concerts and the MTV Music Awards. Celebrities are routinely spotted in Westwood shopping, dining, or taking in a movie. Glamorous movie premieres for Hollywood blockbusters attract top stars to Westwood theaters on what seems to be almost a weekly basis. And that's just in Westwood, with no mention of the famed Sunset Strip bars, Hollywood clubs, trendy restaurants, and chic Beverly Hills boutiques.

For a more refined sort of cultural pursuit, Los Angeles is also the home of the Getty Center, the premier $1-billion museum-cum-cultural center-cum-icon perched in the Brentwood hills just above campus. Other noted museums include the Los Angeles County Museum of Art and the Museum of Contemporary Art, as well as UCLA's own Fowler Museum of Cultural History and the UCLA Hammer Museum. UCLA Performing Arts brings a roster of top international talents to perform, while Broadway productions often find their way to local venues such as the Ahmanson, the Pantages, and the Shubert theaters.

Sports and music fans will find plenty of live athletic events and concerts at the Staples Center, Dodger Stadium, the Rose Bowl, the Great Western Forum, the Hollywood Bowl, and Universal Amphitheater.

Los Angeles is also the home of such top tourist attractions as Disneyland, Universal Studios, Six Flags Magic Mountain, Venice Beach, Mann's Chinese Theater, and the Walk of Fame.

What college experience is complete without at least a couple of road trips to reminisce over with friends for years after? Las Vegas, San Diego, Santa Barbara, the San Francisco Bay Area, and Mexico, for example, are all within half a day's drive away.

And for those whose sights are set even further, Los Angeles International Airport is less than ten miles away, convenient for spring break trips to Mazatlán and summer backpacking tours of Europe.

UCLA is consistently ranked one of the top ten universities in the nation in surveys of academic excellence and is considered—at under $4,225 a year (for in-state students)—a real bargain among the most competitive colleges. However, students—and their families—must still come up with the money as well as cough up an additional several thousand for books and living expenses. This is where financial aid comes in.

More than fifty percent of UCLA students receive some sort of financial aid; the average annual award amount is $8,000. Many also work part time.

Federal, state, and university funds provide four types of aid: scholarships based on grades and other achievements; need-based grants; loans that must be paid back after graduating; and work-study money, which is need-based and earned through part-time employment.

Entering undergraduates can apply for many state and federal scholarships in the scholarship section of their University of California application. Between January 1 and March 2, students must submit the Free Application for Federal Student Aid (FAFSA) to qualify for other forms of financial aid.

FAFSA applications are then evaluated for financial need, which is calculated by subtracting what students and their families can contribute from the estimated cost of education. The expected contribution amount takes into account the student's and parents' total income and assets (excluding home equity), savings, taxes, mandatory living expenses, parents' ages and need for retirement income, number of children and other dependents in the family household, family members in college, and certain unusual financial circumstances.

The university then creates an awards package using several funding sources to cover the balance. Aid packages contain the maximum grant and university scholarship amount for which a student qualifies. Funds are generally distributed evenly over fall, winter, and spring quarter. In most cases, students must maintain at least half-time enrollment to receive aid.

Additionally, there are numerous opportunities for private scholarship, and the financial aid office and other resources can help match students with scholarships. UCLA and Westwood also offer plenty of opportunities for student employment for those who choose to work to help pay for school.

GRADUATES

UCLA graduates receive an education that prepares them for careers in almost any field, to be leaders, newsmakers, decision makers, policy makers, entrepreneurs. Alumni have found jobs in all fields, whether it's in entertainment, sports, the corporate world, politics, or wherever they choose to be.

Some students get recruited or find jobs before graduating. Others find that the Career Center and Alumni Association provide a lot of career planning and networking advice and programs to help them find a job quickly. Many students also go on to graduate or professional school.

SUMMING UP

UCLA really is the best of all worlds. Its prime location in metropolitan Los Angeles near the Pacific Ocean, Hollywood, and Los Angeles International Airport makes it an international gateway for culture and entertainment. The climate here is mild and pleasant all year. UCLA itself, as one of the finest research universities in the world, draws top scholars and scientists from around the globe, prime research dollars, worldwide attention for its cutting-edge research, and a reputation for all-around excellence. Many of its academic programs are ranked in the top ten nationally. Its medical center has been named the best hospital in the western United States for the thirteenth straight year. It is a leader in new technology. UCLA is one of the top athletics schools. It is known for the diversity and quality of its student body.

And UCLA's reach can be felt all over the city, nation, and world, as the campus and its people outreach to those in need, from poverty-stricken inner-city Los Angeles families to war refugees. Both UCLA Extension, which is the largest urban-based continuing education program in the United States, and the Medical Center have several satellite sites to serve those all over the city. Professors conduct research in all parts of the world, and their work—whether it's laying the groundwork for the Internet or finding a cure for AIDS—affects everyone.

Not only that, but UCLA is, from anyone's perspective, a beautiful campus. The handsome red brick and terra-cotta Romanesque buildings at the center of campus evoke distinction and refinement, while some of the newer buildings shout innovation and creativity, and the gorgeous landscaping, striking architecture, and stunning views lend an inherent harmony to the entire campus.

No wonder UCLA is the most sought-after school in the nation!

❏ *Amy Ko, B.A.*

UNIVERSITY OF CHICAGO

 University of Chicago
Chicago, IL 60637

 (773) 702-1234, Admissions: (773) 702-8650
Fax: (773) 702-4199

 Web site: *www.uchicago.edu*

 Enrollment

Full-time ❏ women: 2,324
❏ men: 2,258

Part-time ❏ women: 19
❏ men: 37

INTRODUCING THE UNIVERSITY OF CHICAGO

I was going to begin: "When I look back on my four years at the University of Chicago, they seem to me like a blissful dream." But that is precisely wrong. I should say: "When I look back on my four years at the University of Chicago, they seem to me years of waking up and of being intensely awake." I say "awake" because the University of Chicago, especially its college, is a community committed to the life of the mind, so that inquiry, whether in laboratories or libraries, tends to be intertwined with life.

As one of the world's great universities, the University of Chicago has been shaping higher education—and the intellectual lives of undergraduates—for more than a century. A private institution chartered in 1890, Chicago's 203-acre campus on the shores of Lake Michigan has been home to 78 Nobel Laureates, the largest number affiliated with any American university. Chicago scholars were the first to split the atom, to measure the speed of light, and to develop the field of sociology.

Carrying on this tradition of innovative and provocative thought, Chicago's 4,515 undergraduates form a community of learners who have discovered the pleasure of exploring, taking risks, immersing themselves intellectually, and determining the direction of their own education. They choose Chicago because they want an undergraduate liberal arts curriculum taught by a faculty of renowned scholars and teachers; they seek small classes and spirited discussions (eighty-three percent of classes have fewer than twenty-five students, and the student-faculty ratio is 4:1); they participate in opportunities on and off campus that take their professional and recreational interests to a higher level; they want preparation for the most challenging careers and best graduate schools; and they look to learn outside of the classroom from some of the brightest minds around—other Chicago students.

ADMISSIONS REQUIREMENTS

The Committee on Admissions has no rigid formula for the successful applicant and considers a candidate's entire application—academic and extracurricular records, essays, letters of recommendations, and SAT or ACT scores. A personal interview is encouraged because it provides the candidate with a chance to learn more about the college and lets the college know what may not easily be conveyed in the application.

Though no specific secondary school courses are prescribed, a standard college preparatory program is ideal: four years of English, three to four years of math and laboratory sciences, three or more years of social sciences, and a foreign language. The essays that you are asked to write as part of the application are an opportunity to show your individuality in addition to your ability to write clearly and effectively.

The University of Chicago does not employ numerical cut-offs when evaluating applications for admission. Of the 1,220 students in the Class of 2008, seventy-eight percent graduated in the top ten percent of their high school classes. The middle fifty percent of admitted students had either a combined score between 1360 and 1490 on the SAT or a cumulative score of between 28 and 32 on the ACT. SAT Subject Tests are not required.

Evaluating Applications

The first page of the Chicago application states, "A college application is an imperfect way of communicating your qualifications, talents, and special interests. Still, you should find plenty of room for creativity here as you describe yourself and your accomplishments." The goal in the Admissions Office is to extend its knowledge of a student well beyond a test score or GPA and understand, as much as possible, that student's personal and academic qualities. To that end, each application is read first by a regional counselor, someone who should understand more about the student's high school and its environment. Then, each application is read at least once more (and perhaps three or four times in all), with a final decision rendered by an admissions committee, an associate, or the dean.

For first-year applicants, the following information for admission consideration is required:

- Personal information including extracurricular activities
- Essays—two short-answer responses and one extended essay
- High School Report Form including the transcript and the counselor recommendation
- Teacher Recommendations—one from a math or science teacher and one from an English or social studies teacher (substitutions are not allowed, but you may submit additional recommendations)
- SAT or ACT score (test must be taken by the application deadline)
- Midyear Report Form, due by February 15 online, if at all possible
- Students applying for need-based financial aid need to submit the FAFSA, CSS PROFILE and Financial Aid Application Form 4, which is part of the application.

Students are encouraged to interview if possible. Interviews are conducted on campus, but the school is able to accommodate many requests for alumni interviews in the student's home territory. Although it is not required, an interview is an excellent way for students to share information about themselves that is not easily communicated through the application and to gain a greater understanding of the University of Chicago.

○ Have you ever walked through the aisles of warehouse stores like Costco or Sam's Club and wondered who would buy a jar of mustard a foot and a half tall? *We've* bought it, but it didn't stop us from wondering about other things, like absurd eating contests, impulse buys, excees, unimagined uses for mustard, storage, preservatives, notions of bigness…and dozens of other ideas both silly and serious. Write an essay somehow inspired by superhuge mustard.—Based on a suggestion by Katherine Gold of Cherry Hill High School East, Cherry Hill, NJ

○ How do your feel about Wednesday?—Inspired by Maximilian Pascual Ortega, a graduate of Maine Township High School South, Park Ridge, IL

○ The Sudanese author Tayeb Salih wrote, "Turning to left and right, I found I was halfway between north and south. I was unable to continue, unable to return." If he is unable to choose, the character faces the threat of being frozen in place or torn between two states. Describe a halfway point in your life—a moment between your own kind of "north" and "south." Tell us about your choice, your inability to choose, or perhaps your folly in thinking there was even a choice to be made.—Inspired by Rafi Mottahedeh, a graduate of Deerfield Academy, Deerfield, MA

ACADEMIC LIFE

The atmosphere of shared intellectual excitement is what I have missed most since I left the University of Chicago.

An Educational Ideal

The University of Chicago is dedicated to the proposition that education consists of serious and communal inquiry into such questions, under the guidance of teachers who have reflected at length upon these questions. As one student described it, "This experience is like waking up; via such questions, one is not transported to a theoretical and remote world, but rather finds oneself in the familiar world, revealed by a new light."

A student's University of Chicago education is comprised of a common core of courses, free electives, in-depth study within a major or concentration, and opportunities for research, internships, and overseas study. This academic program allows for both freedom and flexibility while developing a set of shared experiences and languages of discovery.

The Common Core

In Chicago's core, students find new ways of investigating the human and natural worlds through classes in the humanities, social sciences, mathematics, natural sciences, physical sciences, and civilizations. The common core is different from a set of distribution requirements. It provides a fertile common ground of conversation among all students in the college. Not all students have read all of the same books, but almost everyone has acquaintance, for instance, with Plato's *Apology of Socrates*, the *Republic*, writings of Adam Smith, Karl Marx, and Max Weber, some of Shakespeare, and often Thucydides' Peloponnesian War, and Virginia Woolf.

Majors leading to Bachelor of Arts or Bachelor of Science degrees, enable students to specialize in one area in great depth. With more than 2,500 courses available each year, undergraduates choose electives, which allow them to explore their interests more broadly. Students may opt to join faculty in research through the College Research Opportunities Program, or they may design their own research projects.

EXAMPLES OF COMMON CORE COURSES

○ Humanities—Human Being and Citizen; Form/Problem/Event; Readings in Literature; Philosophical Perspectives

○ Social Science—Classics of Social and Political Thought; Self, Culture, and Society; Wealth, Power, and Virtue

○ Civilization Studies—History of Western Civilization; Introduction to East Asian Civilization; Science, Culture, and Society in Western Civilization; Introduction to African Civilization.

Study Abroad

To enhance their on-campus experience, whether for the purpose of an academic project or for language acquisition, many Chicago students study abroad. Choosing from more than forty programs in nineteen countries, students pursue a wide range of interests—fine art, anthropology, and rain forest biology among them. The growing number of Foreign Language Acquisition Grants—seventy-five this past summer—provide funding for students to live and study for at least one quarter in a foreign country. One of the most popular ways to do study abroad at Chicago is by satisfying the core civilization requirement through one of the intensive ten-week programs offered in Athens, Rome, Paris, Barcelona, Vienna, Buenos Aires, Cape Town, and Pune.

Faculty

Above all, it was my excellent teachers who brought me to love the University of Chicago, to love learning, reading, and study, to feel so strongly about the university that I would be asked to write a published essay about it. In your decision about where to go to college, I urge you to consider no factor more important than the presence of caring, excellent teachers.

Of all the college students I have ever met, those students who found caring teachers loved their colleges and their years in college; those who were not blessed with caring teachers were dissatisfied, often downright unhappy.

SOCIAL LIFE AND ACTIVITIES

Campus Activities

Even with the delights and demands of academic life, Chicago undergraduates find time to participate in more than 300 student organizations. *The Chicago Maroon*, one of three student newspapers, got its start in 1892, the year classes began. The Model United Nations Team, Debate Society, and College Bowl Team have all won awards, some at the international level. Improvisational social satire—the brand of wit made famous on *Saturday Night Live*—got its start here and lives on in the Off-Off Campus improv group. Four hundred student actors, playwrights, designers, producers, directors, and technicians stage thirty-five plays annually through University Theater. The music scene is just as broad, with symphony and chamber orchestras, jazz and wind ensembles, *a cappella* groups, and classical and gospel choirs. Other clubs range in variety from "anime" to community service. Chicago's extensive intramural and club sports program involves more than seventy percent of students, and the varsity sports program offers nineteen men's and women's teams participating at the NCAA Division III level.

Another focal point of campus life is the residential house system. Each student is guaranteed housing for four years at Chicago, and students choose from among eleven residence halls.

Coffee Shops

A conversational social life is fostered by many coffee shops on campus. The Reg, Harper Library, the Classics Building, Cobb Hall, the Divinity School, the Business School, and the Reynolds Club all have coffee shops and each offers an ambience and cuisine of its own.

The coffee shop in the Divinity School is run by graduate students who use the proceeds to underwrite their expenses and provide scholarships to needy students. It has food from many of the ethnic restaurants in Hyde Park, including Thai, Mexican, and Middle Eastern dishes. Being in the basement, the student coffee shop has a close and shadowy feel conducive to heartfelt talk. It also sells mugs and T-shirts that boast: "The Divinity School Coffee Shop—Where God Drinks Coffee." The Classics coffee shop offers its food and drinks with a space that has a very high ceiling and a row of high windows at one end that welcomes an abundance of light, which in turn brings out the wood paneling along the walls. The Reynolds Club renovation has turned it into the de facto student center, with lounges, a marketplace, the offices of dozens of student organizations, and football and pool tables installed in the coffee shop upstairs. The coffee shop, along with Einstein's Bagels on the first floor, are open until 2:00 A.M.

Movies

You can also see a movie on the Chicago campus just about any night of the week. The university is home to DOC (short for Documentary Film Group)—the oldest film society in the country, which shows at least one movie every night and more on the weekends when recently released films are featured. On weeknights, they run various series, such as a Kurosawa film or a Western every Tuesday for the whole term. Fire Escape Productions is the filmmaking arm of DOC. The productions are mostly shorts, but in 2002, Fire Escape completed the first feature-length film shot by the group.

Festivals

There are a number of major festivals during the year including Ribs n' Bibs, The Humanities Open House, Kuviasungnerk, Summer Breeze, and the Folk Festival. Kuviasungnerk, which runs for a week during January, is an attempt to beat the cold by getting out into it at six o'clock in the morning. Hundreds and hundreds of students attend various activities, including aikido classes led by sociology professor David Levine. On the final day, this class takes place outside on the lakefront. Until 8:30 or 9:00 A.M., one can get free hot cocoa, coffee, and doughnuts from a stand in the center of the quads. Those hardy souls who come every morning have a T-shirt that proclaims, "I survived Kuviasungnerk!" Summer Breeze is a week of games, dances, and blues and rock performances by the best local bands, and free drinks of all kinds. The Folk Festival draws together folk music performers from around the country and students from throughout the university for a weekend of performances, master classes, and jam sessions. The annual Scavenger Hunt is a huge campus event that has teams circling the Henry Crown Field House with paper clips, shaving their heads, and driving to other states to retrieve items ranging from circus elephants to Canadian traffic signs.

Other Popular Activities

Model United Nations—University of Chicago (or MUNUC), started in the late 1980s by a few independent and very capable students, has blossomed into the largest student organization on campus, hosting an award-winning model-U.N. conference for high school students from around the United States. More than a thousand visitors annually descend on the Palmer House Hilton for a weekend of intensive meetings simulating the activities of the U.N.

The student-run radio station, WHPK 88.5 FM, offers a dizzyingly eclectic variety of programs, from avant-garde rock to political commentary. The theater groups are particularly strong, staging about thirty-five full-scale productions per year. Off-Off Campus is a student improvisation group that continues the tradition begun by the students who went on to found the Second City comedy club. Students can act, direct, produce, and even write their own shows. Because there is no theater major at the university, any student can audition for any role in any play; a science major can direct a show. Yet classes on acting and directing are taught by professionals active in the Chicago scene. The student-run University Theater has internship programs with two professional theaters: the university's professional and critically acclaimed Court Theater and the Steppenwolf Theater. Many students join the University Orchestra, the Chamber Orchestra, the University Chorus, or the Motet Choir, which makes an annual tour during spring break. There are several student-led *a capella* singing groups, including The Unaccompanied Women, The Acafellas, and Rhythm 'n Jews.

Recent years have seen the flourishing of several organizations that help students use their abilities to help Chicago. The university is in the heart of the south side of Chicago, an economically, ethnically diverse region of the city. The Community Service Center was started by students in the early 1990s. The center links hundreds of students with volunteer opportunities around the city. A tutoring program run by the Blue Gargoyle facilitates weekly one-on-one meetings between university students and children who need help in school. Actors from University Theater perform and lead workshops in local schools. Student Teachers run an after-school program with three local elementary schools, where students teach reading and

---

creative writing in discussion courses that they themselves design. Habitat for Humanity regularly brings together large groups of students to build or repair homes, and a program called "Turn A Lot Around" puts students to work alongside residents in cleaning up vacant lots and transforming them into gardens.

Housing

The university guarantees housing for four years for every student. In 2002, a new residence hall, Max Palevsky Residential Commons, opened in the center of campus. Particularly nice about the Chicago housing system is the easy availability of single rooms, even for first-year students, but double rooms are plentiful as well. The Shoreland, with several hundred students, is a renovated luxury hotel with views of Lake Michigan and large apartment-style rooms. Built in the neo-Gothic style, Burton-Judson is the other large dorm, and is particularly sociable, while still having lots of single rooms.

The dorms are subdivided into Houses, some named after famous professors or Chicago luminaries. Each large dorm has a master, usually a senior faculty member, and each house has a resident head, usually a senior graduate student. The masters and resident heads host discussions, trips downtown, and study breaks for the dorm. The resident heads, many of whom are married, provide a steadying influence, and if there are children, their goodwill can be great company after a long day.

About a third of Chicago's students live off campus, but they remain in the Hyde Park neighborhood. This means that almost everyone lives off campus for the fourth year, some also for the third year and even second year. Despite all the hassles of bill paying and grocery shopping, students who live off campus love the independence and self-sufficiency. Affordable apartments are available near campus and one can buy into a dining hall meal plan. The occasional student even lives on the north side, commuting daily to campus, in order to take better advantage of the city.

Chicago—the City

The city of Chicago is one of the original jazz and blues centers of the nation. Anyone with the least taste for blues should visit the Checkerboard Lounge. The Chicago Symphony is world class; tickets to concerts at the newly renovated Orchestra Hall are inexpensive and easy to get, whether for full orchestra concerts or intimate chamber music. The major theaters (the Shubert and the grand old Louis Sullivan-designed Auditorium Theater) put on new and classic plays and musicals. The Chicago Shakespeare Theater is widely acclaimed. There is also an array of small, inexpensive, experimental theaters, several founded by the University of Chicago alumni on the north side, where one can see *Too Much Light Makes the Baby Go Blind* or an avant-garde production of Aeschylus' *Agamemnon*. Chicago is also a city that loves to eat: Chinese (try dim sum at Hong Minh in Chinatown) or Japanese, Thai (four restaurants in Hyde Park alone!), Korean, Vietnamese, Polish, Italian, Indian, French, Cajun, or down-home American.

Students with a taste for professional sports have options year-round, from the Chicago Bulls to the Bears, Cubs, White Sox, and two hockey teams.

It's been years since I left the U of C, but the performances of Shakespeare's Othello *and Sophocles'* Elektra *that I saw at Court Theater still live in my memory.*

Hyde Park

The university's neighborhood, Hyde Park, is a residential community of 41,000 and is located just seven miles from the city's center. Hyde Park is home to more than sixty-five percent of Chicago's faculty and their families and is often cited as a model of cosmopolitan and multiethnic urban living. The neighborhood offers such cultural attractions as the Museum of Science and Industry, the DuSable Museum of African-American History, and right on Chicago's campus, the Oriental Institute Museum, the David and Alfred Smart Museum of Art, the Court Theater, and the Renaissance Society. By bus, train, car, or the university's own shuttle service, downtown Chicago, with its corporate giants, cultural attractions, and ethnic neighborhoods is just fifteen minutes away. Whether students are visiting the festivals, shops, and theaters around the city, exploring the varied cuisines of distinct ethnic communities, or absorbing the neo-Gothic architecture of campus, they continue to live the "life of the mind" for which the university is deservedly famous.

FINANCIAL AID

Chicago is committed to helping students from all economic backgrounds attend the university and makes admissions decisions on a need-blind basis. Furthermore, the University meets one hundred percent of students' demonstrated financial need. More than half of Chicago students receive some form of financial assistance. Students wishing to apply for financial aid should submit the University of Chicago financial aid application along with the Free Application for Federal Student Aid and the Financial Aid PROFILE of the College Scholarship Service (CSS). The University of Chicago also offers purely merit-based College Honors Scholarships and University Scholarships. These range in value from $9,000 to full tuition for four years, and they succeed in attracting some extraordinary students.

GRADUATES

A degree from the University of Chicago can take you anywhere. Graduates work in government, business, law, academia, entertainment, and public service. A surprising number of graduates, about eighty-five percent, will seek to receive a graduate degree within five years of graduating, either in graduate or professional school, and ninety-five percent of graduates say they plan to enter graduate or professional school within five years. As students begin to consider their opportunities and ambitions, the Career and Placement Services (CAPS) office helps students make the transition into the wider world. Their career counselors have information about a whole array of opportunities for further study or employment, in the public or private sector, whether for-profit or nonprofit, and they talk with students to help them figure what their ambitions are, what the next step after graduation should be, and how best to present themselves and their credentials. The CAPS web site (at *http://caps.uchicago.edu*) provides twenty-four-hour access to a range of information, including an internship database with more than 1,000 listings.

Many students start to take advantage of CAPS long before graduation. The University of Chicago has an innovative set of internship programs that reflect the importance that employers of all kinds place on real-world experience. Students work as interns with researchers in several Smithsonian Institutions in and around Washington, D.C., including the Museum of Natural History, the National Portrait Gallery, and the Smithsonian Environmental Research Center. Also in Washington, students participating in the Paul Douglas Internship Program (named after former faculty member and U.S. senator from Illinois, Paul Douglas) worked in each of the Illinois U.S. senators' offices, while others served as White House interns. In Chicago, students selected as Jeff Metcalf interns worked in for-profit firms such as Goldman Sachs, as well as nonprofits, such as the Joffrey Ballet and the Museum of Contemporary Art. Undergraduates selected for the Mayoral Internship Program worked as paid interns in the office of Mayor Richard M. Daley during much of the past academic year.

SUMMING UP

Even the very brightest students do not run out of challenges. The university really has a liberal arts college housed within a world-class research university. The great resources of the research university are in most departments at the students' disposal, and students often have close contact with the world of graduate students. The intellectual diversity of the students and faculty sustains endlessly stimulating debates. The wealth of diversity in the university is complemented by the wealth of diversity in the city: music, theater, shopping, dining, museums, movies, parks, ethnic neighborhoods, night life, and Lake Michigan.

These surroundings enrich and enliven the concentrated atmosphere of the university campus, where learning, discovery, hard work, and thoughtful conversation create an atmosphere that, for an intensely curious student, is exhilarating and inspiring.

❏ *Jonathan Beere, B.A.,*
Melissa Meltzer, University of Chicago

Mike Lovett

	University of Miami **Coral Gables, FL 33146**	**Enrollment**	
	305-284-2211 Fax: 305-284-2507 E-mail: *admission@miami.edu* Web site: *www.miami.edu*	**Full-time** ❏ women: 7,474 ❏ men: 6,850 **Part-time** ❏ women: 873 ❏ men: 473	

INTRODUCING UNIVERSITY OF MIAMI

Palm trees blow gently in the breeze while macaws perch curiously on the branches of giant banyan trees. A manatee, astray from its home, sunbathes in the canal while mischievous ducks chase an ibis looking for food. Inside the buildings nestled in this lush, tropical setting, the serenity disappears into a bustling hotbed of activity. World-renowned geneticists are researching a cure for cancer. Budding journalists are learning to ask the right questions, and musical protégés take advice from Broadway masters including Jerry Herman and Barry

10 Lessons Learned from the Dalai Lama

9 National Football and Baseball Championships—1982, 1983, 1985, 1987, 1989, 1991, 1999, 2001

8 Top States UM Students Hail from: Florida, California, Texas, New York, New Jersey, Massachusetts, Illinois, Pennsylvania

7 Residential Colleges—Mahoney, Pearson, Stanford, Hecht, Eaton, Apartments, University Village

6 Rockin' Concerts—Coldplay, Green Day, All American Rejects, John Mayer, Kanye West, Audioslave and more all have played at the BankUnited Center

5 Presidents in UM History—Ashe, Pearson, King, Foote, Shalala

4 Recent visits from Presidential Candidates—George W. Bush, John Kerry, Howard Dean, Ralph Nader

3 Literary Lectures—Toni Morrison, Maya Angelou, Eli Wiesel

2 Supreme Court Justice Appearances—Chief Justice John Roberts, Justice Edward Breyer

1 Billion Dollars—Raised during UM's Momentum Fundraising Campaign

Brown. Located in Coral Gables, Florida, the University of Miami offers the quaint atmosphere of a city rich in history while positioned just ten minutes from a booming metropolis.

Approximately 10,500 undergraduate students call University of Miami (UM) home. Coming from 49 states and over one hundred foreign countries, the university boasts a diverse student population, and a stroll through the Whitten University Center (UC), the hub of student activity, displays this tapestry of cultural pride. On any given day, the UC patio is transformed into a stage for Cuban cuisine, Asian spoken-word poetry, or vibrant hip-hop dancers.

Ethnic heritage isn't the only thing that UM students take pride in. With a tradition rich in athletics, Hurricane sports bond students both on the field and off. "The U," as sports fans fondly call UM, is a powerhouse. Alumni, faculty, staff, and students alike, joined by the whole community, rally for the Hurricanes during baseball and football games, and bleed orange and green when the basketball team takes to the hoops. The university had the unique opportunity to see athletics play out under different stadium lights when UM's on-campus Lowe Art Museum, hosted "Game Face: What a Female Athlete Looks Like." This photographic exhibit was a portrait of women in sports, exemplifying the importance of Title IX and praising the strong, athletic woman.

The university's ability to blend academics with culture provides an environment that breeds higher learning and intellectual growth. With the launch of "UM Presents," an on-line portal highlighting all the cultural offerings on campus, the university community, as well as UM's neighbors, have a cultural smorgasbord at their fingertips. Promoting events including lectures from UM's renowned faculty to the Frost School of Music's annual extravaganza, Festival Miami, the variety of programs appeals to every taste.

Giving students the opportunity to learn and grow outside of the classroom is one of UM's best attributes, and it clearly enhances the academic experience. It is not unusual for faculty to offer a Thanksgiving dinner to students not traveling home for the holiday. Creating a home away from home, resident faculty in each of the residential colleges will often provide an oven to bake cookies in or simply help students adjust to life on campus. As seniors, students have created lasting relationships with their professors.

At a school like the University of Miami in a city like Miami, in one day students can learn about DNA or Shakespeare and parasail over Biscayne Bay or snorkel in coral reefs. Learning branches out far beyond the classroom as students explore the city and reach higher.

ADMISSIONS REQUIREMENTS

Applying to the college is an exciting time in any student's life. Perusing college brochures in high school guidance counselor's office and looking at university web sites on the Internet is a good way to research prospective schools. Upon opening an admissions brochure from UM, the bright school colors of green and orange and vibrant photos of college life will immediately spark your attention, as will the text listing all UM has to offer students now and, more importantly, their futures.

Meeting the Faces of UM

The first true step in the admissions process, meeting an admissions counselor, will only make you more eager to apply. UM routinely sends counselors around the country to meet with prospective students, and making an appointment is easy. By joining the mailing list through the admissions web site, high school students can see when the counselors will be in their area.

The Ideal Student

Admissions counselors will talk about UM's ideal student. The profile is someone who demonstrates academic talent and a strong sense of personal integrity and has a well-rounded secondary school experience, inside and outside of the classroom. They will also explain that UM receives approximately 19,000 applications every year but strives to keep the size of each freshman class small, around 2,000. The average weighted GPA of an incoming student is 4.2 and the median SAT scores range from 1220 to 1370 (based on

1600). Students who took the ACT scored between 27 and 31 and 68 percent of incoming freshmen ranked in the top 10 percent of their high school class.

The numbers may appear a bit intimidating, but the admissions team looks for well-rounded individuals with a strong personal statement and superior recommendations from their guidance counselors.

Down and Dirty with Applications

After the nerves of applying settle; its time to get down to the busy work. By logging on to the admissions web site, students can find a downloadable application. At the university, there are three options to apply. Students can apply for Early Decision if UM is going to be the first choice; Early Action, which allows students to express serious interest in UM but keep their options open; and Regular Decision. The difference between the three is the timeline in which you learn your acceptance status: Early Decision coming in late December and Early Action and Regular Decision coming in mid-April. Here's a hint: Students who choose Early Decision generally get first pick at housing choices because they will have to mail in their enrollment forms and deposits before everyone else. So if you're absolutely sure of the college you want to attend, keep that in mind.

While applying to UM, students can also decide if they would like to enter into the Honors Program which demands a higher level of study and performance. Students who are accepted are required to have an SAT score of over 1300 and must be in the top 5 percent of their class.

The Campus Visit

Even though reading about universities is a good way to get the basics on what the campus has to offer, nothing can compare to the experience of visiting the campus and seeing first-hand the people and places that make up the institution.

After just a fifteen minute taxi ride from Miami International Airport, students arrive at Stanford Drive, the main entrance to UM, and the campus tour begins.

Greeted by a row of majestic palm trees, UM's campus looks more like Club Med than the stoic brick and mortar universities I was accustomed to up north.

As students explore campus hot spots like the food court, they'll be surprised to see the variety of offerings. Smoothie bars, sushi chefs, salad buffets, Starbucks, and taco stations were bustling with students.

The campus was hopping. Shuttles picked up and dropped off students at several busy locations. The shuttles, aptly named the HurryCanes, not only ran campus routes, but also transported students to and from a neighboring Publix grocery store, Shops at Sunset Place Mall, Crandon Beach, and Coconut Grove, a late night strip popular among college students.

> *After meeting Megan, my admissions counselor, and then seeing the campus myself, I was all Hurricane.*

The admissions process at the University of Miami was easy to follow, and admissions counselors create a personal relationship with each prospective student they meet. After the first discussion, it's apparent that their phones, in-boxes, and doors are always open to any questions or comments applicants might have.

ACADEMIC LIFE

At the University of Miami, there are over 10,000 faculty, staff, and administrators whose main goal is to deliver an exceptional higher education experience. The Coral Gables campus, UM's home base, is the location for its two colleges and six schools that house over 120 bachelor's degree programs within eight undergraduate schools. In addition, the Coral Gables campus houses professional degree programs including the School of Law and School of Architecture. The Rosenstiel School for Marine and Atmospheric Sciences and Miller School of Medicine are located on separate campuses. Many schools require students to enroll in a double major. For example, students majoring in motion pictures through the School of Communication may also major in photography through the College of Arts and Sciences. During their time at UM, a 120-credit hour minimum must be fulfilled, which to a student can seem like an eternity, but four years go by fast, and students leave UM prepared to take on the world.

While attending UM, students typically take twelve to eighteen credits a semester, meaning a majority of students are working diligently to graduate in four years. Classes are small, with a fourteen-to-one student-to-professor ratio. Students usually chose credit hours based on the number of activities they might be involved in, hours worked as a student employee on campus, and classes needed to fulfill their requirements. With the help of an academic advisor, picking classes and staying on track became an easy task.

For some students, studying in Miami may seem like traveling to a different part of the world. International food, dance, clothing, and language pop up all over and are celebrated on campus. Researchers at the Miami European Union Center study how Europe's relationships with America, among other counties, shape the world today, politically and economically. Over at the Center for Hemispheric Policy, panels of experts discuss important issues facing Latin America today. Students are given a chance to interact with researchers and attend conferences and lectures that explore the world around them and leave UM prepared to enter the global market.

For students looking for a real international experience, UM's study-abroad program delivers an experience to last a lifetime. Featuring programs in twenty-eight countries, the study-abroad program whisks students away to the Czech Republic, Australia, England, Singapore, Trinidad and Tobago, Iceland, and Monaco to name a few.

UNIVERSITY OF MIAMI'S SCHOOLS AND COLLEGES

- ○ School of Architecture
- ○ College of Arts and Sciences
- ○ School of Business Administration
- ○ School of Communication
- ○ School of Education
- ○ College of Engineering
- ○ Philip and Patricia Frost School of Music
- ○ School of Nursing and Health Studies
- ○ Graduate School
- ○ School of Law
- ○ Leonard M. Miller School of Medicine
- ○ Rosenstiel School of Marine and Atmospheric Science
- ○ Division of Continuing and International Education

The faculty at the University of Miami is among the best in the country. These knowledgeable individuals aren't just people who assign what seems like endless amounts of textbook reading and grade papers with an iron fist; they are movers and shakers in their professions and areas of research. The most interesting aspect of working with professors who are current practitioners is the blending of academics and real-life experience.

In several public relations classes, group projects were assigned where students were paired with a client (usually business members in our local community) and asked to develop a complete media strategy. This meant conducting focus groups and surveys in the community to find out about the public's knowledge of the client, creating promotional material for distribution, and presenting ideas and solutions.

Hands-on curriculum is evident all over campus. Students in the Frost School of Music have recording studios at their fingertips, and several times a year they sit in on master classes where their form is critiqued by leading entertainment professionals. Motion picture majors are required to write scripts, conduct casting calls, and shoot film to produce short movies. At the end of the spring semester, the Cannes Film Festival provides an opportunity for budding directors to showcase their works to the community. Select films are then taken to Los Angeles for a second premiere through a program that matches students to alumni working in the major movie studios in Hollywood.

UM also focuses on giving students a variety of options when choosing classes. This allows individuals to think outside of the box when picking classes. A biomedical engineering major might find him or herself in the actor's studio in Theatre 101. A finance major, opera major, and visual communications major might sit next to each other in an architecture class. Mixing students from all walks of life, with different interests and views, provides students with a melting pot of academic flavors. This classroom recipe increases student productivity as well as the exchange of ideas.

Mixing students from all walks of life, with different interests and views, provides students with a melting pot of academic flavors.

SOCIAL LIFE AND ACTIVITIES

Students at the University of Miami will find out fast: New York might be the "city that never sleeps" but Miami is the city that never stops the party. And life at UM keeps that motto alive and well. At UM, students party in a million different ways, continuously redefining the word, and not just in the *Animal House* way. Students involved in Salsa Craze heat things up on the dance floor as they learn how to salsa, meringue, and samba twice a week in the University Center. Members of Delta Gamma, just one of the thirteen sororities on campus, participate in Anchor Splash, their annual fund-raising week by holding contests between different Greek and non-Greek organizations, including a "Mr. Anchor Splash" competition. The Rathskeller, UM's on-campus bar and grill, is the home of Hurricane watch-parties, comedy improv hours, and open mike nights. It's a great place to grab a pitcher and burger and hang with friends.

Campus Activism and Community Service

On the campus activism side of student life, UM offers a number of organizations and activities perfect for the community-service-driven individual. Students can visit the Smith Tucker Involvement Center (also known as The STIC) to look at the list of organizations UM has to offer or pop into the Volunteer Services Center to find out where they can help on campus and in the community.

Over 900 University of Miami students participate each year in the National Gandhi Day of Service. Planned by the Council of International Students and Organizations, this joint effort provides the opportunity to give back to the community. In one of the largest student-led volunteer service events in Miami-Dade County, UM teams up with students from other local colleges to volunteer at a number of locations including Citizens for a Better South Florida, the Community Partnership for Homeless, and Camillus House, a local soup kitchen.

Another initiative at UM is STRIVE (Serving Together Reaching Integrity, Values, & Engagement), a select group of University of Miami students that have formed a living community that focuses on leadership and civic engagement. Originating out of the Butler Volunteer Services Center, thirty-one students live together in on-campus apartments, studying and participating in a number of service- and leadership-driven activities. The program includes an academic component that requires students to take classes with curriculum that focuses on building a strong voice in the greater community and are paired with mentors in the faculty.

Athletics

If anyone has any questions about how much athletics are loved and cherished at the University of Miami, they only need to walk around campus during Homecoming weekend. Almost 3,000 alumni from around the country travel back to South Florida to join current students, faculty, and community members to celebrate the University of Miami's Homecoming festivities. UM's annual homecoming parade kicks off the Friday night pregame parties.

Following the parade is one of UM's most cherished traditions, the boat-burning ceremony on UM's own Lake Osceola, in the heart of campus. The boat-burning ceremony involves setting a wood boat on fire in the middle of the lake. The tradition states that if the mast breaks before the boat sinks, UM will win the Homecoming football game.

Football isn't the only sport Hurricane fans go crazy for. Crowds of students cheer on the basketball team at the state-of-the-art BankUnited Center, and each season the stands are packed as the baseball team takes the recently renovated diamond at Mark Light Field located in the Alex Rodriguez Park. Both venues are located on campus, just a few steps from the residential colleges.

Men's sports have a lot of bragging rights, but the women can definitely do their share of talking. Under the tutelage of Coach Katie Meier, the women's basketball team has made a statement in the Atlantic Coast Conference that they are a force to be reckoned with. Women's track also boasts all-star athletes including Lauren Williams, who was the 2005 World Champion, Olympic medalist, and was also honored as a Visa Humanitarian Athlete of the Year by *USA Track & Field*.

Intramural sports are also of big interest to UM students. Flag football and soccer games are played five days a week on the intramural field. The university's Equestrian Team competes in horse shows, displaying their skills in flatwork and jumping.

Life in the City of Miami

The University of Miami is located in the city of Coral Gables, a suburb of Miami-Dade County. For students, this means easy access to everything Miami has to offer. Downtown Miami, South Beach, Key Biscayne, the Design District, and the upscale shopping center Village of Merrick Park are a twenty-minute drive away. Fortunately for students without cars on campus, Miami and Coral Gables offer a number of safe, easy ways to get around town. With a little planning, students can ride the Metrorail (the university has its own stop), city trolleys, or UM's HurryCane shuttles, or use taxi services to any location in Miami.

Students at the University of Miami will find out fast: New York might be the "city that never sleeps," but Miami is the city that never stops the party.

Nightlife in Miami serves up a heaping dose of diversity, appealing to every taste and budget. Whether it is a quick, inexpensive Cuban meal at Versailles, sushi and pad thai at Moon Thai, or plate-throwing Greek cuisine at Taverna Opa, Miami is known for its nightlife as well as its cultural flair. World events such as the Miami International Film Festival, the International Book Fair, the Latin Grammys, and the Winter Music Conference attract tourists from all countries. When you live in Miami, these events are at your doorstep, and the chance to see renowned films, authors, artists, and musicians is a priceless experience.

Safety On Campus and Off

For parents who may worry about sending their kids away to a big city, they need not be concerned. The University of Miami has a number of programs, policies, and procedures in place to ensure students' safety as they find their way in and around campus.

When walking from residential colleges at night, blue light phones located around campus put students instantly in contact with members of UM's Department of Public Safety. Officers are on call to escort anyone around campus and are a constant and reassuring presence. Students hired through the Department of Residence Halls staff a desk in each residential college at night, checking in visitors, with photo I.D. required. This ensures that only students enter the buildings.

UM also takes a proactive approach toward ensuring students' well-being. Educational programs such as Pier 21, organized by the Center for Alcohol and Other Drug Awareness, teach alcohol awareness and responsibility to students. Through the counseling center, the university has a number of programs for students who might be feeling blue. The Student Health Center is opening for students who are under the weather or may just need a flu shot. The on-campus pharmacy provides quick and easy access to medication for students suffering from a cough or cold.

The Wellness Center provides programs for the mind and body. Students can sign up for yoga, healthy cooking classes, aerobic exercises, and a favorite amongst members, Butts and Guts, designed to tone your abs and behind! The Wellness Center is the best gym in town, and it's all yours if you come to UM. All of the various programs on campus are designed to promote a healthy lifestyle, as well as social and personal responsibility.

Looking tanned and toned in the 80-degree weather that comes during February may be a strong allure to students, especially those coming from the north; however, its important to touch on another weather-related phenomenon unique to Miami: hurricanes.

The University of Miami is well prepared to handle a hurricane of any intensity. Hurricane shutters adorn every residential college. Students are given food and beverage during hurricane warnings as well. Staff and administrators in each of the residential colleges keep students informed and aware of changes in the weather, and updates from the university president are e-mailed as new information arrives. Information is also posted on the school's web site, especially for parents who live outside of Florida. A hotline is in place for students, faculty, staff, and parents to call and find out the latest news.

The university administration isn't the only arm of UM involved in hurricane preparation. CERT (Canes Emergency Response Team) is a student-led initiative that serves as a resource for the University and its Coral Gables neighbors during emergency situations such as a hurricane by delivering water and disseminating information to off-campus neighbors. This specially trained group also participates in drills designed to improve basic search and rescue procedures and sharpen the important skills of triaging, treating, and transporting victims. As hurricane season begins, these students are available to even help members of the community put up hurricane shutters.

FINANCIAL AID

It can also be useful to have a finance major sit next to you to tell you how to manage your student loans and financial aid packets each year. That kind of free advice can also be found at UM's Office of Financial Aid or by looking on the department's web site.

The university works with students on a number of levels to provide the maximum amount of tuition assistance possible. Academic scholarships are awarded based on merit and are announced in students' acceptance letters. In 2005–2006, 86 percent of all full-time freshmen and 87 percent of full-time upperclassmen received some form of financial aid. The average freshman was given $23,188 to help pay for school. Need-based grants are awarded and need-based self-help aid such as student loans and jobs through college work-study are also available.

ficiency were taught. I worked for three separate departments on campus, and at each job it was obvious that my supervisors took an active interest in teaching me how to be a productive member of the office staff. They became mentors instead of bosses.

On-campus jobs also provide a networking function as well as a paycheck. My senior year I interned at UM's Media Relations office. This opened up doors to post-college employment, and my peers who interned with me were also able to find jobs based on the skills we learned there. One of our interns received a fantastic job with "Deco Drive," an entertainment program on our local Fox affiliate through my boss's contacts.

GRADUATES

If you think high school went fast, college races by at the speed of light. A blur of late-night cramming sessions at "Club Richter" or the Otto G. Richter Library, spring breaks on South Beach, and football games at the Orange Bowl come rushing back as you step on stage to receive your diploma on the most important day of a student's life, commencement.

Over 2,400 bachelor degrees were awarded in 2004 and just over 155,000 people called UM home in the university's eighty-year history. Alumni of the University of Miami are scattered across all 50 states and in 148 countries.

PROMINENT GRADUATES

Rick Barry, '65, Professional Athlete: UM's all-time leading scorer on the court, Barry is the only player in basketball history to win titles in the NCAA, NBA, and ABA. He is also inducted into the Basketball Hall of Fame.

Gloria Estefan, '78, Entertainer and Producer: An internationally known superstar, Estefan produced No. 1 singles including "Rhythm is Gonna Get You."

While alumni may have left Miami to make their mark on the world, UM is never far from their hearts. The Alumni Association works as a liaison between UM and alumni, reporting on their successes through the Miami Connection. Alumni groups such as the D.C. Canes, a group of alumni residing in Washington, D.C., hold frequent gatherings to watch athletic events and to network. Alumni weekly news is e-mailed out to subscribers several times a year letting UM grads stay updated on what's happening at their alma mater. Administrators at the university also travel around the country giving lectures and speeches about the vision and future of UM.

It isn't unusual for students to interact with grads who return to campus either. UM alumni often participate in career fairs, recruiting students nearing graduation. For example, when the Public Relations Student Society of America, a student group of public relations majors on campus, holds their biannual mixers, a quick glance around the room shows that about half of the attendants are UM grads interested in seeing their fellow Canes succeed in the profession.

If students need assistance jump-starting their career path, the university's Toppel Career Planning and Placement Center is the place to go. Toppel plays host to several major career fairs throughout the academic year as well as to workshops designed to help students by presenting resume critiques, holding mock interviews, and offering brochures and lectures on job-searching techniques. Toppel also supports CaneZone, an on-line portal where students can post resumes and search for employment opportunities. If students are exploring graduate school, they can also visit Toppel to research graduate programs, the application process, and admissions exams. These are free services available to students and alumni.

SUMMING UP

At the University of Miami, students will receive an educational experience that lets students dip their feet into political debates, cultural festivals, intellectual lectures, and athletic events, not to mention the Atlantic

PROMINENT GRADUATES

Roy Firestone, '75, Broadcast Journalist: A personality on ESPN's *Up Close*, Firestone hosts a variety of cable network specials as well.

Jerry Herman, '53, Composer/Lyricist, A revered artist on Broadway, Herman created masterpieces including *Hello Dolly!* and *Mame*. Herman is the recipient of two Tony and Grammy Awards.

Patricia Ireland, '75, Activist, She is former president of the National Organization for Women.

David Alan Isaacs, '71, Producer, He created hit sitcoms including *Cheers* and *Frasier*, and also collaborated with writers for *MASH*.

Duane Johnson, '95, Professional Athlete and Actor, Duane "The Rock" Johnson was a star wrestler in the World Wrestling Federation. He also starred in blockbuster movies that include *The Grindiron Gang* and *The Rundown*.

Suzy Kolber, '86, Broadcast Journalist, A former anchor for Fox Sports, Kolber now reports for ESPN.

Alfred O'Hara, '54, NASA, As a launch director for NASA space shuttles, O'Hara worked on the *Apollo, Skylab,* and the *Apollo-Soyuz* launches.

Sylvester Stallone, '99, Actor, A Hollywood superstar, winning acclaim for his 1976 motion picture *Rocky,* Stallone became one of the highest-paid actors.

Ocean. Its dynamic, tropical location, world-renowned faculty, and the exceptional programs designed to enhance student life make UM a place where a high school student grows and matures into an adult ready to enter the professional world with sophistication and creative spark. The unique mix of tradition and innovation instills pride in students and inspires them to leave their own mark the moment they step on campus. When you graduate from UM, you don't become a statistic, you become part of the legacy, part of the UM family that bonds people from every walk of life. Ask any alumni of UM how this university bonds each student who crosses its campus in an indescribable way, and they're sure to say "You wouldn't understand; it's a Canes Thing."

❏ *Melissa Greco, B.S.*

THE UNIVERSITY OF NORTH CAROLINA AT CHAPEL HILL

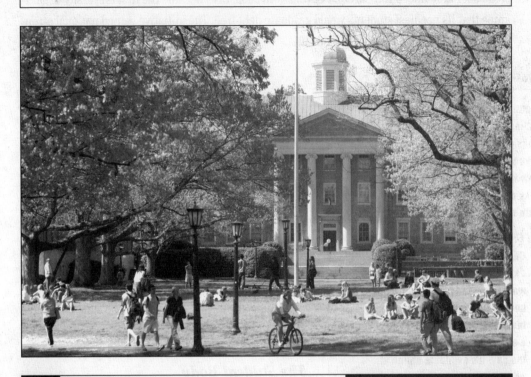

 The University of North Carolina
at Chapel Hill
Chapel Hill, NC 27599-2200

 E-mail: *uadm@email.unc.edu*
Web site: *http://www.unc.edu*

 Enrollment

Full-time ❏ women: 9,322
❏ men: 6,589

Part-time ❏ women: 460
❏ men: 393

INTRODUCING THE UNIVERSITY OF NORTH CAROLINA AT CHAPEL HILL ▭

Carolina is a study in contrasts. Grits 'n' gravy and liberal activism; founded by slave owners but unflinchingly committed to diversity; world renowned yet dedicated to local service. UNC is an engaging mix of sobering social concern and all-night parties, intellect and athleticism, and leadership tempered by tradition. It's a combustible blend that fuels passionate debate, innovation, and introspection.

Chartered in 1789, the University of North Carolina is a child of the Revolution and the first public university in the United States to open its doors just four years later. Now over 210 years old, UNC still blazes trails and champions implausible causes. When the university's chancellor announced the Carolina Covenant in 2003, UNC became the first university to guarantee that its neediest students would graduate debt free. The initiative gained national attention and several universities followed suit.

But what they couldn't imitate was the unwavering commitment to the public good, to the people, that is inherent in all things Carolina. Since its founding, UNC has first and foremost been an institution of the people, an uncommon feat in a field that is increasingly driven by revenue and rankings. The people, for UNC, are not just the residents of North Carolina but each and every student who studies in its halls. Carolina is committed to serving and to educating—not just those who can afford a world-class education, but also those who can no longer afford to live without one.

The Student Body

That commitment to serving a diverse student body is reflected in the classroom, where you're just as likely to sit next to a congressman's son as you are the daughter of a textile worker, where people from all backgrounds dissect and discuss social issues such as female oppression in Third World countries and outsourcing. It's an environment that causes a healthy degree of friction and feeds red-hot academics. UNC consistently ranks among the top universities in the United States and is home to one of the nation's top business schools, the Kenan-Flagler Business School. About eighty percent of Carolina students graduate within five years after meeting a wide range of liberal arts requirements, completing a rigorous study in their academic major, and often studying abroad for a semester.

They are able to do so because Carolina attracts the best and brightest from all walks of life. Three-quarters of recent freshmen ranked in the top ten percent of their high school class, and almost 200 were valedictorians. Among them were students with perfect SAT scores, National Merit finalists, student body presidents, and talented athletes and musicians. With such highly qualified applicants, Carolina's admissions process is extremely competitive, especially among out-of-state students. Less than thirty-seven percent of would-be Tar Heels are admitted each year and competition among out-of-state applicants is especially fierce because state law caps nonresident enrollment at eighteen percent of the student body. That makes an out-of-state admission offer from Carolina one of the hardest to come by in the country.

UNC is academically rigorous, but what makes Carolina a must-attend university is its unparalleled focus on experience gleaned outside the classroom. Carolina has perhaps the most civically engaged student body of any school in the United States. You'll be hard pressed to find students hunkered in the library night after night. Instead, members of the Young Democrats and College Republicans go head to head on listservs and in The Pit, the "unofficial" center of campus. Aspiring journalists pour hours of work into *The Daily Tar Heel*, the campus' award-winning daily newspaper. Students counsel rape victims and build houses, and then head to the athletic fields.

The Campus

They do it all in and around one of the most beautiful college campuses in the nation—from the grassy tree-lined quads to the marbled halls of stately Wilson Library, the chiming Bell Tower to the pink and white blossoms buzzing with bees. Students return to a campus at summer's end that is lush and green and in a few months will be ablaze with the reds, oranges, and yellows of fall. They can always expect a few snow flurries and maybe even an ice day or two, perfect for sledding, snowball fights, and other childhood pastimes far removed from the pressures of mid-terms and papers. And without fail, just as students begin to hate crisp days, the campus bursts into bloom, drawing warmth and sunbathers to the quads.

It's a place made for active lives, punctuated by a handful of lazy, sun-filled days. If college, to you, just means double-majoring and getting out, you'd probably be better off at any number of other schools. Carolina is best savored. Expect to play hard, work harder, and always be on the go. Carolina students, faculty, and administrators are always pressing forward, embracing change, moving at full throttle.

In short—the faint of heart need not apply.

ADMISSIONS REQUIREMENTS

So, you know you want to go to Carolina, but aren't sure how to score one of those coveted fat envelopes. The good news: Carolina has a large admissions staff that pores over applications, considering the unique abilities each candidate would bring to the incoming class. The bad: About 19,000 students competed for less than 3,600 spots last year, which makes admission to Carolina highly competitive—even more so if you're applying from outside North Carolina.

Out-of-state enrollment is limited to eighteen percent of the undergraduate class, or about 650 of the freshman spots any given year. In 2005, more than 10,000 applicants competed for those spots, making an out-of-state offer to attend Carolina one of the toughest to come by in the country. Now that you know the basic numbers, here's a rough guide on how to figure your odds.

Academic Excellence

There's no set formula for success, but a demonstrated record of academic excellence is a must to score an admissions offer from Carolina. The university requires—not suggests—that students have pursued college-preparatory work in high school, and the Admissions Office recommends that students take as many Advanced Placement or International Baccalaureate courses as possible. Carolina requires a high school diploma from an accredited institution and will not accept a GED or other high school equivalency degree for freshman admission. UNC also requires that students complete specific high school course units as follows:

Subject	Units Required	Units Recommended
English	4	4
Math	4	4
Science	3	4
Lab units within these	1	1 or more
Foreign Language	2 (same language)	4 or more
Social Studies	2	3 or more
Academic electives	2	—

Once you are sure you've got the basics covered, it's time to turn your attention to test scores and class rank. Four students with perfect 1600s and 107 National Merit Finalists numbered among the 3,751 incoming freshmen in 2005. That class, on average, posted an SAT score of 1,299, with out-of-state students averaging 1,355. The following table provides a more detailed academic profile of Carolina's 2005 freshman class:

High School Class Rank	Percent of 2005 Freshmen Class
Top 10 percent	73.6 percent
Top 20 percent	92.4 percent

Combined SAT Score**	Percent of 2005 Freshmen Class
1500 and higher	5.3 percent
1400 to 1490	17.7 percent
1300 to 1390	31.1 percent
1200 to 1290	27.5 percent
1100 to 1190	11.9 percent
Below 1100	6.4 percent*

*Note: Students with an SAT under 1100 often are admitted because they have demonstrated outstanding ability in an area outside of testing.

**Based on total score of 1600 for SAT test taken by this class.

It's important to consider that the average SAT scores and class rank of the admitted class have been consistently climbing. And it's equally important to consider that while academic excellence is crucial, admissions officers at Carolina don't base their decisions on test scores and grade point averages alone.

Life Experience

The trump card at Carolina can be summed up in three phrases: demonstrated leadership, a commitment to community service, and diverse life experiences. Particular strength in one area can make up for deficiency in another because, while Carolina values well-rounded students, its focus is on creating a well-rounded class. Carolina's leaders see its eclectic, energized student body as a major strength and as a crucial vehicle for reaching and improving a broad swath of society.

University Chancellor James Moeser puts it this way: "There is a sustained commitment to public service and great potential for leadership. It's by design that we attract people like that." In fact, Moeser and other leaders are so focused on that goal that they recently created an upper-level management position at UNC dedicated solely to studying and cultivating incoming classes. So, don't underestimate the importance of extracurricular activities, strong references, a captivating college essay, and more than a little passion.

UNC is a world-class research institution with humanities at its heart. As such, the faculty strives to produce graduates well versed in both the hard sciences and the arts. Biology majors will graduate with a basic appreciation for Chaucer, and a chemistry set won't be a foreign object to journalism majors. Undergraduates are given ample opportunity to participate in faculty research or projects of their own design, and for a large research institution, faculty members are surprisingly accessible. Carolina is careful to maintain a 14 to 1 student-faculty ratio overall, and even professors in large lecture classes make themselves readily available.

Professors do a great job of making themselves accessible to students and are, in fact, disappointed if students don't take them up on their offer. Right from the start, I got to know some professors well, and those relationships stayed with me throughout my time here.

—*Dan Harrison, 2004, Current Carolina Law Student*

First-Year Seminars

Carolina ensures that students immediately have the opportunity to connect with faculty by offering dozens of intimate, engaging courses called First-Year Seminars. These aren't the 200-person lecture classes of freshman lore. The classes typically are limited to twenty students or fewer and are available only to first-year students, so you won't have to fight upperclassmen for a choice spot. The seminars enable students to study topics that go well beyond the basics and to participate in faculty-led research they traditionally wouldn't tackle until their junior or senior year. The program offers more than 300 courses in 38 departments and schools, though not all classes are available in a given semester. Current topics range from "American Culture in the Era of Ragtime" to "Space Identity and Power in the Middle East" to "Energy Resources for a Hungry Planet." You can check out more online at *http://www.unc.edu/fys*.

General College

Most first-year seminars fulfill course requirements in general education, which is composed of a whole host of courses students must take in the College of Arts and Sciences. All students spend their first two years in the General College where they must fulfill about twenty specific foundations, approaches, and connections requirements, such as Quantitative Reasoning, U.S. Diversity, Literacy and Performing Arts, Historical Analysis, and English Composition and Rhetoric. The course options within each perspective are broad, allowing students to chart their own unique intellectual course.

Students also can place out of some courses or use selected Advanced Placement and International Baccalaureate tests to earn credit. General College credits typically are earned during students' first two years, though some upper-level general education requirements are required during junior and senior years. To meet the requirements of the General College and complete their major on time, students typically carry a manageable course load of twelve to fifteen hours. Full-time students must obtain special permission to carry fewer than twelve hours or more than seventeen.

Majors

UNC offers seventy-one undergraduate majors in nine of thirteen schools. Students typically declare a major heading into their junior year, though students who enter Carolina with college credit, place out of courses, or carry especially heavy loads may begin working on a major earlier. When declaring a major, undergraduates either remain in the College of Arts and Sciences or enter one of four professional schools (dentistry or medi-

TOP TEN MAJORS

In order of descending enrollment:
- ○ Biology
- ○ Journalism and Mass Communication
- ○ Psychology
- ○ Business Administration
- ○ Communication Studies
- ○ Political Science
- ○ English
- ○ Economics
- ○ History
- ○ Exercise and Sport Science

cine), as well as Kenan-Flagler Business School or the schools of education, information and library science, journalism and mass communication, nursing, and public health. The Business and Journalism schools are the most popular schools, and biology, psychology, and political science are among the most popular majors within the College of Arts and Sciences. Political science, psychology, and Romance Languages are all common second majors.

Students can double-major at Carolina or can pursue a major and two minors. Certain majors, such as journalism, require an area of outside concentration. Though rare, students can major in two schools, but because of the intense, focused course load required in most professional schools, they must get special permission to do so.

Global/International Focus

Carolina, over the past few years, has markedly increased its focus on global education — from the study of foreign languages to global issues classes to study abroad. By the end of 2006, the school completed the construction of the Global Education Center, which will bring international studies, resources for study abroad, and international research centers under one roof.

UNC has long had a robust study abroad program that enables students to tailor foreign experience to their academic pursuits and personal interests. Students can choose from over 300 credit-bearing programs in seventy countries and can opt for a semester, a year, or a summer session abroad. UNC students have participated in programs all over the world, including Singapore, Sydney, Cuba, Cairo, Montpellier, and Moscow. Academic eligibility requirements vary from program to program. Numerous programs provide internships and service learning opportunities abroad as well as specialized courses taught by UNC faculty or courses taught at a local university. The extensive program portfolio, combined with UNC's growing emphasis on global education and its new curriculum, has made the university's study abroad program one of the most successful in the United States.

> The Carolina Southeast Asia Summer Program (SEAS) was an opportunity of a lifetime. Truthfully, this was my first time outside of the country, and I was hesitant about leaving home. However, upon my return, I quickly discovered I had not missed very much while being away. The program fostered self-confidence in my academic pursuits. Now, I have an open mind in terms of health, race and ethnic relations, and economic development.

—LyTonya Fowler, UNC Chapel Hill undergraduate, Carolina SEAS Program 2006

According to the Institute of International Education, Carolina has a higher rate of students going abroad than any other public research university nationwide. During the 2003–2004 academic year, 1,362 undergraduates studied abroad. UNC ranked sixth among all public and private research universities for the total number of undergraduate and graduate students going abroad (1,657). Those who have taken time to study abroad say the experience was invaluable for their academic and personal development.

Honors

Accepted applicants are automatically considered for Carolina's Honors Program, which admits about 200 incoming freshman each year. Students not selected for the program can apply during their freshman or sophomore years. Honors classes also are open to students not enrolled in the Honors Program, and although students in the program get first shot at the classes, honors classes rarely fill up before they open to general enrollment. Students not in the program can still graduate with honors by maintaining a high grade point average, usually higher than a 3.2 but determined by individual departments, and by completing an honors thesis senior year. Many students that graduate with honors opt for that route.

SOCIAL LIFE AND ACTIVITIES

The Pit, a brick campus square of sorts, is the social hub of the campus. It's buzzing during class hours with students hawking hundreds of organizations, passing out fliers for upcoming events, or just chatting with friends between classes. Located between the student union, the main dining hall, the campus bookstore, and two libraries, The Pit is the place to see and be seen between dusk and dawn.

After the lights go down, students flock to Franklin Street, the main drag in Chapel Hill, which borders the campus on the north. Franklin Street has dozens of homegrown bars and restaurants, including several microbreweries and lots of options for dining al fresco. Every Halloween, it fills with about 80,000 revelers from across the state for what is billed as the largest block party in the United States. And when UNC beats Duke in men's basketball, students rush the street, setting supervised fires, climbing trees, and just celebrating. "It's the best main street in America," twenty-one-year-old Ike Johnston, a senior, said of Franklin Street. "It's an entire business district in a small town made to satisfy people between ages eighteen and twenty-two."

Student Organizations

Student organizations are as essential to a Carolina education as finals and term papers. Carolina has over 600 officially recognized student organizations, and if you still can't find one that fits your interests, you can launch your own. Social and political organizations, such as the Black Student Movement, Young Democrats, College Republicans, and the Lesbian, Gay, Bisexual, Transgender—are extremely active on campus and pepper The Pit with information on events and initiatives. Those groups play a significant role in campus politics as do members of UNC's large, independent student government. Student Body

President elections, held every February, never fail to produce animated campaigns and a large slate of candidates.

> *With student organizations, whether it's working tech on a play or working sixty hours a week for the student newspaper, chances are you'll come away with a deeper understanding of what you want to do with life, as well as practical experience.*

—*Jennifer Samuels, 2004*

Student Press

Covering it all is a vigorous student press, namely, *The Daily Tar Heel*, the campus' award-winning, independent student newspaper. The DTH is funded entirely through advertising and consistently is recognized as one of the top student dailies in the country. It has produced storied alums such as author Thomas Wolfe and Charles Kuralt of CBS. Carolina also has several publications funded through student fees, including *Blue & White* magazine, *The Carolina Review*, and *The Black Ink*. The journalism school also produces a mostly student-run, award-winning television broadcast program called *Carolina Week*.

Community Service

Students also are active in more direct community service, both on and off campus. The university boasts a sizeable Habitat for Humanity chapter, an influential Campus Y, hundreds of annual service projects and fund-raisers, and an active service-learning program in which students take courses that require off-campus community service component. Carolina's largest annual student fund-raiser, Dance Marathon, is a twenty-four-hour dance marathon. In 2006, 750 dancers raised $201,142 for the N.C. Children's Hospital—both of these were records. The marathon involves hundreds of students from across campus but its volunteer positions are heavily populated by UNC's Greek community.

Greek Life

The Greeks, which are an active part of campus life, sponsor various 5Ks throughout the year and are best known for the Derby Days fund-raiser in the fall and several large parties thrown on the last day of classes each year. The Greek system, which has twenty-two traditional fraternities and nine sororities, eight historically black fraternities and sororities, and fourteen religious and multicultural ones, draws about fourteen percent of

Carolina students. Greek life will provide you with a full social calendar, but you definitely don't have to go Greek to have a fulfilling, active social life at Carolina.

Athletics

Carolina is basketball country, and with five national titles, legendary Coach Dean Smith, and star Michael Jordan to its name, there's no question why. The men in baby blue play a high-octane game and consistently post wins in what is the toughest basketball league in the country, the Atlantic Coast Conference.

I was dragged to my first Carolina men's basketball game. I should have counted myself lucky to have a ticket, but as a native Texan, I was raised on the notion that football reigns supreme. So it was with hesitation that I joined the sea of Carolina blue rolling toward the massive Dean Dome, a building that somehow manages not only to be imposing but also inspiring and irresistible. As the crisp air filled with the electricity of the crowd, a chill ran up my spine. By the time I made it to my seat in the stomping, whooping students' section, I knew it wasn't the cold but rather the first of what would be many encounters with basketball fever.

WHAT'S WITH THE BLUE FOOT?

It's a Tar Heel of course. Carolina's actual mascot is a ram, but its athletic programs universally are known as the Tar Heels. The same nickname also is widely used to indicate a North Carolinian. So what is a Tar Heel? The most common explanation of the nickname dates back to the Civil War. The story more or less goes like this: North Carolina troops were fighting a battle in Virginia alongside other troops from that state. They were taking quite a beating and next thing the Carolina boys knew, the Virginians had retreated. But the North Carolinians fought on, undeterred—and they won. According to lore, the Virginians asked the victorious troops in a condescending tone whether there was anymore tar down in the Old North State. The reply: "No, not a bit; old Jeff's bought it all up. He's going to put it on your heels to make you stick better in the next fight."
Since then, as the legend goes, North Carolinians were known as the Tar Heels for their ability to stick out a fight. As Carolina alumni and administrators are eager to point out, UNC Tar Heels are known for fighting the good fight, not only on the basketball and football field, but in all aspects of life.

Still, if your passion is more lush grass than polished wood, more hurdles than hoops, you're not alone. Carolina—across the board—is an athlete's paradise. The university is home to twenty-eight men's and women's varsity teams, and has dozens of intramural and club teams, including the highly competitive men's club rowing team. Carolina has aggressively implemented Title IX and has some of the most successful women athletes in the country.

In fact, the true Tar Heel dynasty isn't basketball, but women's soccer. The team has brought home eighteen national titles and developed athletes such as soccer celebrity Mia Hamm and her fellow 2004 Olympic Gold medalist, Cat Reddick. The Tar Heel team hosts a soccer camp every summer and has inspired thousands of female athletes nationwide. They have a devoted following and draw some of the largest crowds of any nonrevenue sport at UNC.

If cheering from the stands isn't your idea of athletics, but you don't want the pressure of a varsity team, Carolina still has plenty of options. Most club teams, a step up from intramural competition, travel for games and are relatively well funded through student fees and fund-raisers. For the more casual athlete, the campus offers numerous well-maintained intramural fields, tennis, volleyball, and basketball courts, ropes courses, a golf course, miles of paths and trails, two pools, and state-of-the-art workout facilities.

Chapel Hill and Environs

Chapel Hill is the quintessential college town, complete with stunning lawns and centuries-old homes, a vibrant nightlife, and a progressive, close-knit community. It's home to about 50,000 of the most highly educated people in the state and joins nearby Carrboro—a quirky, charismatic town—in playing host to Carolina students. Chapel Hill and Carrboro are the heart of Orange County, which boasts miles of meandering country roads perfect to unwind and recharge on after a tough day of classes.

Pass up the lush, rolling hills for Interstate 40, which runs through Chapel Hill, and you can be in downtown Raleigh, the state capital, in about thirty minutes or in Durham, home of Duke University, in ten minutes flat. Together, Chapel Hill-Carrboro, Durham, and Raleigh form the Triangle region of North Carolina, a metropolitan area that is home to more than one million people, contains the Raleigh-Durham International Airport, and is internationally renowned for top-notch research and technology. In sum, Chapel Hill offers the charm and safety of a small town with the nearby amenities of a large urban center.

FINANCIAL AID

Carolina consistently rates as a best buy in national publications, meaning it provides a quality education for a relatively low cost. Still, the cost of attendance would be prohibitive for many students, especially out-of-state students, without financial aid. UNC is committed to meeting one hundred percent of students' demonstrated financial need in order to ensure that every qualified student has a shot at a Carolina education, regardless of their finances. The university does so with a combination of scholarships, loans, and federal, state, and university grants, and private gifts.

Students who apply for admission are automatically considered for merit-based scholarships, but you can submit additional information if you are interested in the Robertson Scholarship (see below). To apply for need-based aid, submit the Free Application for Federal Student Aid, or FAFSA, and the CSS/PROFILE no later than March 1. Both forms are available online on the FAFSA and College Board Web sites.

More information about aid at Carolina can be obtained on the Web site for the Office of Scholarships and Student Aid at *http://studentaid.unc.edu/studentaid*. You can also contact the student aid staff Monday through Friday from 9 A.M. to 4 P.M. at (919) 962-8396. The staff is helpful and understanding, and the office's director, who was a low-income, first-generation college student, has been innovative and aggressive in advocating for enhanced access for students with financial need.

Carolina Covenant

One of those innovative ideas was the Carolina Covenant, which is Carolina's promise that its neediest students will graduate debt free. Launched in 2003, the landmark program covers all the costs of education through scholarships, grants, and a ten- to twelve-hour-a-week work-study program. Loans are not part of the picture. To be considered for the Covenant, all you have to do is fill out the standard financial aid forms listed above. Students whose family incomes fall at or below two hundred percent of the federal poverty line will automatically qualify for the Covenant. You can find out more and view profiles of Covenant recipients online at *http://www.unc.edu/carolinacovenant*.

Robertson Scholarship

The Robertson Scholarship is a joint privately funded program hosted by Carolina and Duke University. It is designed to foster collaboration between the two institutions and to allow selected students to benefit from the best of both schools' course offerings and faculty expertise. Thirty students are selected for the program each year; fifteen matriculate at Carolina and fifteen at Duke, though all scholars can attend classes at either campus. Students selected for the program receive full tuition, room, and living stipends at Carolina and a laptop computer. Applicants should exhibit academic excellence, leadership potential, a commitment to community service, and strong ethical principles. For more information, visit *http://www.robertsonscholars.org*.

Morehead Scholars Program

The Morehead Scholarship is a privately funded scholarship program and is the most prestigious honor at Carolina. The program provides a whole host of on- and off-campus enrichment activities and a strong network of mentors and potential employers. The scholarship includes full tuition and fees for four years, a laptop, a fully funded, four-year summer enrichment program that begins the summer before freshman year, and an annual stipend that covers all other normal expenses, including housing, meals, travel, and books. The total estimated value for in-state students is about $80,000 and $140,000 for out-of-state students, because of the different tuition costs.

About forty students are selected for the scholarship each year, which is entirely merit-based. The criteria used to evaluate candidates are: capacities to lead and motivate fellow students, scholastic ability and extracurricular attainments, moral force of character, and physical vigor as shown by participation in sports or in other ways. Students must be nominated by the Admissions Office or a participating school to apply. All schools in North Carolina are eligible to nominate students, and select schools across the United States and Great Britain are eligible. To see if your school can nominate candidates, visit *http://www.moreheadfoundation.org*. If your school isn't on the list, you still can be nominated by the Carolina Admissions Office if you apply by the November 1 deadline.

GRADUATES

Carolina gets in your blood. Whether or not you were a Tar Heel born and bred, like the fight song says, you are a Tar Heel for life when you leave Carolina. That not only means graduates have a deep, lifelong connection to the university, but also that they pursue their dreams with the zeal and character Carolina has taught them. Tar Heels are givers, the lifeblood of countless communities, visionaries, and leaders.

Carolina consistently sends undergraduates on to pursue masters and doctorates at top-notch schools, including Harvard, Stanford, Columbia, and Carolina's own graduate programs. Others have gone on to become highly successful entrepreneurs, teachers, authors, professional athletes, entertainers—you name it—and many venture into politics, particularly in North Carolina.

Carolina has large alumni associations across the United States and a host of devoted alumni who give millions of dollars to the school each year. None will ever forget the main quad in the wee hours of the morning—calm, more than a little balmy, and simply awe-inspiring. None will ever forget screaming until it hurt in the only dome that will ever mean basketball, or the late nights at Linda's and He's Not Here on Franklin Street, and the early mornings learning Spanish in Dey Hall. And they will forever rally 'round the Well, even if only in their hearts, when hope and courage are in short supply.

SUMMING UP

The Carolina experience is part community, part stunning intellect, part dedication, and a pound or two of passion. Add a dose of revelry and adventure and top it off with timeless architecture and rolling lawns. At its core, Carolina offers top athletics, a world-class education, a focus on service and leadership, and a fun-loving student body—and its unique role as a leading public institution makes it a must attend. The university is ever-mindful of its duty to "the people," and as a public school, Carolina educates a far more diverse student body than found at many private schools.

Chapel Hill, which plays host to the university, is a town with a village mentality, and the caring, engagement, and warmth that comes with it. It sprung up around the university and will forever be a university town, but with about 50,000 full-time residents, it's now large enough to offer some "townie" flavor of its own. Step onto Franklin Street, sample the shops, restaurants, and bars, and you'll never want to see a Main Street or First Street again.

All told, Carolina provides the quintessential college experience without the cliché. Expect to get rowdy from time to time, to take your studies seriously and your public duty even more so. Prepare to become a thinker, a leader, and a caretaker of all that has come before.

❏ *Elyse Ashburn, B.A.*

PROMINENT GRADS

- ○ Mia Hamm, 1994, World Famous Women's Soccer Player
- ○ Charles Kuralt, 1965, Beloved CBS News Broadcaster
- ○ James K. Polk, 1818, Only alumnus to serve as U.S. President
- ○ Hugh McColl, 1957, Retired Chairman and CEO of Bank of America
- ○ Michael Jordan, 1986, Perhaps the greatest basketball player ever
- ○ Thomas Wolfe, 1920, Author of "Look Homeward Angel"
- ○ Andy Griffith, 1949, TV Actor, Comedian, Producer, and Grammy-winning Musician
- ○ David Brinkley, 1992, Distinguished TV Journalist
- ○ Marion Jones, 1997, Olympic Track Star
- ○ Davis Love III, 1993, PGA Tour Member

UNIVERSITY OF NOTRE DAME

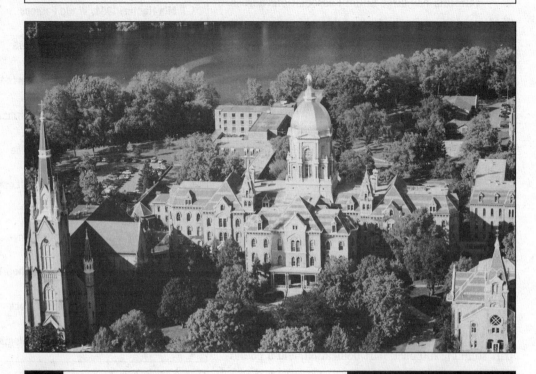

 University of Notre Dame
Notre Dame, IN 46556

 (574) 631-7505

 E-mail: *admissio.1@ND.edu*
Web site: *http://www.nd.edu*

 Enrollment

Full-time ❑ women: 3,877
❑ men: 4,383

INTRODUCING NOTRE DAME

Every year in late August, freshmen converge upon Notre Dame's campus in South
Bend, Indiana, rushing from one freshman orientation event to the next. During the many
dances, the Alumni Hall Tie Dye Party, and the Orientation Mass, a certain phrase resonates
throughout the campus: "the Notre Dame family." This one phrase, which has a slightly different meaning for each student and alum, is a distinctive element of the University of Notre
Dame.

I experienced "the Notre Dame family" immediately during my initial days at the university. I first sensed the friendliness among the students when my parents and I arrived on campus. As we pulled up to my dorm, a number of my hall-mates descended upon our car, fully packed with all the essentials for college, and helped us carry all my stuff to my room. But the Notre Dame family is more than just friendliness; the campus has a sense of togetherness to it. During those first days on campus my parents and I immediately felt at home in my new surroundings and we began to realize that my Notre Dame experience would not only be for me, but would include my parents in many ways as well; they too would become part of the Notre Dame family.

The phrase "Notre Dame family" embodies three of the main characteristics of Notre Dame: community, tradition, and Catholic heritage.

The campus setting makes it easy to foster a close-knit community. With its tree-lined paths and two lakes, the 1,250-acre campus seems to be isolated from the rest of the world. The university is located ninety miles east of Chicago and has more than 130 buildings on campus. The dorms in particular are an integral part of the campus and enhance the feeling of community. Eighty percent of students live on campus, and most remain on campus for three or four years.

Notre Dame's Catholic roots are a vital part of life at the university. Even the buildings on campus, such as Sacred Heart Basilica, the Grotto, and "Touchdown Jesus" on the side of the library, demonstrate the Catholic character and influence at the school. Eighty-five percent of Notre Dame students are Catholic, and the Catholic nature of the school is emphasized in all aspects of life at the university, including classes. In fact, one of the main social activities of the week for dorm residents and off-campus students is Sunday night mass in the dorm chapels.

The Notre Dame family can trace its roots back 162 years to when Fr. Sorin and his fellow Holy Cross religious brothers founded l'Université de Notre Dame du lac (Our Lady of the Lake) in three small log buildings. The campus has grown significantly since that time, but the strong desire to educate students in the classroom and beyond remains. By the time freshmen reach graduation day, they will realize that they are part of a unique group that extends beyond South Bend. And although the students may have different memories of what makes Notre Dame such a special place, each will have been shaped in some way by the elements of the Notre Dame family.

The University of Notre Dame looks for students who are Renaissance individuals—intellectuals, leaders, athletes, artists, and volunteers. Basically, Notre Dame wants the best all-around students.

In a recent freshman class, 11,316 students applied for entrance, 3,581 were admitted, and 1,995 enrolled. On average, the students who enrolled graduated in the top five percent of their senior class; in fact, thirty-four percent ranked one, two, three, four, or five in their class.

As one recent Notre Dame grad put it:

I remember attending a freshman orientation program with my entire freshman class and their families. The Dean of Student Affairs asked those students who had been valedictorians or salutatorians of their high school classes to raise their hands. As I looked around, I was surrounded by a sea of raised arms. That's when I realized my class was packed with students who were all accustomed to being number one.

So, how does Notre Dame evaluate all of the applications it receives every year? There are five areas on which students are judged: high school record, standardized tests, teachers' evaluations, extracurricular accomplishments, and the essays and personal statement submitted with the application.

From a student's high school record, Notre Dame considers the quality of the school's curriculum. Notre Dame recommends that applying students take four years of English, math, science, foreign language, history, and electives. The admissions counselors especially look at students who have pushed themselves by taking honors and AP-level classes, in addition to courses such as precalculus or calculus, chemistry, and physics. A current Notre Dame student said:

The only reason I suffered through physics in high school was so it would be on my transcript when I applied to Notre Dame, even though I knew I was going to be an English major.

Notre Dame also considers a student's class rank, grades, and the academic competition at the high school.

Standardized Tests

Notre Dame requires either the SAT or the ACT and candidly admits it places a great deal of emphasis on standardized tests. The mid fifty percent score ranges of entering freshmen are 1300–1450 (SAT, based on 1600) and 30–33 (ACT).

Recommendations

Because Notre Dame does not interview candidates, teacher recommendations are one way for the admissions counselors to learn about the applicants personally. Students should have a variety of teachers, who have worked with them extensively, write their evaluations.

Extracurricular Activities

As mentioned earlier, Notre Dame seeks enthusiastic students who have developed themselves inside and outside of the classroom; therefore, the university weighs extracurricular activities heavily. Students are judged on leadership positions in clubs and student government, school and community involvement, and special talents. Also, because service work is an important aspect of life at Notre Dame, the university looks for students who have volunteered at social service organizations such as nursing homes, soup kitchens, and day care centers.

Personal Statements

Finally, a student's essays and personal statements are thrown into the evaluation mix; these compositions are vital to providing the admissions counselor with an inside look at the student. For instance, one essay asks students to reflect on how a book, poem, play, or piece of music has influenced their lives. Also, Notre Dame requires two long essays and three shorter essays, which is more than many schools' applications.

Application Plans

Notre Dame has two application plans, Early Action and Regular Action. With Early Action, a good option for people who have exceptional grades and standardized test scores, applications are due the beginning of November. If admitted through Early Action, students do not have to withdraw their applications from other schools and they have until May 1 to inform Notre Dame of their decision. Most students still apply Regular Action, however, in which applications are due at the beginning of January.

International and Minority Students

The student body at Notre Dame is geographically diverse, representing all fifty states, more than 100 countries, and five continents. Notre Dame believes international students add a unique perspective to the campus and make the university an international center of teaching and research; however, due to the Catholic heritage of the school, Notre Dame is not very mixed ethnically. Only about seventeen percent of the student body are minority students.

Similar to many highly competitive colleges, Notre Dame has made a serious commitment to recruiting minority students; for example, Notre Dame hosts two events every year to introduce minority students to life at the school. One is the Fall Open House, which has become a popular event for prospective students. Later in the year, after acceptances are sent out, Notre Dame brings admitted students and their families to Notre Dame for a three-day campus visit to help them with the decision process.

Women

Notre Dame also has increased the number of women in its student body. About five years ago, the ratio of men to women was three to one; now it is almost one to one. To accommodate the increased number of women students, Notre Dame converted some male dorms into female dorms and constructed several new residence halls.

Children of Alums

Part of the reason Notre Dame has maintained its traditions and family feeling is the fact that about twenty-five percent of the students are children of Notre Dame alums. Each year the university aims to admit the appropriate number of daughters and sons of alums to maintain this statistic.

> *Although it is not unusual to have three generations from one family attend the University of Notre Dame, my grandfather, father, and I share a unique experience in that we all graduated exactly thirty years apart ('34, '64, '94). And while it is true we had individual experiences and memories spanning over half a century, we share a timeless bond with every other member who makes up the much larger "Notre Dame family": an overwhelming sense of community, tradition, and pride.*

Visits

For applying students who wish to visit the campus, Notre Dame will arrange an informational meeting with an admissions counselor and an overnight stay in a residence hall with a student host. To get the feeling of attending Notre Dame, the prospective student sits in on classes and eats at the dining hall. The program is a great way for students to experience the campus and decide if Notre Dame is the right fit for them.

ACADEMIC LIFE

For many students, Notre Dame marks the first time they are required to question and articulate their feelings about their faith, social beliefs, and politics. No longer are students asked to simply regurgitate information as they did in high school; instead, as students learn world history, finance, and calculus, they begin to define themselves and what is important to them. A Notre Dame graduate once stated, "In the Notre Dame classroom, the spirit and the intellect culminate."

As a Catholic school, the university could easily expect that students believe only what the Catholic Church teaches, but often, the required theology and philosophy core classes force students to take a serious look at what they believe and why. The Notre Dame learning environment is a unique combination of faith and questioning.

The Colleges and Majors

Notre Dame is divided into five colleges: Arts and Letters (the largest), Business, Science, Engineering, and Architecture. Overall, the most popular majors are political science, finance, and accounting, with majors such as history and economics growing in popularity. Notre Dame also has a strong preprofessional studies program, which combine medical school prerequisite courses with a liberal arts major or additional science classes. Each college also has its own academic organizations and honor societies, including the Arts and Letters Business Society and the Management Club.

First Year of Studies

Before selecting a college, all students are enrolled into the First Year of Studies (FYS), a program created to help freshmen adjust to college-level academics. The FYS assigns each student an advisor, who guides students with course selection, choosing a college and/or a major, and with concerns about classes. The FYS center also provides students with tutors and study groups if necessary. Students must fulfill the core requirements of the FYS before they can enter sophomore year. Usually, students do not have any difficulty completing the required classes since approximately half of each incoming freshman class receives class credit for AP classes and SAT Subject Test scores.

Although taking calculus for a future political science major might seem like sheer agony, Notre Dame adheres to the philosophy of a well-rounded education, and offers its core classes as a way to achieve this purpose. For example, while in the FYS program, all students must complete one semester of Freshman Seminar and Composition and Literature (Comp and Lit). Freshman Seminar is a literature class that addresses any topic the professor selects, from reading Plato's *Republic* the entire semester to studying the subject of leadership through reading books about Ghandi. Comp and Lit is more of a grammar class that focuses on improving the overall structure of a student's writing through rewriting and peer evaluations.

By the end of their sophomore year, students are required to declare a major, but at this point, most students have created a program of study simply by taking electives that interest them.

College Seminar

If students declare Arts and Letters as their college, they are required to complete a unique course called College Seminar, a semester-long class with approximately thirteen to twenty students, guided by an Arts and Letters professor. Each course is built around the academic specialty of the instructor, but all explore the breadth of the liberal arts.

> *My class was lead by Professor T. R. Swartz of the economics department, a man of unmatched energy. The first action he took was to move our class from the uncomfortable, stiff chairs in O'Shaughnessy to the inviting lounge of a residence hall. Next, he limited our writing assignments to one page, exactly, no eight-point fonts and no wide margins. He forced us to write briefly, concisely, and weekly. Our class, a diverse group of students, became fast friends. No one missed class, and it was at 9:00 A.M., which is considered early in college. After an intense year of discussion and thought, T.R. told us, "Choose a theme for your life. Find a purpose and direct your actions toward it." Never in my life have such simple words had such a profound effect on me.*

Faculty

The majority of classes at Notre Dame have fifteen to twenty-five students. With classes that size and a student-teacher ratio of thirteen to one, students and teachers develop close relationships, a crucial element of the educational experience at Notre Dame. Teachers often invite students to their homes for dinner to hold class discussions or simply socialize.

Academics at Notre Dame is a two-part machine, student and teacher, and when they are functioning in sync, they create the spirit of Notre Dame. Professors at the university guide their students, but allow them the necessary freedom to discover their interests and strengths.

Internships

Students have the opportunity to apply for internships that pique their interest, both on and off campus. For example, the local NBC affiliate, WNDU-TV, and the Notre Dame News and Information office offer internships to qualified students. Many students apply to be teachers' assistants their senior year, a rewarding experience that allows upper- and lower-class students to work together closely.

My senior year I had the opportunity to design, implement, and write a thesis in psychology that incorporated my interests in children, minority populations, and psychological experience. Through the university's strong connections to the community (in my case, Head Start of South Bend) and the guidance of the faculty, my work had an established framework in which I could create an experience that was meaningful to me. There was room for individuality and independence within a supportive structure, which is sometimes a tough balance to achieve, but an example of how the academic experience at Notre Dame is broader than the limited space of a classroom.

Study Abroad

Many students go abroad their sophomore or junior year. In fact, among research universities, Notre Dame has the third highest percentage of students engaged in international study programs. Some of the popular year-long programs are in Angers, France; Innsbruck, Austria; and Toledo, Spain. Students who participate in the year-long programs tend to go during their sophomore year and are required to take intensive language courses before they go. The favorite semester-long programs include London; Jerusalem; Santiago, Chile; and Fremantle, Australia. All of the abroad programs are competitive to get into, so often students end up enrolling in other universities' programs, although it does sometimes affect class credit.

Physically Challenged Students

To further diversify Notre Dame academics, the university provides programs to accommodate students with disabilities. For example, students with challenges can get note takers, have extended time on exams, or use textbooks on disk to ensure equal access to all disciplines and facilities.

Libraries

Students also have access to almost three million volumes in the ten libraries located on campus. Most of these facilities have late hours and are open twenty-four hours a day during exams. In addition, there are ten computer clusters throughout the campus, many of which are always open.

Because Notre Dame is a highly competitive college that requires students to put in long hours of studying, it is common to see students heading off to the library on Friday and Saturday nights to do class work. Notre Dame students are dedicated to their education and are willing to put in the extra hours on the weekend if necessary, even if they are only going to be studying on the extremely social second floor of the Hesburgh Library.

After four years of intense learning at Notre Dame, students are armed with the tools of the Notre Dame academic environment—independence, questioning, and discipline—and are prepared to commence learning in the real world.

SOCIAL LIFE AND ACTIVITIES

Students at Notre Dame are as busy with club meetings and sports during the week as they are with their normal course load.

Although Notre Dame does not have a Greek system, students reside in the same dorm throughout their stay at Notre Dame and are often identified by the dorm they live in. For example, it is common to hear students refer to each other by saying, "She lives in Walsh" or "He used to live in Carroll Hall." The dorms organize a large number of student activities, including volunteer tutoring at local schools, dinners with Brother/Sister dorms, and residence hall councils.

Athletics

Tradition is an important aspect of life at Notre Dame, and the most famous tradition at the university is football. From the "1812 Overture" played at the beginning of each game's fourth quarter, to the world's oldest marching band, to the legends of Knute Rockne and the Gipper, "Fightin' Irish" football is rich in tradition. Because of the team's national reputation, many believe Notre Dame is much larger than its average enrollment of 8,300 undergraduates. Overall, the Irish athletic programs annually rank among the top twenty in the nation for both men and women.

Intramural sports are very popular. Each dorm usually offers football (men), flag football (women), basketball, and soccer. Since the majority of students played varsity sports in high school, and many were captains of their teams, intramural sports are extremely competitive. In fact, Notre Dame may be the only school where students play intramural football wearing full gear. Women's flag football is equally competitive; injuries such as concussions, broken wrists, and cuts requiring stitches are not uncommon. In line with Notre Dame's love of football, the championship games for both of these football teams are played at Notre Dame Stadium.

After classes, students work out at the athletic facilities available on campus, including the Rockne Memorial (the Rock), the Joyce Center, Rolfs Sports Recreation Center, Rolfs Aquatic Center, and Loftus Center. Students are able to swim, run on tracks and treadmills, ride stationary bikes, lift weights, or participate in aerobics classes at these fitness centers. In addition, Notre Dame has a new Ben Crenshaw-designed golf course for students and alumni to play on from April through October.

The traditions of Notre Dame extend past the football season. Events such as the Keenan Review, a "talent" show performed by the residents of Keenan Hall; An Tostal, the student spring festival; Bookstore Basketball, the world's largest five-on-five outdoor basketball tournament; and the Blue and Gold game, the spring inter-squad football scrimmage, all contribute to traditional life at Notre Dame.

Volunteering

On the non-athletic side, the Center for Social Concerns (CSC) runs more than thirty-five community service clubs that offer students the opportunity to participate in volunteer programs in the South Bend area, as well as across the country and around the world. About seventy-five percent of the Notre Dame student body participated in programs coordinated through the CSC, including Big Brothers/Big Sisters, Habitat for Humanity, Neighborhood Study Help Program, and Recycling Irish. The CSC epitomizes the Notre Dame spirit. The center uses a holistic method by enhancing students' spiritual and intellectual awareness of today's social realities through service opportunities and seminars. The center also identifies volunteer programs to participate in around the country with service trips to areas such as Appalachia and the inner cities. In addition, each summer, more than 125 Notre Dame alumni clubs sponsor 200 Notre Dame students in Summer Service Projects around the United States. Said a recent graduate, who participated in a Summer Service Project while at Notre Dame:

I spent the summer before my senior year living in a Jersey City homeless shelter for women and their children. I was given the opportunity to see the tough realities of the world. One woman I clearly remember was a twenty-year-old mother who was wise beyond her years, struggling to find a job while being supported by the welfare system. Through her I learned what really matters in life: unconditional love, trust, and spirituality. I didn't need to know anything else.

Special Interest Clubs

Notre Dame has more than twenty special interest clubs including College Republicans, College Democrats, and Knights of Columbus. In addition, the university offers twenty-three ethnic organizations such as the African and American Student Alliance, the Hispanic American Organization, and the Korean Club.

Performing Programs

Although Notre Dame historically has not been known as a performing arts school, that is quickly changing, especially with the construction of a new Performing Arts Center, which opened in fall 2004. Students currently have a variety of programs to choose from. There are a range of music groups, from Shenanigans, a song and dance troupe, to the Liturgical Choir, and nine instrumental music groups, including Concert Band. If students are interested in drama, a number of different troupes put on performances throughout the year, including The Freshmen Four, St. Edward's Hall Players, and the Department of Film, Television, and Theatre, which produces four plays. The relocation of Actors From the London Stage to Notre Dame has prompted a surge in Shakespearean productions on campus.

Publications

For future Pulitzer Prize winners, Notre Dame has several student-run publications: *The Observer*, the daily newspaper; *Scholastic*, the weekly news magazine; and *The Dome*, Notre Dame's yearbook. All of these publications have positions for students interested in copywriting, design, and photography. Students with a strong interest in music have the opportunity to be DJs at WVFI-AM, the alternative music station, and WSND-FM, the classical music station.

Additional special annual events on campus include the Sophomore Literary Festival, the Collegiate Jazz Festival, and the Black Cultural Arts Festival.

Weekend Activities

The weekends offer Notre Dame students plenty of social and recreational activities as well. In the fall, weekends are dominated by Notre Dame football games, both home and away. Students often have family and friends visit on these weekends to tailgate before the game, follow the marching band across campus, and dine by candlelight at the dining halls. Many people say that life at Notre Dame ends after football season, but,

POPULAR SOCIAL EVENTS

- ○ Junior Parents Weekend
- ○ Morrissey Film Festival
- ○ Fisher Regatta
- ○ Beaux Arts Ball
- ○ Glee Club Christmas Concert
- ○ Bengal Bouts

since Notre Dame has joined the Big East, other sports, such as men's and women's soccer, volleyball, hockey, lacrosse, and men's and women's basketball games, have become popular events. In fact, women's basketball games average 7,800 fans since winning the 2001 National Championships.

Although traditional dating is not common at Notre Dame, dorms host dances and formals throughout the school year.

Notre Dame does not allow hard alcohol in dorm rooms, and the university has strict penalties if underage students are caught drinking in the halls or carrying alcohol across campus. On-campus parties usually end by 2:00 A.M. when parietals, or visiting hours, end. As a university that is based on Roman Catholic values, Notre Dame has single-sex dorms and enforces visiting hours. If a student is found in a dorm of the opposite sex after parietals, there are serious consequences.

Upper-class students often host parties at off-campus student housing complexes, such as Campus View and Lafayette Square, or hang out at popular bars, such as Club 23, Corby's, and Legends, the restaurant/bar located on campus.

Many students enjoy dining out on the weekends at favorite local restaurants, such as Macri's Deli for sandwiches, Bruno's for pizza, Rocco's for pasta, and CJ's for burgers. Also, the Student Union Board (SUB) and the Snite Museum show recently released films on campus.

FINANCIAL AID

When compared to other Catholic and private universities that are nationally recognized for academic excellence, the overall costs for Notre Dame tend to be lower.

For a recent academic year, Notre Dame expected tuition and academic fees would be around $33,407, and room and board approximately $8,730. For books, students can expect to pay about $850 per year. To cut back on the cost of books, students often purchase course materials from each other or buy used books from Pandora's Books, located on the corner of Howard Street and Notre Dame Avenue, about three blocks south of campus. The university reminds students to expect costs to increase annually in order to maintain Notre Dame's solid academic environment.

As for personal expenses, the overall cost of living in South Bend is less than in other cities, but students typically spent $1,000 to $1,500 per year for incidentals as well as social and weekend activities, such as going out for dinner, movies, and other social activities.

In the last few years, the university has made aggressive efforts to substantially increase its financial aid funding.

According to Joe Russo, Director of Financial Aid:

> *In 1990, Notre Dame had $5.5 million for financial aid, and in 2003, the amount increased significantly, to more than $78 million. We have now reached the point where every student who gets into Notre Dame can afford to attend Notre Dame and experience the Notre Dame family.*

This growth in funding stems from programs including post-season football bowl games, the Affinity credit card (each time alums use their Notre Dame credit card, money is donated to Notre Dame's financial aid fund), the NBC contract to televise Notre Dame home football games, and licensing income from Notre Dame paraphernalia sold around the United States.

The Package

When a student receives financial aid from Notre Dame, the university works with the student and his or her family to create a financial aid package, often a combination of low-interest loans (Perkins Student Loans and Stafford Student Loans), scholarship money, and work-study. The university encourages work-study for students on financial aid to help cover their personal expenses. Options for on-campus employment include working in the dining halls, computer clusters, at the athletic department, and in the library. Also, the Notre Dame alumni clubs across the country provide hundreds of scholarships annually, now totaling more than $1 million, to incoming students.

Grants and Other Options

As part of Notre Dame's efforts to increase the ethnic and socioeconomic diversity at the school, the university offers the Holy Cross Grants. These scholarship programs are awarded to students from disadvantaged backgrounds.

Other financial aid options include two-, three-, and four-year ROTC scholarships with the Air Force, Army, or Navy (includes Marines). These scholarships sometimes cover full tuition, and books, and provide a $150 monthly stipend. A little more than five percent of Notre Dame's students are on one of the above ROTC scholarships. In fact, Notre Dame's Navy ROTC unit is the second largest in the country (the Naval Academy is first).

To apply for financial aid, students are required to submit the standard Free Application for Federal Student Aid (FAFSA) and the PROFILE of the College Scholarship Service (CSS) by February 15, but are encouraged to file them as early as possible.

GRADUATES

Every home football game, Notre Dame alumni wander around the campus, remembering the days when the university belonged to them. Wearing their green shamrock-covered pants, they visit the bookstore, stop by concession stands, and stroll past their old dorms. As the current students pass the old alums on their way to tailgate, Notre Dame students promise themselves they will never become sentimental graduates, but when graduation day arrives, they find themselves reminiscing about their time at Notre Dame as well. The recent grads might be wearing jeans instead of plaid pants, but suddenly they also become nostalgic about their alma mater. Notre Dame alums are known for being maudlin when it comes to the university, and are the butt of many jokes as a result, but it is difficult to leave Notre Dame and not realize that it is a special place. Once someone attends Notre Dame, whether it was in the 1940s or in the 21st century, that person is always a member. It isn't a coincidence that Notre Dame boasts one of the largest and most loyal alumni networks of any U.S. college. The university has 218 clubs in the United States and fifty-four alumni clubs worldwide.

In 1996 the Office of Institutional Research at Notre Dame conducted a survey of the undergraduate Class of 1986. The survey intended to find how satisfied those graduates were with their Notre Dame educational experience, if they felt prepared for life after college, and if they would select Notre Dame again if they could relive their college experience. In all of the questionnaire areas, student satisfaction indicated that the overwhelming majority (eighty-five to ninety-five percent) of alums had positive and enthusiastic feelings about their experience at Notre Dame.

After graduating from Notre Dame, alumni locate all over the world and enter a wide array of professions. Every year, Notre Dame sends the largest percentage of its graduates into the career world. The most popular fields graduates enter into include, law, marketing and sales, engineering, medicine, and accounting.

Career Center

To help students secure positions in the business world, Notre Dame's Career Center holds seminars about writing résumés and preparing for interviews, and also counsels students on what professional careers fit their interests. The Career Center invites a range of companies to the campus; however, many of the companies tend to be better matches for business and engineering students than for liberal arts majors.

Advanced Degrees

Many students go on to pursue advanced degrees, in law, medicine, MBA programs, or other graduate programs. Almost half of all Notre Dame grads eventually go on to complete at least one advanced degree.

Service Programs

After graduation, social service continues to be an integral part of many students' lives. In recent years, about ten percent of each graduating class has entered into a one- or two-year service program, domestic and abroad. The Center for Social Concerns, which brings numerous postgraduate service programs to campus, advises students on what programs are available and would be a good match in terms of structure, location, and activity. Some of the more popular programs include Jesuit Volunteer Corps, Alliance for Catholic Education (ACE, a Notre Dame-founded program), Inner City Teaching Corps, and the Peace Corps.

Alumni Support

In terms of alumni annual giving, Notre Dame ranks third in the nation, but alumni are dedicated to Notre Dame more than just financially. Approximately 161,000 alums participate in events organized by the alumni clubs, such as golf outings, happy hours, and vacations. There are also activities meant to enhance the spiritual, educational, and professional aspects of alumni's lives. For example, the Alumni Association has started a program that brings graduates back to South Bend to rehab houses in the area and the Chicago Alumni Club frequently hosts networking meetings for graduates.

When a student graduates from Notre Dame and is unclear what area he or she wants to enter or is looking for a career change later in life, the Notre Dame alumni make up a strong support network. Graduates often look to each other for career guidance, resources, and connections, even if they graduated generations apart.

Alums permeate every field worldwide, from politics and the film industry to medical research and education, yet they all share the moral, ethical, and spiritual framework of the Notre Dame family.

SUMMING UP

The plethora of activities, programs, and facilities at Notre Dame allows students to create their own experience while at the university. As the phrase "Notre Dame family" has a different connotation for each student and graduate, so does the "Notre Dame experience." Although the school encourages students to be involved in all aspects of university life, students can choose if they want to focus more on academics, service, student government, or the arts. It is the same for social activities, where there is something for everyone.

The spirit of Notre Dame students and graduates proves that there is something special about the place. The fact that people affiliated with Notre Dame call it a family shows that students and graduates really care about the school and the people involved with it.

When I think about all of my experiences at Notre Dame, a certain image comes to my mind. No matter where we were, at a football game, mass, or special function, every time students and faculty heard the Notre Dame alma mater played, we put our arms around each other and swayed. Friends, strangers, teachers, students—it didn't matter. It was always such a powerful and unifying sight to have everyone together for that moment and exhibiting what the "Notre Dame family" really meant.

All in all, it is the last lines of the Notre Dame alma mater, "Notre Dame, Our Mother," that truly summarize how its students and graduates feel about the school: "And our hearts forever, Love thee, Notre Dame."

❏ *Meghan Case Kelley, B.A.*

UNIVERSITY OF PENNSYLVANIA

 University of Pennsylvania
Philadelphia, PA 19104

 (215) 898-7507
Fax: (215) 898-9670

 E-mail: *info@admissions.upenn.edu*
Web site: *http://www.upenn.edu*

 Enrollment

Full-time ❏ women: 4,810
　　　　　❏ men: 4,735

Part-time ❏ women: 126
　　　　　❏ men: 170

INTRODUCING THE UNIVERSITY OF PENNSYLVANIA

Penn was founded in 1749 as a Charity School intended to provide students with an education based on the ideas of Benjamin Franklin. Franklin's philosophy held that a student's education need not be wholly traditional, but practical as well; he was controversial in his proposal that teaching English was more important than teaching Latin. The resulting curriculum developed during Franklin's forty-year tenure as a trustee included the sciences, mathematics, history, logic, and philosophy. It was later built upon by the creation of the nation's first medical school, business school, and law classes. As America's first university, Penn has remained dedicated to the philosophy under which it was founded, and continues to offer its students and faculty opportunities to achieve in academic, social, and professional worlds.

In 250 years, Penn's student body has grown from a graduating class of seven to a student population of 20,000, half of which are undergraduates. This qualifies Penn as one of the larger schools in the Ivy League; however, the feeling on campus indicates the opposite. The Penn campus is mostly concentrated within a twelve-block area, centered upon Locust Walk, a tree-lined pedestrian walkway that bisects the entire campus in length and connects dormitories, academic facilities, libraries, and recreational spaces. Throughout the campus one can find visual records of Penn's development in West Philadelphia, tracing from the late 1800s through the present, with buildings by former student Frank Furness, professor Louis Kahn, modernist Eero Saarinen, and Penn graduate Robert Venturi. This mix of old and new gives Penn the easily distinguishable impression that characterizes its campus and sets it off from the city surrounding it.

The campus and its urban setting are major parts of student attraction to Penn. While the campus stands in visual contrast from the rest of the city, Penn is neither detached from Philadelphia nor uninvolved in its community. Penn students regularly explore the city, and many participate in community service and tutoring projects in nearby neighborhoods. The city provides an excellent complement to Penn, offering more than one hundred museums and galleries, multiple performing arts venues, top-ranked restaurants and bars, historical sites, and a variety of other attractions for students to take advantage of. Students often spend nights and weekends in historic Old City, Center City (Philadelphia's "downtown"), South Street, and other parts of town, but always return to campus to meet up with friends, do schoolwork, or relax at a campus establishment.

Given its setting and the opportunities offered, Penn practically guarantees that a student will find his or her niche. Penn students come from a variety of backgrounds, and are linked by their appreciation for hard work and academics—that is certainly how they earned their place at the university—but are marked by their ability to balance their education with social and extracurricular pursuits. Students come from fifty states and more than one hundred countries (ten percent of students at Penn are international). Registered student groups serving religion, politics, talents, hobbies, geographic origin, ethnicity, culture, sexuality, and other areas number almost 400, and student interests are so broad that this number continues to grow. This exciting mix of personalities fuels the academic and social environment at Penn, where students seem to take a genuine interest in learning on both sides of the classroom walls.

ADMISSIONS REQUIREMENTS

As the college admissions pool becomes increasingly large, acceptance to Penn is becoming more and more competitive. The hype of Early Decision has resulted in an enlarged ED applicant pool, and in past years Penn has taken up to half of their freshman class from this group. The median SAT falls around 1400, and most freshmen graduated in the top ten percent of their class. In order to remain competitive in this pool, it is necessary to pursue a rigorous high school curriculum.

While the academic program is very important to the application, admissions officers consider more than just letters and numbers. The Penn application gives students a chance to demonstrate personal talents and interests, specific strengths and goals, and any other elements that the applicant feels are important to communicate who they are and what would make them a unique addition to the university. Past essay questions have asked students what fictional character they would most like to meet, what has been one of the greatest challenges they've faced, and of course the one that is most provocative, to include page 217 of one's 300-page autobiography. These questions are deliberately open-ended, allowing students to further demonstrate their personality through their interpretation of the answer.

ADMISSIONS PROCESS

Every year, *The Daily Pennsylvanian* runs an article announcing that Penn's incoming freshmen are the result of its most selective admissions process yet. As a freshman, you read this and gain some confidence for the coming school year—you're more qualified than all of the upper classmen. Then your sophomore year they have an article about the new freshmen, but the numbers are higher and the accomplishments greater.

Penn does not require specific coursework or minimum scores for application, but does look for a student who has maximized his or her high school experience, meaning that they should be taking the most challenging curriculum offered, and should be doing well. Standardized tests are required, and a student must submit either the SAT exam and three SAT Subject Tests *or* the ACT exam. Students are welcome to submit both if they choose. Admissions Officers will consider the highest set of test scores. AP scores may be submitted, and exams may be used for placement or credit.

Note: Though there are no foreign language requirements for application, it is useful to have some background, as there are language proficiency requirements for graduation. This proficiency can be met with one of the more than one hundred languages taught at Penn.

In reviewing all of the required materials, as well as supplementary materials students might have supplied, admissions officers are looking to admit a diverse student body. This diversity applies to academic and extracurricular interests and accomplishments, life experiences, geographic location, cultural background, and any other number of circumstances that might make for a unique candidate. Admissions officers want students that are right for Penn, but also for whom Penn is a good match, and all applicants are asked to discuss why they feel Penn is best for them. The most important elements of the application are breadth and depth of involvement in academics and activities, personal statements, and teacher/school recommendations.

ACADEMIC LIFE

For many students, the start of freshman year at Penn may be a wake-up call. Most students will come from high schools where they were top students, and where they definitely did not have to do much to prove it. Take roughly 2,400 of those students and pool them together with 7,500 sophomores, juniors, and seniors, and an incoming freshman is set for a humbling experience. The upside of this is how much you can learn from your classmates, many of whom may have studied in depth the material you have merely familiarized yourself with. They will have worked in places you'd never thought to work, visited countries you've never thought of visiting, and started clubs and activities unlike any that existed at the school you came from. As a student at Penn, you may learn just as much from your friends as you do in your classes.

Penn provides plenty of support for students and makes efforts to acclimate freshmen to their new environment. Students are assigned peer advisors, faculty advisors, and academic advisors from their undergraduate division. These people can help select courses, plan out future semesters, and ultimately guide the student throughout his or her academic career.

Course Selection

Course registration at Penn could not be any easier or more convenient. After out-phasing written and phone-in methods, students can now do their entire course search, request, and registration through PennInTouch, an on-line system that can also be used to manage tuition, transcripts, student voting, and many other student concerns. After establishing a schedule, students are given what is an equivalent to a "shopping period" known as add/drop, during which they may attend various classes to ultimately finalize their course selection by two weeks into the semester.

Faculty

Almost all courses at Penn are taught by full professors, with the exception of some writing and foreign language classes. Though the average class size is small, larger classes break down into recitation sections led either by professors or grad/Ph.D. students. One way or another, professors stay in close contact with their students—they are not at Penn solely to perform private research and teach graduate students—and most professors are extremely accessible and eager to get to know their students. At the first meeting of a class, professors discuss the materials to be covered and dispense syllabi delineating required materials, exams, and assignments, and most important, any contact information. This may include office location and hours, e-mail, phone number, and additional contacts. All professors are required to keep office hours during which students are invited to stop by with any questions or concerns.

Four Undergraduate Schools

Most students applying to Penn will make their application to one of the four undergraduate schools. These include the College of Arts and Sciences, the Wharton School, the School of Engineering and Applied Science, and the School of Nursing. Joint degree programs offer students a combination of two of the schools, and students may apply to these highly selective programs as well. As few students are taken into these programs, applicants are given the opportunity to request admission to a single-degree program in one of the affiliated schools should they not be accepted for the joint degree program.

> **PENN ACADEMIC FIRSTS**
>
> Penn established the nation's first collegiate business school, the first medical school, the first modern liberal arts curriculum, the first psychology clinic, the first botany department, the first university teaching hospital, the first journalism curriculum, the first chairs of chemistry and psychology, and the first course in the contemporary novel.

Majors

Undergraduates in the College officially select their majors by the end of their sophomore year. The time before this can be used fulfilling language or general requirements as well as coursework for their intended major. The College has a general requirement, consisting of ten classes taken from seven different academic sectors. In addition, all students must also be proficient in a language and fulfill a writing requirement. Graduates of the College are expected to take full advantage of the liberal arts and sciences.

There are more than fifty majors offered in the College. Special programs such as Biological Basis of Behavior (BBB) and Philosophy, Politics, and Economics (PPE) attract students for their multidisciplinary approach. The Annenberg School sponsors a major in Communications through the College, and the Graduate School of Fine Arts supports Fine Arts and Architecture majors. Students with specific interests that are not directly addressed by available majors are allowed to find an advisor and create an individualized major. It is not unusual for students in the College to double major or carry multiple minors.

Students in engineering can opt for a Bachelor of Science (BSE) or a Bachelor of Applied Science (BAS) degree. Those selecting the BSE are usually on a preprofessional tract, which makes up the majority of students in the undergraduate program. The BAS offers a chance for students with an interest in technology who are less sure about their future career to add a liberal arts component to their education. All engineering students take seven courses in the College. The engineering curriculum culminates with a senior design project, which is either an original or continued research project based upon their undergraduate work.

The Wharton School was the first business school in the world, founded with the goal of providing an undergraduate business program that integrated humanities and social sciences. All students in the Wharton School receive a Bachelor of Science in Economics. Students are required to take a set of core requirements including finance, management, accounting, and marketing, and must pursue coursework outside of Wharton as well. Wharton students do not have majors, but concentrations, made up of four course units from one area of study. There are twenty concentrations offered, and just as in the College, students are permitted to individualize their concentration. Often students will pursue more than one concentration; the most popular is finance.

Nursing students all receive a Bachelor of Science in Nursing, qualifying them to directly enter the professional world or continue in a graduate or professional program. Penn's Nursing program is consistently ranked one of the best in the country. Some nurses use their education as a strong premed preparation. With four hospitals in the neighborhood, nursing students are placed in their particular areas of interest for their clinical rotations.

Regardless of which undergraduate school a student chooses to matriculate into, Penn's "One University System" offers the opportunity for students in one school to take classes in any of the other three. In some cases, it is possible to receive a minor or second major in another school. The flexibility of this system allows students to pursue interests outside of their home school, and often eases the concern of students with varied interests. It also enables students, with professor permission, to take graduate-level courses, which can in some cases lead to submatriculation (entry into one of Penn's graduate programs).

Facilities

Students will find that all departments at the university are internationally respected, and that part of the benefit of studying at a large, competitive university is taking advantage of the facilities available. Penn offers sixteen libraries; the two largest and most popular are Van Pelt Library, with its twenty-four-hour study lounge, and the Fisher Fine Arts Library, which is so quiet and beautiful that you'll feel you are disturbing the silence just by shifting your books. In addition to libraries, the university offers a Museum of Archaeology and Anthropology, multiple art galleries, the Institute of Contemporary Art, television and radio stations, performance spaces, an arboretum, a planetarium, and constantly updated computer and science labs. The campus network allows students to have on-line access from everywhere on campus, including dorm rooms, libraries, classrooms, study lounges, the student union, coffee shops, and now with a wireless Ethernet system, certain zones of campus.

Study Abroad

Penn offers opportunities for international programs on six continents and in thirty-nine countries on a semester-long, full-year, or summer basis. In order to make study abroad a viable option for as many students as possible, Penn's Office of International Programs provides much flexibility in arranging for travel. If you are interested in studying somewhere that Penn does not specifically offer a program, you can find a program through another school, get it approved, and arrange to have your credit from participation in that program transferred back to Penn. If a student is receiving financial aid, that package will be applicable to international programs as well. Most students go abroad at some point, usually in their junior year or at least during the summer. There are programs to suit everyone's schedule and goals, and it is a great way to experience some of the things you have studied in the classroom.

I spent the summer between my sophomore and junior years studying in Tokyo. I participated in a language program at a Japanese university, and was able to use those credits toward one of my majors. During that summer, my language skills improved enough that I was able to skip an academic year of language instruction. More importantly, I gained confidence in my language skills and a proper understanding of the practical applications of Japanese. I also had the unique opportunity to travel and explore the culture and sights that I had previously known only in the classroom.

SOCIAL LIFE AND ACTIVITIES

Everyone says that college is a time to learn about oneself. A large part of this self-discovery is facilitated by the people you meet during these four years. Many of my first friends at Penn were people I met during a preorientation program (PennQuest) or were residents of my dorm floor. With time at Penn, one begins to meet more friends through classes, activities, or at parties and other social events. Freshmen will be happy to know that all first-year students are in the same situation as they are and are eager to make new friends.

Residential Life

Housing is arranged according to a system of eleven individual College Houses. It serves as an organizational system as well as a way of breaking students down into smaller groups. Support is found throughout the College House with advising, technical support, and even special residential programs that house people with shared interests. Members of the faculty and staff live within the College Houses as well, operating a host of special events including subsidized trips and activities, study breaks, and educational programs. Within the College Houses, students are divided into groups of about twenty students, each with their own Resident or Graduate Advisor—a current student living in the dorms who provides social support to students and is given a budget to operate small hall functions. The popularity of the College House system and the renovations have made on-campus living more desirable; students frequently retain the room they originally lived in, or stay in their original College House. Many students move off campus as upperclassmen, but can maintain affiliation with the College House they previously lived in.

As a freshman I lived in Penn's oldest dorm, the Quad. I lived in a three-room triple with two other students who were at the time only random names in a packet of housing information. Our freshman hall included students from around the world and of many different backgrounds. It has been interesting to see the different paths that we have explored. There always seems to be some sort of bond between students who have lived together during their first year at Penn.

Orientation

Over the past years, Penn's New Student Orientation program has grown into a week-long event, allowing first-year students to get a feel for the campus before classes actually start. Special events planned just for freshmen include tours of campus and the city, introductions to campus facilities, College House meetings, social events, convocation, and lots of free food. Many upperclassmen return to campus early to attend a few of the events, such as Freshman Performing Arts Night, which offers a sampling of the many performing arts groups on campus. It is a great way to meet new friends, get your questions about campus answered, and begin the year on a positive note.

Penn offers a few preorientation opportunities, including PENNquest (outdoor experience), PENNacle (leadership), and PENNcorp (community service). I participated in PENNquest, where one hundred students are broken into groups of ten for a four-day hike through the Pocono Mountains. Participation in these programs is limited, and there is an application process that is well worth the effort. The programs offer students a chance to meet other freshmen in a unique environment, and secure friendships that can last through the rest of college.

Student Activity Groups

Penn has been dubbed "the social Ivy," a title that it likely deserves, though not for the fraternity-crazy, non-studying image that it seems to imply. Rather, what distinguishes Penn students is their ability to break from studying to explore personal interests, work on extracurriculars, or just catch up with friends. They approach their out-of-class activities with just as much passion as their academic pursuits.

Students at Penn have their choice of hundreds of student activity groups. Though there is certainly not time to get involved in everything, student groups regularly host events for fund-raising, building student interest or awareness, and showing the talents and culture of the students they represent. There is always something to do on campus, and activities of note are major speakers and performers drawn each year through Social Planning and Events Committee (SPEC)-funded events and many special events organized through the Office of Student Life and the Student Activities Committee. Penn students also get involved in community service, much of which is organized through Civic House, and includes tutoring and mentoring programs for West Philadelphia children as well as other issues ranging from community building to social action.

An easy way to make friends with similar interests is to participate in activities. It is okay to test the waters in several different areas. I participated in academic and service groups, planning committees, and varsity athletics. Though I did not stick with all of these activities (and likely if I had, I would not have had time to go to class and graduate), exploring different areas helped to clarify what I did and did not want to do, and also introduced me to other students who became my closest friends.

SPEC

The Social Planning and Events Committee (SPEC) is responsible for the organization of many of Penn's largest events. Connaissance, a SPEC-run committee, funds major speakers in the fall and spring. In recent years a wide range of speakers including Benjamin Netanyahu, Ellen DeGeneres, Gloria Steinem, and shows like "Politically Incorrect" and MTV's "Loveline" appeared. Another group, the Spring Fling Committee organizes a two-day, two-stage concert complete with carnival-like attractions, a craft fair, and a final concert by a major act on Saturday night.

Since most groups at Penn are student run, there are opportunities to gain valuable leadership experience as the head of a student group. There are also chances to get involved in all aspects of student life, including student government, the Nominations and Elections Committee, and the Student Council on Undergraduate Education. Any students representing a common interest can organize and create their own group, and recruitment by various student groups happens throughout the year at orientation events and along Locust Walk.

Athletics

Penn is Division One and in the Ivy League. Three tiers of athletic involvement offer students the choice of varsity, club, or intramural levels. With these choices, students hoping to continue with sports on a level of high participation and competition can join varsity teams, and those looking for a more relaxed involvement can join club teams (which compete with other colleges) or an intramural team. This allows high school athletes to keep up with their sport, but cut down on time commitment, and also gives novices an opportunity to explore new sports, and take their interests to whatever level they desire.

Athletic facilities include three gyms, a tennis pavilion, two pools, squash courts, indoor/outdoor tennis courts, playing fields, an indoor ice rink, rowing tanks, weight rooms, saunas, an all new fitness center, the nation's first two-tier football stadium, and a boathouse on Philadelphia's historic Boathouse Row. Athletic facilities are open for use by students with IDs when not reserved by an athletic team.

Greek Life

About thirty percent of students at Penn are affiliated with the Greek system. Depending on your interests, Greek life includes members of fraternities, sororities, and coed honors and community service-based fraternities. The official rush for Penn's twenty-nine national fraternities and eight national sororities is in the spring, and pledging begins later in the semester. Because many of the rush activities are fun and a good opportunity to meet people, many freshmen get involved in rush even if they are not interested in pledging, and some realize during the process that they would actually like to pledge. One way or the other, Greek life does not dominate campus, and neither does it determine one's friends. Most fraternity and sorority events are open to all students, non-Greeks included. Given that it is such a relaxed system, membership in a Greek organization comes down solely to a matter of personal preference.

The City and Safety

Students at Penn have the benefit of living in one of the country's largest cities. Situated in the middle of the DC-to-Boston megalopolis, the City of Philadelphia offers a full range of amenities, including wonderful bars and restaurants, rich cultural resources, historic landmarks, and an exciting nightlife. Going to school in the nation's fifth-largest city means that there are always many choices for what to do when you are not in class or doing homework. Attractions such as the Philadelphia Museum of Art, the Franklin Institute, and the Mutter Museum are definitely worth exploring. The city attracts many great performers, and has a lively theater and performing arts scene. Every year the Fringe Festival attracts artists and performers to show off their talents in a week of special events. Also of note is First Friday, during which the galleries in Old City stay open late to show off their holdings. There are many great restaurants and bars in the area as well, and Penn runs shuttles down to the festivities to encourage students to explore.

PENN ATHLETICS FACTS

- The Heisman Trophy is named after Penn Coach John Heisman.
- The Penn Relays held on Penn's Franklin Field every April is the world's largest annual track meet.
- The first black American to win an Olympic gold medal (1908) was a Penn grad.
- Penn's football team was the first in the United States to use numbers on its jerseys.

For students concerned with adjusting to urban life, Penn is very proactive. Students are briefed on safety issues when they first come to Penn, and are familiarized with the various levels of security and assistance made available to them. All students are given a photo identification card, which is used to gain access to dormitories, libraries, and other campus buildings. Free walking and driven escorts are available to take students back to their destination. There are a number of proactive measures taken to make sure students feel safe on campus.

FINANCIAL AID

Like all of the schools in the Ivy League, Penn's admissions process is need-blind (for U.S. citizens, permanent residents, Mexicans, and Canadians), meaning that the admissions decision is made without regard to students' ability to pay for their education. There are no athletic or merit-based awards. The financial aid package is entirely need-based, and the university is committed to fulfilling one hundred percent of "demonstrated need." This figure is calculated using several financial forms, and is unique to each student's situation. Almost sixty percent of undergraduate students receive some form of financial aid. Financial assistance packages may include a student loan, a work-study job, and a grant, in addition to funds that might be provided on the federal and state levels. Limited financial aid funds are available to international students from other countries.

PROMINENT GRADS

- Sadie Alexander, First African-American Woman in the United States to earn a Ph.D.
- Harold Prince, Broadway Producer
- Ron Perelman, Financier
- Ed Rendell, Governor of Pennsylvania, Former Mayor of Philadelphia
- Donald Trump, Entrepreneur
- Maury Povich, Talk Show Host
- Andrea Mitchell, News Correspondent
- Harold E. Ford, Jr., U.S. Congressman

GRADUATES

On-campus recruiting starts in the fall of senior year, and many students have accepted job offers by the winter holidays. In recent years, as many as fourteen percent of graduates have gone directly to a graduate program, and statistics show that eighty percent of Penn graduates have received a second degree within ten years of graduation.

After finals and before graduation, senior students have a week of activities known as Senior Week. Most noteworthy is probably the Walnut Walk, a pub-crawl starting in Old City and heading west to Penn's campus, making stops along the way at twenty-one preselected bars. Students take this time to catch up with friends before heading out in the many directions they will take just weeks later.

Graduates of Penn will find that they have received training in more than just their area of study, and many will go on to work in fields very different from their undergraduate studies. If the size of Homecoming and graduation events is any indication of the graduate's appreciation for their alma mater, then applicants should expect great things.

SUMMING UP

The admissions selection process is complex. The best way to know if Penn is right for you is to absorb as much information as possible. Talk to current students, faculty, and alumni, and if possible, make a campus visit, take a tour, and attend an information session. Go to Penn-hosted events in your hometown.

Penn is always changing, but by adding on and improving, not by replacing and forgetting past success. I invite you to explore what Penn has to offer, partially jealous that I won't be able to experience all of the great new things added every year.

❏ *Erik Frey, B.A.*

UNIVERSITY OF RICHMOND

<table>
<tr><td></td><td>**University of Richmond**
Richmond, Virginia 23173</td></tr>
<tr><td></td><td>(804) 289-8640 or (800) 700-1662
Fax: (804) 287-6003</td></tr>
<tr><td></td><td>E-mail: *admissions@richmond.edu*
Web site: *http://www.richmond.edu*</td></tr>
</table>

 Enrollment

Full-time ❏ women: 1,459
             ❏ men: 1,422

Part-time ❏ women: 16
             ❏ men: 23

INTRODUCING THE UNIVERSITY OF RICHMOND

When the characters of the television show, *Dawson's Creek*, began their college search with a campus visit, the producers of the show wanted a location that typified "college." It was no surprise they chose the University of Richmond, a campus that is so picturesque it could pass for a 350-acre movie set. Any camera angle would reveal a place thick with towering Virginia pines and oaks, benches, a huge green lawn where student study, lay out, throw Frisbees, and even attend class al fresco around the centerpiece, ten-acre Westhampton Lake.

—*Rebecca Sadock, Class of 2005, Business Major, Communications Minor*

Founded in 1830, Richmond is the second-oldest private university in Virginia and located only six miles from downtown Richmond. Despite its close proximity to the city, the campus is a world of its own, surrounded by trees and excellent-for-jogging suburban neighborhoods. Richmond began as a Baptist seminary but after about ten years, it added literary studies to the curriculum and began to take the form of a college. Women were first admitted in 1914 and, initially, men and women attended separate colleges under the University of Richmond name: Westhampton College, for women, and Richmond College for men. Today, men and women still have separate student governments, enabling more leadership opportunities, and they maintain their own sets of unique traditions.

In addition to a law school and various masters programs, Richmond has three schools of undergraduate study: the School of Arts and Sciences, the Robins School of Business, and the Jepson School of Leadership Studies. All students, regardless of their field of study or scholar status, are required to take the freshman-year CORE course, a two-semester class aimed at providing a foundation for their education to follow. During CORE, students read challenging texts by authors ranging from Rousseau to Freud to Toni Morrison. Unless they place out, students also must take a required curriculum touching all the major subjects. The required courses aren't restrictive and usually turn Richmond students into jacks of all trades and masters of one or two—their major and minors. Double majors are commonplace at Richmond, as are minors and concentrations. It's not that the course load isn't rigorous—rare is a night when the library isn't crowded— it's just that the students, for the most part, are ambitious.

When students aren't studying or going to class, there are activities, groups and opportunities for every interest. Even after the first week of school, it's easy to find oneself overwhelmed with activities, from the Film and Photography Society to the debate team to virtually every intramural sport. There are six fraternities and eight sororities, a weekly campus newspaper, an on-campus FM radio station, four resident *a cappella* groups, and organizations for almost every religious affiliation, to name only a few. Richmond is also an NCAA Division I, Atlantic 10 Conference school in eighteen varsity sports.

Spider

Richmond is the only college in the United States with a spider as its mascot. And, "spider" quickly becomes part of students' everyday lingo: Spidercard, the convenient debit card for all campus purchases, Spiderbytes (the e-mail bulletin of campus activities), Spider Sports Center (the busy campus recreation and fitness center), Spider athletics (the intercollegiate teams), and, most important, Spider pride, which most students exhibit on a daily basis.

ADMISSIONS REQUIREMENTS

Richmond students do not fit a mold, nor do their academic backgrounds. That said, no formula guarantees admission to the University of Richmond, although, as with most schools of its caliber, a solid transcript, above-average standardized test scores, a record of community involvement, and overall well-roundedness can improve an applicant's chances. Many of its applicants possess such traits in abundance, so Richmond also looks for applicants who display character, eclectic interests, independence, integrity, and diversity, as evidenced by the application essay or recommendations. How have you spent your free time? When have you displayed leadership? What sets you apart from other students of equal academic talent?

For the 2004–2005 school year, Richmond received 6,236 applicants; 2,475 were accepted. Of those accepted, 782 enrolled and sixty percent ranked in the top ten percent of their graduating class. Sixty-four percent of the class of 2008 went to a public high school.

Applicants have the option of taking the SAT or taking the ACT. Last year, most accepted students' SAT scores ranged between 1260 and 1400 (based on 1600; 620–690 Verbal and 630–700 Math) and ACT scores between 27 and 30. The recommended, though not required, high school program goes as follows:

- four years of a foreign language
- four years of English
- four years of mathematics
- four years of laboratory science
- four years of history

Richmond offers student-led tours every day, and prospective students have the option of staying overnight and going to classes, meals, and meetings with current students to get a true feel for campus life.

Early Decision

Applicants who know Richmond is the place for them should consider applying for Early Decision. Two Early Decision plans are available; fall Early Decision applications must be postmarked by November 15, and winter Early Decision applications by January 15. Early Decision applicants not granted admission will either be deferred to Regular admission or denied.

The application statistics of admitted Early and Regular Decision students are similar, so applying Early Decision might be beneficial to those who feel they are on the borderline for admission. For 2004–2005, 389 early decision applications were received, and 178 of those students enrolled.

ACADEMIC LIFE

On any given school night, you can scroll down your buddy list on Instant Messenger, and eight out of ten people's away messages will say something like "library" or "Boatwright" or "music library" or a variety of other affectionate nicknames for one of Richmond's three libraries. There is always a sufficient amount of work to be done, and the libraries—with comfortable chairs, study rooms, flat screen computers, quiet nooks, social areas, and a Starbucks—are the place to do it. All the camaraderie on the first and second floors of the main library, Boatwright, sometimes makes it a fun place to go even when you don't have work . . . at least for a few minutes, until you remember you're in a library.

Five schools comprise the University of Richmond: the School of Arts and Sciences, the Jepson School of Leadership Studies, the Robins School of Business, the School of Law, and the School of Continuing Studies. Richmond also offers a number of graduate programs through its schools of arts and sciences, business, and continuing studies. Among all the schools, there are over 100 majors, minors, and concentrations.

Academics at Richmond are not for slackers. No matter the school or major, students' work loads are, for the most part, consistently rigorous. But, for all the hard work, there is just as much reward and satisfaction. The average class size is sixteen people, and the student-faculty ratio is 10:1. As a result, the professors are very accessible, always willing to answer questions after class, and many times even sharing their home phone numbers. Small class sizes are conducive to dynamic classroom discussion, so if you prefer anonymity, Richmond is not the place.

THE HONOR CODE

"I pledge that I have neither received nor given unauthorized assistance during the completion of this work."
—*University of Richmond Honor Code*

Academic integrity is first and foremost at Richmond, and the implementation of its age-old honor code reflects it. During orientation, students learn the honor code, and they must write it on every assignment, quiz, and test thereafter. The university's forty-member Honor Council ensures that the system is carried out by educating students about the honor code and the consequences of violating it. When students are accused of a violation, they must appear before the Honor Council, where the circumstances of the reported violation are examined and the appropriate discipline decided.

Because of professors' and students' high regard for the honor code, professors are usually lenient with how and where students complete assignments, often allowing them to take tests or quizzes outside or at home.

General Education Program

To further reinforce a solid liberal arts foundation, all students must complete a general education program in the School of Arts and Sciences. This program includes the Core course, expository writing, demonstrated proficiency in a foreign language, plus one course each in math, literary studies, natural science, social analysis, history, and visual or performing arts. Students may place out of some of those requirements with high AP scores, but Core is mandatory.

Jepson School of Leadership Studies

The University of Richmond is home to the first school in the nation devoted entirely to leadership studies. The mission of the Jepson School of Leadership Studies is to develop people who understand the moral responsibility of leadership. Students apply to enter the school, founded in 1992, in their sophomore year, and admission is highly selective. The curriculum is highly diversified and interdisciplinary, though the focus remains ethics, moral reasoning, group interaction, and compatibility, with an experiential service learning component.

After graduation, leadership majors pursue careers in a wide range of fields from healthcare to business to the Peace Corps, and twenty-two percent go on to law school or graduate school.

> *Because of my time at Jepson, I feel amply prepared to go out and change the world. My professors were invaluable in helping me get an internship at the Desmond Tutu Peace Centre in Cape Town, South Africa, last summer.*

—Kate Lowell, Class of 2005, Leadership Studies and Political Science

Examples of courses offered at the Jepson School are Justice and Civil Society, Conflict Resolution, Communicating and Leading, Critical Thinking, Ethics in Leadership, and Ethics of the Novel.

Study Abroad

Almost half of Richmond undergraduates take advantage of one or more of seventy-five study-abroad programs worldwide. Students may opt for a summer, a semester, or an entire year in places ranging from Tibet to Poland. The Office of International Education helps students every step of the way, from finding the best-fitting programs, to making sure students are successfully acclimated, to providing an outlet for them to share their experiences upon returning to Richmond. International Education also offers extensive orientation programs, as well as various activities upon return in order to make the transitions as smooth as possible.

> *Studying abroad in Valencia, Spain, was one of the best things I could have done for myself during college. Richmond was instrumental in helping me choose a program and making my transitions perfect. Also, because Richmond encourages studying abroad so much and so many students take advantage of the opportunity, I had friends all over Europe that I could visit every weekend.*

SOCIAL LIFE AND ACTIVITIES

Having abundant on- and off-campus activities, rare is the time when Richmond students find themselves with nothing to do. There are more than 250 on-campus clubs and organizations to choose from, so students can easily find their time thoroughly occupied by activities ranging from cultural to social to recreational. The only problem, it seems, is deciding in which activities to partake and figuring out how to divide your time among them.

Athletics

Richmond is the only university that hails the Spider as a mascot, and Spider pride runs rampant, especially where athletics are concerned. Richmond is an NCAA Division I and Atlantic 10 Conference member in eighteen varsity sports. One of the most active—and certainly visible—groups on campus, the Richmond Rowdies, comes together for the sole purpose of supporting intercollegiate teams, usually in "rowdy" fashion.

> *When I go to a Richmond basketball game, I feel like I go to a big school, especially when we're playing teams like Arizona or Pittsburgh and the game is being broadcast on ESPN or ESPN2. The players are local celebs, and tons of students and fans from all over the community come to support them for every home game. Richmond basketball—both men's and women's—is one of the greatest things about this school.*

If Division I isn't your desired competition level, there are twenty-four club teams, from soccer to equestrian to Ultimate Frisbee. During 2003–2004, sports club teams collectively raised more than $80,000. In recent years, some club teams traveled as far as Arizona, Michigan, and California to participate in tournaments. In spring 2005, the men and women of the rowing club traveled to London to compete in two regattas and tour England.

FAST FACTS ABOUT STUDENT LIFE

- ○ Around eighty-five percent of undergraduates are from out of state.
- ○ Forty-seven states and more than seventy countries are represented in the student population.
- ○ Fifty-two percent women, 48 percent men.
- ○ Approximately ninety-two percent of students live on-campus all four years of college.

Richmond's athletic facilities include a 9,000-seat basketball arean, football stadium, soccer-track complex, lighted intramural fields, intramural gym, aerobics and weight rooms, indoor swimming pool, tennis, racquetball, and squash courts. The Spider Fitness Center has treadmills, elliptical machines, weights, stair-climbing machines, and various other workout machines. Many students prefer to get their workout via the scenic route—at any time, people walk or run on the path around scenic Westhampton Lake in the center of campus.

The Coordinate System

The University of Richmond is composed of two coordinate colleges: Richmond College, for men, and Westhampton College, for women. Although all degrees say "University of Richmond" and all students eat, attend classes, and participate in clubs and organizations together, men and women each have their own student government, dean's office, residence life staff, and longstanding traditions. Because of the coordinate system, multiple leadership positions are available to students, and the residence life staffs and deans' offices tailor programs to the unique needs of the men and women they serve. Three traditions, each sponsored by one of the coordinate colleges, include

- **Proclamation Night**, when Westhampton first-years sign the honor pledge and write themselves letters about what they hope to achieve during the next four years. At the same time, amid laughter and tears, Westhampton seniors read the letters they wrote to themselves three years earlier.

- First-year men participate in **Investiture**, during which they take a class picture, sign the honor pledge, and hear reflections by selected senior men.

- **Ring Dance** is a celebration sponsored by Westhampton College for its junior women. Participants' families and friends are invited to attend the event held at the sumptuous, five-star Jefferson Hotel. During Ring Dance, fathers escort their daughters down the enormous, 100-foot stairway, while deans announce their majors and minors to the crowd.

Greek Life

Participation in a fraternity or sorority at Richmond is common. More than forty percent of men and fifty percent of women belong to a Greek organization. There are six

WILL

Women Involved in Living and Learning (WILL) is an on-campus organization created to strengthen leadership qualities, foster analytical skills, and increase self-esteem of its undergraduate women members. WILL members take classes culminating in a women, gender, and sexuality studies minor. They also perform one community-service project each semester and attend events and speakers throughout the year. Prominent on campus, WILL members graduate with a heightened sense of women's health issues, current disadvantages facing women and minorities in national and international communities, women and minority history, and topics related to career and family planning. WILL was created in 1980, in response to a study suggesting that the self-confidence of women students plummets during their college years.

fraternities and eight sororities, all nationally affiliated. Richmond is unique in that no housing is designated strictly for specific fraternities or sororities. Fraternities, however, each have a lodge along Fraternity Row, where they host parties about once a weekend.

Before I came to college, I was sure I would never involve myself with a sorority. I had stereotypes of "sorority girls" and I had seen too many Lifetime movies about awful pledging practices. After a few weeks at Richmond, I knew nothing could be further from the truth here. Joining a sorority second semester of my freshman year introduced me to a ton of people I'm confident I wouldn't have otherwise met—or at least gotten so close to—and has also proven itself as an invaluable networking tool, as there are members of my sorority all over the country. Plus, since there isn't Greek housing at Richmond, my joining a sorority hasn't excluded me from anyone, as many of my best friends, roommates, and neighbors are in different sororities or unaffiliated.

Students who think joining a sorority or fraternity is not for them should not worry about feeling excluded. Dozens of other groups, such as club sports, publications, campus radio, student government, and *a cappella* singing, enhance students' social lives. Plus, since students don't rush until second semester, they have time to decide if Greek life is right for them and solidify friendships with people who end up in different fraternities or sororities, or neither. The lack of Greek housing meshes all students together, regardless of their affiliations.

Richmond, Virginia

Students at Richmond enjoy a variety of natural resources and opportunities at their fingertips because of its location in Richmond, Virginia. Though the university is nestled in a safe, suburban, beautiful campus, students need drive only about fifteen minutes to be in the heart of the city. Richmond is home to numerous historic landmarks and neighborhoods, many museums, four professional sports teams, great shopping, and six other colleges and universities. Among students' favorite Richmond offerings:

- **Carytown,** an eclectic, trendy area ten minutes from the university featuring boutiques, specialty stores, and great restaurant options
- **Byrd Theatre,** located in Carytown. Students flock to the Byrd Theatre for its $2 movies. The Byrd, which showed its first film in 1928, can be described only as majestic, with its balconies, high ceiling, and red curtains. Before Saturday night showings, an organist rises out of the orchestra pit and plays traditional favorites.

- **Brown's Island,** a huge outdoor venue in the James River. Musicians of all genres give concerts here during warmer months.
- **Cultural Opportunities,** such as the Richmond Ballet, Richmond Symphony, Virginia Opera, and various traveling Broadway shows, abound in Richmond and play not only at the Modlin Center for the Arts on campus, but also the Landmark Theatre and Carpenter Center downtown. The Virginia Museum of Fine Arts, Virginia Historical Society, and Library of Virginia present standing and traveling exhibits of international acclaim.
- **Byrd and Maymont Parks,** are beautiful, huge parks where students go to relax, play Frisbee, or just stroll. Between the two, stands a Nature Center and small zoo.

Many students land internships in Richmond and, since it is a government center and home to several large corporations, a variety of jobs and internships are always available during the school year and summer. If students can't find what they want in Richmond, D.C., Baltimore, Virginia Beach, and the scenic Blue Ridge Mountains are no more than two hours away.

QUEST

Every two years all Richmond undergraduates have the opportunity to win $25,000 by posing a comprehensive, challenging question. During the Quest competition, students write a question and a 1,500-word essay explaining how that question can be applied to all fields of study. In their rationale, students, who are encouraged to team up with a faculty member, suggest potential courses and speakers. After a question is chosen, for the next two years various courses are modeled after it, events are organized around it, and speakers from all walks of life come to campus to discuss it. The Quest competition was designed to promote deep, interdisciplinary thinking. Since the initial Quest in 1999, the questions have been

1. Is truth in the eye of the beholder?
2. When does discovery inspire change?
3. How do we know which questions to ask?
4. What moves us?

Quest speakers have included Toni Morrison, Carl Bernstein, Lily Tomlin, and numerous other scholars, authors, and artists. Quest classes have included Religion and Presidential Leadership in the Twentieth Century, Cataclysmic Change and the Russian Worldview in Russian Painting, and Victorian Fantasy—New Questions for Nineteenth Century Writers.

FINANCIAL AID

Sixty-eight percent of Richmond students receive some form of financial assistance, whether need-based or merit-based. Richmond prides itself on practicing a need-blind, full-aid admission policy. Qualified students will never be denied admission to Richmond based on ability to pay, and the university promises the financial aid necessary to attend, including grants, loans, and scholarships. Loan burden is capped at $4,000 a year. Richmond is one of fewer than forty schools in the country to meet one hundred percent of undergraduates' demonstrated financial need. Tuition for the 2006–2007 school year comes to $36,550, and with room, board, and fees included, the total cost of attendance is $42,610.

Scholarships and Jobs

Richmond wants the brightest students and doesn't want them to be discouraged from applying because of the sticker price. Hence, there are fifty full tuition merit-based scholarships available to each entering class through the Richmond Scholars Program.

Richmond Scholars Program

One out of every fifteen incoming students at the University of Richmond will receive a full-tuition, merit-scholarship.

Through the generous Richmond Scholars program, the university awards these scholarships to fifty members of every incoming class, each consisting of approximately 750 students. Recipients have demonstrated extraordinary academic achievement, exceptional personal qualities, and potential for ongoing contributions to society.

All domestic and international first-year admission applicants are eligible for consideration.

Richmond Scholars Program Benefits

- Full-tuition scholarship, renewable annually, valued at approximately $140,000 over four years
- Eligibility for a one-time $3,000 grant to support a student-selected activity that enhances the academic experience
- Priority course registration
- Priority housing selection
- Specialty faculty mentors to guide students and help them fulfill their potential
- Complimentary tickets to selected cultural event in the Modlin Center for the Arts

Distinctive Designations Within the Richmond Scholars Program

Some students are selected for the following distinctive scholar designations that exist within this program and may afford additional benefits:

Oldham Scholar

Up to five Richmond Scholars will be designated as Oldham Scholars, and their award will equal the value of a full tuition plus room and board. Over four years, the value of the scholarship for a student designated as an Oldham Scholar will exceed $162,000.

Since 1983, the generosity of alumnus Mr. W. Dortch Oldham and his wife, Sis, has enabled the university to award such scholarships to those incoming students who exemplify the highest scholarship, personal integrity, and potential for leadership.

Science Scholar

Up to five Richmond Scholars demonstrating passion and excellence in scientific discovery in the sciences, mathematics, and computer science are selected for early involvement in undergraduate research.

Oliver Hill Scholar

Up to fifteen Richmond Scholars are invited to participate in this special program that focuses on African Americans, social justice, and challenges that exist in multifaceted global society. Participants receive an additional annual award of $1,000.

Artist Scholar

Up to two Richmond Scholars with extraordinary talent and a clear passion for visual or performing arts are paired with arts faculty mentors to maximize opportunities to develop students' talents.

Richmond Scholar Qualities

Successful candidates demonstrate one or more from the following list of accomplishments and qualities:

- Outstanding and engaged scholarship
- Desire to be at the forefront in the creation and discovery of new knowledge
- Leadership skills
- Desire to be a leader in service to society
- Broad worldview
- Excitement about learning from people who are different from themselves in a diverse community of scholars.
- Recognition of the importance of personal integrity and ethical decision making
- Enthusiastic pursuit of self-improvement
- Desire to make the most of opportunities presented
- Exceptional talent in artistic expression

In addition to the Richmond Scholars programs, Richmond awards numerous other scholarships, for example, to international students, theater and dance students, Virginia

---

residents, and ROTC students, to name only a few. Furthermore, many individual academic departments award need- and merit-based scholarships.

While on campus, students have the option of on-campus jobs. Those not receiving financial aid are still eligible for campus employment and work-study. Jobs range from working in campus catering to the libraries to the front desk at the campus recreational facilities. Students working on campus during the academic year are exempt from Social Security taxes.

GRADUATES

The University of Richmond's Career Development Center (CDC) does everything in its power to ensure postgraduation job satisfaction, as well as resume-building summer employment or research for those who want it. The CDC has a massive database of employers looking for students to fill internships or entry-level positions, from ranch hand in Wyoming to investment banking in New York. Almost forty percent of Richmond graduates pursue graduate school within five years. Academic, prelaw, premed, and preengineering advisors are all specially trained to help students achieve their goals.

> The Career Development Center is one of the University of Richmond's greatest assets. The nucleus of the CDC is its committed, informed, warm, and supportive staff. I cultivated a relationship with the counselors beginning freshman year, and they were instrumental in guiding me through the career development process, introducing me to stimulating internship opportunities, and connecting my interests and major with potential career paths. They instilled in me the ability to recognize and successfully articulate my strengths during the job search and selection process, on a resume or during an interview. The CDC helped me to acquire the knowledge and resources to secure my first-choice job in New York City after graduation.

> —Kaitlin Yapchaian, '04, B.A, Studio Art

The CDC offers walk-in hours every weekday, when current students or young alumni can get resume or cover letter critiques, interview tips, or any kind of career or major advice. The counselors will tell you that over eighty-five percent of jobs are acquired through networking, but they also will be the first to help you establish those networks using a vast online directory of University of Richmond grads in every field all over the world.

"The Real World"

The CDC hosts an annual event where dozens of Richmond graduates, all well-established in their careers, come back to the campus for a weekend to dispense "real world" advice. During The Real World, which markets itself as a networking opportunity, approximately forty graduates from a variety of backgrounds and fields discuss their career paths, how they have gotten where they are, things they wish they had done differently, and anything else students could want to know. Every year, students listen to a keynote speaker and then break out into career-specific groups ranging from entertainment and the arts, to nonprofit organizations, to science-related fields. The Real World always coincides with a Richmond Spider's men's basketball game, so that many students attend the game with the alumni. The Real World often leads to jobs and internships for students, but always results in the advantage of forging a relationship with a knowledgeable expert in a field of your choice.

> *I have a theory that we'll never know if things worked out for the best, so we might as well assume they did. My choice to come to Richmond doesn't force me to make that assumption; it was the perfect place to spend what I consider my most formative four years. I truly believe it couldn't have been better anywhere else. My teachers are my friends and my mentors; my ambitious, eclectic, amazingly intelligent friends are life-long; my communication skills and my confidence in them have increased exponentially; and the knowledge I've acquired here, both in and out of the classroom, has perpetuated a life—my own—of endless curiosity and intellectual pursuit. The classes I've taken and the community service I've done have fostered a new perspective, one of empathy and empowerment. I'm going to miss this place so much—and I might be that random graduate who comes back way too often—but I feel incredibly prepared to go out and find a place for myself in the world.*

Like any place of higher learning, the University of Richmond is not for everyone. For people who embrace opportunities, people who feel satisfied by working hard for a cause, academic or otherwise, and people who want a traditional college experience on a beautiful campus—Richmond is the perfect place.

❏ *Lauren B. Lumsden, B.A.*

	University of Rochester Rochester, NY 14627	Enrollment	
	(585) 275-3221 (888) 822-2256	**Full-time** ❏ women: 2,243 ❏ men: 2,360	
	E-mail: *admit@admissions.rochester.edu* Web site: *http://www.rochester.edu*	**Part-time** ❏ women: 236 ❏ men: 65	

INTRODUCING UNIVERSITY OF ROCHESTER

For students looking for a college combining a tradition of academic excellence and experimental vision with a fresh perspective on training this country's future leaders, the University of Rochester (UR) deserves consideration. It is the smallest research university in the nation. What distinguishes UR from other great private universities is that it puts students in the driver's seat. And for any pothole in college, the university seems to have the patch.

Although UR's main campus (located along the Genesee River and thus known as the River Campus) is a couple of miles away from downtown Rochester, students are engaged with and immersed in the community academically and socially. Recently the school's annual community-service day during first-year orientation was expanded to a two-day event, which included bus tours of the unique neighborhoods, highlighting the great shops and restaurants, and educational workshops, facilitated by community leaders. This outreach has made a difference in the way students perceive their community.

Rochester's transportation system is great. From the U of R you can catch one of several free bus lines that can literally take you any place you would want to go in the city.

—*Ike Howdeshell, '07*

UR's social scene is anything but typical. A Friday night might be filled with an a capella group performance (at last count, there are five), a play at the Todd International Theatre Program, a fraternity party, Southern (yes, Southern) barbecue dinner at Dinosaur Barbeque, or some combination of the above.

Over ninety-eight percent of classes at UR are taught by faculty, not teaching assistants. Faculty members engage students through immersion in small seminar courses, which are common even in the Freshman year. Not only are almost all upper-level courses also small, but most students undertake individualized projects or join research efforts alongside their favorite professor. In part, this close mentorship is why so many UR alumni head to graduate or professional school.

UR provides a red-hot environment for growth and learning, despite a cool climate (with lots of snow in the winter!). For the cold-phobic, the architects of the beautifully planned campus devised a system of tunnels connecting all the main academic buildings on campus. These tunnels keep students warm during the winter months, and the tradition of painting the tunnels with upcoming events keeps students informed as to all that is happening at UR academically and socially. The first spring day—when students come out in droves to bask in the sun while playing Frisbee on the Eastman Quad, picnicking on the Residential Quad, and playing stickball on the Fraternity Quad—makes all the cold worthwhile. In short, UR is a place where students can take control of their education and pursue their dreams.

ADMISSIONS REQUIREMENTS

UR's admissions standards, already very selective, have become even more competitive since the mid-1990s. Still, the process ensures that each applicant is given careful and comprehensive consideration. The admissions office still reviews applications the "old-fashioned" way: one at a time.

Sixty-five percent of incoming students graduated in the top ten percent of their class. UR accepts both SAT and ACT scores. Average SAT scores range from 600 to 720 on the Verbal section and from 620 to 740 on the Math section. Average ACT scores range from 27 to 30. The typical UR student has completed numerous Advanced Placement or International Baccalaureate courses, and has earned an academic unweighted grade point average of 3.75. The admissions committee that reviews each application does not just crunch numbers. They also "value unquantifiable strengths such as initiative, creativity, enthusiasm and leadership." These qualities are best demonstrated through extracurricular and creative activities pursued in depth.

Diversity

Building on the region's legacy of Susan B. Anthony and Frederick Douglass, UR is dedicated to assembling and educating a diverse student body. Fewer than half of Rochester students come from New York. UR's students also hail from over ninety different countries. At least ten percent of the student population consists of students considered to be underrepresented minorities. It primarily creates this diverse community by providing resources to students from different backgrounds. The Office of Minority Student Affairs works with students to make them feel welcome and support them in their academic pursuits. The Early Connections Opportunity Program brings first-year students to school early to acclimate them to the collegiate environment, build community, and develop the requisite skills to be successful at school. The McNair Program encourages low-income, first-generation, and underrepresented minority undergraduates to pursue doctoral degrees. These opportunities, not to mention the dozens of student organizations, create an environment welcoming and challenging to all.

> *The Early Connections Opportunity was a great way . . . to get a close look at what life would be like during a regular semester.*

—*Christabell Catala, '08*

Application Process

UR requires the Common Application, Rochester's Common Application supplement, and any supporting material. The application asks for basic demographic information, a description of achievements and activities, a personal statement, an official school report including transcript, and standardized test scores. All parts of the application are due by January 15.

UR has two Early Decision (ED) options for those set on attending. The first ED plan allows students to apply by November 15 and receive an admissions decision by December. The second ED plan offers applicants another chance to decide that UR is their first-choice: Their applications will then be expedited so that students receive a decision within three weeks of confirmation of the application being complete. Students interested in competing for merit scholarships should note that Part I of the application is due November 15.

Interviews are strongly encouraged and sometimes required when prospective students are visiting campus. Interviews may also be arranged with alumni in different regions or with admissions representatives on off-campus interview days.

ACADEMIC LIFE

At Rochester, students take an entrepreneurial approach to education. Each student seems to be his or her own start-up company, and the school is just a hotbed of academic innovation. To administrators, "knowledge is about self-definition." According to Jody Asbury, Dean of Students, "We urge students to own their education, to learn what they love and give shape to where they live."

Most schools drown their students in at least a year and sometimes two years of a core or distributed curriculum, which restricts their choices in what they study initially. Those schools that often look for uniqueness and self-motivation in their applicants discourage both after the students arrive. The theory for places with a core curriculum are threefold: (1) it will ensure basic competencies to the school's graduates; (2) it will force students to make an informed decision about their course of study; and (3) it will provide the groundwork for future study. The reality is that core curricula are dreaded by many students because course selection becomes more about checking the boxes to meet the requirements than about developing competencies and being well-rounded. Instead of really delving into particular subjects, the core demands a student take introductory courses in many different fields—many of which do not go beyond what would be taught in an AP course. The problem is, of course, that core curricula go against two values many students expect from a liberal education: freedom of learning and depth of study.

UR poses a unique solution to this problem, called the Rochester Curriculum. Instead of starting students with many required introductory-level classes, often in subjects of little interest, UR categorizes the academic disciplines into three major fields: natural sciences, social sciences, and humanities. Before graduating, each student must take three closely related classes within each one of these fields, but the sequence and depth is a matter of individual choice.

From the beginning, each UR student is free to learn what he or she wishes, how he or she wishes. This liberty allows students to assemble modes of analysis from a variety of disciplines. Often students pursue double (or even triple) majors in seemingly incongruent fields because the Rochester Curriculum sparks this curiosity. Ultimately, the impact of the curriculum goes beyond the years spent at UR: the self-determination and originality that UR breeds are traits that are highly regarded by prospective employers who include the university as one of their recruiting grounds.

> ### MUST-TAKE CLASSES (AND WITH THE ROCHESTER CURRICULUM YOU CAN TAKE THEM)
>
> American Sign Language I
> Black Holes, Time Warps and the Large-Scale Structure of the Universe
> Death, Dying, and Beyond
> History of Jazz
> Philosophy, History, and Practice of Non-violence
> Roman Structures: Engineering in the Classical World
> Tap Improvisation and Choreography
> The Ideas of the Greeks
> The New Europe
> Theories of Personality and Psychotherapy

I came to Rochester as a biology student, but took some introductory courses in cognitive science that led me to computer science. I'm now a double degree student, studying both fields.

—*Robert S. Swier*

Still, students must eventually decide on a major course of study. To help them with this process is the extremely accessible Center for Academic Support. And professors' doors are always open to provide academic counsel.

Majors and Certificates

UR is a research institution, with great strengths in science and engineering, but liberal arts, music, and psychology are also popular, and both the political science and economics departments rank in the top fifteen in the country. With over fifty majors to choose from, students master all types of fascinating topics. Students wanting to take an interdisciplinary approach can design their own majors, an opportunity many students pursue.

Additionally, UR offers certificate programs in actuarial studies, Asian studies, biotechnology, international relations, management studies, and Polish and Central European studies. Many students pursue these as great complements to their majors and minors.

Classes and Faculty

"We threw out general education," says Jonathan Burdick, Dean of Admissions. Because of the Rochester Curriculum, the course topics and syllabi seem to be more student-driven. Classes are almost exclusively taught by faculty, and the classes tend to be smaller and discussion-based. On a warm spring day, it is not unusual to see a class gathered in the middle of Eastman Quadrangle—the main academic space—fervently discussing a book they read.

Faculty take their teaching responsibilities seriously, which is unusual at a research university. Ninety-nine percent of Rochester faculty members hold the highest degree in their field. Within the faculty are several Nobel and Pulitzer Prize winners, members of selective academic societies, and authors of widely read publications. Often it is not until after a student is finished with the class that he or she realizes how highly regarded a professor is in the field of study. But for most of the faculty, humility reigns supreme. Open-door policy is not an empty concept. Professors are always welcoming students into their offices and even their homes to provide further instruction, career advice, or personal inspiration.

Other Academic Opportunities

Quest courses allow students to immerse themselves fully in research and projects of great interest. The activities are normally hands-on. They are geared towards first-year students and usually are held with twenty or fewer people.

UR's outstanding Eastern School of Music, School of Medicine and Dentistry, School of Business, and Warner School of Education give undergraduate students access to their special events, courses, and other resources. More excitingly, there are three major and several small guaranteed admission programs that allow applicants to be accepted into the college and given assurance of admission to the respective professional school or master's degree program. This means that at the tender age of eighteen, a student may confidently know where he or she is going to be six or eight years from now. In the case of the Rochester Early Medical Scholars (REMS), a combined B.A./B.S.-M.D. program for exceptional undergraduates, the student would be graduating from medical school and preparing for residency! The Rochester Early Business Scholars program is a six-year B.A./B.S.-M.B.A. program. The Guaranteed Rochester Accelerated Degree in Education (GRADE) is a five-year (4 + 1) B.A./B.S. + M.S. in Education program for students admitted to UR who are interested in becoming educators. It is important to note that admissions to these programs is highly competitive.

UR also encourages students to earn their undergraduate and master's degrees in five years through its original 3-2 programs. The first three years focus on the undergraduate degree, and the last two will fulfill the master's requirements. These 3-2 programs are available in many subject areas, including: business administration, engineering, human development, music education, optics, and public health.

The Take Five Scholars Program is perhaps even more unique. Although most students do not enter into college thinking four years will be insufficient, UR students soon discover that there is so much more to explore. Once one begins work or even graduate

GREAT THINGS TO STUDY WHILE SPENDING A TUITION-FREE FIFTH YEAR AT UR

Take-Five Scholars create their own program. Here's what some past scholars chose:

Gender Differences in Communication

Human and Artificial Intelligence

Contemporary Social Issues: Becoming an Informed Artist

Faith & Power: The Relations between Church and State in Medieval Europe

Grammars of Music and Language: The Translation of Aural and Written Symbols into Meaning

International Relations and Global Perspective

Exploring the Aesthetic Relationships between Buildings and Photographs

China's Ability to Cope with the Influence of Western Culture school, it is far harder, if not impossible, to pursue a side interest. The Take Five Scholars Program makes things easier by providing a tuition-free extra year for students to create their own program and pursue additional study. Since its inception in 1986, 800 students have taken advantage of this unique opportunity.

For those who are in a rush to get to the next thing but want to savor all that UR has to offer, there is the Senior Scholar Program. Seniors, who have completed their requirements save credit hours and major, may pursue a singular project and dedicate all of their time and efforts to its success. The project might be a scientific investigation, a research endeavor, a major publication, or a work of art. Early planning is necessary, but the end result is well worth the hard work during the first three years to be eligible.

Study Abroad

Everything is global these days. UR has been at the forefront of the movement to ensure that every one of its graduates is equipped with a global education. One great way of doing this is by taking advantage of UR's over fifty semester-long and full-year study-abroad programs. For example, they have an Internships in Europe program that allows students to work in places like the House of Commons, the Louvre, and the European Union. Even if you cannot find a UR program that meets your exact wishes, the school is very good at accommodating your preferences, helping you find a program, and ensuring that the credits will transfer. Over seventy percent of the students study abroad and have done so in over seventy countries. Destinations include Australia, Austria, Belgium, China, Costa Rica, Egypt, France, Germany, Ghana, Ireland, Italy, Japan, Kenya, Mexico, New Zealand, Poland, Russia, Spain, Sweden, Taiwan, and the United Kingdom.

SOCIAL LIFE AND ACTIVITIES

Seeing a bored UR student is a rarity. There is too much to do. With a broad swath of 200 active student groups, there seems to be a speaker, debate, dance, or party every night. Students fill their planners with these events, making for a very engaged campus, politically and socially.

But it is sometimes the impromptu events at UR that are the most appreciated: playing Frisbee on Eastman Quad, enjoying a game of stickball in the Fraternity Quad, or taking a cat-nap in Rush Rhees Library. To get a better understanding of what students at UR do when they are not in class, this section will explore where they sleep, what teams they cheer on (or join), how they express their creative side, how students serve their community, how active the Greeks are, and where the students hang off campus.

Renovated Housing

The River Campus provides housing for most of the undergraduates at UR. Eastman School of Music students study and live on a campus in downtown Rochester. The university recently renovated most of its original buildings; all residence halls are now fully wired for voice mail, cable television, and high-speed Internet (T3 lines in every room) access.

New students are expected to live on campus through their sophomore year. The overwhelming majority of students dwell on campus all four years. However, because Rochester is a fun and affordable place to live, UR also arranges nearby housing in the surrounding neighborhoods.

Beyond the convenience of being within walking distance to all classes, study spaces, and university events, living on campus provides a tremendous number of social opportunities. First-year orientation is centered around where you live so that students will have the chance to bond with people on their same hallway and dorm. Every first-year hallway contains upper-class Residential Advisors, D'Lions, and Freshman Fellows, who introduce students to dormitory life, smooth the transition to college, and provide bridges to all that awaits students at UR.

Affinity housing is also available for students with particular lifestyle desires such as quiet-study and coed by random room. For students looking to live with like-minded individuals, UR offers special-interest housing. Examples of these living arrangements include the Music Interest Floor, Drama House, Computer Interest Floor, Health and Home, and the Tiernan Project (community and university service).

Student Groups

Without exception, students participate in and lead a wide array of student groups on campus. There are far too many to list, but, even so, students regularly take the initiative to form new groups to fulfill a perceived need. Groups on campus pursue broad affinity, service, performance, social, political, academic, and social missions on campus. With faculty, administration, alumni, and community support, these groups breathe life into the campus.

Religion

Due to the diverse backgrounds of UR's students and faculty, the school is home to a variety of religious beliefs. Although UR is a secular institution, it provides a number of opportunities to live out one's faith everyday.

The home of religious worship is the uniquely designed Interfaith Chapel on the banks of the Genesee River; the chapel is a place for worship, meditation, and quiet study. As the words above its entrance proclaim, the chapel was built to be a house of prayer for all people. UR contains a number of faith-based communities that offer an opportunity for like-minded students to gather and worship together, such as Hillel, Catholic Newman Community, Buddhist groups, the Muslim Community, the Protestant Community, and the Interfaith Community. UR also has many student-run groups, which lead their fellow students in worship, including the Agape Christian Fellowship, Brothers and Sisters in Christ (B.A.S.I.C.), Campus Crusade for Christ, Inter-Varsity Christian Fellowship, the Hindu Students Association, and the Muslim Students Association.

Religious life on campus is respected by all and often serves as the fulcrum of support and healing for more challenging times.

Sports and Recreation

UR has a tradition of athletic excellence that dates back to its founding in the nine-teenth century. UR incorporates athletics and recreation into its educational mission. Almost all students participate in the university's twenty-two varsity sports, twenty-two club teams, and intramural sports. With sports in the NCAA, UAA (the most geographical-ly diverse Division III conference in the nation), and the Liberty League (formerly the UCAA), students can find athletic competition and pleasure anywhere they go on campus.

In the last four years, eight Rochester teams have competed in the NCAA Division III team championships, highlighted by the men's and women's basketball teams reaching the Division III Final Four in 2002 (men) and 2003 (women). Nine sports have sent individuals to the NCAA Division III Championships. Nineteen sports have been nationally ranked. Additionally, in the past four years, thirteen athletes have earned All-America honors, and eleven have been bestowed Academic All-America honors on the Verizon/CoSIDA Academic All-America team.

Club sports allow athletes to compete against students at other schools in more diverse sports and without the pressure of conference competition.

For those athletes who want to play for the camaraderie or the love of the sport, intramurals provide a great opportunity to get exercise and compete in a more casual environment. With the recent $14.6 million renovation of the Goergen Athletic Center, including a brand new 11,000 square-foot Fitness Center, students have a great place to train and get in shape.

The Arts

The university and its students have long had a love of the performing arts. From student-run performing projects to a cappella groups, a rich and varied artistic tradition means there's always something to do or see.

The university has a number of active theatre groups, and performances are available on campus throughout the year. According to its mission, the International Theatre Program "aims to offer students a comprehensive introduction to the performance aspects and technical demands of theatre by producing four major productions every year." Because there is no stand-alone theatre major (but there is a great theatre concentration in the English department!), students from all different backgrounds and training have the chance to collaborate on these productions.

The world-renowned Eastman School of Music also provides students with voice and music lessons. Moreover, Eastman provides a constant stream of student and community entertainment with its three symphony orchestras, three choral groups, seven jazz ensembles, and an assortment of chamber groups. It also regularly hosts internationally acclaimed musical artists.

A capella groups reign supreme at UR. Currently, five a capella groups offer fantastic shows for students and even do things like provide Valentines Day serenades for someone's sweetheart. Students interested in dance and performance can take advantage of many opportunities at Rochester, in addition to watching dancers and performance groups that visit the university.

UR also serves as a great venue for major performance groups throughout the year. Beyond the university-sponsored events, Rochester sees its share of headlining bands and international tour stops.

Community Service

UR has a proud tradition of serving its surrounding community and instilling in its graduates a call to service that has led alumni to the Peace Corps, Teach for America, and other opportunities.

—Emily Reiss, '08

Most schools have a half-day community service component as part of the mandatory orientation activities. UR's event called Wilson Days is actually a two-day event that engages first-year students in labor, enrichment, engagement, and education. Students walk away from this experience with an appreciation of not only the needs of Rochester but also its assets. This relationship continues throughout the four years with unique programs like Urban Scholars, where students spend the summer working for local governmental agencies and nonprofit organizations and learning about some of the issues surrounding urban decline and revitalization. There is even a nationwide Wilson Day for alumni held every spring.

More than seventy percent of Rochester students continue to volunteer for community service projects sponsored by the university or on their own each semester. A student organization called Community Service Network acts as the clearinghouse for projects, allowing students and student groups to spend their time serving the community, not searching for places to serve. There is also a special-interest housing unit called the Community Living Center, located in an old fraternity house, that allows like-minded individuals to cohabitate.

Fraternities and Sororities

A little less than a quarter of UR undergrads are members of fraternities and sororities. Six of the eleven sororities and ten of the seventeen fraternities enjoy on-campus living space, notably the Fraternity Quad. Because these groups are so close, the administration works carefully with them to ensure they are providing quality academic and social opportunities to members and nonmembers alike.

Although they do not dominate the social life at UR, fraternities and sororities are a great way to develop interpersonally and intrapersonally.

Exploring Rochester, New York

Over one million people live and work in the Rochester metropolitan area. Because of the beauty of its natural landscape, including Lake Ontario and the Finger Lakes region, parks, professional sports teams, planetarium, museums, orchestras, theater companies, and its overall quality of life, Rochester has been ranked among America's most

---

livable cities. Students may not choose to attend UR just to live in Rochester, but students soon discover the gem of the city in which they live and study.

> *There is just so much that the city has to take advantage of. From various specialty restaurants to Blue Cross Arena and its performances, from the Little and Geva Theatres to various nightlife venues, there are countless ways to keep entertained in Rochester.*

> —*Lindsay Dussing, '07*

For many students, Rochester becomes their classroom. Professors regularly take trips to parts of the community for lessons. Other students see Rochester as their playground. For example, Bristol Mountain, a popular ski resort, is only thirty minutes from campus.

> *Every other Saturday, my friends and I catch the 10 A.M. bus to the Public Market. After getting our necessary cups of Saturday morning coffee or steaming cider at Java's, we stroll, watching bundled families in the winter and kids climb giant pumpkins in the fall. We pick up cookies from the Amish stand, lots of fresh fruit and vegetables from local farmers, pasta, a French baguette from the bakery, Brie cheese, and the always the same sweet potato pie for dessert. Back in the dorm, we cook up a delicious dinner and gather around our hodge-podge collection of plates and mugs with the same small group of friends and maybe a guest or two for our ritual meal.*

> —*Lindsey Lewis, '09*

FINANCIAL AID

For the 2006–2007 academic year, total expenses to attend the University of Rochester were $45,823. The Office of Financial Aid works with every admitted student to ensure that the cost of enrollment is not a barrier to attending UR.

> *For a leading university, the U of R works hard to meet students' needs. They worked with me and gave me an offer I couldn't refuse!*

> —*Ike Howdeshell, '07*

- Francis Bellamy, 1876, Author of the Pledge of Allegiance
- Joseph C. Wilson, '31, Founder of Xerox and the man who brought xerography to the world
- D. Carleton Gajdusek, '43, Nobel Prize winner in medicine
- Virginia Dwyer, '43, as AT&T vice president for finance, was highest-ranking woman executive in the country
- Edwin Colodny, '48, Board chairman of COMSAT and former airline executive who transformed Allegheny Airlines into USAir
- D. Allan Bromley, '52, Prominent physicist and chief science advisor to President George H.W. Bush
- Donald Henderson, M.D., '54, Leader of the team that eliminated smallpox worldwide
- Retired Rear Admiral Stuart Platt, '55, in charge of procuring all nuclear-powered submarines and aircraft carriers during the Reagan era; served on the Joint Chiefs of Staff
- George Walker, D.M.A., '56, '57, First living African American composer to win the Pulitzer Prize for music
- Ron Carter, '59, recognized as the greatest jazz bassist today
- Edward Gibson, '59, Astronaut who set an American record for space travel with 84 days in orbit
- Karen Brown, '61, '72 (Ph.D.), Deputy director, National Institute of Standards and Technology
- Barry Meyer, '64, Chairman and chief executive, Warner Brothers

(Continued)

Sixty-eight percent of the student body received need-based aid, and three quarters of students receive aid in total. There are plenty of merit-based scholarships to further reassure prospective students. Even if you do not think you would be eligible for these types of awards, look carefully at the criteria, as UR has many unique scholarships. For example, the Seventh Generation Scholarship provides a $10,000 renewable award for students committed to environmental action and sustainable development, embodying the Hau-de-no-sau-nee values. The PRIS^{2}M Scholarship awards $5,000 per year for four years to outstanding graduates of Rochester high schools who have participated in PRIS2M (Program in Rochester to Interest Students in Science and Math Program). The Youth Orchestra Scholarship is awarded to incoming students who "have demonstrated musical excellence and commitment through participation in a regional youth orchestra and who intend to pursue a significant academic challenge in a discipline other than music."

These are just a small sampling of the many scholarships available. Please keep in mind that there might be earlier deadlines for these scholarships. Also, all applicants desiring merit-based awards should schedule an admission interview.

GRADUATES

Because of this caring and enriching environment, UR produces graduates that go on to do many great things for the school, the community, the country, and the world. The UR Career Center is a tremendous space for students to perfect their resume, sharpen their interviewing skills, network with employers, and find summer and postgraduation jobs. Still, because UR imbues its students with such a fondness for learning, over eighty percent of graduates end up pursuing graduate or professional school.

SUMMING UP

Students at UR are the entrepreneurs of their education. The Rochester Curriculum not only alters the educational formation of every student on campus; it also changes the culture of the campus, with students eager to mold themselves into better people and the world around them a better place. This notion goes right to the heart of the university's motto: *meliora*, meaning "always better," which isn't just a principle to stand on but something with which the university walks every day.

❑ *Matt Wolfe, B.A.*

UNIVERSITY OF SOUTHERN CALIFORNIA

 University of Southern California
Los Angeles, CA 90089

 (213) 740-1111

 Web site: *www.usc.edu*

 Enrollment

Full-time ❏ women: 8,099
           ❏ men: 7,902

Part-time ❏ women: 320
           ❏ men: 408

INTRODUCING USC

Los Angeles is the most vibrant and diverse city in America, bringing together more people from more places than any city in the world. The city is a pulsating nerve center of entertainment, commerce, culture, and ideas. The University of Southern California reads the pulse of its vibrant host city and, in many ways, is a microcosm of the urban giant.

Like Los Angeles, USC offers incredible variation, not only bringing together students of diverse backgrounds, but also nurturing a strong community that encourages innovation and debate. USC offers more majors and minors than any university in the country. Disciplines intersect across campus, giving birth to many interdisciplinary programs. Each contributes to the culture of the school, making USC a melting pot of theories and principles. Coupled with low student-to-faculty ratios, small class sizes, hundreds of student organizations, and cutting-edge research facilities, USC offers the international presence that is expected of a top-tier, private research university.

Los Angeles is perhaps best known as the entertainment capital of the world, and USC contributes to that reputation. USC has a long-running commitment to nurturing growth in culture and the arts. USC offers nationally renowned cinema, theater, and music programs. These schools have trained Academy Award-winning directors, Broadway performers, and award-winning writers. USC has the only college band to have ever recorded a platinum selling album.

While often recognized for its programs in the arts, the arts programs are simply one of many outstanding offerings of the university. USC has a strong scientific research community, one of the top in the country in terms of research dollars awarded each year. Moreover, USC has forged innovative programs, encouraging undergraduate research through faculty-student collaborations. The business programs are equally well known, and USC has developed a national reputation for encouraging entrepreneurship. Likewise, USC has developed programs that combine new technology with new forms of communication, and is a national leader in multimedia and video gaming.

Despite the great academic opportunities offered by the university, USC is not just about classroom life. USC was named *Time Magazine's* "College of the Year" in 2000, because more than half of the student body participate in volunteer programs that help the surrounding Los Angeles community. The city and the school have developed a mutually beneficial give-and-take relationship.

And, of course, let's not forget sports. Like the rest of Los Angeles, known for its many sports teams with strong fan bases, USC has a strong athletic tradition. USC has produced more Olympic athletes than any other university in the country, and USC consistently has nationally ranked sports teams. The cardinal-and-gold-colored blood runs thick in the veins of proud alumni who frequent the campus to cheer on their Trojan athletes.

USC is a university that is innovative and forward-looking, bringing its students the best resources to help them become tomorrow's leaders. Yet, as the university has developed and expanded since its founding in 1880, its foundation has remained untouched. At the core of USC stands a united family—the Trojan Family.

The extended family of USC is a global network made up of thousands of alumni, students, faculty, and staff, as well as the parents of students, children, and grandchildren of alumni, the Board of Trustees, the boards of councilors, donors, athletic fans, and neighborhood partners. Indeed, no university is better known for the vastness of support that its alumni and affiliates provide far beyond the campus gates. But, the uniqueness of the Trojan Family isn't due to its large numbers. Rather, it's the extraordinary closeness and solidarity that is found in this genuinely supportive community. To its members, the term "Trojan Family" is more than a phrase—it represents a promise, a commitment to support that is lifelong and worldwide.

ADMISSIONS REQUIREMENTS

As the Trojan Family has continued to grow and the buzz about USC has spread both nationally and globally, the number of applicants has increased significantly in recent years, making USC one of the "hottest schools in the country" according to *Newsweek Magazine*. In the fall of 2006, the school received 33,979 applications, and was able to admit only 8,634 students, or just about twenty-five percent.

Grades, Test Scores, and Requirements

The median SAT score for the 2006 freshman class was 2054 (1372 on a two-part scale). The average GPA was 3.8 (unweighted). Admission to USC is highly competitive. Successful candidates for admission to USC will have completed a rigorous college preparatory curriculum in high school and will have availed themselves of every academic opportunity open to them.

Application Filing

USC does not use any system of Early Decision, Early Action, or Early Notification in its admissions process. There are three deadlines for filing applications:

- December 10: Deadline for freshmen or transfer students applying for merit scholarship competition of the Baccalaureate/MD program.
- January 10: Final deadline for freshman applications.
- February 1: Final deadline for transfer student applications.

Application forms are available from the USC Admission Office, or prospective students may apply on-line at *www.usc.edu*. The application cost is $65. All freshman applicants are notified by March 31.

Transferring

Another way to get into USC is by transferring from a community college. Many partnership programs are in place between USC and community colleges that help facilitate the transfer process.

ACADEMIC LIFE

At USC, education can be as unique as you are. "What's your major?" is a question of the past. With more majors and minors offered than at any other American university, many USC students do not settle for just one major. In fact, students are encouraged to pursue double-major and -minor opportunities.

"Our ideal is to help students develop the kind of intellectual flexibility needed for life in the twenty-first century that the best thinkers of the European Renaissance displayed." With these words as a backdrop, President Steven B. Sample launched the USC Renaissance Scholars program in the year 2000. The Renaissance Scholars program honors students whose broad interests help them excel academically. Like Leonardo da Vinci, who was equally adept in the arts and the sciences, Renaissance Scholars are students whose majors and minors are from widely separated fields of study. Renaissance Scholars are eligible to compete for the $10,000 Renaissance Scholar Prize that has been specially authorized by the Board of Trustees. Up to ten prizes are awarded every year. (I was awarded a Renaissance Scholar Prize for my major in Business Administration with an emphasis in Information and Operations Management and a minor in Natural Sciences.) Renaissance Scholars have completed hundreds of combinations of majors and minors, ranging from a major in engineering and a minor in cinema to a double major in physics and classics.

Programs of Study

As the Renaissance Scholars program demonstrates, programs of study at USC are both abundant and flexible. With thirty-three college departments in the College of Letters, Arts, and Sciences and seventeen professional schools, USC has interdisciplinary programs galore—and if your dream program is not offered, create it yourself.

- ○ College of Letters, Arts, and Sciences
- ○ Architecture
- ○ Business
- ○ Cinematic Arts
- ○ Communications
- ○ Engineering
- ○ Fine Arts
- ○ Gerontology
- ○ Health Professions
- ○ Music
- ○ Policy, Planning, and Development
- ○ Theatre

At the core of any program of study at USC is the general education program. In addition to major requirements, students must take a class from each of six general education categories and take at least two writing classes (one lower-division and one upper-division). The six general education categories cover broad disciplines such as literature, the arts, science, and social issues. Within each category, students may choose from dozens of classes. The program offers students flexibility on two fronts. By having numerous choices to fulfill each requirement, students can tailor their program to their interests and passions. By reducing the total number of courses in the general education program, students have more elective units available to complete a second major or minor, or just take a fun class.

Elective Classes

When choosing elective classes, Trojan students get to select from some of the best in the country. For example, every semester, Leonard Maltin from "Entertainment Tonight" teaches a weekly cinema class in which he screens a different prerelease motion picture. Following the screening, the class conducts a question-and-answer session with a guest involved in the making of the movie—usually the director, producer, or leading actor.

Every spring, President Steven Sample teams up with Professor Warren Bennis, leadership guru and author of over thirty books, to teach "The Art and Adventure of Leadership." Forty students, hand-selected by Sample and Bennis, study leadership styles of key figures of the modern era, interact with prominent leaders in the classroom, and are challenged to take an introspective look and start developing their leadership styles.

"The Art and Adventure of Leadership" was the highlight of my classroom experience at USC. Class guests included former Massachusetts Governor Michael Dukakis, director Robert Zemeckis, former Los Angeles Mayor Richard Riordan, businessman Eli Broad, and a SWAT team commander. The papers I wrote were read personally by Sample and Bennis and then discussed over small-group luncheons. What other classroom in the country provides students such hands-on access to today's most prominent leaders?

Upper-division Classes

Like general education and elective classes, upper-division classes are also taught by world-renowned faculty. For example, the business school features proven entrepreneurs. And a chief economist for the Securities and Exchange Commission even teaches a class. The engineering school features researchers with many patents on their office walls. The biology department features key contributors to the human genome project. And the music, theatre, cinematic arts, and art schools feature award-winning faculty in their respective fields. Working directly with these distinct leaders provides students access to cutting-edge research in their field of study and connects the classroom community with the outside world.

Collectively, USC's academic programs provide students with the skills, contacts, and knowledge to get their careers off to a running start and help them make significant contributions to their academic, professional, and business communities as they move beyond USC and into the world.

Special Programs

In addition to the broadest selection of academic programs offered by any university, USC also offers several highly selective programs tailored to students with specialized interests. Three of the flagship programs are the Thematic Option program, the Resident Honors Program, and the Baccalaureate/M.D. program.

Thematic Option (TO) has been cited by several college guides as one of the best general education honors programs in the country. Each year, about 200 freshmen participate in the interdisciplinary core curriculum. TO offers small classes with some of the university's best undergraduate teachers and a hand-picked group of writing instructors. The curriculum is organized according to themes rather than by discipline and fulfills all general education requirements.

Resident Honors Program (RHP) allows high-achieving high school seniors to get a head start on their college education. RHP students matriculate into USC a year early and complete their senior year requirements for high school and freshman year simultaneously. Although RHP students attend classes and participate in campus activities like all other students, they are required to stay in the honors dormitory and participate in special group programs to ensure their transition into college is smooth.

The Baccalaureate/M.D. program (BMD) is an eight-year joint undergraduate/medical program designed for students demonstrating a strong interest in pursuing a career as a clinical physician. BMD students are encouraged to pursue "nontraditional premedical" majors and are guaranteed a seat in the Keck School of Medicine of USC upon completion of core classes and passing base grade point average and MCAT requirements. While in the program, BMD students participate in medical research projects and attend programs sponsored by the medical school. By reducing the stress attached to applying to medical school and encouraging students to pursue a broad undergraduate education, BMD students have completed many majors in addition to their premed classes.

As a member of the Baccalaureate/M.D. program, I majored in Business Administration. My classmates' majors included Theater, Classics, History, and Mechanical Engineering. As part of the program, I participated in plastic surgery and stem cell research projects. The program encouraged me to pursue my passions and build a broad foundation coming into medical school. The Keck School of Medicine believes such students have the best potential to be great physicians and develop strong relationships with their patients.

In addition to these flagship programs, other special programs such as undergraduate research grants and study abroad have a wider reach to students. Undergraduate research is encouraged across campus and is a major requirement in some departments. Most students engaging in research join ongoing projects in large laboratories. However, students may design their own research project and apply for a campus grant. Several dozen grants of $2,500 are dedicated for such projects. For students wishing to leave the beautiful weather of Southern California for a semester or two, USC has partnerships with universities around the world. In fact, USC consistently ranks among the top three U.S. universities in international enrollment with more than 5,000 students. While most programs only satisfy elective units, some transfer upper-division credits.

Faculty and Class Size

USC has a small average class size and low faculty-to-student ratio (ten-to-one) that is expected of any top-tier private research university. In fact, while the USC faculty has great academic and intellectual horsepower and field recognition, this is not what distinguishes it from other universities. What distinguishes USC from other top research universities is the faculty's commitment to undergraduate education and the access that is provided to students. Most of the faculty that are in the spotlight for their groundbreaking research and best-selling books also teach undergraduate courses. In addition to normal office hours that professors schedule, several programs subsidize lunches with professors to help students build personal relationships. Meeting professors during "nontraditional" hours such as late-night coffee or weekend activities is not uncommon. In short, USC provides its best academic resources directly to its undergraduate students.

SOCIAL LIFE AND ACTIVITIES

USC's rigorous academic programs are accompanied by equally vigorous social activities. On campus, over six hundred organized clubs support interests ranging from archeology to waterskiing. These clubs compete for students' time with conferences, concerts, and special speakers. An extensive Greek system draws participation from approximately seventeen percent of students. Across campus, hundreds of volunteer opportunities await Trojan students in the heart of Los Angeles. Slightly further away, students can choose from basking on Southern California's sunny beaches, partying in the Hollywood nightlife, or snowboarding on local slopes. And in addition to all of these activities, school spirit runs high as the Trojan faithful swarm in masses to cheer on USC's championship sports programs.

Campus Life

USC has on-campus dormitories and off-campus apartments that house over 6,200 students. In addition to these, thousands of students live in apartments and houses in the streets surrounding the campus. During the day, hundreds of students ride their bicycles around campus and at night the occasional house party can always be found.

Several blocks away from campus are dozens of large Victorian-style houses that have been converted into student housing. My sophomore and junior years, nine of my friends and I teamed up to rent a ten-bedroom house.

Campus is always buzzing with activities. Two activities that attract the most attention are the President's Distinguished Lecture series and student-sponsored Program Board concerts. These bring today's most prominent leaders and most popular bands directly to campus. Hence the mantra, *the world comes to USC*.

During my four years, campus speakers included George H.W. Bush, Colin Powell, Henry Kissinger, Madeline Albright, Margaret Thatcher, and Rosa Parks, and campus concerts included Blink 182, Nelly, Naughty By Nature, Wyclef Jean, and Smash Mouth.

Athletics

The Trojan is one of the most recognized mascots in collegiate athletics. This recognition is supported by athletic excellence—Trojans have won 106 team national championships, three hundred and forty-seven individual NCAA titles, and more Olympic medals than students at any other American university.

Football is perhaps USC's most decorated program: eleven national championships; fifteen unbeaten seasons; seven Heisman Trophy winners (most recently Reggie Bush in 2005); and representation in all but two Super Bowls. One USC football star even won an Oscar for Best Actor! In 1925–26, Marion Morrison played tackle at USC. He later graduated, changed his name to John Wayne, and won the Best Actor award for *True Grit*.

In baseball, USC has won twelve national championships (no other school has more than five), and produced more than ninety major-leaguers, including home-run specialist Mark McGwire and strikeout ace Randy Johnson.

The women's basketball team has produced many stars including Cheryl Miller, Cynthia Cooper, Tina Thompson, and Lisa Leslie, the first woman to slam-dunk in a professional basketball game.

These championship teams are supported by perhaps the most recognized collegiate band in the country. The Trojan Marching Band has performed nationally and is the only collegiate marching band to have corecorded a platinum album, "Tusk" with Fleetwood Mac.

These achievements help explain why the cardinal-and-gold-colored blood runs thick in the veins of proud students and alumni who fill up stadiums and gymnasiums to cheer on their Trojan athletes. On Saturday afternoons in the fall, five generations of Trojans can be found tailgaiting on campus before a football game.

For those wishing to compete on the field, varsity athletics is not always an achievable goal. Two alternatives, intramural and club intercollegiate sports, provide opportunities to play competitive sports. Club sports offer a great opportunity to play intercollegiate sports without the demand of varsity schedules. USC has forty-eight official club teams including crew, rugby, softball, soccer, hockey, lacrosse, equestrian, and polo. But if your favorite sport is not available, form a new team just like we did!

> *My dream of playing varsity volleyball faded when I developed a chronic knee injury in high school. Unwilling to completely abandon the idea of playing competitive volleyball at the collegiate level, I teamed up with seven other freshmen to form the USC men's club volleyball team. That year, we scheduled only a few games and had a mediocre record, but we made progress with every season. By my senior year, we had over twenty games scheduled, were sponsored by Nike, traveled crosscountry to nationals, and were ranked in the Top 25 by the governing body of club volleyball.*

Community Service

More than half of USC students volunteer in community service projects each year. This dedication to the betterment of its surrounding communities earned USC College of the Year honors from *Time Magazine* in 2000. One of the most common volunteer programs is the Joint Educational Program (JEP). Students participating in JEP teach in local schools once a week, often teaching simplified versions of the material learned in their college classes. Other volunteer opportunities include working in food banks and homeless shelters and the Alternative Spring Break program, in which students travel during spring break to low-income neighborhoods and build homes for the community.

Los Angeles Life

USC's backdrop is Los Angeles, perhaps the world's most diversified and exciting city. The opportunities to have fun in the city are endless; the Hollywood nightlife, Santa Monica and Venice beaches, Big Bear and Snow Summit ski slopes, museums, concerts, professional sport teams, and shopping just to name a few. So pick up a map or a travel guide and start exploring!

FINANCIAL AID

With the cost of tuition, room, and board rising, it is not a surprise that more than sixty percent of USC students receive some form of financial aid. According to the Office of Admission and Financial Aid, all students applying for aid at USC are required to fill out both the Free Application for Federal Student Aid (FAFSA) and the CSS Profile to establish eligibility for need-based federal, state, and USC grants as well as federal loans and work-study. USC operates one of the largest financial aid programs in the country.

USC has a long tradition of meeting one hundred percent of the USC-determined financial need for those undergraduate students who satisfy all eligibility requirements and deadlines. Entering students are admitted to the University based on academic achievement, test scores, leadership, and community involvement. Financial need is not a factor in the admission decision for freshmen.

For those students who apply for financial aid, need is measured based on the income and assets information of families collected through the federal FAFSA, the CSS profile, and other required forms. Approximately sixty percent of the freshmen class receives aid based on need. In 2005–2006, the average freshman need-based financial aid award was $29,256. Such awards are made up of grants, work, and student loans.

I held three part-time jobs during my four years at USC: sports clinician with "Kids In Sports," laboratory instructor for Statistics, and grader for Information Technology classes. These jobs helped me earn several thousand dollars a year for my school costs, enabled me to apply skills learned in the classroom, and provided a great break from studying. While working these jobs, I averaged eighteen units a semester, played a club sport, and maintained a healthy social life.

Students are encouraged to apply for merit-based awards. The most notable are the Trustee (full-tuition), Presidential (half-tuition), and Dean's (quarter-tuition) scholarships. More than five hundred of these scholarships are awarded annually, providing one of the largest merit-based scholarship programs in the country. In addition to these programs, USC alumni groups and other organizations provide scholarships for our students.

Part-time jobs are also a good way to manage school costs. Working too many hours is discouraged as it distracts from academic focus, but most students can fulfill their work-study requirements with ten to fifteen hours of work per week.

GRADUATES

Many extraordinarily bright people have attended USC. The school has had more than its fair share of successful entrepreneurs, award-winning artists and performers, politicians, and athletes. Simply providing a long list of USC's all-time stars would be interesting, but probably would not tell much about how the average graduate fares.

USC students pursuing postgraduate education have high acceptance rates into medical, law, and other graduate programs. Those entering directly into the business world are highly sought out by both local and global businesses. USC's career advisement centers orchestrate career and job fairs for the more than 600 companies that recruit on campus. In fact, many Trojan students receive job offers before they graduate from USC. By the end of the fall semester my senior year, I had more formal job offers than I could count on one hand.

In fact, USC graduates are often better candidates than their counterparts at other top schools because of their internship experience. A benefit of attending school in a large urban setting is that many internship opportunities are available with local companies. These internships are either paid or taken for class credit and often lead to full-time job offers.

Regardless of the path that USC graduates choose to take, the Trojan Family is always there to support them. From mentorship and coaching to interviews and job offers, the Trojan Family is an extraordinarily strong network that is genuinely supportive.

PROMINENT GRADS

- Herb Alpert, Musician, Cofounder of A&M Records
- Neil Armstrong, Astronaut (First Man on the Moon)
- Art Buchwald, Pulitzer Prize-winning Columnist, Author
- LeVar Burton, Actor
- Sam Donaldson, Television News Anchor
- Frank Gehry, Architect
- Pat Haden, NFL Quarterback, Rhodes Scholar, TV commentator
- Ron Howard, Film Director
- Robinson Jeffers, Poet
- Swoozie Kurtz, Actress
- Marilyn Horne, Opera Singer
- George Lucas, Filmmaker
- Mark McGwire, Baseball Legend
- John Ritter, Actor
- Norman Schwarzkopf, General (Persian Gulf)
- Michael Tilson Thomas, World-class Conductor, Music Director of San Francisco Symphony
- John Wayne, Actor
- David L. Wolper, Film, Television Producer

Perhaps it is a cliché, but the four years that constitute an undergraduate education are often the most transformative in a person's life. College is time for learning, growing, changing, and reaching.

When I went to college, I was sure I wanted to be a doctor. Once there, I found USC's premedical training programs to be superb, and my science classes taught me much of what I would need to know in order to pursue my goal. Yet, the classes were just the beginning. Through a hospital and clinical internship program, I got to experience what it would be like to be a doctor, spending time in the hospital, working with patients, and observing surgeries. Then, through another program, I had the opportunity to do original research in a world-class biomedical research lab. While I very much enjoyed the experiences in these programs, ironically it was precisely these programs that helped me to realize that I did not want to be a doctor. Since I was a child I had imagined myself in medicine, however, when I experienced it up close, I realized it was not for me. Yet, I was only able to learn this about myself, by having such rich and complete experiences in medicine, the kinds of experiences that few places offer undergraduates. Most students have to wait until medical school to find out if they really will enjoy medicine or not.

Also, at USC, I learned that I could make a difference. USC's emphasis on community service motivated me to volunteer to organize youth sport's leagues in disadvantaged neighborhoods. It was amazing to watch. First, there were a few kids who turned up, then more came. Finally, parents and neighbors came to cheer on the teams. It was wonderful to see people coming together, supporting the kids in their communities, and working to build something special.

The change in my perspective largely came from exposure to the abundance of other opportunities available at USC. Things suddenly became interesting to me that I could never have imagined as a high school senior, simply because I did not know that such opportunities were available and viable. Classes in leadership and entrepreneurship opened a whole new perspective of the world to me. Meeting and actually talking to such leaders as former Massachesetts governor Michael Dukakis, former Los Angeles mayor Richard Riordan, businessman Eli Broad, and director Robert Zemeckis helped me gain a perspective on how I myself thought about leadership. Working with professors in business classes who were not simply theorists, but practitioners, helped bring the business world alive.

When I think about the transformations I went through at USC, those transformations were not just intellectual, but personal and social as well. When I think of the close friendships I developed at USC, I marvel at their diversity. My close friends included a video-game journalist who was syndicated in many languages, an all-American volleyball player, a keyboard player in the jazz band, a first-generation Indian immigrant, friends who like me had grown up in several different countries, an orthodox aspiring rabbi, and a cinema student who had traveled the world. Our backgrounds were incredibly diverse, as were our interests. USC fostered an environment where we could learn from each other and enjoy each other, where we came to see our very diversity as a gift in itself.

Each student's journey through USC is different. Some students come to USC and find that the goals that they thought they wanted to pursue in high school are the goals they do pursue, with USC providing a rich and complex background for them to do it. Others, like me, come to USC to discover that the opportunities USC offers change our goals, as we grow and change in response to the abundance of pursuits available, whether intellectual, social, or community. USC offers many paths, and all of them provide an abundance of opportunities.

USC gives its students the world. The university offers a broad selection of highly regarded academic programs taught by world-renowned faculty dedicated to undergraduate education. The student body is one of the most active in the country, with thriving on-campus organizations, a strong involvement in community service, and a broad array of social events. The sports programs are second to none—all in the most vibrant city in the world. Most important, once you enter USC you become part of the USC family, a network of friends and support that extend across the world, shaping you and supporting you not only in your college years, but for the rest of your life. The Trojan Family extends its arms to you. Fight On!

❏ *Achi Yaffe, B.S.*

UNIVERSITY OF VIRGINIA

Photo by Dan Grogan

 University of Virginia
Charlottesville, VA 22906

 (434) 982-3200
Fax: (434) 924-3587

 E-mail: *undergrad_admission@virginia.edu*
Web site: *http://www.virginia.edu*

 **Enrollment**

Full-time ❏ women: 7,324
          ❏ men: 5,992

Part-time ❏ women: 25
          ❏ men: 29

INTRODUCING UVA

In the fall, Thomas Jefferson's village stretches out before you. The tops of the maple and ash trees lining the evergreen lawn burn with the reds, oranges, and yellows of the East Coast fall. The graceful lines of their trunks are echoed in the rows of white colonnades that frame the lawn and announce the historic pavilions and rooms, still living quarters for popular faculty and honored students. Everywhere, the vast expanse of grass is dotted with picnickers, students studying, mini football games, and picture-snapping tourists. Yet your gaze is drawn past all of this to the north end of the lawn, to the building commanding the entire scene, the world-famous Rotunda. Based on the Roman Pantheon, the sparkling marble of its flowing staircase and regal columns and the elegant arc of its majestic dome ensure that the Rotunda is not only a historical landmark, but one of the most beautiful structures ever to grace a college campus.

> *As I walk to my dreaded test, I smile as I remember that by the time I get out of class, the sun will have set and warm yellow light will be glowing within the many windows surrounding the lawn. I know that on my walk home, I'll feel more like a lucky tourist after closing time than an undergraduate headed to the dining hall.*

Amazing aesthetics, however, is not the reason why UVa has long been known as the "Public Ivy," and why it attracts so many exceptional students and professors. Founded by Thomas Jefferson in 1819, UVa remains one of the highest ranked state-funded institutions in the nation. Offering undergraduate programs in architecture, arts and sciences, commerce, education, engineering and applied science, and nursing, the university continues to operate on its founder's belief in the importance of a solid liberal arts education. Of its 20,368 enrolled students, two-thirds are undergraduates, and while offering the opportunities and diversity of a medium-size school, UVa still has a fairly concentrated main campus area, creating a smaller community feel. In other words, it will be virtually impossible to walk to class without recognizing at least a few faces. The central campus area has 1,160 acres and fifteen libraries. (The overall size is 3,340 acres, with 529 buildings.) Many students and professors also take advantage of the extraordinary new Albert and Shirley Small Special Collections Library, which houses numerous rare historical books and items and also boasts one of the most extensive collections of Thomas Jefferson's effects and documents in the world. Although steeped in history and tradition, UVa remains on the cutting edge of technology, offering computerized library services, Internet access, and a variety of resources, including mainframes, minicomputers, PCs, and a network of printers, which are available to students at the many computer labs around grounds. Courses that use e-mail discussion groups or Internet newsgroup subscriptions to enhance class communication are quite common. Special learning facilities at UVa include a learning resource center, an art gallery, radio and TV stations, and an art museum.

Attending UVa is more than just going through the motions of four years of tests, papers, and parties. It is an experience that will completely consume you. You will be a first-year instead of a freshman, you will live on-grounds instead of on campus, you will be able to write the honor pledge in your sleep, you will learn "The Good Old Song," and you will come to recognize Thomas Jefferson as some sort of deity. At the end of it all, you will be welcomed into one of the most close-knit, active, and supportive alumni networks in the country. But most important, you will have interacted with top-notch professors and students, will have been a part of Jefferson's still thriving vision of public education, and you will have done it all without you or your parents having to face the increasingly terrifying price tag of a private institution.

ADMISSIONS REQUIREMENTS

You've got the grades and the extracurricular activities. You've taken the toughest courses your high school offers, squared away your recommendations, and conquered the SAT. But in front of you lies one of the most comprehensive college applications in the country. There are several short essays as well as one long, open-ended, and intimidating question. Since you've set your heart on UVa, you've done some research and discovered that sweating over these questions is indeed important. The Admissions Committee will be examining each of your responses in detail, giving your whole application the kind of attention it would typically only receive at a small, private school.

Each year, the qualifications of students applying to UVa are more impressive. SAT I scores for a recent freshman class were Verbal—654, Math—671. The average ACT score was 28.

All applicants must take the SAT or the ACT, as well as two SAT Subject Tests of their choice. Although the GED is accepted, most successful candidates have graduated from accredited high schools and have completed sixteen academic courses including four courses of English, four of mathematics beginning with Algebra I, two of physics, biology, or chemistry (three if they are applying to engineering), and two years of a foreign language. AP credits are accepted. Recently about one out of every three applicants was accepted to UVa. You will generally have a slightly better chance if you are from Virginia, or if you fall into the legacy category by being the child of alumni. In any case, if you are seriously considering UVa, then you are probably an excellent student with impressive extracurricular activities, outstanding recommendations, and an eye-catching application essay.

For more than a year, I have worked one on one with a professor who was an expert in my area of interest. I exhausted every resource in the libraries and university archives. I read, researched, wrote, edited, and rewrote, and though I missed some parties and lost some sleep, I gained something else—the realization that UVa honors thesis is an experience I may never want to relive, but it's also one of which I will always be proud.

The distinguished majors program is just one example of the outstanding academic opportunities available at UVa. You can take part in internships, study abroad and accelerated degree programs, B.A.-B.S. degrees in chemistry and physics, dual majors in most arts and sciences programs, student-designed majors and an interdisciplinary major, as well as non-degree study and pass/fail options. A first-year on-grounds honors program and two national honor societies, including Phi Beta Kappa, are available, as are the departmental honors programs. If you take the time to explore the options and pursue your interests, the university is a once-in-a-lifetime shot at an amazing collection of knowledge, talent, and possibility. Ninety percent of the faculty hold Ph.D.s or terminal degrees and many are the recipients of such honors as the Pulitzer Prize, the National Book Award, the Humboldt Award, and Fulbright Fellowships. Graduate students do teach thirty-two percent of the introductory courses, with an average size of fifty students for an entry-level lecture and sixty-two for an introductory lab. Yet the student–faculty ratio remains fifteen to one, and the College of Arts and Sciences specializes in small, discussion-oriented seminars led by full professors. These courses often involve a significant workload, but they also usually cover the professor's favorite subject, from such topics as Native American poetry to cult studies or Civil War culture, and can be extremely informative, interesting, and entertaining.

Course Requirements

Depending on your major, your flexibility to choose electives and select courses will vary. For example, an English major will always have more decisions to make during registration than a premed biochemistry major. However, because UVa focuses on instilling a broad liberal arts background in all of its students, the distribution requirements insure that everyone gets a chance to sample the wide variety of course material offered. All undergraduates must complete twelve hours of mathematics and science, six hours each of humanities, composition, and social sciences, fourteen credits of foreign languages, three hours of historical studies, and three hours of non-Western perspectives. In total, by graduation, students must complete 120 credit hours, including 18 to 42 hours in their major, with a minimum GPA of 2.0.

Majors

English, history, and biology are the strongest majors academically, while commerce, biology, and psychology have the largest enrollments. UVa confers B.A., B.S., B.A.R.H., B.I.S., B.S.C., B.S.N., and B.U.E.P. degrees in addition to master's and doctoral degrees.

Echols Scholars Program

An example of academic opportunity at UVa, the Echols program offers talented students the means to make the most of their scholastic experience. Founded in 1960 by university faculty, the program continues to operate under the guidance of tenured or tenure-track professors who act as special advisors and mentors to the scholars. As an Echols scholar, your only requirement at UVa is to graduate with 120 approved credit hours. A scholar is free from the distribution requirements and even from declaring a major at all. Many scholars use this freedom to focus on "concentrations" in several of their areas of interest, to double major, or to truly invest themselves in a distinguished majors program. Echols scholars also enjoy priority in choosing courses from ISIS, UVa's computerized registration process, and a scholar will usually never have trouble adding into a restricted or full class. The Echols program also encourages richness in more than just the educational areas of college life. First-year scholars live together in adjacent dormitories and special group activities, both academic and social, are offered for scholars of all years. Participation in the Echols Scholars Program is usually based on an invitation process. Every UVa applicant is considered, and approximately ten percent of each entering class is chosen.

Honor Code

> *On my honor as a student, I have neither given nor received aid on this exam.*

You will sign and date this statement hundreds of times if you attend UVa, but what exactly does it mean, and why is it so important? Established in 1842 in order to ease tensions between faculty and students, the Honor System was soon adopted and maintained by the students. Although it has changed to reflect the ideals of the ever-shifting student body, the system remains an integral part of the UVa mind-set. The simple principles of honor establish a network of trust rarely found in a college setting, including unproctored tests, take-home exams, and even check-writing privileges throughout the local community. However, violating such significant trust also means significant consequences. If a student commits a willful, serious act of lying, cheating, or stealing, and is found guilty by a jury of peers, the only possible sanction is a permanent dismissal from the university. Since the system is entirely student-run, you may participate in many different facets, perhaps as a randomly selected juror, an honor committee member, or an honor advisor, counsel, or educator. Regardless of whether you seek it out, rest assured that the Honor System, its benefits and responsibilities, will be an important part of your daily student life.

Pressure and Competition

In general, the students at UVa were serious about academics when they were in high school and by the time they reach Charlottesville, they're even more determined to make the most of their college experience. At the same time though, there is rarely an overwhelming sense of academic pressure and competition. UVa students can usually excel in the classroom without losing their perspective on the larger picture. As one wide-eyed first-year student found out, a sense of humor is often involved in keeping stress under control.

It was 2:00 A.M. in the middle of finals week. I had been buried in my books since early that morning. Despite all my preparation, I was debating not even showing up for my test the next day, I was so sure I was going to fail. Just as I was about to close my book and give up completely, a group of students who had been studying together for hours right next to me suddenly jumped up on top of their table and began an impromptu striptease in the middle of Clemons Library. Pretty soon they had the entire room either participating or cheering them on. When it was over, everyone settled right back down and continued studying. It reminded me that life was not solely about finals. I suddenly realized that I would survive the week. After that, I didn't even mind reopening my books.

SOCIAL LIFE AND ACTIVITIES

At UVa football games, fans of all ages, sporting Cavalier paraphernalia, throng together at the back of the vehicles, imbibing homemade fried chicken, sandwiches, barbecue, beer, and all sorts of other goodies they don't serve at the dining halls. Luckily, my roommate was a legacy student with an entire family of enthusiastic, generous alumni, and I would find myself munching and mingling with the entire clan. A steady stream of students, many showing traditional spirit with their khakis and skirts, others waving banners and various body parts smeared with orange and blue paint, moves through the gates to descend on the bleachers.

Student Body

With their virtually universal appeal, football games are an example of a UVa social event that draws together all different sections of the student body and the local community, both of which have interesting dynamics. Each year, UVa seems to welcome a more diverse entering class. Of the more than 13,000 present undergraduate students, sixty-eight percent are from Virginia, with the rest coming from all fifty states and Washington D.C. and 105 foreign countries, including Canada. Sixty-four percent of the students are white, eight percent are African American, and eleven percent Asian American. Forty-seven percent are Protestant, twenty-three percent are Catholic, and twenty percent claim no religious affiliation.

The Town

Charlottesville itself offers a unique mix of long-time residents and ever-present tourists. Although the city and surrounding Albemarle County have a population of 117,000 people, Charlottesville maintains a small, friendly town feeling. At UVa, you are nestled just east of the Blue Ridge Mountains, only minutes from the homes of Thomas Jefferson, James Madison, and James Monroe, as well as the stunning sights of Shenandoah National Park and Skyline Drive. In short, there's never a problem finding activities when the relatives come to visit. As a student, you'll probably spend a significant amount of social time on "the corner," a group of shops, bookstores, restaurants, and bars within walking distance of grounds, or on the historic downtown pedestrian mall, which has movie theaters, local boutiques, plenty of coffee houses, and even a new ice skating rink.

Clubs and Organizations

While major school activities such as football games, the famous annual Virginia Film Festival, and the traditional Foxfield Races bring everyone together, most students find an outlet for their social lives through one or more of the numerous activities offered on grounds. With more than 300 clubs and organizations to choose from, UVa students tend to be as active outside as they are inside the classroom. One of the more popular social opportunities is the Greek system. An example of deeply rooted tradition at the university, there are over sixty social and service fraternities and sororities in which twenty-eight percent of men and thirty percent of women are involved. Many more make treks to Rugby Road (the site of many of the fraternity and sorority houses) on Thursday, Friday, and Saturday nights, where there is never a shortage of parties.

For those who tire of the Greek scene, there is no shortage of alternative extracurricular pursuits. Aside from academic societies and professional clubs (including the oldest debating society for undergraduates in the nation) there are groups related to art, band, cheerleading, chess, choir, chorale, chorus, computers, dance, drama, culture, film, gay interests, honors, international concerns, photography, and politics. There are religious associations and special interest groups, including UVA-NOW and ROTC. UVa also has a daily newspaper, a weekly news journal, and plenty of student-run special-interest magazines, as well as three radio stations that broadcast on grounds. Another immensely popular organization is Madison House, through which students participate in a variety of community services.

Sports

Finally, activities that require more coordination, such as intramural sports, are also a favorite way to socialize. More than eighty-five percent of students participate in the thirty different sports available. For the more serious and talented athletes, UVa has twelve intercollegiate sports for men and thirteen for women. The university is also a Division I member of the NCAA and competes in the Atlantic Coast Conference. From the recently expanded Scott Stadium and a 15,000 seat arena to be underway in 2006 to four recreation centers (including an aquatic and fitness facility), UVa offers students every opportunity to enhance their bodies as well as their minds.

Basically, on those rare occasions when you don't actually have to be studying something (and those more frequent times when you choose not to study something), you'll find plenty of other agendas you want to pursue. The key is to choose which activities are most important to you and to make sure you allot some of your precious nonacademic time to truly enjoying them.

FINANCIAL AID

Approximately forty-four percent of all undergraduates receive some form of financial aid, including Parents PLUS loans. Aside from Athletic Grants-in-Aid, non-need-based loan programs, and special scholarships, all undergraduate financial aid is based on financial need. Four percent of undergraduates are involved in part-time work-study employment and the average earnings from college work for the school year are $2,277. To qualify for financial aid, entering students must complete and submit a Free Application for Federal Student Aid (FAFSA) and a Financial Aid Statement (FAS) by March 1. A new initiative, "Access UVa" offers loan-free packages for low-income students, caps on need-based loans for all other students, and a commitment to meet 100 percent of need for every student.

GRADUATES

Under a massive oak behind the Rotunda, I, along with the close friends I have made over the last four years, lean together, a blur of caps, gowns, and tassels. The camera snaps one last time before I take my first steps in the procession that marks the end of our undergraduate education. As the May morning stretches lazily towards a steamy afternoon, I descend the steps of the Rotunda and gaze out over the lawn, now overflowing with a colorful mass of proud parents, camera-wielding grandparents, and wide-eyed siblings. Later, at my major ceremony, I hold out my hand and receive the long roll of paper that justifies and attests to all of the cramming, sleepless nights, three-hour finals, and fifteen-page papers of the last few years. Stepping off the stage, no longer a student, I realize that the diploma I clutch is not only a consummation of the past, but what will now also be a powerful key to my future.

In a typical year, UVa awards over 3,000 bachelor's degrees. Among those graduates, the most popular majors are commerce, psychology, economics, history, and foreign affairs. More than 500 companies recruited on grounds last year.

SUMMING UP

So ask yourself, why would you want to attend UVa? Because of its high rankings, its rigorous standards, and its feasible tuition? Obviously. Because you would have the chance to take a poetry seminar with former U.S. poet laureate Rita Dove, or a class on race relations from civil rights activist Julian Bond, or a political science lecture with renowned political analyst Larry Sabato? Of course. Because of the academic opportunities, including honors programs, student-run newspapers, magazines, and radio stations? Absolutely. Or even because of its outstanding Office of Career Planning and Placement, which offers internships, externships, résumé and job search guidance, and even arranges interviews with major companies on grounds? Positively. Maybe because of the richness of UVa's history and tradition, from its creation by one of the most important men in America's past to its unique continuation of distinguished customs such as the student-run honor system or the benevolent and mysterious secret societies? Definitely. Is it because the school is located in the heart of a charming city from which you can drive for ten minutes and be in some of the most beautiful, rural scenery in the country? Certainly. Aside from all of this, you realize that you want to attend UVa because of all the little things, from painting Beta bridge, or attending the Restoration Ball, to working for Madison House, or living in La Maison Française, which make any student who attends this university a member of a community and a part of an experience that stretches far beyond a four-year education.

❏ *Larisa Barry, B.A.*

Vanderbilt University
Nashville, TN 37203-1700

(615) 322-2561; (800) 288-0432
Fax: (615) 343-7765

E-mail: *admission@vanderbilt.edu*
Web site: *www.vanderbilt.edu*

 Enrollment

Full-time ❑ women: 3,228
          ❑ men: 3,018

Part-time ❑ women: 15
          ❑ men: 25

INTRODUCING VANDERBILT

Nestled close to the middle of downtown Nashville, Tennessee, Vanderbilt University has stood as a stronghold of higher education in the southeastern United States since its founding in 1873 by a gift from railroad and shipping magnate Cornelius Vanderbilt. However, led in recent years by an energetic bowtie-wearing chancellor and the most diverse, talented student body in the university's history, "Vandy" has become one of the country's most bustling, engaging undergraduate institutions.

> *I love the metaphor of Vanderbilt being "constantly under construction."*
> *I appreciate the fact that the school seems to have improved itself every time I*
> *visit, and I think these changes reflect Vanderbilt's overall interest in always*
> *evolving toward excellence.*

Characterized by a unique balance of academic rigor and social activity, Vanderbilt has always attracted the nation's top students. These students come to learn in an intimate and diverse academic setting; many of them have multiple majors or do research with their professors. Because it is comprised of four undergraduate schools and several renowned graduate programs, Vanderbilt provides unique opportunities for academic exploration.

Students from all fifty states and ninety countries also bring to campus a buzz of activity. Their wide variety of extracurricular passions range from the more traditional (Division I sports, community service, and student government) to the more obscure (hot air ballooning, bowling, and disc golf). Vandy students traditionally exhibit a thirst for service to the world around them, and over half of the student body also participates in volunteer activities while at Vanderbilt. Every year many students travel to destinations ranging from South Dakota to New York City through the Alternative Spring Break program, which was founded at Vanderbilt.

A walk around Vanderbilt reveals one of the nation's most beautiful campuses. A national arboretum, Vandy's 330 acres are densely populated with leafy limbs under which students (and squirrels) habitually nap, snack, or study. The student body lives amidst the various species of trees and classic red brick buildings of Vanderbilt's campus. Because of this, the university has dedicated dorm space to a variety of housing options, such as a brand new Freshman Commons, including five new and five renovated residence halls. The Freshman Commons is the first phase of a transformative system of college halls, which will amplify the synergy of social and intellectual life on campus.

Though natural beauty has always been an exceptional feature of Vanderbilt's campus, more recent additions to the school have revitalized and supplemented campus life in other ways. In recent years, Vanderbilt has added several buildings to its already generous campus, including a new Student Life Center, renovated classroom buildings, like historic Buttrick Hall, a studio arts building and gallery, and a Hillel center for Jewish life. The university ambitiously plans further progress in hopes of continually enhancing the Vanderbilt experience.

Vanderbilt students are only a mile from flourishing downtown Nashville, and the campus itself rests in the center of the city's trendiest nightlife. Nashville's population of 1.5 million people radiates a vibrant mix of cosmopolitan energy and southern hospitality, which students find both welcoming and invigorating. Metropolitan Nashville also offers Vanderbilt students opportunities for community service, employment, internships, and religious life just outside the campus perimeter.

A challenging and energetic university, Vanderbilt continues to seek students who hope to engage in four years of both academic and social learning. These students will play a vital role not only in contributing to Vanderbilt intellectually and socially, but also in shaping the direction of the university.

ADMISSIONS REQUIREMENTS

A highly competitive institution, Vanderbilt has experienced significant increases in the number, diversity, and academic profile of its freshmen applicants for the last few years. In the 2004–2005 application year, more than 12,100 students applied for around 1,600 freshman spots at Vanderbilt. The average class rank of admitted students was top five percent, and accepted applicants combined exceptional classroom performance with average SAT Critical Reading and Verbal scores ranging between 1300 and 1470.

Application Requirements

An application to Vanderbilt is evaluated on the basis of five components. The first and most important of these components focuses on a student's academic work in high school. Admissions officers look for a high school curriculum of challenging, academic classes (with an emphasis on Honors, Advanced Placement, and International Baccalaureate courses), rather than simply basing their evaluation on grade point average. Additionally, applicants should submit standardized test scores, academic teacher recommendations, a resume of extracurricular pursuits, and the essays requested on the application. Though it publishes its own two-part application, Vanderbilt also accepts the Common Application. Students submitting a Common Application must also complete Vanderbilt's Common Application Supplement.

Standardized Tests

Vanderbilt accepts both the SAT and the ACT. All ACT students must complete the optional writing tests. SAT subject tests are not required for admission; however, they are strongly recommended. These subject tests are used not only for admission evaluation, but may also be used for placement into language, math, and writing classes upon entrance to the university (additional testing times are offered at academic orientations). Vanderbilt additionally requires the TOEFL for overseas applicants whose first language is not English.

Decision Plans

Vanderbilt offers three decision plans: Early Decision I, Early Decision II, and Regular Decision. Created for students who have decided upon Vanderbilt as their first choice, Early Decision is a binding admission plan. Students who apply Early Decision sign a contract to attend Vanderbilt and agree to withdraw all other applications if accepted. Early Decision I applications are due by November 1 with notification mailed by December 15. Early Decision II and Regular Decision applicants must be postmarked by January 3. Early Decision II students receive notification by February 15, and Regular Decision students receive notification by April 1.

ENGAGE

Since the fall of 2006, Vanderbilt has offered a unique opportunity for freshman applicants. Through the ENGAGE (Early Notification of Guaranteed Admission for Graduate Education) Scholars Program, a select group of admitted freshmen also receive early admission to the Vanderbilt graduate or professional school of their choice.

The program offers exceptional opportunities for personal and academic growth; for example, the ENGAGE Scholars Program guarantees at least one paid summer internship in addition to providing research and practical experience. Faculty in each field mentor the Scholars, and Scholars also have access to specific and unique programming available only to students in the ENGAGE program.

ENGAGE currently partners with Vanderbilt's graduate and professional schools in divinity, education, engineering, law, management, medicine, and nursing. Freshman applicants must meet the appropriate deadlines. After these applications are reviewed, finalists are invited to campus to interview with the designated graduate or professional school.

Vanderbilt welcomes the chance to encourage students to explore a liberal arts curriculum while pursuing ambitious goals for work and study beyond their undergraduate experience.

Under the umbrella of Vanderbilt University lie four undergraduate schools: College of Arts and Science, Peabody College of Education and Human Development, School of Engineering, and Blair School of Music. With its four undergraduate schools and distinguished graduate programs in law, medicine, business, divinity, nursing, and education, Vanderbilt is uniquely suited to provide its students with lavish opportunity to explore and research many fields of study. Though all four undergraduate schools have varying academic requirements, every undergraduate at Vanderbilt has access to the courses and resources of the entire university. It is even possible to major in one school and minor or double major in another. As a result, at least one-third of Vanderbilt students have multiple majors, many create their own interdisciplinary programs, and all enjoy the opportunity to learn from a diverse academic community.

For me, the best part of academics at Vanderbilt was how learning was integrated across the curriculum and even outside it. I had an interdisciplinary major (Public Policy Studies) and minor (European Studies). Having this broad academic background that was an integrated whole rather that a collection of disparate pieces gave me a better leg up in the workplace after graduation, but more than that it prepared me for life in the "real world."

College of Arts and Science

The oldest and largest undergraduate school at Vanderbilt, the College of Arts and Science offers students a broad, liberal arts education, based on a multidisciplinary curriculum in humanities, natural science, social science, languages, and math. Students begin fulfilling this core curriculum in their first year and are not required to declare a major until the spring of their second year. Thus, broad exploration and multidisciplinary study characterize the Arts and Science student.

The college is home to several interdisciplinary institutes and centers as well as the Honor Scholars program. Additionally, all freshmen in Arts and Science are required to take a freshman seminar. These courses are typically designed around the faculty's unique interests, with a strong additional focus on writing and enrollment limited to fifteen freshmen.

Engineering School

The first private school in the South to offer a degree in engineering, the Vanderbilt School of Engineering boasts exceptional progress in recent years. For example, the school's new facilities offer every possible learning tool for students in the field of engineering, including wireless connection, interactive computer classrooms, and advanced research and computer labs. Additionally, Engineering faculty have recently claimed several notable awards in their fields. Vanderbilt Engineering students also take required courses in liberal arts, and thus, are highly sought after by corporations as well as graduate schools. Of those engineering graduates seeking employment in a recent year, ninety-five percent had jobs within six months of graduation.

Peabody College of Education and Human Development

Consistently ranked in the top five education schools in the nation, Peabody College is home to the education and human development majors at Vanderbilt. With its focus on experiential learning across the lifespan, Peabody requires internship and field placements for most of its majors. The most popular undergraduate major at Vanderbilt—Human and Organizational Development—resides in Peabody College. This major requires a one-semester internship, which many students choose to complete in New York, San Francisco, and other approved cities. Students in the education majors find themselves in classroom settings from the beginning of their Vanderbilt experience, thus guaranteeing superb preparation for work upon graduation. Peabody has produced several renowned programs, including the progressive Head Start program, and it also boasts the top Special Education program in the nation.

Blair School of Music

Vanderbilt is only one of a small handful of top-tier private universities to boast an accredited undergraduate school of music. The Blair School of Music addresses music through a broad array of academic, pedagogical, and performing activities. Each student auditions as a part of the admissions process and chooses to study performance (including all orchestral instruments), composition/theory, musical arts, or musical arts/teacher education. The Blair School features not only gifted student performers, but also a prestigious faculty of musicians; both students and faculty enrich the campus with frequent performances at Vanderbilt and in the greater Nashville community. In 2002, the Martha Rivers Ingram Center for the Performing Arts opened as Blair's performance wing. This breathtaking facility includes a 618-seat performance hall with full staging capabilities, in addition to generous rehearsal, administrative, and studio space.

> *One of the greatest opportunities I had as a student at Blair was getting to see the Nashville Symphony perform frequently. Seeing my clarinet professor on stage with my music theory professor and the teacher of my ear training class and then being able to dialogue about the performance with them the next day in class was a priceless experience for a music major.*

Faculty

A prestigious research institution, Vanderbilt employs many professors who have received and are receiving notable recognition in their fields. However, professors at Vanderbilt truly enjoy both the teaching and the research aspects of their profession. In fact, many professors choose Vanderbilt because it is a school where they can focus on teaching relationships in addition to conducting excellent research. To this end, almost all of the professors hold office hours, and they continually make themselves available via e-mail, phone, or appointment. Vandy boasts a 9:1 student to faculty ratio; in contrast to many research universities, Vanderbilt can also boast that ninety-five percent of a typical undergraduate's courses are taught by professors. With such personal attention, undergraduates never doubt that the faculty at Vanderbilt genuinely care about their students.

Classes

The prestigious learning environment at Vanderbilt feels intimate not only because of the faculty, but also because of the small class sizes. With an average class size of nineteen, Vanderbilt's undergraduate schools keep almost every class (ninety-eight percent) below fifty students, and a majority of them (seventy-eight percent) below twenty five students. In some classes, graduate students assist professors as teaching assistants by leading small group breakout sections and conducting review sessions. Professors also work hard to keep classes lively and challenging. For example, a sunny spring day at Vanderbilt usually smiles on several classes discussing the day's material on the grassy lawns of the campus.

Recently, in order to continue challenging students and attracting prestigious faculty, Vanderbilt has placed a renewed focus on interdisciplinary study and research funding. Undergraduates at Vandy have continually increasing exposure to teaching and research in cutting-edge fields. In keeping with this pedagogical philosophy, the head of one of Vanderbilt's newest interdisciplinary departments (a renowned scientist) also taught a freshman seminar last year.

Study Abroad

Approximately forty percent of Vanderbilt students study abroad at some point in their Vanderbilt careers. These students take advantage of Vanderbilt's unique partnerships in various countries, usually for one or two semesters of junior year, or for summer study. Vanderbilt has home-base programs in several countries, including England, Spain, Italy, France, and Germany. Participants in the Vanderbilt Study Abroad programs are guaranteed that their financial aid packages will translate to the Study Abroad semester or year, and courses in the Vanderbilt programs have been evaluated for transferal of credit. Additionally, Vanderbilt belongs to a consortium of schools through which students can find alternative programs that may be better suited to their interests. Many students take advantage of Study Abroad opportunities to further proficiency in language as well as cultural knowledge and experience. Vanderbilt encourages students from all undergraduate schools to pursue studies abroad when possible.

My semester in Leeds, England, unquestionably changed my life. Thanks to the ease with which Vandy transferred my financial aid and academic credits, I was free to enjoy the experience without any headaches. I will never forget reading novels for my Victorian Lit class while the sheep slipped by me outside the train window—I traveled a great deal and learned so much about the world!

Graduate Study

Vanderbilt offers applicants unique academic opportunities for graduate study. For example, the university now offers a handful of select freshman applicants direct admission to Vanderbilt graduate programs through the ENGAGE program. Second, Vandy students have the opportunity to apply early to the Vanderbilt business and medical programs. The medical school accepts a select number of Vanderbilt undergraduates at the end of their sophomore year. These students do not take the MCATs and proceed directly to Vanderbilt's Medical School upon graduation. The Owen Graduate School of Management accepts undergraduates in their junior year at Vanderbilt; these students complete their undergraduate studies in addition to an M.B.A. in five years. In 2006, the College of Arts and Science also began 4+1 programs, which result in the Master's degree in five years in many disciplines.

The Honor Code

> *"Today I give you two examinations, one in trigonometry and one in honesty. I hope you pass them both, but if you fail one, let it be trigonometry."*
> —M. Madison Garratt

The Honor Code governs student integrity at Vanderbilt University. A rich tradition at Vanderbilt, the Honor Code allows faculty and students to learn in a flexible and trusting environment.

Since 1875, Vanderbilt students have pledged, "I pledge on my honor that I have neither given nor received aid on this examination." As a result, students and faculty alike are free to operate in a trusting way with each other. Professors will often give take-home exams or leave the room during exams.

Commitment to the Honor Code begins with all freshmen participating in a discussion and signing of the Code during fall orientation. The pages of signatures hang in Sarratt Student Center, framed as a reminder to students of their oath and to the Vanderbilt community of its reputation for integrity.

The Honor Council, a group of Vanderbilt students, investigates violations and assigns consequences. These students also help disseminate information regarding the Honor Code and its applications to student life.

SOCIAL LIFE AND ACTIVITIES

Although Vanderbilt students pursue academic success vigorously, they also pour vast amounts of energy and time into extracurricular pursuits. This balance of academic and social pursuits brings a friendly and energetic feel to campus life.

Student Organizations

Nearly all of Vanderbilt's 1,400-plus organizations are open to all students, who can join at any point in their Vanderbilt careers. These organizations cater to a variety of interests, and they facilitate speakers, special events, community service projects and various other campus activities.

Sarratt Student Center, the hub of campus life, houses office space, mailboxes, meeting areas, and even faculty advisors for these campus organizations. Additionally, the Sarratt Student Center is a sprawling home to student study spaces, a cinema, several dining options, the bookstore, the post office, and a convenience store called Varsit/Market. Because of the involved nature of campus life at Vanderbilt, the Student Center daily buzzes with activity. On a sunny day, students congregate to advertise events, sell tickets, and socialize on "The Wall."

> *When people ask me to describe my life as an undergraduate at Vanderbilt, I often say "busy!" From the moment I took my first tour of campus, I loved the fact that Vanderbilt was filled with people who had as much energy as I did. The experience of living, studying, organizing, serving, performing, growing, and relaxing with my fellow students provided me with rich growth and deep friendships, both of which are still part of my life today.*

Athletics

A member of the Southeastern Conference, Vanderbilt offers Division I athletics in addition to club and intramural sports. Vanderbilt University maintains a proud tradition of Black and Gold (the school colors) in intercollegiate sports, including six men's and ten women's varsity teams. Students enjoy attending games to cheer and to socialize. Vandy has enjoyed tremendous success in basketball (both men's and women's basketball teams advanced to the Sweet Sixteen in 2004), baseball, golf, tennis, soccer, women's swimming, and women's lacrosse. Vanderbilt athletes strive for excellence both on the field/court and in the classroom.

Vandy students also enjoy the chance to compete against other colleges at the club level. Among popular favorites are the Ultimate Frisbee, crew, and rugby teams. These teams travel to tournaments and often function as tight-knit social groups.

At the intracollegiate level, Vanderbilt students participate in intramurals. The largest student organization, Vanderbilt intramurals offer seasonal sports such as basketball, football, soccer, volleyball, and water polo for men's, women's, and coed teams.

Intramural facilities and individual fitness facilities are located in the Student Recreation Center at Vanderbilt. The Rec Center contains weights, cardio machines, indoor and outdoor tracks, basketball courts, racquetball and squash courts, aerobics and yoga facilities, a climbing wall, an indoor pool, Ping-Pong tables, and a café in addition to the intramural fields. Additionally, the Outdoor Recreational Program at Vanderbilt hosts weekend trips to various parks for climbing, hiking, kayaking, and spelunking. Students can also borrow equipment and take courses in outdoor skills through this program. Every year, the Outdoor Rec plans a hike through the Grand Canyon during spring break, and a ski trip to Colorado over Christmas break.

> *Vanderbilt attracted me as an athlete and a student, a combination offering that no other university could match. Challenged daily on the football field, playing against national title contenders, I also relished the chance to compete daily in the classroom against the brightest minds in the country. From a chancellor who strives to "win" in every aspect of the university, to coaches and players who respect and honor academic commitments and accomplishments, the entire athletic community at Vanderbilt pursues victories on the field without losing sight of other academic and social victories to be won off the field.*

Residence Life

Because all undergraduates are required to live on campus, the students who choose to attend Vanderbilt quickly become enmeshed in the Vanderbilt community. Beginning in 2008, all freshmen will live together in the new Freshman Commons without regard to undergraduate school. This complex facilitates relationships between the incoming, diverse freshman class as they embark on their Vanderbilt careers. Critical to the first year experience is the new Vanderbilt Visions orientation program. Lasting from move-in day through spring break, first year students meet weekly in small groups, which are team-taught by a professor and trained upper-class students to discuss issues of transition and Vanderbilt community traditions.

After freshman year, Vanderbilt offers students a wide range of housing options on campus. For example, McTyeire International House promotes the study of foreign language by requiring students to speak French, German, Spanish, Chinese, or Japanese while in the dorm and at specific events. McTyeire residents also plan activities pertaining to the culture and nations associated with their language. Alternatively, Vanderbilt offers a hall dedicated to philosophy and the fine arts, as well as a group of ten-person houses dedicated to community service projects. All students at Vanderbilt have access to various arrangements of single rooms, shared rooms, and suites throughout their four years. Students are not allowed to bring cars to campus until sophomore year. Vanderbilt's walking campus accommodates the needs of students through campus access to laundry facilities, dining options, and a chapel.

Orientation Programs

One of Vanderbilt's strengths lies in its dedication to facilitating new students' transitions to college life. Vanderbilt offers a series of programs to this end. First, accepted students can attend an optional Summer Academic Orientation. This two-day, summer program is divided by undergraduate school and offers incoming freshmen a chance to decode their academic requirements, register for classes, and meet other students. Many students have met roommates through the Summer Academic Orientation Program, and all students are thrilled by the opportunity to complete academic registration before moving to campus in the fall.

On move-in day, freshmen and their families find themselves overcome by hordes of identically T-shirted VUCeptors, who insist on carrying boxes, refrigerators, backpacks, and anything else they can find. These hardworking VUCeptors then pair up with faculty members to usher groups of twenty freshmen through their first year of Vanderbilt life.

Finally, Vanderbilt offers optional early orientation programs to incoming freshmen. These programs have gained enormous popularity in recent years, and have now expanded to include five themed options. Themes center around outdoor activities and skills, service, leadership, and diversity. These programs seek to provide orientation, transition, and fun for incoming Vanderbilt students.

Alternative Spring Break

The original program of its kind, Vanderbilt's Alternative Spring Break (ASB) annually sends students into needy communities over spring break. Vanderbilt ASB is also one of the largest programs in the country. In 2005, over 350 students traveled to nearly thirty destinations across the United States, Canada, and Mexico to face issues ranging from Native American issues to urban violence. The ASB Executive Board states, "Our mission is to promote critical thinking, social action and continued community involvement by combining education and direct service on the local, regional, national and international levels."

Greek Life

While Greek life plays a significant role at Vanderbilt, less than half of the student body participates in fraternities or sororities. Unlike most southern schools, Vandy offers a deferred recruitment process. New member recruitment occurs during the spring semester of freshman year, giving new students a chance to adjust to college life and make friends in the fall semester. Students at Vanderbilt can choose from nineteen fraternities and twelve sororities, including Asian, Hispanic, and historically black Greek organizations. All parties are open to the entire student body, and only officers (usually around six) live in the Greek houses on campus.

Nashville

Although students from outside the South may tiptoe with curiosity into Nashville, they are certain to fall in love with the city soon after arriving. "Music City" claims the country's "third coast," featuring musicians from many genres and backgrounds, who can be seen performing all over the city. In addition to its renowned live music scene, Nashville boasts a rich cultural and educational heritage. Sixteen other universities call Nashville home, as do the only exact replica of Greece's Parthenon, the Frist Center for the Visual Arts, the Tennessee government and state capital, the NFL's Tennessee Titans, and the NHL's Nashville Predators. Nashville also features diversity usually reserved for more sizable cities, with the largest Kurdish population in the United States and thriving Asian, Hispanic, and African communities.

Vanderbilt's location near downtown Nashville provides easy access to Nashville's best restaurants and hottest night spots, and students often walk to nearby parks. When Vandy students need to get away for a weekend, Nashville also provides an ideal location from which to travel, as it is served by an international airport featuring service from seventeen airlines, and easy access to three major interstate highways.

FINANCIAL AID

Vanderbilt awards both need-based and merit-based financial aid. To qualify for need-based financial aid, applicants must complete the Free Application for Federal Student Aid (FAFSA) form in addition to the CSS PROFILE form by February 1. Based on the need indicated by these forms, the Office of Student Financial Aid awards financial aid packages that include a combination of federal and institutional grants, student loans, and work-study.

Additionally, Vanderbilt awards annually over two hundred merit-based scholarships in each of the four undergraduate schools. These scholarships are awarded based on a student's application for admission and are not related to financial need.

○ Tom Schulman, '72, Academy Award-winning screenwriter *(Dead Poet's Society)*

○ Albert Gore, Jr., '77, Former Vice-President of the United States

○ Tipper Gore, '76, Wife of Former Vice-President

○ Amy Grant, '82, Award-winning Recording Artist

○ Will Perdue,'88, ESPN Radio Commentator; Former NBA World Champion with Chicago Bulls and San Antonio Spurs

○ Fred Thompson,'67, Movie, TV Actor, Former U.S. Senator

○ Dr. Norman Shumway,'49, Transplant Pioneer at Stanford

○ Lamar Alexander, '62, Current U.S. Senator from Tennessee, Former Secretary of Education, Former Governor of Tennessee

○ Ann S. Moore, '71, CEO and Chairwoman, Time Inc.

○ James Neal, '57, Watergate Counsel

○ Bill Purcell, '79, Mayor, Metropolitan Nashville-Davidson County

○ Perry Wallace, '70, SEC's First African-American Basketball Player, Law Professor, Washington, D.C.

○ Sam Feist, '91, Senior Executive Producer, CNN

○ The Late Grantland Rice, '01 (1901), Legendary Sportswriter

○ James Patterson, '70, Best-selling Crime-Suspense Novelist

○ The Late Robert Penn Warren, '25, Author and Three-Time Pulitzer Prize Winner *(All The Kings Men)*

○ Dr. Mildred Stahlman, '46, Neonatology Pioneer at Vanderbilt

○ Dr. Thomas Frist, Jr., '61, Chairman, Founder, Hospital Corporation of America

○ Chantelle Anderson, '03, Two-time First Team All-American

Over sixty percent of Vanderbilt University receives some form of financial aid. The average award in 2005–2006 was around $30,924.

GRADUATES

The original gates of Vanderbilt University, still located at the main entrance to campus, have ushered generations of Vanderbilt students into the world with great success. Vanderbilt graduates are equipped with strong analytical, critical thinking and writing skills, and they have many options upon graduation.

The Career Center at Vanderbilt assists students in the job search. Career counselors offer standard services such as resume review, and recruiters also come on campus to conduct information sessions and interviews at the Career Center. In fact, more than 250 recruiters came to campus in a recent year. Vandy students also have access to career testing, an alumni mentor search engine, and career workshops.

While the majority of Vanderbilt graduates enter the workforce upon graduation, a significant number also attend graduate programs. Vanderbilt's rigorous academics and excellent reputation make it a wonderful springboard for further education. Approximately thirty percent of Vanderbilt graduates attend graduate school immediately following graduation; law and medicine are two popular options for postgraduate study. Over time, more than two-thirds of Vanderbilt graduates pursue further studies.

SUMMING UP

The perfect blend of social activity and academic rigor, Vanderbilt offers prospective students a chance to explore, engage in, and enjoy the college experience. Its spacious lawns, beckoning benches, and shady branches create a comfortable and lovely home for the university's increasingly diverse and talented student body. In the classroom, students thrive under the expert and personal instruction of Vanderbilt's faculty. Outside the classroom, Vanderbilt students continue to affect the world through involvement and service, both in their years on campus and in their lives beyond the gates of Vanderbilt.

A blossoming community, Vanderbilt University offers all students a chance to experience four years of challenge, vitality, and change.

❏ *Lauren (Nicole) Shaub, B.A.*

VASSAR COLLEGE

 Vassar College
Poughkeepsie, NY 12601

 (845) 437-7300, (800) 827-7270
Fax: (845) 437-7063

 E-mail: *admissions@vassar.edu*
Web site: *http://www.vassar.edu*

 Enrollment

Full-time ❑ women: 1,422
❑ men: 960

Part-time ❑ women: 23
❑ men: 19

INTRODUCING VASSAR

Like many a good college story, this one begins with beer.

In 1861 a philanthropist brewer created a college for women in the Hudson Valley, bestowing upon it both his name and his broad-minded, forward-thinking spirit. The founder? Matthew Vassar.

On welcoming its first students on September 26, 1865, Vassar College stood out immediately as an institution where a woman could receive an education as diverse and full as that of any man. For the first time, women could take courses in art history, astronomy, chemistry, geology, mathematics, music, and physical education with some of the most prominent scholars of the era, such as astronomer Maria Mitchell and music historian Frederick Louis Ritter. Significantly, it chose rose and gray as its school colors, an eloquent visual representation of the dawning of women's education through the gray of their previous intellectual life. Throughout the years, first as a women's college and since 1969 a coed institution, Vassar has upheld and sustained this tradition of academic rigor, fierce independence, and zeal for experimentation.

Yet Vassar has never feared change, often embracing it in radical ways. In 1966, brother university Yale invited Vassar to merge campuses. After much debate among students and administration, Vassar refused the offer. Instead, it made the revolutionary decision to accept men in 1969, thus becoming, rather appropriately, the first of the Seven Sisters colleges to move to coeducation. Yet such is the power of the "Vassar girl" image that many people even now believe the school is all women. It couldn't be farther from the truth; men comprise approximately forty percent of the varied student body. Having established the standard for higher education for women, Vassar now serves as the paradigm for true coeducation.

VASSAR TRADITIONS

- **Afternoon tea:** A simple spread of tea and cookies in Main's Rose Parlor.
- **Convocation:** Incoming seniors ascend to the top of Main to announce themselves with a ritual ringing of the bell. Your camera is a must for the stunning view.
- **Daisy Chain:** Group of sophomore women and men who bear a chain of daisies during Commencement.
- **Founder's Day:** All-day annual celebration in late April celebrating Matthew Vassar's birthday. Must be seen to be believed.
- **Nilda's Cookies:** Favorite Retreat snack from a local baker, the famed Nilda. A sign reminds you not to stick them in the toaster.
- **Primal Scream:** At midnight before exam week, students congregate in the residential quad to scream. Cathartic.
- **Serenading:** Honoring/roast of the seniors at the beginning of the year with songs from each dorm and class. Water guns and silly string are *de rigueur*.
- **Vassar Devil:** Devil's food cake with vanilla ice cream, hot fudge, and marshmallow sauce. Its lesser-known angel-food cousin is, naturally, the Vassar Angel.

The Campus and Traditions

Located seventy miles north of (and an easy train ride from) New York City in the middle of the Hudson Valley, Vassar retains an intriguing mix of custom and advance. Its famously breathtaking 1,000-acre campus, set in suburban Poughkeepsie, juxtaposes nineteenth-century architecture and gorgeous New England foliage with modern edifices and cutting-edge technology. Students still enjoy some of the rituals of their predecessors—afternoon tea in the Main Parlor, the decadent chocolate dessert known as the Vassar Devil—while participating in newer additions—underclassmen serenading the seniors, the pre-exam week Primal Scream. They still major in English, political science, biology, and psychology, and participate in student government, intramural sports, and the newspaper, but vary their schedules with courses in American studies, Gaelic, music performance, and urban studies, and meetings with their ethnic students' clubs, film societies, and improv groups. And that's not counting their fieldwork, independent projects, and study abroad. Or their work-study programs, meals with friends at the dining center, a famous Nilda's Cookie (don't stick them in the toaster!) with a professor, a visit to the Frances Lehman Loeb Art Center, a walk around Sunset Lake, or nights at campus pub Matthew's Mug. A challenge, perhaps, but the motivated students of Vassar embrace it wholeheartedly, maintaining a well-rounded life of high academic performance and lively extracurricular activities.

Study Body

Highly selective, this liberal arts college attracts a refreshingly diverse student body, where individualism and tolerance are bywords. The small population allows everyone to, if not know, at least recognize everyone else, from "the guy on the unicycle" to "the girl who bought my cube fridge last spring." With its ratio of nine students for every one professor, class sizes reflect this, allowing for friendly working relationships that often continue beyond the course and even graduation. It also permits the exploration of a variety of academic interests via student-designed majors, independent study, and research partnerships.

From 1865 until the present day, Vassar has remained at the forefront of liberal arts institutions with its boldness, innovation, and strength, positioning itself as a leading force in higher education.

Who knew that beer could do a college good?

ADMISSIONS REQUIREMENTS

So you've read all the glossy brochures, checked out the Web site, had Coke and hors d'oeuvres at an informational function, talked with a representative, and maybe even visited the school. And you've decided that, yes, Vassar is for you.

Now for the important part—applying.

Although Vassar students form a diverse community, they all share a background of high academic achievement. For the class of 2010, the admissions committee accepted a record low of 30 percent of the 6,075 applications submitted, the third-largest pool in college history. Of those accepted, 670 students (36.6 percent) enrolled.

The class of 2010 had a particularly strong academic profile. Nearly ninety percent of them came from the top twenty percent of their graduating class, while forty-four percent were in the top five percent. Their average SAT score was 1380 and their average grade point average was an unweighted A–.

Naturally, Vassar does not require every candidate to present the same credentials, but they do expect applicants to have taken the most rigorous course load available to them. A qualified student ideally will have elected to take four years of English, mathematics, laboratory science, history or social science, and foreign language. If available, most of those courses will be at the accelerated, honors, Advanced Placement, or International Baccalaureate level.

The Application

To apply for fall admission to the freshman class, candidates may apply via Vassar's own on-line application, through the Common Application, or by traditional paper means. Students must take either the SAT, as well as two SAT subject tests, or the ACT. All tests should be taken no later than December of senior year. In addition to the $60 fee and usual information forms, the application requires a personal essay and an analytical writing sample of two to five pages. Optional is "Your Space," a section so legendary that it once boasted its own T-shirt at the campus bookstore. As promised, the blank space presents an opportunity for students to express themselves outside of an academic context, as actual personalities rather than just grades and numbers.

For students who know that Vassar is their first choice, there are two Early Decision deadlines: November 15, with notification in mid-December, and January 1, with notification by February 1. The application for regular admission is due by January 1, with notification about April 1st.

Vassar's Office of Admission Web site, located at *http://admissions.vassar.edu/*, includes further information about the school, admission policies, campus tours, inquiry forms, and more.

Transfer Students

As Vassar accepts only a fairly small number of transfer students each year, the transfer application process is very competitive. Applicants from two- or four-year institutions must have at least one year of liberal arts coursework that reflects a high level of achievement. Vassar's Transfer Application is available through the Admission Office and on-line on their Web site. The application deadline for the spring semester is November 1, for the fall semester, it is March 15.

International Students

Vassar actively recruits international students. Nine percent of the student body has either foreign or dual citizenship, representing nearly fifty different countries. Answers to a list of questions of special interest to international students is available on the Vassar admission Web site. To apply for admission to the freshman class, international candidates use the same application forms as American students.

ACADEMIC LIFE

I don't think you fully realize the extent of what Scotty has done at Vassar.... [S]he has raised herself from a poor scholar to a very passable one.... We have every reason to cheer for our baby.

—*F. Scott Fitzgerald to Zelda Fitzgerald, on their daughter Frances Scott Fitzgerald '42*

Vassar students love their work. "The history department," declared a student proudly, "is filled with geniuses." Though he was describing his concentration, it's a sentiment echoed across the student body about their respective disciplines. Nominal requirements, abundant course offerings, engaging faculty, small class sizes, cutting-edge resources, and intellectual freedom blend to create the ideal academic setting for eager students.

Requirements

In keeping with its belief in independence and flexibility, Vassar minimizes academic requirements: thirty-four credits to graduate, as well as fulfillment of the freshman course (a writing-intensive introduction to a particular discipline), foreign language, and quantitative skill requirements. Each major also comes with its own structure, usually a range of ten to seventeen courses.

Students must declare a major by the end of sophomore year, taking one of four paths: concentration in a department such as history or French, an interdepartmental program such as biochemistry or Victorian studies, a multidisciplinary program such as urban studies or cognitive science, or an individually developed course of study in the independent program. The most popular majors are English, psychology, and political science. In addition, students can opt to take a correlate sequence (similar to a minor) of six courses in a variety of areas.

Credits can also be earned by other academic means. Most departments offer fieldwork internships, which enable students to apply the theories of their discipline in a practical setting. Students have accepted internships locally or in Albany or New York City during the school year or across the United States during the summer. It's possible to study elsewhere for a semester or a year, either through Vassar's exchange or Junior Year Abroad programs. Students have gone to colleges such as Amherst, Dartmouth, Howard, Morehouse, Smith, Wellesley, and Wesleyan or to countries in nearly every continent.

VASSAR COURSES

- Africana Studies 275: Caribbean Discourse
- Biology 356: Aquatic Ecology
- Computer Science 379: Computer Animation: Art, Science, and Criticism
- Economics 220: The Political Economy of Health Care
- English 261: The Literary Revival in Ireland, 1885–1922
- Film 216: Genre: Romantic Comedy
- German Studies 101: Vampires, Lunatics, and Cyborgs: Exploring the Uncanny Recesses of the Romantic Consciousness
- Music 219: Electronic Music
- Philosophy 125: Symbolic Logic
- Psychology 343: States of Conciousness
- Urban Studies 350: New York City as a Social Laboratory

Faculty

At some institutions, professors are distinguished but unapproachable. Not so at Vassar.

Class sizes run small; average enrollment is twenty-one for an introductory course, sixteen for intermediate courses, and ten for advanced courses. This allows professors and students to develop rapport in and out of the classroom, reducing the teacher-pupil structure to colleague status. Professors maintain regular office hours for anyone who needs to work out the knots in a paper or project or just wants to chat; as a student noted: "The professors are readily available to talk about anything from that day's lecture to future career paths." Further, students often work one-on-one with professors on research projects, and professors typically regard students as junior colleagues and collaborators. In fact, it's not uncommon for Vassar faculty to know all their students personally or to enjoy lunch with them in the Retreat. One graduate recalled his thesis advisor taking him out for a celebratory drink after he submitted the manuscript. But don't let this casualness fool you; the academics are as demanding as the professors are accessible. Many Vassar students who have gone on to advanced study have remarked on how well their upper-division courses prepared them for graduate-level work.

Advisors

Vassar's advising system benefits from these small class sizes. Based on their academic interests, entering students are assigned faculty pre-major advisors until they decide on a major. Once they do so, they select a departmental or program advisor, who assists students in registering for courses every semester, ensures that requirements are being met, and provides help with any academic questions or issues. Students often choose the major advisor, as well as advisors for senior or independent work, based on personal experience with the professors or on common intellectual interests. The classroom ratio gives students a chance to see a professor's teaching style and personality and gauge whether it will mesh with a dream project.

I took classes with Professors Joyce and Zlotnick as a junior and loved the experience so much that I had them advise me on some independent and senior work. From proposal level to completion, they were super, just great choices. I used to joke that they were my English Department parents. To this day, I consider them mentors.

SOCIAL LIFE AND ACTIVITIES

This might not be the stuff that college descriptions are made of, but I still think it's important to recognize how sweet it is to live in an arboretum. Walking through Japanese maples after the rain doesn't feel nearly as trite as it sounds.

With just 2,400 or so students, Vassar projects a strong sense of community, an intimate unity rarely found at other institutions. Everyone knows each other by face, if not by name, making a simple walk around campus resemble a Three, no, a *Two* Degrees of Separation map. Despite diversity in background or character, students are open enough to find common ground and to accept differences, leading to a welcoming and varied social scene. One graduate remarked, "As cheesy as it sounds, the best thing about Vassar is the people. The students are smart, interesting, quirky, and generally don't take themselves too seriously."

Residences

As soon as new students walk onto campus, the dorms receive them with open arms into the Vassar community. In the first tentative weeks and beyond, it becomes a familiar, welcoming space; often the friends made in the dorms remain friends for life.

Nearly the entire student body lives on campus; nine traditional residence halls, a co-op, and three sets of apartment-style housing accommodate them. Populated with mostly freshmen, sophomores, and juniors, each residence hall comes with its own broad characterization: posh Cushing, homey Davison, party dorm Josselyn, central Main, all-women Strong. Each comes with its own activities, faculty resident House Fellow (often with their families), and student leaders. Particularly important is the Student Fellow, an upperclassman mentor assigned to a group of incoming freshmen, who can provide assistance, comfort, and answers when necessary.

VASSAR ON THE SCREEN

Most people know Vassar through movie or television references. Some of the more famous:

- *A Day at the Races* (1937): To the remark "But that's a girls' college," Groucho Marx provides the useful retort: "I found that out the third year when I tried out for the swim team."
- *Some Like It Hot* (1959): Sugar Kane (Marilyn Monroe) pretends to be a Vassar girl in order to impress millionaire Junior (Tony Curtis).
- *The Group* (1966): Based on the novel by Mary McCarthy, '33, the film echoes the traditions and hallmarks of Vassar in its depiction of a similar institution.
- *The Simpsons* (1989–present): The best-known source of Vassar references. Second-grade prodigy Lisa often expresses a desire to become a Brewer.
- *Don't Tell Mom the Babysitter's Dead* (1991): Sue Ellen (Christina Applegate) finds doors opening to her when she pretends to be a Vassar grad.
- *Kicking and Screaming* (1995): Written and directed by alum Noah Baumbach, this indie focuses on a Vassar-like school. A favorite with students, who enjoy picking out all the similarities.

Most seniors opt to live with four or five friends in the partly furnished, campus-owned complexes known as the Terrace Apartments (TAs), Town Houses (THs), and South Commons. Providing an alternative to the traditional residence halls, the experience gives upperclassmen a real-world taste of apartment living and, even more importantly, a last chance to be together before graduating.

> *If I could go back to any time in my life, it would be to senior year when I lived in D-block [of the THs] with all my friends.*

Activities

At about 100 and counting, the myriad clubs and organizations available to students provide a gateway to an even larger section of the Vassar community. Always changing and expanding, the groups cover areas from the literary (*Helicon, Miscellany News, Spectator*) and performing arts (*a cappella*, drama, film, photography, radio) to ethnic (Asian Student Alliance, Black Student Union, Poder Latino) and cultural groups (Feminist Majority Leadership Alliance, Queer Coalition) and from politics (Student Activist Union, Students for a Free Tibet) and traditional student government (Vassar Student Association [VSA]) to activities (hiking, juggling, snowboarding) and service (EMS, Listening Center). If nothing appeals to you, ask around before submitting a proposal to the VSA; chances are, someone else shares your interest.

Athletics

Over the past decade, Vassar's athletic program has grown and flourished. A Division III school, the college has twenty-five varsity teams (thirteen for women and twelve for men), as well as a variety of club sports and intramural leagues.

Recently renovated and expanded, Walker Field House encompasses a 42,250-square-foot floor space with a new tennis/multipurpose playing surface, six-lane Olympic-size swimming pool and diving well, and a sports medicine area. An adjoining 53,000-square-foot athletic facility has a wood-floor gymnasium, elevated running track, and 5,000-square-foot fitness space. In addition, a new dance studio and dance theater, golf course, outdoor tennis courts, and a multitude of fields are available for sporting and recreational play.

On-campus Entertainment

Vassar has given over more space than ever to students, providing them with further choices for their leisure hours. The restored second floor of the Students' Building has become a place for students to lounge around on couches and to congregate for special campus-wide events and activities. Another recent addition, the Atrium Juice Bar, serves gourmet food and drinks at the Athletics and Fitness Center. These new recreational centers join an old favorite, the College Center, in entertaining students.

Located in Main Building, the College Center is, as the name suggests, fundamental to Vassar life. Nearly everyone passes through at least once a day to look in their mailbox, buy a textbook or a burgundy-and-gray T-shirt from the bookstore, check e-mail at a computer terminal, grab a quick Starbucks coffee from the Kiosk and a snack from the Retreat before running off to class, get $20 from the ATM to pay for that beer (if you're—ahem—legal) at the campus pub, Matthew's Mug, or enjoy a laugh with friends while people watching outside.

The various campus groups and organizations are always good for entertainment as well. Any day or night of the week, a student can go to a play or a film, attend a Wyclef Jean or a Dar Williams concert, listen to a guest lecture by Tom Hanks or Robert F. Kennedy, Jr., check out an exhibit at the Frances Lehman Loeb Art Center, take a walk around Sunset Lake, cheer for the Brewers at a soccer game or tennis match, and much more.

Or you could even venture off-campus.... .

Off-campus Entertainment

Although possible to keep a car on campus, many students don't. Fortunately, the immediate area around Vassar has become increasingly college-friendly in the last few years, especially as many merchants now accept Vassar debit accounts. Cafés and ethnic restaurants have sprung up within walking distance, complementing student favorites: Baby Cakes bakery, Juliet Café and Billiards restaurant, and Three Arts bookstore. Standbys such as the Acropolis Diner and The Dutch Cabin remain almost extensions of the school. In addition, hourly shuttles on the weekends go to the Galleria Mall.

For those lucky enough to have a car (or know someone who does), any of the towns around the Hudson Valley make for a good day trip. Hyde Park has the Franklin D. Roosevelt Presidential Library, but the town's constant stream of visitors has as much to do with the Culinary Institute of America, the perfect place for a celebratory meal. (Around Commencement, see how many of your fellow diners you know.) Small and artsy, Rhinebeck has eclectic shops, good food, and a tiny yet great independent cinema. And, just across the Hudson River are the Catskill Mountains, the Shawangunks (best climbing on the East Coast), and the infamous village of Woodstock.

Want to inject a little more urban energy into upstate living? Farther afield but no less exciting lies New York City, a mere hour and 3/4 away by train. The Hudson line of the Metro North Railroad begins in Poughkeepsie and ends in Manhattan's Grand Central Station, so there's no fear of sleeping through a connection. Not that you'd want to: for an average of $25, the round-trip journey provides an amazing scenic glimpse of the Hudson Valley. Once in Manhattan, take advantage of the cultural scene: museums, Broadway plays, bars, restaurants, and shopping.

FINANCIAL AID

Though many stereotype Vassar as a rich kid's domain, fifty-five percent of its students receive financial aid and fifty percent are awarded need-based scholarships. Committed to providing education to qualified students regardless of financial circumstance, Vassar awards more than $25 million annually in scholarships in addition to federal and state aid. Vassar meets one hundred percent of the demonstrated need of all admitted students.

Financial aid packages can include government and other non-Vassar grants or scholarships, loans, campus jobs, and Vassar scholarships. The standard package for freshmen who demonstrate need after outside grants and scholarships includes a Stafford Loan and a campus job allocation. Students with need that exceeds these resources receive a Vassar scholarship to cover the full extent of their calculated financial need. The average total financial aid award to first-year students in 2006 was $28,891. The Office of Student Employment gives financial aid students first priority for job placements, which range from academic or administrative office work to campus security.

Deadlines for financial aid play a significant role in receiving a package, as Vassar must review a large number of aid applications every year. Apply as early as possible, regardless of acceptance notification. The deadline for freshman financial aid applications, complete with the PROFILE and FAFSA, is February 1, with notification of aid decisions in early April.

GRADUATES

It's a (hopefully) sunny day in late May. You've moved the tassel to the other side, accepted the diploma, tossed the mortarboard in the air, and completed the final walk out of the Amphitheater. Now what?

In a typical Vassar graduating class, seventy-one percent of graduates will have employment, while another twenty percent will enter graduate school within six months of commencement. How do you figure out which one you will be? Vassar is there to help.

Within five years of graduation, approximately eighty percent of Vassar graduates opt for graduate or professional school. The Office for Fellowship and Preprofessional Advising assists current students and alumnae/i as they apply to graduate, medical, law, and business schools. They also help students compete for fellowships, grants, prizes, and scholarships awarded by foundations, organizations, and schools, as well as for the $150,000 in graduate fellowships awarded annually by Vassar itself. Graduates consistently win Fulbrights, Mellons, National Science Foundation grants, Rhodes, Watsons, and more.

A leader in producing doctoral candidates, Vassar also has graduates accepted regularly at top-ranked schools of medicine, law, business, and edu-

PROMINENT GRADS

- Ellen Swallow Richards, 1870, Founder of Ecology
- Crystal Eastman, '03, Coauthor of the Equal Rights Amendment
- Edna St. Vincent Millay, '17, Pulitzer Prize-winning Poet
- Mary Steichen Calderone, '25, "Grandmother" of Sex Education
- Rear Admiral Grace Murray Hopper, '28, Inventor of the Compiler and Coinventor of the Computer Language COBOL
- Mary McCarthy, '33, Pulitzer Prize-winning Author
- Elizabeth Bishop, '34, Pulitzer Prize-winning Poet
- Vera Cooper Rubin, '48, Senior Astronomer at the Carnegie Institute's Department of Terrestrial Magnetism, Discoverer of "Dark Matter"
- Mary Oliver, '54, Pulitzer Prize-winning Poet
- Elizabeth Titus-Putnam, '55, Founder of the Student Conservation Association
- Sau Lan Wu, '63, High-Energy Particle Physicist, Codiscoverer of Gluon
- Geraldine Laybourne, '69, Creator of *Nickelodeon* and *Nick at Nite,* President of Oxygen Media, Inc.
- Meryl Streep, '71, Academy Award-winning Actress
- Jane Smiley, '71, Pulitzer Prize-winning Author
- Paula Madison, '74, President and General Manager of KNBC-TV in Los Angeles

- Richard W. Roberts, '74, U.S. Federal District Judge, District of Columbia
- Geraldine Laybourne, '69, President and CEO, Oxygen Media
- Eben Ostby, '77, Technical Academy Award-winner for *A Bug's Life*
- Lloyd Braun, '80, Concept Developer of *The Sopranos* and *Desperate Housewives,* now Head of Media and Entertainment at Yahoo
- John Carlstrom, '81, MacArthur Fellow and Astrophysicist, Codesigner of D.A.S.I. (Degree Angular Scale Interferometer) at the South Pole
- Lisa Kudrow, '85, Costar of *Friends* and star of "The Comeback"
- John Gatins, '90, Screenwriter and Director of *Dreamer*
- Stacy London, '91, Fashion Guru, Costar of *What Not To Wear*
- Noah Baumbach, '91, Director and Screenwriter, *The Squid and the Whale*
- Adam Green, '95, Founder of Rocking the Boat
- Ethan Zohn, '96, *Survivor: Africa* Winner and Cofounder of Grassroot Soccer
- Jessi Klein, '97, named "Best Female Stand Up in 2003" by "Emerging Comics of New York"

cation at rates significantly higher than the national average. In 2003, medical schools accepted seventy-eight percent of Vassar seniors who applied, as opposed to the national average of fifty percent; graduates have gone on to Columbia, Stanford, University of Pennsylvania, University of Chicago, and Yale. Law schools took ninety percent of Vassar applicants in 2003; among these schools were Columbia, Georgetown, Harvard, NYU, Stanford, and UCLA.

Careers

Not interested in more school? Try the Office of Career Development. Beginning in freshman year and continuing beyond graduation, Career Development offers a number of services, programs, and resources to help students navigate the job market. There's no need to have a career plan in mind; the office welcomes anyone who needs assistance. It provides help with anything from deciding on a major to working on résumés and interview skills. They can arrange for an internship for credit through the Office of Field Work or a "shadowing" opportunity through the Previews Program or facilitate a connection between students and employers through on- and off-campus job recruitment. Perhaps its most valuable resource is the Career Advisory Program (CAP), a database of more than 8,000 alumnae/i who have volunteered to give advice on finding jobs and internships in specific fields to current students and graduates.

Just as the smallness of the student body creates a sense of community, Vassar's alumnae/i association, the AAVC, maintains this feeling after graduation through class reunions, regional clubs, and groups. However, even without the 34,000-member-strong organization, you can go anywhere in the world knowing that, inevitably, there will be a fellow Vassar alum not far away.

> *A couple of years ago, I went to England for a vacation. I'd been in the country for all of five minutes, when I spotted a guy I'd known from a bunch of my classes at the other end of the customs line!*

SUMMING UP

> *What you can take away from Vassar is a taste for excellence that needn't diminish.*

—*Meryl Streep, '71, commencement speech to the Class of 1983*

When I think of my time in college, it reminds me of a photo montage where tiny images take shape into a larger one—thousands of memories forming a unique Vassar experience. Of course, some stand out more than others: certain classes and professors, thesis, friends. Probably most people say the same of their college years. Maybe they've had similar experiences—sneaking into the faculty lounge at midnight and cleaning out the fridge, films at professors' homes, potato peeling on our front stoop, tossing texts out a window postexam—but mine have that goofy nostalgia that hits all Vassar alums. Having expected to miss the old alma mater in a jaded, ironic sort of way, we find ourselves looking back with this golden, idyllic *Brideshead Revisited—This Side of Paradise* feeling.

Academically and culturally, Vassar's fearlessness, integrity, and strength contribute to its deserved standing as one of the finest colleges in the world. Yet its ability to forge such loyalty and respect in all its students can't be dismissed out of hand. As early as the application process, Vassar sees us not only as students, but also as individuals; in return, we regard it not only as a school, but also as a home.

❑ *Kelley Kawano, B.A.*

WAKE FOREST UNIVERSITY

✉ **Wake Forest University**
Winston-Salem, NC 27109

☎ (336) 758-5201

🌐 E-mail: *admissions@wfu.edu*
Web site: *http://www.wfu.edu*

🚹🚺 **Enrollment**

Full-time ❏ women: 2,160
❏ men: 2,076

Part-time ❏ women: 36
❏ men: 60

INTRODUCING WAKE FOREST UNIVERSITY

Wake Forest is a small, liberal arts institution that offers the resources of a much larger university. The school boasts thirty-seven majors, study-abroad programs in five continents, three libraries with nearly 1.8 million volumes, and big-time Atlantic Coast Conference sports, but the average undergraduate class size is just nineteen and professors almost always know all their students' names. Only a handful of classes are taught by graduate students, and large lecture halls are virtually nonexistent. Faculty members are very committed both to teaching and getting to know their students. Though many faculty members have also conducted outstanding research, their focus is clearly on undergraduates.

The university has more than 4,200 undergraduate students. While long-considered a respected regional institution, the school has gained national recognition in the last twenty-five years, hovering in or near the top twenty-five in major college rankings and cranking out eleven Rhodes Scholars over the last twenty years. Though the private school tuition can be steep for many families, the school has a broad merit scholarships program, attracting top students from around the country with partial and full scholarships for academic achievement, leadership, and distinction in the performing arts.

The campus is set on 340-acres in Winston-Salem, N C, on the edge of the foothills of the Blue Ridge Mountains. The campus is a roughly fifteen-minute walk from end to end, and students won't make it across without running into a few familiar faces. Most students live on campus all four years, shaping a close-knit and friendly community. The campus has been recognized as one of the most beautiful in the country. In the spring, it teems with daffodils and flowering dogwoods; in the fall, students enjoy warm afternoons under the changing leaves of ash trees on the main quad. Wait Chapel, which has hosted two presidential debates, most recently in 2000, anchors the campus.

The university was founded by the Baptist State Convention of North Carolina in 1834, but cut formal ties to the convention in 1986. Though the school is more than 170 years old, the Georgian-style campus just celebrated its fiftieth anniversary. The university was founded in Wake County, North Carolina, about two hours east of its present location, but opened in Winston-Salem in 1956 on land donated by the Reynolds family (of tobacco company fame) and with money from a family foundation.

Winston-Salem is a city of about 227,000. The downtown, about four miles from campus, has undergone a rebirth over the last five years and now hosts an annual film festival, monthly art gallery hops, and a warm-weather outdoor concert series with performances three nights a week. Old tobacco warehouses are being renovated as loft apartments, and with the addition of new bars and restaurants, downtown's nightlife is growing. The city is home to five other colleges, among them Winston-Salem State University and the North Carolina School of the Arts, and is home to the headquarters of Reynolds American, Sara Lee, Hanes, and Krispy Kreme. The city is less than a forty-five-minute drive from two state parks that offer great trails for day-hikers and gorgeous views of the North Carolina Piedmont.

The university's motto is *Pro Humanitate*, and this is emphasized throughout campus life. Most students do some kind of volunteer service, whether it's providing English as a Second Language, tutoring at a local elementary school, or working at an AIDS hospice. The university sponsors several service trips over the winter break, sending students to work with the destitute and dying in Calcutta and to build schools in Vietnam. The university also sponsors "Project Pumpkin," which brings more than 1,500 children from community agencies to campus to trick-or-treat in residence halls and play festival games with costumed undergrads.

Other campus traditions include the Lovefeast, a candlelit Christmas service grounded in the area's Moravian traditions and held annually in Wait Chapel, and "Rolling the Quad," a postgame celebration for big athletic wins that involves covering the quad's trees in toilet paper and leaves nearby dorms woefully undersupplied for the remainder of the weekend following Saturday victories. During exam weeks, faculty and staff take to the kitchens of a campus dining hall to serve a late night breakfast of pancakes and scrambled eggs to weary students, even carrying their trays for them as they wait in line.

ADMISSIONS REQUIREMENTS

Admission to Wake Forest has become increasingly competitive. Applications jumped by more than nineteen percent from 2004–2005 to 2005–2006. Of the 7,500 students who applied for fall 2006 admission, about thirty-eight percent were accepted. The middle fifty percent of students scored from 1280 to 1400 on the SAT I, and thirty-five percent of current freshmen were in the top five percent of their high school class.

The 2006 entering class of 1,126 students hailed from forty-four different states and fourteen foreign countries. Twenty-three percent of the entering class was from North Carolina, with New Jersey, Pennsylvania, New York, and Virginia rounding out the most represented states. Increasing the racial and ethnic diversity has been a priority for the admissions office, and the 2006 class had the highest ever number of minority students at seventeen percent. *Black Enterprise* magazine ranked Wake Forest twenty-second on its 2006 list of "50 Top Colleges for African Americans."

Director of Undergraduate Admissions Martha Allman said students seeking admission to Wake Forest should take the most strenuous curriculum available that they can manage. "Bloom where you're planted," she said. In addition to SAT scores and class rankings, the admissions office looks at an applicant's recommendations, leadership record, and enrollment in Advanced Placement or honor courses. They also make heavy use of essays and short-answer questions on the admissions application. Students must write two essays and respond to short-answer prompts like "What outrages you?" and "Describe yourself in fifty words or less." "We're looking for students who look outside themselves," Allman said. "The student who is tuned into what is going on around them, the student who is interested in many things. We are looking at students who are compassionate [and] students who have done community service, and not just as a resume builder." The university began accepting ACT scores for the first time for the fall 2006 class.

The university accepts the Common Application, though a supplement is required. Early Decision applications require an early decision agreement and must be received by November 15. The Regular Admission deadline is January 15, though students who want to be considered for the university's most generous scholarships should submit their applications, as well as a separate scholarship application, by December 1. Several of the merit-based scholarships also require an on-campus interview for finalists. Though not required, Allman said she encourages other students to set up interviews as well.

Finally, Allman offers this piece of advice to students: Don't spread yourselves too thin. "I think there has been a push to talk about well roundedness of students and that has caused high school students to think, 'I have to play four sports, and I have to be in orchestra, and I have to be in all these clubs.'" she said. "Your first priority should be your school work, then pick a few things that you really enjoy, that you're really good at, and spend your extracurricular time there. Don't just resume build."

ACADEMIC LIFE

Students not-so-affectionately refer to the university as "Work Forest." Classes are small, most range from about ten to thirty students, so professors expect a lot and notice when you don't show up. Most are strict about attendance and expect participation, and professors, not graduate students, teach every class. The ten-to-one student-to-faculty ratio means professors have time for individual students. With the exception of some introductory science and communication classes, professors will be the ones grading your papers. Professors have scheduled office hours, but most have open-door policies where students are free to stop by any time. Faculty members, of whom eighty-nine percent hold Ph.D.s, enjoy teaching, and undergraduates get the kind of personal attention that only graduate students may get at larger universities. Expect a few invitations to dinner at professors' houses.

Curriculum

The backbone of a Wake Forest degree is a liberal arts curriculum, and students are required to take a broad range of courses in the humanities and sciences. Among the

---

requirements are courses in a foreign language, fine arts and literature, as well as classes in mathematics or the natural sciences and two courses in health and exercise. All freshmen are required to take a freshman seminar, a small class that covers topics like the analytical methods of Sherlock Holmes, the rise of the computer game culture, and the intent and interpretations of the Bill of Rights. Most students complete the liberal arts requirements in their first two years, spending their junior and senior years on electives and courses for their majors and minors.

For students unsure of what they'd like to study, the required classes provide a chance to explore existing interests or discover new ones. Michelle Sikes, a 2007 graduate and the university's most recent Rhodes Scholar, called the liberal arts curriculum one of the university's strongest points. Sikes chose her mathematical-economics major after taking an economics course to satisfy one of the liberal arts requirements. She said she'd always loved math, and in economics she found "a way to use math that was helpful and applicable to the real world."

Wake has such a broad curriculum that they make you take that you really have to be able to do well in everything from science and math to reading and writing in foreign languages.

—*Michelle Sikes, '2007, Rhodes Scholar*

The student who comes to Wake Forest intent on applying to medical school may very well end up a biology major, or he or she might switch tracks to philosophy after discovering a love of Rousseau in a required course.

Students can earn a B.A. or B.S. in thirty-seven majors. The most popular are communication, business, psychology, political science, biology, economics, and English. The university also offers thirty-one minors, plus an additional nineteen interdisciplinary minors in areas like cultural resource preservation, Latin-American studies, neuroscience, and health policy and administration. Professors welcome suggestions for new minors or courses of study. Students can apply to the Calloway School of Business and Accountancy in the spring of their sophomore year. The school offers majors in accounting, business, finance, and mathematical business. Accounting students can earn their bachelor's and master's in accounting in five years, and the program's graduates have ranked either first or second in the nation for the highest pass rate on the CPA exam over the last five years. The Calloway School was ranked seventeenth on *Business Week* magazine's list of top fifty undergraduate business schools.

The Calloway School of Business and Accountancy moved into a new 57,000-square-foot facility in 2004. The Kirby Hall, home to the Calloway Center of Business, Mathematics and Computer Science, was a $14 million project, which added an entirely new building connected to what is known as West Hall. In addition to Calloway, the building also houses mathematics, computer science, and the Center for Undergraduate Entrepreneurship. Motivated students can graduate with honors in their major by writing a thesis or completing an independent project. Wake Forest also gives students the opportunities and the funding to do research or complete independent projects at home or abroad over the summer. Recent projects have involved working on women's health issues in Peru, researching religious sites in India, and completing an internship at Florida's Dolphin Research Center. The university has also begun a Washington, DC, program that allows students to earn credit while interning and living in the nation's capital for a semester.

Study Abroad

Wake Forest strongly encourages its students to spend a semester or a summer exploring another part of the world. About sixty percent of Wake Forest students study abroad, placing the school fourth among major universities according to the 2006 Open Doors report from the Institute of International Education. The university owns houses in the Hampstead neighborhood of London, on the Grand Canal in Venice, and in the Nineteenth District of Vienna. In these programs, a university professor, and often his or her family, lives with a group of students who are taught two classes by the Wake Forest professor and two by native professors. The programs have a four-day-a-week class schedule and a two-week mid-semester break, leaving plenty of time for travel within the host country or beyond. Wake Forest also has exchange programs with universities in Dijon, France; Salamanca, Spain; and Beijing, China. For those who don't want to spend a full semester abroad, summer study opportunities include a cultural anthropology program in Nepal, Arabic courses in Morocco, and an opportunity to learn about tropical diversity in Peru. Students may also choose to study with a program that is not affiliated with Wake Forest and then transfer the credits earned. The Center for International Studies provides excellent assistance in helping students find the programs that are right for them, as well as work out the logistics of transferring credits or carrying financial aid abroad. It also offers study-abroad scholarships that can be applied to travel or other expenses.

I sat on the lush grass of Regent Park's Primrose Hill and gazed at the central London skyline in the distance. Not a bad place to study for a few hours, I thought.

I spent four months at Wake Forest's Worrell House over a spring semester. Fifteen students, along with a professor and her family, shared the four-story home at the edge of London's Hampstead neighborhood.

Our theater course, a standard for every group that studies at Worrell House, included performances each week in London's West End theater district, oftentimes with some of the best seats in the house. We also took in shows by the Royal Shakespeare Company on a class trip to Stratford-upon-Avon and toured the New Globe Theatre in London.

An art class brought weekly lectures from the director of one of the world's largest collections of British art with separate trips to London's galleries led by another professor. Our political science courses took us through the halls of Parliament and into London's courtrooms.

The four-day-a-week class schedule left time for weekend trips to places like Edinburgh, Bath, Cardiff, and Paris, and my two-week spring break spanned four countries. I rowed a boat around a lake in Madrid's El Parque del Retiro, went to a Mass led by the Pope in Rome, and woke up from an overnight train ride with a view of the sun rising over the Mediterranean Sea.

When I flew to London, it was the first time I'd ever been on a plane. I returned four months later with plenty of stamps in my passport and a new view of the world.

Technology

All students receive a laptop computer with a CD burner and DVD player as well as an all-in-one color printer/scanner/copier as part of their tuition. At the beginning of the junior year, each student trades in the old laptop for an upgraded model and keeps that computer upon graduation. In addition to the university's professionally staffed computer helpline, Resident Technology Advisors, computer-savvy students trained to address any problems with the laptops are available in each dorm. Students can access the Internet from almost anywhere on campus, twenty-four hours a day via the campus-wide, high-speed, wireless network.

SOCIAL LIFE AND ACTIVITIES

Wake Forest is tucked into a suburban area of the city, so there are few off-campus entertainment options that students can walk to. As such, most of the university's social activities are centered on campus. The Greek system is a major part of campus life; about thirty-three percent of men are affiliated with a fraternity, and fifty-three percent of women are affiliated with a sorority. The Greek system is very integrated into the campus as a whole. Students who choose to live with their fraternity or sorority members do so in blocks of on-campus housing rather than in mansions tagged with Greek letters, and many members choose not to live with their organizations at all. On weekend nights, Greek groups sponsor parties open to all students in their lounges, and students can hop back and forth across the quad from one party to another.

The campus provides plenty of cultural options, both student-produced and professional. There is rarely a night when there isn't a play, concert, poetry reading, or lecture to attend. The Secrest Artists Series brings internationally renowned performers like violin virtuoso Itzhak Perlman, mezzo-soprano Denyce Graves, and Doc Severinsen and his Big Band to campus, with free tickets for students. Student Union draws popular big-name acts to Wait Chapel, with past performers including Dave Matthews, Guster, Nickel Creek, Ben Folds, and comedians Lewis Black, Adam Sandler, and Kevin Nealon. There are student-produced plays, a cappella concerts, ethnic festivals, discounted movie screenings, and art gallery exhibitions. Several times a year, the Lilting Banshees campus comedy troupe mocks Wake Forest life in its midnight sketch-comedy shows.

CAMPUS TRADITIONS

Rolling the Quad: After major athletic victories, students and sometimes faculty and staff send rolls of toilet paper flying over the ash trees of the university's main quad. Billowing toilet paper never looked so beautiful.

Project Pumpkin: This annual volunteer event brings more than 1,500 children from community agencies to trick-or-treat in dorm rooms and play games set up in residence hall lounges and across the quad. Most undergraduate students dress up to join in the festivities.

Lovefeast: This candle lit service in Wait Chapel honors the area's Moravian heritage and tradition. Students and community members sing carols and partake in the traditional feast of sweet buns and coffee.

Brain Piccolo Cancer Fund Drive: Student groups raise money for the Comprehensive Cancer Center of Wake Forest University in honor of Piccolo, a former Wake Forest football player and member of the Chicago Bears whose friendship with African-American teammate Gale Sayers and death from cancer at the age of twenty-six inspired the movie *Brian's Song*. Through events like Dance-A-Thons, races, and silent auctions, Greek groups raise more than $50,000 annually for the fund.

The white lights of luminaries lined the quad, right up to the steps of Wait Chapel where a bright Moravian star hung above. Inside, students and Winston-Salem residents were gathering for the annual Lovefeast, a Christmas celebration honoring the area's Moravian heritage.

Wake Forest's Lovefeast began in 1965 and has become the largest in North America. There was something about the simple beauty of this service that brought me back every year.

Servers, who might be classmates or your professors, passed out sweet buns and coffee to the more than 2,000 people who packed the chapel.

The chapel was darkened as the choir led carols. Each worshipper held a beeswax candle. A single flame became thousands as it was passed from candle to candle, across each row, then back to the next. It sometimes gave me goosebumps.

For the final carol, "Joy to the World," everyone held their candles high, thousands of tiny points of light brightening the darkness and warming the soul.

North Carolina's mild climate means that lots of campus socializing happens outdoors. In warm weather, which is really all but a few months of the year, students hang out on the university's main quad or on nearby Davis Field, where wooden swings hang from tree branches. Reynolda Gardens, just a short path through the woods away from campus, offers study spots in the formal garden and nearby fields. The garden's running trails are heavily used by the health-conscious student body. Students are also free to use the campus track, tennis courts, indoor and outdoor basketball courts, and pool. There are also several sand volleyball courts scattered around campus. The Miller Center offers weights and cardiovascular machines, and for a small fee students can attend an unlimited number of aerobics, yoga, spinning, and other classes. The university's campus recreation department opened the university's first climbing wall for students, faculty and staff in Reynolds Gymnasium.

Off campus, the city's Borders and Barnes and Noble bookstores are favorite study spots. Fourth Street, downtown's main drag, offers dining options ranging from pizza to Thai food to brewery fare and boasts an occasional independent film series. Trade Street has become a funky arts destination, with its gallery hops and concert series. The city has a number of local theater companies and also began hosting the River Run International Film Festival, an annual film festival, several years ago. Ziggy's, less than a mile from campus, brings in local and national music acts. For upperclassmen, bars in the city's West End and on Burke Street are popular hangouts. Hanes Mall, about a fifteen-minute drive from campus, houses many familiar national retail chains. There are easy day-trips to several state parks with great hiking. For security, gates at the campus's vehicle entranceways close at 10 P.M. every night, though students, faculty, and staff with parking passes can come and go freely at all hours. Visitors must register with guards at the two gatehouses.

Housing and Dining

More than seventy percent of students live on campus. The university guarantees housing for eight semesters, and students are required to live on campus for their first two years. Upperclassmen wishing to live off campus must apply to do so, but many choose to stay on campus in apartment-style housing. Polo Residence Hall, which opened in 1998, consists of townhouse-style apartments. In four-person units, each student gets his or her own bedroom and shares a kitchen, living room, and two bathrooms. Two-person apartments have a single bedroom, a living area, bathroom, and kitchenette. Student apartments are older but provide two-person units with two bedrooms and a shared bathroom, kitchenette, and living area surrounding a courtyard. Upperclassmen are usually also able to secure single rooms in suites on the quad. Housing for underclassmen is hall or suite-style, with most students in double-occupancy rooms. All rooms are air-conditioned and all the university's dorms are co-educational. First-year students have the option of living in Johnson Hall, a substance-free residence hall in which students have agreed to refrain from smoking and alcohol use.

Groups of students may also apply for Theme Housing within the university's residence halls or in university-owned houses across the street from campus. Theme Housing is aimed at allowing students with common educational or extracurricular interests to live together. Current themes include acting, physical fitness, environmentally friendly living, tolerance, and technology. Groups interested in applying for Theme Housing must have a mission statement and a plan for how their theme house will benefit the university and community. For those students who do want to live off campus, there are plenty of apartment complexes a short drive from the university and off-campus housing is generally inexpensive, unlike that of major college towns. There are also rental homes available along streets adjacent to campus.

All students who live on campus must have a meal plan; options vary by class standing and residence hall. The university's main dining hall was recently renovated. Its official name is The Fresh Food Company, but students know the sunken dining hall as "The Pit." Offerings there include fresh salads and deli sandwiches, Italian dishes, burgers and hot subs off the grill, fresh ethnic entrees, and traditional Southern favorites. The Benson University Center offers Pizza Hut, Chick-fil-A, and Panera bagels. Benson is also home to Shorty's, a campus pub of sorts that offers Starbucks coffee and, for students twenty-one and over, beer on tap. It is a fun place to watch a game and often hosts student musicians. The Magnolia Room, open for lunch on weekdays, offers buffet-style dining with white tablecloths, cloth napkins, and great views. It's a great place to meet friends for a leisurely lunch between classes and serves some of the best sweet tea around. Other campus dining options include a Subway, a small food court near the Worrell Professional Center, and a convenience store for students who want to do some cooking of their own.

Clubs and Organizations

There are 125 on-campus organizations, from Gospel Choir to Aviation Club to men's and women's Ultimate Frisbee teams, to cater to students with varied interests. There are a range of religious groups, with several offering on-campus services, and a cappella groups of all stripes. The Volunteer Service Corps sponsors outreach programs and can help match students up with local agencies. It also sponsors international service trips over winter break and domestic spring break trips in which students have helped with environmental clean-up and worked in homeless shelters. Intramural sports are also popular, with twenty sports for men and sixteen for women. The student-run newspaper, *The Old Gold and Black*, comes out every Thursday and has won several national awards. Students also publish *The Howler* yearbook, several literary and poetry magazines, and a journal of scholarly essays. If there isn't a group that suits your interest, start one yourself. Student Government handles all budget requests for student organizations and decides how the money is doled out.

Athletics

Wake Forest is the smallest school in the Atlantic Coast Conference and the third smallest school in the country to field a Division I football team, but its sports programs have enjoyed huge success. The school's basketball team, which has cranked out NBA stars like Josh Howard, Tim Duncan, and Chris Paul, has often been ranked in the top twenty-five. The golf program has turned out stars like Arnold Palmer, Curtis Strange, and Jay Haas and has earned three national championships. The football team finished the 2006 season as ACC Champions, earning an appearance in the BCS Orange Bowl, which drew the largest gathering of alumni in Wake Forest history. The field hockey team won three consecutive national championships from 2002 to 2004 and played in the national championship title game in 2006. And both the men's and women's soccer teams finished their 2006 seasons in the top twenty-five. The university's 2006 fall sports success even attracted national attention, with *USA Today* recently profiling the athletics program under the headline "Tiny Wake Forest turns its size into an asset."

Students get free tickets to all home games. Fall brings tailgates and football at Groves Stadium, and winter brings the ACC basketball season, when fans clad in gold and black tie-dyes fill Lawrence Joel Memorial Coliseum to watch the Deacs take on the likes of Duke and UNC—Chapel Hill. Big athletic victories merit "Rolling the Quad," as students—and sometimes a few professors—cover the ash trees of the university's main lawn with long ribbons of white toilet paper. The university also prides itself on its high graduation rate for student athletes. Of Division I schools with football programs, Wake Forest has the best graduation rate in the nation at ninety-six percent.

> **SO WHAT IS DEMON DEACON ANYWAY?**
>
> **Wake Forest was originally known as the Tigers.**
> **By the 1920s, fans referred to Wake Forest as the "Baptists" or the "Old Gold & Black," the school colors.**
> **The editor of the student newspaper coined the nickname "Demon Deacons" in a 1923 article about a football game against Trinity (now Duke), noting Wake Forest's "devilish" play and fighting spirit.**

FINANCIAL AID

Wake Forest is part of a group of top schools committed to a need-blind admissions policy, meaning ability to pay is not considered when an admissions decision is made. Though Wake Forest has been recognized as a value among elite private schools, costs of attendance are still high. Sixty-three percent of undergraduates receive some type of financial assistance, with thirty-six percent receiving need-based aid. For the 2005–2006 academic year, students with need received an average of $17,300 in scholarship and grant funds. The university also offers work-study positions to help students cover the costs of attendance, and about thirty percent of undergraduates work part-time.

The university has a broad and generous merit scholarships program, with top scholarships covering the full costs of tuition and attendance, allowances for books and other needs, and summer grants for individual study projects. Some scholarships are awarded on the basis of pure merit, others consider merit with other factors, like whether the student is part of a historically underrepresented group or is a North Carolina resident. Other scholarships are awarded for outstanding leadership, entrepreneurship, written or oral communication skills, community service, or talent in the arts.

- A. R. Ammons, Poet
- Richard Burr, U.S. Senator
- James Cain, U.S. Ambassador to Denmark
- Evelyn "Pat" Foote, Retired Brigadier General, U.S. Army
- A1 Hunt, Managing Editor for Government Reporting, Bloomberg News
- Penelope Niven, Biographer
- Maria Henson, Pulitzer Prize-winning Journalist
- Billy Packer, Sports Commentator
- Lee Norris, Actor, *One Tree Hill*
- Arnold Palmer, Professional Golfer
- Brian Piccolo, Professional Football Player
- Tim Duncan, Professional Basketball Player
- Will D. Campbell, Author
- Marc Blucas, Actor, *First Daughter* and *The Alamo*
- Jim Perdue, Chairman, CEO, Perdue Farms
- Charles Ergen, Chairman, CEO, EchoStar
- Ken Thompson, Chairman, CEO, Wachovia
- Chris Paul, Professional Basketball Player
- Curtis Strange, Professional Golfer
- W. J. Cash, Author

In an average class, eighty-eight percent of students graduate in five years or less. Within six months of graduation about thirty percent of graduates are enrolled in graduate or professional school and sixty percent are employed. Advising is available for prelaw and premedical students. In a recent year, sixty-eight percent of those applying to medical school were accepted, more than twenty percentage points higher than the national average. About sixty percent of those applying to law schools were accepted.

For students deciding on potential career paths, the Office of Career Services provides a resource center packed with career information, an Alumni Career Assistance Program that hooks students up with alums employed in various professions, and helps in finding internships. For those actively searching for jobs or internships, the office helps students prepare by offering individual job search counseling, resume consultations, and mock interviews. Career Services also organizes on-campus job and graduate school fairs and recruiting opportunities and keeps a database of job openings. It also holds networking forums in several major cities across the country.

Many other students opt to spend a year or two after graduation in service. Programs like Teach for America and Americorps are particularly popular. The university ranked eleventh among schools with fewer than 5,000 undergraduates on the Peace Corps' 2006 list of top-producing colleges and universities. The university also has a program dedicated to helping current undergraduates or recent grads apply for postgraduate scholarship and fellowship programs, like the Rhodes, Truman, and Fulbright scholarships.

SUMMING UP

Wake Forest is a place with a strong sense of community where undergraduate students feel like they truly matter. Professors and staff really get to know the students here, and students often form lasting relationships with faculty members. Professors show up on more than a few wedding invitation lists of graduates. Motivated students can excel here and leave an impact. Past students founded a nonprofit organization that assists African hospitals, helped create new interdisciplinary minors, and started campus traditions like the Lovefeast and winter-break service trips. Academic coursework is rigorous but rewarding, and opportunities for students to push themselves intellectually are plentiful, from writing an honors thesis in your major to designing and receiving funding for a summer project. Professors are extremely accessible to undergraduates, and teaching remains the priority for faculty members.

One drawback of this small Southern school is that the student body tends to be somewhat racially homogenous. Though minority recruitment has been a priority for the admissions office and the school's minority population has been growing, the percentage of students who are part of minority racial or ethnic groups still hovers at fifteen percent. And although the university's suburban location is scenic, it can sometimes feel isolating, especially for students without a car. Winston-Salem provides plenty of entertainment options, but students have to drive, not walk, to just about all of them spread out across the city. If you're looking for a college town experience, Wake Forest is probably not the right place for you.

But if you're looking for a place where you'll have the amenities and resources of a large university without the feeling that you're part of a faceless crowd, give Wake Forest a good look. When you're sitting in the five-story windowed atrium of the Z. Smith Reynolds Library, cheering the Deacs on at an ACC basketball game, or mulling over the varied course offerings for the spring semester, you'll feel like you're at a much larger institution. But when you run into your freshman-year English professor just before graduation and he remembers not only your name, but your hometown, you'll realize you're at a place like few others. Under the magnolia trees and clear-blue Carolina sky, you'll find the best of both worlds here.

❏ *Lisa Hoppenjans, B.A.*

WASHINGTON AND LEE UNIVERSITY

 Washington and Lee University
Lexington, VA 24450

 Enrollment

 (540) 458-8710
Fax: (540) 458-8062

Full-time ❑ women: 866
❑ men: 877

 E-mail: *admissions@wlu.edu*
Web site: *http://www.wlu.edu*

Part-time ❑ women: 11
❑ men: 10

INTRODUCING WASHINGTON AND LEE

On a crisp fall afternoon in Virginia, students walk up the grassy slope to Washington and Lee's colonnade, rows of white columns that define the face of the campus's red brick buildings. The students walk in the shadows of the columns and climb the worn steps of Payne Hall. Just inside their classroom is a bronze plaque commemorating the space where General Robert E. Lee took his oath of office as president of the school in 1865. The open windows frame more students passing along the back campus. Some enter Leyburn Library, a wide complex of concrete and brick. Others open the doors to the Great Hall of the Science Center;

vaulted, sky-lit ceilings expose balconies for each of the floors above, where more students move to and from completely modern classrooms and laboratories.

As these students cross Washington and Lee University's picturesque campus, they see its balance of the old and the new—traditions and changes. Founded in 1749, the university boasts a long and rich history. The school won critical support in 1796 when George Washington donated $20,000 to its endowment. (Washington's gift was the largest ever made to a private American school at the time, and the sum continues to pay a portion of every student's tuition.) The school was known as Washington College at the end of the Civil War, when Robert E. Lee assumed its presidency. Lee led the college through far-reaching changes until his death in 1870. Washington and Lee students cherish Lee for his educational reforms: joining the college with a local law school, instituting classes in business and economics, creating the first college-level journalism program, and establishing the seeds of the student-governed Honor System. Those century-old innovations are now traditions that make Washington and Lee the fine liberal arts institution it is today. The university maintains these traditions and follows Lee's example, always initiating change. The last decade has witnessed additions to the curriculum, complete revitalization of the fraternity system, and construction of new facilities for the fine arts, athletics, and the sciences. A new fitness center opened in Fall 2002, along with the newly renovated journalism school, and the new John W. Elrod University Commons opened in Fall 2003. The year 2006 saw the inaugural season of Wilson Hall, the new music and art facility.

Students at Washington and Lee call their school "W&L," and their love for W&L is as loyal as their love for Lee. One former student admits:

> *I called home crying a few times during my freshman year because I was so grateful to my parents for giving me the opportunity to come to W&L.*

National surveys routinely rank W&L students among the happiest in the country. When naming what makes them happy, every student generation names the same strong traditions: a small student body of 1,770 that is truly a community, intimate classes averaging around sixteen students, a faculty dedicated to students and to teaching, and an Honor System that creates a society of trust where no student will lie, cheat, or steal.

The small town of Lexington, Virginia forms the backdrop for all of this student bliss. Although only 7,000 residents live in Lexington year-round, students from Washington and Lee and its neighbor, the Virginia Military Institute, add substantially to the town's true population. (The two schools add much to the town through their cultural and athletic programs as well.) One politics major notes:

> *The scenic, safe surroundings have allowed me to make W&L a home away from home, to enjoy the college experience without the worries and distractions of a big school or a big city.*

W&L students become active citizens of Lexington as "big brothers" or "big sisters" to local youths, as coaches for Little League teams, as members of church congregations, and as participants in outreach groups such as Habitat for Humanity and the Nabors Service League.

Although all W&L students call Lexington "home," they journey from all corners of the United States to get there. Only fourteen percent of undergraduates hail from Virginia. Other well-represented states include Florida, Georgia, Maryland, New Jersey, New York, Pennsylvania, and Texas. It surprises many to learn that the student body includes nearly as many from California as from Kentucky or Connecticut. W&L truly has a national student body to match its national reputation. An intensified effort to recruit international students has resulted in attracting young men and women of nearly fifty citizenships.

ADMISSIONS REQUIREMENTS

Word is out—magazines rank W&L one of the nation's premiere liberal arts institutions year after year. Its academic reputation, small size, and pure beauty attract an increasing number of applicants with increasingly stronger credentials. Because space in Washington and Lee's student body is limited, gaining admittance to the university has become increasingly difficult.

A glance at Washington and Lee's admissions statistics confirms just how selective the school has become. Of the 4,215 students who applied for admission into a recent class, only 1,150 were admitted, yielding a freshman class of 450 (228 men, 222 women). These enrolling students achieved remarkable scores on their standardized tests. The middle fifty percent range of their SAT scores spanned 1330–1450; the same range of ACT scores was 28–31. These freshmen earned an average rank in class above ninety-three percent of their high school classmates. Forty-five were valedictorians or salutatorians; thirty-seven were National Merit Scholars or Finalists.

These facts certainly portray W&L's selectivity, but they do not illustrate the great care that its Admissions Office takes in reviewing all applications. Washington and Lee believes that the high school record is the surest sign of a student's potential for success in college. Admissions officers read every student's transcript, weighing grades against the difficulty of the curriculum. Successful applicants typically have strong grades in rigorous college-preparatory or Advanced Placement classes. Standardized tests are used as a uniform measurement in comparing students who often come from schools with drastically different curricula and grading scales. W&L also strives to evaluate each student's character and personality through essays and recommendations. In hopes of finding future members of the school's athletic teams, cultural groups, and student committees, W&L's Admissions Office further judges applicants by their extracurricular pursuits.

Interviews

Proof of Washington and Lee's genuine interest in getting to know applicants lies in the fact that it continues to offer personal interviews. Interviews and student-guided tours may be scheduled by calling the Admissions Office. For students who cannot travel to Lexington for a meeting with an admissions officer, interviews with alumni admissions program representatives are available in most major cities in the United States (*http://admissions.wlu.edu/app*).

Requirements

W&L's admissions requirements are clear and straightforward. Applicants must submit the Common Application (*www.commonapp.org*), or they may use W&L's own paper forms. Those using W&L's paper application should complete Part I of the application for admission, this preliminary application asks for biographical information. After receiving Part I from applicants, W&L then sends Part II of the application. It includes transcript forms, two teacher recommendation forms, and guidelines for the submission of supplemental information (including an essay). Applicants should submit the SAT or the ACT with its writing section, plus two SAT Subject Exams in different subjects. The Regular Decision deadline for submission of applications is January 15. Students can expect replies from Washington and Lee in early April. All application forms are available on-line at *http://admissions.wlu.edu*.

Early Decision

For students who want to attend Washington and Lee above all other schools, there are two binding Early Decision options. Early Decision applicants must acknowledge that Washington and Lee is their first choice and that they will attend if admitted. Early Decision applications are due by November 15 for Early Decision I or January 2 for Early Decision II. W&L delivers notice by December 22 for E.D. I or February 1 for E.D. II. Admitted students happily claim a coveted place in the freshman class. W&L defers consideration of those who are not admitted until the regular admissions process.

Another admissions deadline remains for applicants who want to vie for the university's many generous Honor Scholarships. These students complete an additional essay and submit their applications by December 15. W&L invites finalists to visit the campus during the late winter; the Admissions Office notifies scholarship recipients in early April.

ACADEMIC LIFE

Nothing shapes life at Washington and Lee more than its Honor System. The Honor System dates back to Lee's simple demand that all of his students act honorably. Today, a committee of elected students (known as the Executive Committee) administers the Honor System, informing freshmen of its guidelines and enforcing its principles. The system is built upon trust; it holds that students who lie, cheat, or steal are not trustworthy and, therefore, not welcome in the Washington and Lee community. For that reason, there is only one sanction for any student found guilty of an honor violation: permanent removal from the student body.

Because the Honor System works so well, Washington and Lee students enjoy freedoms that would be impossible at other universities. All academic buildings on the W&L campus, including the library, remain open twenty-four hours a day. Since professors trust that cheating will not occur, students take unproctored tests and exams. Students even schedule their own exams during week-long exam periods. It is possible that every student in an English class could take the same exam in a different place at a different time; students are trusted not to discuss the content of their exams with their classmates. These freedoms extend beyond the classroom as well.

I constantly leave money in my backpack right in the middle of campus without giving a moment's thought to its security.

Classes

If there is one thing that defines all colleges, it must be the classroom. Today, many college classrooms are cavernous, badly lit lecture halls. A professor or, more likely, a teaching assistant speaks through a microphone to hundreds of students seated in row after row of identical chairs. W&L defines the classroom differently. Its students enjoy small, intimate classes that are never taught by a graduate student or a teaching assistant. A large class at W&L might contain thirty-five students. Average classes number fourteen to seventeen. Many upperclassmen take seminar classes with fewer than ten other students. They all might sit around a single table with their professor, creating the kind of personal, in-depth interaction that is a W&L hallmark.

Professors

Small classes allow students to get to know their professors as people, and vice versa.

Teachers here seem to relish the opportunity to get to know the students, even if they realize that that particular student will only be taking that one class from them. Within your major, every professor knows you and begs you to take their classes. It's rather flattering.

An alumnus remembers similar experiences:

I never lost my awe of my professors, but I really came to rely on many of them as friends. Of course, that made the stakes higher. I always felt that I had to do my best work because I didn't want to disappoint them.

Professors keep long office hours so that they can meet with students outside of class. Most professors do not have strict attendance guidelines, but, because classes are so small, every student learns that an absence gets noticed. Although it may be unheard of at other universities, W&L students enjoy eating dinner occasionally at professors' homes.

Curriculum

Despite Washington and Lee's small size, the university offers a startlingly varied curriculum that a *Washington Post* article described as "the envy of many larger institutions." Committed to the ideal of a liberal arts education, W&L requires all students to meet general education requirements in composition; literature; a foreign language; the fine arts, history, philosophy, and religion; science and mathematics; the social sciences; and physical education. Most students meet these requirements by the end of their sophomore year. They spend their junior and senior years fulfilling a major course of study and exploring elective classes.

Students divide their time between the university's College of Arts and Sciences which includes the School of Journalism (or "J-School"), and the Ernest Williams II School of Commerce, Economics, and Politics (or "C-School"). W&L's broad curriculum allows it to offer majors in subjects not commonly taught in outer top colleges, such as accounting, business, engineering, East Asian languages and literature, geology, and neuroscience. Students may earn Bachelor of Arts or Bachelor of Science degrees, in addition to Bachelor of Science degrees with Special Attainments in Chemistry and Bachelor of Science degrees with Special Attainments in Commerce. The Shepherd Program for the Interdisciplinary Study of Poverty as well as the Society and the Professions Studies in Applied Ethics are among W&L's unique, crosscurricular courses of study, along with formal non-major programs in African American studies, environmental studies, global stewardship, and women's studies. Undergraduates also benefit from the presence of W&L's top-ranked school of law. Some law courses are open to undergrads, and most special events and guest lectures welcome them, as well.

Study Areas

W&L students spread all over the campus to study. Carrels in Leyburn Library may be reserved on the first day of classes. Confident in the Honor System, students leave texts and notebooks in their carrels for the entire school year. Other students study in the libraries located in the Science Center, Journalism School, or Commerce School. Because academic buildings stay open twenty-four hours a day, an occasional student may "pull an all-nighter" while working in a classroom. Students compose their papers on computers in computer labs located in most academic buildings. Every dormitory room is connected to the university computer network, and wireless zones around campus allow students to get on-line wherever they might be studying.

W&L classes typically demand considerable reading and writing. Students quickly learn that no skill proves more valuable than the ability to write clearly and concisely; professors expect nothing less. Classes and workloads may be tough, but the academic mood at Washington and Lee never becomes cutthroat.

> *W&L may have competitive admissions, but students here enjoy learning more through cooperation and collaboration with peers.*

This mood may be due, in part, to the Honor System. Students trust one another. They do not compete against one another; they compete against themselves.

The Academic Year

W&L has a unique academic year consisting of a twelve-week fall term, a twelve-week winter term, and a six-week spring term. Most students take four classes in the fall, four classes in the winter, and two classes in the spring. The spring term allows for a kind of academic flexibility that is truly uncommon. In years past, students in English classes spent the term studying five of Faulkner's novels in great detail. Those in botany classes traveled to the American West to examine its indigenous fauna. Members of economics classes journeyed to the financial centers of Europe to learn about the European Economic Community, while politics majors interned in Washington, D.C. Because the spring term closes the school year, students who study abroad or serve in internships for the term may continue to do so throughout the summer. Students who stay at W&L enjoy compressed classes, along with beautiful weather for reading outdoors or tubing down the Maury River.

SOCIAL LIFE AND ACTIVITIES

Phil Flickinger, a 1997 graduate of Washington and Lee, has published a collection of his cartoons that appeared in W&L's student newspapers. Entitled *Invasion of the Bug-Eyed Preppies,* the book captures many of the quirks of social life at W&L. Flickinger's most revealing cartoon juxtaposes two groups—"Generation X" and "Generation Lex." "Generation X" is a frowning, shaggy group of tattooed and pierced slackers. "Generation Lex" is a group of Lexington, Virginia's W&L students—straitlaced and smartly dressed. One W&L male in the cartoon asks, "Has anyone seen my Duckheads?"

Like most humor, this cartoon evokes a great deal of truth by use of stereotypes. Of course, every member of Generation X does not have a skateboard and a navel ring. Likewise, every student at W&L does not fit the cartoon's notion of a preppy. For every rule or stereotype, there are exceptions. It may be true that most W&L students are more conservative than their peers at other schools. Nevertheless, W&L's student body contains a strong mix of "ambitious, on-the-ball" individuals who pursue differing interests with differing attitudes. Somehow, they all seem bound by a single thread.

> *I still maintain that in no other school can one find such a classy group of well brought-up individuals. Everyone respects one another to an amazing degree.*

Residences

All W&L freshmen live in one of four freshman dormitories and take their meals in a contemporary common dining room in the Elrod Commons, the Marketplace. Sophomores live on campus, too, in upperclass dorms and apartments, fraternity houses, and separate houses for groups such as the Outing Club, International Club, and Spanish Club. Juniors and seniors may live on campus, though many choose to live off campus. Apartments above downtown stores provide many options for students, as do legendary student homes with colorful names like Fishbait, Munster, Windfall, the Batcave, Jacob's Ladder, and Amityville. All students enjoy the majestic beauty of the surrounding Shenandoah Valley and Blue Ridge Mountains, which provide every imaginable outdoor activity.

The Greeks

Seventy-five percent of W&L men and women are in one of thirteen fraternities or five sororities. Many fraternities and sororities engage in volunteer efforts, such as tutoring elementary students, cleaning up nature trails, organizing food blood drives, and working for the local emergency services. Their social events aren't exclusive affairs, but welcome all students, Greek and non-Greek alike. Friendships between members of different organizations are common, as are friendships between Greek members and independent students. Fraternity and sorority houses are owned by the university and are clean and well-maintained.

Other Organizations

For a small school, Washington and Lee supports an impressive array of civic, cultural, and athletic organizations to meet every student's interests. The Society for the Arts, for example, sponsors dramatic performances and readings of student poetry and fiction. The General Activities Board brings bands and comedians to campus. W&L's many journalism majors contribute to two rival student newspapers, the traditional *Ring-tum Phi* and the more winsome *Trident*. The Contact Committee presents debates and lectures by nationally-known visitors. Through club and intramural sports, choral groups, an orchestra, college Democrats, college Republicans, religious organizations, and service groups, any W&L student finds fulfilling diversions and relationships outside of class.

MEN'S VARSITY SPORTS

- Cross-Country
- Football
- Soccer
- Basketball
- Swimming
- Indoor Track
- Wrestling
- Baseball
- Golf
- Lacrosse
- Tennis
- Track and Field

WOMEN'S VARSITY SPORTS

- Cross-Country
- Soccer
- Tennis
- Volleyball
- Basketball
- Swimming
- Indoor Track
- Lacrosse
- Tennis
- Track and Field
- Equestrian
- Field Hockey

Sports

Many Washington and Lee students also choose to participate in varsity sports. W&L's Generals compete in Division III sports through the Old Dominion Athletic Conference, maintaining sterling academic and athletic records. Recently, 194 of W&L's 400 varsity athletes achieved GPAs of 3.5 or better. The Generals have had ten conference championship teams, seventeen All-American athletes, nine conference players of the year, and seventy-nine first-team all-conference players. For ten of the last twelve years, W&L teams won the ODAC Commissioner's Cup for the best all-around athletic program. Football and lacrosse remain the perennial favorites of spectators at W&L, attracting large and vocal crowds.

Popular Events

Among W&L's most popular events are two campus-wide bonanzas: the Fancy Dress Ball and Mock Convention. A black-tie ball attended by students, alumni, and faculty,

Fancy Dress (or "FD") is a yearly affair that celebrated its centennial in 2007. A student committee sponsors a concert on a Friday evening, followed by the ball on a Saturday night. Festivities fill the weekend, making for a marathon that only the most excited students can complete. Mock Convention (or "Mock Con") occurs with equal flair every four years. Organized to predict the presidential candidate for the political party out of office, Mock Con approximates an actual political convention on a grand scale. Students form state delegations and spend countless hours in research. They succeed in predicting candidates at an uncanny rate. The 1992 Mock Democratic Convention accurately selected Bill Clinton as its nominee. The 1996 Mock Republican Convention garnered live coverage on C-SPAN. House Speaker Newt Gingrich addressed the crowd of Washington and Lee students, and Bob Dole spoke to the assembly via phone when he accepted the convention's nomination. The 2000 mock convention predicted the nomination of George W. Bush, and the 2004 convention correctly chose John Kerry.

FINANCIAL AID

Washington and Lee uses student tuition dollars as efficiently and fairly as any university in the country. At many schools, students and their families pay inflated tuitions; one full-paying student's cost of attending school also includes a portion of the fees necessary to educate another student who receives financial aid. In other words, students subsidize other students' tuitions. At W&L, most financial aid dollars are drawn from grants and endowment, so the cost of attendance at W&L is often lower than the cost of attending other highly selective colleges. For a small school offering a world-class education, W&L is clearly a tremendous value. W&L students and their families find that the university possesses an intimate academic setting that rivals any other—at an extremely competitive cost.

No one will claim that the annual tuition and room and board is small change, however. The cost of any college education exceeds the budgets and imaginations of many American families. Washington and Lee strives to make tuition costs affordable by offering generous financial aid packages to students whenever possible.

W&L's admissions process is need-blind, so a student's ability to pay tuition is never a part of the admissions decision. W&L's Financial Aid Office, upon learning of a student's admission, works to ensure that a student's financial needs can be met.

In order to reach its goal of meeting a student's financial needs, W&L's Financial Aid Office requires that a student's family fill out the College Scholarship Service Financial Aid Profile. The CSS Profile may be found online. The Financial Aid Office strongly recommends submission of the profile by mid-January. Doing so will ensure receipt of all student information by mid-February. Additionally, W&L's Financial Aid Office requires a student's family to provide tax returns from the two previous tax years. W&L's priority deadline for submitting all required Financial Aid application materials is March 1st. Applicants and their parents are strongly encouraged to review the detailed instructions about making application for financial aid on W&L's web site – *http://wlu.edu/financialaid.*

Students applying through W&L's Early Decision program may obtain a financial aid estimate by registering with the College Scholarship Service in October and submitting forms through CSS in mid-November.

Because any college financial aid process may prove frustrating and confusing, W&L's Admissions Office recommends early, careful planning for any student's family. The Financial Aid Office takes great care in addressing each family's personal and individual needs.

Apart from its need-based aid programs, Washington and Lee also awards numerous merit-based scholarships every year. Ranging from partial tuition awards to scholarships that cover full tuition, room, and board, W&L's Honor Scholarships reward students who possess great academic and personal promise. Therefore, finalists must meet and exceed the university's admissions standards in addition to demonstrating potential campus leadership. Recipients carry their scholarships throughout their four-year tenure at Washington and Lee, provided they establish a minimum 3.0 grade-point average and maintain a personal record fitting an Honor Scholar. Students who wish to apply for these awards must submit their applications along with an additional Honor Scholarship essay by December 15.

Washington and Lee also sponsors Finalists in the National Merit Scholarship Competition. National Merit Finalists who are admitted to the university and designate Washington and Lee as their first choice of colleges with the National Merit Finalist Scholarship Corporation will receive up to $7,000 yearly.

GRADUATES

The percentage of freshmen who return to Washington and Lee for their sophomore years stands as a sure, impressive sign of student contentment: typically ninety-five percent of freshmen return to W&L as sophomores. A more impressive sign is the number of W&L students who enter as freshmen and graduate four years later. Typically between

PROMINENT GRADS

- Lloyd Dobyns, News Commentator
- Joseph Goldstein, Nobel Prize Winner
- Bill Johnston, President of the New York Stock Exchange
- David Low, Astronaut
- Roger Mudd, Journalist
- Cy Twombly, Artist
- Tom Wolfe, Author

eighty-five and ninety percent graduate on schedule. Clearly, Washington and Lee students stay at the university, and they stay happy. In an age when many college students need five years to earn a degree, the vast majority of W&L students find both adequate advisement and access to the classes they need in order to graduate in four years.

Traditionally, W&L produces a high percentage of history, biology, and economics majors. That so many students should favor history at W&L, given the university's own long history, should be no surprise. The university's numerous biology majors include many who regularly establish a stellar record in gaining admittance to medical schools. Economics majors typically carry their expert training from W&L's Commerce School into the business world.

All Washington and Lee students receive excellent advice from the Career Services Office. The Career Services Office provides mock interview and résumé-review services. Students use the office's complete resources to research potential employers. The Office welcomes over 100 companies to interview W&L students for jobs and summer internships every year. It further organizes off-campus interviews and enlists students in job fairs through the Selective Liberal Arts Consortium and Big Apple Recruiting Consortium. These job fairs enable W&L students to meet employers in major American cities. The Career Services Office has an internship exchange with twenty-five top liberal arts colleges, which produces over 6,000 internship listings each year.

The Career Services Office also tracks W&L students as they leave W&L for employment and graduate school. Its report for the class of 2005 shows sixty-seven percent of graduates in employment, along with twenty-three percent seeking postbaccalaureate degrees. A slim five percent either were seeking employment or were content taking time off after graduation. The report reveals that large numbers of working graduates found positions in business, banking and finance, government, journalism, or education. Of the 2003 graduates who decided to pursue advanced degrees, thirty-five percent entered general graduate schools, thirty-two percent entered law school, and twenty-three percent entered medical school. Other students began studies in dental, veterinary, engineering, and business schools.

Because students come from all parts of the country to attend Washington and Lee, they also disperse themselves across the map after graduation. Recent trends show increasing numbers of W&L graduates moving to New York City, Washington, Charlotte, and Atlanta for work. In every city, existing alumni association chapters support and welcome new graduates.

Washington and Lee alumni share a unique experience that creates "an immediate bond" between them. They treasure their undergraduate memories and remain fiercely loyal to their alma mater. One graduate describes a revelation about the nature of Washington and Lee alumni this way:

> *I have a W&L trident decal on the back of my car, and I was at the gas station one day when a stranger asked me what it was. I explained that it was the symbol for my school, Washington and Lee University. The stranger said, "Oh, I thought maybe it was a sign for some kind of cult." I laughed, and then, the more I thought about it, the more I realized the stranger wasn't necessarily wrong. W&L is a kind of cult—but in a good way. We all believe very strongly in the same ideals and we all have a strong sense of belonging to a very special place.*

SUMMING UP

Washington and Lee's four freshman dormitories form a cluster on the edge of campus. Baker, Davis, and Gilliam dorms face one another, creating a horseshoe; students gather in its "quad" every day. Just across the street, Graham-Lees—the oldest of the four dorms—overlooks the Baker-Davis-Gilliam quad. An arched breezeway passes through the building; on the left, a marble step between two columns is clearly worn more than the rest. Superstition holds that freshmen must walk up this step, between the columns, or risk failing their first test. Millions of feet have kept the tradition.

Just next door to Graham-Lees dormitory is the Lee House. Robert E. Lee built this home when he was the president of the school, and presidents of Washington and Lee have lived there ever since. Freshman voices can be heard in the Lee House as they echo from the dormitories. A past president joked that, although he preferred classical music, he could not help becoming familiar with the musical tastes of each freshman class.

That the president of the university lives so close to the freshman class demonstrates something wonderful about Washington and Lee: The person who runs the school shares the same block with those who are just learning the school's nuances. There is a continuity from the top of the administration to the bottom of the student body, and this continuity permeates the entire university. There is a sense of familiarity and camaraderie. Washington and Lee students cherish this camaraderie and guard it closely long after they leave the quaint streets of Lexington.

❑ *Cameron Howell, B.A.*

WASHINGTON UNIVERSITY IN ST. LOUIS

Washington University in St. Louis
St. Louis, MO 63130-4899

(314) 935-6000
Fax: (314) 935-4290, (800) 638-0700

E-mail: *admissions@wustl.edu*
Web site: *http://admissions.wustl.edu*

Enrollment

Full-time ❏ women: 3,146
❏ men: 3,023

Part-time ❏ women: 767
❏ men: 530

INTRODUCING WASH. U.

From modest beginnings as a regional university, Washington University in St. Louis has emerged as a national leader in undergraduate and graduate education. The university now draws approximately ninety percent of students from outside of Missouri, with students from all fifty states, two U.S. territories, the District of Columbia, and over sixty countries. Nearly sixty percent of the students come from more than 500 miles away, making this one of the most geographically diverse universities in the world. As a medium-sized university, Wash. U. provides the perfect combination of a friendly smaller campus with the resources of a large university. Visitors will notice a unique spirit of camaraderie. Some might attribute it to midwestern friendliness, but more likely it is the product of the common desire to learn that pervades the campus.

Washington University's Danforth Campus is set on a hill overlooking Forest Park, one of the nation's largest urban parks. The World's Fair brought international ambassadors and exhibits to the park in 1904, and Brookings Hall served as a gathering place much as it does for students today. From this vantage point, seven miles west of downtown St. Louis, the offices, restaurants, theaters, and stadiums nearly blend into the horizon. Known for the majestic Gateway Arch, St. Louis offers a variety of cultural experiences from concerts and theater performances to Cardinals baseball games and the second largest Mardi Gras celebration in the nation.

I applied to schools all over the country. But when it came time to choose, I realized that Washington U. was everything I wanted in a university. After visiting, I found out that Washington U. has much better programs and gives me so many more choices than any other school I had applied to. I can take classes in chemistry, presidential rhetoric, or political science while I focus on photography. There's just an unbelievable amount of options.

—*Zachary Gitlin*
College of Arts & Sciences, 2008

Students can choose from four undergraduate colleges: Arts & Sciences, Business, Design and Visual Arts (including Architecture, Art), and Engineering. (There are also graduate programs in these colleges, plus those in Law, Medicine, Occupational Therapy, Physical Therapy, and Social Work.) The choices don't end there. Many students opt to pursue combined studies through double majors, minors, or dual-degree programs. It is easy to pursue multiple interests even if they involve two different undergraduate schools of the university. Flexibility is a key component of an education at Washington University. Faculty advisors guide students on a path that explores a variety of interests.

Wash. U. provides a dynamic, challenging academic environment. Students can choose from unique courses such as "The Cultural History of the Robot" and "Strangers and Savages, Aliens and Outcasts." Opportunities to learn don't end in the classroom either. Research projects are open to undergraduates, and every year many students choose to travel and study abroad through a university-sponsored program.

Technology helps Wash. U. students develop skills for learning that will make them successful later in their careers. In addition to resources located in the libraries, the university offers wireless access to the Internet in many locations as well as computer labs in the residential colleges and other campus locations, and direct Internet access in each residence hall room. Most courses offer an on-line element whether it is a home page, tutorials, or the interactive on-line learning environment called Prometheus.

Improvements are also taking place on the campus landscape—new buildings are sprouting up every year. In recent years, Whitaker Hall for Biomedical Engineering and a new Earth and Planetary Sciences Building opened on campus, Olin Library completed renovations that include a popular Internet cafe. Washington has a commitment to improvement, and it shows.

> *At the College of Architecture we get a really strong foundation to work from, regardless of any changes of technology in the future. And I love my professors. Sometimes when we work on projects late at night or on weekends, they stop by to check on us or even bring us snacks. We have tremendous respect for them and for their knowledge and skills, but they make themselves very approachable and available for us.*

—Eun Grace Choi
College of Architecture, 2007

However, the real value comes from students. At Wash. U., students set high academic standards for themselves, but they also enjoy participating in community service, playing Frisbee in the Swamp, and going to parties at one of twelve fraternities. Social, cultural, political, and religious groups design programs to educate and entertain their fellow students. Ursa's, a corner cafe that accepts university meal cards, offers a patio where students meet on warm afternoons. Issues of *Student Life*, the 128-year-old student newspaper, can be seen on tables and in backpacks all over campus. Whether students choose to live in a Residential College, the Village, a fraternity, or a university-owned apartment, they will enjoy the benefits of a close community.

ADMISSIONS REQUIREMENTS

With over 22,000 applications in a recent year, Wash. U. is becoming increasingly competitive. To compete, students must pursue a challenging combination of courses and extracurricular activities. Admissions officers look at course selection and grades, recommendations, essays, extracurricular activities, and standardized tests.

Academic excellence, demonstrated by transcripts and test scores, is only the first step in the admissions process. At Washington U., applicants must also show how they have challenged themselves or pursued a personal talent. Initiative—taking honors, AP and IB courses when available, conducting independent research, or leading a team—separates high achievers. Recommendation letters and essay responses are the best methods for applicants to emphasize their unique qualities.

Admissions Deadlines

Either the SAT or the ACT is required and should be taken in the fall of senior year, if not earlier. Early Decision applications are accepted by November 15, whereas regular decision applications are due by January 15. Regular admission decisions are mailed on April 1.

Admission Procedures by School

General admission procedures require sending a high school transcript, which should include the following:

- 4 years of English
- 4 years of mathematics (calculus is recommended)
- 3–4 years of history and social sciences
- 3–4 years of laboratory sciences
- at least 2 years of foreign language

High school courses should reflect preparation for the program you are pursuing. For instance, students interested in the sciences, engineering, or the premedicine program should have preparation in chemistry, physics, calculus, and biology. Art and Architecture students have the option of providing a portfolio, which should include drawings from direct observation and a variety of media. A strong academic background is essential for success at Washington University, but it must be combined with a desire to seek out challenges.

> *I like it that you can take classes in any school — art, business, arts and sciences. I like it open-ended, since I don't know what I'm going to do. I came here for a liberal arts education, and that's what I'm doing. It's really easy to come in contact with professors ranked high in their field. I meet important people on a day-to-day basis."*

—Daniel Gealy
College of Arts & Sciences, 2009

ACADEMIC LIFE

Flexibility is central to academics at Wash. U. Students are encouraged to pursue their interests even when they change; multiple interests are not only tolerated but encouraged. It is common to have a double major, even in different schools of the university. Sixty percent of students earn a major and minor or more than one major. Some students even choose to design their own major. With over ninety programs and 1,500 courses offered, no wonder students get excited about multiple subjects. Wash. U. students experience self-discovery by taking challenging classes in many divisions, working with renowned professors, and using their analytical skills.

Preparation

Many students receive credit for AP, honors, or IB courses taken during high school. In addition, placement exams are offered for areas such as foreign language and mathematics. Even when credit is not awarded, honors courses are beneficial in the admissions process because they represent a student's desire to be challenged.

Unique Opportunities

Many students begin their studies with optional freshman seminars and special programs, such as the Mind, Brain, and Behavior program, which prepares students for research during sophomore year. FOCUS seminars, concentrating on controversial issues in society, are also popular. Wash. U. is a pioneer in combined studies, with majors such as Philosophy, Neuroscience, and Psychology (PNP) and American Culture Studies. The University Scholars Program is another unique opportunity, in which students apply for both undergraduate and graduate study at Washington University in specific areas. University Scholars work with a faculty mentor who guides them toward their desired graduate studies.

Academic Schedule

The school year is organized into two semesters, with a wide selection of courses also offered during the summer. Students typically take about fifteen credit hours (or five classes) per semester. By junior and senior year, many students are able to schedule classes with Fridays off. One of the only required courses at Wash. U. is writing 1, a freshman-level writing course. Writing provides the foundation for communication in nearly all disciplines, so its importance is stressed early. Later, course selection is guided by each undergraduate school. In Arts & Sciences, classes are chosen through a cluster system. Core courses cover the following areas:

- Physical and natural sciences and mathematics
- Social and behavioral sciences
- Textual and historical studies
- Languages and the arts

> *I really wanted to come to Washington University because of how easy it is to combine studies and majors between schools. I'm a double major in art and engineering, specializing in visual communications and computer science. I was really impressed by how extensive the wireless network is and how much we use the Internet in conjunction with the classroom.*

—Joyce Santos
College of Art; School of Engineering & Applied Science, 2008

Faculty

Professors at Washington U. are leaders in their fields, engaged in research but also interested in sharing their knowledge with undergraduates. They enjoy teaching. Professors have been honored with awards that include the Nobel Prize and Pulitzer Prize. Yet, professors are approachable and accessible in and out of the classroom. Frequently, students and professors meet to continue a classroom discussion, discuss a paper, or clarify information before an exam. Some undergraduates pursue research, working closely with a faculty mentor. Research is not constrained to laboratory science either. Opportunities exist in a variety of fields, from anthropology to economics.

> *I feel that undergraduates at Washington U. have been very well taken care of. I was at once struck by the school's beauty. Because they were offering these scholarship opportunities, I knew they place a special emphasis on academic achievement. When I interviewed with the professors I saw that I wasn't just going to be a number. I was a writer. I was a reader. I was a scholar—someone to be challenged and engaged.*

—Laura Quek
College of Arts & Sciences, 2007

Classes

As in the selection of a major, class options are numerous and flexible. Students in the undergraduate schools are encouraged to take classes from the other schools. An architecture student may take an engineering class in computer science, while a political science major takes management in the business school.

Classes at Washington challenge students to think analytically, to become problem solvers, and relate ideas to the big picture. More than eighty percent of classes have fewer than twenty-four students, encouraging personal attention from the professor and a prominent role in discussion. Classes can be larger the first year, especially in introductory courses that provide a prerequisite for many majors. By senior year, students find themselves in much smaller classes, among a community of their peers. Classes provide solid preparation for graduate school or a career by emphasizing communication skills and critical thinking.

Advisors

Students are automatically assigned to a four-year academic advisor upon arrival. Advisors are guides and resources for self-discovery. They help students achieve their goals and outline a career path, but they rely on students to challenge themselves. Freshmen also are given a peer advisor, an upper-class student who can provide assistance in making the transition to college. Once a student declares a major, he or she chooses a major advisor. Major advisors have experience and knowledge in their fields and can be especially helpful in discussing career options.

Learning Beyond the Classroom

Outside the classroom walls, experiential learning shapes the Wash. U. experience. Many students participate in internships, whether they are during the summer or the school year. The Career Center maintains relationships with many companies to facilitate internships for students.

Study-abroad programs are available for every discipline, and are typically completed during junior year. Programs include economics at the London School of Economics, business in Hong Kong, and health care in France.

Ultimately, it is the daily experiences of the university—interacting with peers, conducting research, or joining a student group—that complete the learning experience.

Resources

With more than 3.6 million books, periodicals, and government publications, Wash. U. libraries provide excellent resources for research—including wireless Internet access. Electronic resources are also plentiful with subscriptions to many electronic journals and databases available through a campus Internet connection. In addition, all campus rooms are supplied with in-room data connections, and each residential college has its own computer lab. Courses in computer science and electronic media are also available for interested students even if they are not students in the School of Engineering.

The most recent additions to the Wash. U. landscape, the Earth and Planetary Sciences Building, offer state-of-the-art equipment for students interested in biomedical engineering and in geology and the space sciences, respectively. Soon a new dorm under construction in the residence hall area will offer students additional living options.

Campus events such as lectures, readings, and conferences are another asset to an education at Wash. U. The Assembly Series is a regular lecture program during the academic year. In recent years speakers on campus have included NAACP Chairman Julian Bond, former Supreme Court Justice Sandra Day O'Connor, *New York Times* columnist Tom Friedman, the Dalai Lama of Tibet, Hillary Rodham Clinton, Bill Gates, and a number of U.S. Presidents..

Educational services such as the Writing Center, the International House, and the Disability Resource Center offer help to students. Students can discuss an essay with a peer tutor or simply brainstorm ideas at the Writing Center. International students benefit from English Language Programs courses and assistance with the transition to life in the United States. Even a student who breaks a wrist can be assisted with note-takers from the Disability Resource Center ready to fill in while the student heals.

SOCIAL LIFE AND ACTIVITIES

> *It's important to look beyond your classes and schoolwork to find out what your true passions are. Especially as a freshman, you should take advantage of opportunities to join extracurricular groups. You can use these experiences to choose a major, to choose classes, and to guide your career choices.*

—*Brittany Jackson*
College of Arts & Sciences, 2008

Leadership

Leadership at Washington University is apparent both in and out of the classroom. Students may develop as leaders through group projects in the business school, teamwork in intramural basketball, or as an elected class representative. Avenues for developing leadership skills include meeting with other student leaders in the Student Group Council, attending leadership conferences, or participating in workshops during the Women's Leadership Training Initiative. The most valuable learning experience for many students is simply diving into a leadership position. Advisors in the Office of Student Activities are available for support, but student leaders make the real decisions for their groups.

Elected positions in the Congress of the South 40 (CS40), the North Side Association, and Student Union (SU) are highly sought after. These governing organizations allow students to influence important issues that shape the Wash. U. community. CS40 and the North Side Association are the government bodies for the residential areas of campus, known as the South 40 and the Village. Student Union, the primary student governmental body, allocates nearly $2 million in activities funds to student groups in addition to representing student concerns to the administration. Students here have power to make a difference.

Academic/Preprofessional Organizations

Academic organizations provide an opportunity to meet with students and faculty who share your interests. Groups such as the Biomedical Engineers Society, Pre-Med Society, and American Institute of Graphic Arts allow students to discuss their career interests and learn from a community of their peers. Honorary groups recognize outstanding students and bring them together to help the community. For example, the sophomore honorary, Lock & Chain, hosts the biannual book sale.

Community Service

Surveys indicate fifty-seven percent of students at Wash. U. participate in community service, whether on campus or in the St. Louis community. Volunteer opportunities range from teaching children about environmental issues to serving food to those in need. Community service also means raising money for charities through Greek philanthropies or events such as Dance Marathon, a day of entertainment benefiting the Children's Miracle Network. The Campus Y offers many programs for students interested in volunteering, including hosting the Special Olympics at the Athletic Complex. While some students are enjoying Caribbean beaches, other students choose an alternative spring break, devoting one week to community service projects such as building homes for low-income families.

Greek Life

Fraternities and sororities complement life at Wash. U. by providing social activities, community service, brotherhood, and sisterhood. About twenty-five percent of students belong to one of twelve fraternities or six sororities. Rush takes place at the beginning of the second semester, so students have a chance to learn about Greek life well before joining. Fraternities have on-campus houses, managed by the university. Sororities have suites to gather for meetings or relaxation, but no traditional living quarters on campus. "Greeks" at Wash. U. are not in an isolated community. Fraternities and sororities provide a supportive social structure for students, but most "Greek" students maintain or develop relationships with "non-Greek" students throughout their time at Wash. U.

I like to be involved and active. Washington University has given me a lot of opportunities to find organizations that I want to get involved in. I'm on the campus interview team, president of CHIMES junior honorary, and class council secretary. The opportunities, resources, and experiences have helped me grow into a well-grounded person and given me a strong foundation for success in the future.

—Sara Anne Morris
Olin School of Business, 2007

Social Events and Performances

While students at Wash. U. work hard, they also take time to relax. Social events such as concerts, acts by comedians, and a weekly happy hour are popular among students.

Artistic performances are abundant. Wash. U. is known for its excellent *a cappella* groups—male, female, coed, ethnic, cultural, classical, gospel—you name it. The Performing Arts Department puts on up to six productions a year. A battle of the bands called Sounds of the Swamp features student bands in a showcase of Wash. U. talent.

Walk In Lay Down, better known as WILD, is a Wash. U. tradition and the most highly attended event every semester. For one day, the Quad is filled with free food, drinks, games, music, and people. Students, faculty, and staff come together to celebrate both the beginning and end of the academic year. The day culminates with a headlining band, which is kept secret until about a week before the event.

Thurtene

The oldest student-run carnival in the nation, Thurtene, is a Wash. U. community service tradition. A junior honor organization called Thurtene organizes the carnival for one weekend in April each year, complete with a Ferris wheel, cotton candy, and games. Fraternities and sororities team up to build and decorate playhouses, or "facades," to perform plays and musicals written by students. Not only the university's students, faculty, and staff enjoy the carnival, but families from the St. Louis community also join in the fun. All of the proceeds from ticket sales are donated to local charities.

Media

Wash. U. students use media for artistic expression, to convey opinions, or to entertain others, and at the same time they gain valuable real-life experience. The university TV station (WUTV) and radio station (KWUR) are student-run and feature student broadcasters, actors, and DJs. Written publications highlight the talents of student writers. *Student Life*, one of the nation's oldest independent student newspapers, is a forum for dialogue on controversial issues as well as a way to find out what is happening on campus. Literary magazines feature student essays, short stories, poems, photographs, and drawings.

Cultural and Religious Groups

Cultural groups offer a community for people with similar backgrounds while educating others about diverse traditions, values, and lifestyles. Annual performances such as the Indian celebration of Diwali and the Lunar New Year Festival create long lines of students waiting at the box office for tickets.

Religious organizations such as Hillel and the Catholic Student Center create a home away from home for many students. These organizations not only offer religious services, but also fellowship with other students, community service projects, and contact with St. Louis.

Political Activism

Political groups on both sides of the spectrum are active on campus, and they encourage students to discuss issues by sponsoring debates and voting drives. In 2004, the second U.S. Presidential Debate, featuring George W. Bush and John Kerry, was hosted at the Washington University Athletic Complex. Students participated as volunteers and were admitted into the audience.

I visited Washington U. during high school, and it was really because of the campus and people that I wound up here. I enjoy having the amazing variety of opportunities available. I'm a pitcher on the women's softball team. I've juggled fire with the juggling club.

—Laurel Sagartz
School of Engineering & Applied Science, 2007

Sports

Wash. U. is an NCAA Division III school and founding member of the University Athletic Association (UAA). No athletic scholarships are offered, which means that athletes are dedicated to both academics and athletics. Student athletes are students first, athletes second. Eighteen varsity sports are offered, and Wash. U. has had championship success in almost every one. In 2003–2004, the women's volleyball team has captured a record-setting eight NCAA Division III national championships.

Club and intramural sports are popular among students because they allow exercise, competition, and camaraderie without the time commitment of varsity sports. More than seventy-five percent of students have participated in at least one intramural sport. Some unusual sports such as Ultimate Frisbee and inner-tube water polo are included in the intramural choices.

Sports and recreation facilities at Washington are comprehensive. The Athletic Complex includes an indoor and outdoor track, a swimming pool, basketball court, tennis courts, racquetball courts, and more. The South 40 Fitness Center provides a place to work out just steps away from most of the residence halls. The tree-lined paths and golf course of Forest Park are just across the street.

St. Louis is known as a great sports city, so even professional sports fanatics can be happy at Wash. U. With teams such as the St. Louis Rams, Cardinals, and Blues, games take place year-round. Busch Stadium is easily accessible from Wash. U. via the MetroLink, and both peer advisors and resident advisors are known to take their groups to sports games on occasion.

On Campus

Freshmen generally live in double or triple rooms on a coed floor of between twenty-five and fifty students. These freshman floors are a learning experience for everyone, and become a supportive community for many. Early in the fall semester, groups of bright-eyed freshmen can be seen walking together on the way to dinner or a party. Fourteen new residence halls have been built since 1998.

Off Campus

Situated near Forest Park, the university provides access to museums, recreational facilities, and the St. Louis Zoo, nearly all of which have free admission. Just on the other side of the park is the Washington University School of Medicine in the Central West End, one of the young, hip areas of St. Louis. Full of vintage clothing stores, every type of ethnic restaurant, and several coffee shops, the Central West End is the perfect place to sit back with friends over a cup of java and discuss the last campus speaker or the results of the chemistry mid-term.

Nearby Clayton, the financial district and county government center, offers opportunities for summer internships or simply a romantic dinner at an Italian restaurant, followed by a stroll through an art gallery. A bit further in the other direction, downtown St. Louis offers history and entertainment. Every student should visit the Gateway Arch sometime during his or her four years, but other attractions such as jazz clubs, Union Station (a historic, restored train station that features a beautiful hotel, shops, and restaurants), and the Anheuser-Busch brewery (world's largest) deserve some attention.

CAMPUS FOOD

With 16 Bon Appétit dining locations on campus, convenience is a major factor in student satisfaction. Ursa's, a cafe with retro style, includes pool tables, computers, and board games. The Bear's Den, another campus food location, stays open until 3:00 A.M. on weekends to accommodate late-night snacking. National food chains such as Subway, Krispy Kreme, and Starbucks contribute to the variety in food options. Efforts are made to inform students about nutritional content and portion size through the dining services web site. Perhaps the most successful feature of the dining program is the simplest, as each student ID includes a magnetic strip that automatically deducts food "points" from the student's account at any food location on campus.

For students interested in seeing more of St. Louis, university shuttles, the MetroLink light rail system, MetroBus, taxicabs, rental cars, and upperclassmen are viable options. Movie theaters, grocery stores, and restaurants are all accessible by train, bus, or shuttle. Areas such as the Loop, a district famous for its shops, restaurants, and bars, is within walking distance of the university. Students can be found at Fitz's—a local root beer brewery—one of the local bookstores, or the famous St. Louis Bread Company.

FINANCIAL AID

Most students receive some form of financial assistance through scholarships, student loans, and part-time employment. All scholarships are awarded based on merit, yet some are given on both merit and need. Both the College Scholarship Service (CSS) PROFILE and the Free Application for Federal Student Aid (FAFSA) are acceptable to apply for need-based financial assistance. Army and Air Force ROTC Scholarships are another option. Payment plans with monthly tuition installments and long-term, low-interest loans are available for parents.

Employment

Students have access to numerous campus jobs whether or not they have applied for financial assistance. Approximately half of all students work part-time on campus. These students can be found in laboratories, administrative offices, libraries, theaters, the Athletic Complex, and the bookstore.

Scholarships

The University provides more than $53 million each year in scholarships to undergraduates, including both merit-based and need-based scholarships. More information is available from the admissions Web site (*admissions.wustl.edu*).

The most popular majors for a recent year's graduating class included biology, psychology, engineering, and business. Graduates found jobs around the country and around the world. Every year employers seek out the combination of skills developed at Washington University.

Students have access to the Washington University Career Centers, where the staff is ready to critique a résumé, discuss a career search, or provide career resources. Career preparation covers all four years with seminars ranging from "How to Find an Internship" to "Interviewing Skills." Approximately 250 companies recruited on campus in a recent year including Microsoft, Gap Inc., and Goldman Sachs. Wash. U. also offers an opportunity to build connections with alumni through a database called Career Connections.

An education at Wash. U. fosters a continued desire for learning, and many students choose to continue with graduate study. In fact, thirty percent of the Class of 2006 planned to graduate school immediately, and eighty-five percent said they planned further graduate or professional education some time in the future. Wash. U. prepares students for success in master's degree and Ph.D. programs. Some students even pursue further study in one of the graduate programs offered through the university's eight schools.

I chose Washington University because of the unique opportunities offered here. Washington U. encourages students to broaden their horizons, to go beyond the scope of their chosen disciplines and expand their minds. I was attracted to both the academic excellence here and the encouraging atmosphere. Most of all, I like the cooperation and the partnerships I've formed. We all work together and learn from each other. This helps build friendships and widens my horizons.

—Nikhail Aggarwal
School of Engineering & Applied Science, 2008

○ **Clark Clifford, Former Secretary of Defense**

○ **Ken Cooper, Pulitzer Prize-winning Journalist**

○ **David Garroway, Host of NBC-TV's** *Today Show*

○ **Frank Gladney, Founder of 7-UP**

○ **A.E. Hotchner, Novelist and Playwright**

○ **John F. McDonnell, Former CEO of McDonnell Douglas**

○ **Shepherd Mead, Playwright**

○ **Condé Nast,** *Vogue* **Publisher**

○ **Mike Peters, Pulitzer Prize-winning Editorial Cartoonist**

○ **Harold Ramis, Screenwriter famous for** *Ghostbusters* **and** *Animal House*

○ **Earl Sutherland, Nobel Laureate in Medicine**

○ **James Thompson, Former Governor of Illinois**

○ **Tennessee Williams, Playwright**

○ **William H. Webster, Former Director of FBI and CIA**

SUMMING UP

From the friendly smiles on the oak-lined paths to the group study sessions in Ursa's Cafe, visitors pick up an atmosphere of community at Wash. U. This atmosphere extends into the classroom, where professors are eager to share their knowledge and students are engaged in active analysis. Flexibility is also prevalent in the selection of classes, majors, and extracurricular activities. Students with initiative can define their own experience, and Wash. U. has the resources to support innovative thinking. Professors who lead in their field, the latest technology, and the surrounding city of St. Louis all create opportunities for learning. Still, much self-discovery takes place outside of the classroom—in residence halls, at student group meetings, and even at social events. The size and location of Washington U. make it a perfect fit for students who don't want to be lost in the crowd but are excited by the opportunities at a medium-sized university.

❏ *Joyce Lawrence, B.S. B.A.*

 Webb Institute
Glen Cove, NY 11542-1398

 (516) 671-2213
Fax: (516) 708-WEBB

 E-mail: *admissions@webb-institute.edu*
Web site: *http://www.webb-institute.edu*

 Enrollment

Full-time ❑ women: 17
❑ men: 70

INTRODUCING WEBB INSTITUTE

Welcome to Webb Institute, one of the most unusual colleges in the world, but also one of the best. Let's set some things straight from the start:

- Webb Institute was founded in 1889 by millionaire William H. Webb, one of the preeminent shipbuilders of the mid-nineteenth century, the era of the clipper ships.
- The purpose of the school is to advance the art and science of shipbuilding in the United States by training promising young people for careers in that field; thus, Webb confers only

one undergraduate degree: a Bachelor of Science in Naval Architecture and Marine Engineering.

- The Webb program is a full, four-year, intense engineering education.
- All students receive a full-tuition scholarship for all four years. (Yes, it's an almost-free education; the only costs are room, board, and books.)
- The Webb campus is a mansion on Long Island Sound.
- Only about eighty students attend in total, with a maximum of twenty-six in a class.
- All Webb students have two months of practical work experience every winter, for a total of at least eight months experience upon graduation.
- All Webb sophomores sail on ships for their winter work term, most overseas to the Caribbean, Europe, and Asia.
- Webb graduates are highly regarded in the maritime industry and eagerly recruited.
- Webb's placement rate is one hundred percent.
- Graduates are regularly accepted into master's programs at schools with prestigious graduate programs such as MIT and Stanford.
- Webb is not a military school; it is a completely private institution, focusing primarily on the needs of the commercial shipbuilding market; therefore, students have no obligations to the school on goverment upon graduation.
- The Webb degree is readily transferable to a wide range of other engineering disciplines, not only shipbuilding.
- Webb is fully accredited.

To sum up, Webb Institute is one of the best (if not the best) engineering schools in the country, it's basically free, and it happens to focus on ships. If you have never heard of Webb, don't worry—many of the students presently attending didn't know about it either until their senior year in high school, when they received an introductory brochure in the mail! But don't let Webb's small size and apparent obscurity fool you: Webb may be one of the best-kept secrets in academia, but certainly not in the maritime industry. If you are interested in getting a great job right out of college, with little debt, and you are smart and willing to work hard to learn about engineering in shipbuilding, then read on.

ADMISSIONS REQUIREMENTS

The admissions form asks basic questions, such as, "Who are you? Where do you live? What do you like to do?" Other paperwork includes teacher evaluations, high school transcript, college transcript, if you have taken any courses at the college level, and proof of citizenship or green card. That's about it. Many students say the Webb application was the easiest one they filled out.

What kind of student does Webb want? The school was founded to entice the brightest and best young people in the United States to pursue careers in shipbuilding, mainly by offering them a great education at no cost; therefore, Webb has set very high standards for prospective freshmen. Applicants must be in the top ten percent of their high school class and have a minimum GPA of 3.5. They must also take both the SAT and the SAT Subject Tests in Mathematics Level I or II, and Physics or Chemistry. A minimum score of 600 Verbal and 660 Math on the SAT is required. Applicants must either be United States citizens, native-born or naturalized, or hold a green card showing permanent residency and have attended a secondary school in the United States or its possessions or territories.

Webb also wants people who will do well in the Webb environment, with particular regard to the smallness of the school and the academic emphasis on ships and engineering. This means that people who are well-rounded and have at least some social skills are preferable to those who just sit in a corner and stare at the wall. Also, prospective freshmen must show dedication at least to engineering, if not to shipbuilding specifically. These qualities show through in the extracurricular activities that an applicant lists on the form and through the required personal interview with the president of the school.

A couple of side notes are in order here. First, Webb accepts incoming students only as freshmen; in other words, there is no transferring from another school into the upper classes of Webb. Second, Webb does not give any Advanced Placement credit. So, in short, everyone starts out equally at Webb. However, this fact should not discourage Webb wannabees from taking AP classes in high school, particularly calculus, because it may give them a slight edge in admissions (as well as make the first-semester race through integrals a little easier).

So what are an applicant's chances of acceptance? They are better than they might first appear, considering that only twenty-five freshmen are admitted each year. Stephen Ostendorff, the Director of Student Services and Admissions, describes the admissions process from his perspective in this way: First, the qualified students are separated from the unqualified students, based upon their application forms and SAT scores. This first cut typically narrows down the applicant pool to about seventy. Next, Steve starts inviting the top prospects to the school for interviews; as they accept, the marginally qualified students are dropped from the bottom of the list. Over thirty of the seventy are invited for interviews, because sometimes after the interview, the school realizes that the prospective student is not right for it or the prospective student realizes Webb is not right for him or her. Steve said the really tough decisions are about the students in the "forty-to-fifty" range. These students are qualified, but ultimately some are not pursued because of the high yield among the top thirty applicants. In summary, then, if an applicant meets Webb's academic standards, he or she stands greater than a fifty/fifty chance of acceptance. Then if that applicant is invited to interview and really wants to go to Webb, he or she stands a very good chance of getting in.

There's one last item about admissions: It is Webb's policy not to discriminate on the basis of race, creed, gender, or physical handicap, but does have physical and mental requirements due to the strenuous nature of the winter work and curricular program. This fact is important to keep in mind, especially when visiting the campus, because one quickly realizes that the vast majority of students are white males. However, female and minority students historically have not had any major problems with the students or the school. Webb's mission is to educate the best people, period. Basically, if you're a minority and you don't mind being in the minority, Webb is still a fine school for you to consider attending.

ACADEMIC LIFE

Webb doesn't teach you how to be smart. You're already smart when you come here. Webb teaches you how to work.

Webb is a hard school. There is no doubt about it. Nobody flies through Webb; everybody suffers alike. But that's what makes it good, and the 146 credits required to graduate (that's more than eighteen credits per semester) is only the tip of the iceberg. Add multiple field trips, highly respected faculty both in engineering and humanities classes, two months of practical work experience each year, and projects that few other schools dare to attempt—such as the senior thesis and the preliminary design of a large ship—and you begin to get the bigger picture. The incredible amount of learning and work that Webb crams into four years is what makes the school dear to alumni, and the alumni dear to employers.

Courses

Webb Institute confers only one undergraduate degree—the Bachelor of Science in Naval Architecture and Marine Engineering. Everyone takes the same technical classes over the course of four years. There are about six classes per semester, on average, with one being a humanities class. Freshman year, the courses are mostly basic scientific courses, such as calculus, physics, and chemistry, as found in any good engineering school. Sophomore year, more fundamental engineering courses are presented, such as fluid dynamics, strength of materials, and thermodynamics. Then in the junior year, study tends toward more field-related work, beginning with ship resistance and propulsion and including ship structural analysis, ship auxiliary and steam systems, electrical engineering, and ship maneuverability. Finally, in the senior year, the courses are almost all marine-related and involve huge projects such as ship design, ship's lines, machinery arrangement, propeller design, and a senior thesis of the student's choosing. Despite the above trends, one of the many unique aspects of Webb is that naval architecture and marine engineering courses are presented throughout the four-year program, as early as first-semester freshman year. This tactic helps to keep students interested and to prepare them (especially freshmen and sophomores) for their winter work jobs.

There tend to be two kinds of students at Webb: those who are interested in small pleasure and utility craft and those who prefer to deal with large ocean-going commercial and military vessels. The Webb curriculum distinctly favors the latter; however, the engineering and marine fundamentals learned often can be transferred to the design of smaller boats. The small craft design course in the junior year helps this transition, and discussion of small craft technologies, such as fiberglass hulls, is included in other classes.

Disciplines

Another good point about the Webb curriculum is that it is quite streamlined, yet still broadbased. This apparent dichotomy is possible because of the nature of naval architecture and marine engineering. Consider all the disciplines involved in designing a ship. First, there is the hull moving through the water; the study of this action involves knowledge of hydrodynamics (and even aerodynamics—a modern rudder is a type of wing). Next, there is the hull itself; the design of adequate structural integrity requires a good understanding of the principles of civil engineering. Then there are the guts of the ship—all the machinery and electrical equipment. The design of these systems requires, for example, knowledge of combustion and heat transfer (chemical engineering), engines and other auxiliary machinery (mechanical engineering), and ship electrical power distribution and electronic control systems (electrical engineering). Elements of all these various disciplines must be learned, but in only one, four-year degree program. Therefore, to accelerate the learning process, only the highlights of each discipline are discussed. The fundamental engineering principles are taught first, followed by those aspects pertaining to shipbuilding (for example, the use of steel and fiberglass). Irrelevant aspects (such as concrete) are reserved for independent study. This somewhat narrow approach can be maddening to people with purely scientific interests, but is great for those with an engineering inclination who "just want to use it."

Humanities

> *When students grow sick of ships, they can take a break and work on their humanities classes.*

There is one humanities class each semester. Standard topics range from technical communications to U.S. foreign policy to ethics. Occasionally, students are able to have some choice in what humanities courses they take, such as during the first semester of junior year, when the class, interacting with the faculty, decides on topics for three to four electives. Professor Richard Harris, the sole full-time humanities professor currently at Webb, teaches several of the Webb courses, and the rest are taught by adjuncts, many of whom are fairly well-known in their fields. Through all these classes, Webb students can broaden their horizons and hone their communication skills, as much as is possible from a highly technical program. As alumni attest, many employers are impressed with the excellent writing and speaking abilities of Webb graduates.

Classrooms and Faculty

One of the big benefits of Webb is how conducive the environment is to learning. Each class (such as the sophomores) has its own classroom, with a workstation in it for each student. Almost all the classes are held in these four classrooms; the students stay put and the professors are the ones who have to run to their next class! Classes begin at 9:00 A.M. and go to noon; after an hour of lunch, they continue until three. On Monday mornings, there is a special one-hour lecture by a guest speaker from industry. Although these arrangements may be reminiscent of third grade with Mrs. Hoag, there is nothing elementary about the faculty or the lectures. The student-to-faculty ratio is around seven to one. All the Webb professors have earned master's degrees, and several have earned doctorates. The small class size and common coursework enable the professors to gauge how much the students know and how much remains to be covered. Students often interrupt the lectures with questions, which the professors welcome, as this promotes understanding and allows the professors to move swiftly over the simple stuff and dwell more on the difficult material. After classes, the professors are readily available to answer further questions and to help students with problems.

Library, Computers, and Labs

After classes are done for the day, many students work together in the classroom, or in the Livingston Library, which is open twenty-four hours a day (like the rest of the campus) and contains one of the best collections on naval architecture and marine engineering in the country. All students are given laptops when they enter Webb and the campus facilities are completely covered by a wireless network with full Internet access. High-quality printers and a high-speed plotter are available, as well as a photocopier—all for free. The student-run bookstore provides everything else necessary, from notebook paper to rulers to coffee mugs. Laboratory equipment is not always state-of-the-art, but it is adequate. There are chemistry, materials science, and physics laboratories in the basement of the main building, and marine engineering, fluids, and electrical engineering laboratories in the Haeberle Laboratory building. Special equipment in the Haeberle Laboratory includes a complete boiler/turbine steam system, two diesel engines with dynamometer, and a flow channel.

The Towing Tank

The pride of Webb is the Robinson Model Basin. This basin is a long tank of water in which scale models of ships' hulls are towed and their performance variables are measured. Significant recent research in the basin includes testing of commercial and military hull form, yachts, and systematic study of high-speed multi hulls.

Workload

It is appropriate at this point to emphasize the intense workload at Webb. Four hours per night tends to be the typical amount of time spent on homework, but it can often be much higher than that. Pulling all-nighters for major projects and even regular homework assignments is all too common. Most of the work is not overly difficult; it's just that there's so much of it that it takes forever to do. How to handle all that pressure is one of the major lessons that students learn at Webb. The other one is how to work together to have a shot at getting all the work done.

> *What do you call the guy who graduates last in the class? A naval architect!*

Winter Work Program

L ast but certainly not least is the winter work program. To understand this program, you must first understand Webb's unusual calendar year, which runs as follows: Fall semester starts at the end of August and goes until winter break; spring semester starts at the beginning of March and goes until late June. This arrangement leaves two two-month breaks in the year: January through February and July through August. The summer break is just that—time off that's free of scholastic obligations. For the winter break, however, all students are required to work at jobs that are related to the maritime industry, sort of like co-op jobs or internships. The school finds jobs with shipyards for freshmen who work hands-on as apprentices doing welding, fitting, etc. For sophomores, the school arranges berths on merchant ships, where the students work as cadet observers in the engine rooms and on decks, doing routine maintenance. Of course, one of the perks is that students get to travel, sometimes even overseas to the Caribbean, Europe, or Asia, depending on the particular ship. Junior and senior year, however, students are on their own and must find maritime, engineering-related jobs. Most students get jobs in shipyard engineering departments or separate design or consulting offices, though a wide range of opportunities exists because Webb is fairly broad on what it considers marine-related work. Increasingly, students are going international, finding jobs all over the world. Thus, by the time a student graduates from Webb, he or she has first-hand experience of how a ship is designed and engineered, how it is physically constructed, and how it is operated at sea. This knowledge is invaluable to employers, especially when some competing graduates from other naval architecture schools have never even set foot on a deck!

SOCIAL LIFE AND ACTIVITIES

> *Most Webbies laugh sarcastically when someone mentions social life at Webb.*

It is most unfortunate: a stellar social life is one of those things that students generally have to give up when they come to Webb for their college education. There is just no way that a school averaging around eighty undergraduates can offer the same amount of social diversity and opportunity that, say, a state school with 20,000 students can offer. This hard fact, coupled with the intense technical workload that Webb requires and (for many male students, at least) the realization that, in some years, you can count the female students on two hands and a foot, tends to make life at Webb seem almost monastic at times.

The above view is overly pessimistic, however. On those rare moments when you're through with your work and you finally have time to look around you, Webb is actually a great place to live. There is an active choral group and a theatrical troupe for students' artistic outlets. From the campus, to sports, to the student organization, to being directly on Long Island Sound, to the City of Glen Cove, to nearby New York City, Webb has many positive attractions to enjoy.

The Campus

For starters, life at Webb is about as comfortable as a middle-class undergrad could hope for. The Webb campus is the former estate of Herbert L. Pratt, who is irrelevant to our story here except for the fact that he owned a really nice house on a really nice piece of property in a really nice area, and now it's Webb's. More specifically, Webb's mansion is located on twenty-six acres of prime waterfront property on beautiful Long Island Sound, in an area nicknamed the "Gold Coast" because of all the rich people who built their lavish estates here back in the Roaring Twenties.

Think The Great Gatsby, *and you'll have a pretty good idea of the look of the place. Or, if you haven't read that book, you can watch the movie* Batman Forever *and look for Webb as the exterior of Wayne Manor; the outdoor shots were filmed here in 1994!*

The main building is the mansion, of course. It houses all the important things on its three floors, including all four classrooms in the wings, undergraduate male residence, dining room, library, the academic laboratories, lecture hall, laundry room, computer room, faculty offices, and administrative offices. What this means is that a male student can stay completely indoors for whole weeks at a time (though this is not recommended). The female undergraduate students, on the other hand, have their dorm rooms on the second floor of the nearby Robinson Model Basin, so they are forced to get fresh air every day as they stroll a few yards over to the main building for classes and meals. Both male and female rooms are relatively spacious and are adequately furnished, with two students per room being typical. Phone jacks and TV hookups are in each room. All in all, it's a nice place to live.

Conveniences

What are really nice are all the conveniences that Webb offers. The food service provides three meals a day during the week and brunch and dinner on weekends, and the chefs do an excellent job (honestly, this is the best college food in the universe). Little things like free soap, a linen service, fifty-cent washers and dryers, free laundry detergent and bleach, and ample parking for all students (including freshmen) make life just that much easier. Also, the Student Organization (S.O.) services are particularly helpful. The S.O. treasury allows students to cash checks and make deposits and withdrawals. The S.O. kitchen allows students to refrigerate and microwave their own food. The S.O. bookstore has just about every academic tool necessary for classes. Other facilities include the S.O. garage, wood shop, and machine shop. All these services are accessible twenty-four hours a day. Almost anything a person needs to live and work comfortably can be found on campus, which is a big plus for students without cars.

The S.O.

The Student Organization merits further explanation. Basically, students govern themselves, and to a degree not found at most other schools. All students are members of the S.O. and agree to abide by the S.O. Handbook and the Honor Code. The handbook lays out all the chairmanships and rules, and the Honor Code forbids stealing, cheating, etc. Such documents are not peculiar to Webb; many schools have them. What is different about Webb is that students actually govern themselves by these rules, for the most part. Thus, a tour of Webb will reveal unusual practices, such as dorm rooms with locks operated only from the inside, attic storage of students' belongings, books and calculators left on classroom desks and library tables, and the aforementioned twenty-four-hour-a-day access to almost every public room and building on campus. This freedom does not mean that Webb is unsafe, however. During the day, everyone is everywhere on campus, and with only eighty-some students, everybody knows everybody who should be there. A student Officer of the Day is also on duty to greet guests. At night, hired security patrols the campus. In short, Webb has not had any serious crimes in a long, long while, and any minor offenses are usually dealt with by the S.O. Honor Council and the school administration. Thus, students at Webb don't have to worry like students at other schools do about the safety of themselves and their belongings.

Sports

There are many sports and activities at Webb to help students eat up all their free time. For athletics, Webb belongs to the Hudson Valley Men's Athletic Conference, a sports league of small schools in the area. (Although it says Men's Athletic Conference, women are welcome to and often do play on the teams—it's really more like coed sports.) Many students play sports which include basketball and volleyball (played in the gymnasium), soccer (on Thorpe Field), tennis (on the two courts on campus), sailing, and cross-country. For sailing, Webb owns several 420s for competition on the Sound, in addition to Lasers and two motor-boats—all for qualified students to use. For personal fitness, Webb has some weight equipment in the gym; also, students can use the Glen Cove YMCA at no cost, with its complete weight room, pool, and gym. Actually, since Webb athletics are run primarily by the students, if students want to start a sport not currently offered, they can form a team, call up other schools in the area that have the sport, and, Presto! there's competition.

> *Look, Ma, I'm playing college basketball!*

The above description may make talented athletes and sports enthusiasts cringe when they read it. Admittedly, you'll never see Webb in the NCAA basketball final four or in the Rose Bowl. However, the general informality of Webb athletics does not mean that athletes do not play hard or that competition is not fierce and fun. All of the Webb teams have won several games in their recent seasons. The sailing team is particularly good and regularly places highly in regattas, occasionally beating schools like Cornell and the U.S. Naval Academy. And this success is all achieved with ordinary students, not elite athletes. Many students who would not otherwise ever play intercollegiate sports can show up for practices and then proceed to beat the tar out of teams from schools ten times larger. Or, if that's not your style, you can play on an intermural team and just beat the tar out of your roommate.

Social Events

Webb has several social events throughout the year, both large and small, formal and informal. A small event may be an evening of eating, drinking, and shooting pool and the breeze in the student pub while a local guy plucks out some songs on his guitar. Big events include Homecoming, Parents Weekend, the Beach, Halloween and Christmas parties, and the biggest one of all—Webbstock. Webbstock is held on a Saturday in June, just before the school year is out, and entails six or seven bands (some of them famous), free drinks and food, and all sorts of sports, games, and activities out on the terraces under the hot sun in front of the blue Sound. It's quite an experience.

Off Campus

Finally, some reports indicate that there is life outside of Webb. Glen Cove is a quiet suburban town, with a movie theater, various stores, several different churches and houses of worship, public beaches and parks, and the all-important Taco Bell (it stays open the latest). Students with musical talent are welcome to join the North Shore Symphony Orchestra. In addition, students can hop on the Long Island Rail Road and be at Pennsylvania Station in midtown Manhattan in under an hour and a half. Of course, if you have a car, all of Long Island and New York City is within a couple of hours driving time, at most. Students also participate in the Solar Splash Competition. The students work all year on a solar electric boat and then travel to the competition, which has recently been in Buffalo and Arkansas. So, in summary, there are a lot of fun things to do at Webb, both on and off campus, if you have the time...*if you have the time.*

FINANCIAL AID

Financial aid can be very simple at Webb. First of all, Webb provides a full-tuition scholarship to all students; this is possible because of a huge endowment created by the beneficence of William Webb and the generous contributions of others. Thus, the only major expenses are about $7,000 a year for room and board (living in a mansion is not cheap!) and about $300 to $700 per semester for books (though for the first semester of freshman year it's more like $900 for books). However, Webb Institute is dedicated to providing whatever financial aid is necessary to allow all students to attend, because that was one of William Webb's original stipulations when he founded the school and donated his millions to it. First of all, Webb participates in the Pell Grant program and the Family Federal Educational Loan program, which includes Plus and Stafford loans. Any further needs are met with Webb's various own scholarships. The bottom line is that graduates from Webb don't have the tens of thousands of dollars worth of debt to pay off that many graduates from other top-notch schools do, and any debt that Webbies do incur is small and easily paid off with the high starting salaries that Webb graduates procure.

GRADUATES

After four excruciating years, it's nice to know that you can get into just about any graduate school in the country or go straight into industry with a high-paying job and a promising future. Webb's record is one-hundred-percent placement, even in an industry that has been shrinking in the United States for the past couple of decades. And, by the way, ships aren't in any danger of extinction! That kind of security is really hard to beat in an era of corporate downsizing.

First of all, let's reiterate: Webb is NOT a military school. There are no obligations whatsoever upon graduation, not even to stay in the maritime industry. You're free to do as you please with your life.

The next question, of course, is, "What do you do with a degree in naval architecture and marine engineering?" It's a good question, with a multitude of answers. Webbies always seem to be in demand at shipyards across the country, where they do engineering work as they design the ships of the future. Independent design and consulting offices offer attractive jobs with many different kinds of technical work. The offshare industry needs (and pays well for) Webb graduates. Just about any shore-based maritime work is open for graduates, since the Webb degree covers many different areas of learning. Outside of the maritime industry, there are many engineering jobs for which Webb graduates are qualified, especially if they obtain a master's degree in the particular field. Actually, Webb graduates are not even limited to engineering; business, managerial, and finance positions seem to be popular destinations among the alumni. Basically, the rule of thumb seems to be that as long as there is a maritime industry, Webb graduates will always have jobs.

To be completely honest, the demand for Webb grads does not rest solely on the quality of the Webb education, no matter how good it is. In reality, the way many Webb students get jobs for winter work and after graduation is by calling up Webb alumni who work at the particular companies of interest. Many of the key people in the maritime industry are Webb alumni, and they are usually more than willing to help a fellow Webbie get a job. This reality may sound slightly like a "good-ol'-boy" network, but many times even graduates from other schools admit that Webbies are the best.

If graduates don't want to go into the maritime industry, or if they know they want to be in research or management, graduate school becomes an attractive option. Almost every year one or more graduates go to MIT to pursue either technical degrees in areas such as hydrodynamics, or a maritime business degree in Ocean Systems Management. Many graduates obtain an MBA within five to ten years after graduation. Almost any field is open for Webb graduates to study; however, some graduate studies may require the completion of a few pre-requisite courses.

One last point about graduating from Webb: The maritime industry is an international field. What this means is that if you would like to work overseas, there are many opportunities, even for winter work. For example, recently students have worked in Sweden, Greece, and Australia. The possibilities are endless!

SUMMING UP

Webb Institute is a rare school; and like many rare things, it is invaluable, if you can recognize and appreciate it. Admittedly, Webb is not for everybody. It is a hard, taxing, and focused school. It's like being in the Marine Corps for the mind. But the status and opportunity that come with a degree from Webb certainly make it all worthwhile. A Webb education is a top-notch education, certainly better for engineering than any Ivy League or technical school—and the price just can't be beat. So, if you have the interest in ships, the smarts, and the stamina necessary to make it through Webb, by all means, DO IT! It may very well be the most accelerating four years your career will ever see.

❏ *Alan Bolind, B.S.*

 Wellesley College
106 Central Street
Wellesley, MA 02481

 (781) 283-1000
Fax: (781) 283-3678

 E-mail: *admission@wellesley.edu*
Web site: *http://www.wellesley.edu*

 Enrollment

Full-time ❏ women: 2,215

INTRODUCING WELLESLEY

Wellesley's unofficial motto is to "educate women who will make a difference in the world." And if there's one thing a Wellesley education will give you, it's a sense of empowerment that you have the skills, confidence, and know-how to succeed at anything you choose.

Consistently ranked among the top five liberal arts colleges in the nation, Wellesley offers its students a serious intellectual environment combined with a fun, all-women atmosphere. It's not uncommon to find friends gossiping until early morning, baking cookies together while cramming for an exam, or crowded around the dorm television on Thursday nights for a study break.

Wellesley is a college where the emphasis is on you. You'll never be a number at Wellesley; all of your professors will know you by your name and the quality of your work. Student opinions not only count but are actively solicited, from determining which professors receive tenure, to selecting your commencement speaker, to campus and dorm governance issues.

My first year at Wellesley, several students were chosen to help select the next president of the college. And our input didn't stop there! The new president asked us to call her by her first name, Diana, and always said hello when we saw her walking across campus or jogging around the lake. She also came to many of the college's activities, from attending school plays, soccer games, and student body meetings, to greeting trick-or-treaters at her home on Halloween. She gave us the feeling she really cared, and she did.

Part of Wellesley's charm also comes from its surroundings. Nestled in the suburb of Wellesley, Massachusetts, twelve miles outside of Boston, the college is located on a 500-acre campus that boasts one of the most spectacular settings in New England. Students often spend their weekends canoeing on Lake Waban, reading on Green Beach, or "traying" down Severance Green in the snow.

But during the week, students focus almost exclusively on their work. Wellesley is a teaching college rather than a research university, so students receive plenty of individual attention. Professors hold extensive office hours and some will even bake brownies for class or have students over to their homes. Every professor assigns and grades papers and exams; no graduate students compete for your attention or evaluate your work.

English, psychology, and economics are among the most popular majors, although students dabble in everything from economics of Third World countries to sports medicine to Greek art. Many students choose to double-major, while others will select a minor, often a foreign language. Students can take only fourteen of their thirty-two credits in their major, so they are forced to broaden their education beyond a few departments.

Outside of the classroom, students spend much of their time participating in sports, college government, music groups, dee-jaying at the college radio station, and exploring Boston.

While Wellesley is not a party school, social opportunities abound if you're determined and aggressive. On campus, very few students choose not to participate in an extracurricular activity. And if your favorite activity on campus doesn't exist, simply propose it to college government—chances are, it will be approved.

An open mind is one of the crucial elements of being a Wellesley student, and the colleges stresses racial, ethnic, and religious diversity among its students. While most women call the mid-Atlantic home, students come from all fifty states and hail from more than sixty-five countries. Although everyone is required to take a course from the multicultural curriculum, students often learn best about other cultures and customs from spending time with one another in the dorms.

> *I went to the Divali, or "festival of lights," dinner with one of my friends sophomore year. She was dressed in a beautiful Indian robe and took part in a traditional dance like I had never seen before. Afterwards, we had home-cooked dishes from Indian recipes that were both exotic and delicious. It was a wonderful, eye-opening experience.*

The dorms each have their own distinct character and it's easy to get to know both older and younger students, since dorms are not separated by class.

All in all, you'll work hard at Wellesley, but you'll never regret it. Wellesley will push you to your intellectual and physical limits, but you'll finish college with excellent preparation for whatever next step you choose to take. Wellesley may drive you crazy as a student, but as an alumna, you'll realize it was the best decision you've ever made.

ADMISSIONS REQUIREMENTS

As Wellesley's profile has risen in recent years, the percentage of students admitted has declined from fifty percent to about thirty-four percent. But if you have a strong academic record, are motivated and enthusiastic, and know you want to attend a top school, Wellesley should be an easy choice.

Since the college believes a diverse student body is important, Wellesley seeks to bring together a group of individuals who enrich the school by their different experiences, races, ethnicities, religions, geographic backgrounds, and interests. Approximately forty-four percent of the student body is white, twenty-five percent is Asian, and thirteen percent is African American, Latino, and Native American and eight percent are international students. While sixty-four percent have attended public high schools, the other thirty-four percent have gone to private schools and one percent have been home-schooled.

Decision Plans

The college offers three decision plans for prospective students, each with different deadlines and each geared toward a different kind of applicant. All, require the standard application fee of $50, although the fee is waived for online applicants and in cases of financial need.

- *Early Decision* is designed for women who are sure they want to attend Wellesley; about one-fifth of incoming students are accepted under this plan. If you think you might fall into this category, it's best to visit the college early, attend a few classes, meet some professors, and arrange an overnight stay with a student in her dorm room. The Early Decision deadline falls on November 1, so you must take the SAT or ACT by October. The advantage of this plan is that you'll know by the winter holidays whether you've been admitted or deferred to the regular application pool. The only disadvantage is that the decision is binding, so if accepted, you must withdraw your applications from all other schools.

- For students who are strongly considering Wellesley but aren't sure they want to commit to the Early Decision program, the *Early Evaluation* plan has a deadline of January 1. You'll receive a letter by the end of February that indicates your chances of acceptance, but the final decision is not sent out until April. Early Evaluation is a smart plan for people who want to know how realistic their chances of admission are without having to pledge to one school.

- Finally, Wellesley offers a *Traditional Regular Decision* plan. Applications are due January 15, so you can take standardized tests through December of your senior year. Again, the Board of Admissions will notify you of its decision in April. Students placed on the wait list will also be notified at this time.

After you've chosen which plan is right for you, it's time to think about assembling your application package.

Application Requirements

Wellesley requires its applicants to take either the ACT (with Writing) or SAT and two SAT Subject Tests (recommended one to be quantitative). In a recent incoming class, first-year students typically scored between 600 and 700 on the Math section and between 600 and 800 on the Verbal section of the SAT I.

Of course, standardized tests are only one part of your Wellesley application. High school grades are equally, if not more, important. Ninety-five percent of incoming students were in the top quarter of their class; all ranked in the top half. You'll also need two academic teacher recommendations. It's best to choose teachers who know you well from the classroom and extracurricular activities, and who can easily talk about your abilities, development as a student, personality, and potential as a Wellesley woman.

Along with the regular admissions paperwork, Wellesley requires a personal essay. The essay is one of the most crucial parts of the application because it tells the admission board who you are, what you think, and why you would make a good candidate for Wellesley. It's also a chance for you to stand out from everybody else and tout your achievements. Remember, students, professors, and admissions officers are reading your essay, so your chances are best if you gear it toward a general audience.

Finally, Wellesley recommends, but does not require, an admissions interview. Try to have the interview on campus, so you can get the flavor of the school. Remember, the interview is not just a chance for the admissions officers to learn more about you, but for you to learn more about Wellesley. If you can't make it up to Boston, you can meet with an alumna in your area.

Applying to college seemed like a daunting process, but the Wellesley students and professors I met were so encouraging I felt as though they really wanted me there. The admissions office also went out of its way. When my parents and I arrived late for the campus tour, a student took us individually to our tour group and showed us sights along the way. The experience was actually symbolic of my years at Wellesley—everyone makes an extra effort to help each other out and is always supportive.

A few other points: AP credits (up to a total of four credits) are accepted, provided you score a four or five on most tests. Interviews are required of transfer students, as are high school and college transcripts, and SAT scores. Students applying from abroad must take the college boards and submit scores from their native countries' college entrance exams. Furthermore, a TOEFL exam is strongly recommended for students whose native language is not English.

ACADEMIC LIFE

One of the best things about a Wellesley education is the opportunity to study a broad array of topics. Wellesley's curriculum offers up a plate of anything and everything, but leaves the choice to you. The college provides major and minor programs of study in more than thirty departments and programs.

When I was a first-year student at Wellesley, my parents told me they had a few requirements of their own: I should take art history, economics, history, and a course in Shakespeare while in college. I put them off until junior and senior years—what a mistake! I regretted not minoring in history. And now when I go to art museums, I understand so much more—the time period, the artist's purposes, and color schemes.

Courses

Before students can graduate, they must meet some basic requirements. All students must complete thirty-two units of credits (usually one credit per course), at least eight of which are in your major. You also must maintain a 2.0, or C, average. In addition, all students must elect nine courses drawn from eight substantive and skill-based categories; a multicultural class; an expository writing course; one year of physical education; and demonstrated proficiency in a foreign language. Students must also complete four 300-level, or the most specialized, courses, at least two of which are in your major, to ensure you have in-depth knowledge in several subjects. If this all sounds daunting, it's not. Remember, you have eight semesters to spread these classes out. Most professors would advise, however, that you complete these courses during your first two years at Wellesley, so you can concentrate on completing your major and travel abroad during your junior and senior years.

Beyond the requirements, though, you can break your own academic path at Wellesley, including devising your own major and the courses needed to complete it. It's wise to experiment with a wide variety of offerings; many students find they have strong interests in subjects as different as English and physics, and love spending hours poring over books in the Reserve Room, but also relish nights spent stargazing at the Observatory. The college offers many courses without prerequisites, so you don't have to be a whiz at something before you walk into the classroom.

Faculty

The strongest aspect of Wellesley's academic life is its professors. The 305 faculty members are about evenly split between men and women, all of whom hold degrees in their fields from the top schools. And with a faculty-student ratio of nine to one, you'll not only know but most likely become friends with your professors.

Although research is considered a vital part of any professor's résumé, Wellesley professors are at the college principally because they want to teach, not because they want to do research. This means they'll know you by name and grade your work, and that you'll have valuable personal contacts when it comes time to ask for career advice and graduate school recommendations. They'll also take an interest in your life outside the classroom: how the soccer team did, if your family is visiting for Family Weekend, and when your theater production will be appearing on campus. At Wellesley, the average course size ranges from fifteen to twenty-five students, depending on the type of class.

A SAMPLING OF COURSES AT WELLESLEY

- Artificial Intelligence
- Trade and Migration
- The Victorian Novel
- Women of Russia: A Portrait Gallery
- Comparative Physiology and Anatomy of Vertebrates with Laboratory
- Islamic Society in Historical Perspective
- Race and Ethnicity in American Literature
- Vergil's *Aeneid*
- Conservatism and Liberalism in Contemporary American Politics
- Government Policy: Its Effect on the Marketplace
- Christianity and the Third World
- Sociology of the Family
- Paris: City of Light
- Techniques of Acting
- Psychology of Language
- Paleontology with Laboratory
- Presidential-Congressional Relations
- African American Feminism
- Renaissance Art in Venice and in Northern Italy
- New Literatures: Lesbian and Gay Writing in America

> *My parents recently visited Wellesley and had lunch with one of my professors. Even though I graduated several years ago, he jumped at the chance to meet them again and spent an hour and a half reminiscing with them about my years as a student and sharing personal stories. It was a great experience that I doubt would have happened at any other school.*

Another advantage of such an intimate class setting is that you'll have a unique chance to engage in truly intellectual debates that will often last more than the regular seventy minutes of class time. Professors also go out of their way to bring some of the brightest minds in their field to campus to meet with students in group settings, answer your questions, and spur your curiosity.

Course Load

The course load at Wellesley is not easy, but it is manageable. You can expect to stay up late reading Chaucer, spend your Sunday afternoons in the laboratory running chemistry experiments, and devote your mornings to practicing French in the language lab. But you'll be surprised at how much you come to enjoy each of these experiences, and you'll still have plenty of time left to participate in extracurricular activities and enjoy a healthy social life.

After their first year, Wellesley students are allowed to elect up to five courses a semester; they can also audit classes and take courses pass/fail. The college's Honor Code allows students to schedule their own exams at the end of the semester. While this option allows you to take finals at your own pace, self-discipline in studying is a must.

Honors Program

For those who want to dive deeper into a particular academic area, the college offers an honors program for seniors. Provided students meet a high GPA in their major and choose an appropriate topic for study, they can work with several professors to complete a year-long thesis, thus qualifying for departmental honors. Students can also qualify for Latin Honors, based on their grade point average, which are recognized at graduation.

Exchange Program

Wellesley offers many opportunities for students to study outside the campus borders— ranging from cross-registering for a course at MIT to spending a year or semester at a university in Mexico, Korea, or France. Other programs include exchanges at Spelman College in Georgia, Mills College in California, and the Twelve College Exchange.

A number of intensive courses in other countries are offered during the three-week January winter session.

SOCIAL LIFE AND ACTIVITIES

Clubs

From the rugby team to the Canada Club to the more traditional activities such as the campus newspaper and student government, it's all yours for the taking at Wellesley.

Wellesley prides itself on offering just about any activity its students could want. If you're a dancer or singer, a literary lover, or a philosophy guru, there's a club for you. In all, Wellesley offers about 170 student groups and most have no membership requirements or dues—those are included in your annual student activity fee.

While these clubs will take as much of your time as you let them, they will also comprise some of your fondest college memories. You'll share the experience of running an organization together, from top to bottom, and learn both management and organizational skills far superior to those you'd get out of most internships. Few Wellesley students participate in no clubs at all; on average, students participate in at least one or two groups each year.

As a resident advisor my sophomore year, I was both the leader on my floor and part of a management team that arranged activities for my fellow dorm-mates. When the resident advisors met each Wednesday night, we'd talk about our individual problems and successes, and the direction we wanted to help take the dorm in. It was a wonderful chance to be a team player, see the impact our decisions had on our peers, and learn from their feedback.

Wellesley encourages first-year students to participate in all activities. Most clubs thrive on the energy and enthusiasm new students bring; they're also a great way to meet Wellesley women of all ages. A student activities' night is held at the beginning of each school year, so you can check out clubs that sound interesting. The new Wang Campus Center is the base of extracurricular life, although most activities take students everywhere from campus to the entire northeast corridor.

Sports

Wellesley also offers a variety of sports teams that compete with other Seven Sisters and regional schools, including soccer, basketball, volleyball, swimming, lacrosse, golf, softball, cross-country, and tennis. The college prides itself on graduating well-rounded individuals, so students are encouraged to take part in sports, whether on a varsity or intramural level. And with the Nannerl O. Keohane Sports Center on campus, that's not hard to do. The Keohane Sports Center, named after Wellesley's eleventh president, includes an indoor track, pool, sauna, basketball and tennis courts, and weight room. In the fall and spring, students also canoe on Lake Waban and row on the Charles River in Boston.

I took golf during my junior year at Wellesley and loved it! We played on the college's beautiful course across the street from campus and learned all about the strokes and various clubs. The best part, though, was that we were able to laugh together about our mistakes as beginners but also able to actually play nine holes when the semester ended!

Dorms

While clubs and sports are a great way to meet other students, dorms provide the most natural setting for getting to know your Wellesley sisters. Almost all students live in the dorms, and on-campus housing for four years is guaranteed, with most juniors and seniors living in single rooms. Some students live in co-ops, cooking their own food and living in a relaxed residential system. In most dorms, though, resident directors, house presidents, first-year coordinators, and resident advisors plan activities, from showing videos to having leaf-jumping parties, to holding study breaks complete with café lattes and Milano cookies. A favorite activity of the year is Holiday Dinner, where seniors dress in their gowns, students gather to sing songs, and the dining halls prepare a fabulous feast, complete with the college's own peppermint stick pie.

Wellesley does not have a Greek system, but students with interests in art, music, and Shakespeare can join one of the four society houses on campus. The groups arrange campus-wide lectures and events, as well as provide another social outlet for members.

Parties

Keep in mind that Wellesley is not a party school, but that doesn't mean there aren't parties on campus. The opportunities also are there if you want to attend parties on campus or at Boston area colleges and universities each weekend, go clubbing, or be a sister at a fraternity house. While many first-year students do all of the above, older students often spend weekends on campus, listening to comedians and musicians at Punch's Alley, the campus pub; taking advantage of the college theater; seeing classic 1980s movies at the Film Society; and just enjoying each other's company. As with most other things at Wellesley, you create the path you want to take.

FINANCIAL AID

College these days is expensive, but one of Wellesley's most important priorities is maintaining its need-blind admissions policy. More than half of Wellesley students receive some form of financial aid. In 1999 the college boosted its financial aid program by offering more grants instead of loans.

A Wellesley education costs about $42,000 per year, including tuition, room, board, and the student activity and facilities fees. Students in Massachusetts must enroll in a health insurance program. The average yearly financial aid package was recently close to $28,000.

While a financial aid award depends on a student's need, the college provides aid for about sixty percent of first-year students and fifty-nine percent of all students.

Payment Plans

Wellesley offers three payment plans to help students pay for their education:

- The semester payment plan allows students and their families to pay tuition and other expenses twice each year; this program is generally recommended for parents who are using savings to pay for college or have loans guaranteed at very favorable rates.
- The ten-month payment plan assists families who are using current earnings to pay for tuition in five installments.
- The prepaid tuition stabilization plan allows families to pay the entire cost of a Wellesley education upon entrance to the school. This program sets the cost of tuition at the first-year rate and will not reflect any subsequent increases during the course of the student's education.

Students who are interested in obtaining financial aid must submit their most recent income tax returns, along with the FAFSA or Wellesley's own financial statement. The deadline for financial aid applications is January 15.

Working on Campus

To raise money for their education, many students work on campus in activities ranging from being a guard in the college's Davis Museum and Cultural Center, to working as an assistant in one of the departments, to working in a dining hall. The average annual intake from these jobs is about $2,000. It's also a great way to meet fellow students, work along-side your professors or administrators, and spend time enjoying the campus.

Loans and Grants

Wellesley also offers four types of loans to incoming students: the federal Stafford Loan, the federal Perkins Loan, the Wellesley College Student's Aid Society Loan, and the Wellesley College Loan program.

The federal Stafford and Perkins loans are repayable starting six months after graduation. While the Stafford Loan has a variable interest rate that is set each summer for the upcoming year, the Perkins Loan has a set interest rate of five percent and is available to students who demonstrate high financial need.

The Wellesley College Student's Aid Society Loan is a low-interest loan that must be repaid within five years and nine months of graduation. The Wellesley College Loan program, which is geared toward international students, requires payments twice a year following graduation.

Wellesley also offers grants from the college's funds and from the federal Supplemental Opportunity Grant Program. In addition, students who think they may be eligible for state grants and the federal Pell Grant should contact the financial aid office, which verifies students' enrollment and eligibility.

Finally, financial awards from outside organizations are calculated into the work-loan-grant program administered by the college. The Students' Aid Society also provides professional and winter clothing, emergency loans, and supplies for students receiving aid.

GRADUATES

Chances are you've heard of some of Wellesley's most famous graduates: former First Lady and Senator Hillary Rodham Clinton, former Secretary of State Madeleine Korbel Albright, and screenwriter/director Nora Ephron (of *When Harry Met Sally* and *Sleepless in Seattle* fame), to name just a few. But in truth, whether they're famous or not, most Wellesley alumnae are very successful at (and very happy with) what they do.

Wellesley graduates about 580 to 620 students each year, with about half of them choosing to go on to graduate school or other study, and about half going into the working world. Ninety-three percent of students graduate within six years of enrollment. Many students choose a career in business, often starting out as a management consultant at a high-powered Manhattan or Boston firm. Other popular careers include education, law, journalism, and medicine. Teach for America is the number one employer for recent grads.

More than 150 companies and non-profit organizations, ranging from Microsoft to Smith Barney, recruit on campus each year. Students find that the recruiting process is a great way to learn more about these companies, practice their interviewing skills, and, of course, land that all-important first job. Because Wellesley graduates are so successful, most companies return year after year.

The college also offers a well-staffed Center for Work and Service to assist students about postgraduation plans. From advice on polishing up your résumé to helping you apply for fellowship programs, the center's employees are knowledgeable and accessible. The center also pairs up students and mentors for a day-long "shadow" program in January, and keeps a database with names of alumnae all over the world who have offered to share their professional insights. The Wellesley alumnae network is extensive, powerful, and accessible.

- Madeleine Albright, former US Secretary of State
- Katharine Lee Bates, Professor, Author, *America the Beautiful*
- Michelle Caruso-Cabrera, MSNBC Journalist
- Hillary Rodham Clinton, Former First Lady, U.S. Senator from New York
- Marjory Stoneman Douglas, Environmentalist
- Wendy Lee Gramm, Former Chair, Commodities Futures Trading Commission
- Mildred McAfee Horton, Founder of WAVES
- Madame Chiang Kai-shek, Nationalist Chinese Leader
- Nannerl O. Keohane, Political Scientist, President of Duke University
- Ali McGraw, Actress
- Pamela Melroy, NASA Astronaut
- Cokie Roberts, Journalist
- Diane Sawyer, Journalist
- Vivian Pinn, Director of National Institutes of Health

The alumnae association provides several programs for juniors and seniors, too, including a mentoring night, where students share dinner and conversation with alumnae in the Boston area who have similar career interests. In addition, the association sponsors workshops on buying a car, renting an apartment, finding a job, and generally making it on your own.

I went to the mentoring night my senior year, and sat around an alumna's living room chatting about our common interest in journalism. One alum, Jean Dietz, had been a correspondent for The Boston Globe. *Another, Callie Crossley, was a producer with the ABC newsmagazine, 20/20. It was great to hear about their experiences as successful women in journalism, and they were genuinely interested in helping me start my career.*

Many Wellesley alumnae have been pathbreakers in their careers and all of them want to see you succeed; you'll find that this support network of more than 36,000 women worldwide will follow you wherever you go and is always ready to lend a hand.

Once you leave Wellesley, you'll find that all your networks of career support are still available to help you, and that local alumnae clubs throughout the world sponsor events, from happy hours, hayrides, and Sunday afternoon teas to lectures by professors who are visiting the area and pizza nights with prospective students. Graduates also serve on the Board of Trustees, as advisors to various groups, and as admissions representatives. But the best part of being a graduate may be taking part in the reunion parades, where graduates dress in their class colors, take part in Stepsinging—a favorite college tradition—have a chance to revisit the campus in the spring, and catch up with their friends.

SUMMING UP

Although Wellesley women are diverse in their interests, backgrounds, and personalities, all of them share the experience of having attended the top women's college in the country. Wellesley offers its students the opportunity to expand their minds, challenge their limits, and learn to be meaningful leaders in a changing world.

Wellesley women share more than an education, though. From Flower Sunday in September, when sophomores give their "little sisters," or first-year students, a daisy as a sign of welcome and friendship, to commencement, when seniors pop champagne corks together, Wellesley develops in its students a sense of sisterhood, a camaraderie that can only be shared at a women's college. While students may complain about a lack of social life during their four years there, they will also revel in the chance to study without distraction and to be completely in the company of a group of outstanding women. As a favorite campus saying goes, "Not a girls' school without men, but a women's college without boys."

The campus is also a sanctuary, a safe and secure atmosphere, where you will find yourself enveloped by the beautiful Massachusetts environment.

Professors are there to offer a hand as well; many of them have been known to spend an hour or more with each student during office hours. As a student, you'll not only learn facts and figures, but how to analyze and apply that information to other problems. Your professors will challenge you to become active thinkers and participants in and out of the classroom, by sharing your enthusiasm and success, offering advice, and also becoming lifelong friends.

Wellesley is a college where you will be known by your first name, whether you're the college president, a professor, or a student. You can also choose whether to be the student body president or just a member of the student body. You become empowered because you make the decisions and you shape your future.

If you have a preconceived notion of a women's college, chances are it's not true at Wellesley—the college is not a bastion of lesbianism, nor a stronghold of left-wing, radical feminism. It's also not a place for meek-mannered women. What Wellesley is, is a supportive environment that gives its students a sense of self-esteem, accomplishment, and the ability to apply that knowledge and confidence elsewhere. What Wellesley does is to successfully educate women who do, time and time again, make a difference in the world.

❏ *Mary Lynn F. Jones, B.A.*

WESLEYAN UNIVERSITY

Photo by Nancy Wolz

Wesleyan University
Middletown, CT 06459

(860) 685-3000
Fax: (860) 685-3001

E-mail: *admissions@wesleyan.edu*
Web site: *www.wesleyan.edu/admission*

 Enrollment

Full-time ❑ women: 1,389
          ❑ men: 1,401

INTRODUCING WESLEYAN

Wesleyan students feel a unique bond with one another that goes beyond school spirit. When you meet someone who went to Wes you feel like you know them already, in the sense that you've both shared in the discovery of some wonderful secret.

For years, Wesleyan has been one of America's best-kept educational secrets, but it seems that the word is getting out. Increasing numbers of applicants are realizing that Wesleyan's unparalleled academics and unique student body make for a college experience unsurpassed elsewhere. Its top-notch faculty includes some of the best in the country in both research and teaching, and the students are driven by the inner desire to work hard and to have fun. To add to this, Wesleyan is a college on the edge of the future, with an administration and a president, Douglas J. Bennet, committed to leading Wesleyan with vision, demonstrating the value of a liberal arts education to the world.

Three things set Wesleyan apart from the rest: size, academic intensity, and its student body. Wesleyan is a small-to-medium liberal arts college (2,700 undergraduates) set on a beautiful and spacious New England campus, comparable to schools like Amherst and Williams. But as a thriving research university, with a small population of 150 graduates, the productivity and distinction of Wesleyan faculty in research rival that of faculty at much larger institutions. Because of its unique size, undergraduate students make use of graduate resources and enjoy small seminar-sized classes and opportunities to personally get to know professors.

Many students choose Wes over the Ivy League for its intellectual environment, which differs from other competitive schools in one key quality: While students at other universities are often encouraged to compete against others, Wesleyan students only compete to do better than they did last week. Wes students feel comfortable helping each other with work, and talking about intellectual ideas even (gasp!) outside the classroom.

Wesleyan fosters independence—its approach to liberal arts education encourages undergraduates to invest deeply in their courses of study, without mandating a set of core courses that every student must slog through. What students do have in common is *passion*— they are passionate about their studies, passionate about their artistic endeavors, and passionate about their politics. "The greatest thing that Wesleyan did for me was help me define my own education," said one graduating senior. This might seem daunting to some, but Wesleyan students rise to the occasion.

You're in a place where no one tells you how to live, how to dress, or (heaven forbid) what to think—academically or otherwise. I tend to see it as a challenge.

ADMISSIONS REQUIREMENTS

There is no question that Wesleyan is one of America's "hot" schools. The Office of Admissions has seen a nineteen percent increase in applications since 1996. Only twenty-eight percent of those who applied in a recent year were admitted.

What students should apply? Make no mistake: Wesleyan is academically rigorous; in general, applicants have performed extraordinarily well in high school. Of a recent class, sixty-eight percent ranked in the top ten percent of their high school class. Seventy-one percent took biology, chemistry, and physics in high school. As with many colleges, the high school transcript is considered the most important element of the application, but Wesleyan prides itself on taking the time to get to know each applicant as a person and not as a series of numbers, weighing heavily the personal essay, recommendations, and interview. Median SAT scores are Verbal—700, Math—700, Writing—690, ACT—30. The SAT or ACT is required, as are two SAT Subject Tests.

Students at Wesleyan are stellar beyond SAT scores, grades, and lists of activities. They are intellectually curious, take initiative, and have proved that they will contribute to the Wesleyan community. A recent freshman class included a student who was the first female member of her high school football team, an award-winning playwright, a nationally ranked chess player, and a student who started a midnight basketball program in his hometown. Every year, there are many students who excel as starting players on varsity sports teams, leaders of high school student bodies, and active volunteers in their communities. Applicants to Wes must prove that they have made use of the resources and options available in high school, and plan to continue to be active and engaged in college.

For the student who is serious about Wesleyan, applying Early Decision provides a slight edge in the application process. It is encouraged only for those who have selected Wes as the top choice. Admittance to Wesleyan ED is binding.

ACADEMIC LIFE

It took me a while to get used to the demanding academic schedule at Wesleyan. But when I did, I really came to realize what makes it so special. As well as one-on-one attention from my professors, I really benefited from their scholarship. I began to learn with my professors, rather than from them.

Wesleyan has earned a reputation as one of the finest schools in the country for good reason: its professors are top scholars and teachers, and its students take initiative and have a passion for learning. Wesleyan differs from other top-ranked institutions, however, in the depth of its commitment to fostering the pursuit of individual intellectual interests.

Course Offerings

The breadth of offerings at Wesleyan is outstanding. Typical liberal arts disciplines such as history, English, and physics exist side by side with such departments as molecular biology and biochemistry (MB & B), East Asian studies, and film studies.

I was amazed when, in my senior year of high school, I found the Wesleyan course catalog in our guidance center. I thought I might have to go to a huge state university to take the range of courses I was interested in, but Wesleyan had it all—from Oceanography to Linguistics, Archaeology to Film—I felt that I'd finally found a school that would keep pace with my interests.

Wesleyan's unique course offerings include "Autobiographical and Professional Choice," "Philosophical Foundations of Economic Justice," "Conservation Aquatic Ecosystems," and "Western Movies: Myth, Ideology, and Genre." Another of Wesleyan's major strengths is its arts curriculum; introductory courses are open to all and most graduating seniors, regardless of their majors, have taken at least one dance, studio art, or music course. Popular choices include Introduction to Drawing, West African Dance, and Worlds of Music.

The free and open aspect of the Wesleyan curriculum goes beyond the arts. Because there are very few classes reserved only for majors, students can follow many interests and not feel blocked out of classes. So how does a student decide which four or five classes a semester to take from over 900 courses in 39 departments and programs and 45 major fields of study? Upon arrival on the campus, each student is assigned a faculty advisor. The FA works with the student to define an academic mission and choose classes, all via Wesleyan's high-tech and student-friendly on-line course registration system.

FYI Classes

From the very first semester, academic exploration at Wesleyan is encouraged. Freshmen are prioritized for admittance to a host of small, intellectually rigorous seminars known as First-Year Initiatives, or FYI classes. The first two years at Wesleyan are generally reserved for exploration of the wide-ranging curriculum. To fulfill Wesleyan's General Education Expectations (GenEds), students must take at least three courses (from at least two different departments) in each of three categories: humanities and arts, social and behavioral sciences, and natural sciences and mathematics. The vast majority of Wesleyan students fulfill these expectations without ever trying, though it is possible to opt out of the Expectations with a valid academic reason.

Majors

A student's final two years at Wesleyan are when he or she can truly delve into a chosen course of study. Majors are declared at the end of the sophomore year. The most-declared majors at Wes are English, psychology, and government, but double-majoring is common, and more students triple-major than one might imagine. Interdepartmental majors such as psychology-sociology, African American studies, medieval studies, and East Asian studies are popular, and the American studies department at Wes is considered to be one of the finest undergraduate programs in the country—housed in the Center for the Americas with Latin American studies. Students may also, with faculty approval, create a university major, joining two or more areas of study not already conjoined under the auspices of an interdepartmental major. Wesleyan also features two special interdisciplinary majors that must be declared during freshman year, the College of Letters (COL), which combines literature, history, philosophy, and foreign languages, and the College of Social Studies (CSS), combining history, government, philosophy, and economics (sometimes called the "College of Suicidal Sophomores," in reference to its demanding sophomore year schedule of a ten-page paper a week).

Study Abroad

Many students (almost fifty percent) choose to augment their on-campus experience at Wesleyan by taking one or two semesters abroad or away from campus. With the assistance of the Office of International Affairs, students can study abroad in Wesleyan programs in France, Germany, Italy, Mexico, and Spain. Wesleyan also has special relationships with programs in Japan and China, and students go to any of the other 140 programs approved by the Office of International Studies. Wesleyan is also part of the Twelve College Exchange Program, a group of prestigious New England colleges that offers exchanges for the semester or year.

The Thesis

The grand finale of a student's academic life at Wesleyan is often the completion of a thesis. Though it is only through the optional thesis process that a student can earn university honors (there is a separate Phi Beta Kappa selection process), many students choose to do a thesis simply to fulfill personal intellectual goals. The most common theses at Wesleyan are year-long research projects, producing papers that range in length from 30 to 45 pages in the sciences to 100 to 160 pages in English or history. Dance, theater, and music majors perform their theses for the Wesleyan community, while studio arts majors participate in a three-week gallery exhibition and the thesis films constitute a special slate of screenings at the end of the semester.

Faculty

The Wesleyan faculty is outstanding and engaging. In recent studies, Wesleyan professors have tipped the scales in scholarship—the science faculty has received more outside funding from prestigious sources such as NSF and NIH than their peers at any comparable institution, and the economics department is renowned as one of the best in the country. Unlike many larger institutions, however, the most productive scholars at Wesleyan are often highly regarded as the best teachers. All of the more than 300 full-time faculty members teach undergraduates. Professors frequently structure classes around their current interests and research, allowing for timely, engaging classroom discussion. Students frequently become involved in helping professors with research and have often co-authored papers with their professors. Professors are generally accessible and meet with their students informally outside of class. The faculty includes jazz musician and MacArthur Fellowship winner, Anthony Braxton; film authority, Jeanine Basinger; international terrorism expert, Martha Crenshaw; former *Art Bulletin* editor, John Paoletti; award-winning American studies scholar, Richard Slotkin,; experimental music composer, Alvin Lucier; prominent DNA researcher, David Beveridge; and noted historian of China; Vera Schwarcz.

Despite the depth and breadth of the curriculum, students may find they wish to explore a subject not covered by any class offered. In that event, they may, in consultation with a faculty member, design a tutorial to study the subject they are interested in. Recent student-organized tutorials have included topics in Native American studies, literature seminars focusing on American novelists Don DeLillo and Anne Rice, and a survey of "Complexity Theory."

Facilities

It is nearly impossible for any single student to exhaust Wesleyan's academic resources, but it may be even more difficult to exhaust its physical resources. Wesleyan's modern, technologically adaptable classroom space is enhanced by several fine computer labs, e-mail and Internet connections in each dorm room, and more lab space in the Science Center per student than any other science research institution in the country. Olin Library, the university's largest library, has one million volumes including a music library and a rare book collection (including a Shakespeare First Folio). The Smith Room on the first floor is a popular place to meet friends in the evening, and the small, quiet study rooms on the second and third floors are for those who prefer dead silence (many seniors who write honors theses get their own thesis carrels, small private rooms, many with window views). The Information Commons on the first floor is another popular place for students to gather when they work together or individually on various academic projects. Students can use on-site desktop computers and printers or bring their own laptops while having access in a centralized area to library reference resources, information technology, and a network of academic resources on campus. Across the street from Olin, the Science Library houses science-oriented materials along with the Cutter Collection, an eclectic collection of one family's turn-of-the-century books, and a small natural history museum. Across campus in the Center for the Arts (CFA), the Davison Art Center is a national landmark that houses the art library and 10,000 prints by old masters and modern artists.

SOCIAL LIFE AND ACTIVITIES

The variety of Wesleyan's academic life is equaled, if not exceeded, by the variety of its social life. There is a popular theory at Wesleyan that if you get any students into conversation, you will find that they do something fascinating—from leading the Ultimate Frisbee team to directing a short film. It is a place teeming with students who are interested in living in a charged environment. Each week, the student body hosts a wide variety of activities ranging from dance performances to sports games to live music, and it is not uncommon to attend several of such different events in one day.

Although Middletown is located thirty minutes from New Haven, thirty minutes from Hartford, and two hours from New York City and Boston, Wesleyan students often don't feel the need to venture very far to have fun, and the focus of the social life is located on campus. Middletown has a variety of restaurants popular with students (it can be difficult to get a table at O'Rourke's Diner on a Sunday morning, where students have entertained Clint Eastwood and Allen Ginsberg), but for nightlife Wesleyan sticks close to home. Walk around the campus grounds on a weekend night and you will see bands performing in the West Co Café, plays at the Paricelli '92 Theater, movies at the Goldsmith Family Cinema at the Center for Film Studies, and hip-hop shows at student venues.

Parties

There are as many different kinds of parties as there are kinds of people—gatherings ranging from house parties to all-campus parties to dorm parties to parties sponsored by student groups. Often parties have themes: a costume party in LoRise, an eighties dance at Psi Upsilon fraternity, or a swing ball to celebrate the Senior Film Festival. Parties range from small and intimate to large and loud, but they are never exclusive, and never focused exclusively around drinking. Often a group such as the Black and Latino Brotherhood or the women's rugby team will sponsor a campus event that attracts a broad cross section of students. Each year, two large musical events—Fall Ball and Spring Fling—attract big-name bands to campus. Recently featured were Andrew WK, Talib Kweli, Saul Williams, Immortal Technique, Cee-Lo, and Welfare Poets.

The first year at Wes is the only year social activities are arranged; after orientation, students plan their own social calendars. In general, the more adventurous students are, the more events they will attend and the more people they will meet. Friendships grow out of social events, residential life, classes, clubs, and sports teams. While Wesleyan students don't go on traditional "dates," a couple might meet at Klekolo, a local cafe, or drive to the always-open Athenian Diner.

I try to go to as many things I can and meet as many people I can, but there's always more—I'm always reluctant to go away for the weekend, because I'm afraid I'll miss something.

Dining on Campus

Dining on campus underwent a complete renaissance for the fall of 2007. Brand new dining facilities are the anchors of the new 110,000-square-foot Usdan University Center. Two new dining halls that seat more than 300 people each are adjacent to a state-of-the-art dining marketplace with a brick oven pizza oven, a Mongolian grill, a deli, and a salad bar, as well as kosher and vegan serving stations. Students have views of Foss Hill, a popular student hangout, and Andrus Field, where the football and baseball teams play.

The University

The University Center also houses a first floor café with soups, sandwiches, salads, and coffee. The third floor will feature a more upscale dining room for lunches with faculty and staff. Students will still be able to use their meal plan elsewhere on campus at Summerfields and Weswings, or at one of the eating clubs located in the fraternity houses. Always handy is Weshop, the campus grocery store which stocks fresh produce, name-brand foods, and organic and vegan choices; students can make purchases there using their dining points.

Housing

Wesleyan is one of the only schools I know of where freshmen can live in a single if they want to; in fact, it's one of the reasons I chose to go there. I value that students are allowed that independence even from day one.

Wesleyan housing is prime real estate compared to some other schools. On-campus housing is guaranteed all four years, and can range from traditional freshman residence halls to small New England houses on tree-lined streets. All undergraduates live on campus. Most first-year students live in residence halls in double rooms. Upperclassmen either elect to stay in the residence halls or live in apartments, townhouses, New England clapboard houses, or special interest houses, which include everything from German House to Science House to Womanist House. These houses sponsor educational and social events for the whole campus.

Fraternities and Sororities

Fraternities are an option for housing and also for social life: five percent of students are involved in the six fraternities (some coed) and two sororities on campus. The Mystical Seven and The Skull and Serpent, secret societies both located on Wyllys Avenue at the gateway to the Center for the Arts, date from the early 1900s and are shrouded in mystery, but no one lives here. (We think.)

Organizations

Wesleyan students like to get involved. They serve on every university committee, organize orientation and graduation, and independently allocate funds to more than 200 student organizations, which include groups devoted to politics, athletics, and artistic and cultural interests. Fifteen student publications are sent to press at least once a semester, ranging from the school newspaper, the *Argus*, to magazines of fiction, humor, women's issues, activism, and poetry. Students are also responsible for the wide variety of lecturers and artists who visit campus. WESU-FM, the campus radio station, is something to be proud of, not just because it is the oldest continuously operating college radio station in the country, but because it plays cool music and anyone can become a DJ.

Athletics

Although many people do not know it until they visit campus, Wesleyan's Freeman Athletic Center (affectionately nicknamed "The Palace") is one of the finest college athletic centers in New England. Completed in 1990 at the cost of $22 million and recently upgraded with a $13 million addition, the athletic complex has the 1,200-seat Silloway Gymnasium, a fifty-meter pool, a 200-meter indoor track (with four indoor tennis courts), the Spurrier-Snyder Rink for ice skating activities, the eight-court Rosenbaum Squash Center, and campus also is home to a 5,000-seat football stadium overlooked by Olin Library, a new synthetic turf field, sixteen hard-surfaced indoor tennis courts, a 400-meter outdoor track, and many fields for practice and play. The Macomber Boathouse on the Connecticut River is home for both men's and women's crew. Athletics at the Wesleyan are first-rate and interest top athletes: fifteen men's varsity and fourteen women's varsity athletic teams compete at the Division III level. About sixty percent of students are involved in some sort of organized athletics with popular club and intramural activities complementing varsity opportunities. Over the last five years teams in women's basketball, and men's and women's volleyball have all qualified for NCAA tournament play. Numerous other individuals have earned spots at NCAA Championships in swimming, track and field, and wrestling with a handful of All-Americans.

FINANCIAL AID

If you are applying to colleges and are also in need of financial aid, keep this in mind: Wesleyan continues to hold firm to need-blind admissions, meaning that Wesleyan admits students without knowledge of their financial need. Recently, when several schools around the country gave up their need-blind programs, Wesleyan students led the country's college students in protest of this change in policy.

Wesleyan awards aid to all admitted students to the full extent of demonstrated need. Wesleyan is generous with financial aid; most students receiving aid from Wesleyan get a package that includes a grant, student loans, and work-study jobs. However, the university has rolled back student loan expectations thirty percent, starting with the class of 2004. Grants are substituted for the loans.

Tuition at Wesleyan is not cheap. To pay the full amount required—not to mention the other costs in room, board, and personal expenses—about half of the student body receives financial aid, the average package being $23,433 for 2005–2006.

GRADUATES

Education at Wesleyan is more about learning to live your life than memorizing the vagaries of some obscure academic discipline. Wesleyan is the definitive liberal arts college—here, students learn how to think critically, write clearly, and make informed decisions. Graduates can succeed in any situation; they are flexible, creative, and roll with the punches. It is not uncommon for English majors to become computer programmers, psychology majors to go to law school, economics majors to go to film school, and music majors to become math teachers.

There is no single field of endeavor pursued by the majority of Wesleyan grads. Of a recent class, thirty-five percent of students are in business, thirteen percent are in law school or law-related fields, twelve percent are in education, thirteen percent are in grad school, thirteen percent in medicine or health, and twelve percent in the arts. While Wesleyan had the country's second highest number of seniors applying to the Peace Corps, the top three employers hiring students from the class of 2006 were Morgan Stanley, Mitchell Madison Group, and Teach for America.

As for continuing education after Wesleyan, about fifteen percent of students go to graduate school immediately after graduation. Five years after graduation, about seventy-five percent will have gone to some kind of graduate school, and acceptance rates to professional schools remain close to ninety percent. In addition to formal schooling, Wesleyan graduates have also won more Watson Fellowships for self-designed student projects than any other school in the country. Graduates have recently pursued such topics as "The Practice of Movement: Nomadic Domestic Architecture" and "Understanding Cross-Cultural Health Care for Refugees."

Wesleyan students spend plenty of time visiting the excellent library and friendly staff of the Career Resource Center (CRC), which helps students plan ahead for leaving campus, even in the first year of college. With help from the CRC, many students opt for internships over January break and in the summer, often with Wesleyan alumni or parents in their field of interest. Wesleyan has a tight network of alumni and parents in the field who can also help in the latter years at Wesleyan by providing informational interviews and even offering jobs.

PROMINENT GRADS

- Dana Delany, Actress
- Daniel Handler (aka Lemony Snicket), Author
- John Kickenlooper, Mayor of Denver, Colorado
- Herb Kelleher, Executive Chairman and Former President and CEO, Southwest Airlines
- Sebastian Junger, Author
- Jay Levy, AIDS Researcher
- Daphne Kwok, Executive Director, Angel Island Immigration Station Foundation
- Jonathan Schwartz, President and CEO, Sun Microsystems
- Ted Shaw, Director-Counsel and President, NAACP Legal Defense and Educational Fund
- Beverly Daniel Tatum, President, Spelman College
- Laura Walker, President and CEO, WNYC Radio
- Joss Whedon, Film and Television Director
- Dar Williams, Folksinger

SUMMING UP

So, picture this: It's fall in New England, the air is crisp, your ears are red from the slight bite of the cold, and the leaves of the trees are slowly turning the bright color of fire. You walk from the Campus Center to the steps of Olin Library, one of the oldest buildings on campus, where students have gathered in the afternoon sun to chat and read. You enter the building and follow the hall leading to the front face of the building, the north side of massive arched windows overlooking the football field, and take a seat in the Information Commons.

From here, one has the best view of what Wesleyan has to offer. Across the football field is the old Fayerweather Gymnasium, which is in the process of being transformed to house a ballroom and theater and dance rehearsal studios. Beyond that (and beyond the Office of Admissions, which has to be seen to be believed), is the Center for the Arts, where generations of students have also learned to play the Javanese Gamalon, an instrument so large it takes twenty people to play. To the west is Foss Hill, a definite social center of campus, and to the east is the scenic and historic college row, where it all began.

Here you can get a vision for Wesleyan's future. The room you are in, the north room of Olin Library, built in 1985, encompasses the original face of the historic building, designed by Henry Bacon in 1831. The addition is more than an architectural element; it is a symbol of the past and future of Wesleyan. Founded as a small Methodist college for men in the early nineteenth century on the principles of community and the value of a liberal arts education, Wesleyan has held fast to these values, at the same time that it has built on, renovated, and transformed the school into a modern small university. It has seen coeducation, racial tension, peace rallies, and firebombings—few American schools have seen as much change. But at the same time, Wesleyan has still remained consistent—just as the old bricks of Olin Library have always faced the football field, the school has always been leading the pack—a place where high-quality students and top-notch faculty gather to learn and explore.

Wesleyan is unique because it attracts vibrant, open-minded, creative students, and because it rewards these students for pursuing intellectual interests and outside pursuits with vigor. At the same time that they engage students in the classroom, Wesleyan's faculty contributes high-level scholarship and is made up of dedicated and caring teachers. Wesleyan has a small-college atmosphere, yet it is a place where students are challenged to make new discoveries about themselves and others. Because of this, it will always be the special place, the undiscovered secret, the definitive liberal arts education of the twenty-first century. Take a moment to discover it for yourself.

❏ *Stacy Theberge, B.A.*

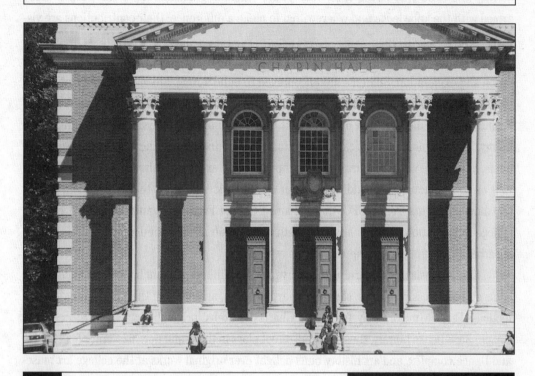

 Williams College
Williamstown, MA 01267

 (413) 597-2211

 E-mail: *admission@williams.edu*
Web site: *http://www.williams.edu*

Enrollment

Full-time ❏ women: 1,033
❏ men: 967

Part-time ❏ women: 20
❏ men: 13

INTRODUCING WILLIAMS COLLEGE

Nestled in the purple mountains of the Berkshires lies Williams College, a small, private, liberal arts institution with an undergraduate population of around 2,000 students. The community is close-knit, the campus idyllic, the student body brimming with an almost tangible excitement for learning and life. These are students who work hard *and* play hard, devoting serious attention to courses and extracurriculars alike; the result is a campus that hums with activity and academic fervor. After four years, Williams graduates leave the Purple Valley armed with the knowledge and wherewithal to make a difference; their contributions are visible across the spectrum.

Founded in 1793, Williams exemplifies the liberal arts *modus operandi* of experimentation and exploration. Students are encouraged to build strong, broad foundations and then to construct spires soaring into the unknown. In this fashion, students can both pursue familiar interests and discover new ones; it is not uncommon to find a physics major taking music theory, for example, or a political science student spending time in the geology lab. Most students, as well, are vigorously involved in campus life and extracurriculars and don't hesitate to take on several activities in addition to their coursework. With more than 116 student groups on campus, ranging from WUFO, the Williams Ultimate Frisbee Organization, to WCFM, the college radio station, there is always something to pique interest, and students are quick to spearhead new groups as campus interests evolve.

The enthusiasm for learning that pervades the Williams student body is matched by the college's boundless resources, state-of-the-art facilities, and some of the world's premier collections. English majors may fawn over Charles Dickens' original *Pickwick Papers* in the Chapin Rare Books Library, theatre lovers direct plays in the brand new '62 Center for Theatre and Dance complex, and art history buffs delight over original works at the college art museum and the Sterling and Francine Clark Art Institute just down the road. The college frequently brings in guest lecturers and artists to enrich campus life, and recent years have seen noteworthies like Philip Glass, Werner Herzog, and Salman Rushdie alighting at the lectern for an evening's dalliance.

Williams prides itself on its commitment to excellence and being well rounded, and this promise is most evident in the breadth and depth of the student body itself. Williams students hail from nearly all fifty states and more than forty-five different countries. About a third are American students of color, more than forty percent receive some type of financial aid, and the division between public and private school students is about 60:40. The spectrum of interests and experiences represented on campus creates a richly diverse environment, where students have great potential to learn from one another and strengthen themselves. Though social groups—as at most colleges—do tend to form based on participation in activities, most Williams students move easily beyond rigid associations, resulting in a friendly, open social atmosphere.

U.S. President James Garfield (class of 1856), speaking of his former professor and early college president Mark Hopkins, once remarked, "The ideal college is Mark Hopkins on one end of a log and a student on the other." To this day, the metaphor lives on; with one of the lowest faculty-student ratios in the country; Williams brings students and professors closer, both in and out of the classroom. Williams professors are not only distinguished scholars but also passionate teachers, and students are top priority. Discussions in class often spill over into debates in the local coffee shop, or a class dinner at a professor's home, and office hours—at all hours—are the norm.

Just as students are central in the college's academic life, so are they in determining the future of the college. When Williams abolished fraternities in the 1960s and then went coed in the 1970s, students participated in the decision-making process. Today, students are a vital part of nearly every administrative committee on campus, helping shape campus social life, enforce the honor code, and even oversee the dining halls. Students hold real responsibilities at Williams, and it is this trust and partnership, this collaborative climate, that defines the college.

ADMISSIONS REQUIREMENTS

There is no such thing as a "typical" Williams student. As one of the most competitive colleges in the nation, Williams is highly selective, and the Admissions Office prides itself on shaping a class diverse in interests, experience, and ability. The only shared trait—perhaps, even, an archetype—of accepted students is a *joie de vivre*, an enthusiasm for learning and seeking out challenges that electrifies the Williams campus.

Of course, passion is merely the icing on the cake; Williams is forced to turn down four out of every five students who apply and therefore must hold very high standards for admission. Williams requires high school transcripts and standardized test scores from all applicants, including results from either the SAT or the ACT (with writing) and three SAT Subject Tests. If a student submits the SAT, Admissions will consider his or her best score on each section (math, verbal, writing); if he or she takes the ACT, the school will look at the student's best composite score. Although Williams considers grades and test scores to be just two of many admissions criteria, it should be noted that most who are admitted are high achievers, taking the most challenging course load offered at their schools; in a recent class, fifty-five percent scored 700 or higher on the SAT verbal, and fifty-six percent scored 700 or higher on the SAT math.

Even so, Williams does not fill its class solely from lists of high school valedictorians and perfect SAT scores. It is rare that a student will get in strictly on academic achievement; the Admissions Committee looks for students who balance academics with a commitment to other pursuits. In the same way that applicants should take the time to get to know the college beyond its statistics, Williams wants a fully realized rendering of its applicants, rather than a schematic of test scores and GPA.

The best way to get to know Williams is to visit and actually spend time on campus meeting students and professors. The Admissions Office offers student-run tours and information sessions every day and will also arrange for prospective students to stay overnight in a dorm to experience residential, social, and academic life at Williams firsthand.

Williams offers both Early and Regular Decision. If Williams is your first-choice school, you may submit your application for early consideration, along with an agreement that, if accepted, you will withdraw all other applications and not apply further. The Early Decision application deadline is November 10, and notification is mailed by December 15.

Applicants not accepted under Early Decision will ordinarily be deferred for reconsideration under the Regular Decision plan. Students with qualifications below Williams's general admission standards, however, will receive final notification in December. Regular Decision applications are due January 1, and decisions are mailed by the first week of April. Accepted candidates must reply by May 1, and acceptances are always contingent upon students finishing the current school year in good standing.

ACADEMIC LIFE

As a true liberal arts institution, Williams pairs a rich academic tradition with a modern focus on experimental learning. The old disciplines are still evident in the framework, to be sure; one can still read the classics in their original Latin and Greek, play out elaborate rhetorical battles in a philosophy class, and digest the great canonical works of literature and art. Take, for example, the English lecture course "Introduction to the Novel," a survey of some of the classics (Faulkner, Joyce, Nabokov), or the yearlong survey course in Western art and architecture, which, according to rumor, is the most popular selection Williams offers. To supplement this grand academic tradition, however, there are all sorts of new and surprising options: a forensic science class complete with staged crime scenes; an interdisciplinary music/English class explicating the careers of Bob Dylan, Joni Mitchell, and The Beatles; a tutorial on satire. While the fundamental education model remains the same, the subjects and requirements have changed, and students are, more than ever, in charge of their own academic paths.

With a 4-1-4 calendar, Williams divides its year into two twelve-week semesters, with a four-week period in January, Winter Study, sandwiched between. Students must complete four courses per semester and a single class each Winter Study to graduate. There are no specific course requirements (no single class is mandatory); to encourage exploration of different subjects, however, all courses are assigned to one of three academic divisions, and students must pass three courses from each division in order to graduate. Division I includes the arts and humanities; Division II consists of the social sciences, such as economics, history, and psychology; Division III is comprised of the natural sciences, including chemistry, biology, physics, and math. Students must also take one class in a non-Western tradition and complete classes that fulfill specific competencies in writing and quantitative studies. With such flexible guidelines, it is easy for students to focus on subjects that interest them while still exploring a broad, liberal arts education.

WINTER STUDY

While other college students lounge around with several extra weeks of holiday vacation, Williams students use the month of January to take the "work hard, play hard" atmosphere at Williams to a whole new level. During these four weeks, students are required to take a single class, which can range from introductory figure drawing to research projects in molecular biology. Some students plan "99s," or independent studies, and others journey abroad with professors, completing service projects in Guatemala or exploring art and music in Vienna. The possibilities presented by Winter Study are endless, and students enjoy the relief it offers from the normal academic course load—relief often found in a day or two (or twelve) spent skiing at the nearby resorts.

Students do not need to declare a major until the end of their sophomore year, affording plenty of time to choose a discipline. The major generally consists of nine to eleven courses, usually culminating in a senior seminar or capstone course. Within the major, students are often given more specific guidelines to diversify their studies; English majors, for example, are required to take courses in three different time periods (pre-1700, 1700–1900, post-1900), to gain a better understanding of literary movements across time.

Williams's lenient course requirements have led to a growing tendency to double major, something now done by about a third of the students. Interestingly enough, most students who double major do so in noncomplementary divisions: history and biology, math and music, English and chemistry. These students believe that double majoring, rather than going against the grain of the liberal arts education, is not only great preparation for the balancing act of the real world but allows for freedom of choice down the road.

Something happens during Williams classes. Whether it is a professor's nuanced summation, a classmate's probing question, your own search for words, or maybe just the image or text in front of you, something causes a trapdoor to open under your feet. The world is harrowingly fresh again. It caused many a late night conversation and even more frequently a smile.

—Nicholas S. Anderson,
'06, art history major

STUDYING OFF CAMPUS

About one third of Williams students choose to study off campus for either a semester or a full year, usually as juniors. In addition to helping place students in a wide variety of study abroad programs, Williams sponsors three off-campus programs of its own. The Williams-Exeter Programme at England's Oxford University allows roughly twenty juniors each year to become full-time Oxford students, taking tutorial classes and living together in a college-owned house. At Williams-Mystic, a semester-long program at Mystic Seaport in Connecticut, students are immersed in an interdisciplinary study of the sea, taking field trips to the Puget Sound or California coast and spending ten days living on a tall ship. Williams in New York, which debuted Fall 2005, is a semester of intensive fieldwork in the mainstream institutions of New York City, in conjunction with companion courses taught by Williams faculty and local professors alike.

Williams courses are generally small and discussion-oriented, with the exception of a few large, lecture-based introductory courses; even these usually have a separate lab or discussion section that requires student participation. Students are expected to read and learn material outside of class, developing their own take on ideas before coming to lecture. Exams are largely based on problem solving and critical thinking and require students to build upon concepts learned during the course; multiple-choice tests and their ilk are virtually nonexistent.

Students who wish to pursue honors can complete a senior thesis. Under the supervision of a faculty sponsor, a student works independently for either one or two semesters, completing a substantial written work that must be presented and defended in front of a faculty panel. No senior assignment is required for graduation.

I felt overwhelmed at Williams a lot. Concepts seemed far too complex for me to understand completely; papers seemed too long to write; projects seemed too daunting to finish. I discovered, however, that if I just got started on something and put enough effort into it, I could see it through, no matter how difficult it seemed. I don't know if that's a good lesson for the real world or not, but I do know that it has emboldened me to try many new things, and to never let my uncertainty stand in my way.

—Alden Robinson, '06,
American studies major

Faculty

Williams faculty members are at the college because they primarily want to teach undergraduates, and their motivation invigorates the classroom. Although most of them are brilliant researchers (ninety-six percent have their terminal degree), they put students first and make themselves available both in and out of the classroom. Almost every class is taught by a professor, and teaching assistants are used primarily to help grade routine assignments and help direct review sessions.

The fact that Williams professors are so accessible is sometimes a shock for students who are not used to engaging their teachers. They not only make office hours and appointments available for students with academic questions, but they become advisors on everything from postgraduate plans to personal issues. Professors also keep involved in campus life, some even joining intramural sports.

In addition to teaching, Williams professors produce an impressive amount of scholarship, for which they regularly receive national attention and major grants. Many professors, as well, will take on students to assist them over the summer and during the year, giving students valuable research experience; in recent years, hundreds of students have participated.

Residential Life

The close-knit atmosphere of the college is made even more evident through its housing system. The majority of Williams students live in campus housing—in fact, the option to live off-campus or in a co-operative house is only available to seniors—and the dormitories are kept clean, comfortable, and up-to-date with frequent renovations. Housing is comprised of single and double rooms, arranged in suites, with generous common space throughout.

First-year students live in "entries" of approximately twenty-five students, headed by a pair of Junior Advisors (JAs). Unlike the Residential Advisors of most colleges, JAs are unpaid, are more along the lines of mentors than a police force, and are integral to a first-year student's transition process. Entries often appear cult-like, especially around dinnertime, when large crowds of first-years traipse into the dining halls and commandeer three or four tables at a time, and the connections forged among entrymates are often the strongest of a student's career.

Williams dormitories and co-ops are further organized into "neighborhoods," a recent housing change aimed to extend the entry experience to upper-class students. Through the neighborhood system, students are assigned to one of four clusters of dorms, geographically located across campus, and live in that cluster over the next four years. Within neighborhoods, students are free to choose where they live and can "pick in" with groups of friends each year in a housing lottery. With diversity across campus as a primary goal, Williams has no fraternities, sororities, or special-interest housing.

A lot of people say that much of the Williams education takes place outside the classroom. They're right—we learn through our sports, our clubs, our performances, and so forth—but many people overlook the best education of all: our classmates. My friends astounded me by the depth with which they involved themselves in their studies, and the passion with which they spoke of them. I broadened my understanding of the world not just through my academic work, but also through late-night study/chat sessions in my dorm. Knowledge, at Williams, is truly contagious, and it was a privilege to have my classmates infect me with it.

—*Alden Robinson, '06,*
American studies major

SOCIAL LIFE AND ACTIVITIES

With a student body composed of individuals who did *everything* in high school, it is no wonder that the campus is full of an almost frenetic energy. Though the college is small, there is always something going on, and students keep themselves very busy. As Williamstown itself offers few entertainment options (the "town," in students' minds, is often distilled to Spring Street, a one-way thoroughfare located at the heart of campus, crowded with restaurants and shops), social life is student-driven and mostly confined to campus. Few regularly leave town on weekends, so students get to know each other well and support each other in their athletic events, concerts, and performances. The administration contributes to campus life by providing funding for lectures, concerts, parties, and movies to keep the place lively.

> *The best thing about Williams is that there is such a wide variety of things to do for fun. You could run from one of the dining hall's amazing theme dinners to a Berkshire Symphony Orchestra concert to an improv comedy show to a dance party with your friends all within the span of a few hours, and then do it all again the following night with an entirely different set of activities. The only problem is figuring out how to squeeze everything in!*

—*Mary Beth Anzovino, '06, chemistry major*

Williams students never hesitate to organize new clubs and groups, especially with the help of student activities funding, if they find their interests aren't met. As a result, the number of recognized clubs and student groups on campus grows each year, and now tops one hundred; with so many options to choose from, it's not hard to find something to do in your free time.

Very few teams or clubs restrict membership, and there is no Greek system, so just about everything is open to everyone. Among the largest groups are the swing dancing club and the Williams Outing Club (WOC), which sponsors outdoor activities. The Minority Coalition, comprised of groups supporting students from minority backgrounds, sponsors campus-wide celebrations like Black History Month and Coming Out Days. Students can voice their opinions and spur changes in campus life through College Council and in writing for the weekly campus

Foliage season in the Berkshires fills local hotels with pilgrimaging New Englanders; Williams students, however, have the privilege of a full autumnal panorama simply while walking to and from class. In fact, the college annually celebrates its picturesque location—a tradition dating back over a hundred years—with Mountain Day. On an unannounced Friday morning in October, students will wake to the sound of the chapel bells and a message from the college president canceling all classes. Students, faculty, and staff pack lunches (or pick up a brown bag lunch, complete with trail mix, at the dining hall) and make their way up the nearby Stony Ledge. At the top, with an uninhibited view of Mount Greylock (the state's highest point, at over 3,400 feet), they enjoy apple cider and donuts, musical performances from student groups, and the joy of being outdoors on a crisp, fall, New England afternoon.

newspaper, *The Record*, and about forty percent of students regularly do community service. Music is also popular, and students can participate at any level, whether it is through beginners' music lessons or as part of the Berkshire Symphony, a group made up of professional musicians, faculty, and students. Other popular groups include the jazz ensemble and the Kusika African drumming and dance ensemble, not to mention a full range of a cappella groups, singing everything from pop to madrigals.

For those interested in sports (and about forty percent of Williams students are), Williams has over more than thirty-two varsity squads and even more intramural organizations, including an equestrian team, a figure-skating club, and water polo. Moreover, Williams's teams are consistently among the nation's best in NCAA Division III and play a major role in shaping school spirit, drawing huge crowds—especially when Williams is playing its nemesis, Amherst.

In terms of a party scene, Williams tends toward smaller parties hosted in dorms, rather than formal all-campus blowouts—except for the big weekends of Homecoming, Winter Carnival, and Spring Fling. Regular weekend parties are hosted in the larger dorms and tend to be standard keg parties with a DJ. A stricter party policy instituted in the past few years has limited the amount of alcohol at these events and has made training with security officers and health counselors mandatory for all party hosts. Still, students who want to drink usually have no trouble finding alcohol, while students who do not drink are not pressured to do so.

FINANCIAL AID

With the annual inflation of tuition prices, college is growing increasingly expensive. Williams, with comprehensive fees totaling $40,300, is one of the nation's priciest, but at the same time Williams goes out of its way to make it financially viable for all accepted students to attend. Furthermore, Williams is one of a handful of schools with a need-blind admissions policy—a student's ability to pay is never factored into an admissions decision—and pledges to meet 100 percent of the demonstrated need of its students, both American and international.

Williams' financial aid packages are awarded on a need basis; it offers no merit-based scholarships. Instead, the Financial Aid Office evaluates each family individually, considering size, the number of students in college, income, and assets before determining how much the family can pay. The resulting aid package will cover the entire difference between the cost of the student's education and the expected family contribution, in a combination of grants, loans, and campus employment. Students are expected to contribute some of their summer earnings toward their payment.

Being a financial aid student at Williams carries no stigma at all. In a recent year, almost fifty percent of the incoming class received some type of financial aid. The average annual award to first-year students in 2005–2006 was $31,419. Financial aid students are expected to work part-time on campus, and their earnings are included in their annual award; many first-year students work in the dining halls, while upper-class students do everything from manning the library reference desks, to working in a professor's lab, to writing news releases for the Office of Public Affairs or the Sports Information Office.

GRADUATES

With today's competitive job market, many might question the value of a broad, liberal arts education. A Williams education, however, in addition to its intellectual perks, carries a lot of weight in the real world, and one's Williams degree becomes a certain kind of pedigree. Williams graduates are seen as movers, shakers, thinkers, communicators, and leaders, and employers recognize that those qualities translate neatly into the ability to learn quickly, meet challenges, and get results—a skill set that is hard to ignore.

A Williams education is good preparation for nearly any career path, and graduates have proven this by making names for themselves in professions as diverse as education, journalism, scientific research, public service, business, and the arts. Just as the college encourages and facilitates the stretching of academic boundaries, a Williams degree allows graduates to pursue fields or projects that most interest them, and to switch between fields with relative ease. Many Williams grads go on to more schooling, with many earning professional degrees in law, medicine, and business, and some earning their master's or Ph.D.

On campus, students can research potential career options and build resumes through

---

- William Bennett, Former Secretary of Education
- Arne Carlson, Former Minnesota Governor
- Stephen Case, Chairman, AOL-Time Warner
- Dominick Dunne, Writer
- John Frankenheimer, Movie and TV Director
- James Garfield, Twentieth President of the United States
- Richard Helms, Former CIA Director
- Elia Kazan, Director and Writer
- Thomas Krens, Guggenheim Museum Director
- Arthur Levitt, Former SEC Chairman
- Stacey Schiff, Pulitzer Prize Winner
- Stephen Sondheim, Composer and Lyricist
- George Steinbrenner, New York Yankees Owner
- Fay Vincent, Former Major League Baseball Commissioner
- Martha Williamson, Executive Producer, *Touched by an Angel*

the Office of Career Counseling (OCC). The OCC hosts a variety of on-campus recruiters, offers mock interview sessions, and assists students with resumes and cover letters. It also puts on alumni panels and career fairs in underrepresented areas, such as nonprofits, publishing, and government service.

An invaluable asset for graduates is the vast Williams alumni network, often affectionately called the Williams Mafia. Most alumni are incredibly enthusiastic about helping out a fellow Eph, and having contacts in the workforce has proven to be a great help to new graduates.

After leaving Williams, graduates are welcomed into the fold of the Williams Society of Alumni, the first such group in North America. In the 1820s, the group revitalized the college after half of the students and faculty left to form Amherst; today, it remains one of the most active alumni associations in the country. Not only do generous graduates donate annually, helping Williams continue expanding and evolving its programs and facilities, but alumni are also active in campus life, often returning to teach Winter Study classes or take on students for summer internships. As the burgeoning crowds at Homecoming reveal, once you enter the Purple Valley, you never truly leave.

SUMMING UP

Williams is built upon and around its students, and they are all the happier for it. The resources available are first-rate, the faculty are among the most distinguished in the nation, and the staff is world-class. But in making lively classroom discussion to organizing nearly all campus events and activities to voicing issues and directing the future of the college, Williams's students make the campus the passionate, vibrant place that it is.

Just as there is no "typical" Williams student, the Williams experience is different for everyone who attends; the college is a place where students are expected to create their own paths, both inside the classroom and out. Williams is a place where students seek out and overcome their toughest obstacles, growing and learning with every challenge; they know how to accept help and are generous in offering it to others.

Students work hard and set ambitious goals, but they also know how to put things in perspective, making room for friends and recreation. Even in the face of an all-night study session or hefty research assignment, there is always time for a midnight trip to the snack bar or an hour's respite in the common room. It is these shared moments that are often at the heart of the Williams experience.

In the end, what you get out of Williams is what you put into it: yourself. And even though your time spent in the Purple Valley is, sadly, finite, it is an experience that makes the impression of a lifetime.

❑ *Jennifer Linnan, B.A.*

YALE UNIVERSITY

Yale University
Office of Undergraduate Admission
P.O. Box 208234
New Haven, CT 06520-8234

(203) 432-9300
Fax: (203) 432-9392

E-mail: *undergraduate.admissions@yale.edu*
Web site: *http://www.yale.edu*

 Enrollment

Full-time ❑ women: 2,609
❑ men: 2,707

INTRODUCING YALE

If you've decided to attend Yale, "Where are you going to school?" can be a complicated question. If you're like most Yale students, you're so excited about coming to the school that you'll want to jump out and say "Yale!" loud and clear, eyes and cheeks aglow. But answering the question so directly provokes many different reactions, based on Yale's reputation as one of the finest universities in the world. So students and even alumni practice several indirect responses, including "New Haven" (there are a handful of other colleges and universities here;

just read the exit sign for "Yale Univ." and "Albertus Magnus"); "Connecticut" (a state with MANY colleges), and the even more vague "Back East."

Like many of the questions that hold great import before you begin college, this one soon fades into oblivion. A freshman will quickly observe and follow the pattern set by the undergraduate body: Everyone is too busy taking maximum advantage of the university's vast resources to boast or even think about Yale's reputation. The 1998 yearbook is titled *Unlimited Capacity*. Indeed, students are in overdrive most of the time. Yale's unwavering commitment to undergraduate education, the residential college system, and the breadth of academic and extracurricular opportunities are central tenets of the Yale experience. These are the reasons why Yalies have chosen Yale, not for its reputation, and not for its location in the small New England city (though it seems more of a town) of New Haven, Connecticut.

Yalies joke about the question "Where do you go to school?" because Yale is not simply where people go to school. It is a community, and the happiest members of that community are those who actively participate in it. Many students remember being hit with the Yale fever almost immediately upon arriving on campus—that's how tangible the sense of community is.

On my first walk around the campus, I just knew that this was where I wanted to go to college. Students were rushing to get to class, while I was struggling to read my campus map that was torn and wrinkled by a strong wind (which I've now come to recognize as a robust sea breeze from the nearby Long Island Sound). Then a student stopped and asked me if I needed directions. I wound up going to his English class, where he introduced me to his professor. Then he took me to Durfee's Sweet Shop, and directed me to other buildings he thought I'd want to see. All his enthusiasm and helpfulness got me hooked. Now I look out for maps blowing in the wind, and am always glad for the chance to talk to prospective students—even after almost four years here, a couple of labor strikes, and a housing crunch.

ADMISSIONS REQUIREMENTS

Ask students what they know about admissions and you're likely to hear that the hardest thing about Yale is getting in. Look past that casual statement, however, to recognize a deeper truth: There's no set formula for admission to a place that seeks to maintain a diverse student body. As the Admissions Committee says on its web page (*http://www.yale.edu/admit/*), the two basic questions it brings to the process are "Who is likely to make the most of Yale's resources?" and "Who will contribute significantly to the Yale community?" It's a complex approach, one designed to select a class of motivated, energetic achievers with broad interests and skills, all of whom are enticed by the opportunities Yale offers both in and out of the classroom.

Beyond that stated mission, applicants should be aware of several general facts:

- First, admission is extremely competitive, as the committee aims for a class of approximately 1,250 from over 21,000 applicants.
- Second, while there are no official score cut-offs and applicants' test results vary widely, medians on the Verbal and Mathematics parts of the SAT generally fall in between 700 and 790, and ACT composites in the low 30s.
- Third, the great majority of Yalies (ninety-five percent) placed in the top tenth of their high school class; a distinguished record in a demanding college preparatory program may compensate for modest standardized test scores, but the reverse is usually not true.
- Fourth, the committee is searching for students with some less tangible qualities suggested by the various documents in their applications. Some successful candidates are well rounded, while others have specialized talents, some have displayed leadership capabilities in extracurricular activities while others have shown dedication to an after-school job, but all, hopefully, show a capacity for involvement, commitment, and personal growth.
- Finally, Yale has a need-blind admissions policy for both U.S. and international students, meaning that an applicant's financial circumstances will not be given any weight during the admission process. You won't be rejected because you apply for financial aid, as Yale is strongly committed to the idea of equality of opportunity, seeking to shape a class of students from all parts of the country and all segments of society. In addition, Yale recently announced a $7.5 million increase in undergraduate financial aid, which will reduce the amount that Yale expects a student to contribute to his or her education by $13,780 over four years.

The admissions process produces a class that reflects Yale's interest in diversity, not only in academic and extracurricular interests but also in ethnicity and geographical distribution. Today, minority students comprise nearly twenty-seven percent of the student body, and Yalies hail from all fifty states and over seventy countries. Be prepared to meet people of all cultural, social, and financial backgrounds, and also be prepared to meet people who have worn Yale blue since birth—"legacies" make up around ten percent of each class.

Early Action

Applicants who are certain that Yale is their first choice may want to take advantage of the single choice Early Action program. As with Early Action programs elsewhere, an Early Action application to Yale is not a binding commitment from the student. Interested students should submit a complete application by November 1. In mid-December the committee will respond with an acceptance or denial of admission, or a deferral, which postpones the final decision until April, when all applicants are notified.

Being admitted to Yale signals the Admission Committee's faith in the applicant's ability to be a successful Yale student. Does that mean that admission is, in fact, the hardest part of Yale? Well, all students have to face that question on their own. Yalies tend to make life hard on themselves by pursuing their academics and activities so intensely—clearly they have proven their stamina by the time they graduate.

ACADEMIC LIFE

I've found that the amount of work at Yale varies from student to student, from course to course, from semester to semester, and even from night to night. My two roommates major in the sciences, and have a pretty consistent work load: a bunch of problem sets and lab reports each week. I'm a history major, which means that I've always got a lot of reading to try to keep up with, but my busy periods are more sporadic—basically the few times a semester I have papers due, when my life can get totally crazy. It seems that whether they put in the effort seven days a week, or just seven times a semester, all Yale students develop an ability to instantaneously calculate when they'll have to go to sleep to get that recommended eight hours.

In 1701 ten Connecticut clergymen met in the town of Branford, each with a gift of books to contribute for the founding of the college in Saybrook on the Connecticut River that would become Yale. From those forty folios, the university's holdings have grown to include over twelve million volumes; the extensive library system is the seventh largest research library in the world. A library is the heart of any learning institution, and the prominence of Yale's collections (not to mention the imposing sight of Sterling Memorial Library's Gothic tower looming over the central campus) reminds students that while they may spend countless hours dashing around to eagerly explore extracurricular interests, their intellectual development is paramount.

To foster that development, Yale has always remained committed to the idea of a liberal arts education. According to one faculty report, "Our object is not to teach that which is peculiar to any one of the professions, but to lay the foundation which is common to them all…" Those words were written in 1828, and they still characterize the Yale philosophy today. Simply put, Yale wants to teach you how to think. The university doesn't have career-oriented fields of study—if you want to major in communications or marketing, for example, look elsewhere—but, instead, aims to provide students with the tools to succeed in any field.

Majors and Workload

What you *can* major in is any of almost seventy disciplines, from astronomy to film studies to Russian. Yale also allows you to double-major and, if you can convince a faculty committee that it's necessary and that you're up to the challenge, to design your own major. In a recent year, the most popular fields of study were history, biology, economics, and political science.

Yale has no required courses, but employs a framework of distributional requirements to make sure that students explore a sufficient diversity of subjects. Each course is placed in one of four distributional groups—languages and literature; the humanities (including history, art, music, philosophy, and other disciplines); the social sciences; and mathematics, science, and engineering. Each student must take at least twelve classes from outside the distribu-tional group that includes the major and at least three in each of the remaining distributional groups. Students must also improve their proficiency in a foreign language, a requirement that can be satisfied by completing a foreign language course at Yale. While most colleges require a normal four-year course load of thirty-two credits, a Yale degreerequires thirty-six, a source of pride for Yalies, meaning students spend some semesters managing five courses simultaneously.

It's a lot to grasp at first, and it's no surprise that the structure of a Yale education means things can get pretty hectic and intense at times. However, the system makes perfect sense from a liberal arts perspective, giving students the freedom and responsibility to shape their academic careers, while guaranteeing a certain amount of breadth of study in addition to the depth one experiences in a major. As an added incentive to explore, some courses can be taken Credit/D/Fail, which means that a grade of C or above will show up as a "CR" on one's transcript. Many Yalies grumble about the various distributional requirements, but if you press them, most will admit they're glad they took that English or geology course that initially seemed so unconnected to their interests, because it exposed them to different people and different ways of thinking.

"Shopping" for Classes

These notions of academic exploration, freedom, and responsibility are embodied in Yale's unique shopping period, the first two weeks of each semester, in which students shop for classes. Most colleges require students to preregister for classes, but Yale allows its students to attend any course offered at the start of the semester, filling out their schedules only after hearing the professors and perusing the syllabi. Shopping period is a great opportunity to shape an interesting schedule while trying to balance the various times, demands (tests, papers, problem sets), and sizes (seminars, small and large lectures) of the classes. For some, shopping period can literally be a life-changing experience—one student dropped in on an introductory architecture lecture sophomore year, found himself enthralled by the professor, and spent the next two years immersed in blueprints and models. Many professors dislike shopping period, since they start off the semester with no idea of how many students will eventually take their classes, but students will tell you it's one of the best things about the Yale experience.

Reading Week

The end-of-term equivalent to shopping period is reading week, a week between the end of classes and the start of finals that makes Yale students the envy of their peers at most other institutions. Ideally a time to pause, reflect, and study in preparation for finals, it's more often a time of late-night paper writing and catching up on reading not completed on time. Studying, of course, includes study breaks, and reading week is also a time of catching up with friends before winter break and summer vacation.

Faculty

Yale's graduate schools are well respected, but the college remains the physical, intellectual, and even emotional center of Yale. The student-to-faculty ratio is 7:1 and only nine percent of classes have fifty or more students. As a leading research institution attracting scholars of international renown in every field, Yale expects its faculty to put time and energy into teaching undergraduates. Faculty members welcome the opportunity to share their enthusiasm with students, and many of Yale's most distinguished senior professors teach introductory courses. Some have attained cult status and attract hundreds of students.

Yale is not merely a place for academic excellence. In fact, many students won't even cite the academic environment as the most important aspect of their college years. It is academic excellence, however, that makes the Yale experience and reputation so distinctive and attracts so many applicants each year.

SOCIAL LIFE AND ACTIVITIES

Freshman Orientation

The first few days of freshman year lay the groundwork for a rich and intricate life outside of the classroom. They may begin with a seven-day hiking trip in the Catskills or Berkshires or a two-day retreat at a nearby summer camp. About a third of the class takes part in these programs, known as FOOT (Freshman Outdoor Orientation Trip) and Freshperson Conference. Even though their duration is brief, and students scatter in all directions once classes begin, many alumni of these orientation programs have reunions throughout college. The FOOT program has recently started an electronic listserve for alumni to share their most recent hiking adventures.

The day these programs end, Camp Yale—the official freshman orientation—begins. Wearing navy T-shirts that announce, "Ask me for help," freshman counselors—seniors who have gone through a rigorous training program to serve as peer advisors to the freshman class, and who live with them—stand outside of the entryways on Old Campus to meet their new charges. At convocation, the president addresses the freshman class. This is followed by a reception at his house. Finally, the upperclassmen get their chance to meet and greet, during a bazaar of undergraduate activities. Before classes have even begun, organization leaders line the sidewalks of Old Campus to recruit freshmen. The freshman counselors also hold meetings with their counselees where they go over the course selection process and review many of the resources available to students, from a twenty-four-hour shuttle bus to free condoms to professional counseling.

This flurry of activity during the first few days exemplifies Yale's commitment to its undergraduates. As soon as students arrive, they are part of the community, and are asked to become active in it. There are many different levels of support and orientation; students manage their way through the array of decisions and opportunities differently. Some will visit their freshman counselor every day, while others will turn to upperclassmen or to their faculty advisor. Freedom and choice prevail; Yale expects and relies on students to act responsibly.

Residential Colleges

The primary way to identify new students at Yale is by the residential college. A couple of months before school starts, every incoming student is randomly assigned to one of twelve residential colleges, an affiliation that lasts throughout one's four years at Yale, and beyond. The college system breaks down each class of approximately 1,240 students into much smaller and more intimate units of approximately 100 students who live and eat together. Ideally, during the time students live there, this place feels like home, and has many of the amenities one could wish for: television rooms, libraries, music practice rooms, climbing walls, darkrooms, a sauna (in Calhoun College), computer rooms, even performance spaces and printing presses.

Each college has a master, a faculty member who lives with his or her family in the master's house. In addition to their professorial duties of teaching and research, the master oversees the social life of the college—intramural teams, dances, tailgates, and arts festivals, for instance. The master eats regularly in the dining hall and invites students frequently into his or her home, sometimes for the relaxed social interchange of a study break or the chance to meet an author, politician, or other dignitary during a Master's Tea (recent guests have included Spike Lee, Edward Norton, and Meryl Streep). The residential college deans also live in the college and oversee the freshman counselors and the academic lives of students. A dean must approve a student's schedule, and is the only person authorized to grant a student a "dean's excuse" for not meeting academic deadlines.

While most freshmen live on Old Campus together, and are encouraged to bond as a class, they also participate fully in residential college life. At the beginning of their sophomore year, students move into their colleges. There they room with classmates, but live in a section or on a hallway with juniors and seniors. In randomly assigning students to residential colleges, Yale's aim is to create twelve microcosms of the larger undergraduate community. Students with different interests and backgrounds—and, outside of the residential college, entirely different lives—live and learn side by side. Students have the option of transferring to another residential college.

About fifteen percent of students decide to live off campus, though Yale recently instituted a new policy that requires undergraduates to live on campus for two years.

The residential college system could be described as part of Yale's infrastructure. During commencement, all students graduate in a ceremony on Old Campus, but return to their residential colleges to receive their diplomas. Most "class notes" in the monthly *Yale Alumni Magazine*, which all graduates of the college automatically receive, identify people by their college. It is an extremely efficient way to give students the best of both worlds at Yale—the resources of a large research university, with the attention, support, and sense of community of a small liberal arts college.

SEVEN THINGS YOU CAN DO AT YALE

- ○ Climb the steps to the top of Harkness Tower
- ○ Take a walk through Grove Street Cemetery
- ○ Take a trip to the Whitlock Book Barn
- ○ Go apple-picking at Bishop's Orchard
- ○ Picnic on the top of East Rock
- ○ Spend an afternoon reading on the Divinity School lawn
- ○ Compete in intramural coed inner tube water polo

Athletics

The residential colleges also create an infrastructure for students to participate in athletics. Intramurals are recreational and everyone in the college, regardless of previous experience, is encouraged to participate. Competitions between the colleges usually take place in the afternoon or evening, and results are tallied on a weekly basis as residential colleges strive for the Tyng Cup, awarded at the end of the year to the college with the most points. Less publicly fought for but nonetheless a source of college pride is the Gimbel Cup, awarded annually to the residential college with the highest grade point

average. Lastly, there's the Tang Cup, awarded to college teams in a one-day competition organized in association with the fraternities. Because of the residential college system, fraternities and sororities are not a major social force at Yale, but they do exist, and provide community service and social outlets for the students who participate.

Clubs and Organizations

Of course, many other communities and affiliations abound at Yale—the ones students create and choose for themselves. There are twelve possible responses to the question, "What college are you in?" There are hundreds of possible responses to the next-important question, "What do you do?" On any given weeknight during dinner, a group of students is planning their next singing jam, magazine deadline, political debate, student rally, chamber orchestra recital, juggling demonstration, Habitat for Humanity project, or play auditions. There's a club for chess players, engineers, anglophiles, and polar bears (those who dare to swim in the Long Island Sound during the winter). There's scripted comedy, improv comedy, and published comedy, not to mention many student-produced comic strips. There's opera, klezmer, and black spiritual music, available live and on CD. It's exhausting to even think of how many options are available—and even more exhausting to recognize that students spend large portions of their time sustaining these organizations. Over 300 groups register with the Yale College Dean's Office, including fifteen *a cappella* groups (from the tuxedoed Whiffenpoofs to the Dylan-inspired Tangled Up In Blue), forty undergraduate publications (including the Yale Daily News, the oldest college daily), and two dozen cultural groups.

You will never lack for something to do on the Yale campus, and if you ever did find yourself in that position, you would do as many have done before you: start your own group for your own hobby. If you're not copyediting final pages into the wee hours of the morning, you're trying to figure out how to see your friends in their three separate productions. Most likely, you'll see the productions back to back and then do your copyediting. One cannot measure a student's devotion, nor can one imagine a limit to a student's energy. The majority of students aren't merely involved in a group, they're leading one. Only during reading period, the week before final exams start, does the campus start to settle down. The kiosks all over campus, usually plastered with posters advertising events, begin to look bare as the libraries swell with students for the first time all semester.

> *Sometimes I wish I could take a semester off from classes, given my other commitments. Filofaxes are for professionals, but many people at Yale have them just to keep track of the meetings and dinners they take part in. I try to take my classes on Tuesdays and Thursdays so I have three full free days to work my campus job, do my activities, and study. I feel wired all of the time, but everyone does. There's this frenetic energy or buzz on campus that's very difficult to escape. If I'm not doing something, I feel like a slacker. It's difficult to find time just to hang out, though luckily, I see my friends regularly, since most of them are involved in the same groups. During vacations, I sleep. A lot.*

New Haven

New Haven, a moderate-sized port city, is about ninety minutes away from New York. That's far enough away to make New Haven part of New England, and not a New York offshoot. To call it a port city is perhaps misleading, since its days as a prosperous center of shipping and industry are long past. New Haven, designated as an All American City in 1998 and recognized as the cultural capital of Connecticut, would be much worse off without Yale, and while town-gown relations have sometimes been strained in Yale's history, today their interaction is characterized by collaboration and cooperation. Yale is the city's largest contributor of real estate taxes, donates over $2 million a year to the city's fire services, is the city's biggest employer, and the university has joined forces with the city to build a new economic base—the latest goal is to utilize Yale's academic resources to develop a profit-minded Biotechnology center within the city. Completely revitalized Broadway and Chapel Street shopping districts—a component of Yale's community investment program—feature many locally-owned shops and several national anchor stores such as J. Crew, Urban Outfitters, Barnes & Noble, and Au Bon Pain.

The campus is a few miles from Long Island Sound, and refreshing sea breezes can still be felt, even if you have to climb one of the towers on campus to see the water. Beach towns along the Connecticut coast, though difficult to visit if you don't have a car, offer antique shops, fresh seafood, and farms for hayrides and apple picking. Sleeping Giant State Park is a twenty-minute bike ride away. In short, though the campus is adjacent to neighborhoods of different income levels, many of the pastoral diversions completely absent from a big city campus are quite accessible to Yale students. Far from hiding in their dorm rooms in the walled-in court-yards of green lawns and shady trees, students are aware and caring of their surroundings. Over sixty-five percent of the students pursue community service projects in New Haven. The locked gates and visibility of both Yale and New Haven police patrols don't seem to bother students, but do serve to keep students safe.

The Elm City birthplace of President George W. Bush, may not be as nationally recognized as cities that host other Ivy League schools, its charms grow on students, who often decide to stay in New Haven during the summers or attend graduate school at Yale. The small portion of students who do stick to campus life exclusively miss out on a modest but eclectic music and arts scene, and treasures like the first and best hamburger (Louis's Lunch), the best fried donuts and pigs-in-a-blanket (The Yankee Doodle), and, of course, the first pizza in the U.S. (Pepe's, and its rival, Sally's located in Wooster Square—about a twenty-minute walk from campus). The chance to get involved and be useful to the city fosters a civic identity that graduates carry with them. Last year, more than 100 seniors took jobs with Teach for America and the Peace Corps.

FINANCIAL AID

In its admissions process Yale may be need-blind, but no one should be blind to the financial realities connected with attendance. The actual cost of attending college varies from student to student. There are the following usual expenses: tuition and fees, room and board, books, and personal expenses, and a yearly hospitalization coverage fee and other optional and incidental expenses.

The basis of all financial aid awards at Yale is the student's "demonstrated financial need," the difference between the estimated cost of attendance and the expected family contribution. For a recent academic year, more than sixty percent of all undergraduates qualified to receive financial assistance in the form of scholarships, grants, low-interest educational loans, and work-study from all sources. Yale does not offer academic or athletic scholarships or any other type of special scholarship that is not based on demonstrated need. More than $59.9 million in university-controlled need-based aid was offered to forty-five percent of the undergraduate student body.

The expected contribution is determined by the Financial Aid Office, which analyzes the FAFSA, CSS Financial Aid Profile, and other forms submitted by the family, and measures the family's ability to contribute toward Yale's costs.

Packages

After consideration of these factors, the university offers financial aid in the form of a package with two basic components: "self-help" (a combination of term-time employment and educational loans) and "gift aid," which covers any need beyond that covered by self-help. While other types of loans are available, the primary source of long-term, low-interest loans is the federal Stafford Loan Program, for which citizens or permanent residents of the United States are eligible. Students who apply for financial aid will automatically be considered for all types of "gift aid," which consists of scholarships from the university, as well as Yale alumni clubs, and from endowed and federal funds, including federal Supplemental Educational Opportunity Grants, administered by the university. Additionally, Yale participates in a number of financing options that can assist families in paying for college, whether or not the family is determined to have demonstrated financial need.

Jobs

> *It helped me pay for college, but my job (in a campus office that doesn't interact much with students) also became something I really enjoyed. The truth is, when you spend your whole day surrounded by eighteen- to twenty-two-year-olds, sometimes it's nice to be around people who aren't students or professors, people who drive into New Haven for the day. It was basic office work, but it was good to have an enforced break from academics and the intensity of the Yale experience.*

On-campus jobs (available also to students not on financial aid, though aid recipients have priority) offer a wide variety of opportunities. Students fill positions as dining hall workers, library clerks, laboratory assistants, research assistants, and aides to residential college masters. Jobs also abound in various campus offices. Recently, wage rates for university jobs ranged from $10.90 for entry-level positions to over fifteen dollars per hour for dining hall workers. A large number of Yale students balance school and employment.

For more in-depth information on financing a Yale education, including an example of a financial aid award, check out *http://www.yale.edu/admit/financing.html*.

GRADUATES

It's difficult enough to describe the intense experience of four years at Yale. Once they enter the world at large, Yalies go off to do a multitude of impressive things. Part of Yale's mission is to train leaders, and Yale's alumni do lead, as U.S. presidents (five attended Yale), company CEOs, academics, journalists, lawyers, and advocates. Living in New Haven, a city where volunteerism can make such a difference, is a life-shaping experience for students, many of whom later gravitate to public service in government or nonprofit organizations. The diversity of Yale's student body, and the breadth of its academic offerings, prepares graduates for diverse careers. A sampling of recent graduates should give you an idea: investment banker, Peace Corps volunteer, reporter in Indonesia, computer programmer, book publicist, teacher. When alumni reach out to one another, they continue to learn from their classmates' endeavors.

The Association of Yale Alumni oversees a network of more than 125 local Yale Clubs and associations that have a mission to connect and reconnect the alumni to the university. These groups also involve alumni volunteers in the admissions process, as they are charged with interviewing students in their area and filling out evaluation forms. Many local groups host receptions for admitted students. Fund-raising is carried out by the Alumni Fund, a separate organization that can boast one of the highest participation rates of the Ivy League. The university recently launched a $3 billion capital campaign, largely fueled by the generosity of its alumni. That alumni are devoted and loyal is a good sign of the quality of the experience they had during their time here.

Yalies enjoy coming back to campus. Twice yearly, over 200 alumni, elected as delegates by their local associations, convene in New Haven to address the latest news and developments at Yale and discuss alumni affairs. Some fly in from as far away as Switzerland and Hong Kong. Reunions bring thousands more back to campus in the spring, for a weekend of dancing, dining, and catching up. Many current students work during reunions, and have the extra treat of meeting alums who lived in their residential college or perhaps took a class with the same instructor. Recently, the university has embarked on "A Day with Yale" program, which puts administrators and faculty members on the road to share their knowledge and talents with the alumni population.

An alumni gathering would not be complete without the spirited singing of the alma mater, "Bright College Years." The lyrics sum up the immense loyalty and nostalgia shared by Yale graduates.

PROMINENT GRADS

- William F. Buckley, Writer
- George H.W. Bush, U.S. President
- George W. Bush, U.S. President
- Jodie Foster, Actress/Director
- Charles Ives, Composer
- Joseph I. Lieberman, U.S. Senator
- Sinclair Lewis, Nobel Prize-winning Author
- Maya Lin, Architect
- Henry Luce, *Time* and *Life Magazine* Founder
- David McCullough, Historian
- Samuel F.B. Morse, Telegraph and Morse Code Inventor
- Gene Siskel, Movie Critic
- William Howard Taft, U.S. President
- Garry Trudeau, "Doonesbury" creator
- Arthur Watson, IBM Founder
- Thornton Wilder, Pulitzer Prize-winning Playwright

Bright College years, with pleasure rife,
The shortest, gladdest years of life;
How swiftly are ye gliding by!
Oh, why doth time so quickly fly?

Oh, let us strive that ever we
May let these words our watch-cry be,
Where'er upon life's sea we sail:
"For God, for Country, and for Yale!"

SUMMING UP

Go to the "front door" of the Yale World Wide Web site (*http://www.yale.edu/*) and you may see a Yale campus scene or famous building. As Yale embarks on its fourth century, the same mingling of past and future is palpable on the campus. For example, students' increasing use of e-mail occurs in the computer center located in the basement of Connecticut Hall, the university's oldest building, and wireless Internet is available in most dining halls and libraries. While the university remains committed to perpetuating its traditional strengths, it also allows its energetic and intellectually enthusiastic student body to lead it toward a new future.

❏ *Amanda Gordon, B.A.*
❏ *Seth Oltman, B.A.*

STRATEGIES

by
Rachel Weimerskirch

APPLICATION STRATEGIES

1. Use the application as a chance to best present yourself on paper.

....

2. Make your essay shine.

....

3. Give yourself time to meet your deadlines.

....

4. Remember all the housekeeping details.

....

5. Apply to schools that feel right for you.

....

1. USE THE APPLICATION AS A CHANCE TO BEST PRESENT YOURSELF ON PAPER

- CONSIDER THE COMPETITION: If you're an admissions officer, a typical day might look something like this: over your mug of morning coffee, you're peering at a stack of hundreds—maybe thousands—of applications from all over the world. SATs, GPAs, and other acronyms are standards to consider in determining the strongest candidates. After the numbers are crunched, who will catch your eye and hold your interest? Sometimes even the straight A student/captain of the hockey team/organizer of a program at a homeless shelter won't make the cut—unless, of course, he or she knows how to paint his or her own self-portrait in the most flattering light.

- APPROACH THE APPLICATION AS AN OPPORTUNITY: For the applicant, the application doesn't have to be daunting—or a chore. Think of it as one of life's rare opportunities to design your own image. Applying to college can really stress you out, or applying to college can be an opportunity to re-create yourself for an audience of admissions officers who are looking for someone original, creative, and stellar. They are looking for that edge, that extra something beyond the mainstream that tells them you are right for their school and that their school is a match for you.

- IT'S ALL ABOUT YOU: It's sometimes hard to flaunt your good qualities, throwing modesty to the wind, but this time, piece together all of your valuable high school accomplishments and brag about them—loud! Be specific about all of your leadership roles, your significant contributions to an area of interest. Were you president of a student body? Editor-in-chief of a newspaper? A rated athlete? Have you been recognized as an All-State or an MVP? Did you organize others in support of a cause? Write about and emphasize the activities that inspire you. They'll serve as vibrant colors for your self-portrait.

- TO SUPPLEMENT OR NOT TO SUPPLEMENT: If you've been visited by the muse, some colleges welcome supplementary material. Sending original poetry, music, or art may help to introduce a fuller picture of you as a person. If something means a lot to you, send it, but be brutal in your selections—pick only the best of your best.

  Other schools clearly request only materials that adhere to application requirements. Read carefully to determine whether or not supplementary materials will be accepted and considered. Don't provide an original score of your aspiring Broadway musical if the school isn't going to consider it a factor in your acceptance.

2. MAKE YOUR ESSAY SHINE

- SEE IT AS YOUR SPACE: A memorable essay is one of the best ways to reveal the true you. What is not on the application that you would like the college or university to know? If the stack of applications you face seems to reduce you to a list of activities, grades, and courses, use the freedom that the essay gives you to choose your topic and to use your voice.

- THE WRITING IMPULSE: Write about your passions; they will speak for you and allow your voice to shout through the paper. Use the essay questions to let the college get to know you as a person.

3. GIVE YOURSELF TIME TO MEET YOUR DEADLINES

- PROCRASTINATION WILL ALWAYS GET YOU DOWN: In the line-up of college application tasks, pacing is one of the most important strategies. Give yourself a realistic timeline when devising a schedule for yourself. You don't want to run out of energy before you reach the finish line.

- CREATE A PLAN OF ATTACK: Maybe you want to dive head first into the application that has the earliest deadline, devoting all of your after-school hours until you polish it off. Or perhaps you will begin with the application to your first-choice school so that you can dedicate your freshest enthusiasms to number one on your wish list. Whatever way you begin, be sure that you remain on top of the required dates of submission—not just for the application proper, but for the test scores, letters of recommendation, and so on. (Remember that colleges might have different dates for specific tests; some require more SAT Subject Tests than others, for example.) A college application is a many-layered process. Sometimes each layer contains a different date to consider.

- INVEST IN A CALENDAR: It doesn't hurt to write down on a calendar all of the important dates for each school. You can color code according to school or according to layers (for example, dates for letters of recommendation can be sea green while dates for the registration of appropriate tests can be periwinkle). Make the application process a priority.

4. REMEMBER ALL THE HOUSEKEEPING DETAILS

- PROOFREAD… If you take your time, you'll make sure that details are not overlooked. (Did I sign the application? Did I send the University of Chicago a check made payable to

Colgate?) Go beyond Spell Check and really proofread your work carefully until you are sure it's in its best form.

- …AND PROOFREAD AGAIN WITH SOMEONE ELSE'S EYES: After you have read and reread your essay and application, you may feel too close to it to catch any missing commas. Show it to some objective observers who will see it with fresh eyes—counselors, Mom, Dad, teachers, those who know you well. They will see it for the first time, just as an admissions officer will. If the application is striking, they may even discover something about you that they didn't know before.

- TYPE, DON'T WRITE: Maybe your third-grade teacher worked your fingers to the bone practicing your penmanship, but your perfect script will not make it for the reader who is looking at countless other applications. Your essay should be computer-generated. For the application, taking the extra time to line up those little lines and boxes to a typewriter or word processor is worth the effort.

5. APPLY TO SCHOOLS THAT FEEL RIGHT FOR YOU

- CHOOSE THE SCHOOL TO WHICH YOU'RE GUARANTEED TO BE ACCEPTED WITH THE SAME CARE SPENT SELECTING YOUR DREAM SCHOOL: While you read on and on about the selectivity of schools and about the importance of really impressing those to which you have chosen to apply, don't forget that you are, in a sense, interviewing the schools almost as much as they are interviewing you. An application is a hefty investment of yourself. Each school you choose should be one that you can see yourself attending, whether it's choice number one or choice number five. Each application should be tailored to the school where it will end its journey. Keep your schools in mind as you complete their applications. The application—and the school—should bring out your best points—carefully, thoughtfully, honestly, and creatively.

ESSAY-WRITING STRATEGIES

1. What does the college want in your essay? That is the question.

....

2. Start rough. Then refine.

....

3. Pen to paper (or fingers to keyboard): The write stuff about you.

....

4. Organize.

....

5. Trust the power of the written word. Trust yourself.

....

> *When you write, you lay out a line of words. The line of words is a miner's pick, a wood-carver's gouge, a surgeon's probe. You wield it, and it digs a path you follow. Soon you find yourself deep in new territory. Is it a dead end, or have you located the real subject? You will know tomorrow, or this time next year.*

— *Annie Dillard*
From The Writing Life. *Harper and Row, 1989.*

What you write now in your personal statements and essays *will* determine tomorrow. Don't stop short of inspiring work. It could help open the door to your dream school.

1. WHAT DOES THE COLLEGE WANT IN YOUR ESSAY? THAT IS THE QUESTION

- ASSESS YOUR OPTIONS FOR THE ESSAY QUESTION: Some colleges and universities provide specific questions to direct your essay writing. You may be asked to offer your views on a particular topic or issue. ("If you could change anything in the world, what would you change and how?" or "Describe an experience that changed you.") Others leave the essay topic relatively open-ended and personal, allowing you the somewhat daunting task: "Tell us about *you*."

  Whether you decide to comment on the state of the Union or to recount an inspirational volunteer job, you often have a few essay questions from which to choose. Study the question that feels most comfortable to you and pick it apart to plan your approach.

- GET TO THE HEART OF THE QUESTION: You are anxious to write your college essay about that one life-changing moment. How do you fit that experience into an answer to the college's question? It's a good idea to look into what is being asked, address the question directly, and elaborate on your answer to their query with some interesting experiences of your own. The questions offered on the application are meant for you to choose in order to let the college get to know you better, so mold the question to you personally. If you discuss the topics that are asked in the question of your choice and describe personal experiences, you can't go wrong.

2. START ROUGH, THEN REFINE

- CREATE AN OUTLINE/ROUGH DRAFT: First, organize your thoughts around your topic and outline some important points that you plan to stress. Start with a draft that captures your feelings and images, then return to it again and again to make it lucid and refined.

- DO NOT BE AFRAID OF CHANGE: Elizabeth Bishop worked through multiple drafts for each of her poems, and her revisions filled pages at times. The most inspiring of poets, bards, novelists, and essayists are unafraid to "kill a few of their babies," as they say in the literary world. All well-written material reaches fluidity through revision and change. Don't let the raw emotion of your personal statement be the only strength that makes it impressive. Editing for content, making changes, and reorganizing your thoughts will enhance the quality of your writing. Admissions officers will be unimpressed by writing that is anything less than careful and thoughtful.

3. PEN TO PAPER (OR FINGERS TO KEYBOARD): THE WRITE STUFF ABOUT YOU

- HAVE FUN WITH IT (BUT DON'T BUY INTO GIMMICKS): You are looking for that edge in your essay that will attract the attention of admission officers who have read more essays than they can count. Something about you is unique and outstanding. Enjoy the chance to use your voice creatively, without simply boasting about your good qualities. Let the admissions officers know you by telling a well-written story and completely selling yourself.

    One admissions officer at a top college claims that it is the essay that makes or breaks an application in her mind, and if a student has the ability to take over a creative written space with an essay that sticks with her, she's sold. An applicant who writes succinctly, well, and with a twist impresses her. A student who wrote about his track career and sent his old track shoes attached to the essay did not.

- HONESTY IS THE BEST POLICY: The old adage is true: write what you know. Don't be afraid to be honest and to be yourself.

4. ORGANIZE

- KEEP THE SCHOOL IN MIND WHEN WRITING ABOUT YOURSELF: The essay can be a further exploration of why you are right for that particular school and why that school is right for you. In reflecting on who you are right now, you will also be able to look forward to what you wish to become through your experiences at your future school.

- REDUCE, REUSE, RECYCLE: If something has inspired you to create a piece that really speaks about you, adapt it to fit into various college applications. It's okay to use one essay for more than one school. After all, the admissions officers at Yale rarely compare specifics with the admissions officers at Berkeley. Some essay topics and questions are flexible enough so that you can tailor your essay to more than one school. You are attracted to these schools for reasons that are personal and specific. The essay is your chance to let them know the things about you that fit with the things you like about them. You are not cheating if you say the same thing about yourself to more than one admissions office.
- DON'T FORGET THE FINISHING TOUCHES: Type the essay. Check the spelling. Correct margins and punctuation. Have several readers look it over for you. Sounds like a drill, but neatness and care can't hurt.

5. TRUST THE POWER OF THE WRITTEN WORD. TRUST YOURSELF

- LET YOUR ESSAY SPEAK FOR YOU: Writing is a powerful tool. Unlike speaking in an interview or filling in boxes on an application, writing a personal statement or answering an essay question allows you to think, plan, and revise an interesting, articulate presentation of yourself. Be as complete as possible and don't be afraid to take risks by telling your own story. Discussing a personal experience takes strength—the chance to use your voice is a gift; wrap it in language and give it to the college of your choice. They'll open it carefully and, if they remember it, it is a gift that will bring many happy returns.

FINANCING
STRATEGIES

❑   ❑

1. Know what is expected of you.

....

2. Set a timetable and get an early start.

....

3. Explore every possible source of funding.

....

4. Lean on you.

....

5. College is worth the investment!

....

Regardless of your family's income, college is no small feat. The cost of tuition, room and board, books, travel, and related expenses continues to rise in an intimidating, discouraging way. Applying for financial aid is the first step in scaling that monetary hurdle. In all cases, no matter what your income bracket, applying for financial aid is definitely the first sign of a smart, bright, college-bound student.

1. KNOW WHAT IS EXPECTED OF YOU

- GET THE FACTS: Don't just stare at that pile of tax returns and financial information. As with all things, the best place to begin is at the beginning. Sharpen your number two pencils, but before you start, make sure you remember these guidelines:

> Males must be registered for the draft when applying for aid.
> Don't leave blanks on any financial aid form, whether it is for the school, the agency, or a loan.
> Sign and keep copies of all forms. Send only originals.
> Include the correct processing fees.

- DEFINE YOUR TERMS: You'll need to know the language before you travel through the process of financial aid. There is a dizzying amount of terms and acronyms (the financial aid world loves acronyms). Consider this your official dictionary of Financial Aid Jargon (FAJ).

Acknowledgment Report: Notification to the student after the need form has been received by a processing agency.

College Scholarship Service (CSS): Service that analyzes family need and contribution.

Expected Family Contribution (EFC): Amount determined by the federal government that your family should have accessible to help pay for school; used in determining your eligibility for grants and loans.

Free Application for Federal Student Aid (FAFSA): Free federal application that must be filed to determine eligibility for federal student loans.

Financial Aid Forms (FAF): Forms processed by the College Scholarship Service of the College Board to determine your family's financial need and contribution; results are sent by the CSS to colleges and universities.

Information Request Form: Form that the federal government may send to ask for further or corrected information before granting a federal Pell Grant.

Payment Voucher: Part Three of the Student Aid Report; submitted to the school financial aid officer to determine the Pell Grant amount.

Student Aid Report (SAR): Official notification of federal Pell Grant eligibility, usually received by the student and the school four to six weeks after submission of the application.

Verification: Process of checking financial aid applications for accuracy.

2. SET A TIMETABLE AND GET AN EARLY START

- JANUARY: Gather all of the necessary financial aid forms from your schools and from processing agencies. Collect the documents and information that you will need to complete these required forms (such as tax returns, bank statements, and so on). Send your completed forms to the processors soon after January 1.

- FEBRUARY: Three to six weeks after submitting your application, its receipt will be confirmed via mail. A report will follow that will outline your family's expected contribution and eligibility for aid. Look for the SAR, which you will submit to the school you ultimately choose to attend. Discuss the results with your family and direct any questions you have to your financial aid officer.

- MARCH–JULY: Colleges and universities make financial aid decisions at this time, so be sure that your application is complete. The financial aid award letter from your school indicates the amount of aid you will receive for the year, including all federal grants and loans, outside awards, and state aid. Sign and return a copy of the letter if you accept the school's package. If you need more assistance or have questions about the offer, contact the school's aid officer now. Don't wait!

3. EXPLORE EVERY POSSIBLE SOURCE OF FUNDING

- PARENTS: Figure out ahead of time what role your family will play in helping to finance your education.

- THE FEDS: Despite cuts and obstacles, the government still provides most of the aid that is awarded to college students.

- THE STATE: Many states offer need- and merit-based aid. Inquire into your home base resources for the college-bound.

- COLLEGES AND UNIVERSITIES: Check the philosophy of the schools to which you are applying. Need-blind? (The school does not consider financial need in admissions.)

Need-sensitive? (The school considers financial need only when deliberating over candidates after subsidiary funds have been allocated.) How is aid distributed? Will your freshman year aid package be guaranteed for four years? Don't be afraid to pose the tough questions to the financial aid director or advisor. Paying for college is one of the most important investments you will make. You have the right to be an educated consumer.

- PRIVATE ORGANIZATIONS AND FOUNDATIONS: If you have particular talents or aspirations, examine organizations that award merit-based aid. Many organizations offer assistance to students heading towards a certain major or grant help to high school seniors from a specific area. Investigate all your options at your local library.

4. LEAN ON YOU

- WORK IT...BORROW IT: Students have the responsibility of thinking about saving a bit in high school, finding summer jobs, taking out loans, and working during college. Many financial aid packages include on-campus jobs. Both on- and off-campus work is not only lucrative for spending money and tuition money, it can provide valuable experiences that contribute to more than just your payment plan.

5. COLLEGE IS WORTH THE INVESTMENT!

- DON'T FEAR THE NUMBERS: It more than adds up. What you get for your money is often priceless. The degree equals the architecture of a life and a future. The major yields connections and expertise in a field that excites you. The experience gained in obtaining that slip of paper written in Latin can be so rich and full and once-in-a-lifetime, it almost doesn't hurt to make the loan payments afterwards. Almost. Because, in a perfect world, the fine-tuning of our minds wouldn't cost a penny. Until we reach that glorious place, it pays to plan a way to make the refinement of our mental sensibilities as affordable as possible.

STUDY
STRATEGIES

1. Time management: the key to staying on top.

2. Establish blocks of time for each commitment.

3. Learn to love your classes.

4. Plan ahead.

5. Prioritize!

It is two o'clock in the morning. You have just stumbled back to your dorm room after a late rehearsal for a production headed by a very serious senior director. Your legs are still sore from rugby tryouts earlier in the week. That psychology assignment is due tomorrow afternoon, but you have to finish it in the twenty-four-hour computer lab tonight because you have to work at the café in the morning. Your roommate is still awake, waiting to hear your advice on this great-new-somebody he or she just met.

Now what are you going to do to make sure that all of the high school preparation, careful application work, diligent essay-writing, hard-won financial aid, and lofty aspirations will play out successfully on the stage of this collegiate experience?

1. TIME MANAGEMENT: THE KEY TO STAYING ON TOP

- FINDING THE BALANCE: College is a nonstop mélange of experiences. Juggling studies with social life, extracurricular activities, jobs, and friends can be harrowing. The idea is to enjoy each facet of your life to the fullest, without losing sight of important priorities.

  You know yourself. Try not to take on too much if you are the kind of student who needs as little distraction as possible. Try not to take on too little if you thrive on a tight schedule to keep yourself motivated and challenged. Above all, develop a schedule that will focus on your classes, with occasional varied, diverse, and interesting demands on your time.

- THE FILOFAX SYNDROME: Electronic planners and little black books are no longer accessories to be found only in the boardrooms of corporate America. They can be spotted peeking out of many a backpack, tucked away among Henry James novels in dorm rooms, and present on the desks at student government meetings. College students aren't kidding about "penciling you in." It's often wise to keep track of your commitments in writing. You'd be surprised how much easier deadlines, meetings, and social events fall in beside each other when you can see them written in front of you.

2. ESTABLISH BLOCKS OF TIME FOR EACH COMMITMENT

- BREAK UP THE DAYS OF THE WEEK: Set aside chunks of time that you regularly spend dedicating yourself to your classes. Just as you would make a work schedule at any job, you should have an academic work schedule that you attempt to follow. You are your own boss, so punch in for physics on Monday evenings after dinner, English lit on Tuesday mornings before practice, and so on.

You won't have to set your academic plan in stone. In fact, you'll need plenty of flexibility (for the weeks when you have an English paper due, but no physics lab because you finished it early). The point is to promise yourself that you have blocks of time solely for the subjects you are studying each semester.

- USE THE IN-BETWEEN HOURS: Maybe on Thursdays you have two hours in mid-afternoon between your seminar and your art class. You could fill those two hours with errands that you've been meaning to take care of. You could score two extra hours in the library researching a project. You could finish a problem set or run to the gym to work out. It's important to steal the hours in your day that are sandwiched between other commitments. That precious time can be easily lost in the Bermuda Triangle where time runs when you are busy and thirsty for more hours in the day. Instead, grab it and put it to good use before it gets away. Making each moment count is the key. (That doesn't mean you can't use those hours to meet a friend for coffee. A little R and R is definitely a priority, too.)

3. LEARN TO LOVE YOUR CLASSES

- ELECT PASSIONS: Not every class of your college career will change your life, but you will definitely move from high school chem labs and single-sex phys ed to more engaging academic pursuits. You'll find flexibility, even within the requirements. Your major will allow you to focus on something that you feel strongly about, while still dabbling in areas that are new and challenging.

- EXPERIMENT. PUSH YOURSELF. TRY NEW THINGS: If you have no idea what a cognitive science course called "Time" could possibly cover, but the idea of meeting to discuss such a broad subject fascinates you, take it! If you love the humanities, make sure you take a science as well. And if you admire art with the eye of a true aesthete, but you can't draw to save your life, make sure you sign up for basic life drawing at some point in your college career. Studying something that falls outside of your main line of interest is an excellent way to spice up your classwork.

- THIS IS A RICH, RARE TIME: Even when the work load brings you down and your calendar is filled with deadlines for papers, exams, presentations, and projects, try not to forget how lucky you are to have this time in your life. You are being asked to study, to work, to grow, to expand your mind, and to look through frames of reference and windows that you have never experienced before now. College is a precious opportunity. Covet your right to acquire so much knowledge in such an individual way.

4. PLAN AHEAD

- LOOK AT THE SYLLABUS: Early in the term, your professors will provide careful plans of what they will cover throughout the semester. Most professors let you know right away the important dates to remember, required readings, and class topics for the duration of the course. The class syllabus can jump-start your timeline for the final paper, or allow you to stay on top of things for the midterm project. Check the syllabus in the beginning of the course for all of your classes. You can coordinate the crunch times (such as those times before breaks when every professor assigns work as if his or hers is your only class!). Knowing ahead of time allows you to be prepared for the avalanches. When you are prepared and you have stocked your research and your resources, it becomes easier to successfully weather any academic storm.
- MEET THE PROFESSOR AND/OR THE TA: Know the professor's office hours and take advantage of them. Find out if professors or assistants are accessible via e-mail or phone and contact them frequently to talk about your work, your ideas, your progress.

5. PRIORITIZE!

- MAKE CLASSES NUMBER ONE: Want to do well in college? Then make college classes your first, most important priority and look out for number one. You will be making room in your life for lots of things: jobs, volunteerism, sports, clubs and activities, friends, dating…the list goes on and on. Believe it or not, there are enough hours in the day to get to everything. Although it is impossible to accomplish all that you think you might want to try between freshman and senior year, it is feasible to try everything and still succeed academically. Just make sure that the library becomes an important part of your week (and yes, sometimes your weekend, too!) and get your priorities in order.

A MOST COMPETITIVE COMPARISON

SCHOOL	NUMBER OF APPLI- CATIONS	ACCEPTED	ENROLLED	M/F RATIO	SAT I SCORES			COSTS
					VERBAL	MATH	COMB.	
Amherst College	6,281	1,176	431	50/50	700	700	1400	$41,590
Barnard College	n/av	n/av	n/av	3/97	n/av	n/av	n/av	$38,000
Bates College	4,356	1,272	490	49/51	675	680	1355	$42,100
Boston College	n/av	n/av	n/av	48/52	n/av	n/av	n/av	$41,600
Bowdoin College	5,026	1,232	478	48/52	700	700	1400	$41,660
Brandeis University	7,343	2,794	739	44/56	680	690	1370	$41,551
Brown University	16,911	2,587	1,475	46/54	720	720	1440	$42,015
California Institute of Technology	n/av	n/av	n/av	70/30	n/av	n/av	n/av	$36,123
Carleton College	5,036	1,471	542	47/53	n/av	n/av	n/av	$40,467
Carnegie Mellon University	n/av	n/av	n/av	60/40	n/av	n/av	n/av	$32,700
Case Western Reserve University	7,181	4,916	1,162	59/41	600	690	1350	$37,314
Claremont McKenna College	3,734	786	271	54/46	700	700	1400	$42,920
Colby College	3,874	1,454	511	46/54	680	680	1350	$41,770
Colgate University	8,008	2,168	729	51/49	666	681	1347	$41,170
College of New Jersey	7,300	3,289	1,236	42/58	630	650	1280	$15,120 (in-state) $18,315 (out-of-state)
College of the Holy Cross	4,744	2,270	723	45/55	632	634	1266	$40,664

All figures relate to a recent freshman class except the Male/Female Ratio numbers, which reflect the entire undergraduate student body for a recent class. Figures are either as published in *Barron's Profiles of American Colleges, 27th Edition* or in the essay portion of this book.

SCHOOL	NUMBER OF APPLI-CATIONS	ACCEPTED	ENROLLED	M/F RATIO	SAT I SCORES			COSTS
					VERBAL	MATH	COMB.	
College of William and Mary	5,700	n/av	n/av	44/56	n/av	n/av	n/av	$14,147 (in-state) $23,186 (out-of-state)
Columbia University/ Columbia College	15,793	1,693	1,024	48/52	720	710	1430	$42,584
Columbia University/ School of Engineering and Applied Science (SEAS)	2,332	1,040	315	73/27	700	760	1460	$42,584
Connecticut College	4,183	1,477	492	40/60	670	660	1330	$41,975 (includes room and board)
Cooper Union for the Advancement of Science and Art	2,301	308	228	64/36	670	700	1370	$38,500
Cornell University	24,452	6,621	3,108	50/50	680	710	1390	$41,717
Dartmouth College	11,734	2,173	1,077	50/50	713	719	1432	$39,465
Davidson College	4,258	1,146	463	50/50	680	680	1360	$36,825
Duke University	18,090	3,995	1,724	52/48	720	720	1460	$41,239
Emory University	12,011	4,395	1,259	42/58	670	690	1360	$40,546
George Washington University	19,406	7,275	2,411	44/56	650	650	1360	$48,820
Georgetown University	15,285	3,286	1,551	46/54	n/av	n/av	n/av	$43,183
Hamilton College	4,189	1,502	498	50/50	690	680	1370	$41,660
Harvard College	n/av	n/av	n/av	53/47	n/av	n/av	n/av	$45,860
Harvey Mudd College	1,899	683	195	71/29	720	760	1480	$42,352
Haverford College	3,112	816	316	47/53	690	690	1380	$41,600
Johns Hopkins University	11, 274	3,907	1,133	54/46	685	710	1395	$42,044
Kenyon College	3,929	1,420	441	48/52	670	660	1330	$39,500
Lafayette College	n/av	n/av	n/av	52/48	n/av	n/av	na/v	$39.267
Macalester College	4,317	1,893	491	42/58	700	670	1370	$36,500

SCHOOL	NUMBER OF APPLI-CATIONS	ACCEPTED	ENROLLED	M/F RATIO	SAT I SCORES VERBAL	MATH	COMB.	COSTS
Massachusetts Institute of Technology	10,440	1,494	996	57/43	730	780	1510	$41,800
Middlebury College	5,254	1,241	555	48/52	740	730	1470	$42,120 (tuition only)
New York University	34,509	12,662	n/av	39/61	680	690	1370	$43,170
Northwestern University	n/av	n/av	n/av	47/53	n/av	n/av	n/av	$37,595
Oberlin College	4,553	2,016	792	44/56	698	663	1361	$40,904
Occidental College	5,121	2,086	436	43/57	640	650	1290	$40,185
Pomona College	n/av	n/av	n/av	50/50	730	720	1450	$40,774
Princeton University	16,529	1,826	1,230	54/46	n/av	n/av	n/av	$40,213
Reed College	2,646	1,200	353	45/55	710	670	1380	$41,106
Rice University	8,106	1,802	727	52/48	n/av	n/av	n/av	$32,290
Scripps College	1,836	847	234	all women	690	670	1360	$41,000
Smith College	n/av	n/av	n/av	all women	660	640	1300	$41,474
Stanford University	20,192	2,426	1,633	53/47	n/av	n/av	n/av	$41,557
Swarthmore College	4,085	917	389	48/52	730	710	1400	$41,280
Tufts University	15,536	4,398	1,365	49/51	50	n/av	n/av	$42,018
Tulane University	17,572	7,867	1,602	49/51	n/av	n/av	n/av	$41,098
United States Military Academy	n/av	n/av	n/av	86/14	n/av	n/av	n/av	$0
United States Naval Academy	4,769	1,450	1,245	86/14	650	670	1320	$0
University of California at Los Angeles	42,224	11,361	4,422	43/57	630	670	1300	$17,681 (in-state) $24,882 (out-of-state)
University of Chicago	9,011	3,628	1,205	49/51	n/av	n/av	n/av	$42,360
University of Miami	18,812	8,679	2,277	47/53	n/av	n/av	n/av	$38,397
University of North Carolina at Chapel Hill	18,414	6,736	3,751	42/58	643	656	1299	$11,129 (in-state) $18,411 (out-of-state)

SCHOOL	NUMBER OF APPLI-CATIONS	ACCEPTED	ENROLLED	M/F RATIO	SAT I SCORES			COSTS
					VERBAL	MATH	COMB.	
University of Notre Dame	11,317	3,582	1,995	53/47	667	693	1360	$39,552
University of Pennsylvania	18,824	3,913	2,552	50/50	700	720	1420	$41,766
University of Richmond	5,778	2,743	772	49/51	n/av	n/av	n/av	$40,510
University of Rochester	n/av	n/av	n/av	49/51	637	667	1,304	$41,135
University of Southern California	31,634	8,418	2,741	50/50	668	690	1358	$41,618
University of Virginia	15,657	5,898	3,112	45/55	660	670	1330	$13,759 (in-state) $24,114 (out-of-state)
Vanderbilt University	11,663	4,115	1,622	48/52	n/av	n/av	n/av	$41,986
Vassar College	6,314	1,803	650	40/60	770	686	1456	$41,700
Wake Forest University	7,494	2,882	1,120	49/51	n/av	n/av	n/av	$38,290
Washington and Lee University	3,948	1,136	467	50/50	690	690	1380	$38,880
Washington University In St. Louis	21,515	4,044	1,388	48/52	n/av	n/av	n/av	$42,106
Webb Institute	110	33	22	80/20	680	740	1420	$8,340 (room and board—no tuition)
Wellesely College	4,466	1,463	605	all women	700	685	1385	$41,030
Wesleyan University	6,879	1,902	717	50/50	700	700	1400	$42,122
Williams College	5,822	1,095	536	48/52	710	710	1420	$40,311
Yale University	19,451	1,880	1,321	51/49	750	750	1500	$41,000

COLLEGE SUMMARIES

COLLEGE SUMMARIES

COLLEGE SUMMARY INDEX

❑ **Amherst College**, at first glance, is a picturesque New England liberal arts college. But beyond the red brick and fall foliage are the people who make the college what it is—the top-notch faculty, the accessible administration, the successful alumni, and most importantly, the energetic and expressive students. Collectively, those who make Amherst what it is give to the school its character, effort, and intellect, and receive in turn, the character, effort, and intellect of their fellow colleagues and students, making Amherst more than an academic institution, but a community.

❑ **Barnard College** is an independent college for women partnered with Columbia University and located in New York City. The 2,300 undergraduates pursue a broad variety of liberal arts majors. Graduation requirements are flexibly structured so students can fashion a course of study to meet their needs. Those interested in professional or graduate schools in law, business, medicine, or other areas are advised on appropriate courses. Over 2,500 internships are available to students through the Career Development Office, which also sponsors on-campus recruitment and workshops. Eighty or so student organizations are complemented by those at Columbia University, offering a wealth of activity and opportunity for leadership and involvement; varsity athletes compete in Division I.

Barnard's unique combination of strengths—a commited faculty of teacher-scholars, full access to the resources of a great university, and the abundant offerings of New York City—make it an excellent choice for young women interested in an urban setting and an excellent, well-rounded education.

❑ **Bates College** is small, friendly, yet academically excellent. Bates does not require standardized test scores for admission. It is strongly committed to a program of broad education including the humanities and the sciences. The student body and faculty are unusually supportive and inclusive. One example is the absence of fraternities and sororities. Bates continues to be committed to providing an environment in which students can excel. A Bates education extends beyond the walls of academic buildings, and is formed in the integration of academics, athletics, study abroad, and activities. Located midway between the Atlantic coastline and the mountains, the school offers a broad choice of sports and outdoor activities.

❏ **Boston College** is a Catholic and Jesuit university dedicated to the highest standards of undergraduate education, offering opportunities for intellectual and personal growth by combining gifted students, a nationally reknowned faculty, first-rate facilities, and a premier location with an educational mission devoted to academic, professional, and spiritual development of its community. Following in the footsteps of St. Ignatius' centuries-old academic tradition, Boston College attempts to develop "men and women in service for others" through a curriculum that focuses on a wide range of intellectual pursuits through the lenses of justice and social responsibility.

❏ **Bowdoin College** is a coed liberal arts college situated on the coast of Maine just north of Portland. The 212-year-old school offers courses in everything from neuroscience to English literature, Chinese to art history, and while the academic emphasis is always on learning for learning's sake, Bowdoin continues to prepare its graduates to be leaders in all fields. Well known for its athletic prowess and distinguished alumni, Bowdoin is also forward-looking, with many newly constructed dormitories and state-of-the-art science and theater facilities. Perhaps best known for its strong ties to Maine and that state's pragmatic sensibilities, Bowdoin continues to produce graduates who gracefully navigate their way through the world with a solid grounding in the arts, science, world cultures, and the spirit of volunteerism.

❏ **Brandeis University** is the youngest private research university in the nation. It combines the faculty and resources of a world-class research institution with the intimacy and personal attention of a small liberal arts college. Located in Waltham, Massachusetts, on 235 attractive suburban acres, Brandeis is in an ideal location just nine miles west of Boston. Both in and out of the classroom, Brandeis provides a dynamic environment for students. While academically challenging, the curriculum can be tailored to each student need after ensuring that general requirements are met. With $3,200 undergraduates, more than 250 official clubs and organizations, and an active student body, extracurricular life on campus leaves little else to be desired. Graduates leave with a well-rounded liberal arts education and a degree from a university well known and respected in academic and professional communities, and they are instilled with a strong commitment to social justice.

❏ A **Brown University** education offers the perfect combination of flexibility and rigor. Students are free to choose their own academic path, and whatever they decide, they can't go wrong, for there are challenging, vibrant educational experiences wherever you turn at Brown. Brown is also a true university-college where students benefit from close contact with professors. At Brown, bright, self-directed students get the freedom and support they need to realize their full academic potential.

❏ **The California Institute of Technology**, better known as Caltech, is one of the world's preeminent research universities packaged in a small-school environment. Caltech is at the forefront of scientific research, with thirty-one Nobel prizes won by Caltech faculty and alumni over its 100-year history. At the same time, it enrolls only 913 undergraduates and employs 300 professorial faculty. Located on a beautiful campus in Pasadena, California, Caltech students live in intimate student houses that promote a laid-back southern California lifestyle. The academics at Caltech are anything but laid back though, with every student required to learn quantum mechanics and multivariable calculus by their sophomore year. If a student has a true passion for science, then Caltech is the place to be. Caltech provides the consummate learning experience. Caltech is probably the only school where the Ph.Ds outnumber the undergraduates, and research is a part of everyday life; more than half of students spend a summer doing research on campus before they graduate. A Caltech education prepares students for science at the highest level, and more Caltech graduates go on to earn doctorates in engineering and science than from any other university in the country.

❏ **Carleton College,** Many Carls will admit that the reason why they chose to go to this small liberal arts school in the middle of the Midwest is the people Carleton attracts, including professors, staff members, and students. Most students will also admit that it wasn't the orange gelatin dessert with carrot shavings that sometimes makes its way into the dining hall, or the −20 degree wind chill that often creeps up in the winter months. While they might hail from thousands of different backgrounds, Carls are an intensely intellectual and academically curious bunch, often going above and beyond classroom requirements because a certain topic sparks an interest. The vast majority of classes at Carleton are very demanding, and the academic atmosphere is intense, but not competitive. Students also place great importance on getting an education outside of the classroom, whether it is on the frisbee field, during a conversation in a dorm room, or at a student-organized meeting. Carls want to learn from and teach their peers in a community where many different viewpoints are respected. From the first day of freshman year, students of this highly selective but still slightly obscure small liberal arts college can learn from, support, and have fun with each other, and that is certainly not a small opportunity.

❏ Students come to **Carnegie Mellon** to pursue the richness of an academic and artistic community comprised of seven distinct colleges. Through our liberal/professional mission, students acquire depth and breadth of knowledge, creativity and intellectual playfulness, critical judgment, independent learning, and resourcefulness. They graduate as the innovative leaders and problem-solvers of tomorrow.

❏ **Case Western Reserve University** is known primarily as a technical school. People are attracted by its excellent engineering and science programs. What is perhaps less well known is that Case has equally excellent liberal arts programs, and the entire Case curriculum easily ranks among the most competitive in the country. With a campus integrated into Cleveland's metropolitan framework, Case provides opportunities for students that aren't available at colleges wedged among such entities as museums, theater, music, film, dance, food, and lots more. To top it off, Case offers excellent financial aid packages that, as long as students keep their grades up, can help take a significant chunk out of their total tuition and other expenses. With a revamped undergraduate curriculum, incoming students at Case can expect one of the highest degrees of academic freedom available.

❏ **Claremont McKenna College**, a small liberal arts college of 1,140 students, is known for its focus on leadership across curricula and for its strong political science and economics departments. Located east of Los Angeles, Claremont McKenna is part of the Claremont consortium, a group of seven institutions that share facilities and resources. CMC students choose the college for its strong community feeling within the greater environment of the consortium, excellent professors who place an emphasis on teaching, and for the strong preparation for careers in public service and the professions.

❏ Located in the heart of Maine, **Colby College** is a beautiful and surprisingly interesting place, and it's getting better all the time. Though small—the student body remains at about 1,800—it is a thriving cultural and intellectual center. Since its inception in 1813, it has also enjoyed a history of pioneering achievements in liberal arts education, from being one of the first schools to admit women (1871), to the introduction of one of the first African-American studies program in the nation (1973), to initiatives such as the Integrated Studies curriculum established in 1997. Located within driving distance of mountains, lakes, and Maine's scenic coast, the remote campus especially appeals to lovers of the outdoors, while the flourishing arts community seems to keep the less physically adventuresome more than satisfied. If you're looking for a small, prestigious school with challenging academics, easy-to-join sports and arts scenes, a truly warm sense of community, and a lot of room in which to grow, then this is the one.

❏ **Colgate University** is a small, liberal arts university nestled in the hills of upstate New York. A rigorous curriculum combined with a nurturing faculty creates maximum opportunities for academic growth and success. Campus culture is lively, hosting a competitive Division I athletic program, an active artistic scene, and a strong tradition of community involvement. Colgate prepares its graduates to be lifelong learners in an ever-changing economy, equipped with a broad knowledge base and a sense of world citizenship to succeed on whatever career path they choose.

❏ **The College of New Jersey**, originally established as a teachers' college, is now the state's most competitive public academic powerhouse. With seven schools, cutting-edge programs and state-of-the-art facilities, the diverse learning environment is unparalleled in excellence and value. Proud of its commitment to public service, the college experience centers heavily on community, both on campus and off, providing students with a variety of ways to get involved and become leaders in their communities. TCNJ is located in suburban Ewing, New Jersey, just outside of the state capital of Trenton, and is just minutes away from all the arts and entertainment the East Coast has to offer.

❑ **College of the Holy Cross** is highly respected for its superior undergraduate academic programs, excellent faculty, and the intelligence, imagination, and achievements of its students. It is also well known for its strong, well-supported, and enthusiastic commitment to the principle of educating men and women for others, in a community that generates a strong feeling of belonging and a vital sense of loyalty. Holy Cross is a place to learn how to learn, and not a place to seek job training. The fundamental purpose of the college is not to train students for specific occupations but to inform the mind and to foster clear thought and expression through the balanced study of the arts and the sciences.

❑ The **College of William and Mary** is a small public university with a primary focus on developing a strong undergraduate education and experience for its students. The college, the second oldest college in the country, is known as "The Alma Mater of a Nation" for a reason—it is steeped in history. Its beautifully laid-out campus sits out adjacent to Colonial Williamsburg and meshes with the rest of picturesque Williamsburg. William and Mary emphasizes the development of responsibility and motivation in its students by providing personalized support in every capacity but also allowing students the freedom to control their own living, learning, and social environments. William and Mary challenges its students to be the best they can be at everything they are involved in while at the College. This type of well-rounded training proves to be essential to students upon graduation and entering the work world.

❑ **Columbia University/Columbia College**, one of four undergraduate schools at Columbia University, distinguishes itself academically with its core curriculum—a series of required classes concentrating on the great Western contributions in art, philosophy, music, and literature to the modern world. With the core, students learn how to merge information in the classroom with knowledge from New York City, where Columbia is located. Visits to museums, musical performances, and art galleries become standard learning fare with the core. The Columbia student's four-year experience is also constantly enhanced by the exciting world of New York; Broadway, Museum Mile, Central Park, Greenwich Village, and Wall Street are all just a subway ride away. The college also boasts a diverse student population, outstanding faculty who are leaders in their fields, and over seventy different majors and concentrations in fifty-four academic departments.

❑ Attending **Columbia University/SEAS** means being in the presence of knowledge-seeking people. Of course, Columbia offers an excellent academic experience, but it also draws its students to learning, and to sharing the educationally diverse life experiences of a metropolitan environment. It is virtually impossible to describe Columbia and do justice to its reputation. Not only is acceptance to Columbia testimony of hard work prior to college, but it is also evidence that you are eager to be challenged in all aspects of life while being supported by a strong community.

❑ **Connecticut College** is the gem of all New England liberal arts colleges. The "Connecticut College Experience" goes beyond the consumption of knowledge, to inventing creative solutions to questions in any given academic field. Located on the coastline, halfway between Boston and New York City, this small, yet diverse environment put liberal arts into action. It pushes students to activate the knowledge they have gained and apply it to the world. With a longstanding Honor Code, Connecticut College remains academically rigorous, socially conscious, and offers some of the most unique study abroad and internship opportunities in the world.

❑ The three schools of the **Cooper Union for the Advancement of Science and Art** provide students of architecture, art, and engineering an unparalleled education. The education combines specialized education in the major with courses in the humanities and social sciences. Cooper's challenging atmosphere and caring professors offers possibilities for personal growth and development. Located in the heart of the East Village (in Manhattan), Cooper offers its students wonderful opportunities for exploration, social endeavors, extracurricular activities, and entertainment.

❑ **Cornell University**, an Ivy League school and land-grant college located in the scenic Finger Lakes region of Central New York, is home to 13,500 undergraduates pursuing studies in more than eighty majors in the university's seven small to mid-sized undergraduate colleges: Agriculture and Life Sciences, Architecture, Art and Planning; Arts and Sciences; Engineering; Hotel Administration, Human Ecology; and Industrial and Labor Relations. Cornell students come from all fifty states and more than one hundred twenty countries. Special features of the university include a world-renowned faculty; an outstanding undergraduate research program; twenty libraries; superb research and teaching faculties; a large, diverse study abroad program; more than 800 student organizations, thirty- six varsity sports; and a graduation rate close to ninety-two percent.

❑ **Dartmouth College**, the only college in the eight Ivy League schools, is distinguished by its flexible calendar system, focus on undergraduates, and community spirit. Known for its top-notch academics, Dartmouth offers small classes, close faculty-student relationships, and a host of research opportunities. Dartmouth students take three classes per ten-week term, are required to spend their sophomore summer on campus, and have the opportunity to take part in more than forty study abroad programs. With its diverse but intimate atmosphere, Dartmouth breeds some of the highest student satisfaction rates in the country.

❑ Dedicated to undergraduate teaching and research, **Davidson College** is a premier academic institution where ideas flourish, honor matters, and character counts. Intent on developing the whole person, the staff and faculty of Davidson College create a supportive environment in which discussions thrive and passions ignite. Davidson's rigorous liberal arts curriculum challenges students to explore their interests and discover new strengths. At Davidson, students meet the challenges of demanding professors, a variety of diverse and interesting community activities, and a strong Honor Code that forms a community based on mutual trust and respect.

❑ The momentum and pulse of energy that run through **Duke University** mirror the explosive growth of North Carolina's Triangle area—Raleigh, Chapel Hill, and Durham, Duke's home—and the famous Research Triangle Park it helped to create. A residential campus, Duke's rise in national preeminence is a result of its diverse, inquisitive student body working with renowned scholars in Duke's world-class programs and medical center. Independent studies and out-of-class learning experiences complement a demanding liberal arts or engineering curriculum. Duke's continuing push for excellence is coupled with an intimate feeling of community that encourages collaboration and student development. A wealth of club activities, top-notch athletics, and community service top off the opportunities for student involvement. Intellectually active students, engaged faculty, and the most spectacular campus environment in the country make for an idyllic setting to learn and grow during the undergraduate years.

❏ **Emory University** is located fifteen minutes from downtown Atlanta, on a lush campus in suburban Druid Hills. The close-knit, yet diverse, campus community is a nurturing environment for students, with a supportive faculty who are extremely accessible and happy to help students get the most from their Emory experience. There is a plethora of academic, cultural and social outlets for Emory students and the students' academic drive and active social life blend to provide a quintessential college experience for those who are willing to work hard and play hard. The university is extremely supportive of students' postgraduate plans and assists collegians in any way they can to help them land jobs, fellowships, and admission to advanced degree programs. Intellectually active and diverse students, engaged faculty, and a spectacular setting ranks Emory among the nation's elite and is an idyllic setting for students to learn and grow in their collegiate years.

❏ The **George Washington University** is a place constantly moving forward. A strong academic reputation continues to grow thanks to large increases in research funding; academic and residential space is growing thanks to increased popularity and attendance class after class. The opportunities available to students for social and professional engagement are constantly growing due to the university's premiere location. The diversity and culture present in Washington, D.C., is echoed by the liberal and engaging learning environment that GW's faculty create, offering to students a college experience that challenges, motivates, and equips students to enter successful careers at home and abroad.

❏ Founded in 1789, the same year the U.S. Constitution took effect, **Georgetown University**, is the nation's oldest Catholic university. What began as Georgetown College, a small gathering of twelve students and a handful of professors, has grown into a major international university that includes four undergraduate schools, respected graduate programs, a law school, and a medical school. The vision of Georgetown founder John Carroll, S.J., still guides the university in its commitment to Catholic, Jesuit education in the liberal arts tradition, with respect for diversity and open dialogue in pursuit of truth.

❏ **Hamilton College** is far more than a college on a hilltop—it is a community. It is a place where fewer than 2,000 undergraduates work closely with their professors and fellow students to acquire a solid liberal arts education with an emphasis on effective oral and written communication skills. It is a place where students' spare time and energy are the impetus behind a wide variety of extracurricular and social activities. And it is a place where students can develop a strong sense of self and of the whole as they realize their individuality, establish lifelong friendships, and take responsibility for and pride in their inimitable role in a vibrant and close-knit community. Because they eat, sleep, work, talk, play, and breathe Hamilton for four years, Hamilton students develop a unique sense of camaraderie that tends to extend well beyond their time on the Hill.

❏ Founded in 1636, **Harvard University/Harvard College** is the oldest college in the United States. Harvard is home to the world's largest university library system, a world-renowned faculty, and a student body of many talents and interests. Located in Cambridge, Massachusetts, Harvard offers its undergraduates a broad liberal arts education and the exciting urban atmosphere of Boston, one of America's great college towns.

❏ Located in Claremont, California, **Harvey Mudd College** is a small school of 730 students with a rigorous curriculum and a narrow academic focus on engineering, science, and mathematics. The curriculum consists of six majors (engineering, math, computer science, biology, chemistry, and physics) three interdisciplinary programs (mathematical biology, computer science and math, and chemistry and biology), and a large humanities/social science department. The college has a broad academic approach with an emphasis on the humanities and social sciences as well as core science, math, and engineering principals. The residential campus is vibrant with a student body that is widely talented, dynamic, and eccentric, in addition to being academically gifted. HMC is bolstered by its participation in The Claremont Colleges Consortium, which gives Mudd students access to academic resources, course offerings, athletics, and other opportunities that could not otherwise be supported by a small technical college. The student-run Honor Code demands integrity and honesty from every student. Students at Mudd would be able to more fully enjoy the beaches, mountains, and nightlife of Southern California if they were not so caught up in getting a fine education and having a great time without ever leaving the campus.

❑ **Haverford College** has emerged as one of the top private colleges in the country. Drawing on a distinguished faculty, small classroom environment, and the resources of a tri-college partnership, Haverford is an excellent educational experience. An effective and comprehensive Honor Code provides a background of trust and respect that students take seriously and carry with them after graduation. Ten miles outside of Philadelphia, Haverford has a small, but thriving social life, a wealth of extracurricular activities, and an education that will last a lifetime.

❑ An expansive research university with a small undergraduate population, **Johns Hopkins University** boasts top-ranked programs in the Humanities, Social Sciences, Natural Sciences, and Engineering. Attracting an intellectually rich, diverse, and involved group of students each year, the university and its philosophy of education are founded upon the notions of exploration and inquiry. Research, internship, and study abroad experiences allow students access to Baltimore and beyond, preparing them to be successful leaders and global citizens.

❑ **Kenyon College,** the first private college founded in the state of Ohio, is an institution dedicated to the study of the liberal arts and sciences. Students are encouraged to develop their individual talents while working to understand the greater world through deliberate study of the broad array of academic disciplines offered. The college funds research for science majors and generously supports faculty who engage in one-on-one research with students in other academic disciplines. At this diverse, highly residential college, Kenyon students live on campus full-time and housing is guaranteed all four years. Social life is dominated by the residential nature of the school. Students rarely leave for an entire weekend off campus. Nearly thirty percent of students choose to play a varsity sport at the Division III level. Additionally, students participate in more than 150 organizations and clubs, ranging from publications to student government to community service. A Kenyon education is excellent preparation for professional or graduate-level education, and just over seventy percent of Kenyon graduates will eventually enroll in graduate-level study after leaving the college.

❑ **Lafayette College** is located high atop College Hill in Easton, Pennsylvania. The college of everyone's dreams, its beautiful architecture, perfectly manicured grounds, cutting-edge technology, and the most inspiring and energetic students and faculty make Lafayette one of the most desirable liberal arts college in the United States. A small college with large-college resources, Lafayette is most notable for propelling students into advanced research, encouraging student leaders, and building well-rounded students. Most important, Lafayette helps students fulfill their dreams.

❑ **Macalester College** is an academically excellent college of about 1,900 students that successfully integrates internationalism, multiculturalism, and civic engagement with a top-notch liberal arts education. Macalester's location in a vibrant residential neighborhood of St. Paul, Minnesota, and just minutes from the downtowns of each Twin City, offers unlimited opportunities for community service, internships, and leisure activities. Macalester's campus life provides exciting academic, research, athletic, and extracurricular prospects. Furthermore, Mac's excellent professors are deeply committed to undergraduate education and students. Undoubtedly, a Mac education is the ultimate preparation for success in academia, law, medicine, social service, and business. But more importantly, Mac is an exceptional environment of life-altering enlightenment, life-changing experiences and lifelong friendships.

❑ It's tough to get accepted at **Massachusetts Institute of Technology**—and the academic life is even more challenging. It's expensive—but financial aid is reliable. With a reputation for science and engineering, MIT surprises some with its highly rated economics, philosophy, and music departments (among others). Whether you go on to graduate or professional school, or confront the job market, a degree from MIT will serve you very well.

❑ **Middlebury College** is tucked in a bucolic spot between the Green and Adirondack mountains and is a haven for passionate, active, and engaged students seeking academic rigor and social satisfaction. Middlebury's academic and cocurricular offerings accommodate the great diversity of students who elect to spend four years in a visually inspiring if off-the-beaten-track setting. With particular renown for foreign language instruction, international studies, and environmental studies, Middlebury offers strength across the curriculum and is constantly enhancing facilities and curricular resources in an endless pursuit to become, as a former college president once put it, "a better version of itself."

❏ **New York University** is a private, urban research university located in the heart of New York City. Prominent faculty and driven, independent students make NYU a premier institution for an undergraduate education strongly founded in the liberal arts. The university encourages hands-on learning both in and out of the classroom, through internships, undergraduate research, and study abroad opportunities. NYU's location in the Greenwich Village neighborhood of Manhattan allows for a social life of constant stimulation and endless opportunity for the college student and nouveau New Yorker. The time, energy, and money spent on NYU will not go unrewarded, as the school has a placement rate of over ninety percent into a full-time job or graduate program within three months of graduation. NYU has something for everyone. If you are an open-minded, independent, driven person willing to take up the reins and seek out what it is you desire from life, NYU is the place for you.

❏ **Northwestern** students enjoy an usually broad choice of academic opportunities, given Northwestern's size. With more than eighty academic concentrations in six undergraduate schools and a variety of interdisciplinary programs, Northwestern offers an impressive range of studies that allows students flexibility and choice. As a result, Northwestern students at all levels learn from and do research with outstanding faculty members in many fields while collaborating with fellow students both in and out of the classroom. In addition, because of Northwestern's emphasis on effective communication, regardless of area of study, you will learn to think analytically, write clearly and speak persuasively, thereby preparing you for positions of responsibility and leadership. Finally, Northwestern draws strength and vitality from Chicago, one of the world's great cities, located just south of the undergraduate campus in Evanston. Students enjoy Chicago's outstanding intellectual, professional, social, and cultural opportunities. Northwestern students can make their undergraduate experience be pretty much anything they want, given the range of academic, social, and cultural choices that exist. For most students, that means four years of great education—and some really fun times with good friends.

❏ **Oberlin College** is a small, academically rigorous liberal arts college located thirty-five miles west of Cleveland, Ohio. Oberlin's student population peaks at approximately 2,800 students, so small classes and close relationships with professors are the norm.

Oberlin is as well known for its exceptional liberal arts education as it is for its strong science curriculum, with professors working at the top tier of their respective disciplines and a brand-new, state-of-the-art science center. In addition to Oberlin's College of Arts and Sciences, the campus is home to the Oberlin Conservatory of Music, the oldest continuously operating conservatory in the United States. Oberlin's Conservatory is renowned internationally as a professional music school of the highest caliber. Among its illustrious alumni are writer, composer, and saxophonist James McBride, and mezzo-soprano Denyce Graves.

❏ **Occidental College** is an intimate liberal arts institution located on a beautiful, tree-filled campus in the Eagle Rock neighborhood of Los Angeles. The student body at Oxy is one of the most diverse in the nation, in all respects, and students here pair deep intellectual curiosity with a desire to apply their knowledge toward addressing real-world problems and concerns. Coursework is uniformly rigorous, and classes are vital and lively—professors here love to teach, class sizes are small, and students in all disciplines find that faculty serve as willing mentors and advocates. Research opportunities abound for interested undergraduate students. The campus bustles with activity—concerts, speakers, dance recitals, club events, parties, debates, sports games—and students fan out to explore LA's inexhaustible menu of music, theater, art, dance, food, nightlife, and culture.

❏ **Pomona College** is a small, academically rigorous liberal arts college located thirty-five miles from Los Angeles. It is the largest of the Claremont Colleges, a consortium of five undergraduate colleges and two graduate universities that share some facilities and work together to provide their students with classroom and extracurricular opportunities. Graduates can rely on their perception, analysis, and communication skills to go anywhere they want and do whatever they dream.

❏ **Princeton University's** commitment to undergraduate education sets it apart from other universities of comparable stature. Because the world-class faculty concentrates on undergraduates, students have a high degree of flexibility in designing academic programs and remarkable access to professors for precepts and independent study. In fact, the culmination of the Princeton undergraduate career, the senior thesis, gives every student a chance to work one-on-one with an advising professor on a level that is often not achieved in graduate school programs. In addition to the extraordinary academic experience, Princeton also provides social and extracurricular activities that create a rich and rewarding experience for gifted students of diverse backgrounds and interests.

❏ **Reed College** in Portland, Oregon, provides creative, intellectual, and open-minded students with a rigorous and classical education in the liberal arts and sciences. Students and professors work closely in an environment of trust and collaboration, promoting independent thinking and a liberal spirit of inquiry and research. Every graduate completes a year-long senior thesis, a culmination of his or her academic program and a testimony to the passion for learning that Reed students bring to their education. With no NCAA or varsity athletics, fraternities or sororities, campus life promotes the tremendous diversity of students' interests, from the traditional to out-of-the-box. Reed values a desire for knowledge and awareness both for personal fulfillment as well as for the creation of an undergraduate community that balances individual freedom with personal responsibility.

❏ **Rice University** is one of the youngest and most dynamic of America's highly competitive universities. The university is focused on teaching and research for both undergraduates and graduate students, and is frequently touted as one of the best values in higher education today. The intimate community at Rice is distinguished by its inclusive residential college system that fosters the exchange of cultures and ideas among students as well as student-faculty interactions. Located on a wooded campus in Houston, Texas, the university also benefits from the resources of the fourth-largest city in the country.

❏ **Scripps College** combines the close-knit community of a residential campus with the expanded resources of the Claremont Consortium. With its strength in interdisciplinary fields, Scripps offers students a well-rounded education, one each student can pursue in her own unique way. The women who attend the college work hard and are always willing to offer support to fellow students. After completing the rigorous workweek, students have the advantage of soaking up some California sun, even in the middle of December. If a student has a specific academic, athletic, or social interest, she is sure to find it somewhere at Scripps and will probably find a few lifelong friends along the way.

❏ **Smith College.** While a number of women's colleges have begun admitting men or become absorbed into coeducational universities, Smith College has grown into the largest independent women's college in the country. The school sits on a 125-acre campus at the center of Northampton, a small town that enjoys a vibrant cultural scene, and is often compared to major cities such as Boston, its neighbor 90 miles to the east. Smith's green campus, ivy-covered buildings, hiking trails, and majestic trees are easy on the eye. And the close-knit community, where professors and students are often on a first-name basis, helps to develop students' entire character. Smith has consistently ranked among the top liberal arts schools in the country to turn out Fulbright Scholars. Alumnae are leaders in fields as varied as engineering, film, medicine, and art.

❏ **Stanford University's** dynamic environment challenges its undergraduates to cultivate their strengths as scholars and human beings. Offering everything from archaeology classes in South America to the Stanford Linear Accelerator Center exploring the subatomic universe to the nation's highest ranked community service program, Stanford gives its students unlimited access to the world's wealth of opportunities. Add to that a beautiful, sprawling 8,800-acre campus designed by Frederick Law Olmsted, and a nationally recognized athletic program, and you have the ideal undergraduate experience.

❏ A small liberal arts and engineering school renowned for its immoderately long reading lists and breakneck pace, **Swarthmore College** is situated within a serene, green, 357-acre campus outside Philadelphia. Its students are of remarkable intellect, imagination, diversity, and commitment to social change. Classes are quite small—most with fifteen students or fewer—and focused heavily on writing, reading, and lab work. Juniors and seniors may choose to be part of its unique External Examination program, taking even smaller, double-credit seminars for two years, and eventually being evaluated by a panel of professors from other universities. When they finally come out of the libraries, Swarthmore students are part of a small, almost familial social scene, characterized by on-campus parties and lots of dorm bonding.

❏ **Tufts University** is a medium-sized major research university situated on a picturesque campus just outside of downtown Boston. A university that embodies the best aspects of small liberal arts colleges and large research universities, Tufts is a close-knit and diverse community of scholars, activists, and leaders who use their intellects to create solutions to real-world problems. Small, discussion-based classes, accessible professors, and an emphasis on discovery through student-initiated research characterize the campus' academic environment. In addition to their studies, students lead balanced lives by participating in more than 200 student organizations and taking advantage of the cultural stimulation found in nearby Boston, the biggest college town in the entire country.

❏ **Tulane University,** located in the heart of uptown New Orleans, couples the charm and mystique of Deep South culture with a world-class liberal arts education. The laid-back, encouraging, and extremely talented faculty provide students individual guidance and support. The myriad academic and social activities range from student-led organizations, leadership opportunities, and innovative academic and scholarship programs to Mardi Gras, Jazz Fest, and Saints Football. Tulane not only gives students the tools to make knowledgeable decisions and solve complex problems, it grants them humor to cope with their mistakes. Tulane rewards students for working hard while making an effort to impress that work isn't everything. The oak-filled campus and tropical weather embrace students who are eager to gain knowledge from a top-tier university while providing public service to help rebuild one of the nation's most culturally significant cities.

❏ **The U.S. Military Academy at West Point**, the nation's oldest service academy, is a four-year, federally funded program, aimed at developing commissioned leaders of character for our army and our nation. The West Point experience is one that is unforgettable. It "stretches your intellect, develops your self-confidence and overall potential, and prepares you for an important leadership role while serving the nation." The academy challenges cadets intellectually, physically, and militarily. The program is tough, the rewards are many, and the opportunities are endless. At West Point "much of the history we teach was made by people we taught."

❏ **The U.S. Naval Academy** is the Navy's and Marine Corps' four-year undergraduate educational institution. Established in 1845, it prepares young men and women for careers as officers in both the navy and marine corps. Graduates earn a bachelor of science degree in one of nineteen majors in engineering, mathematics, applied sciences, social sciences, and the humanities. Tuition, room, and board are paid for by the federal government. As repayment, all graduates incur a five-year service obligation as either naval or marine corps officers after graduation.

❏ **The University of California, Los Angeles (UCLA)**, is consistently ranked among America's top ten universities. UCLA educates 37,000 undergraduate and graduate students annually and is California's largest and most comprehensive university. Naturally, being the high achiever that it is, UCLA is not satisfied being excellent in only one or two areas. A well-rounded school, UCLA boasts the nation's top-ranked athletics program, premier facilities, a wealth of student programs and campus traditions, and incredible student diversity. And the university continually strives to find new ways to grow and be innovative in fulfilling its missions of teaching, research, and service. One of nine campuses in the University of California's public school system, UCLA is located in the heart of some of Los Angeles' most affluent areas in the college town of Westwood.

❏ **The University of Chicago** relishes intellectual intensity, expressed both through hard work and through sincere conversation. The ideal student is, like a Renaissance man or woman or a Ciceronian rhetorician, a complete person, with a well-rounded education, a wide-ranging curiosity, and a deep-driving commitment to civic life. Social life tends to be low-key and friendly, without emphasis on drinking, large parties, or status. All students must complete the common core, a unique curriculum developed and taught by leading professors, but complemented by a specialized concentration, sometimes in a traditional discipline, sometimes designed by the student. Athletics and student activities, particularly community involvement, help students to flourish and to practice the ethical ideals and social theories articulated by the great books of the common core.

❏ **The University of Miami** (UM) offers the perks of a small, intimate campus life with the excitement and culture of a large city. Nestled in tropical South Florida, UM is known for its world-class research facilities, diverse student population, and powerhouse athletics. UM recruits top faculty whose professional experience is as compelling as their devotion to students. UM's Coral Gables campus houses two colleges and six schools that offer over 120 bachelor degree programs within eight undergraduate schools Attracting top students from almost every state in the United States and over one hundred foreign countries, UM has a diverse population and programs and activities to suit every interest. When graduates leave UM, they leave prepared, having taken interdisciplinary courses geared to encourage a well-rounded education.

❑ **The University of North Carolina at Chapel Hill** provides the quintessential college experience without the cliché. Expect to get rowdy from time to time, to take your studies seriously and your public duty even more so. Prepare to become a thinker, a leader, and a caretaker of all that has come before. The University of North Carolina, chartered in 1789, is the first public university in the United States to open its doors. In the more than 200 years since, Carolina has attracted the best and brightest from all walks of life, and it is steadfast in its commitment to serving a diverse student body. UNC consistently ranks among the top universities in the United States, but what truly makes it a must-attend university is its unparalleled focus on experience gleaned outside the classroom. Carolina has perhaps the most civically engaged student body of any school in the United States. So, if college, to you, means double-majoring and rushing off to grad school in three years, you'd probably be better off at any number of other schools. Carolina is best savored. Expect to play hard, work harder—and always be on the go.

❑ **The University of Notre Dame** is a private research university located in South Bend, Indiana. One of the most prestigious Catholic universities in the country, Notre Dame is known for its family-like environment and loyal alumni network. Students are active participants in community service projects, athletics, and dorm-based activities. Notre Dame is deeply rooted in tradition and heritage that extends beyond the football season.

❑ Located in Philadelphia, the **University of Pennsylvania** is the nation's first university. Each of its four undergraduate schools offers a liberal arts-influenced education reflective of the ideals of Penn's founder, Benjamin Franklin. Students will find flexibility in their coursework, providing them with a strong grounding in the liberal arts, as well as the education necessary to gain expertise in its many internationally respected departments. Penn offers the opportunity to achieve both in and out of the classroom, making it the ideal place to further one's academic and extracurricular interests.

❑ **University of Richmond** is a beautiful, academically challenging private university conveniently situated in one of the country's most historic cities: Richmond, Virginia. Even though the university's location in a state capital is conducive to internships, shopping, cultural opportunities, and more, Richmond's safe, secluded campus maintains an atmosphere that emanates "college." At any given time, there are students studying on the greens, running around the lake, walking to one of the three on-campus libraries, playing Frisbee, or shuffling off to class. Richmond is large enough to offer all the amenities of a larger university—NCAA Division I athletics, a campus radio station, a plethora of classes and majors, and a vast alumni network—and it is also small enough that students feel empowered to become involved and lead all of the above. If you thrive on classroom discussion and debate, if you are independent and like being involved, if you want the amenities of a big city and a traditional college environment, and if you like to have fun and be intellectually satisfied, the University of Richmond is the place to spend your next four years.

❑ **University of Rochester** has seen moderate growth in recent years, producing graduates ready to lead and serve the world. Rochester provides innovative, tailored opportunities for undergraduate students on a beautifully planned campus in a warm and collegial community. About 4,100 undergraduate students on campus take control of their education through the unique Rochester Curriculum, which boasts first-year seminars, self-designed courses of study, and no core curriculum. Students are further engaged by leading student organizations, researching alongside professors, and serving and learning more about the Rochester community. With the world-class Eastman School of Music, several top-ten academic departments, a caring administration, and a friendly and enriching faculty, Rochester is truly a distinct place to learn and grow.

❑ **The University of Southern California**, the oldest private research university in Southern California, offers highly ranked programs in business, cinematic arts, engineering, and fine arts, as well as in its College of Letters, Arts, and Sciences. USC is recognized for interdisciplinary research, and is particularly strong in communication and multimedia technologies. Undergraduates are encouraged to take advantage of an exceptional array of majors and minors by studying topics that are widely separated across the academic landscape. Its focus on service-learning was spotlighted in 2000, when *Time* magazine named USC its "College of the Year." On the sports front, in addition to a nationally ranked football program, USC has produced more Olympian athletes than any other American university. It also attracts more international students than any other American university. With Los Angeles—a global center for culture, science, technology, and trade—as its backdrop, USC offers unmatched social and cultural opportunities as well as internships and other learning experiences.

❑ **The University of Virginia** is an institution famous for the rigor and quality of its academics, the richness of its history, and the beauty of its architecture and setting. With a total of over 20,000 enrolled students, UVa maintains its status as the public ivy by offering an outstanding liberal arts education, and attracting superior faculty as well as students. Wahoos become part of Thomas Jefferson's legacy as they pursue their studies in an intimate academic community and maintain that community through the student-run Honor System and government. UVa is nestled amidst rolling farmland just minutes from the Blue Ridge mountains in the friendly, bustling city of Charlottesville, Virginia.

❑ **Vanderbilt University** is a home not only to lavish lawns, shady branches, and many squirrels, but also to undergraduates who engage in all aspects of the college experience. A thriving institution located in the heart of downtown Nashville, Vanderbilt boasts an unparalleled blend of academic rigor and social activity. Students at Vanderbilt enjoy access to four undergraduate schools and several renowned graduate programs, and Vanderbilt encourages exploration within and across its many academic disciplines. Outside the classroom, Vanderbilt students reside in a vibrant on-campus community in which they participate through community service and campus involvement. Balancing social activity and academic rigor, Vanderbilt students explore, engage, and grow in a challenging, prestigious, and hospitable undergraduate community.

❏ Founded in 1865 in upstate New York, **Vassar College** quickly gained a reputation for its innovative approach to education. Throughout its history, it has maintained and broadened this commitment to academic rigor and independent thinking. Coeducational and highly selective, this liberal arts school unites a small yet diverse student population with a dedicated faculty to create a friendly community within the classroom and beyond. In addition, a wide range of activities and athletics allow students to excel in all areas of college life. To this day, Vassar remains a distinctive, original institution of the highest standard.

❏ **Wake Forest University** is a small liberal arts institution located on a scenic campus in Winston-Salem, North Carolina. With fewer than 4,500 undergraduates, the school boasts small classes taught by professors dedicated to teaching and providing students with personal attention. But the university remains committed to providing the amenities and resources of larger schools, offering study-abroad programs in five continents, the excitement of Atlantic Coast Conference athletics, and a national reputation for academic achievement. The university's broad merit scholarships program attracts top students from around the country.

❏ Located in the heart of Virginia's beautiful Shenandoah Valley, **Washington and Lee University** takes its name from two great American generals who shaped the school in its early history. In 1796 George Washington made his era's largest donation to a private American institution when he awarded $20,000 to the fledgling college. Robert E. Lee served as the school's president after the Civil War. Today, Washington and Lee University exemplifies the value of a liberal arts education. Its student body of 1,770 undergraduates comes from all parts of the United States to enjoy small classes, personal interaction with an excellent faculty, a varied and challenging curriculum, and an Honor System that creates an environment of trust.

❏ **Washington University in St. Louis** is a medium-sized university, large enough to provide the highest quality professors, facilities, and academic opportunities, but small enough for students to receive individual guidance. Washington attracts some of the best students from across the country to its undergraduate divisions, which include Arts & Sciences, Art, Architecture, Business, and Engineering. Students are encouraged to pursue a variety of academic and extracurricular interests, and above all to challenge themselves. Opportunities exist on-campus and in St. Louis for students interested in community service, leadership, athletics, music, and numerous other activities. Nearby neighborhoods offer the best entertainment and cultural experiences in the city, but the campus is just far enough away from downtown to enjoy grassy fields and a spectacular view of Forest Park. Visitors to the University often notice the friendly atmosphere on campus, students saying hello to each other on the paths and conversing in depth with renowned professors. Students here thrive in a diverse environment where cooperation creates a stimulating intellectual community and a fun social scene both on and off campus.

❏ **Webb Institute** is the oldest school devoted to naval architecture and marine engineering (shipbuilding) in the United States. Founded and endowed in 1889 by millionaire and shipbuilder William H. Webb, the school is located in Glen Cove, New York, on Long Island Sound. Its rigorous, four-year engineering program focuses on the fundamentals of commercial ship design. Each of the approximately eighty students receives a full-tuition scholarship for all four years, regardless of need; students pay only for room, board, and books. Financial aid for these costs is available. Each winter, students gain two months of practical work experience in a shipyard, on board a ship, or in a design firm. Finally, Webb's placement rate is one hundred percent, with graduates either attending graduate school or entering the maritime or other industries.

❏ **Wellesley College** educates women who will be smart, successful, and concerned leaders of their communities. Wellesley provides valuable hands-on experiences, from allowing students to run organizations to engaging their professors and peers in intellectual debates both in and out of the classroom. Nestled just outside of Boston in the town of Wellesley, Massachusetts, the college offers both on-campus activities and easy access to a large city. The nine-to-one faculty-student ratio means students receive individual attention, while the all-women's environment produces a strong sense of sisterhood in a supportive atmosphere. But the best part of the Wellesley experience is the deep friendships students form as the college pushes them to excel and develop to their potential.

❑ **Wesleyan University** is a small liberal arts college in Connecticut that attracts vibrant, open-minded, and creative students. Its nationally recognized professors are tops in their fields, and within a small-college atmosphere, they reward students for pursuing intellectual interests with rigor. Students tend to keep busy; they work hard at their studies, have fun, and explore outside the classroom. Wesleyan is a great place for students to grow and learn in a comfortable, open atmosphere.

❑ **Williams College** is a small, liberal arts college located in the Berkshires. Despite its world-class facilities and nationally acclaimed faculty, the college is defined by its students. Students direct their own academic paths, both inside and outside of the classroom, enjoying a proliferation of extracurricular activities, a culturally rich area, and the beauty of the surrounding mountains. Students are given tremendous responsibility and also tend to be motivated by their own goals instead of grades. Living together in such a small, close-knit community for four years creates lasting friendships and one of the most loyal groups of alumni in the world.

❑ **Yale University's** superior academic program, together with a unique residential college system and energetic extracurricular atmosphere, offer students a place to expand their minds, explore their interests, and have fun juggling it all. The atmosphere is intense, but in diverse ways; Yalies work and play hard. While they enjoy the resources of a great research university, they enjoy even more the focus on undergraduate education that exists at Yale. The vision and excellence of the students provide an education in itself, creating hundreds of tight-knit communities within the larger social structure. Yale is a place to be dazzled by peers and professors, a place that graduates continue to remember with fondness long after they have graduated.

AUTHOR BIOGRAPHIES

❑ AUTHOR BIOGRAPHIES ❑

INDEX

AMHERST COLLEGE ❑ **Molly Lyons,** class of '97, has worked an editorial assistant at *Elle Decor Magazine*.

BARNARD COLLEGE ❑ **Catherine Webster** has served as assistant dean at Barnard. She has served Barnard as first-year class dean, associate director of the Pre-College Program, and director of the First-Year Focus Program. She holds M.A. degrees from New York University (in French literature) and Columbia's Teachers College (in College Student Personnel Administration) and a B.A. from Columbia College, where she was a member of the first coeducational class.

BATES COLLEGE ❑ **Christopher Byrne** graduated from Bates in 1997 with a Bachelor of Science degree majoring in biology. Chris was a four-year member of the varsity lacrosse team. He has conducted research on leukemia at the Dana Farber Cancer Institute, and planned to go on to medical school.

BOSTON COLLEGE ❑ **Matthew J. Kita** graduated from Boston College in 1998 with a Bachelor of Arts degree in political science. While at BC, he was a member of several performing ensembles, including the Boston College Marching Band. After graduation, he earned his Master of Arts degree in Higher Education Policy from the University of Maryland, and is currently working on his Juris Doctorate at the University of Houston Law Center.

BOWDOIN COLLEGE ❑ **Nathaniel Vinton** was an English major at Bowdoin and earned High Honors for his work on Herman Melville. He spoke at his graduation in 2001 and was a candidate for the Rhodes Scholarship. Currently a staff writer at *Ski Racing Magazine* (assigned to the U.S. ski team beat), he is looking for any freelance writing assignments, and can be reached at *nathanielvinton@yahoo.com*.

BRANDEIS UNIVERSITY ❑ **Joshua F. A. Peck**, class of '02, graduated with high honors from Brandeis University. While at Brandeis, he was elected to two consecutive terms as Student Union President. Currently, he works as a Legislative Correspondent for Congressman Steve Rothman in Washington, D.C.

BIOGRAPHIES

BROWN UNIVERSITY ❏ **Michelle Walson** graduated from Brown *magna cum laude* in 1999 with an A.B. in English and American literature and honors in creative writing. She served as the arts editor for Brown's weekly newspaper and was a four-year member of the Brown University Chorus. Recently, she worked for a PBS documentary series in Boston and is applying to graduate programs in television and film production.

CALIFORNIA INSTITUTE OF TECHNOLOGY ❏ **Ted Jou**, class of 2003, double majored at Caltech in Applied Mathematics and Business Economics and Management. He contributed to Barron's during his senior year while serving as president of the undergraduate student body. While at Caltech, he served on the student government Board of Directors for two years and was a regular contributor to the student newspaper.

CARLETON COLLEGE ❏ **Erika Lewis** graduated from Carleton in 2006 with a B.A. in English. After graduation, she learned the fine art of making delicious espresso drinks and interned at *MSP Communications*, a magazine firm in Minneapolis, MN. She is currently a Teach for America corps member in New Mexico.

CARNEGIE MELLON UNIVERSITY ❏ **Jessica Demers** graduated from Carnegie Mellon in 1999 with a B.A. in professional writing. She is a satellite coordinator at CNN in Atlanta. While at Carnegie Mellon, she worked as a Sleeping Bag Weekend student coordinator through the Office of Admission.

CASE WESTERN RESERVE UNIVERSITY ❏ **Charles Onyett** graduated from Case in May 2004 with a B.A. in English and minors in philosophy and psychology. Perhaps his most notable contribution to Case was his internship at *Case Magazine* during his senior year. He is in the process of applying to graduate programs to pursue a writing degree. In the meantime, he freelances for various publications and Web sites, reads a lot of books, and occasionally watches awful movies on television while laughing hysterically.

CLAREMONT MCKENNA COLLEGE ❏ **Sarah Ciaccia** graduated from Claremont McKenna College in 2003 with a dual degree in Government and Literature. She is the recipient of a Rotary Ambassadorial Scholarship and is currently studying in Bologna, Italy.

COLBY COLLEGE ❏ **Kate Bolick**, class of 1995, majored in American Studies and minored in Creative Writing. After graduation, she worked as an editor at *The Atlantic Monthly*, before accepting a fellowship to pursue a master's degree in Cultural Reporting and Criticism at New York University. Currently she is a freelance writer living in New York; her essays and book reviews have appeared in *The Atlantic*, *The Boston Globe*, *Newsday*, and *Vogue*.

COLGATE UNIVERSITY ❏ **Stephanie Wortel,** graduated magna cum laude from Colgate in 2006 as an astronomy-physics major. During her time at Colgate, Stephanie had a four-year volunteer involvement on the staff of the Dean of First Year Students, worked extensively revitalizing the student theatre community through Masque and Triangle, and performed in numerous choral concerts, vocal recitals, and theatrical productions. Stephanie in numerous choral concerts, vocal recitals, and theatrical productions. Stephanie currently resides in New York City, pursuing a career in professional performance..

THE COLLEGE OF NEW JERSEY ❏ **Emily L. Weiss** graduated from The College of New Jersey in 2003 with a B.A. in English. A journalism and professional writing minor, she spent much of her time working on the school's on-line magazine, *unbound*, as well as writing for the school newspaper, *The Signal*. She is continuing her tenure at TCNJ on the opposite side of the fence, currently working in the Office of College and Community Relations. Emily is also an active member of the Hawthorne (New Jersey) Caballeros Drum and Bugle Corps.

COLLEGE OF THE HOLY CROSS ❏ **Tim Keller** graduated with an A.B. in economics and served a year in the Jesuit Volunteer Corps where he taught an entrepreneurial business class to "at-risk" youth in Southern California. A native of the Midwest, he recently moved to Charlotte, NC, where he now works at Bank of America Securities, LLC.

COLLEGE OF WILLIAM AND MARY ❑ **Matthew Scranton** graduated in 2006 with a B.A. in history with a geology minor. He spent much of his time volunteering in the Office of Admissions as an intern and tour guide. Matt was also the Assistant Director of the Student Mentoring Program, a four-year member of the Rugby team, and the President and Co-Founder of a not-for-profit group and was selected as the student speaker for the 2006 Commencement. He is currently a Peace Corps Volunteer serving in Chongqing, China.

COLUMBIA UNIVERSITY/COLUMBIA COLLEGE ❑ **Anna Lisa Raya** graduated from Columbia College in 1995 with a bachelor's degree in English. One year later, she earned her master's in journalism from Columbia's Graduate School of Journalism, where she also received the Richard T. Baker award for magazine writing. While a CC student, she became active in many Latino student organizations, dabbled in photography, and worked on a student-run magazine for fashion enthusiasts. She has served as a deputy news editor at *People* magazine in New York City.

COLUMBIA UNIVERSITY/SEAS ❑ **Kelly Lenz** received her B.S. in biomedical engineering from Columbia University's Fu Foundation's School of Engineering and Applied Science. She has served as the project coordinator of the New York City Multidisciplinary Child Fatality Review, a project funded by New York State, managed by Medical and Health Research for New York City, Inc. (MHRA), and cosponsored by the New York City Office of the Chief Medical Examiner. In addition to having a strong background in the sciences, Kelly is also an alumna of Fiorello H. La Guardia High School of Music and Art and the Performing Arts, with a major in vocal performance.

CONNECTICUT COLLEGE ❑ While an undergraduate at Connecticut College, **Jennifer De Leon** took advantage of several study abroad and work experiences and was able to travel to twelve different countries including Vietnam, France, and Nigeria. With a B.A. in International Relations and as a recipient of an International Studies Certificate, she worked as a congressional aide for Congressman Edward J. Markey in Boston, Massachusetts, during her first year out of college. Now she is a third-grade teacher in San Jose, California, as part of the Teach For America AmeriCorps program. She is currently working toward her Masters in the Art of Teaching and Learning through the Center for Teaching Excellence and Social Justice at the University of San Francisco School of Education.

COOPER UNION ❏ **Dalia Levine** graduated from Cooper in 2002 with a Bachelor's of Engineering in Chemical Engineering. While serving on the Senior Class Council she helped fund-raise for the Class Gift and helped organize the Senior Bash party. She has also been copresident of Kesher (Hillel) and a vice-president of American Institute of Chemical Engineering. She served on the Resident Hall Association and as a Resident Assistant. Currently, she works for Merck & Co., Inc.

CORNELL UNIVERSITY ❏ **Laura Barrantes** graduated from the College of Arts and Sciences in 1997 as a government major. While at Cornell, she was cochair of the Orientation Steering Committee, a member of the Senior Honor Society of the Quill and Dagger, a Cornell Tradition Fellow, a member of Alpha Phi Omega National Service Fraternity, and a Cornell National Scholar. She has served as one of the reunion chairs for the class and has worked in Washington, D.C., with the American Political Science Association.

DARTMOUTH COLLEGE ❏ **Suzanne Leonard** graduated from Dartmouth in 1996 with a double major in English and psychology. While at school, she studied abroad in Madrid and London, had an internship with *Psychology Today*, and was involved with the *Dartmouth Alumni Magazine*. After graduating, she attended the Radcliffe publishing course in Cambridge, Massachusetts. She has worked as an editorial assistant at *Fitness* magazine, lived in Brooklyn, and contemplated a move to graduate school in England.

DAVIDSON COLLEGE ❏ **Page Neubert**, '01, graduated cum laude with an A.B. in English and holds an M.A. in creative writing from the Bread Loaf School of English through Middlebury College. She works for the Robin Hood Foundation in New York City.

DUKE UNIVERSITY ❑ **John Tolsma**, served as student body president during the 1994–1995 academic year. After working as an executive aide for Lamar Alexander's 1996 presidential bid, he attended the J.D./M.B.A. program at Harvard Law and Business Schools.

EMORY UNIVERSITY ❑ **Alyssa Abkowitz** received a B.A. in anthropology and journalism from Emory University in 2004. While at school, she studied abroad in Kenya and Tanzania, interned at *National Geographic Traveler* as an American Society of Magazine Editors internship recipient, and was the Features editor of *The Emory Wheel*. Currently, she's a staff writer at *Creative Loafing*, Atlanta's alternative newsweekly. She is planning to move to D.C. in the near future to pursue an M.A. at American University in international affairs.

THE GEORGE WASHINGTON UNIVERSITY ❑ **Jeremiah Davis** graduated from GW in 2003 with a B.A., *summa cum laude*, in English literature. He currently serves as a Presidential Administrative Fellow for the university, working on an M.P.H. in Health Policy ('05) and working as the Director of the school's outdoor and environmental education program. As an undergraduate, he was a Presidential Academic Scholar, Symposium Member of the University Honors Program, and member of Phi Beta Kappa; he served as Vice-President and President of the campus chapter of Habitat for Humanity, volunteered at the Bread for the City clinic, and worked both as a Community Specialist in the residence halls as well as a Writing Center Tutor. He is preparing to enter medical school in the fall of 2005.

GEORGETOWN UNIVERSITY ❑ **Meaghan M. Keeler** graduated magna cum laude from the Walsh School of Foreign Service with a concentration in International Politics in 2002. She was actively involved in student government, the Senior Class Committee, Leadership Programs, and HoyaSibs Weekend. Meaghan is currently employed as an events coordinator at a non-profit firm, Women in International Security. She plans to return to graduate school for a masters degree in International Affairs.

HAMILTON COLLEGE ❑ **Jennifer Kostka** graduated summa cum laude from Hamilton College in 2004 with a concentration in English and a minor in French. While at Hamilton, she was a member of the Residence Hall Council, secretary of the Emerson Literary Society, copyeditor for *The Spectator,* senior tutor at the Writing Center, and publications intern in the Office of Communications and Development. In addition, she was the winner of the Frederick Reese Wagner prize scholarship in English and was a two-time recipient of the Kellogg Essay prize for excellence in writing. She is currently working at a college textbook publishing company in Boston where she works primarily on English and World Language titles. She has continued to stay connected to the Hamilton community by joining the Boston chapter of Hamilton's GOLD (Graduates of the Last Decade) Alumni Association.

HARVARD UNIVERSITY/HARVARD COLLEGE ❏ **Brooke Earley** received an A.B. in history *magna cum laude* from Harvard and Radcliffe Colleges in 1994 and an M.Ed. from Harvard University in 1998. She has worked as an admissions officer and freshman advisor at Harvard and Radcliffe.

HARVEY MUDD COLLEGE ❏ **Erik Ring** majored in engineering and graduated from Harvey Mudd in 1996. He has lived and worked in Irvine, California, and his work keeps him in front of a computer most of the time. Running, backpacking, tennis, and his pet turtle Curly keep him busy the rest of the time.

HAVERFORD COLLEGE ❏ **Steve Manning** graduated in 1996 from Haverford, where he majored in history and played baseball and basketball. He has worked at the college in the publications office, writing the alumni magazine and maintaining the Haverford home page.

JOHNS HOPKINS UNIVERSITY ❏ **Amy Brokl** graduated from Hopkins in 2003 with a B.A. in English and the History of Art. Over the course of her four years, she served on the Commission for Undergraduate Education and the Orientation executive staff, alternating with time spent on the lacrosse field and out in Baltimore. She also gave interviews for the Office of Undergraduate Admissions and assisted with its alumni volunteers, a job that proved a natural segue to her current position as an associate director.

KENYON COLLEGE ❑ **Adam Sapp** is a 2002 graduate of Kenyon College. After receiving his B.A. in history at Kenyon, he worked as reporter for a newspaper in northern Ohio for four months before pursuing work at Claremont McKenna College in Claremont, California. He is currently the Associate Dean of Admission and Financial Aid at Claremont McKenna College.

LAFAYETTE COLLEGE ❑ **Jodi Morgen**, class of 1997, has worked as an interactive copywriter and has lived in New York City. After achieving in such challenges as Student Government President and movie critic for *The Lafayette*, Jodi has experienced great success writing advertising on the Internet, most notably banner ads that read "Win! Win! Win!"

MACALESTER COLLEGE ❑ **Noah Palm** graduated *summa cum laude* from Macalester College with a Bachelor of Arts in Biology with an emphasis on Immunology and Microbiology. Noah participated heavily in research and teaching while at Mac. He chose to continue his studies in biology by pursuing a Doctorate in Immunobiology at Yale University.

MASSACHUSETTS INSTITUTE OF TECHNOLOGY ❑ **Stacy McGeever,** SB '93, majored in mathematics and computer science at MIT.

MIDDLEBURY COLLEGE ❑ **Devin B. Zatorski** graduated from Middlebury College in 2004 with a joint degree in English and political science. He was editor-in-chief of *The Middlebury Campus* newspaper and studied abroad in Edinburgh, Scotland, where he conducted research for the Green Party in the Scottish Parliament. More importantly, he went snow-shoeing with a dean, dined at many professors' homes, and met even more for coffee at The Grille. Devin is associate editor at the Advisory Board Company in Washington, D.C. where he manages a daily news service for health care industry executives. He has also worked on the justice beat at ABC News and as a researcher at the entertainment-driven *USA Weekend Magazine*. He credits liberal arts education with inspiring his round-about path in journalism. Reach him at *zatorskde@advisory.com*

NEW YORK UNIVERSITY ❏ **Eric Muroski** graduated from NYU in 2002 with a double major in playwriting and literature from the Gallatin School of Individualized Study. He is the copresident of a New York City-based theater production company that gives new talent a forum in which to present their art. He also recently held a professional position in the NYU Undergraduate Admissions Office and is now enrolled in a graduate acting program.

NORTHWESTERN UNIVERSITY ❏ **Kristen Acimovic** graduated *cum laude* and with departmental honors from Northwestern in 2002 with a B.A. in English Literature. While at Northwestern, Kristen was an R.A., an intern, a sorority member, and a volunteer. She is currently a freelance writer in New York City.

OBERLIN COLLEGE ❏ **Sue Angell** graduated from Oberlin College with a B.A. in 1999. She majored in English and religion, concentrating on medieval literature and ancient Christianity. Since graduating, she has worked for Oberlin's Office of College Relations as a staff writer and editor.

OCCIDENTAL COLLEGE ❏ **Steven Barrie-Anthony** graduated from Occidental College in 2004 with a B.A. in religious studies and then headed off to work as a staff feature writer with the *Los Angeles Times*. At the *Times* he developed the technology and arts/culture beat, examining the effects of communication technology on person and society, and covered art, architecture, music, the movie business, and literature. In 2006, he returned to Oxy as a research fellow in religious studies, and also serves as the journalist-in-residence at NewSchools Venture Fund, a San Francisco philanthropy foundation dedicated to supporting educational entrepreneurship in underserved communities.

POMONA COLLEGE ❏ **Christina Caldwell** graduated from Pomona College in 1994 with an international relations degree, then moved to northern Virginia to help defeat Oliver North's bid for the U.S. Senate. She later worked in Boston, Massachusetts, for the U.S. Department of Education, helping colleges, universities, and trade schools around New England to implement the William D. Ford Federal Direct Student Loan program.

BIOGRAPHIES

PRINCETON UNIVERSITY ❏ **M. Kathryn Taylor** majored in English at Princeton and graduated in 1974. After receiving her M.A. from the University of Pennsylvania, she left the academic world for a career in banking. In 1987 she returned to teaching and for several years was chairman of the English department at the Baldwin School in Bryn Mawr, Pennsylvania. She has combined part-time teaching with freelance writing. Her clients have included corporations, banks, law firms, nonprofit arts organizations, and schools, including Princeton, where she has done writing assignments for the Alumni Council, the Office of Communications and Publications, and the *Princeton Alumni Weekly*. Her essays have also appeared in the *Philadelphia Inquirer Sunday Magazine*.

REED COLLEGE ❏ **Christopher Moses**, graduated from Reed in 2002, also serving as student body president that year. His senior history thesis investigated Wampanoag Indian and English interactions on colonial Martha's Vineyard. Chris hopes to become a furniture-making, typeface-designing historian, and is currently applying to Ph.D. programs.

RICE UNIVERSITY ❏ **Michol McMillian Ecklund**, a native of Stillwater, Oklahoma, graduated *cum laude* from Rice University in 1997 with a Bachelor of Arts degree and a triple major in Political Science, Economics, and Managerial Studies. While at Rice, she was a varsity cheerleader, Director of the Student Admissions Council, and a statistics tutor. Michol graduated from Harvard Law School in 2000 and is currently a senior tax attorney with Marathon Oil Company in Houston.

SCRIPPS COLLEGE ❏ **Lindsey Galloway** recently graduated from Scripps College with a B.A. in English and gender and women's studies, finishing her thesis on historical novels by contemporary women writers. She has interned at *U.S. News and World Report* and Denver's city magazine *5280* and has also written for the Scripps alumnae magazine and college newspaper *Voice*.

SMITH COLLEGE ❏ **April Simpson** double majored in American studies and government and graduated cum laude. Following commencement, she interned on the education desk of *The New York Times* before entering a one-year reporting position at the *Boston Globe*.

STANFORD UNIVERSITY ❑ **Gabriela Gutierrez** graduated from Stanford in 2002, having majored in Religious Studies, and English and French Literatures. After serving as Assistant Director of Undergraduate Admissions at Stanford, she traveled widely until settling in Mexico, where she now lives and works.

SWARTHMORE COLLEGE ❑ **Sylvia Weedman** graduated from Swarthmore with high honors in 1997. A history major and a political science minor, she was the codirector of the Writing Associate program and wrote for the campus newspaper, *The Phoenix*, and the humor magazine, *Spike*. She has worked as an assistant editor at *The American Prospect* magazine in Cambridge, Massachusetts.

TUFTS UNIVERSITY ❑ **Adam Goodman** graduated from Tufts in 2003 with highest honors and a degree in history. While on campus, he participated in the Institute for Global Leadership's EPIIC program, wrote a column for *The Tufts Daily*, and founded the Tufts Table Tennis Club. After spending three years as an Assistant Director of Admissions and Multicultural Recruitment at Tufts, Adam accepted a job in the Rio Grande Valley along the Mexican border, where he currently works as a history teacher at IDEA College Preparatory.

TULANE UNIVERSITY ❑ **Casey Haugner** graduated from Newcomb College of Tulane University in 2005 with a B.A. in English, creative writing. She then went on to graduate from Tulane's A.B. Freeman School of Business with an MBA in finance and management in 2006. She is currently working in Washington DC, where she does marketing and communications for Deloitte's global public sector, and misses New Orleans terribly.

U.S. MILITARY ACADEMY ❑ **Lt. Megan Scanlon** received her B.S. in 1997 from the U.S. Military Academy at West Point. While at West Point, she studied law and systems engineering, and also played on the women's lacrosse team. Megan has been stationed at Fort Eustis, Virginia, training as an army transportation corps officer.

U.S. NAVAL ACADEMY ❑ **Anthony Holds**, Servidas, is a surface warfare officer in the U.S. Navy for 5 years. After his graduation from the U.S. Naval Academy in May of 1997, he worked as the music department coordinator at the academy for seven months. He then completed a stint in Newport, Rhode Island, at the navy's Surface Warfare Officer School. Upon graduation from that training program, he entered the operational fleet as a division officer onboard a navy ship. Holds recently appeared on Broadway in the show "Dracula" and is pursuing a career as an actor/singer.

UNIVERSITY OF CALIFORNIA, LOS ANGELES (UCLA) ❑ **Amy Ko** is a 1997 graduate of UCLA with degrees in English and sociology.

UNIVERSITY OF CHICAGO ❑ **Jonathan Beere** graduated from the University of Chicago in 1995 with a concentration in history, philosophy, and social studies of science and medicine. He studied classics at Oxford University as a Rhodes Scholar. He has pursued a Ph.D. in philosophy at Princeton.

UNIVERSITY OF MIAMI ❑ **Melissa Greco** graduated in 2005 with a B.S. in Communication. She currently works for the university's Media Relations Department where she serves as the Media Editorial Coordinator. Like a true Miamian, she enjoys Cuban food and sunny afternoons on the beach. She would like to thank Annette Herrera and Margot Winick for their words and wisdom on all things UM.

UNIVERSITY OF NORTH CAROLINA AT CHAPEL HILL ❑ **Elyse Ashburn** graduated from The University of North Carolina in 2004 with a degree in journalism and mass communication. While at Carolina, she served as editor-in-chief of the student newspaper *The Daily Tar Heel* and interned at the *St. Petersburg Times* and *The Atlanta Journal-Constitution*. She currently works as a reporter for the *News & Record* in Greensboro, N.C.

UNIVERSITY OF NOTRE DAME ❑ **Meghan Kelley**, '95, was a history and American studies major at the University of Notre Dame and resided in Walsh Hall for three years. While in school, Meghan was active with the Center for Social Concerns, and intramural sports, and studied in London her junior year. After graduation, Meghan volunteered with Boys Hope/Girls Hope and has worked in public relations in Chicago.

UNIVERSITY OF PENNSYLVANIA ❑ **Erik Frey** graduated in 2002 with majors in Architecture and Asian and Middle Eastern Studies and respective concentrations in Design and Japanese. At Penn, he was involved in the Connaissance and Spring Fling committees, the American Institute of Architecture Students, and several other extracurriculars. Since graduation, he has been working, taking post-bac classes, and concentrating on selecting a graduate program.

UNIVERSITY OF RICHMOND ❑ **Lauren B. Lumsden**, as she writes this, is preparing to graduate from the University of Richmond in May 2005 with a degree in journalism and minors in Spanish and women's studies. She plans to go to New York City but what she will actually do there, she has no idea; there are too many choices and she's incredibly indecisive. At Richmond, Lauren was a DJ on WDCE campus radio, a member of Kappa Kappa Gamma sorority, a participant in Women Involved in Living and Learning, and a member of the Film and Photography Society. Her favorite things include ice cream, knitting, eBay, Pedro Almodovar films, the *Facebook*, and her friends.

UNIVERSITY OF ROCHESTER ❑ **Matt Wolfe** graduated from the University of Rochester in 2003 with a Bachelor of Arts Degree in political science and economics (Honors), minoring in Legal Studies and attaining International Relations and Management Studies certificates. At UR, Matt was involved in community service, the Catholic Newman Community, the Delta Kappa Epsilon fraternity, intramural sports, and theatre. In college, he spent a semester working as a research assistant in the British House of Commons and studying in London. After graduation, Matt served two years through Teach for America, educating students with special needs at Augustine Middle School (New Orleans, LA). Currently, Matt is pursuing a joint-degree in law and public policy (J.D./M.P.P.) at the Duke University School of Law and Terry Sanford Institute of Public Policy.

UNIVERSITY OF SOUTHERN CALIFORNIA ❏ **Achi Yaffe** graduated from USC in 2001 with a B.S. in Business Administration and a minor in Natural Sciences. At USC, he was the cocaptain of the men's club volleyball team, a member of the Baccalaureate/M.D. program, and a Renaissance Scholar. Achi worked as a business analyst with McKinsey & Company, out of their Los Angeles and Tel Aviv offices. He then went on to study for his MBA at Harvard Business School.

UNIVERSITY OF VIRGINIA ❏ **Larisa Barry** graduated with a B.A. from UVa with a distinguished major in English and a minor in French in 1997. She has worked as an assistant editor with an environmental consulting firm in Arlington, Virginia.

VANDERBILT UNIVERSITY ❏ **Lauren (Nicole) Shaub** graduated from Vanderbilt in 2001 with a B.A. in English and Communication Studies. Upon graduation, she worked for two years as an Admissions Counselor at Vanderbilt, and is currently completing an M.Ed. in Counseling Psychology full-time at Teachers College (Columbia University) in New York.

VASSAR COLLEGE ❏ An English major, **Kelley Kawano** graduated from Vassar College in 2000. She served as editor-in-chief of *Asian Quilt* and appeared prominently in Vassar's students of color and college viewbooks. After four years with Random House's Web development division and writing for the online magazine *Bold Type*, she returned to school. Currently a doctoral student in literature at the Graduate Center at City University of New York, Kelley teaches writing.

WAKE FOREST UNIVERSITY ❏ **Lisa Hoppenjans** is a 2003 graduate, who majored in political science and minored in journalism. At Wake Forest she furiously cheered on the basketball team, worked long nights for the campus newspaper, and spent a semester studying at the university's house in London. She is a reporter with *The News & Observer* of Raleigh, North Carolina.

WASHINGTON AND LEE UNIVERSITY ❏ **Cameron Howell** was born and raised in Columbia, South Carolina. He graduated from Washington and Lee University in 1994 and has resided in Charlottesville, Virginia.

WASHINGTON UNIVERSITY IN ST. LOUIS ❏ **Joyce Lawrence**, B.S.B.A. '04, graduated with majors in marketing and international business and a minor in psychology. She is currently living in San Diego and attending the Masters in pacific International Affairs Program at University of California San Diego.

WEBB INSTITUTE ❏ **Alan Bolind** holds a Bachelor of Science in naval architecture and marine engineering. While at Webb he played soccer during his freshman year and was later on the yearbook staff. At graduation, his plans for the future included Webb graduate school.

WELLESLEY COLLEGE ❏ **Mary Lynn Jones** served as editor-in-chief of *The Wellesley News* and graduated from Wellesley College in 1996 with departmental honors in political science. She received her M.S.J. from the Columbia University Graduate School of Journalism in 1997. Mary Lynn has been a staff writer at *The Hill* newspaper in Washington, D.C., covering the Senate and lobbying.

WESLEYAN UNIVERSITY ❏ **Stacy Theberge**, '95, majored in English at Wesleyan, and spent many hours researching an out-of-print novel and rollerblading down Wyllys Avenue. She has lived in Los Angeles, and would like to thank Morgan Fahey, '95, Henry Myers, '95, and Sadia Shepard, '97 for contributing to this article.

WILLIAMS COLLEGE ❏ **Jennifer Linnan** graduated in 2006 with a double major in chemistry and English. At Williams, she was a copyeditor for *The Williams Record*, wrote news and event releases for the Office of Public Affairs, and performed with the Williams Percussion Ensemble. She currently lives in New York City.

YALE UNIVERSITY ❏ **Amanda Gordon** has worked as an assistant editor at *Glamour Magazine* and has been active in planning activities and editing a newsletter for New York-area Yale alumni. She graduated in 1994 with a B.A. in English. At Yale she worked in the Admissions Office, the Dean's Office, and the Master's Office of Ezra Stiles College.

❏ **Seth Oltman** graduated from Yale in 1997 with a B.A. in history. At Yale he edited the *Yale Record* (a humor magazine) and *Urim v'Tumim* (a Jewish journal), tutored at a local elementary school, and worked for four years at the Yale University Press. He has been an editorial assistant at *Chief Executive Magazine*.

❑ INDEX BY STATE ❑

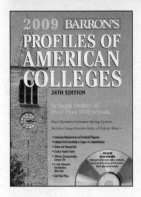
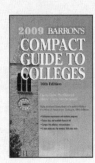